HOLT SCIENCE & TECHNOLOGY

Earth
Science

HOLT, RINEHART AND WINSTON

A Harcourt Education Company

Orlando • **Austin** • New York • San Diego • Toronto • London

Acknowledgments

Contributing Authors

Kathleen Meehan Berry
Science Chairman
Canon-McMillan School
  District
Canonsburg, Pennsylvania

Robert H. Fronk, Ph.D.
Professor
Science and Mathematics
  Education Department
Florida Institute of
  Technology
Melbourne, Florida

**Mary Kay Hemenway,
  Ph.D.**
*Research Associate and Senior
  Lecturer*
Department of Astronomy
The University of Texas at
  Austin
Austin, Texas

Kathleen Kaska
*Former Life and Earth Science
  Teacher and Science
  Department Chair*

Peter E. Malin, Ph.D.
Professor of Geology
Division of Earth and
  Ocean Sciences
Duke University
Durham, North Carolina

Karen J. Meech, Ph.D.
Astronomer
Institute for Astronomy
University of Hawaii
Honolulu, Hawaii

**Robert J. Sager, M.S., J.D.,
  L.G.**
*Coordinator and Professor of
  Earth Science*
Pierce College
Lakewood, Washington

Inclusion Specialist

Karen Clay
*Inclusion Specialist
  Consultant*
Boston, Massachusetts

Safety Reviewer

Jack Gerlovich, Ph.D.
Associate Professor
School of Education
Drake University
Des Moines, Iowa

Academic Reviewers

David M. Armstrong, Ph.D.
Professor
Ecology and Evolutionary
  Biology
University of Colorado
Boulder, Colorado

Kenneth H. Brink, Ph.D.
*Senior Scientist and Physical
  Oceanography Director*
Coastal Ocean Institute
  and Rinehart Coastal
  Research Center
Woods Hole Oceanographic
  Institution
Woods Hole, Massachusetts

John Brockhaus, Ph.D.
*Professor of Geospatial
  Information Science and
  Director of Geospatial
  Information Science
  Program*
Department of Geography
  and Environmental
  Engineering
United States Military
  Academy
West Point, New York

Dan Bruton, Ph.D.
Associate Professor
Department of Physics and
  Astronomy
Stephen F. Austin State
  University
Nacogdoches, Texas

Wesley N. Colley, Ph.D.
Lecturer
Department of Astronomy
University of Virginia
Charlottesville, Virginia

Roger J. Cuffey, Ph.D.
Professor of Paleontology
Department of Geosciences
Pennsylvania State
  University
University Park,
  Pennsylvania

Turgay Ertekin, Ph.D.
*Professor and Chairman of
  Petroleum and Natural Gas
  Engineering*
Energy and Geo-
  Environmental
  Engineering
Pennsylvania State
  University
University Park,
  Pennsylvania

Deborah Hanley, Ph.D.
Meteorologist
State of Florida
Department of Agriculture
  and Consumer Services
Division of Forestry
Tallahassee, Florida

**Mary Kay Hemenway,
  Ph.D.**
*Research Associate and Senior
  Lecturer*
Astronomy Department
The University of Texas
Austin, Texas

Richard N. Hey, Ph.D.
Professor of Geophysics
Department of Geophysics
  & Planetology
University of Hawaii at
  Manoa
Honolulu, Hawaii

Ken Hon, Ph.D.
*Associate Professor of
  Volcanology*
Geology Department
University of Hawaii at Hilo
Hilo, Hawaii

Susan Hough, Ph.D.
Scientist
United States Geological
  Survey (USGS)
Pasadena, California

Steven A. Jennings, Ph.D.
Associate Professor
Geography and
  Environmental Studies
University of Colorado at
  Colorado Springs
Colorado Springs, Colorado

Acknowledgments
continued on page 846

Contents in Brief

Contents

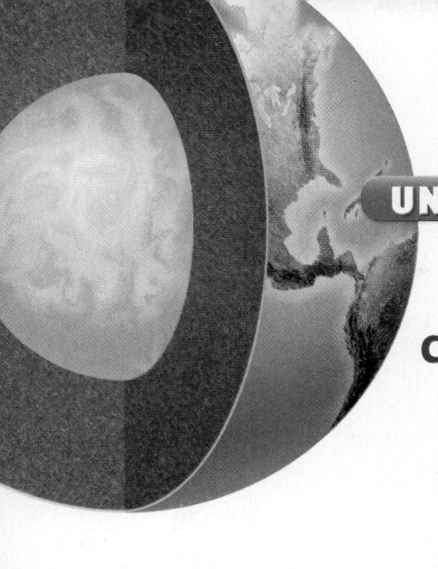

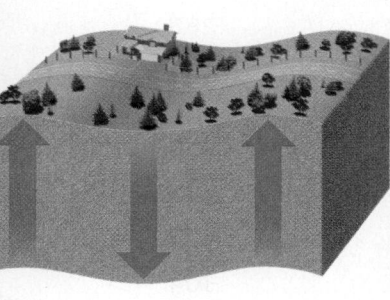

Contents   vii

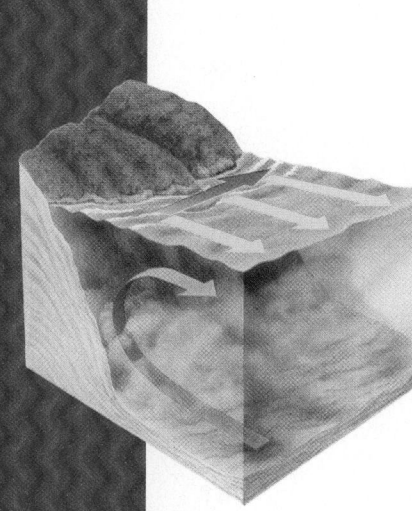

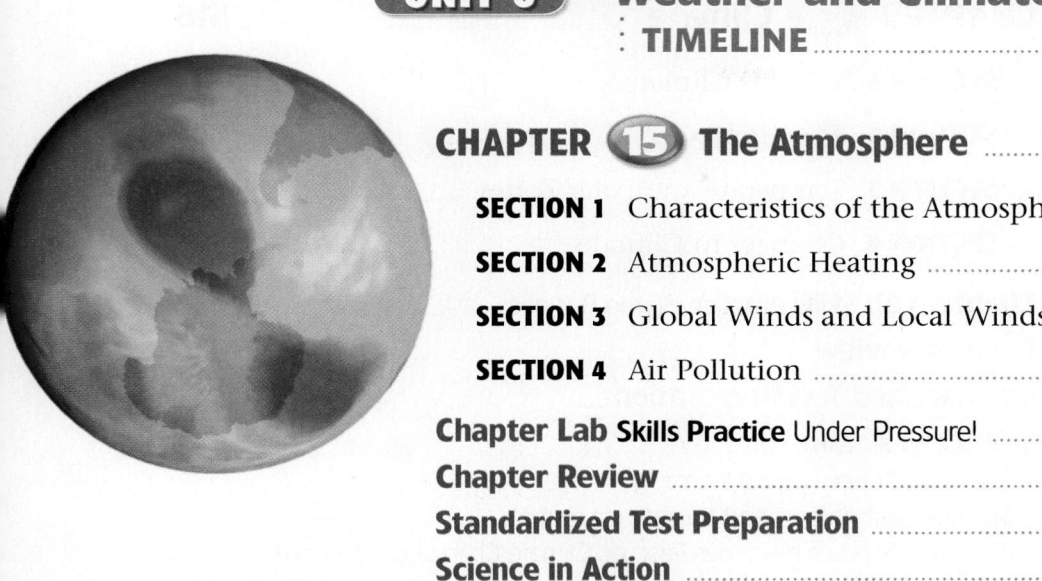

Contents **xi**

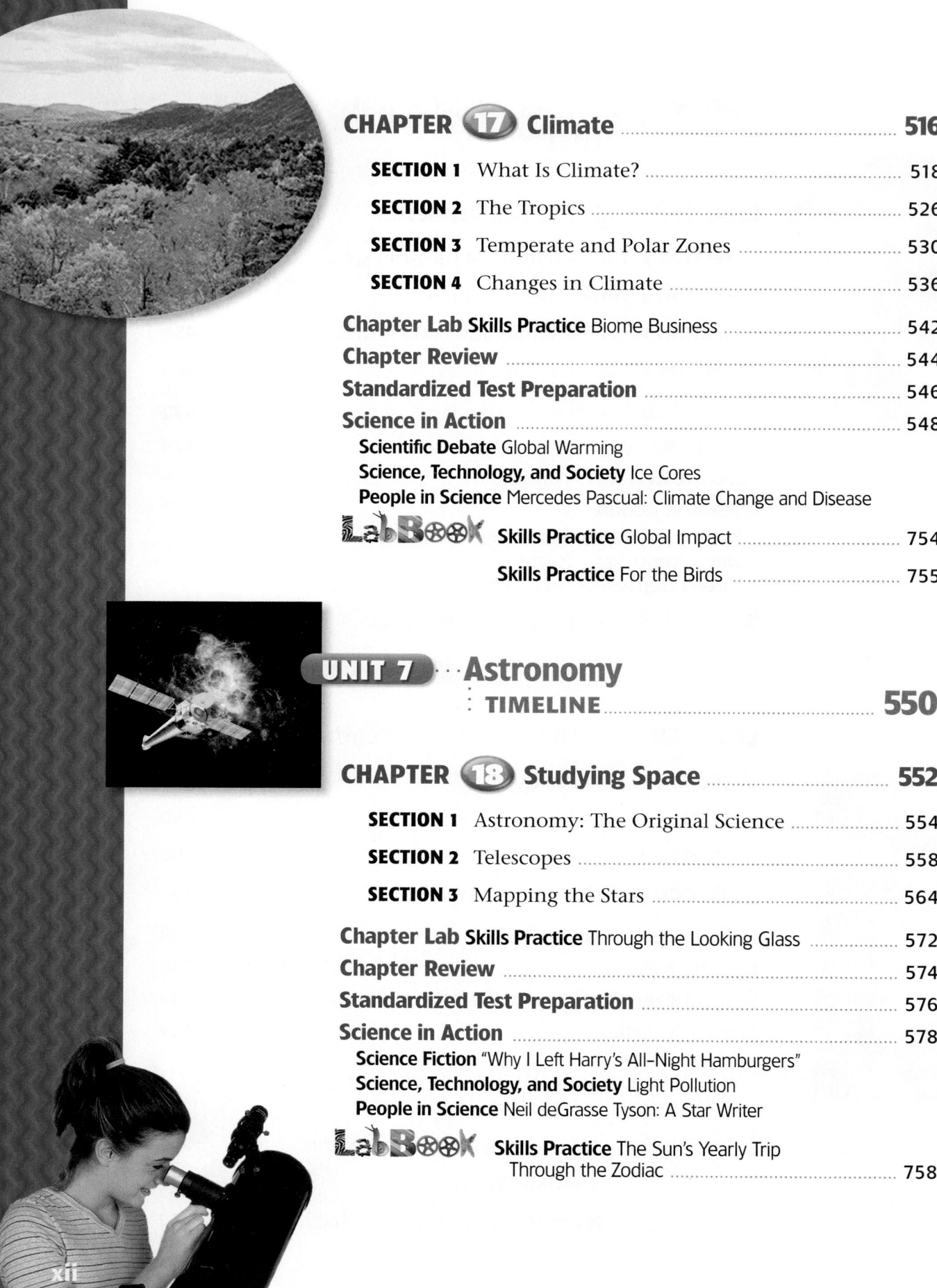

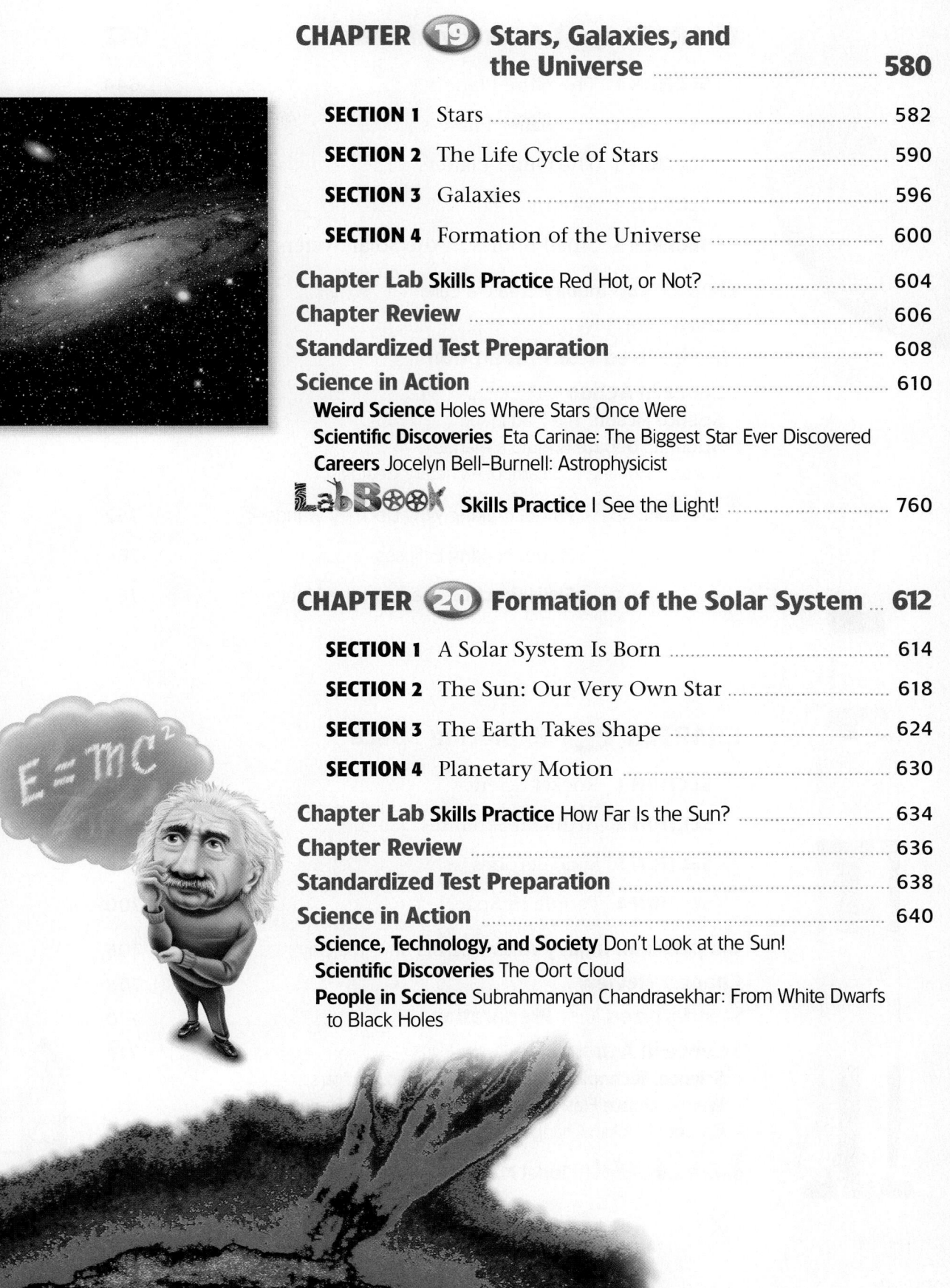

$E = mc^2$

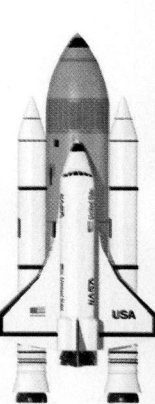

Chapter Labs and LabBook

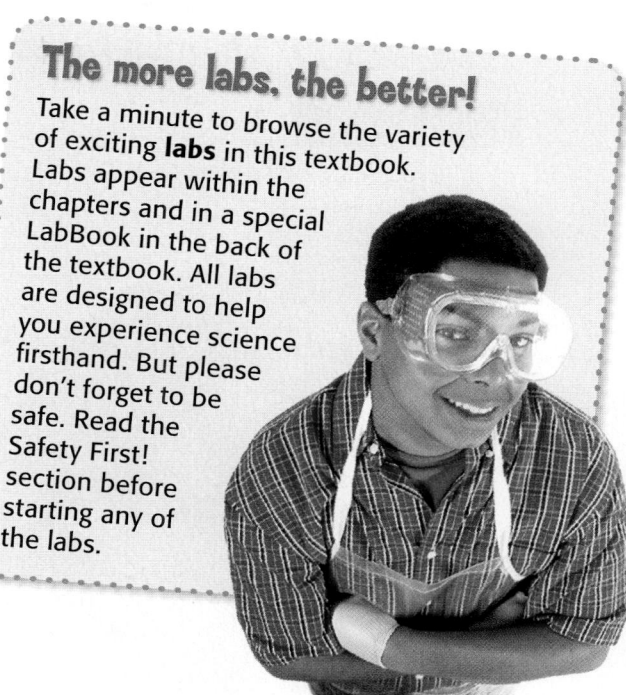

The more labs, the better!

Take a minute to browse the variety of exciting **labs** in this textbook. Labs appear within the chapters and in a special LabBook in the back of the textbook. All labs are designed to help you experience science firsthand. But please don't forget to be safe. Read the Safety First! section before starting any of the labs.

Start your engines with an activity!

Get motivated to learn by doing the two activities at the beginning of each chapter. The **Pre-Reading Activity** helps you organize information as you read the chapter. The **Start-up Activity** helps you gain scientific understanding of the topic through hands-on experience.

PRE-READING ACTIVITY

FOLDNOTES

START-UP ACTIVITY

READING STRATEGY

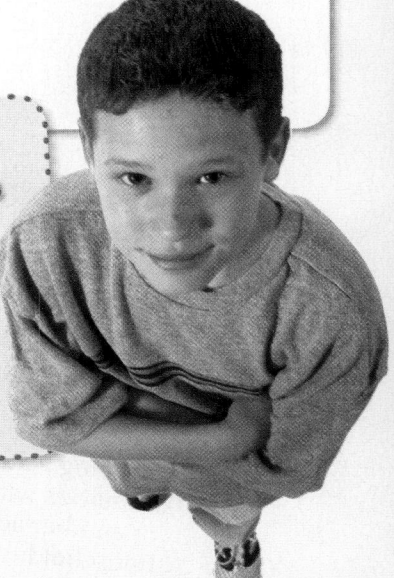

Remembering what you read doesn't have to be hard!

A **Reading Strategy** at the beginning of every section provides tips to help you remember and/or organize the information covered in the section.

Quick Lab

School to Home

Activity

Science brings you closer together!

Bring science into your home by doing **School-to-Home Activities** with a parent or another adult in your household.

INTERNET ACTIVITY

Get caught in the Web!

Go to **go.hrw.com** for **Internet Activities** related to each chapter. To find the Internet Activity for a particular chapter, just type in the keyword listed below.

MATH PRACTICE

MATH FOCUS

Science and math go hand in hand.

The **Math Focus** and **Math Practice** items show you many ways that math applies directly to science and vice versa.

Connection to...

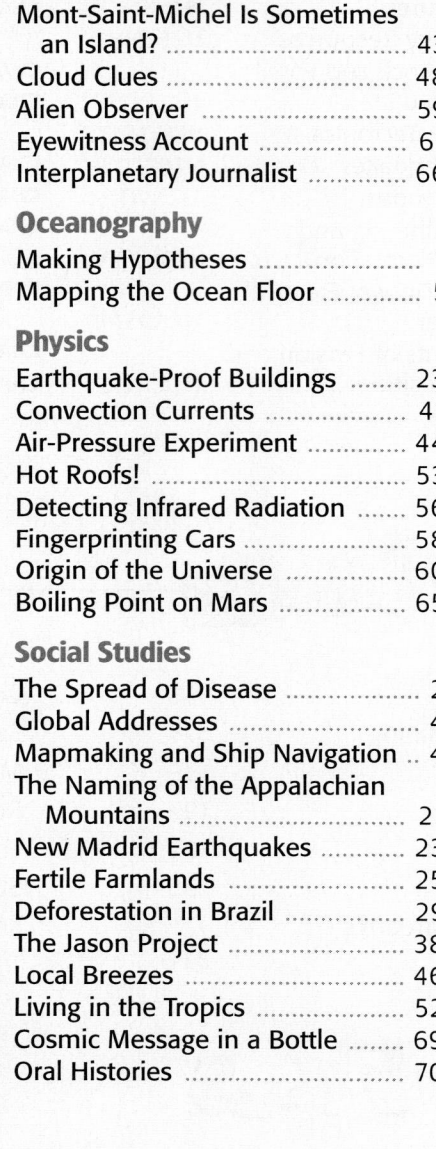

One subject leads to another.

You may not realize it at first, but different subjects are related to each other in many ways. Each **Connection** explores a topic from the viewpoint of another discipline. In this way, all of the subjects you learn about in school merge to improve your understanding of the world around you.

Science in Action

Science moves beyond the classroom!

Read **Science in Action** articles to learn more about science in the real world. These articles will give you an idea of how interesting, strange, helpful, and action packed science is. At the end of each chapter, you will find three short articles. And if your thirst is still not quenched, go to **go.hrw.com** for in-depth coverage.

How to Use Your Textbook

Your Roadmap for Success with Holt Science and Technology

Reading Warm-Up

A Reading Warm-Up at the beginning of every section provides you with the section's objectives and key terms. The objectives tell you what you'll need to know after you finish reading the section.

Key terms are listed for each section. Learn the definitions of these terms because you will most likely be tested on them. Each key term is highlighted in the text and is defined at point of use and in the margin. You can also use the glossary to locate definitions quickly.

STUDY TIP Reread the objectives and the definitions to the key terms when studying for a test to be sure you know the material.

Get Organized

A Reading Strategy at the beginning of every section provides tips to help you organize and remember the information covered in the section. Keep a science notebook so that you are ready to take notes when your teacher reviews the material in class. Keep your assignments in this notebook so that you can review them when studying for the chapter test.

SECTION 1

READING WARM-UP

Objectives
- Describe how moving water shapes the surface of the Earth by the process of erosion.
- Explain how water moves through the water cycle.
- Describe a watershed.
- Explain three factors that affect the rate of stream erosion.
- Identify four ways that rivers are described.

Terms to Learn

erosion   divide
water cycle   channel
tributary   load
watershed

READING STRATEGY

Reading Organizer As you read this section, create an outline of the section. Use the headings from the section in your outline.

erosion the process by which wind, water, ice, or gravity transports soil and sediment from one location to another

Figure 1 The Grand Canyon is located in northwestern Arizona. The canyon formed over millions of years as running water eroded the rock layers. (In some places, the canyon is now 29 km wide.)

The Active River

If you had fallen asleep with your toes dangling in the Colorado River 6 million years ago and you had woken up today, your toes would be hanging about 1.6 km (about 1 mi) above the river!

The Colorado River carved the Grand Canyon, shown in **Figure 1**, by washing billions of tons of soil and rock from its riverbed. The Colorado River made the Grand Canyon by a process that can take millions of years.

Rivers: Agents of Erosion

Six million years ago, the area now known as the Grand Canyon was nearly as flat as a pancake. The Colorado River cut down into the rock and formed the Grand Canyon over millions of years through a process called erosion. **Erosion** is the process by which soil and sediment are transported from one location to another. Rivers are not the only agents of erosion. Wind, rain, ice, and snow can also cause erosion.

Because of erosion caused by water, the Grand Canyon is now about 1.6 km deep and 446 km long. In this section, you will learn about stream development, river systems, and the factors that affect the rate of stream erosion.

Reading Check Describe the process that created the Grand Canyon. *(See the Appendix for answers to Reading Checks.)*

308   Chapter 11   The Flow of Fresh Water

Be Resourceful — Use the Web

SCILINKS.

Internet Connect boxes in your textbook take you to resources that you can use for science projects, reports, and research papers. Go to scilinks.org, and type in the SciLinks code to get information on a topic.

go.hrw.com

Visit go.hrw.com Find worksheets, **Current Science**® magazine articles online, and other materials that go with your textbook at **go.hrw.com.** Click on the textbook icon and the table of contents to see all of the resources for each chapter.

Figure 4 *A mountain stream, such as the one at left, at Kenai Peninsula in Alaska, flows rapidly and has more erosive energy. A river on a flat plain, such as the Kuskowim River in Alaska, shown below, flows slowly and has less erosive energy.*

Stream Erosion

As a stream forms, it erodes soil and rock to make a channel. A **channel** is the path that a stream follows. When a stream first forms, its channel is usually narrow and steep. Over time, the stream transports rock and soil downstream and makes the channel wider and deeper. When streams become longer and wider, they are called *rivers*. A stream's ability to erode is influenced by three factors: gradient, discharge, and load.

Gradient

Figure 4 shows two photos of rivers with very different gradients. *Gradient* is the measure of the change in elevation over a certain distance. A high gradient gives a stream or river more erosive energy...

Discharge

The amount...

tributary a stream that flows into a lake or into a larger stream

watershed the area of land that is drained by a water system

divide the boundary between drainage areas that have streams that flow in opposite directions

channel the path that a stream follows

Use the Illustrations and Photos

Art shows complex ideas and processes. Learn to analyze the art so that you better understand the material you read in the text.

Tables and graphs display important information in an organized way to help you see relationships.

A picture is worth a thousand words. Look at the photographs to see relevant examples of science concepts that you are reading about.

Answer the Section Reviews

Section Reviews test your knowledge of the main points of the section. Critical Thinking items challenge you to think about the material in greater depth and to find connections that you infer from the text.

STUDY TIP When you can't answer a question, reread the section. The answer is usually there.

Do Your Homework

Your teacher may assign worksheets to help you understand and remember the material in the chapter.

STUDY TIP Don't try to answer the questions without reading the text and reviewing your class notes. A little preparation up front will make your homework assignments a lot easier. Answering the items in the Chapter Review will help prepare you for the chapter test.

SECTION Review

Summary

- Rivers cause erosion by removing and transporting soil and rock from the riverbed.
- The water cycle is the movement of Earth's water from the ocean to the atmosphere to the land and back to the ocean.
- A river system is made up of a network of streams and rivers.
- A watershed is a region that collects runoff water that then becomes part of a river or a lake.
- A stream with a high gradient has more energy for eroding soil and rock.
- When a stream's discharge increases, its erosive energy also increases.
- A stream with a load of large particles has a higher rate of erosion than a stream with a dissolved load.
- A developing river can be described as youthful, mature, old, or rejuvenated.

Using Key Terms

1. Use each of the following terms in a separate sentence: *erosion, water cycle, tributary, watershed, divide, channel,* and *load.*

Understanding Key Ideas

2. Which of the following drains a watershed?
   a. a divide
   b. a drainage basin
   c. a tributary
   d. a water system
3. Describe how the Grand Canyon was formed.
4. Draw the water cycle. In your drawing, label *condensation, precipitation,* and *evaporation.*
5. What are three factors that affect the rate of stream erosion?
6. Which stage of river development is characterized by flat flood plains?

Critical Thinking

7. **Making Inferences** How does the water cycle help develop river systems?
8. **Making Comparisons** How do youthful rivers, mature rivers, and old rivers differ?

Interpreting Graphics

Use the pie graph below to answer the questions that follow.

Distribution of Water in the World

Water underground, in soil, and in air 0.5%

Rivers and lakes 0.2%

Polar ice caps 2.3%

Oceans 97%

9. Where is most of the water in the world found?
10. In what form is the majority of the world's fresh water?

NSTA
Developed and maintained by the
National Science Teachers Association

For a variety of links related to this chapter, go to www.scilinks.org
Topic: Rivers and Streams
SciLinks code: HSM1316

315

Visit Holt Online Learning

If your teacher gives you a special password to log onto the Holt Online Learning site, you'll find your complete textbook on the Web. In addition, you'll find some great learning tools and practice quizzes. You'll be able to see how well you know the material from your textbook.

Visit CNN Student News

You'll find up-to-date events in science at **cnnstudentnews.com.**

SAFETY FIRST!

Exploring, inventing, and investigating are essential to the study of science. However, these activities can also be dangerous. To make sure that your experiments and explorations are safe, you must be aware of a variety of safety guidelines. You have probably heard of the saying, "It is better to be safe than sorry." This is particularly true in a science classroom where experiments and explorations are being performed. Being uninformed and careless can result in serious injuries. Don't take chances with your own safety or with anyone else's.

The following pages describe important guidelines for staying safe in the science classroom. Your teacher may also have safety guidelines and tips that are specific to your classroom and laboratory. Take the time to be safe.

Safety Rules!

Start Out Right

Always get your teacher's permission before attempting any laboratory exploration. Read the procedures carefully, and pay particular attention to safety information and caution statements. If you are unsure about what a safety symbol means, look it up or ask your teacher. You cannot be too careful when it comes to safety. If an accident does occur, inform your teacher immediately regardless of how minor you think the accident is.

If you are instructed to note the odor of a substance, wave the fumes toward your nose with your hand. Never put your nose close to the source.

Safety Symbols

All of the experiments and investigations in this book and their related worksheets include important safety symbols to alert you to particular safety concerns. Become familiar with these symbols so that when you see them, you will know what they mean and what to do. It is important that you read this entire safety section to learn about specific dangers in the laboratory.

Eye protection

Clothing protection

Hand safety

Heating safety

Electric safety

Chemical safety

Animal safety

Sharp object

Plant safety

xxvi

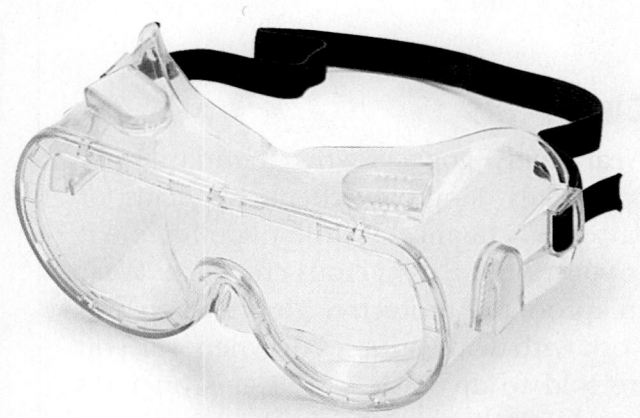

Eye Safety

Wear safety goggles when working around chemicals, acids, bases, or any type of flame or heating device. Wear safety goggles any time there is even the slightest chance that harm could come to your eyes. If any substance gets into your eyes, notify your teacher immediately and flush your eyes with running water for at least 15 minutes. Treat any unknown chemical as if it were a dangerous chemical. Never look directly into the sun. Doing so could cause permanent blindness.

Avoid wearing contact lenses in a laboratory situation. Even if you are wearing safety goggles, chemicals can get between the contact lenses and your eyes. If your doctor requires that you wear contact lenses instead of glasses, wear eye-cup safety goggles in the lab.

Safety Equipment

Know the locations of the nearest fire alarms and any other safety equipment, such as fire blankets and eyewash fountains, as identified by your teacher, and know the procedures for using the equipment.

Neatness

Keep your work area free of all unnecessary books and papers. Tie back long hair, and secure loose sleeves or other loose articles of clothing, such as ties and bows. Remove dangling jewelry. Don't wear open-toed shoes or sandals in the laboratory. Never eat, drink, or apply cosmetics in a laboratory setting. Food, drink, and cosmetics can easily become contaminated with dangerous materials.

Certain hair products (such as aerosol hair spray) are flammable and should not be worn while working near an open flame. Avoid wearing hair spray or hair gel on lab days.

Sharp/Pointed Objects

Use knives and other sharp instruments with extreme care. Never cut objects while holding them in your hands. Place objects on a suitable work surface for cutting.

Be extra careful when using any glassware. When adding a heavy object to a graduated cylinder, tilt the cylinder so that the object slides slowly to the bottom.

Heat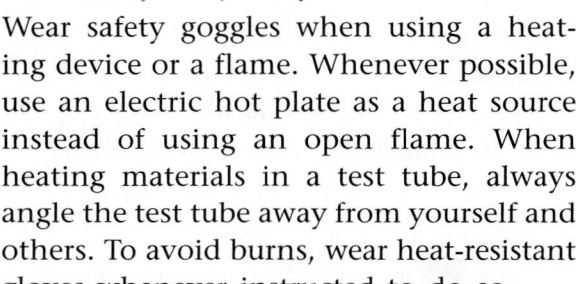

Wear safety goggles when using a heating device or a flame. Whenever possible, use an electric hot plate as a heat source instead of using an open flame. When heating materials in a test tube, always angle the test tube away from yourself and others. To avoid burns, wear heat-resistant gloves whenever instructed to do so.

Electricity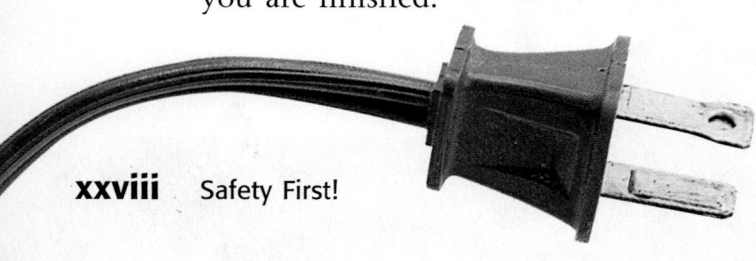

Be careful with electrical cords. When using a microscope with a lamp, do not place the cord where it could trip someone. Do not let cords hang over a table edge in a way that could cause equipment to fall if the cord is accidentally pulled. Do not use equipment with damaged cords. Be sure that your hands are dry and that the electrical equipment is in the "off" position before plugging it in. Turn off and unplug electrical equipment when you are finished.

Chemicals

Wear safety goggles when handling any potentially dangerous chemicals, acids, or bases. If a chemical is unknown, handle it as you would a dangerous chemical. Wear an apron and protective gloves when you work with acids or bases or whenever you are told to do so. If a spill gets on your skin or clothing, rinse it off immediately with water for at least 5 minutes while calling to your teacher.

Never mix chemicals unless your teacher tells you to do so. Never taste, touch, or smell chemicals unless you are specifically directed to do so. Before working with a flammable liquid or gas, check for the presence of any source of flame, spark, or heat.

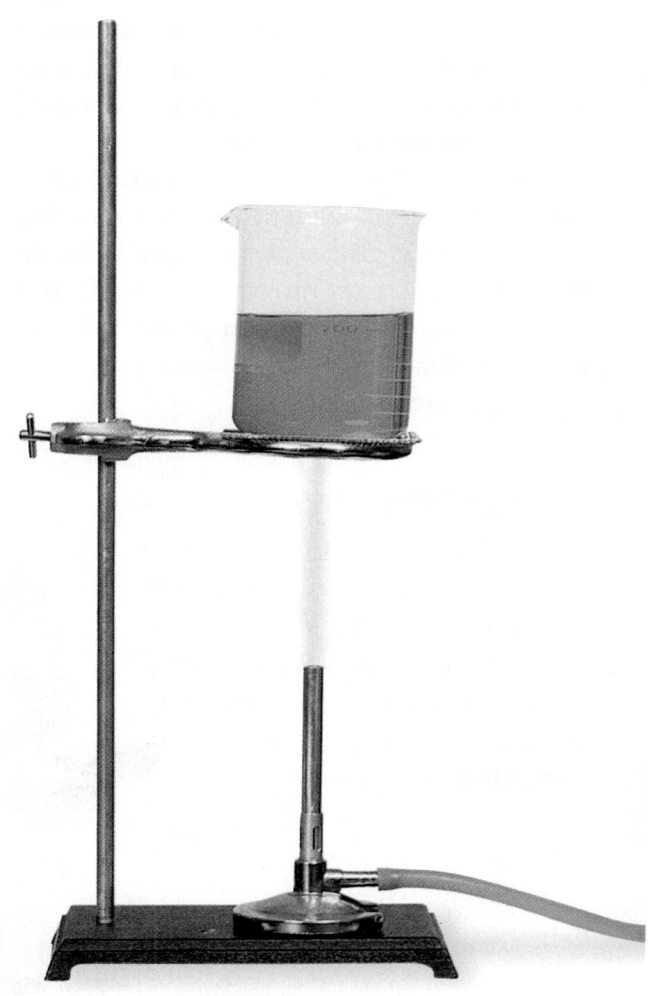

Animal Safety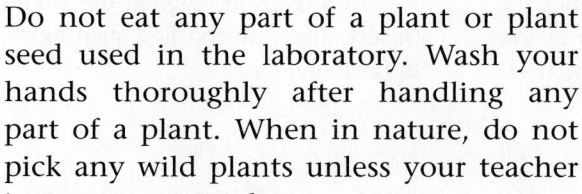

Always obtain your teacher's permission before bringing any animal into the school building. Handle animals only as your teacher directs. Always treat animals carefully and respectfully. Wash your hands thoroughly after handling any animal.

Plant Safety

Do not eat any part of a plant or plant seed used in the laboratory. Wash your hands thoroughly after handling any part of a plant. When in nature, do not pick any wild plants unless your teacher instructs you to do so.

Glassware

Examine all glassware before use. Be sure that glassware is clean and free of chips and cracks. Report damaged glassware to your teacher. Glass containers used for heating should be made of heat-resistant glass.

UNIT 1

TIMELINE

Introduction to Earth Science

In this unit, you will start your own investigation of the planet Earth and of the regions of space beyond it. But first you should prepare yourself by learning about the tools and methods used by Earth scientists. As you can imagine, it is not easy to study something as large as the Earth or as far away as Venus. Yet Earth scientists study these planets and more. The timeline shown here identifies a few of the events that have helped shape our understanding of the Earth.

1669

Nicolaus Steno accurately describes the process by which living organisms become fossils.

1904

Roald Amundsen determines the position of the magnetic north pole.

1922

Roy Chapman Andrews discovers fossilized dinosaur eggs in the Gobi Desert. They are the first such eggs to be found.

fossilized dinosaur eggs in the Gobi Desert

1962

By reaching an altitude of over 95 km, the *X-15* becomes the first fixed-wing plane to reach space.

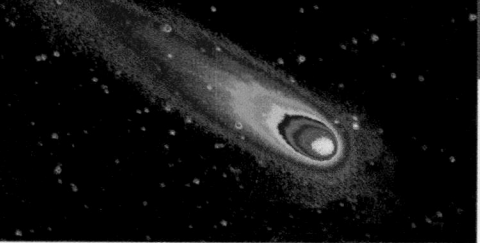

1758

Halley's comet makes a reappearance, which confirms Edmond Halley's 1705 prediction. The comet reappeared 16 years after Halley's death.

1799

The Rosetta stone is discovered in Egypt. It enables scholars to decipher Egyptian hieroglyphics.

1896

The first modern Olympic Games are held in Athens, Greece.

1943

The volcano Paricutín grows more than 200 m tall during its first two weeks of eruption.

Paricutín Volcano

1960

The first weather satellite, *TIROS I,* is launched by the United States.

1970

The first Earth Day is celebrated in the United States on April 22.

1990

The Hubble Space Telescope is launched into orbit. Three years later, faulty optics are repaired during a space walk.

1994

China begins construction of Three Gorges Dam, the world's largest dam. Designed to control the Yangtze River, the dam will supply an estimated 84 billion kilowatt-hours of hydroelectric power per year.

2002

A new order of insects—*Mantophasmatodea*—is found both preserved in 45 million−year−old amber and living in southern Africa.

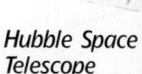

Hubble Space Telescope

1

The World of Earth Science

About the PHOTO

What is that man doing? Ricardo Alonso, a geologist in Argentina, is measuring the footprints left by a dinosaur millions of years ago. Taking measurements is just one way that scientists collect data to answer questions and test hypotheses.

PRE-READING ACTIVITY

FOLDNOTES **Key-Term Fold** Before you read the chapter, create the FoldNote entitled "Key-Term Fold" described in the **Study Skills** section of the Appendix. Write a key term from the chapter on each tab of the key-term fold. Under each tab, write the definition of the key term.

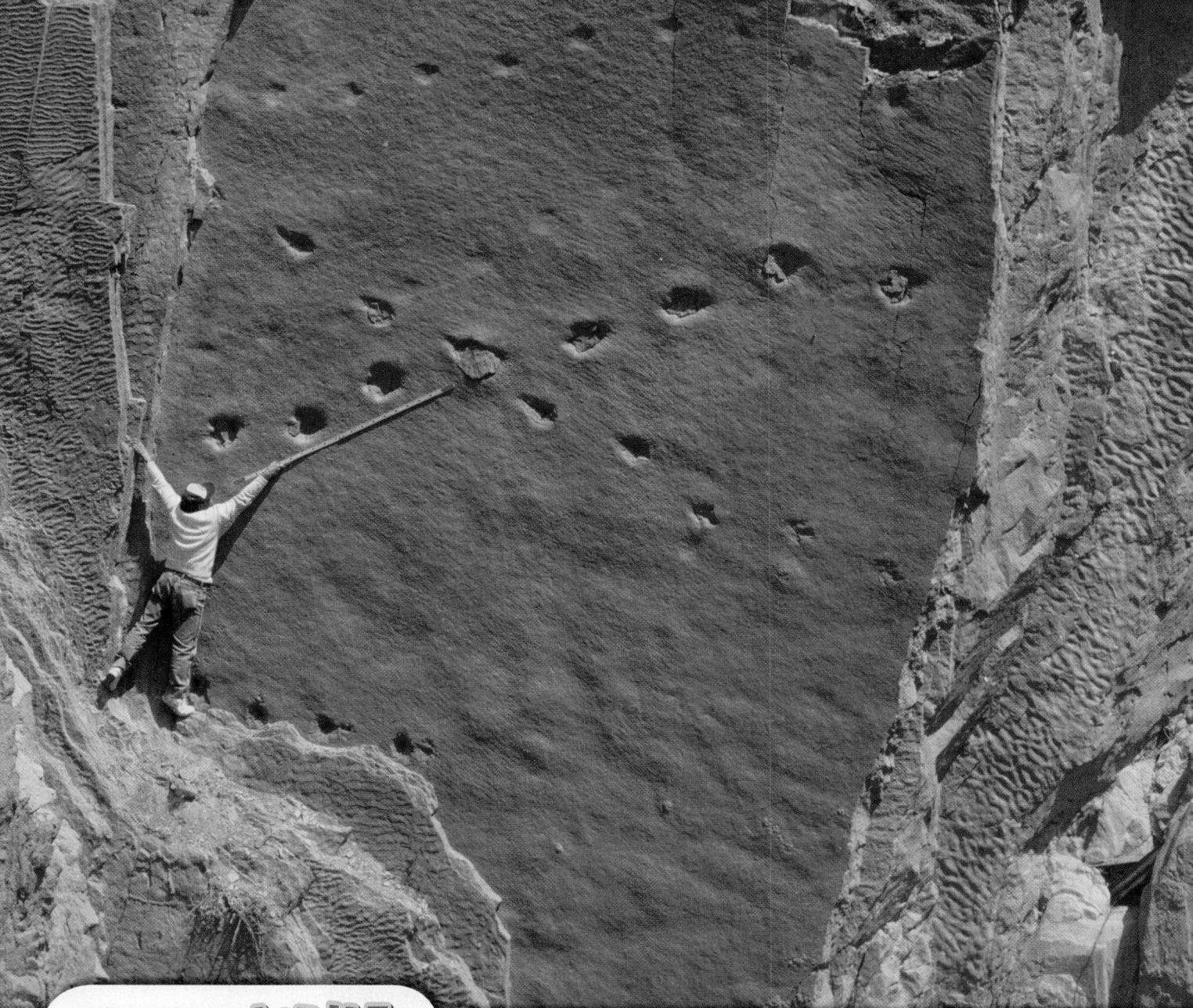

START-UP ACTIVITY

Mission Impossible?

In this activity, you will do some creative thinking to solve what might seem like an impossible problem.

Procedure

1. Examine an **index card.** Your mission is to fit yourself through the card. You can only tear and fold the card. You cannot use tape, glue, or anything else to hold the card together.

2. Brainstorm with a partner ways to complete your mission. Then, record your plan.

3. Test your plan. Did it work? If necessary, get **another index card** and try again. Record your new plan and the results.

4. Share your plans and results with your classmates.

Analysis

1. Why was it helpful to come up with a plan in advance?

2. How did testing your plan help you complete your mission?

3. How did sharing your ideas with your classmates help you complete your mission? What did your classmates do differently?

Branches of Earth Science

Planet Earth! How can anyone study something as large and complicated as our planet?

One way is to divide the study of the Earth into smaller areas of study. In this section, you will learn about some of the most common areas of study. You will also learn about some of the people that work within these areas.

Geology—Science That Rocks

The study of the origin, history, and structure of the Earth and the processes that shape the Earth is called **geology**. Everything that has to do with the solid Earth is part of geology.

Most geologists specialize in a particular aspect of the Earth. For example, a *volcanologist* is a geologist who studies volcanoes. Are earthquakes more to your liking? Then, you could be a *seismologist,* a geologist who studies earthquakes. How about digging up dinosaurs? You could be a *paleontologist,* a geologist who studies fossils. These are only a few of the careers you could have as a geologist.

Some geologists become highly specialized. For example, geologist Robert Fronk, at the Florida Institute of Technology, explores the subsurface of Earth by scuba diving in underwater caves in Florida and the Bahamas. Underwater caves often contain evidence that sea level was once much lower than it is now. The underwater caves shown in **Figure 1** contain *stalagmites* and *stalactites*. These formations develop from minerals in water that drips in air-filled caves. When Fronk sees these kinds of geologic formations in underwater caves, he knows that the caves were once above sea level.

geology the study of the origin, history, and structure of the Earth and the processes that shape the Earth

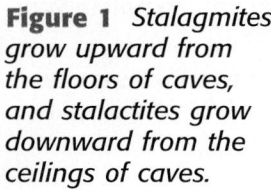

Figure 1 *Stalagmites grow upward from the floors of caves, and stalactites grow downward from the ceilings of caves.*

Oceanography—Water, Water Everywhere

The scientific study of the sea is called **oceanography.** Special areas of oceanography include physical oceanography, biological oceanography, geological oceanography, and chemical oceanography. Physical oceanographers study physical features of the ocean such as waves and currents to see how they affect weather patterns and aquatic life. Biological oceanographers study the plants and animals that live in the ocean. Geological oceanographers study and explore the ocean floor for clues to the Earth's history. Chemical oceanographers study amounts and distributions of natural and human-made chemicals in the ocean.

✔ **Reading Check** Describe four special areas of oceanography. (*See the Appendix for answers to Reading Checks.*)

Exploring the Ocean Floor

Not long ago, people studied the ocean only from the surface. But as technology has advanced, scientists have worked with engineers to build miniature research submarines to go practically anywhere in the oceans.

John Trefry is an oceanographer who studies the ocean floor in a minisub called *Alvin.* Using the *Alvin,* Trefry can travel 2.4 km below the surface of the ocean. At this depth, Trefry can explore an interesting new world. One of the most exciting sights Trefry has seen is a black smoker. As shown in **Figure 2,** *black smokers* are rock chimneys on the ocean floor that spew black clouds of minerals. Black smokers are a kind of *hydrothermal vent,* which is a crack in the ocean floor that releases very hot water from beneath the Earth's surface. The minerals and hot water from these vents support a beautiful and exotic biological community. The aquatic life includes blood-red tube worms that are 3.5 m long, clams that are 30 cm in diameter, and blind white crabs.

oceanography the scientific study of the sea

How Hot Is 300°C?

1. Use a **thermometer** to measure the air temperature in the room in degrees Celsius. Record your reading.

2. Hold the thermometer near a **heat source** in the room, such as a light bulb or a heating vent. Be careful not to burn yourself. Record your reading.

3. How do the temperatures you recorded compare with the 300°C temperature of the water from a black smoker?

Figure 2 *Black smokers, such as this one seen through the window of* Alvin, *can reach temperatures up to 300°C!*

Figure 3 *This image, made from several satellite photos, traces Hurricane Andrew's path at three locations from the Atlantic Ocean (right) to the Gulf of Mexico (left).*

Meteorology—It's a Gas!

meteorology the scientific study of the Earth's atmosphere, especially in relation to weather and climate

The study of the Earth's atmosphere, especially in relation to weather and climate, is called **meteorology.** When you ask, "Is it going to rain today?" you are asking a meteorological question. One of the most common careers in meteorology is weather forecasting. Sometimes, knowing what the weather will be like makes our lives more comfortable. Sometimes, our lives depend on these forecasts.

Hurricanes

In 1928, a major hurricane hit Florida and killed 1,836 people. In contrast, a hurricane of similar strength—Hurricane Andrew, shown in **Figure 3**—hit Florida in 1992 and killed 48 people. Why were there far fewer deaths in 1992? Two major reasons were hurricane tracking and weather forecasting.

Meteorologists began tracking Hurricane Andrew on Monday, August 17, 1992. By the following Sunday morning, most people in southern Florida had left the coast. The National Hurricane Center had warned them that Andrew was headed their way. The hurricane caused a lot of damage. However, it killed very few people, thanks to meteorologists' warnings.

Figure 4 *These meteorologists are risking their lives to gather data about tornadoes.*

Tornadoes

An average of 780 tornadoes touch down each year in the United States. What do you think about a meteorologist who chases tornadoes as a career? Howard Bluestein does just that. He predicts where tornadoes are likely to form. He then drives to within a couple of kilometers of the site to gather data, as shown in **Figure 4.** By gathering data this way, scientists such as Bluestein hope to understand tornadoes better. The better scientists understand tornadoes, the better scientists can predict how tornadoes will behave.

Astronomy—Far, Far Away

How do you study things that are beyond Earth? Astronomers can answer this question. **Astronomy** is the study of the universe. Astronomers study stars, asteroids, planets, and everything else in space.

Because most things in space are too far away to study directly, astronomers depend on technology to help them study objects in space. Optical telescopes are one way astronomers study objects in space. Optical telescopes have been used for hundreds of years. Galileo built an optical telescope in 1609. But optical telescopes are not the only kind of telescope astronomers use.

Optical telescopes need light to see objects, such as planets and comets. However, some objects do not give off light or are too far away to be seen with an optical telescope. Instead of detecting the visible light waves, radio telescopes, such as the one in **Figure 5,** detect radio waves. Radio waves are not visible like light waves are, but data from radio waves form patterns. From these patterns, astronomers can make images to learn more about the objects in space.

Star Struck

Astronomers spend much of their time studying stars. Astronomers estimate that there are more than 100 billion billion stars—that is a lot of stars! The most familiar star in the universe is the sun. The sun is the closest star to the Earth. For this reason, astronomers have studied the sun more than other stars.

Reading Check What do astronomers study?

astronomy the study of the universe

Lots of Zeros!

Astronomers estimate that there are more than 100 billion billion stars! One billion written out in numerals looks like this: 1,000,000,000.

How many zeros do you need in order to write 100 billion billion in numerals? To find out, multiply 1 billion by 1 billion, and then multiply your answer by 100. Count the zeros in the final answer.

Now, time how long it takes you to count to 100. How long would it take you to count to 100 a billion billion times?

Figure 5 *Radio telescopes receive radio waves from objects in space.*

Special Branches of Earth Science

In addition to the main branches of Earth science, there are branches that depend heavily on other areas of science. Earth scientists often find themselves in careers that rely on life science, chemistry, physics, and many other areas of science.

Environmental Science

The study of how humans interact with the environment is called *environmental science.* As shown in **Figure 6,** one task of an environmental scientist is to determine how humans affect the environment. Environmental science relies on geology, life science, chemistry, and physics to help preserve Earth's resources and to teach others how to use them wisely.

Figure 6 *This environmental scientist is measuring chemicals in the water to look for traces of urban or industrial pollution.*

Ecology

By studying the relationships between organisms and their surroundings, scientists can better understand the behavior of these organisms. An *ecologist* is a person who studies a community of organisms and their nonliving environment. Ecologists work in many fields, such as wildlife management, agriculture, forestry, and conservation.

Geochemistry

Geochemistry combines the studies of geology and chemistry. *Geochemists,* such as the one in **Figure 7,** specialize in the chemistry of rocks, minerals, and soil. By studying the chemistry of these materials, geochemists can determine the economic value of the materials. Geochemists also can determine what the environment was like when the rocks first formed. Additionally, geochemists study the distribution and effect of chemicals added to the environment by human activity.

Figure 7 *This geochemist is taking rock samples from the field so she can perform chemical analyses of them in a laboratory.*

Geography and Cartography

Physical geographers, who are educated in geology, biology, and physics, study the surface features of Earth. *Cartographers* make maps of those features by using aerial and satellite photos, and computer mapping systems. Have you ever wondered why cities are located where they are? Often, the location of a city is determined by geography. Many cities, such as the one in **Figure 8,** were built near bodies of water because boats were used for transporting people and trade items. Rivers and lakes also provide communities with water for drinking and for raising crops and animals.

✓ Reading Check What do cartographers do?

Figure 8 *The Mississippi River helped St. Louis become the large city it is today.*

SECTION
Review

Summary

- The four major branches of Earth science are geology, oceanography, meteorology, and astronomy.

- Other areas of science that are linked to Earth science are environmental science, geochemistry, ecology, geography, and cartography.

- Some careers that are associated with branches of Earth science are volcanologist, seismologist, paleontologist, oceanographer, meteorologist, and astronomer.

Using Key Terms

1. Use each of the following terms in a separate sentence: *geology, oceanography,* and *astronomy*.

Understanding Key Ideas

2. Which of the following Earth scientists would study tornadoes?
   a. a geologist
   b. an oceanographer
   c. a meteorologist
   d. an astronomer

3. On which major branch of Earth science does geochemistry rely?
   a. geology
   b. oceanography
   c. meteorology
   d. astronomy

4. List the major branches of Earth science.

5. In which major branch of Earth science would a scientist study black smokers?

6. List two branches of Earth science that rely heavily on other areas of science. Explain how the branches rely on the other areas of science.

7. List and describe three Earth science careers.

Math Skills

8. Each week, a volcanologist reads 80 pages in a book about volcanoes. In a 4-week period, how many pages will the volcanologist read?

Critical Thinking

9. **Making Inferences** If you were a *hydrogeologist,* what kind of work would you do?

10. **Identifying Relationships** Explain why an ecologist might need to understand geology.

11. **Applying Concepts** Explain how an airline pilot would use Earth science in his or her career.

SCI**LINKS**.

NSTA
Developed and maintained by the National Science Teachers Association

For a variety of links related to this chapter, go to www.scilinks.org

Topic: Branches of Earth Science
SciLinks code: HSM0191

Scientific Methods in Earth Science

Imagine that you are standing in a thick forest on the bank of a river. Suddenly, you hear a booming noise, and you feel the ground begin to shake.

You notice a creature's head looming over the treetops. The creature's head is so high that its neck must be 20 m long! Then, the entire animal comes into view. You now understand why the ground is shaking. The giant animal is *Seismosaurus hallorum* (SIEZ moh SAWR uhs hah LOHR uhm), the "earth shaker," illustrated in **Figure 1.**

Learning About the Natural World

The description of the *Seismosaurus hallorum* is not based on imagination alone. Scientists have been studying dinosaurs since the 1800s. Scientists gather bits and pieces of information about dinosaurs and their environment. Then, they re-create what dinosaurs might have been like 150 million years ago. But how do scientists put it all together? How do they know if they have discovered a new species? Asking questions like these is the beginning of a process scientists use to learn more about the natural world.

Reading Check How do scientists begin to learn about the natural world? (*See the Appendix for answers to Reading Checks.*)

Figure 1 Seismosaurus hallorum *is one of the largest dinosaurs known.*

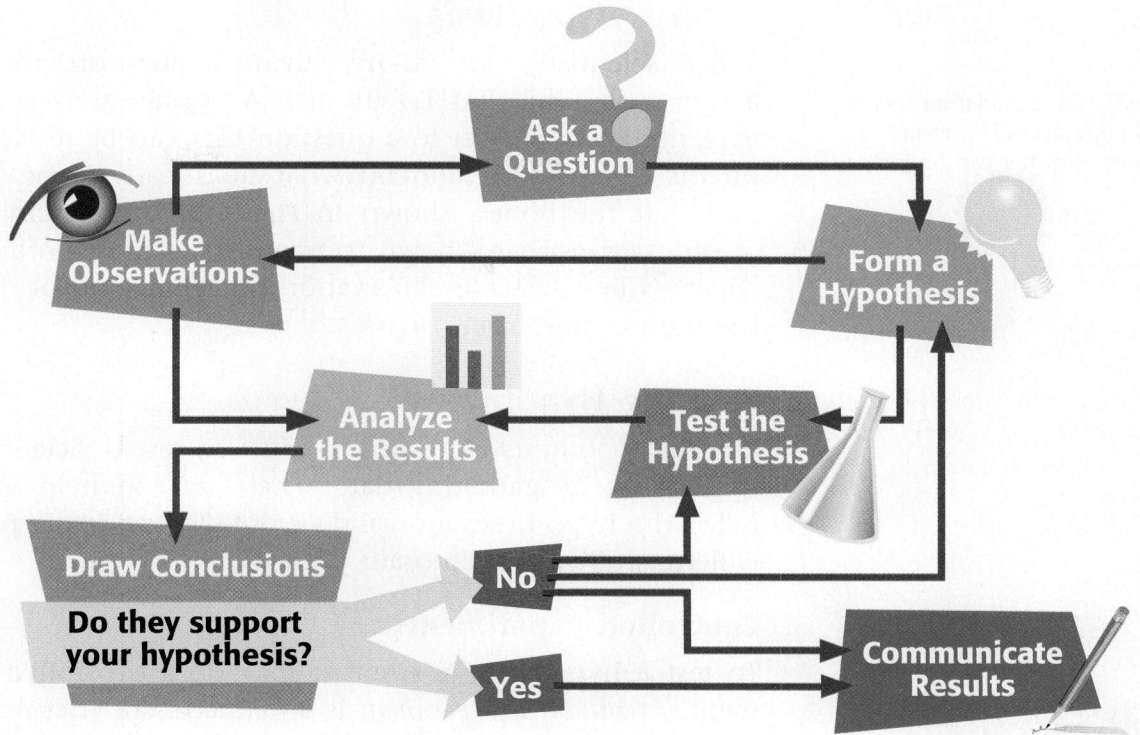

Figure 2 *Steps of scientific methods are illustrated in this flowchart. Notice that there are several ways to follow the paths.*

What Are Scientific Methods?

When scientists observe the natural world, they often think of a question or problem. But scientists don't just guess answers. Instead, they follow a series of steps called *scientific methods.* **Scientific methods** are a series of steps that scientists use to answer questions and solve problems. The most basic steps are shown in **Figure 2.**

Although scientific methods have several steps, there is not a set procedure. Scientists may use all of the steps or just some of the steps. They may even repeat some of the steps or do them in a different order. The goal of scientific methods is to come up with reliable answers and solutions. Scientists use scientific methods to gain insight into the problems they investigate.

scientific methods a series of steps followed to solve problems

Ask a Question

Asking a question helps focus the purpose of an investigation. For example, David D. Gillette, a scientist who studies fossils, examined some bones found by hikers in New Mexico in 1979. He could tell they were bones of a dinosaur. But he didn't know what kind of dinosaur. Gillette may have asked, "What kind of dinosaur did these bones come from?" Gillette knew that in order to answer this question, he would have to use scientific methods.

Form a Hypothesis

When scientists want to investigate a question, they form a hypothesis (hie PAHTH uh sis). A **hypothesis** is a possible explanation or answer to a question that can be tested. Based on his observations and on what he already knew, Gillette said that the bones, shown in **Figure 3,** came from a kind of dinosaur not yet known to scientists. This hypothesis was Gillette's best testable explanation for what kind of dinosaur the bones came from.

Test the Hypothesis

Once a hypothesis is formed, it must be tested. Scientists test hypotheses by gathering data. The data can help scientists tell if the hypotheses are valid or not. To test his hypothesis, Gillette studied the dinosaur bones.

Controlled Experiments

To test a hypothesis, a scientist may do a controlled experiment. A *controlled experiment* is an experiment that tests only one factor, or *variable,* at a time. All other variables remain constant. By changing only one variable, scientists can see the results of just that one change. If more than one variable is changed, scientists cannot easily determine which variable caused the outcome. For example, let's say you tried to make a gelatin fruit mold, but the gelatin would not harden. The next time you made the gelatin fruit mold, you take out the oranges and pineapples. The gelatin might harden this time, but you won't know whether the pineapples or the oranges caused the gelatin not to harden the first time.

For another activity related to this chapter, go to **go.hrw.com** and type in the keyword **HZ5WESW.**

Figure 3 *Gillette and his team had to carefully dig out the bones before taking them to the laboratory for further study.*

Making Observations

Controlled experiments are important for testing hypotheses. Some scientists, however, often depend more on observations than experiments to test their hypotheses. Because scientists cannot always control all variables, some scientists often observe nature and collect large amounts of data. Gillette took hundreds of measurements of the dinosaur bones, as illustrated in **Figure 4.** He compared his measurements with those of bones from known dinosaurs. He also visited museums and talked with other scientists.

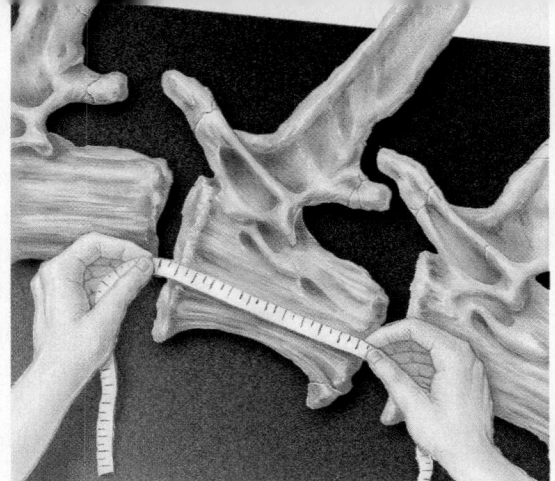

Figure 4 *Gillette observed and measured the dinosaur bones to test his hypothesis.*

Keeping Accurate Records

When testing a hypothesis, a scientist's expectations can affect what he or she actually observes. For this reason, it is important for scientists to keep clear, honest, and accurate records of their experiments and observations. Scientists should present findings supported by scientific data, not by opinions. When possible, scientists will repeat experiments to verify their findings. A hypothesis cannot be examined usefully in a scientific way without enough data. Just one example is never enough to prove something true. However, one example could prove that something is not true.

Analyze the Results

Once scientists finish their tests, they must analyze the results. Scientists often make tables and graphs to organize and summarize their data. When Gillette analyzed his results, he found that the bones of the mystery dinosaur did not match the bones of any known dinosaur. The bones were either too large or too different in shape.

✓ Reading Check Why would scientists create graphs and tables of their data?

CONNECTION TO Oceanography

WRITING SKILL **Making Hypotheses** Scientists exploring the Texas Gulf Coast have discovered American Indian artifacts that are thousands of years old. The odd thing is that the artifacts were buried in the sea floor several meters below sea level. These artifacts had not been moved since they were originally buried. If American Indian artifacts are several meters below sea level, the question to ask is, "Why are they there?" In your **science journal,** form a hypothesis that answers this question. Remember, your hypothesis must be stated in such a way that it can be tested using scientific methods.

Earth Shaker!
One foot is equal to 0.305 m. If a *Seismosaurus hallorum* was 45 m long, how long is the *Seismosaurus hallorum* in inches?

Draw Conclusions

After carefully analyzing the results of their tests, scientists must conclude whether the results supported the hypothesis. Hypotheses are valuable even if they turn out not to be true. If a hypothesis is not supported by the tests, scientists may repeat the investigation to check for errors. Or they may ask new questions and form new hypotheses.

Based on all his studies, Gillette concluded that the bones found in New Mexico were indeed from an unknown dinosaur. This dinosaur, shown in **Figure 5,** was probably 45 m long and weighed between 60 and 100 tons. The creature certainly fit the name Gillette gave it—*Seismosaurus hallorum,* the "earth shaker."

Communicate Results

After finishing an investigation, scientists communicate their results. In this way, scientists share with others what they have learned. Science depends on the sharing of information. Scientists share information by writing reports for scientific journals and giving lectures on their results.

Gillette shared his discovery of *Seismosaurus* at a press conference at the New Mexico Museum of Natural History and Science. He later sent a report that described his investigation to the *Journal of Vertebrate Paleontology*.

When a scientist reveals new evidence, other scientists will evaluate the evidence. They will review the experimental procedure, the data from the experiments, and the reasoning behind explanations. This questioning of evidence and explanations is part of scientific inquiry. Scientists know that their results may be questioned by other scientists. They also understand that data aren't always interpreted the same way by two people. In some cases, another scientist may have published different results on the same topic. In this case, scientists may come to different conclusions. When there is disagreement, scientists will further investigate to find the truth.

✓ Reading Check Why is it important for the scientific community to review new evidence?

Figure 5 *This model of the skeleton of* Seismosaurus hallorum *is based on Gillette's research. The darker-colored bones are those that have been found so far.*

2 m

Case Closed?

Even after results are reviewed and accepted by the scientific community for publication, the investigation of the topic may not be finished. New evidence may become available. The scientist may change the hypothesis based on the new evidence. In other cases, the scientist may have more questions that arise from the original evidence. For example, with the discovery of the *Seismosaurus,* Gillette may have wondered what the *Seismosaurus* ate. What environment did it live in? How did it become extinct? As shown in **Figure 6,** Gillette continues to use scientific methods to answer these questions.

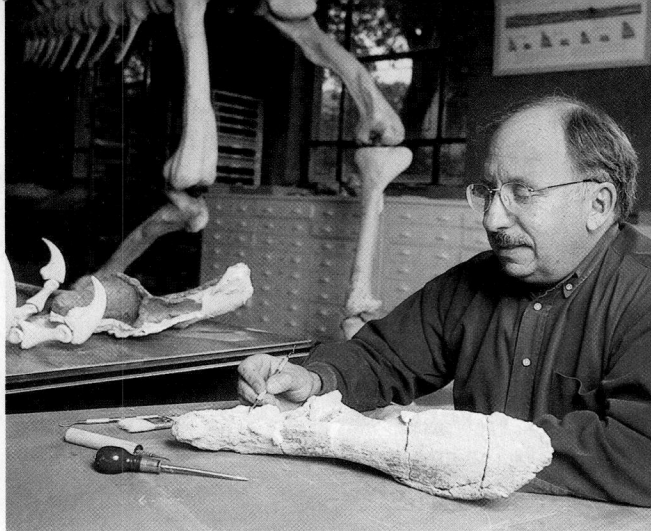

Figure 6 *Gillette continues to study the bones of* Seismosaurus *for new insights into the past.*

SECTION
Review

Summary

- Scientists begin to learn about the natural world by asking questions.

- The steps of scientific methods are to ask a question, form a hypothesis, test the hypothesis, analyze the results, draw conclusions, and communicate results.

- Communicating results allows the evidence to be reviewed for accuracy by other scientists.

- Scientific investigations often lead people to ask new questions about the topic.

Using Key Terms

1. Use the following terms in the same sentence: *scientific method* and *hypothesis*.

Understanding Key Ideas

2. Which of the following is NOT part of scientific methods?
   a. ask a question
   b. test the hypothesis
   c. analyze results
   d. close the case

3. Which of the following is the step in scientific methods in which a scientist uses a controlled experiment?
   a. form a hypothesis
   b. test the hypothesis
   c. analyze results
   d. communicate results

4. Explain how scientists use more than imagination to form answers about the natural world.

5. Why do scientists communicate the results of their investigations?

6. For what reason might a scientist change his or her hypothesis after it has already been accepted?

Math Skills

7. If the *Seismosaurus*'s neck is 20 m long and the scientist studying *Seismosaurus* is 2 m long, how many scientists, lined up head to toe, would it take to equal the length of a *Seismosaurus* neck?

Critical Thinking

8. **Applying Concepts** Why might two scientists develop different hypotheses based on the same observations? Explain.

9. **Evaluating Hypotheses** Explain why Gillette's hypothesis—that the bones came from a kind of dinosaur unknown to science—is a testable hypothesis.

SCiLINKS®

NSTA
Developed and maintained by the
National Science Teachers Association

For a variety of links related to this chapter, go to www.scilinks.org

Topic: Scientific Methods
SciLinks code: HSM1359

Scientific Models

For your next science project, you will be studying volcanoes. To help you learn more about volcanoes, your teacher suggests using baking soda, vinegar, and clay. How can this help you learn about volcanoes?

Baking soda, vinegar, and clay were the materials used to make the model of the volcano shown in **Figure 1.** By building a model, you can learn more about how volcanoes work.

Types of Scientific Models

A pattern, plan, representation, or description designed to show the structure or workings of an object, system, or concept is a **model.** Models are used to help us understand the natural world. With a model, a scientist can explain or analyze an object, system, or concept in more detail. Models can be used to represent things that are too small to see, such as atoms, or too large to completely see, such as the Earth or the solar system. Models can also be used to explain the past and present and to predict the future. There are three major types of scientific models—physical, mathematical, and conceptual.

Physical Models

Physical models are models that you can touch. Model airplanes, cars, and dolls are all physical models. Physical models often look like the real thing. However, physical models have limitations. For example, a doll is a model of a baby, but a doll does not act like a baby.

Figure 1 *The model volcano looks a little bit like the real volcano, but the model cannot destroy acres of forests with hot lava!*

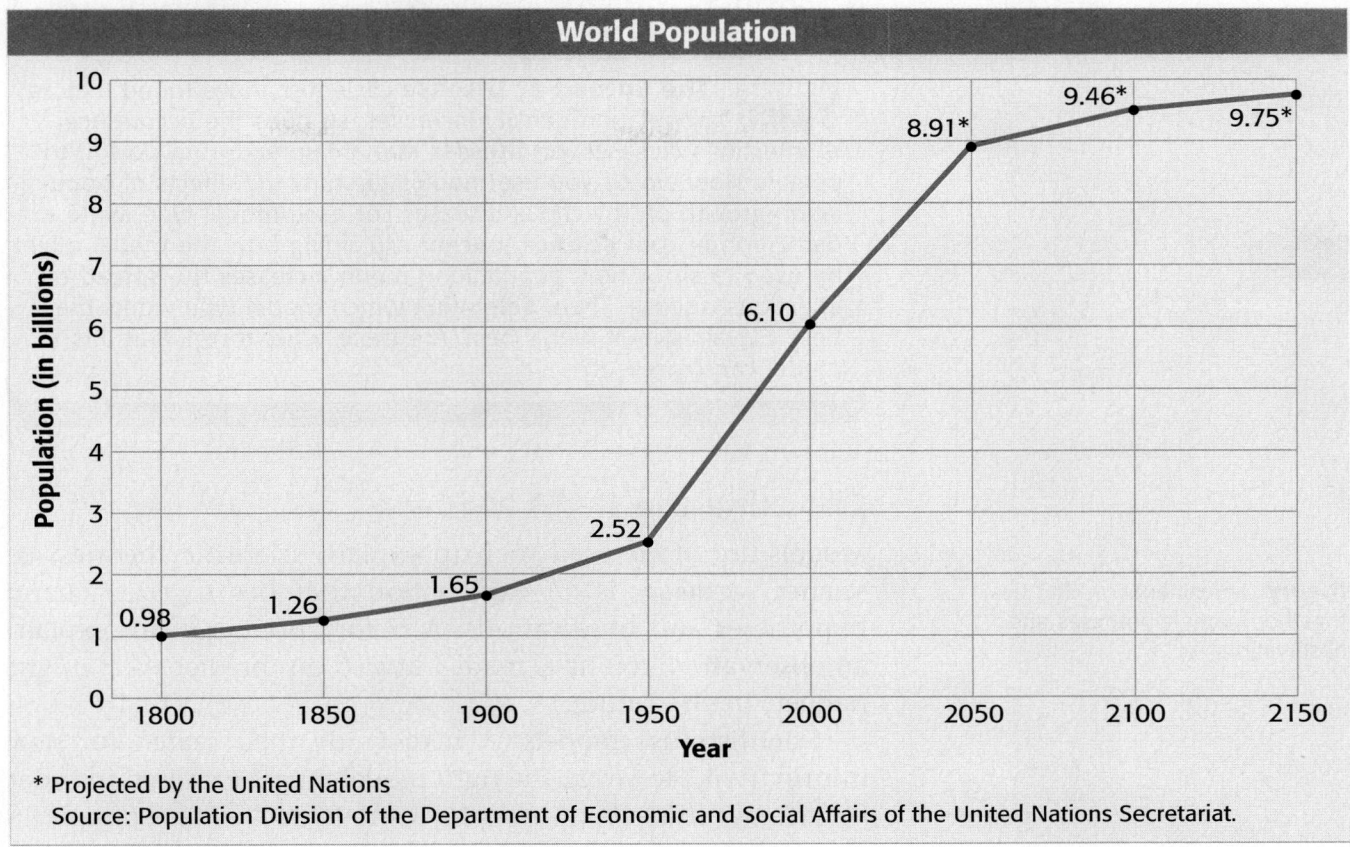

World Population

Population (in billions)

0.98 — 1800
1.26 — 1850
1.65 — 1900
2.52 — 1950
6.10 — 2000
8.91* — 2050
9.46* — 2100
9.75* — 2150

Year

* Projected by the United Nations
  Source: Population Division of the Department of Economic and Social Affairs of the United Nations Secretariat.

Figure 2 *This graph shows human population growth predicted by a mathematical model run on a computer.*

Mathematical Models

A *mathematical model* is made up of mathematical equations and data. Some mathematical models are simple. These models allow you to calculate things such as how far a car will go in an hour or how much you would weigh on the moon. Other models are so complex that computers are needed to process them. Look at **Figure 2.** Scientists used a mathematical model to predict population growth in the world. There are many variables that affect population growth. A computer helped process these variables into a model scientists could use.

Conceptual Models

The third type of model is a *conceptual model*. Some conceptual models are systems of ideas. Others are based on making comparisons with familiar things to help illustrate or explain an idea. One example of a conceptual model is the big bang theory. The *big bang theory* is an explanation of the structure of the universe. Conceptual models are composed of many hypotheses. Each hypothesis is supported through scientific methods.

Reading Check What is the big bang theory? (*See the Appendix for answers to Reading Checks.*)

Choosing the Right Model

theory an explanation that ties together many hypotheses and observations

Models are often used to help explain scientific theories. In science, a **theory** is an explanation that ties together many hypotheses and observations. A theory not only can explain an observation you have made but also can predict what might happen in the future.

Scientists use models to help guide their search for new information. However, the right model must be chosen in order for the scientist to be able to learn from it. For example, a physical model is useful to understand objects that are too small or too large to see completely. In these cases, a model can help you picture the thing in your mind.

The information that scientists gather by using models can help support a theory or show it to be wrong. Models can be changed or replaced. These changes happen when new observations are made that lead scientists to change their theories. For example, **Figure 3** shows that as scientists' knowledge of the Earth changed, so did the Earth's model.

Figure 3 *Scientists' model of Earth changed as new information was gathered.*

Climate Models

Scientists who study the Earth's atmosphere have developed mathematical climate models to try to imitate Earth's climate. A climate model is like a complicated recipe with thousands of ingredients. One important ingredient is the level of carbon dioxide in the atmosphere. Other ingredients are land and ocean-water temperatures around the globe as well as information about clouds, cloud cover, snow, ice cover, and ocean currents.

You may be wondering how a model can be created with so much data. Because of the development of more powerful computers, scientists are able to process large amounts of data from many different variables, as shown in **Figure 4.** These mathematical models do not make exact predictions about future climates, but they do estimate what might happen. Someday, these models may help scientists prevent serious climate problems, such as global warming or another ice age.

Figure 4 *This meteorologist is using a high-speed supercomputer to do climate modeling.*

✓ *Reading Check* Why is a climate model complicated?

SECTION Review

Summary

- Models are used to help us understand the natural world.
- There are three types of models: physical models, mathematical models, and conceptual models.
- Scientists must choose the right type of model to learn about a topic.
- A climate model is a mathematical model with so many variables that powerful computers are needed to process the data.

Using Key Terms

1. In your own words, write a definition for each of the following terms: *model* and *theory*.

Understanding Key Ideas

2. Which of the following types of models are systems of ideas?
   a. physical models
   b. mathematical models
   c. conceptual models
   d. climate models

3. Why do scientists use models?

4. Describe the three types of models.

5. Which type of model would you use to study objects that are too small to be seen? Explain.

6. Describe why the climate model is a mathematical model.

Math Skills

7. A model of a bridge is 1 m long and 2.5% of the actual size of the bridge. How long is the actual bridge?

Critical Thinking

8. **Analyzing Ideas** Describe one advantage of physical models.

9. **Applying Concepts** What type of model would you use to study an earthquake? Explain.

Measurement and Safety

Have you ever used your hand or your foot to measure the length of an object?

At one time, standardized units were based on parts of the body. Long ago, in England, the standard for an inch was three grains of barley. Using such units was not a very accurate way to measure things because they were based on objects that varied in size. Recognizing the need for a global measurement system, the French Academy of Sciences developed a system in the late 1700s. Over the next 200 years, the metric system, now called the *International System of Units* (SI), was refined.

Using the International System of Units

Today, most scientists and other people in almost all countries use the International System of Units. One advantage of using SI measurements is that all scientists can share and compare their observations and results. Another advantage of the SI is that all units are based on the number 10, which is a number that is easy to use in calculations. **Table 1** contains the commonly used SI units.

✓ *Reading Check* Why was the International System of Units developed? (*See the Appendix for answers to Reading Checks.*)

Table 1	Common SI Units and Conversions	
Length	**meter (m)**	
	kilometer (km)	1 km = 1,000 m
	decimeter (dm)	1 dm = 0.1 m
	centimeter (cm)	1 cm = 0.01 m
	millimeter (mm)	1 mm = 0.001 m
	micrometer (µm)	1 µm = 0.000001 m
	nanometer (nm)	1 nm = 0.000000001 m
Volume	**cubic meter (m³)**	
	cubic centimeter (cm³)	$1 \text{ cm}^3 = 0.000001 \text{ m}^3$
	liter (L)	$1 \text{ L} = 1 \text{ dm}^3 = 0.001 \text{ m}^3$
	milliliter (mL)	$1 \text{ mL} = 0.001 \text{ L} = 1 \text{ cm}^3$
Mass	**kilogram (kg)**	
	gram (g)	1 g = 0.001 kg
	milligram (mg)	1 mg = 0.000 001 kg
Temperature	**kelvin (K)**	
	Celsius (°C)	0°C = 273 K
		100°C = 373 K

Length

To measure length, a scientist uses meters (m). A **meter** is the basic SI unit of length. You may remember that SI units are based on the number 10. If you divide 1 m into 100 parts, for example, each part equals 1 cm. In other words, a centimeter equals one-hundredth of a meter. Some objects are so tiny that smaller units must be used. To describe the length of microscopic objects, scientists use micrometers (μm) or nanometers (nm). To describe the length of larger objects, scientists use kilometers (km).

Volume

Imagine that you are a scientist who needs to move some fossils to a museum. How many fossils will fit into a crate? The answer depends on the volume of the crate and the volume of each fossil. **Volume** is the measure of the size of a body or region in three-dimensional space.

The volume of a liquid is often given in liters (L). Liters are based on the meter. A cubic meter ($1 \ m^3$) is equal to 1,000 L. So, 1,000 L will fit into a box measuring 1 m on each side. The volume of a large, solid object is given in cubic meters. The volumes of smaller objects can be given in cubic centimeters (cm^3) or cubic millimeters (mm^3). To calculate the volume of a box-shaped object, multiply the object's length by its width and then multiply by its height.

The length, height, and width of irregularly shaped objects, such as rocks and fossils, are difficult to measure accurately. However, the volume of an irregularly shaped object can be determined by measuring the volume of liquid that the object displaces. The student in **Figure 1** is using a graduated cylinder to measure the volume of water a rock displaces.

meter the basic unit of length in the SI (symbol, m)

volume a measure of the size of a body or region in three-dimensional space

Taking Measurements

With a parent, measure the width of your kitchen table, using your hands as a unit of measure. First, use your own hand to determine the width of the table. Then, have your parent use his or her hand to measure the width of the table. Compare your measurement with that of your parent. Was the number of units the same? Explain why it is important to use standard units of measurement.

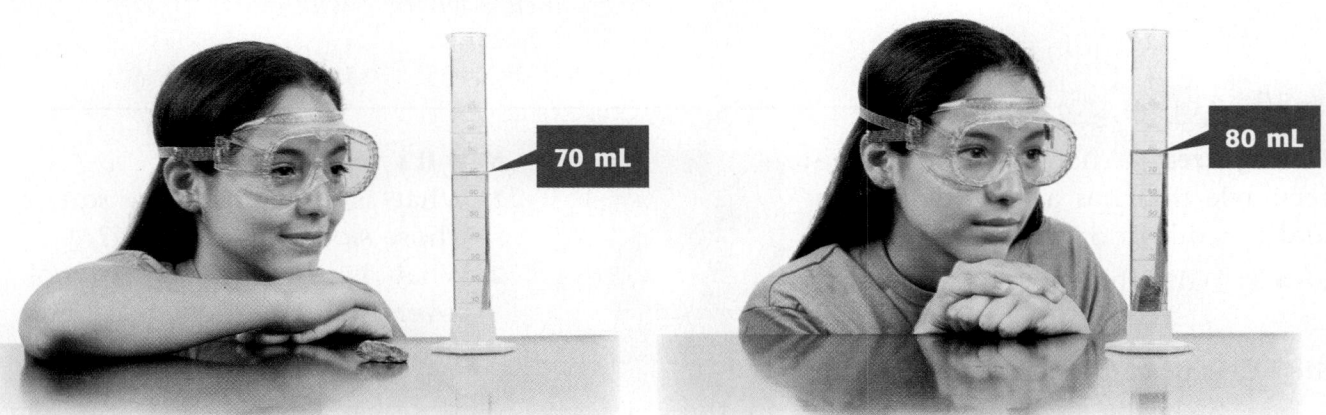

Figure 1 *This graduated cylinder contains 70 mL of water. After the rock was added, the water level moved to 80 mL. Because the rock displaced 10 mL of water and because 1 mL = 1 cm^3, the volume of the rock is 10 cm^3.*

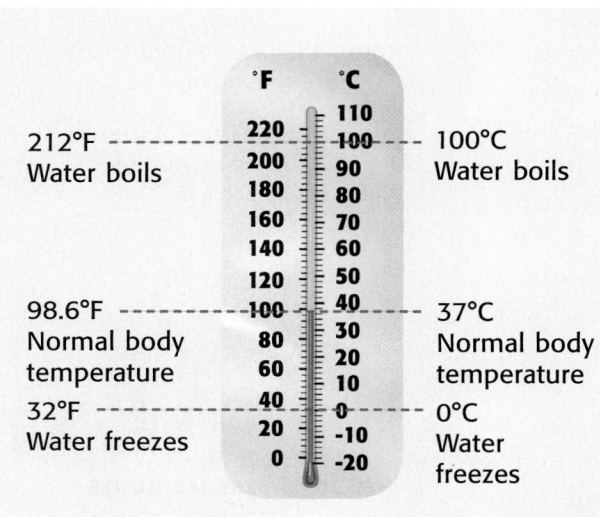

Figure 2 *This thermometer shows the relationship between degrees Fahrenheit and degrees Celsius.*

mass a measure of the amount of matter in an object

temperature a measure of how hot (or cold) something is

area a measure of the size of a surface or a region

Mass

A measure of the amount of matter in an object is **mass**. The kilogram (kg) is the basic unit for mass. The kilogram is used to describe the mass of things such as boulders. But many common objects are not so large. Grams (g) are used to describe the mass of smaller objects, such as an apple. One thousand grams equals 1 kg. The mass of large objects, such as an elephant, is given in metric tons. A metric ton equals 1,000 kg.

Temperature

Temperature is the measure of how hot (or cold) something is. You are probably used to describing temperature with degrees Fahrenheit (°F). For example, if your body temperature is 101°F, you have a fever. Scientists, however, usually use degrees Celsius (°C). The thermometer in **Figure 2** shows the relationship between degrees Fahrenheit and degrees Celsius. The kelvin, the SI base unit for temperature, is also used in science.

Area

How much paper would you need to cover the top of your desk? To answer this question, you must find the area of the desk. **Area** is a measure of how much surface an object has. The units for area are square units, such as square meters (m²), square centimeters (cm²), and square kilometers (km²). To calculate the area of a square or rectangle, first measure the length and width. Then, use the following equation:

$$area = length \times width$$

Finding Area What is the area of a rectangle that has a length of 4 cm and a width of 5 cm?

Step 1: Write the equation for area.

$$area = length \times width$$

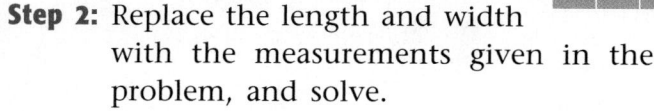

Step 2: Replace the length and width with the measurements given in the problem, and solve.

$$area = 4 \text{ cm} \times 5 \text{ cm} = 20 \text{ cm}^2$$

Now It's Your Turn
1. What is the area of a square whose sides measure 5 m?
2. What is the area of a book cover that is 22 cm wide and 28 cm long?

Density

The ratio of the mass of a substance to the volume of the substance is the substance's **density**. Because density is the ratio of mass to volume, units often used for density are grams per milliliter (g/mL) and grams per cubic centimeter (g/cm^3). You can calculate density by using the following equation:

$$density = \frac{mass}{volume}$$

Safety Rules!

Science is exciting and fun, but it can also be dangerous. Always follow your teacher's instructions. Before starting any scientific investigation, obtain your teacher's permission. Read the lab procedures completely and carefully before you start. Pay attention to safety information and caution statements. **Figure 3** shows the safety symbols that are used in this book.

✓ **Reading Check** What should you do before you start a scientific investigation?

Figure 3   Safety Symbols

Eye protection

Clothing protection

Hand safety

Heating safety

Electric safety

Sharp object

Chemical safety

Animal safety

Plant safety

density the ratio of the mass of a substance to the volume of the substance

SECTION Review

Summary

- The SI is the standard system of measurement used by scientists around the world.
- The basic SI units of measurement for length, volume, mass, and temperature are the meter, liter, kilogram, and kelvin, respectively.
- Safety rules must be followed at all times during a scientific investigation.

Using Key Terms

The statements below are false. For each statement, replace the underlined term to make a true statement.

1. The length multiplied by the width of an object is the <u>density</u> of the object.

2. The measure of the amount of matter in an object is the <u>area</u>.

Understanding Key Ideas

3. Which of the following SI units is most often used to measure length?
   a. meter
   b. liter
   c. gram
   d. degrees Celsius

4. What are two benefits of using the International System of Units?

5. At what temperature in degrees Celsius does water freeze?

6. Why is it important to follow safety rules?

Math Skills

7. Find the density of an object that has a mass of 34 g and a volume of 14 mL.

Critical Thinking

8. **Making Comparisons** Which weighs more: a pound of feathers or a pound of lead? Explain.

SCI LINKS

NSTA
Developed and maintained by the National Science Teachers Association

For a variety of links related to this chapter, go to www.scilinks.org

Topic: Systems of Measurement
SciLinks code: HSM1490

Model-Making Lab

Using Scientific Methods

Geologists often use a technique called core sampling to learn what underground rock layers look like. This technique involves drilling several holes in the ground in different places and taking samples of the underground rock or soil. Geologists then compare the samples from each hole at each depth to construct a diagram that shows the bigger picture.

In this activity, you will model the process geologists use to diagram underground rock layers. You will first use modeling clay to form a rock-layer model. You will then exchange models with a classmate, take core samples, and draw a diagram of your classmate's rock layers.

OBJECTIVES

Design a model to demonstrate core sampling.

Create a diagram of a classmate's model by using the core sample method.

MATERIALS

- knife, plastic
- modeling clay, three or four colors
- pan or box, opaque
- pencil, unsharpened
- pencils or markers, three or four colors
- PVC pipe, 1/2 in.

SAFETY

- Form a plan for your rock layers. Make a sketch of the layers. Your sketch should include the colors of clay in several layers of varying thicknesses. Note: Do not let the classmates who will be using your model see your plan.

- In the pan or box, mold the clay into the shape of the lowest layer in your sketch.

- Repeat the procedure described in the second bullet for each additional layer of clay. Exchange your rock-layer model with a classmate.

Ask a Question

1 Can unseen features be revealed by sampling parts of the whole?

Form a Hypothesis

2 Form a hypothesis about whether taking core samples from several locations will give a good indication of the entire hidden feature.

Test the Hypothesis

3 Choose three places on the surface of the clay to drill holes. The holes should be far apart and in a straight line. (Do not remove the clay from the pan or box.)

4 Slowly push the PVC pipe through all the layers of clay. Slowly remove the pipe.

5 Gently push the clay out of the pipe with an unsharpened pencil. This clay is a core sample.

6 Draw the core sample, and record your observations. Be sure to use a different color of pencil or marker for each layer.

7 Repeat steps 4–6 for the next two core samples. Make sure your drawings are side by side and in the same order as the samples in the model.

Analyze the Results

1 **Examining Data** Look at the pattern of rock layers in each of your core samples. Think about how the rock layers between the core samples might look. Then, make a diagram of the rock layers.

2 **Organizing Data** Complete your diagram by coloring the rest of each rock layer.

Draw Conclusions

3 **Evaluating Data** Use the plastic knife to cut the clay model along a line connecting the three holes. Remove one side of the model so that you can see the layers.

4 **Evaluating Models** How well does your rock-layer diagram match the model? Explain.

5 **Evaluating Methods** What are some limitations of your diagram as a model of the rock layers?

6 **Drawing Conclusions** Do your conclusions support your hypothesis? Explain your answer.

Applying Your Data

List two ways that the core-sampling method could be improved.

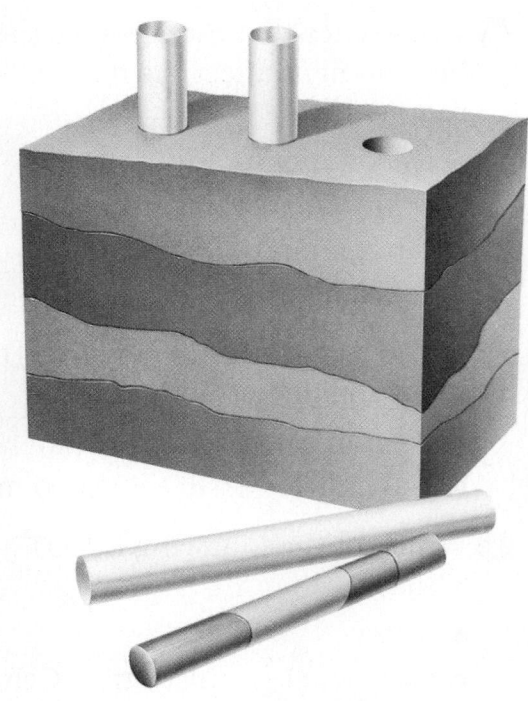

Chapter Review

USING KEY TERMS

Complete each of the following sentences by choosing the correct term from the word bank.

geology
astronomy
scientific methods
hypothesis

1 The study of the origin, history, and structure of the Earth and the processes that shape the Earth is called ___.

2 An explanation that is based on prior scientific research or observations and that can be tested is called a(n) ___.

3 ___ are a series of steps followed to solve problems.

UNDERSTANDING KEY IDEAS

Multiple Choice

4 The science that uses geology to study how humans affect the natural environment is
a. paleontology.
b. environmental science.
c. cartography.
d. volcanology.

5 A pencil measures 14 cm long. How many millimeters long is it?
a. 1.4 mm
c. 1,400 mm
b. 140 mm
d. 1,400,000 mm

6 Which of the following is NOT an SI unit?
a. meter
c. liter
b. foot
d. degrees Celsius

7 Which of the following is a limitation of models?
a. They are large enough to be seen.
b. They do not act exactly like the thing they model.
c. They are smaller than the thing they model.
d. They use familiar things to model unfamiliar things.

8 Gillette's hypothesis was
a. supported by his results.
b. not supported by his results.
c. based only on observations.
d. based only on what he already knew.

Short Answer

9 Why would scientific investigations lead to new scientific investigations?

10 How and why do scientists use models?

11 What are three types of models? Give an example of each.

12 What problems could occur if scientists didn't communicate the results of their investigations?

13 What problems could occur if there were not an International System of Units?

14 Which safety symbols would you expect to see for an experiment that requires the use of acid?

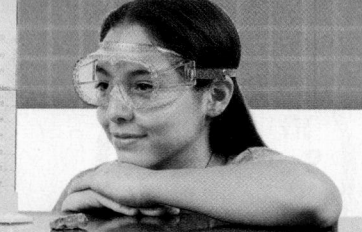

CRITICAL THINKING

15 **Concept Mapping** Use the following terms to create a concept map: *Earth science, scientific methods, hypothesis, problem, question, experiment,* and *observations.*

16 **Analyzing Processes** Why do you not need to complete the steps of scientific methods in a specific order?

17 **Evaluating Conclusions** Why might two scientists working on the same problem draw different conclusions?

18 **Analyzing Methods** Scientific methods often begin with observation. How does observation limit what scientists can study?

19 **Making Comparisons** A rock that contains fossil seashells might be studied by scientists in at least two branches of Earth science. Name those branches. Why did you choose those two branches?

INTERPRETING GRAPHICS

Use the graph below to answer the questions that follow.

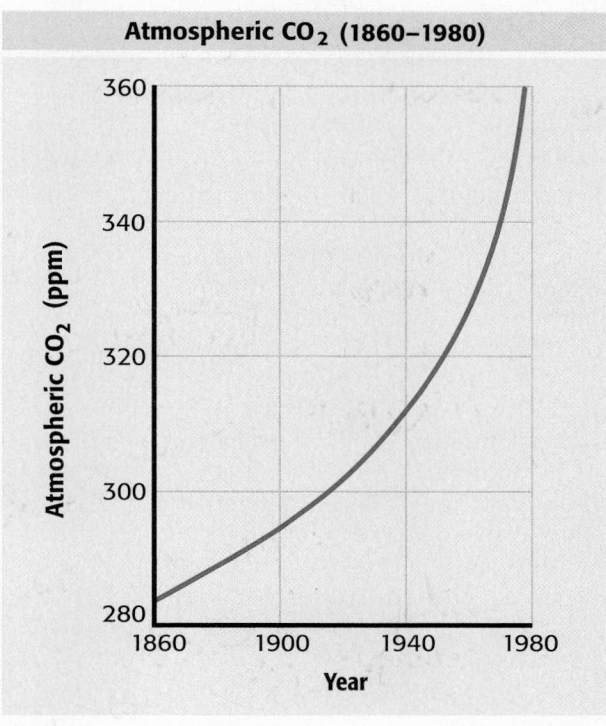

Atmospheric CO_2 (1860–1980)

20 Has the amount of CO_2 in the atmosphere increased or decreased since 1860?

21 The line on the graph is curved. What does this curve indicate?

22 Was the rate of change in the level of CO_2 between 1940 and 1960 higher or lower than it was between 1880 and 1900? How can you tell?

23 What conclusions can you draw from reading this graph?

Standardized Test Preparation

Read each of the passages below. Then, answer the questions that follow each passage.

Passage 1 Scientists look for answers by asking questions. For instance, scientists have wondered if there is some relationship between Earth's core and Earth's magnetic field. To form their hypothesis, scientists started with what they knew: Earth has a dense, solid inner core and a molten outer core. They then created a computer model to simulate how Earth's magnetic field is generated. The model predicted that Earth's inner core spins in the same direction as the rest of the Earth but slightly faster than the surface. If that hypothesis is correct, it might explain how Earth's magnetic field is generated. But how could the researchers test the hypothesis? Because scientists couldn't drill down to the core, they had to get their information indirectly. They decided to track seismic waves created by earthquakes.

1. In the passage, what does *simulate* mean?
- **A** to look or act like
- **B** to process
- **C** to calculate
- **D** to predict

2. According to the passage, what do scientists wonder?
- **F** if the Earth's inner core was molten
- **G** if there was a relationship between Earth's core and Earth's magnetic field
- **H** if the Earth had a solid outer core
- **I** if computers could model the Earth's core

3. What did the model predict?
- **A** The Earth's outer core is molten.
- **B** The Earth's inner core is molten.
- **C** The Earth's inner core spins in the same direction as the rest of the Earth.
- **D** The Earth's outer core spins in the same direction as the rest of the Earth.

Passage 2 Scientists analyzed seismic data for a 30-year period. They knew that seismic waves traveling through the inner core along a north-south path travel faster than waves passing through it along an east-west line. Scientists searched seismic data records to see if the orientation of the "fast path" for seismic waves changed over time. They found that in the last 30 years, the direction of the "fast path" for seismic waves had indeed shifted. This is strong evidence that Earth's core does travel faster than the surface, and it strengthens the hypothesis that the spinning core creates Earth's magnetic field.

1. In the passage, what does *orientation* mean?
- **A** speed
- **B** direction
- **C** magnetic field
- **D** intensity

2. What evidence did scientists find?
- **F** The Earth's core does travel faster than the surface.
- **G** The "fast path" does not change.
- **H** Seismic waves travel faster along an east-west line.
- **I** The spinning core does not create the Earth's magnetic field.

3. What do scientists hypothesize about the Earth's magnetic field?
- **A** It was found in the last 30 years.
- **B** It travels faster along a north-south path.
- **C** It is losing its strength.
- **D** It is created by the spinning core.

The table below contains data that shows the relationship between volume and pressure. Use the table to answer the questions that follow.

Volume (L)	Pressure (kPa)
0.5	4,960
1.0	2,480
2.0	1,240
3.0	827

1. What is the pressure when the volume is 2.0 L?

A 4,960 kPa

B 2,480 kPa

C 1,240 kPa

D 827 kPa

2. What is the volume when the pressure is 827 kPa?

F 0.5 L

G 1.0 L

H 2.0 L

I 3.0 L

3. What is the change in pressure when the volume is increased from 0.5 L to 1.0 L?

A 4,960 kPa

B 2,480 kPa

C 1,240 kPa

D 0.50 kPa

4. Which of the following patterns best describes the data?

F When the volume is doubled, the pressure is tripled.

G When the volume is tripled, the pressure is cut in half.

H As the volume increases, the pressure remains the same.

I As the volume increases, the pressure decreases.

Read each question below, and choose the best answer.

1. The original design for a boat shows a rectangular shape that is 5 m long and 1.5 m wide. If the design is reduced to 3.4 m long and 1 m wide, by how much does the area of the boat decrease?

A 1.7 m^2

B 4.1 m^2

C 7.5 m^2

D 9.2 m^2

2. If *density = mass/volume,* what is the density of an object that has a mass of 50 g and a volume of 2.6 cm^3?

F 0.052 cm^3/g

G 19.2 g/cm^3

H 47.4 g/cm^3

I 130 g/cm^3

3. During a chemical change, two separate pieces of matter combined into one. The mass of the final product is 82 g. The masses of the original pieces must equal the final product's mass. What are the possible masses of the original pieces of matter?

A 2 g and 18 g

B 2 g and 41 g

C 12 g and 8 g

D 42 g and 40 g

4. An adult *Seismosaurus hallorum* weighs 82 tons. A baby *Seismosaurus hallorum* weighs 46 tons. The weight of the baby *Seismosaurus hallorum* is what percentage of the weight of the adult *Seismosaurus hallorum*?

F 24%

G 44%

H 56%

I 98%

Standardized Test Preparation

Science in Action

Science, Technology, and Society

A "Ship" That Flips?

Does your school's laboratory have doors on the floor or tables bolted sideways to the walls? A lab like this exists, and you can find it floating in the ocean. *FLIP, or Floating Instrument Platform*, is a 108 m long ocean research vessel that can tilt 90°. *FLIP* is towed to an area that scientists want to study. To flip the vessel, empty chambers within the vessel are filled with water. The *FLIP* begins tilting until almost all of the vessel is underwater. Having most of the vessel below the ocean's surface stabilizes the vessel against wind and waves. Scientists can collect accurate data from the ocean, even during a hurricane!

Social Studies ACTiViTY

Design your own *FLIP*. Make a map on poster board. Draw the layout of a living room, bathroom, and bedroom before your *FLIP* is tilted 90°. Include entrances and walkways to use when *FLIP* is not flipped.

Weird Science

It's Raining Fish and Frogs

What forms of precipitation have you seen fall from the sky? Rain, snow, hail, sleet, or fish? Wait a minute! Fish? Fish and frogs might not be a form of precipitation, but as early as the second century, they have been reported to fall from the sky during rainstorms. Scientists theorize that tornadoes or waterspouts that suck water into clouds can also suck up unsuspecting fish, frogs, or tadpoles that are near the surface of the water. After being sucked up into the clouds and carried a few miles, these reluctant travelers then rain down from the sky.

Language Arts ACTiViTY

WRITING SKILL You are a reporter for your local newspaper. On a rainy day in spring, while driving to work, you witness a downpour of frogs and fish. You pull off to the side of the road and interview other witnesses. Write an article describing this event for your local newspaper.

Sue Hendrickson

Paleontologist Could you imagine having a job in which you spent all day digging in the dirt? This is just one of Sue Hendrickson's job descriptions. But Hendrickson does not dig up flowers. Hendrickson is a paleontologist, and she digs up dinosaurs! Her most famous discovery is the bones of a *Tyrannosaurus rex*. *T. rex* is one of the largest meat-eating dinosaurs. It lived between 65 million and 85 million years ago. Walking tall at 6 m, *T. rex* was approximately 12.4 m long and weighed between 5 and 7 tons. Hendrickson's discovery is the most complete set of bones ever found of the *T. rex*. The dinosaur was named Sue to honor Hendrickson for her important find. From these bones, Hendrickson and other scientists have been able to learn more about the dinosaur, including how it lived millions of years ago. For example, Hendrickson and her team of scientists found the remains of Sue's last meal, part of a a duck-billed, plant-eating dinosaur called *Edmontosaurus* that weighed approximately 3.5 tons!

Math Activity

ACTIVITY

The *T. rex* named Sue weighed 7 tons and the *Edmontosaurus* weighed 3.5 tons. How much smaller is *Edmontosaurus* than Sue? Express your answer as a percentage.

go.hrw.com

To learn more about these Science in Action topics, visit go.hrw.com and type in the keyword **HZ5WESF.**

Current Science

Check out Current Science® articles related to this chapter by visiting go.hrw.com. Just type in the keyword HZ5CS01.

Maps as Models of the Earth

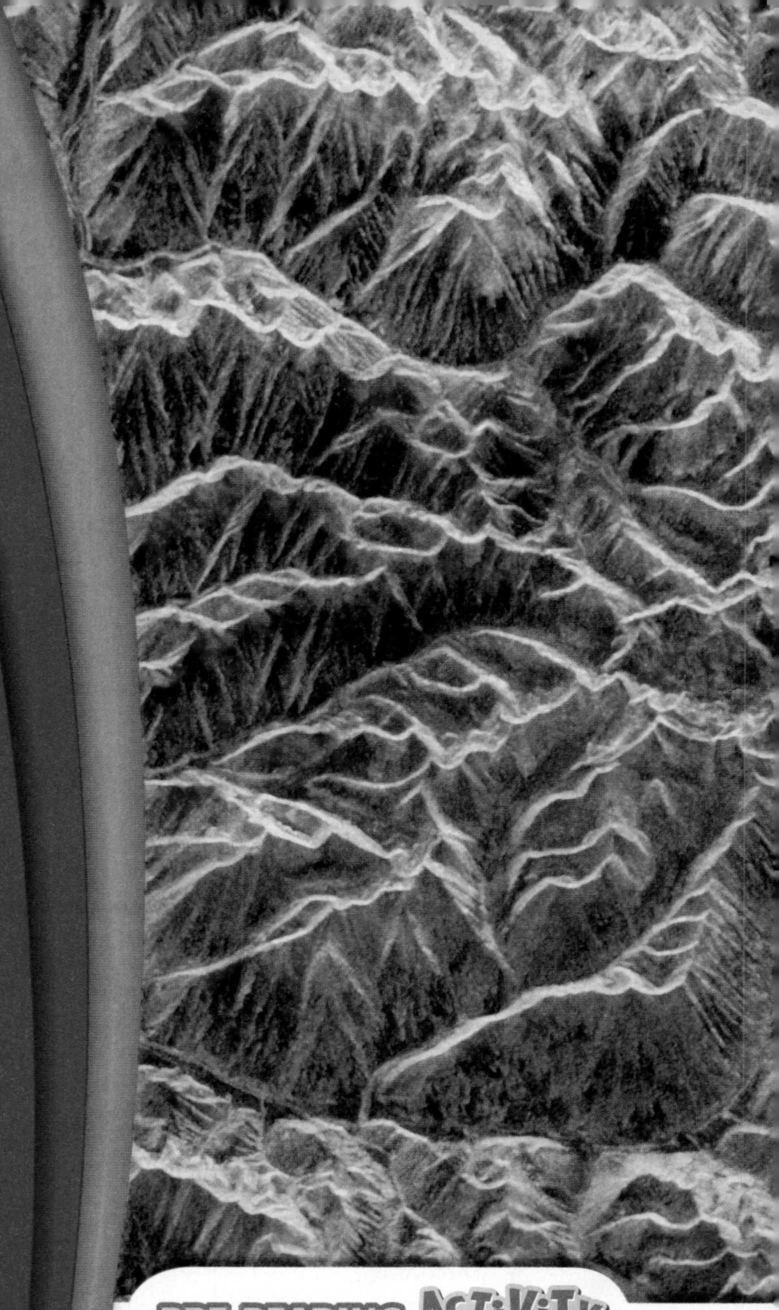

About the PHOTO

No ordinary camera took this picture! In fact, a camera wasn't used at all. This image is a radar image of a mountainous area of Tibet. It was taken from the space shuttle. Radar imaging is a method that scientists use to map areas of the Earth from far above the Earth's surface.

PRE-READING ACTIVITY

FOLDNOTES **Three-Panel Flip Chart**
Before you read the chapter, create the FoldNote entitled "Three-Panel Flip Chart" described in the **Study Skills** section of the Appendix. Label the flaps of the three-panel flip chart with "Cylindrical projection," "Conical projection," and "Azimuthal projection." As you read the chapter, write information you learn about each category under the appropriate flap.

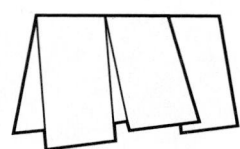

START-UP ACTIVITY

Follow the Yellow Brick Road

In this activity, you will not only learn how to read a map but you will also make a map that someone else can read.

Procedure

1. Use a **computer drawing program or colored pencils and paper** to draw a map that shows how to get from your classroom to another place in your school, such as the gym. Make sure you include enough information for someone unfamiliar with your school to find his or her way.

2. After you finish drawing your map, switch maps with a partner. Examine your classmate's map, and try to figure out where the map is leading you.

Analysis

1. Is your map an accurate picture of your school? Explain your answer.

2. What could you do to make your map better? What are some limitations of your map?

3. Compare your map with your partner's map. How are your maps alike? How are they different?

You Are Here

Have you ever noticed the curve of the Earth's surface? You probably haven't. When you walk across the Earth, it does not appear to be curved. It looks flat.

Over time, ideas about Earth's shape have changed. Maps reflected how people saw the world and what technology was available. A **map** is a representation of the features of a physical body such as Earth. If you look at Ptolemy's (TAHL uh meez) world map from the second century, as shown in **Figure 1,** you might not know what you are looking at. Today satellites give us more accurate images of the Earth. In this section, you will learn how early scientists knew Earth was round long before pictures from space were taken. You will also learn how to find location and direction on Earth's surface.

What Does Earth Really Look Like?

The Greeks thought of Earth as a sphere almost 2,000 years before Christopher Columbus made his voyage in 1492. The observation that a ship sinks below the horizon as it sails into the distance supported the idea of a spherical Earth. If Earth were flat, the ship would not sink below the horizon.

Eratosthenes (ER uh TAHS thuh NEEZ), a Greek mathematician, wanted to know the size of Earth. In about 240 BCE, he calculated Earth's circumference using math and observations of the sun. There were no satellites or computers back then. We now know his calculation was wrong by only 6,250 km!

READING WARM-UP

Objectives

- Explain how a magnetic compass can be used to find directions on Earth.
- Explain the difference between true north and magnetic north.
- Compare latitude and longitude.
- Explain how latitude and longitude is used to locate places on Earth.

Terms to Learn

map	latitude
true north	equator
magnetic declination	longitude
	prime meridian

READING STRATEGY

Reading Organizer As you read this section, create an outline of the section. Use the headings from the section in your outline.

map a representation of the features of a physical body such as Earth

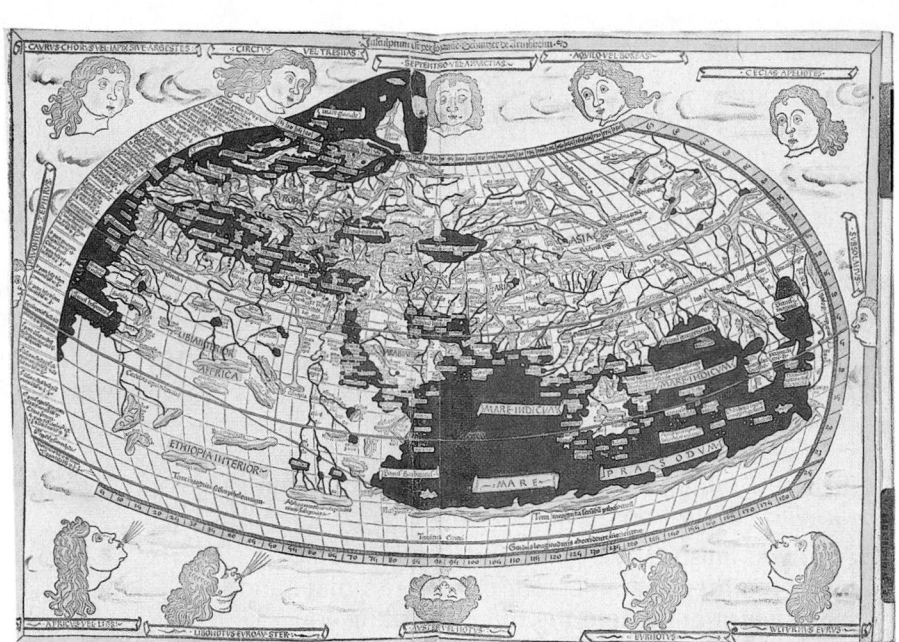

Figure 1 *This map shows what explorers thought the world looked like 1,800 years ago.*

Figure 2 *The North Pole is a good reference point for describing locations in North America.*

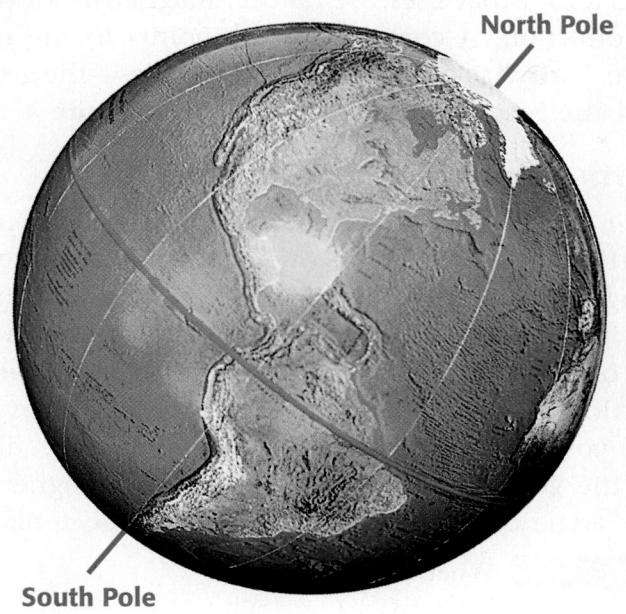

North Pole

South Pole

SCHOOL to HOME

WRITING SKILL **Columbus's Voyage**

Did Christopher Columbus discover that Earth was a sphere only after he completed his voyage in 1492? Or did he know before he left? With a parent, use the Internet or the library to find out more information about Columbus's voyage. Then, write a paragraph describing what you learned.

ACTiViTY

Finding Direction on Earth

When giving directions to your home, you might name a landmark, such as a grocery store, as a reference point. A *reference point* is a fixed place on the Earth's surface from which direction and location can be described.

The Earth is spherical, so it has no top, bottom, or sides for people to use as reference points for determining locations on its surface. However, the Earth does rotate, or spin, on its axis. The Earth's axis is an imaginary line that runs through the Earth. At either end of the axis is a geographic pole. The North and South Poles are used as reference points when describing direction and location on the Earth, as shown in **Figure 2.**

✓ *Reading Check* **What is a reference point?** (*See the Appendix for answers to Reading Checks.*)

Cardinal Directions

A reference point alone will not help you give good directions. You will need to be able to describe how to get to your home from the reference point. You will need to use the directions north, south, east, and west. These directions are called *cardinal directions.* Using cardinal directions is much more precise than saying "Turn left," "Go straight," or "Turn right." So, you may tell a friend to walk a block north of the gas station to get to your home. To use cardinal directions properly, you will need a compass, shown in **Figure 3.**

Figure 3 *A compass shows the cardinal directions north, south, east and west, as well as combinations of these directions.*

Using a Compass

A magnetic compass will show you which direction is north. A *compass* is a tool that uses the natural magnetism of the Earth to show direction. A compass needle points to the magnetic north pole. Earth has two different sets of poles—the geographic poles and the magnetic poles, as shown in **Figure 4.**

True North and Magnetic Declination

Remember that the Earth's geographic poles are on either end of the Earth's axis. Earth has its own magnetic field, which produces magnetic poles. Earth's magnetic poles are not lined up exactly with Earth's axis. So, there is a difference between the locations of Earth's magnetic and geographic poles. **True north** is the direction to the geographic North Pole. When using a compass, you need to make a correction for the difference between the geographic North Pole and the magnetic north pole. The angle of correction is called **magnetic declination.**

✓ **Reading Check** What is true north?

true north the direction to the geographic North Pole

magnetic declination the difference between the magnetic north and the true north

Figure 4 *Unlike the geographic poles, which are always in the same place, the magnetic poles have changed location throughout the history of the Earth.*

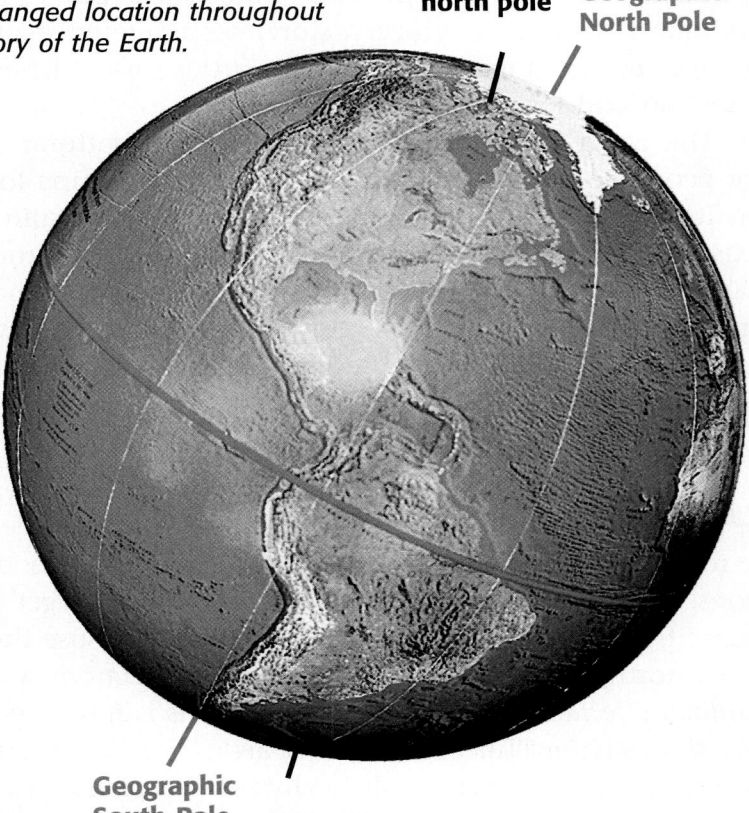

Magnetic north pole

Geographic North Pole

Geographic South Pole

Magnetic south pole

Making a Compass

1. Do this lab outside. Carefully rub a **steel sewing needle** against a **magnet** in the same direction 40 times.

2. Float a **1 cm × 3 cm piece of tissue paper** in a **bowl of water.**

3. Place the needle in the center of the tissue paper.

4. Compare your compass with a **regular compass.** Are both compasses pointing in the same direction?

5. How would you improve your compass?

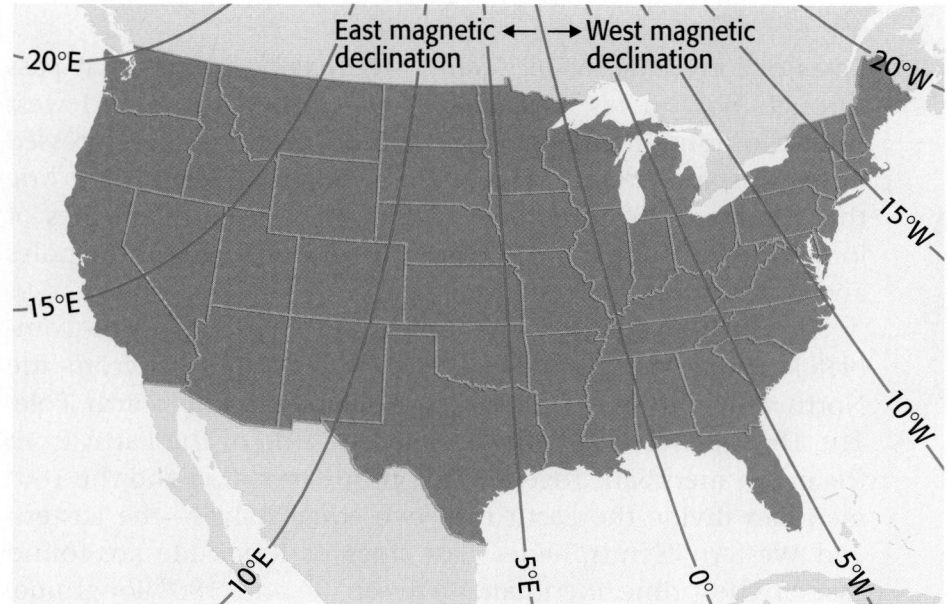

East magnetic ←——→ West magnetic
declination declination

20°E

20°W

15°W

15°E

10°W

10°E

5°E

0°

5°W

Figure 5 *The blue lines on the map connect points that have the same magnetic declination.*

Using Magnetic Declination

Magnetic declination is measured in degrees east or west of true north. Magnetic declination has been determined for different points on the Earth's surface. Once you know the declination for your area, you can use a compass to determine true north. This correction is like the correction you would make to the handlebars of a bike with a bent front wheel. You have to turn the handlebars a certain amount to make the bicycle go straight. **Figure 5** shows a map of the magnetic declination of the United States. What is the approximate magnetic declination of your city or town?

Finding Locations on the Earth

All of the houses and buildings in your neighborhood have addresses that give their location. But how would you find the location of something such as a city or an island? These places can be given an "address" using *latitude* and *longitude*. Latitude and longitude are shown by intersecting lines on a globe or map that allow you to find exact locations.

Latitude

Imaginary lines drawn around the Earth parallel to the equator are called lines of latitude, or *parallels*. **Latitude** is the distance north or south from the equator. Latitude is expressed in degrees, as shown in **Figure 6.** The **equator** is a circle halfway between the North and South Poles that divides the Earth into the Northern and Southern Hemispheres. The equator represents 0° latitude. The North Pole is 90° north latitude, and the South Pole is 90° south latitude.

latitude the distance north or south from the equator; expressed in degrees

equator the imaginary circle halfway between the poles that divides the Earth into the Northern and Southern Hemispheres

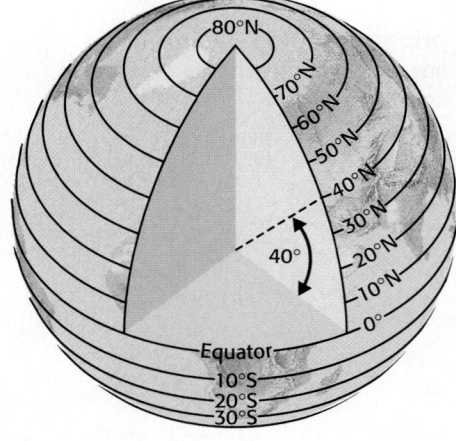

Figure 6 *Degrees latitude are a measure of the angle made by the equator and the location on the Earth's surface, as measured from the center of the Earth.*

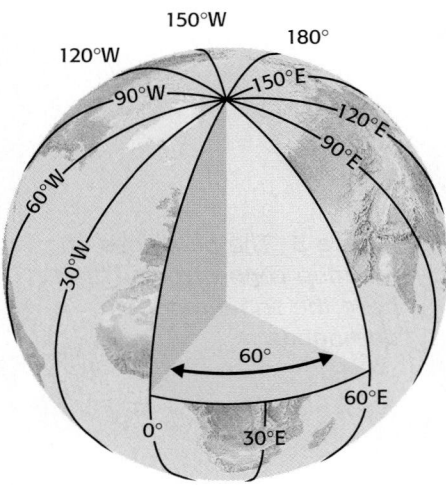

150°W
180°
120°W
90°W
150°E
120°E
60°W
90°E
30°W
60°
60°E
0°
30°E

Figure 7 *Degrees longitude are a measure of the angle made by the prime meridian and the location on the Earth's surface, as measured from the center of the Earth.*

longitude the distance east and west from the prime meridian; expressed in degrees

prime meridian the meridian, or line of longitude, that is designated as 0° longitude

Longitude

Lines of longitude, or *meridians*, are imaginary lines that pass through both poles. **Longitude** is the distance east and west from the prime meridian. Like latitude, longitude is expressed in degrees, as shown in **Figure 7.** The **prime meridian** is the line that represents 0° longitude. Unlike lines of latitude, lines of longitude are not parallel. Lines of longitude touch at the poles and are farthest apart at the equator.

Unlike the equator, the prime meridian does not completely circle the globe. The prime meridian runs from the North Pole through Greenwich, England, to the South Pole. The 180° meridian lies on the opposite side of the Earth from the prime meridian. Together, the prime meridian and the 180° meridian divide the Earth into two equal halves—the Eastern and Western Hemispheres. East lines of longitude are found east of the prime meridian, between 0° and 180° longitude. West lines of longitude are found west of the prime meridian, between 0° and 180° longitude.

Using Latitude and Longitude

Points on the Earth's surface can be located by using latitude and longitude. Lines of latitude and lines of longitude cross and form a grid system on globes and maps. This grid system can be used to find locations north or south of the equator and east or west of the prime meridian.

Figure 8 shows you how latitude and longitude can be used to find the location of your state capital. First, locate the star representing your state capital on the appropriate map. Then, use the lines of latitude and longitude closest to your state capital to estimate its approximate latitude and longitude.

✓ **Reading Check** Which set of imaginary lines are referred to as meridians: lines of latitude or lines of longitude?

CONNECTION TO Social Studies

Global Addresses You can find the location of any place on Earth by finding the coordinates of the place, or latitude and longitude, on a globe or a map. Using a globe or an atlas, find the coordinates of the following cities:

New York, New York	Madrid, Spain
Sao Paulo, Brazil	Paris, France
Sydney, Australia	Cairo, Egypt

Then, find the latitude and longitude coordinates of your own city. Can you find another city that shares the same latitude as your city? Can you find another city that shares the same longitude?

ACTiViTY

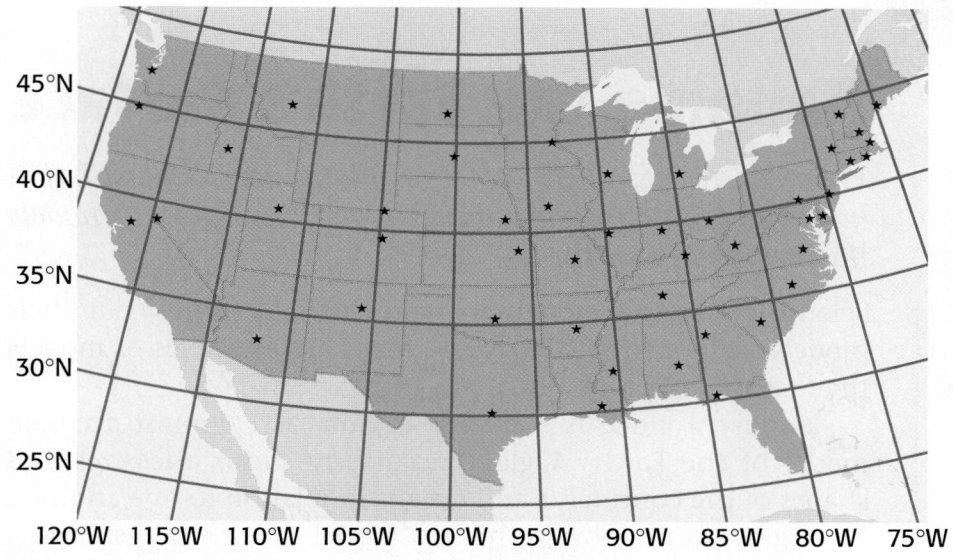

Figure 8 *The grid pattern formed by lines of latitude and longitude allows you to pinpoint any location on the Earth's surface.*

SECTION Review

Summary

- Magnetic compasses are used to find direction on Earth's surface. A compass needle points to the magnetic north pole.

- True north is the direction to the geographic North Pole, which never changes. The magnetic north pole may change over time. Magnetic declination is the difference between true north and magnetic north.

- Latitude and longitude help you find locations on a map or a globe. Lines of latitude run east and west. Lines of longitude run north and south through the poles. These lines cross and form a grid system on globes and maps.

Using Key Terms

1. Use each of the following terms in a separate sentence: *latitude, longitude, equator,* and *prime meridian.*

2. In your own words, write a definition for the term *true north.*

Understanding Key Ideas

3. The geographic poles are
   a. used as reference points when describing direction and location on Earth.
   b. formed because of the Earth's magnetic field.
   c. at either end of the Earth's axis.
   d. Both (a) and (c)

4. How are lines of latitude and lines of longitude alike? How are they different?

5. How can you use a magnetic compass to find directions on Earth?

6. What is the difference between true north and magnetic north?

7. How do lines of latitude and longitude help you find locations on the Earth's surface?

Math Skills

8. The distance between 40°N latitude and 41°N latitude is 69 mi. What is this distance in km? (Hint: 1 km = 0.621 mi)

Critical Thinking

9. **Applying Concepts** While exploring the attic, you find a treasure map. The map shows that the treasure is buried at 97°N and 188°E. Explain why this location is incorrect.

10. **Making Inferences** When using a compass to explore an area, why do you need to know an area's magnetic declination?

SCILINKS®

NSTA
Developed and maintained by the
National Science Teachers Association

For a variety of links related to this chapter, go to www.scilinks.org

Topic: Latitude and Longitude
SciLinks code: HSM0854

Mapping the Earth's Surface

What do a teddy bear, a toy airplane, and a plastic doll have in common besides being toys? They are all models that represent real things.

Scientists also use models to represent real things, but their models are not toys. Globes and maps are examples of models that scientists use to study the Earth's surface.

Because a globe is a sphere, a globe is the most accurate model of the Earth. A globe accurately shows the sizes and shapes of the continents and oceans in relation to one another. But a globe is not always the best model to use when studying the Earth's surface. A globe is too small to show many details, such as roads and rivers. It is much easier to show details on maps. But how do you show the Earth's curved surface on a flat surface? Keep reading to find out.

A Flat Sphere?

A map is a flat representation of the Earth's curved surface. However, when you move information from a curved surface to a flat surface, you lose some accuracy. Changes called *distortions* happen in the shapes and sizes of landmasses and oceans on maps. Direction and distance can also be distorted. Consider the example of the orange peel shown in **Figure 1.**

✓ **Reading Check** What are distortions on maps? (*See the Appendix for answers to Reading Checks.*)

Figure 1 *If you remove and flatten the peel from an orange, the peel will stretch and tear. Notice how shapes as well as distances between points on the peel are distorted.*

Map Projections

Mapmakers use map projections to move the image of Earth's curved surface onto a flat surface. No map projection of Earth can show the surface of a sphere in the correct proportions. All flat maps have distortion. However, a map showing a smaller area, such as a city, has less distortion than a map showing a larger area, such as the world.

To understand how map projections are made, think of Earth as a translucent globe that has a light inside. If you hold a piece of paper against the globe, shadows appear on the paper. These shadows show marks on the globe, such as continents, oceans, and lines of latitude and longitude. The way the paper is held against the globe determines the kind of map projection that is made. The most common map projections are based on three shapes—cylinders, cones, and planes.

Cylindrical Projection

A map projection that is made when the contents of the globe are moved onto a cylinder of paper is called a **cylindrical projection** (suh LIN dri kuhl proh JEK shuhn). The most common cylindrical projection is called a *Mercator projection* (muhr KAYT uhr proh JEK shuhn). The Mercator projection shows the globe's latitude and longitude lines as straight lines. Equal amounts of space are used between longitude lines. Latitude lines are spaced farther apart north and south of the equator. Because of the spacing, areas near the poles look wider and longer on the map than they look on the globe. In **Figure 2,** Greenland appears almost as large as Africa!

INTERNET ACTIVITY

For another activity related to this chapter, go to **go.hrw.com** and type in the keyword **HZ5MAPW.**

cylindrical projection a map projection that is made by moving the surface features of the globe onto a cylinder

---

Figure 2 Cylindrical Projection

This cylindrical projection is a Mercator projection. It is accurate near the equator but distorts areas near the North and South Poles.

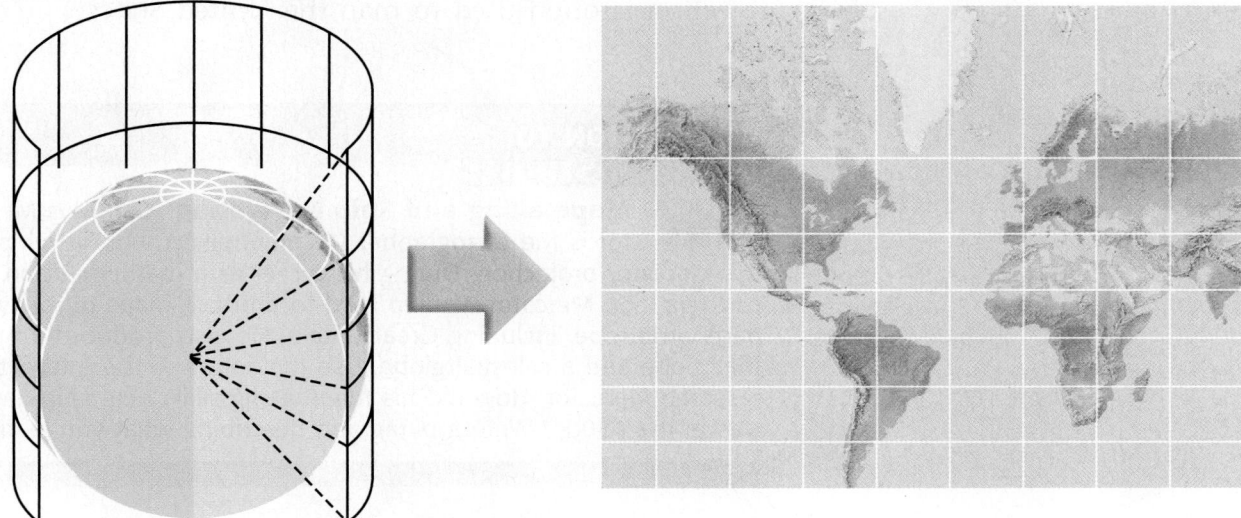

Figure 3 Conic Projection

A series of conic projections can be used to map a large area. Because each cone touches the globe at a different latitude, conic projections reduce distortion.

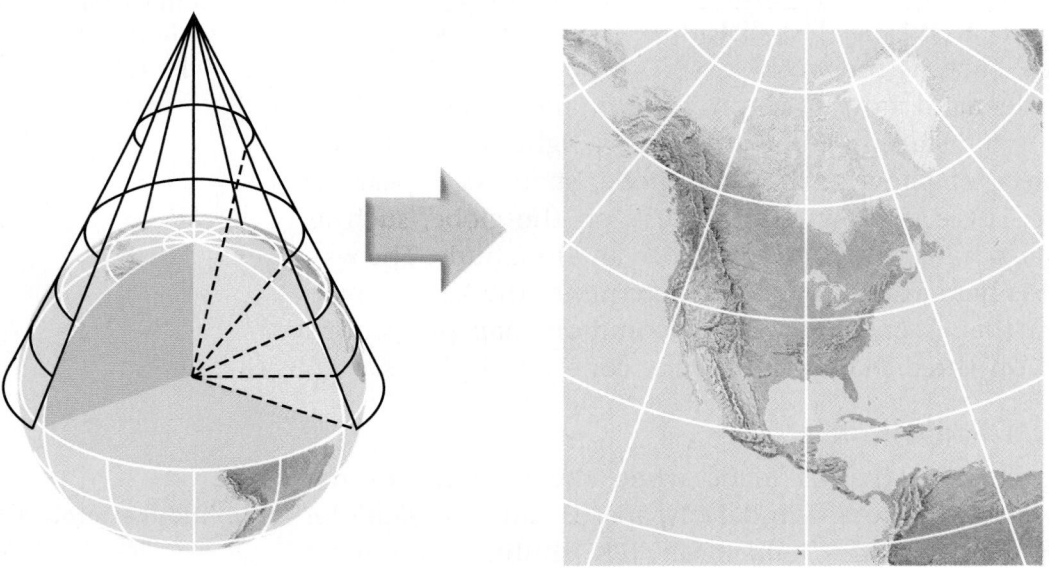

Conic Projection

conic projection a map projection that is made by moving the surface features of the globe onto a cone

A map projection that is made by moving the contents of the globe onto a cone is a **conic projection,** shown in **Figure 3.** This cone is then unrolled to form a flat plane.

The cone touches the globe at each line of longitude but at only one line of latitude. There is no distortion along the line of latitude where the globe touches the cone. Areas near this line of latitude are distorted less than other areas are. Because the cone touches many lines of longitude and only one line of latitude, conic projections are best for mapping large masses of land that have more area east to west. For example, a conic projection is often used to map the United States.

CONNECTION TO Social Studies

WRITING SKILL **Mapmaking and Ship Navigation** Gerardus Mercator is the cartographer (or mapmaker) who developed the Mercator projection. During his career as a mathematician and cartographer, Mercator worked hard to produce maps of many parts of Europe, including Great Britain. He also produced a terrestrial globe and a celestial globe. Use the library or the Internet to research Mercator. How did his mapmaking skills help ship navigators in the 1500s? Write a paragraph describing what you learn.

Figure 4 Azimuthal Projection

On this azimuthal projection, distortion increases as you move farther from the North Pole.

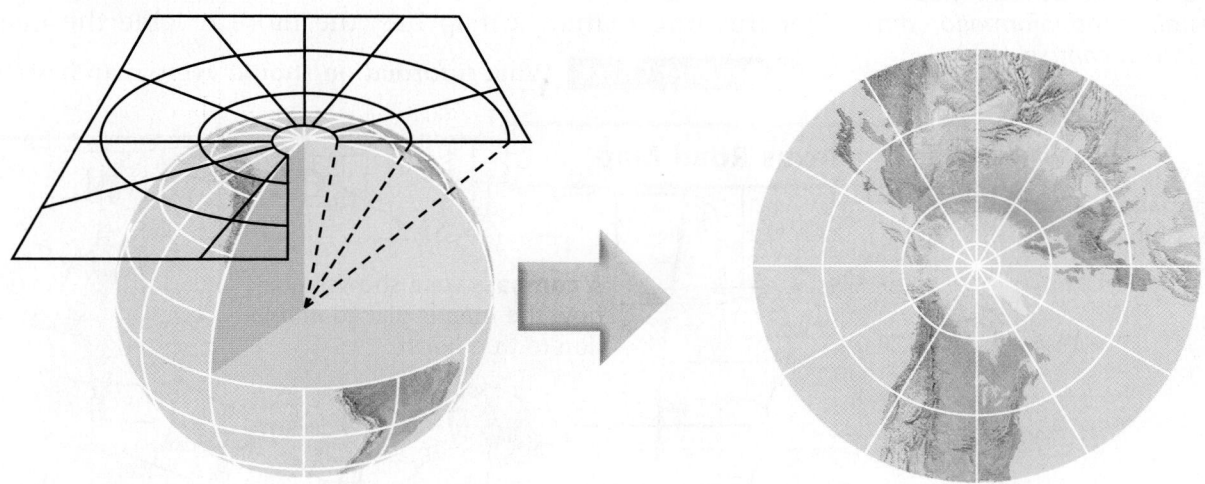

Azimuthal Projection

An **azimuthal projection** (AZ uh MYOOTH uhl proh JEK shuhn) is a map projection that is made by moving the contents of the globe onto a flat plane. Look at **Figure 4.** On an azimuthal projection, the plane touches the globe at only one point. There is little distortion at this point of contact. The point of contact for an azimuthal projection is usually one of the poles. However, distortion of direction, distance, and shape increases as you move away from the point of contact. Azimuthal projections are most often used to map areas of the globe that are near the North and South Poles.

azimuthal projection a map projection that is made by moving the surface features of the globe onto a plane

✓ *Reading Check* **How are azimuthal and conic projections alike? How are they different?**

Equal-Area Projection

A map projection that shows the area between the latitude and longitude lines the same size as that area on a globe is called an *equal-area projection*. Equal-area projections can be made by using cylindrical, conic, or azimuthal projections. Equal-area projections are often used to map large land areas, such as continents. The shapes of the continents and oceans are distorted on equal-area projections. But because the scale used on equal-area projections is constant throughout the map, this type of projection is good for determining distance on a map. **Figure 5** is an example of an equal-area projection.

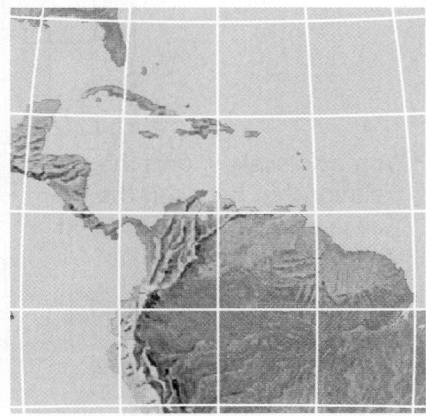

Figure 5 *Equal-area projections are useful for determining distance on a map.*

Information Shown on Maps

Regardless of the kind of map you are reading, the map should contain the information shown in **Figure 6.** This information includes a title, a compass rose, a scale, a legend, and a date. Unfortunately, not all maps have all this information. The more of this information a map has, the more reliable the map is.

✓ **Reading Check** What information should every map have?

Figure 6 *This Texas road map includes all of the information that a map should contain.*

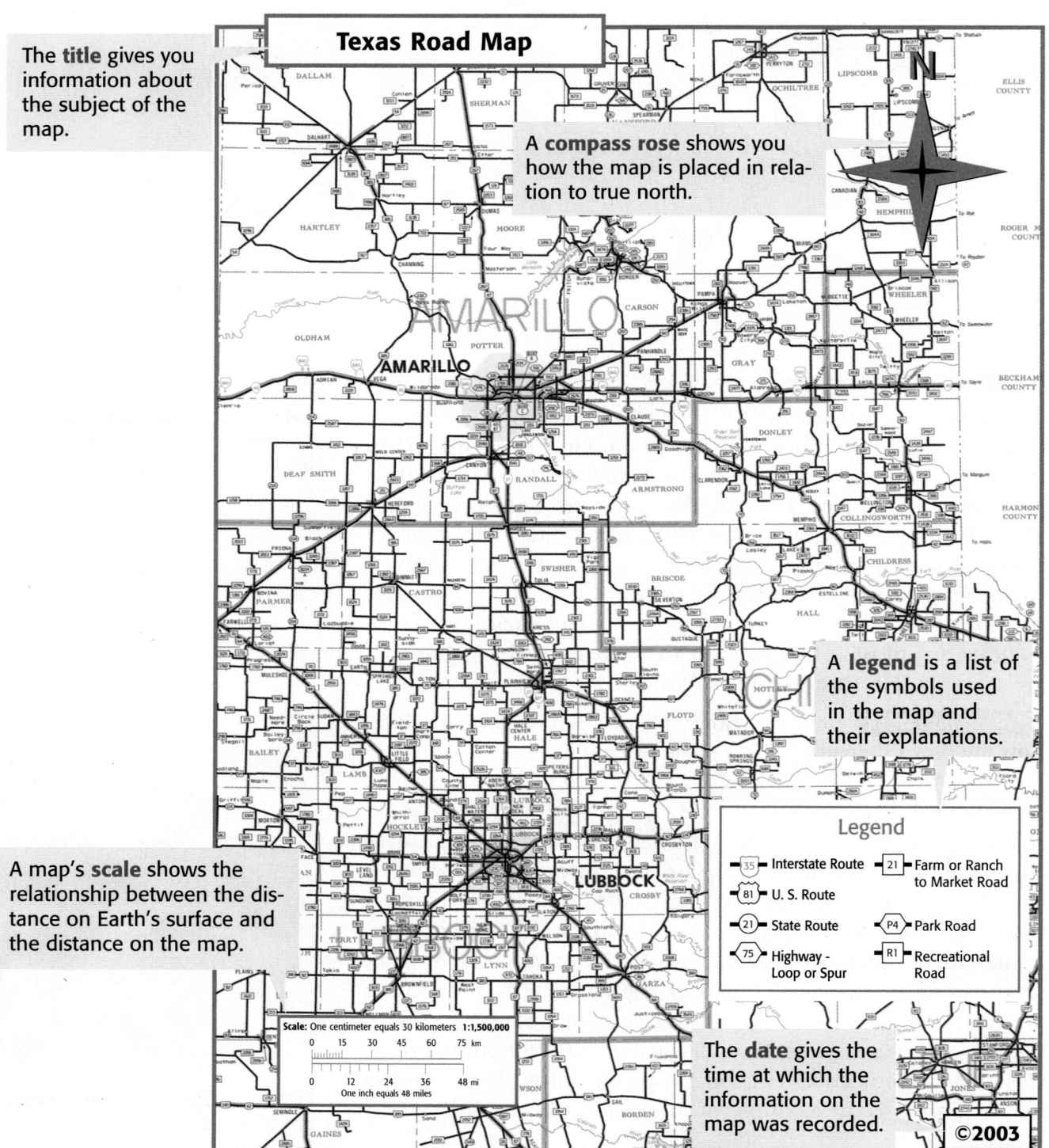

The **title** gives you information about the subject of the map.

A **compass rose** shows you how the map is placed in relation to true north.

A **legend** is a list of the symbols used in the map and their explanations.

A map's **scale** shows the relationship between the distance on Earth's surface and the distance on the map.

The **date** gives the time at which the information on the map was recorded.

Texas Road Map

Legend

35 Interstate Route		21 Farm or Ranch to Market Road	
81 U. S. Route		P4 Park Road	
21 State Route		R1 Recreational Road	
75 Highway - Loop or Spur			

Scale: One centimeter equals 30 kilometers 1:1,500,000

0   15   30   45   60   75 km

0   12   24   36   48 mi
One inch equals 48 miles

©2003

Modern Mapmaking

For many centuries mapmakers relied on the observations of explorers to make maps. Today, however, mapmakers have far more technologically advanced tools for mapmaking.

Many of today's maps are made by remote sensing. **Remote sensing** is a way to collect information about something without physically being there. Remote sensing can be as basic as putting cameras on airplanes. However, many mapmakers rely on more sophisticated technology, such as satellites.

remote sensing the process of gathering and analyzing information about an object without physically being in touch with the object

Remote Sensing and Satellites

The image shown in **Figure 7** is a photograph taken by a satellite. Satellites can also detect energy that your eyes cannot. Remote sensors gather data about energy coming from Earth's surface and send the data back to receiving stations on Earth. A computer is then used to process the information to make a picture you can see.

Remote Sensing Using Radar

Radar is a tool that uses waves of energy to map Earth's surface. Waves of energy are sent from a satellite to the area being observed. The waves are then reflected from the area to a receiver on the satellite. The distance and the speed in which the waves travel to the area and back are measured and analyzed to create a map of the area. The waves used in radar can move through clouds and water. Because of this ability, radar has been used to map the surface of Venus, whose atmosphere is thick and cloudy.

Figure 7 *Satellites can produce very detailed images of the Earth's surface. The satellite that took this picture was 423 mi above the Earth's surface!*

Figure 8 *This tiny GPS unit may come in handy if you are ever lost.*

Global Positioning System

Did you know that satellite technology can actually help you from getting lost? The *global positioning system* (GPS) can help you find where you are on Earth. GPS is a system of orbiting satellites that send radio signals to receivers on Earth. The receivers calculate a given place's latitude, longitude, and elevation.

GPS was invented in the 1970s by the U.S. Department of Defense for military use. However, during the last 30 years, GPS has made its way into people's daily lives. Mapmakers use GPS to verify the location of boundary lines between countries and states. Airplane and boat pilots use GPS for navigation. Businesses and state agencies use GPS for mapping and environmental planning. Many new cars have GPS units that show information on a screen on the dashboard. Some GPS units are small enough to wear on your wrist, as shown in **Figure 8,** so you can know your location anywhere you go!

Geographic Information Systems

Mapmakers now use geographic information systems to store, use, and view geographic information. A *geographic information system*, or GIS, is a computerized system that allows a user to enter different types of information about an area. This information is entered and stored as layers. The user can then use the stored information to make complex analyses or display maps. **Figure 9** shows three GIS images of Seattle, Washington.

✓ **Reading Check** Explain how information is stored using GIS.

Figure 9 *The images at right show the location of sewer lines, roads, and parks in Seattle, Washington.*

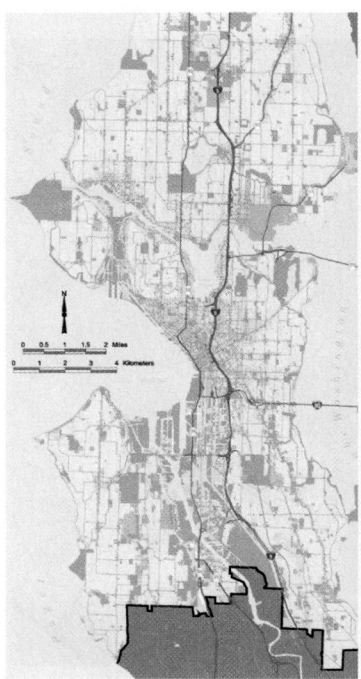

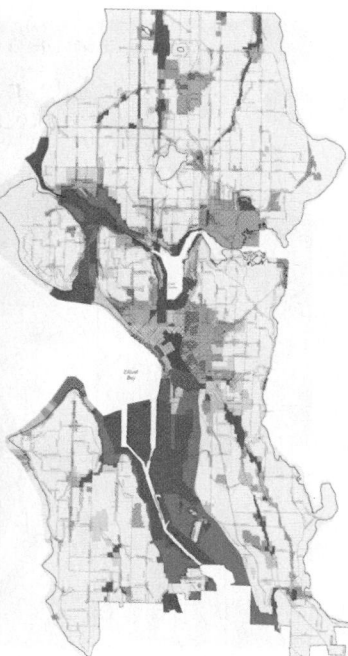

SECTION
Review

Summary

- When information is moved from a curved surface to a flat surface, distortion occurs.
- Three main types of projections are used to show Earth's surface on a flat map: cylindrical, conic, and azimuthal projections.
- Equal-area maps are used to show the area of a piece of land in relation to the area of other landmasses and oceans.
- Maps should contain a title, a scale, a legend, a compass rose, and a date.

- Modern mapmakers use remote sensing technology, such as satellites and radar.
- The Global positioning system, or GPS, is a system of satellites that can help you determine your location no matter where you are.
- Geographical information systems, or GIS, are computerized systems that allow mapmakers to store and use many types of data about an area.

Using Key Terms

1. In your own words, write a definition for each of the following terms: *cylindrical projection, azimuthal projection,* and *conic projection.*

Understanding Key Ideas

2. Which of the following map projections is most often used to map the United States?
   a. cylindrical projection
   b. conic projection
   c. azimuthal projection
   d. equal-area projection

3. List five things found on maps. Explain how each thing is important to reading a map.

4. Describe how GPS can help you find your location on Earth.

5. Why is radar useful when mapping areas that tend to be covered in clouds?

Critical Thinking

6. **Analyzing Ideas** Imagine you are a mapmaker. You have been asked to map a landmass that has more area from east to west than from north to south. What type of map projection would you use? Explain.

7. **Making Inferences** Imagine looking at a map of North America. Would this map have a large scale or a small scale? Would a map of your city have a large scale or a small scale? Explain.

Interpreting Graphics

Use the map below to answer the questions that follow.

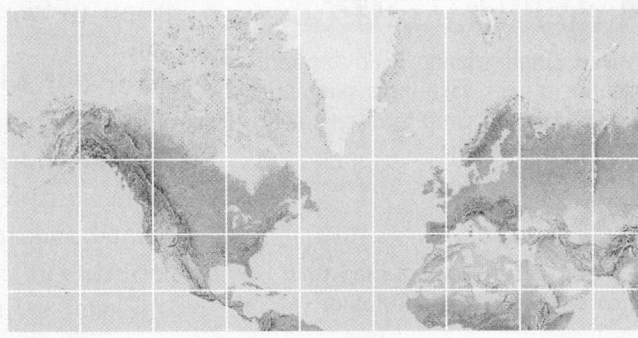

8. What type of projection was used to make this map?

9. Which areas of this map are the most distorted? Explain.

10. Which areas of this map are the least distorted? Explain.

SCILINKS®

NSTA
Developed and maintained by the
National Science Teachers Association

For a variety of links related to this chapter, go to www.scilinks.org

Topic: Mapmaking
SciLinks code: HSM0909

Topographic Maps

Imagine you are going on a camping trip in the wilderness. To be prepared, you want to take a compass and a map. But what kind of map should you take? Because there won't be any roads in the wilderness, you can forget about a road map. Instead, you will need a topographic map.

A **topographic map** (TAHP uh GRAF ik MAP) is a map that shows surface features, or topography (tuh PAHG ruh fee), of the Earth. Topographic maps show both natural features, such as rivers, lakes, and mountains, and features made by humans, such as cities, roads, and bridges. Topographic maps also show elevation. **Elevation** is the height of an object above sea level. The elevation at sea level is 0. In this section, you will learn how to read a topographic map.

Elements of Elevation

The United States Geological Survey (USGS), a federal government agency, has made topographic maps for most of the United States. These maps show elevation in feet (ft) rather than in meters, the SI unit usually used by scientists.

Contour Lines

On a topographic map, *contour lines* are used to show elevation. **Contour lines** are lines that connect points of equal elevation. For example, one contour line would connect points on a map that have an elevation of 100 ft. Another line would connect points on a map that have an elevation of 200 ft. **Figure 1** illustrates how contour lines appear on a map.

READING WARM-UP

Objectives

● Explain how contour lines show elevation and landforms on a map.

● Explain how the relief of an area determines the contour interval used on a map.

● List the rules of contour lines.

Terms to Learn

topographic map
elevation
contour line
contour interval
relief
index contour

READING STRATEGY

Paired Summarizing Read this section silently. In pairs, take turns summarizing the material. Stop to discuss ideas that seem confusing.

topographic map a map that shows the surface features of Earth

elevation the height of an object above sea level

contour line a line that connects points of equal elevation

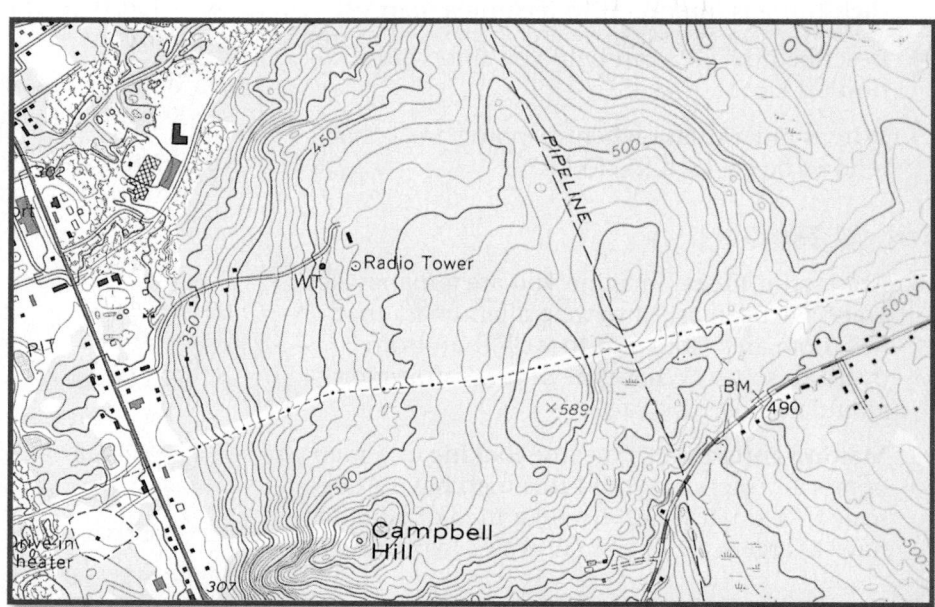

Figure 1 *Because contour lines connect points of equal elevation, the shape of the contour lines reflects the shape of the land.*

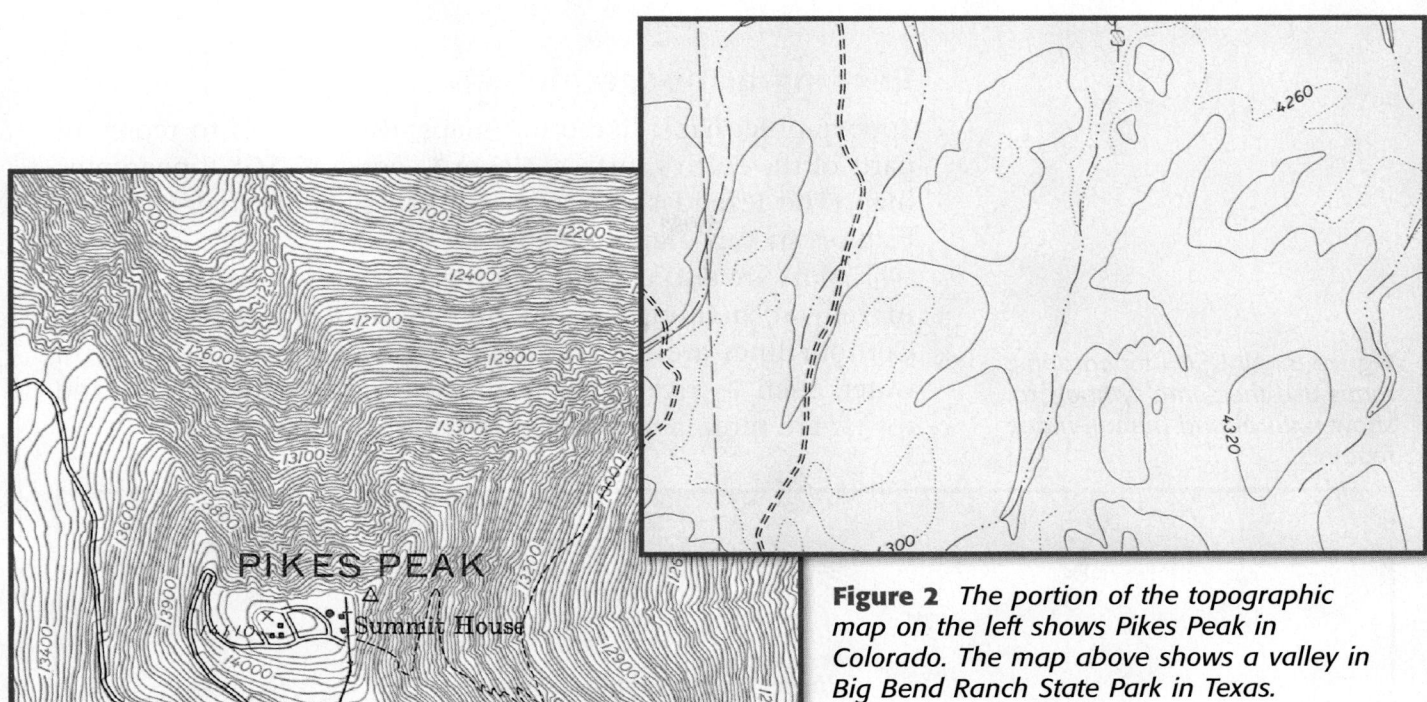

Figure 2 *The portion of the topographic map on the left shows Pikes Peak in Colorado. The map above shows a valley in Big Bend Ranch State Park in Texas.*

Contour Interval

The difference in elevation between one contour line and the next is called the **contour interval.** For example, a map with a contour interval of 20 ft would have contour lines every 20 ft of elevation change, such as 0 ft, 20 ft, 40 ft, and 60 ft. A mapmaker chooses a contour interval based on the area's relief. **Relief** is the difference in elevation between the highest and lowest points of the area being mapped. Because the relief of an area with mountains is large, the relief might be shown on a map using a large contour interval, such as 100 ft. However, a flat area has small relief and might be shown on a map by using a small contour interval, such as 10 ft.

The spacing of contour lines also indicates slope, as shown in **Figure 2.** Contour lines that are close together show a steep slope. Contour lines that are spaced far apart show a gentle slope.

Index Contour

On USGS topographic maps, an index contour is used to make reading the map easier. An **index contour** is a darker, heavier contour line that is usually every fifth line and that is labeled by elevation. Find an index contour on both of the topographic maps shown in **Figure 2.**

✓ *Reading Check* **What is an index contour?** (*See the Appendix for answers to Reading Checks.*)

contour interval the difference in elevation between one contour line and the next

relief the variations in elevation of a land surface

index contour on a map, a darker, heavier contour line that is usually every fifth line and that indicates a change in elevation

CONNECTION TO Oceanography

Mapping the Ocean Floor
Oceanographers use topographic maps to map the topography of the ocean floor. Use the Internet or the library to find a topographic map of the ocean floor. How are maps of the ocean floor similar to maps of the continents? How are they different?

Reading a Topographic Map

Topographic maps, like other maps, use symbols to represent parts of the Earth's surface. **Figure 3** shows a USGS topographic map. The legend shows some of the symbols that represent features in topographic maps.

Colors are also used to represent features of Earth's surface. In general, buildings, roads, bridges, and railroads are black. Contour lines are brown. Major highways are red. Bodies of water, such as rivers, lakes, and oceans are blue. Cities and towns are pink, and wooded areas are green.

Figure 3 *All USGS topographic maps use the same symbols to show natural and human-made features.*

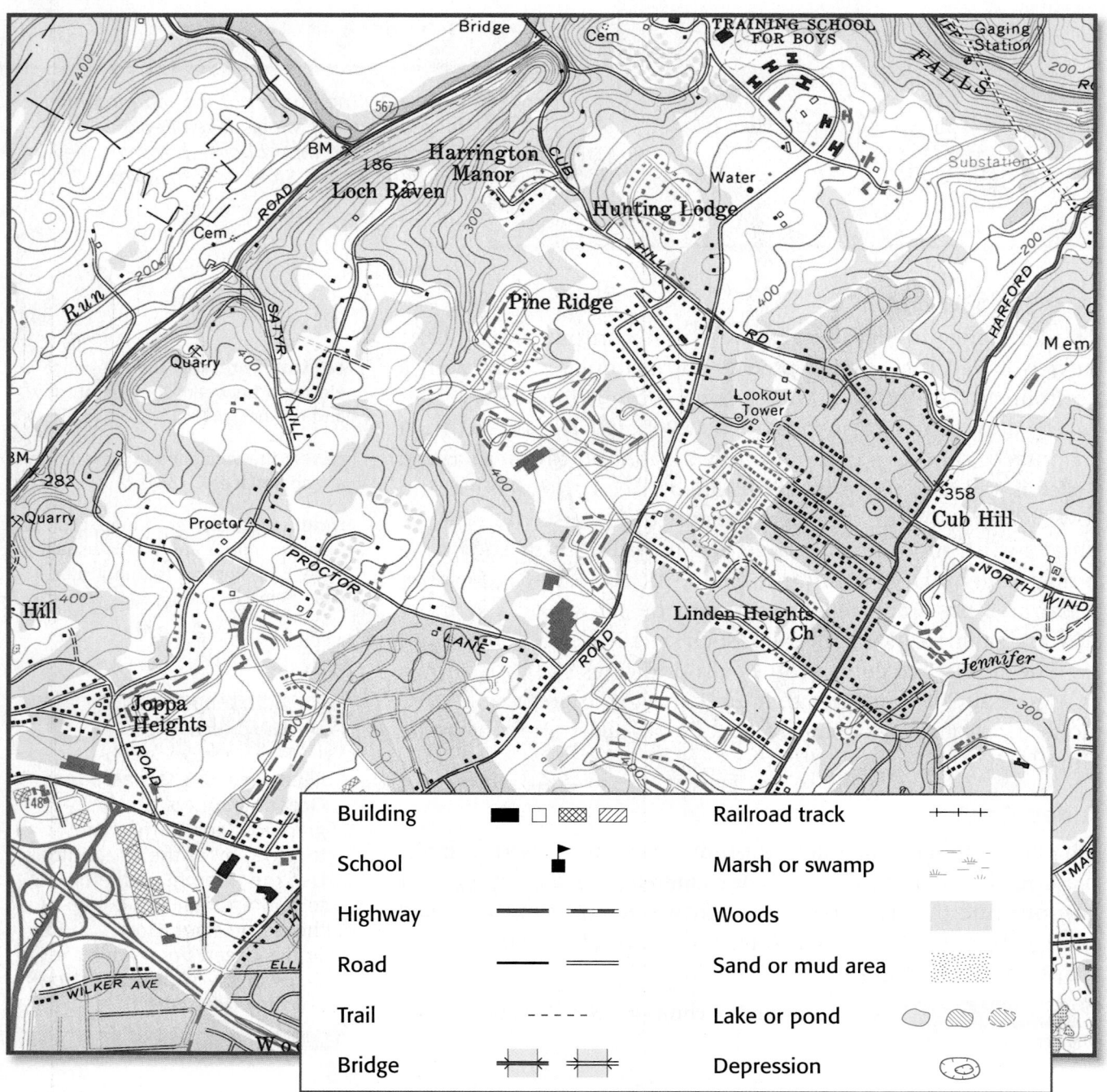

Building	■ □ ▨ ▨	Railroad track	+++++
School	⚑	Marsh or swamp	
Highway	━━━ ━ ━	Woods	
Road	─── ═══	Sand or mud area	
Trail	- - - - -	Lake or pond	
Bridge		Depression	

The Golden Rules of Contour Lines

Contour lines are the key to explaining the size and shape of landforms on a topographic map. Reading a topographic map takes training and practice. The following rules will help you understand how to read topographic maps:

- Contour lines never cross. All points along a contour line represent one elevation.
- The spacing of contour lines depends on slope characteristics. Contour lines that are close together show a steep slope. Contour lines that are far apart show a gentle slope.
- Contour lines that cross a valley or stream are V shaped. The V points toward the area of highest elevation. If a stream or river flows through the valley, the V points upstream.
- The tops of hills, mountains, and depressions are shown by closed circles. Depressions are marked with short, straight lines inside the circle that point downslope to the depression.

CONNECTION TO Environmental Science

Endangered Species State agencies, such as the Texas Parks and Wildlife Department, use topographic maps to mark where endangered plant and animal species are. By marking the location of the endangered plants and animals, these agencies can record and protect these places. Use the Internet or another source to find out if there is an agency in your state that tracks endangered species by using topographic maps.

SECTION Review

Summary

- Contour lines are used to show elevation and landforms by connecting points of equal elevation.
- The contour interval is determined by the relief of an area.
- Contour lines never cross. Contour lines that cross a valley or a stream are V shaped and point upstream. The tops of hills, mountains, and depressions are shown by closed circles.

Using Key Terms

1. In your own words, write a definition for each of the following terms: *topographic map, contour interval,* and *relief.*

Understanding Key Ideas

2. An index contour
   a. is a heavier contour line that shows a change in elevation.
   b. points in the direction of higher elevation.
   c. indicates a depression.
   d. indicates a hill.

3. How do topographic maps represent the Earth's surface?

4. How does the relief of an area determine the contour interval used on a map?

5. What are the rules of contour lines?

Math Skills

6. The contour line at the base of a hill reads 90 ft. There are five contour lines between the base of the hill and the top of the hill. If the contour interval is 30 ft, what is the elevation of the highest contour line?

Critical Thinking

7. **Making Inferences** Why isn't the highest point on a hill represented by a contour line?

SCiLINKS

NSTA
Developed and maintained by the National Science Teachers Association

For a variety of links related to this chapter, go to www.scilinks.org

Topic: Topographic Maps
SciLinks code: HSM1536

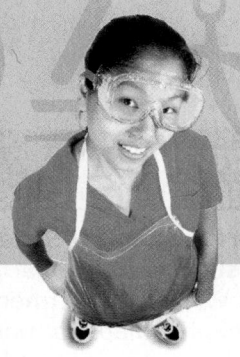

Skills Practice Lab

OBJECTIVES

Construct a tool to measure the circumference of the Earth.

Calculate the circumference of the Earth.

MATERIALS

- basketball
- books or notebooks (2)
- calculator (optional)
- clay, modeling
- flashlight or small lamp
- meterstick
- pencils, unsharpened (2)
- protractor
- ruler, metric
- string, 10 cm long
- tape, masking
- tape measure

SAFETY

Round or Flat?

Eratosthenes thought of a way to measure the circumference of Earth. He came up with the idea when he read that a well in southern Egypt was entirely lit by the sun at noon once each year. He realized that to shine on the entire surface of the well water, the sun must be directly over the well. At the same time, in a city just north of the well, a tall monument cast a shadow. Thus, Eratosthenes reasoned that the sun could not be directly over both the monument and the well at noon on the same day. In this experiment, you will see how Eratosthenes' way of measuring works.

Ask a Question

1. How could I use Eratosthenes' method of investigation to measure the size of the Earth?

Form a Hypothesis

2. Formulate a hypothesis that answers the question above. Record your hypothesis.

Test the Hypothesis

3. Set the basketball on a table. Place a book or notebook on either side of the basketball to hold the ball in place. The ball represents Earth.

4 Use modeling clay to attach a pencil to the "equator" of the ball so that the pencil points away from the ball.

5 Attach the second pencil to the ball at a point that is 5 cm above the first pencil. This second pencil should also point away from the ball.

6 Use a meterstick to measure 1 m away from the ball. Mark the 1 m position with masking tape. Label the position "Sun." Hold the flashlight so that its front edge is above the masking tape.

7 When your teacher turns out the lights, turn on your flashlight and point it so that the pencil on the equator does not cast a shadow. Ask a partner to hold the flashlight in this position. The second pencil should cast a shadow on the ball.

8 Tape one end of the string to the top of the second pencil. Hold the other end of the string against the ball at the far edge of the shadow. Make sure that the string is tight. But be careful not to pull the pencil over.

9 Use a protractor to measure the angle between the string and the pencil. Record this angle.

10 Use the following formula to calculate the experimental circumference of the ball.

$$Circumference = \frac{360° \times 5 \text{ cm}}{\text{angle between pencil and string}}$$

11 Record the experimental circumference you calculated in step 10. Wrap the tape measure around the ball's equator to measure the actual circumference of the ball. Record this circumference.

Analyze the Results

1 **Examining Data** Compare the experimental circumference with the actual circumference.

2 **Analyzing Data** What could have caused your experimental circumference to differ from the actual circumference?

3 **Analyzing Data** What are some of the advantages and disadvantages of taking measurements this way?

Draw Conclusions

4 **Evaluating Methods** Was Eratosthenes' method an effective way to measure Earth's circumference? Explain your answer.

Chapter Review

USING KEY TERMS

For each pair of terms, explain how the meanings of the terms differ.

1 *true north* and *magnetic north*

2 *latitude* and *longitude*

3 *equator* and *prime meridian*

4 *cylindrical projection* and *azimuthal projection*

5 *contour interval* and *index contour*

6 *global positioning system* and *geographic information system*

UNDERSTANDING KEY IDEAS

Multiple Choice

7 A point whose latitude is 0° is located on the

  a. North Pole.

  b. equator.

  c. South Pole.

  d. prime meridian.

8 The distance in degrees east or west of the prime meridian is

  a. latitude.

  b. declination.

  c. longitude.

  d. projection.

9 Widely spaced contour lines indicate a

  a. steep slope.

  b. gentle slope.

  c. hill.

  d. river.

10 The most common map projections are based on three geometric shapes. Which of the following geometric shapes is NOT one of the three geometric shapes?

  a. cylinder

  b. square

  c. cone

  d. plane

11 A cylindrical projection is distorted near the

  a. equator.

  b. poles.

  c. prime meridian.

  d. date line.

12 What is the relationship between the distance on a map and the actual distance on Earth called?

  a. legend

  b. elevation

  c. relief

  d. scale

13 ___ is the height of an object above sea level.

  a. Contour interval

  b. Elevation

  c. Declination

  d. Index contour

Short Answer

14 List four methods that modern mapmakers use to make accurate maps.

15 Why is a map legend important?

16 Why does Greenland appear so large in relation to other landmasses on a map made using a cylindrical projection?

17 What is the function of contour lines on a topographic map?

18 How can GPS help you find your location on Earth?

19 What is GIS?

CRITICAL THINKING

20 **Concept Mapping** Use the following terms to create a concept map: *maps, legend, map projection, map parts, scale, cylinder, title, cone, plane, date,* and *compass rose.*

21 **Making Inferences** One of the important parts of a map is its date. Why is the date important?

22 **Analyzing Ideas** Why is it important for maps to have scales?

23 **Applying Concepts** Imagine that you are looking at a topographic map of the Grand Canyon. Would the contour lines be spaced close together or far apart? Explain your answer.

24 **Analyzing Processes** How would a GIS system help a team of engineers plan a new highway system for a city?

25 **Making Inferences** If you were stranded in a national park, what kind of map of the park would you want to have with you? Explain your answer.

INTERPRETING GRAPHICS

Use the topographic map below to answer the questions that follow.

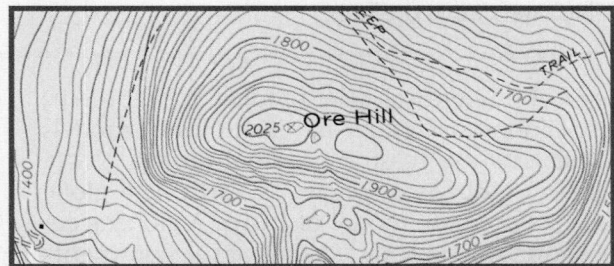

26 What is the elevation change between two adjacent lines on this map?

27 What type of relief does this area have?

28 What surface features are shown on this map?

29 What is the elevation at the top of Ore Hill?

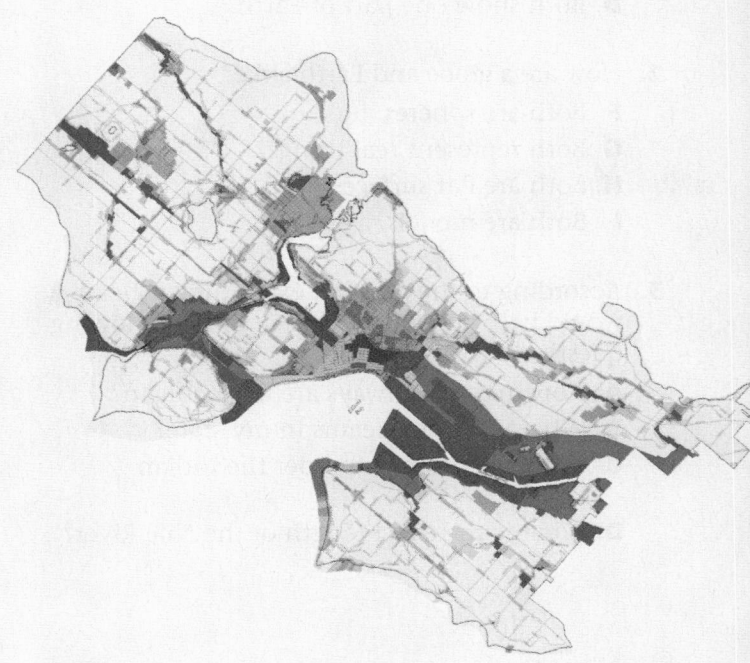

Standardized Test Preparation

Read each of the passages below. Then, answer the questions that follow each passage.

Passage 1 Scientists use models to represent things. Globes and maps are examples of models that scientists use to study Earth's surface.

Because a globe is a sphere, as Earth is, a globe is the most accurate model of Earth. A globe accurately shows the sizes and shapes of the continents and oceans in relation to one another. But a globe is not always the best model to use when studying Earth's surface. For example, a globe is too small to show a lot of detail, such as roads and rivers. It is much easier to show details on maps. Maps can show the whole Earth or parts of it.

1. According to the passage, how are a globe and a map alike?
   A Both show a lot of detail.
   B Both are used to study the size of Earth's oceans.
   C Both are models used to the study Earth's surface.
   D Both show one part of Earth.

2. How are a globe and Earth alike?
   F Both are spheres.
   G Both represent real things.
   H Both are flat surfaces.
   I Both are models.

3. According to the passage, examining a globe would help you answer which of the following questions?
   A How many highways are in Michigan?
   B Where are the streams in my state?
   C Which continents border the Indian Ocean?
   D What is the exact length of the Nile River?

Passage 2 The names of many geographic locations in the United States are <u>rich</u> in description and national history. Names such as Adirondack and Chesapeake come from Native American languages. Some names, such as New London, Baton Rouge, and San Francisco, reflect European naming traditions. Other names, such as Stone Mountain and Long Island, provide a description of the area. The mapping efforts in the United States that took place after the Civil War often led to multiple names for one location. But mapmakers and scientists needed consistent names of locations for their studies. In 1890, the U.S. Board on Geographic Names was formed. This board determines and maintains location names.

1. In the passage, what does *rich* mean?
   A wealthy
   B abundant
   C incomplete
   D thick

2. Which of the following statements is true?
   F Mapmakers enjoyed using multiple names for the same location.
   G The U.S. Board on Geographic Names determines the name for an area.
   H Names such as Baton Rouge and San Francisco describe the physical area.
   I All geographic names came from Native American languages.

3. What can you infer from the passage?
   A Mapmakers name locations after themselves.
   B Scientists used descriptions of the physical area as names for locations.
   C The U.S. Board on Geographic Names now determines the names for locations.
   D Today, many locations in the United States have several names.

Use each figure below to answer the question that follows each figure.

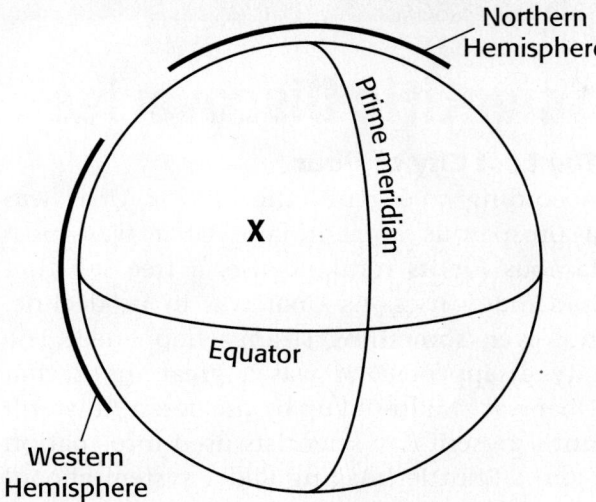

Northern Hemisphere
Prime meridian
X
Equator
Western Hemisphere

1. An X shows the location of a field investigation study site. Which of the following pairs of terms accurately describes the location of the X on the map?

A Northern Hemisphere; Western Hemisphere

B Northern Hemisphere; Eastern Hemisphere

C Southern Hemisphere; Eastern Hemisphere

D Southern Hemisphere; Western Hemisphere

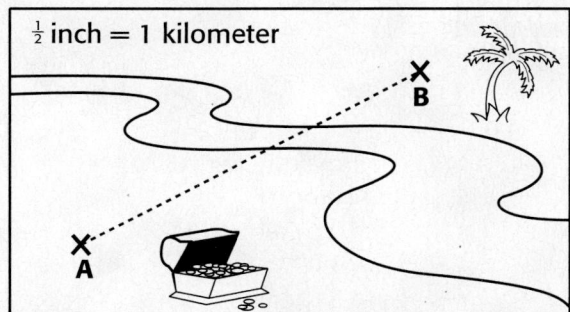

½ inch = 1 kilometer

X B

X A

2. The map above shows the distance from point A to point B. According to this map, what is the actual distance from point A to point B?

F 1 km

G 2 km

H 4 km

I 6 km

Read each question below, and choose the best answer.

1. Greenland's area is approximately 2 million square kilometers. The area of Africa is approximately 15 times the area of Greenland. What is the approximate area of Africa?

A 30 million square kilometers

B 17 million square kilometers

C 13 million square kilometers

D 7.5 million square kilometers

2. A satellite is 264 km above Earth's surface. What is this measurement expressed in meters?

F 264,000 m

G 26,400 m

H 2,640 m

I 0.264 m

3. On a topographic map, every fifth contour line is a darker line, or *index contour*. How many index contours are there in a series of 50 contour lines?

A 8

B 9

C 10

D 11

4. Juan and Maria hike up a mountain. Maria is at an elevation of 4.3 km. Juan is at an elevation of 2.7 km. What is the difference between their elevations?

F 1.6 km

G 2.6 km

H 6.0 km

I 7.0 km

5. The North Pole is 90°N latitude. If you drew a line from the North Pole to the center of Earth and a line from a point on the equator to the center of Earth, what kind of angle would the two lines form at Earth's center?

A acute

B obtuse

C equilateral

D right

Science in Action

Scientific Discoveries

The Lost City of Ubar

According to legend, the city of Ubar was a prosperous ancient city. Ubar was most famous for its frankincense, a tree sap that had many uses. As Ubar was in its decline, however, something strange happened. The city disappeared! It was a great myth that Ubar was swallowed up by the desert. It wasn't until present-day scientists used information from a Shuttle Imaging Radar system aboard the space shuttle that this lost city was found! Using radar, scientists were able to "see" beneath the huge dunes of the desert, where they finally found the lost city of Ubar.

Science, Technology, and Society

Geocaching

Wouldn't it be exciting to go on a hunt for buried treasure? Thousands of people around the world participate in geocaching, which is an adventure game for GPS users. In this adventure game, individuals and groups of people put caches, or hidden treasures, in places all over the world. Once the cache is hidden, the coordinates of the cache's location are posted on the Internet. Then, geocaching teams compete to find the cache. Geocaching should only be attempted with parental supervision.

Roads appear as purple lines on this computer-generated remote-sensing image.

Social Studies ACTIVITY

WRITING SKILL Ubar was once a very wealthy, magnificent city. Its riches were built on the frankincense trade. Research the history of frankincense, and write a paragraph describing how frankincense was used in ancient times and how it is used today.

Language Arts ACTIVITY

Why was the word *geocaching* chosen for this adventure game? Use the Internet or another source to find the origin and meaning of the word *geocaching*.

Matthew Henson

Arctic Explorer Matthew Henson was born in Maryland in 1866. His parents were freeborn sharecroppers. When Henson was a young boy, his parents died. He then went to look for work as a cabin boy on a ship. Several years later, Henson had traveled around the world and had become educated in the areas of geography, history, and mathematics. In 1898, Henson met U.S. Naval Lieutenant Robert E. Peary. Peary was the leader of Arctic expeditions between 1886 and 1909.

Peary asked Henson to accompany him as a navigator on several trips, including trips to Central America and Greenland. One of Peary's passions was to be the first person to reach the North Pole. It was Henson's vast knowledge of mathematics and carpentry that made Peary's trek to the North Pole possible. In 1909, Henson was the first person to reach the North Pole. Part of Henson's job as navigator was to drive ahead of the party and blaze the first trail. As a result, he often arrived ahead of everyone else. On April 6, 1909, Henson reached the approximate North Pole 45 minutes ahead of Peary. Upon his arrival, he exclaimed, "I think I'm the first man to sit on top of the world!"

Math ACTIVITY

On the last leg of their journey, Henson and Peary traveled 664.5 km in 16 days! On average, how far did Henson and Peary travel each day?

To learn more about these Science in Action topics, visit go.hrw.com and type in the keyword **HZ5MAPF**.

Current Science

Check out Current Science® articles related to this chapter by visiting go.hrw.com. Just type in the keyword **HZ5CS02**.

UNIT 2

TIMELINE

Earth's Resources

In this unit, you will learn about the basic components of the solid Earth—rocks and the minerals from which they are made. You will also learn about other resources the Earth contains. The ground beneath your feet is a treasure-trove of interesting materials, some of which are very valuable. Secrets of Earth's history are also hidden within the ground's depths. This timeline shows some of the events that have occurred through human history as scientists have come to understand more about our planet.

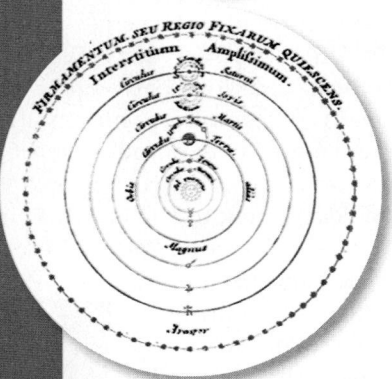

1543
Nicolaus Copernicus argues that the sun rather than the Earth is the center of the universe.

1860
Fossil remains of *Archaeopteryx,* a species that may link reptiles and birds, are discovered in Germany.

1936
Hoover Dam is completed. This massive hydroelectric dam, standing more than 221 m, required 3.25 million cubic yards of concrete to build.

1975
Tabei Junko of Japan becomes the first woman to successfully climb Mount Everest, 22 years after Edmund Hillary and Tenzing Norgay first conquered the mountain in 1953.

1681

The dodo, a flightless bird, is driven to extinction by the actions of humans.

1739

Georg Brandt identifies a new element and names it cobalt.

1848

James Marshall discovers gold at Sutter's Mill, in California, beginning the California gold rush. Prospectors during the gold rush of the following year are referred to as "forty-niners."

1947

Willard F. Libby develops a method of dating prehistoric objects by using radioactive carbon.

1955

Using 1 million pounds of pressure per square inch and temperatures of more than 1,700°C, General Electric creates the first artificial diamonds from graphite.

1969

Apollo 11 astronauts Neil Armstrong and Edwin "Buzz" Aldrin bring 22 kg of moon rocks and soil back to the Earth.

1989

Russian engineers drill a borehole 12 km into the Earth's crust. The borehole is more than 3 times deeper than the deepest mine shaft.

1997

Sojourner, a roving probe on Mars, investigates a Martian boulder nicknamed Yogi.

1999

A Japanese automaker introduces the first hybrid car into the U.S. market.

3

Minerals of the Earth's Crust

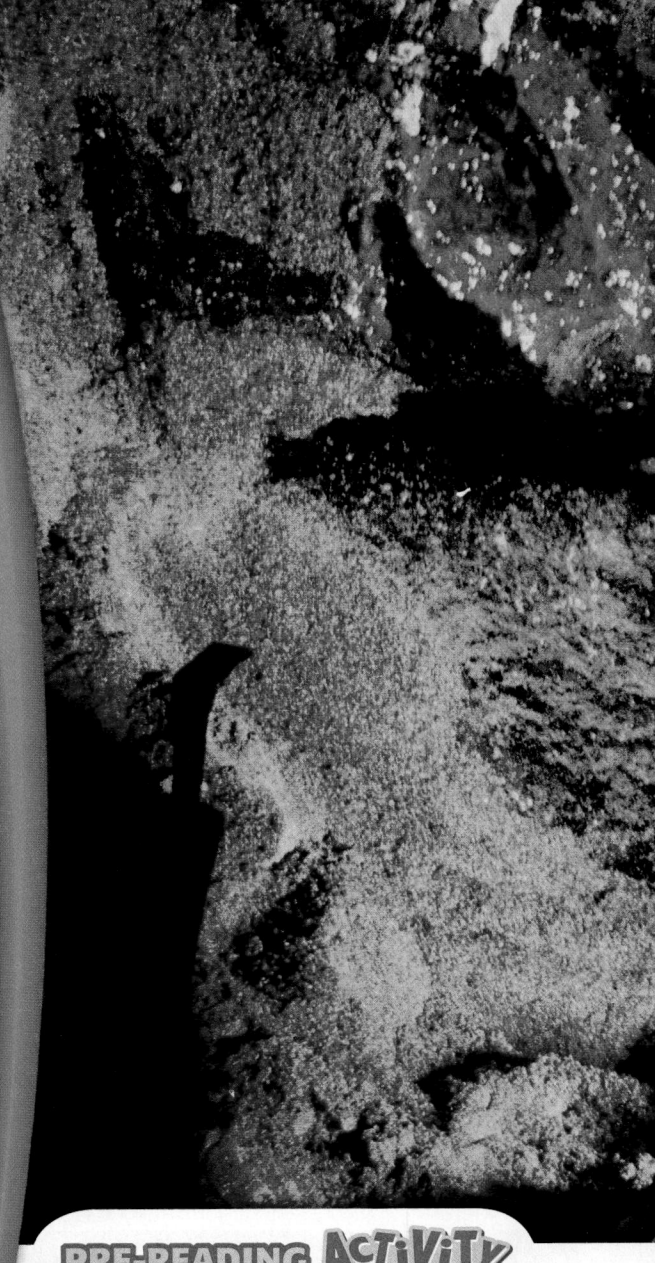

About the PHOTO

Fluorescence is the ability that some minerals have to glow under ultraviolet light. The beauty of mineral fluorescence is well represented at the Sterling Hill Mine in Franklin, New Jersey. In this picture taken at the mine, minerals in the rock glow as brightly as if they had been freshly painted by an artist.

PRE-READING ACTIVITY

Graphic Organizer

Concept Map Before you read the chapter, create the graphic organizer entitled "Concept Map" described in the **Study Skills** section of the Appendix. As you read the chapter, fill in the concept map with details about minerals.

STARTUP ACTIVITY

What Is Your Classroom Made Of?

One of the properties of minerals is that minerals are made from nonliving material. Complete the following activity to see if you can determine whether items in your classroom are made from living or nonliving materials.

Procedure

1. On a **sheet of paper,** make two columns. Label one column "Materials made from living things." Label the second column "Materials made from nonliving things."

2. Look around your classroom. Choose a variety of items to put on your list. Some items that you might select are your clothing, your desk, books, notebook paper, pencils, the classroom windows, doors, walls, the ceiling, and the floor.

3. With a partner, discuss each item that you have chosen. Decide into which column each item should be placed. Write down the reason for your decision.

Analysis

1. Are most of the items that you chose made of living or nonliving materials?

What Is a Mineral?

You may think that all minerals look like gems. But, in fact, most minerals look more like rocks. Does this mean that minerals are the same as rocks? Well, not really. So, what's the difference?

For one thing, rocks are made of minerals, but minerals are not made of rocks. A **mineral** is a naturally formed, inorganic solid that has a definite crystalline structure.

Mineral Structure

By answering the four questions in **Figure 1,** you can tell whether an object is a mineral. If you cannot answer "yes" to all four questions, you don't have a mineral. Three of the four questions may be easy to answer. The question about crystalline structure may be more difficult. To understand what crystalline structure is, you need to know a little about the elements that make up a mineral. **Elements** are pure substances that cannot be broken down into simpler substances by ordinary chemical means. All minerals contain one or more of the 92 naturally occurring elements.

Is it nonliving material?
A mineral is inorganic, meaning it isn't made of living things.

Is it a solid?
Minerals can't be gases or liquids.

Does it have a crystalline structure?
Minerals are crystals, which have a repeating inner structure that is often reflected in the shape of the crystal. Minerals generally have the same chemical composition throughout.

Is it formed in nature?
Crystalline materials made by people aren't classified as minerals.

Figure 1 *The answers to these four questions will determine whether an object is a mineral.*

Atoms and Compounds

Each element is made of only one kind of atom. An *atom* is the smallest part of an element that has all the properties of that element. Like other substances, minerals are made up of atoms of one or more elements.

Most minerals are made of compounds of several different elements. A **compound** is a substance made of two or more elements that have been chemically joined, or bonded. Halite, NaCl, for example, is a compound of sodium, Na, and chlorine, Cl, as shown in **Figure 2.** A few minerals, such as gold and silver, are composed of only one element. A mineral that is composed of only one element is called a *native element.*

✓ **Reading Check** How does a compound differ from an element? (*See the Appendix for answers to Reading Checks.*)

Crystals

Solid, geometric forms of minerals produced by a repeating pattern of atoms that is present throughout the mineral are called **crystals.** A crystal's shape is determined by the arrangement of the atoms within the crystal. The arrangement of atoms in turn is determined by the kinds of atoms that make up the mineral. Each mineral has a definite crystalline structure. All minerals can be grouped into crystal classes according to the kinds of crystals they form. **Figure 3** shows how the atomic structure of gold gives rise to cubic crystals.

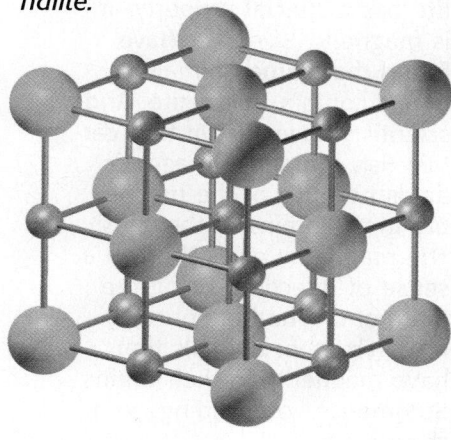

Figure 2 *When atoms of sodium (purple) and chlorine (green) join, they form a compound commonly known as rock salt, or the mineral halite.*

mineral a naturally formed, inorganic solid that has a definite crystalline structure

element a substance that cannot be separated or broken down into simpler substances by chemical means

compound a substance made up of atoms of two or more different elements joined by chemical bonds

crystal a solid whose atoms, ions, or molecules are arranged in a definite pattern

Figure 3   Composition of the Mineral Gold

The mineral gold is composed of gold atoms arranged in a crystalline structure.

Crystals of the mineral gold

The atomic structure of gold

The crystal structure of gold

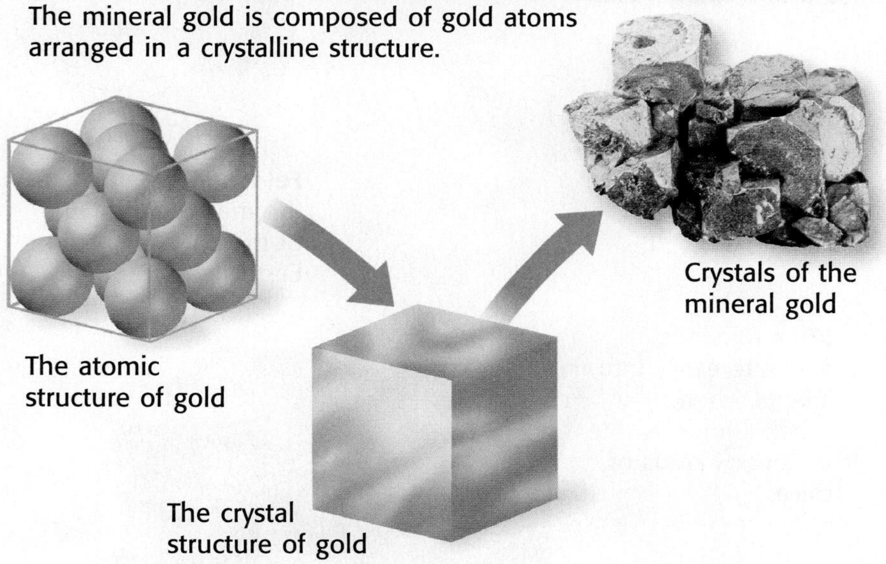

Two Groups of Minerals

The most common classification of minerals is based on chemical composition. Minerals are divided into two groups based on their chemical composition. These groups are the silicate minerals and the nonsilicate minerals.

Silicate Minerals

Silicon and oxygen are the two most common elements in the Earth's crust. Minerals that contain a combination of these two elements are called **silicate minerals.** Silicate minerals make up more than 90% of the Earth's crust. The rest of the Earth's crust is made up of nonsilicate minerals. Silicon and oxygen usually combine with other elements, such as aluminum, iron, magnesium, and potassium, to make up silicate minerals. Some of the more common silicate minerals are shown in **Figure 4.**

Nonsilicate Minerals

Minerals that do not contain a combination of the elements silicon and oxygen form a group called the **nonsilicate minerals.** Some of these minerals are made up of elements such as carbon, oxygen, fluorine, and sulfur. **Figure 5** on the following page shows the most important classes of nonsilicate minerals.

✔ **Reading Check** How do silicate minerals differ from nonsilicate minerals?

silicate mineral a mineral that contains a combination of silicon, oxygen, and one or more metals

nonsilicate mineral a mineral that does not contain compounds of silicon and oxygen

---

Figure 4 Common Silicate Minerals

Quartz is the basic building block of many rocks.

Feldspar minerals are the main component of most rocks on the Earth's surface.

Mica minerals separate easily into sheets when they break. Biotite is one of several kinds of mica.

Figure 5 Classes of Nonsilicate Minerals

Native elements are minerals that are composed of only one element. Some examples are copper, Cu, gold, Au, and silver, Ag. Native elements are used in communications and electronics equipment.

Copper

Oxides are compounds that form when an element, such as aluminum or iron, combines chemically with oxygen. Oxide minerals are used to make abrasives, aircraft parts, and paint.

Corundum

Carbonates are minerals that contain combinations of carbon and oxygen in their chemical structure. We use carbonate minerals in cement, building stones, and fireworks.

Calcite

Sulfates are minerals that contain sulfur and oxygen, SO_4. Sulfates are used in cosmetics, toothpaste, cement, and paint.

Gypsum

Halides are compounds that form when fluorine, chlorine, iodine, or bromine combine with sodium, potassium, or calcium. Halide minerals are used in the chemical industry and in detergents.

Fluorite

Sulfides are minerals that contain one or more elements, such as lead, iron, or nickel, combined with sulfur. Sulfide minerals are used to make batteries, medicines, and electronic parts.

Galena

SECTION Review

Summary

- A mineral is a naturally formed, inorganic solid that has a definite crystalline structure.
- Minerals may be either elements or compounds.
- Mineral crystals are solid, geometric forms that are produced by a repeating pattern of atoms.
- Minerals are classified as either silicate minerals or nonsilicate minerals based on the elements of which they are composed.

Using Key Terms

1. In your own words, write a definition for each of the following terms: *element*, *compound*, and *mineral*.

Understanding Key Ideas

2. Which of the following minerals is a nonsilicate mineral?
   a. mica
   b. quartz
   c. gypsum
   d. feldspar

3. What is a crystal, and what determines a crystal's shape?

4. Describe the two major groups of minerals.

Math Skills

5. If there are approximately 3,600 known minerals and about 20 of the minerals are native elements, what percentage of all minerals are native elements?

Critical Thinking

6. **Applying Concepts** Explain why each of the following is not considered a mineral: water, oxygen, honey, and teeth.

7. **Applying Concepts** Explain why scientists consider ice to be a mineral.

8. **Making Comparisons** In what ways are sulfate and sulfide minerals the same. In what ways are they different?

Developed and maintained by the National Science Teachers Association

For a variety of links related to this chapter, go to www.scilinks.org

Topic: Gems
SciLinks code: HSM0640

Identifying Minerals

If you closed your eyes and tasted different foods, you could probably determine what the foods are by noting properties such as saltiness or sweetness. You can also determine the identity of a mineral by noting different properties.

In this section, you will learn about the properties that will help you identify minerals.

READING WARM-UP

Objectives

- Identify seven ways to determine the identity of minerals.
- Explain special properties of minerals.

Terms to Learn

luster	fracture
streak	hardness
cleavage	density

READING STRATEGY

Reading Organizer As you read this section, create an outline of the section. Use the headings from the section in your outline.

Color

The same mineral can come in a variety of colors. For example, in its purest state quartz is clear. Samples of quartz that contain various types of and various amounts of impurities, however, can be a variety of colors.

Besides impurities, other factors can change the appearance of minerals. The mineral pyrite, often called fool's gold, normally has a golden color. But if pyrite is exposed to air and water for a long period, it can turn brown or black. Because of factors such as impurities, color usually is not the best way to identify a mineral.

Luster

luster the way in which a mineral reflects light

The way a surface reflects light is called **luster.** When you say an object is shiny or dull, you are describing its luster. Minerals have metallic, submetallic, or nonmetallic luster. If a mineral is shiny, it has a metallic luster. If the mineral is dull, its luster is either submetallic or nonmetallic. The different types of lusters are shown in **Figure 1.**

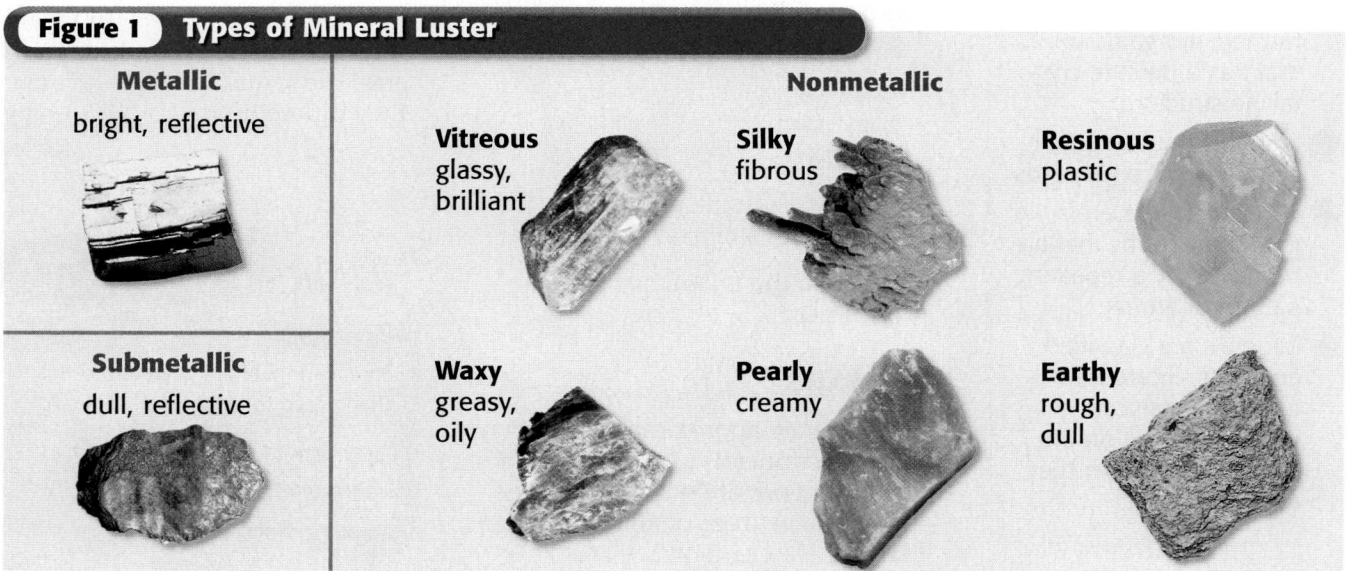

Figure 1 Types of Mineral Luster

Metallic
bright, reflective

Submetallic
dull, reflective

Nonmetallic

Vitreous
glassy, brilliant

Waxy
greasy, oily

Silky
fibrous

Pearly
creamy

Resinous
plastic

Earthy
rough, dull

Streak

The color of a mineral in powdered form is called the mineral's **streak.** A mineral's streak can be found by rubbing the mineral against a piece of unglazed porcelain called a *streak plate.* The mark left on the streak plate is the streak. The streak is a thin layer of powdered mineral. The color of a mineral's streak is not always the same as the color of the mineral sample. The difference between color and streak is shown in **Figure 2.** Unlike the surface of a mineral sample, the streak is not affected by air or water. For this reason, using streak is more reliable than using color in identifying a mineral.

✓ **Reading Check** Why is using streak more reliable in identifying a mineral than using color is? (*See the Appendix for answers to Reading Checks.*)

Cleavage and Fracture

Different types of minerals break in different ways. The way a mineral breaks is determined by the arrangement of its atoms. **Cleavage** is the tendency of some minerals to break along smooth, flat surfaces. **Figure 3** shows the cleavage patterns of the minerals mica and halite.

Fracture is the tendency of some minerals to break unevenly along curved or irregular surfaces. One type of fracture is shown in **Figure 4.**

Figure 2 *The color of the mineral hematite may vary, but hematite's streak is always red-brown.*

streak the color of the powder of a mineral

cleavage the splitting of a mineral along smooth, flat surfaces

fracture the manner in which a mineral breaks along either curved or irregular surfaces

Figure 3 *Cleavage varies with mineral type.*

Mica breaks easily into distinct sheets. ▶

Halite breaks at 90° angles in three directions.
▼

Figure 4 *This sample of quartz shows a curved fracture pattern called* conchoidal fracture *(kahn KOYD uhl FRAK chuhr).*

Figure 5 Mohs Hardness Scale

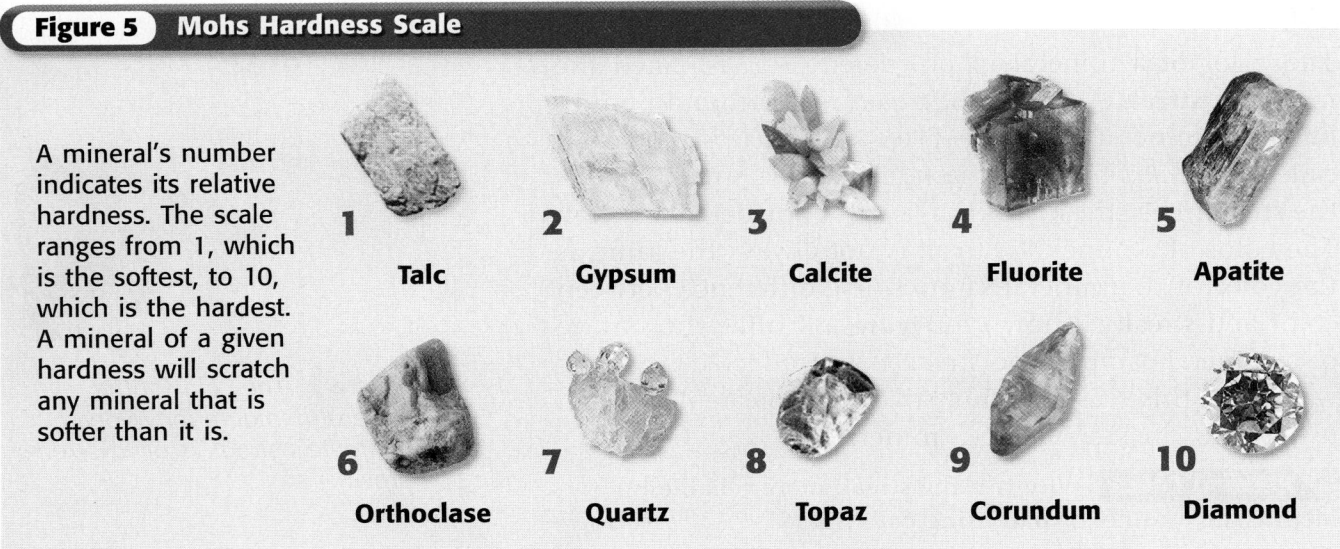

A mineral's number indicates its relative hardness. The scale ranges from 1, which is the softest, to 10, which is the hardest. A mineral of a given hardness will scratch any mineral that is softer than it is.

1 Talc
2 Gypsum
3 Calcite
4 Fluorite
5 Apatite
6 Orthoclase
7 Quartz
8 Topaz
9 Corundum
10 Diamond

hardness a measure of the ability of a mineral to resist scratching

density the ratio of the mass of a substance to the volume of the substance

Hardness

A mineral's resistance to being scratched is called **hardness**. To determine the hardness of minerals, scientists use *Mohs hardness scale,* shown in **Figure 5.** Notice that talc has a rating of 1 and diamond has a rating of 10. The greater a mineral's resistance to being scratched is, the higher the mineral's rating is. To identify a mineral by using Mohs scale, try to scratch the surface of a mineral with the edge of one of the 10 reference minerals. If the reference mineral scratches your mineral, the reference mineral is harder than your mineral.

✓ *Reading Check* How would you determine the hardness of an unidentified mineral sample?

Density

If you pick up a golf ball and a table-tennis ball, which will feel heavier? Although the balls are of similar size, the golf ball will feel heavier because it is denser. **Density** is the measure of how much matter is in a given amount of space. In other words, density is a ratio of an object's mass to its volume. Density is usually measured in grams per cubic centimeter. Because water has a density of 1 g/cm^3, it is used as a reference point for other substances. The ratio of an object's density to the density of water is called the object's *specific gravity.* The specific gravity of gold, for example, is 19. So, gold has a density of 19 g/cm^3. In other words, there is 19 times more matter in 1 cm^3 of gold than in 1 cm^3 of water.

Scratch Test

1. You will need a **penny,** a **pencil,** and your **finger-nail.** Which one of these three materials is the hardest?

2. Use your fingernail to try to scratch the graphite at the tip of a pencil.

3. Now try to scratch the penny with your fingernail.

4. Rank the three materials in order from softest to hardest.

Special Properties

Some properties are particular to only a few types of minerals. The properties shown in **Figure 6** can help you quickly identify the minerals shown. To identify some properties, however, you will need specialized equipment.

Figure 6   Special Properties of Some Minerals

Fluorescence
Calcite and fluorite glow under ultraviolet light. The same fluorite sample is shown in ultraviolet light (top) and in white light (bottom).

Chemical Reaction
Calcite will become bubbly, or "fizz," when a drop of weak acid is placed on it.

Optical Properties
A thin, clear piece of calcite placed over an image will cause a double image.

Magnetism
Both magnetite and pyrrhotite are natural magnets that attract iron.

Taste
Halite has a salty taste.

Radioactivity
Minerals that contain radium or uranium can be detected by a Geiger counter.

SECTION Review

Summary

● Properties that can be used to identify minerals are color, luster, streak, cleavage, fracture, hardness, and density.

● Some minerals can be identified by special properties they have, such as taste, magnetism, fluorescence, radioactivity, chemical reaction, and optical properties.

Using Key Terms

1. Use each of the following terms in a separate sentence: *luster, streak,* and *cleavage.*

Understanding Key Ideas

2. Which of the following properties of minerals is expressed in numbers?
   a. fracture
   b. cleavage
   c. hardness
   d. streak

3. How do you determine a mineral's streak?

4. Briefly describe the special properties of minerals.

Math Skills

5. If a mineral has a specific gravity of 5.5, how much more matter is there in 1 cm^3 of this mineral than in 1 cm^3 of water?

Critical Thinking

6. **Applying Concepts** What properties would you use to determine whether two mineral samples are different minerals?

7. **Applying Concepts** If a mineral scratches calcite but is scratched by apatite, what is the mineral's hardness?

8. **Analyzing Methods** What would be the easiest way to identify calcite?

SCiLINKS®

NSTA
Developed and maintained by the National Science Teachers Association

For a variety of links related to this chapter, go to www.scilinks.org

Topic: Identifying Minerals
SciLinks code: HSM0782

The Formation, Mining, and Use of Minerals

If you wanted to find a mineral, where do you think you would look?

Minerals form in a variety of environments in the Earth's crust. Each of these environments has a different set of physical and chemical conditions. Therefore, the environment in which a mineral forms determines the mineral's properties. Environments in which minerals form may be on or near the Earth's surface or deep beneath the Earth's surface.

READING WARM-UP

Objectives

● Describe the environments in which minerals form.

● Compare the two types of mining.

● Describe two ways to reduce the effects of mining.

● Describe different uses for metallic and nonmetallic minerals.

Terms to Learn

ore
reclamation

READING STRATEGY

Discussion Read this section silently. Write down questions that you have about this section. Discuss your questions in a small group.

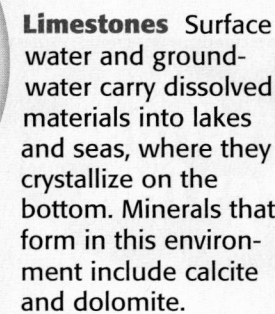

Limestones Surface water and ground-water carry dissolved materials into lakes and seas, where they crystallize on the bottom. Minerals that form in this environment include calcite and dolomite.

Evaporating Salt Water When a body of salt water dries up, minerals such as gypsum and halite are left behind. As the salt water evaporates, these minerals crystallize.

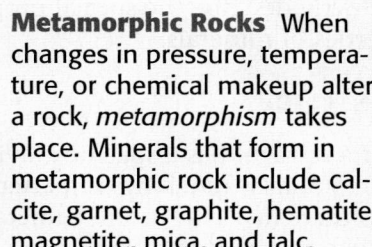

Metamorphic Rocks When changes in pressure, temperature, or chemical makeup alter a rock, *metamorphism* takes place. Minerals that form in metamorphic rock include calcite, garnet, graphite, hematite, magnetite, mica, and talc.

INTERNET ACTIVITY

For another activity related to this chapter, go to go.hrw.com and type in the keyword **HZ5MINW.**

Hot-Water Solutions
Groundwater works its way downward and is heated by magma. It then reacts with minerals to form a hot liquid solution. Dissolved metals and other elements crystallize out of the hot fluid to form new minerals. Gold, copper, sulfur, pyrite, and galena form in such hot-water environments.

Pegmatites As magma moves upward, it can form teardrop-shaped bodies called *pegmatites.* The mineral crystals in pegmatites become extremely large, sometimes growing to several meters across! Many gemstones, such as topaz and tourmaline, form in pegmatites.

Plutons As magma rises upward through the crust, it sometimes stops moving before it reaches the surface and cools slowly, forming millions of mineral crystals. Eventually, the entire magma body solidifies to form a *pluton.* Mica, feldspar, magnetite, and quartz are some of the minerals that form from magma.

MATH PRACTICE

Surface Coal Mining

Producing 1 metric ton of coal requires that up to 30 metric tons of earth be removed first. Some surface coal mines produce up to 50,000 metric tons of coal per day. How many metric tons of earth might have to be removed in order to mine 50,000 metric tons of coal?

ore a natural material whose concentration of economically valuable minerals is high enough for the material to be mined profitably

Mining

Many kinds of rocks and minerals must be mined to extract the valuable elements they contain. Geologists use the term **ore** to describe a mineral deposit large enough and pure enough to be mined for profit. Rocks and minerals are removed from the ground by one of two methods—surface mining or sub-surface mining. The method miners choose depends on how close to the surface or how far down in the Earth the mineral is located.

Surface Mining

When mineral deposits are located at or near the surface of the Earth, surface-mining methods are used to remove the minerals. Types of surface mines include open pits, surface coal mines, and quarries.

Open-pit mining is used to remove large, near-surface deposits of economically important minerals such as gold and copper. As shown in **Figure 1,** ore is mined downward, layer by layer, in an open-pit mine. Explosives are often used to break up the ore. The ore is then loaded into haul trucks and transported from the mine for processing. Quarries are open pits that are used to mine building stone, crushed rock, sand, and gravel. Coal that is near the surface is removed by surface coal mining. Surface coal mining is sometimes known as strip mining because the coal is removed in strips that may be as wide as 50 m and as long as 1 km.

Figure 1 *In open-pit mines, the ore is mined downward in layers. The stair-step excavation of the walls keeps the sides of the mine from collapsing. Giant haul trucks (inset) are used to transport ore from the mine.*

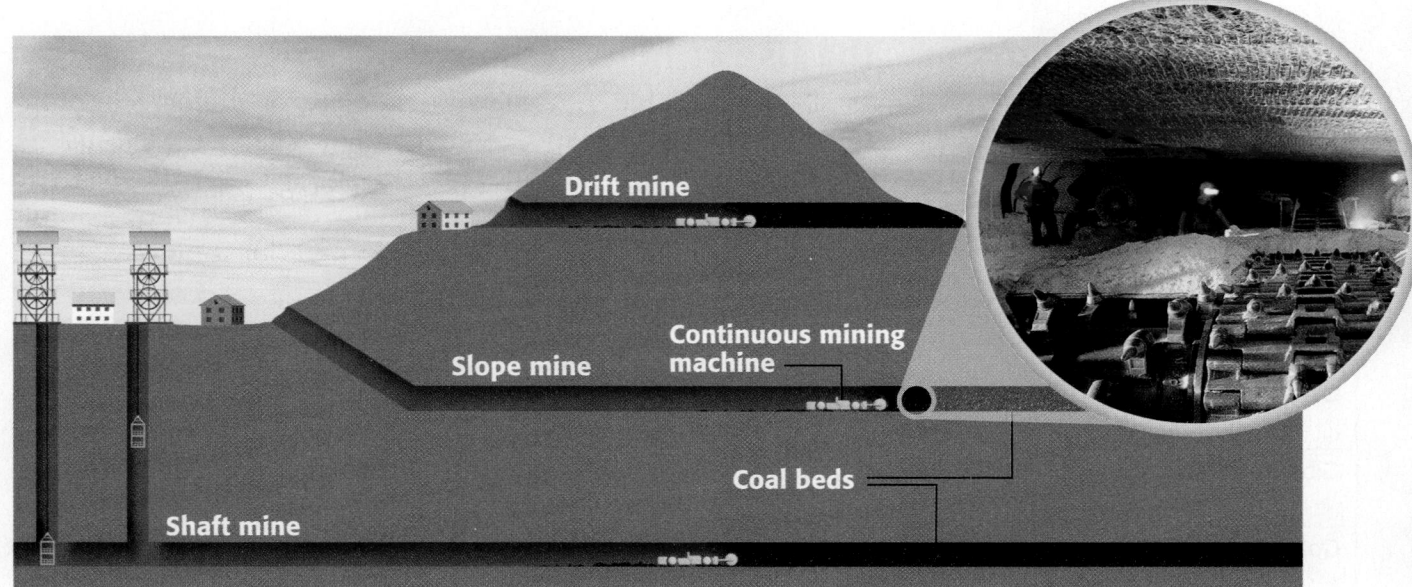

Drift mine

Continuous mining machine

Slope mine

Coal beds

Shaft mine

Subsurface Mining

Subsurface mining methods are used when mineral deposits are located too deep within the Earth to be surface mined. Subsurface mining often requires that passageways be dug into the Earth to reach the ore. As shown in **Figure 2,** these passageways may be dug horizontally or at an angle. If a mineral deposit extends deep within the Earth, however, a vertical shaft is sunk. This shaft may connect a number of passageways that intersect the ore at different levels.

 **Reading Check** Compare surface and subsurface mining. (*See the Appendix for answers to Reading Checks.*)

Responsible Mining

Mining gives us the minerals we need, but it may also create problems. Mining can destroy or disturb the habitats of plants and animals. Also, the waste products from a mine may get into water sources, which pollutes surface water and groundwater.

Mine Reclamation

One way to reduce the potential harmful effects of mining is to return the land to its original state after the mining is completed. The process by which land used for mining is returned to its original state or better is called **reclamation.** Reclamation of mined public and private land has been required by law since the mid-1970s. Another way to reduce the effects of mining is to reduce our need for minerals. We reduce our need for minerals by recycling many of the mineral products that we currently use, such as aluminum.

Figure 2 *Subsurface mining is the removal of minerals or other materials from deep within the Earth. Passageways must be dug underground to reach the ore. Machines such as continuous mining machines (inset) are used to mine ore in subsurface mines.*

reclamation the process of returning land to its original condition after mining is completed

SCHOOL to HOME

Recycling Minerals at Home

With your parent, locate products in your home that are made of minerals. Decide which of these products could be recycled. In your **science journal,** make a list of the products that could be recycled to save minerals.

The Use of Minerals

As shown in **Table 1,** some minerals are of major economic and industrial importance. Some minerals can be used just as they are. Other minerals must be processed to get the element or elements that the minerals contain. **Figure 3** shows some processed minerals used to make the parts of a bicycle.

Table 1	Common Uses of Minerals
Mineral	**Uses**
Copper	electrical wire, plumbing, coins
Diamond	jewelry, cutting tools, drill bits
Galena	batteries, ammunition
Gibbsite	cans, foil, appliances, utensils
Gold	jewelry, computers, spacecraft, dentistry
Gypsum	wallboards, plaster, cement
Halite	nutrition, highway de-icer, water softener
Quartz	glass, computer chips
Silver	photography, electronics products, jewelry
Sphalerite	jet aircraft, spacecraft, paints

Metallic Minerals

Some minerals are metallic. Metallic minerals have shiny surfaces, do not let light pass through them, and are good conductors of heat and electricity. Metallic minerals can be processed into metals that are strong and do not rust. Other metals can be pounded or pressed into various shapes or stretched thinly without breaking. These properties make metals desirable for use in aircraft, automobiles, computers, communications and electronic equipment, and spacecraft. Examples of metallic minerals that have many industrial uses are gold, silver, and copper.

Nonmetallic Minerals

Other minerals are nonmetals. Nonmetallic minerals have shiny or dull surfaces, may let light pass through them, and are good insulators of electricity. Nonmetallic minerals are some of the most widely used minerals in industry. For example, calcite is a major component of concrete, which is used in building roads, buildings, bridges, and other structures. Industrial sand and gravel, or silica, have uses that range from glassmaking to producing computer chips.

Figure 3 Some Materials Used in the Parts of a Bicycle

Handlebars titanium from ilmenite

Frame aluminum from bauxite

Spokes iron from magnetite

Pedals beryllium from beryl

Gemstones

Some nonmetallic minerals, called *gemstones*, are highly valued for their beauty and rarity rather than for their usefulness. Important gemstones include diamond, ruby, sapphire, emerald, aquamarine, topaz, and tourmaline. An example of a diamond is shown in **Figure 4.** Color is the most important characteristic of a gemstone. The more attractive the color is, the more valuable the gem is. Gemstones must also be durable. That is, they must be hard enough to be cut and polished. The mass of a gemstone is expressed in a unit known as a *carat*. One carat is equal to 200 mg.

✓ **Reading Check** In your own words, define the term *gemstone*.

Figure 4 *The Cullinan diamond, at the center of this scepter, is part of the largest diamond ever found.*

SECTION Review

Summary

- Environments in which minerals form may be located at or near the Earth's surface or deep below the surface.
- The two types of mining are surface mining and subsurface mining.
- Two ways to reduce the effects of mining are the reclamation of mined land and the recycling of mineral products.
- Some metallic and nonmetallic minerals have many important economic and industrial uses.

Using Key Terms

Complete each of the following sentences by choosing the correct term from the word bank.

    ore   reclamation

1. _____ is the process of returning land to its original condition after mining is completed.

2. _____ is the term used to describe a mineral deposit that is large enough and pure enough to be mined for profit.

Understanding Key Ideas

3. Which of the following conditions is NOT important in the formation of minerals?

    a. presence of groundwater

    b. evaporation

    c. volcanic activity

    d. wind

4. What are the two main types of mining, and how do they differ?

5. List some uses of metallic minerals.

6. List some uses of nonmetallic minerals.

Math Skills

7. A diamond cutter has a raw diamond that weighs 19.5 carats and from which two 5-carat diamonds will be cut. How much did the raw diamond weigh in milligrams? How much will each of the two cut diamonds weigh in milligrams?

Critical Thinking

8. **Analyzing Ideas** How does reclamation protect the environment around a mine?

9. **Applying Concepts** Suppose you find a mineral crystal that is as tall as you are. What kinds of environmental factors would cause such a crystal to form?

Developed and maintained by the National Science Teachers Association

For a variety of links related to this chapter, go to www.scilinks.org

Topic: Mining Minerals
SciLinks code: HSM0968

Skills Practice Lab

OBJECTIVES

Calculate the density and specific gravity of a mineral.

Explain how density and specific gravity can be used to identify a mineral specimen.

MATERIALS

- balance
- beaker, 400 mL
- galena sample
- pyrite sample
- ring stand
- spring scale
- string
- water, 400 mL

SAFETY

Galena

Pyrite

Is It Fool's Gold?
A Dense Situation

Have you heard of fool's gold? Maybe you've seen a piece of it. This mineral is actually pyrite, and it was often passed off as real gold. However, there are simple tests that you can do to keep from being tricked. Minerals can be identified by their properties. Some properties, such as color, vary from sample to sample. Other properties, such as density and specific gravity, remain consistent across samples. In this activity, you will try to verify the identity of some mineral samples.

Ask a Question

1. How can I determine if an unknown mineral is not gold or silver?

Form a Hypothesis

2. Write a hypothesis that is a possible answer to the question above. Explain your reasoning.

Test the Hypothesis

3. Copy the data table. Use it to record your observations.

Observation Chart		
Measurement	**Galena**	**Pyrite**
Mass in air (g)		
Weight in air (N)		
Volume of mineral (mL)		
Weight in water (N)		

DO NOT WRITE IN BOOK

4. Find the mass of each sample by laying the mineral on the balance. Record the mass of each sample in your data table.

5. Attach the spring scale to the ring stand.

6. Tie a string around the sample of galena, and leave a loop at the loose end. Suspend the galena from the spring scale, and find its mass and weight in air. Do not remove the sample from the spring scale yet. Enter these data in your data table.

7. Fill a beaker halfway with water. Record the beginning volume of water in your data table.

8. Carefully lift the beaker around the galena until the mineral is completely submerged. Be careful not to splash any water out of the beaker! Do not allow the mineral to touch the beaker.

9. Record the new volume and weight in your data table.

10. Subtract the original volume of water from the new volume to find the amount of water displaced by the mineral. This is the volume of the mineral sample itself. Record this value in your data table.

11. Repeat steps 6–10 for the sample of pyrite.

Analyze the Results

1. **Constructing Tables** Copy the data table below. (Note: 1 mL = 1 cm³)

Density Data Table

Mineral	Density (g/cm³)	Specific gravity
Silver	10.5	10.5
Galena	DO NOT WRITE IN BOOK	
Pyrite		
Gold	19.0	19.0

2. **Organizing Data** Use the following equations to calculate the density and specific gravity of each mineral, and record your answers in your data table.

$$density = \frac{mass\ in\ air}{volume}$$

$$specific\ gravity = \frac{weight\ in\ air}{weight\ in\ air - weight\ in\ water}$$

Draw Conclusions

3. **Drawing Conclusions** The density of pure gold is 19 g/cm³. How can you use this information to prove that your sample of pyrite is not gold?

4. **Drawing Conclusions** The density of pure silver is 10.5 g/cm³. How can you use this information to prove that your sample of galena is not silver?

5. **Applying Conclusions** If you found a gold-colored nugget, how could you find out if the nugget was real gold or fool's gold?

Chapter Review

1 Use each of the following terms in a separate sentence: *element, compound,* and *mineral.*

For each pair of terms, explain how the meanings of the terms differ.

2 *color* and *streak*

3 *mineral* and *ore*

4 *silicate mineral* and *nonsilicate mineral*

UNDERSTANDING KEY IDEAS

Multiple Choice

5 Which of the following properties of minerals does Mohs scale measure?

a. luster
b. hardness
c. density
d. streak

6 Pure substances that cannot be broken down into simpler substances by ordinary chemical means are called

a. molecules.
b. elements.
c. compounds.
d. crystals.

7 Which of the following properties is considered a special property that applies to only a few minerals?

a. luster
b. hardness
c. taste
d. density

8 Silicate minerals contain a combination of the elements

a. sulfur and oxygen.
b. carbon and oxygen.
c. iron and oxygen.
d. silicon and oxygen.

9 The process by which land used for mining is returned to its original state is called

a. recycling.
b. regeneration.
c. reclamation.
d. renovation.

10 Which of the following minerals is an example of a gemstone?

a. mica
b. diamond
c. gypsum
d. copper

Short Answer

11 Compare surface and subsurface mining.

12 Explain the four characteristics of a mineral.

13 Describe two environments in which minerals form.

14 List two uses for metallic minerals and two uses for nonmetallic minerals.

15 Describe two ways to reduce the effects of mining.

16 Describe three special properties of minerals.

CRITICAL THINKING

17 Concept Mapping Use the following terms to create a concept map: *minerals, calcite, silicate minerals, gypsum, carbonates, nonsilicate minerals, quartz,* and *sulfates.*

18 Making Inferences Imagine that you are trying to determine the identity of a mineral. You decide to do a streak test. You rub the mineral across the streak plate, but the mineral does not leave a streak. Has your test failed? Explain your answer.

19 Applying Concepts Why would cleavage be important to gem cutters, who cut and shape gemstones?

20 Applying Concepts Imagine that you work at a jeweler's shop and someone brings in some gold nuggets for sale. You are not sure if the nuggets are real gold. Which identification tests would help you decide whether the nuggets are gold?

21 Identifying Relationships Suppose you are in a desert. You are walking across the floor of a dry lake, and you see crusts of cubic halite crystals. How do you suppose the halite crystals formed? Explain your answer.

INTERPRETING GRAPHICS

The table below shows the temperatures at which various minerals melt. Use the table below to answer the questions that follow.

Melting Points of Various Minerals	
Mineral	**Melting Point (°C)**
Mercury	−39
Sulfur	+113
Halite	801
Silver	961
Gold	1,062
Copper	1,083
Pyrite	1,171
Fluorite	1,360
Quartz	1,710
Zircon	2,500

22 According to the table, what is the approximate difference in temperature between the melting points of the mineral that has the lowest melting point and the mineral that has the highest melting point?

23 Which of the minerals listed in the table do you think is a liquid at room temperature?

24 Pyrite is often called *fool's gold*. Using the information in the table, how could you determine if a mineral sample is pyrite or gold?

25 Convert the melting points of the minerals shown in the table from degrees Celsius to degrees Fahrenheit. Use the formula °F = (9/5 × °C) + 32.

Standardized Test Preparation

READING

Read each of the passages below. Then, answer the questions that follow each passage.

Passage 1 In North America, copper was mined at least 6,700 years ago by the ancestors of the Native Americans who live on Michigan's upper peninsula. Much of this mining took place on Isle Royale, an island in Lake Superior. These <u>ancient</u> people removed copper from the rock by using stone hammers and wedges. The rock was sometimes heated first to make breaking it up easier. Copper that was mined was used to make jewelry, tools, weapons, fish hooks, and other objects. These objects were often marked with designs. The Lake Superior copper was traded over long distances along ancient trade routes. Copper objects have been found in Ohio, Florida, the Southwest, and the Northwest.

1. In the passage, what does *ancient* mean?
   A young
   B future
   C modern
   D early

2. According to the passage, what did the ancient copper miners do?
   F They mined copper in Ohio, Florida, the Southwest, and the Northwest.
   G They mined copper by cooling the rock in which the copper was found.
   H They mined copper by using stone tools.
   I They mined copper for their use only.

3. Which of the following statements is a fact according to the passage?
   A Copper could be shaped into different objects.
   B Copper was unknown outside of Michigan's upper peninsula.
   C Copper could be mined easily from the rock in which it was found.
   D Copper could not be marked with designs.

Passage 2 Most mineral names end in *-ite*. The <u>practice</u> of so naming minerals dates back to the ancient Romans and Greeks, who added *-ites* and *-itis* to common words to indicate a color, a use, or the chemistry of a mineral. More recently, mineral names have been used to honor people, such as scientists, mineral collectors, and even rulers of countries. Other minerals have been named after the place where they were discovered. These place names include mines, quarries, hills, mountains, towns, regions, and even countries. Finally, some minerals have been named after gods in Greek, Roman, and Scandinavian mythology.

1. In the passage, what does *practice* mean?
   A skill
   B custom
   C profession
   D use

2. According to the passage, the ancient Greeks and Romans did not name minerals after what?
   F colors
   G chemical properties
   H people
   I uses

3. Which of the following statements is a fact according to the passage?
   A Minerals are sometimes named for the country in which they are discovered.
   B Minerals are never named after their collectors.
   C All mineral names end in *-ite*.
   D All of the known minerals were named by the Greeks and Romans.

A sample of feldspar was analyzed to find out what it was made of. The graph below shows the results of the analysis. Use the graph below to answer the questions that follow.

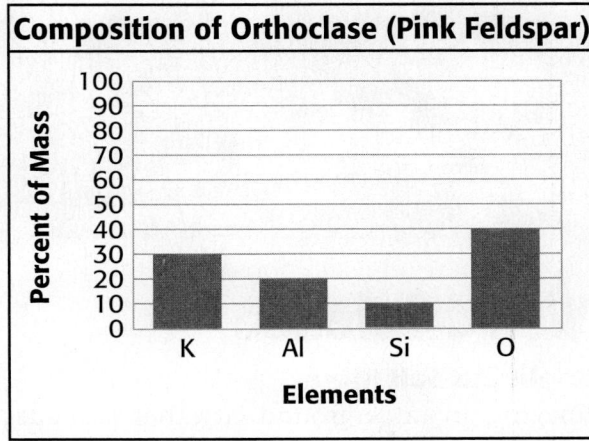

Composition of Orthoclase (Pink Feldspar)

1. The sample consists of four elements: potassium, K, aluminum, Al, silicon, Si, and oxygen, O. Which element makes up the largest percentage of your sample?

   A potassium

   B aluminum

   C silicon

   D oxygen

2. Silicate minerals, such as feldspar, contain a combination of silicon and oxygen. What percentage of your sample is composed of silicon and oxygen combined?

   F 30%

   G 40%

   H 50%

   I 70%

3. If your sample has a mass of 10 g, how many grams of oxygen does it contain?

   A 1 g

   B 2 g

   C 4 g

   D 8 g

4. Your sample of orthoclase has a hardness of 6. Which of the following minerals will scratch your sample?

   F gypsum

   G corundum

   H calcite

   I apatite

Read each question below, and choose the best answer.

1. Gold classified as 24-karat is 100% gold. Gold classified as 18-karat is 18 parts gold and 6 parts another, similar metal. The gold is therefore 18/24, or 3/4, pure. What is the percentage of pure gold in 18-karat gold?

   A 10%

   B 25%

   C 50%

   D 75%

2. Gold's specific gravity is 19. Pyrite's specific gravity is 5. What is the difference in the specific gravities of gold and pyrite?

   F 8 g/cm^3

   G 10 g/cm^3

   H 12 g/cm^3

   I 14 g/cm^3

3. In a quartz crystal, there is one silicon atom for every two oxygen atoms. So, the ratio of silicon atoms to oxygen atoms is 1:2. If there were 8 million oxygen atoms in a sample of quartz, how many silicon atoms would there be in the sample?

   A 2 million

   B 4 million

   C 8 million

   D 16 million

Science in Action

Science Fiction

"The Metal Man" by Jack Williamson

In a dark, dusty corner of Tyburn College Museum stands a life-sized statue of a man. Except for its strange greenish color, the statue looks quite ordinary. But if you look closely, you will see the perfect detail of the hair and skin. On the statue's chest, you will also see a strange mark—a dark crimson shape with six sides. No one knows how the statue ended up in the dark corner. But most people in Tyburn believe that the metal man is, or once was, Professor Thomas Kelvin of Tyburn College's geology department. Read for yourself the strange story of Professor Kelvin and the Metal Man, which is in the *Holt Anthology of Science Fiction*.

Language Arts ACTIVITY

WRITING SKILL Read "The Metal Man" by Jack Williamson. Write a short essay explaining how the ideas in the story are related to what you are learning.

Weird Science

Wieliczka Salt Mine

Imagine an underground city that is made entirely of salt. Within the city are churches, chapels, rooms of many kinds, and salt lakes. Sculptures of biblical scenes, saints, and famous historical figures carved from salt are found throughout the city. Even chandeliers of salt hang from the ceilings. Such a city is located 16 km southeast of Krakow, Poland, inside the Wieliczka (VEE uh LEETS kuh) Salt Mine. As the mine grew over the past 700 years, it turned into an elaborate underground city. Miners constructed chapels to patron saints so they could pray for a safe day in the mine. Miners also developed superstitions about the mine. So, images that were meant to bring good luck were carved in salt. In 1978, the mine was added to UNESCO's list of endangered world heritage sites. Many of the sculptures in the mine have begun to dissolve because of the humidity in the air. Efforts to save the treasures in the mine from further damage were begun in 1996.

Social Studies ACTIVITY

WRITING SKILL Research some aspect of the role of salt in human history. For example, subjects might include the Saharan and Tibetan salt trade or the use of salt as a form of money in ancient Poland. Report your findings in a one-page essay.

People in Science

Jamie Hill

The Emerald Man Jamie Hill was raised in the Brushy Mountains of North Carolina. While growing up, Hill gained firsthand knowledge of the fabulous green crystals that could be found in the mountains. These green crystals were emeralds. Emerald is the green variety of the silicate mineral beryl and is a valuable gemstone. Emerald crystals form in pockets, or openings, in rock known as *pegmatite*.

Since 1985, Hill has been searching for pockets containing emeralds in rock near the small town of Hiddenite, North Carolina. He has been amazingly successful. Hill has discovered some spectacular emerald crystals. The largest of these crystals weighs 858 carats and is on display at the North Carolina Museum of Natural Science. Estimates of the total value of the emeralds that Hill has discovered so far are well in the millions of dollars. Hill's discoveries have made him a celebrity, and he has appeared both on national TV and in magazines.

Math ACTIVITY

An emerald discovered by Jamie Hill in 1999 was cut into a 7.85-carat stone that sold for $64,000 per carat. What was the total value of the cut stone?

go.hrw.com

To learn more about these Science in Action topics, visit go.hrw.com and type in the keyword **HZ5MINF.**

Current Science

Check out Current Science® articles related to this chapter by visiting go.hrw.com. Just type in the keyword **HZ5CS03.**

Rocks: Mineral Mixtures

About the PHOTO

Irish legend claims that the mythical hero Finn MacCool built the Giant's Causeway, shown here. But this rock formation is the result of the cooling of huge amounts of molten rock. As the molten rock cooled, it formed tall pillars separated by cracks called *columnar joints*.

PRE-READING ACTIVITY

Graphic Organizer

Spider Map Before you read the chapter, create the graphic organizer entitled "Spider Map" described in the **Study Skills** section of the Appendix. Label the circle "Rock." Create a leg for each of the sections in this chapter. As you read the chapter, fill in the map with details about the material presented in each section of the chapter.

START-UP ACTIVITY

Classifying Objects

Scientists use the physical and chemical properties of rocks to classify rocks. Classifying objects such as rocks requires looking at many properties. Do this exercise for some classification practice.

Procedure

1. Your teacher will give you a **bag** containing **several objects.** Examine the objects, and note features such as size, color, shape, texture, smell, and any unique properties.

2. Develop three different ways to sort these objects.

3. Create a chart that organizes objects by properties.

Analysis

1. What properties did you use to sort the items?

2. Were there any objects that could fit into more than one group? How did you solve this problem?

3. Which properties might you use to classify rocks? Explain your answer.

The Rock Cycle

You know that paper, plastic, and aluminum can be recycled. But did you know that the Earth also recycles? And one of the things that Earth recycles is rock.

READING WARM-UP

Objectives

● Describe two ways rocks have been used by humans.

● Describe four processes that shape Earth's features.

● Describe how each type of rock changes into another type as it moves through the rock cycle.

● List two characteristics of rock that are used to help classify it.

Terms to Learn

rock cycle   deposition
rock   composition
erosion   texture

READING STRATEGY

Reading Organizer As you read this section, make a flowchart of the steps of the rock cycle.

Scientists define **rock** as a naturally occurring solid mixture of one or more minerals and organic matter. It may be hard to believe, but rocks are always changing. The continual process by which new rock forms from old rock material is called the **rock cycle.**

The Value of Rock

Rock has been an important natural resource as long as humans have existed. Early humans used rocks as hammers to make other tools. They discovered that they could make arrowheads, spear points, knives, and scrapers by carefully shaping rocks such as chert and obsidian.

Rock has also been used for centuries to make buildings, monuments, and roads. **Figure 1** shows how rock has been used as a construction material by both ancient and modern civilizations. Buildings have been made out of granite, limestone, marble, sandstone, slate, and other rocks. Modern buildings also contain concrete and plaster, in which rock is an important ingredient.

✓ *Reading Check* **Name some types of rock that have been used to construct buildings.** (*See the Appendix for answers to Reading Checks.*)

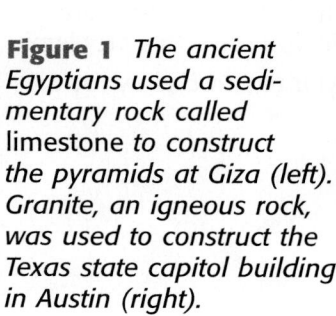

Figure 1 *The ancient Egyptians used a sedimentary rock called* limestone *to construct the pyramids at Giza (left). Granite, an igneous rock, was used to construct the Texas state capitol building in Austin (right).*

Processes That Shape the Earth

Certain geological processes make and destroy rock. These processes shape the features of our planet. These processes also influence the type of rock that is found in a certain area of Earth's surface.

Weathering, Erosion, and Deposition

The process in which water, wind, ice, and heat break down rock is called *weathering*. Weathering is important because it breaks down rock into fragments. These rock and mineral fragments are the sediment of which much sedimentary rock is made.

The process by which sediment is removed from its source is called **erosion.** Water, wind, ice, and gravity can erode and move sediments and cause them to collect. **Figure 2** shows an example of the way land looks after weathering and erosion.

The process in which sediment moved by erosion is dropped and comes to rest is called **deposition.** Sediment is deposited in bodies of water and other low-lying areas. In those places, sediment may be pressed and cemented together by minerals dissolved in water to form sedimentary rock.

Heat and Pressure

Sedimentary rock made of sediment can also form when buried sediment is squeezed by the weight of overlying layers of sediment. If the temperature and pressure are high enough at the bottom of the sediment, the rock can change into metamorphic rock. In some cases, the rock gets hot enough to melt. This melting creates the magma that eventually cools to form igneous rock.

How the Cycle Continues

Buried rock is exposed at the Earth's surface by a combination of uplift and erosion. *Uplift* is movement within the Earth that causes rocks inside the Earth to be moved to the Earth's surface. When uplifted rock reaches the Earth's surface, weathering, erosion, and deposition begin.

rock a naturally occurring solid mixture of one or more minerals or organic matter

rock cycle the series of processes in which a rock forms, changes from one type to another, is destroyed, and forms again by geological processes

erosion the process by which wind, water, ice, or gravity transports soil and sediment from one location to another

deposition the process in which material is laid down

Figure 2 *Bryce Canyon, in Utah, is an excellent example of how the processes of weathering and erosion shape the face of our planet.*

Illustrating the Rock Cycle

You have learned about various geological processes, such as weathering, erosion, heat, and pressure, that create and destroy rock. The diagram on these two pages illustrates one way that sand grains can change as different geological processes act on them. In the following steps, you will see how these processes change the original sand grains into sedimentary rock, metamorphic rock, and igneous rock.

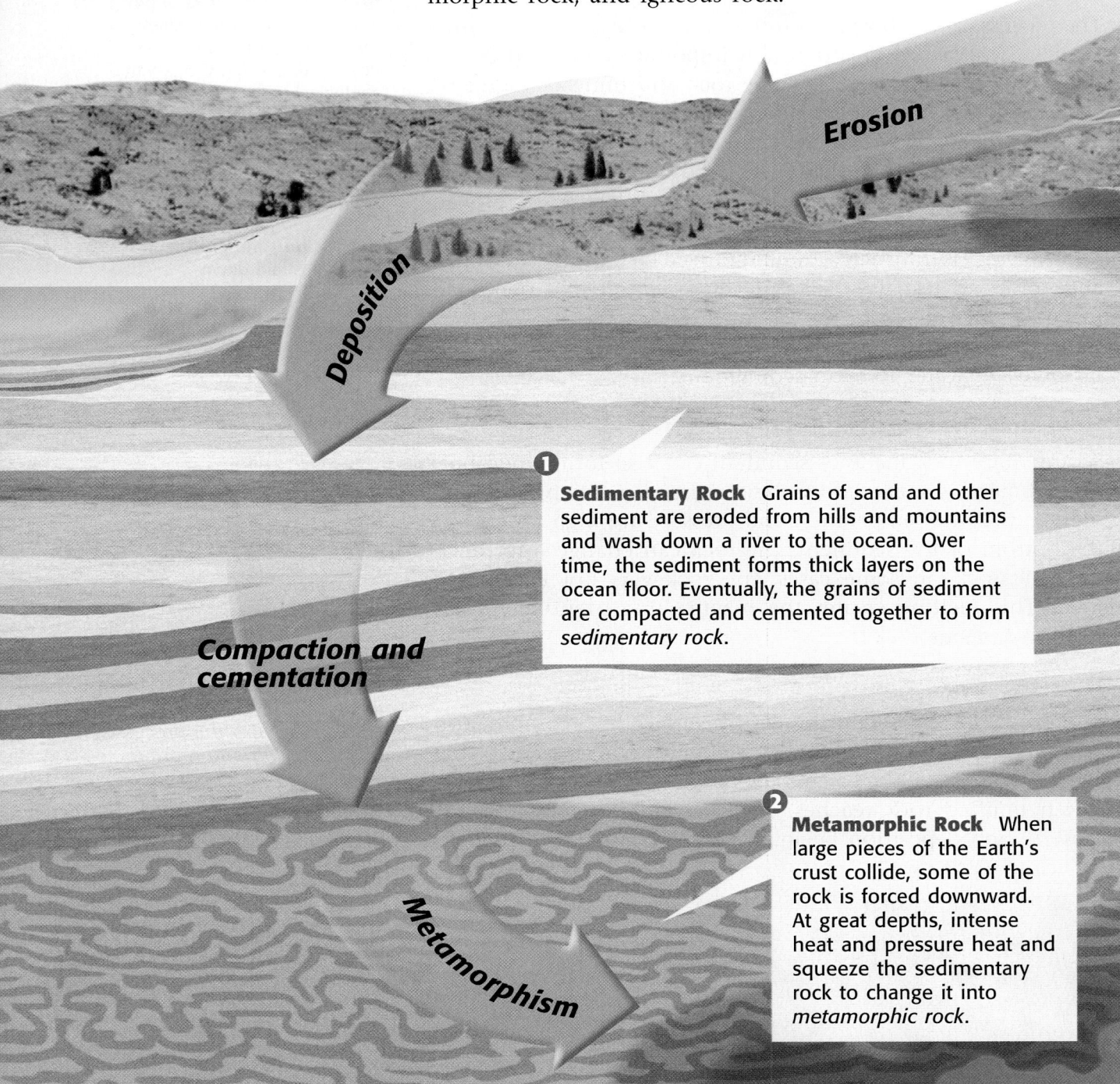

Erosion

Deposition

Compaction and cementation

Metamorphism

❶ **Sedimentary Rock** Grains of sand and other sediment are eroded from hills and mountains and wash down a river to the ocean. Over time, the sediment forms thick layers on the ocean floor. Eventually, the grains of sediment are compacted and cemented together to form *sedimentary rock*.

❷ **Metamorphic Rock** When large pieces of the Earth's crust collide, some of the rock is forced downward. At great depths, intense heat and pressure heat and squeeze the sedimentary rock to change it into *metamorphic rock*.

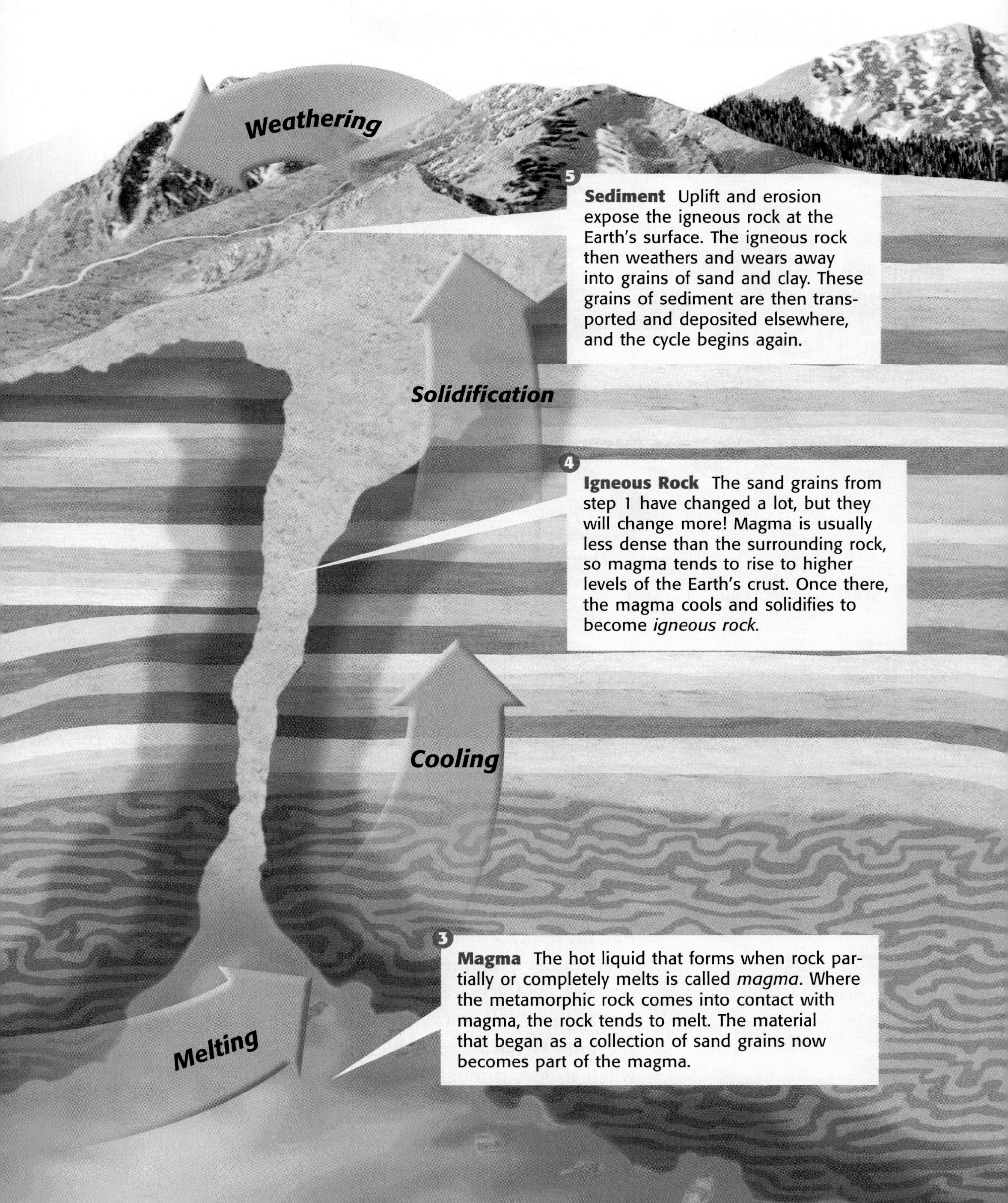

Weathering

5

Sediment Uplift and erosion expose the igneous rock at the Earth's surface. The igneous rock then weathers and wears away into grains of sand and clay. These grains of sediment are then transported and deposited elsewhere, and the cycle begins again.

Solidification

4

Igneous Rock The sand grains from step 1 have changed a lot, but they will change more! Magma is usually less dense than the surrounding rock, so magma tends to rise to higher levels of the Earth's crust. Once there, the magma cools and solidifies to become *igneous rock*.

Cooling

3

Magma The hot liquid that forms when rock partially or completely melts is called *magma*. Where the metamorphic rock comes into contact with magma, the rock tends to melt. The material that began as a collection of sand grains now becomes part of the magma.

Melting

Figure 3 The Rock Cycle

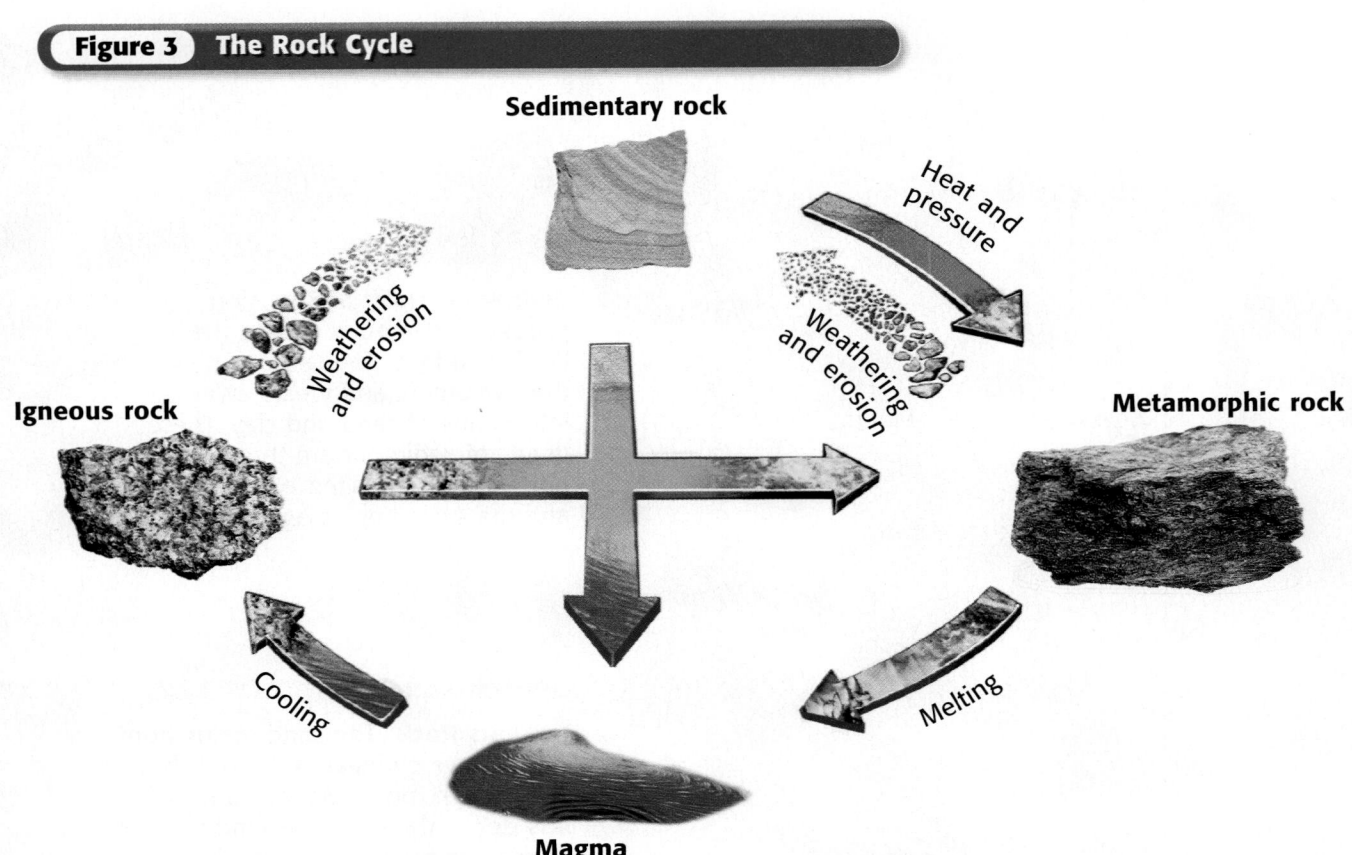

Sedimentary rock

Heat and pressure

Weathering and erosion

Weathering and erosion

Igneous rock

Metamorphic rock

Cooling

Melting

Magma

Round and Round It Goes

You have seen how different geological processes can change rock. Each rock type can change into one of the three types of rock. For example, igneous rock can change into sedimentary rock, metamorphic rock, or even back into igneous rock. This cycle, in which rock is changed by geological processes into different types of rock, is known as the rock cycle.

Rocks may follow various pathways in the rock cycle. As one rock type is changed to another type, several variables, including time, heat, pressure, weathering, and erosion may alter a rock's identity. The location of a rock determines which natural forces will have the biggest impact on the process of change. For example, rock at the Earth's surface is primarily affected by forces of weathering and erosion, whereas deep inside the Earth, rocks change because of extreme heat and pressure. **Figure 3** shows the different ways rock may change when it goes through the rock cycle and the different forces that affect rock during the cycle.

✓ *Reading Check* What processes change rock deep within the Earth?

Rock Classification

You have already learned that scientists divide all rock into three main classes based on how the rock formed: igneous, sedimentary, and metamorphic. But did you know that each class of rock can be divided further? These divisions are also based on differences in the way rocks form. For example, all igneous rock forms when magma cools and solidifies. But some igneous rocks form when magma cools *on* the Earth's surface, and others form when magma cools deep *beneath* the surface. Therefore, igneous rock can be divided again based on how and where it forms. Sedimentary and metamorphic rocks are also divided into groups. How do scientists know how to classify rocks? They study rocks in detail using two important criteria—composition and texture.

Composition

The minerals a rock contains determine the **composition** of that rock, as shown in **Figure 4.** For example, a rock made of mostly the mineral quartz will have a composition very similar to that of quartz. But a rock made of 50% quartz and 50% feldspar will have a very different composition than quartz does.

✔ **Reading Check** What determines a rock's composition?

What's in It?

Assume that a granite sample you are studying is made of 30% quartz and 55% feldspar by volume. The rest is made of biotite mica. What percentage of the sample is biotite mica?

composition the chemical makeup of a rock; describes either the minerals or other materials in the rock

---

Figure 4 Two Examples of Rock Composition

The composition of a rock depends on the minerals the rock contains.

Limestone

95% Calcite — 5% Aragonite

Granite

10% Biotite mica
35% Quartz — 55% Feldspar

Figure 5 **Three Examples of Sedimentary Rock Texture**

Fine-grained

Siltstone

Medium-grained

Sandstone

Coarse-grained

Conglomerate

Texture

texture the quality of a rock that is based on the sizes, shapes, and positions of the rock's grains

The size, shape, and positions of the grains that make up a rock determine a rock's **texture.** Sedimentary rock can have a fine-grained, medium-grained, or coarse-grained texture, depending on the size of the grains that make up the rock. Three samples of textures are shown in **Figure 5.** The texture of igneous rock can be fine-grained or coarse-grained, depending on how much time magma has to cool. Based on the degree of temperature and pressure a rock is exposed to, metamorphic rock can also have a fine-grained or coarse-grained texture.

The texture of a rock can provide clues as to how and where the rock formed. Look at the rocks shown in **Figure 6.** The rocks look different because they formed in very different ways. The texture of a rock can reveal the process that formed it.

✔ *Reading Check* Give three examples of sedimentary rock textures.

Figure 6 **Texture and Rock Formation**

Basalt, a fine-grained igneous rock, forms when lava that erupts onto Earth's surface cools rapidly.

Sandstone, a medium-grained sedimentary rock, forms when sand grains deposited in dunes, on beaches, or on the ocean floor are buried and cemented.

Summary

- Rock has been an important natural resource for as long as humans have existed. Early humans used rock to make tools. Ancient and modern civilizations have used rock as a construction material.

- Weathering, erosion, deposition, and uplift are all processes that shape the surface features of the Earth.

- The rock cycle is the continual process by which new rock forms from old rock material.

- The sequence of events in the rock cycle depends on processes, such as weathering, erosion, deposition, pressure, and heat, that change the rock material.

- Composition and texture are two characteristics that scientists use to classify rocks.

- The composition of a rock is determined by the minerals that make up the rock.

- The texture of a rock is determined by the size, shape, and positions of the grains that make up the rock.

Using Key Terms

Complete each of the following sentences by choosing the correct term from the word bank.

rock	composition
rock cycle	texture

1. The minerals that a rock is made of determine the ___ of that rock.

2. ___ is a naturally occurring, solid mixture of crystals of one or more minerals.

Understanding Key Ideas

3. Sediments are transported or moved from their original source by a process called
   a. deposition.
   b. erosion.
   c. uplift.
   d. weathering.

4. Describe two ways that rocks have been used by humans.

5. Name four processes that change rock inside the Earth.

6. Describe four processes that shape Earth's surface.

7. Give an example of how texture can provide clues as to how and where a rock formed.

Critical Thinking

8. **Making Comparisons** Explain the difference between texture and composition.

9. **Analyzing Processes** Explain how rock is continually recycled in the rock cycle.

Interpreting Graphics

10. Look at the table below. Sandstone is a type of sedimentary rock. If you had a sample of sandstone that had an average particle size of 2 mm, what texture would your sandstone have?

Classification of Clastic Sedimentary Rocks	
Texture	**Particle size**
coarse grained	> 2 mm
medium grained	0.06 to 2 mm
fine grained	< 0.06 mm

SCiLINKS®

NSTA
Developed and maintained by the National Science Teachers Association

For a variety of links related to this chapter, go to www.scilinks.org

Topic: Composition of Rock
SciLinks code: HSM0327

Igneous Rock

Where do igneous rocks come from? Here's a hint: The word igneous *comes from a Latin word that means "fire."*

Igneous rock forms when hot, liquid rock, or *magma,* cools and solidifies. The type of igneous rock that forms depends on the composition of the magma and the amount of time it takes the magma to cool.

Origins of Igneous Rock

Igneous rock begins as magma. As shown in **Figure 1,** there are three ways magma can form: when rock is heated, when pressure is released, or when rock changes composition.

When magma cools enough, it solidifies to form igneous rock. Magma solidifies in much the same way that water freezes. But there are also differences between the way magma freezes and the way water freezes. One main difference is that water freezes at 0°C. Magma freezes between 700°C and 1,250°C. Also, liquid magma is a complex mixture containing many melted minerals. Because these minerals have different melting points, some minerals in the magma will freeze or become solid before other minerals do.

READING WARM-UP

Objectives

● Describe three ways that igneous rock forms.

● Explain how the cooling rate of magma affects the texture of igneous rock.

● Distinguish between igneous rock that cools within Earth's crust and igneous rock that cools at Earth's surface.

Terms to Learn

intrusive igneous rock
extrusive igneous rock

READING STRATEGY

Reading Organizer As you read this section, make a table comparing intrusive rock and extrusive rock.

Figure 1 The Formation of Magma

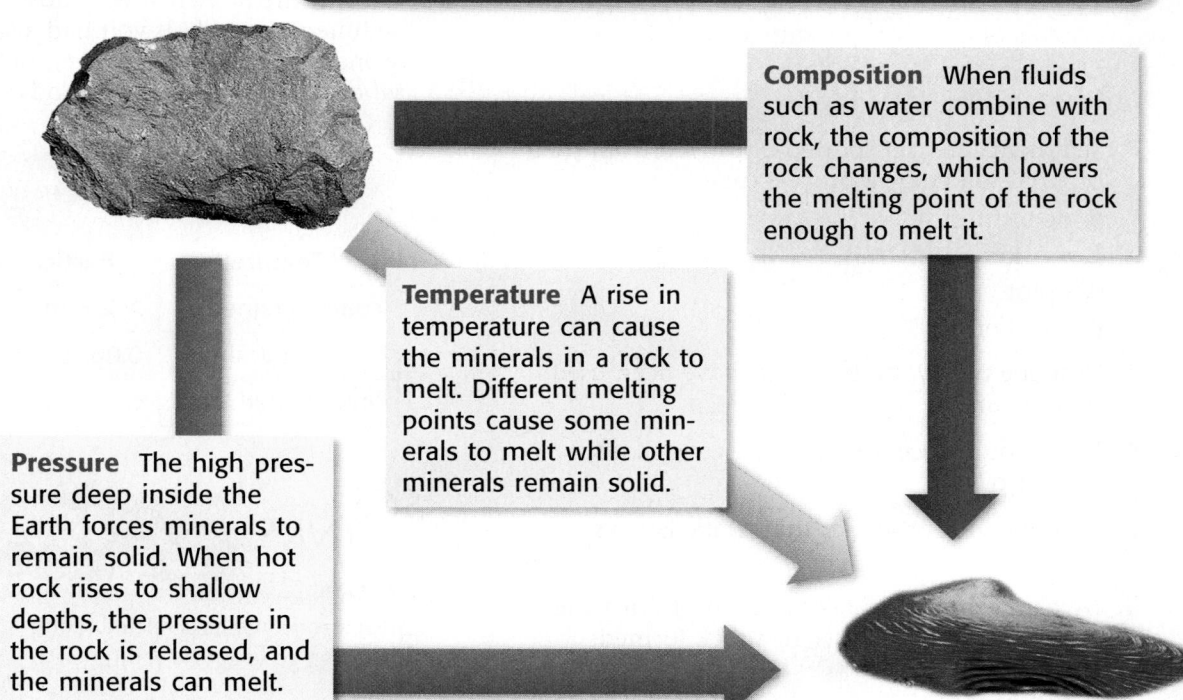

Composition When fluids such as water combine with rock, the composition of the rock changes, which lowers the melting point of the rock enough to melt it.

Temperature A rise in temperature can cause the minerals in a rock to melt. Different melting points cause some minerals to melt while other minerals remain solid.

Pressure The high pressure deep inside the Earth forces minerals to remain solid. When hot rock rises to shallow depths, the pressure in the rock is released, and the minerals can melt.

Figure 2 Igneous Rock Texture

	Coarse-grained	Fine-grained
Felsic	Granite	Rhyolite
Mafic	Gabbro	Basalt

Composition and Texture of Igneous Rock

Look at the rocks in **Figure 2.** All of the rocks are igneous rocks even though they look different from one another. These rocks differ from one another in what they are made of and how fast they cooled.

The light-colored rocks are less dense than the dark-colored rocks are. The light-colored rocks are rich in elements such as aluminum, potassium, silicon, and sodium. These rocks are called *felsic rocks.* The dark-colored rocks, called *mafic rocks,* are rich in calcium, iron, and magnesium, and poor in silicon.

Figure 3 shows what happens to magma when it cools at different rates. The longer it takes for the magma or lava to cool, the more time mineral crystals have to grow. The more time the crystals have to grow, the larger the crystals are and the coarser the texture of the resulting igneous rock is.

In contrast, the less time magma takes to cool, the less time crystals have to grow. Therefore, the rock that is formed will be fine grained. Fine-grained igneous rock contains very small crystals, or if the cooling is very rapid, it contains no crystals.

✓ Reading Check Explain the difference between felsic rock and mafic rock. (*See the Appendix for answers to Reading Checks.*)

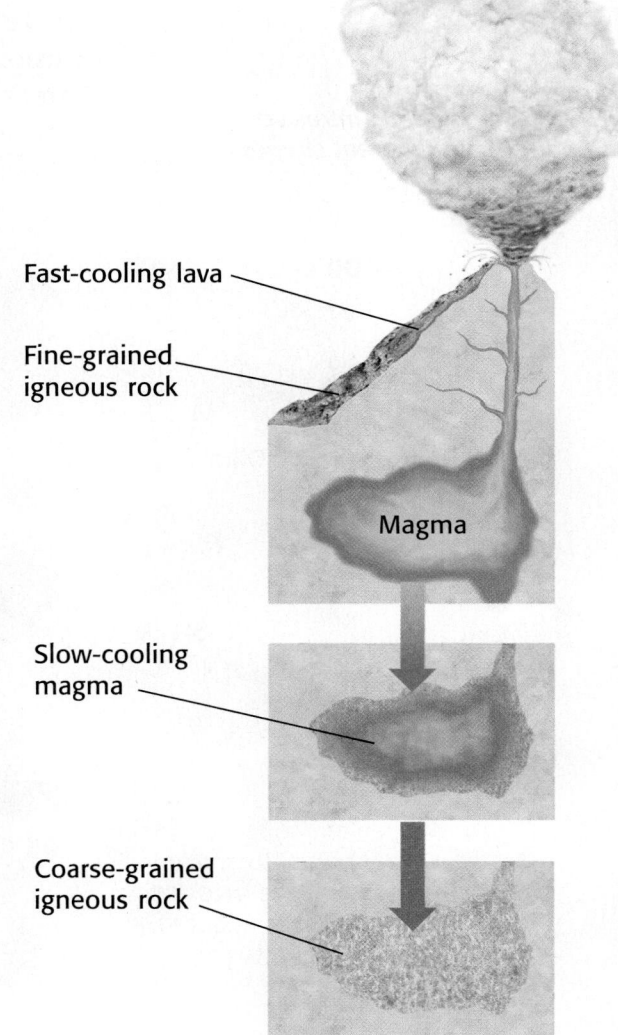

Figure 3 *The amount of time it takes for magma or lava to cool determines the texture of igneous rock.*

Fast-cooling lava

Fine-grained igneous rock

Magma

Slow-cooling magma

Coarse-grained igneous rock

For another activity related to this chapter, go to **go.hrw.com** and type in the keyword **HZ5RCKW.**

intrusive igneous rock rock formed from the cooling and solidification of magma beneath the Earth's surface

Figure 4 *Igneous intrusive bodies have different shapes and sizes.*

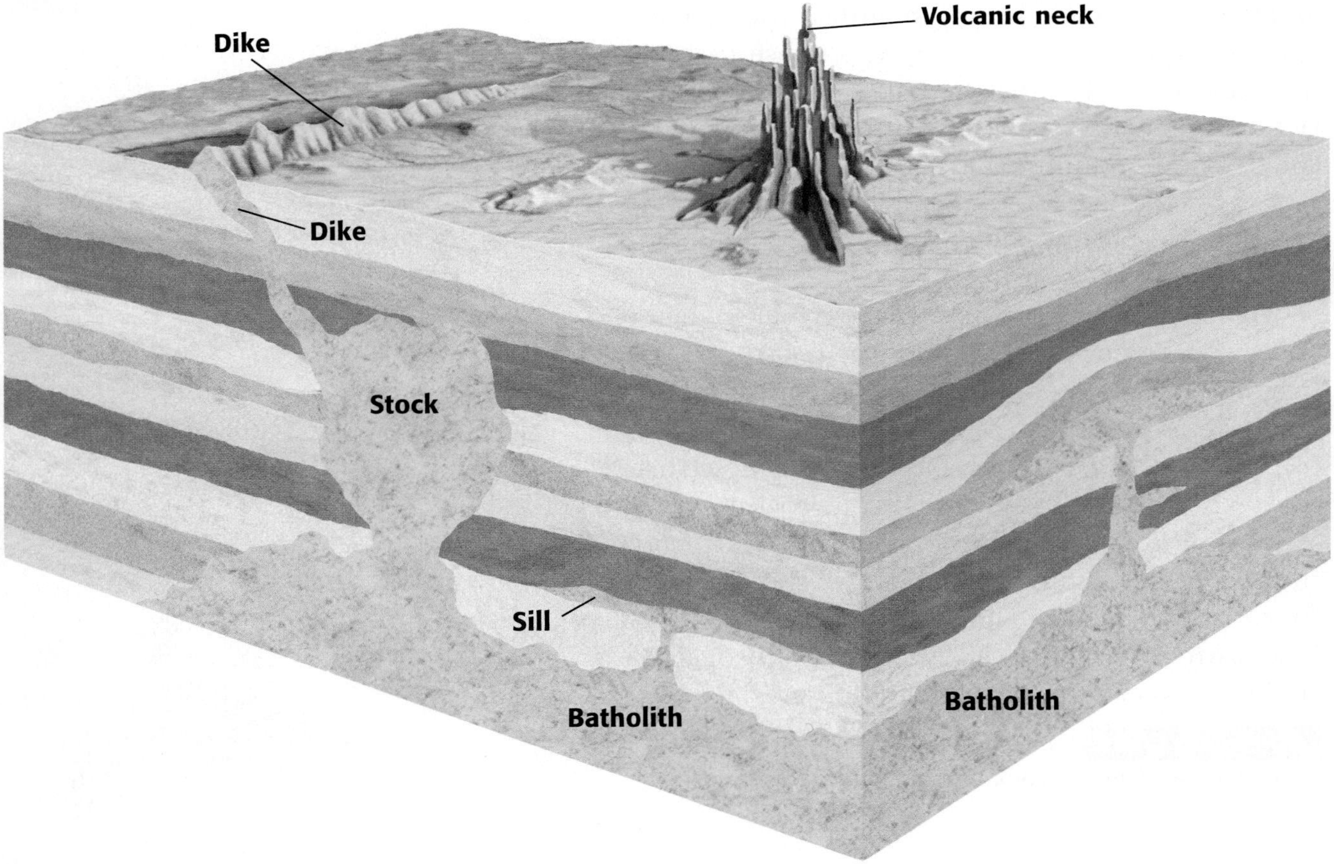

Igneous Rock Formations

Igneous rock formations are located above and below the surface of the Earth. You may be familiar with igneous rock formations that were caused by lava cooling on the Earth's surface, such as volcanoes. But not all magma reaches the surface. Some magma cools and solidifies deep within the Earth's crust.

Intrusive Igneous Rock

When magma *intrudes,* or pushes, into surrounding rock below the Earth's surface and cools, the rock that forms is called **intrusive igneous rock.** Intrusive igneous rock usually has a coarse-grained texture because it is well insulated by surrounding rock and cools very slowly. The minerals that form are large, visible crystals.

Masses of intrusive igneous rock are named for their size and shape. Common intrusive shapes are shown in **Figure 4.** *Plutons* are large, irregular-shaped intrusive bodies. The largest of all igneous intrusions are *batholiths. Stocks* are intrusive bodies that are exposed over smaller areas than batholiths. Sheetlike intrusions that cut across previous rock units are called *dikes,* whereas *sills* are sheetlike intrusions that are oriented parallel to previous rock units.

Dike

Volcanic neck

Dike

Stock

Sill

Batholith

Batholith

Extrusive Igneous Rock

Igneous rock that forms from magma that erupts, or extrudes, onto the Earth's surface is called **extrusive igneous rock.** Extrusive rock is common around volcanoes. It cools quickly on the surface and contains very small crystals or no crystals.

When lava erupts from a volcano, a *lava flow* forms. **Figure 5** shows an active lava flow. Lava does not always flow from volcanoes. Sometimes lava erupts and flows from long cracks in the Earth's crust called *fissures*. Lava flows from fissures on the ocean floor at places where tension is causing the ocean floor to be pulled apart. This lava cools to form new ocean floor. When a large amount of lava flows out of fissures onto land, the lava can cover a large area and form a plain called a *lava plateau*. Pre-existing landforms are often buried by these lava flows.

✔ Reading Check How does new ocean floor form?

Figure 5 *An active lava flow is shown in this photo. When exposed to Earth's surface conditions, lava quickly cools and solidifies to form a fine-grained igneous rock.*

extrusive igneous rock rock that forms as a result of volcanic activity at or near the Earth's surface

---

SECTION Review

Summary

- Igneous rock forms when magma cools and hardens.
- The texture of igneous rock is determined by the rate at which the rock cools.
- Igneous rock that solidifies at Earth's surface is extrusive. Igneous rock that solidifies within Earth's surface is intrusive.
- Shapes of common igneous intrusive bodies include batholiths, stocks, sills, and dikes.

Using Key Terms

1. In your own words, write a definition for each of the following terms: *intrusive igneous rock* and *extrusive igneous rock*.

Understanding Key Ideas

2. ___ is an example of a coarse-grained, felsic, igneous rock.
   a. Basalt
   b. Gabbro
   c. Granite
   d. Rhyolite

3. Explain three ways in which magma can form.

4. What determines the texture of igneous rocks?

Math Skills

5. The summit of a granite batholith has an elevation of 1,825 ft. What is the height of the batholith in meters?

Critical Thinking

6. **Making Comparisons** Dikes and sills are both types of igneous intrusive bodies. What is the difference between a dike and a sill?

7. **Predicting Consequences** An igneous rock forms from slow-cooling magma deep beneath the surface of the Earth. What type of texture is this rock most likely to have? Explain.

SCI**LINKS**

N**STA**
Developed and maintained by the National Science Teachers Association

For a variety of links related to this chapter, go to www.scilinks.org

Topic: Igneous Rock
SciLinks code: HSM0783

Sedimentary Rock

Have you ever tried to build a sand castle at the beach? Did you ever wonder where the sand came from?

Sand is a product of weathering, which breaks rock into pieces. Over time, sand grains may be compacted, or compressed, and then cemented together to form a rock called *sandstone*. Sandstone is just one of many types of sedimentary rock.

Origins of Sedimentary Rock

Wind, water, ice, sunlight, and gravity all cause rock to physically weather into fragments. Through the process of erosion, these rock and mineral fragments, called *sediment*, are moved from one place to another. Eventually, the sediment is deposited in layers. As new layers of sediment are deposited, they cover older layers. Older layers become compacted. Dissolved minerals, such as calcite and quartz, separate from water that passes through the sediment to form a natural cement that binds the rock and mineral fragments together into sedimentary rock.

Sedimentary rock forms at or near the Earth's surface. It forms without the heat and pressure that are involved in the formation of igneous and metamorphic rocks.

The most noticeable feature of sedimentary rock is its layers, or **strata.** A single, horizontal layer of rock is sometimes visible for many miles. Road cuts are good places to observe strata. **Figure 1** shows the spectacular views that sedimentary rock formations carved by erosion can provide.

READING WARM-UP

Objectives

● Describe the origin of sedimentary rock.

● Describe the three main categories of sedimentary rock.

● Describe three types of sedimentary structures.

Terms to Learn

strata
stratification

READING STRATEGY

Reading Organizer As you read this section, create an outline of this section. Use the headings from the section in your outline.

Figure 1 *The red sandstone "monuments" for which Monument Valley in Arizona has been named are the products of millions of years of erosion.*

Figure 2 Classification of Clastic Sedimentary Rock

Conglomerate   Sandstone   Siltstone   Shale

Coarse grained ←——————————————————————→ Fine grained

Composition of Sedimentary Rock

Sedimentary rock is classified by the way it forms. *Clastic sedimentary rock* forms when rock or mineral fragments, called *clasts,* are cemented together. *Chemical sedimentary rock* forms when minerals crystallize out of a solution, such as sea water, to become rock. *Organic sedimentary rock* forms from the remains of once-living plants and animals.

strata layers of rock (singular, *stratum*)

Clastic Sedimentary Rock

Clastic sedimentary rock is made of fragments of rocks cemented together by a mineral such as calcite or quartz. **Figure 2** shows how clastic sedimentary rock is classified according to the size of the fragments from which the rock is made. Clastic sedimentary rocks can have coarse-grained, medium-grained, or fine-grained textures.

Chemical Sedimentary Rock

Chemical sedimentary rock forms from solutions of dissolved minerals and water. As rainwater slowly makes its way to the ocean, it dissolves some of the rock material it passes through. Some of this dissolved material eventually crystallizes and forms the minerals that make up chemical sedimentary rock. Halite, one type of chemical sedimentary rock, is made of sodium chloride, NaCl, or table salt. Halite forms when sodium ions and chlorine ions in shallow bodies of water become so concentrated that halite crystallizes from solution.

✓ Reading Check How does a chemical sedimentary rock such as halite form? (*See the Appendix for answers to Reading Checks.*)

CONNECTION TO Language Arts

WRITING SKILL **Salty Expressions** The word salt is used in many expressions in the English language. Some common examples include "the salt of the earth," "taken with a grain of salt," not worth his salt," "the salt of truth," "rubbing salt into a wound," and "old salt." Use the Internet or another source to research one these expressions. In your research, attempt to find the origin of the expression. Write a short paragraph that summarizes what you found.

Organic Sedimentary Rock

Most limestone forms from the remains, or *fossils*, of animals that once lived in the ocean. For example, some limestone is made of the skeletons of tiny organisms called *coral*. Coral are very small, but they live in huge colonies called *reefs*, shown in **Figure 3.** Over time, the skeletons of these sea animals, which are made of calcium carbonate, collect on the ocean floor. These animal remains eventually become cemented together to form *fossiliferous limestone* (FAH suhl IF uhr uhs LIEM STOHN).

Corals are not the only animals whose remains are found in fossiliferous limestone. The shells of mollusks, such as clams and oysters, commonly form fossiliferous limestone. An example of fossiliferous limestone that contains mollusks is shown in **Figure 4.**

Another type of organic sedimentary rock is *coal*. Coal forms underground when partially decomposed plant material is buried beneath sediment and is changed into coal by increasing heat and pressure. This process occurs over millions of years.

Figure 3 *Ocean animals called* coral *create huge deposits of limestone. As they die, their skeletons collect on the ocean floor.*

Figure 4   **The Formation of Organic Sedimentary Rock**

Marine organisms, such as brachiopods, get the calcium carbonate for their shells from ocean water. When these organisms die, their shells collect on the ocean floor and eventually form fossiliferous limestone (inset). Over time, huge rock formations that contain the remains of large numbers of organisms, such as brachiopods, form.

Sedimentary Rock Structures

Many features can tell you about the way sedimentary rock formed. The most important feature of sedimentary rock is stratification. **Stratification** is the process in which sedimentary rocks are arranged in layers. Strata differ from one another depending on the kind, size, and color of their sediment.

Sedimentary rocks sometimes record the motion of wind and water waves on lakes, oceans, rivers, and sand dunes in features called *ripple marks*, as shown in **Figure 5**. Structures called *mud cracks* form when fine-grained sediments at the bottom of a shallow body of water are exposed to the air and dry out. Mud cracks indicate the location of an ancient lake, stream, or ocean shoreline. Even raindrop impressions can be preserved in fine-grained sediments, as small pits with raised rims.

Reading Check What are ripple marks?

Figure 5 *These ripple marks were made by flowing water and were preserved when the sediments became sedimentary rock. Ripple marks can also form from the action of wind.*

stratification the process in which sedimentary rocks are arranged in layers

---

SECTION Review

Summary

- Sedimentary rock forms at or near the Earth's surface.
- Clastic sedimentary rock forms when rock or mineral fragments are cemented together.
- Chemical sedimentary rock forms from solutions of dissolved minerals and water.
- Organic limestone forms from the remains of plants and animals.
- Sedimentary structures include ripple marks, mud cracks, and raindrop impressions.

Using Key Terms

1. In your own words, write a definition for each of the following terms: *strata* and *stratification*.

Understanding Key Ideas

2. Which of the following is an organic sedimentary rock?
   a. chemical limestone
   b. shale
   c. fossiliferous limestone
   d. conglomerate

3. Explain the process by which clastic sedimentary rock forms.

4. Describe the three main categories of sedimentary rock.

Math Skills

5. A layer of a sedimentary rock is 2 m thick. How many years did it take for this layer to form if an average of 4 mm of sediment accumulated per year?

Critical Thinking

6. **Identifying Relationships** Rocks are classified based on texture and composition. Which of these two properties would be more important for classifying clastic sedimentary rock?

7. **Analyzing Processes** Why do you think raindrop impressions are more likely to be preserved in fine-grained sedimentary rock rather than in coarse-grained sedimentary rock?

SCiLINKS

NSTA
Developed and maintained by the National Science Teachers Association

For a variety of links related to this chapter, go to www.scilinks.org

Topic: Sedimentary Rock
SciLinks code: HSM1365

Metamorphic Rock

Have you ever watched a caterpillar change into a butterfly? Some caterpillars go through a biological process called metamorphosis in which they completely change their shape.

Rocks can also go through a process called *metamorphism*. The word *metamorphism* comes from the Greek words *meta,* which means "changed," and *morphos,* which means "shape." Metamorphic rocks are rocks in which the structure, texture, or composition of the rock have changed. All three types of rock can be changed by heat, pressure, or a combination of both.

Origins of Metamorphic Rock

The texture or mineral composition of a rock can change when its surroundings change. If the temperature or pressure of the new environment is different from the one in which the rock formed, the rock will undergo metamorphism.

The temperature at which most metamorphism occurs ranges from 50°C to 1,000°C. However, the metamorphism of some rocks takes place at temperatures above 1,000°C. It seems that at these temperatures the rock would melt, but this is not true of metamorphic rock. It is the depth and pressure at which metamorphic rocks form that allows the rock to heat to this temperature and maintain its solid nature. Most metamorphic change takes place at depths greater than 2 km. But at depths greater than 16 km, the pressure can be 4,000 times greater than the pressure of the atmosphere at Earth's surface.

Large movements within the crust of the Earth cause additional pressure to be exerted on a rock during metamorphism. This pressure can cause the mineral grains in rock to align themselves in certain directions. The alignment of mineral grains into parallel bands is shown in the metamorphic rock in **Figure 1.**

Figure 1 *This metamorphic rock is an example of how mineral grains were aligned into distinct bands when the rock underwent metamorphism.*

Contact metamorphism

Sedimentary rock

Magma

Regional metamorphism

Contact Metamorphism

One way rock can undergo metamorphism is by being heated by nearby magma. When magma moves through the crust, the magma heats the surrounding rock and changes it. Some minerals in the surrounding rock are changed into other minerals by this increase in temperature. The greatest change takes place where magma comes into direct contact with the surrounding rock. The effect of heat on rock gradually decreases as the rock's distance from the magma increases and as temperature decreases. *Contact metamorphism* occurs near igneous intrusions, as shown in **Figure 2.**

Regional Metamorphism

When pressure builds up in rock that is buried deep below other rock formations or when large pieces of the Earth's crust collide with each other, *regional metamorphism* occurs. The increased pressure and temperature causes rock to become deformed and chemically changed. Unlike contact metamorphism, which happens near bodies of magma, regional metamorphism occurs over thousands of cubic kilometers deep within Earth's crust. Rocks that have undergone regional metamorphism are found beneath most continental rock formations.

✓ Reading Check Explain how and where regional metamorphism takes place. (*See the Appendix for answers to Reading Checks.*)

Stretching Out

1. Sketch the crystals in granite rock on a **piece of paper** with a **black-ink pen.** Be sure to include the outline of the rock, and fill it in with different crystal shapes.

2. Flatten some **plastic play putty** over your drawing, and slowly peel it off.

3. After making sure that the outline of your granite has been transferred to the putty, squeeze and stretch the putty. What happened to the crystals in the granite? What happened to the granite?

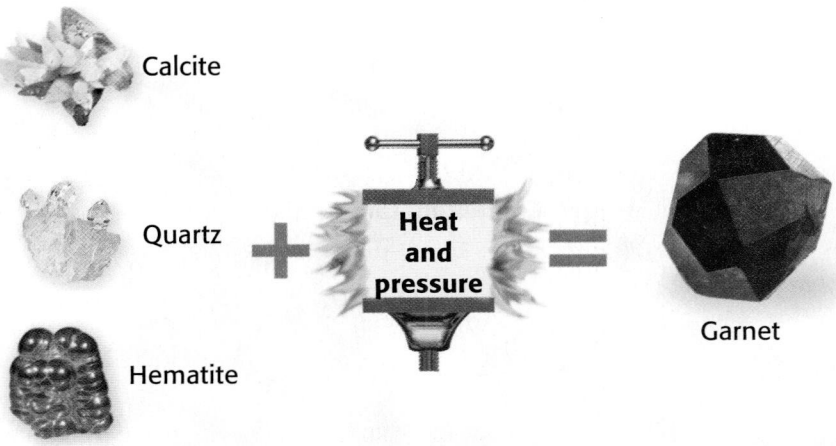

Figure 3 *The minerals calcite, quartz, and hematite combine and recrystallize to form the metamorphic mineral garnet.*

Calcite

Quartz

Hematite

Heat and pressure

Garnet

Making a Rock Collection

With a parent, try to collect a sample of each class of rock described in this chapter. You may wish to collect rocks from road cuts or simply collect pebbles from your garden or driveway. Try to collect samples that show the composition and texture of each rock. Classify the rocks in your collection, and bring it to class. With other members of the class, discuss your rock samples and see if they are accurately identified.

ACTIVITY

Composition of Metamorphic Rock

Metamorphism occurs when temperature and pressure inside the Earth's crust change. Minerals that were present in the rock when it formed may not be stable in the new temperature and pressure conditions. The original minerals change into minerals that are more stable in these new conditions. Look at **Figure 3** to see an example of how this change happens.

Many of these new minerals form only in metamorphic rock. As shown in **Figure 4,** some metamorphic minerals form only at certain temperatures and pressures. These minerals, known as *index minerals,* are used to estimate the temperature, depth, and pressure at which a rock undergoes metamorphism. Index minerals include biotite mica, chlorite, garnet, kyanite, muscovite mica, sillimanite, and staurolite.

Reading Check What is an index mineral?

Figure 4 *Scientists can understand a metamorphic rock's history by observing the minerals the rock contains. For example, a metamorphic rock that contains garnet formed at a greater depth and under greater heat and pressure than a rock that contains only chlorite.*

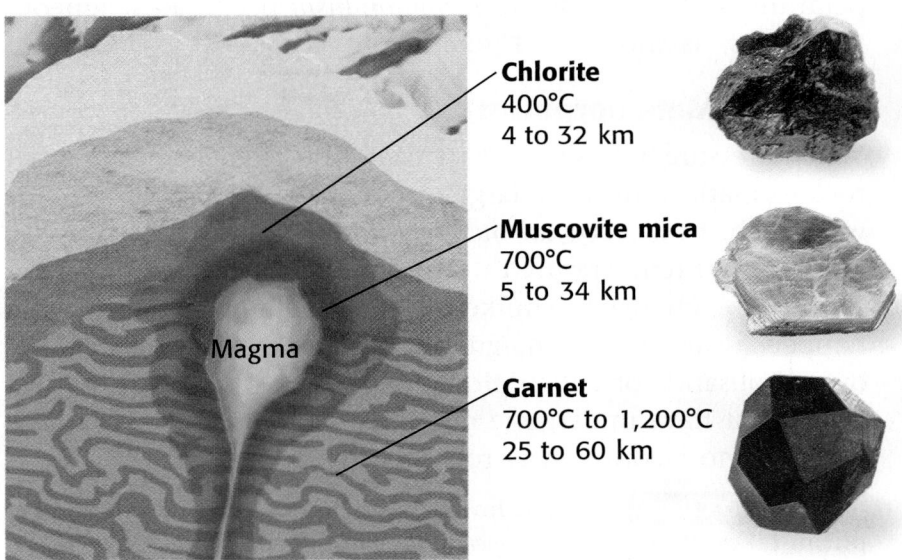

Magma

Chlorite
400°C
4 to 32 km

Muscovite mica
700°C
5 to 34 km

Garnet
700°C to 1,200°C
25 to 60 km

Textures of Metamorphic Rock

You have learned that texture helps scientists classify igneous and sedimentary rock. The same is true of metamorphic rock. All metamorphic rock has one of two textures—foliated or nonfoliated. Take a closer look at each of these types of metamorphic rock to find out how each type forms.

Foliated Metamorphic Rock

The texture of metamorphic rock in which the mineral grains are arranged in planes or bands is called **foliated.** Foliated metamorphic rock usually contains aligned grains of flat minerals, such as biotite mica or chlorite. Look at **Figure 5.** Shale is a sedimentary rock made of layers of clay minerals. When shale is exposed to slight heat and pressure, the clay minerals change into mica minerals. The shale becomes a foliated metamorphic rock called *slate.*

Metamorphic rocks can become other metamorphic rocks if the environment changes again. If slate is exposed to more heat and pressure, the slate can change into rock called *phyllite.* When phyllite is exposed to heat and pressure, it can change into *schist.*

If metamorphism continues, the arrangement of minerals in the rock changes. More heat and pressure cause minerals to separate into distinct bands in a metamorphic rock called *gneiss* (NIES).

foliated the texture of metamorphic rock in which the mineral grains are arranged in planes or bands

Sedimentary shale

Slate

Phyllite

Figure 5 *The effects of metamorphism depend on the heat and pressure applied to the rock. Here you can see what happens to shale, a sedimentary rock, when it is exposed to more and more heat and pressure.*

Schist

Gneiss

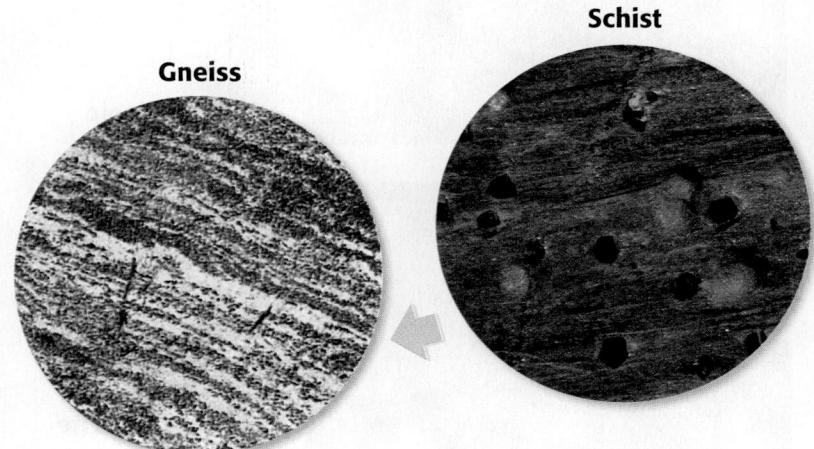

WRITING SKILL **Metamorphosis** The term *metamorphosis* means "change in form." When some animals undergo a dramatic change in the shape of their body, they are said to have undergone a metamorphosis. As part of their natural life cycle, moths and butterflies go through four stages. After they hatch from an egg, they are in the larval stage in the form of a caterpillar. In the next stage, they build a cocoon or become a chrysalis. This stage is called the *pupal stage*. They finally emerge into the adult stage of their life, in which they have wings, antennae, and legs! Research other animals that undergo a metamorphosis, and summarize your findings in a short essay.

nonfoliated the texture of metamorphic rock in which the mineral grains are not arranged in planes or bands

Nonfoliated Metamorphic Rock

The texture of metamorphic rock in which the mineral grains are not arranged in planes or bands is called **nonfoliated**. Notice that the rocks shown in **Figure 6** do not have mineral grains that are aligned. This lack of aligned mineral grains is the reason these rocks are called *nonfoliated rocks*.

Nonfoliated rocks are commonly made of one or only a few minerals. During metamorphism, the crystals of these minerals may change in size or the mineral may change in composition in a process called *recrystallization*. The quartzite and marble shown in **Figure 6** are examples of sedimentary rocks that have recrystallized during metamorphism.

Quartz sandstone is a sedimentary rock made of quartz sand grains that have been cemented together. When quartz sandstone is exposed to the heat and pressure, the spaces between the sand grains disappear as the grains recrystallize to form quartzite. Quartzite has a shiny, glittery appearance. Like quartz sandstone, it is made of quartz. But during recrystallization, the mineral grains have grown larger than the original grains in the sandstone.

When limestone undergoes metamorphism, the same process that happened to the quartz happens to the calcite, and the limestone becomes marble. The calcite crystals in the marble are larger than the calcite grains in the original limestone.

Figure 6 Two Examples of Nonfoliated Metamorphic Rock

Marble and quartzite are nonfoliated metamorphic rocks. As you can see in the views through a microscope, the mineral crystals are not well aligned.

Marble

Quartzite

Metamorphic Rock Structures

Like igneous and sedimentary rock, metamorphic rock also has features that tell you about its history. In metamorphic rocks, these features are caused by deformation. *Deformation* is a change in the shape of a rock caused by a force placed on it. These forces may cause a rock to be squeezed or stretched.

Folds, or bends, in metamorphic rock are structures that indicate that a rock has been deformed. Some folds are not visible to the naked eye. But, as shown in **Figure 7,** some folds may be kilometers or even hundreds of kilometers in size.

✔ **Reading Check** How are metamorphic rock structures related to deformation?

Figure 7 *These large folds occur in metamorphosed sedimentary rock along Saglet Fiord in Labrador, Canada.*

SECTION Review

Summary

- Metamorphic rocks are rocks in which the structure, texture, or composition has changed.

- Two ways rocks can undergo metamorphism are by contact metamorphism and regional metamorphism.

- As rocks undergo metamorphism, the original minerals in a rock change into new minerals that are more stable in new pressure and temperature conditions.

- Foliated metamorphic rock has mineral crystals aligned in planes or bands, whereas nonfoliated rocks have unaligned mineral crystals.

- Metamorphic rock structures are caused by deformation.

Using Key Terms

1. In your own words, define the following terms: *foliated* and *nonfoliated.*

Understanding Key Ideas

2. Which of the following is not a type of foliated metamorphic rock?
   a. gneiss
   b. slate
   c. marble
   d. schist

3. Explain the difference between contact metamorphism and regional metamorphism.

4. Explain how index minerals allow a scientist to understand the history of a metamorphic rock.

Math Skills

5. For every 3.3 km a rock is buried, the pressure placed upon it increases 0.1 gigapascal (100 million pascals). If rock undergoing metamorphosis is buried at 16 km, what is the pressure placed on that rock? (Hint: The pressure at Earth's surface is .101 gigapascal.)

Critical Thinking

6. **Making Inferences** If you had two metamorphic rocks, one that has garnet crystals and the other that has chlorite crystals, which one could have formed at a deeper level in the Earth's crust? Explain your answer.

7. **Applying Concepts** Which do you think would be easier to break, a foliated rock, such as slate, or a nonfoliated rock, such as quartzite? Explain.

8. **Analyzing Processes** A mountain range is located at a boundary where two tectonic plates are colliding. Would most of the metamorphic rock in the mountain range be a product of contact metamorphism or regional metamorphism? Explain.

SCiLINKS®

NSTA
Developed and maintained by the National Science Teachers Association

For a variety of links related to this chapter, go to www.scilinks.org

Topic: Metamorphic Rock
SciLinks code: HSM0949

Skills Practice Lab

Let's Get Sedimental

How do we determine if sedimentary rock layers are undisturbed? The best way to do this is to be sure that fine-grained sediments near the top of a layer lie above coarse-grained sediments near the bottom of the layer. This lab activity will show you how to read rock features that will help you distinguish individual sedimentary rock layers. Then, you can look for the features in real rock layers.

OBJECTIVES

Model the process of sedimentation.

Determine whether sedimentary rock layers are undisturbed.

MATERIALS

- clay
- dropper pipet
- gravel
- magnifying lens
- mixing bowl, 2 qt
- sand
- scissors
- soda bottle with a cap, plastic, 2 L
- soil, clay rich, if available
- water

SAFETY

Procedure

1. In a mixing bowl, thoroughly mix the sand, gravel, and soil. Fill the soda bottle about one-third full of the mixture.

2. Add water to the soda bottle until the bottle is two-thirds full. Twist the cap back onto the bottle, and shake the bottle vigorously until all of the sediment is mixed in the rapidly moving water.

3. Place the bottle on a tabletop. Using the scissors, carefully cut the top off the bottle a few centimeters above the water, as shown. The open bottle will allow water to evaporate.

4. Immediately after you set the bottle on the tabletop, describe what you see from above and through the sides of the bottle.

5. Do not disturb the container. Allow the water to evaporate. (You may speed up the process by carefully using the dropper pipet to siphon off some of the clear water after you allow the container to sit for at least 24 hours.) You may also set the bottle in the sun or under a desk lamp to speed up evaporation.

6. After the sediment has dried and hardened, describe its surface.

7. Carefully lay the container on its side, and cut a wide, vertical strip of plastic down the length of the bottle to expose the sediments in the container. You may find it easier if you place pieces of clay on either side of the container to stabilize it. (If the bottle is clear along its length, this step may not be required.)

8. Brush away the loose material from the sediment, and gently blow on the surface until it is clean. Examine the surface, and record your observations.

Analyze the Results

1 **Identifying Patterns** Do you see anything through the side of the bottle that could help you determine if a sedimentary rock is undisturbed? Explain your answer.

2 **Identifying Patterns** Can you observe a pattern of deposition? If so, describe the pattern of deposition of sediment that you observe from top to bottom.

3 **Explaining Events** Explain how these features might be used to identify the top of a sedimentary layer in real rock and to decide if the layer has been disturbed.

4 **Identifying Patterns** Do you see any structures through the side of the bottle that might indicate which direction is up, such as a change in particle density or size?

5 **Identifying Patterns** Use the magnifying lens to examine the boundaries between the gravel, sand, and silt. Do the size of the particles and the type of sediment change dramatically in each layer?

Draw Conclusions

6 **Making Predictions** Imagine that a layer was deposited directly above the sediment in your bottle. Describe the composition of this new layer. Will it have the same composition as the mixture in steps 1–5 in the Procedure?

Applying Your Data

With your class or with a parent, visit an outcrop of sedimentary rock. Apply the information that you have learned in this lab to see if you can determine whether the sedimentary rock layers are disturbed or undisturbed.

Chapter Review

USING KEY TERMS

1 In your own words, write a definition for the term *rock cycle*.

Complete each of the following sentences by choosing the correct term from the word bank.

stratification   foliated
extrusive igneous rock   texture

2 The ___ of a rock is determined by the sizes, shapes, and positions of the minerals the rock contains.

3 ___ metamorphic rock contains minerals that are arranged in plates or bands.

4 The most characteristic property of sedimentary rock is ___.

5 ___ forms plains called *lava plateaus*.

UNDERSTANDING KEY IDEAS

Multiple Choice

6 Sedimentary rock is classified into all of the following main categories except

a. clastic sedimentary rock.

b. chemical sedimentary rock.

c. nonfoliated sedimentary rock.

d. organic sedimentary rock.

7 An igneous rock that cools very slowly has a ___ texture.

a. foliated

b. fine-grained

c. nonfoliated

d. coarse-grained

8 Igneous rock forms when

a. minerals crystallize from a solution.

b. sand grains are cemented together.

c. magma cools and solidifies.

d. mineral grains in a rock recrystallize.

9 A ___ is a common structure found in metamorphic rock.

a. ripple mark   c. sill

b. fold   d. layer

10 The process in which sediment is removed from its source and transported is called

a. deposition.   c. weathering.

b. erosion.   d. uplift.

11 Mafic rocks are

a. light-colored rocks rich in calcium, iron, and magnesium.

b. dark-colored rocks rich in aluminum, potassium, silica, and sodium.

c. light-colored rocks rich in aluminum, potassium, silica, and sodium.

d. dark-colored rocks rich in calcium, iron, and magnesium.

Short Answer

12 Explain how composition and texture are used by scientists to classify rocks.

13 Describe two ways a rock can undergo metamorphism.

14 Explain why some minerals only occur in metamorphic rocks.

15 Describe how each type of rock changes as it moves through the rock cycle.

16 Describe two ways rocks were used by early humans and ancient civilizations.

CRITICAL THINKING

17 **Concept Mapping** Use the following terms to construct a concept map: *rocks, metamorphic, sedimentary, igneous, foliated, nonfoliated, organic, clastic, chemical, intrusive,* and *extrusive.*

18 **Making Inferences** If you were looking for fossils in the rocks around your home and the rock type that was closest to your home was metamorphic, do you think that you would find many fossils? Explain your answer.

19 **Applying Concepts** Imagine that you want to quarry, or mine, granite. You have all of the equipment, but you have two pieces of land to choose from. One area has a granite batholith underneath it. The other has a granite sill. If both intrusive bodies are at the same depth, which one would be the better choice for you to quarry? Explain your answer.

20 **Applying Concepts** The sedimentary rock coquina is made up of pieces of seashells. Which of the three kinds of sedimentary rock could coquina be? Explain your answer.

21 **Analyzing Processes** If a rock is buried deep inside the Earth, which geological processes cannot change the rock? Explain your answer.

INTERPRETING GRAPHICS

The bar graph below shows the percentage of minerals by mass that compose a sample of granite. Use the graph below to answer the questions that follow.

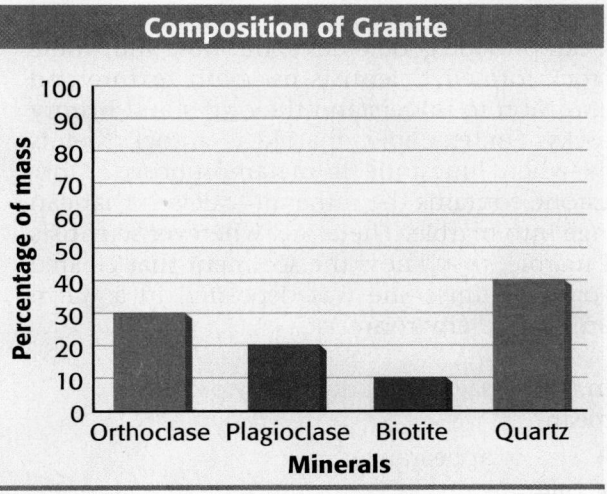

22 Your rock sample is made of four minerals. What percentage of each mineral makes up your sample?

23 Both plagioclase and orthoclase are feldspar minerals. What percentage of the minerals in your sample of granite are not feldspar minerals?

24 If your rock sample has a mass of 10 g, how many grams of quartz does it contain?

25 Use paper, a compass, and a protractor or a computer to make a pie chart. Show the percentage of each of the four minerals your sample of granite contains. (Look in the Appendix of this book for help on making a pie chart.)

READING

Read each of the passages below. Then, answer the questions that follow each passage.

Passage 1 The texture and composition of a rock can provide good clues about how and where the rock formed. Scientists use both texture and composition to understand the <u>origin</u> and history of rocks. For example, marble is a rock that is made when limestone is metamorphosed. Only limestone contains the mineral—calcite—that can change into marble. Therefore, wherever scientists find marble, they know the sediment that created the original limestone was deposited in a warm ocean or lake environment.

1. In the passage, what does the word *origin* mean?

A size or appearance

B age

C location or surroundings

D source or formation

2. Based on the passage, what can the reader conclude?

F Marble is a sedimentary rock.

G Limestone is created by sediments deposited in warm ocean or lake environments.

H Marble is a rock that is made when sandstone has undergone metamorphism.

I In identifying a rock, the texture of a rock is more important than the composition of the rock.

3. What is the main idea of the passage?

A Scientists believe marble is the most important rock type to study.

B Scientists study the composition and texture of a rock to determine how the rock formed and what happened after it formed.

C Some sediments are deposited in warm oceans and lakes.

D When limestone undergoes metamorphism, it creates marble.

Passage 2 Fulgurites are a rare type of natural glass found in areas that have quartz-rich sediments, such as beaches and deserts. A <u>tubular</u> fulgurite forms when a lightning bolt strikes material such as sand and melts the quartz into a liquid. The liquid quartz cools and solidifies quickly, and a thin, glassy tube is left behind. Fulgurites usually have a rough outer surface and a smooth inner surface. Underground, a fulgurite may be shaped like the roots of a tree. The fulgurite branches out with many arms that trace the zigzag path of the lightning bolt. Some fulgurites are as short as your little finger, but others stretch 20 m into the ground.

1. In the passage, what does the word *tubular* mean?

A flat and sharp

B round and long

C funnel shaped

D pyramid shaped

2. From the information in the passage, what can the reader conclude?

F Fulgurites are formed above ground.

G Sand contains a large amount of quartz.

H Fulgurites are most often very small.

I Fulgurites are easy to find in sandy places.

3. Which of the following statements best describes a fulgurite?

A Fulgurites are frozen lightning bolts.

B Fulgurites are rootlike rocks.

C Fulgurites are glassy tubes found in deserts.

D Fulgurites are natural glass tubes formed by lightning bolts.

Use the diagram below to answer the questions that follow.

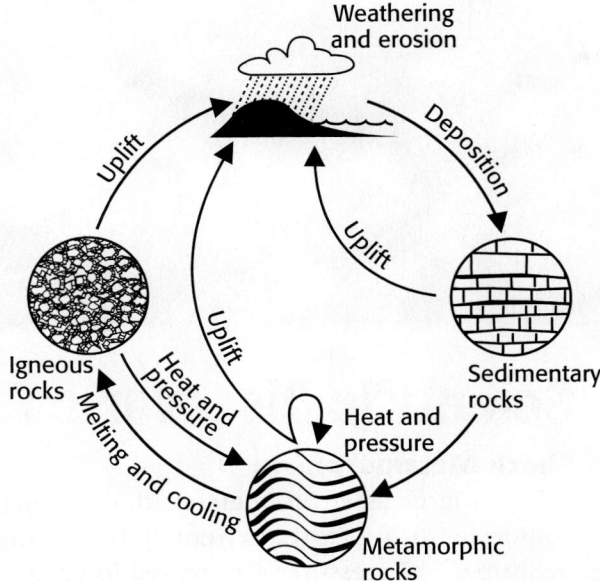

Weathering and erosion

Uplift

Deposition

Uplift

Igneous rocks

Heat and pressure

Uplift

Melting and cooling

Heat and pressure

Sedimentary rocks

Metamorphic rocks

1. According to the rock cycle diagram, which of the following statements is true?

A Only sedimentary rock gets weathered and eroded.

B Sedimentary rocks are made from metamorphic, igneous, and sedimentary rock fragments and minerals.

C Heat and pressure create igneous rocks.

D Metamorphic rocks are created by melting and cooling.

2. A rock exists at the surface of the Earth. What would be the next step in the rock cycle?

F cooling

G weathering

H melting

I metamorphism

3. Which of the following processes brings rocks to Earth's surface, where they can be eroded?

A burial

B deposition

C uplift

D weathering

4. Which of the following is the best summary of the rock cycle?

F Each type of rock gets melted. Then the magma turns into igneous, sedimentary, and metamorphic rock.

G Magma cools to form igneous rock. Then, the igneous rock becomes sedimentary rock. Sedimentary rock is heated and forms metamorphic rock. Metamorphic rock melts to form magma.

H All three rock types weather to create sedimentary rock. All three rock types melt to form magma. Magma forms igneous rock. All three types of rock form metamorphic rock because of heat and pressure.

I Igneous rock is weathered to create sedimentary rock. Sedimentary rock is melted to form igneous rock. Metamorphic rock is weathered to form igneous rock.

MATH

Read each question below, and choose the best answer.

1. Eric has 25 rocks he has collected as a science project for class. Nine rocks are sedimentary, 10 are igneous, and 6 are metamorphic. If Eric chooses a rock at random, what is the probability that he will choose an igneous rock?

A 1/2

B 2/5

C 3/8

D 1/15

2. At a mineral and fossil show, Elizabeth bought two quartz crystals that cost $2.00 each and four trilobite fossils that cost $3.50 each. Which equation can be used to describe c, the total cost of her purchase?

F $c = (2 \times 4) + (2.00 \times 3.50)$

G $c = (2 \times 2.00) + (4 \times 3.50)$

H $c = (4 \times 2.00) + (2 \times 3.50)$

I $c = (2 + 2.00) + (4 + 3.50)$

Standardized Test Preparation

Science in Action

Science, Technology, and Society

The Moai of Easter Island

Easter island is located in the Pacific Ocean more than 3,200 km from the coast of Chile. The island is home to mysterious statues that were carved from volcanic ash. The statues, called *moai,* have human heads and large torsos. The average moai weighs 14 tons and is more than 4.5 m tall, though some are as tall as 10 m! Altogether, 887 moai have been discovered. How old are the moai? Scientists believe that the moai were built between 500 and 1,000 years ago. What purpose did moai serve for their creators? The moai may have been religious symbols or gods.

Social Studies ACTIVITY

WRITING SKILL Research another ancient society or civilization, such as the ancient Egyptians, who are believed to have used stone to construct monuments to their gods or to important people. Report your findings in a short essay.

Scientific Discoveries

Shock Metamorphism

When a large asteroid, meteoroid, or comet collides with the Earth, extremely high temperatures and pressures are created in Earth's surface rock. These high pressures and temperatures cause minerals in the surface rock to shatter and recrystallize. The new minerals that result from this recrystallization cannot be created under any other conditions. This process is called *shock metamorphism.*

When large objects from space collide with the Earth, craters are formed by the impact. However, impact craters are not always easy to find on Earth. Scientists use shock metamorphism as a clue to locate ancient impact craters.

Language Arts ACTIVITY

WRITING SKILL The impact site caused by the asteroid strike in the Yucatán 65 million years ago has been named the Chicxulub (cheeks OO loob) structure. Research the origin of the name Chicxulub, and report your findings in a short paper.

Careers

Robert L. Folk

Petrologist For Dr. Robert Folk, the study of rock takes place on the microscopic level. Dr. Folk is searching for tiny life-forms he has named nannobacteria, or dwarf bacteria, in rock. *Nannobacteria* may also be spelled *nanobacteria*. Because nannobacteria are so incredibly small, only 0.05 to 0.2 μm in diameter, Folk must use an extremely powerful 100,000× microscope, called a *scanning electron microscope*, to see the shape of the bacteria in rock. Folk's research had already led him to discover that a certain type of Italian limestone is produced by bacteria. The bacteria were consuming the minerals, and the waste of the bacteria was forming the limestone. Further research led Folk to the discovery of the tiny nannobacteria. The spherical or oval-shaped nannobacteria appeared as chains and grapelike clusters. From his research, Folk hypothesized that nannobacteria are responsible for many inorganic reactions that occur in rock. Many scientists are skeptical of Folk's nannobacteria. Some skeptics believe that the tiny size of nannobacteria makes the bacteria simply too small to contain the chemistry of life. Others believe that nannobacteria actually represent structures that do not come from living things.

Math Activity

If a nannobacterium is 1/10 the length, 1/10 the width, and 1/10 the height of an ordinary bacterium, how many nannobacteria can fit within an ordinary bacterium? (Hint: Draw block diagrams of both a nannobacterium and an ordinary bacterium.)

To learn more about these Science in Action topics, visit go.hrw.com and type in the keyword **HZ5RCKF.**

Current Science

Check out Current Science® articles related to this chapter by visiting go.hrw.com. Just type in the keyword **HZ5CS04.**

5

Energy Resources

About the PHOTO

Would you believe that this house is made from empty soda cans and old tires? Well, it is! *The Castle,* named by its designer, architect Mike Reynolds, and located in Taos, New Mexico, not only uses recycled materials but also saves Earth's energy resources. All of the energy used to run this house comes directly from the sun, and the water used for household activities is rainwater.

PRE-READING ACTIVITY

Graphic Organizer

Comparison Table Before you read the chapter, create the graphic organizer entitled "Comparison Table" described in the **Study Skills** section of the Appendix. Label the columns with an energy resource from the chapter. Label the rows with "Pros" and "Cons." As you read the chapter, fill in the table with details about the pros and cons of each energy resource.

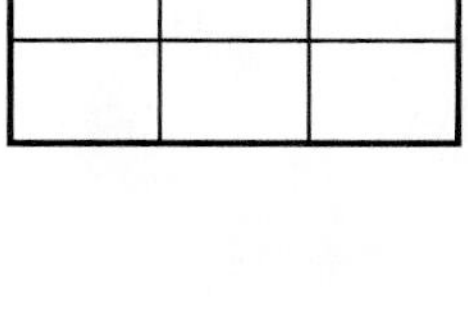

START-UP ACTIVITY

What Is the Sun's Favorite Color?

Try the following activity to see which colors are better than others at absorbing the sun's energy.

Procedure

1. Obtain **at least five balloons** that are different colors but the same size and shape. One of the balloons should be white, and one should be black. Do not inflate the balloons.

2. Place **several small ice cubes** in each balloon. Each balloon should contain the same amount of ice.

3. Line up the balloons on a flat, uniformly colored surface that receives direct sunlight. Make sure that all of the balloons receive the same amount of sunlight and that the openings in the balloons are not facing directly toward the sun.

4. Record the time that it takes the ice to melt completely in each of the balloons. You can tell how much ice has melted in each balloon by pinching the balloons open and then gently squeezing the balloon.

Analysis

1. In which balloon did the ice melt first? Why?

2. What color would you paint a device used to collect solar energy? Explain your answer.

Natural Resources

What does the water you drink, the paper you write on, the gasoline used in the cars you ride in, and the air you breathe have in common?

Water, trees used to make paper, crude oil used to make gasoline, and air are just a few examples of Earth's resources. Can you think of other examples of Earth's resources?

Earth's Resources

The Earth provides almost everything needed for life. For example, the Earth's atmosphere provides the air you breathe, maintains air temperatures, and produces rain. The oceans and other waters of the Earth give you food and needed water. The solid part of the Earth gives nutrients, such as potassium, to the plants you eat. These resources that the Earth provides for you are called natural resources.

A **natural resource** is any natural material that is used by humans. Examples of natural resources are water, petroleum, minerals, forests, and animals. Most resources are changed and made into products that make people's lives more comfortable and convenient, as shown in **Figure 1.** The energy we get from many of these resources, such as gasoline and wind, ultimately comes from the sun's energy.

READING WARM-UP

Objectives

● Describe how humans use natural resources.

● Compare renewable resources with nonrenewable resources.

● Explain three ways that humans can conserve natural resources.

Terms to Learn

natural resource
renewable resource
nonrenewable resource
recycling

READING STRATEGY

Reading Organizer As you read this section, make a concept map by using the terms above.

Figure 1 Natural Resources

This pile of lumber is made of wood, which comes from trees.

The gasoline in this can is made from oil pumped from the Earth's crust.

Electrical energy generated by these wind turbines ultimately comes from the sun's energy.

Figure 2 *Trees and fresh water are just a few of the renewable resources available on Earth.*

Renewable Resources

Some natural resources can be renewed. A **renewable resource** is a natural resource that can be replaced at the same rate at which the resource is used. **Figure 2** shows two examples of renewable resources. Although many resources are renewable, they still can be used up before they can be renewed. Trees, for example, are renewable. However, some forests are being cut down faster than new forests can grow to replace them.

✓ *Reading Check* **What is a renewable resource?** (*See the Appendix for answers to Reading Checks.*)

Nonrenewable Resources

Not all of Earth's natural resources are renewable. A **nonrenewable resource** is a resource that forms at a rate that is much slower than the rate at which it is consumed. Coal, shown in **Figure 3,** is an example of a nonrenewable resource. It takes millions of years for coal to form. Once coal is used up, it is no longer available. Petroleum and natural gas are other examples of nonrenewable resources. When these resources become scarce, humans will have to find other resources to replace them.

natural resource any natural material that is used by humans, such as water, petroleum, minerals, forests, and animals

renewable resource a natural resource that can be replaced at the same rate at which the resource is consumed

nonrenewable resource a resource that forms at a rate that is much slower than the rate at which it is consumed

Figure 3 *The coal used in the industrial process shown here is not quickly replaced by natural processes.*

Conserving Natural Resources

Whether the natural resources you use are renewable or nonrenewable, you should be careful how you use them. To conserve natural resources, you should try to use them only when necessary. For example, leaving the faucet on while brushing your teeth wastes clean water. Turning the faucet on only to rinse your brush saves water that you may need for other uses.

Conserving resources also means taking care of the resources even when you are not using them. For example, it is important to keep lakes, rivers, and other water resources free of pollution. Polluted lakes and rivers can affect the water you drink. Also, polluted water resources can harm the plants and animals, including humans, that depend on them to survive.

Energy Conservation

The energy we use to heat our homes, drive our cars, and run our computers comes from natural resources. The way in which we choose to use energy on a daily basis affects the availability of the natural resources. Most of the natural resources that provide us energy are nonrenewable resources. So, if we don't limit our use of energy now, the resources may not be available in the future.

As with all natural resources, conserving energy is important. You can conserve energy by being careful to use only the resources that you need. For example, turn lights off when you are not using them. And make sure the washing machine is full before you start it, as shown in **Figure 4.** You can also ride a bike, walk, or take a bus because these methods use fewer resources than a car does.

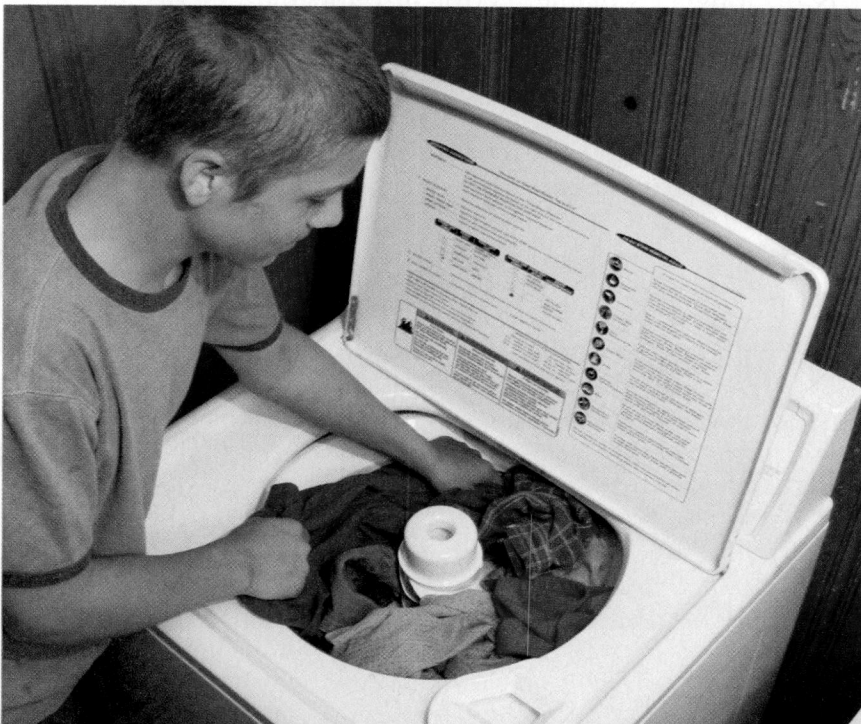

Figure 4 *Making sure the washing machine is full before running it is one way you can avoid wasting natural resources.*

Reduce, Reuse, Recycle

Another way to conserve natural resources is to recycle, as shown in **Figure 5. Recycling** is the process of reusing materials from waste or scrap. Recycling reduces the amount of natural resources that must be obtained from the Earth. For example, recycling paper reduces the number of trees that must be cut down to make new paper products. Recycling also conserves energy. Though energy is required to recycle materials, it takes less energy to recycle an aluminum can than it does to make a new one!

Newspaper, aluminum cans, most plastic containers, and cardboard boxes can be recycled. Most plastic containers have a number on them. This number informs you whether the item can be recycled. Plastic products with the numbers 1 and 2 can be recycled in most communities. Check with your community's recycling center to see what kinds of materials the center recycles.

✔ **Reading Check** What are some kinds of products that can be recycled?

recycling the process of recovering valuable or useful materials from waste or scrap; the process of reusing some items

Figure 5 *You can recycle many household items to help conserve natural resources.*

SECTION Review

Summary

- We use natural resources such as water, petroleum, and lumber to make our lives more comfortable and convenient.

- Renewable resources can be replaced within a relatively short period of time, but nonrenewable resources may take thousands or even millions of years to form.

- Natural resources can be conserved by using only what is needed, taking care of resources, and recycling.

Using Key Terms

1. Use each of the following terms in a separate sentence: *natural resource, renewable resource, nonrenewable resource,* and *recycling.*

Understanding Key Ideas

2. How do humans use most natural resources?

3. Which of the following is a renewable resource?
   a. oil
   b. water
   c. coal
   d. natural gas

4. Describe three ways to conserve natural resources.

Math Skills

5. If a faucet dripped for 8.6 h and 3.3 L of water dripped out every hour, how many liters of water dripped out altogether?

Critical Thinking

6. **Making Inferences** How does human activity affect Earth's renewable and nonrenewable resources?

7. **Applying Concepts** List five products you regularly use that can be recycled.

8. **Making Inferences** Why is the availability of some renewable resources more of a concern now than it was 100 years ago?

SCLINKS®

NSTA
Developed and maintained by the
National Science Teachers Association

For a variety of links related to this chapter, go to www.scilinks.org

Topic: Natural Resources
SciLinks code: HSM1015

Fossil Fuels

How does a sunny day 200 million years ago relate to your life today?

Chances are that if you traveled to school today or used a product made of plastic, you used some of the energy from sunlight that fell on Earth several hundred million years ago. Life as you know it would be very different without the fuels or products formed from plants and animals that lived alongside the dinosaurs.

Energy Resources

The fuels we use to run cars, ships, planes, and factories and to generate electrical energy, shown in **Figure 1,** are energy resources. *Energy resources* are natural resources that humans use to generate energy. Most of the energy we use comes from a group of natural resources called fossil fuels. A **fossil fuel** is a nonrenewable energy resource formed from the remains of plants and animals that lived long ago. Examples of fossil fuels include petroleum, coal, and natural gas.

Energy is released from fossil fuels when they are burned. For example, the energy from burning coal in a power plant is used to produce electrical energy. However, because fossil fuels are a nonrenewable resource, once they are burned, they are gone. Therefore, like other resources, fossil fuels need to be conserved. In the 21st century, societies will continue to explore alternatives to fossil fuels. But they will also focus on developing more-efficient ways to use these fuels.

fossil fuel a nonrenewable energy resource formed from the remains of organisms that lived long ago; examples include oil, coal, and natural gas

Figure 1 *Light produced from electrical energy can be seen in this satellite image taken from space.*

Figure 2 *Some refineries use a process called* distillation *to separate petroleum into various types of petroleum products.*

Types of Fossil Fuels

All living things are made up of the element carbon. Because fossil fuels are formed from the remains of plants and animals, all fossil fuels are made of carbon, too. Most of the carbon in fossil fuels exists as hydrogen-carbon compounds called *hydrocarbons*. But different fossil fuels have different forms. Fossil fuels may exist as liquids, gases, or solids.

Liquid Fossil Fuels: Petroleum

A liquid mixture of complex hydrocarbon compounds is called **petroleum.** Petroleum is also commonly known as *crude oil*. Petroleum is separated into several kinds of products in refineries, such as the one shown in **Figure 2.** Examples of fossil fuels separated from petroleum are gasoline, jet fuel, kerosene, diesel fuel, and fuel oil.

More than 40% of the world's energy comes from petroleum products. Petroleum products are the main fuel for forms of transportation, such as airplanes, trains, boats, and ships. Crude oil is so valuable that it is often called *black gold*.

petroleum a liquid mixture of complex hydrocarbon compounds; used widely as a fuel source

natural gas a mixture of gaseous hydrocarbons located under the surface of the Earth, often near petroleum deposits; used as a fuel

Gaseous Fossil Fuels: Natural Gas

A gaseous mixture of hydrocarbons is called **natural gas.** Most natural gas is used for heating, but it is also used for generating electrical energy. Your kitchen stove may be powered by natural gas. Some motor vehicles, such as the van in **Figure 3,** use natural gas as fuel. An advantage of using natural gas is that using it causes less air pollution than using oil does. However, natural gas is very flammable. Gas leaks can lead to fires or deadly explosions.

Methane, CH_4, is the main component of natural gas. But other components, such as butane and propane, can be separated from natural gas, too. Butane and propane are often used as fuel for camp stoves and outdoor grills.

Figure 3 *Vehicles powered by natural gas are becoming more common.*

✓ Reading Check What is natural gas most often used for? (*See the Appendix for answers to Reading Checks.*)

Figure 4 *This coal is being gathered so that it may be burned in the power plant shown in the background.*

coal a fossil fuel that forms underground from partially decomposed plant material

INTERNET ACTIVITY

For another activity related to this chapter, go to **go.hrw.com** and type in the keyword **HZ5ENRW.**

Solid Fossil Fuels: Coal

The solid fossil fuel that humans use most is coal. **Coal** is a fossil fuel that is formed underground from partially decomposed plant material. Coal was once the major source of energy in the United States. People burned coal in stoves to heat their homes. They also used coal in transportation. Many trains in the 1800s and early 1900s were powered by coal-burning steam locomotives.

As cleaner energy resources became available, people reduced their use of coal. People began to use coal less because burning coal produces large amounts of air pollution. Now, people use forms of transportation that use oil instead of coal as fuel. In the United States, coal is now rarely used as a fuel for heating. However, many power plants, such as the one shown in **Figure 4,** burn coal to generate electrical energy.

✓ Reading Check In the 1800s and early 1900s, what was coal most commonly used for?

CONNECTION TO Chemistry

Hydrocarbons Both petroleum and natural gas are made of compounds called *hydrocarbons*. A hydrocarbon is an organic compound that contains only carbon and hydrogen. A molecule of propane, C_3H_8, a gaseous fossil fuel, contains three carbons and eight hydrogens. Using a molecular model set, create a model of a propane molecule. (Hint: Each carbon atom should have four bonds, and each hydrogen atom should have one bond.)

ACTIVITY

How Do Fossil Fuels Form?

All fossil fuels form from the buried remains of ancient organisms. But different kinds of fossil fuels form in different ways and from different kinds of organisms.

Petroleum and Natural Gas Formation

Petroleum and natural gas form mainly from the remains of microscopic sea organisms. When these organisms die, their remains settle on the ocean floor. There, the remains decay, are buried, and become part of the ocean sediment. Over time, the sediment slowly becomes rock, trapping the decayed remains. Through physical and chemical changes over millions of years, the remains become petroleum and gas. Gradually, more rocks form above the rocks that contain the fossil fuels. Under the pressure of overlying rocks and sediments, the fossil fuels can move through permeable rocks. *Permeable rocks* are rocks that allow fluids, such as petroleum and gas, to move through them. As shown in **Figure 5,** these permeable rocks become reservoirs that hold petroleum and natural gas.

The formation of petroleum and natural gas is an ongoing process. Part of the remains of today's sea life will become petroleum and natural gas millions of years from now.

Rock Sponge

1. Place **samples of sandstone, limestone,** and **shale** in separate **Petri dishes.**
2. Place **five drops of light machine oil** on each rock sample.
3. Observe and record the time required for the oil to be absorbed by each of the rock samples.
4. Which rock sample absorbed the oil fastest? Why?
5. Based on your findings, describe a property that allows fossil fuels to be easily removed from reservoir rock.

Figure 5 *Petroleum and gas move through permeable rock. Eventually, these fuels are collected in reservoirs. Rocks that are folded upward are excellent fossil-fuel traps.*

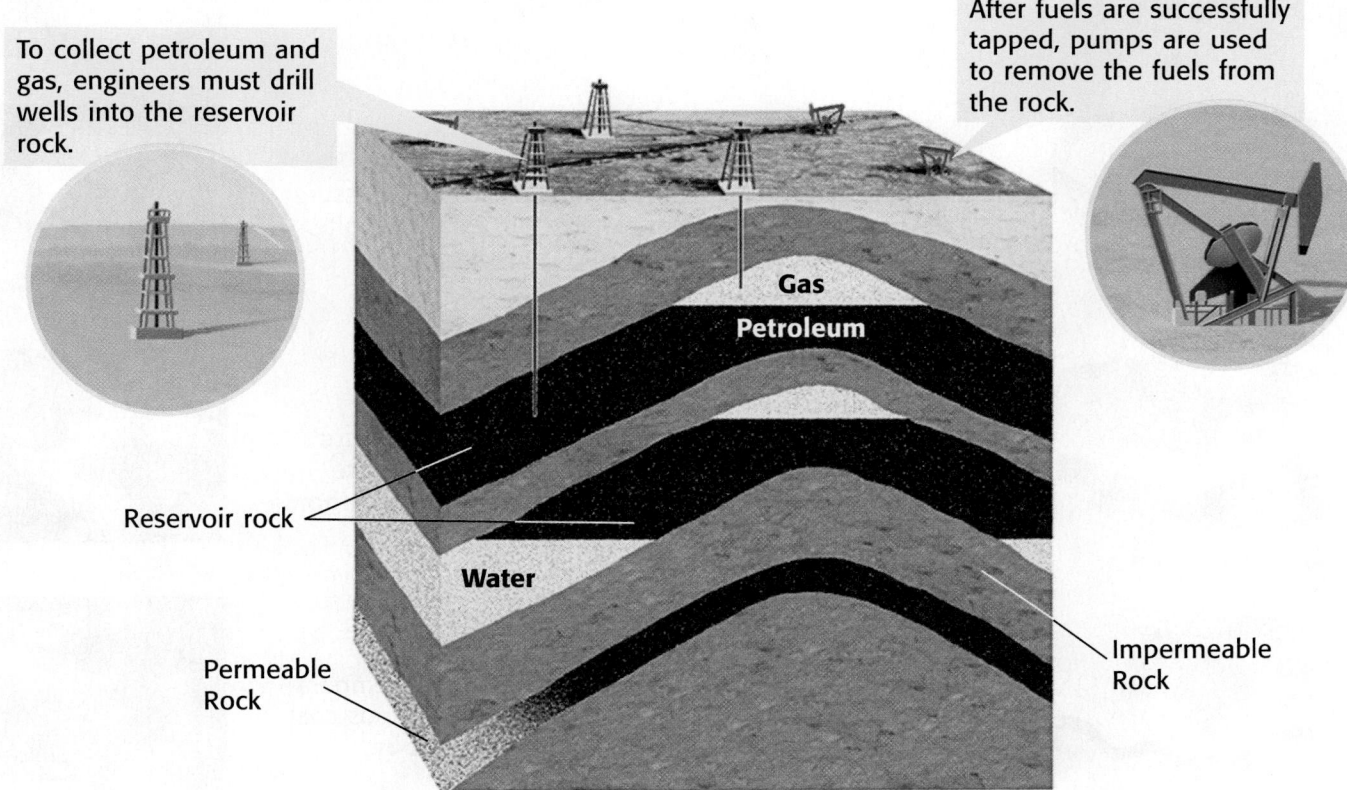

To collect petroleum and gas, engineers must drill wells into the reservoir rock.

After fuels are successfully tapped, pumps are used to remove the fuels from the rock.

Gas

Petroleum

Reservoir rock

Water

Permeable Rock

Impermeable Rock

Coal Formation

Coal forms differently from the way petroleum and natural gas form. Coal forms underground from decayed swamp plants over millions of years. When the plants die, they sink to the bottom of the swamp. This begins the process of coal formation.

The four stages of coal formation, as shown in **Figure 6,** are peat, lignite, bituminous coal, and anthracite. Peat is a form of coal in which the remains of plants are only partially decomposed. Over time, the peat is buried under sediment. Water and gases are squeezed out of the peat. Pressure and high temperature then turn the peat into lignite. The process by which pressure and temperature increase due to the deposition of sediment creates different forms of coal. The percentage of carbon increases with each stage of coal formation. The higher the carbon content is, the more cleanly the material burns. Pollution controls can remove most of the pollutants produced by burning coal. However, when burned, all grades of coal pollute the air.

Figure 6 **Coal Formation**

Stage 1: Peat
Bacteria and fungi change sunken swamp plants into peat. Peat is about **60% carbon.**

Stage 2: Lignite
Sediment buries the peat, which increases the pressure and temperature. The peat slowly changes into lignite, which is about **70% carbon.**

Stage 3: Bituminous Coal
As the lignite becomes more buried, the temperature and pressure continue to increase. Eventually, lignite turns into bituminous coal, which is about **80% carbon.**

Stage 4: Anthracite
As bituminous coal becomes more buried, the temperature and pressure continue to increase. Bituminous coal turns into anthracite, which is about **90% carbon.**

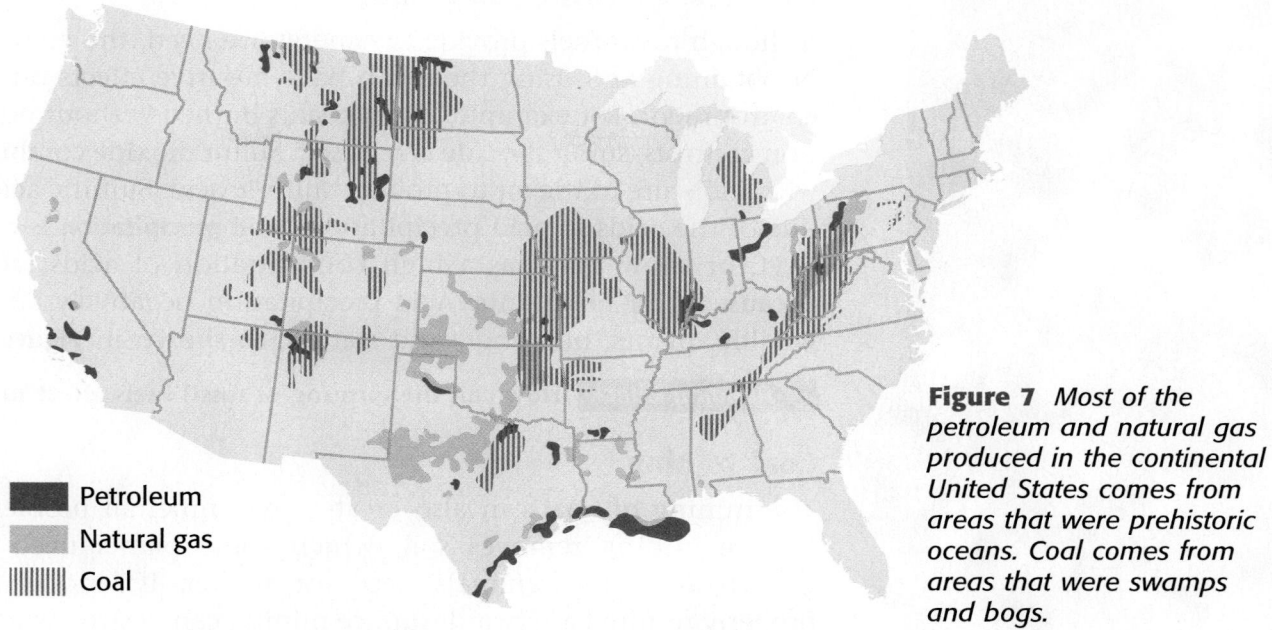

Petroleum

Natural gas

|||||||||| Coal

Figure 7 *Most of the petroleum and natural gas produced in the continental United States comes from areas that were prehistoric oceans. Coal comes from areas that were swamps and bogs.*

Where Are Fossil Fuels Found?

Fossil fuels are found in many parts of the world. Some fossil fuels are found on land, while other fossil fuels are found beneath the ocean. As shown in **Figure 7,** the United States has large reserves of petroleum, natural gas, and coal. Despite its large reserves of petroleum, the United States imports petroleum as well. About one-half of the petroleum used by the United States is imported from the Middle East, South America, Africa, Canada, and Mexico.

How Do We Obtain Fossil Fuels?

Humans use several methods to remove fossil fuels from the Earth's crust. The kind and location of fuel determine the method used to remove the fuel. People remove petroleum and natural gas from Earth by drilling wells into rock that contains these resources. Oil wells exist on land and in the ocean. For offshore drilling, engineers mount drills on platforms that are secured to the ocean floor or that float at the ocean's surface. **Figure 8** shows an offshore oil rig.

People obtain coal either by mining deep beneath Earth's surface or by surface mining. Surface mining, also known as *strip mining,* is the process by which soil and rock are stripped from the Earth's surface to expose the underlying coal that is to be mined.

Reading Check How are natural gas and petroleum removed from Earth?

Figure 8 *Large oil rigs, some of which are more than 300 m tall, operate offshore in many places, such as the Gulf of Mexico and the North Sea.*

1994

1935

Figure 9 *Notice how this statue looked before the effects of acid precipitation.*

acid precipitation precipitation, such as rain, sleet, or snow, that contains a high concentration of acids, often because of the pollution of the atmosphere

smog photochemical haze that forms when sunlight acts on industrial pollutants and burning fuels

Problems with Fossil Fuels

Although fossil fuels provide the energy we need, the methods of obtaining and using them can have negative effects on the environment. For example, when coal is burned without pollution controls, sulfur dioxide is released. Sulfur dioxide combines with moisture in the air to produce sulfuric acid. Sulfuric acid is one of the acids in acid precipitation. **Acid precipitation** is rain, sleet, or snow that has a high concentration of acids, often because of air pollutants. Acid precipitation negatively affects wildlife, plants, buildings, and statues, as shown in **Figure 9.**

✓ *Reading Check* How can the burning of fossil fuels affect rain?

Coal Mining

The mining of coal can also create environmental problems. Surface mining removes soil, which some plants need for growth and some animals need for shelter. If land is not properly restored afterward, surface mining can destroy wildlife habitats. Coal mining can also lower water tables and pollute water supplies. The potential for underground mines to collapse endangers the lives of miners.

Petroleum Problems

Producing, transporting, and using petroleum can cause environmental problems and endanger wildlife. In June 2000, the carrier, *Treasure,* sank off the coast of South Africa and spilled more than 400 tons of oil. The toxic oil coated thousands of blackfooted penguins, as shown in **Figure 10.** The oil hindered the penguins from swimming and catching fish for food.

Smog

Burning petroleum products causes an environmental problem called smog. **Smog** is photochemical haze that forms when sunlight acts on industrial pollutants and burning fuels. Smog is particularly serious in cities such as Houston and Los Angeles as a result of millions of automobiles that burn gasoline. Also, mountains that surround Los Angeles prevent the wind from blowing pollutants away.

Figure 10 *The oil spilled from the carrier,* Treasure, *endangered the lives of many animals including the blackfooted penguins.*

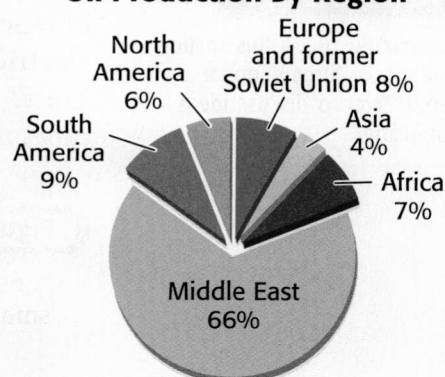

SECTION Review

Summary

- Energy resources are resources that humans use to produce energy.
- Petroleum is a liquid fossil fuel that is made of hydrocarbon compounds.
- Natural gas is a gaseous fossil fuel that is made of hydrocarbon compounds.
- Coal is a solid fossil fuel that forms from decayed swamp plants.
- Petroleum and natural gas form from decayed sea life on the ocean floor.

- Fossil fuels are found all over the world. The United States imports half of the petroleum it uses from the Middle East, South America, Africa, Mexico, and Canada.
- Fossil fuels are obtained by drilling oil wells, mining below Earth's surface, and strip mining.
- Acid precipitation, smog, water pollution, and the destruction of wildlife habitat are some of the environmental problems that are created by the use of fossil fuels.

Using Key Terms

1. Use each of the following terms in a separate sentence: *energy resource, fossil fuel, petroleum, natural gas, coal, acid precipitation,* and *smog.*

Understanding Key Ideas

2. Which of the following stages of coal formation contains the highest carbon content?
   a. lignite
   b. anthracite
   c. peat
   d. bituminous coal

3. Name a solid fossil fuel, a liquid fossil fuel, and a gaseous fossil fuel.

4. Briefly describe how petroleum and natural gas form.

5. How do we obtain petroleum and natural gas?

6. Describe the advantages and disadvantages of fossil fuel use.

Critical Thinking

7. **Making Comparisons** What is the difference between the organic material from which coal forms and the organic material from which petroleum and natural gas form?

8. **Making Inferences** Why can't carpooling and using mass-transit systems eliminate the problems associated with fossil fuels?

Interpreting Graphics

Use the pie chart below to answer the questions that follow.

Oil Production by Region

North America 6%
Europe and former Soviet Union 8%
South America 9%
Asia 4%
Africa 7%
Middle East 66%

Source: International Energy Agency.

9. Which region produces the most oil?

10. If the total sales of oil in 2002 were $500 billion, what was the value of the oil produced in North America?

SC*i*LINKS®

NSTA
Developed and maintained by the
National Science Teachers Association

For a variety of links related to this chapter, go to www.scilinks.org

Topic: Fossil Fuels
SciLinks code: HSM0614

Alternative Resources

What would your life be like if you couldn't play video games, turn on lights, microwave your dinner, take a hot shower, or take the bus to school?

READING WARM-UP

Objectives

- Describe alternatives to the use of fossil fuels.
- List advantages and disadvantages of using alternative energy resources.

Terms to Learn

nuclear energy
chemical energy
solar energy
wind power
hydroelectric energy
biomass
gasohol
geothermal energy

READING STRATEGY

Paired Summarizing Read this section silently. In pairs, take turns summarizing the material. Stop to discuss ideas that seem confusing.

Most of your energy needs and the energy needs of others are met by the use of fossil fuels. Yet, there are two main problems with fossil fuels. First, the availability of fossil fuels is limited. Fossil fuels are nonrenewable resources. Once fossil fuels are used up, new supplies won't be available for thousands—or even millions—of years.

Second, obtaining and using fossil fuels has environmental consequences. To continue to have access to energy and to overcome pollution, we must find alternative sources of energy.

Splitting the Atom: Fission

The energy released by a fission or fusion reaction is **nuclear energy.** *Fission* is a process in which the nuclei of radioactive atoms are split into two or more smaller nuclei, as shown in **Figure 1.** When fission takes place, a large amount of energy is released. This energy can be used to generate electrical energy. The SI unit for all forms of energy is the joule. However, electrical energy and nuclear energy is often measured in megawatts (MW).

Figure 1 **Fission**

A neutron from a uranium-235 atom splits the nucleus into two smaller nuclei called *fission products* and two or more neutrons.

Uranium-235

Neutron

Neutron

Barium-142

Energy

Krypton-91

Pros and Cons of Fission

Nuclear power plants provide alternative sources of energy that do not have the problems that fossil fuels do. So, why don't we use nuclear energy more instead of using fossil fuels? Nuclear power plants produce dangerous radioactive wastes. Radioactive wastes must be removed from the plant and stored until their radioactivity decreases to a harmless level. But nuclear wastes can remain dangerously radioactive for thousands of years. These wastes must be stored in an isolated place where the radiation that they emit cannot harm anyone.

Another problem with nuclear power plants is the potential for accidental release of radiation into the environment. A release could happen if the plant overheats. If a plant's cooling system were to stop working, the plant would overheat. Then, its reactor could melt, and a large amount of radiation could escape into the environment. In addition, towers like the one shown in **Figure 2,** keep hot water from potentially disrupting the local ecosystem.

Figure 2 *Cooling towers are used to cool water leaving a nuclear power plant before the water is released into the environment.*

Combining Atoms: Fusion

Another method of getting energy from nuclei is fusion, shown in **Figure 3.** *Fusion* is the joining of two or more nuclei to form a larger nucleus. This process releases a large amount of energy and happens naturally in the sun.

The main advantage of fusion is that it produces few dangerous wastes. The main disadvantage of fusion is that very high temperatures are required for the reaction to take place. No known material can withstand such high temperatures. Therefore, the reaction must happen within a special environment, such as a magnetic field. Controlled fusion reactions have been limited to laboratory experiments.

nuclear energy the energy released by a fission or fusion reaction; the binding energy of the atomic nucleus

✓ **Reading Check** What is the advantage of producing energy through fusion? (*See the Appendix for answers to Reading Checks.*)

Figure 3 Fusion

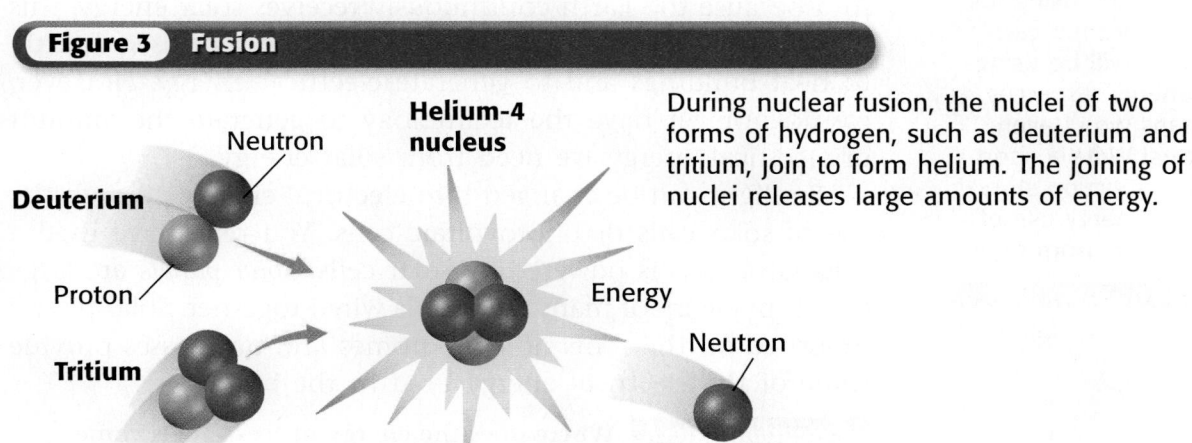

During nuclear fusion, the nuclei of two forms of hydrogen, such as deuterium and tritium, join to form helium. The joining of nuclei releases large amounts of energy.

Figure 4 *This image shows a prototype of a fuel-cell car. Power from fuel cells may be commonly used in the future.*

chemical energy the energy released when a chemical compound reacts to produce new compounds

solar energy the energy received by the Earth from the sun in the form of radiation

Chemical Energy

When you think of fuel for an automobile, you most likely think of gasoline. However, not all vehicles are fueled by gasoline. Some vehicles, such as the one shown in **Figure 4,** are powered by energy that is generated by fuel cells. Fuel cells power automobiles by converting **chemical energy** into electrical energy by reacting hydrogen and oxygen into water. One advantage of using fuel cells as energy sources is that fuel cells do not create pollution. The only byproduct of fuel cells is water. Fuel cells are also more efficient than internal combustion engines are.

The United States has been using fuel cells in space travel since the 1960s. Fuel cells have provided space crews with electrical energy and drinking water. One day, fuel-cell technology may be used to generate electrical energy in buildings, ships, and submarines, too.

Solar Energy

Almost all forms of energy, such as the energy of fossil fuels, come from the sun. The energy received by the Earth from the sun in the form of radiation is **solar energy.** The Earth receives more than enough solar energy to meet all of our energy needs. And because the Earth continuously receives solar energy, this energy is a renewable resource. Solar energy can be used directly to heat buildings and to generate electrical energy. However, we do not yet have the technology to generate the amount of electrical energy we need from solar energy.

Sunlight can be changed into electrical energy through the use of solar cells or photovoltaic cells. You may have used a calculator that is powered by solar cells. *Solar panels* are large panels made up of many solar cells wired together. Solar panels mounted on the roofs of some homes and businesses provide some of the electrical energy used in the buildings.

✓ Reading Check Where does the energy of fossil fuels come from?

Solar Heating

Solar energy is also used for direct heating through solar collectors. *Solar collectors* are dark-colored boxes that have glass or plastic tops. A common use of solar collectors is to heat water, as shown in **Figure 5.** More than 1 million solar water heaters have been installed in the United States. Solar water heaters are especially common in Florida and California.

Pros and Cons of Solar Energy

One of the best things about solar energy is that it doesn't produce pollution. Also, solar energy is renewable, because it comes from the sun. However, some climates don't have enough sunny days to benefit from solar energy. Also, although solar energy is free, solar cells and solar collectors are more expensive to make than other energy systems are. The cost of installing a complete solar-power system in a house can be one-third of the total cost of the house.

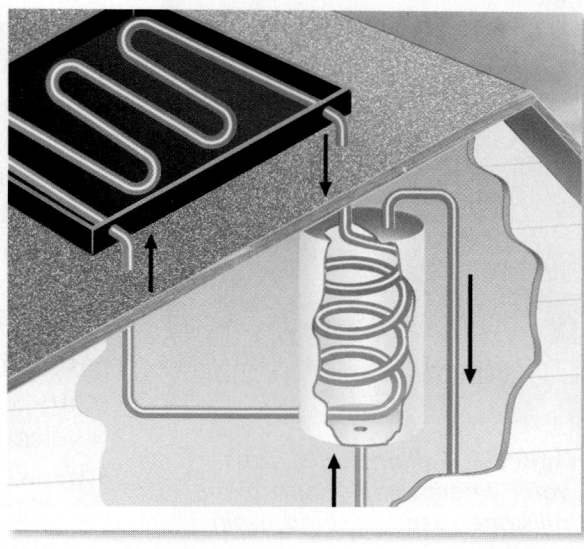

Figure 5 *The liquid in the solar collector is heated by the sun. Then, the liquid is pumped through tubes that run through a water heater, which causes the temperature of the water to increase.*

Wind Power

Wind is made indirectly by solar energy through the uneven heating of air. Energy can be harnessed from wind. **Wind power** is the use of a windmill to drive an electric generator. Clusters of wind turbines, like the ones shown in **Figure 6,** can generate a significant amount of electrical energy. Wind energy is renewable, and it doesn't cause any pollution. However, in many areas, the wind isn't strong enough or frequent enough to create energy on a large scale.

wind power the use of a windmill to drive an electric generator

Figure 6 *Wind turbines take up only a small part of the ground's surface. As a result, the land on wind farms can be used for more than one purpose.*

137

Figure 7 *Falling water turns water wheels, which turn giant millstones used to grind grain into flour.*

hydroelectric energy electrical energy produced by falling water

Figure 8 *Falling water turns turbines inside hydroelectric dams and generates electrical energy for millions of people.*

Hydroelectric Energy

Humans have used the energy of falling water for thousands of years. Water wheels, such as the one shown in **Figure 7,** have been around since ancient times. In the early years of the Industrial Revolution, water wheels provided energy for many factories. Today, the energy of falling water is used to generate electrical energy. Electrical energy produced by falling water is called **hydroelectric energy.**

Pros and Cons of Hydroelectric Energy

After the dam is built, hydroelectric energy is inexpensive and causes little pollution. It is renewable because water constantly cycles from water sources to the air, to the land, and back to the water source. But like wind energy, hydroelectric energy is not available everywhere. It can be produced only where large volumes of falling water can be harnessed. Huge dams, such as the one in **Figure 8,** must be built on major rivers to capture enough water to generate significant amounts of electrical energy.

Using more hydroelectric energy could reduce the demand for fossil fuels, but there are trade-offs. Building the large dams necessary for hydroelectric power plants often destroys other resources, such as forests and wildlife habitats. For example, hydroelectric dams on the lower Snake and Columbia Rivers in Washington state disrupt the migratory paths of local populations of salmon and steelhead. Large numbers of these fish die each year because their migratory path is disrupted. Dams can also decrease water quality and create erosion problems.

Reading Check Why is hydroelectric energy renewable?

Power from Plants

Plants are similar to solar collectors. Both absorb energy from the sun and store it for later use. Leaves, wood, and other parts of plants contain the stored energy. Even the dung of plant-grazing animals is high in stored energy. These sources of energy are called biomass. **Biomass** is organic matter that can be a source of energy.

Burning Biomass

Biomass energy can be released in several ways. The most common way is to burn biomass. Approximately 70% of people living in developing countries, about half the world population, burn wood or charcoal to heat their homes and cook their food. In contrast, about 5% of the people in the United States heat and cook this way. Scientists estimate that the burning of wood and animal dung accounts for approximately 14% of the world's total energy use. **Figure 9** shows a woman who is preparing cow dung that will be dried and used for fuel.

Gasohol

Biomass material can also be changed into liquid fuel. Plants that contain sugar or starch can be made into alcohol. The alcohol can be burned as a fuel. Or alcohol can be mixed with gasoline to make a fuel called **gasohol.** More than 1,000 L of alcohol can be made from 1 acre of corn. But people in the United States use a large amount of fuel for their cars. And the alcohol produced from about 40% of one corn harvest in the United States would provide only 10% of the fuel used in our cars! Biomass is a renewable source of energy. However, producing biomass requires land that could be used for growing food.

biomass organic matter that can be a source of energy

gasohol a mixture of gasoline and alcohol that is used as a fuel

Miles per Acre

Imagine that you own a car that runs on alcohol made from corn that you grow. You drive your car about 15,000 mi per year, and you get 240 gal of alcohol from each acre of corn that you process. If your car has a gas mileage of 25 mi/gal, how many acres of corn must you process to fuel your car for a year?

Figure 9 *In many parts of the world where firewood is scarce, people burn animal dung for energy.*

Energy from Within Earth

If you have ever seen a volcanic eruption, you know how powerful the Earth can be. The energy produced by the heat within Earth is called **geothermal energy.**

Geothermal Energy

In some areas, groundwater is heated by *magma,* or melted rock. Often, the heated groundwater becomes steam. *Geysers* are natural vents that discharge this steam or water in a column into the air. The steam and hot water can also escape through wells drilled into the rock. From these wells, geothermal power plants can harness the energy from within Earth by pumping the steam and hot water, as shown in **Figure 10.** The world's largest geothermal power plant in California, called *The Geysers,* produces electrical energy for 1.7 million households.

Geothermal energy can also be used to heat buildings. In this process, hot water and steam are used to heat a fluid. Then, this fluid is pumped through a building in order to heat the building. Buildings in Iceland are heated from the country's many geothermal sites in this way.

✓ **Reading Check** How do geothermal power plants obtain geothermal energy from the Earth?

geothermal energy the energy produced by heat within the Earth

Figure 10 How a Geothermal Power Plant Works

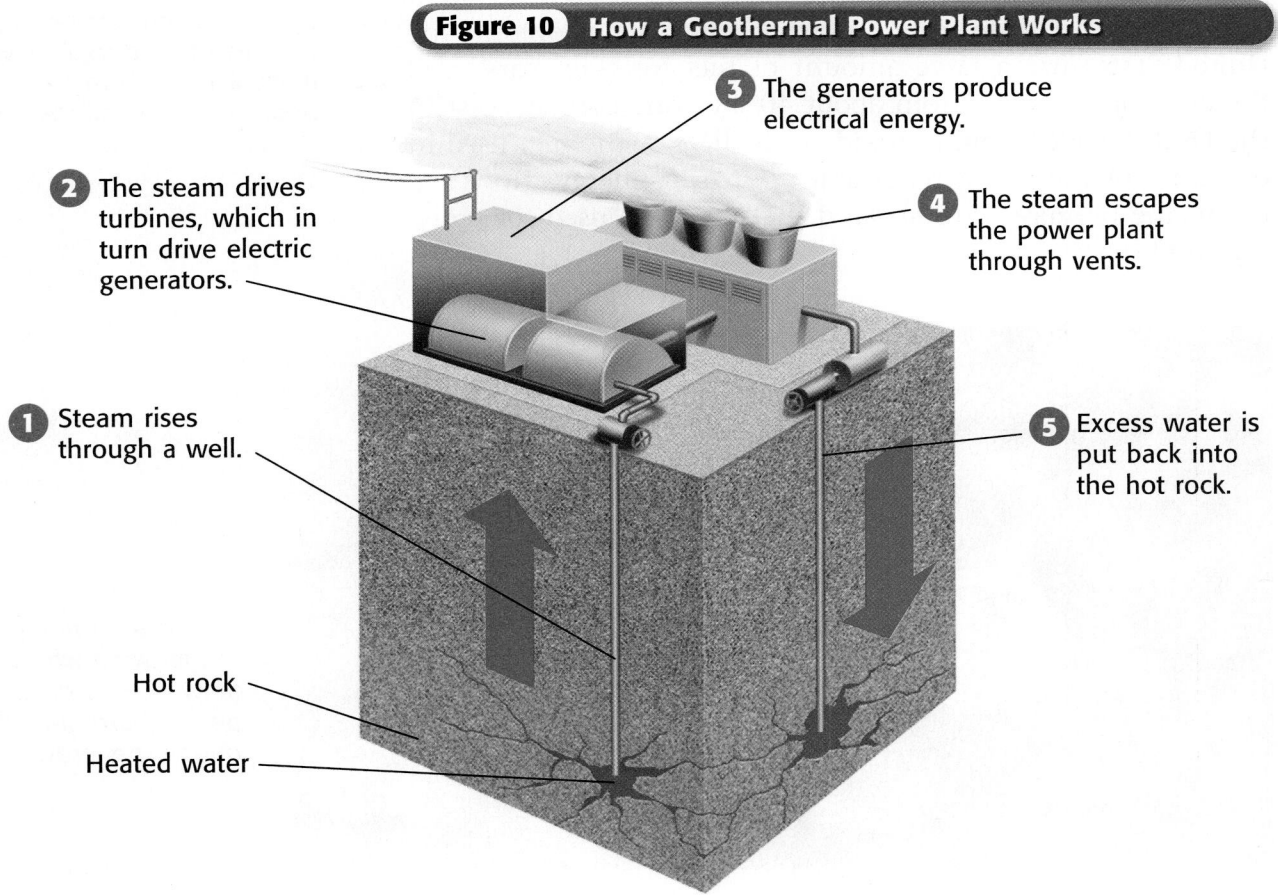

2 The steam drives turbines, which in turn drive electric generators.

3 The generators produce electrical energy.

4 The steam escapes the power plant through vents.

1 Steam rises through a well.

5 Excess water is put back into the hot rock.

Hot rock

Heated water

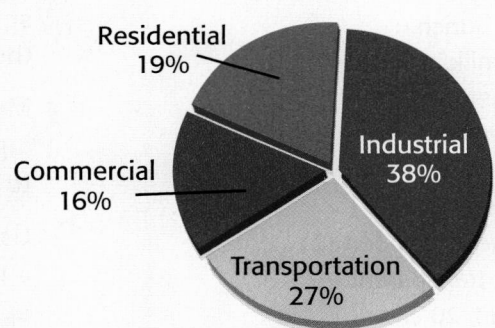

Summary

- Nuclear energy can be released by fission, and or fusion. The byproduct of fission is radioactive waste.
- For fusion to take place, extremely high temperatures are required.
- Fuel cells combine hydrogen and oxygen to produce electrical energy. Fuel cells release water as a byproduct.
- Solar energy is a renewable resource that doesn't emit pollution. However, solar panels and solar collectors are expensive.
- Wind power is a renewable resource that doesn't emit pollution. However, wind energy cannot be generated in all areas.
- Hydroelectric energy is a cheap, renewable resource that causes little pollution. However, it is available only in some areas.
- Burning biomass and gasohol can release energy, but not enough to meet all of our energy needs.
- Geothermal energy comes from the Earth but is available only in certain areas.

Using Key Terms

1. In your own words, write a definition for each of the following terms: *nuclear energy, solar energy, wind power, hydroelectric energy, biomass, gasohol,* and *geothermal energy.*

Understanding Key Ideas

2. Which of the following alternative resources requires hydrogen and oxygen to produce energy?
   a. fuel cells
   b. solar energy
   c. nuclear energy
   d. geothermal energy

3. Describe two ways of using solar energy.

4. Where is the production of hydroelectric energy practical?

5. Describe two ways to release biomass energy.

6. Describe two ways to use geothermal energy.

Critical Thinking

7. **Analyzing Methods** If you were going to build a nuclear power plant, why wouldn't you build it in the middle of a desert?

8. **Predicting Consequences** If an alternative resource could successfully replace crude oil, how might the use of that resource affect the environment?

Interpreting Graphics

Use the graph below to answer the questions that follow.

How Energy Is Used in the United States

Residential 19%
Industrial 38%
Commercial 16%
Transportation 27%

Source: International Energy Agency.

9. What is the total percentage of energy that is used for commercial and industrial purposes?

10. What is the total percentage of energy that is not used for residential purposes?

SCiLINKS®

NSTA
Developed and maintained by the
National Science Teachers Association

For a variety of links related to this chapter, go to www.scilinks.org

Topic: Renewable Resources
SciLinks code: HSM1291

Make a Water Wheel

Lift Enterprises is planning to build a water wheel that will lift objects like a crane does. The president of the company has asked you to modify the basic water wheel design so that the water wheel will lift objects more quickly.

Ask a Question

1 What factors influence the rate at which a water wheel lifts a weight?

Form a Hypothesis

2 Change the question above into a statement to formulate a testable hypothesis.

Test the Hypothesis

3 Build a water wheel model. Measure and mark a 5 × 5 cm square on an index card. Cut the square out of the card. Fold the square in half to form a triangle.

4 Measure and mark a line 8 cm from the bottom of the plastic jug. Use scissors to cut along this line. (Your teacher may need to use a safety razor to start this cut for you.)

5 Use the paper triangle you made in step 3 as a template. Use a permanent marker to trace four triangles onto the flat parts of the top section of the plastic jug. Cut the triangles out of the plastic to form four fins.

6 Use a thumbtack to attach one corner of each plastic fin to the round edge of the cork, as shown below. Make sure the fins are equally spaced around the cork.

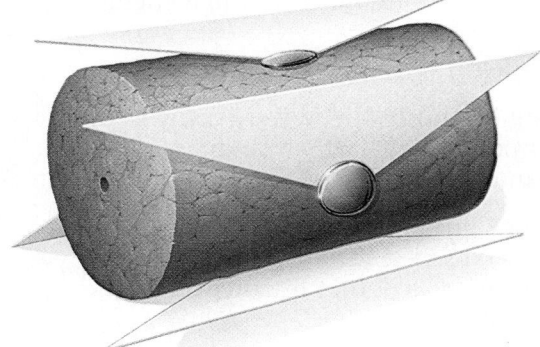

OBJECTIVES

Create a model of a water wheel.

Determine factors that influence the rate at which a water wheel lifts a weight.

MATERIALS

- bottle, soda, 2 L, filled with water
- card, index, 3 × 5 in.
- clay, modeling
- coin
- cork
- glue
- hole punch
- jug, milk, plastic
- marker, permanent, black
- meterstick
- safety razor (for teacher)
- scissors
- skewers, wooden (2)
- tape, transparent
- thread, 20 cm
- thumbtacks (5)
- watch or clock that indicates seconds

SAFETY

7 Press a thumbtack into one of the flat sides of the cork. Jiggle the thumbtack to widen the hole in the cork, and then remove the thumbtack. Repeat on the other side of the cork.

8 Place a drop of glue on one end of each skewer. Insert the first skewer into one of the holes in the end of the cork. Insert the second skewer into the hole in the other end of the cork.

9 Use a hole punch to carefully punch two holes in the bottom section of the plastic jug. Punch each hole 1 cm from the top edge of the jug, directly across from one another.

10 Carefully push the skewers through the holes, and suspend the cork in the center of the jug. Attach a small ball of clay to the end of each skewer. The balls should be the same size.

11 Tape one end of the thread to one skewer on the outside of the jug, next to the clay ball. Wrap the thread around the clay ball three times. (As the water wheel turns, the thread should wrap around the clay. The other ball of clay balances the weight and helps to keep the water wheel turning smoothly.)

12 Tape the free end of the thread to a coin. Wrap the thread around the coin, and tape it again.

13 Slowly pour water from the 2 L bottle onto the fins so that the water wheel spins. What happens to the coin? Record your observations.

14 Lower the coin back to the starting position. Add more clay to the skewer to increase the diameter of the wheel. Repeat step 13. Did the coin rise faster or slower this time?

15 Lower the coin back to the starting position. Modify the shape of the clay, and repeat step 13. Does the shape of the clay affect how quickly the coin rises? Explain your answer.

16 What happens if you remove two of the fins from opposite sides? What happens if you add more fins?

17 Experiment with another fin shape. How does a different fin shape affect how quickly the coin rises?

Analyze the Results

1 **Examining Data** What factors influence how quickly you can lift the coin? Explain.

Draw Conclusions

2 **Drawing Conclusions** What recommendations would you make to the president of Lift Enterprises to improve the water wheel?

Chapter Review

USING KEY TERMS

The statements below are false. For each statement, replace the underlined term to make a true statement.

1 A liquid mixture of complex hydrocarbon compounds is called <u>natural gas</u>.

2 Energy that is released when a chemical compound reacts to produce a new compound is called <u>nuclear energy</u>.

For each pair of terms, explain how the meanings of the terms differ.

3 *solar energy* and *wind power*

4 *biomass* and *gasohol*

UNDERSTANDING KEY IDEAS

Multiple Choice

5 Which of the following resources is a renewable resource?

a. coal   c. oil

b. trees   d. natural gas

6 Which of the following fuels is NOT made from petroleum?

a. jet fuel

b. lignite

c. kerosene

d. fuel oil

7 Peat, lignite, and anthracite are all forms of

a. petroleum.

b. natural gas.

c. coal.

d. gasohol.

8 Which of the following factors contributes to smog?

a. automobiles

b. sunlight

c. mountains surrounding urban areas

d. All of the above

9 Which of the following resources is produced by fusion?

a. solar energy

b. natural gas

c. nuclear energy

d. petroleum

10 To produce energy, nuclear power plants use a process called

a. fission.

b. fusion.

c. fractionation.

d. None of the above

11 A solar-powered calculator uses

a. solar collectors.

b. solar panels.

c. solar mirrors.

d. solar cells.

Short Answer

12 How does acid precipitation form?

13 If sunlight is free, why is electrical energy from solar cells expensive?

14 Describe three ways that humans use natural resources.

15 Explain how fossil fuels are found and obtained.

CRITICAL THINKING

16 Concept Mapping Use the following terms to create a concept map: *fossil fuels, wind energy, energy resources, biomass, renewable resources, solar energy, nonrenewable resources, natural gas, gasohol, coal,* and *oil.*

17 Predicting Consequences How would your life be different if fossil fuels were less widely available?

18 Evaluating Assumptions Are fossil fuels nonrenewable? Explain.

19 Evaluating Assumptions Why do we need to conserve renewable resources even though they can be replaced?

20 Evaluating Data What might limit the productivity of a geothermal power plant?

21 Identifying Relationships Explain why the energy we get from many of our resources ultimately comes from the sun.

22 Applying Concepts Describe the different ways you can conserve natural resources at home.

23 Identifying Relationships Explain why coal usually forms in different locations from where petroleum and natural gas form.

24 Applying Concepts Choose an alternative energy resource that you think should be developed more. Explain the reason for your choice.

INTERPRETING GRAPHICS

Use the graph below to answer the questions that follow.

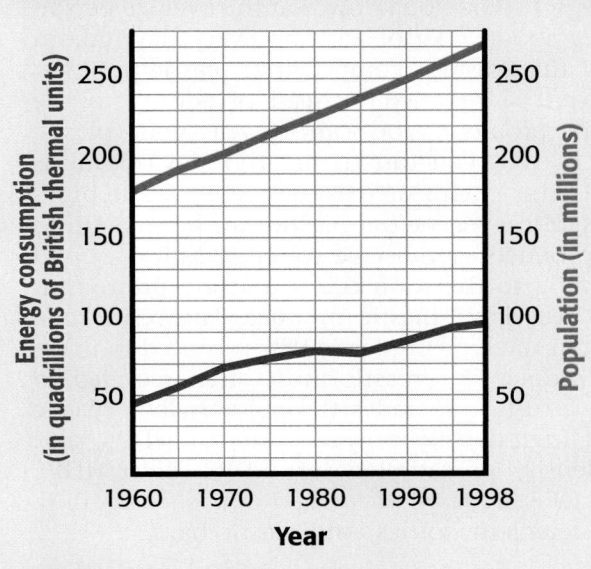

Energy Consumption and Population Growth in the United States

Source: U.S. Department of Energy.

25 How many British thermal units were consumed in 1970?

26 In what year was the most energy consumed?

27 Why do you think that energy consumption has not increased at the same rate as the population has increased?

READING

Read each of the passages below. Then, answer the questions that follow each passage.

Passage 1 Did you know that the average person creates about 2 kg of garbage every day? About 7% of this waste is <u>composed</u> of plastic products that can be recycled. Instead of adding to the landfill problem, you can recycle your plastic trash so that you can sit on it. Today, plastic is recycled into items such as park benches and highchairs. However, before plastic can be made into new products, it must be sorted. Plastic is sorted according to the resin codes that are printed on every recyclable plastic product. The resin code tells you the type of plastic that was used to make the product. The plastic most often recycled to make furniture includes the polyethylene plastic called high-density polyethylene, or HDPE, and low-density polyethylene, or LDPE. Both HDPE and LDPE are used to make items such as milk jugs, detergent bottles, and plastic bags.

1. In the passage, what does *composed* mean?
  A processed into
  B formed
  C crushed
  D melted

2. According to the passage, plastic products
  F can be recycled into highchairs.
  G can be recycled into cars.
  H cannot be recycled.
  I cause environmental problems.

3. According to the passage, which of the following statements is a fact?
  A The average person creates 7 kg of waste every day.
  B The average person weighs 7 kg.
  C LDPE can be used to make milk jugs, detergent bottles, plastic bags, and grocery bags.
  D Recycled plastics are too weak to be made into furniture.

Passage 2 You may have heard of the great California gold rush. In 1849, thousands of people moved west to California hoping to strike gold. But you may not have heard about another rush, which occurred 10 years later. What lured people to northwestern Pennsylvania in 1859? The thrill of striking oil did! However, people were using oil long before 1859. People started using oil as early as 3000 BCE. In Mesopotamia, oil was used to waterproof ships. The Egyptians and Chinese <u>utilized</u> oil as a medicine. It was not until the late 1700s and early 1800s that people began to use oil as a fuel for lamps to light homes and factories. Today, oil is most commonly used in transportation.

1. In the passage, what does *utilized* mean?
  A processed
  B drank
  C burned
  D used

2. According to the passage, which of the following statements is true?
  F Oil can be used to waterproof ships.
  G Oil wasn't discovered until 3000 BCE.
  H Oil was first used in Pennsylvania as a medicine.
  I Oil was used in transportation as early as 1849.

3. According to the passage, which of the following statements is a fact?
  A In 1849, people moved to Pennsylvania for a gold rush.
  B In 1649, people used oil to light homes and factories.
  C In 1849, people moved to California to find gold.
  D In 1849, people did not have any use for oil.

Below is a pie chart of how various energy resources meet the world's energy needs. Use this pie chart to answer the questions that follow.

World Usage of Energy Resources

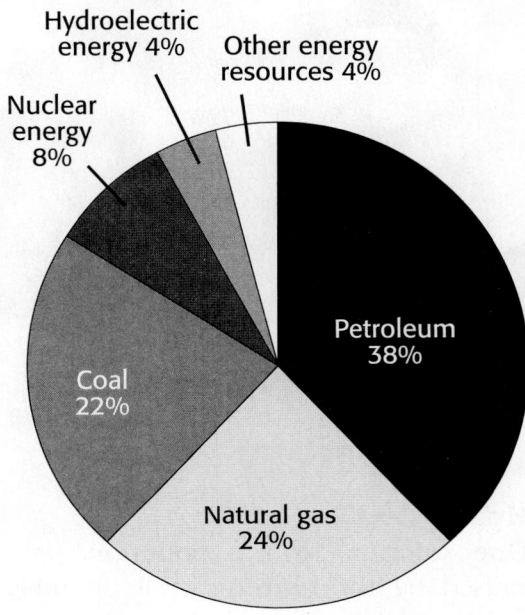

Hydroelectric energy 4%

Other energy resources 4%

Nuclear energy 8%

Petroleum 38%

Coal 22%

Natural gas 24%

1. What percentage of the energy used in the world comes from coal?

   A 22%

   B 24%

   C 28%

   D 38%

2. What percentage of the energy used in the world comes from fossil fuels?

   F 54%

   G 84%

   H 96%

   I 100%

3. What is the total percentage of energy used for resources that do not include fossil fuels?

   A 3%

   B 16%

   C 24%

   D 64%

Read each question below, and choose the best answer.

1. The ratio of the number of kilograms of aluminum recycled to the number of kilograms of newspaper recycled by a seventh-grade class is 34 to 170. What is this ratio written as a decimal?

   A 0.02

   B 0.2

   C 0.5

   D 5

2. Peat is about 60% carbon. Approximately how many kilograms of carbon would a 130 kg sample of peat contain?

   F 7.8 kg

   G 52 kg

   H 78 kg

   I 780 kg

3. If a 24 kg sample of anthracite is examined and 21.6 kg of carbon is found in the sample, what percentage of the sample is carbon?

   A 90%

   B 10%

   C 9%

   D 2.4%

4. Cora's car runs on alcohol made from corn. Cora drives her car 12,000 km per year, and her car's gas mileage is 30 km/L. If 200 L of alcohol can be obtained from each acre of corn that is processed, about how many acres of corn would Cora have to process to fuel her car for a year?

   F 1 acre

   G 2 acres

   H 8 acres

   I 50 acres

Standardized Test Preparation

Science in Action

Scientific Debate

The Three Gorges Dam

Dams provide hydroelectric energy, drinking water, and food for crops. Unfortunately, massive dam projects flood scenic landscapes and disrupt the environment around the dam. For example, the Three Gorges dam in China has displaced almost 2 million people living in the project area. Opponents of the project claim that the dam will also increase pollution levels in the Yangtze River. However, supporters of the dam say it will control flooding and provide millions of people with hydroelectric power. Engineers estimate that the dam's turbines will produce enough electrical energy to power a city 10 times the size of Los Angeles, California.

Science, Technology, and Society

Hybrid Cars

One solution to the pollution problem caused by the burning of fossil fuels for transportation purposes is to develop cars that depend less on fossil fuels. One such car is called a *hybrid*. Instead of using only gasoline for energy, a hybrid car uses gasoline and electricity. Because of its special batteries, the hybrid needs less gasoline to run than a car powered only by gasoline does. Some hybrids can have a gas mileage of as much as 45 mi/gal! Already, there are several models on the market to choose from. In the near future, you might see more hybrid cars on the roads.

Language Arts ACTIVITY

WRITING SKILL Find out more about another dam project. Develop your own opinion on the project. What do you think the best outcome would be? Create a fictional story that expresses this outcome.

Math ACTIVITY

Charlie's truck has a gas mileage of 17 mi/gal. Charlie drives his truck an average of 12,000 mi per year. Then, he sells the truck and buys a new hybrid car that has a gas mileage of 45 mi/gal. If gasoline costs $1.40 per gallon, how much money will Charlie save in a year by driving the hybrid car instead of his truck?

Careers

Fred Begay

Nuclear Physicist Generating energy by combining atoms is called *fusion*. This process is being developed by nuclear physicists, such as Dr. Fred Begay, at the Department of Energy's Los Alamos National Laboratory. Begay hopes to someday make fusion an alternative energy resource. Because fusion is the process that generates energy in the sun, Begay uses NASA satellites to study the sun. Begay explains that it is necessary to develop skills in abstract reasoning to study fusion. As a Navajo, Begay developed these skills while growing up at his Navajo home in Towaoc, Colorado, where his family taught him about nature. Today, Begay uses his skills not only to help develop a new energy resource but also to mentor Native American and minority students. In 1999, Begay won the Distinguished Scientist Award from the Society for Advancement of Chicanos and Native Americans in Science.

Social Studies ACTIVITY

Research the lifestyle of Native Americans before 1900. Then, create a poster that compares resources that Native Americans used before 1900 with resources that many people use today.

To learn more about these Science in Action topics, visit go.hrw.com and type in the keyword HZ5ENRF.

Current Science

Check out Current Science® articles related to this chapter by visiting go.hrw.com. Just type in the keyword HZ5CS05.

6

The Rock and Fossil Record

About the  PHOTO

This extremely well preserved crocodile fossil has been out of water for 49 million years. Its skeleton was collected in an abandoned mine pit in Messel, Germany.

PRE-READING ACTIVITY

FOLDNOTES **Layered Book** Before you read the chapter, create the FoldNote entitled "Layered Book" described in the **Study Skills** section of the Appendix. Label the tabs of the layered book with "Earth's history," "Relative dating," "Absolute dating," "Fossils," and "Geologic time." As you read the chapter, write information you learn about each category under the appropriate tab.

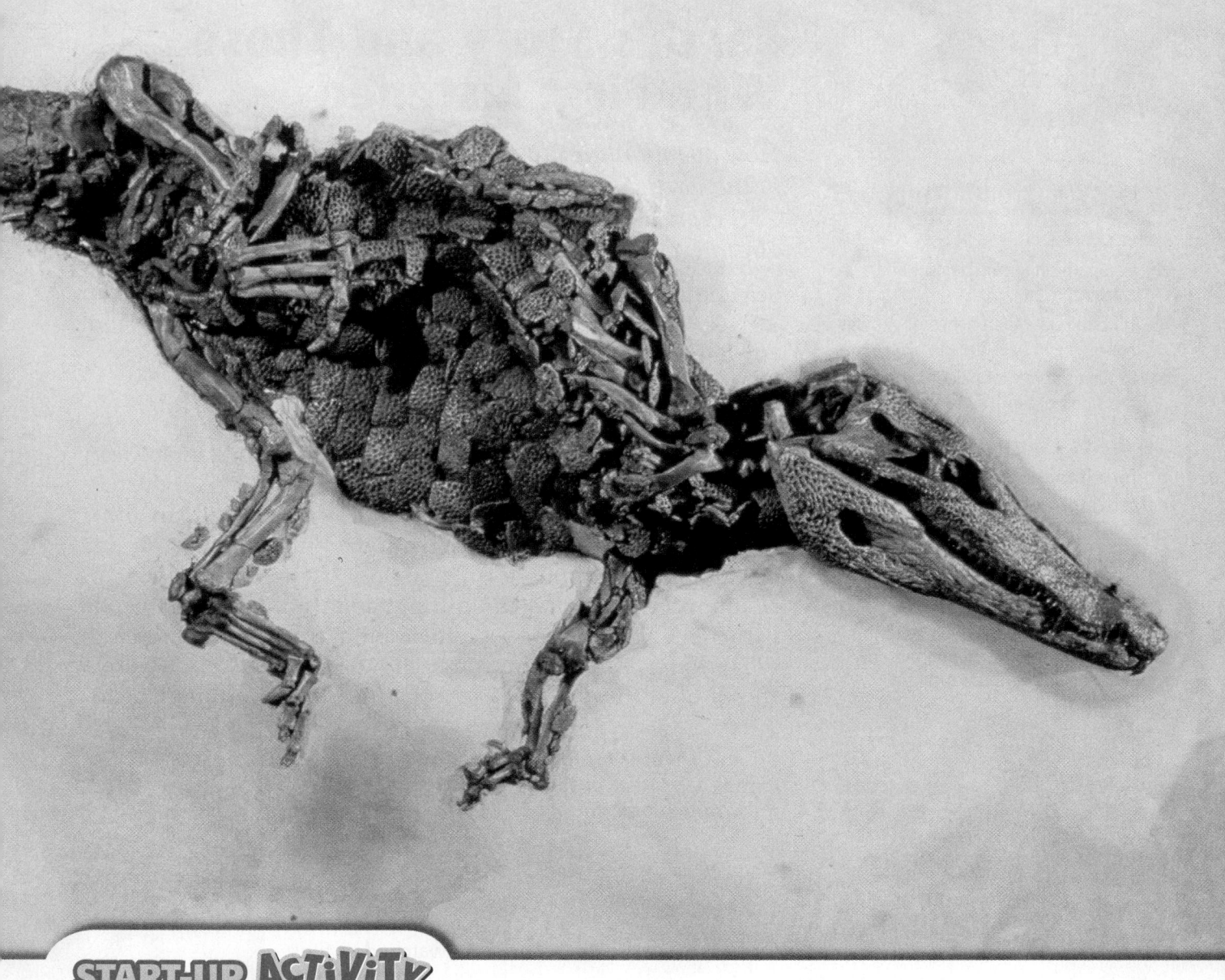

Making Fossils

How do scientists learn from fossils? In this activity, you will study "fossils" and identify the object that made each.

Procedure

1. You and three or four of your classmates will be given **several pieces** of **modeling clay** and a **paper sack** containing a few **small objects.**

2. Press each object firmly into a piece of clay. Try to leave a "fossil" imprint showing as much detail as possible.

3. After you have made an imprint of each object, exchange your model fossils with another group.

4. On a **sheet of paper,** describe the fossils you have received. List as many details as possible. What patterns and textures do you observe?

5. Work as a group to identify each fossil, and check your results. Were you right?

Analysis

1. What kinds of details were important in identifying your fossils? What kinds of details were not preserved in the imprints? For example, can you tell the materials from which the objects are made or their color?

2. Explain how scientists follow similar methods when studying fossils.

Earth's Story and Those Who First Listened

How do mountains form? How is new rock created? How old is the Earth? Have you ever asked these questions? Nearly 250 years ago, a Scottish farmer and scientist named James Hutton did.

Searching for answers to his questions, Hutton spent more than 30 years studying rock formations in Scotland and England. His observations led to the foundation of modern geology.

The Principle of Uniformitarianism

In 1788, James Hutton collected his notes and wrote *Theory of the Earth.* In *Theory of the Earth,* he stated that the key to understanding Earth's history was all around us. In other words, processes that we observe today—such as erosion and deposition—remain uniform, or do not change, over time. This assumption is now called uniformitarianism. **Uniformitarianism** is the idea that the same geologic processes shaping the Earth today have been at work throughout Earth's history. **Figure 1** shows how Hutton developed the idea of uniformitarianism.

Figure 1 *Hutton observed gradual, uniform geologic change.*

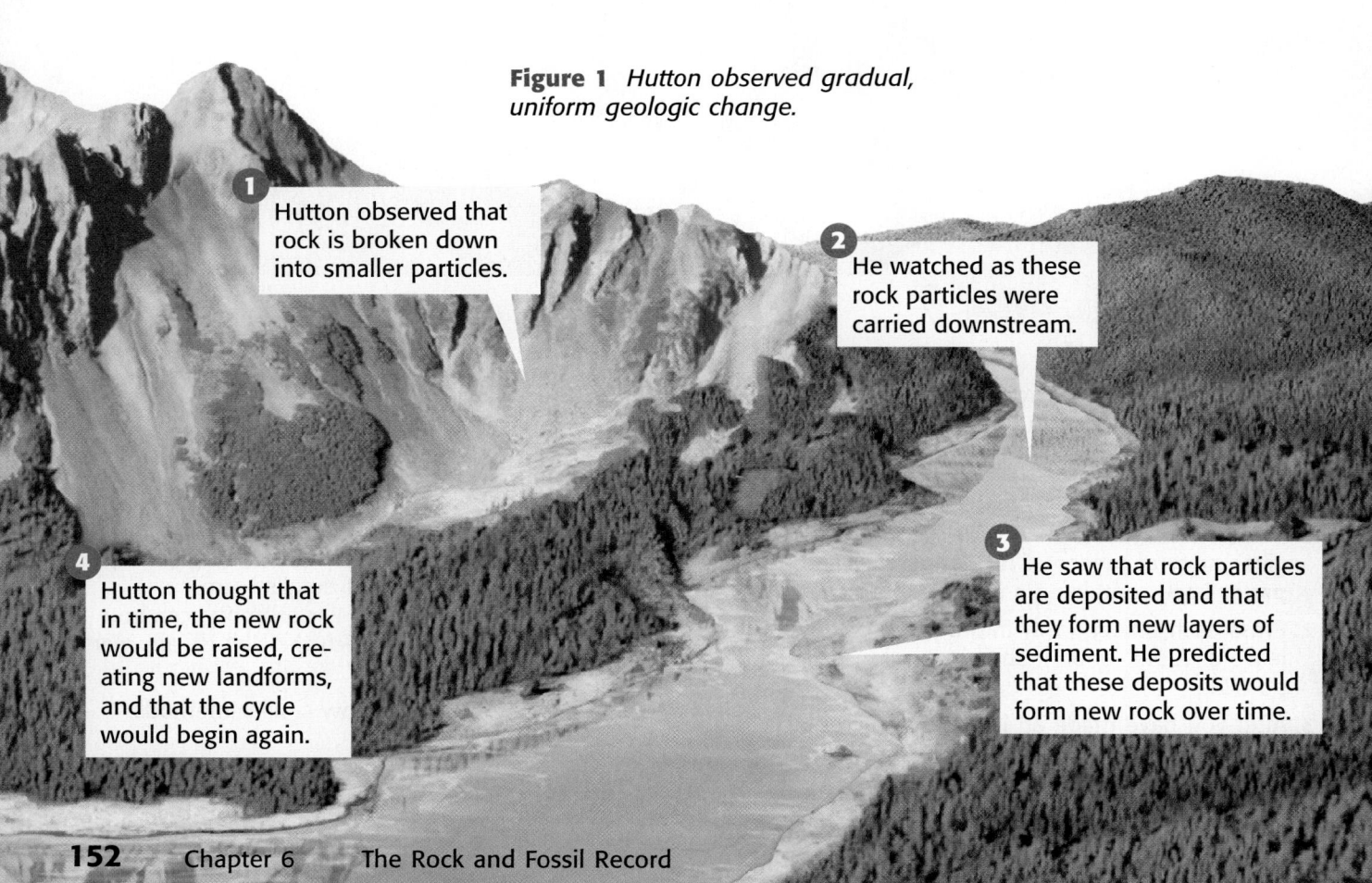

1 Hutton observed that rock is broken down into smaller particles.

2 He watched as these rock particles were carried downstream.

3 He saw that rock particles are deposited and that they form new layers of sediment. He predicted that these deposits would form new rock over time.

4 Hutton thought that in time, the new rock would be raised, creating new landforms, and that the cycle would begin again.

Figure 2 *This photograph shows Siccar Point on the coast of Scotland. Siccar Point is one of the places where Hutton observed results of geologic processes that would lead him to form his principle of uniformitarianism.*

Uniformitarianism Versus Catastrophism

Hutton's theories sparked a scientific debate by suggesting that Earth was much older than previously thought. In Hutton's time, most people thought that Earth was only a few thousand years old. A few thousand years was not nearly enough time for the gradual geologic processes that Hutton described to have shaped our planet. The rocks that he observed at Siccar Point, shown in **Figure 2,** were deposited and folded, indicating a long geological history. To explain Earth's history, most scientists supported catastrophism. **Catastrophism** is the principle that states that all geologic change occurs suddenly. Supporters of catastrophism thought that Earth's features, such as its mountains, canyons, and seas, formed during rare, sudden events called *catastrophes.* These unpredictable events caused rapid geologic change over large areas—sometimes even globally.

√ Reading Check According to catastrophists, what was the rate of geologic change? (*See the Appendix for answers to Reading Checks.*)

A Victory for Uniformitarianism

Despite Hutton's work, catastrophism remained geology's guiding principle for decades. Only after the work of British geologist Charles Lyell did people seriously consider uniformitarianism as geology's guiding principle.

From 1830 to 1833, Lyell published three volumes, collectively titled *Principles of Geology,* in which he reintroduced uniformitarianism. Armed with Hutton's notes and new evidence of his own, Lyell successfully challenged the principle of catastrophism. Lyell saw no reason to doubt that major geologic change happened at the same rate in the past as it happens in the present—gradually.

uniformitarianism a principle that states that geologic processes that occurred in the past can be explained by current geologic processes

catastrophism a principle that states that geologic change occurs suddenly

CONNECTION TO Biology

WRITING SKILL **Darwin and Lyell** The theory of evolution was developed soon after Lyell introduced his ideas, which was no coincidence. Lyell and Charles Darwin were good friends, and their talks greatly influenced Darwin's theories. Similar to uniformitarianism, Darwin's theory of evolution proposes that changes in species occur gradually over long periods of time. Write a short essay comparing uniformitarianism and evolution.

Modern Geology—A Happy Medium

During the late 20th century, scientists such as Stephen J. Gould challenged Lyell's uniformitarianism. They believed that catastrophes do, at times, play an important role in shaping Earth's history.

Today, scientists realize that neither uniformitarianism nor catastrophism accounts for all geologic change throughout Earth's history. Although most geologic change is gradual and uniform, catastrophes that cause geologic change have occurred during Earth's long history. For example, huge craters have been found where asteroids and comets are thought to have struck Earth in the past. Some scientists think one such asteroid strike, approximately 65 million years ago, may have caused the dinosaurs to become extinct. **Figure 3** is an imaginary re-creation of the asteroid strike that is thought to have caused the extinction of the dinosaurs. The impact of this asteroid is thought to have thrown debris into the atmosphere. The debris spread around the entire planet and rained down on Earth for decades. This global debris cloud may have blocked the sun's rays, causing major changes in the global climate that doomed the dinosaurs.

Reading Check How can a catastrophe affect life on Earth?

Figure 3 *Today, scientists think that sudden events are responsible for some changes during Earth's past. An asteroid hitting Earth, for example, may have led to the extinction of the dinosaurs about 65 million years ago.*

Paleontology—The Study of Past Life

The history of the Earth would be incomplete without a knowledge of the organisms that have inhabited our planet and the conditions under which they lived. The science involved with the study of past life is called **paleontology.** Scientists who study this life are called *paleontologists.* The data paleontologists use are fossils. Fossils are the remains of organisms preserved by geologic processes. Some paleontologists specialize in the study of particular organisms. Invertebrate paleontologists study animals without backbones, whereas vertebrate paleontologists, such as the scientist in **Figure 4,** study animals with backbones. Paleobotanists study fossils of plants. Other paleontologists reconstruct past ecosystems, study the traces left behind by animals, and piece together the conditions under which fossils were formed. As you see, the study of past life is as varied and complex as Earth's history itself.

Figure 4 *Edwin Colbert was a 20th-century vertebrate paleontologist who made important contributions to the study of dinosaurs.*

paleontology the scientific study of fossils

SECTION Review

Summary

- Uniformitarianism assumes that geologic change is gradual. Catastrophism is based on the idea that geologic change is sudden.

- Modern geology is based on the idea that gradual geologic change is interrupted by catastrophes.

- Using fossils to study past life is called *paleontology.*

Using Key Terms

1. Use each of the following terms in a separate sentence: *uniformitarianism, catastrophism,* and *paleontology.*

Understanding Key Ideas

2. Which of the following words describes change according to the principle of uniformitarianism?
   a. sudden
   b. rare
   c. global
   d. gradual

3. What is the difference between uniformitarianism and catastrophism?

4. Describe how the science of geology has changed.

5. Give one example of catastrophic global change.

6. Describe the work of three types of paleontologists.

Math Skills

7. An impact crater left by an asteroid strike has a radius of 85 km. What is the area of the crater? (Hint: The area of a circle is πr^2.)

Critical Thinking

8. **Analyzing Ideas** Why is uniformitarianism considered to be the foundation of modern geology?

9. **Applying Concepts** Give an example of a type of recent catastrophe.

SCiLINKS®

NSTA

Developed and maintained by the National Science Teachers Association

For a variety of links related to this chapter, go to www.scilinks.org

Topic: Earth's Story
SciLinks code: HSM0450

Relative Dating: Which Came First?

Imagine that you are a detective investigating a crime scene. What is the first thing you would do?

You might begin by dusting the scene for fingerprints or by searching for witnesses. As a detective, you must figure out the sequence of events that took place before you reached the crime scene.

Geologists have a similar goal when investigating the Earth. They try to determine the order in which events have happened during Earth's history. But instead of relying on fingerprints and witnesses, geologists rely on rocks and fossils to help them in their investigation. Determining whether an object or event is older or younger than other objects or events is called **relative dating.**

The Principle of Superposition

Suppose that you have an older brother who takes a lot of photographs of your family and piles them in a box. Over the years, he keeps adding new photographs to the top of the stack. Think about the family history recorded in those photos. Where are the oldest photographs—the ones taken when you were a baby? Where are the most recent photographs—those taken last week?

Layers of sedimentary rock, such as the ones shown in **Figure 1,** are like stacked photographs. As you move from top to bottom, the layers are older. The principle that states that younger rocks lie above older rocks in undisturbed sequences is called **superposition.**

Figure 1 *Rock layers are like photos stacked over time—the younger ones lie above the older ones.*

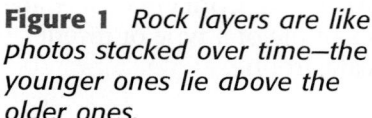

Disturbing Forces

Not all rock sequences are arranged with the oldest layers on the bottom and the youngest layers on top. Some rock sequences are disturbed by forces within the Earth. These forces can push other rocks into a sequence, tilt or fold rock layers, and break sequences into movable parts. Sometimes, geologists even find rock sequences that are upside down! The disruptions of rock sequences pose a challenge to geologists trying to determine the relative ages of rocks. Fortunately, geologists can get help from a very valuable tool—the geologic column.

The Geologic Column

To make their job easier, geologists combine data from all the known undisturbed rock sequences around the world. From this information, geologists create the geologic column, as illustrated in **Figure 2.** The **geologic column** is an ideal sequence of rock layers that contains all the known fossils and rock formations on Earth, arranged from oldest to youngest.

Geologists rely on the geologic column to interpret rock sequences. Geologists also use the geologic column to identify the layers in puzzling rock sequences.

Reading Check List two ways in which geologists use the geologic column. (*See the Appendix for answers to Reading Checks.*)

relative dating any method of determining whether an event or object is older or younger than other events or objects

superposition a principle that states that younger rocks lie above older rocks if the layers have not been disturbed

geologic column an arrangement of rock layers in which the oldest rocks are at the bottom

---

Figure 2 **Constructing the Geologic Column**

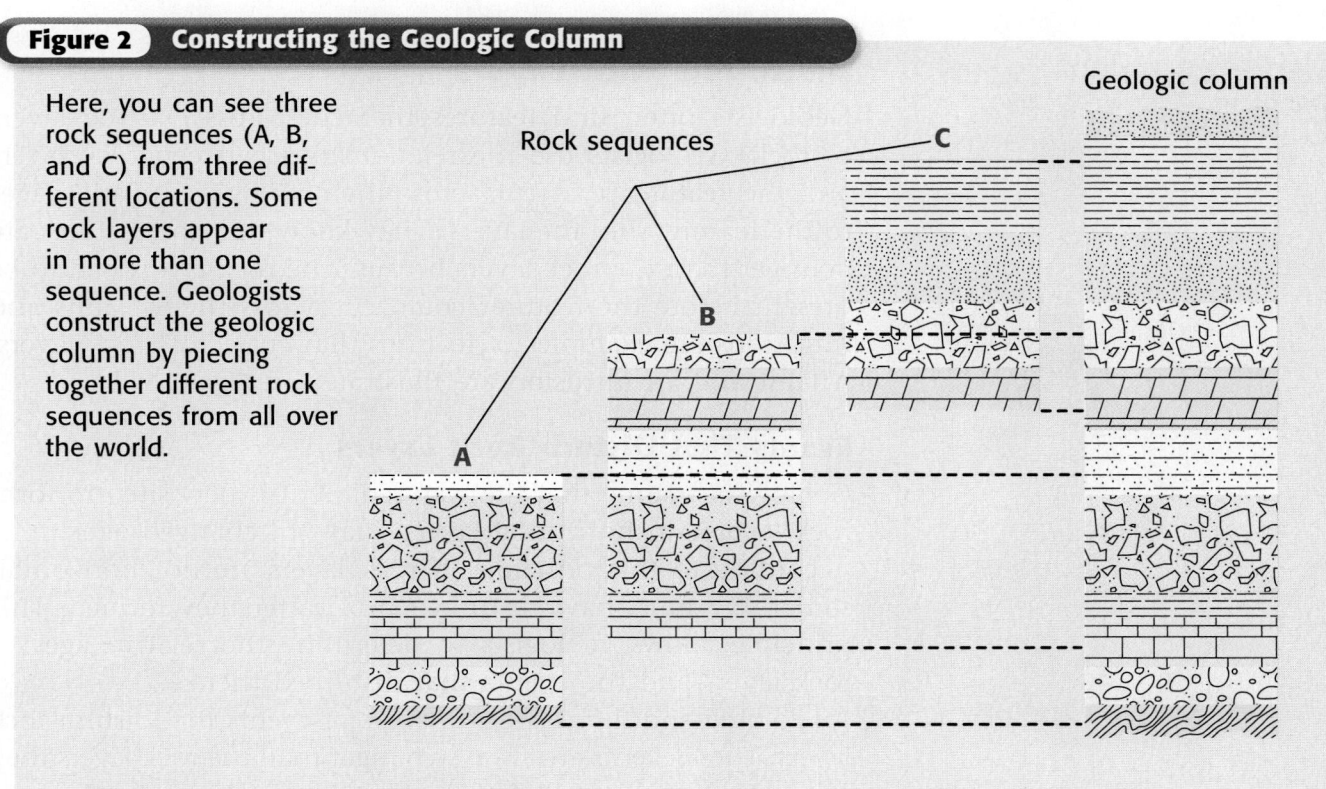

Here, you can see three rock sequences (A, B, and C) from three different locations. Some rock layers appear in more than one sequence. Geologists construct the geologic column by piecing together different rock sequences from all over the world.

Rock sequences

Geologic column

Figure 3 How Rock Layers Become Disturbed

Fault A *fault* is a break in the Earth's crust along which blocks of the crust slide relative to one another.

Intrusion An *intrusion* is molten rock from the Earth's interior that squeezes into existing rock and cools.

Folding *Folding* occurs when rock layers bend and buckle from Earth's internal forces.

Tilting *Tilting* occurs when internal forces in the Earth slant rock layers.

Disturbed Rock Layers

Geologists often find features that cut across existing layers of rock. Geologists use the relationships between rock layers and the features that cut across them to assign relative ages to the features and the layers. They know that the features are younger than the rock layers because the rock layers had to be present before the features could cut across them. Faults and intrusions are examples of features that cut across rock layers. A fault and an intrusion are illustrated in **Figure 3.**

Events That Disturb Rock Layers

Geologists assume that the way sediment is deposited to form rock layers—in horizontal layers—has not changed over time. According to this principle, if rock layers are not horizontal, something must have disturbed them after they formed. This principle allows geologists to determine the relative ages of rock layers and the events that disturbed them.

Folding and tilting are two types of events that disturb rock layers. These events are always younger than the rock layers they affect. The results of folding and tilting are shown in **Figure 3.**

Gaps in the Record—Unconformities

Faults, intrusions, and the effects of folding and tilting can make dating rock layers a challenge. Sometimes, layers of rock are missing altogether, creating a gap in the geologic record. To think of this another way, let's say that you stack your newspapers every day after reading them. Now, let's suppose you want to look at a paper you read 10 days ago. You know that the paper should be 10 papers deep in the stack. But when you look, the paper is not there. What happened? Perhaps you forgot to put the paper in the stack. Now, imagine a missing rock layer instead of a missing newspaper.

Missing Evidence

Missing rock layers create breaks in rock-layer sequences called unconformities. An **unconformity** is a surface that represents a missing part of the geologic column. Unconformities also represent missing time—time that was not recorded in layers of rock. When geologists find an unconformity, they must question whether the "missing layer" was never present or whether it was somehow removed. **Figure 4** shows how *nondeposition,* or the stoppage of deposition when a supply of sediment is cut off, and *erosion* create unconformities.

unconformity a break in the geologic record created when rock layers are eroded or when sediment is not deposited for a long period of time

✓ **Reading Check** Define the term unconformity.

Figure 4 How Unconformities Are Created

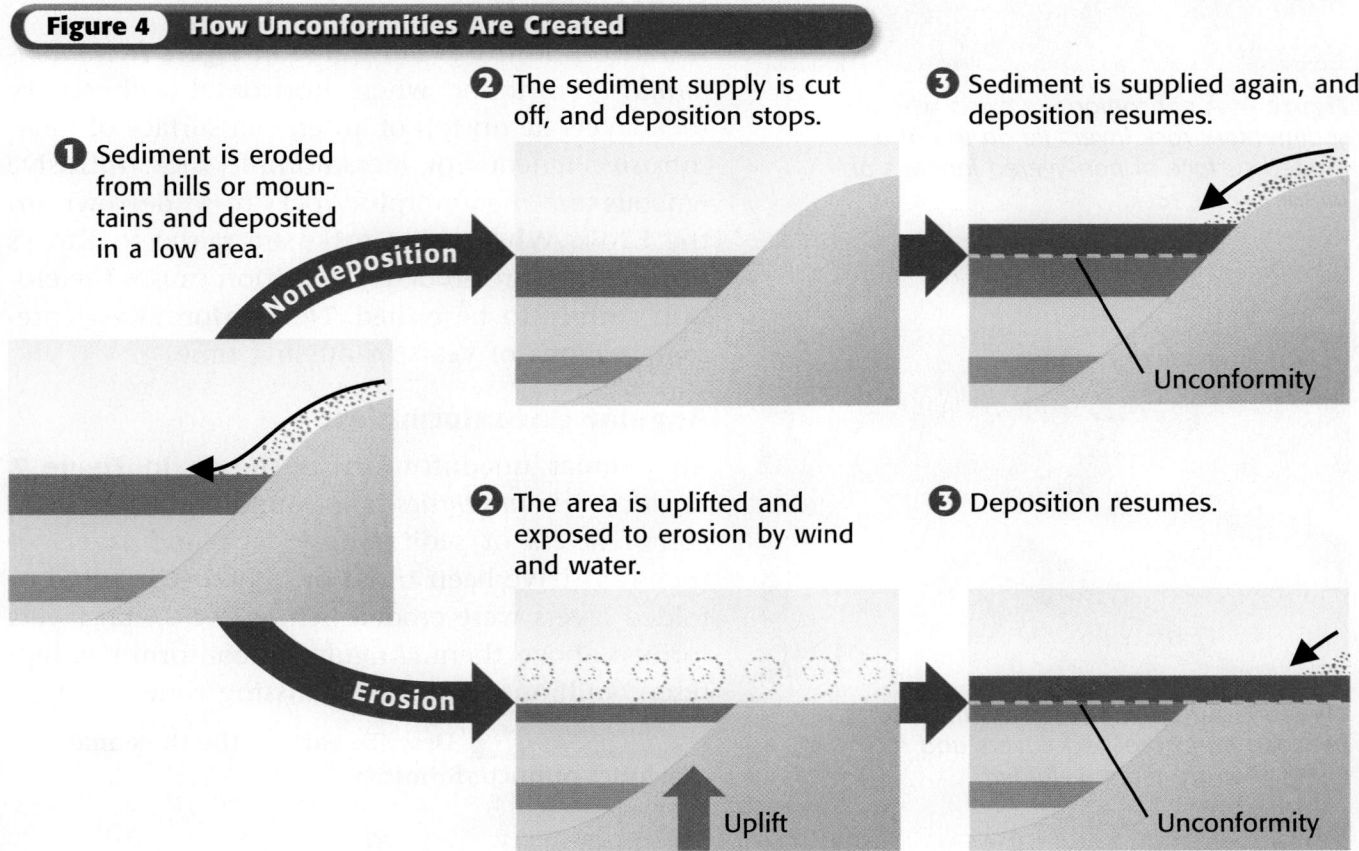

❶ Sediment is eroded from hills or mountains and deposited in a low area.

Nondeposition

❷ The sediment supply is cut off, and deposition stops.

❸ Sediment is supplied again, and deposition resumes.

Unconformity

Erosion

❷ The area is uplifted and exposed to erosion by wind and water.

Uplift

❸ Deposition resumes.

Unconformity

Types of Unconformities

Most unconformities form by both erosion and nondeposition. But other factors can complicate matters. To simplify the study of unconformities, geologists place them into three major categories: disconformities, nonconformities, and angular unconformities. The three diagrams at left illustrate these three categories.

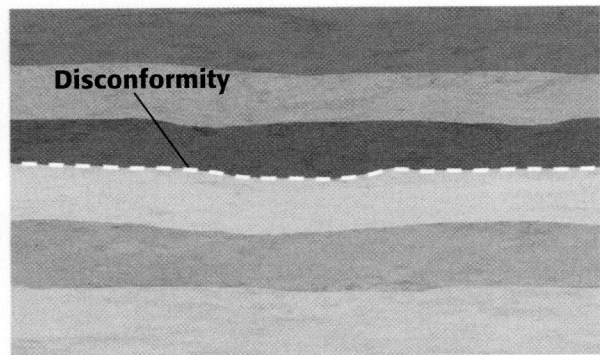

Figure 5 *A disconformity exists where part of a sequence of parallel rock layers is missing.*

Disconformities

The most common type of unconformity is a disconformity, which is illustrated in **Figure 5.** *Disconformities* are found where part of a sequence of parallel rock layers is missing. A disconformity can form in the following way. A sequence of rock layers is uplifted. Younger layers at the top of the sequence are removed by erosion, and the eroded material is deposited elsewhere. At some future time, deposition resumes, and sediment buries the old erosion surface. The disconformity that results shows where erosion has taken place and rock layers are missing. A disconformity represents thousands to many millions of years of missing time.

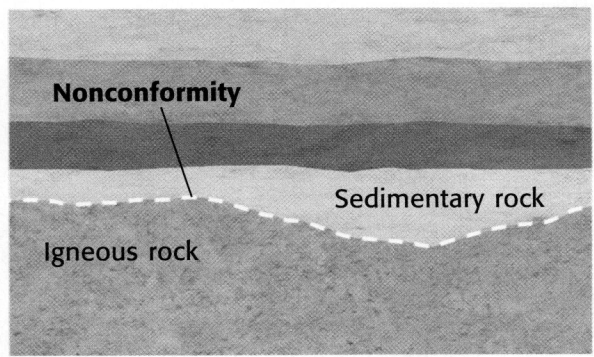

Figure 6 *A nonconformity exists where sedimentary rock layers lie on top of an eroded surface of nonlayered igneous or metamorphic rock.*

Nonconformities

A nonconformity is illustrated in **Figure 6.** *Nonconformities* are found where horizontal sedimentary rock layers lie on top of an eroded surface of older intrusive igneous or metamorphic rock. Intrusive igneous and metamorphic rocks form deep within the Earth. When these rocks are raised to Earth's surface, they are eroded. Deposition causes the erosion surface to be buried. Nonconformities represent millions of years of missing time.

Angular Unconformities

An angular unconformity is shown in **Figure 7.** *Angular unconformities* are found between horizontal layers of sedimentary rock and layers of rock that have been tilted or folded. The tilted or folded layers were eroded before horizontal layers formed above them. Angular unconformities represent millions of years of missing time.

✔ **Reading Check** Describe each of the three major categories of unconformities.

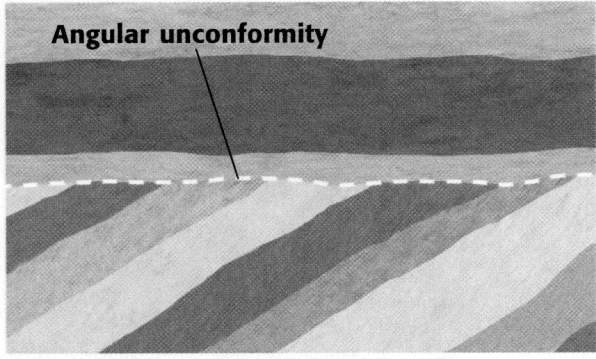

Figure 7 *An angular unconformity exists between horizontal rock layers and rock layers that are tilted or folded.*

Rock-Layer Puzzles

Geologists often find rock-layer sequences that have been affected by more than one of the events and features mentioned in this section. For example, as shown in **Figure 8,** intrusions may squeeze into rock layers that contain an unconformity. Determining the order of events that led to such a sequence is like piecing together a jigsaw puzzle. Geologists must use their knowledge of the events that disturb or remove rock-layer sequences to help piece together the history of Earth as told by the rock record.

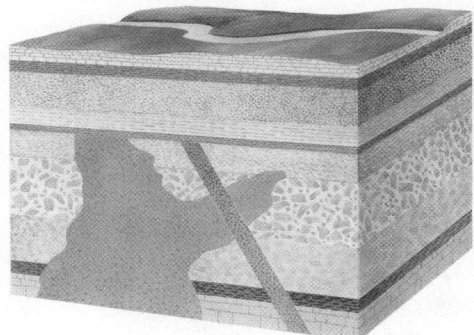

Figure 8 *Rock-layer sequences are often disturbed by more than one rock-disturbing feature.*

SECTION Review

Summary

- Geologists use relative dating to determine the order in which events happen.
- The principle of superposition states that in undisturbed rock sequences, younger layers lie above older layers.
- Folding and tilting are two events that disturb rock layers. Faults and intrusions are two features that disturb rock layers.
- The known rock and fossil record is indicated by the geologic column.
- Geologists examine the relationships between rock layers and the structures that cut across them in order to determine relative ages.

Using Key Terms

1. In your own words, write a definition for each of the following terms: *relative dating, superposition,* and *geologic column.*

Understanding Key Ideas

2. Molten rock that squeezes into existing rock and cools is called a(n)
   a. fold.
   b. fault.
   c. intrusion.
   d. unconformity.

3. List two events and two features that can disturb rock-layer sequences.

4. Explain how physical features are used to determine relative ages.

Critical Thinking

5. **Analyzing Concepts** Is there a place on Earth that has all the layers of the geologic column? Explain.

6. **Analyzing Ideas** Disconformities are hard to recognize because all of the layers are horizontal. How does a geologist know when he or she is looking at a disconformity?

Interpreting Graphics

Use the illustration below to answer the question that follows.

7. If the top rock layer were eroded and deposition later resumed, what type of unconformity would mark the boundary between older rock layers and the newly deposited rock layers?

SCi LINKS

NSTA
Developed and maintained by the
National Science Teachers Association

For a variety of links related to this chapter, go to www.scilinks.org

Topic: Relative Dating
SciLinks code: HSM1288

SECTION 3

Absolute Dating: A Measure of Time

READING WARM-UP

Objectives
- Describe how radioactive decay occurs.
- Explain how radioactive decay relates to radiometric dating.
- Identify four types of radiometric dating.
- Determine the best type of radiometric dating to use to date an object.

Terms to Learn
absolute dating
isotope
radioactive decay
radiometric dating
half-life

READING STRATEGY

Reading Organizer As you read this section, make a concept map by using the terms above.

Have you ever heard the expression "turning back the clock"? With the discovery of the natural decay of uranium in 1896, French physicist Henri Becquerel provided a means of doing just that. Scientists could use radioactive elements as clocks to measure geologic time.

The process of establishing the age of an object by determining the number of years it has existed is called **absolute dating.** In this section, you will learn about radiometric dating, which is the most common method of absolute dating.

Radioactive Decay

To determine the absolute ages of fossils and rocks, scientists analyze isotopes of radioactive elements. Atoms of the same element that have the same number of protons but have different numbers of neutrons are called **isotopes.** Most isotopes are stable, meaning that they stay in their original form. But some isotopes are unstable. Scientists call unstable isotopes *radioactive.* Radioactive isotopes tend to break down into stable isotopes of the same or other elements in a process called **radioactive decay. Figure 1** shows an example of how radioactive decay occurs. Because radioactive decay occurs at a steady rate, scientists can use the relative amounts of stable and unstable isotopes present in an object to determine the object's age.

Figure 1 Radioactive Decay

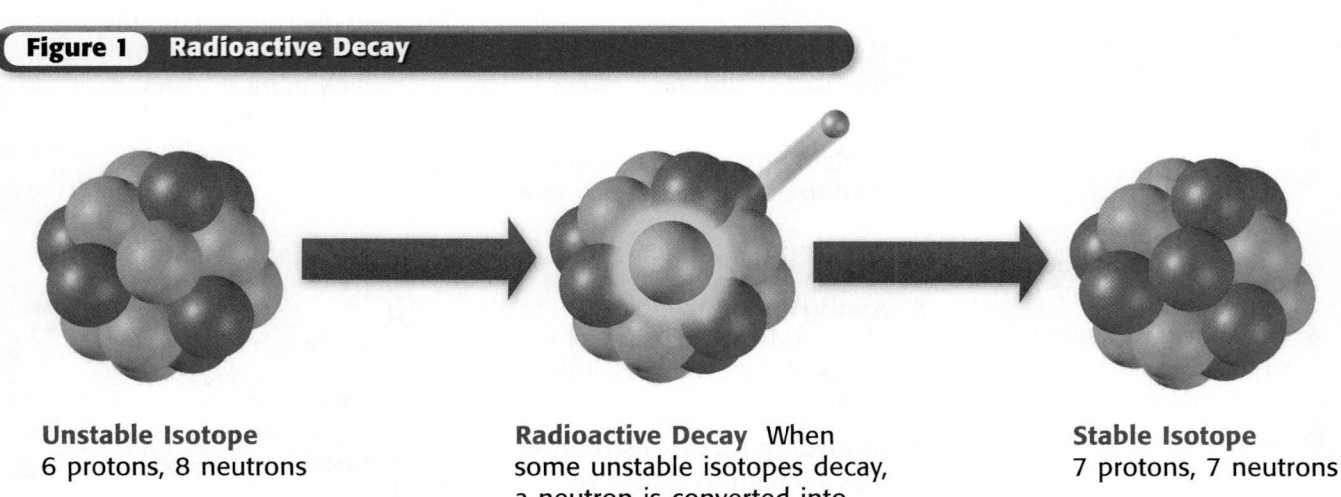

Unstable Isotope
6 protons, 8 neutrons

Radioactive Decay When some unstable isotopes decay, a neutron is converted into a proton. In the process, an electron is released.

Stable Isotope
7 protons, 7 neutrons

Dating Rocks—How Does It Work?

In the process of radioactive decay, an unstable radioactive isotope of one element breaks down into a stable isotope. The stable isotope may be of the same element or, more commonly, a different element. The unstable radioactive isotope is called the *parent isotope*. The stable isotope produced by the radioactive decay of the parent isotope is called the *daughter isotope*. The radioactive decay of a parent isotope into a stable daughter isotope can occur in a single step or a series of steps. In either case, the rate of decay is constant. Therefore, to date rock, scientists compare the amount of parent material with the amount of daughter material. The more daughter material there is, the older the rock is.

Radiometric Dating

If you know the rate of decay for a radioactive element in a rock, you can figure out the absolute age of the rock. Determining the absolute age of a sample, based on the ratio of parent material to daughter material, is called **radiometric dating.** For example, let's say that a rock sample contains an isotope with a half-life of 10,000 years. A **half-life** is the time that it takes one-half of a radioactive sample to decay. So, for this rock sample, in 10,000 years, half the parent material will have decayed and become daughter material. You analyze the sample and find equal amounts of parent material and daughter material. This means that half the original radioactive isotope has decayed and that the sample must be about 10,000 years old.

What if one-fourth of your sample is parent material and three-fourths is daughter material? You would know that it took 10,000 years for half the original sample to decay and another 10,000 years for half of what remained to decay. The age of your sample would be 2 × 10,000, or 20,000, years. **Figure 2** shows how this steady decay happens.

✓ **Reading Check** What is a half-life? (*See the Appendix for answers to Reading Checks.*)

absolute dating any method of measuring the age of an event or object in years

isotope an atom that has the same number of protons (or the same atomic number) as other atoms of the same element do but that has a different number of neutrons (and thus a different atomic mass)

radioactive decay the process in which a radioactive isotope tends to break down into a stable isotope of the same element or another element

radiometric dating a method of determining the age of an object by estimating the relative percentages of a radioactive (parent) isotope and a stable (daughter) isotope

half-life the time needed for half of a sample of a radioactive substance to undergo radioactive decay

Figure 2 *After every half-life, the amount of parent material decreases by one-half.*

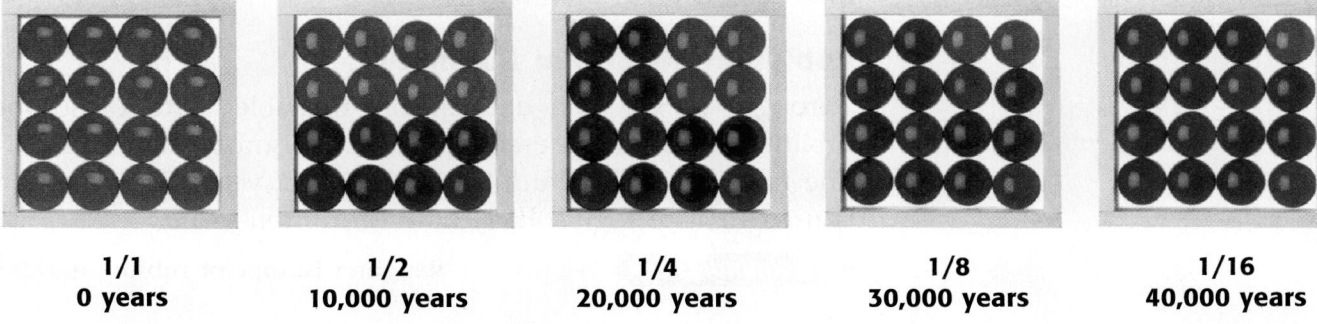

| 1/1 | 1/2 | 1/4 | 1/8 | 1/16 |
| 0 years | 10,000 years | 20,000 years | 30,000 years | 40,000 years |

Figure 3 *This burial mound at Effigy Mounds resembles a snake.*

Types of Radiometric Dating

Imagine traveling back through the centuries to a time before Columbus arrived in America. You are standing along the bluffs of what will one day be called the Mississippi River. You see dozens of people building large mounds. Who are these people, and what are they building?

The people you saw in your time travel were Native Americans, and the structures they were building were burial mounds. The area you imagined is now an archaeological site called Effigy Mounds National Monument. **Figure 3** shows one of these mounds.

According to archaeologists, people lived at Effigy Mounds from 2,500 years ago to 600 years ago. How do archaeologists know these dates? They have dated bones and other objects in the mounds by using radiometric dating. Scientists use different radiometric-dating techniques based on the estimated age of an object. As you read on, think about how the half-life of an isotope relates to the age of the object being dated. Which technique would you use to date the burial mounds?

Potassium-Argon Method

One isotope that is used for radiometric dating is potassium-40. Potassium-40 has a half-life of 1.3 billion years, and it decays to argon and calcium. Geologists measure argon as the daughter material. This method is used mainly to date rocks older than 100,000 years.

Uranium-Lead Method

Uranium-238 is a radioactive isotope that decays in a series of steps to lead-206. The half-life of uranium-238 is 4.5 billion years. The older the rock is, the more daughter material (lead-206) there will be in the rock. Uranium-lead dating can be used for rocks more than 10 million years old. Younger rocks do not contain enough daughter material to be accurately measured by this method.

Rubidium-Strontium Method

Through radioactive decay, the unstable parent isotope rubidium-87 forms the stable daughter isotope strontium-87. The half-life of rubidium-87 is 49 billion years. This method is used to date rocks older than 10 million years.

Reading Check What is the daughter isotope of rubidium-87?

Carbon-14 Method

The element carbon is normally found in three forms, the stable isotopes carbon-12 and carbon-13 and the radioactive isotope carbon-14. These carbon isotopes combine with oxygen to form the gas carbon dioxide, which is taken in by plants during photosynthesis. As long as a plant is alive, new carbon dioxide with a constant carbon-14 to carbon-12 ratio is continually taken in. Animals that eat plants contain the same ratio of carbon isotopes.

Once a plant or an animal dies, however, no new carbon is taken in. The amount of carbon-14 begins to decrease as the plant or animal decays, and the ratio of carbon-14 to carbon-12 decreases. This decrease can be measured in a laboratory, such as the one shown in **Figure 4.** Because the half-life of carbon-14 is only 5,730 years, this dating method is used mainly for dating things that lived within the last 50,000 years.

Figure 4 *Some samples containing carbon must be cleaned and burned before their age can be determined.*

SECTION Review

Summary

- During radioactive decay, an unstable isotope decays at a constant rate and becomes a stable isotope of the same or a different element.

- Radiometric dating, based on the ratio of parent to daughter material, is used to determine the absolute age of a sample.

- Methods of radiometric dating include potassium-argon, uranium-lead, rubidium-strontium, and carbon-14 dating.

Using Key Terms

1. Use each of the following terms in a separate sentence: *absolute dating, isotope,* and *half-life.*

Understanding Key Ideas

2. Rubidium-87 has a half-life of
   a. 5,730 years.
   b. 4.5 billion years.
   c. 49 billion years.
   d. 1.3 billion years.

3. Explain how radioactive decay occurs.

4. How does radioactive decay relate to radiometric dating?

5. List four types of radiometric dating.

Math Skills

6. A radioactive isotope has a half-life of 1.3 billion years. After 3.9 billion years, how much of the parent material will be left?

Critical Thinking

7. **Analyzing Methods** Explain why radioactive decay must be constant in order for radiometric dating to be accurate.

8. **Applying Concepts** Which radiometric-dating method would be most appropriate for dating artifacts found at Effigy Mounds? Explain.

For a variety of links related to this chapter, go to www.scilinks.org

Topic: Absolute Dating
SciLinks code: HSM0003

Looking at Fossils

Descending from the top of a ridge in the badlands of Argentina, your expedition team suddenly stops. You look down and realize that you are walking on eggshells— dinosaur eggshells!

A paleontologist named Luis Chiappe had this experience. He had found an enormous dinosaur nesting ground.

Fossilized Organisms

The remains or physical evidence of an organism preserved by geologic processes is called a **fossil.** Fossils are most often preserved in sedimentary rock. But as you will see, other materials can also preserve evidence of past life.

Fossils in Rocks

When an organism dies, it either immediately begins to decay or is consumed by other organisms. Sometimes, however, organisms are quickly buried by sediment when they die. The sediment slows down decay. Hard parts of organisms, such as shells and bones, are more resistant to decay than soft tissues are. So, when sediments become rock, the hard parts of animals are much more commonly preserved than are soft tissues.

Fossils in Amber

Imagine that an insect is caught in soft, sticky tree sap. Suppose that the insect gets covered by more sap, which quickly hardens and preserves the insect inside. Hardened tree sap is called *amber.* Some of our best insect fossils are found in amber, as shown in **Figure 1.** Frogs and lizards have also been found in amber.

Reading Check Describe how organisms are preserved in amber. (*See the Appendix for answers to Reading Checks.*)

READING WARM-UP

Objectives

- Describe five ways that different types of fossils form.
- List three types of fossils that are not part of organisms.
- Explain how fossils can be used to determine the history of changes in environments and organisms.
- Explain how index fossils can be used to date rock layers.

Terms to Learn

fossil
trace fossil
mold
cast
index fossil

READING STRATEGY

Reading Organizer As you read this section, create an outline of the section. Use the headings from this section in your outline.

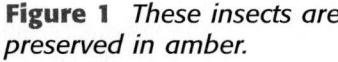
Figure 1 *These insects are preserved in amber.*

Figure 2 *Scientist Vladimir Eisner studies the upper molars of a 20,000-year-old woolly mammoth found in Siberia, Russia. The almost perfectly preserved male mammoth was excavated from a block of ice in October 1999.*

Petrifaction

Another way that organisms are preserved is by petrifaction. *Petrifaction* is a process in which minerals replace an organism's tissues. One form of petrifaction is called permineralization. *Permineralization* is a process in which the pore space in an organism's hard tissue—for example, bone or wood—is filled up with mineral. Another form of petrifaction is called *replacement,* a process in which the organism's tissues are completely replaced by minerals. For example, in some specimens of petrified wood, all of the wood has been replaced by minerals.

fossil the remains or physical evidence of an organism preserved by geological processes

Fossils in Asphalt

There are places where asphalt wells up at the Earth's surface in thick, sticky pools. The La Brea asphalt deposits in Los Angeles, California, for example, are at least 38,000 years old. These pools of thick, sticky asphalt have trapped and preserved many kinds of organisms for the past 38,000 years. From these fossils, scientists have learned about the past environment in southern California.

Frozen Fossils

In October 1999, scientists removed a 20,000-year-old woolly mammoth frozen in the Siberian tundra. The remains of this mammoth are shown in **Figure 2.** Woolly mammoths, relatives of modern elephants, became extinct approximately 10,000 years ago. Because cold temperatures slow down decay, many types of frozen fossils are preserved from the last ice age. Scientists hope to find out more about the mammoth and the environment in which it lived.

CONNECTION TO Environmental Science

WRITING SKILL **Preservation in Ice** Subfreezing climates contain almost no decomposing bacteria. The well-preserved body of John Torrington, a member of an expedition that explored the Northwest Passage in Canada in the 1840s, was uncovered in 1984. His body appeared much as it did at the time he died, more than 160 years earlier. Research another well-preserved discovery, and write a report for your class.

Figure 3 *These dinosaur tracks are located in Arizona. They leave a trace of a dinosaur that had longer legs than humans do.*

trace fossil a fossilized mark that is formed in soft sediment by the movement of an animal

mold a mark or cavity made in a sedimentary surface by a shell or other body

cast a type of fossil that forms when sediments fill in the cavity left by a decomposed organism

Other Types of Fossils

Besides their hard parts—and in rare cases their soft parts—do organisms leave behind any other clues about their existence? What other evidence of past life do paleontologists look for?

Trace Fossils

Any naturally preserved evidence of animal activity is called a **trace fossil.** Tracks like the ones shown in **Figure 3** are a fascinating example of a trace fossil. These fossils form when animal footprints fill with sediment and are preserved in rock. Tracks reveal a lot about the animal that made them, including how big it was and how fast it was moving. Parallel track-ways showing dinosaurs moving in the same direction have led paleontologists to hypothesize that dinosaurs moved in herds.

Burrows are another trace fossil. Burrows are shelters made by animals, such as clams, that bury in sediment. Like tracks, burrows are preserved when they are filled in with sediment and buried quickly. A *coprolite* (KAHP roh LIET), a third type of trace fossil, is preserved animal dung.

Molds and Casts

Molds and casts are two more examples of fossils. A cavity in rock where a plant or animal was buried is called a **mold.** A **cast** is an object created when sediment fills a mold and becomes rock. A cast shows what the outside of the organism looked like. **Figure 4** shows two types of molds from the same organism—and internal mold and an external mold.

Reading Check How are a cast and a mold different?

Figure 4 *This photograph shows two molds from an ammonite. The image on the left is the internal mold of the ammonite, which formed when sediment filled the ammonite's shell, which later dissolved away. The image on the right is the external mold of the ammonite, which preserves the external features of the shell.*

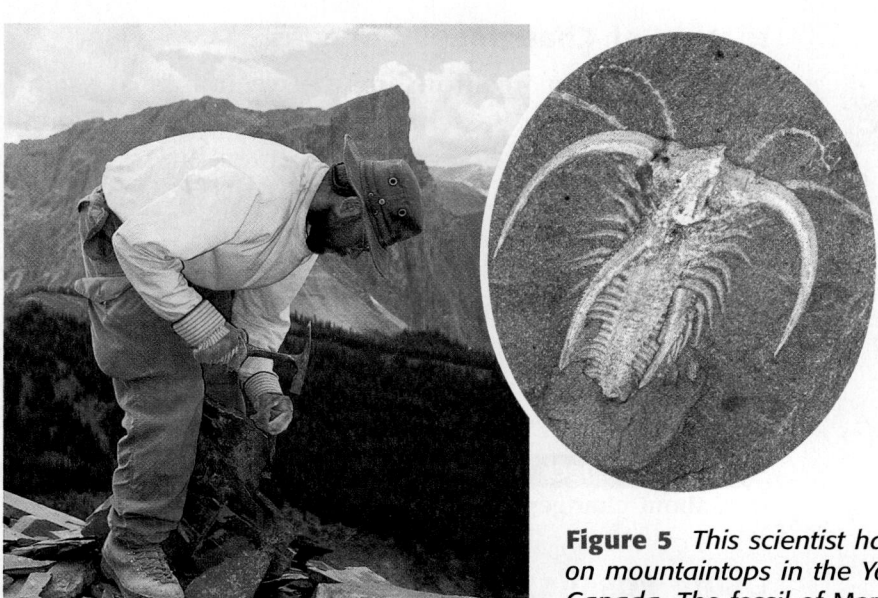

Figure 5 *This scientist has found marine fossils on mountaintops in the Yoho National Park in Canada. The fossil of* Marrella, *shown above, tells the scientist that these rocks were pushed up from below sea level millions of years ago.*

Using Fossils to Interpret the Past

Think about your favorite outdoor place. Now, imagine that you are a paleontologist at the same site 65 million years from now. What types of fossils would you dig up? Based on the fossils you found, how would you reconstruct this place?

The Information in the Fossil Record

The fossil record offers only a rough sketch of the history of life on Earth. Some parts of this history are more complete than others. For example, scientists know more about organisms that had hard body parts than about organisms that had soft body parts. Scientists also know more about organisms that lived in environments that favored fossilization. The fossil record is incomplete because most organisms never became fossils. And of course, many fossils have yet to be discovered.

History of Environmental Changes

Would you expect to find marine fossils on the mountaintop shown in **Figure 5**? The presence of marine fossils means that the rocks of these mountaintops in Canada formed in a totally different environment—at the bottom of an ocean.

The fossil record reveals a history of environmental change. For example, marine fossils help scientists reconstruct ancient coastlines and the deepening and shallowing of ancient seas. Using the fossils of plants and land animals, scientists can reconstruct past climates. They can tell whether the climate in an area was cooler or wetter than it is at present.

Make a Fossil

1. Find a **common object,** such as a shell, a button, or a pencil, to use to make a mold. Keep the object hidden from your classmates.

2. To create a mold, press the items down into **modeling clay** in a **shallow pan or tray.**

3. Trade your tray with a classmate's tray, and try to identify the item that made the mold.

4. Describe how a cast could be formed from your mold.

Fossil Hunt

Go on a fossil hunt with your family. Find out what kinds of rocks in your local area might contain fossils. Take pictures or draw sketches of your trip and any fossils that you find.

index fossil a fossil that is found in the rock layers of only one geologic age and that is used to establish the age of the rock layers

History of Changing Organisms

By studying the relationships between fossils, scientists can interpret how life has changed over time. For example, older rock layers contain organisms that often differ from the organisms found in younger rock layers.

Only a small fraction of the organisms that have existed in Earth's history have been fossilized. Because the fossil record is incomplete, it does not provide paleontologists with a continuous record of change. Instead, they look for similarities between fossils, or between fossilized organisms and their closest living relatives, and try to fill in the blanks in the fossil record.

✓ Reading Check How do paleontologists fill in missing information about changes in organisms in the fossil record?

Using Fossils to Date Rocks

Scientists have found that particular types of fossils appear only in certain layers of rock. By dating the rock layers above and below these fossils, scientists can determine the time span in which the organisms that formed the fossils lived. If a type of organism existed for only a short period of time, its fossils would show up in a limited range of rock layers. These types of fossils are called index fossils. **Index fossils** are fossils of organisms that lived during a relatively short, well-defined geologic time span.

Ammonites

To be considered an index fossil, a fossil must be found in rock layers throughout the world. One example of an index fossil is the fossil of a genus of ammonites (AM uh NIETS) called *Tropites*, shown in **Figure 6.** *Tropites* was a marine mollusk similar to a modern squid. It lived in a coiled shell. *Tropites* lived between 230 million and 208 million years ago and is an index fossil for that period of time.

Figure 6 Tropites *is a genus of coiled ammonites.* Tropites *existed for only about 20 million years, which makes this genus a good index fossil.*

Trilobites

Fossils of a genus of trilobites (TRIE loh BIETS) called *Phacops* are another example of an index fossil. Trilobites are extinct. Their closest living relative is the horseshoe crab. Through the dating of rock, paleontologists have determined that *Phacops* lived approximately 400 million years ago. So, when scientists find *Phacops* in rock layers anywhere on Earth, they assume that these rock layers are also approximately 400 million years old. An example of a *Phacops* fossil is shown in **Figure 7.**

✓ **Reading Check** Explain how fossils of *Phacops* can be used to establish the age of rock layers.

Figure 7 *Paleontologists assume that any rock layer containing a fossil of the trilobite* Phacops *is about 400 million years old.*

SECTION Review

Summary

- Fossils are the remains or physical evidence of an organism preserved by geologic processes.

- Fossils can be preserved in rock, amber, asphalt, and ice and by petrifaction.

- Trace fossils are any naturally preserved evidence of animal activity. Tracks, burrows, and coprolites are examples of trace fossils.

- Scientists study fossils to determine how environments and organisms have changed over time.

- An index fossil is a fossil of an organism that lived during a relatively short, well-defined time span. Index fossils can be used to establish the age of rock layers.

Using Key Terms

Complete each of the following sentences by choosing the correct term from the word bank.

cast	index fossils
mold	trace fossils

1. A ___ is a cavity in rock where a plant or animal was buried.

2. ___ can be used to establish the age of rock layers.

Understanding Key Ideas

3. Fossils are most often preserved in

   a. ice.

   b. amber.

   c. asphalt.

   d. rock.

4. Describe three types of trace fossils.

5. Explain how an index fossil can be used to date rock.

6. Explain why the fossil record contains an incomplete record of the history of life on Earth.

7. Explain how fossils can be used to determine the history of changes in environments and organisms.

Math Skills

8. If a scientist finds the remains of a plant between a rock layer that contains 400 million–year-old *Phacops* fossils and a rock layer that contains 230 million–year-old *Tropites* fossils, how old could the plant fossil be?

Critical Thinking

9. **Making Inferences** If you find rock layers containing fish fossils in a desert, what can you infer about the history of the desert?

10. **Identifying Bias** Because information in the fossil record is incomplete, scientists are left with certain biases concerning fossil preservation. Explain two of these biases.

SCILINKS

NSTA
Developed and maintained by the National Science Teachers Association

For a variety of links related to this chapter, go to www.scilinks.org

Topic: Looking at Fossils
SciLinks code: HSM0886

Time Marches On

How old is the Earth? Well, if the Earth celebrated its birthday every million years, there would be 4,600 candles on its birthday cake! Humans have been around only long enough to light the last candle on the cake.

Try to think of the Earth's history in "fast-forward." If you could watch the Earth change from this perspective, you would see mountains rise up like wrinkles in fabric and quickly wear away. You would see life-forms appear and then go extinct. In this section, you will learn that geologists must "fast-forward" the Earth's history when they write or talk about it. You will also learn about some incredible events in the history of life on Earth.

Geologic Time

Shown in **Figure 1** is the rock wall at the Dinosaur Quarry Visitor Center in Dinosaur National Monument, Utah. Contained within this wall are approximately 1,500 fossil bones that have been excavated by paleontologists. These are the remains of dinosaurs that inhabited the area about 150 million years ago. Granted, 150 million years seems to be an incredibly long period of time. However, in terms of the Earth's history, 150 million years is little more than 3% of the time our planet has existed. It is a little less than 4% of the time represented by the Earth's oldest known rocks.

Figure 1 *Bones of dinosaurs that lived about 150 million years ago are exposed in the quarry wall at Dinosaur National Monument in Utah.*

Figure 2 Well-preserved plant and animal fossils are common in the Green River formation. Clockwise from the upper right are a fossil leaf, a dragonfly, a fish, and a turtle.

The Rock Record and Geologic Time

One of the best places in North America to see the Earth's history recorded in rock layers is in Grand Canyon National Park. The Colorado River has cut the canyon nearly 2 km deep in some places. Over the course of 6 million years, the river has eroded countless layers of rock. These layers represent almost half, or nearly 2 billion years, of Earth's history.

Reading Check How much geologic time is represented by the rock layers in the Grand Canyon? (*See the Appendix for answers to Reading Checks.*)

The Fossil Record and Geologic Time

Figure 2 shows sedimentary rocks that belong to the Green River formation. These rocks, which are found in parts of Wyoming, Utah, and Colorado, are thousands of meters thick. These rocks were once part of a system of ancient lakes that existed for a period of millions of years. Fossils of plants and animals are common in these rocks and are very well preserved. Burial in the fine-grained lake-bed sediments preserved even the most delicate structures.

INTERNET ACTIVITY

For another activity related to this chapter, go to **go.hrw.com** and type in the keyword **HZ5FOSW**.

Phanerozoic Eon

(543 million years ago to the present)
The rock and fossil record mainly represents the Phanerozoic eon, which is the eon in which we live.

Proterozoic Eon

(2.5 billion years ago to 543 million years ago)
The first organisms with well-developed cells appeared during this eon.

Archean Eon

(3.8 billion years ago to 2.5 billion years ago)
The earliest known rocks on Earth formed during this eon.

Hadean Eon

(4.6 billion years ago to 3.8 billion years ago)
The only rocks that scientists have found from this eon are meteorites and rocks from the moon.

Geologic Time Scale

Era	Period	Epoch	Millions of years ago
Cenozoic	Quaternary	Holocene	0.01
		Pleistocene	1.8
	Tertiary	Pliocene	5.3
		Miocene	23.8
		Oligocene	33.7
		Eocene	54.8
		Paleocene	65
Mesozoic	Cretaceous		144
	Jurassic		206
	Triassic		248
Paleozoic	Permian		290
	Pennsylvanian		323
	Mississippian		354
	Devonian		417
	Silurian		443
	Ordovician		490
	Cambrian		543

PHANEROZOIC EON

PROTEROZOIC EON — 2,500

ARCHEAN EON — 3,800

HADEAN EON — 4,600

Figure 3 *The geologic time scale accounts for Earth's entire history. It is divided into four major parts called eons. Dates given for intervals on the geologic time scale are estimates.*

The Geologic Time Scale

The geologic column represents the billions of years that have passed since the first rocks formed on Earth. Altogether, geologists study 4.6 billion years of Earth's history! To make their job easier, geologists have created the geologic time scale. The **geologic time scale,** which is shown in **Figure 3,** is a scale that divides Earth's 4.6 billion–year history into distinct intervals of time.

Reading Check Define the term *geologic time scale*.

Divisions of Time

Geologists have divided Earth's history into sections of time, as shown on the geologic time scale in **Figure 3.** The largest divisions of geologic time are **eons** (EE AHNZ). There are four eons—the Hadean eon, the Archean eon, the Proterozoic eon, and the Phanerozoic eon. The Phanerozoic eon is divided into three **eras,** which are the second-largest divisions of geologic time. The three eras are further divided into **periods,** which are the third-largest divisions of geologic time. Periods are divided into **epochs** (EP uhks), which are the fourth-largest divisions of geologic time.

The boundaries between geologic time intervals represent shorter intervals in which visible changes took place on Earth. Some changes are marked by the disappearance of index fossil species, while others are recognized only by detailed paleontological studies.

The Appearance and Disappearance of Species

At certain times during Earth's history, the number of species has increased or decreased dramatically. An increase in the number of species often comes as a result of either a relatively sudden increase or decrease in competition among species. *Hallucigenia,* shown in **Figure 4,** appeared during the Cambrian period, when the number of marine species greatly increased. On the other hand, the number of species decreases dramatically over a relatively short period of time during a mass extinction event. **Extinction** is the death of every member of a species. Gradual events, such as global climate change and changes in ocean currents, can cause mass extinctions. A combination of these events can also cause mass extinctions.

geologic time scale the standard method used to divide the Earth's long natural history into manageable parts

eon the largest division of geologic time

era a unit of geologic time that includes two or more periods

period a unit of geologic time into which eras are divided

epoch a subdivision of a geologic period

extinction the death of every member of a species

Figure 4 Hallucigenia, *named for its "bizarre and dreamlike quality," was one of numerous marine organisms to make its appearance during the early Cambrian period.*

Figure 5 *Jungles were present during the Paleozoic era, but there were no birds singing in the trees and no monkeys swinging from the branches. Birds and mammals didn't evolve until much later.*

The Paleozoic Era—Old Life

The Paleozoic era lasted from about 543 million to 248 million years ago. It is the first era well represented by fossils.

Marine life flourished at the beginning of the Paleozoic era. The oceans became home to a diversity of life. However, there were few land organisms. By the middle of the Paleozoic, all modern groups of land plants had appeared. By the end of the era, amphibians and reptiles lived on the land, and insects were abundant. **Figure 5** shows what the Earth might have looked like late in the Paleozoic era. The Paleozoic era came to an end with the largest mass extinction in Earth's history. Some scientists believe that ocean changes were a likely cause of this extinction, which killed nearly 90% of all species.

The Mesozoic Era—The Age of Reptiles

The Mesozoic era began about 248 million years ago. The Mesozoic is known as the *Age of Reptiles* because reptiles, such as the dinosaurs shown in **Figure 6,** inhabited the land.

During this time, reptiles dominated. Small mammals appeared about the same time as dinosaurs, and birds appeared late in the Mesozoic era. Many scientists think that birds evolved directly from a type of dinosaur. At the end of the Mesozoic era, about 15% to 20% of all species on Earth, including the dinosaurs, became extinct. Global climate change may have been the cause.

Reading Check Why is the Mesozoic known as the *Age of Reptiles?*

Figure 6 *Imagine walking in the desert and bumping into these fierce creatures! It's a good thing humans didn't evolve in the Mesozoic era, which was dominated by dinosaurs.*

The Cenozoic Era—The Age of Mammals

The Cenozoic era, as shown in **Figure 7,** began about 65 million years ago and continues to the present. This era is known as the *Age of Mammals.* During the Mesozoic era, mammals had to compete with dinosaurs and other animals for food and habitat. After the mass extinction at the end of the Mesozoic era, mammals flourished. Unique traits, such as regulating body temperature internally and bearing young that develop inside the mother, may have helped mammals survive the environmental changes that probably caused the extinction of the dinosaurs.

Figure 7 *Thousands of species of mammals evolved during the Cenozoic era. This scene shows species from the early Cenozoic era that are now extinct.*

SECTION Review

Summary

- The geologic time scale divides Earth's 4.6 billion–year history into distinct intervals of time. Divisions of geologic time include eons, eras, periods, and epochs.

- The boundaries between geologic time intervals represent visible changes that have taken place on Earth.

- The rock and fossil record represents mainly the Phanerozoic eon, which is the eon in which we live.

- At certain times in Earth's history, the number of life-forms has increased or decreased dramatically.

Using Key Terms

1. Use each of the following terms in the same sentence: *era, period,* and *epoch.*

Understanding Key Ideas

2. The unit of geologic time that began 65 million years ago and continues to the present is the
   a. Holocene epoch.
   b. Cenozoic era.
   c. Phanerozoic eon.
   d. Quaternary period.

3. What are the major time intervals represented by the geologic time scale?

4. Explain how geologic time is recorded in rock layers.

5. What kinds of environmental changes cause mass extinctions?

Critical Thinking

6. **Making Inferences** What future event might mark the end of the Cenozoic era?

7. **Identifying Relationships** How might a decrease in competition between species lead to the sudden appearance of many new species?

Interpreting Graphics

8. Look at the illustration below. On the Earth-history clock shown, 1 h equals 383 million years, and 1 min equals 6.4 million years. In millions of years, how much more time is represented by the Proterozoic eon than by the Phanerozoic eon?

Phanerozoic eon   Hadean eon

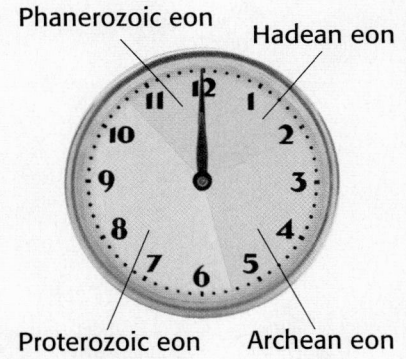

Proterozoic eon   Archean eon

SCILINKS®

NSTA
Developed and maintained by the
National Science Teachers Association

For a variety of links related to this chapter, go to www.scilinks.org

Topic: Geologic Time
SciLinks code: HSM0668

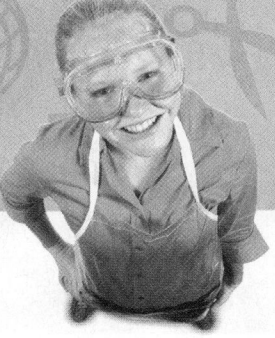

Model-Making Lab

How Do You Stack Up?

According to the principle of superposition, in undisturbed sequences of sedimentary rock, the oldest layers are on the bottom. Geologists use this principle to determine the relative age of the rocks in a small area. In this activity, you will model what geologists do by drawing sections of different rock outcrops. Then, you will create a part of the geologic column, showing the geologic history of the area that contains all of the outcrops.

Procedure

1. Use a metric ruler and a pencil to draw four boxes on a blank piece of paper. Each box should be 3 cm wide and at least 6 cm tall. (You can trace the boxes shown on the next page.)

2. With colored pencils, copy the illustrations of the four outcrops on the next page. Copy one illustration in each of the four boxes. Use colors and patterns similar to those shown.

3. Pay close attention to the contact between layers—straight or wavy. Straight lines represent bedding planes, where deposition was continuous. Wavy lines represent unconformities, where rock layers may be missing. The top of each outcrop is incomplete, so it should be a jagged line. (Assume that the bottom of the lowest layer is a bedding plane.)

4. Use a black crayon or pencil to add the symbols representing fossils to the layers in your drawings. Pay attention to the shapes of the fossils and the layers that they are in.

5. Write the outcrop number on the back of each section.

6. Carefully cut the outcrops out of the paper, and lay the individual outcrops next to each other on your desk or table.

7. Find layers that have the same rocks and contain the same fossils. Move each outcrop up or down to line up similar layers next to each other.

8. If unconformities appear in any of the outcrops, there may be rock layers missing. You may need to examine other sections to find out what fits between the layers above and below the unconformities. Leave room for these layers by cutting the outcrops along the unconformities (wavy lines).

9 Eventually, you should be able to make a geologic column that represents all four of the outcrops. It will show rock types and fossils for all the known layers in the area.

10 Tape the pieces of paper together in a pattern that represents the complete geologic column.

Analyze the Results

1 **Examining Data** How many layers are in the part of the geologic column that you modeled?

2 **Examining Data** Which is the oldest layer in your column? Which rock layer is the youngest? How do you know? Describe these layers in terms of rock type or the fossils they contain.

3 **Classifying** List the fossils in your column from oldest to youngest. Label the youngest and oldest fossils.

4 **Analyzing Data** Look at the unconformity in outcrop 2. Which rock layers are partially or completely missing? How do you know?

Draw Conclusions

5 **Drawing Conclusions** Which (if any) fossils can be used as index fossils for a single layer? Why are these fossils considered index fossils? What method(s) would be required to determine the absolute age of these fossils?

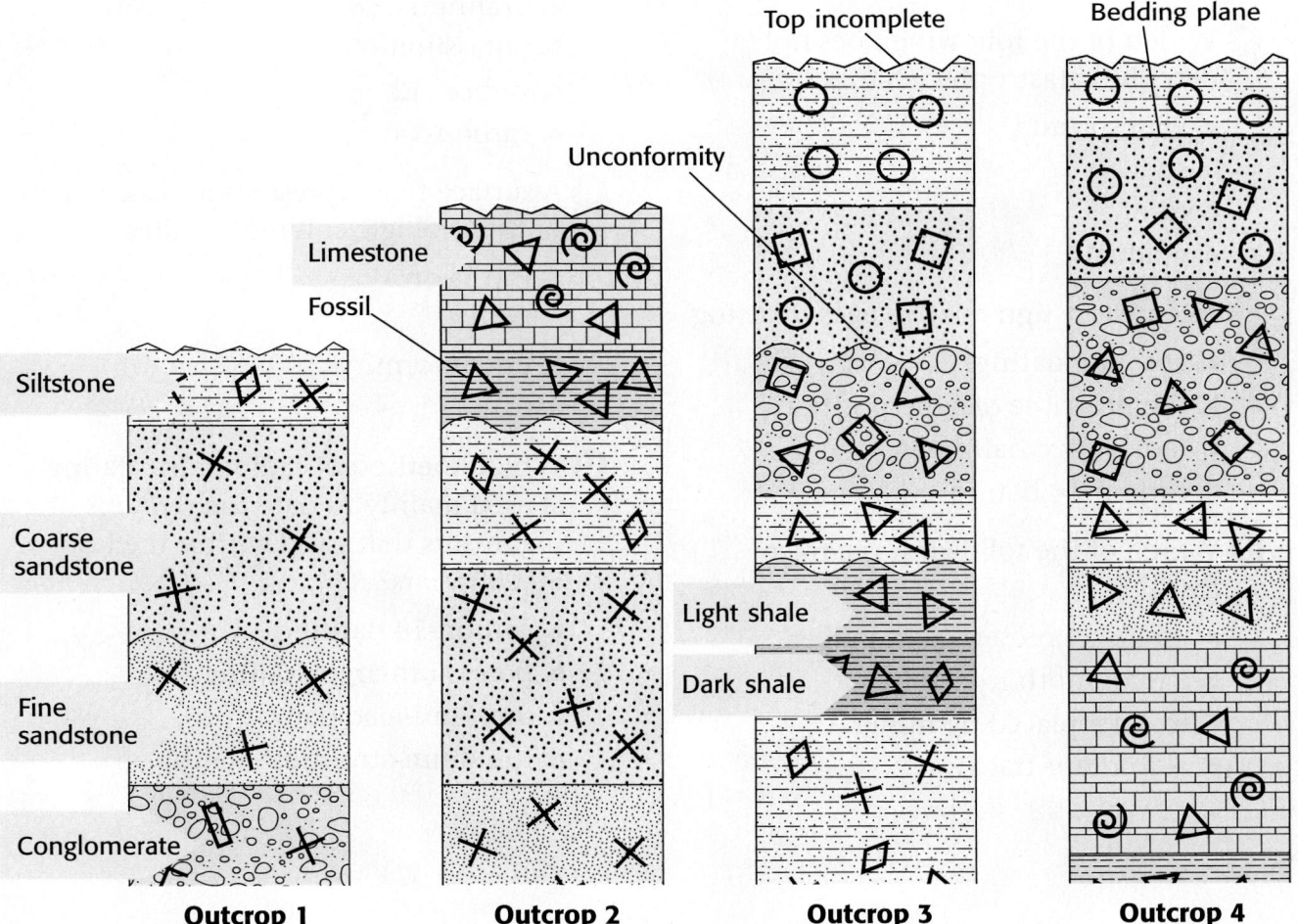

Outcrop 1   Outcrop 2   Outcrop 3   Outcrop 4

Chapter Review

USING KEY TERMS

1 In your own words, write a definition for each of the following terms: *superposition*, *geologic column*, and *geologic time scale*.

For each pair of terms, explain how the meanings of the terms differ.

2 *uniformitarianism* and *catastrophism*

3 *relative dating* and *absolute dating*

4 *trace fossil* and *index fossil*

UNDERSTANDING KEY IDEAS

Multiple Choice

5 Which of the following does not describe catastrophic change?

a. widespread

b. sudden

c. rare

d. gradual

6 Scientists assign relative ages by using

a. absolute dating.

b. the principle of superposition.

c. radioactive half-lives.

d. carbon-14 dating.

7 Which of the following is a trace fossil?

a. an insect preserved in amber

b. a mammoth frozen in ice

c. wood replaced by minerals

d. a dinosaur trackway

8 The largest divisions of geologic time are called

a. periods.

b. eras.

c. eons.

d. epochs.

9 Rock layers cut by a fault formed

a. after the fault.

b. before the fault.

c. at the same time as the fault.

d. There is not enough information to determine the answer.

10 Of the following isotopes, which is stable?

a. uranium-238

b. potassium-40

c. carbon-12

d. carbon-14

11 A surface that represents a missing part of the geologic column is called a(n)

a. intrusion.

b. fault.

c. unconformity.

d. fold.

12 Which method of radiometric dating is used mainly to date the remains of organisms that lived within the last 50,000 years?

a. carbon-14 dating

b. potassium-argon dating

c. uranium-lead dating

d. rubidium-strontium dating

Short Answer

13 Describe three processes by which fossils form.

14 Identify the role of uniformitarianism in Earth science.

15 Explain how radioactive decay occurs.

16 Describe two ways in which scientists use fossils to determine environmental change.

17 Explain the role of paleontology in the study of Earth's history.

CRITICAL THINKING

18 **Concept Mapping** Use the following terms to create a concept map: *age, half-life, absolute dating, radioactive decay, radiometric dating, relative dating, superposition, geologic column,* and *isotopes*.

19 **Applying Concepts** Identify how changes in environmental conditions can affect the survival of a species. Give two examples.

20 **Identifying Relationships** Why do paleontologists know more about hard-bodied organisms than about soft-bodied organisms?

21 **Analyzing Processes** Why isn't a 100 million–year-old fossilized tree made of wood?

INTERPRETING GRAPHICS

Use the diagram below to answer the questions that follow.

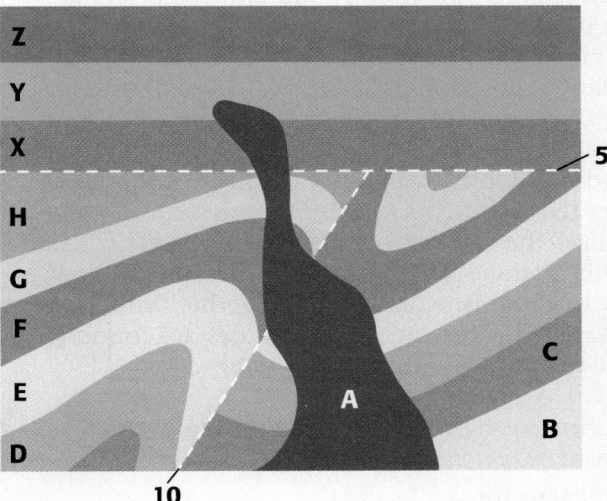

22 Is intrusion A younger or older than layer X? Explain.

23 What feature is marked by 5?

24 Is intrusion A younger or older than fault 10? Explain.

25 Other than the intrusion and faulting, what event happened in layers **B, C, D, E, F, G,** and **H**? Number this event, the intrusion, and the faulting in the order that they happened.

Standardized Test Preparation

Read each of the passages below. Then, answer the questions that follow each passage.

Passage 1 Three hundred million years ago, the region that is now Illinois had a different climate than it does today. Swamps and shallow bays covered much of the area. No fewer than 500 species of plants and animals lived in this environment. Today, the remains of these organisms are found beautifully preserved within nodules. Nodules are round or oblong structures usually composed of cemented sediments that sometimes contain the fossilized hard parts of plants and animals. The Illinois nodules are <u>exceptional</u> because the soft parts of organisms are found together with hard parts. For this reason, these nodules are found in fossil collections around the world.

1. In the passage, what is the meaning of the word *exceptional*?

  A beautiful

  B extraordinary

  C average

  D large

2. According to the passage, which of the following statements about nodules is correct?

  F Nodules are rarely round or oblong.

  G Nodules are usually composed of cemented sediment.

  H Nodules are not found in present-day Illinois.

  I Nodules always contain fossils.

3. Which of the following is a fact in the passage?

  A The Illinois nodules are not well known outside of Illinois.

  B Illinois has had the same climate throughout Earth's history.

  C Both the hard and soft parts of organisms are preserved in the Illinois nodules.

  D Fewer than 500 species of plants and animals have been found in Illinois nodules.

Passage 2 In 1995, paleontologist Paul Sereno and his team were working in an unexplored region of Morocco when they made an <u>astounding</u> find—an enormous dinosaur skull! The skull measured approximately 1.6 m in length, which is about the height of a refrigerator. Given the size of the skull, Sereno concluded that the skeleton of the animal it came from must have been about 14 m long—about as big as a school bus. The dinosaur was even larger than *Tyrannosaurus rex*! The newly discovered 90 million–year-old predator most likely chased other dinosaurs by running on large, powerful hind legs, and its bladelike teeth meant certain death for its prey.

1. In the passage, what does the word *astounding* mean?

  A important

  B new

  C incredible

  D one of a kind

2. Which of the following is evidence that the dinosaur described in the passage was a predator?

  F It had bladelike teeth.

  G It had a large skeleton.

  H It was found with the bones of a smaller animal nearby.

  I It is 90 million years old.

3. What types of information do you think that fossil teeth provide about an organism?

  A the color of its skin

  B the types of food it ate

  C the speed that it ran

  D the mating habits it had

Use the graph below to answer the questions that follow.

Read each question below, and choose the best answer.

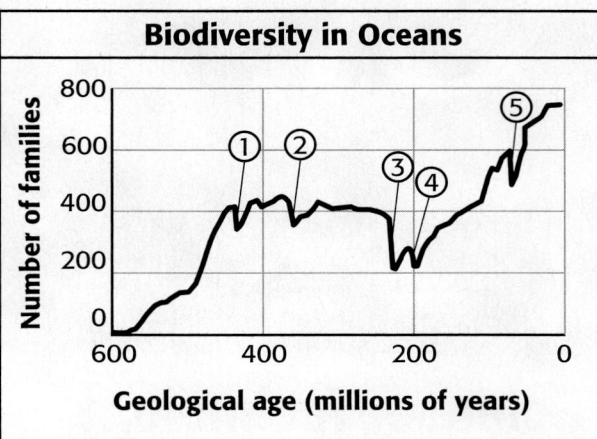

Biodiversity in Oceans

1. At which point in Earth's history did the greatest mass-extinction event take place?
   - **A** at point 1, the Ordovician-Silurian boundary
   - **B** at point 3, the Permian-Triassic boundary
   - **C** at point 4, the Triassic-Jurassic boundary
   - **D** at point 5, the Cretaceous-Tertiary boundary

2. Immediately following the Cretaceous-Tertiary extinction, represented by point 5, approximately how many families of marine organisms remained in the Earth's oceans?
   - **F** 200 marine families
   - **G** 300 marine families
   - **H** 500 marine families
   - **I** 700 marine families

3. Approximately how many million years ago did the Ordovician-Silurian mass-extinction event, represented by point 1, take place?
   - **A** 200 million years ago
   - **B** 250 million years ago
   - **C** 350 million years ago
   - **D** 420 million years ago

1. Carbon-14 is a radioactive isotope with a half-life of 5,730 years. How much carbon-14 would remain in a sample that is 11,460 years old?
   - **A** 12.5%
   - **B** 25%
   - **C** 50%
   - **D** 100%

2. If a sample contains an isotope with a half-life of 10,000 years, how old would the sample be if 1/8 of the original isotope remained in the sample?
   - **F** 20,000 years
   - **G** 30,000 years
   - **H** 40,000 years
   - **I** 50,000 years

3. If a sample contains an isotope with a half-life of 5,000 years, how old would the sample be if 1/4 of the original isotope remained in the sample?
   - **A** 10,000 years
   - **B** 20,000 years
   - **C** 30,000 years
   - **D** 40,000 years

4. If Earth history spans 4.6 billion years and the Phanerozoic eon was 543 million years, what percentage of Earth history does the Phanerozoic eon represent?
   - **F** about 6%
   - **G** about 12%
   - **H** about 18%
   - **I** about 24%

5. Humans live in the Holocene epoch. If the Holocene epoch has lasted approximately 10,000 years, what percentage of the Quaternary period, which began 1.8 million years ago, is represented by the Holocene?
   - **A** about 0.0055%
   - **B** about 0.055%
   - **C** about 0.55%
   - **D** about 5.5%

Standardized Test Preparation

Science in Action

Scientific Debate

Feathered Dinosaurs

One day in 1996, a Chinese farmer broke open a rock he found in the bed of an ancient dry lake. What he found inside the rock became one of the most exciting paleontological discoveries of the 20th century. Preserved inside were the remains of a dinosaur. The dinosaur had a large head; powerful jaws; sharp, jagged teeth; and, most important of all, a row of featherlike structures along the backbone. Scientists named the dinosaur *Sinosauropteryx*, or "Chinese dragon wing." *Sinosauropteryx* and the remains of other "feathered" dinosaurs recently discovered in China have led some scientists to hypothesize that feathers evolved through theropod (three-toed) dinosaurs. Other paleontologists disagree. They believe the structures along the backbone of these dinosaurs are not feathers but the remains of elongated spines, like those that run down the head and back of an iguana.

Science, Technology, and Society

DNA and a Mammoth Discovery

In recent years, scientists have unearthed several mammoths that had been frozen in ice in Siberia and other remote northern locations. Bones, fur, food in the stomach, and even dung have all been found in good condition. Some scientists hoped that DNA extracted from the mammoths might lead to the cloning of this animal, which became extinct about 10,000 years ago. But the DNA might not be able to be duplicated by scientists. However, DNA samples may nevertheless help scientists understand why mammoths became extinct. One theory about why mammoths became extinct is that they were killed off by disease. Using DNA taken from fossilized mammoth bone, hair, or dung, scientists can check to see if it contains the DNA of a disease-causing pathogen that led to the extinction of the mammoths.

Language Arts ACTiViTY

Paleontologists often give dinosaurs names that describe something unusual about the animal's head, body, feet, or size. These names have Greek or Latin roots. Research the names of some dinosaurs, and find out what the names mean. Create a list of dinosaur names and their meanings.

Math ACTiViTY

The male Siberian mammoth reached a height of about 3 m at the shoulder. Females reached a height of about 2.5 m at the shoulder. What is the ratio of the maximum height of a female Siberian mammoth to the height of a male Siberian mammoth?

People in Science

Lizzie May

Amateur Paleontologist For Lizzie May, summer vacations have meant trips into the Alaskan wilderness with her stepfather, geologist/paleontologist Kevin May. The purpose of these trips has not been for fun. Instead, Kevin and Lizzie have been exploring the Alaskan wilderness for the remains of ancient life—dinosaurs, in particular.

At age 18, Lizzie May has gained the reputation of being Alaska's most famous teenage paleontologist. It is a reputation that is well deserved. To date, Lizzie has collected hundreds of dinosaur bones and located important sites of dinosaur, bird, and mammal tracks. In her honor and as a result of her hard work in the field, scientists named the skeleton of a dinosaur discovered by the Mays "Lizzie." "Lizzie" is a duckbill dinosaur, or hadrosaur, that lived approximately 90 million years ago. "Lizzie" is the oldest dinosaur ever found in Alaska and one of the earliest known duckbill dinosaurs in North America.

The Mays have made other, equally exciting discoveries. On one summer trip, Kevin and Lizzie located six dinosaur and bird track sites that dated back 97 million to 144 million years. On another trip, the Mays found a fossil marine reptile more than 200 million years old—an ichthyosaur—that had to be removed with the help of a military helicopter. You have to wonder what other exciting adventures are in store for Lizzie and Kevin!

Social Studies ACTIVITY

WRITING SKILL Lizzie May is not the only young person to have made a mark in dinosaur paleontology. Using the Internet or another source, research people such as Bucky Derflinger, Johnny Maurice, Brad Riney, and Wendy Sloboda, who as young people made contributions to the field of dinosaur study. Write a short essay summarizing your findings.

To learn more about these Science in Action topics, visit go.hrw.com and type in the keyword **HZ5FOSF**.

Current Science

Check out Current Science® articles related to this chapter by visiting go.hrw.com. Just type in the keyword HZ5CS06.

UNIT 3

TIMELINE

The Restless Earth

In this unit, you will learn what a dynamic planet the Earth is. Earth's landmasses are changing position continuously as they travel across Earth's surface on tremendous blocks of rock. As these blocks collide with each other, mountain ranges are formed. As these blocks pull apart, magma is released from below, sometimes explosively in volcanic eruptions. When these blocks grind slowly past one another, long breaks in the Earth are created, where devastating earthquakes can take place. This timeline shows some of the events that have occurred as scientists have tried to understand our dynamic Earth.

1864

Jules Verne's *A Journey to the Center of the Earth* is published. In this fictional story, the heroes enter and exit the Earth through volcanoes.

1912

Alfred Wegener proposes his theory of continental drift.

1979

Volcanoes are discovered on Io, one of Jupiter's moons.

1980

Mount St. Helens erupts after an earthquake triggers a landslide on the volcano's north face.

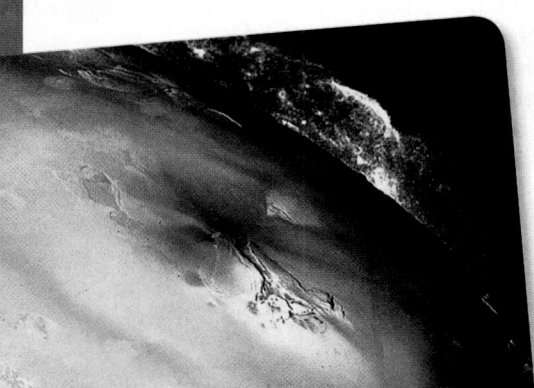

Io, one of Jupiter's moons

1883

When Krakatau erupts, more than 36,000 people are killed.

1896

Henry Ford builds his first car.

The Quadricycle, Henry Ford's first car

1906

San Francisco burns in the aftermath of an earthquake.

1935

Charles Richter devises a system of measuring the magnitude of earthquakes.

1951

Color television programming is introduced in the United States.

1962

A worldwide network of seismographs is established.

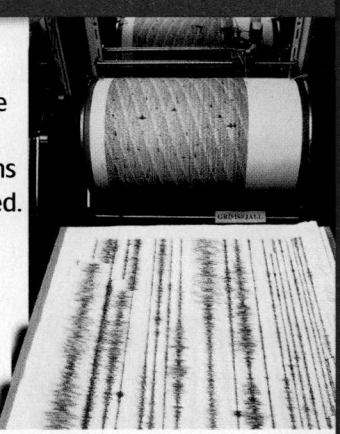

1982

Compact discs (CDs) and compact-disc players are made available to the public.

1994

An eight-legged robot named Dante II descends into the crater of an active volcano in Alaska.

Dante II

1997

The population of the Caribbean island of Montserrat dwindles to less than half its original size as frequent eruptions of the Soufriere Hills volcano force evacuations.

2003

An earthquake of magnitude 4.6 strikes Alabama. It is one of the largest earthquakes ever recorded for this area.

7

Plate Tectonics

About the PHOTO

The San Andreas fault stretches across the California landscape like a giant wound. The fault, which is 1,000 km long, breaks the Earth's crust from Northern California to Mexico. Because the North American plate and Pacific plate are slipping past one another along the fault, many earthquakes happen.

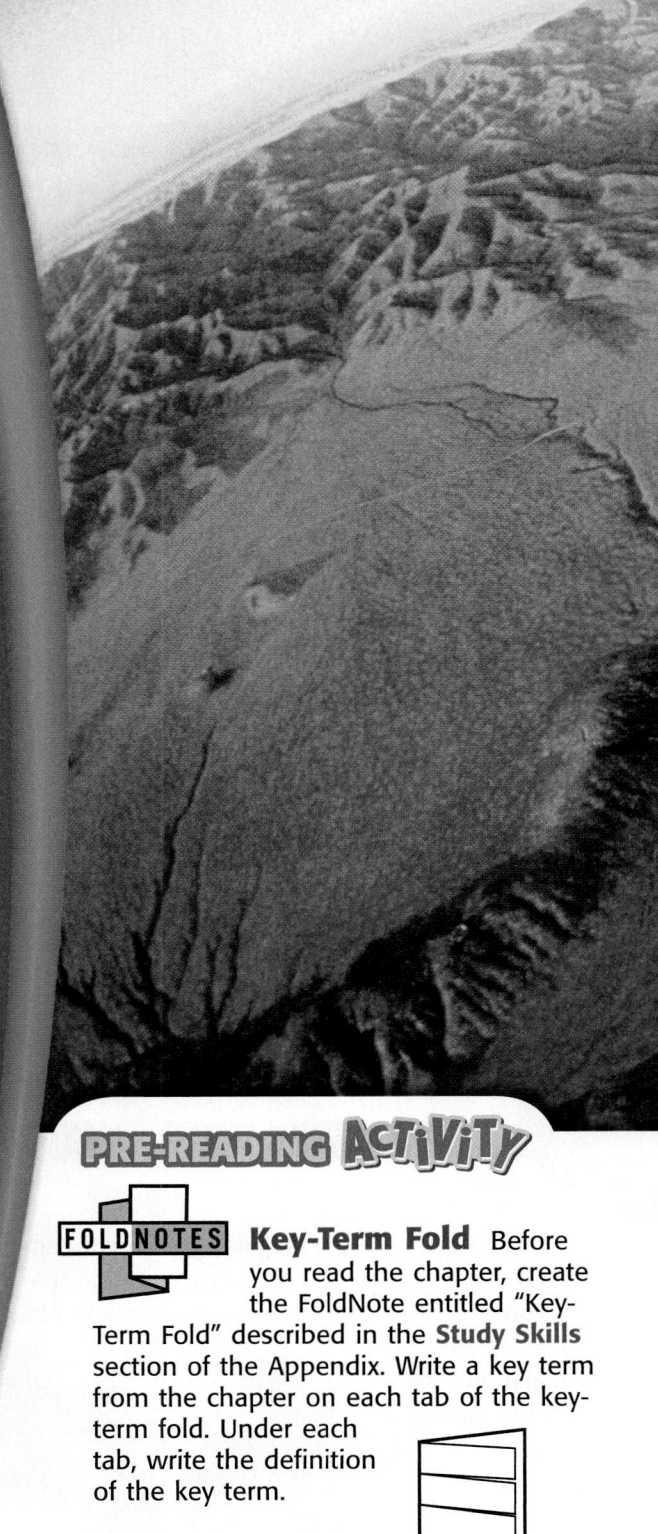

PRE-READING ACTIVITY

FOLDNOTES **Key-Term Fold** Before you read the chapter, create the FoldNote entitled "Key-Term Fold" described in the **Study Skills** section of the Appendix. Write a key term from the chapter on each tab of the key-term fold. Under each tab, write the definition of the key term.

START-UP ACTIVITY

Continental Collisions

As you can see, continents not only move but can also crash into each other. In this activity, you will model the collision of two continents.

Procedure

1. Obtain **two stacks of paper** that are each about 1 cm thick.

2. Place the two stacks of paper on a **flat surface,** such as a desk.

3. Very slowly, push the stacks of paper together so that they collide. Continue to push the stacks until the paper in one of the stacks folds over.

Analysis

1. What happens to the stacks of paper when they collide with each other?

2. Are all of the pieces of paper pushed upward? If not, what happens to the pieces that are not pushed upward?

3. What type of landform will most likely result from this continental collision?

Inside the Earth

If you tried to dig to the center of the Earth, what do you think you would find? Would the Earth be solid or hollow? Would it be made of the same material throughout?

Actually, the Earth is made of several layers. Each layer is made of different materials that have different properties. Scientists think about physical layers in two ways—by their composition and by their physical properties.

The Composition of the Earth

The Earth is divided into three layers—the crust, the mantle, and the core—based on the compounds that make up each layer. A *compound* is a substance composed of two or more elements. The less dense compounds make up the crust and mantle, and the densest compounds make up the core. The layers form because heavier elements are pulled toward the center of the Earth by gravity, and elements of lesser mass are found farther from the center.

The Crust

The outermost layer of the Earth is the **crust.** The crust is 5 to 100 km thick. It is the thinnest layer of the Earth.

As **Figure 1** shows, there are two types of crust—continental and oceanic. Both continental crust and oceanic crust are made mainly of the elements oxygen, silicon, and aluminum. However, the denser oceanic crust has almost twice as much iron, calcium, and magnesium, which form minerals that are denser than those in the continental crust.

READING WARM-UP

Objectives

- Identify the layers of the Earth by their composition.
- Identify the layers of the Earth by their physical properties.
- Describe a tectonic plate.
- Explain how scientists know about the structure of Earth's interior.

Terms to Learn

crust	asthenosphere
mantle	mesosphere
core	tectonic plate
lithosphere	

READING STRATEGY

Reading Organizer As you read this section, create an outline of the section. Use the headings from the section in your outline.

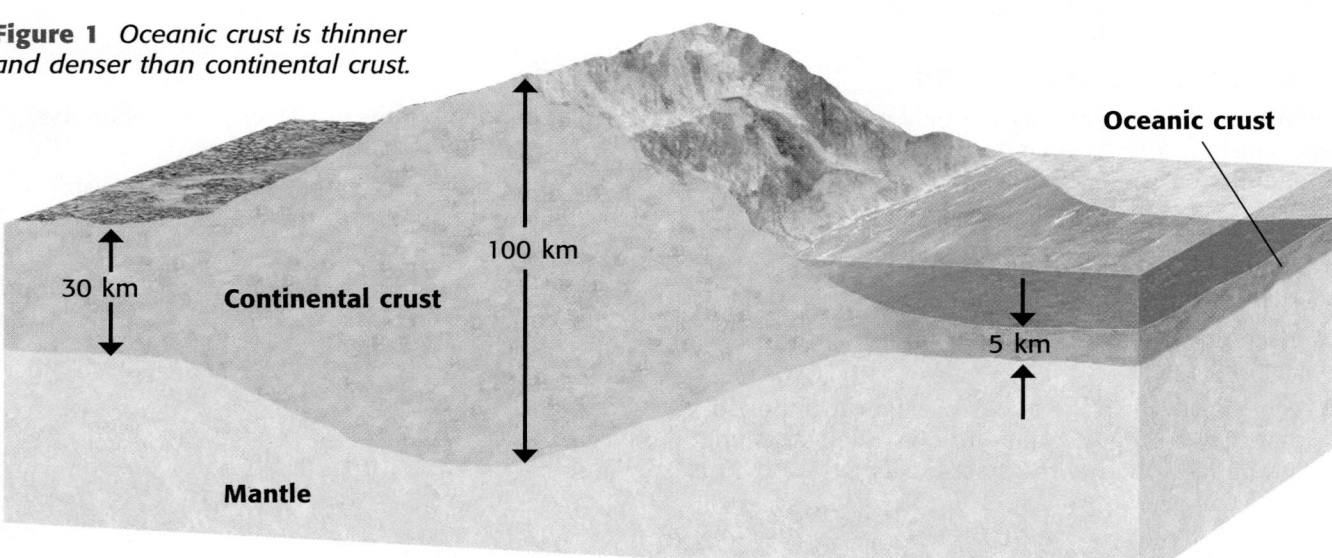

Figure 1 *Oceanic crust is thinner and denser than continental crust.*

Oceanic crust

30 km

100 km

Continental crust

5 km

Mantle

The Mantle

The layer of the Earth between the crust and the core is the **mantle.** The mantle is much thicker than the crust and contains most of the Earth's mass.

No one has ever visited the mantle. The crust is too thick to drill through to reach the mantle. Scientists must draw conclusions about the composition and other physical properties of the mantle from observations made on the Earth's surface. In some places, mantle rock pushes to the surface, which allows scientists to study the rock directly.

As you can see in **Figure 2,** another place scientists look for clues about the mantle is the ocean floor. Magma from the mantle flows out of active volcanoes on the ocean floor. These underwater volcanoes have given scientists many clues about the composition of the mantle. Because the mantle has more magnesium and less aluminum and silicon than the crust does, the mantle is denser than the crust.

Figure 2 *Volcanic vents on the ocean floor, such as this vent off the coast of Hawaii, allow magma to rise up through the crust from the mantle.*

The Core

The layer of the Earth that extends from below the mantle to the center of the Earth is the **core.** Scientists think that the Earth's core is made mostly of iron and contains smaller amounts of nickel but almost no oxygen, silicon, aluminum, or magnesium. As shown in **Figure 3,** the core makes up roughly one-third of the Earth's mass.

crust the thin and solid outermost layer of the Earth above the mantle

mantle the layer of rock between the Earth's crust and core

core the central part of the Earth below the mantle

Reading Check Briefly describe the layers that make up the Earth. (*See the Appendix for answers to Reading Checks.*)

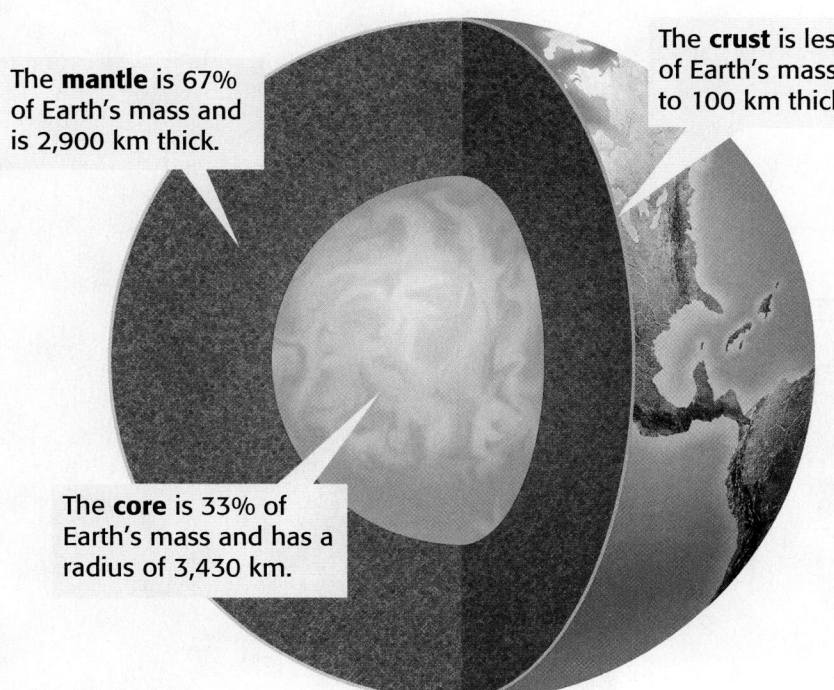

The **mantle** is 67% of Earth's mass and is 2,900 km thick.

The **crust** is less than 1% of Earth's mass and is 5 to 100 km thick.

The **core** is 33% of Earth's mass and has a radius of 3,430 km.

Figure 3 *The Earth is made up of three layers based on the composition of each layer.*

Using Models

Imagine that you are building a model of the Earth that will have a radius of 1 m. You find out that the average radius of the Earth is 6,380 km and that the thickness of the lithosphere is about 150 km. What percentage of the Earth's radius is the lithosphere? How thick (in centimeters) would you make the lithosphere in your model?

The Physical Structure of the Earth

Another way to look at the Earth is to examine the physical properties of its layers. The Earth is divided into five physical layers—the lithosphere, asthenosphere, mesosphere, outer core, and inner core. As shown in the figure below, each layer has its own set of physical properties.

✓ **Reading Check** What are the five physical layers of the Earth?

Lithosphere The outermost, rigid layer of the Earth is the **lithosphere.** The lithosphere is made of two parts—the crust and the rigid upper part of the mantle. The lithosphere is divided into pieces called *tectonic plates*.

Asthenosphere The **asthenosphere** is a plastic layer of the mantle on which pieces of the lithosphere move. The asthenosphere is made of solid rock that flows very slowly.

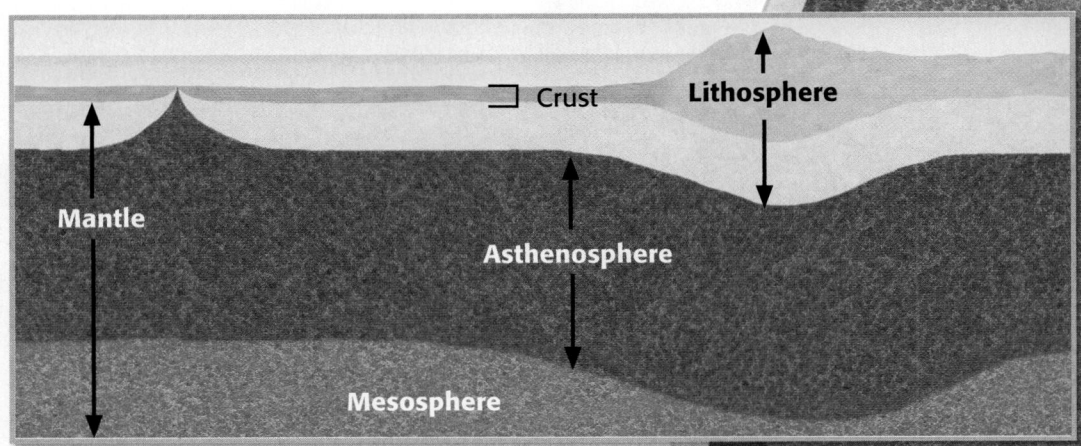

Crust

Lithosphere

Mantle

Asthenosphere

Mesosphere

lithosphere the solid, outer layer of the Earth that consists of the crust and the rigid upper part of the mantle

asthenosphere the soft layer of the mantle on which the tectonic plates move

mesosphere the strong, lower part of the mantle between the asthenosphere and the outer core

Mesosphere Beneath the asthenosphere is the strong, lower part of the mantle called the **mesosphere.** The mesosphere extends from the bottom of the asthenosphere to the Earth's core.

Lithosphere
15–300 km

Asthenosphere
250 km

Mesosphere
2,550 km

Outer Core The Earth's core is divided into two parts—the outer core and the inner core. The outer core is the liquid layer of the Earth's core that lies beneath the mantle and surrounds the inner core.

Inner Core The inner core is the solid, dense center of our planet that extends from the bottom of the outer core to the center of the Earth, which is about 6,380 km beneath the surface.

Outer core
2,200 km

Inner core
1,230 km

Tectonic Plates

Pieces of the lithosphere that move around on top of the asthenosphere are called **tectonic plates**. But what exactly does a tectonic plate look like? How big are tectonic plates? How and why do they move around? To answer these questions, begin by thinking of the lithosphere as a giant jigsaw puzzle.

A Giant Jigsaw Puzzle

All of the tectonic plates have names, some of which you may already know. Some of the major tectonic plates are named on the map in **Figure 4.** Notice that each tectonic plate fits together with the tectonic plates that surround it. The lithosphere is like a jigsaw puzzle, and the tectonic plates are like the pieces of a jigsaw puzzle.

Notice that not all tectonic plates are the same. For example, compare the size of the South American plate with that of the Cocos plate. Tectonic plates differ in other ways, too. For example, the South American plate has an entire continent on it and has oceanic crust, but the Cocos plate has only oceanic crust. Some tectonic plates, such as the South American plate, include both continental and oceanic crust.

tectonic plate a block of lithosphere that consists of the crust and the rigid, outermost part of the mantle

Major Tectonic Plates

1. Pacific plate
2. North American plate
3. Cocos plate
4. Nazca plate
5. South American plate
6. African plate
7. Eurasian plate
8. Indian plate
9. Australian plate
10. Antarctic plate

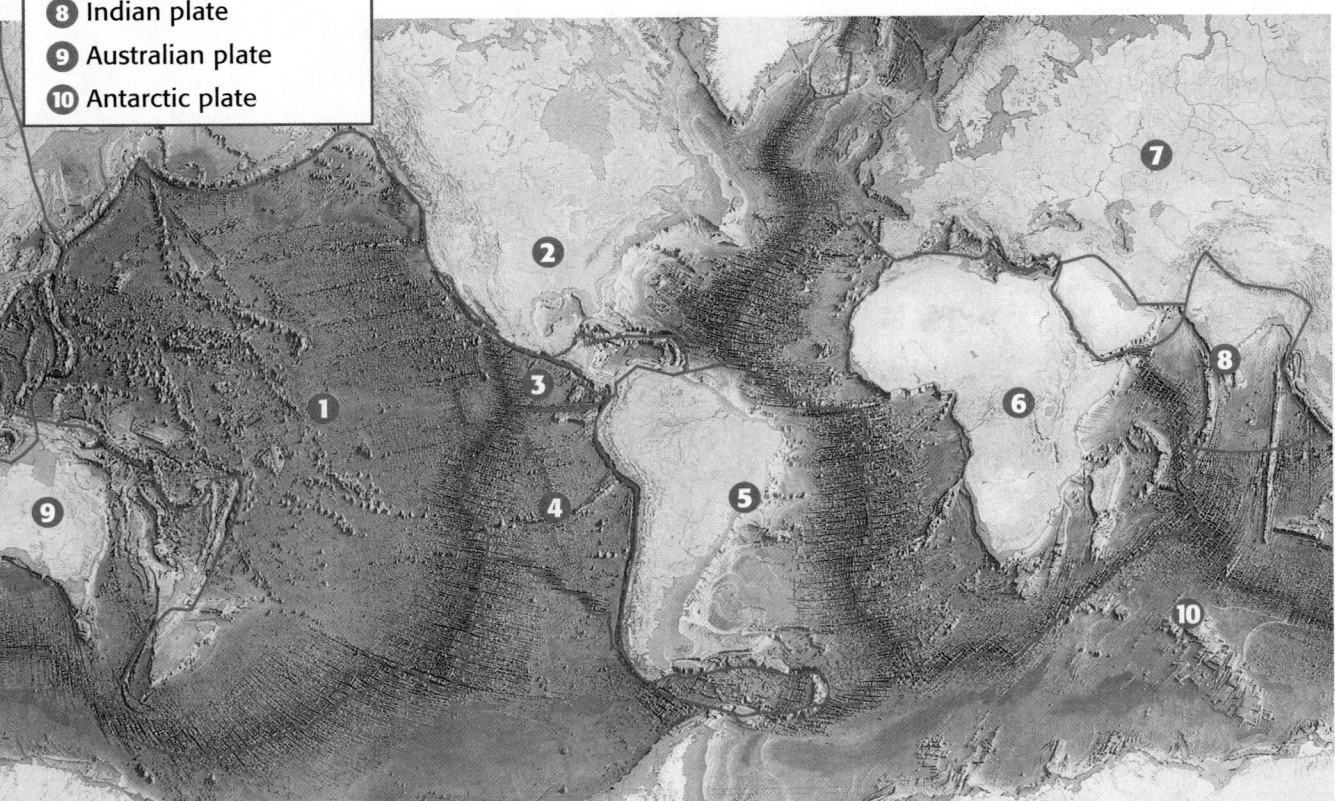

Figure 4 *Tectonic plates fit together like the pieces of a giant jigsaw puzzle.*

Figure 5 The South American Plate

This image shows what you might see if you could lift the South American plate out of its position between other tectonic plates.

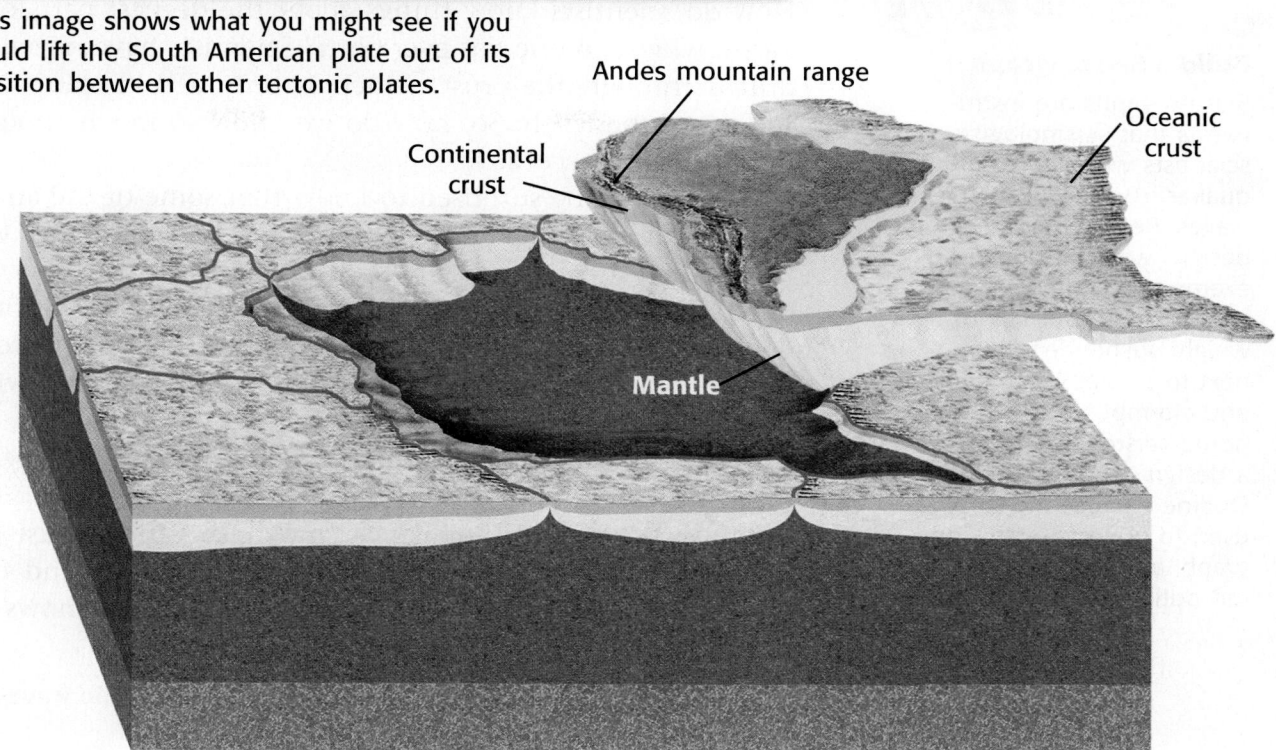

Andes mountain range

Continental crust

Oceanic crust

Mantle

A Tectonic Plate Close-Up

What would a tectonic plate look like if you could lift it out of its place? **Figure 5** shows what the South American plate might look like if you could. Notice that this tectonic plate not only consists of the upper part of the mantle but also consists of both oceanic crust and continental crust. The thickest part of the South American plate is the continental crust. The thinnest part of this plate is in the mid-Atlantic Ocean.

Like Ice Cubes in a Bowl of Punch

Think about ice cubes floating in a bowl of punch. If there are enough cubes, they will cover the surface of the punch and bump into one another. Parts of the ice cubes are below the surface of the punch and displace the punch. Large pieces of ice displace more punch than small pieces of ice. Tectonic plates "float" on the asthenosphere in a similar way. The plates cover the surface of the asthenosphere, and they touch one another and move around. The lithosphere displaces the asthenosphere. Thick tectonic plates, such as those made of continental crust, displace more asthenosphere than do thin plates, such as those made of oceanic lithosphere.

Reading Check Why do tectonic plates made of continental lithosphere displace more asthenosphere than tectonic plates made of oceanic lithosphere do?

Quick Lab

Tectonic Ice Cubes

1. Take the bottom half of a clear, **2 L soda bottle** that has been cut in half. Make sure that the label has been removed.

2. Fill the bottle with **water** to about 1 cm below the top edge of the bottle.

3. Get **three pieces of irregularly shaped ice** that are small, medium, and large.

4. Float the ice in the water, and note how much of each piece is below the surface of the water.

5. Do all pieces of ice float mostly below the surface? Which piece is mostly below the surface? Why?

Mapping the Earth's Interior

How do scientists know things about the deepest parts of the Earth, where no one has ever been? Scientists have never even drilled through the crust, which is only a thin skin on the surface of the Earth. So, how do we know so much about the mantle and the core?

Would you be surprised to know that some of the answers come from earthquakes? When an earthquake happens, vibrations called *seismic waves* are produced. Seismic waves travel at different speeds through the Earth. Their speed depends on the density and composition of material that they pass through. For example, a seismic wave traveling through a solid will go faster than a seismic wave traveling through a liquid.

When an earthquake happens, machines called *seismographs* measure the times at which seismic waves arrive at different distances from an earthquake. Seismologists can then use these distances and travel times to calculate the density and thickness of each physical layer of the Earth. **Figure 6** shows how seismic waves travel through the Earth.

✓ **Reading Check** What are some properties of seismic waves?

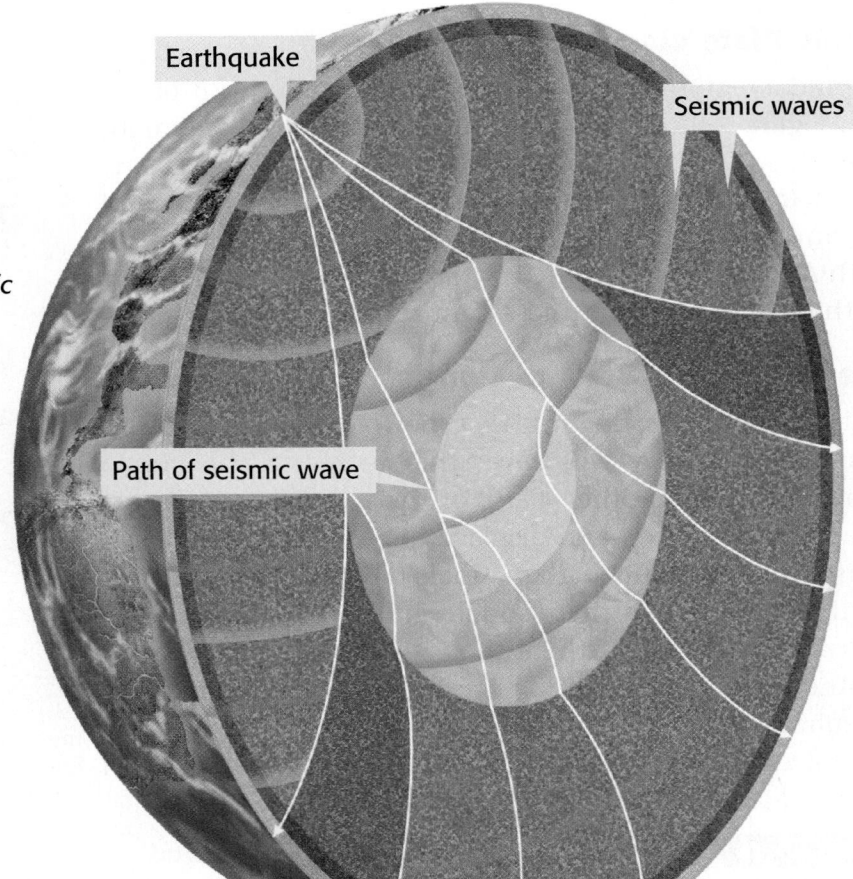

Figure 6 *By measuring changes in the speed of seismic waves that travel through Earth's interior, seismologists have learned that the Earth is made of different layers.*

Earthquake

Seismic waves

Path of seismic wave

Summary

- The Earth is made up of three layers—the crust, the mantle, and the core—based on chemical composition. Less dense compounds make up the crust and mantle. Denser compounds make up the core.

- The Earth is made up of five main physical layers: the lithosphere, the asthenosphere, the mesosphere, the outer core, and the inner core.

- Tectonic plates are large pieces of the lithosphere that move around on the Earth's surface.

- The crust in some tectonic plates is mainly continental. Other plates have only oceanic crust. Still other plates include both continental and oceanic crust.

- Thick tectonic plates, such as those in which the crust is mainly continental, displace more asthenosphere than do thin plates, such as those in which the crust is mainly oceanic.

- Knowledge about the layers of the Earth comes from the study of seismic waves caused by earthquakes.

Using Key Terms

For each pair of terms, explain how the meanings of the terms differ.

1. *crust* and *mantle*

2. *lithosphere* and *asthenosphere*

Understanding Key Ideas

3. The part of the Earth that is molten is the
   a. crust.
   b. mantle.
   c. outer core.
   d. inner core.

4. The part of the Earth on which the tectonic plates move is the
   a. lithosphere.
   b. asthenosphere.
   c. mesosphere.
   d. crust.

5. Identify the layers of the Earth by their chemical composition.

6. Identify the layers of the Earth by their physical properties.

7. Describe a tectonic plate.

8. Explain how scientists know about the structure of the Earth's interior.

Interpreting Graphics

9. According to the wave speeds shown in the table below, which two physical layers of the Earth are densest?

Speed of Seismic Waves in Earth's Interior	
Physical layer	**Wave speed**
Lithosphere	7 to 8 km/s
Asthenosphere	7 to 11 km/s
Mesosphere	11 to 13 km/s
Outer core	8 to 10 km/s
Inner core	11 to 12 km/s

Critical Thinking

10. **Making Comparisons** Explain the difference between the crust and the lithosphere.

11. **Analyzing Ideas** Why does a seismic wave travel faster through solid rock than through water?

SCILINKS®

NSTA
Developed and maintained by the
National Science Teachers Association

For a variety of links related to this chapter, go to www.scilinks.org
Topic: Composition of the Earth; Structure of the Earth
SciLinks code: HSM0329; HSM1468

Restless Continents

Have you ever looked at a map of the world and noticed how the coastlines of continents on opposite sides of the oceans appear to fit together like the pieces of a puzzle? Is it just coincidence that the coastlines fit together well? Is it possible that the continents were actually together sometime in the past?

READING WARM-UP

Objectives

● Describe Wegener's hypothesis of continental drift.

● Explain how sea-floor spreading provides a way for continents to move.

● Describe how new oceanic lithosphere forms at mid-ocean ridges.

● Explain how magnetic reversals provide evidence for sea-floor spreading.

Terms to Learn

continental drift
sea-floor spreading

READING STRATEGY

Paired Summarizing Read this section silently. In pairs, take turns summarizing the material. Stop to discuss ideas that seem confusing.

Wegener's Continental Drift Hypothesis

One scientist who looked at the pieces of this puzzle was Alfred Wegener (VAY guh nuhr). In the early 1900s, he wrote about his hypothesis of *continental drift*. **Continental drift** is the hypothesis that states that the continents once formed a single landmass, broke up, and drifted to their present locations. This hypothesis seemed to explain a lot of puzzling observations, including the observation of how well continents fit together.

Continental drift also explained why fossils of the same plant and animal species are found on continents that are on different sides of the Atlantic Ocean. Many of these ancient species could not have crossed the Atlantic Ocean. As you can see in **Figure 1,** without continental drift, this pattern of fossils would be hard to explain. In addition to fossils, similar types of rock and evidence of the same ancient climatic conditions were found on several continents.

✓ **Reading Check** How did fossils provide evidence for Wegener's hypothesis of continental drift? (*See the Appendix for answers to Reading Checks.*)

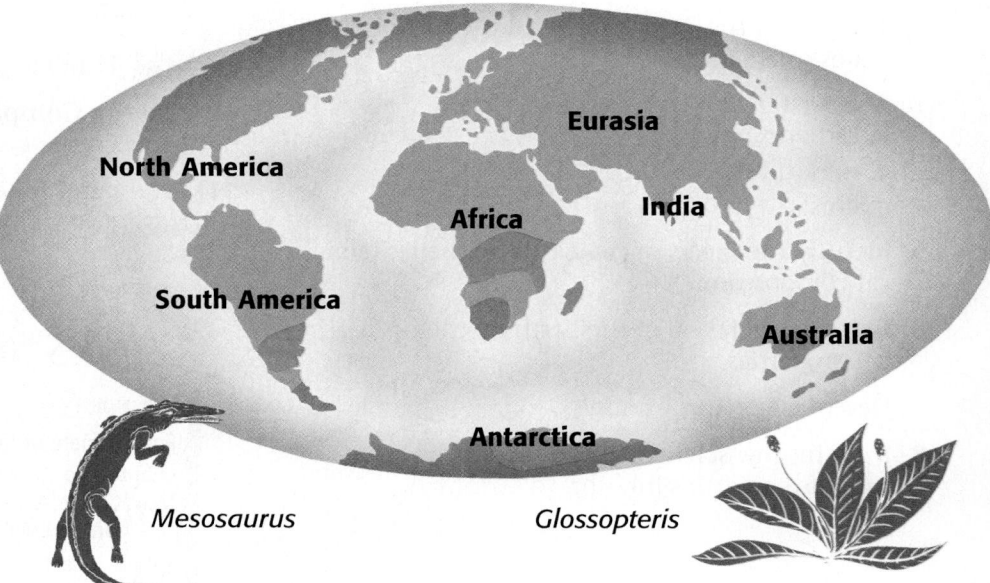

Figure 1 *Fossils of* Mesosaurus, *a small, aquatic reptile, and* Glossopteris, *an ancient plant species, have been found on several continents.*

North America

Eurasia

Africa

India

South America

Australia

Antarctica

Mesosaurus

Glossopteris

Figure 2   The Drifting Continents

245 Million Years Ago
Pangaea existed when some of the earliest dinosaurs were roaming the Earth. The continent was surrounded by a sea called *Panthalassa*, which means "all sea."

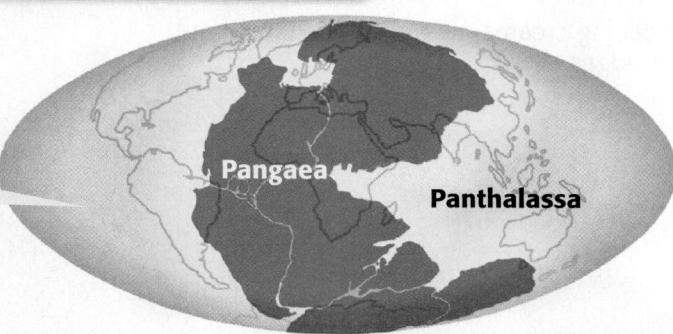

180 Million Years Ago
Gradually, Pangaea broke into two big pieces. The northern piece is called *Laurasia*. The southern piece is called *Gondwana*.

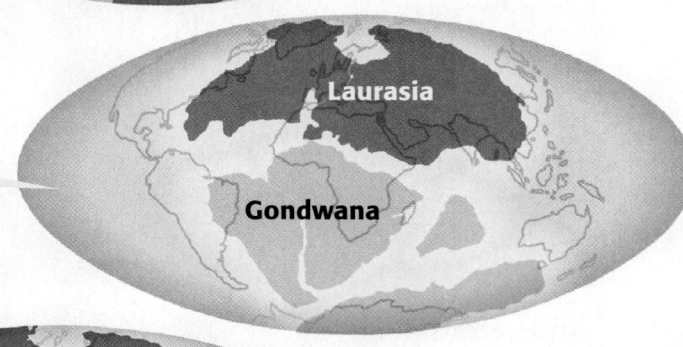

65 Million Years Ago
By the time the dinosaurs became extinct, Laurasia and Gondwana had split into smaller pieces.

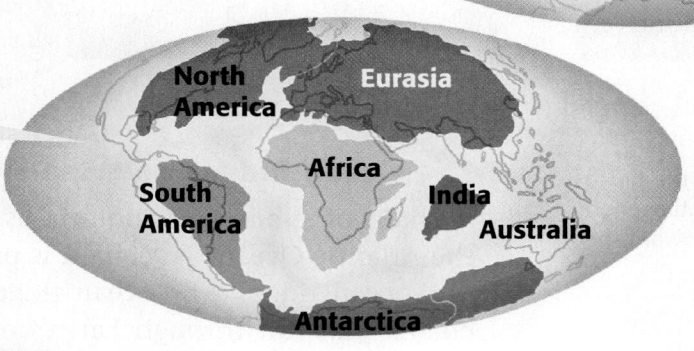

The Breakup of Pangaea

Wegener made many observations before proposing his hypothesis of continental drift. He thought that all of the present continents were once joined in a single, huge continent. Wegener called this continent *Pangaea* (pan JEE uh), which is Greek for "all earth." We now know from the hypothesis of plate tectonics that Pangaea existed about 245 million years ago. We also know that Pangaea further split into two huge continents—Laurasia and Gondwana—about 180 million years ago. As shown in **Figure 2,** these two continents split again and formed the continents we know today.

continental drift the hypothesis that states that the continents once formed a single landmass, broke up, and drifted to their present locations

Sea-Floor Spreading

When Wegener put forth his hypothesis of continental drift, many scientists would not accept his hypothesis. From the calculated strength of the rocks, it did not seem possible for the crust to move in this way. During Wegener's life, no one knew the answer. It wasn't until many years later that evidence provided some clues to the forces that moved the continents.

Figure 3 Sea-Floor Spreading

Sea-floor spreading creates new oceanic lithosphere at mid-ocean ridges.

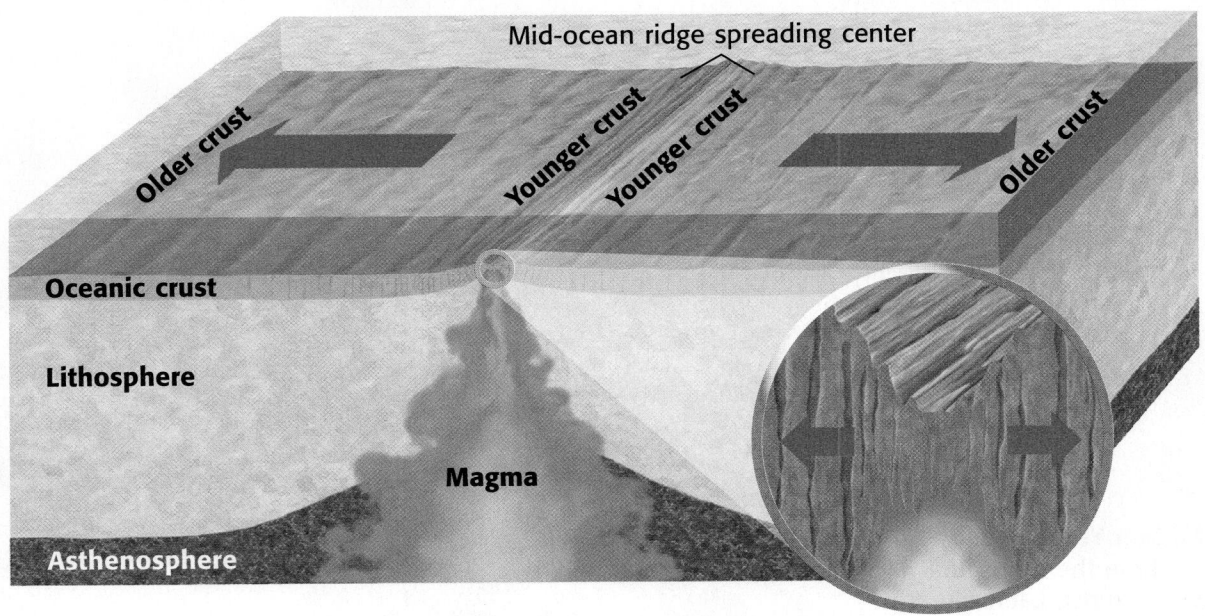

Mid-Ocean Ridges and Sea-Floor Spreading

A chain of submerged mountains runs through the center of the Atlantic Ocean. The chain is part of a worldwide system of mid-ocean ridges. Mid-ocean ridges are underwater mountain chains that run through Earth's ocean basins.

Mid-ocean ridges are places where sea-floor spreading takes place. **Sea-floor spreading** is the process by which new oceanic lithosphere forms as magma rises toward the surface and solidifies. As the tectonic plates move away from each other, the sea floor spreads apart and magma fills in the gap. As this new crust forms, the older crust gets pushed away from the mid-ocean ridge. As **Figure 3** shows, the older crust is farther away from the mid-ocean ridge than the younger crust is.

sea-floor spreading the process by which new oceanic lithosphere forms as magma rises toward the surface and solidifies

Evidence for Sea-Floor Spreading: Magnetic Reversals

Some of the most important evidence of sea-floor spreading comes from magnetic reversals recorded in the ocean floor. Throughout Earth's history, the north and south magnetic poles have changed places many times. When the poles change places, the polarity of Earth's magnetic poles changes, as shown in **Figure 4.** When Earth's magnetic poles change places, this change is called a *magnetic reversal.*

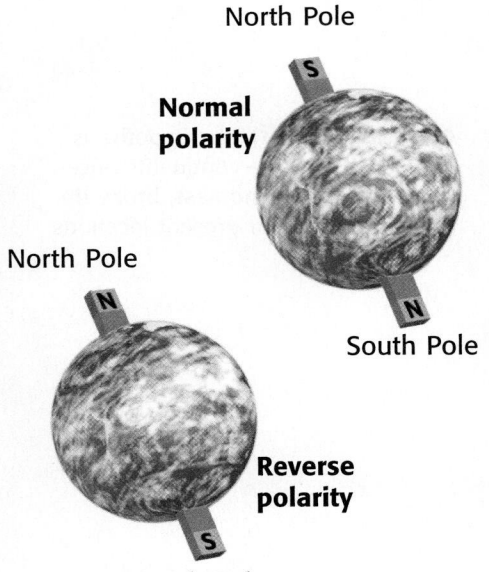

Figure 4 *The polarity of Earth's magnetic field changes over time.*

Magnetic Reversals and Sea-Floor Spreading

The molten rock at the mid-ocean ridges contains tiny grains of magnetic minerals. These mineral grains contain iron and are like compasses. They align with the magnetic field of the Earth. When the molten rock cools, the record of these tiny compasses remains in the rock. This record is then carried slowly away from the spreading center of the ridge as sea-floor spreading occurs.

As you can see in **Figure 5,** when the Earth's magnetic field reverses, the magnetic mineral grains align in the opposite direction. The new rock records the direction of the Earth's magnetic field. As the sea floor spreads away from a mid-ocean ridge, it carries with it a record of magnetic reversals. This record of magnetic reversals was the final proof that sea-floor spreading does occur.

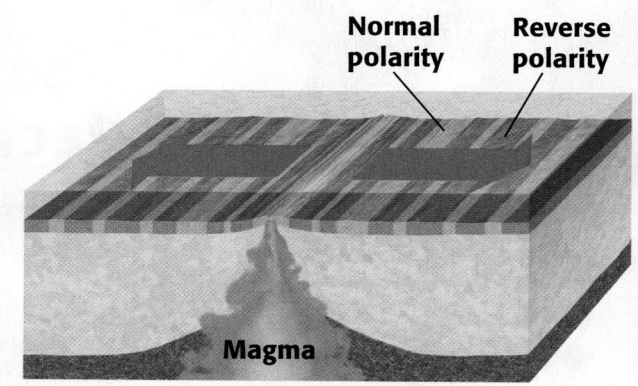

Normal polarity **Reverse polarity**

Magma

Figure 5 *Magnetic reversals in oceanic crust are shown as bands of light blue and dark blue oceanic crust. Light blue bands indicate normal polarity, and dark blue bands indicate reverse polarity.*

✓ **Reading Check** How is a record of magnetic reversals recorded in molten rock at mid-ocean ridges?

SECTION
Review

Summary

- Wegener hypothesized that continents drift apart from one another and have done so in the past.
- The process by which new oceanic lithosphere forms at mid-ocean ridges is called sea-floor spreading.
- As tectonic plates separate, the sea floor spreads apart and magma fills in the gap.
- Magnetic reversals are recorded over time in oceanic crust.

Using Key Terms

1. In your own words, write a definition for each of the following terms: *continental drift* and *sea-floor spreading*.

Understanding Key Ideas

2. At mid-ocean ridges,
   a. the crust is older.
   b. sea-floor spreading occurs.
   c. oceanic lithosphere is destroyed.
   d. tectonic plates are colliding.

3. Explain how oceanic lithosphere forms at mid-ocean ridges.

4. What is magnetic reversal?

Math Skills

5. If a piece of sea floor has moved 50 km in 5 million years, what is the yearly rate of sea-floor motion?

Critical Thinking

6. **Identifying Relationships** Explain how magnetic reversals provide evidence for sea-floor spreading.

7. **Applying Concepts** Why do bands indicating magnetic reversals appear to be of similar width on both sides of a mid-ocean ridge?

8. **Applying Concepts** Why do you think that old rocks are rare on the ocean floor?

SCILINKS.

NSTA
Developed and maintained by the National Science Teachers Association

For a variety of links related to this chapter, go to www.scilinks.org

Topic: Tectonic Plates
SciLinks code: HSM1497

The Theory of Plate Tectonics

It takes an incredible amount of force to move a tectonic plate! But where does this force come from?

As scientists' understanding of mid-ocean ridges and magnetic reversals grew, scientists formed a theory to explain how tectonic plates move. **Plate tectonics** is the theory that the Earth's lithosphere is divided into tectonic plates that move around on top of the asthenosphere. In this section, you will learn what causes tectonic plates to move. But first you will learn about the different types of tectonic plate boundaries.

Tectonic Plate Boundaries

A boundary is a place where tectonic plates touch. All tectonic plates share boundaries with other tectonic plates. These boundaries are divided into three types: convergent, divergent, and transform. The type of boundary depends on how the tectonic plates move relative to one another. Tectonic plates can collide, separate, or slide past each other. Earthquakes can occur at all three types of plate boundaries. The figure below shows examples of tectonic plate boundaries.

READING WARM-UP

Objectives
- Describe the three types of tectonic plate boundaries.
- Describe the three forces thought to move tectonic plates.
- Explain how scientists measure the rate at which tectonic plates move.

Terms to Learn

plate tectonics
convergent boundary
divergent boundary
transform boundary

READING STRATEGY

Brainstorming The key idea of this section is plate tectonics. Brainstorm words and phrases related to plate tectonics.

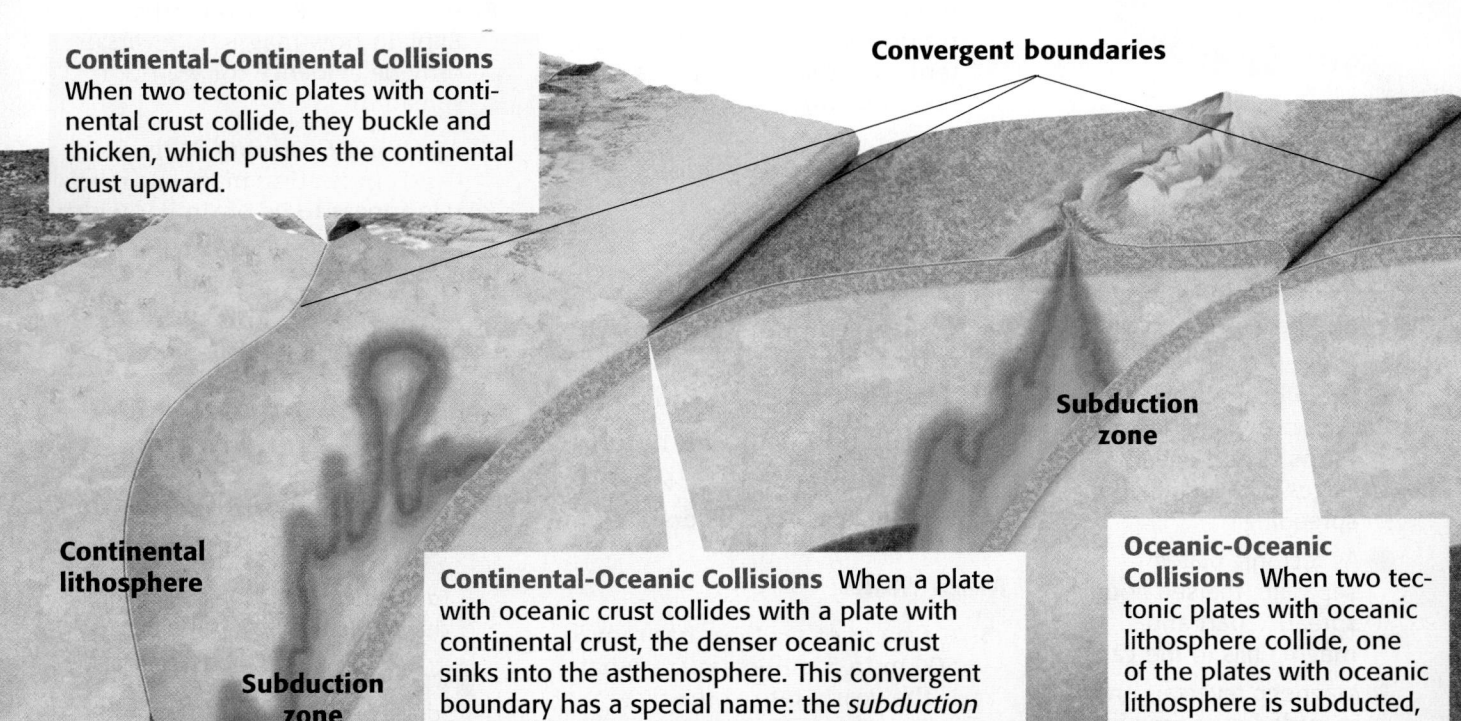

Continental-Continental Collisions
When two tectonic plates with continental crust collide, they buckle and thicken, which pushes the continental crust upward.

Convergent boundaries

Subduction zone

Continental lithosphere

Subduction zone

Continental-Oceanic Collisions When a plate with oceanic crust collides with a plate with continental crust, the denser oceanic crust sinks into the asthenosphere. This convergent boundary has a special name: the *subduction zone*. Old ocean crust gets pushed into the asthenosphere, where it is remelted and recycled.

Oceanic-Oceanic Collisions When two tectonic plates with oceanic lithosphere collide, one of the plates with oceanic lithosphere is subducted, or sinks, under the other plate.

Convergent Boundaries

When two tectonic plates collide, the boundary between them is a **convergent boundary.** What happens at a convergent boundary depends on the kind of crust at the leading edge of each tectonic plate. The three types of convergent boundaries are continental-continental boundaries, continental-oceanic boundaries, and oceanic-oceanic boundaries.

Divergent Boundaries

When two tectonic plates separate, the boundary between them is called a **divergent boundary.** New sea floor forms at divergent boundaries. Mid-ocean ridges are the most common type of divergent boundary.

Transform Boundaries

When two tectonic plates slide past each other horizontally, the boundary between them is a **transform boundary.** The San Andreas Fault in California is a good example of a transform boundary. This fault marks the place where the Pacific and North American plates are sliding past each other.

✓ **Reading Check** Define the term *transform boundary.* (*See the Appendix for answers to Reading Checks.*)

plate tectonics the theory that explains how large pieces of the Earth's outermost layer, called *tectonic plates,* move and change shape

convergent boundary the boundary formed by the collision of two lithospheric plates

divergent boundary the boundary between two tectonic plates that are moving away from each other

transform boundary the boundary between tectonic plates that are sliding past each other horizontally

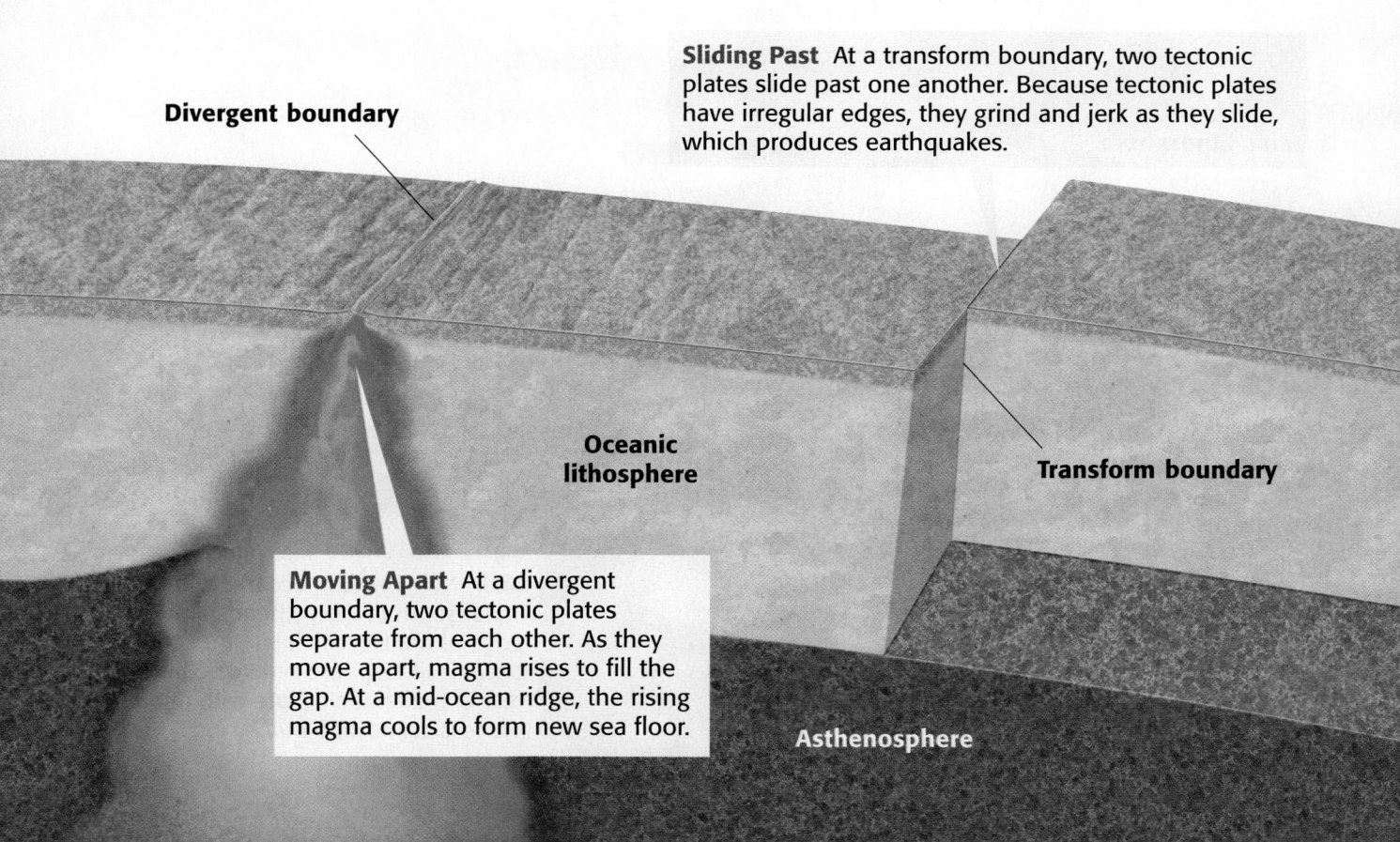

Divergent boundary

Sliding Past At a transform boundary, two tectonic plates slide past one another. Because tectonic plates have irregular edges, they grind and jerk as they slide, which produces earthquakes.

Oceanic lithosphere

Transform boundary

Moving Apart At a divergent boundary, two tectonic plates separate from each other. As they move apart, magma rises to fill the gap. At a mid-ocean ridge, the rising magma cools to form new sea floor.

Asthenosphere

Possible Causes of Tectonic Plate Motion

You have learned that plate tectonics is the theory that the lithosphere is divided into tectonic plates that move around on top of the asthenosphere. What causes the motion of tectonic plates? Remember that the solid rock of the asthenosphere flows very slowly. This movement occurs because of changes in density within the asthenosphere. These density changes are caused by the outward flow of thermal energy from deep within the Earth. When rock is heated, it expands, becomes less dense, and tends to rise to the surface of the Earth. As the rock gets near the surface, the rock cools, becomes more dense, and tends to sink. **Figure 1** shows three possible causes of tectonic plate motion.

✓ **Reading Check** What causes changes in density in the asthenosphere?

Figure 1 **Three Possible Driving Forces of Plate Tectonics**

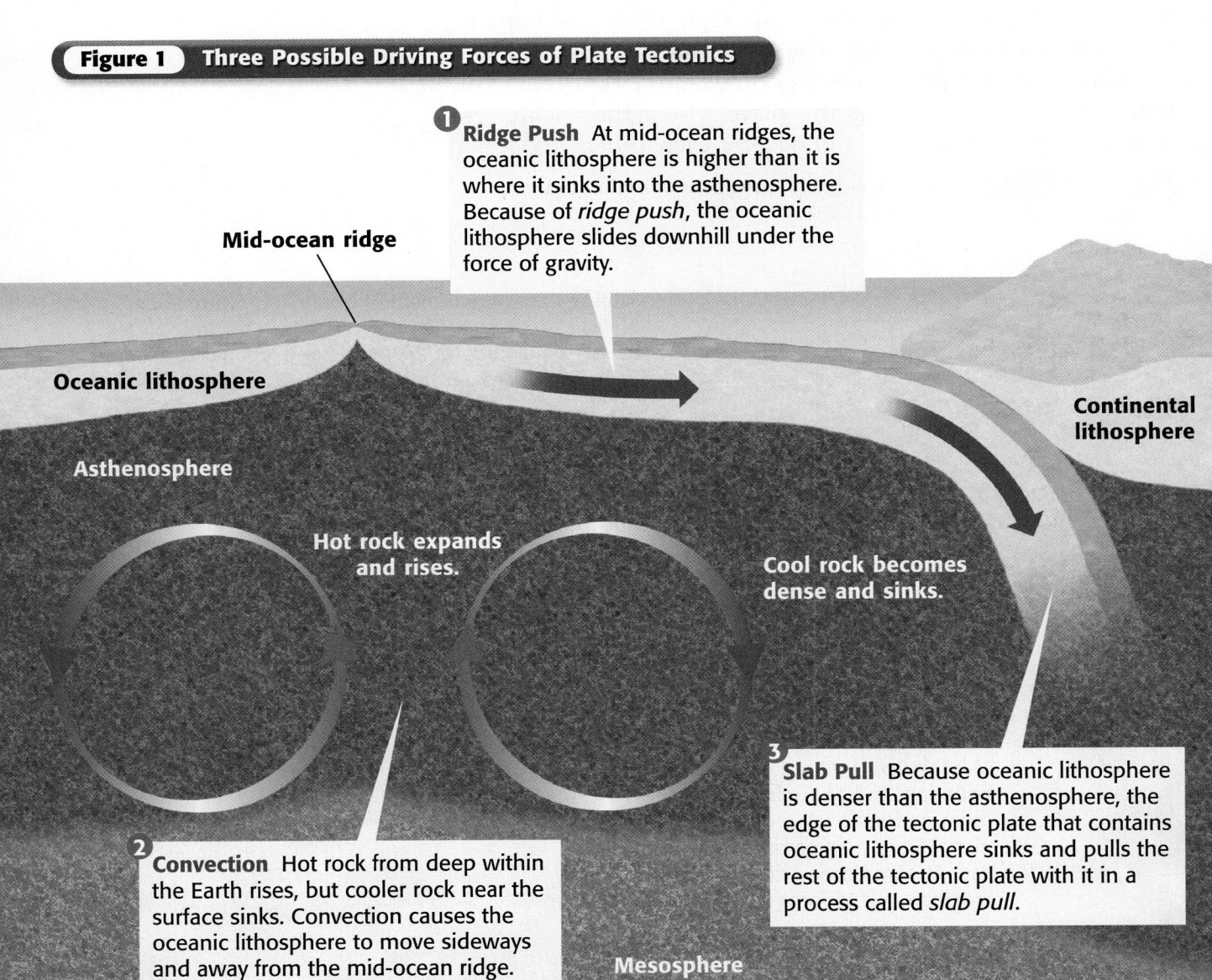

1 Ridge Push At mid-ocean ridges, the oceanic lithosphere is higher than it is where it sinks into the asthenosphere. Because of *ridge push*, the oceanic lithosphere slides downhill under the force of gravity.

Mid-ocean ridge

Oceanic lithosphere

Asthenosphere

Continental lithosphere

Hot rock expands and rises.

Cool rock becomes dense and sinks.

3 Slab Pull Because oceanic lithosphere is denser than the asthenosphere, the edge of the tectonic plate that contains oceanic lithosphere sinks and pulls the rest of the tectonic plate with it in a process called *slab pull*.

2 Convection Hot rock from deep within the Earth rises, but cooler rock near the surface sinks. Convection causes the oceanic lithosphere to move sideways and away from the mid-ocean ridge.

Mesosphere

Tracking Tectonic Plate Motion

How fast do tectonic plates move? The answer to this question depends on many factors, such as the type and shape of the tectonic plate and the way that the tectonic plate interacts with the tectonic plates that surround it. Tectonic plate movements are so slow and gradual that you can't see or feel them—the movement is measured in centimeters per year.

The Global Positioning System

Scientists use a system of satellites called the *global positioning system* (GPS), shown in **Figure 2,** to measure the rate of tectonic plate movement. Radio signals are continuously beamed from satellites to GPS ground stations, which record the exact distance between the satellites and the ground station. Over time, these distances change slightly. By recording the time it takes for the GPS ground stations to move a given distance, scientists can measure the speed at which each tectonic plate moves.

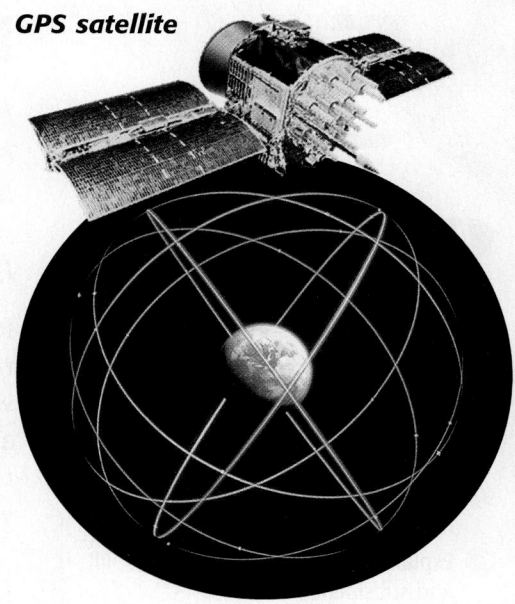

GPS satellite

Figure 2 *The image above shows the orbits of the GPS satellites.*

SECTION Review

Summary

- Boundaries between tectonic plates are classified as convergent, divergent, or transform.

- Ridge push, convection, and slab pull are three possible driving forces of plate tectonics.

- Scientists use data from a system of satellites called the global positioning system to measure the rate of motion of tectonic plates.

Using Key Terms

1. In your own words, write a definition for the term *plate tectonics*.

Understanding Key Ideas

2. The speed a tectonic plate moves per year is best measured in

   a. kilometers per year.

   b. centimeters per year.

   c. meters per year.

   d. millimeters per year.

3. Briefly describe three possible driving forces of tectonic plate movement.

4. Explain how scientists use GPS to measure the rate of tectonic plate movement.

Math Skills

5. If an orbiting satellite has a diameter of 60 cm, what is the total surface area of the satellite? (Hint: *surface area* = $4\pi r^2$)

Critical Thinking

6. **Identifying Relationships** When convection takes place in the mantle, why does cool rock material sink and warm rock material rise?

7. **Analyzing Processes** Why does oceanic crust sink beneath continental crust at convergent boundaries?

Developed and maintained by the National Science Teachers Association

For a variety of links related to this chapter, go to www.scilinks.org

Topic: Plate Tectonics
SciLinks code: HSM1171

Deforming the Earth's Crust

Have you ever tried to bend something, only to have it break? Take long, uncooked pieces of spaghetti, and bend them very slowly but only a little. Now, bend them again, but this time, bend them much farther and faster. What happened?

How can a material bend at one time and break at another time? The answer is that the stress you put on the material was different each time. *Stress* is the amount of force per unit area on a given material. The same principle applies to the rocks in the Earth's crust. Different things happen to rock when different types of stress are applied.

Deformation

The process by which the shape of a rock changes because of stress is called *deformation*. In the example above, the spaghetti deformed in two different ways—by bending and by breaking. **Figure 1** illustrates this concept. The same thing happens in rock layers. Rock layers bend when stress is placed on them. But when enough stress is placed on rocks, they can reach their elastic limit and break.

Compression and Tension

The type of stress that occurs when an object is squeezed, such as when two tectonic plates collide, is called **compression.** When compression occurs at a convergent boundary, large mountain ranges can form.

Another form of stress is *tension*. **Tension** is stress that occurs when forces act to stretch an object. As you might guess, tension occurs at divergent plate boundaries, such as mid-ocean ridges, when two tectonic plates pull away from each other.

✓ **Reading Check** How do the forces of plate tectonics cause rock to deform? (*See the Appendix for answers to Reading Checks.*)

READING WARM-UP

Objectives

● Describe two types of stress that deform rocks.

● Describe three major types of folds.

● Explain the differences between the three major types of faults.

● Identify the most common types of mountains.

● Explain the difference between uplift and subsidence.

Terms to Learn

compression   fault
tension   uplift
folding   subsidence

READING STRATEGY

Discussion Read this section silently. Write down questions that you have about this section. Discuss your questions in a small group.

 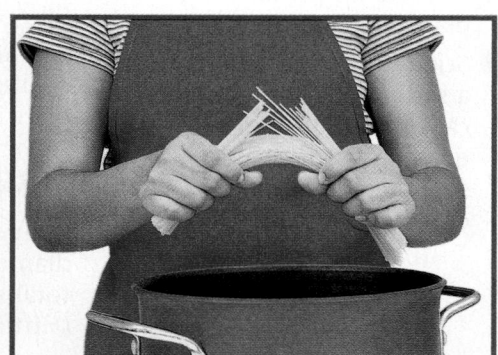

Figure 1 *When a small amount of stress is placed on uncooked spaghetti, the spaghetti bends. Additional stress causes the spaghetti to break.*

Figure 2 Folding: When Rock Layers Bend Because of Stress

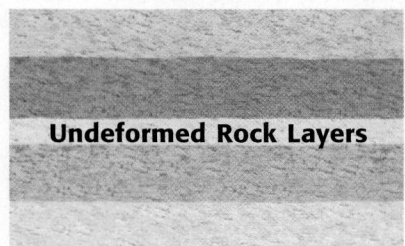
Unstressed

Undeformed Rock Layers

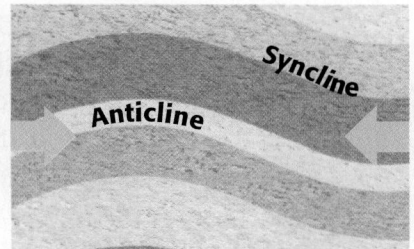
Horizontal stress

Syncline

Anticline

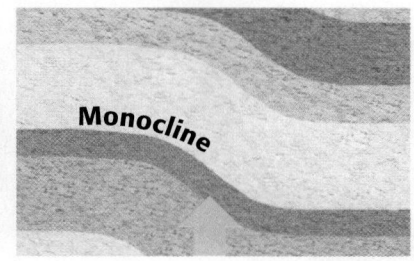
Vertical stress

Monocline

Folding

The bending of rock layers because of stress in the Earth's crust is called **folding.** Scientists assume that all rock layers started as horizontal layers. So, when scientists see a fold, they know that deformation has taken place.

Types of Folds

Depending on how the rock layers deform, different types of folds are made. **Figure 2** shows the two most common types of folds—*anticlines*, or upward-arching folds, and *synclines,* downward, troughlike folds. Another type of fold is a *monocline.* In a monocline, rock layers are folded so that both ends of the fold are horizontal. Imagine taking a stack of paper and laying it on a table. Think of the sheets of paper as different rock layers. Now put a book under one end of the stack. You can see that both ends of the sheets are horizontal, but all of the sheets are bent in the middle.

Folds can be large or small. The largest folds are measured in kilometers. Other folds are also obvious but are much smaller. These small folds can be measured in centimeters. **Figure 3** shows examples of large and small folds.

compression stress that occurs when forces act to squeeze an object

tension stress that occurs when forces act to stretch an object

folding the bending of rock layers due to stress

Figure 3 *The large photo shows mountain-sized folds in the Rocky Mountains. The small photo shows a rock that has folds smaller than a penknife.*

Fault

Footwall

Hanging wall

Figure 4 *The position of a fault block determines whether it is a hanging wall or a footwall.*

fault a break in a body of rock along which one block slides relative to another

Faulting

Some rock layers break when stress is applied to them. The surface along which rocks break and slide past each other is called a **fault.** The blocks of crust on each side of the fault are called *fault blocks*.

When a fault is not vertical, understanding the difference between its two sides—the *hanging wall* and the *footwall*—is useful. **Figure 4** shows the difference between a hanging wall and a footwall. Two main types of faults can form. The type of fault that forms depends on how the hanging wall and footwall move in relationship to each other.

Normal Faults

A *normal fault* is shown in **Figure 5.** When a normal fault moves, it causes the hanging wall to move down relative to the footwall. Normal faults usually occur when tectonic forces cause tension that pulls rocks apart.

Reverse Faults

A *reverse fault* is shown in **Figure 5.** When a reverse fault moves, it causes the hanging wall to move up relative to the footwall. This movement is the reverse of a normal fault. Reverse faults usually happen when tectonic forces cause compression that pushes rocks together.

✓ *Reading Check* How does the hanging wall in a normal fault move in relation to a reverse fault?

Figure 5 **Normal and Reverse Faults**

Normal Fault When rocks are pulled apart because of tension, normal faults often form.

Reverse Fault When rocks are pushed together by compression, reverse faults often form.

Figure 6 *The photo at left is a normal fault. The photo at right is a reverse fault.*

Telling the Difference Between Faults

It's easy to tell the difference between a normal fault and a reverse fault in drawings with arrows. But what types of faults are shown in **Figure 6**? You can certainly see the faults, but which one is a normal fault, and which one is a reverse fault? In the top left photo in **Figure 6,** one side has obviously moved relative to the other side. You can tell this fault is a normal fault by looking at the order of sedimentary rock layers. If you compare the two dark layers near the surface, you can see that the hanging wall has moved down relative to the footwall.

Strike-Slip Faults

A third major type of fault is called a *strike-slip fault.* An illustration of a strike-slip fault is shown in **Figure 7.** *Strike-slip faults* form when opposing forces cause rock to break and move horizontally. If you were standing on one side of a strike-slip fault looking across the fault when it moved, the ground on the other side would appear to move to your left or right. The San Andreas Fault in California is a spectacular example of a strike-slip fault.

Quick Lab

Modeling Strike-Slip Faults

1. Use **modeling clay** to construct a box that is 6 in. × 6 in. × 4 in. Use different colors of clay to represent different horizontal layers.

2. Using **scissors,** cut the box down the middle. Place **two 4 in. × 6 in. index cards** inside the cut so that the two sides of the box slide freely.

3. Using gentle pressure, slide the two sides horizontally past one another.

4. How does this model illustrate the motion that occurs along a strike-slip fault?

Figure 7 *When rocks are moved horizontally by opposing forces, strike-slip faults often form.*

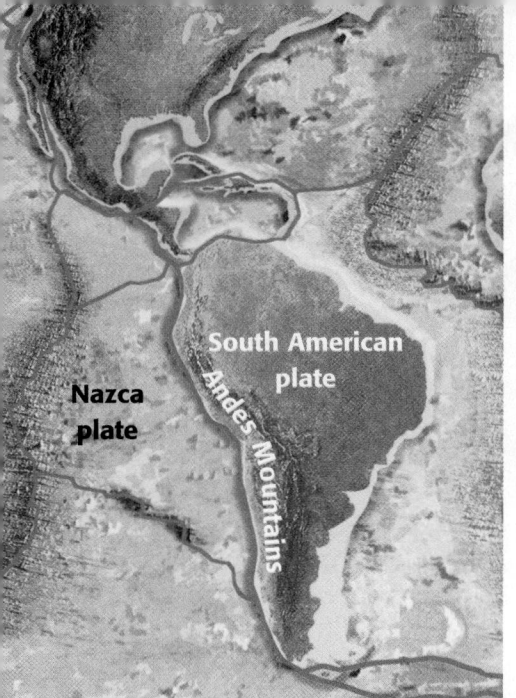

Figure 8 *The Andes Mountains formed on the edge of the South American plate where it converges with the Nazca plate.*

Plate Tectonics and Mountain Building

You have just learned about several ways the Earth's crust changes because of the forces of plate tectonics. When tectonic plates collide, land features that start as folds and faults can eventually become large mountain ranges. Mountains exist because tectonic plates are continually moving around and colliding with one another. As shown in **Figure 8,** the Andes Mountains formed above the subduction zone where two tectonic plates converge.

When tectonic plates undergo compression or tension, they can form mountains in several ways. Take a look at three of the most common types of mountains—folded mountains, fault-block mountains, and volcanic mountains.

Folded Mountains

The highest mountain ranges in the world are made up of folded mountains. These ranges form at convergent boundaries where continents have collided. *Folded mountains* form when rock layers are squeezed together and pushed upward. If you place a pile of paper on a table and push on opposite edges of the pile, you will see how folded mountains form.

An example of a folded mountain range that formed at a convergent boundary is shown in **Figure 9.** About 390 million years ago, the Appalachian Mountains formed when the landmasses that are now North America and Africa collided. Other examples of mountain ranges that consist of very large and complex folds are the Alps in central Europe, the Ural Mountains in Russia, and the Himalayas in Asia.

Reading Check Explain how folded mountains form.

Figure 9 *The Appalachian Mountains were once as tall as the Himalaya Mountains but have been worn down by hundreds of millions of years of weathering and erosion.*

Figure 10 *When the crust is subjected to tension, the rock can break along a series of normal faults, which creates fault-block mountains.*

Fault-Block Mountains

When tectonic forces put enough tension on the Earth's crust, a large number of normal faults can result. *Fault-block mountains* form when this tension causes large blocks of the Earth's crust to drop down relative to other blocks. **Figure 10** shows one way that fault-block mountains form.

When sedimentary rock layers are tilted up by faulting, they can produce mountains that have sharp, jagged peaks. As shown in **Figure 11,** the Tetons in western Wyoming are a spectacular example of fault-block mountains.

Volcanic Mountains

Most of the world's major volcanic mountains are located at convergent boundaries where oceanic crust sinks into the asthenosphere at subduction zones. The rock that is melted in subduction zones forms magma, which rises to the Earth's surface and erupts to form *volcanic mountains.* Volcanic mountains can also form under the sea. Sometimes these mountains can rise above the ocean surface to become islands. The majority of tectonically active volcanic mountains on the Earth have formed around the tectonically active rim of the Pacific Ocean. The rim has become known as the *Ring of Fire.*

CONNECTION TO Social Studies

WRITING SKILL **The Naming of the Appalachian Mountains** How did the Appalachian Mountains get their name? It is believed that the Appalachian Mountains were named by Spanish explorers in North America during the 16th century. It is thought that the name was taken from a Native American tribe called *Appalachee,* who lived in northern Florida. Research other geological features in the United States, including mountains and rivers, whose names are of Native American origin. Write the results of your research in a short essay.

Figure 11 *The Tetons formed as a result of tectonic forces that stretched the Earth's crust and caused it to break in a series of normal faults.*

For another activity related to this chapter, go to **go.hrw.com** and type in the keyword **HZ5TECW.**

uplift the rising of regions of the Earth's crust to higher elevations

subsidence the sinking of regions of the Earth's crust to lower elevations

Uplift and Subsidence

Vertical movements in the crust are divided into two types—uplift and subsidence. The rising of regions of Earth's crust to higher elevations is called **uplift.** Rocks that are uplifted may or may not be highly deformed. The sinking of regions of Earth's crust to lower elevations is known as **subsidence** (suhb SIED'ns). Unlike some uplifted rocks, rocks that subside do not undergo much deformation.

Uplifting of Depressed Rocks

The formation of mountains is one type of uplift. Uplift can also occur when large areas of land rise without deforming. One way areas rise without deforming is a process known as *rebound*. When the crust rebounds, it slowly springs back to its previous elevation. Uplift often happens when a weight is removed from the crust.

Subsidence of Cooler Rocks

Rocks that are hot take up more space than cooler rocks. For example, the lithosphere is relatively hot at mid-ocean ridges. The farther the lithosphere is from the ridge, the cooler and denser the lithosphere becomes. Because the oceanic lithosphere now takes up less volume, the ocean floor subsides.

Tectonic Letdown

Subsidence can also occur when the lithosphere becomes stretched in rift zones. A *rift zone* is a set of deep cracks that forms between two tectonic plates that are pulling away from each other. As tectonic plates pull apart, stress between the plates causes a series of faults to form along the rift zone. As shown in **Figure 12,** the blocks of crust in the center of the rift zone subside.

Figure 12 *The East African Rift, from Ethiopia to Kenya, is part of a divergent boundary, but you can see how the crust has subsided relative to the blocks at the edge of the rift zone.*

SECTION Review

Summary

- Compression and tension are two forces of plate tectonics that can cause rock to deform.
- Folding occurs when rock layers bend because of stress.
- Faulting occurs when rock layers break because of stress and then move on either side of the break.
- Mountains are classified as either folded, fault-block, or volcanic depending on how they form.

- Mountain building is caused by the movement of tectonic plates. Folded mountains and volcanic mountains form at convergent boundaries. Fault-block mountains form at divergent boundaries.
- Uplift and subsidence are the two types of vertical movement in the Earth's crust. Uplift occurs when regions of the crust rise to higher elevations. Subsidence occurs when regions of the crust sink to lower elevations.

Using Key Terms

For each pair of key terms, explain how the meanings of the terms differ.

1. *compression* and *tension*

2. *uplift* and *subsidence*

Understanding Key Ideas

3. The type of fault in which the hanging wall moves up relative to the footwall is called a

   a. strike-slip fault.

   b. fault-block fault.

   c. normal fault.

   d. reverse fault.

4. Describe three types of folds.

5. Describe three types of faults.

6. Identify the most common types of mountains.

7. What is rebound?

8. What are rift zones, and how do they form?

Critical Thinking

9. **Predicting Consequences** If a fault occurs in an area where rock layers have been folded, which type of fault is it likely to be? Why?

10. **Identifying Relationships** Would you expect to see a folded mountain range at a mid-ocean ridge? Explain your answer.

Interpreting Graphics

Use the diagram below to answer the questions that follow.

11. What type of fault is shown in the diagram?

12. At what kind of tectonic boundary would you most likely find this fault?

SCiLINKS

NSTA
Developed and maintained by the
National Science Teachers Association

For a variety of links related to this chapter, go to www.scilinks.org

Topic: Faults; Mountain Building
SciLinks code: HSM0566; HSM0999

Model-Making Lab

Convection Connection

Some scientists think that convection currents within the Earth's mantle cause tectonic plates to move. Because these convection currents cannot be observed directly, scientists use models to simulate the process. In this activity, you will make your own model to simulate tectonic plate movement.

OBJECTIVES

Model convection currents to simulate plate tectonic movement.

Draw conclusions about the role of convection in plate tectonics.

MATERIALS

- craft sticks (2)
- food coloring
- gloves, heat-resistant
- hot plates, small (2)
- pan, aluminum, rectangular
- pencil
- ruler, metric
- thermometers (3)
- water, cold
- wooden blocks

SAFETY

Ask a Question

1. How can I make a model of convection currents in the Earth's mantle?

Form a Hypothesis

2. Turn the question above into a statement in which you give your best guess about what factors will have the greatest effect on your convection model.

Test the Hypothesis

3. Place two hot plates side by side in the center of your lab table. Be sure that they are away from the edge of the table.

4. Place the pan on top of the hot plates. Slide the wooden blocks under the pan to support the ends. Make sure that the pan is level and secure.

5. Fill the pan with cold water. The water should be at least 4 cm deep. Turn on the hot plates, and put on your gloves.

6. After a minute or two, tiny bubbles will begin to rise in the water above the hot plates. Gently place two craft sticks on the water's surface.

7. Use the pencil to align the sticks parallel to the short ends of the pan. The sticks should be about 3 cm apart and near the center of the pan.

8. As soon as the sticks begin to move, place a drop of food coloring in the center of the pan. Observe what happens to the food coloring.

9. With the help of a partner, hold one thermometer bulb just under the water at the center of the pan. Hold the other two thermometers just under the water near the ends of the pan. Record the temperatures.

10. When you are finished, turn off the hot plates. After the water has cooled, carefully empty the water into a sink.

Analyze the Results

1. **Explaining Events** Based on your observations of the motion of the food coloring, how does the temperature of the water affect the direction in which the craft sticks move?

Draw Conclusions

2. **Drawing Conclusions** How does the motion of the craft sticks relate to the motion of the water?

3. **Applying Conclusions** How does this model relate to plate tectonics and the movement of the continents?

4. **Applying Conclusions** Based on your observations, what can you conclude about the role of convection in plate tectonics?

Applying Your Data

Suggest a substance other than water that might be used to model convection in the mantle. Consider using a substance that flows more slowly than water.

Chapter Review

USING KEY TERMS

1 Use the following terms in the same sentence: *crust, mantle,* and *core*.

Complete each of the following sentences by choosing the correct term from the word bank.

asthenosphere   uplift
tension   continental drift

2 The hypothesis that continents can drift apart and have done so in the past is known as ___.

3 The ___ is the soft layer of the mantle on which the tectonic plates move.

4 ___ is stress that occurs when forces act to stretch an object.

5 The rising of regions of the Earth's crust to higher elevations is called ___.

UNDERSTANDING KEY IDEAS

Multiple Choice

6 The strong, lower part of the mantle is a physical layer called the

a. lithosphere.

b. mesosphere.

c. asthenosphere.

d. outer core.

7 The type of tectonic plate boundary that forms from a collision between two tectonic plates is a

a. divergent plate boundary.

b. transform plate boundary.

c. convergent plate boundary.

d. normal plate boundary.

8 The bending of rock layers due to stress in the Earth's crust is known as

a. uplift.

b. folding.

c. faulting.

d. subsidence.

9 The type of fault in which the hanging wall moves up relative to the footwall is called a

a. strike-slip fault.

b. fault-block fault.

c. normal fault.

d. reverse fault.

10 The type of mountain that forms when rock layers are squeezed together and pushed upward is the

a. folded mountain.

b. fault-block mountain.

c. volcanic mountain.

d. strike-slip mountain.

11 Scientists' knowledge of the Earth's interior has come primarily from

a. studying magnetic reversals in oceanic crust.

b. using a system of satellites called the *global positioning system*.

c. studying seismic waves generated by earthquakes.

d. studying the pattern of fossils on different continents.

Short Answer

12 Explain how scientists use seismic waves to map the Earth's interior.

13 How do magnetic reversals provide evidence of sea-floor spreading?

14 Explain how sea-floor spreading provides a way for continents to move.

15 Describe two types of stress that deform rock.

16 What is the global positioning system (GPS), and how does GPS allow scientists to measure the rate of motion of tectonic plates?

CRITICAL THINKING

17 **Concept Mapping** Use the following terms to create a concept map: *sea-floor spreading, convergent boundary, divergent boundary, subduction zone, transform boundary,* and *tectonic plates.*

18 **Applying Concepts** Why does oceanic lithosphere sink at subduction zones but not at mid-ocean ridges?

19 **Identifying Relationships** New tectonic material continually forms at divergent boundaries. Tectonic plate material is also continually destroyed in subduction zones at convergent boundaries. Do you think that the total amount of lithosphere formed on the Earth is about equal to the amount destroyed? Why?

20 **Applying Concepts** Folded mountains usually form at the edge of a tectonic plate. How can you explain folded mountain ranges located in the middle of a tectonic plate?

INTERPRETING GRAPHICS

Imagine that you could travel to the center of the Earth. Use the diagram below to answer the questions that follow.

Composition	Structure
Crust (50 km)	Lithosphere (150 km)
Mantle (2,900 km)	Asthenosphere (250 km)
	Mesosphere (2,550 km)
Core (3,430 km)	Outer core (2,200 km)
	Inner core (1,228 km)

21 How far beneath the Earth's surface would you have to go before you were no longer passing through rock that had the composition of granite?

22 How far beneath the Earth's surface would you have to go to find liquid material in the Earth's core?

23 At what depth would you find mantle material but still be within the lithosphere?

24 How far beneath the Earth's surface would you have to go to find solid iron and nickel in the Earth's core?

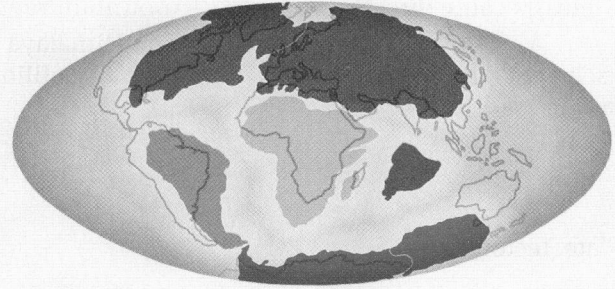

Standardized Test Preparation

Read each of the passages below. Then, answer the questions that follow each passage.

Passage 1 The Deep Sea Drilling Project was a program to retrieve and research rocks below the ocean to test the hypothesis of sea-floor spreading. For 15 years, scientists studying sea-floor spreading <u>conducted</u> research aboard the ship *Glomar Challenger*. Holes were drilled in the sea floor from the ship. Long, cylindrical lengths of rock, called *cores,* were obtained from the drill holes. By examining fossils in the cores, scientists discovered that rock closest to mid-ocean ridges was the youngest. The farther from the ridge the holes were drilled, the older the rock in the cores was. This evidence supported the idea that sea-floor spreading creates new lithosphere at mid-ocean ridges.

1. In the passage, what does *conducted* mean?
- **A** directed
- **B** led
- **C** carried on
- **D** guided

2. Why were cores drilled in the sea floor from the *Glomar Challenger*?
- **F** to determine the depth of the crust
- **G** to find minerals in the sea-floor rock
- **H** to examine fossils in the sea-floor rock
- **I** to find oil and gas in the sea-floor rock

3. Which of the following statements is a fact according to the passage?
- **A** Rock closest to mid-ocean ridges is older than rock at a distance from mid-ocean ridges.
- **B** One purpose of scientific research on the *Glomar Challenger* was to gather evidence for sea-floor spreading.
- **C** Fossils examined by scientists came directly from the sea floor.
- **D** Evidence gathered by scientists did not support sea-floor spreading.

Passage 2 The Himalayas are a range of mountains that is 2,400 km long and that <u>arcs</u> across Pakistan, India, Tibet, Nepal, Sikkim, and Bhutan. The Himalayas are the highest mountains on Earth. Nine mountains, including Mount Everest, the highest mountain on Earth, are more than 8,000 m tall. The formation of the Himalaya Mountains began about 80 million years ago. A tectonic plate carrying the Indian subcontinent collided with the Eurasian plate. The Indian plate was driven beneath the Eurasian plate. This collision caused the uplift of the Eurasian plate and the formation of the Himalayas. This process is continuing today.

1. In the passage, what does the word *arcs* mean?
- **A** forms a circle
- **B** forms a plane
- **C** forms a curve
- **D** forms a straight line

2. According to the passage, which geologic process formed the Himalaya Mountains?
- **F** divergence
- **G** subsidence
- **H** strike-slip faulting
- **I** convergence

3. Which of the following statements is a fact according to the passage?
- **A** The nine tallest mountains on Earth are located in the Himalaya Mountains.
- **B** The Himalaya Mountains are located within six countries.
- **C** The Himalaya Mountains are the longest mountain range on Earth.
- **D** The Himalaya Mountains formed more than 80 million years ago.

The illustration below shows the relative velocities (in centimeters per year) and directions in which tectonic plates are separating and colliding. Arrows that point away from one another indicate plate separation. Arrows that point toward one another indicate plate collision. Use the illustration below to answer the questions that follow.

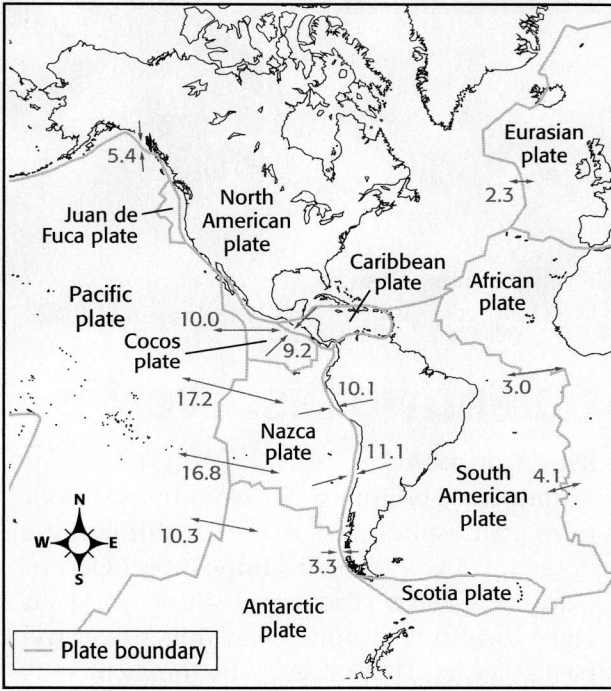

1. Between which two tectonic plates does spreading appear to be the fastest?

   A the Australian plate and the Pacific plate

   B the Antarctic plate and the Pacific plate

   C the Nazca plate and the Pacific plate

   D the Cocos plate and the Pacific plate

2. Where do you think mountain building is taking place?

   F between the African plate and the South American plate

   G between the Nazca plate and the South American plate

   H between the North American plate and the Eurasian plate

   I between the African plate and the North American plate

Read each question below, and choose the best answer.

1. The mesosphere is 2,550 km thick, and the asthenosphere is 250 km thick. If you assume that the lithosphere is 150 km thick and that the crust is 50 km thick, how thick is the mantle?

   A 2,950 km

   B 2,900 km

   C 2,800 km

   D 2,550 km

2. If a seismic wave travels through the mantle at an average velocity of 8 km/s, how many seconds will the wave take to travel through the mantle?

   F 318.75 s

   G 350.0 s

   H 362.5 s

   I 368.75 s

3. If the crust in a certain area is subsiding at the rate of 2 cm per year and has an elevation of 1,000 m, what elevation will the crust have in 10,000 years?

   A 500 m

   B 800 m

   C 1,200 m

   D 2,000 m

4. Assume that a very small oceanic plate is located between a mid-ocean ridge and a subduction zone. At the ridge, the plate is growing at a rate of 5 km every 1 million years. At the subduction zone, the plate is being destroyed at a rate of 10 km every 1 million years. If the oceanic plate is 100 km across, how long will it take the plate to disappear?

   F 100 million years

   G 50 million years

   H 20 million years

   I 5 million years

Standardized Test Preparation

Science in Action

Science, Technology, and Society

Using Satellites to Track Plate Motion

When you think of laser beams firing, you may think of science fiction movies. However, scientists use laser beams to determine the rate and direction of motion of tectonic plates. From ground stations on Earth, laser beams are fired at several small satellites orbiting 5,900 km above Earth. From the satellites, the laser beams are reflected back to ground stations. Differences in the time it takes signals to be reflected from targets are measured over a period of time. From these differences, scientists can determine the rate and direction of plate motion.

Social Studies ACTiViTY

WRITING SKILL Research a society that lives at an active plate boundary. Find out how the people live with dangers such as volcanoes and earthquakes. Include your findings in a short report.

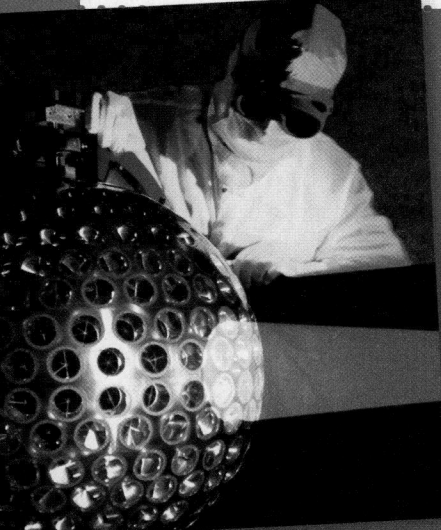

This scientist is using a laser to test one of the satellites that will be used to track plate motion.

Scientific Discoveries

Megaplumes

Eruptions of boiling water from the sea floor form giant, spiral disks that twist through the oceans. Do you think it's impossible? Oceanographers have discovered these disks at eight locations at mid-ocean ridges over the past 20 years. These disks, which may be tens of kilometers across, are called *megaplumes*. Megaplumes are like blenders. They mix hot water with cold water in the oceans. Megaplumes can rise hundreds of meters from the ocean floor to the upper layers of the ocean. They carry gases and minerals and provide extra energy and food to animals in the upper layers of the ocean.

Language Arts ACTiViTY

WRITING SKILL Did you ever wonder about the origin of the name *Himalaya*? Research the origin of the name *Himalaya*, and write a short report about what you find.

Alfred Wegener

Continental Drift Alfred Wegener's greatest contribution to science was the hypothesis of continental drift. This hypothesis states that continents drift apart from one another and have done so in the past. To support his hypothesis, Wegener used geologic, fossil, and glacial evidence gathered on both sides of the Atlantic Ocean. For example, Wegener recognized similarities between rock layers in North America and Europe and between rock layers in South America and Africa. He believed that these similarities could be explained only if these geologic features were once part of the same continent.

Although continental drift explained many of his observations, Wegener could not find scientific evidence to develop a complete explanation of how continents move. Most scientists were skeptical of Wegener's hypothesis and dismissed it as foolishness. It was not until the 1950s and 1960s that the discoveries of magnetic reversals and sea-floor spreading provided evidence of continental drift.

Math Activity

The distance between South America and Africa is 7,200 km. As new crust is created at the mid-ocean ridge, South America and Africa are moving away from each other at a rate of about 3.5 cm per year. How many millions of years ago were South America and Africa joined?

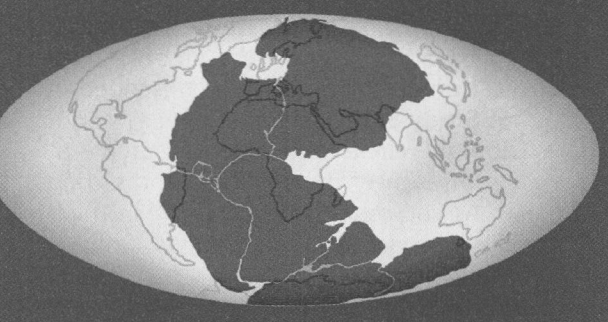

To learn more about these Science in Action topics, visit go.hrw.com and type in the keyword **HZ5TECF**.

Current Science

Check out Current Science® articles related to this chapter by visiting go.hrw.com. Just type in the keyword **HZ5CS07**.

Earthquakes

About the

On January 17, 1995, an earthquake of magnitude 7.0 shook the area in and around Kobe, Japan. Though the earthquake lasted for less than a minute, more than 5,000 people lost their lives and another 300,000 people were left homeless. More than 200,000 buildings were damaged or destroyed. Large sections of the elevated Hanshin Expressway, shown in the photo, toppled when the columns supporting the expressway failed. The expressway passed over ground that was soft and wet, where the shaking was stronger and longer lasting.

PRE-READING ACTIVITY

Graphic Organizer

Spider Map Before you read the chapter, create the graphic organizer entitled "Spider Map" described in the **Study Skills** section of the Appendix. Label the circle "Earthquakes." Create a leg for each of the sections in this chapter. As you read the chapter, fill in the map with details about the material presented in each section of the chapter.

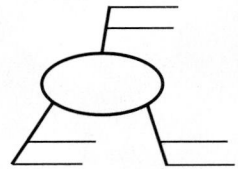

START-UP ACTIVITY

Bend, Break, or Shake

In this activity, you will test different materials in a model earthquake setting.

Procedure

1. Gather a **small wooden stick,** a **wire clothes hanger,** and a **plastic clothes hanger.**

2. Draw a straight line on a **sheet of paper.** Use a **protractor** to measure and draw the following angles from the line: 20°, 45°, and 90°.

3. Put on your **safety goggles.** Using the angles that you drew as a guide, try bending each item 20° and then releasing it. What happens? Does it break? If it bends, does it return to its original shape?

4. Repeat step 3, but bend each item 45°. Repeat the test again, but bend each item 90°.

Analysis

1. How do the different materials' responses to bending compare?

2. Where earthquakes happen, engineers use building materials that are flexible but that do not break or stay bent. Which materials from this experiment would you want building materials to behave like? Explain your answer.

What Are Earthquakes?

Have you ever felt the earth move under your feet? Many people have. Every day, somewhere within this planet, an earthquake is happening.

The word *earthquake* defines itself fairly well. But there is more to earthquakes than just the shaking of the ground. An entire branch of Earth science, called **seismology** (siez MAHL uh jee), is devoted to studying earthquakes. Earthquakes are complex, and they present many questions for *seismologists,* the scientists who study earthquakes.

Where Do Earthquakes Occur?

Most earthquakes take place near the edges of tectonic plates. *Tectonic plates* are giant pieces of Earth's thin, outermost layer. Tectonic plates move around on top of a layer of plastic rock. **Figure 1** shows the Earth's tectonic plates and the locations of recent major earthquakes.

Tectonic plates move in different directions and at different speeds. Two plates can push toward or pull away from each other. They can also slip slowly past each other. As a result of these movements, numerous features called faults exist in the Earth's crust. A *fault* is a break in the Earth's crust along which blocks of the crust slide relative to one another. Earthquakes occur along faults because of this sliding.

READING WARM-UP

Objectives

● Explain where earthquakes take place.

● Explain what causes earthquakes.

● Identify three different types of faults that occur at plate boundaries.

● Describe how energy from earthquakes travels through the Earth.

Terms to Learn

seismology   P waves
deformation   S waves
elastic rebound
seismic waves

READING STRATEGY

Paired Summarizing Read this section silently. In pairs, take turns summarizing the material. Stop to discuss ideas that seem confusing.

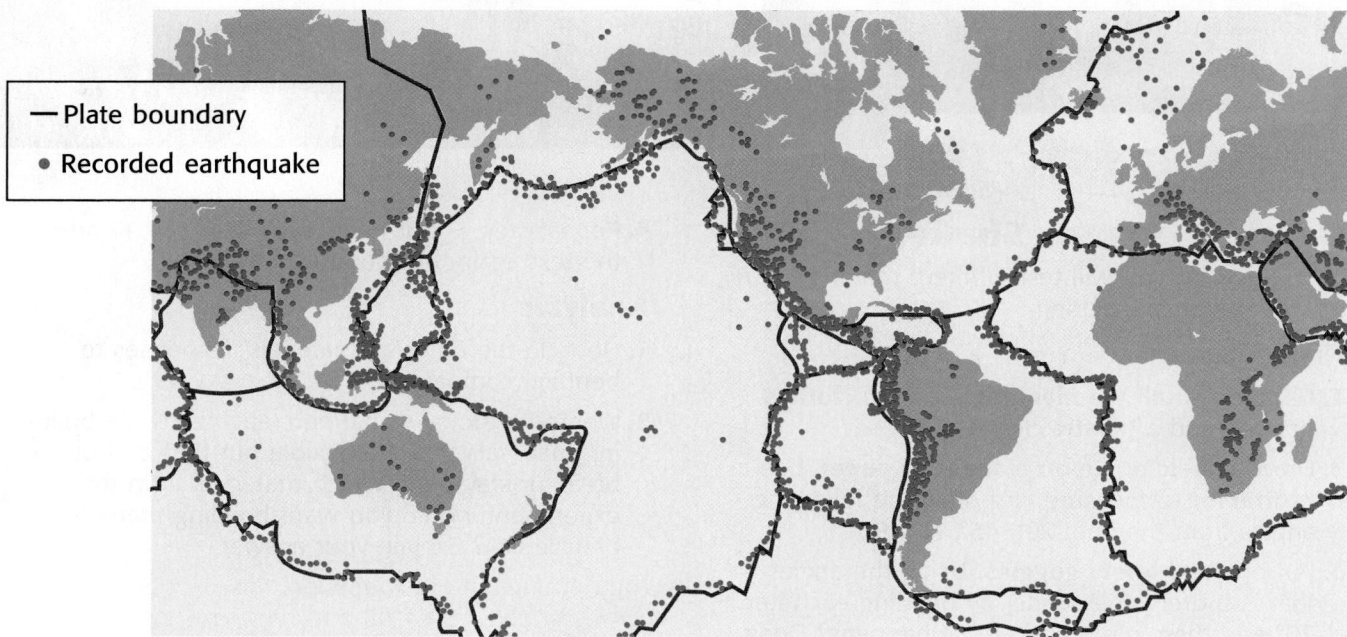

— Plate boundary
● Recorded earthquake

Figure 1 *The largest and most active earthquake zone lies along the plate boundaries surrounding the Pacific Ocean.*

What Causes Earthquakes?

As tectonic plates push, pull, or slip past each other, stress increases along faults near the plates' edges. In response to this stress, rock in the plates deforms. **Deformation** is the change in the shape of rock in response to stress. Rock along a fault deforms in mainly two ways. It deforms in a plastic manner, like a piece of molded clay, or in an elastic manner, like a rubber band. *Plastic deformation,* which is shown in **Figure 2,** does not lead to earthquakes.

Elastic deformation, however, does lead to earthquakes. Rock can stretch farther without breaking than steel can, but rock will break at some point. Think of elastically deformed rock as a stretched rubber band. You can stretch a rubber band only so far before it breaks. When the rubber band breaks, it releases energy. Then, the broken pieces return to their unstretched shape.

Figure 2 *This road cut is adjacent to the San Andreas Fault in southern California. The rocks in the cut have undergone deformation because of the continuous motion of the fault.*

Elastic Rebound

The sudden return of elastically deformed rock to its original shape is called **elastic rebound.** Elastic rebound is like the return of the broken rubber-band pieces to their unstretched shape. Elastic rebound occurs when more stress is applied to rock than the rock can withstand. During elastic rebound, energy is released. Some of this energy travels as seismic waves. These seismic waves cause an earthquake, as shown in **Figure 3.**

Reading Check How does elastic rebound relate to earthquakes? (*See the Appendix for answers to Reading Checks.*)

seismology the study of earthquakes

deformation the bending, tilting, and breaking of the Earth's crust; the change in the shape of rock in response to stress

elastic rebound the sudden return of elastically deformed rock to its undeformed shape

Figure 3 Elastic Rebound and Earthquakes

Before earthquake

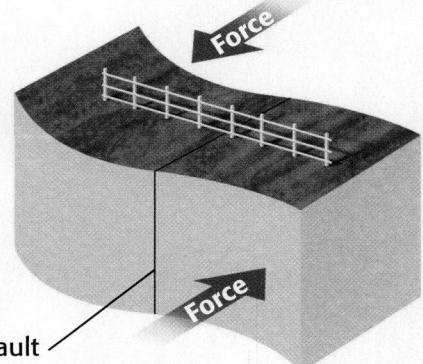

Fault

① Tectonic forces push rock on either side of the fault in opposite directions, but the rock is locked together and does not move. The rock deforms in an elastic manner.

After earthquake

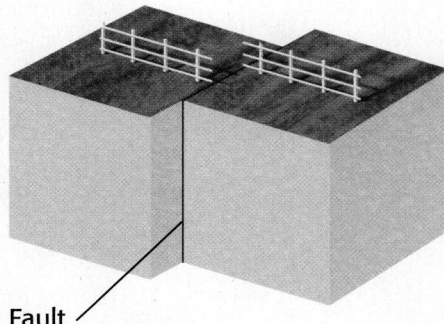

Fault

② When enough stress is applied, the rock slips along the fault and releases energy.

Faults at Tectonic Plate Boundaries

A specific type of plate motion takes place at different tectonic plate boundaries. Each type of motion creates a particular kind of fault that can produce earthquakes. Examine **Table 1** and the diagram below to learn more about plate motion.

Table 1 Plate Motion and Fault Types	
Plate motion	**Major fault type**
Transform	strike-slip fault
Convergent	reverse fault
Divergent	normal fault

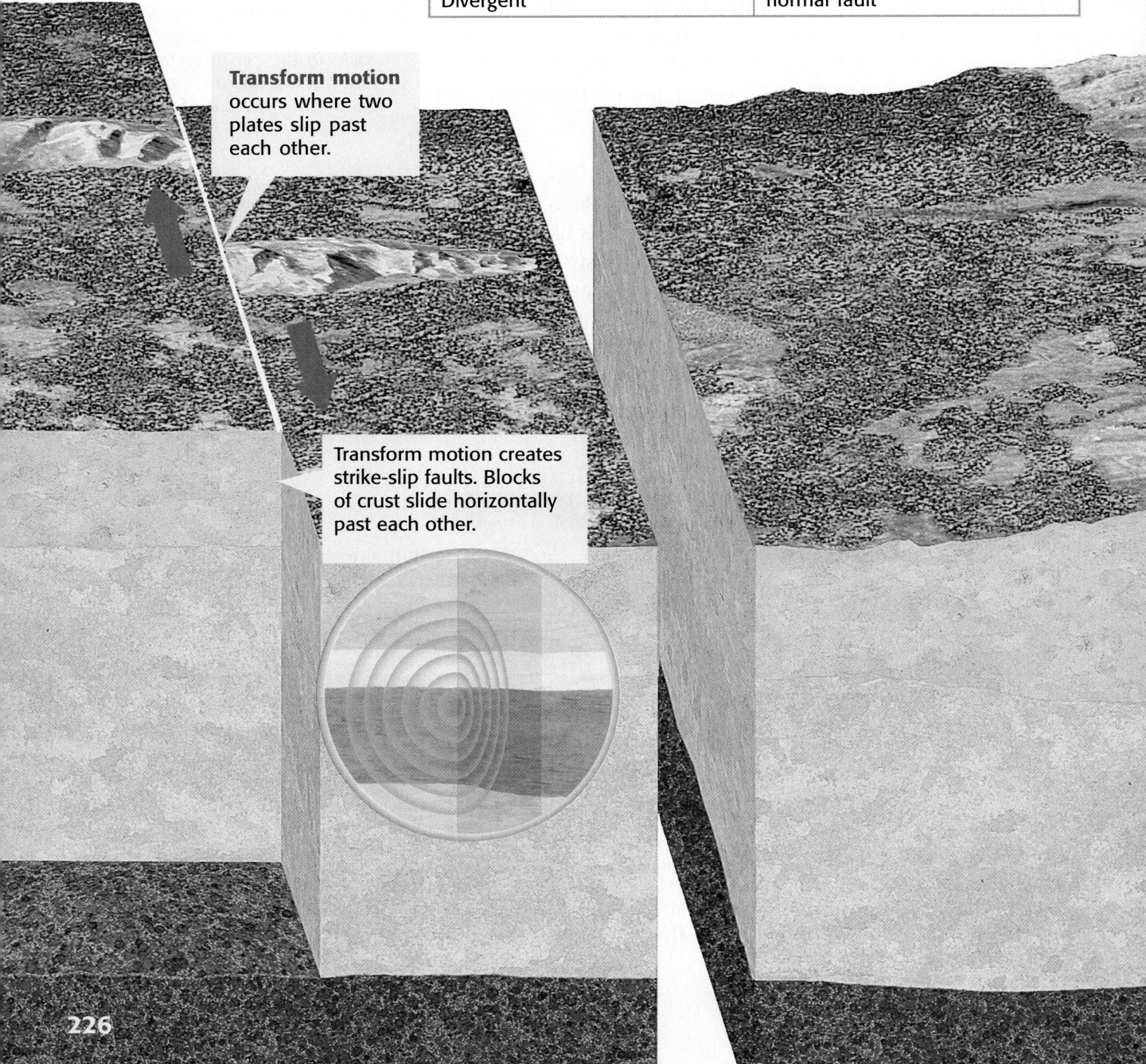

Transform motion occurs where two plates slip past each other.

Transform motion creates strike-slip faults. Blocks of crust slide horizontally past each other.

Earthquake Zones

Earthquakes can happen both near Earth's surface or far below it. Most earthquakes happen in the earthquake zones along tectonic plate boundaries. Earthquake zones are places where a large number of faults are located. The San Andreas Fault Zone in California is an example of an earthquake zone. But not all faults are located at tectonic plate boundaries. Sometimes, earthquakes happen along faults in the middle of tectonic plates.

✓ **Reading Check** Where are earthquake zones located?

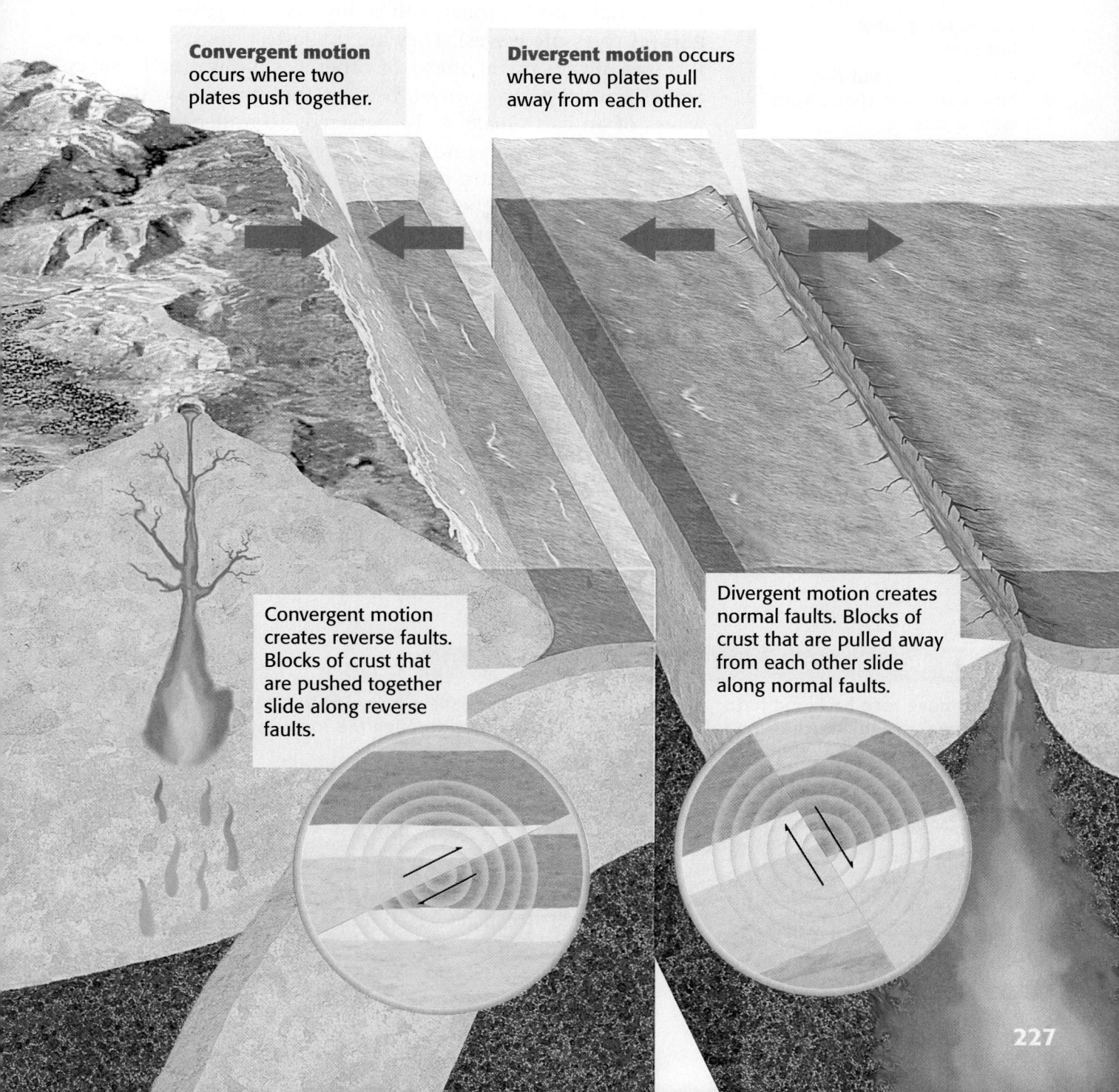

Convergent motion occurs where two plates push together.

Divergent motion occurs where two plates pull away from each other.

Convergent motion creates reverse faults. Blocks of crust that are pushed together slide along reverse faults.

Divergent motion creates normal faults. Blocks of crust that are pulled away from each other slide along normal faults.

Quick Lab

Modeling Seismic Waves

1. Stretch a **spring toy** lengthwise on a **table.**

2. Hold one end of the spring while a partner holds the other end. Push your end toward your partner's end, and observe what happens.

3. Repeat step 2, but this time shake the spring from side to side.

4. Which type of seismic wave is represented in step 2? in step 3?

---

seismic wave a wave of energy that travels through the Earth, away from an earthquake in all directions

P wave a seismic wave that causes particles of rock to move in a back-and-forth direction

S wave a seismic wave that causes particles of rock to move in a side-to-side direction

How Do Earthquake Waves Travel?

Waves of energy that travel through the Earth are called **seismic waves.** Seismic waves that travel through the Earth's interior are called *body waves*. There are two types of body waves: P waves and S waves. Seismic waves that travel along the Earth's surface are called *surface waves*. Each type of seismic wave travels through Earth's layers in a different way and at a different speed. Also, the speed of a seismic wave depends on the kind of material the wave travels through.

P Waves

Waves that travel through solids, liquids, and gases are called **P waves** (pressure waves). They are the fastest seismic waves, so P waves always travel ahead of other seismic waves. P waves are also called *primary waves,* because they are always the first waves of an earthquake to be detected. To understand how P waves affect rock, imagine a cube of gelatin sitting on a plate. Like most solids, gelatin is an elastic material. It wiggles if you tap it. Tapping the cube of gelatin changes the pressure inside the cube, which momentarily deforms the cube. The gelatin then reacts by springing back to its original shape. This process is how P waves affect rock, as shown in **Figure 4.**

S Waves

Rock can also be deformed from side to side. After being deformed from side to side, the rock springs back to its original position and S waves are created. **S waves,** or shear waves, are the second-fastest seismic waves. S waves shear rock side to side, as shown in **Figure 4,** which means they stretch the rock sideways. Unlike P waves, S waves cannot travel through parts of the Earth that are completely liquid. Also, S waves are slower than P waves and always arrive later. Thus, another name for S waves is *secondary waves.*

Figure 4 **Body Waves**

P waves move rock back and forth, which squeezes and stretches the rock, as they travel through the rock.

Direction of wave travel

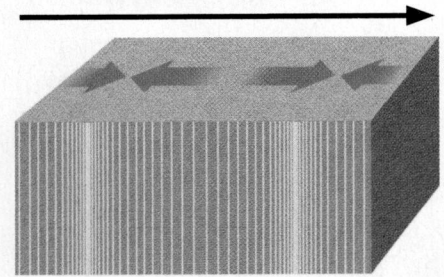

S waves shear rock side to side as they travel through the rock.

Direction of wave travel

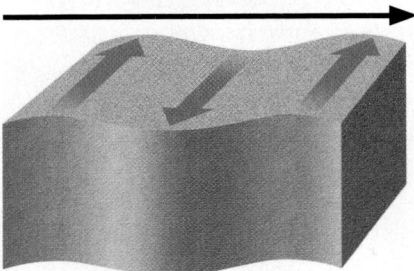

Surface Waves

Surface waves move along the Earth's surface and produce motion mostly in the upper few kilometers of Earth's crust. There are two types of surface waves. One type of surface wave produces motion up, down, and around, as shown in **Figure 5.** The other type produces back-and-forth motion like the motion produced by S waves. Surface waves are different from body waves in that surface waves travel more slowly and are more destructive.

Reading Check Explain the differences between surface waves and body waves.

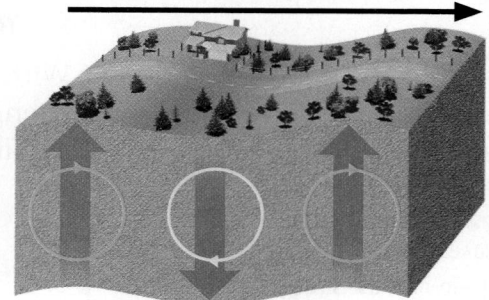

Figure 5   Surface Waves

Surface waves move the ground much like ocean waves move water particles.

Direction of wave travel

SECTION Review

Summary

- Earthquakes occur mainly near the edges of tectonic plates.

- Elastic rebound is the direct cause of earthquakes.

- Three major types of faults occur at tectonic plate boundaries: normal faults, reverse faults, and strike-slip faults.

- Earthquake energy travels as body waves through the Earth's interior or as surface waves along the surface of the Earth.

Using Key Terms

Complete each of the following sentences by choosing the correct term from the word bank.

Deformation	P waves
Elastic rebound	S waves

1. _____ is the change in shape of rock due to stress.

2. _____ always travel ahead of other waves.

Understanding Key Ideas

3. Seismic waves that shear rock side to side are called
   a. surface waves.
   b. S waves.
   c. P waves.
   d. Both (b) and (c)

4. Where do earthquakes occur?

5. What is the direct cause of earthquakes?

6. Describe the three types of plate motion and the faults that are characteristic of each type of motion.

7. What is an earthquake zone?

Math Skills

8. A seismic wave is traveling through the Earth at an average rate of speed of 8 km/s. How long will it take the wave to travel 480 km?

Critical Thinking

9. **Applying Concepts** Given what you know about elastic rebound, why do you think some earthquakes are stronger than others?

10. **Identifying Relationships** Why are surface waves more destructive to buildings than P waves or S waves are?

11. **Identifying Relationships** Why do you think the majority of earthquake zones are located at tectonic plate boundaries?

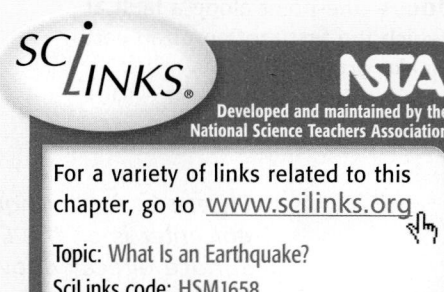

SCiLINKS.

NSTA

Developed and maintained by the
National Science Teachers Association

For a variety of links related to this chapter, go to www.scilinks.org

Topic: What Is an Earthquake?
SciLinks code: HSM1658

Earthquake Measurement

Imagine walls shaking, windows rattling, and glassware and dishes clinking and clanking. After only seconds, the vibrating stops and the sounds die away.

Within minutes, news reports give information about the strength, the time, and the location of the earthquake. You are amazed at how scientists could have learned this information so quickly.

READING WARM-UP

Objectives

- Explain how earthquakes are detected.
- Describe how to locate an earthquake's epicenter.
- Explain how the strength of an earthquake is measured.
- Explain how the intensity of an earthquake is measured.

Terms to Learn

seismograph   epicenter
seismogram   focus

READING STRATEGY

Reading Organizer As you read this section, create an outline of the section. Use the headings from the section in your outline.

seismograph an instrument that records vibrations in the ground and determines the location and strength of an earthquake

seismogram a tracing of earthquake motion that is created by a seismograph

epicenter the point on Earth's surface directly above an earthquake's starting point, or focus

focus the point along a fault at which the first motion of an earthquake occurs

Locating Earthquakes

How do seismologists know when and where earthquakes begin? They depend on earthquake-sensing instruments called seismographs. **Seismographs** are instruments located at or near the surface of the Earth that record seismic waves. When the waves reach a seismograph, the seismograph creates a seismogram. A **seismogram** is a tracing of earthquake motion and is created by a seismograph.

Determining Time and Location of Earthquakes

Seismologists use seismograms to calculate when an earthquake began. Seismologists find an earthquake's start time by comparing seismograms and noting the differences in arrival times of P waves and S waves. Seismologists also use seismograms to find an earthquake's epicenter. An **epicenter** is the point on the Earth's surface directly above an earthquake's starting point. A **focus** is the point inside the Earth where an earthquake begins. **Figure 1** shows the location of an earthquake's epicenter and its focus.

✓ *Reading Check* How do seismologists determine an earthquake's start time? (*See the Appendix for answers to Reading Checks.*)

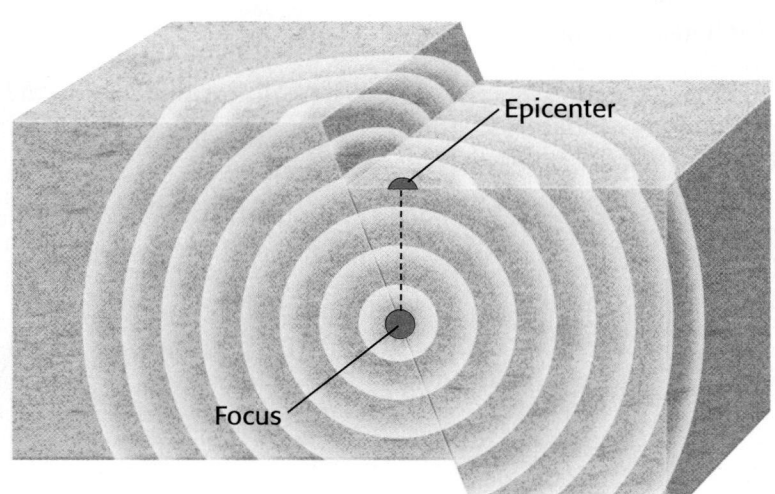

Epicenter

Focus

Figure 1 *An earthquake's epicenter is on the Earth's surface directly above the earthquake's focus.*

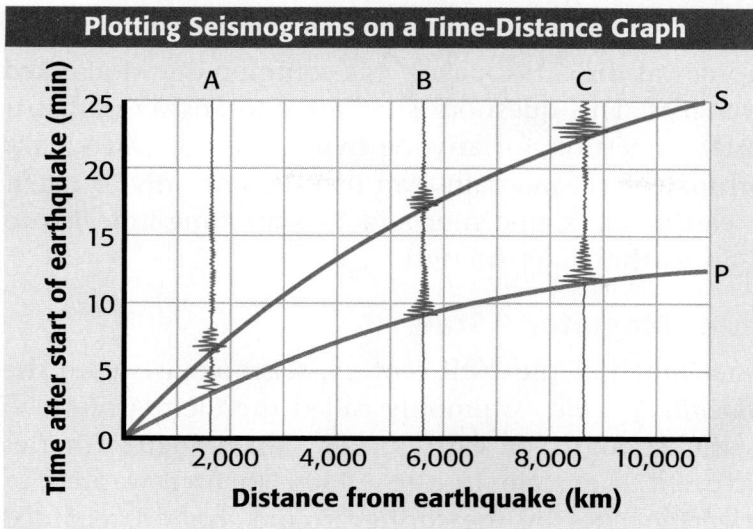

Plotting Seismograms on a Time-Distance Graph

A B C S

Time after start of earthquake (min)

25
20
15
10
5
0

2,000 4,000 6,000 8,000 10,000

P

Distance from earthquake (km)

Figure 2 *After identifying P and S waves, seismologists can use the time difference to determine an earthquake's start time and the distance from the epicenter to each station. The vertical axis tells how much time passed between the start of the earthquake and the arrival of seismic waves at a station. The horizontal axis tells the distance between a station and the earthquake's epicenter.*

The S-P Time Method

Perhaps the simplest method by which seismologists find an earthquake's epicenter is the *S-P time method*. The first step in this method is to collect several seismograms of the same earthquake from different locations. Then, the seismograms are placed on a time-distance graph. The seismogram tracing of the first P wave is lined up with the P-wave time-distance curve, and the tracing of the first S wave is lined up with the S-wave curve, as shown in **Figure 2.** The distance of each station from the earthquake can be found by reading the horizontal axis. After finding out the distances, a seismologist can locate an earthquake's epicenter, as shown in **Figure 3.**

Figure 3 **Finding an Earthquake's Epicenter**

1 A circle is drawn around a seismograph station. The radius of the circle equals the distance from the seismograph to the epicenter. (This distance is taken from the time-distance graph.)

2 When a second circle is drawn around another seismograph station, the circle overlaps the first circle in two spots. One of these spots is the earthquake's epicenter.

3 When a circle is drawn around a third seismograph station, all three circles intersect in one spot—the earthquake's epicenter. In this case, the epicenter was in San Francisco.

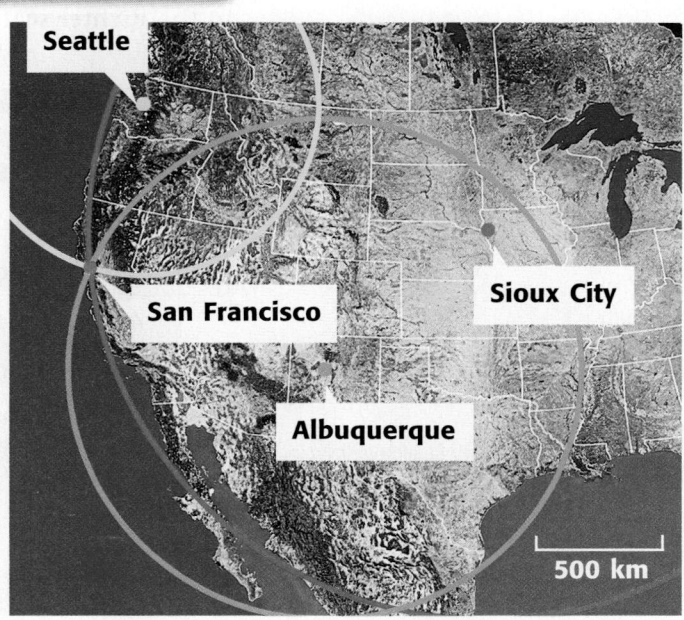

Seattle

San Francisco

Sioux City

Albuquerque

500 km

Measuring Earthquake Strength and Intensity

"How strong was the earthquake?" is a common question asked of seismologists. This question is not easy to answer. But it is an important question for anyone living near an earthquake zone. Fortunately, seismograms can be used not only to determine an earthquake's epicenter and its start time but also to find out an earthquake's strength.

The Richter Magnitude Scale

Throughout much of the 20th century, seismologists used the *Richter magnitude scale*, commonly called the Richter scale, to measure the strength of earthquakes. Seismologist Charles Richter created the scale in the 1930s. Richter wanted to compare earthquakes by measuring ground motion recorded by seismograms at seismograph stations.

Earthquake Ground Motion

A measure of the strength of an earthquake is called *magnitude*. The Richter scale measures the ground motion from an earthquake and adjusts for distance to find its strength. Each time the magnitude increases by one unit, the measured ground motion becomes 10 times larger. For example, an earthquake with a magnitude of 5.0 on the Richter scale will produce 10 times as much ground motion as an earthquake with a magnitude of 4.0. Furthermore, an earthquake with a magnitude of 6.0 will produce 100 times as much ground motion (10 × 10) as an earthquake with a magnitude of 4.0. **Table 1** shows the differences in the estimated effects of earthquakes with each increase of one unit of magnitude.

Reading Check How are magnitude and ground motion related in the Richter scale?

Table 1 Effects of Different-Sized Earthquakes	
Magnitude	**Estimated effects**
2.0	can be detected only by seismograph
3.0	can be felt at epicenter
4.0	can be felt by most people in the area
5.0	causes damage at epicenter
6.0	can cause widespread damage
7.0	can cause great, widespread damage

Modified Mercalli Intensity Scale

A measure of the degree to which an earthquake is felt by people and the amount of damage caused by the earthquake, if any, is called *intensity*. Currently, seismologists in the United States use the Modified Mercalli Intensity Scale to measure earthquake intensity. This scale is a numerical scale that uses Roman numerals from I to XII to describe increasing earthquake intensity levels. An intensity level of I describes an earthquake that is not felt by most people. An intensity level of XII indicates total damage of an area. **Figure 4** shows the type of damage caused by an earthquake that has a Modified Mercalli intensity level of XI.

Because the effects of an earthquake vary from place to place, any earthquake will have more than one intensity value. Intensity values are usually higher near an earthquake's epicenter.

Figure 4 *Intensity values for the 1906 San Francisco earthquake varied from place to place. The maximum intensity level was XI.*

SECTION Review

Summary

- Seismologists detect seismic waves and record them as seismograms.
- The S-P time method is the simplest method to use to find an earthquake's epicenter.
- Seismologists use the Richter scale to measure an earthquake's strength.
- Seismologists use the Modified Mercalli Intensity Scale to measure an earthquake's intensity.

Using Key Terms

1. In your own words, write a definition for each of the following terms: *epicenter* and *focus*.

Understanding Key Ideas

2. What is the difference between a seismograph and a seismogram?

3. Explain how earthquakes are detected.

4. Briefly explain the steps of the S-P time method for locating an earthquake's epicenter.

5. Why might an earthquake have more than one intensity value?

Math Skills

6. How much more ground motion is produced by an earthquake of magnitude 7.0 than by an earthquake of magnitude 4.0?

Critical Thinking

7. **Making Inferences** Why is a 6.0 magnitude earthquake so much more destructive than a 5.0 magnitude earthquake?

8. **Identifying Bias** Which do you think is the more important measure of earthquakes, strength or intensity? Explain.

9. **Making Inferences** Do you think an earthquake of moderate magnitude can produce high Modified Mercalli intensity values?

SCiLINKS®

NSTA
Developed and maintained by the
National Science Teachers Association

For a variety of links related to this chapter, go to www.scilinks.org

Topic: Earthquake Measurement
SciLinks code: HSM0452

Earthquakes and Society

Imagine that you are in class and the ground begins to shake beneath your feet. What do you do?

Seismologists are not able to predict the exact time when and place where an earthquake will occur. They can, at best, make forecasts based on the frequency with which earthquakes take place. Therefore, seismologists are always looking for better ways to forecast when and where earthquakes will happen. In the meantime, it is important for people in earthquake zones to be prepared before an earthquake strikes.

Earthquake Hazard

Earthquake hazard is a measurement of how likely an area is to have damaging earthquakes in the future. An area's earthquake-hazard level is determined by past and present seismic activity. The map in **Figure 1** shows that some areas of the United States have a higher earthquake-hazard level than others do. This variation is caused by differences in seismic activity. The greater the seismic activity, the higher the earthquake-hazard level. The West Coast, for example, has a very high earthquake-hazard level because it has a lot of seismic activity.

Look at the map. What earthquake-hazard level or levels are shown in the area in which you live? How do the hazard levels of nearby areas compare with your area's hazard level?

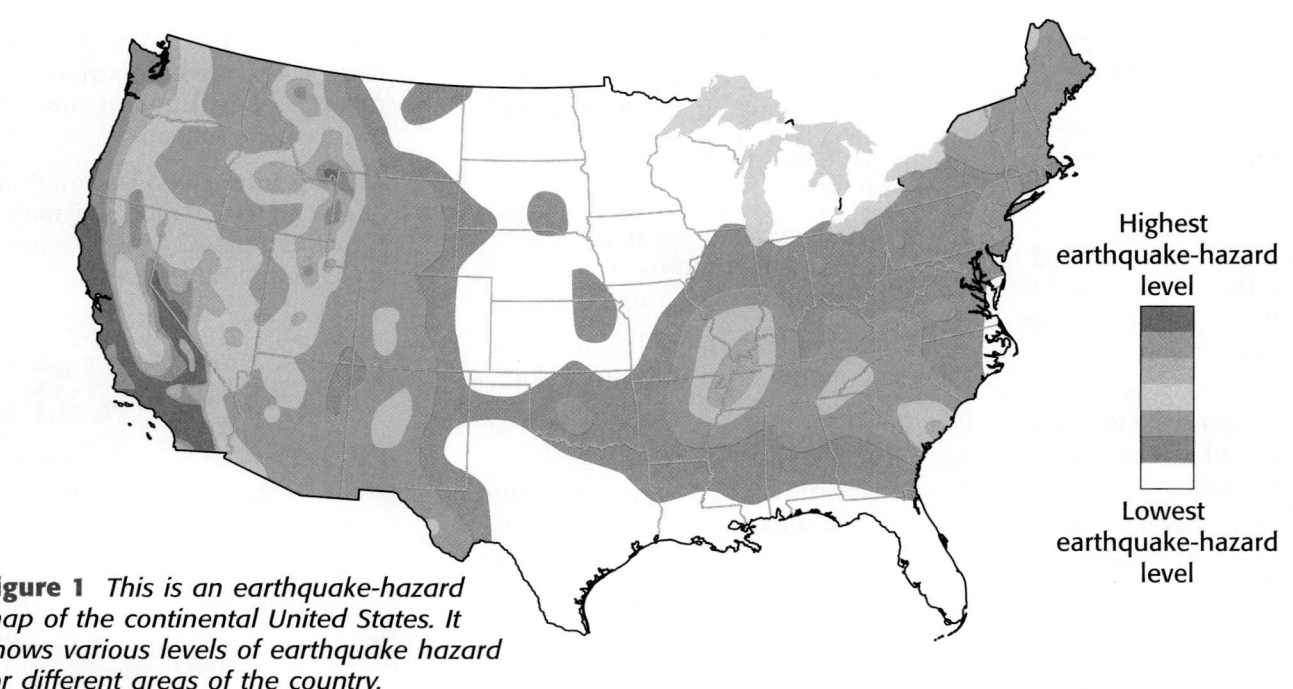

Highest
earthquake-hazard
level

Lowest
earthquake-hazard
level

Figure 1 *This is an earthquake-hazard map of the continental United States. It shows various levels of earthquake hazard for different areas of the country.*

Table 1 Worldwide Earthquake Frequency (Based on Observations Since 1900)

Descriptor	Magnitude	Average number annually
Great	8.0 and higher	1
Major	7.0–7.9	18
Strong	6.0–6.9	120
Moderate	5.0–5.9	800
Light	4.0–4.9	about 6,200
Minor	3.0–3.9	about 49,000
Very minor	2.0–2.9	about 365,000

Earthquake Forecasting

Forecasting when and where earthquakes will occur and their strength is difficult. By looking carefully at areas of seismic activity, seismologists have discovered some patterns in earthquakes that allow them to make some general predictions.

Strength and Frequency

Earthquakes vary in strength. And you can probably guess that earthquakes don't occur on a set schedule. But what you may not know is that the strength of earthquakes is related to how often they occur. **Table 1** provides more detail about this relationship worldwide.

The relationship between earthquake strength and frequency is also at work on a local scale. For example, each year approximately 1.6 earthquakes with a magnitude of 4.0 on the Richter scale occur in the Puget Sound area of Washington State. Over this same time period, approximately 10 times as many earthquakes with a magnitude of 3.0 occur in this area. Scientists use these statistics to make forecasts about the strength, location, and frequency of future earthquakes.

Reading Check What is the relationship between the strength of earthquakes and earthquake frequency? (*See the Appendix for answers to Reading Checks.*)

The Gap Hypothesis

Another method of forecasting an earthquake's strength, location, and frequency is based on the gap hypothesis. The **gap hypothesis** is a hypothesis that states that sections of active faults that have had relatively few earthquakes are likely to be the sites of strong earthquakes in the future. The areas along a fault where relatively few earthquakes have occurred are called **seismic gaps.**

For another activity related to this chapter, go to **go.hrw.com** and type in the keyword **HZ5EQKW.**

gap hypothesis a hypothesis that is based on the idea that a major earthquake is more likely to occur along the part of an active fault where no earthquakes have occurred for a certain period of time

seismic gap an area along a fault where relatively few earthquakes have occurred recently but where strong earthquakes have occurred in the past

Figure 2   A Seismic Gap on the San Andreas Fault

This diagram shows a cross section of the San Andreas Fault. Note how the seismic gap was filled by the 1989 Loma Prieta earthquake and its aftershocks. *Aftershocks* are weaker earthquakes that follow a stronger earthquake.

- Earthquakes prior to 1989 earthquake

- 1989 earthquake and aftershocks

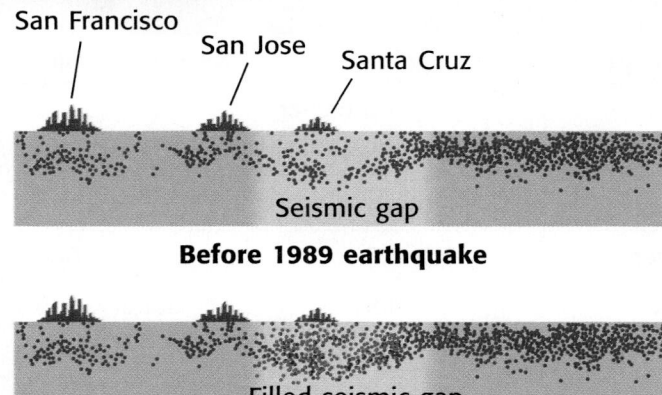

San Francisco   San Jose   Santa Cruz

Seismic gap

Before 1989 earthquake

Filled seismic gap

After 1989 earthquake

Using the Gap Hypothesis

Not all seismologists believe the gap hypothesis is an accurate method of forecasting earthquakes. But some seismologists think the gap hypothesis helped forecast the approximate location and strength of the 1989 Loma Prieta earthquake in the San Francisco Bay area. The seismic gap that they identified is illustrated in **Figure 2.** In 1988, these seismologists predicted that over the next 30 years there was a 30% chance that an earthquake with a magnitude of at least 6.5 would fill this seismic gap. Were they correct? The Loma Prieta earthquake, which filled in the seismic gap in 1989, measured 6.9 on the Richter scale. Their prediction was very close, considering how complicated the forecasting of earthquakes is.

Figure 3 *During the January 17, 1995, earthquake, the fronts of entire buildings collapsed into the streets of Kobe, Japan.*

Earthquakes and Buildings

Figure 3 shows what can happen to buildings during an earthquake. These buildings were not designed or constructed to withstand the forces of an earthquake.

Today, older structures in seismically active places, such as California, are being made more earthquake resistant. The process of making older structures more earthquake resistant is called *retrofitting*. A common way to retrofit an older home is to securely fasten it to its foundation. Steel can be used to strengthen structures made of brick.

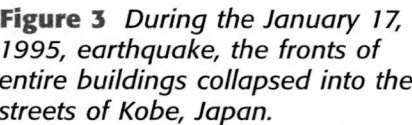 **Reading Check** Explain the meaning of the term *retrofitting*.

Earthquake-Resistant Buildings

A lot has been learned from building failure during earthquakes. Armed with this knowledge, architects and engineers use the newest technology to design and construct buildings and bridges to better withstand earthquakes. Carefully study **Figure 4** to learn more about this modern technology.

Figure 4 Earthquake-Resistant Building Technology

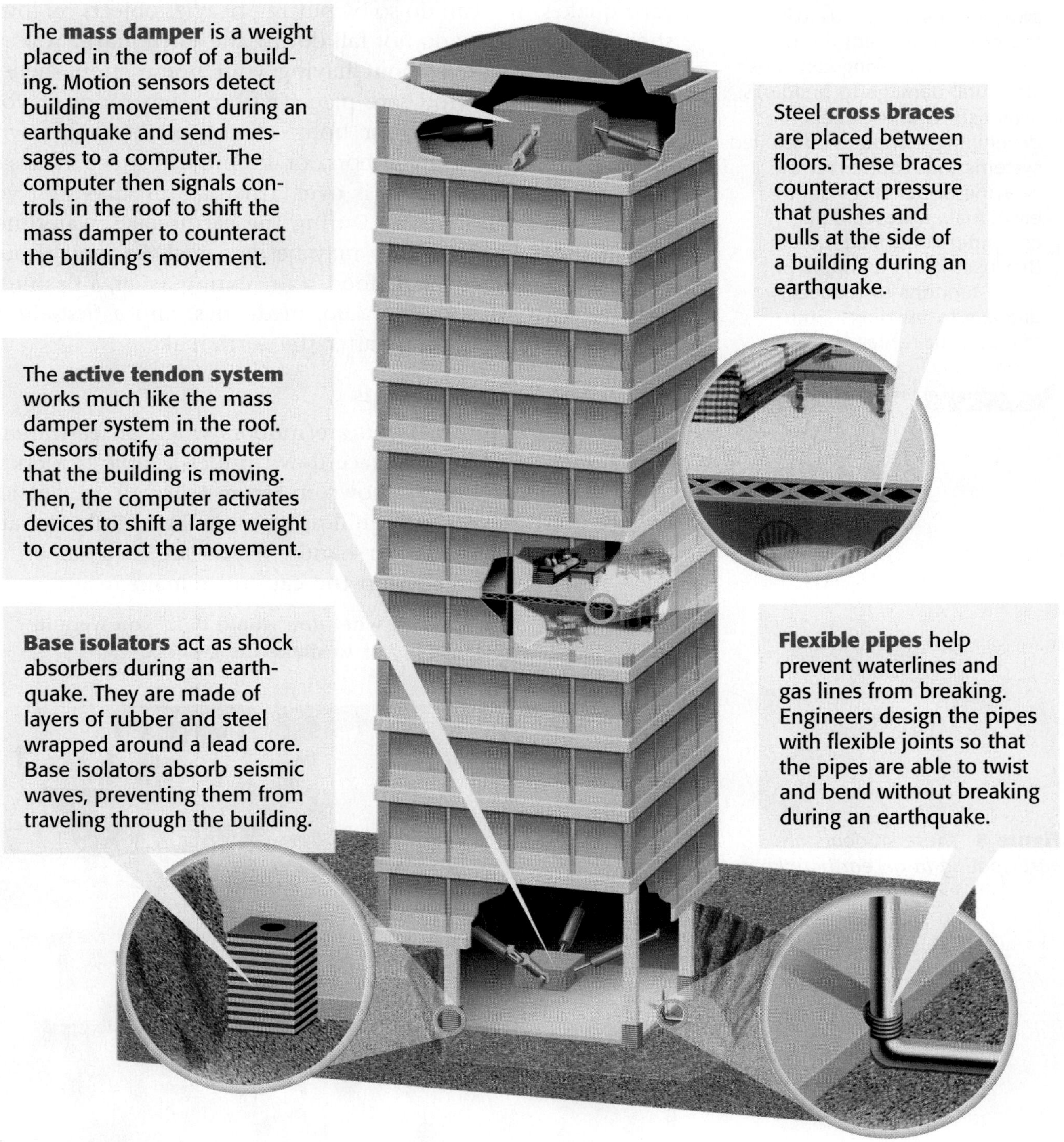

The **mass damper** is a weight placed in the roof of a building. Motion sensors detect building movement during an earthquake and send messages to a computer. The computer then signals controls in the roof to shift the mass damper to counteract the building's movement.

Steel **cross braces** are placed between floors. These braces counteract pressure that pushes and pulls at the side of a building during an earthquake.

The **active tendon system** works much like the mass damper system in the roof. Sensors notify a computer that the building is moving. Then, the computer activates devices to shift a large weight to counteract the movement.

Base isolators act as shock absorbers during an earthquake. They are made of layers of rubber and steel wrapped around a lead core. Base isolators absorb seismic waves, preventing them from traveling through the building.

Flexible pipes help prevent waterlines and gas lines from breaking. Engineers design the pipes with flexible joints so that the pipes are able to twist and bend without breaking during an earthquake.

Earthquake Proof Buildings During earthquakes, buildings often sway from side to side when the ground beneath them moves. This swaying can cause structural damage to buildings. Scientists and engineers are developing computer-controlled systems that counteract the swaying of buildings during earthquakes. Research a computer-controlled system that uses mass dampers or active tendons to reduce damage to buildings. Summarize your research in a short essay.

Are You Prepared for an Earthquake?

If you live in an area where earthquakes are common, there are many things you can do to protect yourself and your property from earthquakes. Plan ahead so that you will know what to do before, during, and after an earthquake. Stick to your plan as closely as possible.

Before the Shaking Starts

The first thing you should do is safeguard your home against earthquakes. You can do so by putting heavier objects on lower shelves so that they do not fall during the earthquake. You can also talk to a parent about having your home strengthened. Next, you should find safe places within each room of your home and outside of your home. Then, make a plan with others (your family, neighbors, or friends) to meet in a safe place after the earthquake is over. This plan ensures that you will all know who is safe. During the earthquake, waterlines, power lines, and roadways may be damaged. So, you should store water, nonperishable food, a fire extinguisher, a flashlight with batteries, a portable radio, medicines, and a first-aid kit in a place you can access after the earthquake.

When the Shaking Starts

The best thing to do if you are indoors when an earthquake begins is to crouch or lie face down under a table or desk in the center of a room, as shown in **Figure 5.** If you are outside, lie face down away from buildings, power lines, and trees and cover your head with your hands. If you are in a car on an open road, you should stop the car and remain inside.

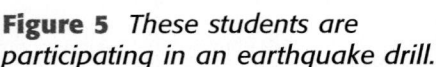 **Reading Check** Explain what you would do if you were in class and an earthquake began to shake the ground.

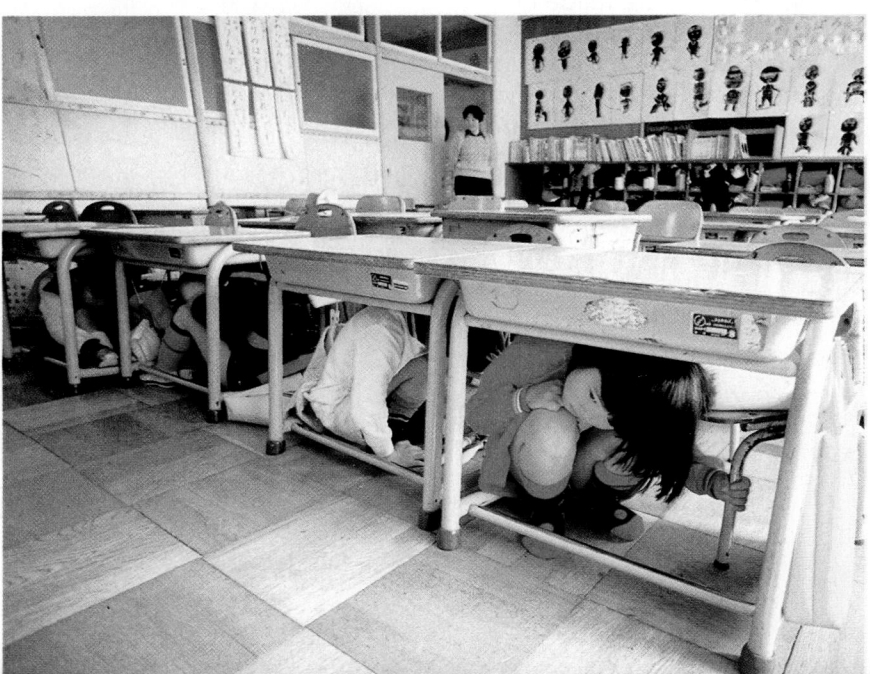

Figure 5 *These students are participating in an earthquake drill.*

After the Shaking Stops

Being in an earthquake is a startling and often frightening experience for most people. After being in an earthquake, you should not be surprised to find yourself and others puzzled about what took place. You should try to calm down and get your bearings as quickly as possible. Then, remove yourself from immediate danger, such as downed power lines, broken glass, and fire hazards. Always stay out of damaged buildings, and return home only when you are told that it is safe to do so by someone in authority. Be aware that there may be aftershocks, which may cause more damage to structures. Recall your earthquake plan, and follow it.

SCHOOL to HOME

Disaster Planning

With your parent, create a plan that will protect your family in the event of a natural disaster, such as an earthquake. The plan should include steps to take before, during, and after a disaster. Present your disaster plan in the form of an oral report to your class.

ACTIVITY

SECTION Review

Summary

- Earthquake hazard is a measure of how likely an area is to have earthquakes in the future.
- Seismologists use their knowledge of the relationship between earthquake strength and frequency and of the gap hypothesis to forecast earthquakes.
- Homes and buildings and bridges can be strengthened to decrease earthquake damage.
- People who live in earthquake zones should safeguard their home against earthquakes.

Using Key Terms

1. In your own words, write a definition for each of the following terms: *gap hypothesis* and *seismic gap*.

Understanding Key Ideas

2. A weight that is placed on a building to make the building earthquake resistant is called a(n)
   a. active tendon system.
   b. cross brace.
   c. mass damper.
   d. base isolator.

3. How is an area's earthquake-hazard level determined?

4. Compare the strength and frequency method with the gap hypothesis method for predicting earthquakes.

5. What is a common way of making homes more earthquake resistant?

6. Describe four pieces of technology that are designed to make buildings earthquake resistant.

7. Name five items that you should store in case of an earthquake.

Math Skills

8. Of the approximately 420,000 earthquakes recorded each year, about 140 have a magnitude greater than 6.0. What percentage of total earthquakes have a magnitude greater than 6.0?

Critical Thinking

9. **Evaluating Hypotheses** Seismologists predict that there is a 20% chance that an earthquake of magnitude 7.0 or greater will fill a seismic gap during the next 50 years. Is the hypothesis incorrect if the earthquake does not happen? Explain your answer.

10. **Applying Concepts** Why is a large earthquake often followed by numerous aftershocks?

SCILINKS

NSTA
Developed and maintained by the National Science Teachers Association

For a variety of links related to this chapter, go to www.scilinks.org

Topic: Earthquakes and Society
SciLinks code: HSM0455

Inquiry Lab

Quake Challenge

In many parts of the world, people must have earthquakes in mind when they construct buildings. Each building must be designed so that the structure is protected during an earthquake. Architects have greatly improved the design of buildings since 1906, when an earthquake and the fires it caused destroyed much of San Francisco. In this activity, you will use marshmallows and toothpicks to build a structure that can withstand a simulated earthquake. In the process, you will discover some of the ways a building can be built to withstand an earthquake.

OBJECTIVES

Build a model of a structure that can withstand a simulated earthquake.

Evaluate ways in which you can strengthen your model.

MATERIALS

- gelatin, square, approximately 8 × 8 cm
- marshmallows (10)
- paper plate
- toothpicks (10)

SAFETY

Ask a Question

1 What features help a building withstand an earthquake? How can I use this information to build my structure?

Form a Hypothesis

2 Brainstorm with a classmate to design a structure that will resist the simulated earthquake. Write two or three sentences to describe your design. Explain why you think your design will be able to withstand a simulated earthquake.

Test the Hypothesis

3 Follow your design to build a structure using the toothpicks and marshmallows.

4 Set your structure on a square of gelatin, and place the gelatin on a paper plate.

5 Shake the square of gelatin to test whether your building will remain standing during a quake. Do not pick up the gelatin.

6 If your first design does not work well, change it until you find a design that does. Try to determine why your building is falling so that you can improve your design each time.

7 Sketch your final design.

8. After you have tested your final design, place your structure on the gelatin square on your teacher's desk.

9. When every group has added a structure to the teacher's gelatin, your teacher will simulate an earthquake by shaking the gelatin. Watch to see which buildings withstand the most severe quake.

Analyze the Results

1. **Explaining Events** Which buildings were still standing after the final earthquake? What features made them more stable?

2. **Analyzing Results** How would you change your design in order to make your structure more stable?

Draw Conclusions

3. **Evaluating Models** This was a simple model of a real-life problem for architects. Based on this activity, what advice would you give to architects who design buildings in earthquake zones?

4. **Evaluating Models** What are some limitations of your earthquake model?

5. **Making Predictions** How could your research have an impact on society?

Chapter Review

USING KEY TERMS

1 Use each of the following terms in a separate sentence: *seismic wave*, *P wave*, and *S wave*.

For each pair of terms, explain how the meanings of the terms differ.

2 *seismograph* and *seismogram*

3 *epicenter* and *focus*

4 *gap hypothesis* and *seismic gap*

UNDERSTANDING KEY IDEAS

Multiple Choice

5 When rock is ___, energy builds up in it. Seismic waves occur as this energy is ___.

a. plastically deformed, increased

b. elastically deformed, released

c. plastically deformed, released

d. elastically deformed, increased

6 Reverse faults are created

a. by divergent plate motion.

b. by convergent plate motion.

c. by transform plate motion.

d. All of the above

7 The last seismic waves to arrive are

a. P waves.

b. body waves.

c. S waves.

d. surface waves.

8 If an earthquake begins while you are in a building, the safest thing for you to do is

a. to run out into an open space.

b. to get under the strongest table, chair, or other piece of furniture.

c. to call home.

d. to crouch near a wall.

9 How many major earthquakes (magnitude 7.0 to 7.9) happen on average in the world each year?

a. 1

b. 18

c. 120

d. 800

10 ___ counteract pressure that pushes and pulls at the side of a building during an earthquake.

a. Base isolators

b. Mass dampers

c. Active tendon systems

d. Cross braces

Short Answer

11 Can the S-P time method be used with one seismograph station to locate the epicenter of an earthquake? Explain your answer.

12 Explain how the Richter scale and the Modified Mercalli Intensity Scale are different.

13 What is the relationship between the strength of earthquakes and earthquake frequency?

14 Explain the way that different seismic waves affect rock as they travel through it.

15 Describe some steps you can take to protect yourself and your property from earthquakes.

CRITICAL THINKING

16 Concept Mapping Use the following terms to create a concept map: *focus, epicenter, earthquake start time, seismic waves, P waves,* and *S waves.*

17 Identifying Relationships Would a strong or light earthquake be more likely to happen along a major fault where there have not been many recent earthquakes? Explain. (Hint: Think about the average number of earthquakes of different magnitudes that occur annually.)

18 Applying Concepts Japan is located near a point where three tectonic plates converge. What would you imagine the earthquake-hazard level in Japan to be? Explain why.

19 Applying Concepts You learned that if you are in a car during an earthquake and are out in the open, it is best to stay in the car. Can you think of any situation in which you might want to leave a car during an earthquake?

20 Identifying Relationships You use gelatin to simulate rock in an experiment in which you are investigating the way different seismic waves affect rock. In what ways is your gelatin model limited?

INTERPRETING GRAPHICS

The graph below illustrates the relationship between earthquake magnitude and the height of tracings on a seismogram. Charles Richter initially formed his magnitude scale by comparing the heights of seismogram readings for different earthquakes. Use the graph below to answer the questions that follow.

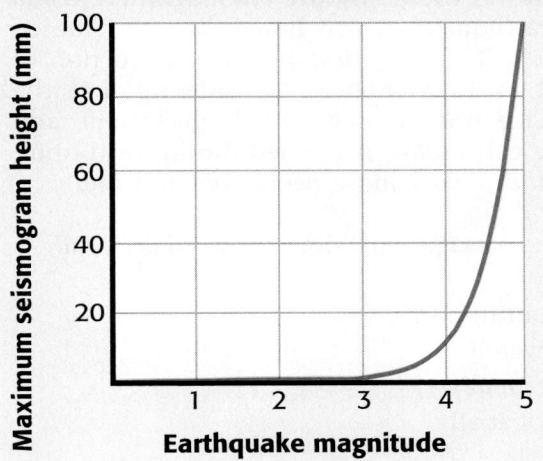

Seismogram Height Vs. Earthquake Magnitude

21 According to the graph, what would the magnitude of an earthquake be if its maximum seismogram height is 10 mm?

22 According to the graph, what is the difference in maximum seismogram height (in mm) between an earthquake of magnitude 4.0 and an earthquake of magnitude 5.0?

23 Look at the shape of the curve on the graph. What does this tell you about the relationship between seismogram heights and earthquake magnitudes? Explain.

Standardized Test Preparation

Read each of the passages below. Then, answer the questions that follow each passage.

Passage 1 At 5:04 P.M. on October 14, 1989, life in California's San Francisco Bay area seemed normal. While 62,000 fans filled Candlestick Park to watch the third game of the World Series, other people were rushing home from a day's work. By 5:05 P.M., the area had changed <u>drastically</u>. The area was rocked by the 6.9 magnitude Loma Prieta earthquake, which lasted 20 s and caused 68 deaths, 3,757 injuries, and the destruction of more than 1,000 homes. Considering that the earthquake was of such a high magnitude and that the earthquake happened during rush hour, it is amazing that more people did not die.

1. In the passage, what does the word *drastically* mean?

   A continuously

   B severely

   C gradually

   D not at all

2. Which of the following statements about the Loma Prieta earthquake is false?

   F The earthquake happened during rush hour.

   G The earthquake destroyed more than 1,000 homes.

   H The earthquake lasted for 1 min.

   I The earthquake had a magnitude of 6.9.

3. Which of the following statements is a fact in the passage?

   A Thousands of people were killed in the Loma Prieta earthquake.

   B The Loma Prieta earthquake happened during the morning rush hour.

   C The Loma Prieta earthquake was a light to moderate earthquake.

   D The Loma Prieta earthquake occurred during the 1989 World Series.

Passage 2 In the United States, seismologists use the Modified Mercalli Intensity Scale to measure the intensity of earthquakes. Japanese seismologists, however, use the Shindo scale to measure earthquake intensity. Earthquakes are <u>assigned</u> a number between 1 and 7 on the scale. Shindo 1 indicates a slight earthquake. Such an earthquake is felt by few people, usually people who are sitting. Shindo 7 indicates a severe earthquake. An earthquake that causes great destruction, such as the earthquake that struck Kobe, Japan, in January 1995, would be classified as Shindo 7.

1. In the passage, what does the word *assigned* mean?

   A named

   B voted

   C given

   D chosen

2. Which of the following statements about the Shindo scale is true?

   F The Shindo scale is used to measure earthquake strength.

   G The Shindo scale, which ranges from 1 to 7, is used to rank earthquake intensity.

   H The Shindo scale is the same as the Modified Mercalli Intensity Scale.

   I Seismologists all over the world use the Shindo scale.

3. Which of the following is a fact in the passage?

   A American seismologists use the Richter scale instead of the Shindo scale.

   B Japanese seismologists measure the intensity of large earthquakes only.

   C The Kobe earthquake was too destructive to be given a Shindo number.

   D Shindo 1 indicates a slight earthquake.

Use the graph below to answer the questions that follow.

Read each question below, and choose the best answer.

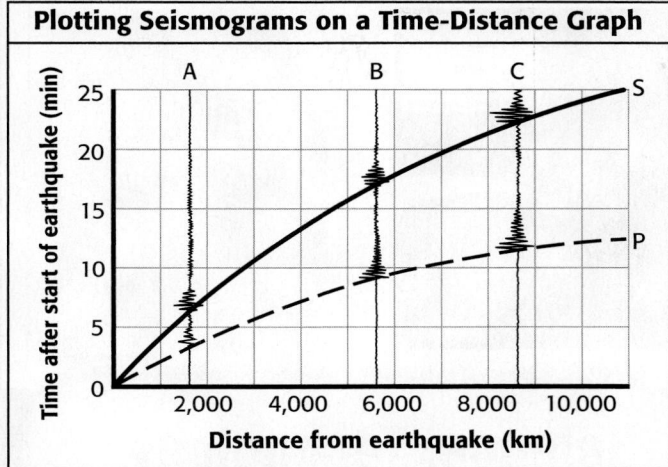

Plotting Seismograms on a Time-Distance Graph

1. According to the seismogram, which waves travel the **fastest**?

   A P waves travel the fastest.

   B S waves travel the fastest.

   C P waves and S waves travel at the same speed.

   D The graph does not show how fast P waves and S waves travel.

2. What is the approximate difference in minutes between the time the first P waves arrived at station B and the time the first S waves arrived at station B?

   F 22 1/2 min

   G 10 1/2 min

   H 8 min

   I 3 min

3. Station A is approximately how much closer to the epicenter than station B is?

   A 1,800 km

   B 4,000 km

   C 5,800 km

   D 8,600 km

1. If a seismic wave travels at a rate of 12 km/s, how far will it travel away from the earthquake in 1 min?

   A 7,200 km

   B 720 km

   C 72 km

   D 7.2 km

2. If a P wave travels a distance of 70 km in 10 s, what is its speed?

   F 700 km/s

   G 70 km/s

   H 7 km/s

   I 0.7 km/s

3. Each time the magnitude of an earthquake increases by 1 unit, the amount of energy released is 31.7 times greater. How much greater is the energy for a magnitude 7.0 earthquake than a magnitude 5.0 earthquake?

   A 31,855 times as strong

   B 63.4 times as strong

   C 634 times as strong

   D 1,005 times as strong

4. An approximate relationship between earthquake magnitude and frequency is that when magnitude increases by 1.0, 10 times fewer earthquakes occur. Thus, if 150 earthquakes of magnitude 2.0 happen in your area this year, about how many 4.0 magnitude earthquakes will happen in your area this year?

   F 50

   G 10

   H 2

   I 0

5. If an average of 421,140 earthquakes occur annually, what percentage of these earthquakes are minor earthquakes if 49,000 minor earthquakes occur annually?

   A approximately .01%

   B approximately .12%

   C approximately 12%

   D approximately 86%

Science in Action

SAFOD PILOT HOLE

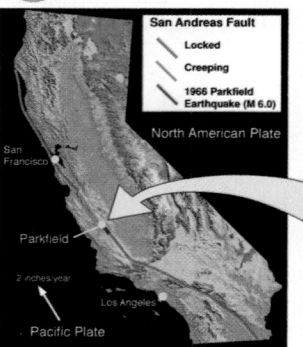

San Andreas Fault
Locked
Creeping
1966 Parkfield Earthquake (M 6.0)

North American Plate

San Francisco

Parkfield

2 inches/year

Los Angeles

Pacific Plate

Surface Trace of San Andreas Fault

1.4 MILES

SAFOD Drilling Target

Source: Martyn Unsworth

Weird Science

Can Animals Predict Earthquakes?

Is it possible that animals close to the epicenter of an earthquake are able to sense changes in their environment? And should we be paying attention to such animal behavior? As long ago as the 1700s, unusual animal activity prior to earthquakes has been recorded. Examples include domestic cattle seeking higher ground and zoo animals refusing to enter their shelters at night. Other animals, such as lizards, snakes, and small mammals, evacuate their underground burrows, and wild birds leave their usual habitats. These events occur days, hours, or even minutes before an earthquake.

Science, Technology, and Society

San Andreas Fault Observatory at Depth (SAFOD)

Seismologists are creating an underground observatory in Parkfield, California, to study earthquakes along the San Andreas Fault. The observatory will be named the San Andreas Fault Observatory at Depth (SAFOD). A deep hole will be drilled directly into the fault zone near a point where earthquakes of magnitude 6.0 have been recorded. Instruments will be placed at the bottom of the hole, 3 to 4 km beneath Earth's surface. These instruments will make seismological measurements of earthquakes and measure the deformation of rock.

Language Arts ACTiViTY

WRITING SKILL Create an illustrated field guide of animal activity to show how animal activity can predict earthquakes. Each illustration must have a paragraph that describes the activity of a specific animal.

Social Studies ACTiViTY

Research the great San Francisco earthquake of 1906. Find images of the earthquake on the Internet and download them, or cut them out of old magazines. Create a photo collage of the earthquake that shows San Francisco before and after the earthquake.

Hiroo Kanamori

Seismologist Hiroo Kanamori is a seismologist at the California Institute of Technology in Pasadena, California. Dr. Kanamori studies how earthquakes occur and tries to reduce their impact on our society. He also analyzes what the effects of earthquakes on oceans are and how earthquakes create giant ocean waves called *tsunamis* (tsoo NAH meez). Tsunamis are very destructive to life and property when they reach land. Kanamori has discovered that even some weak earthquakes can cause powerful tsunamis. He calls these events *tsunami earthquakes,* and he has learned to predict when tsunamis will form. In short, when tectonic plates grind together slowly, special waves called *long-period seismic waves* are created. When Kanamori sees a long-period wave recorded on a seismogram, he knows a tsunami will form. Because long-period waves travel faster than tsunamis, they arrive at recording stations earlier. When an earthquake station records an earthquake, information about that earthquake is provided to a tsunami warning center. The center determines if the earthquake may cause a tsunami and, if so, issues a tsunami warning to areas that may be affected.

Math ACTIVITY

An undersea earthquake causes a tsunami to form. The tsunami travels across the open ocean at 800 km/h. How long will the tsunami take to travel from the point where it formed to a coastline 3,600 km away?

To learn more about these Science in Action topics, visit **go.hrw.com** and type in the keyword **HZ5EQKF.**

Current Science

Check out Current Science® articles related to this chapter by visiting go.hrw.com. Just type in the keyword HZ5CS08.

9

Volcanoes

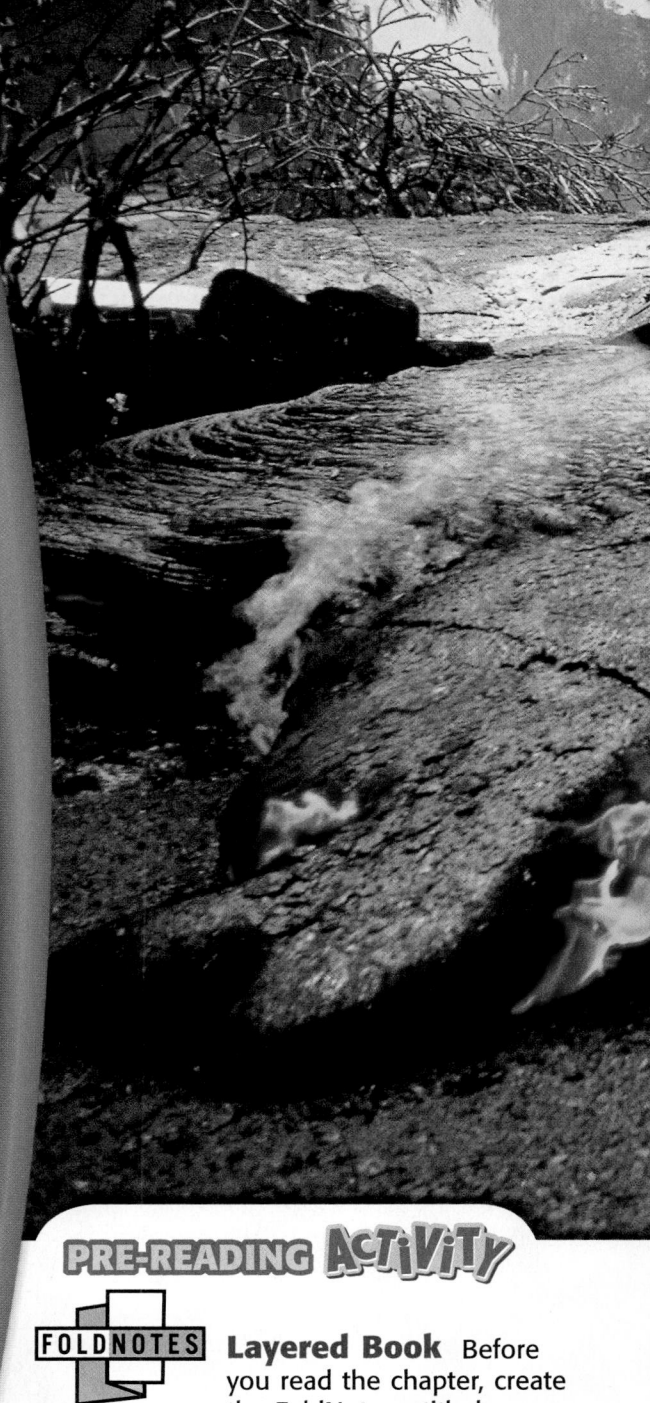

About the PHOTO

When you think of a volcanic eruption, you probably think of a cone-shaped mountain exploding and sending huge clouds of ash into the air. Some volcanic eruptions do just that! Most volcanic eruptions, such as the one shown here, which is flowing over a road in Hawaii, are slow and quiet. Volcanic eruptions happen throughout the world, and they play a major role in shaping the Earth's surface.

PRE-READING ACTIVITY

FOLDNOTES **Layered Book** Before you read the chapter, create the FoldNote entitled "Layered Book" described in the **Study Skills** section of the Appendix. Label the tabs of the layered book with "Volcanic eruptions," "Effects of eruptions," and "Causes of eruptions." As you read the chapter, write information you learn about each category under the appropriate tab.

START-UP ACTIVITY

Anticipation

In this activity, you will build a simple model of a volcano and you will try to predict an eruption.

Procedure

1. Place **10 mL of baking soda** on a **sheet of tissue.** Fold the corners of the tissue over the baking soda, and place the tissue packet in a **large pan.**

2. Put **modeling clay** around the top edge of a **funnel.** Press that end of the funnel over the tissue packet to make a tight seal.

3. After you put on **safety goggles,** add **50 mL of vinegar** and **several drops of liquid dish soap** to a **200 mL beaker** and stir.

4. Predict how long it will take the volcano to erupt after the liquid is poured into the funnel. Then, carefully pour the liquid into the funnel, and use a **stopwatch** to measure how long the volcano takes to begin erupting.

Analysis

1. Based on your observations, explain what happened to cause the eruption.

2. How accurate was your prediction? By how many seconds did the class predictions vary?

3. How do the size of the funnel opening and the amount of baking soda and vinegar affect the amount of time that the volcano takes to erupt?

Volcanic Eruptions

Think about the force released when the first atomic bomb exploded during World War II. Now imagine an explosion 10,000 times stronger, and you will get an idea of how powerful a volcanic eruption can be.

The explosive pressure of a volcanic eruption can turn an entire mountain into a billowing cloud of ash and rock in a matter of seconds. But eruptions are also creative forces—they help form fertile farmland. They also create some of the largest mountains on Earth. During an eruption, molten rock, or *magma,* is forced to the Earth's surface. Magma that flows onto the Earth's surface is called *lava.* **Volcanoes** are areas of Earth's surface through which magma and volcanic gases pass.

Nonexplosive Eruptions

At this moment, volcanic eruptions are occurring around the world—on the ocean floor and on land. Nonexplosive eruptions are the most common type of eruption. These eruptions produce relatively calm flows of lava, such as those shown in **Figure 1.** Nonexplosive eruptions can release huge amounts of lava. Vast areas of the Earth's surface, including much of the sea floor and the Northwest region of the United States, are covered with lava from nonexplosive eruptions.

volcano a vent or fissure in the Earth's surface through which magma and gases are expelled

Figure 1   Examples of Nonexplosive Eruptions

Sometimes, nonexplosive eruptions can spray lava into the air. Lava fountains, such as this one, pulse with the pressure of escaping gases.

The speed of a lava flow can range from a slow creep to as fast as 60 km/h.

250

Explosive Eruptions

Explosive eruptions, such as the one shown in **Figure 2,** are much rarer than nonexplosive eruptions. However, the effects of explosive eruptions can be incredibly destructive. During an explosive eruption, clouds of hot debris, ash, and gas rapidly shoot out from a volcano. Instead of producing lava flows, explosive eruptions cause molten rock to be blown into tiny particles that harden in the air. The dust-sized particles, called *ash,* can reach the upper atmosphere and can circle the Earth for years. Larger pieces of debris fall closer to the volcano. An explosive eruption can also blast millions of tons of lava and rock from a volcano. In a matter of seconds, an explosive eruption can demolish an entire mountainside, as shown in **Figure 3.**

Reading Check List two differences between explosive and nonexplosive eruptions. (*See the Appendix for answers to Reading Checks.*)

Figure 2 *In what resembles a nuclear explosion, volcanic ash rockets skyward during the 1990 eruption of Mount Redoubt in Alaska.*

Figure 3 *Within seconds, the 1980 eruption of Mount St. Helens in Washington State caused the side of the mountain to collapse. The blast scorched and flattened 600 km² of forest.*

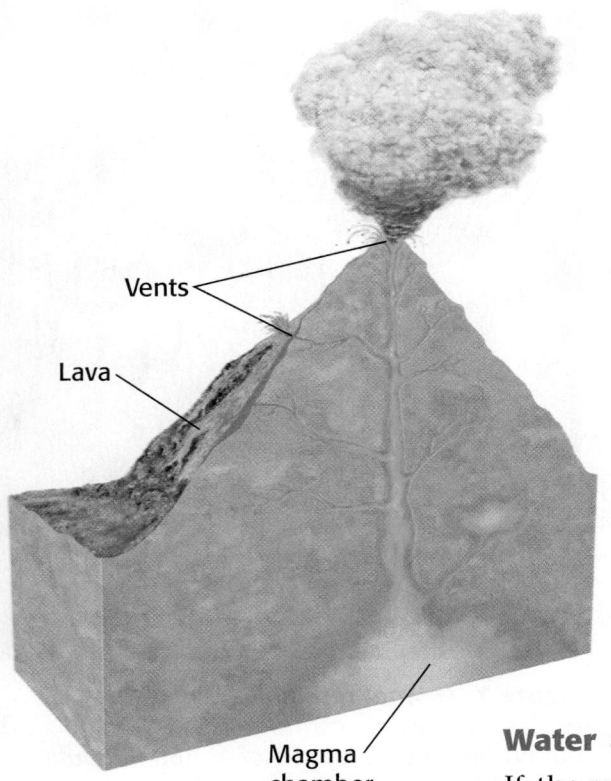

Vents

Lava

Magma chamber

Figure 4 *Volcanoes form when lava is released from vents.*

magma chamber the body of molten rock that feeds a volcano

vent an opening at the surface of the Earth through which volcanic material passes

What Is Inside a Volcano?

If you could look inside an erupting volcano, you would see the features shown in **Figure 4.** A **magma chamber** is a body of molten rock deep underground that feeds a volcano. Magma rises from the magma chamber through cracks in the Earth's crust to openings called **vents.** Magma is released from the vents during an eruption.

What Makes Up Magma?

By comparing the composition of magma from different eruptions, scientists have made an important discovery. The composition of the magma affects how explosive a volcanic eruption is. The key to whether an eruption will be explosive lies in the silica, water, and gas content of the magma.

Water and Magma Are an Explosive Combination

If the water content of magma is high, an explosive eruption is more likely. Because magma is underground, it is under intense pressure and water stays dissolved in the magma. If the magma quickly moves to the surface, the pressure suddenly decreases and the water and other compounds, such as carbon dioxide, become gases. As the gases expand rapidly, an explosion can result. This process is similar to what happens when you shake a can of soda and open it. When a can of soda is shaken, the CO_2 dissolved in the soda is released and pressure builds up. When the can is opened, the soda shoots out, just as lava shoots out of a volcano during an explosive eruption. In fact, some lava is so frothy with gas when it reaches the surface that its solid form, called *pumice,* can float in water!

Silica-Rich Magma Traps Explosive Gases

Magma that has a high silica content also tends to cause explosive eruptions. Silica-rich magma has a stiff consistency. It flows slowly and tends to harden in a volcano's vents. As a result, it plugs the vent. As more magma pushes up from below, pressure increases. If enough pressure builds up, an explosive eruption takes place. Stiff magma also prevents water vapor and other gases from easily escaping. Gas bubbles trapped in magma can expand until they explode. When they explode, the magma shatters and ash and pumice are blasted from the vent. Magma that contains less silica has a more fluid, runnier consistency. Because gases escape this type of magma more easily, explosive eruptions are less likely to occur.

✓ Reading Check How do silica levels affect an eruption?

What Erupts from a Volcano?

Magma erupts as either lava or pyroclastic (PIE roh KLAS tik) material. *Lava* is liquid magma that flows from a volcanic vent. *Pyroclastic material* forms when magma is blasted into the air and hardens. Nonexplosive eruptions produce mostly lava. Explosive eruptions produce mostly pyroclastic material. Over many years—or even during the same eruption—a volcano's eruptions may alternate between lava and pyroclastic eruptions.

Types of Lava

The viscosity of lava, or how lava flows, varies greatly. To understand viscosity, remember that a milkshake has high viscosity and a glass of milk has low viscosity. Lava that has high viscosity is stiff. Lava that has low viscosity is more fluid. The viscosity of lava affects the surface of a lava flow in different ways, as shown in **Figure 5.** *Blocky lava* and *pahoehoe* (puh HOY HOY) have a high viscosity and flow slowly. Other types of lava flows, such as *aa* (AH AH) and *pillow lava,* have lower viscosities and flow more quickly.

CONNECTION TO
Social Studies

Fertile Farmlands Volcanic ash helps create some of the most fertile farmland in the world. Use a world map and reference materials to find the location of volcanoes that have helped create farmland in Italy, Africa, South America, and the United States. Make an illustrated map on a piece of poster board to share your findings.

ACTIVITY

Figure 5 Four Types of Lava

Aa is so named because of the painful experience of walking barefoot across its jagged surface. This lava pours out quickly and forms a brittle crust. The crust is torn into jagged pieces as molten lava continues to flow underneath.

Pahoehoe lava flows slowly, like wax dripping from a candle. Its glassy surface has rounded wrinkles.

Pillow lava forms when lava erupts underwater. As you can see here, this lava forms rounded lumps that are the shape of pillows.

Blocky lava is cool, stiff lava that does not travel far from the erupting vent. Blocky lava usually oozes from a volcano and forms jumbled heaps of sharp-edged chunks.

Figure 6 Four Types of Pyroclastic Material

Volcanic bombs are large blobs of magma that harden in the air. The shape of this bomb was caused by the magma spinning through the air as it cooled.

Lapilli, which means "little stones" in Italian, are pebblelike bits of magma that hardened before they hit the ground.

Volcanic ash forms when the gases in stiff magma expand rapidly and the walls of the gas bubbles explode into tiny, glasslike slivers. Ash makes up most of the pyroclastic material in an eruption.

Volcanic blocks, the largest pieces of pyroclastic material, are pieces of solid rock erupted from a volcano.

Types of Pyroclastic Material

Pyroclastic material forms when magma explodes from a volcano and solidifies in the air. This material also forms when powerful eruptions shatter existing rock. The size of pyroclastic material ranges from boulders that are the size of houses to tiny particles that can remain suspended in the atmosphere for years. **Figure 6** shows four types of pyroclastic material: volcanic bombs, volcanic blocks, lapilli (lah PIL IE), and volcanic ash.

✓ **Reading Check** Describe four types of pyroclastic material.

Modeling an Explosive Eruption

1. Inflate a **large balloon,** and place it in a **cardboard box.**

2. Spread a **sheet** on the floor. Place the box in the middle of the sheet. Mound a thin layer of **sand** over the balloon to make a volcano that is taller than the edges of the box.

3. Lightly mist the volcano with **water.** Sprinkle **tempera paint** on the volcano until the volcano is completely covered.

4. Place **small objects** such as **raisins** randomly on the volcano. Draw a sketch of the volcano.

5. Put on your **safety goggles.** Pop the balloon with a **pin.**

6. Use a **metric ruler** to calculate the average distance that 10 grains of sand and 10 raisins traveled.

7. How did the relative weight of each type of material affect the average distance that the material traveled?

8. Draw a sketch of the exploded volcano.

Pyroclastic Flows

One particularly dangerous type of volcanic flow is called a *pyroclastic flow*. Pyroclastic flows are produced when enormous amounts of hot ash, dust, and gases are ejected from a volcano. This glowing cloud of pyroclastic material can race downhill at speeds of more than 200 km/h—faster than most hurricane-force winds! The temperature at the center of a pyroclastic flow can exceed 700°C. A pyroclastic flow from the eruption of Mount Pinatubo is shown in **Figure 7.** Fortunately, scientists were able to predict the eruption and a quarter of a million people were evacuated before the eruption.

Figure 7 *The 1991 eruption of Mount Pinatubo in the Philippines released terrifying pyroclastic flows.*

SECTION Review

Summary

- Volcanoes erupt both explosively and nonexplosively.
- Magma that has a high level of water, CO_2, or silica tends to erupt explosively.
- Lava can be classified by its viscosity and by the surface texture of lava flows.
- Pyroclastic material, such as ash and volcanic bombs, forms when magma solidifies as it travels through the air.

Using Key Terms

1. In your own words, write a definition for each of the following terms: *volcano, magma chamber,* and *vent.*

Understanding Key Ideas

2. Which of the following factors influences whether a volcano erupts explosively?
   a. the concentration of volcanic bombs in the magma
   b. the concentration of phosphorus in the magma
   c. the concentration of aa in the magma
   d. the concentration of water in the magma

3. How are lava and pyroclastic material classified? Describe four types of lava.

4. Which produces more pyroclastic material: an explosive eruption or a nonexplosive eruption?

5. Explain how the presence of silica and water in magma increases the chances of an explosive eruption.

6. What is a pyroclastic flow?

Math Skills

7. A sample of magma is 64% silica. Express this percentage as a simplified fraction.

Critical Thinking

8. **Analyzing Ideas** How is an explosive eruption similar to opening a can of soda that has been shaken? Be sure to describe the role of carbon dioxide.

9. **Making Inferences** Predict the silica content of aa, pillow lava, and blocky lava.

10. **Making Inferences** Explain why the names of many types of lava are Hawaiian but the names of many types of pyroclastic material are Italian and Indonesian.

For a variety of links related to this chapter, go to www.scilinks.org

Topic: Volcanic Eruptions
SciLinks code: HSM1616

Effects of Volcanic Eruptions

In 1816, Chauncey Jerome, a resident of Connecticut, wrote that the clothes his wife had laid out to dry the day before had frozen during the night. This event would not have been unusual except that the date was June 10!

At that time, residents of New England did not know that the explosion of a volcanic island on the other side of the world had severely changed the global climate and was causing "The Year Without a Summer."

Volcanic Eruptions and Climate Change

The explosion of Mount Tambora in 1815 blanketed most of Indonesia in darkness for three days. It is estimated that 12,000 people died directly from the explosion and 80,000 people died from the resulting hunger and disease. The global effects of the eruption were not felt until the next year, however. During large-scale eruptions, enormous amounts of volcanic ash and gases are ejected into the upper atmosphere.

As volcanic ash and gases spread throughout the atmosphere, they can block enough sunlight to cause global temperatures to drop. The Tambora eruption affected the global climate enough to cause food shortages in North America and Europe. More recently, the eruption of Mount Pinatubo, shown in **Figure 1,** caused average global temperatures to drop by as much as 0.5°C. Although this may seem insignificant, such a shift can disrupt climates all over the world.

✓ Reading Check How does a volcanic eruption affect climate? *(See the Appendix for answers to Reading Checks.)*

READING WARM-UP

Objectives

● Explain how volcanic eruptions can affect climate.
● Compare the three types of volcanoes.
● Compare craters, calderas, and lava plateaus.

Terms to Learn

crater
caldera
lava plateau

READING STRATEGY

Paired Summarizing Read this section silently. In pairs, take turns summarizing the material. Stop to discuss ideas that seem confusing.

Figure 1 *Ash from the eruption of Mount Pinatubo blocked out the sun in the Philippines for several days. The eruption also affected global climate.*

Different Types of Volcanoes

Volcanic eruptions can cause profound changes in climate. But the changes to Earth's surface caused by eruptions are probably more familiar. Perhaps the best known of all volcanic landforms are the volcanoes themselves. The three basic types of volcanoes are illustrated in **Figure 2.**

Shield Volcanoes

Shield volcanoes are built of layers of lava released from repeated nonexplosive eruptions. Because the lava is very runny, it spreads out over a wide area. Over time, the layers of lava create a volcano that has gently sloping sides. Although their sides are not very steep, shield volcanoes can be enormous. Hawaii's Mauna Kea, the shield volcano shown here, is the tallest mountain on Earth. Measured from its base on the sea floor, Mauna Kea is taller than Mount Everest.

Cinder Cone Volcanoes

Cinder cone volcanoes are made of pyroclastic material usually produced from moderately explosive eruptions. The pyroclastic material forms steep slopes, as shown in this photo of the Mexican volcano Paricutín. Cinder cones are small and usually erupt for only a short time. Paricutín appeared in a cornfield in 1943 and erupted for only nine years before stopping at a height of 400 m. Cinder cones often occur in clusters, commonly on the sides of other volcanoes. They usually erode quickly because the pyroclastic material is not cemented together.

Composite Volcanoes

Composite volcanoes, sometimes called *stratovolcanoes,* are one of the most common types of volcanoes. They form from explosive eruptions of pyroclastic material followed by quieter flows of lava. The combination of both types of eruptions forms alternating layers of pyroclastic material and lava. Composite volcanoes, such as Japan's Mount Fuji (shown here), have broad bases and sides that get steeper toward the top. Composite volcanoes in the western region of the United States include Mount Hood, Mount Rainier, Mount Shasta, and Mount St. Helens.

Figure 2 Three Types of Volcanoes

Shield volcano

Cinder cone volcano

Composite volcano

Figure 3 *A crater, such as this one in Kamchatka, Russia, forms around the central vent of a volcano.*

crater a funnel-shaped pit near the top of the central vent of a volcano

caldera a large, semicircular depression that forms when the magma chamber below a volcano partially empties and causes the ground above to sink

Other Types of Volcanic Landforms

In addition to volcanoes, other landforms are produced by volcanic activity. These landforms include craters, calderas, and lava plateaus. Read on to learn more about these landforms.

Craters

Around the central vent at the top of many volcanoes is a funnel-shaped pit called a **crater.** An example of a crater is shown in **Figure 3.** During less explosive eruptions, lava flows and pyroclastic material can pile up around the vent creating a cone with a central crater. As the eruption stops, the lava that is left in the crater often drains back underground. The vent may then collapse to form a larger crater. If the lava hardens in the crater, the next eruption may blast it away. In this way, a crater becomes larger and deeper.

Calderas

Calderas can appear similar to craters, but they are many times larger. A **caldera** is a large, semicircular depression that forms when the chamber that supplies magma to a volcano partially empties and the chamber's roof collapses. As a result, the ground above the magma chamber sinks, as shown in **Figure 4.** Much of Yellowstone Park is made up of three large calderas that formed when volcanoes collapsed between 1.9 million and 0.6 million years ago. Today, hot springs, such as Old Faithful, are heated by the thermal energy left over from those events.

✓ Reading Check How do calderas form?

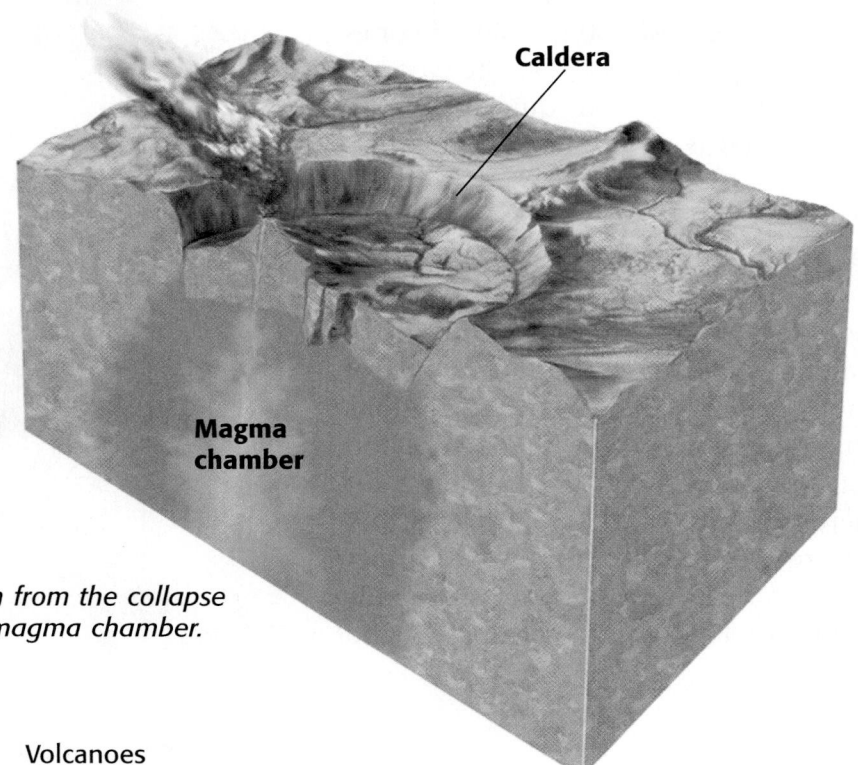

Caldera

Magma chamber

Figure 4 *Calderas form from the collapse of the roof overlying a magma chamber.*

Lava Plateaus

The most massive outpourings of lava do not come from individual volcanoes. Most of the lava on Earth's surface erupted from long cracks, or *rifts,* in the crust. In this type of eruption, runny lava can pour out for millions of years and spread over huge areas. A landform that results from repeated eruptions of lava spread over a large area is called a **lava plateau.** The Columbia River Plateau, part of which is shown in **Figure 5,** is a lava plateau that formed between 17 million and 14 million years ago in the northwestern region of the United States. In some places, the Columbia River Plateau is 3 km thick.

Figure 5 *The Columbia River Plateau formed from a massive outpouring of lava that began 17 million years ago.*

lava plateau a wide, flat landform that results from repeated nonexplosive eruptions of lava that spread over a large area

---

SECTION Review

Summary

- The large volumes of gas and ash released from volcanic eruptions can affect climate.
- Shield volcanoes result from many eruptions of relatively runny lava.
- Cinder cone volcanoes result from mildly explosive eruptions of pyroclastic material.
- Composite volcanoes result from alternating explosive and nonexplosive eruptions.
- Craters, calderas, and lava plateaus are volcanic landforms.

Using Key Terms

Complete each of the following sentences by choosing the correct term from the word bank.

    caldera   crater

1. A ___ is a funnel-shaped hole around the central vent.

2. A ___ results when a magma chamber partially empties.

Understanding Key Ideas

3. Which type of volcano results from alternating explosive and nonexplosive eruptions?
   a. composite volcano
   b. cinder cone volcano
   c. rift-zone volcano
   d. shield volcano

4. Why do cinder cone volcanoes have narrower bases and steeper sides than shield volcanoes do?

5. Why does a volcano's crater tend to get larger over time?

Math Skills

6. The fastest lava flow recorded was 60 km/h. A horse can gallop as fast as 48 mi/h. Could a galloping horse outrun the fastest lava flow?
   (Hint: 1 km = 0.621 mi)

Critical Thinking

7. **Making Inferences** Why did it take a year for the effects of the Tambora eruption to be experienced in New England?

For a variety of links related to this chapter, go to www.scilinks.org

Topic: Volcanic Effects
SciLinks code: HSM1615

Causes of Volcanic Eruptions

More than 2,000 years ago, Pompeii was a busy Roman city near the sleeping volcano Mount Vesuvius. People did not see Vesuvius as much of a threat. Everything changed when Vesuvius suddenly erupted and buried the city in a deadly blanket of ash that was almost 20 ft thick!

Today, even more people are living on and near active volcanoes. Scientists closely monitor volcanoes to avoid this type of disaster. They study the gases coming from active volcanoes and look for slight changes in the volcano's shape that could indicate that an eruption is near. Scientists know much more about the causes of eruptions than the ancient Pompeiians did, but there is much more to be discovered.

The Formation of Magma

Understanding how magma forms helps explain why volcanoes erupt. Magma forms in the deeper regions of the Earth's crust and in the uppermost layers of the mantle where the temperature and pressure are very high. Changes in pressure and temperature cause magma to form.

Pressure and Temperature

Part of the upper mantle is made of very hot, puttylike rock that flows slowly. The rock of the mantle is hot enough to melt at Earth's surface, but it remains a puttylike solid because of pressure. This pressure is caused by the weight of the rock above the mantle. In other words, the rock above the mantle presses the atoms of the mantle so close together that the rock cannot melt. As **Figure 1** shows, rock melts when its temperature increases or when the pressure on the rock decreases.

Figure 1 *The curved line indicates the melting point of a rock. As pressure decreases and temperature increases, the rock begins to melt.*

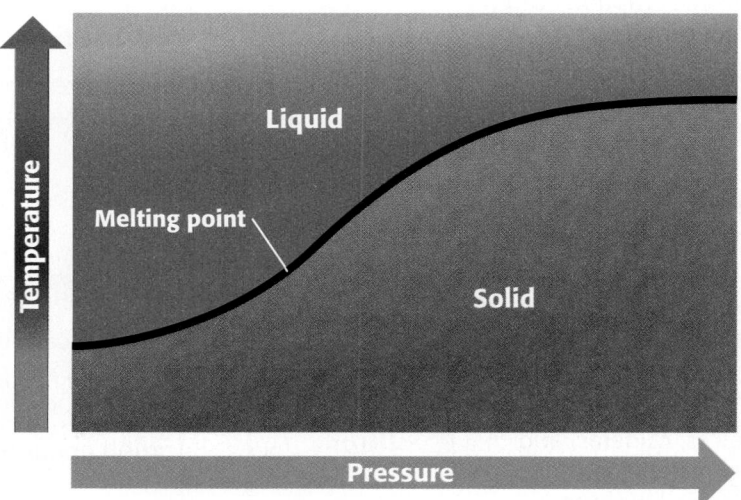

Magma Formation in the Mantle

Because the temperature of the mantle is fairly constant, a decrease in pressure is the most common cause of magma formation. Magma often forms at the boundary between separating tectonic plates, where pressure is decreased. Once formed, the magma is less dense than the surrounding rock, so the magma slowly rises toward the surface like an air bubble in a jar of honey.

Where Volcanoes Form

The locations of volcanoes give clues about how volcanoes form. The map in **Figure 2** shows the location of some of the world's major active volcanoes. The map also shows the boundaries between tectonic plates. A large number of volcanoes lie directly on tectonic plate boundaries. In fact, the plate boundaries surrounding the Pacific Ocean have so many volcanoes that the area is called the *Ring of Fire*.

Tectonic plate boundaries are areas where tectonic plates either collide, separate, or slide past one another. At these boundaries, it is possible for magma to form and travel to the surface. About 80% of active volcanoes on land form where plates collide, and about 15% form where plates separate. The remaining few occur far from tectonic plate boundaries.

Reading Check Why are most volcanoes on plate boundaries? *(See the Appendix for answers to Reading Checks.)*

Quick Lab

Reaction to Stress

1. Make a pliable "rock" by pouring **60 mL of water** into a **plastic cup** and adding **150 mL of cornstarch**, 15 mL at a time. Stir well each time.

2. Pour half of the cornstarch mixture into a **clear bowl**. Carefully observe how the "rock" flows. Be patient—this process is slow!

3. Scrape the rest of the "rock" out of the cup with a **spoon**. Observe the behavior of the "rock" as you scrape.

4. What happened to the "rock" when you let it flow by itself? What happened when you put stress on the "rock"?

5. How is this pliable "rock" similar to the rock of the upper part of the mantle?

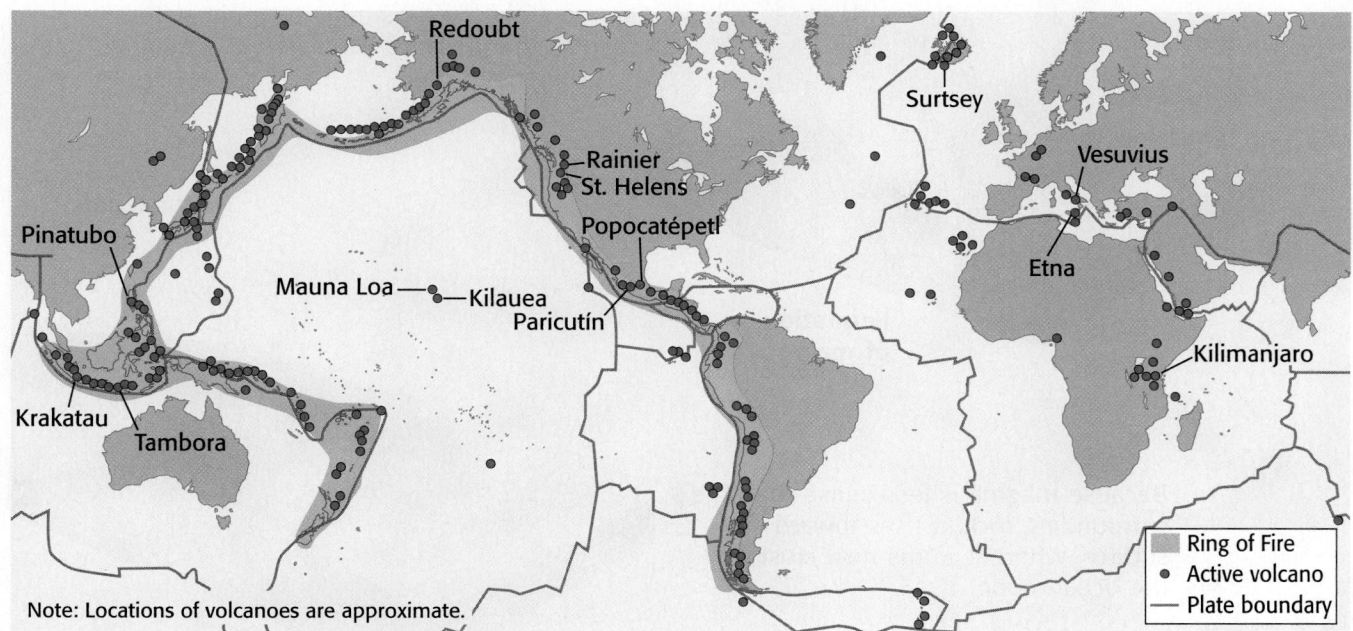

Note: Locations of volcanoes are approximate.

Figure 2 *Tectonic plate boundaries are likely places for volcanoes to form. The Ring of Fire contains nearly 75% of the world's active volcanoes on land.*

How Hot Is Hot?

Inside the Earth, magma can reach a burning-hot 1,400°C! You may be more familiar with Fahrenheit temperatures, so convert 1,400°C to degrees Fahrenheit by using the formula below.

°F = (°C ÷ 5 × 9) + 32

What is the temperature in degrees Fahrenheit?

rift zone an area of deep cracks that forms between two tectonic plates that are pulling away from each other

When Tectonic Plates Separate

At a *divergent boundary,* tectonic plates move away from each other. As tectonic plates separate, a set of deep cracks called a **rift zone** forms between the plates. Mantle rock then rises to fill in the gap. When mantle rock gets closer to the surface, the pressure decreases. The pressure decrease causes the mantle rock to melt and form magma. Because magma is less dense than the surrounding rock, it rises through the rifts. When the magma reaches the surface, it spills out and hardens, creating new crust, as shown in **Figure 3.**

Mid-Ocean Ridges Form at Divergent Boundaries

Lava that flows from undersea rift zones produces volcanoes and mountain chains called *mid-ocean ridges.* Just as a baseball has stitches, the Earth is circled with mid-ocean ridges. At these ridges, lava flows out and creates new crust. Most volcanic activity on Earth occurs at mid-ocean ridges. While most mid-ocean ridges are underwater, Iceland, with its volcanoes and hot springs, was created by lava from the Mid-Atlantic Ridge. In 1963, enough lava poured out of the Mid-Atlantic Ridge near Iceland to form a new island called *Surtsey.* Scientists watched this new island being born!

Figure 3   How Magma Forms at a Divergent Boundary

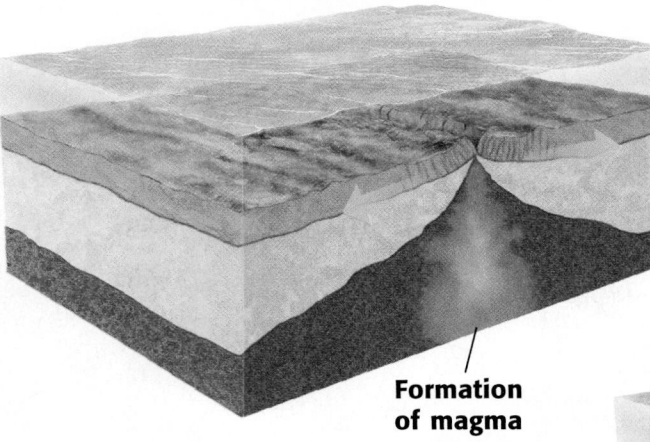

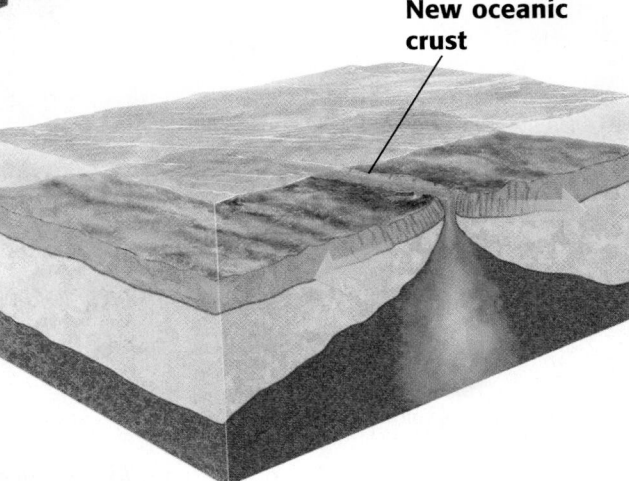

◀ Mantle material rises to fill the space opened by separating tectonic plates. As the pressure decreases, the mantle begins to melt.

New oceanic crust

Formation of magma

Because magma is less dense than the surrounding rock, it rises toward the surface, where it forms new crust on the ocean floor. ▶

Figure 4 How Magma Forms at a Convergent Boundary

Oceanic crust

Continental crust

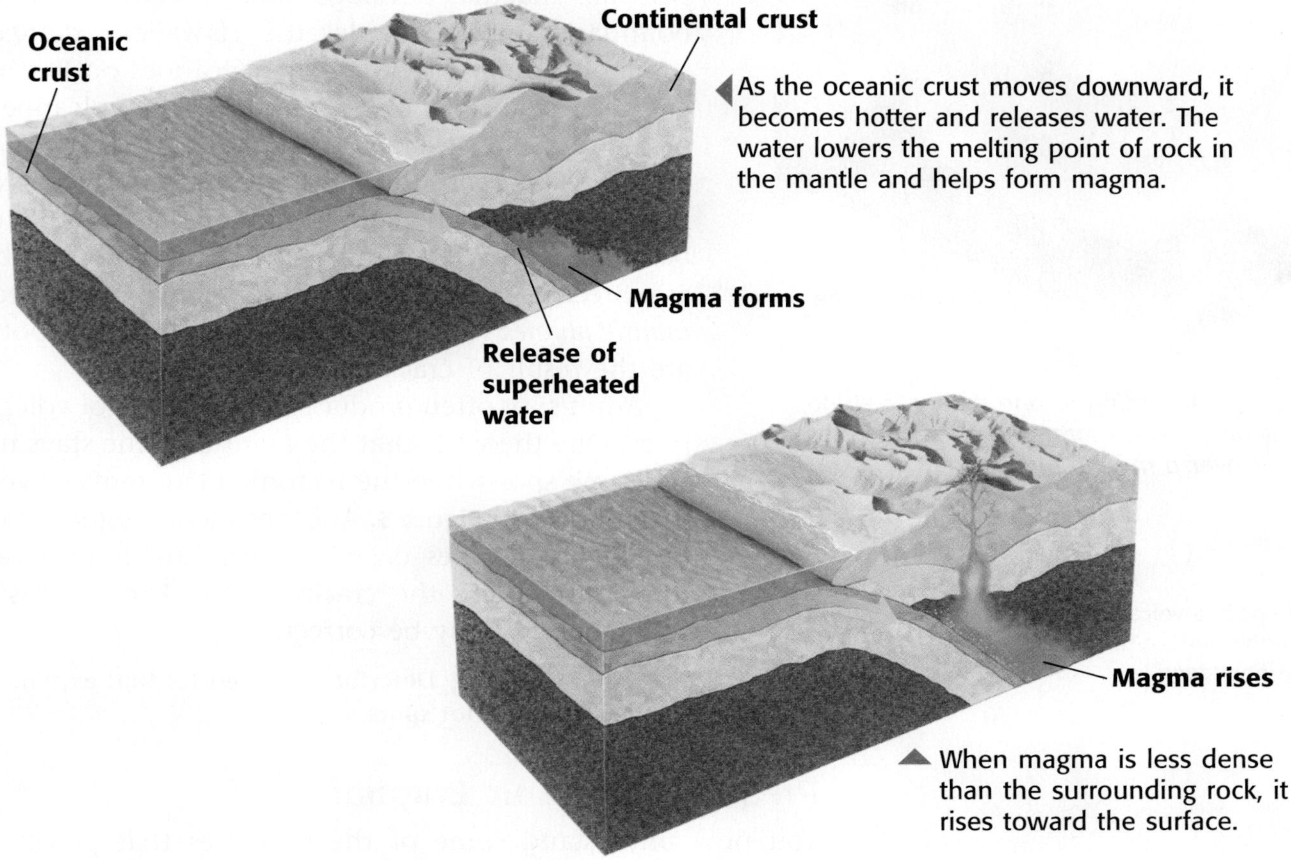

◀ As the oceanic crust moves downward, it becomes hotter and releases water. The water lowers the melting point of rock in the mantle and helps form magma.

Magma forms

Release of superheated water

Magma rises

▲ When magma is less dense than the surrounding rock, it rises toward the surface.

When Tectonic Plates Collide

If you slide two pieces of notebook paper into one another on a flat desktop, the papers will either buckle upward or one piece of paper will move under the other. This is similar to what happens at a convergent boundary. A *convergent boundary* is a place where tectonic plates collide. When an oceanic plate collides with a continental plate, the oceanic plate usually slides underneath the continental plate. The process of *subduction,* the movement of one tectonic plate underneath another, is shown in **Figure 4.** Oceanic crust is subducted because it is denser and thinner than continental crust.

Subduction Produces Magma

As the descending oceanic crust scrapes past the continental crust, the temperature and pressure increase. The combination of increased heat and pressure causes the water contained in the oceanic crust to be released. The water then mixes with the mantle rock, which lowers the rock's melting point, causing it to melt. This body of magma can rise to form a volcano.

✓ *Reading Check* How does subduction produce magma?

Tectonic Models

Create models of convergent and divergent boundaries by using materials of your choice. Have your teacher approve your list before you start building your model at home with a parent. In class, use your model to explain how each type of boundary leads to the formation of magma.

ACTiViTY

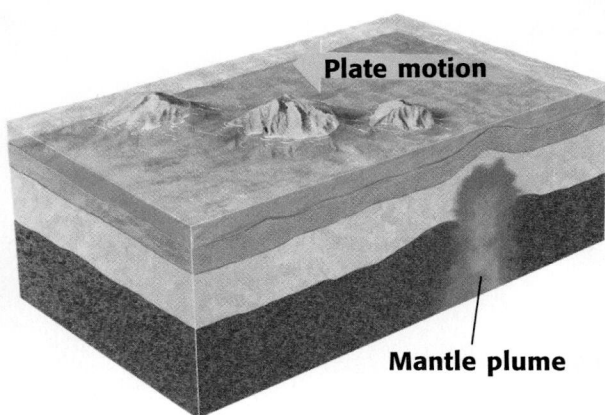

Figure 5 *According to one theory, a string of volcanic islands forms as a tectonic plate passes over a mantle plume.*

hot spot a volcanically active area of Earth's surface far from a tectonic plate boundary

Figure 6 *As if being this close to an active volcano is not dangerous enough, the gases being collected are extremely poisonous.*

Hot Spots

Not all magma develops along tectonic plate boundaries. For example, the Hawaiian Islands, some of the most well-known volcanoes on Earth, are nowhere near a plate boundary. The volcanoes of Hawaii and several other places on Earth are known as *hot spots*. **Hot spots** are volcanically active places on the Earth's surface that are far from plate boundaries. Some scientists think that hot spots are directly above columns of rising magma, called *mantle plumes*. Other scientists think that hot spots are the result of cracks in the Earth's crust.

A hot spot often produces a long chain of volcanoes. One theory is that the mantle plume stays in the same spot while the tectonic plate moves over it, as shown in **Figure 5.** Another theory argues that hot-spot volcanoes occur in long chains because they form along the cracks in the Earth's crust. Both theories may be correct.

✓ Reading Check Describe two theories that explain the existence of hot spots.

Predicting Volcanic Eruptions

You now understand some of the processes that produce volcanoes, but how do scientists predict when a volcano is going to erupt? Volcanoes are classified in three categories. *Extinct volcanoes* have not erupted in recorded history and probably never will erupt again. *Dormant volcanoes* are currently not erupting, but the record of past eruptions suggests that they may erupt again. *Active volcanoes* are currently erupting or show signs of erupting in the near future. Scientists study active and dormant volcanoes for signs of a future eruption.

Measuring Small Quakes and Volcanic Gases

Most active volcanoes produce small earthquakes as the magma within them moves upward and causes the surrounding rock to shift. Just before an eruption, the number and intensity of the earthquakes increase and the occurrence of quakes may be continuous. Monitoring these quakes is one of the best ways to predict an eruption.

As **Figure 6** shows, scientists also study the volume and composition of volcanic gases. The ratio of certain gases, especially that of sulfur dioxide, SO_2, to carbon dioxide, CO_2, may be important in predicting eruptions. Changes in this ratio may indicate changes in the magma chamber below.

Measuring Slope and Temperature

As magma moves upward prior to an eruption, it can cause the Earth's surface to swell. The side of a volcano may even bulge as the magma moves upward. An instrument called a *tiltmeter* helps scientists detect small changes in the angle of a volcano's slope. Scientists also use satellite technology such as the Global Positioning System (GPS) to detect the changes in a volcano's slope that may signal an eruption.

One of the newest methods for predicting volcanic eruptions includes using satellite images. Infrared satellite images record changes in the surface temperature and gas emissions of a volcano over time. If the site is getting hotter, the magma below is probably rising!

INTERNET ACTIVITY

For another activity related to this chapter, go to **go.hrw.com** and type in the keyword **HZ5VOLW**.

SECTION Review

Summary

- Temperature and pressure influence magma formation.
- Most volcanoes form at tectonic boundaries.
- As tectonic plates separate, magma rises to fill the cracks, or rifts, that develop.
- As oceanic and continental plates collide, the oceanic plate tends to subduct and cause the formation of magma.
- To predict eruptions, scientists study the frequency and type of earthquakes associated with the volcano as well as changes in slope, changes in the gases released, and changes in the volcano's surface temperature.

Using Key Terms

1. Use each of the following terms in a separate sentence: *hot spot* and *rift zone*.

Understanding Key Ideas

2. If the temperature of a rock remains constant but the pressure on the rock decreases, what tends to happen?
   a. The temperature increases.
   b. The rock becomes liquid.
   c. The rock becomes solid.
   d. The rock subducts.

3. Which of the following words is a synonym for *dormant*?
   a. predictable
   b. active
   c. dead
   d. sleeping

4. What is the Ring of Fire?

5. Explain how convergent and divergent plate boundaries cause magma formation.

6. Describe four methods that scientists use to predict volcanic eruptions.

7. Why does a oceanic plate tend to subduct when it collides with a continental plate?

Math Skills

8. If a tectonic plate moves at a rate of 2 km every 1 million years, how long would it take a hot spot to form a chain of volcanoes 100 km long?

Critical Thinking

9. **Making Inferences** New crust is constantly being created at mid-ocean ridges. So, why is the oldest oceanic crust only about 150 million years old?

10. **Identifying Relationships** If you are studying a volcanic deposit, would the youngest layers be more likely to be found on the top or on the bottom? Explain your answer.

SCI LINKS

Developed and maintained by the National Science Teachers Association

For a variety of links related to this chapter, go to www.scilinks.org

Topic: What Causes Volcanoes?
SciLinks code: HSM1654

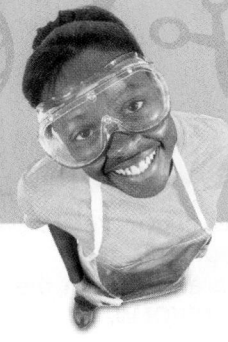

Skills Practice Lab

Volcano Verdict

You will need to pair up with a partner for this exploration. You and your partner will act as geologists who work in a city located near a volcano. City officials are counting on you to predict when the volcano will erupt next. You and your partner have decided to use limewater as a gas-emissions tester. You will use this tester to measure the levels of carbon dioxide emitted from a simulated volcano. The more active the volcano is, the more carbon dioxide it releases.

OBJECTIVES

Build a working apparatus to test carbon dioxide levels.

Test the levels of carbon dioxide emitted from a model volcano.

MATERIALS

- baking soda, 15 mL
- bottle, drinking, 16 oz
- box or stand for plastic cup
- clay, modeling
- coin
- cup, clear plastic, 9 oz
- graduated cylinder
- limewater, 1 L
- straw, drinking, flexible
- tissue, bathroom (2 sheets)
- vinegar, white, 140 mL
- water, 100 mL

SAFETY

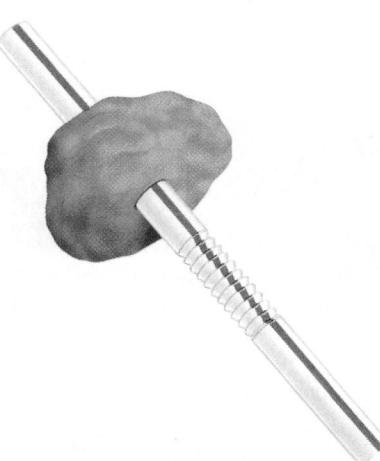

Procedure

1. Put on your safety goggles, and carefully pour limewater into the plastic cup until the cup is three-fourths full. You have just made your gas-emissions tester.

2. Now, build a model volcano. Begin by pouring 50 mL of water and 70 mL of vinegar into the drink bottle.

3. Form a plug of clay around the short end of the straw, as shown at left. The clay plug must be large enough to cover the opening of the bottle. Be careful not to get the clay wet.

4. Sprinkle 5 mL of baking soda along the center of a single section of bathroom tissue. Then, roll the tissue, and twist the ends so that the baking soda can't fall out.

5 Drop the tissue into the drink bottle, and immediately put the short end of the straw inside the bottle to make a seal with the clay.

6 Put the other end of the straw into the limewater, as shown at right.

7 You have just taken your first measurement of gas levels from the volcano. Record your observations.

8 Imagine that it is several days later and you need to test the volcano again to collect more data. Before you continue, toss a coin. If it lands heads up, go to step 9. If it lands tails up, go to step 10. Write down the step that you follow.

9 Repeat steps 1–7. This time, add 2 mL of baking soda to the vinegar and water. (Note: You must use fresh water, vinegar, and limewater.) Write down your observations. Go to step 11.

10 Repeat steps 1–7. This time, add 8 mL of baking soda to the vinegar and water. (Note: You must use fresh water, vinegar, and limewater.) Write down your observations. Go to step 11.

11 Return to step 8 once. Then, answer the questions below.

Analyze the Results

1 **Explaining Events** How do you explain the difference in the appearance of the limewater from one trial to the next?

2 **Recognizing Patterns** What does the data that you collected indicate about the activity in the volcano?

Draw Conclusions

3 **Evaluating Results** Based on your results, do you think it would be necessary to evacuate the city?

4 **Applying Conclusions** How would a geologist use a gas-emissions tester to predict volcanic eruptions?

Chapter Review

USING KEY TERMS

For each pair of terms, explain how the meanings of the terms differ.

1 *caldera* and *crater*

2 *lava* and *magma*

3 *lava* and *pyroclastic material*

4 *vent* and *rift*

5 *cinder cone volcano* and *shield volcano*

UNDERSTANDING KEY IDEAS

Multiple Choice

6 The type of magma that tends to cause explosive eruptions has a

  a. high silica content and high viscosity.
  b. high silica content and low viscosity.
  c. low silica content and low viscosity.
  d. low silica content and high viscosity.

7 Lava that flows slowly to form a glassy surface with rounded wrinkles is called

  a. aa lava.
  b. pahoehoe lava.
  c. pillow lava.
  d. blocky lava.

8 Magma forms within the mantle most often as a result of

  a. high temperature and high pressure.
  b. high temperature and low pressure.
  c. low temperature and high pressure.
  d. low temperature and low pressure.

9 What causes an increase in the number and intensity of small earthquakes before an eruption?

  a. the movement of magma
  b. the formation of pyroclastic material
  c. the hardening of magma
  d. the movement of tectonic plates

10 If volcanic dust and ash remain in the atmosphere for months or years, what do you predict will happen?

  a. Solar reflection will decrease, and temperatures will increase.
  b. Solar reflection will increase, and temperatures will increase.
  c. Solar reflection will decrease, and temperatures will decrease.
  d. Solar reflection will increase, and temperatures will decrease.

11 At divergent plate boundaries,

  a. heat from Earth's core causes mantle plumes.
  b. oceanic plates sink, which causes magma to form.
  c. tectonic plates move apart.
  d. hot spots cause volcanoes.

12 A theory that helps explain the causes of both earthquakes and volcanoes is the theory of

  a. pyroclastics.
  b. plate tectonics.
  c. climatic fluctuation.
  d. mantle plumes.

Short Answer

13 How does the presence of water in magma affect a volcanic eruption?

14 Describe four clues that scientists use to predict eruptions.

15 Identify the characteristics of the three types of volcanoes.

16 Describe the positive effects of volcanic eruptions.

17 **Concept Mapping** Use the following terms to create a concept map: *volcanic bombs, aa, pyroclastic material, pahoehoe, lapilli, lava,* and *volcano.*

18 **Identifying Relationships** You are exploring a volcano that has been dormant for some time. You begin to keep notes on the types of volcanic debris that you see as you walk. Your first notes describe volcanic ash. Later, your notes describe lapilli. In what direction are you most likely traveling—toward the crater or away from the crater? Explain your answer.

19 **Making Inferences** Loihi is a submarine Hawaiian volcano that might grow to form a new island. The Hawaiian Islands are located on the Pacific plate, which is moving northwest. Considering how this island chain may have formed, where do you think the new volcanic island will be located? Explain your answer.

20 **Evaluating Hypotheses** What evidence could confirm the existence of mantle plumes?

INTERPRETING GRAPHICS

The graph below illustrates the average change in temperature above or below normal for a community over several years. Use the graph below to answer the questions that follow.

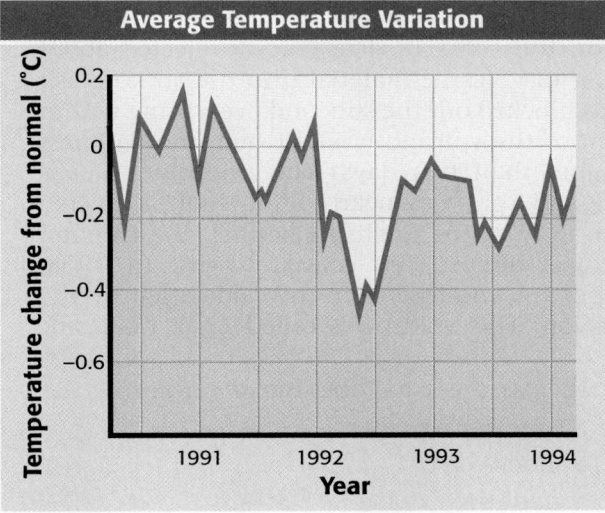

21 If the variation in temperature over the years was influenced by a major volcanic eruption, when did the eruption most likely take place? Explain.

22 If the temperature were measured only once each year (at the beginning of the year), how would your interpretation be different?

READING

Read each of the passages below. Then, answer the questions that follow each passage.

Passage 1 When the volcanic island of Krakatau in Indonesia exploded in 1883, a shock wave sped around the world seven times. The explosion was probably the loudest sound in recorded human history. What caused this enormous explosion? Most likely, the walls of the volcano ruptured, and ocean water flowed into the magma chamber of the volcano. The water instantly turned into steam, and the volcano exploded with the force of 100 million tons of TNT. The volcano ejected about 18 km³ of volcanic material into the air. The ash clouds blocked out the sun, and everything within 80 km of the volcano was plunged into darkness for more than two days. The explosion caused a <u>tsunami</u> that was nearly 40 m high. Detected as far away as the English Channel, the tsunami destroyed almost 300 coastal towns. In 1928, another volcano rose from the caldera left by the explosion. This volcano is called <u>Anak</u> Krakatau.

1. In the passage, what does *tsunami* mean?
  A a large earthquake
  B a shock wave
  C a giant ocean wave
  D a cloud of gas and dust

2. According to the passage, what was the size of the Krakatau explosion probably the result of?
  F pyroclastic material rapidly mixing with air
  G 100 million tons of TNT
  H an ancient caldera
  I the flow of water into the magma chamber

3. What does the Indonesian word *anak* probably mean?
  A father
  B child
  C mother
  D grandmother

Passage 2 Yellowstone National Park in Montana and Wyoming contains three overlapping calderas and evidence of the <u>cataclysmic</u> ash flows that erupted from them. The oldest eruption occurred 1.9 million years ago, the second eruption happened 1.3 million years ago, and the most recent eruption occurred 0.6 million years ago. Seismographs regularly detect the movement of magma beneath the caldera, and the hot springs and geysers of the park indicate that a large body of magma lies beneath the park. The geology of the area shows that major eruptions occurred about once every 0.6 or 0.7 million years. Thus, a devastating eruption is long overdue. People living near the park should be evacuated immediately.

1. In the passage, what does *cataclysmic* mean?
  A nonexplosive
  B ancient
  C destructive
  D characterized by ash flows

2. Which of the following clues are evidence of an active magma body beneath the park?
  F cataclysmic ash flows
  G the discovery of seismoclasts
  H minor eruptions
  I seismograph readings

3. Which of the following contradicts the author's conclusion that an eruption is "long overdue"?
  A Magma has been detected beneath the park.
  B With a variation of 0.1 million years, an eruption may occur in the next 100,000 years.
  C The composition of gases emitted indicates that an eruption is near.
  D Seismographs have detected the movement of magma.

INTERPRETING GRAPHICS

The map below shows some of the Earth's major volcanoes and the tectonic plate boundaries. Use the map below to answer the questions that follow.

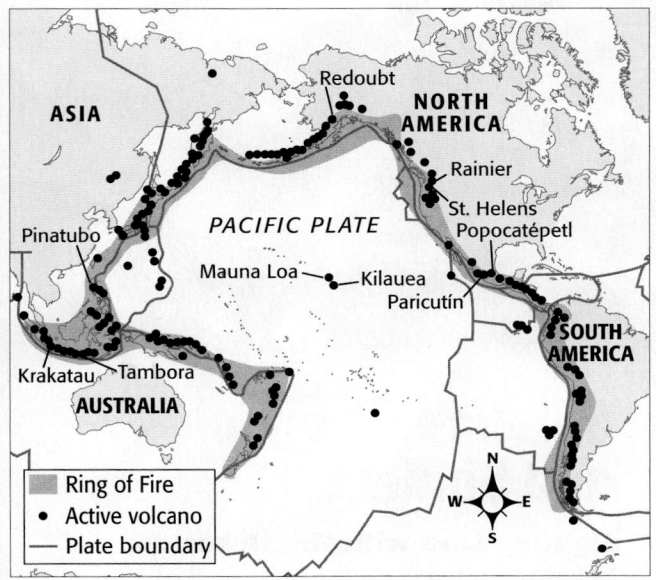

1. If ash from Popocatépetl landed on the west coast of the United States, what direction did the ash travel?

   A northeast

   B northwest

   C southeast

   D southwest

2. Why aren't there any active volcanoes in Australia?

   F Australia is not located on a plate boundary.

   G Australia is close to Krakatau and Tambora.

   H Australia is near a plate boundary.

   I Australia is near a rift zone.

3. If a scientist traveled along the Ring of Fire from Mt. Redoubt to Krakatau, which of the following most accurately describes the directions in which she traveled?

   A west, southeast, east

   B west, southeast, west

   C west, southwest, east

   D west, southwest, west

MATH

Read each question below, and choose the best answer.

1. Midway Island is 1,935 km northwest of Hawaii. If the Pacific plate is moving to the northwest at a rate of 9 cm per year, how long ago was Midway Island over the hot spot that formed the island?

   A 215,000 years

   B 2,150,000 years

   C 21,500,000 years

   D 215,000,000 years

2. In the first year that the Mexican volcano Paricutín appeared in a cornfield, it grew 360 m. The volcano stopped growing at about 400 m. What percentage of the volcano's total growth occurred in the first year?

   F 67%

   G 82%

   H 90%

   I 92%

3. A pyroclastic flow is moving down a hill at 120 km/h. If you lived in a town 5 km away, how much time would you have before the flow reached your town?

   A 2 min and 30 s

   B 1 min and 21 s

   C 3 min and 12 s

   D 8 min and 3 s

4. The Columbia River plateau is a lava plateau that contains 350,000 km³ of solidified lava. The plateau took 3 million years to form. What was the average rate of lava deposition each century?

   F 0.116 km³

   G 11.6 km³

   H 116 km³

   I 11,600 km³

Standardized Test Preparation

Science in Action

Weird Science

Pele's Hair

It is hard to believe that the fragile specimen shown below is a volcanic rock. This strange type of lava, called *Pele's hair,* forms when volcanic gases spray molten rock high into the air. When conditions are right, the lava can harden into strands of volcanic glass as thin as a human hair. This type of lava is named after Pele, the Hawaiian goddess of volcanoes. Several other types of lava are named in Pele's honor. Pele's tears are tear-shaped globs of volcanic glass often found at the end of strands of Pele's hair. Pele's diamonds are green, gemlike stones found in hardened lava flows.

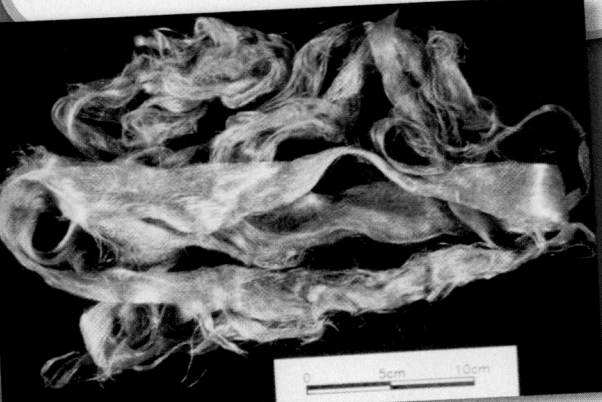

Language Arts ACTIVITY

Volcanic terms come from many languages. Research some volcanic terms on the Internet, and create an illustrated volcanic glossary to share with your class.

Science, Technology, and Society

Fighting Lava with Fire Hoses

What would you do if a 60 ft wall of lava was advancing toward your home? Most people would head for safety. But when an eruption threatened to engulf the Icelandic fishing village of Heimaey in 1973, some villagers held their ground and fought back. Working 14-hour days in conditions so hot that their boots would catch on fire, villagers used fire-hoses to spray sea water on the lava flow. For several weeks, the lava advanced toward the town, and it seemed as if there was no hope. But the water eventually cooled the lava fast enough to divert the flow and save the village. It took 5 months and about 1.5 billion gallons of water to fight the lava flow. When the eruption stopped, villagers found that the island had grown by 20%!

Social Studies ACTIVITY

WRITING SKILL To try to protect the city of Hilo, Hawaii, from an eruption in 1935, planes dropped bombs on the lava. Find out if this mission was successful, and write a report about other attempts to stop lava flows.

Tina Neal

Volcanologist Would you like to study volcanoes for a living? Tina Neal is a volcanologist at the Alaska Volcano Observatory in Anchorage, Alaska. Her job is to monitor and study some of Alaska's 41 active volcanoes. Much of her work focuses on studying volcanoes in order to protect the public. According to Neal, being near a volcano when it is erupting is a wonderful adventure for the senses. "Sometimes you can get so close to an erupting volcano that you can feel the heat, hear the activity, and smell the lava. It's amazing! In Alaska, erupting volcanoes are too dangerous to get very close to, but they create a stunning visual display even from a distance."

Neal also enjoys the science of volcanoes. "It's fascinating to be near an active volcano and become aware of all the chemical and physical processes taking place. When I'm watching a volcano, I think about everything we understand and don't understand about what is happening. It's mind-boggling!" Neal says that if you are interested in becoming a volcanologist, it is important to be well rounded as a scientist. So, you would have to study math, geology, chemistry, and physics. Having a good understanding of computer tools is also important because volcanologists use computers to manage a lot of data and to create models. Neal also suggests learning a second language, such as Spanish. In her spare time, Neal is learning Russian so that she can better communicate with research partners in Kamchatka, Siberia.

Math ACTIVITY

The 1912 eruption of Mt. Katmai in Alaska could be heard 5,620 km away in Atlanta, Georgia. If the average speed of sound in the atmosphere is 342 m/s, how many hours after the eruption did the citizens of Atlanta hear the explosion?

To learn more about these Science in Action topics, visit go.hrw.com and type in the keyword **HZ5VOLF.**

Current Science

Check out Current Science® articles related to this chapter by visiting go.hrw.com. Just type in the keyword HZ5CS09.

UNIT 4

TIMELINE

Reshaping the Land

In this unit, you will learn about how the surface of the Earth is continuously reshaped. There is a constant struggle between the forces that build up the Earth's land features and the forces that break them down. This timeline shows some of the events that have occurred in this struggle as natural changes in the Earth's features took place.

320
Million years ago
Vast swamps along the western edge of the Appalachian Mountains are buried by sediment and form the largest coal fields in the world.

6
Million years ago
The Colorado River begins to carve the Grand Canyon, which is roughly 2 km deep today.

10,000
years ago
The Great Lakes form at the end of the last Ice Age.

1930
Carlsbad Caverns National Park is established. It features the nation's deepest limestone cave and one of the largest underground chambers in the world.

Carlsbad Caverns

280
Million years ago

The shallow inland sea that covered much of what is now the upper midwestern United States fills with sediment and disappears.

140
Million years ago

The mouth of the Mississippi River is near present-day Cairo, Illinois.

65
Million years ago

Dinosaurs become extinct.

1775

The Battle of Bunker Hill, a victory for the Colonials, takes place on a drumlin, a tear-shaped mound of sediment that was formed by an ice-age glacier 10,000 years earlier.

1879

Cleopatra's Needle, a granite obelisk, is moved from Egypt to New York City. Within the next 100 years, the weather and pollution severely damage the 3,000-year-old monument.

1987

An iceberg twice the size of Rhode Island breaks off the edge of Antarctica's continental glacier.

1998

Hong Kong opens a new airport on an artificially enlarged island. Almost 350 million cubic meters of rock and soil were deposited in the South China Sea to form the over 3,000-acre island.

2002

A NASA study finds that the arctic ice cap is melting at a rate of 9% per decade. At this rate, the ice cap could melt during this century.

10

Weathering and Soil Formation

About the PHOTO

Need a nose job, Mr. President? The carving of Thomas Jefferson that is part of the Mount Rushmore National Memorial is having its nose inspected by a National Parks worker. The process of weathering has caused cracks to form in the carving of President Jefferson. National Parks workers use a sealant to protect the memorial from moisture, which can cause further cracking.

PRE-READING ACTIVITY

FOLDNOTES **Key-Term Fold** Before you read the chapter, create the FoldNote entitled "Key-Term Fold" described in the **Study Skills** section of the Appendix. Write a key term from the chapter on each tab of the key-term fold. Under each tab, write the definition of the key term.

START-UP ACTIVITY

What's the Difference?

In this chapter, you will learn about the processes and rates of weathering. Complete this activity to learn about how the size and surface area of a substance affects how quickly the substance breaks down.

Procedure

1. Fill **two small containers** about half full with **water.**
2. Add **one sugar cube** to one container.
3. Add **1 tsp of granulated sugar** to the other container.
4. Using **one spoon for each container,** stir the water and sugar in each container at the same rate.
5. Using a **stopwatch,** measure how long it takes for the sugar to dissolve in each container.

Analysis

1. Did the sugar dissolve at the same rate in both containers? Explain why or why not.
2. Do you think one large rock or several smaller rocks would wear away faster? Explain your answer.

Weathering

If you have ever walked along a trail, you might have noticed small rocks lying around. Where did these rocks come from?

These smaller rocks came from larger rocks that were broken down. **Weathering** is the process by which rock materials are broken down by the action of physical or chemical processes.

Mechanical Weathering

If you were to crush one rock with another rock, you would be demonstrating one type of mechanical weathering. **Mechanical weathering** is the breakdown of rock into smaller pieces by physical means. Agents of mechanical weathering include ice, wind, water, gravity, plants, and even animals.

Ice

The alternate freezing and thawing of soil and rock, called *frost action,* is a form of mechanical weathering. One type of frost action, *ice wedging,* is shown in **Figure 1.** Ice wedging starts when water seeps into cracks during warm weather. When temperatures drop, the water freezes and expands. The ice then pushes against the sides of the crack. This causes the crack to widen.

weathering the process by which rock materials are broken down by the action of physical and chemical processes

mechanical weathering the breakdown of rock into smaller pieces by physical means

Figure 1   Ice Wedging

The granite in the photo has been broken down by repeated ice wedging, which is shown below.

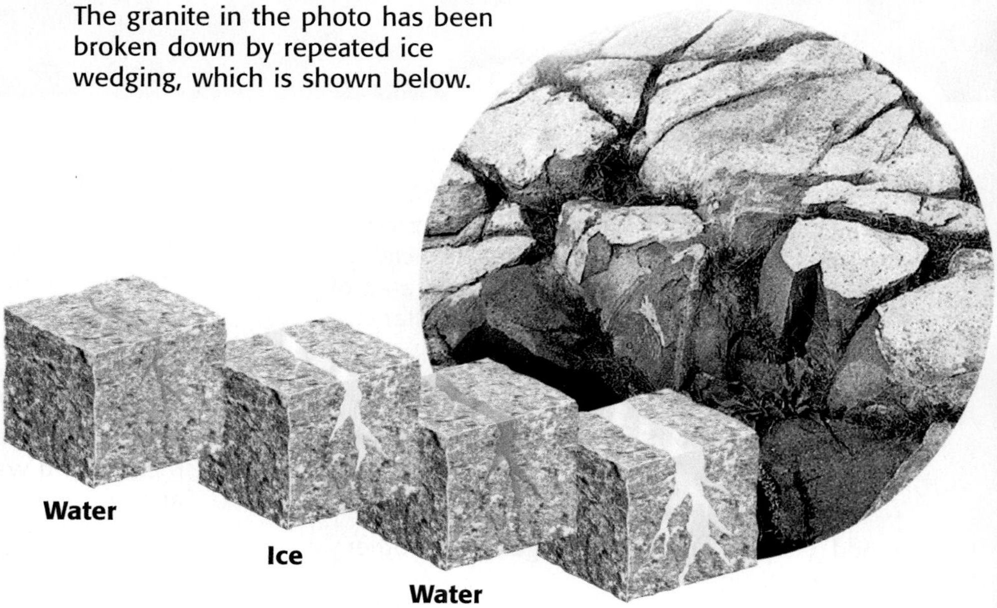

Water

Ice

Water

Ice

Figure 2   Three Forms of Abrasion

These river rocks are rounded because they have been tumbled in the riverbed by fast-moving water for many years.

This rock has been shaped by blowing sand. Such rocks are called ventifacts.

Rocks grind against each other in a rock slide, which creates smaller and smaller rock fragments.

Abrasion

As you scrape a piece of chalk against a board, particles of the chalk rub off to make a line on the board and the piece of chalk wears down and becomes smaller. The same process, called *abrasion*, happens with rocks. **Abrasion** is the grinding and wearing away of rock surfaces through the mechanical action of other rock or sand particles.

Wind, Water, and Gravity

Abrasion can happen in many ways, as shown in **Figure 2.** When rocks and pebbles roll along the bottom of swiftly flowing rivers, they bump into and scrape against each other. The weathering that occurs eventually causes these rocks to become rounded and smooth.

Wind also causes abrasion. When wind blows sand and silt against exposed rock, the sand eventually wears away the rock's surface. The figure above (center) shows what this kind of sandblasting can do to a rock.

Abrasion also occurs when rocks fall on one another. You can imagine the forces rocks exert on each other as they tumble down a mountainside. In fact, anytime one rock hits another, abrasion takes place.

✓ Reading Check Name three things that can cause abrasion.
(See the Appendix for answers to Reading Checks.)

abrasion the grinding and wearing away of rock surfaces through the mechanical action of other rock or sand particles

Figure 3 *Although they grow slowly, tree roots are strong enough to break solid rock.*

Plants

You may not think of plants as being strong, but some plants can easily break rocks. Have you ever seen sidewalks and streets that are cracked because of tree roots? Roots don't grow fast, but they certainly are powerful! Plants often send their roots into existing cracks in rocks. As the plant grows, the force of the expanding root becomes so strong that the crack widens. Eventually, the entire rock can split apart, as shown in **Figure 3.**

Animals

Believe it or not, earthworms cause a lot of weathering! They burrow through the soil and move soil particles around. This exposes fresh surfaces to continued weathering. Would you believe that some kinds of tropical worms move an estimated 100 metric tons of soil per acre every year? Almost any animal that burrows causes mechanical weathering. Ants, worms, mice, coyotes, and rabbits are just some of the animals that contribute to weathering. **Figure 4** shows some of these animals in action. The mixing and digging that animals do often contribute to another type of weathering, called *chemical weathering*. You will learn about this type of weathering next.

✓ Reading Check List three animals that can cause weathering.

Figure 4 *Animals that live in the soil, such as moles, prairie dogs, insects, worms, and gophers, cause a lot of weathering. When the animals burrow in the ground, they break up soil and loosen rocks to be exposed to further weathering.*

Figure 5 — Chemical Weathering of Granite

After thousands of years of chemical weathering, even hard rock, such as granite, can turn to sediment.

1 Rain, weak acids, and air chemically weather granite.

2 The bonds between mineral grains weaken as weathering proceeds.

3 When granite is weathered, it makes sand and clay, also called sediment.

Chemical Weathering

The process by which rocks break down as a result of chemical reactions is called **chemical weathering.** Common agents of chemical weathering are water, weak acids, and air.

Water

If you drop a sugar cube into a glass of water, the sugar cube will dissolve after a few minutes. This process is an example of chemical weathering. Even hard rock, such as granite, can be broken down by water. But, it just may take thousands of years. **Figure 5** shows how granite is chemically weathered.

Acid Precipitation

Rain, sleet, or snow, that contains a high concentration of acids is called **acid precipitation.** Precipitation is naturally acidic. However, acid precipitation contains more acid than normal precipitation. The high level of acidity can cause very rapid weathering of rock. Small amounts of sulfuric and nitric acids from natural sources, such as volcanoes, can make precipitation acidic. However, acid precipitation can also be caused by air pollution from the burning of fossil fuels, such as coal and oil. When these fuels are burned, they give off gases, including sulfur oxides, nitrogen oxides, and carbon oxides. When these compounds combine with water in the atmosphere, they form weak acids, which then fall back to the ground in rain and snow. When the acidity is too high, acid precipitation can be harmful to plants and animals.

chemical weathering the process by which rocks break down as a result of chemical reactions

acid precipitation rain, sleet, or snow, that contains a high concentration of acids

CONNECTION TO Chemistry

Acidity of Precipitation
Acidity is measured by using a pH scale, the units of which range from 0 to 14. Solutions that have a pH of less than 7 are acidic. Research some recorded pH levels of acid rain. Then, compare these pH levels with the pH levels of other common acids, such as lemon juice and acetic acid.

Figure 6 *Acid in groundwater has weathered limestone to form Carlsbad Caverns, in New Mexico.*

Acids in Groundwater

In certain places groundwater contains weak acids, such as carbonic or sulfuric acid. These acids react with rocks in the ground, such as limestone. When groundwater comes in contact with limestone, a chemical reaction occurs. Over a long period of time, the dissolving of limestone forms karst features, such as caverns. The caverns, like the one shown in **Figure 6,** form from the eating away of the limestone.

Acids in Living Things

Another source of acids that cause weathering might surprise you. Take a look at the lichens in **Figure 7.** Lichens produce acids that can slowly break down rock. If you have ever taken a walk in a park or forest, you have probably seen lichens growing on the sides of trees or rocks. Lichens can also grow in places where some of the hardiest plants cannot. For example, lichens can grow in deserts, in arctic areas, and in areas high above timberline, where even trees don't grow.

Figure 7 *Lichens, which consist of fungi and algae living together, contribute to chemical weathering.*

Quick Lab

Acids React!

1. Ketchup is one example of a food that contains weak acids, which react with certain substances. Take a **penny** that has a dull appearance, rub **ketchup** on it for several minutes.

2. Rinse the penny.

3. Where did all the grime on the penny go?

4. How is this process similar to what happens to a rock when it is exposed to natural acids during weathering?

Air

The car shown in **Figure 8** is undergoing chemical weathering due to the air. The oxygen in the air is reacting with the iron in the car, causing the car to rust. Water speeds up the process. But the iron would rust even if no water were present. Scientists call this process oxidation.

Oxidation is a chemical reaction in which an element, such as iron, combines with oxygen to form an oxide. This common form of chemical weathering is what causes rust. Old cars, aluminum cans, and your bike can experience oxidation if left exposed to air and rain for long periods of time.

Reading Check What can cause oxidation?

Figure 8 *Rust is a result of chemical weathering.*

SECTION Review

Summary

- Ice wedging is a form of mechanical weathering in which water seeps into rock cracks and then freezes and expands.
- Wind, water, and gravity cause mechanical weathering by abrasion.
- Animals and plants cause mechanical weathering by turning the soil and breaking apart rocks.
- Water, acids, and air chemically weather rock by weakening the bonds between mineral grains of the rock.

Using Key Terms

1. In your own words, write a definition for each of the following terms: *weathering, mechanical weathering, abrasion, chemical weathering* and *acid precipitation*.

Understanding Key Ideas

2. Which of the following things cannot cause mechanical weathering?
   a. water
   b. acid
   c. wind
   d. animals

3. List three things that cause chemical weathering of rocks.

4. Describe three ways abrasion occurs in nature.

5. Describe the similarity in the ways tree roots and ice mechanically weather rock.

6. Describe five sources of chemical weathering.

Critical Thinking

7. **Making Inferences** Why does acid precipitation weather rocks faster than normal precipitation?

8. **Making Comparisons** Compare the weather processes that affect a rock on top of a mountain and a rock buried beneath the ground.

Math Skills

9. Substances that have a pH of less than 7 are acidic. For each pH unit lower, the acidity is ten times greater. For example, normal precipitation is slightly acidic at a 5.6 pH. If acid precipitation were measured at 4.6 pH, it would be 10 times more acidic than normal precipitation. How many times more acidic would precipitation at 3.6 pH be than normal precipitation?

Rates of Weathering

Have you ever seen a cartoon in which a character falls off a cliff and lands on a ledge? Ledges exist in nature because the rock that the ledge is made of weathers more slowly than the surrounding rock.

Weathering is a process that takes a long time. However, some rock will weather faster than other rock. The rate at which a rock weathers depends on climate, elevation, and the makeup of the rock.

Differential Weathering

Hard rocks, such as granite, weather more slowly than softer rocks, such as limestone. **Differential weathering** is a process by which softer, less weather resistant rocks wear away and leave harder, more weather resistant rocks behind.

Figure 1 shows a landform that has been shaped by differential weathering. Devils Tower was once a mass of molten rock deep inside an active volcano. When the molten rock cooled and hardened, it was protected from weathering by the outer rock of the volcano. After thousands of years of weathering, the soft outer parts of the volcano have worn away. The harder, more resistant rock is all that remains.

Figure 1 *The illustration is an artist's idea of how the original volcano may have looked. The photo inset shows Devils Tower as it appears today.*

The Shape of Rocks

Weathering takes place on the outer surface of rocks. Therefore, the more surface area that is exposed to weathering, the faster the rock will be worn down. A large rock has a large surface area. But a large rock also has a large volume. Because of the large rock's volume, the large rock will take a long time to wear down.

If a large rock is broken into smaller fragments, weathering of the rock happens much more quickly. The rate of weathering increases because a smaller rock has more surface area to volume than a larger rock has. So, more of a smaller rock is exposed to the weathering process. **Figure 2** shows this concept in detail.

differential weathering the process by which softer, less weather resistant rocks wear away and leave harder, more weather resistant rocks behind

✓ **Reading Check** How does an increase in surface area affect the rate of weathering? (*See the Appendix for answers to Reading Checks.*)

Figure 2 Total Surface Area to Volume

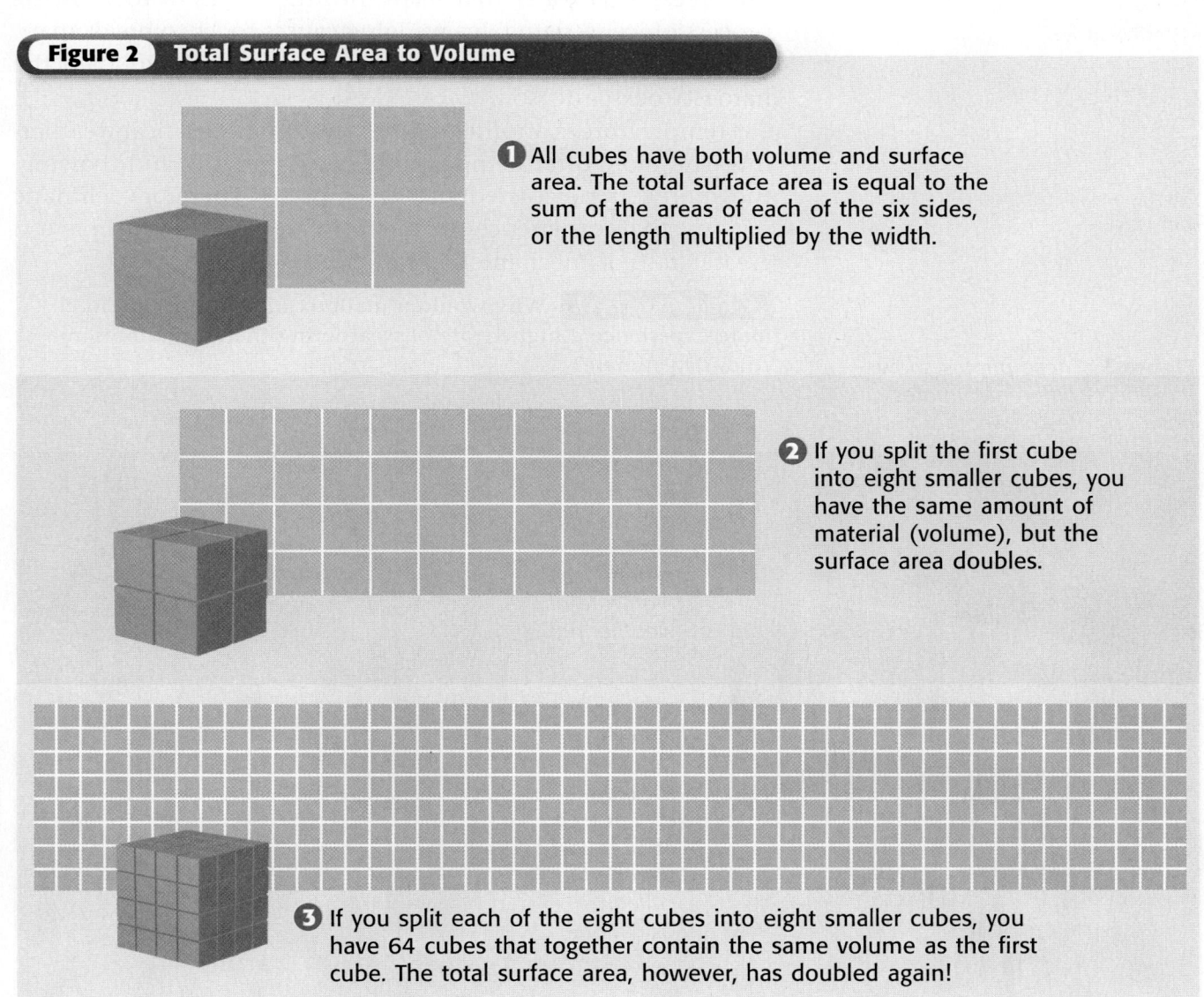

❶ All cubes have both volume and surface area. The total surface area is equal to the sum of the areas of each of the six sides, or the length multiplied by the width.

❷ If you split the first cube into eight smaller cubes, you have the same amount of material (volume), but the surface area doubles.

❸ If you split each of the eight cubes into eight smaller cubes, you have 64 cubes that together contain the same volume as the first cube. The total surface area, however, has doubled again!

Weathering and Climate

The rate of weathering in an area is greatly affected by the climate of that area. *Climate* is the average weather condition in an area over a long period of time. For example, the two mailboxes shown in **Figure 3** are in two different climates. The mailbox on the left is in a dry climate. The mailbox on the right is in a warm, humid climate. As you can see, the mailbox in the warm, humid climate is rusty.

Temperature and Water

The rate of chemical weathering happens faster in warm, humid climates. The rusty mailbox has experienced a type of chemical weathering called oxidation. Oxidation, like other chemical reactions, happens at a faster rate when temperatures are higher and when water is present.

Water also increases the rate of mechanical weathering. The freezing of water that seeps into the cracks of rocks is the process of ice wedging. Ice wedging causes rocks to break apart. Over time, this form of weathering can break down even the hardest rocks into soil.

Temperature is another major factor in mechanical weathering. The more often temperatures cause freezing and thawing, the more often ice wedging takes place. Therefore, climatic regions that experience frequent freezes and thaws have a greater rate of mechanical weathering.

Reading Check Why would a mailbox in a warm, humid climate experience a higher rate of weathering than a mailbox in a cold, dry climate?

Figure 3 These photos show the effects different climates can have on rates of weathering.

◄ This mailbox is in a dry climate and does not experience a high rate of weathering.

This mailbox ▶ is in a warm, humid climate. It experiences a high rate of chemical weathering called oxidation.

Weathering and Elevation

Just like everything else, mountains are exposed to air and water. As a result, mountain ranges are weathered down. Weathering happens on mountains in the same way it does everywhere else. However, as shown in **Figure 4,** rocks at higher elevations, as on a mountain, are exposed to more wind, rain, and ice than the rocks at lower elevations are. This increase in wind, rain, and ice at higher elevations causes the peaks of mountains to weather faster.

Gravity affects weathering, too. The steepness of mountain slopes increases the effects of mechanical and chemical weathering. Steep slopes cause rainwater to quickly run off the sides of mountains. The rainwater carries the sediment down the mountain's slope. This continual removal of sediment exposes fresh rock surfaces to the effects of weathering. New rock surfaces are also exposed to weathering when gravity causes rocks to fall away from the sides of mountains. The increased surface area means weathering happens at a faster rate.

Reading Check Why do mountaintops weather faster than rocks at sea level?

Figure 4 *The ice, rain, and wind that these mountain peaks are exposed to cause them to weather at a fast rate.*

SECTION Review

Summary

- Hard rocks weather more slowly than softer rocks.
- The more surface area of a rock that is exposed to weathering, the faster the rock will be worn down.
- Chemical weathering occurs faster in warm, humid climates.
- Weathering occurs faster at high elevations because of an increase in ice, rain, and wind.

Using Key Terms

1. In your own words, write a definition for the term *differential weathering.*

Understanding Key Ideas

2. A rock will have a lower rate of weathering when the rock
   a. is in a humid climate.
   b. is a very hard rock, such as granite.
   c. is at a high elevation.
   d. has more surface area exposed to weathering.

3. How does surface area affect the rate of weathering?

4. How does climate affect the rate of weathering?

5. Why does the peak of a mountain weather faster than the rocks at the bottom of the mountain?

Math Skills

6. The surface area of an entire cube is 96 cm². If the length and width of each side are equal, what is the length of one side of the cube?

Critical Thinking

7. **Making Inferences** Does the rate of chemical weathering increase or stay the same when a rock becomes more mechanically weathered? Why?

SCiLINKS.

NSTA
Developed and maintained by the
National Science Teachers Association

For a variety of links related to this chapter, go to www.scilinks.org

Topic: Rates of Weathering
SciLinks code: HSM1269

From Bedrock to Soil

Most plants need soil to grow. But what exactly is soil? Where does it come from?

READING WARM-UP

Objectives

- Describe the source of soil.
- Explain how the different properties of soil affect plant growth.
- Describe how various climates affect soil.

Terms to Learn

soil   soil structure
parent rock   humus
bedrock   leaching
soil texture

READING STRATEGY

Prediction Guide Before you read this section, write the title of each heading in this section. Next, under each heading, write what you think you will learn.

The Source of Soil

To a scientist, **soil** is a loose mixture of small mineral fragments, organic material, water, and air that can support the growth of vegetation. But not all soils are the same. Because soils are made from weathered rock fragments, the type of soil that forms depends on the type of rock that weathers. The rock formation that is the source of mineral fragments in the soil is called **parent rock.**

Bedrock is the layer of rock beneath soil. In this case, the bedrock is the parent rock because the soil above it formed from the bedrock below. Soil that remains above its parent rock is called *residual soil.*

Soil can be blown or washed away from its parent rock. This soil is called *transported soil.* **Figure 1** shows one way that soil is moved from one place to another. Both wind and the movement of glaciers are also responsible for transporting soil.

✓ **Reading Check** What is soil formed from? (*See the Appendix for answers to Reading Checks.*)

soil a loose mixture of rock fragments, organic material, water, and air that can support the growth of vegetation

parent rock a rock formation that is the source of soil

bedrock the layer of rock beneath soil

Figure 1 *Transported soil may be moved long distances from its parent rock by rivers, such as this one.*

Figure 2 Soil Texture

The proportion of these different-sized particles in soil determine the soil's texture.

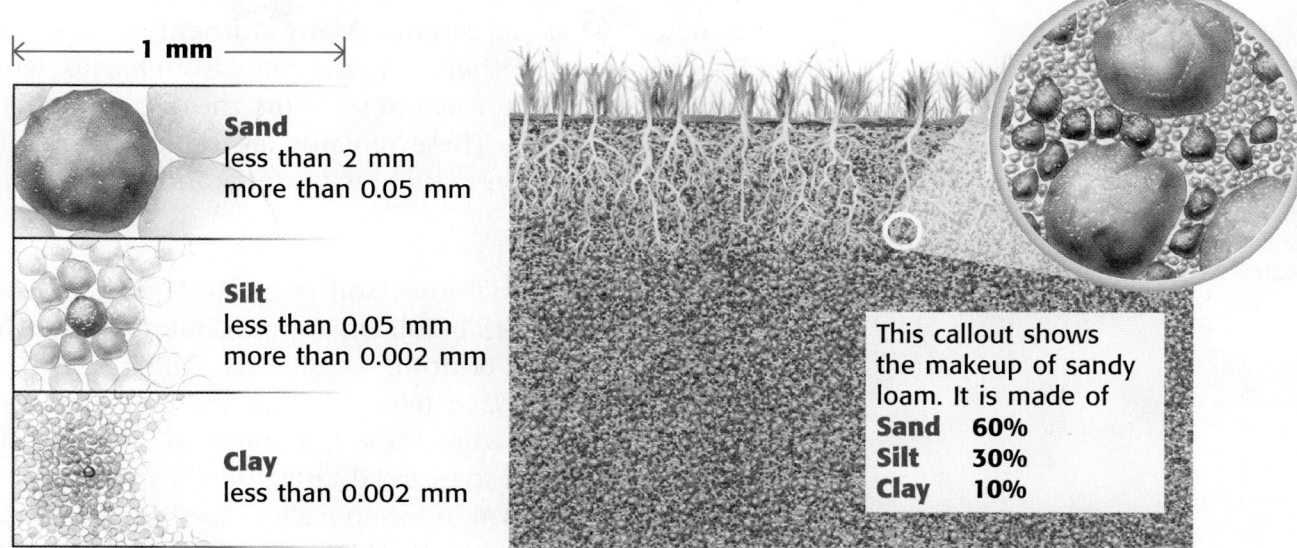

Sand
less than 2 mm
more than 0.05 mm

Silt
less than 0.05 mm
more than 0.002 mm

Clay
less than 0.002 mm

This callout shows the makeup of sandy loam. It is made of
Sand **60%**
Silt **30%**
Clay **10%**

Soil Properties

Some soils are great for growing plants. Other soils can't support the growth of plants. To better understand soil, you will next learn about its properties, such as soil texture, soil structure, and soil fertility.

Soil Texture and Soil Structure

Soil is made of different-sized particles. These particles can be as large as 2 mm, such as sand. Other particles can be too small to see without a microscope. **Soil texture** is the soil quality that is based on the proportions of soil particles. **Figure 2** shows the soil texture for a one type of soil.

Soil texture affects the soil's consistency. Consistency describes a soil's ability to be worked and broken up for farming. For example, soil texture that has a large proportion of clay can be hard and difficult for farmers to break up.

Soil texture influences the *infiltration,* or ability of water to move through soil. Soil should allow water to get to the plants' roots without causing the soil to be completely saturated.

Water and air movement through soil is also influenced by soil structure. **Soil structure** is the arrangement of soil particles. Soil particles are not always evenly spread out. Often, one type of soil particle will clump in an area. A clump of one type of soil can either block water flow or help water flow, which affects soil moisture.

soil texture the soil quality that is based on the proportions of soil particles.

soil structure the arrangement of soil particles

Soil Fertility

Nutrients in soil, such as iron, are necessary for plants to grow. Some soils are rich in nutrients. Other soils may not have many nutrients or are not able to supply the nutrients to the plants. A soil's ability to hold nutrients and to supply nutrients to a plant is described as *soil fertility*. Many nutrients in soil come from the parent rock. Other nutrients come from **humus,** which is the organic material formed in soil from the decayed remains of plants and animals. These remains are broken down into nutrients by decomposers, such as bacteria and fungi.

Soil Horizons

Because of the way soil forms, soil often ends up in a series of layers, with humus-rich soil on top, sediment below that, and bedrock on the bottom. Geologists call these layers *horizons*. The word *horizon* tells you that the layers are horizontal. **Figure 3** shows what these horizons can look like. You can see these layers in some road cuts.

The top layer of soil is often called the *topsoil*. Topsoil contains more humus than the layers below it. The humus is rich in the nutrients plants need to be healthy. This is why good topsoil is necessary for farming.

humus the dark, organic material formed in soil from the decayed remains of plants and animals

leaching the removal of substances that can be dissolved from rock, ore, or layers of soil due to the passing of water

 **Figure 3** Soil Horizons

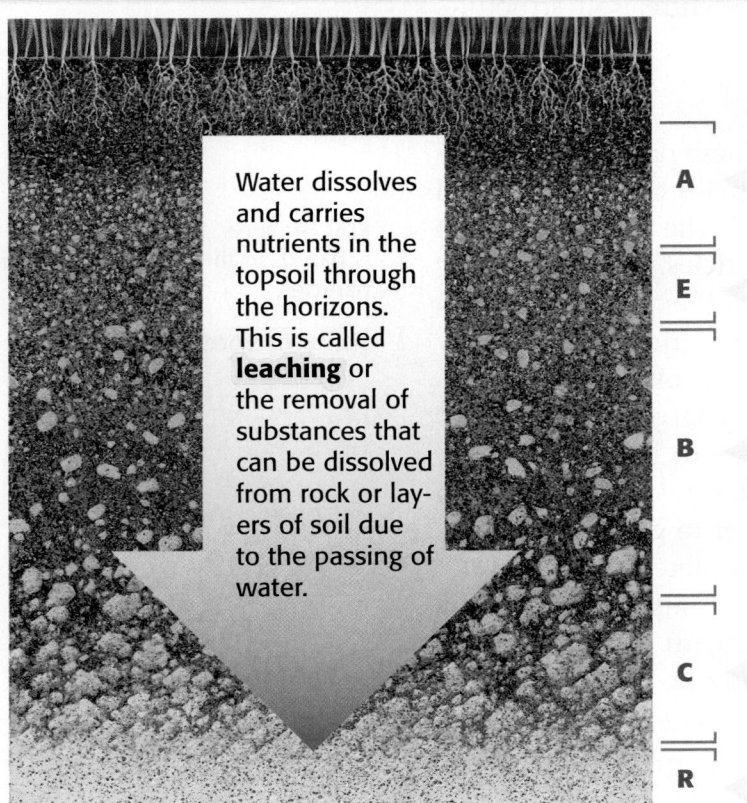

Water dissolves and carries nutrients in the topsoil through the horizons. This is called **leaching** or the removal of substances that can be dissolved from rock or layers of soil due to the passing of water.

A This horizon consists of the topsoil. Topsoil contains more humus than any other soil horizon. Soil in forests often has an O horizon. The O horizon is made up of litter from dead plants and animals.

E This horizon experiences intense leaching of nutrients.

B This horizon collects the dissolved substances and nutrients deposited from the upper horizons.

C This horizon is made of partially weathered bedrock.

R This horizon is made of bedrock that has little or no weathering.

Soil pH

Soils can be acidic or basic. The pH scale is used to measure how acidic or basic a soil is and ranges from 0 to 14. The midpoint, which is 7, is neutral. Soil that has a pH below 7 is acidic. Soil that has a pH above 7 is basic.

The pH of a soil influences how nutrients dissolve in the soil. For example, plants are unable to take up certain nutrients from soils that are basic, or that have a high pH. Soils that have a low pH can restrict other important nutrients from hungry plants. Because different plants need different nutrients, the right pH for a soil depends on the plants growing in it.

Soil and Climate

Soil types vary from place to place. One reason for this is the differences in climate. As you read on, you will see that climate can make a difference in the types of soils that develop around the world.

Tropical Rain Forest Climates

Take a look at **Figure 4.** In tropical rain forest climates, the air is very humid and the land receives a large amount of rain. Because of warm temperatures, crops can be grown year-round. The warm soil temperature also allows dead plants and animals to decay easily. This provides rich humus to the soil.

Because of the lush plant growth, you may think that tropical rain forest soils are the most nutrient-rich in the world. However, tropical rain forest soils are nutrient poor. The heavy rains in this climate leach precious nutrients from the topsoil into deeper layers of soil. The result is that tropical topsoil is very thin. Another reason tropical rain forest soil is nutrient poor is that the lush vegetation has a great demand for nutrients. The nutrients that aren't leached away are quickly taken up by plants and trees that live off the soil.

✓ **Reading Check** Why is the topsoil in tropical rain forests thin?

CONNECTION TO Social Studies

WRITING SKILL **Deforestation in Brazil** In Brazil, rain forests have been cut down at an alarmingly high rate, mostly by farmers. However, tropical rain forest topsoil is very thin and is not suitable for long-term farming. Research the long-term effects of deforestation on the farmers and indigenous people of Brazil. Then, write a one page report on your findings.

Figure 4 *Lush tropical rain forests have surprisingly thin topsoil.*

Desert Climates

While tropical climates get a lot of rain, deserts get less than 25 cm a year. Leaching of nutrients is not a problem in desert soils. But the lack of rain causes many other problems, such as very low rates of chemical weathering and less ability to support plant and animal life. A low rate of weathering means soil is created at a slower rate.

Some water is available from groundwater. Groundwater can trickle in from surrounding areas and seep to the surface. But as soon as the water is close to the surface, it evaporates. So, any materials that were dissolved in the water are left behind in the soil. Without the water to dissolve the minerals, the plants are unable to take them up. Often, the chemicals left behind are various types of salts. These salts can sometimes become so concentrated that the soil becomes toxic, or poisonous, even to desert plants! Death Valley, shown in **Figure 5,** is a desert that has toxic levels of salt in the soil.

Figure 5 *The salty conditions of desert soils make it difficult for many plants to survive.*

Temperate Forest and Grassland Climates

Much of the continental United States has a temperate climate. An abundance of weathering occurs in temperate climates. Temperate areas get enough rain to cause a high level of chemical weathering, but not so much that the nutrients are leached out of the soil. Frequent changes in temperature lead to frost action. As a result, thick, fertile soils develop, as shown in **Figure 6.**

Temperate soils are some of the most-productive soils in the world. In fact, the midwestern part of the United States has earned the nickname "breadbasket" for the many crops the region's soil supports.

✓ Reading Check Which climate has the most-productive soil?

INTERNET ACTIVITY

For another activity related to this chapter, go to **go.hrw.com** and type in the keyword **HZ5WSFW.**

Figure 6 *The rich soils in areas that have a temperate climate support a vast farming industry.*

Arctic Climates

Arctic areas have so little precipitation that they are like cold deserts. In arctic climates, as in desert climates, chemical weathering occurs very slowly. So, soil formation also occurs slowly. Slow soil formation is why soil in arctic areas, as shown in **Figure 7,** is thin and unable to support many plants.

Arctic climates also have low soil temperatures. At low temperatures, decomposition of plants and animals happens more slowly or stops completely. Slow decomposition limits the amount of humus in the soil, which limits the nutrients available. These nutrients are necessary for plant growth.

Figure 7 *Arctic soils, such as the soil along Denali Highway, in Alaska, cannot support lush vegetation.*

SECTION Review

Summary

- Soil is formed from the weathering of bedrock.
- Soil texture affects how soil can be worked for farming and how well water passes through it.
- The ability of soil to provide nutrients so that plants can survive and grow is called *soil fertility*.
- The pH of a soil influences which nutrients plants can take up from the soil.
- Different climates have different types of soil, depending on the temperature and rainfall.

Using Key Terms

1. Use each of the following terms in a separate sentence: *soil, parent rock, bedrock, soil texture, soil structure, humus,* and *leaching*.

Understanding Key Ideas

2. Which of the following soil properties influences soil moisture?
   a. soil horizon
   b. soil fertility
   c. soil structure
   d. soil pH

3. Which of the following soil properties influences how nutrients can be dissolved in soil?
   a. soil texture
   b. soil fertility
   c. soil structure
   d. soil pH

4. When is parent rock the same as bedrock?

5. What is the difference between residual and transported soils?

6. Which climate has the most thick, fertile soil?

7. How does soil temperature influence arctic soil?

Math Skills

8. If a soil sample is 60% sand particles and has 30 million particles of soil, how many of those soil particles are sand?

Critical Thinking

9. **Identifying Relationships** In which type of climate would leaching be more common— tropical rain forest or desert?

10. **Making Comparisons** Although arctic climates are extremely different from desert climates, their soils may be somewhat similar. Explain why.

Soil Conservation

Believe it or not, soil can be endangered, just like plants and animals. Because soil takes thousands of years to form, it is not easy to replace.

If we do not take care of our soils, we can ruin them or even lose them. Soil is a resource that must be conserved. **Soil conservation** is a method to maintain the fertility of the soil by protecting the soil from erosion and nutrient loss.

The Importance of Soil

Soil provides minerals and other nutrients for plants. If the soil loses these nutrients, then plants will not be able to grow. Take a look at the plants shown in **Figure 1.** The plants on the right look unhealthy because they are not getting enough nutrients. There is enough soil to support the plant's roots, but the soil is not providing them with the food they need. The plants on the left are healthy because the soil they live in is rich in nutrients.

All animals get their energy from plants. The animals get their energy either by eating the plants or by eating animals that have eaten plants. So, if plants can't get their nutrients from the soil, animals can't get their nutrients from plants.

✓ **Reading Check** Why is soil important? (*See the Appendix for answers to Reading Checks.*)

Housing

Soil also provides a place for animals to live. The region where a plant or animal lives is called its *habitat.* Earthworms, grubs, spiders, ants, moles, and prairie dogs all live in soil. If the soil disappears, so does the habitat for these animals.

soil conservation a method to maintain the fertility of the soil by protecting the soil from erosion and nutrient loss

Figure 1 *Both of these photos show the same crop, but the soil in the photo on the right is poor in nutrients.*

Water Storage

Soil is also extremely important to plants for water storage. Without soil to hold water, plants would not get the moisture or the nutrients they need. Soil also keeps water from running off, flowing elsewhere, and possibly causing flooding.

Soil Damage and Loss

What would happen if there were no soil? Soil loss is a serious problem around the world. Soil damage can lead to soil loss. Soil can be damaged from overuse by poor farming techniques or by overgrazing. Overused soil can lose its nutrients and become infertile. Plants can't grow in soil that is infertile. Without plants to hold and help cycle water, the area can become a desert. This process, formally known as *desertification,* is called *land degradation*. Without plants and moisture, the soil can be blown or washed away.

Soil Erosion

When soil is left unprotected, it can be exposed to erosion. **Erosion** is the process by which wind, water, or gravity transport soil and sediment from one location to another. **Figure 2** shows Providence Canyon, which was formed from the erosion of soil when trees were cut down to clear land for farming. Roots from plants and trees are like anchors to the soil. Roots keep topsoil from being eroded. Therefore, plants and trees protect the soil. By taking care of the vegetation, you also take care of the soil.

Making Soil

Suppose it takes 500 years for 2 cm of new soil to form in a certain area. But the soil is eroding at a rate of 1 mm per year. Is the soil eroding faster than it can be replaced? Explain.

erosion the process by which wind, water, ice, or gravity transport soil and sediment from one location to another

Figure 2 *Providence Canyon has suffered soil erosion from the cutting of forests for farmland.*

Figure 3 **Soil Conservation Techniques**

Contour plowing helps prevent erosion from heavy rains.

Terracing prevents erosion from heavy rains on steep hills.

No-till farming prevents erosion by providing cover that reduces water runoff.

Soybeans are a **cover crop** which restores nutrients to soil.

Contour Plowing and Terracing

If farmers plowed rows so that they ran up and down hills, what might happen during a heavy rain? The rows would act as river valleys and channel the rainwater down the hill, which would erode the soil. To prevent erosion in this way, a farmer could plow across the slope of the hills. This is called contour plowing. In *contour plowing,* the rows act as a series of dams instead of a series of rivers. **Figure 3** shows contour plowing and three other methods of soil conservation. If the hills are really steep, farmers can use *terracing.* Terracing changes one steep field into a series of smaller, flatter fields. *No-till farming,* which is the practice of leaving old stalks, provides cover from rain. The cover reduces water runoff and slows soil erosion.

Cover Crop and Crop Rotation

In the southern United States, during the early 1900s, the soil had become nutrient poor by the farming of only one crop, cotton. George Washington Carver, the scientist shown in **Figure 4,** urged farmers to plant soybeans and peanuts instead of cotton. Some plants, such as soybeans and peanuts, helped to restore important nutrients to the soil. These plants are called cover crops. *Cover crops* are crops that are planted between harvests to replace certain nutrients and prevent erosion. Cover crops prevent erosion by providing cover from wind and rain.

Another way to slow down nutrient depletion is through *crop rotation.* If the same crop is grown year after year in the same field, certain nutrients become depleted. To slow this process, a farmer can plant different crops. A different crop will use up less nutrients or different nutrients from the soil.

Reading Check What can soybeans and peanuts do for nutrient-poor soil?

Figure 4 *George Washington Carver taught soil conservation techniques to farmers.*

SECTION Review

Summary

- Soil is important for plants to grow, for animals to live in, and for water to be stored.
- Soil erosion and soil damage can be prevented by contour plowing, terracing, using cover crop, and practicing crop rotation.

Using Key Terms

1. In your own words, write a definition for each of the following terms: *soil conservation* and *erosion.*

Understanding Key Ideas

2. What are three important benefits that soil provides?

3. Practicing which of the following soil conservation techniques will replace nutrients in the soil?

   a. cover crop use
   b. no-till farming
   c. terracing
   d. contour plowing

4. How does crop rotation benefit soil?

5. List four methods of soil conservation, and describe how each helps prevent the loss of soil.

Math Skills

6. Suppose it takes 500 years to form 2 cm of new soil without erosion. If a farmer needs at least 35 cm of soil to plant a particular crop, how many years will the farmer need to wait before planting his or her crop?

Critical Thinking

7. **Applying Concepts** Why do land animals, even meat eaters, depend on soil to survive?

Developed and maintained by the National Science Teachers Association

For a variety of links related to this chapter, go to www.scilinks.org

Topic: Soil Conservation
SciLinks code: HSM1409

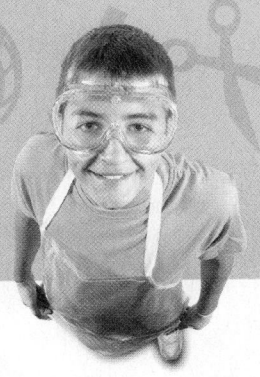

Model-Making Lab

OBJECTIVES

Design a model to understand how abrasion breaks down rocks.

Evaluate the effects of abrasion.

MATERIALS

- bottle, plastic, wide-mouthed, with lid, 3 L
- graph paper or computer
- markers
- pieces of limestone, all about the same size (24)
- poster board
- tap water

SAFETY

Rockin' Through Time

Wind, water, and gravity constantly change rocks. As wind and water rush over the rocks, the rocks may be worn smooth. As rocks bump against one another, their shapes change. The form of mechanical weathering that occurs as rocks collide and scrape together is called *abrasion*. In this activity, you will shake some pieces of limestone to model the effects of abrasion.

Ask a Question

1 How does abrasion break down rocks? How can I use this information to identify rocks that have been abraded in nature?

Form a Hypothesis

2 Formulate a hypothesis that answers the questions above.

Test the Hypothesis

3 Copy the chart on the next page onto a piece of poster board. Allow enough space to place rocks in each square.

4 Lay three of the limestone pieces on the poster board in the area marked "0 shakes." Be careful not to bump the poster board after you have added the rocks.

5 Place the remaining 21 rocks in the 3 L bottle. Then, fill the bottle halfway with water.

6 Close the lid of the bottle securely. Shake the bottle vigorously 100 times.

7 Remove three rocks from the bottle, and place them on the poster board in the box that indicates the number of times the rocks have been shaken.

8 Repeat steps 6 and 7 six times until all of the rocks have been added to the board.

Analyze the Results

1. **Examining Data** Describe the surface of the rocks that you placed in the area marked "0 shakes." Are they smooth or rough?

2. **Describing Events** How did the shape of the rocks change as you performed this activity?

3. **Constructing Graphs** Using graph paper or a computer, construct a graph, table, or chart that describes how the shapes of the rocks changed as a result of the number of times they were shaken.

Draw Conclusions

4. **Drawing Conclusions** Why did the rocks change?

5. **Evaluating Results** How did the water change during the activity? Why did it change?

6. **Making Predictions** What would happen if you used a much harder rock, such as granite, for this experiment?

7. **Interpreting Information** How do the results of this experiment compare with what happens in a river?

Rocks Table	
0 shakes	100 shakes
200 shakes	300 shakes
400 shakes	500 shakes
600 shakes	700 shakes

Chapter Review

USING KEY TERMS

1 In your own words, write a definition for each of the following terms: *abrasion* and *soil texture*.

2 Use each of the following terms in a separate sentence: *soil conservation* and *erosion*.

For each pair of terms, explain how the meanings of the terms differ.

3 *mechanical weathering* and *chemical weathering*

4 *soil* and *parent rock*

UNDERSTANDING KEY IDEAS

Multiple Choice

5 Which of the following processes is a possible effect of water?

a. mechanical weathering
b. chemical weathering
c. abrasion
d. All of the above

6 In which climate would you find the fastest rate of chemical weathering?

a. a warm, humid climate
b. a cold, humid climate
c. a cold, dry climate
d. a warm, dry climate

7 Which of the following properties does soil texture affect?

a. soil pH
b. soil temperature
c. soil consistency
d. None of the above

8 Which of the following properties describes a soil's ability to supply nutrients?

a. soil structure
b. infiltration
c. soil fertility
d. consistency

9 Soil is important because it provides

a. housing for animals.
b. nutrients for plants.
c. storage for water.
d. All of the above

10 Which of the following soil conservation techniques prevents erosion?

a. contour plowing
b. terracing
c. no-till farming
d. All of the above

Short Answer

11 Describe the two major types of weathering.

12 Why is Devils Tower higher than the surrounding area?

13 Why is soil in temperate forests thick and fertile?

14 What can happen to soil when soil conservation is not practiced?

15 Describe the process of land degradation.

16 How do cover crops help prevent soil erosion?

CRITICAL THINKING

17 Concept Mapping Use the following terms to create a concept map: *weathering, chemical weathering, mechanical weathering, abrasion, ice wedging, oxidation,* and *soil.*

18 Analyzing Processes Heat generally speeds up chemical reactions. But weathering, including chemical weathering, is usually slowest in hot, dry climates. Why?

19 Making Inferences Mechanical weathering, such as ice wedging, increases surface area by breaking larger rocks into smaller rocks. Draw conclusions about how mechanical weathering can affect the rate of chemical weathering.

20 Evaluating Data A scientist has a new theory. She believes that climates that receive heavy rains all year long have thin topsoil. Given what you have learned, decide if the scientist's theory is correct. Explain your answer.

21 Analyzing Processes What forms of mechanical and chemical weathering would be most common in the desert? Explain your answer.

22 Applying Concepts If you had to plant a crop on a steep hill, what soil conservation techniques would you use to prevent erosion?

23 Making Comparisons Compare the weathering processes in a warm, humid climate with those in a dry, cold climate.

INTERPRETING GRAPHICS

The graph below shows how the density of water changes when temperature changes. The denser a substance is, the less volume it occupies. In other words, as most substances get colder, they contract and become denser. But water is unlike most other substances. When water freezes, it expands and becomes less dense. Use the graph below to answer the questions that follow.

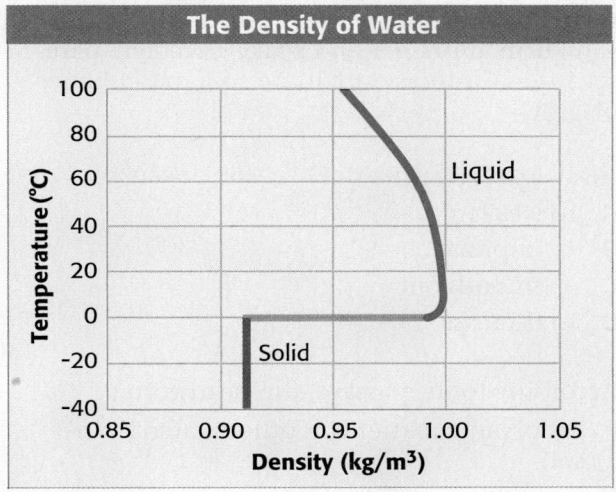

24 Which has the greater density: water at 40°C or water at −20°C?

25 How would the line in the graph look if water behaved like most other liquids?

26 Which substance would be a more effective agent of mechanical weathering: water or another liquid? Why?

READING

Read each of the passages below. Then, answer the questions that follow each passage.

Passage 1 Earthworms are very important for forming soil. As they search for food by digging tunnels in the soil, they expose rocks and minerals to the effects of weathering. Over time, this process makes new soil. And as the worms dig tunnels, they mix the soil, which allows air and water and smaller organisms to move deeper into the soil. Worms have huge appetites. They eat organic matter and other materials in the soil. One earthworm can eat an amount equal to about half its body weight each day! Eating all of that food means that earthworms leave behind a lot of waste. Earthworm wastes, called *castings,* are very high in nutrients and make excellent natural fertilizer. Castings enrich the soil and <u>enhance</u> plant growth.

1. In the passage, what does *enhance* mean?
   A to weaken
   B to improve
   C to smooth out
   D to decrease

2. According to the passage, the earthworms
   F eat organic matter and other materials in soil.
   G do not have much of an appetite.
   H love to eat castings.
   I cannot digest organic matter in soil.

3. Which of the following statements is a fact according to the passage?
   A Earthworms are not important for forming soil.
   B Earthworms only eat organic matter in the soil.
   C An earthworm can eat an amount that equals half its body weight each day.
   D Earthworms eat little food but leave behind a lot of waste.

Passage 2 Worms are not the only living things that help create soil. Plants also play a part in the weathering process. As the roots of plants grow and seek out water and nutrients, they help break large rock fragments into smaller ones. Have you ever seen a plant growing in a crack in the sidewalk? As the plant grows, its roots spread into tiny cracks in the sidewalk. These roots apply pressure to the cracks, and over time, the cracks get bigger. As the plants make the cracks bigger, ice wedging can occur more readily. As the cracks expand, more water runs into them. When the water freezes, it expands and presses against the walls of the crack, which makes the crack even larger. Over time, the weathering caused by water, plants, and worms helps break down rock to form soil.

1. How do plants make it easier for ice wedging to occur?
   A Plant roots block the cracks and don't allow water to enter.
   B Plant roots provide moisture to cracks.
   C Plant roots make the cracks larger, which allows more water to enter the cracks.
   D Plants absorb excess water from cracks.

2. For ice wedging to occur,
   F water in cracks must freeze.
   G plant roots must widen cracks.
   H acid is needed.
   I water is not needed.

3. Which of the following statements is a fact according to the passage?
   A Plant roots can strangle earthworms.
   B Earthworms eat plant roots.
   C Plant roots cannot crack sidewalks.
   D Plant roots break large rock fragments into smaller ones.

The graph below shows the average yearly rainfall in five locations. Use the graph below to answer the questions that follow.

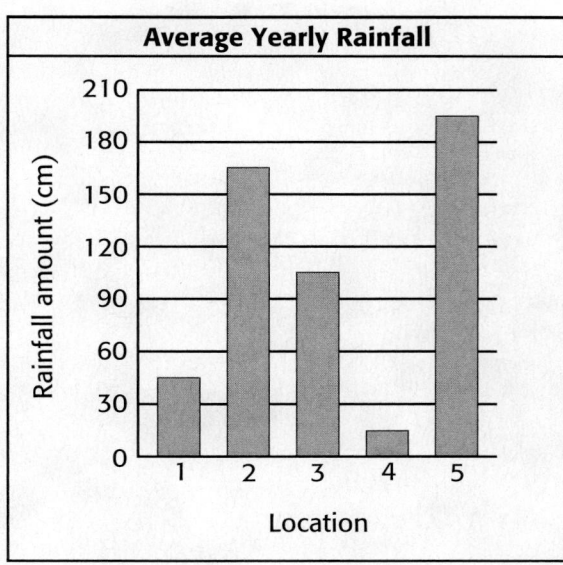

Average Yearly Rainfall

1. Which location has the **most** average yearly rainfall?

   A 1

   B 2

   C 4

   D 5

2. At which location would you expect to find the **most** chemical weathering?

   F 1

   G 3

   H 4

   I 5

3. At which location would you expect to find the **least** amount of chemical weathering?

   A 2

   B 3

   C 4

   D 5

Read each question below, and choose the best answer.

1. If an earthworm that weighs 1.5 g eats an amount equal to half its body weight in a day, how much does the earthworm eat in 1 week?

   A 10.5 g

   B 7 g

   C 5.25 g

   D 1.5 g

2. Calculate the surface area of a cube that measures 3 cm by 3 cm.

   F 9 cm

   G 9 cm^2

   H 54 cm

   I 54 cm^2

3. If a mountain peak weathers away 2 cm every 6 years, how many years will the mountain peak take to weather away 1 m?

   A 8 years

   B 12 years

   C 180 years

   D 300 years

4. The rock ledge that lies under a waterfall erodes about 3 cm each year. How much of the rock will erode over a period of 18 months?

   F 4.5 cm

   G 6 cm

   H 21 cm

   I 54 cm

5. A garden shop charges $0.30 for each ground-cover seedling. How many seedlings can you buy for $6.00?

   A 5 seedlings

   B 18 seedlings

   C 20 seedlings

   D 200 seedlings

Science in Action

Science, Technology, and Society

Flying Fertilizer

Would you believe that dust from storms in large deserts can be transported over the oceans to different continents? Dust from the Gobi Desert in China has traveled all the way to Hawaii! In many cases, the dust is a welcome guest. Iron in dust from the Sahara, a desert in Africa, fertilizes the canopies of South American rain forests. In fact, research has shown that the canopies of Central and South American rain forests get much of their nutrients from dust from the Sahara!

Social Studies ACTIVITY

Find pictures on the Internet or in magazines that show how people in rain forests live. Make a poster by using the pictures you find.

Scientific Discoveries

Strange Soil

Mysterious patterns of circles, polygons, and stripes were discovered in the soil in remote areas in Alaska and the Norwegian islands. At first, scientists were puzzled by these strange designs in remote areas. Then, the scientists discovered that these patterns were created by the area's weathering process, which includes cycles of freezing and thawing. When the soil freezes, the soil expands. When the soil thaws, the soil contracts. This process moves and sorts the particles of the soil into patterns.

Language Arts ACTIVITY

WRITING SKILL Write a creative short story describing what life would be like if you were a soil circle on one of these remote islands.

People in Science

J. David Bamberger

Habitat Restoration J. David Bamberger knows how important taking care of the environment is. Therefore, he has turned his ranch into the largest habitat restoration project in Texas. For Bamberger, restoring the habitat started with restoring the soil. One way Bamberger restored the soil was to manage the grazing of the grasslands and to make sure that grazing animals didn't expose the soil. Overgrazing causes soil erosion. When cattle clear the land of its grasses, the soil is exposed to wind and rain, which can wash the topsoil away.

Bamberger also cleared his land of most of the shrub, *juniper*. Juniper requires so much water per day that it leaves little water in the soil for the grasses and wildflowers. The change in the ranch since Bamberger first bought it in 1959 is most obvious at the fence-line border of his ranch. Beyond the fence is a small forest of junipers and little other vegetation. On Bamberger's side, the ranch is lush with grasses, wildflowers, trees, and shrubs.

Math ACTIVITY

Bamberger's ranch is 2,300 hectares. There are 0.405 hectares in 1 acre. How many acres is Bamberger's ranch?

go.hrw.com

To learn more about these Science in Action topics, visit go.hrw.com and type in the keyword **HZ5WSFF.**

Current Science

Check out Current Science® articles related to this chapter by visiting go.hrw.com. Just type in the keyword **HZ5CS10.**

11

The Flow of Fresh Water

About the  PHOTO

You can hear the roar of Iguaçu (EE gwah SOO) Falls for miles. The Iguaçu River travels more than 500 km across Brazil before it tumbles off the edge of a volcanic plateau in a series of 275 individual waterfalls. Over the past 20,000 years, erosion has caused the falls to move 28 km upstream.

PRE-READING ACTIVITY

FOLDNOTES **Booklet** Before you read the chapter, create the FoldNote entitled "Booklet" described in the **Study Skills** section of the Appendix. Label each page of the booklet with a main idea from the chapter. As you read the chapter, write what you learn about each main idea on the appropriate page of the booklet.

START-UP ACTIVITY

Stream Weavers

Do the following activity to learn how streams and river systems develop.

Procedure

1. Begin with enough **sand** and **gravel** to fill the bottom of a **rectangular plastic washtub.**

2. Spread the gravel in a layer at the bottom of the washtub. On top of the gravel, place a layer of sand that is 4 cm to 6 cm deep. Add more sand to one end of the washtub to form a slope.

3. Make a small hole in the bottom of a **paper cup.** Attach the cup to the inside wall of the tub with a **clothespin.** The cup should be placed at the end that has more sand.

4. Fill the cup with **water,** and observe the water as it moves over the sand. Use a **magnifying lens** to observe features of the stream more closely.

5. Record your observations.

Analysis

1. At the start of your experiment, how did the moving water affect the sand?

2. As time passed, how did the moving water affect the sand?

3. Explain how this activity modeled the development of streams. In what ways was the model accurate? How was it inaccurate?

The Active River

If you had fallen asleep with your toes dangling in the Colorado River 6 million years ago and you had woken up today, your toes would be hanging about 1.6 km (about 1 mi) above the river!

The Colorado River carved the Grand Canyon, shown in **Figure 1,** by washing billions of tons of soil and rock from its riverbed. The Colorado River made the Grand Canyon by a process that can take millions of years.

Rivers: Agents of Erosion

Six million years ago, the area now known as the Grand Canyon was nearly as flat as a pancake. The Colorado River cut down into the rock and formed the Grand Canyon over millions of years through a process called erosion. **Erosion** is the process by which soil and sediment are transported from one location to another. Rivers are not the only agents of erosion. Wind, rain, ice, and snow can also cause erosion.

Because of erosion caused by water, the Grand Canyon is now about 1.6 km deep and 446 km long. In this section, you will learn about stream development, river systems, and the factors that affect the rate of stream erosion.

✓ **Reading Check** Describe the process that created the Grand Canyon. (*See the Appendix for answers to Reading Checks.*)

erosion the process by which wind, water, ice, or gravity transports soil and sediment from one location to another

Figure 1 *The Grand Canyon is located in northwestern Arizona. The canyon formed over millions of years as running water eroded the rock layers. (In some places, the canyon is now 29 km wide.)*

The Water Cycle

Have you ever wondered how rivers keep flowing? Where do rivers get their water? Learning about the water cycle, shown in **Figure 2,** will help you answer these questions. The **water cycle** is the continuous movement of Earth's water from the ocean to the atmosphere to the land and back to the ocean. The water cycle is driven by energy from the sun.

water cycle the continuous movement of water from the ocean to the atmosphere to the land and back to the ocean

Figure 2 The Water Cycle

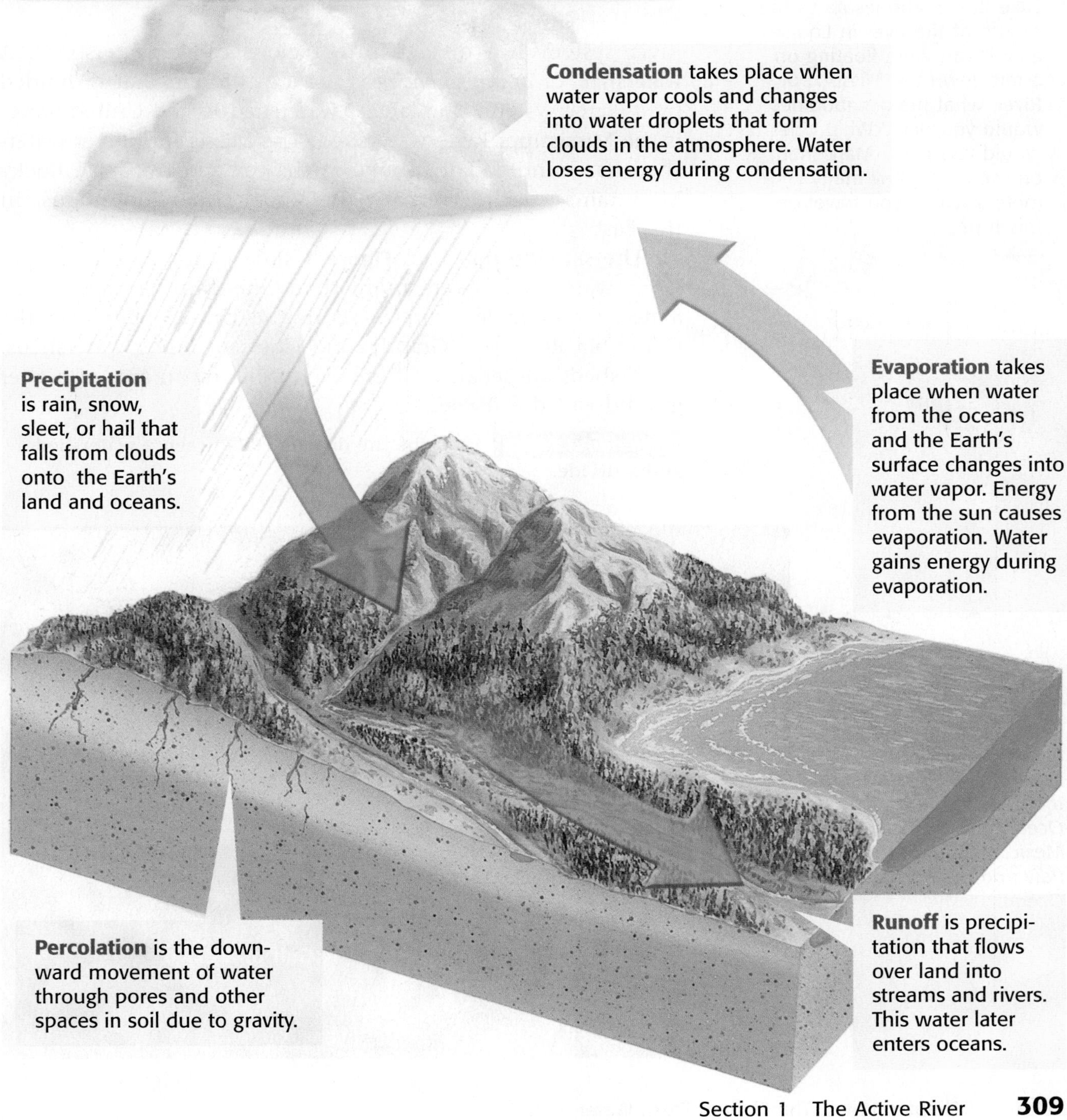

Condensation takes place when water vapor cools and changes into water droplets that form clouds in the atmosphere. Water loses energy during condensation.

Precipitation is rain, snow, sleet, or hail that falls from clouds onto the Earth's land and oceans.

Evaporation takes place when water from the oceans and the Earth's surface changes into water vapor. Energy from the sun causes evaporation. Water gains energy during evaporation.

Percolation is the downward movement of water through pores and other spaces in soil due to gravity.

Runoff is precipitation that flows over land into streams and rivers. This water later enters oceans.

Floating down the River

Study a map of the United States at home with a parent. Find the Mississippi River. Imagine that you are planning a rafting trip down the river. On the map, trace the route of your trip from Lake Itasca, Minnesota to the mouth of the river in Louisiana. If you were floating on a raft down the Mississippi River, what major tributaries would you pass? What cities would you pass? Mark them on the map. How many kilometers would you travel on this trip?

River Systems

The next time you take a shower, notice that individual drops of water join together to become small streams. These streams join other small streams and form larger ones. Eventually, all of the water flows down the drain. Every time you shower, you create a model river system—a network of streams and rivers that drains an area of its runoff. Just as the shower forms a network of flowing water, streams and rivers form a network of flowing water on land. A stream that flows into a lake or into a larger stream is called a **tributary.**

Watersheds

River systems are divided into regions called watersheds. A **watershed,** or *drainage basin,* is the area of land that is drained by a water system. The largest watershed in the United States is the Mississippi River watershed. The Mississippi River watershed has hundreds of tributaries that extend from the Rocky Mountains, in the West, to the Appalachian Mountains, in the East.

The satellite image in **Figure 3** shows that the Mississippi River watershed covers more than one-third of the United States. Other major watersheds in the United States are the Columbia River, Rio Grande, and Colorado River watersheds. Watersheds are separated from each other by an area of higher ground called a **divide.**

Reading Check Describe the difference between a watershed and a divide.

Figure 3 *The Continental Divide runs through the Rocky Mountains. It separates the watersheds that flow into the Atlantic Ocean and the Gulf of Mexico from those that flow into the Pacific Ocean.*

Figure 4 *A mountain stream, such as the one at left, at Kenai Peninsula in Alaska, flows rapidly and has more erosive energy. A river on a flat plain, such as the Kuskokwim River in Alaska, shown below, flows slowly and has less erosive energy.*

Stream Erosion

As a stream forms, it erodes soil and rock to make a channel. A **channel** is the path that a stream follows. When a stream first forms, its channel is usually narrow and steep. Over time, the stream transports rock and soil downstream and makes the channel wider and deeper. When streams become longer and wider, they are called *rivers*. A stream's ability to erode is influenced by three factors: gradient, discharge, and load.

Gradient

Figure 4 shows two photos of rivers with very different gradients. *Gradient* is the measure of the change in elevation over a certain distance. A high gradient gives a stream or river more erosive energy to erode rock and soil. A river or stream that has a low gradient has less energy for erosion.

Discharge

The amount of water that a stream or river carries in a given amount of time is called *discharge*. The discharge of a stream increases when a major storm occurs or when warm weather rapidly melts snow. As the stream's discharge increases, its erosive energy and speed and the amount of materials that the stream can carry also increase.

Reading Check What factors cause a stream to flow faster?

tributary a stream that flows into a lake or into a larger stream

watershed the area of land that is drained by a water system

divide the boundary between drainage areas that have streams that flow in opposite directions

channel the path that a stream follows

Calculating a Stream's Gradient

If a stream starts at an elevation of 4,900 m and travels 450 km downstream to a lake that is at an elevation of 400 m, what is the stream's gradient? (Hint: Subtract the final elevation from the starting elevation, and divide by 450. Don't forget to keep track of the units.)

load the materials carried by a stream

Load

The materials carried by a stream are called the stream's **load.** The size of a stream's load is affected by the stream's speed. Fast-moving streams can carry large particles. Rocks and pebbles bounce and scrape along the bottom and sides of the stream bed. Thus, the size of a stream's load also affects its rate of erosion. The illustration below shows the three ways that a stream can carry its load.

A stream can bounce large materials, such as pebbles and boulders, along the stream bed. These rocks are called the **bed load.**

A stream can carry small rocks and soil in suspension. These materials, called the **suspended load,** make the river look muddy.

The **dissolved load** is material carried in solution, which means that the material is dissolved in the water. Sodium and calcium are some of the materials in the dissolved load.

The Stages of a River

In the early 1900s, William Morris Davis developed a model for the stages of river development. According to his model, rivers evolve from a youthful stage to an old-age stage. He thought that all rivers erode in the same way and at the same rate.

Today, scientists support a different model that considers factors of stream development that differ from those considered in Davis's model. For example, because different materials erode at different rates, one river may develop more quickly than another river. Many factors, including climate, gradient, and load, influence the development of a river. Scientists no longer use Davis's model to explain river development, but they still use many of his terms to describe a river. These terms describe a river's general features, not a river's actual age.

Youthful Rivers

A youthful river, such as the one shown in **Figure 5,** erodes its channel deeper rather than wider. The river flows quickly because of its steep gradient. Its channel is narrow and straight. The river tumbles over rocks in rapids and waterfalls. Youthful rivers have very few tributaries.

Mature Rivers

A mature river, as shown in **Figure 6,** erodes its channel wider rather than deeper. The gradient of a mature river is not as steep as that of a youthful river. Also, a mature river has fewer falls and rapids. A mature river is fed by many tributaries. Because of its good drainage, a mature river has more discharge than a youthful river.

Reading Check What are the characteristics of a mature river?

CONNECTION TO Language Arts

Huckleberry Finn Mark Twain's famous book, *The Adventures of Huckleberry Finn,* describes the life of a boy who lived on the Mississippi River. Mark Twain's real name was Samuel Clemens. Do research to find out why Clemens chose to use the name Mark Twain and how the name relates to the Mississippi River.

▲ **Figure 5** *This youthful river is located in Yellowstone National Park in Wyoming. Rapids and falls are found where the river flows over hard, resistant rock.*

◄ **Figure 6** *A mature river, such as this one in the Amazon basin of Peru, curves back and forth. The bends in the river's channel are called* meanders.

Figure 7 *This old river is located in New Zealand.*

Old Rivers

An old river has a low gradient and little erosive energy. Instead of widening and deepening its banks, the river deposits rock and soil in and along its channel. Old rivers, such as the one in **Figure 7,** are characterized by wide, flat *flood plains*, or valleys, and many bends. Also, an old river has fewer tributaries than a mature river because the smaller tributaries have joined together.

Rejuvenated Rivers

Rejuvenated (ri JOO vuh NAYT ed) rivers are found where the land is raised by tectonic activity. When land rises, the river's gradient becomes steeper, and the river flows more quickly. The increased gradient of a rejuvenated river allows the river to cut more deeply into the valley floor. Steplike formations called *terraces* often form on both sides of a stream valley as a result of rejuvenation. Can you find the terraces in **Figure 8**?

Reading Check How do rejuvenated rivers form?

Figure 8 *This rejuvenated river is located in Canyonlands National Park in Utah.*

Summary

- Rivers cause erosion by removing and transporting soil and rock from the riverbed.

- The water cycle is the movement of Earth's water from the ocean to the atmosphere to the land and back to the ocean.

- A river system is made up of a network of streams and rivers.

- A watershed is a region that collects runoff water that then becomes part of a river or a lake.

- A stream with a high gradient has more energy for eroding soil and rock.

- When a stream's discharge increases, its erosive energy also increases.

- A stream with a load of large particles has a higher rate of erosion than a stream with a dissolved load.

- A developing river can be described as youthful, mature, old, or rejuvenated.

Using Key Terms

1. Use each of the following terms in a separate sentence: *erosion, water cycle, tributary, watershed, divide, channel,* and *load*.

Understanding Key Ideas

2. Which of the following drains a watershed?
   a. a divide
   b. a drainage basin
   c. a tributary
   d. a water system

3. Describe how the Grand Canyon was formed.

4. Draw the water cycle. In your drawing, label *condensation, precipitation,* and *evaporation*.

5. What are three factors that affect the rate of stream erosion?

6. Which stage of river development is characterized by flat flood plains?

Critical Thinking

7. **Making Inferences** How does the water cycle help develop river systems?

8. **Making Comparisons** How do youthful rivers, mature rivers, and old rivers differ?

Interpreting Graphics

Use the pie graph below to answer the questions that follow.

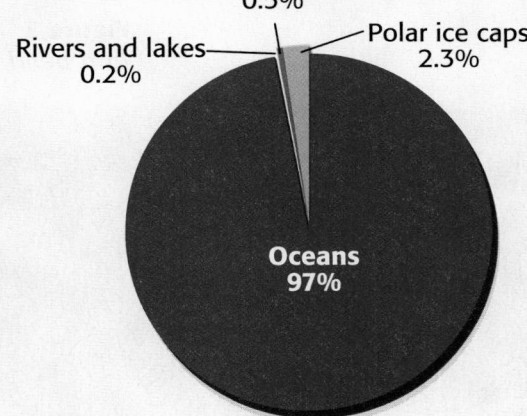

Distribution of Water in the World

Water underground, in soil, and in air
0.5%

Rivers and lakes
0.2%

Polar ice caps
2.3%

Oceans
97%

9. Where is most of the water in the world found?

10. In what form is the majority of the world's fresh water?

Developed and maintained by the National Science Teachers Association

For a variety of links related to this chapter, go to www.scilinks.org

Topic: Rivers and Streams
SciLinks code: HSM1316

Stream and River Deposits

If your job were to carry millions of tons of soil across the United States, how would you do it? You might use a bulldozer or a dump truck, but it would still take you a long time. Did you know that rivers do this job every day?

Rivers erode and move enormous amounts of material, such as soil and rock. Acting as liquid conveyor belts, rivers often carry fertile soil to farmland and wetlands. Although erosion is a serious problem, rivers also renew soils and form new land. As you will see in this section, rivers create some of the most impressive landforms on Earth.

Deposition in Water

You have learned how flowing water erodes the Earth's surface. After rivers erode rock and soil, they drop, or *deposit*, their load downstream. **Deposition** is the process in which material is laid down or dropped. Rock and soil deposited by streams are called *sediment*. Rivers and streams deposit sediment where the speed of the water current decreases. **Figure 1** shows this type of deposition.

READING WARM-UP

Objectives

- Describe the four different types of stream deposits.
- Describe how the deposition of sediment affects the land.

Terms to Learn

deposition   alluvial fan
delta   floodplain

READING STRATEGY

Prediction Guide Before reading this section, write the title of each heading in this section. Next, under each heading, write what you think you will learn.

Figure 1 *This photo shows erosion and deposition at a bend, or meander, of a river in Alaska.*

Deposition occurs along the inside bank of the bend, where the water flows slower.

Erosion occurs along the outside bank of the bend, where the water flows faster.

Placer Deposits

Heavy minerals are sometimes deposited at places in a river where the current slows down. This kind of sediment is called a *placer deposit* (PLAS uhr dee PAHZ it). Some placer deposits contain gold. During the California gold rush, which began in 1849, many miners panned for gold in the placer deposits of rivers, as shown in **Figure 2.**

Delta

A river's current slows when a river empties into a large body of water, such as a lake or an ocean. As its current slows, a river often deposits its load in a fan-shaped pattern called a **delta.** In **Figure 3,** you can see an astronaut's view of the Nile Delta. A delta usually forms on a flat surface and is made mostly of mud. These mud deposits form new land and cause the coastline to grow. The world's deltas are home to a rich diversity of plant and animal life.

If you look back at the map of the Mississippi River watershed, you can see where the Mississippi Delta has formed. It has formed where the Mississippi River flows into the Gulf of Mexico. Each of the fine mud particles in the delta began its journey far upstream. Parts of Louisiana are made up of particles that were transported from places as far away as Montana, Minnesota, Ohio, and Illinois!

Reading Check What are deltas made of? (*See the Appendix for answers to Reading Checks.*)

Figure 2 *Miners rushed to California in the 1850s to find gold. They often found it in the bends of rivers in placer deposits.*

deposition the process in which material is laid down

delta a fan-shaped mass of material deposited at the mouth of a stream

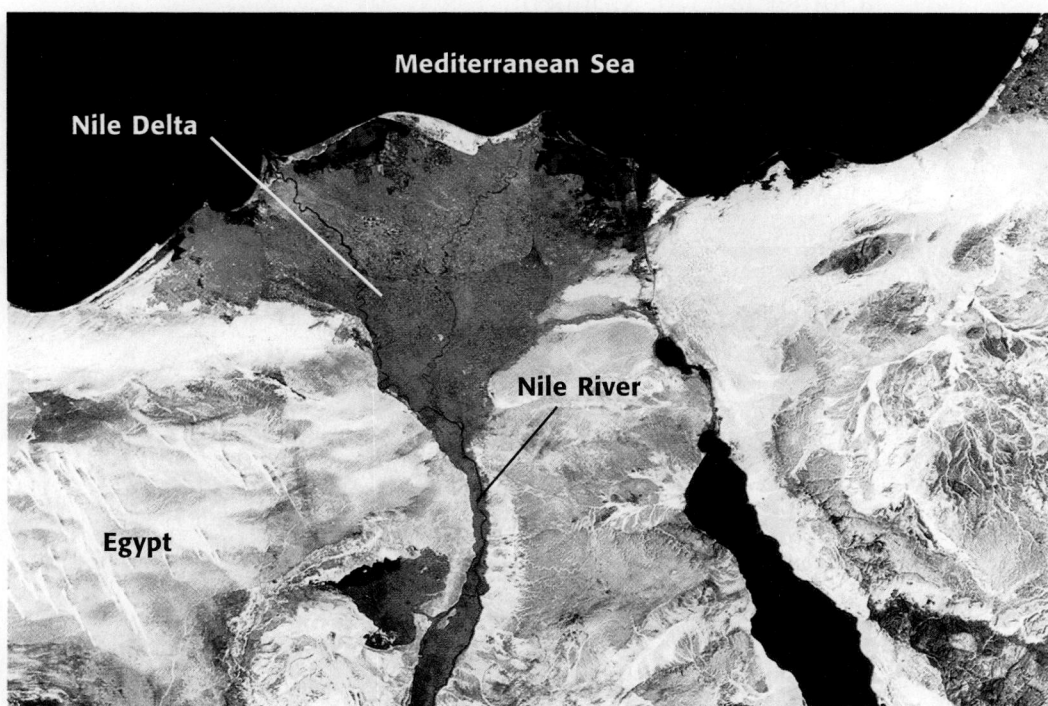

Figure 3 *As sediment is dropped at the mouth of the Nile River, in Egypt, a delta forms.*

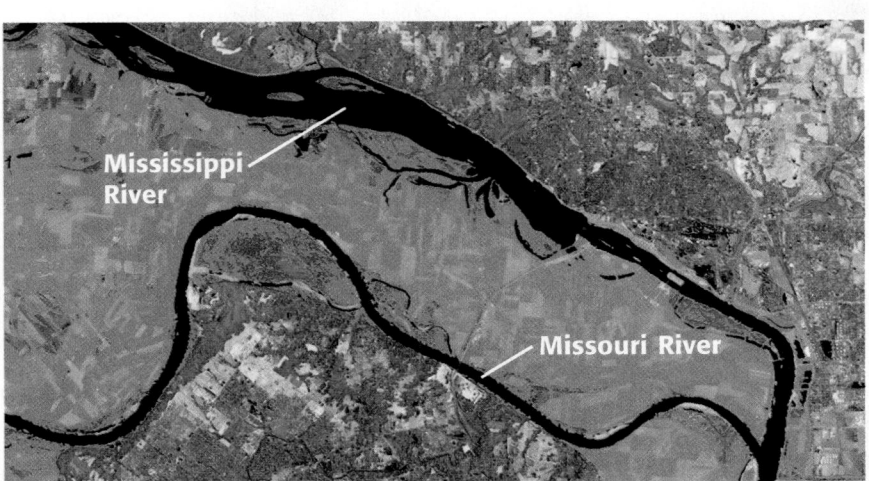

Figure 4 *An alluvial fan, like this one at Death Valley in California, forms when an eroding stream changes rapidly into a depositing stream.*

alluvial fan a fan-shaped mass of material deposited by a stream when the slope of the land decreases sharply

floodplain an area along a river that forms from sediments deposited when the river overflows its banks

Deposition on Land

When a fast-moving mountain stream flows onto a flat plain, the stream slows down very quickly. As the stream slows down, it deposits sediment. The sediment forms an alluvial fan, such as the one shown in **Figure 4. Alluvial fans** are fan-shaped deposits that, unlike deltas, form on dry land.

Floodplains

During periods of high rainfall or rapid snow melt, a sudden increase in the volume of water flowing into a stream can cause the stream to overflow its banks. The area along a river that forms from sediment deposited when a river overflows its banks is called a **floodplain.** When a stream floods, a layer of sediment is deposited across the flood plain. Each flood adds another layer of sediment.

Flood plains are rich farming areas because periodic flooding brings new soil to the land. However, flooding can cause damage, too. When the Mississippi River flooded in 1993, farms were destroyed, and entire towns were evacuated. **Figure 5** shows an area north of St. Louis, Missouri, that was flooded.

Figure 5 *The normal flow of the Mississippi River and Missouri River is shown in black. The area that was flooded when both rivers spilled over their banks in 1993 is shaded red.*

Flooding Dangers

The flooding of the Mississippi River in 1993 caused damage in nine states. But floods can damage more than property. Many people have lost their lives to powerful floods. As shown in **Figure 6,** flash flooding can take a driver by surprise. However, there are ways that floods can be controlled.

One type of barrier that can be built to help control flooding is called a *dam*. A dam is a barrier that can redirect the flow of water. A dam can prevent flooding in one area and create an artificial lake in another area. The water stored in the artificial lake can be used to irrigate farmland during droughts and provide drinking water to local towns and cities. The stored water can also be used to generate electricity.

Overflow from a river can also be controlled by a barrier called a *levee*. A levee is the buildup of sediment deposited along the channel of a river. This buildup helps keep the river inside its banks. People often use sandbags to build artificial levees to control water during serious flooding.

Reading Check List two ways that the flow of water can be controlled.

Figure 6 *Cars driven on flooded roads can easily be carried down to deeper, more dangerous water.*

SECTION Review

Summary

- Sediment forms several types of deposits.
- Sediments deposited where a river's current slows are called *placer deposits.*
- A delta is a fan-shaped deposit of sediment where a river meets a large body of water.
- Alluvial fans can form when a river deposits sediment on land.
- Flooding brings rich soil to farmland but can also lead to property damage and death.

Using Key Terms

1. In your own words, write a definition for each of the following terms: *deposition* and *flood plain.*

Understanding Key Ideas

2. Which of the following forms at places in a river where the current slows?
   a. a placer deposit
   b. a delta
   c. a flood plain
   d. a levee

3. Which of the following can help to prevent a flood?
   a. a placer deposit
   b. a delta
   c. a flood plain
   d. a levee

4. Where do alluvial fans form?

5. Explain why flood plains are both good and bad areas for farming.

Math Skills

6. A river flows at a speed of 8 km/h. If you floated on a raft in this river, how far would you have traveled after 5 h?

Critical Thinking

7. **Identifying Relationships** What factors increase the likelihood that sediment will be deposited?

8. **Making Comparisons** How are alluvial fans and deltas similar?

SCiLINKS®

NSTA

Developed and maintained by the National Science Teachers Association

For a variety of links related to this chapter, go to www.scilinks.org

Topic: Stream Deposits
SciLinks code: HSM1458

Water Underground

Imagine that instead of turning on a faucet to get a glass of water, you pour water from a chunk of solid rock! This idea may sound crazy, but millions of people get their water from within rock that is deep underground.

Although you can see some of Earth's water in streams and lakes, you cannot see the large amount of water that flows underground. The water located within the rocks below the Earth's surface is called *groundwater*. Groundwater not only is an important resource but also plays an important role in erosion and deposition.

The Location of Groundwater

Surface water seeps underground into the soil and rock. This underground area is divided into two zones. Rainwater passes through the upper zone, called the *zone of aeration.* Farther down, the water collects in an area called the *zone of saturation.* In this zone, the spaces between the rock particles are filled with water.

These two zones meet at a boundary known as the **water table,** shown in **Figure 1.** The water table rises during wet seasons and falls during dry seasons. In wet regions, the water table can be at or just beneath the soil's surface. In dry regions, such as deserts, the water table may be hundreds of meters beneath the ground.

Reading Check Describe where the zone of aeration is located. *(See the Appendix for answers to Reading Checks.)*

water table the upper surface of underground water; the upper boundary of the zone of saturation

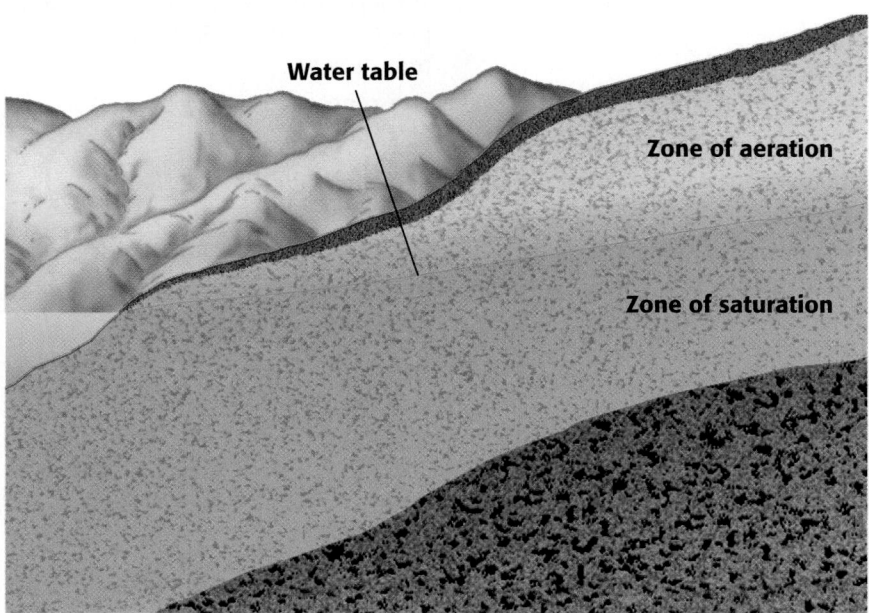

Figure 1 *The water table is the upper surface of the zone of saturation.*

Aquifers

A rock layer that stores groundwater and allows the flow of groundwater is called an **aquifer.** An aquifer can be described by its ability to hold water and its ability to allow water to pass freely through it.

Porosity

The more open spaces, or pores, between particles in an aquifer, the more water the aquifer can hold. The percentage of open space between individual rock particles in a rock layer is called **porosity.**

Porosity is influenced by the differences in sizes of the particles in the rock layer. If a rock layer contains many particles of different sizes, it is likely that small particles will fill up the different-sized empty spaces between large particles. Therefore, a rock layer with particles of different sizes has a low percentage of open space between particles and has low porosity. On the other hand, a rock layer containing same-sized particles has high porosity. This rock layer has high porosity because smaller particles are not present to fill the empty space between particles. So, there is more open space between particles.

Permeability

If the pores of a rock layer are connected, groundwater can flow through the rock layer. A rock's ability to let water pass through is called **permeability.** A rock that stops the flow of water is *impermeable*.

The larger the particles are, the more permeable the rock layer is. Because large particles have less surface area relative to their volume than small particles do, large particles cause less friction. *Friction* is a force that causes moving objects to slow down. Less friction allows water to flow more easily through the rock layer, as shown in **Figure 2.**

aquifer a body of rock or sediment that stores groundwater and allows the flow of groundwater

porosity the percentage of the total volume of a rock or sediment that consists of open spaces

permeability the ability of a rock or sediment to let fluids pass through its open spaces, or pores

For another activity related to this chapter, go to **go.hrw.com** and type in the keyword **HZ5DEPW.**

Figure 2 *Large particles, shown at left, have less total surface area—and so cause less friction—than small particles, shown at right, do.*

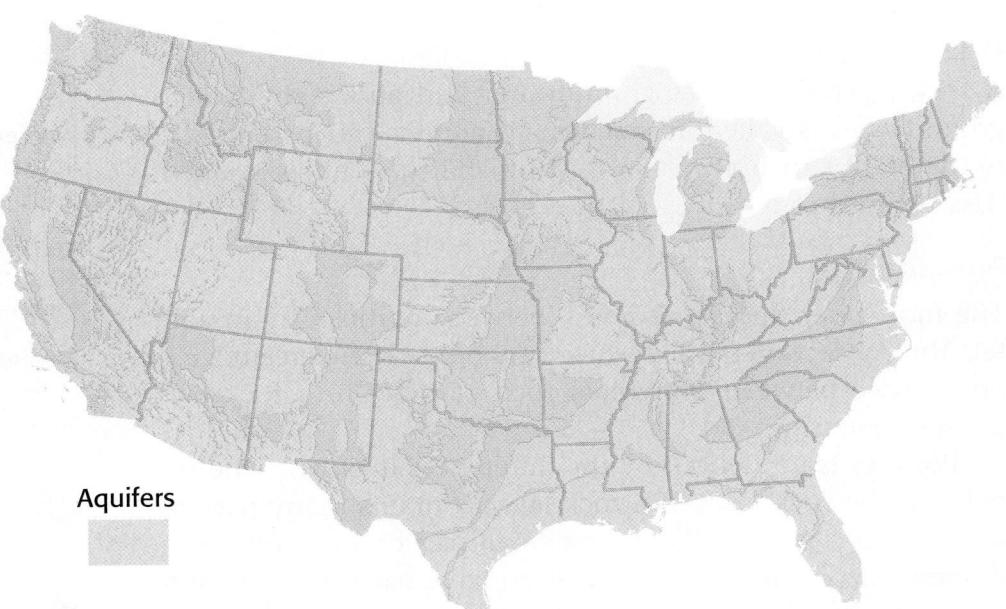

Figure 3 *This map shows aquifers in the United States (excluding Alaska and Hawaii).*

Aquifers

recharge zone an area in which water travels downward to become part of an aquifer

Water Conservation

Did you know that water use in the United States has been reduced by 15% in the last 20 years? This decrease is due in part to the conservation efforts of people like you. Work with a parent to create a water budget for your household. Figure out how much water your family uses every day. Identify ways to reduce your water use, and then set a goal to limit your water use over the course of a week.

Aquifer Geology and Geography

The best aquifers usually form in permeable materials, such as sandstone, limestone, or layers of sand and gravel. Some aquifers cover large underground areas and are an important source of water for cities and agriculture. The map in **Figure 3** shows the location of the major aquifers in the United States.

Recharge Zones

Like rivers, aquifers depend on the water cycle to maintain a constant flow of water. The ground surface where water enters an aquifer is called the **recharge zone.** The size of the recharge zone depends on how permeable rock is at the surface. If the surface rock is permeable, water can seep down into the aquifer. If the aquifer is covered by an impermeable rock layer, water cannot reach the aquifer. Construction of buildings on top of the recharge zone can also limit the amount of water that enters an aquifer.

Reading Check What factors affect the size of the recharge zone?

Springs and Wells

Groundwater movement is determined by the slope of the water table. Like surface water, groundwater tends to move downslope, toward lower elevations. If the water table reaches the Earth's surface, water will flow out from the ground and will form a *spring*. Springs are an important source of drinking water. In areas where the water table is higher than the Earth's surface, lakes will form.

Artesian Springs

A sloping layer of permeable rock sandwiched between two layers of impermeable rock is called an *artesian formation*. The permeable rock is an aquifer, and the top layer of impermeable rock is called a *cap rock,* as shown in **Figure 4.** Artesian formations are the source of water for artesian springs. An **artesian spring** is a spring whose water flows from a crack in the cap rock of the aquifer. Artesian springs are sometimes found in deserts, where they are often the only source of water.

Most springs have cool water. However, some springs have hot water. The water becomes hot when it flows deep in the Earth, because Earth's temperature increases with depth. The temperature of some hot springs can reach 50°C!

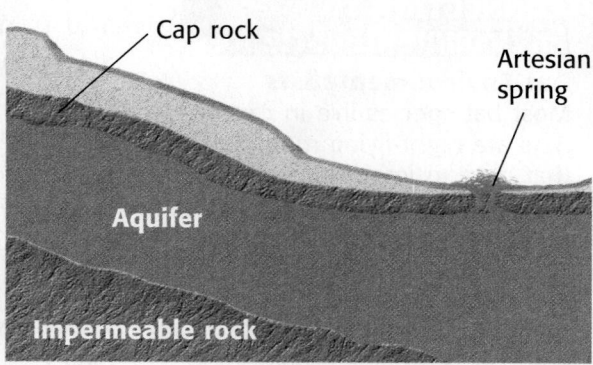

Figure 4 *Artesian springs form when water from an aquifer flows through cracks in the cap rock of an artesian formation.*

Wells

A human-made hole that is deeper than the level of the water table is called a *well.* If a well is not deep enough, as shown in **Figure 5,** it will dry up when the water table falls below the bottom of the well. Also, if an area has too many wells, groundwater can be removed too rapidly. If groundwater is removed too rapidly, the water table will drop, and all of the wells will run dry.

artesian spring a spring whose water flows from a crack in the cap rock over the aquifer

✓ Reading Check How deep must a well be to reach water?

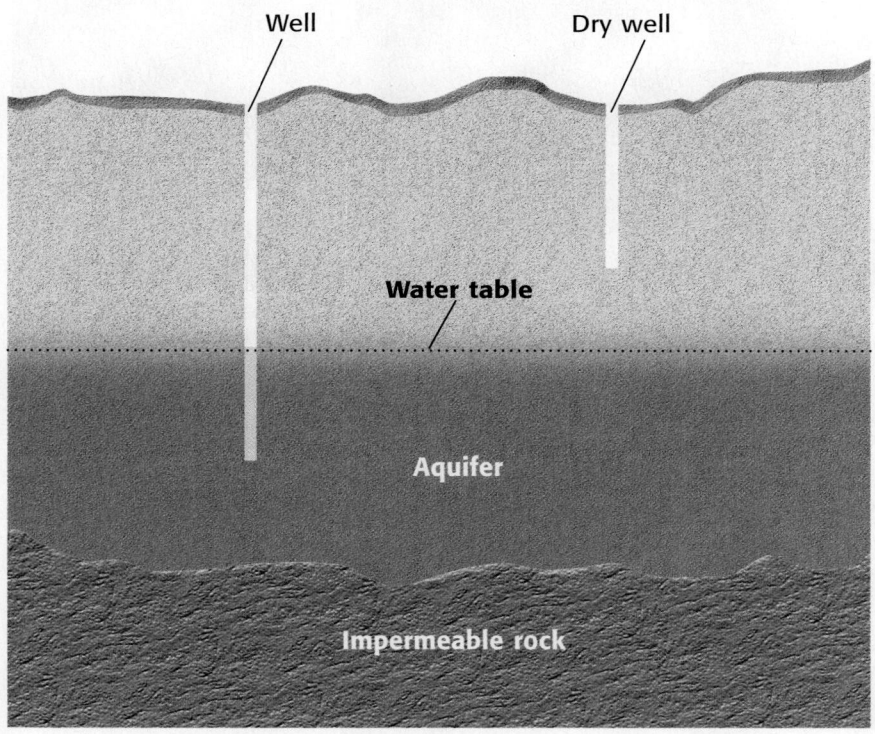

Figure 5 *A well must be drilled deep enough so that when the water table drops, the well still contains water.*

CONNECTION TO Environmental Science

Bat Environmentalists

Most bat species live in caves. Bats are night-flying mammals that play an important role in the environment. Bats eat vast quantities of insects. Many bat species also pollinate plants and distribute seeds. Can you think of other animals that eat insects, pollinate plants, and distribute seeds? Create a poster that includes pictures of these other animals.

Underground Erosion and Deposition

As you have learned, rivers cause erosion when water removes and transports rock and soil from its banks. Groundwater can also cause erosion. However, groundwater causes erosion by dissolving rock. Some groundwater contains weak acids, such as carbonic acid, that dissolve the rock. Also, some types of rock, such as limestone, dissolve in groundwater more easily than other types do.

When underground erosion happens, caves can form. Most of the world's caves formed over thousands of years as groundwater dissolved the limestone of the cave sites. Some caves, such as the one shown in **Figure 6,** reach spectacular proportions.

Cave Formations

Although caves are formed by erosion, they also show signs of deposition. Water that drips from a crack in a cave's ceiling leaves behind deposits of calcium carbonate. Sharp, icicle-shaped features that form on cave ceilings are known as *stalactites* (stuh LAK tiets). Water that falls to the cave's floor adds to cone-shaped features known as *stalagmites* (stuh LAG MIETS). If water drips long enough, the stalactites and stalagmites join to form a *dripstone column.*

Reading Check What process causes the formation of stalactites and stalagmites?

Figure 6 *At Carlsbad Caverns in New Mexico, underground passages and enormous "rooms" have been eroded below the surface of the Earth.*

Stalactite

Stalagmite

Sinkholes

When the water table is lower than the level of a cave, the cave is no longer supported by the water underneath. The roof of the cave can then collapse, which leaves a circular depression called a *sinkhole*. Surface streams can "disappear" into sinkholes and then flow through underground caves. Sinkholes often form lakes in areas where the water table is high. Central Florida is covered with hundreds of round sinkhole lakes. **Figure 7** shows how the collapse of an underground cave can affect a landscape.

Figure 7 *The damage to this city block shows the effects of a sinkhole in Winter Park, Florida.*

SECTION Review

Summary

- The water table is the boundary between the zone of aeration and the zone of saturation.
- Porosity and permeability describe an aquifer's ability to hold water and ability to allow water to flow through.
- Springs are a natural way that water reaches the surface. Wells are made by humans.
- Caves and sinkholes form from the erosion of limestone by groundwater.

Using Key Terms

1. Use the following terms in the same sentence: *water table, aquifer, porosity,* and *artesian spring.*

Understanding Key Ideas

2. Which of the following describes an aquifer's ability to allow water to flow through?
   a. porosity
   b. permeability
   c. geology
   d. recharge zone

3. What is the water table?

4. Describe how particles affect the porosity of an aquifer.

5. Explain the difference between an artesian spring and other springs.

6. Name a feature that is formed by underground erosion.

7. Name two features that are formed by underground deposition.

8. What type of weathering process causes underground erosion?

Math Skills

9. Groundwater in an area flows at a speed of 4 km/h. How long would it take the water to flow 10 km to its spring?

Critical Thinking

10. **Predicting Consequences** Explain how urban growth might affect the recharge zone of an aquifer.

11. **Making Comparisons** Explain the difference between a spring and a well.

12. **Analyzing Relationships** What is the relationship between the zone of aeration, the zone of saturation, and the water table?

Using Water Wisely

Did you know that you are almost 65% water? You depend on clean, fresh drinking water to maintain that 65% of you. But there is a limited amount of fresh water available on Earth. Only 3% of Earth's water is drinkable.

And of the 3% of Earth's water that is drinkable, 75% is frozen in the polar icecaps. This frozen water is not readily available for our use. Therefore, it is important that we protect our water resources.

Water Pollution

Surface water, such as the water in rivers and lakes, and groundwater can be polluted by waste from cities, factories, and farms. Pollution is the introduction of harmful substances into the environment. Water can become so polluted that it can no longer be used or can even be deadly.

Point-Source and Nonpoint-Source Pollution

Pollution that comes from one specific site is called **point-source pollution.** For example, a leak from a sewer pipe is point-source pollution. In most cases, this type of pollution can be controlled because its source can be identified.

    Nonpoint-source pollution, another type of pollution, is pollution that comes from many sources. This type of pollution is much more difficult to control because it does not come from a single source. Most nonpoint-source pollution reaches bodies of water by runoff. The main sources of nonpoint-source pollution are street gutters, fertilizers, eroded soils and silt from farming and logging, drainage from mines, and salts from irrigation. **Figure 1** shows an example of a source of nonpoint-source pollution.

✓ **Reading Check** What type of pollution is the hardest to control? (*See the Appendix for answers to Reading Checks.*)

point-source pollution pollution that comes from a specific site

nonpoint-source pollution pollution that comes from many sources rather than from a single, specific site

Figure 1 *The runoff from this irrigation system could collect pesticides and other pollutants. The result would be nonpoint-source pollution.*

Figure 2 *Waste from farm animals can seep into groundwater and cause nitrate pollution.*

Health of a Water System

You might not realize it, but water quality affects your quality of life as well as other organisms that depend on water. Therefore, it is important to understand how the properties of water influence water quality.

Dissolved Oxygen

Just as you need oxygen to live, so do fish and other organisms that live in lakes and streams. The oxygen dissolved in water is called *dissolved oxygen,* or DO. Levels of DO that are below 4.0 mg/L in fresh water can cause stress and possibly death for organisms in the water.

Pollutants such as sewage, fertilizer runoff, and animal waste can decrease DO levels. Temperature changes also affect DO levels. For example, cold water holds more oxygen than warm water does. Facilities such as nuclear power plants can increase the temperature of lakes and rivers when they use the water as a cooling agent. Such an increase in water temperature is called *thermal pollution*, which causes a decrease in DO levels.

Nitrates

Nitrates are naturally occurring compounds of nitrogen and oxygen. Small amounts of nitrates in water are normal. However, elevated nitrate levels in water can be harmful to organisms. An excess of nitrates in lakes and rivers can also lower DO levels. As shown in **Figure 2,** nitrate pollution can come from animal wastes or fertilizers that seep into groundwater.

Alkalinity

Alkalinity refers to the water's ability to neutralize acid. Acid rain and other acid wastes can harm aquatic life. A pH below 6.0 is too acidic for most aquatic life. Water with a higher alkalinity can better protect organisms from acid.

Measuring Alkalinity

1. Identify two water sources from which to collect water samples.

2. Fill a **plastic cup** with water from one source. Fill a **second plastic cup** with water from the second source. Label each cup with its source.

3. Using a **pH test kit,** test the pH of each sample.

4. Follow the instructions in the test kit, and determine the pH of each of the two samples. Record your observations.

5. What did the results for the two samples indicate about the two sources?

6. Use **water test kits** to measure DO and nitrate levels in the two water samples, and discuss your results.

Cleaning Polluted Water

When you flush the toilet or watch water go down the shower drain, do you ever wonder where the water goes? If you live in a city or large town, the water flows through sewer pipes to a sewage treatment plant. **Sewage treatment plants** are facilities that clean the waste materials out of water. These plants help protect the environment from water pollution. They also protect us from diseases that are easily transmitted through dirty water.

sewage treatment plant a facility that cleans the waste materials found in water that comes from sewers or drains

Primary Treatment

When water reaches a sewage treatment plant, it is cleaned in two ways. First, it goes through a series of steps known as *primary treatment*. In primary treatment, dirty water is passed through a large screen to catch solid objects, such as paper, rags, and bottle caps. The water is then placed in a large tank, where smaller particles, or sludge, can sink and be filtered out. These particles include things such as food, coffee grounds, and soil. Any floating oils and scum are skimmed off the surface.

Secondary Treatment

After undergoing primary treatment, the water is ready for *secondary treatment*. In secondary treatment, the water is sent to an aeration tank, where it is mixed with oxygen and bacteria. The bacteria feed on the wastes and use the oxygen. The water is then sent to another settling tank, where chlorine is added to disinfect the water. The water is finally released into a water source—a river, a lake, or the ocean. **Figure 3** shows the major components of a sewage treatment plant.

Figure 3 *If you live in a city, the water used in your home most likely ends up at a sewage treatment plant, where the water is cleaned.*

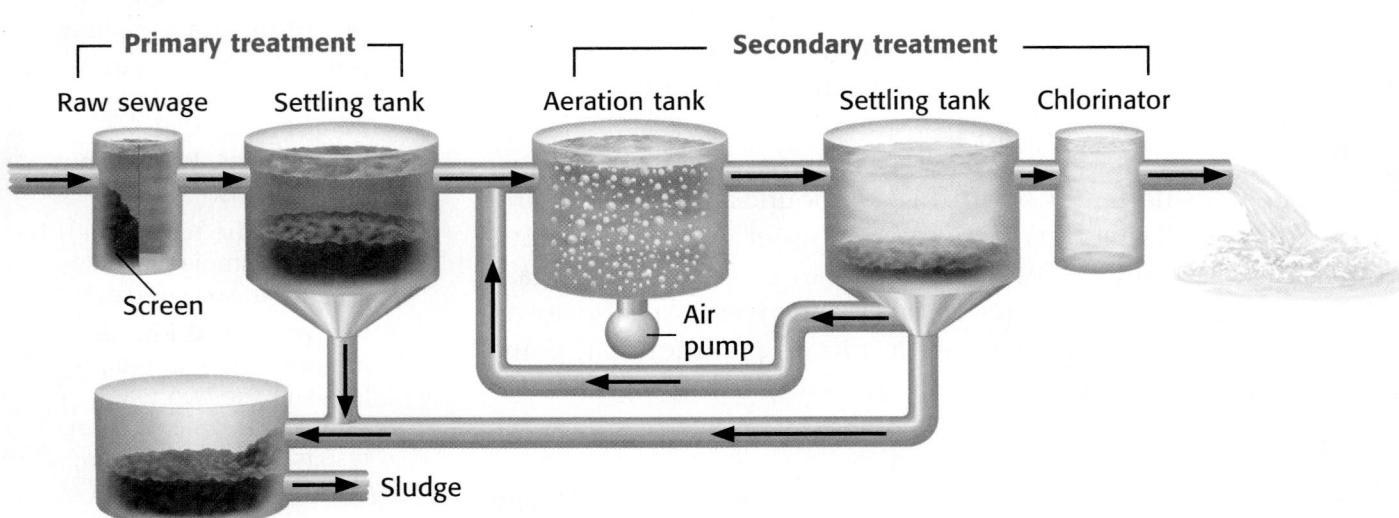

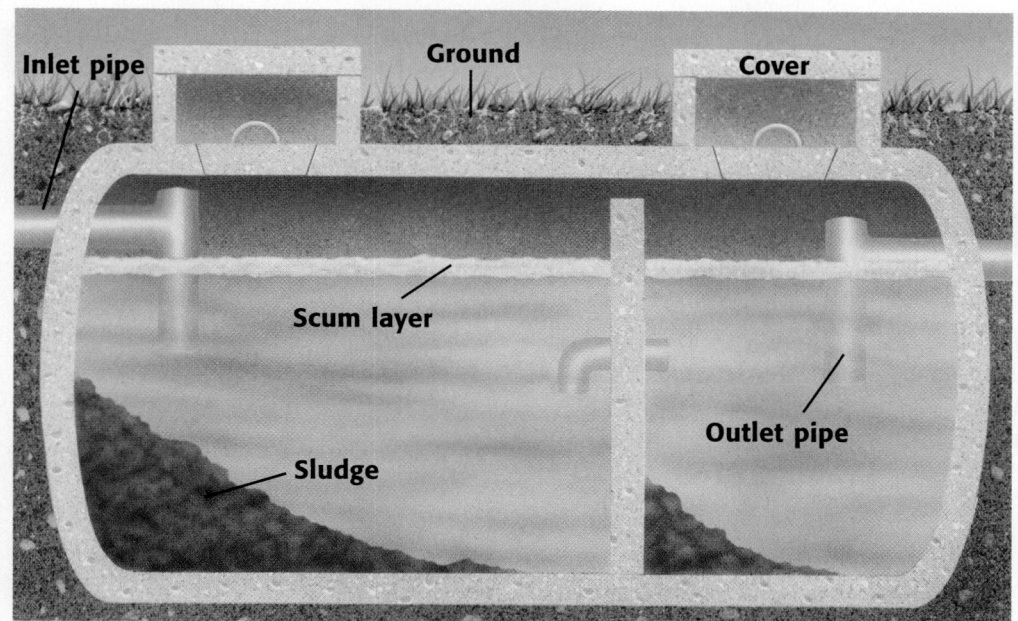

Inlet pipe   Ground   Cover

Scum layer

Sludge

Outlet pipe

Figure 4 *Most septic tanks must be cleaned out every few years in order to work properly.*

Another Way to Clean Wastewater

If you live in an area that does not have a sewage treatment plant, your house probably uses a septic tank. **Figure 4** shows an example of a septic tank. A **septic tank** is a large underground tank that cleans the wastewater from a household. Wastewater flows from the house into the tank, where the solids sink to the bottom. Bacteria break down these wastes on the bottom of the tank. The water flows from the tank into a group of buried pipes. Then, the buried pipes, called a *drain field,* distribute the water. Distributing the water enables the water to soak into the ground.

septic tank a tank that separates solid waste from liquids and that has bacteria that break down the solid waste

Where the Water Goes

Think of some ways that you use water in your home. Do you water the lawn? Do you do the dishes? The graph in **Figure 5** shows how an average household in the United States uses water. Notice that less than 8% of the water we use in our homes is used for drinking. The rest is used for flushing toilets, doing laundry, bathing, and watering lawns and plants.

The water we use in our homes is not the only way water is used. More water is used in industry and agriculture than in homes.

✓ **Reading Check** What percentage of water in our homes is used for drinking?

Bathing, toilet flushing, and laundry
60%

Lawn watering, car washing, and pool maintenance
32%

8%

Drinking, cooking, washing dishes, running a garbage disposal

Figure 5 *The average household in the United States uses about 100 gal of water per day. This pie graph shows some common uses of these 100 gal.*

Water in Industry

About 19% of water used in the world is used for industrial purposes. Water is used to manufacture goods, cool power stations, clean industrial products, extract minerals, and generate energy for factories.

Because water resources have become expensive, many industries are trying to conserve, or use less, water. One way industries conserve water is by recycling it. In the United States, most of the water used in factories is recycled at least once. At least 90% of this recycled water can be treated and returned to surface water.

Water in Agriculture

The Ogallala aquifer is the largest known aquifer in North America. The map in **Figure 6** shows that the Ogallala aquifer runs beneath the ground through eight states, from South Dakota to Texas. The Ogallala aquifer provides water for approximately one-fifth of the cropland in the United States. Farming is the largest user of water in the Western United States. Recently, the water table in the aquifer has dropped so low that some scientists say that it would take at least 1,000 years to replenish the aquifer if it were no longer used.

Most of the water that is lost during farming is lost through evaporation and runoff. New technology, such as drip irrigation systems, has helped conserve water in agriculture. A drip irrigation system delivers small amounts of water directly to plant roots. This system allows plants to absorb the water before the water has a chance to evaporate or become runoff.

✓ Reading Check How does the drip irrigation system help conserve water?

Agriculture in Israel

From 1950 to 1980, Israel reduced the amount of water used in agriculture from 83% to 5%. Israel did so primarily by switching from overhead sprinklers to drip irrigation. A small farm uses 10,000 L of water per day for overhead sprinkler irrigation. How much water would the farm save in 1 year by using a drip irrigation system that uses 75% less water than a sprinkler system?

Figure 6 *Because the Ogallala aquifer has been such a good source of groundwater, it has become overused. The water table has dropped more than 30 m in some areas.*

Conserving Water at Home

There are many ways that people can conserve water at home. For example, many people save water by installing low-flow shower heads and low-flush toilets, because these items use much less water. To avoid watering lawns, some people plant only native plants in their yards. Native plants grow well in the local climate and don't need extra watering.

Your behavior can also help you conserve water. For example, you can take shorter showers. You can avoid running the water while brushing your teeth. And when you run the dishwasher, make sure it is full, as shown in **Figure 7.**

✓ Reading Check List ways in which you can conserve water in your home.

Figure 7 *Run the dishwasher only when it is full.*

SECTION Review

Summary

- Point-source pollution and nonpoint-source pollution are two kinds of water pollution.

- Pollutants can decrease oxygen levels and increase nitrate levels in water. These changes can cause harm to plants, animals, and humans.

- Wastewater can be treated by sewage treatment plants and septic systems.

- Water can be conserved by using only the water that is needed, by recycling water, and by using drip irrigation systems.

Using Key Terms

1. Use each of the following terms in a separate sentence: *point-source pollution, nonpoint-source pollution, sewage treatment plant,* and *septic tank.*

Understanding Key Ideas

2. Which of the following can help protect fish from acid rain?
   a. dissolved oxygen
   b. nitrates
   c. alkalinity
   d. point-source pollution

3. What type of wastewater treatment can be used for an individual home?
   a. sewage treatment plant
   b. primary treatment
   c. secondary treatment
   d. septic tank

4. Which kind of water pollution is often caused by runoff of fertilizers?

5. Describe what DO is.

6. What factors affect the level of dissolved oxygen in water?

7. Describe how water is conserved in industry.

Math Skills

8. If 25% of water used in your home is used to water the lawn and you used a total of 95 gal of water today, how many gallons of water did you use to water the lawn?

Critical Thinking

9. **Making Inferences** How do bacteria help break down the waste in water treatment plants?

10. **Applying Concepts** Other than examples listed in this section, what are some ways you can conserve water?

11. **Making Inferences** Why is it better to water your lawn at night instead of during the day?

SCiLINKS.

NSTA
Developed and maintained by the
National Science Teachers Association

For a variety of links related to this chapter, go to www.scilinks.org
Topic: Water Pollution and Conservation
SciLinks code: HSM1630

Model-Making Lab

Water Cycle—What Goes Up . . .

Why does a bathroom mirror fog up? Where does water go when it dries up? Where does rain come from? These questions relate to the major parts of the water cycle—condensation, evaporation, and precipitation. In this activity, you will make a model of the water cycle.

Procedure

1. Use the graduated cylinder to pour 50 mL of water into the beaker. Note the water level in the beaker.

2. Put on your safety goggles and gloves. Place the beaker securely on the hot plate. Turn the heat to medium, and bring the water to a boil.

3. While waiting for the water to boil, practice picking up and handling the glass plate or watch glass with the tongs. Hold the glass plate a few centimeters above the beaker, and tilt it so that the lowest edge of the glass is still above the beaker.

4. Observe the glass plate as the water in the beaker boils. Record the changes you see in the beaker, in the air above the beaker, and on the glass plate held over the beaker. Write down any changes you see in the water.

OBJECTIVES

Design a model that follows the same processes as those of the water cycle.

Identify each stage of the water cycle in the model.

MATERIALS

- beaker
- gloves, heat-resistant
- graduated cylinder
- hot plate
- plate, glass, or watch glass
- tap water, 50 mL
- tongs or forceps

SAFETY

5 Continue until you have observed steam rising off the water, the glass plate becoming foggy, and water dripping from the glass plate.

6 Carefully set the glass plate on a counter or other safe surface as directed by your teacher.

7 Turn off the hot plate, and allow the beaker to cool. Move the hot beaker with gloves or tongs if you are directed to do so by your teacher.

Analyze the Results

1 **Constructing Charts** Copy the illustration shown above. On your sketch, draw and label the water cycle as it happened in your model. Include arrows and labels for *evaporation, condensation,* and *precipitation*.

2 **Analyzing Results** Compare the water level in the beaker now with the water level at the beginning of the experiment. Was there a change? Explain why or why not.

Draw Conclusions

3 **Making Predictions** If you had used a scale or a balance to measure the mass of the water in the beaker before and after this activity, would the mass have changed? Explain.

4 **Analyzing Charts** How is your model similar to the Earth's water cycle? On your sketch of the illustration, label where the processes shown in the model reflect the Earth's water cycle.

5 **Drawing Conclusions** When you finished this experiment, the water in the beaker was still hot. What stores much of the energy in the Earth's water cycle?

Applying Your Data

As rainwater runs over the land, the water picks up minerals and salts. Do these minerals and salts evaporate, condense, and precipitate as part of the water cycle? Where do they go?

Chapter Review

USING KEY TERMS

The statements below are false. For each statement, replace the underlined term to make a true statement.

1 A stream that flows into a lake or into a larger stream is a <u>water cycle</u>.

2 The area along a river that forms from sediment deposited when the river overflows is a <u>delta</u>.

3 A rock's ability to let water pass through it is called <u>porosity</u>.

For each pair of terms, explain how the meanings of the terms differ.

4 *divide* and *watershed*

5 *artesian springs* and *wells*

6 *point-source pollution* and *nonpoint-source pollution*

UNDERSTANDING KEY IDEAS

Multiple Choice

7 Which of the following processes is not part of the water cycle?

 a. evaporation

 b. percolation

 c. condensation

 d. deposition

8 Which features are common in youthful river channels?

 a. meanders

 b. flood plains

 c. rapids

 d. sandbars

9 Which depositional feature is found at the coast?

 a. delta

 b. flood plain

 c. alluvial fan

 d. placer deposit

10 Caves are mainly a product of

 a. erosion by rivers.

 b. river deposition.

 c. water pollution.

 d. erosion by groundwater.

11 Which of the following is necessary for aquatic life to survive?

 a. dissolved oxygen

 b. nitrates

 c. alkalinity

 d. point-source pollution

12 During primary treatment at a sewage treatment plant,

 a. water is sent to an aeration tank.

 b. water is mixed with bacteria and oxygen.

 c. dirty water is passed through a large screen.

 d. water is sent to a settling tank where chlorine is added.

Short Answer

13 Identify and describe the location of the water table.

14 Explain how surface water enters an aquifer.

15 Why are caves usually found in limestone-rich regions?

CRITICAL THINKING

16 **Concept Mapping** Use the following terms to create a concept map: *zone of aeration, zone of saturation, water table, gravity, porosity,* and *permeability*.

17 **Identifying Relationships** What is water's role in erosion and deposition?

18 **Analyzing Processes** What are the features of a river channel that has a steep gradient?

19 **Analyzing Processes** Why is groundwater hard to clean?

20 **Evaluating Conclusions** How can water be considered both a renewable and a nonrenewable resource? Give an example of each case.

21 **Analyzing Processes** Does water vapor lose or gain energy during the process of condensation? Explain.

The hydrograph below illustrates data collected on river flow during field investigations over a period of 1 year. The discharge readings are from the Yakima River, in Washington. Use the hydrograph below to answer the questions that follow.

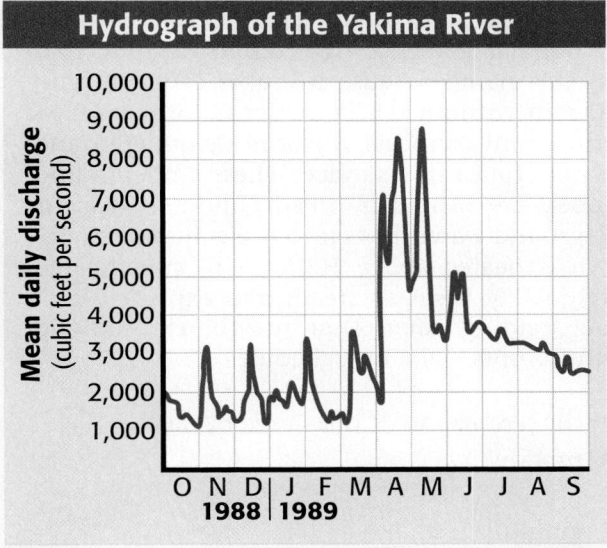

22 In which months is there the highest river discharge?

23 Why is there such a high river discharge during these months?

24 What might cause the peaks in river discharge between November and March?

Standardized Test Preparation

Read each of the passages below. Then, answer the questions that follow each passage.

Passage 1 In parts of Yellowstone National Park, boiling water from deep in the ground blasts into the sky. These blasts of steam come from lakes of strange-colored boiling mud that gurgle and hiss. These features are called geysers. Yellowstone's most popular geyser is named Old Faithful. It is given this name because it erupts every 60 min to 70 min without fail. A geyser is formed when a narrow vent connects one or more underground chambers to Earth's surface. These underground chambers are heated by nearby molten rock. As underground water flows into the vent and chambers, it is heated above 100°C. This superheated water quickly turns to steam and explodes, projecting <u>scalding</u> water 60 m into the air. And Old Faithful erupts right on schedule!

1. In the passage, what does *scalding* mean?
   A muddy
   B burning
   C gurgling
   D steaming

2. According to the passage, what happens to underground water when geysers form?
   F It is heated by molten rock.
   G It is cycled to Earth's center.
   H It travels 60 m through vents.
   I It is poured into volcanoes.

3. Which of the following is a fact in the passage?
   A Old Faithful erupts every 60 min.
   B Old Faithful is located in Yellowstone National Park.
   C There are six geysers at Yellowstone National Park.
   D Molten rock explodes from geysers.

Passage 2 In the Mississippi Delta, long-legged birds step lightly through the marsh and hunt fish or frogs for breakfast. Hundreds of species of plants and animals start another day in this fragile ecosystem. This delta ecosystem is in danger of being destroyed. The threat comes from efforts to make the river more useful. Large portions of the river bottom were <u>dredged</u> to deepen the river for ship traffic. Underwater channels were built to control flooding. What no one realized was that sediments that once formed new land now passed through the channels and flowed out into the ocean. Those river sediments had once replaced the land that was lost every year to erosion. Without them, the river can't replace land lost to erosion. So, the Mississippi River Delta is shrinking. By 1995, more than half of the wetlands were already gone—swept out to sea by waves along the Louisiana coast.

1. In the passage, what does *dredged* mean?
   A moved to the side
   B circulated
   C cleaned
   D scooped up

2. Based on the passage, which of the following statements about the Mississippi River is true?
   F The river never floods.
   G The river is not wide enough for ships.
   H The river's delicate ecosystem is in danger.
   I The river is disappearing.

3. Which of the following is a fact in the passage?
   A By 1995, more than half of the Mississippi River was gone.
   B Underwater channels controlled flooding.
   C Channels help form new land.
   D Sediment cannot replace lost land.

The chart below shows four wells drilled at different depths. Use the chart below to answer the questions that follow.

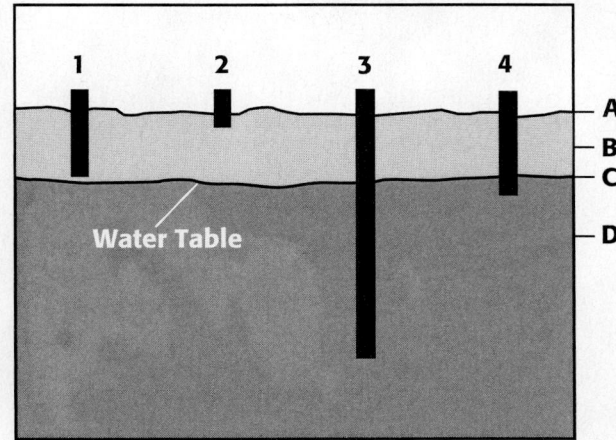

1. A well-drilling company offers the four types of wells shown in the chart. Which well is most likely to be a reliable source of groundwater?

A 1

B 2

C 3

D 4

2. If the area experienced heavy rains, toward which level would the water table move?

F The water table would move toward level B.

G The water table would move toward level D.

H The water table would stay at level C.

I The water table will be gone.

3. If the water table moves to level D, which wells will still be able to provide water?

A all wells

B wells 1 and 2

C well 3

D wells 3 and 4

4. Which well is most likely to be an unreliable source of groundwater?

F 1

G 2

H 3

I 4

Read each question below, and choose the best answer.

1. A river flows at a speed of 10 km/h. If a boat travels upstream at a speed of 15 km/h, how far will it travel in 3 h?

A 10 km

B 15 km

C 20 km

D 25 km

2. Water contamination is often measured in parts per million (ppm). If the concentration of a pollutant is 5 ppm, there are 5 parts of the pollutant in 1 million parts of water. If the concentration of gasoline is 3 ppm in 2,000,000 L of water, how many liters of gasoline are in the water?

F 3 L

G 6 L

H 9 L

I 10 L

3. One family uses 70 L of water a day for showering. If everyone in the family agreed to shorten his or her shower from 10 min to 5 min, how many liters of water would be saved each day?

A 5 L

B 10 L

C 35 L

D 70 L

4. A family uses 800 L of water per day. Of those 800 L, 200 L are used for flushing the toilet. Calculate the percentage of water that the family uses to flush the toilet.

F 25%

G 30%

H 50%

I 60%

5. A river flows at a speed of 8 km/h. If you floated on a raft in this river, how far will you have traveled after 5 h?

A 5 km

B 16 km

C 40 km

D 80 km

Science in Action

Weird Science

Secret Lake

Would you believe there is a freshwater lake more than 3 km below an Antarctic glacier near the South Pole? It is surprising that Lake Vostok can remain in a liquid state at a place where the temperature can fall below –50°C. Scientists believe that the intense pressure from the overlying ice heats the lake and keeps it from freezing. Geothermal energy, which is the energy within the surface of the Earth, also contributes to warmer temperatures. The other unique thing about Lake Vostok is the discovery of living microbes under the glacier that covers the lake!

Language Arts ACTiViTY

Look up the word *geothermal* in the dictionary. What is the meaning of the roots *geo-* and *-thermal*? Find other words in the dictionary that begin with the root *geo-*.

Scientific Discoveries

Sunken Forests

Imagine having your own little secret forest. In Ankarana National Park, in Madagascar, there are plenty of them. Within the limestone mountain of the park, caves have formed from the twisting path of the flowing groundwater. In many places in the caves, the roof has collapsed to form a sinkhole. The light that now shines through the collapsed roof of the cave has allowed miniature sunken forests to grow. Each sunken forest has unique characteristics. Some have crocodiles. Others have blind cavefish. You can even find some species that can't be found anywhere else in the world!

Social Studies ACTiViTY

Find out how Madagascar's geography contributes to the biodiversity of the island nation. Make a map of the island that highlights some of the unique forms of life found there.

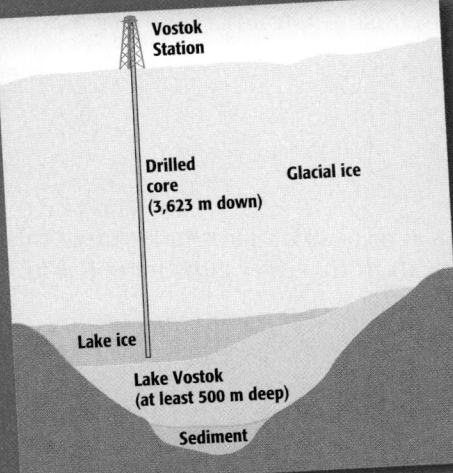

Vostok
Station

Drilled core
(3,623 m down)

Glacial ice

Lake ice

Lake Vostok
(at least 500 m deep)

Sediment

Rita Colwell

A Water Filter for All Did you ever drink a glass of water through a piece of cloth? Dr. Rita Colwell, director of the National Science Foundation, has found that filtering drinking water through a cloth can actually decrease the number of disease-causing bacteria in the water. This discovery is very important for the people of Bangladesh, where deadly outbreaks of cholera are frequent. People are usually infected by the cholera bacteria by drinking contaminated water. Colwell knew that filtering the water would remove the bacteria. The water would then be safe to drink. Unfortunately, filters were too expensive for most of the people to buy. Colwell tried filtering the water with a sari. A sari is a long piece of colorful cloth that many women in Bangladesh wear as skirtlike cloth. Filtering the water with the sari cloth did the trick. The amount of cholera bacteria in the water was reduced. Fewer people contracted cholera, and many lives were saved!

Math Activity

With the cloth water-filter method, there was a 48% reduction in the occurrence of cholera. If there were 125 people out of 100,000 who contracted cholera before the cloth-filter method was used, how many people per 100,000 contracted cholera after using the cloth-filter method?

To learn more about these Science in Action topics, visit go.hrw.com and type in the keyword **HZ5DEPF.**

Current Science

Check out Current Science® articles related to this chapter by visiting go.hrw.com. Just type in the keyword HZ5CS11.

12

Agents of Erosion and Deposition

About the PHOTO

The results of erosion can often be dramatic.
For example, this sinkhole formed in a parking
lot in Atlanta, Georgia, when water running
underground eventually caused the surface of
the land to collapse.

PRE-READING ACTIVITY

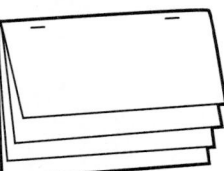

FOLDNOTES **Layered Book** Before
you read the chapter, create
the FoldNote entitled "The
Layered Book" described in the **Study
Skills** section of the Appendix. Label the
tabs of the layered book with "Shoreline
erosion and deposition," "Wind erosion and deposition," and "Erosion and
deposition by ice." As
you read the chap-
ter, write information
you learn about each
category under the
appropriate tab.

START-UP ACTIVITY

Making Waves

Above ground or below, water plays an important role in the erosion and deposition of rock and soil. A shoreline is a good example of how water shapes the Earth's surface by erosion and deposition. Did you know that shorelines are shaped by crashing waves? Build a model shoreline, and see for yourself!

Procedure

1. Make a shoreline by adding **sand** to one end of a **washtub**. Fill the washtub with **water** to a depth of 5 cm. Sketch the shoreline profile (side view), and label it "A."

2. Place a **block** at the end of the washtub opposite the beach.

3. Move the block up and down very slowly to create small waves for 2 min. Sketch the new shoreline profile, and label it "B."

4. Now, move the block up and down more rapidly to create large waves for 2 min. Sketch the new shoreline profile, and label it "C."

Analysis

1. Compare the three shoreline profiles. What is happening to the shoreline?

2. How do small waves and large waves erode the shoreline differently?

Shoreline Erosion and Deposition

Think about the last time you were at a beach. Where did all of the sand come from?

Two basic ingredients are necessary to make sand: rock and energy. The rock is usually available on the shore. The energy is provided by waves that travel through water. When waves crash into rocks over long periods of time, the rocks are broken down into smaller and smaller pieces until they become sand.

As you read on, you will learn how wave erosion and deposition shape the shoreline. A **shoreline** is simply the place where land and a body of water meet. Waves usually play a major role in building up and breaking down the shoreline.

Wave Energy

As the wind moves across the ocean surface, it produces ripples called *waves*. The size of a wave depends on how hard the wind is blowing and how long the wind blows. The harder and longer the wind blows, the bigger the wave.

The wind that results from summer hurricanes and severe winter storms produces large waves that cause dramatic shoreline erosion. Waves may travel hundreds or even thousands of kilometers from a storm before reaching the shoreline. Some of the largest waves to reach the California coast are produced by storms as far away as Australia. So, the California surfer in **Figure 1** can ride a wave that formed on the other side of the Pacific Ocean!

Figure 1 *Waves produced by storms on the other side of the Pacific Ocean propel this surfer toward a California shore.*

Wave Trains

When you drop a pebble into a pond, is there just one ripple? Of course not. Waves, like ripples, don't move alone. As shown in **Figure 2,** waves travel in groups called *wave trains.* As wave trains move away from their source, they travel through the ocean water uninterrupted. But when waves reach shallow water, the bottom of the wave drags against the sea floor, slowing the wave down. The upper part of the wave moves more rapidly and grows taller. When the top of the wave becomes so tall that it cannot support itself, it begins to curl and break. These breaking waves are known as *surf.* Now you know how surfers got their name. The *wave period* is the time interval between breaking waves. Wave periods are usually 10 to 20 s long.

Figure 2 *Because waves travel in wave trains, they break at regular intervals.*

The Pounding Surf

Look at **Figure 3,** and you will get an idea of how sand is made. A tremendous amount of energy is released when waves break. A crashing wave can break solid rock and throw broken rocks back against the shore. As the rushing water in breaking waves enters cracks in rock, it helps break off large boulders and wash away fine grains of sand. The loose sand picked up by waves wears down and polishes coastal rocks. As a result of these actions, rock is broken down into smaller and smaller pieces that eventually become sand.

shoreline the boundary between land and a body of water

✓ **Reading Check** How do waves help break down rock into sand? (*See the Appendix for answers to Reading Checks.*)

Counting Waves

If the wave period is 10 s, approximately how many waves reach a shoreline in a day? (Hint: Calculate how many waves occur in an hour, and multiply that number by the number of hours in a day.)

Figure 3 *Breaking waves crash against the rocky shore, releasing their energy.*

Wave Erosion

Wave erosion produces a variety of features along a shoreline. *Sea cliffs* are formed when waves erode and undercut rock to produce steep slopes. Waves strike the base of the cliff, which wears away the soil and rock and makes the cliff steeper. The rate at which the sea cliffs erode depends on the hardness of the rock and the energy of the waves. Sea cliffs made of hard rock, such as granite, erode very slowly. Sea cliffs made of soft rock, such as shale, erode more rapidly, especially during storms.

Figure 4 **Coastal Landforms Created by Wave Erosion**

Sea stacks are offshore columns of resistant rock that were once connected to the mainland. In these instances, waves have eroded the mainland, leaving behind isolated columns of rock.

Sea arches form when wave action continues to erode a sea cave, cutting completely through the rock.

Sea caves form when waves cut large holes into fractured or weak rock along the base of sea cliffs. Sea caves are common in cliffs composed of sedimentary rock.

Shaping a Shoreline

Much of the erosion responsible for landforms you might see along the shoreline takes place during storms. Large waves generated by storms release far more energy than normal waves do. This energy is so powerful that it is capable of removing huge chunks of rock. **Figure 4** shows some of the major landscape features that result from wave erosion.

For another activity related to this chapter, go to **go.hrw.com** and type in the keyword **HZ5ICEW.**

✓ **Reading Check** Why are large waves more capable of removing large chunks of rock from a shoreline than normal waves are?

Headlands are finger-shaped projections that form when cliffs made of hard rock erode more slowly than surrounding rock. On many shorelines, hard rock will form headlands, and the softer rock will form beaches or bays.

Wave-cut terraces form when a sea cliff is worn back, producing a nearly level platform beneath the water at the base of the cliff.

England

U.S. Virgin Islands

Hawaii

Figure 5 *Beaches are made of different types of material deposited by waves.*

beach an area of the shoreline made up of material deposited by waves

Wave Deposits

Waves carry a variety of materials, including sand, rock fragments, dead coral, and shells. Often, this material is deposited on a shoreline, where it forms a beach.

Beaches

You would probably recognize a beach if you saw one. However, scientifically speaking, a **beach** is any area of the shoreline made up of material deposited by waves. Some beach material is also deposited by rivers.

Compare the beaches shown in **Figure 5.** Notice that the colors and textures vary. They vary because the type of material found on a beach depends on its source. Light-colored sand is the most common beach material. Much of this sand comes from the mineral quartz. But not all beaches are made of light-colored sand. For example, on many tropical islands, such as the Virgin Islands, beaches are made of fine, white coral material. Some Florida beaches are made of tiny pieces of broken seashells. Black sand beaches in Hawaii are made of eroded volcanic lava. In areas where stormy seas are common, beaches are made of pebbles and boulders.

Reading Check Where does beach material come from?

Wave Angle and Sand Movement

The movement of sand along a beach depends on the angle at which the waves strike the shore. Most waves approach the beach at a slight angle and retreat in a direction more perpendicular to the shore. This movement of water is called a longshore current. A *longshore current* is a water current that moves the sand in a zigzag pattern along the beach, as you can see in **Figure 6.**

Figure 6 *When waves strike the shoreline at an angle, sand migrates along the beach in a zigzag path.*

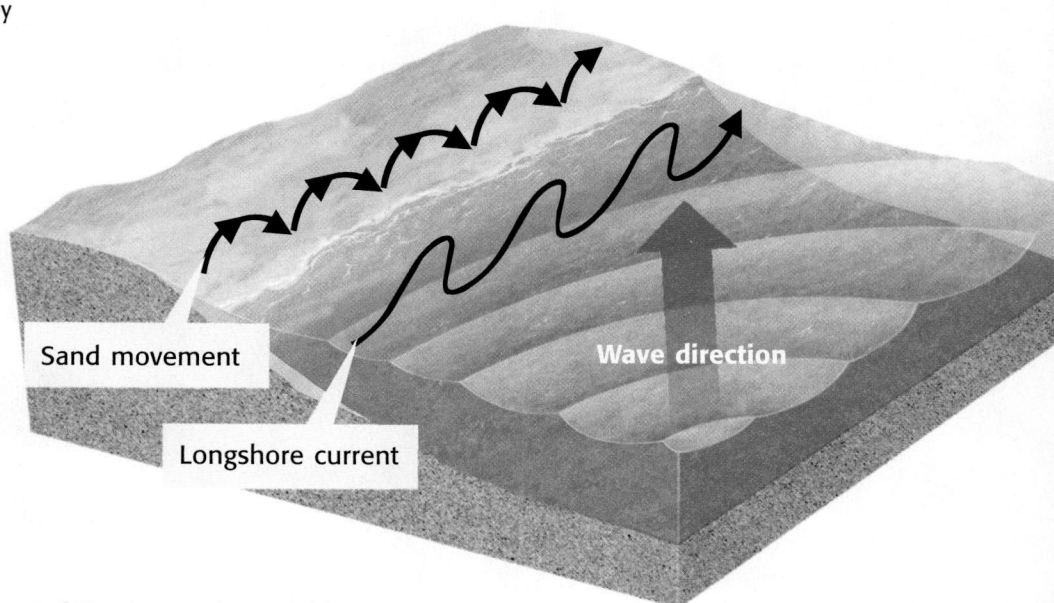
Sand movement

Longshore current

Wave direction

Offshore Deposits

Waves moving at an angle to the shoreline push water along the shore and create longshore currents. When waves erode material from the shoreline, longshore currents can transport and deposit this material offshore, which creates landforms in open water. A *sandbar* is an underwater or exposed ridge of sand, gravel, or shell material. A *barrier spit* is an exposed sandbar that is connected to the shoreline. Cape Cod, Massachusetts, shown in **Figure 7,** is an example of a barrier spit. A barrier island is a long, narrow island usually made of sand that forms offshore parallel to the shoreline.

Figure 7 *A barrier spit, such as Cape Cod, Massachusetts, occurs when an exposed sandbar is connected to the shoreline.*

SECTION Review

Summary

- As waves break against a shoreline, rock is broken down into sand.

- Six shoreline features created by wave erosion include sea cliffs, sea stacks, sea caves, sea arches, headlands, and wave-cut terraces.

- Beaches are made from material deposited by waves.

- Longshore currents cause sand to move in a zigzag pattern along the shore.

Using Key Terms

Complete each of the following sentences by choosing the correct term from the word bank.

　　shoreline　　　beach

1. A ___ is an area made up of material deposited by waves.

2. An area in which land and a body of water meet is a ___.

Understanding Key Ideas

3. Which of the following is a result of wave deposition?
   a. sea arch
   b. sea cave
   c. barrier spit
   d. headland

4. How do wave deposits affect a shoreline?

5. Describe how sand moves along a beach.

6. What are six shoreline features created by wave erosion?

7. How can the energy of waves traveling through water affect a shoreline?

8. Would a small wave or a large wave have more energy? Explain your answer.

Math Skills

9. Imagine that there is a large boulder on the edge of a shoreline. If the wave period is 15 s long, how many times is the boulder hit in a year?

Critical Thinking

10. **Applying Concepts** Not all beaches are made from light-colored sand. Explain why this statement is true.

11. **Making Inferences** How can severe storms over the ocean affect shoreline erosion and deposition?

12. **Making Predictions** How could a headland change in 250 years? Describe some of the features that may form.

Developed and maintained by the National Science Teachers Association

For a variety of links related to this chapter, go to www.scilinks.org

Topic: Wave Erosion
SciLinks code: HSM1638

Wind Erosion and Deposition

Have you ever been working outside and had a gusty wind blow an important stack of papers all over the place?

Do you remember how fast and far the papers traveled and how long it took to pick them up? Every time you caught up with them, they were on the move again. If this has happened to you, then you have seen how wind erosion works. As an agent of erosion, the wind removes soil, sand, and rock particles and transports them from one place to another.

Certain locations are more vulnerable to wind erosion than others. An area with little plant cover can be severely affected by wind erosion because plant roots anchor sand and soil in place. Deserts and coastlines that are made of fine, loose rock material and have little plant cover are shaped most dramatically by the wind.

The Process of Wind Erosion

Wind moves material in different ways. In areas where strong winds occur, material is moved by saltation. **Saltation** is the skipping and bouncing movement of sand-sized particles in the direction the wind is blowing. As you can see in **Figure 1,** the wind causes the particles to bounce. When moving sand grains knock into one another, some grains bounce up in the air, fall forward, and strike other sand grains. These impacts cause other grains to roll and bounce forward.

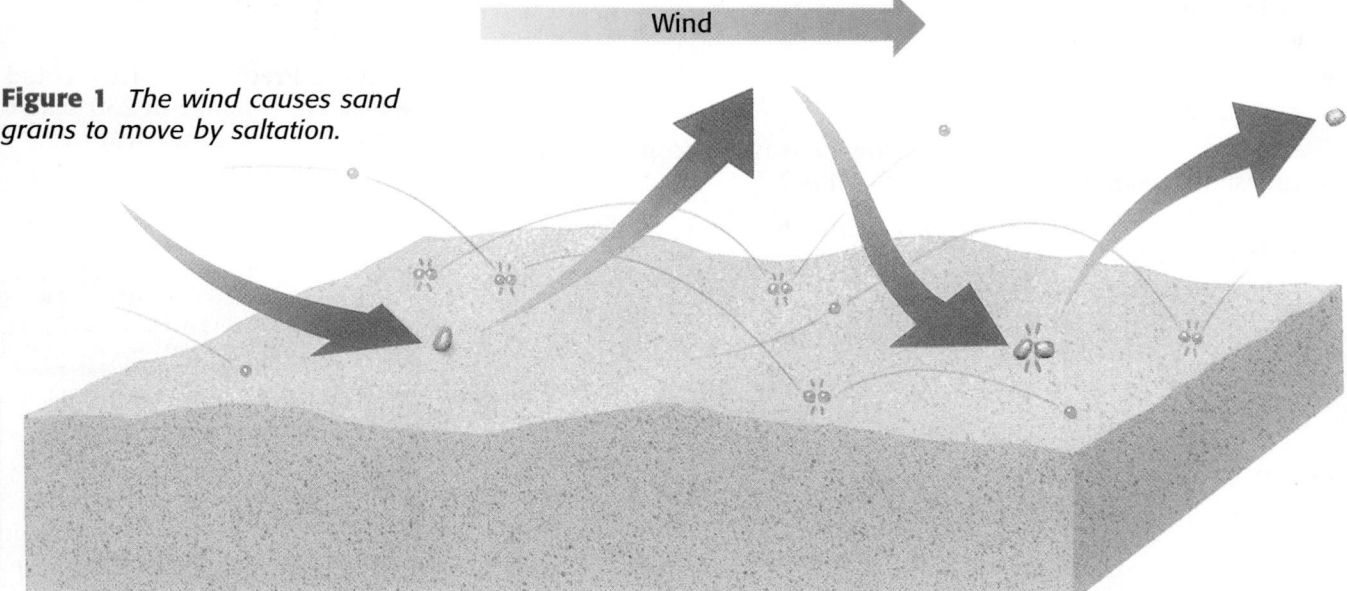

Wind

Figure 1 *The wind causes sand grains to move by saltation.*

Figure 2 *Desert pavement, such as that found in the Painted Desert in Arizona, forms when wind removes all the fine materials.*

Deflation

The removal of fine sediment by wind is called **deflation.** During deflation, wind removes the top layer of fine sediment or soil and leaves behind rock fragments that are too heavy to be lifted by the wind. Deflation may cause *desert pavement,* which is a surface consisting of pebbles and small broken rocks. An example of desert pavement is shown in **Figure 2.**

Have you ever blown on a layer of dust while cleaning off a dresser? If you have, you may have noticed that in addition to your face getting dirty, a little scooped-out depression formed in the dust. Similarly, in areas where there is little vegetation, the wind may scoop out depressions in the landscape. These depressions are called *deflation hollows.*

Reading Check Where do deflation hollows form? (*See the Appendix for answers to Reading Checks.*)

Abrasion

The grinding and wearing down of rock surfaces by other rock or sand particles is called **abrasion.** Abrasion commonly happens in areas where there are strong winds, loose sand, and soft rocks. The blowing of millions of sharp sand grains creates a sandblasting effect. This effect helps to erode, smooth, and polish rocks.

saltation the movement of sand or other sediments by short jumps and bounces that is caused by wind or water

deflation a form of wind erosion in which fine, dry soil particles are blown away

abrasion the grinding and wearing away of rock surfaces through the mechanical action of other rock or sand particles

Making Desert Pavement

1. Spread a mixture of **dust, sand,** and **gravel** on an **outdoor table.**
2. Place an **electric fan** at one end of the table.
3. Put on **safety goggles** and a **filter mask.** Aim the fan across the sediment. Start the fan on its lowest speed. Record your observations.
4. Turn the fan to a medium speed. Record your observations.
5. Finally, turn the fan to a high speed to imitate a desert windstorm. Record your observations.
6. What is the relationship between the wind speed and the size of the sediment that is moved?
7. Does the remaining sediment fit the definition of desert pavement?

loess very fine sediments deposited by the wind

dune a mound of wind-deposited sand that keeps its shape even though it moves

Wind-Deposited Materials

Much like rivers, the wind also carries sediment. And just as rivers deposit their loads, the wind eventually drops all the material it carries. The amount and the size of particles the wind can carry depend on the wind speed. The faster the wind blows, the more material and the heavier the particles it can carry. As wind speed slows, heavier particles are deposited first.

Loess

Wind can deposit extremely fine material. Thick deposits of this windblown, fine-grained sediment are known as **loess** (LOH ES). Loess feels like the talcum powder a person may use after a shower.

Because wind carries fine-grained material much higher and farther than it carries sand, loess deposits are sometimes found far away from their source. Many loess deposits came from glacial sources during the last Ice Age. In the United States, loess is present in the Midwest, along the eastern edge of the Mississippi Valley, and in eastern Oregon and Washington.

Dunes

When the wind hits an obstacle, such as a plant or a rock, the wind slows down. As it slows, the wind deposits, or drops, the heavier material. The material collects, which creates an additional obstacle. This obstacle causes even more material to be deposited, forming a mound. Eventually, the original obstacle becomes buried. The mounds of wind-deposited sand are called **dunes.** Dunes are common in sandy deserts and along the sandy shores of lakes and oceans. **Figure 3** shows a large dune in a desert area.

Figure 3 *Dunes migrate in the direction of the wind.*

The Movement of Dunes

Dunes tend to move in the direction of strong winds. Different wind conditions produce dunes in various shapes and sizes. A dune usually has a gently sloped side and a steeply sloped side, or *slip face,* as shown in **Figure 4.** In most cases, the gently sloped side faces the wind. The wind is constantly transporting material up this side of the dune. As sand moves over the crest, or peak, of the dune, it slides down the slip face, creating a steep slope.

Reading Check In what direction do dunes move?

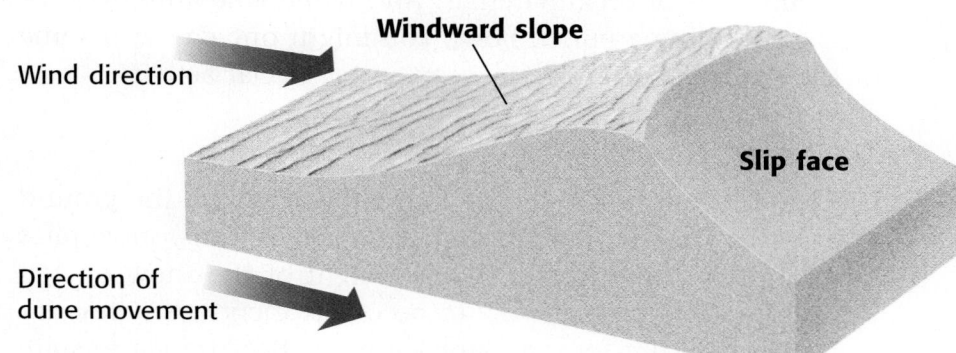

Wind direction

Windward slope

Slip face

Direction of dune movement

Figure 4 *Dunes are formed from material deposited by wind.*

SECTION Review

Summary

- Areas with little plant cover and desert areas covered with fine rock material are more vulnerable than other areas to wind erosion.

- Saltation is the process in which sand-sized particles move in the direction of the wind.

- Three landforms that are created by wind erosion and deposition are desert pavement, deflation hollows, and dunes.

- Dunes move in the direction of the wind.

Using Key Terms

In each of the following sentences, replace the incorrect term with the correct term from the word bank.

dune   saltation
deflation   abrasion

1. <u>Deflation hollows</u> are mounds of wind-deposited sand.

2. The removal of fine sediment by wind is called <u>abrasion</u>.

Understanding Key Ideas

3. Which of the following landforms is the result of wind deposition?
   a. deflation hollow
   b. desert pavement
   c. dune
   d. abrasion

4. Describe how material is moved in areas where strong winds blow.

5. Explain the process of abrasion.

Math Skills

6. If a dune moves 40 m per year, how far does it move in 1 day?

Critical Thinking

7. **Identifying Relationships** Explain the relationship between plant cover and wind erosion.

8. **Applying Concepts** If you climbed up the steep side of a sand dune, is it likely that you traveled in the direction the wind was blowing?

Developed and maintained by the National Science Teachers Association

For a variety of links related to this chapter, go to www.scilinks.org

Topic: Wind Erosion
SciLinks code: HSM1669

Erosion and Deposition by Ice

Can you imagine an ice cube that is the size of a football stadium? Well, glaciers can be even bigger than that.

A **glacier** is an enormous mass of moving ice. Because glaciers are very heavy and have the ability to move across the Earth's surface, they are capable of eroding, moving, and depositing large amounts of rock materials. And while you will never see a glacier chilling a punch bowl, you might one day visit some of the spectacular landscapes carved by glacial activity!

Glaciers—Rivers of Ice

Glaciers form in areas so cold that snow stays on the ground year-round. In polar regions and at high elevations, snow piles up year after year. Over time, the weight of the snow on top causes the deep-packed snow to become ice crystals. These ice crystals eventually form a giant ice mass. Because glaciers are so massive, the pull of gravity causes them to flow slowly, like "rivers of ice." In this section, you will learn about two main types of glaciers, alpine and continental.

Alpine Glaciers

Alpine glaciers form in mountainous areas. One common type of alpine glacier is a valley glacier. Valley glaciers form in valleys originally created by stream erosion. As these glaciers slowly flow downhill, they widen and straighten the valleys into broad U shapes as shown in **Figure 1.**

✓ **Reading Check** **Where do alpine glaciers form?** (*See the Appendix for answers to Reading Checks.*)

glacier a large mass of moving ice

Figure 1 *Alpine glaciers start as snowfields in mountainous areas.*

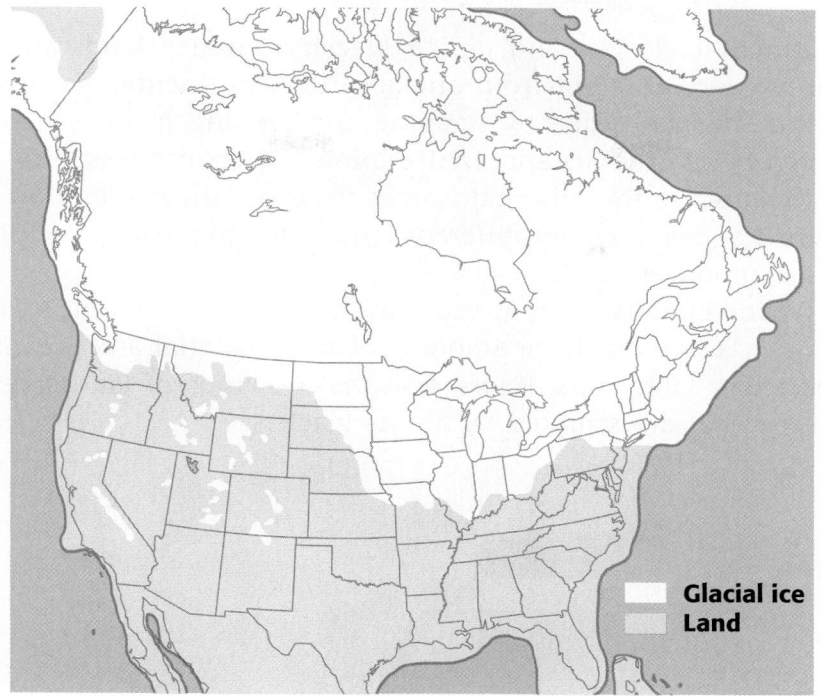

Figure 2 *Eleven U.S. states were covered by ice during the last glacial ice period. Because much of the Earth's water was frozen in glaciers, sea levels fell. Blue lines show the coastline at that time.*

Glacial ice
Land

Continental Glaciers

Not all glaciers are true "rivers of ice." In fact, some glaciers spread across entire continents. These glaciers, called *continental glaciers*, are huge, continuous masses of ice. The largest continental glacier in the world covers almost all of Antarctica. This ice sheet is approximately one and a half times the size of the United States. It is so thick—more than 4,000 m in places—that it buries everything but the highest mountain peaks.

Glaciers on the Move

When enough ice builds up on a slope, the ice begins to move downhill. Thick glaciers move faster than thin glaciers, and the steeper the slope is, the faster the glaciers will move. Glaciers move in two ways: by sliding and by flowing. A glacier slides when its weight causes the ice at the bottom of the glacier to melt. As the water from a melting ice cube causes the ice cube to travel across a table, the water from the melting ice causes a glacier to move forward. A glacier also flows slowly as ice crystals within the glacier slip over each other. Think of placing a deck of cards on a table and then tilting the table. The top cards will slide farther than the lower cards. Similarly, the upper part of the glacier flows faster than the base.

Glacier movement is affected by climate. As the Earth cools, glaciers grow. About 10,000 years ago, a continental glacier covered most of North America, as shown in **Figure 2.** In some places, the ice sheet was several kilometers thick!

Speed of a Glacier

An alpine glacier is estimated to be moving forward at 5 m per day. Calculate how long the ice will take to reach a road and campground located 0.5 km from the front of the advancing glacier. (Hint: 1 km = 1,000 m)

Landforms Carved by Glaciers

Continental glaciers and alpine glaciers produce landscapes that are very different from one another. Continental glaciers smooth the landscape by scraping and eroding features that existed before the ice appeared. Alpine glaciers carve out rugged features in the mountain rocks through which they flow. **Figure 3** shows the very different landscapes that each type of glacier produces.

Alpine glaciers, such as those in the Rocky Mountains and the Alps, carve out large amounts of rock material and create spectacular landforms. **Figure 4** shows the kinds of landscape features that are sculpted by alpine glaciers.

Figure 3 Landscapes Created by Glaciers

Continental glaciers smooth and flatten the landscape.

Alpine glaciers carved out this rugged landscape. ▶

Figure 4 Landscape Features Carved by Alpine Glaciers

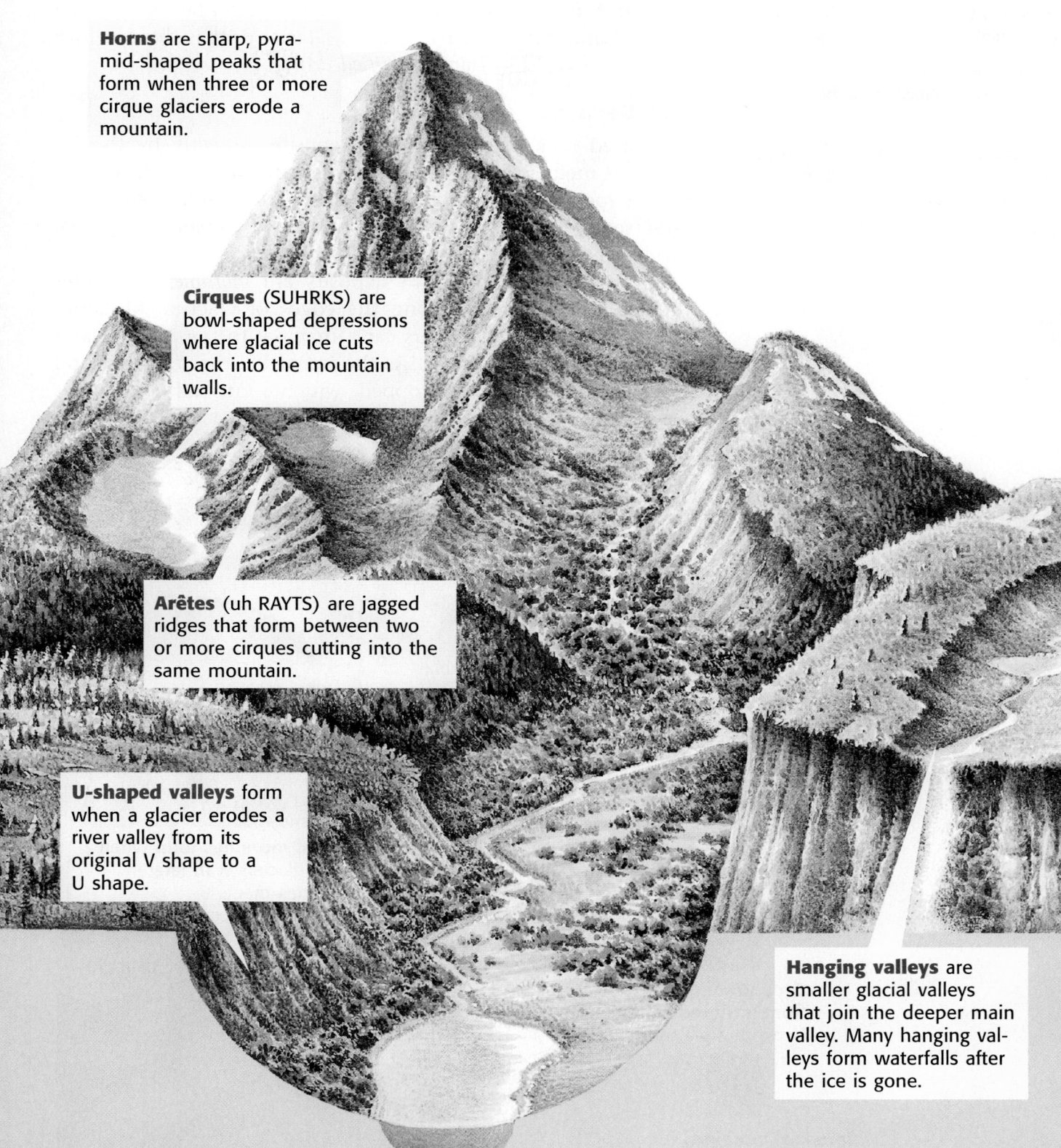

Horns are sharp, pyramid-shaped peaks that form when three or more cirque glaciers erode a mountain.

Cirques (SUHRKS) are bowl-shaped depressions where glacial ice cuts back into the mountain walls.

Arêtes (uh RAYTS) are jagged ridges that form between two or more cirques cutting into the same mountain.

U-shaped valleys form when a glacier erodes a river valley from its original V shape to a U shape.

Hanging valleys are smaller glacial valleys that join the deeper main valley. Many hanging valleys form waterfalls after the ice is gone.

Types of Glacial Deposits

As a glacier melts, it drops all the material it is carrying. **Glacial drift** is the general term used to describe all material carried and deposited by glaciers. Glacial drift is divided into two main types, *till* and *stratified drift*.

Till Deposits

Unsorted rock material that is deposited directly by the ice when it melts is called **till**. *Unsorted* means that the till is made up of rock material of different sizes—from large boulders to fine sediment. When the glacier melts, the unsorted material is deposited on the surface of the ground.

The most common till deposits are *moraines*. Moraines generally form ridges along the edges of glaciers. Moraines are produced when glaciers carry material to the front of and along the sides of the ice. As the ice melts, the sediment and rock it is carrying are dropped, which forms different types of moraines. The various types of moraines are shown in **Figure 5.**

glacial drift the rock material carried and deposited by glaciers

till unsorted rock material that is deposited directly by a melting glacier

stratified drift a glacial deposit that has been sorted and layered by the action of streams or meltwater

Figure 5 **Types of Moraines**

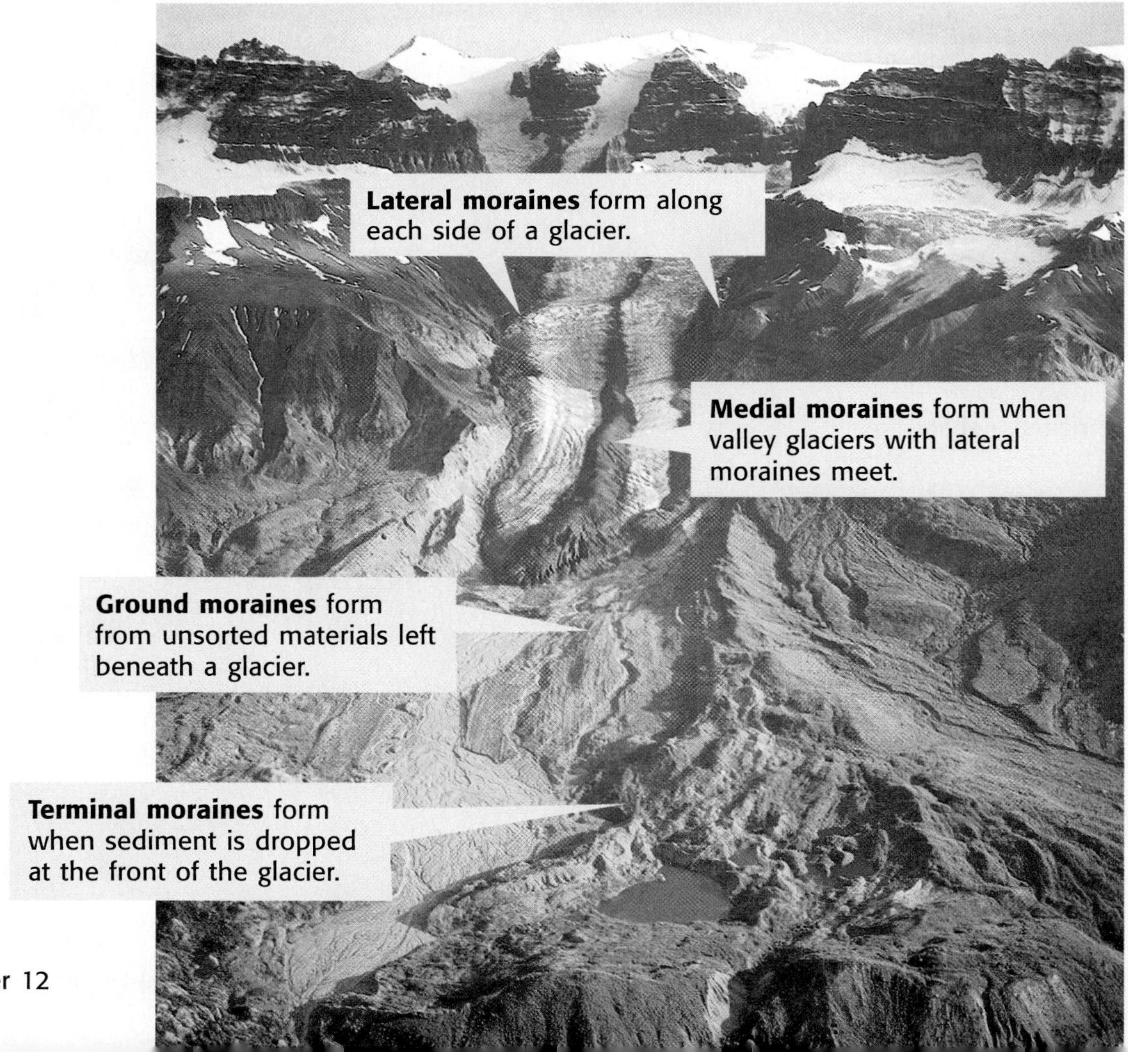

Lateral moraines form along each side of a glacier.

Medial moraines form when valley glaciers with lateral moraines meet.

Ground moraines form from unsorted materials left beneath a glacier.

Terminal moraines form when sediment is dropped at the front of the glacier.

Stratified Drift

When a glacier melts, streams form that carry rock material away from the shrinking glacier. A glacial deposit that is sorted into layers based on the size of the rock material is called **stratified drift.** Streams carry sorted material and deposit it in front of the glacier in a broad area called an *outwash plain.* Sometimes, a block of ice is left in the outwash plain when a glacier retreats. As the ice melts, sediment builds up around the block of ice, and a depression called a *kettle* forms. Kettles commonly fill with water to form lakes or ponds, as **Figure 6** shows.

✓ *Reading Check* Explain the difference between a till deposit and stratified drift.

Figure 6 *Kettle lakes form in outwash plains and are common in states such as Minnesota.*

SECTION Review

Summary

- Alpine glaciers form in mountainous areas. Continental glaciers spread across entire continents.

- Glaciers can move by sliding or by flowing.

- Alpine glaciers can carve cirques, arêtes, horns, U-shaped valleys, and hanging valleys.

- Two types of glacial drift are till and stratified drift.

- Four types of moraines are lateral, medial, ground, and terminal moraines.

Using Key Terms

Complete each of the following sentences by choosing the correct term from the word bank.

glacial drift	glacier
stratified drift	till

1. A glacial deposit that is sorted into layers based on the size of the rock material is called ___.

2. ___ is all of the material carried and deposited by glaciers.

3. Unsorted rock material that is deposited directly by the ice when it melts is ___.

4. A ___ is an enormous mass of moving ice.

Understanding Key Ideas

5. Which of the following is not a type of moraine?
   a. lateral
   b. horn
   c. ground
   d. medial

6. Explain the difference between alpine and continental glaciers.

7. Name five landscape features formed by alpine glaciers.

8. Describe two ways in which glaciers move.

Math Skills

9. A recent study shows that a glacier in Alaska is melting at a rate of 23 ft per year. At what rate is the glacier melting in meters? (Hint: 1 ft = 0.3 m)

Critical Thinking

10. **Analyzing Ideas** Explain why continental glaciers smooth the landscape and alpine glaciers create a rugged landscape.

11. **Applying Concepts** How can a glacier deposit both sorted and unsorted material?

12. **Applying Concepts** Why are glaciers such effective agents of erosion and deposition?

SCLINKS

NSTA
Developed and maintained by the
National Science Teachers Association

For a variety of links related to this chapter, go to www.scilinks.org

Topic: Glaciers
SciLinks code: HSM0675

The Effect of Gravity on Erosion and Deposition

Did you know that the Appalachian Mountains may have once been almost five times as tall as they are now? Why are they shorter now? Part of the answer lies in the effect that gravity has on all objects on Earth.

Although you can't see it, the force of gravity is also an agent of erosion and deposition. Gravity not only influences the movement of water and ice but also causes rocks and soil to move downslope. **Mass movement** is the movement of any material, such as rock, soil, or snow, downslope. Whether mass movement happens rapidly or slowly, it plays a major role in shaping the Earth's surface.

Angle of Repose

If dry sand is piled up, it will move downhill until the slope becomes stable. The *angle of repose* is the steepest angle, or slope, at which loose material will not slide downslope. This is demonstrated in **Figure 1.** The angle of repose is different for each type of surface material. Characteristics of the surface material, such as its size, weight, shape, and moisture level, determine at what angle the material will move downslope.

mass movement a movement of a section of land down a slope

Figure 1 *If the slope on which material rests is less than the angle of repose, the material will stay in place. If the slope is greater than the angle of repose, the material will move downslope.*

Rapid Mass Movement

The most destructive mass movements happen suddenly and rapidly. Rapid mass movement can be very dangerous and can destroy everything in its path.

Rock Falls

While driving along a mountain road, you may have noticed signs along the road that warn of falling rocks. A **rock fall** happens when loose rocks fall down a steep slope. Steep slopes are sometimes created to make room for a road in mountainous areas. Loosened and exposed rocks above the road tend to fall as a result of gravity. The rocks in a rock fall can range in size from small fragments to large boulders.

Landslides

Another type of rapid mass movement is a landslide. A **landslide** is the sudden and rapid movement of a large amount of material downslope. A *slump,* shown in **Figure 2,** is the most common type of landslide. Slumping occurs when a block of material moves downslope over a curved surface. Heavy rains, deforestation, construction on unstable slopes, and earthquakes increase the chances that a landslide will happen. **Figure 3** shows a landslide in India.

✔**Reading Check** What is a slump? (*See the Appendix for answers to Reading Checks.*)

Figure 2 *A slump is a type of landslide that occurs when a block of land becomes detached and slides downhill.*

rock fall a group of loose rocks that fall down a steep slope

landslide the sudden movement of rock and soil down a slope

Figure 3 *This landslide in Bombay, India, happened after heavy monsoon rains.*

Figure 4 *This photo shows one of the many mudflows that have occurred in California during rainy winters.*

mudflow the flow of a mass of mud or rock and soil mixed with a large amount of water

Figure 5 *This lahar overtook the city of Kyushu in Japan.*

Mudflows

A rapid movement of a large mass of mud is a **mudflow.** Mudflows happen when a large amount of water mixes with soil and rock. The water causes the slippery mass of mud to flow rapidly downslope. Mudflows commonly happen in mountainous regions when a long dry season is followed by heavy rains. Deforestation and the removal of ground cover can often result in devastating mudflows. As you can see in **Figure 4,** a mudflow can carry trees, houses, cars, and other objects that lie in its path.

Lahars

Volcanic eruptions or heavy rains on volcanic ash can produce some of the most dangerous mudflows. Mudflows of volcanic origin are called *lahars*. Lahars can travel at speeds greater than 80 km/h and can be as thick as cement. On volcanoes with snowy peaks, an eruption can suddenly melt a great amount of ice. The water from the ice liquefies the soil and volcanic ash to produce a hot mudflow that rushes downslope. **Figure 5** shows the effects of a massive lahar in Japan.

Reading Check Explain how a lahar occurs.

Slow Mass Movement

Sometimes, you don't even notice mass movement happening. Although rapid mass movements are visible and dramatic, slow mass movements happen a little at a time. However, because slow mass movements occur more frequently, more material is moved collectively over time.

Creep

Even though most slopes appear to be stable, they are actually undergoing slow mass movement, as shown in **Figure 6.** The extremely slow movement of material downslope is called **creep.** Many factors contribute to creep. Water loosens soil and allows it to move freely. In addition, plant roots act as a wedge that forces rocks and soil particles apart. Burrowing animals, such as gophers and groundhogs, also loosen rock and soil particles. In fact, rock and soil on every slope travels slowly downhill.

Figure 6 *Bent tree trunks are evidence that creep is happening.*

creep the slow downhill movement of weathered rock material

SECTION Review

Summary

- Gravity causes rocks and soil to move downslope.
- If the slope on which material rests is greater than the angle of repose, mass movement will occur.
- Four types of rapid mass movement are rock falls, landslides, mudflows, and lahars.
- Water, plant roots, and burrowing animals can cause creep.

Using Key Terms

Complete each of the following sentences by choosing the correct term from the word bank.

creep	mass movement
mudflow	rock fall

1. A ___ occurs when a large amount of water mixes with soil and rock.

2. The extremely slow movement of material downslope is called ___.

Understanding Key Ideas

3. Which of the following is a factor that affects creep?
   a. water
   b. burrowing animals
   c. plant roots
   d. All of the above.

4. How is the angle of repose related to mass movement?

Math Skills

5. If a lahar is traveling at 80 km/h, how long will it take the lahar to travel 20 km?

Critical Thinking

6. **Identifying Relationships** Which types of mass movement are most dangerous to humans? Explain your answer.

7. **Making Inferences** How does deforestation increase the likelihood of mudflows?

SCILINKS

NSTA

Developed and maintained by the National Science Teachers Association

For a variety of links related to this chapter, go to www.scilinks.org

Topic: Mass Movements
SciLinks code: HSM0917

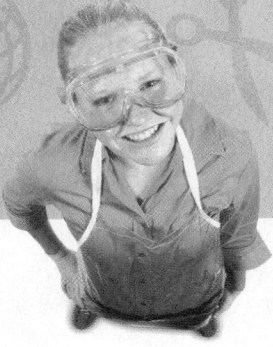

Model-Making Lab

Gliding Glaciers

A glacier is a large, moving mass of ice. Glaciers are responsible for shaping many of Earth's natural features. Glaciers are set in motion by the pull of gravity and by the gradual melting of the glacier. As a glacier moves, it changes the landscape by eroding the surface over which it passes.

Part A: Getting in the Groove

Procedure

The material that is carried by a glacier erodes Earth's surface by gouging out grooves called *striations*. Different materials have varying effects on the landscape. In this activity, you will create a model glacier with which to demonstrate the effects of glacial erosion by various materials.

1. Fill one margarine container with sand to a depth of 1 cm. Fill another margarine container with gravel to a depth of 1 cm. Leave the third container empty. Fill the containers with water.

2. Put the three containers in a freezer, and leave them there overnight.

3. Retrieve the containers from the freezer, and remove the three ice blocks from the containers.

4. Use a rolling pin to flatten the modeling clay.

5. Hold the ice block from the third container firmly with a towel, and press as you move the ice along the length of the clay. Do this three times. In a notebook, sketch the pattern that the ice block makes in the clay.

OBJECTIVES

Build a model of a glacier.

Demonstrate the effects of glacial erosion by various materials.

Observe the effect of pressure on the melting rate of a glacier.

MATERIALS

- brick (3)
- clay, modeling (2 lb)
- container, empty large margarine (3)
- freezer
- graduated cylinder, 50 mL
- gravel (1 lb)
- pan, aluminum rectangular (3)
- rolling pin, wood
- ruler, metric
- sand (1 lb)
- stopwatch
- towel, small hand
- water

6 Repeat steps 4 and 5 using the ice block that contains sand.

7 Repeat steps 4 and 5 using the ice block that contains gravel.

Analyze the Results

1 **Describing Events** Did any material from the clay become mixed with the material in the ice blocks? Explain.

2 **Describing Events** Was any material from the ice blocks deposited on the clay surface? Explain.

3 **Examining Data** What glacial features are represented in your clay model?

Draw Conclusions

4 **Evaluating Data** Compare the patterns formed by the three model glaciers. Do the patterns look like features carved by alpine glaciers or by continental glaciers? Explain.

Part B: Melting Away

Procedure

As the layers of ice build up and a glacier gets larger, a glacier will eventually begin to melt. The water from the melted ice allows a glacier to move forward. In this activity, you'll explore the effect of pressure on the melting rate of a glacier.

1 If possible, make three identical ice blocks without any sand or gravel in them. If that is not possible, use the ice blocks from Part A. Place one ice block upside down in each pan.

2 Place one brick on top of one of the ice blocks. Place two bricks on top of another ice block. Do not put any bricks on the third ice block.

3 After 15 min, remove the bricks from the ice blocks.

4 Using the graduated cylinder, measure the amount of water that has melted from each ice block.

5 Observe and record your findings.

Analyze the Results

1 **Analyzing Data** Which ice block produced the most water?

2 **Explaining Events** What did the bricks represent?

3 **Analyzing Results** What part of the ice blocks melted first? Explain.

Draw Conclusions

4 **Interpreting Information** How could you relate this investigation to the melting rate of glaciers? Explain.

Applying Your Data

Replace the clay with different materials, such as soft wood or sand. How does each ice block affect the different surface materials? What types of surfaces do the different materials represent?

Chapter Review

USING KEY TERMS

For each pair of terms, explain how the meanings of the terms differ.

1 *shoreline* and *longshore current*

2 *beaches* and *dunes*

3 *deflation* and *saltation*

4 *continental glacier* and *alpine glacier*

5 *stratified drift* and *till*

6 *mudflow* and *creep*

UNDERSTANDING KEY IDEAS

Multiple Choice

7 *Surf* refers to
  a. large storm waves in the open ocean.
  b. giant waves produced by hurricanes.
  c. breaking waves near the shoreline.
  d. small waves on a calm sea.

8 When waves cut completely through a headland, a ___ is formed.
  a. sea cave
  b. sea arch
  c. wave-cut terrace
  d. sandbar

9 A narrow strip of sand that is formed by wave deposition and is connected to the shore is called a
  a. barrier spit.
  b. sandbar.
  c. wave-cut terrace.
  d. headland.

10 A wind-eroded depression is called a
  a. deflation hollow.
  b. desert pavement.
  c. dune.
  d. dust bowl.

11 What term describes all types of glacial deposits?
  a. glacial drift
  b. dune
  c. till
  d. outwash

12 Which of the following is NOT a landform created by an alpine glacier?
  a. cirque
  b. deflation hollow
  c. horn
  d. arête

13 What is the term for a mass movement that is of volcanic origin?
  a. lahar
  b. slump
  c. creep
  d. rock fall

14 Which of the following is a slow mass movement?
  a. mudflow
  b. landslide
  c. creep
  d. rock fall

Short Answer

15 Why do waves break when they near the shore?

16 Why are some areas more affected by wind erosion than other areas are?

17 What kind of mass movement happens continuously, day after day?

18 In what direction do sand dunes move?

19 Describe the different types of glacial moraines.

20 **Concept Mapping** Use the following terms to create a concept map: *deflation*, *strong winds*, *saltation*, *dune*, and *desert pavement*.

21 **Making Inferences** How do humans increase the likelihood that wind erosion will occur?

22 **Identifying Relationships** If the large ice sheet covering Antarctica were to melt completely, what type of landscape would you expect Antarctica to have?

23 **Applying Concepts** You are a geologist who is studying rock to determine the direction of flow of an ancient glacier. What clues might help you determine the glacier's direction of flow?

24 **Applying Concepts** You are interested in purchasing a home that overlooks the ocean. The home that you want to buy sits atop a steep sea cliff. Given what you have learned about shoreline erosion, what factors would you take into consideration when deciding whether to buy the home?

The graph below illustrates coastal erosion and deposition at an imaginary beach over a period of 8 years. Use the graph below to answer the questions that follow.

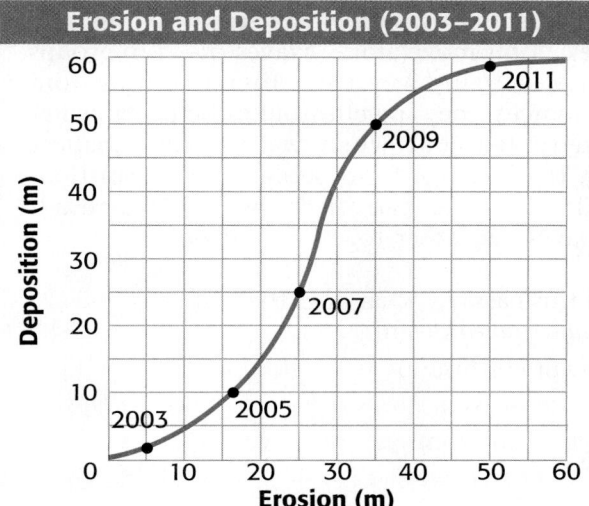

Erosion and Deposition (2003–2011)

25 What is happening to the beach over time?

26 In what year does the amount of erosion equal the amount of deposition?

27 Based on the erosion and deposition data for 2005, what might happen to the beach in the years that follow 2005?

Standardized Test Preparation

Read each of the passages below. Then, answer the questions that follow each passage.

Passage 1 When you drop a pebble into a pond, is there just one ripple? Of course not. Waves, like ripples, don't move alone. Waves travel in groups called wave <u>trains</u>. As wave trains move away from their sources, they travel through the ocean water <u>uninterrupted</u>. But when waves reach shallow water, they change form because the ocean floor crowds the lower part of the wave. As a result, the waves get closer together and taller.

1. In this passage, what does the word *uninterrupted* mean?

    A not continuous

    B not broken

    C broken again

    D not interpreted

2. In this passage, what does the word *train* mean?

    F to teach someone a skill

    G the part of a gown that trails behind the person who is wearing the gown

    H a series of moving things

    I a series of railroad cars

3. According to the passage, what is the cause of taller waves?

    A shallow water

    B deep ocean water

    C rippling

    D wave trains

4. If certain waves are short and far apart, which of the following can be concluded?

    F The waves are approaching the shore.

    G The waves are moving toward their source.

    H The waves were interrupted.

    I The waves are in deep ocean water.

Passage 2 Winter storms create powerful waves that crash into cliffs and break off pieces of rock that fall into the ocean. On February 8, 1998, unusually large waves crashed against the cliffs along Broad Beach Road in Malibu, California. Eventually, the ocean-eroded cliffs <u>buckled</u>, which caused a landslide. One house collapsed into the ocean, and two more houses dangled on the edge of the cliff's newly eroded face. Powerful waves, buckled cliffs, and landslides are part of the ongoing natural process of coastal erosion that is taking place along the California shoreline and along similar shorelines throughout the world.

1. In this passage, what does *buckled* mean?

    A tightened

    B collapsed

    C formed

    D heated up

2. Which of the following describes how this coastal area was damaged?

    F The area was damaged by collapsing houses.

    G The area was damaged an earthquake.

    H The area was damaged by ocean currents.

    I The area was damaged by unusually large waves produced by a winter storm.

3. Which of the following can be concluded from this passage?

    A This area may have landslides in the future.

    B This area is safe from future landslides.

    C This type of landslide is common only to the California coastline.

    D Erosion in this area happens very rarely.

Use each figure below to answer the questions that follow each figure.

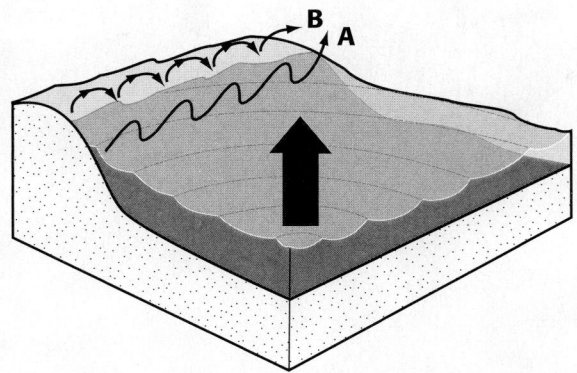

1. In the illustration, what does A label?
   A wave direction
   B wave amplitude
   C wavelength
   D a longshore current

2. In the illustration, what does B label?
   F wave direction
   G wave period
   H the movement of sand
   I a longshore current

3. What process created the landform in the illustration above?
   A erosion by waves
   B saltation
   C abrasion
   D deposition by waves

Read each question below, and choose the best answer.

1. Wind erosion caused a deflation hollow that was circular in shape. The hollow is 100 m wide. What is the circumference of this deflation hollow?
   A 31.4 m
   B 62.8 m
   C 314 m
   D 628 m

2. A homeowner needs to buy and plant 28 trees to prevent wind erosion. Each tree costs $29.99. What is a reasonable estimate for the total cost of these trees before tax?
   F a little more than $200
   G a little less than $600
   H a little less than $900
   I a little more than $1,000

Use the equation below to answer the questions that follow.

$$\frac{number\ of\ waves}{per\ minute} = \frac{60\ s}{wave\ period\ (s)}$$

3. If the wave period is 15 s, how many waves occur in 1 min?
   A 4
   B 60
   C 75
   D 240

4. If the wave period is 30 s, how many waves occur in 1 min?
   F 1
   G 2
   H 3
   I 5

5. If 480 waves broke in 40 min, what is the wave period?
   A 5 s
   B 12 s
   C 15 s
   D 20 s

Science in Action

Weird Science

Long-Runout Landslides

At 4:10 A.M. on April 29, 1903, the town of Frank, Canada, was changed forever when disaster struck without warning. An enormous chunk of limestone fell suddenly from the top of nearby Turtle Mountain. In less than two minutes, the huge mass of rock buried most of the town! Landslides such as the Frank landslide are now known as *long-runout landslides*. Most landslides travel a horizontal distance that is less than twice the vertical distance that they have fallen. But long-runout landslides carry enormous amounts of rock and thus can travel many times farther than they fall. The physics of long-runout landslides are still a mystery to scientists.

Scientific Discoveries

The Lost Squadron

During World War II, an American squadron of eight planes crash-landed on the ice of Greenland. The crew was rescued, but the planes were lost. After the war, several people tried to find the "Lost Squadron." Finally, in 1988, a team of adventurers found the planes by using radar. The planes were buried by 40 years of snowfall and had become part of the Greenland ice sheet! When the planes were found, they were buried under 80 m of glacial ice. Incredibly, the team tunneled down through the ice and recovered a plane. The plane is now named Glacier Girl, and it still flies today!

Math ACTIVITY

The Frank landslide traveled 4 km in 100 s. Calculate this speed in meters per second.

Language Arts ACTIVITY

WRITING SKILL The crew of the Lost Squadron had to wait 10 days to be rescued by dog sled. Imagine that you were part of the crew—what would you have done to survive? Write a short story describing your adventure on the ice sheet of Greenland.

Johan Reinhard

High-Altitude Anthropologist Imagine discovering the mummified body of a girl from 500 years ago! In 1995, while climbing Mount Ampato, one of the tallest mountains in the Andes, Johan Reinhard made an incredible discovery—the well-preserved mummy of a young Inca girl. The recent eruption of a nearby volcano had caused the snow on Mount Ampato to melt and uncover the mummy. The discovery of the "Inca Ice Maiden" gave scientists a wealth of new information about Incan culture. Today, Reinhard considers the discovery of the Inca Ice Maiden his most exciting moment in the field.

Johan Reinhard is an anthropologist. Anthropologists study the physical and cultural characteristics of human populations. Reinhard studied anthropology at the University of Arizona and at the University of Vienna, in Austria. Early in his career, Reinhard worked on underwater archeology projects in Austria and Italy and on projects in the mountains of Nepal and Tibet. He soon made mountains and mountain peoples the focus of his career as an anthropologist. Reinhard spent 10 years in the highest mountains on Earth, the Himalayas. There, he studied the role of sacred mountains in Tibetan religions. Now, Reinhard studies the culture of the ancient Inca in the Andes of South America.

Social Studies ACTIVITY

Find out more about the Inca Ice Maiden or about Ötzi, a mummy that is more than 5,000 years old that was found in a glacier in Italy. Create a poster that summarizes what scientists have learned from these discoveries.

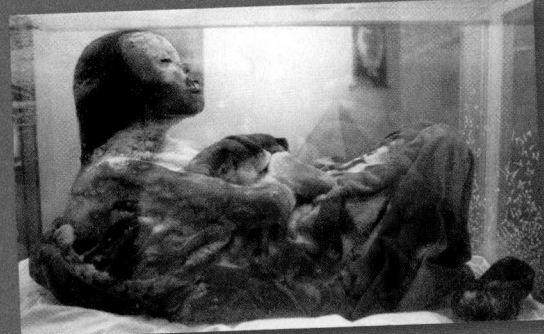

The Inca Ice Maiden was buried under ice and snow for more than 500 years.

To learn more about these Science in Action topics, visit go.hrw.com and type in the keyword **HZ5ICEF.**

Current Science

Check out Current Science® articles related to this chapter by visiting go.hrw.com. Just type in the keyword **HZ5CS12.**

UNIT 5

TIMELINE

Oceanography

In this unit, you will learn about the Earth's oceans and the physical environments that they contain. Together, the oceans form the largest single feature on the Earth. In fact, they cover approximately 70% of the Earth's surface. The oceans not only serve as home for countless living organisms but also affect life on land. This timeline presents some milestones in the exploration of Earth's oceans. Take a deep breath, and dive in!

1851
Herman Melville's novel *Moby Dick* is published.

1938
A coelacanth is discovered in the Indian Ocean near South Africa. Called a fossil fish, the coelacanth was thought to have been extinct for 60 million years.

1978
Louise Brown, the first "test-tube baby," is born in England.

1986
Commercial whaling is temporarily stopped by the International Whaling Commission, but some whaling continues.

1872

The *HMS Challenger* begins its four-year voyage. Its discoveries lay the foundation for the science of oceanography.

1914

The Panama Canal, which links the Atlantic Ocean with the Pacific Ocean, is completed.

1927

Charles Lindbergh completes the first nonstop solo airplane flight over the Atlantic Ocean.

1943

Jacques Cousteau and Émile Gagnan invent the aqualung, a breathing device that allows divers to freely explore the silent world of the oceans.

1960

Jacques Piccard and Don Walsh dive to a record 10,916 m below sea level in their bathyscaph *Trieste*.

1977

Thermal vent communities of organisms that exist without sunlight are discovered on the ocean floor.

1994

The completion of the tunnel under the English Channel makes train and auto travel between Great Britain and France possible.

1998

Ben Lecomte of Austin, Texas, successfully swims across the Atlantic Ocean from Massachusetts to France, a distance of 5,980 km. His record-breaking feat takes 73 days.

2001

Researchers find that dolphins, like humans and the great apes, can recognize themselves in mirrors.

13

Exploring the Oceans

About the

Are two heads better than one? Although it may look like this reef lizardfish has two heads, it's actually swallowing another fish whole! Reef lizardfish are commonly found in the Western Pacific Ocean. Unlike most other types of lizardfish, the reef lizardfish prefers to rest on hard surfaces and is usually seen in pairs.

PRE-READING ACTIVITY

FOLDNOTES **Layered Book** Before you read the chapter, create the FoldNote entitled "Layered Book" described in the **Study Skills** section of the Appendix. Label the tabs of the layered book with "Characteristics of ocean water," "The ocean floor," "Ocean zones," and "Resources from the ocean." As you read the chapter, write information you learn about each category under the appropriate tab.

START-UP ACTiViTY

Exit Only?

To study what life underwater would be like, scientists sometimes live in underwater laboratories. How do these scientists enter and leave these labs? Believe it or not, the simplest way is through a hole in the lab's floor. You might think water would come in through the hole, but it doesn't. How is this possible? Do the following activity to find out.

Procedure

1. Fill a **large bowl** about two-thirds full of **water.**

2. Turn a **clear plastic cup** upside down.

3. Slowly guide the cup straight down into the water. Be careful not to guide the cup all the way to the bottom of the bowl. Also, be careful not to tip the cup.

4. Record your observations.

Analysis

1. How does the air inside the cup affect the water below the cup?

2. How do your findings relate to the hole in the bottom of an underwater research lab?

Earth's Oceans

What makes Earth so different from Mars? What does Earth have that Mercury doesn't?

Earth stands out from the other planets in our solar system primarily for one reason—71% of the Earth's surface is covered with water. Most of Earth's water is found in the global ocean. The global ocean is divided by the continents into four main oceans. The divisions of the global ocean are shown in **Figure 1.** The ocean is a unique body of water that plays many parts in regulating Earth's environment.

Divisions of the Global Ocean

The largest ocean is the *Pacific Ocean*. It flows between Asia and the Americas. The volume of the *Atlantic Ocean*, the second-largest ocean, is about half the volume of the Pacific. The *Indian Ocean* is the third-largest ocean. The *Arctic Ocean* is the smallest ocean. This ocean is unique because much of its surface is covered by ice. Therefore, the Arctic Ocean has not been fully explored.

READING WARM-UP

Objectives

- List the major divisions of the global ocean.
- Describe the history of Earth's oceans.
- Identify the properties of ocean water.
- Describe the interactions between the ocean and the atmosphere.

Terms to Learn

salinity
water cycle

READING STRATEGY

Discussion Read this section silently. Write down questions that you have about this section. Discuss your questions in a small group.

Figure 1 *The global ocean is divided by the continents into four main oceans.*

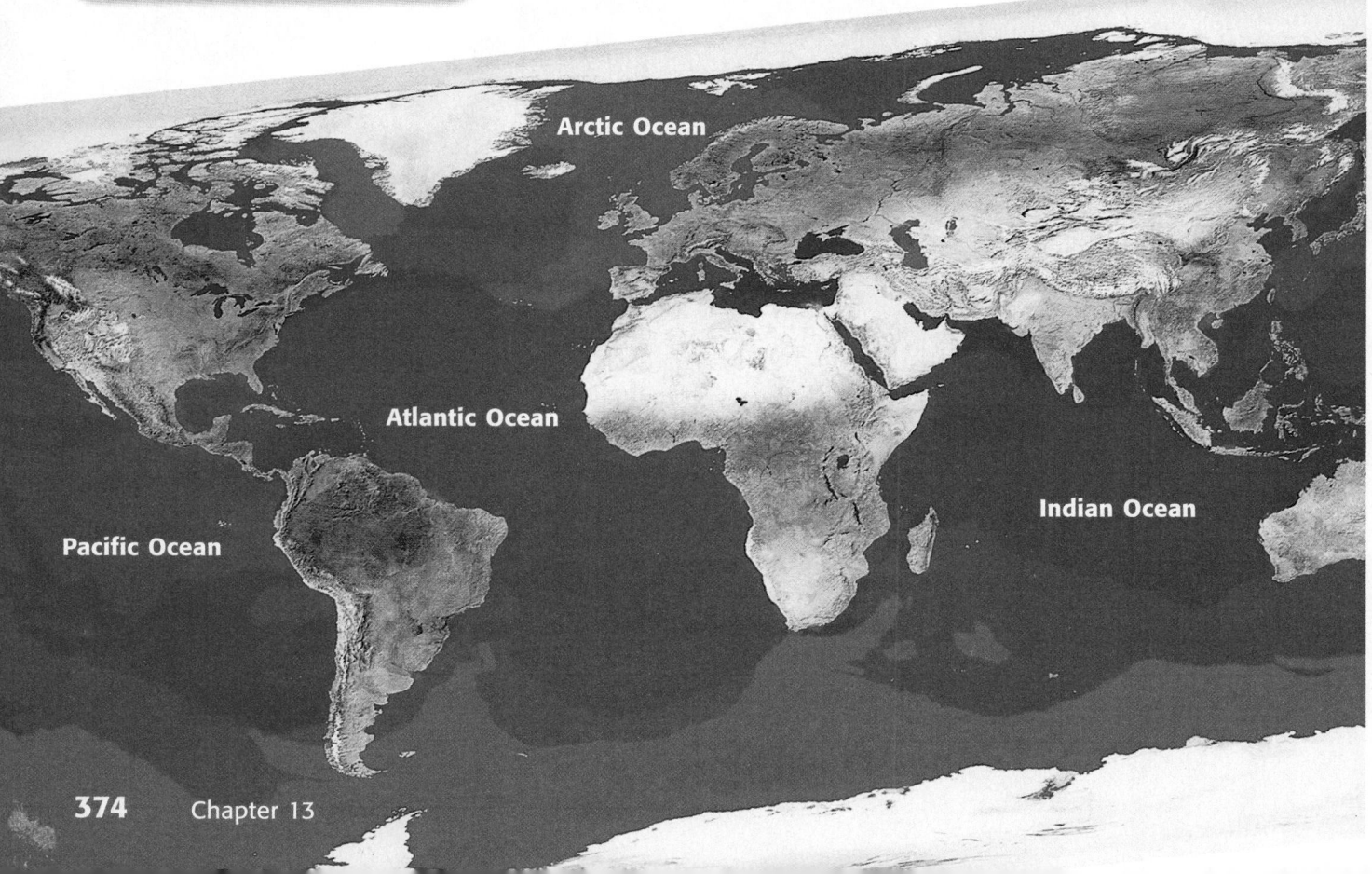

Arctic Ocean

Atlantic Ocean

Indian Ocean

Pacific Ocean

Figure 2   The History of Earth's Oceans

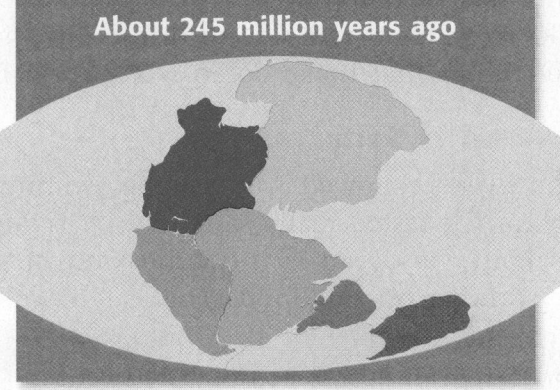

About 245 million years ago

The continents were one giant landmass called Pangaea. The oceans were one giant body of water called Panthalassa.

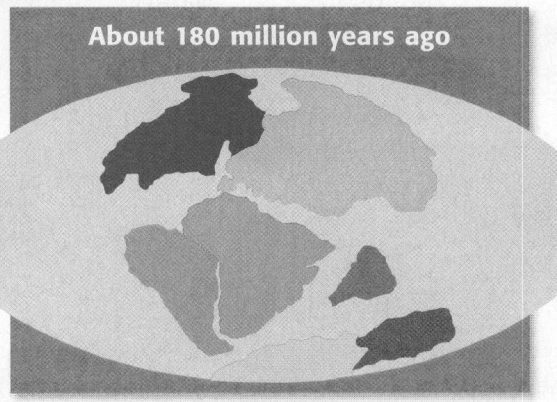

About 180 million years ago

As Pangaea broke apart, the North Atlantic Ocean and the Indian Ocean began to form.

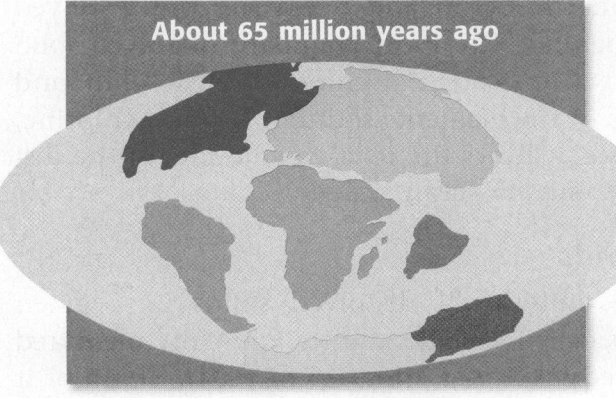

About 65 million years ago

The South Atlantic Ocean was much smaller than it is today.

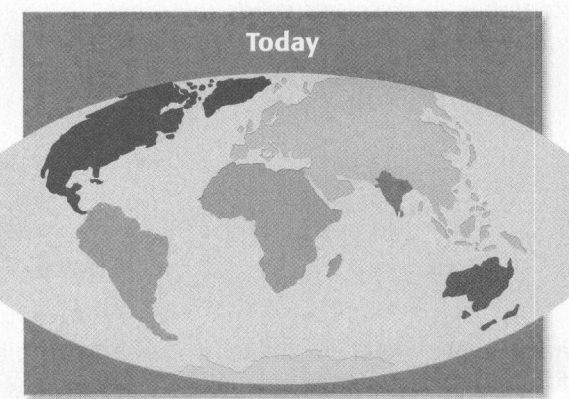

Today

The continents continue to move at a rate of 1 to 10 cm per year. The Pacific Ocean is getting smaller. However, the other oceans are growing.

How Did the Oceans Form?

About 4.5 billion years ago, Earth was a very different place. There were no oceans. Volcanoes spewed lava, ash, and gases all over the planet. The volcanic gases began to form Earth's atmosphere. Meanwhile, Earth was cooling. Sometime before 4 billion years ago, Earth cooled enough for water vapor to condense. This water began to fall as rain. The rain filled the deeper levels of Earth's surface, and the first oceans began to form.

The shape of the Earth's oceans has changed a lot over time. Much has been learned about the oceans' history. Some of this history is shown in **Figure 2.**

Reading Check How did the first oceans begin to form on **Earth?** (*See the Appendix for answers to Reading Checks.*)

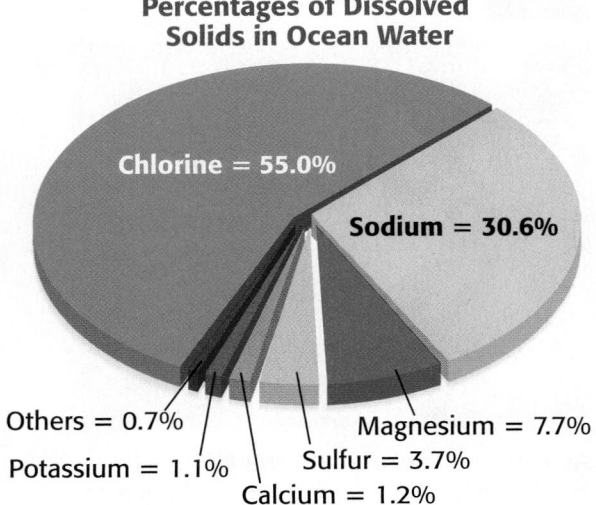

Percentages of Dissolved Solids in Ocean Water

Chlorine = 55.0%

Sodium = 30.6%

Others = 0.7%

Potassium = 1.1%

Calcium = 1.2%

Sulfur = 3.7%

Magnesium = 7.7%

Figure 3 *This pie graph shows the relative percentages of dissolved solids (by mass) in ocean water.*

salinity a measure of the amount of dissolved salts in a given amount of liquid

Characteristics of Ocean Water

You know that ocean water is different from the water that flows from your sink at home. For one thing, ocean water is not safe to drink. But there are other things that make ocean water special.

Ocean Water Is Salty

Have you ever swallowed water while swimming in the ocean? It tasted really salty, didn't it? Most of the salt in the ocean is the same kind of salt that we sprinkle on our food. This salt is called *sodium chloride.*

Salts have been added to the ocean for billions of years. As rivers and streams flow toward the oceans, they dissolve various minerals on land. The running water carries these dissolved minerals to the ocean. At the same time, water is *evaporating* from the ocean and is leaving the dissolved solids behind. The most abundant dissolved solid in the ocean is sodium chloride. This compound consists of the elements sodium, Na, and chlorine, Cl. **Figure 3** shows the relative amounts of the dissolved solids in ocean water.

Chock-Full of Solids

A measure of the amount of dissolved solids in a given amount of liquid is called **salinity.** Salinity is usually measured as grams of dissolved solids per kilogram of water. Think of it this way: 1 kg (1,000 g) of ocean water can be evaporated to 35 g of dissolved solids, on average. Therefore, if you evaporated 1 kg of ocean water, 965 g of fresh water would be removed and 35 g of solids would remain.

Climate Affects Salinity

Some parts of the ocean are saltier than others. Coastal water in places with hotter, drier climates typically has a higher salinity. Coastal water in cooler, more humid places typically has a lower salinity. One reason for this difference is that heat increases the evaporation rate. Evaporation removes water but leaves salts and other dissolved solids behind. Salinity levels are also lower in coastal areas that have a cooler, more humid climate because more fresh water from streams and rivers runs into the ocean in these areas.

Reading Check Why does coastal water in places with hotter, drier climates typically have a higher salinity than coastal water in places with cooler, more humid climates?

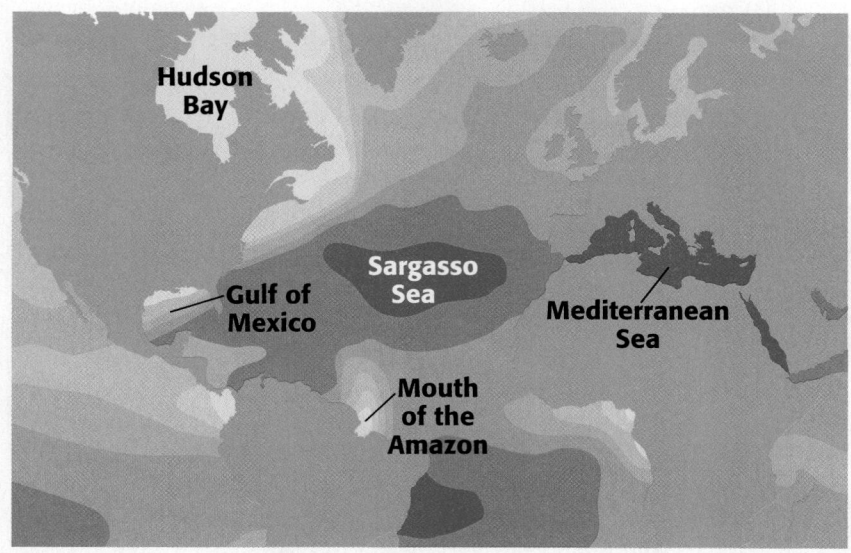
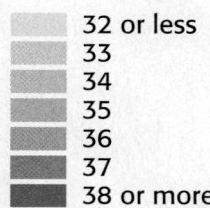

Proportion of salt per
1,000 parts of sea water

	32 or less
	33
	34
	35
	36
	37
	38 or more

Figure 4 *Salinity varies in different parts of the ocean because of variations in evaporation, circulation, and freshwater inflow.*

Water Movement Affects Salinity

Another factor that affects ocean salinity is water movement. Some parts of the ocean, such as bays, gulfs, and seas, move less than other parts. Parts of the open ocean that do not have currents running through them can also be slow moving. Slower-moving areas of water develop higher salinity. **Figure 4** shows salinity differences in different parts of the ocean.

Temperature Zones

The temperature of ocean water decreases as depth increases. However, this temperature change does not happen gradually from the ocean's surface to its bottom. Water in the ocean can be divided into three layers by temperature. As **Figure 5** shows, the temperature at the surface is much warmer than the average temperature of ocean water.

Figure 5   Temperature Zones in the Ocean

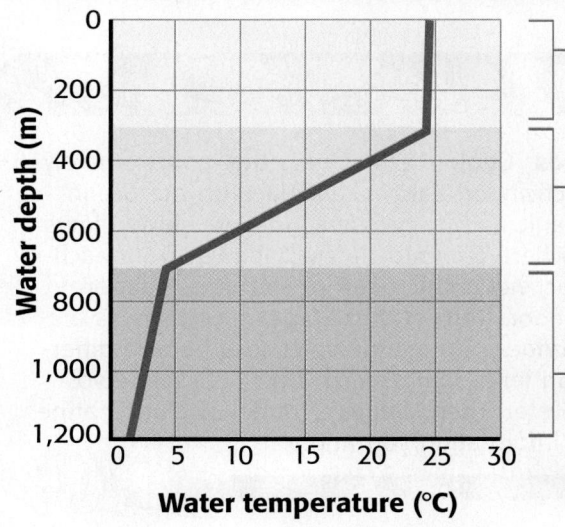

Surface zone The *surface zone* is the warm, top layer of ocean water. It can extend to 300 m below sea level. Sunlight heats the top 100 m of the surface zone. Surface currents mix the heated water with cooler water below.

Thermocline The *thermocline* is the second layer of ocean water. It can extend from 300 m below sea level to about 700 m below sea level. In the thermocline, temperature drops with increased depth faster than it does in the other two zones.

Deep zone The *deep zone* is the bottom layer that extends from the base of the thermocline to the bottom of the ocean. The temperature in this zone can range from 1°C to 3°C.

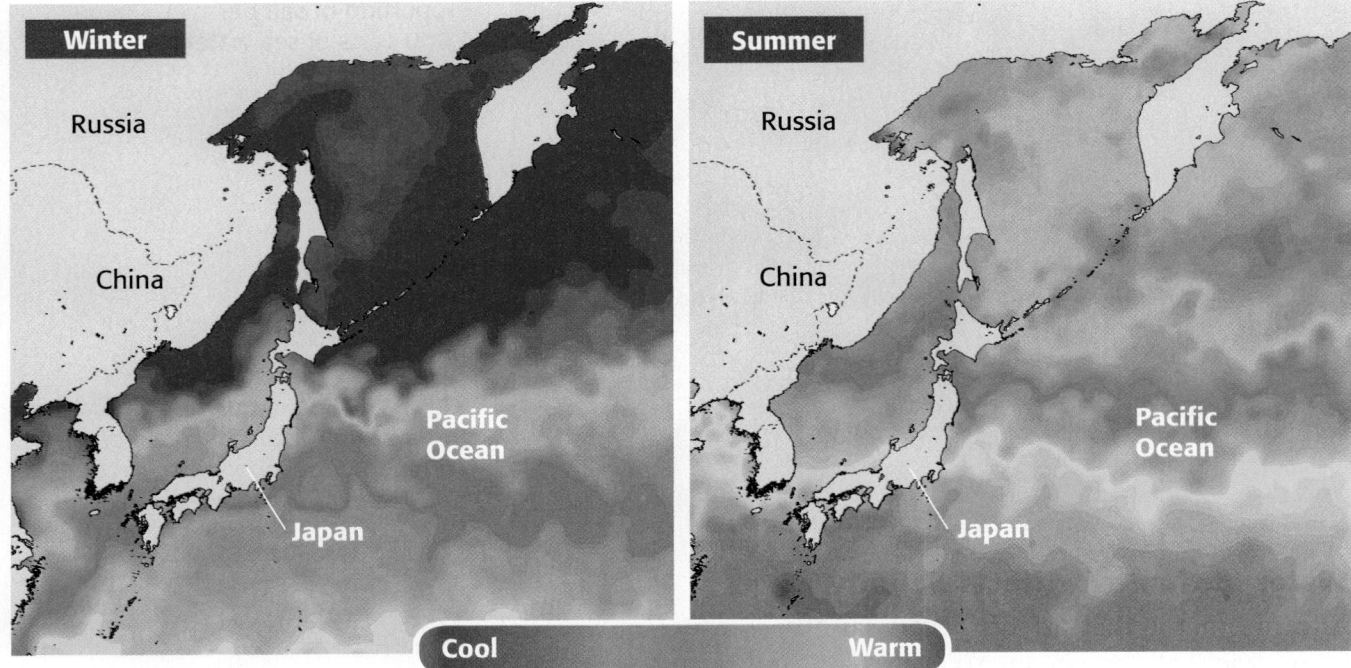

Winter		Summer
Russia		Russia
China		China
Pacific Ocean		Pacific Ocean
Japan		Japan

Cool   Warm

Figure 6 *These satellite images show that the surface temperatures in the northern Pacific Ocean change with the seasons.*

Surface Temperature Changes

If you live near the coast, you may know how different a swim in the ocean feels in December than it feels in July. Temperatures in the surface zone vary with latitude and the time of year. Surface temperatures range from 1°C near the poles to about 24°C near the equator. Parts of the ocean along the equator are warmer because they receive more direct sunlight per year than areas closer to the poles. However, both hemispheres receive more direct sunlight during their summer seasons. Therefore, the surface zone is heated more in the summer. **Figure 6** shows how surface-zone temperatures vary depending on the time of year.

✓ **Reading Check** Why are parts of the ocean along the equator warmer than those closer to the poles?

CONNECTION TO Geology

Submarine Volcanoes Geologists estimate that approximately 80% of the volcanic activity on Earth takes place on the ocean floor. Most of the volcanic activity occurs as magma slowly flows onto the ocean floor where tectonic plates pull away from each other. Other volcanic activity is the result of volcanoes that are located on the ocean floor. Both of these types of volcanoes are called *submarine volcanoes*. Submarine volcanoes behave differently than volcanoes on land do. Research how submarine volcanoes behave underwater. Then, create a model of a submarine volcano based on the information you find.

ACTIVITY

The Ocean and the Water Cycle

If you could sit on the moon and look down at Earth, what would you see? You would notice that Earth's surface is made up of three basic components—water, land, and clouds (air). All three are part of a process called the water cycle, as shown in **Figure 7.** The **water cycle** is the continuous movement of water from the ocean to the atmosphere to the land and back to the ocean. The ocean is an important part of the water cycle because nearly all of Earth's water is in the ocean.

water cycle the continuous movement of water from the ocean to the atmosphere to the land and back to the ocean

Figure 7 The Water Cycle

Condensation As water vapor rises into the atmosphere, it cools and interacts with dust particles. Eventually, the water vapor turns to liquid water. This change from a gas to a liquid is called *condensation.*

Evaporation The sun heats liquid water, causing it to rise into the atmosphere as water vapor. This physical change from a liquid to a gas is called *evaporation.* Water evaporates directly from oceans, lakes, rivers, falling rain, plants, animals, and other sources.

Precipitation When water droplets become heavy enough, they fall back to Earth's surface as precipitation. *Precipitation* is solid or liquid water that falls to Earth. Most precipitation falls directly back into the ocean.

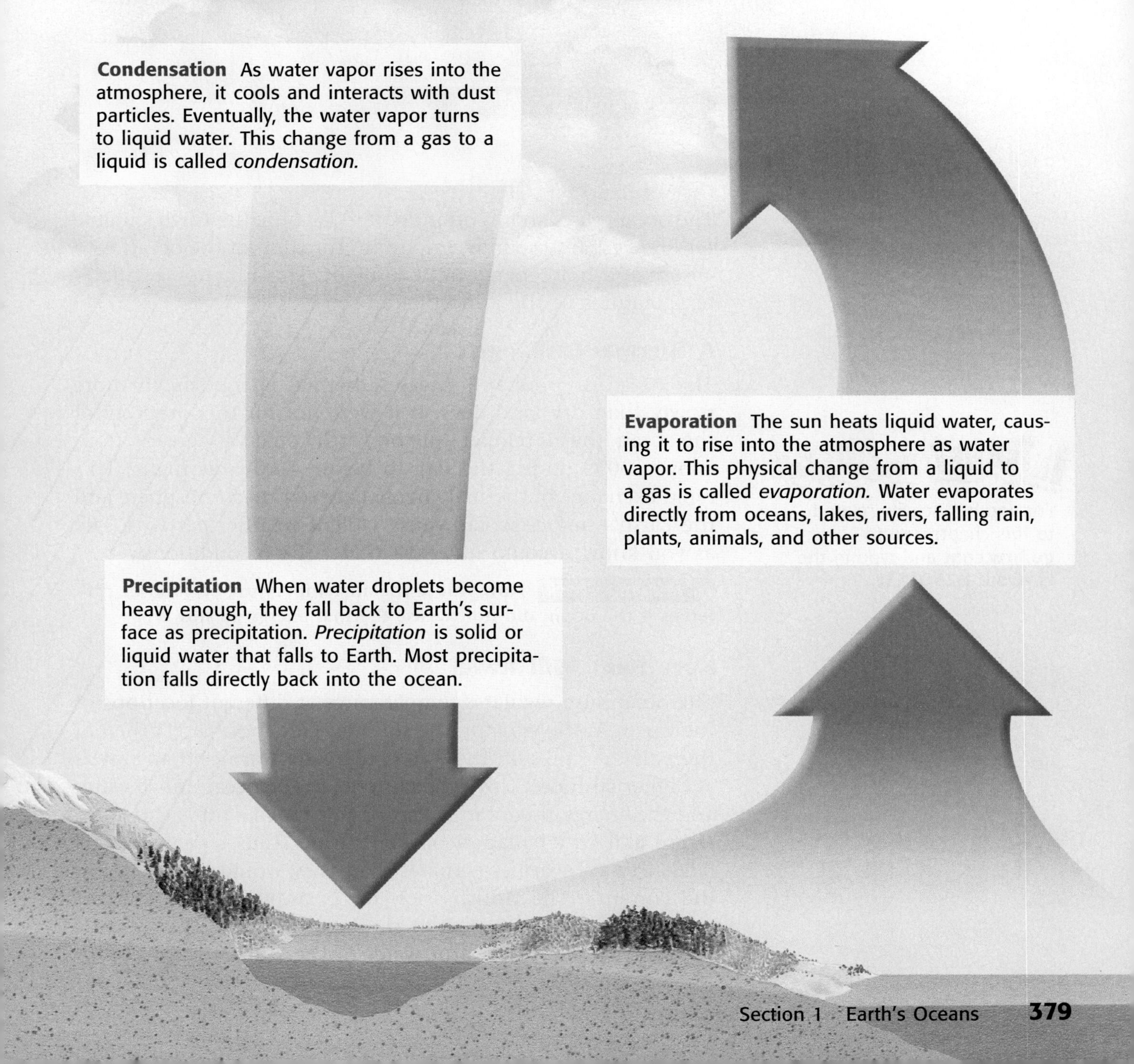

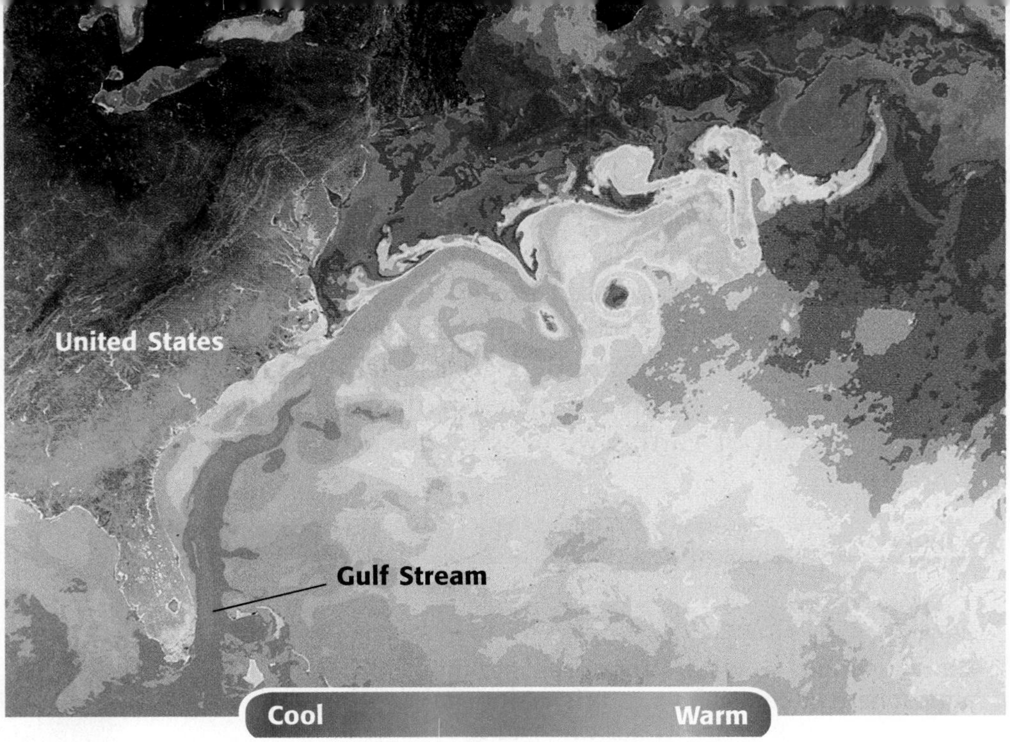

Figure 8 *This infrared satellite image shows the Gulf Stream moving warm water from lower latitudes to higher latitudes.*

United States

Gulf Stream

Cool   Warm

A Global Thermostat

The ocean plays an important part in keeping the Earth suitable for life. Perhaps the most important function of the ocean is to absorb and hold energy from sunlight. This function regulates temperatures in the atmosphere.

A Thermal Exchange

The ocean absorbs and releases thermal energy much more slowly than dry land does. If it were not for this property of the ocean, the air temperature on Earth could vary greatly from above 100°C during the day to below −100°C at night. This rapid exchange of thermal energy between the atmosphere and the Earth's surface would cause violent weather patterns. Life as you know it could not exist under these conditions.

✓ **Reading Check** How would the air temperature on land be different if the ocean did not release thermal energy so slowly?

Have Heat, Will Travel

The ocean also regulates temperatures at different locations of the Earth. At the equator, the sun's rays are more direct than at the poles. As a result, the waters there are warmer than waters at higher latitudes. However, currents in the ocean move water and the energy it contains. Part of this movement is shown in **Figure 8.** This circulation of warm water causes some coastal lands to have warmer climates than they would have without the currents. The British Isles, for example, have a warmer climate than most regions at the same latitude. This warmer climate is due to the warm water of the Gulf Stream.

For another activity related to this chapter, go to **go.hrw.com** and type in the keyword **HZ5OCEW.**

SECTION
Review

Summary

- The global ocean is divided by the continents into four main oceans: Pacific Ocean, Atlantic Ocean, Indian Ocean, and Arctic Ocean.

- The four oceans as we know them today formed within the last 300 million years.

- Salts have been added to the ocean for billions of years. Salinity is a measure of the amount of dissolved salts in a given weight or mass of liquid.

- The three temperature zones of ocean water are the surface zone, the thermocline, and the deep zone.

- The water cycle is the continuous movement of water from the ocean to the atmosphere to the land and back to the ocean. The ocean plays the largest role in the water cycle.

- The ocean stabilizes Earth's weather conditions by absorbing and holding thermal energy.

Using Key Terms

1. In your own words, write a definition for each of the following terms: *salinity* and *water cycle*.

Understanding Key Ideas

2. The top layer of ocean water that extends to 300 m below sea level is called the
   a. deep zone.
   b. surface zone.
   c. Gulf Stream.
   d. thermocline.

3. Name the major divisions of the global ocean.

4. Explain how Earth's first oceans formed.

5. Why is the ocean an important part of the water cycle?

6. Between which two steps of the water cycle does the ocean fit?

Critical Thinking

7. **Making Inferences** Describe how the ocean plays a role in stabilizing Earth's weather conditions.

8. **Identifying Relationships** List one factor that affects salinity in the ocean and one factor that affects ocean temperatures. Explain how each factor affects salinity or temperature.

Interpreting Graphics

Use the image below to answer the questions that follow.

2 Condensation 1 Evaporation 3 Precipitation

9. At which stage would solid or liquid water fall to the Earth?

10. At which stage would the sun's energy cause liquid to rise into the atmosphere as water vapor?

SCiLINKS®

NSTA
Developed and maintained by the
National Science Teachers Association

For a variety of links related to this chapter, go to www.scilinks.org

Topic: Exploring Earth's Oceans
SciLinks code: HSM0557

The Ocean Floor

What lies at the bottom of the ocean? How deep is the ocean?

These questions were once unanswerable. By using new technology, scientists have learned a lot about the ocean floor. Scientists have discovered landforms on the ocean floor and have measured depths for almost the entire ocean floor.

Studying the Ocean Floor

Sending people into deep water to study the ocean floor can be risky. Fortunately, there are other ways to study the deep ocean. These ways include surveying from the ocean surface and from high above in space.

Seeing by Sonar

Sonar stands for *sound navigation and ranging*. This technology is based on the echo-ranging behavior of bats. Scientists use sonar to determine the ocean's depth by sending sound pulses from a ship down into the ocean. The sound moves through the water, bounces off the ocean floor, and returns to the ship. The deeper the water is, the longer the round trip takes. Scientists then calculate the depth by multiplying half the travel time by the speed of sound in water (about 1,500 m/s). This process is shown in **Figure 1.**

READING WARM-UP

Objectives

● Describe technologies for studying the ocean floor.

● Identify the two major regions of the ocean floor.

● Classify subdivisions and features of the two major regions of the ocean floor.

Terms to Learn

continental shelf   rift valley
continental slope   seamount
continental rise   ocean trench
abyssal plain
mid-ocean ridge

READING STRATEGY

Reading Organizer As you read this section, create an outline of the section. Use the headings from the section in your outline.

Figure 1   Ocean Floor Mapping with Sonar

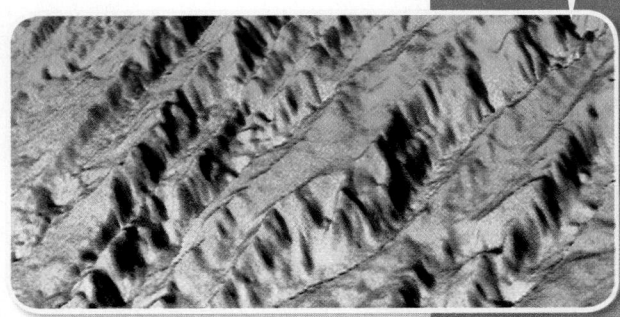

3 Scientists use sonar signals to make a *bathymetric profile,* which is a map of the ocean floor that shows the ocean's depth.

Oceanography via Satellite

In the 1970s, scientists began studying Earth from satellites in orbit around the Earth. In 1978, scientists launched the satellite *Seasat*. This satellite focused on the ocean, sending images back to Earth that allowed scientists to measure the direction and speed of ocean currents.

Studying the Ocean with *Geosat*

Geosat, once a top-secret military satellite, has been used to measure slight changes in the height of the ocean's surface. Different underwater features, such as mountains and trenches, affect the height of the water above them. Scientists measure the different heights of the ocean surface and use the measurements to make detailed maps of the ocean floor. Maps made using satellite measurements, such as the map in **Figure 2,** can cover much more territory than maps made using ship-based sonar readings.

Reading Check How do scientists use satellites to make detailed maps of the ocean floor? (*See the Appendix for answers to Reading Checks.*)

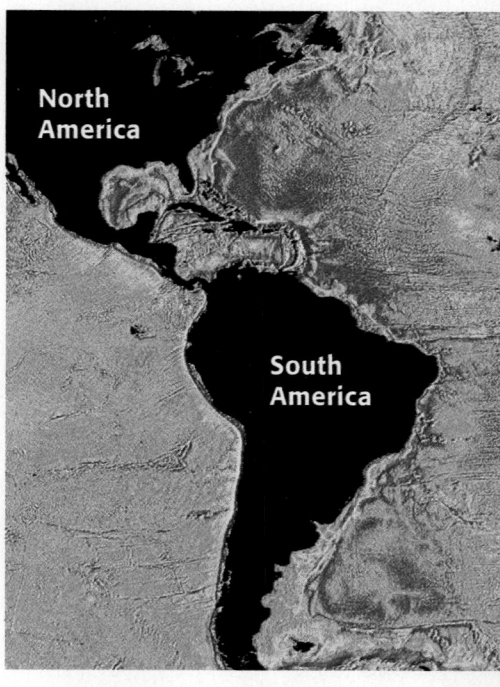

Figure 2 *This map was generated by satellite measurements of different heights of the ocean surface.*

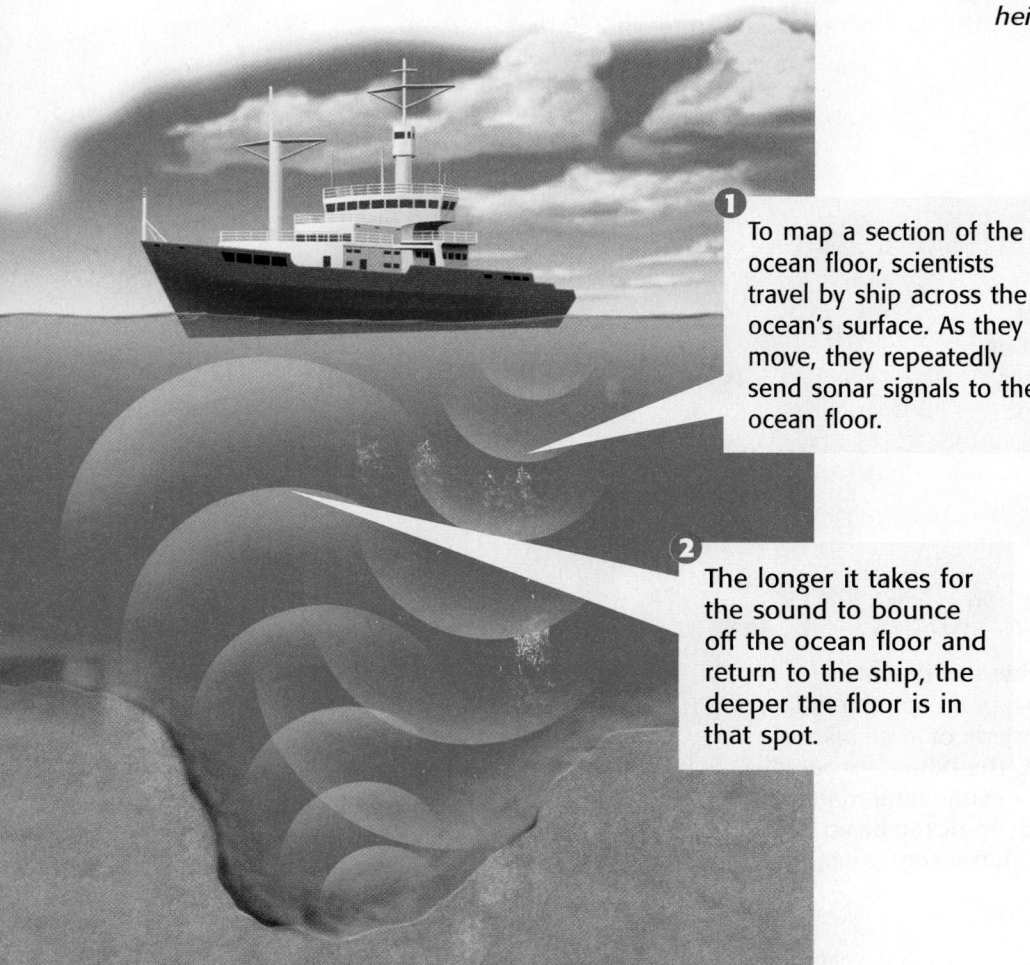

❶ To map a section of the ocean floor, scientists travel by ship across the ocean's surface. As they move, they repeatedly send sonar signals to the ocean floor.

❷ The longer it takes for the sound to bounce off the ocean floor and return to the ship, the deeper the floor is in that spot.

continental shelf the gently sloping section of the continental margin located between the shoreline and the continental slope

continental slope the steeply inclined section of the continental margin located between the continental rise and the continental shelf

continental rise the gently sloping section of the continental margin located between the continental slope and the abyssal plain

abyssal plain a large, flat, almost level area of the deep-ocean basin

Revealing the Ocean Floor

Can you imagine being an explorer assigned to map uncharted areas on the planet? You might think that there are not many uncharted areas left because most of the land has already been explored. But what about the bottom of the ocean?

The ocean floor is not a flat surface. If you could go to the bottom of the ocean, you would see a number of impressive features. You would see the world's longest mountain chain, which is about 64,000 km (40,000 mi) long as well as canyons deeper than the Grand Canyon. And because it is underwater and some areas are so deep, much of the ocean floor is still not completely explored.

✓ **Reading Check** How long is the longest mountain chain in the world? Where is it located?

Figure 3 The Ocean Floor

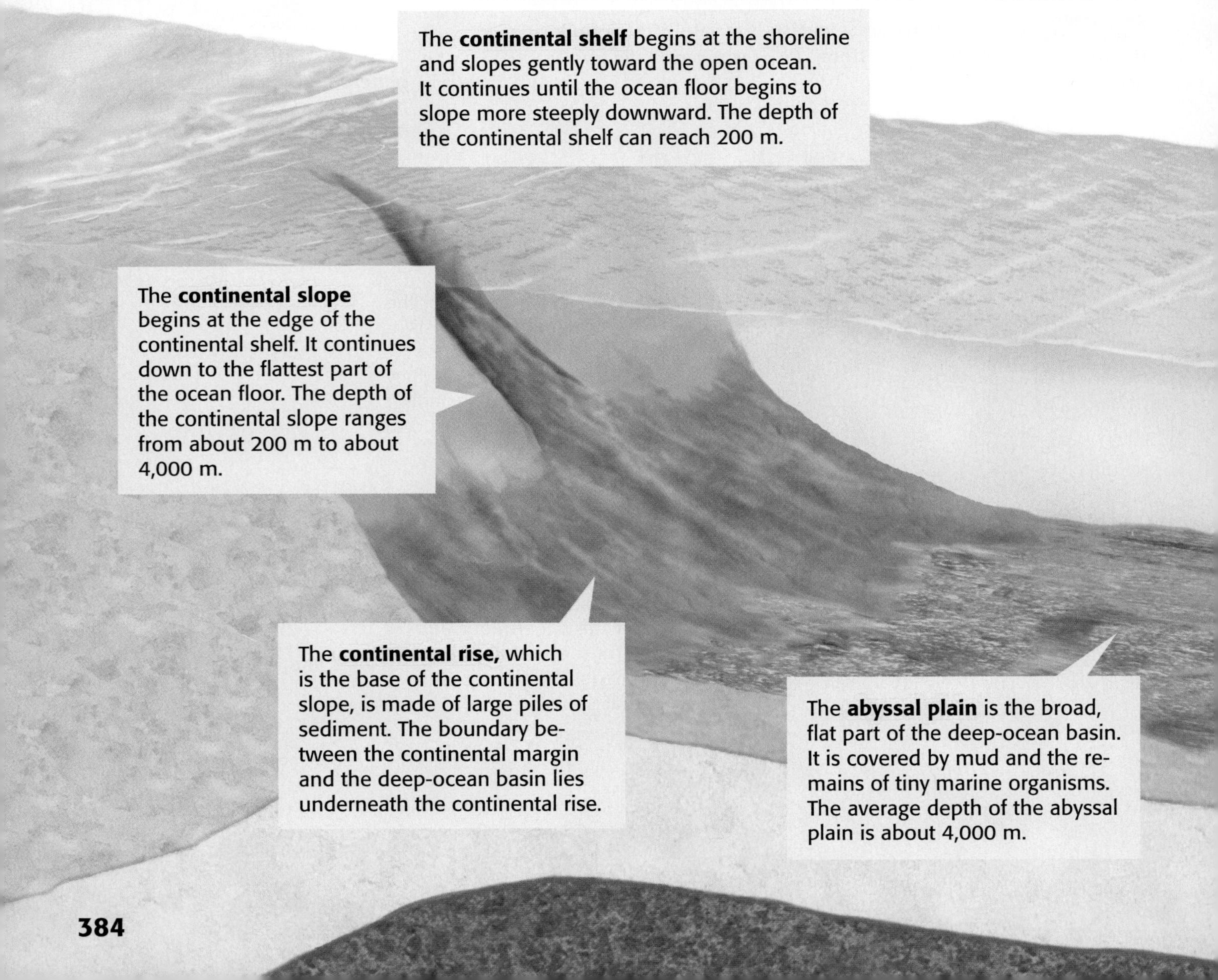

The **continental shelf** begins at the shoreline and slopes gently toward the open ocean. It continues until the ocean floor begins to slope more steeply downward. The depth of the continental shelf can reach 200 m.

The **continental slope** begins at the edge of the continental shelf. It continues down to the flattest part of the ocean floor. The depth of the continental slope ranges from about 200 m to about 4,000 m.

The **continental rise,** which is the base of the continental slope, is made of large piles of sediment. The boundary between the continental margin and the deep-ocean basin lies underneath the continental rise.

The **abyssal plain** is the broad, flat part of the deep-ocean basin. It is covered by mud and the remains of tiny marine organisms. The average depth of the abyssal plain is about 4,000 m.

Regions of the Ocean Floor

If you journeyed to the ocean floor, you would first notice two major regions. The *continental margin* is made of continental crust, and the *deep-ocean basin* is made of oceanic crust. Imagine that the ocean is a giant swimming pool. The continental margin is the shallow end of the pool, and the deep-ocean basin is the deep end of the pool. The figure below shows how these two regions are subdivided.

Underwater Real Estate

As you can see in **Figure 3** below, the continental margin is subdivided into the continental shelf, the continental slope, and the continental rise. These divisions are based on depth and changes in slope. The deep-ocean basin consists of the abyssal (uh BIS uhl) plain, mid-ocean ridges, rift valleys, and ocean trenches. All of these features form near the boundaries of Earth's *tectonic plates*. On parts of the deep-ocean basin that are not near plate boundaries, there are thousands of seamounts. Seamounts are submerged volcanic mountains on the ocean floor.

Reading Check What are the subdivisions of the continental margin?

mid-ocean ridge a long, undersea mountain chain that forms along the floor of the major oceans

rift valley a long, narrow valley that forms as tectonic plates separate

seamount a submerged mountain on the ocean floor that is at least 1,000 m high and that has a volcanic origin

ocean trench a steep, long depression in the deep-sea floor that runs parallel to a chain of volcanic islands or a continental margin

Mid-ocean ridges are mountain chains that form where tectonic plates pull apart. This pulling motion creates cracks in the ocean floor called *rift zones*. As rifts form, magma rises to fill the spaces. Heat from the magma causes the crust on either side of the rifts to expand, which forms the ridges.

As mountains build up, a **rift valley** forms between them in the rift zone.

Seamounts are individual mountains of volcanic material. They form where magma pushes its way through or between tectonic plates. If a seamount builds up above sea level, it becomes a volcanic island.

Ocean trenches are huge cracks in the deep-ocean basin. Ocean trenches form where one oceanic plate is pushed beneath a continental plate or another oceanic plate.

Exploring the Ocean with Underwater Vessels

Just as astronauts explore space with rockets, scientists explore the oceans with underwater vessels. These vessels contain the air that the explorers need to breathe and all of the scientific instruments that the explorers need to study the oceans.

Piloted Vessels: *Alvin* and *Deep Flight*

One research vessel used to travel to the deep ocean is called *Alvin*. *Alvin* is 7 m long and can reach some of the deepest parts of the ocean. Scientists have used *Alvin* for many underwater missions, including searches for sunken ships, the recovery of a lost hydrogen bomb, and explorations of the sea floor. In 1977, scientists aboard *Alvin* discovered an oasis of life around hydrothermal vents near the Galápagos Islands. Ecosystems near hydrothermal vents are unique because some organisms living around the vent do not rely on photosynthesis for energy. Instead, these organisms rely on chemicals in the water as their source of energy.

Another modern vessel that scientists use to explore the deep ocean is an underwater airplane called *Deep Flight*. This vessel, shown in **Figure 4,** moves through the water in much the same way that an airplane moves through the air. Future models of *Deep Flight* will be designed to transport pilots to the deepest parts of the ocean, which are more than 11,000 m deep.

Reading Check Why is the ecosystem discovered by *Alvin* unique?

CONNECTION TO Social Studies

The JASON Project The JASON project, started by oceanographer Dr. Robert Ballard, allows students and teachers to take part in virtual field trips to some of the most exotic locations on Earth. Using satellite links and the Internet, students around the world have participated in scientific expeditions to places such as the Galápagos Islands, the Sea of Cortez, and deep-sea hydrothermal vents. Using the Internet, research where the JASON project is headed to next!

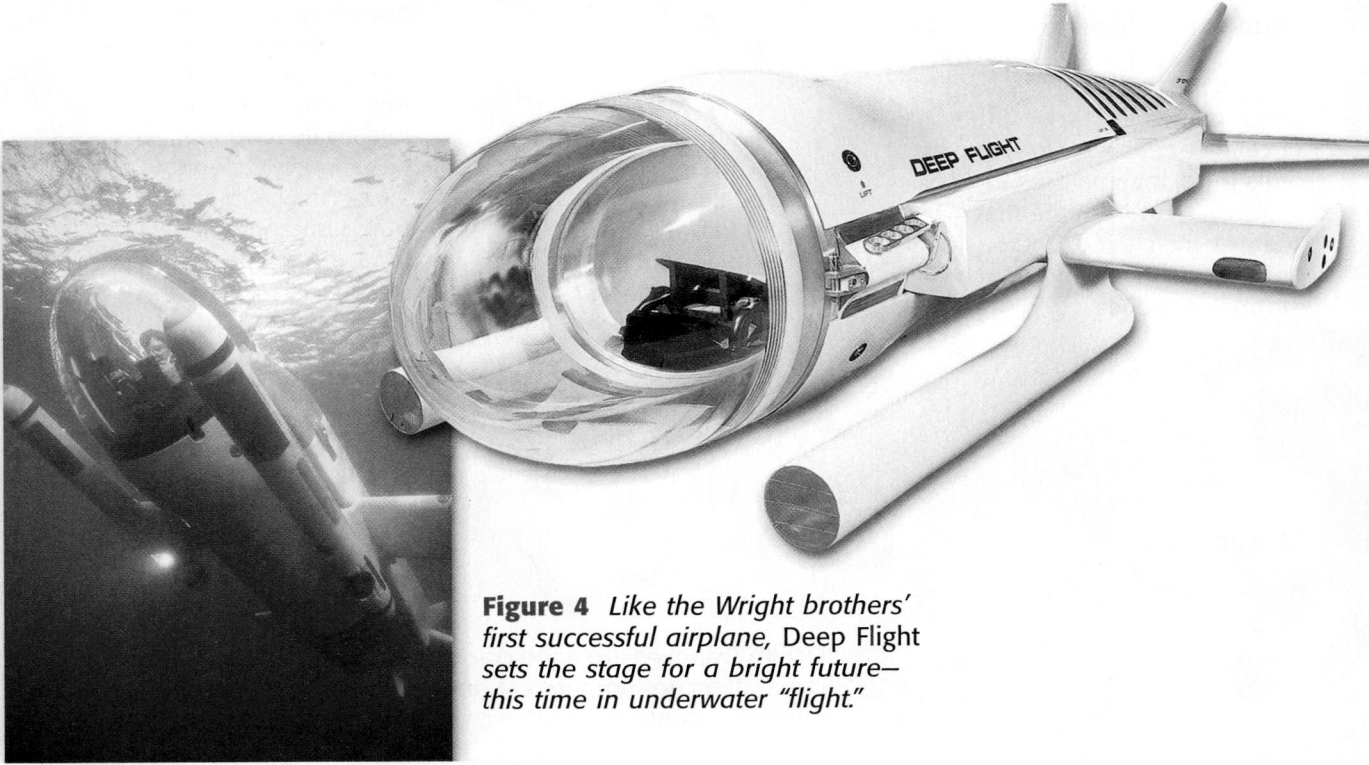

Figure 4 *Like the Wright brothers' first successful airplane, Deep Flight sets the stage for a bright future— this time in underwater "flight."*

Robotic Vessels: *JASON II* and *Medea*

Exploring the deep ocean by using piloted vessels is expensive and can be very dangerous. For these reasons, scientists use robotic vessels to explore the ocean. One interesting robot team consists of *JASON II* and *Medea*. These robots are designed to withstand pressures much greater than those found in the deepest parts of the ocean. *JASON II* is "flown" by a pilot at the surface and is used to explore the ocean floor. *Medea* is attached to *JASON II* with a tether and explores above the sea floor. In the future, unpiloted "drone" robots shaped like fish may be used. Another robot under development uses the ocean's thermal energy for power. These robots could explore the ocean for years and send data to scientists at the surface.

SECTION Review

Summary

- Scientists study the ocean floor from the surface using sonar and satellites.

- The ocean floor is divided into two regions—the continental margin and the deep-ocean basin.

- The continental margin consists of the continental shelf, the continental slope, and the continental rise.

- The deep-ocean basin consists of the abyssal plain, mid-ocean ridges, rift valleys, seamounts, and ocean trenches.

- Scientists explore the ocean from below the surface by using piloted vessels and robotic vessels.

Using Key Terms

For each pair of terms, explain how the meanings of the terms differ.

1. *continental shelf* and *continental slope*

2. *abyssal plain* and *ocean trench*

3. *mid-ocean ridge* and *seamount*

Understanding Key Ideas

4. Sonar is a technology based on the
   a. *Geosat* satellite.
   b. surface currents in the ocean.
   c. zones of the ocean floor.
   d. echo-ranging behavior of bats.

5. List the two major regions of the ocean floor.

6. Describe the subdivisions of the continental margin.

7. List three technologies for studying the ocean floor, and explain how they are used.

8. List three underwater missions that *Alvin* has been used for.

9. Explain how *Jason II* and *Medea* are used to explore the ocean.

10. Describe how a bathymetric profile is made.

Math Skills

11. Air pressure at sea level is 1 atmosphere (atm). Underwater, pressure increases by 1 atm every 10 m of depth. For example, at a depth of 10 m, water pressure is 2 atm. What is the pressure at 100 m?

Critical Thinking

12. **Making Comparisons** How is exploring the oceans similar to exploring space?

13. **Applying Concepts** Is the ocean floor a flat surface? Explain your answer.

Developed and maintained by the National Science Teachers Association

For a variety of links related to this chapter, go to www.scilinks.org

Topic: The Ocean Floor
SciLinks code: HSM1062

Life in the Ocean

In which part of the ocean does an octopus live? And where do dolphins spend most of their time?

Just as armadillos and birds occupy very different places on Earth, octopuses and dolphins live in very different parts of the ocean. Trying to study life in the oceans can be a challenge for scientists. The oceans are so large that many forms of marine life have not been discovered, and there are many more organisms that scientists know little about. To make things easier, scientists classify marine organisms into three main groups.

The Three Groups of Marine Life

The three main groups of marine life, as shown in **Figure 1,** are plankton, nekton, and benthos. Marine organisms are placed into one of these three groups according to where they live and how they move.

Organisms that float or drift freely near the ocean's surface are called **plankton.** Most plankton are microscopic. Plankton are divided into two groups—those that are plant-like (*phytoplankton*) and those that are animal-like (*zooplankton*). Organisms that swim actively in the open ocean are called **nekton.** Types of nekton include mammals, such as whales, dolphins, and sea lions, as well as many varieties of fish. **Benthos** are organisms that live on or in the ocean floor. There are many types of benthos, such as crabs, starfish, worms, coral, sponges, seaweed, and clams.

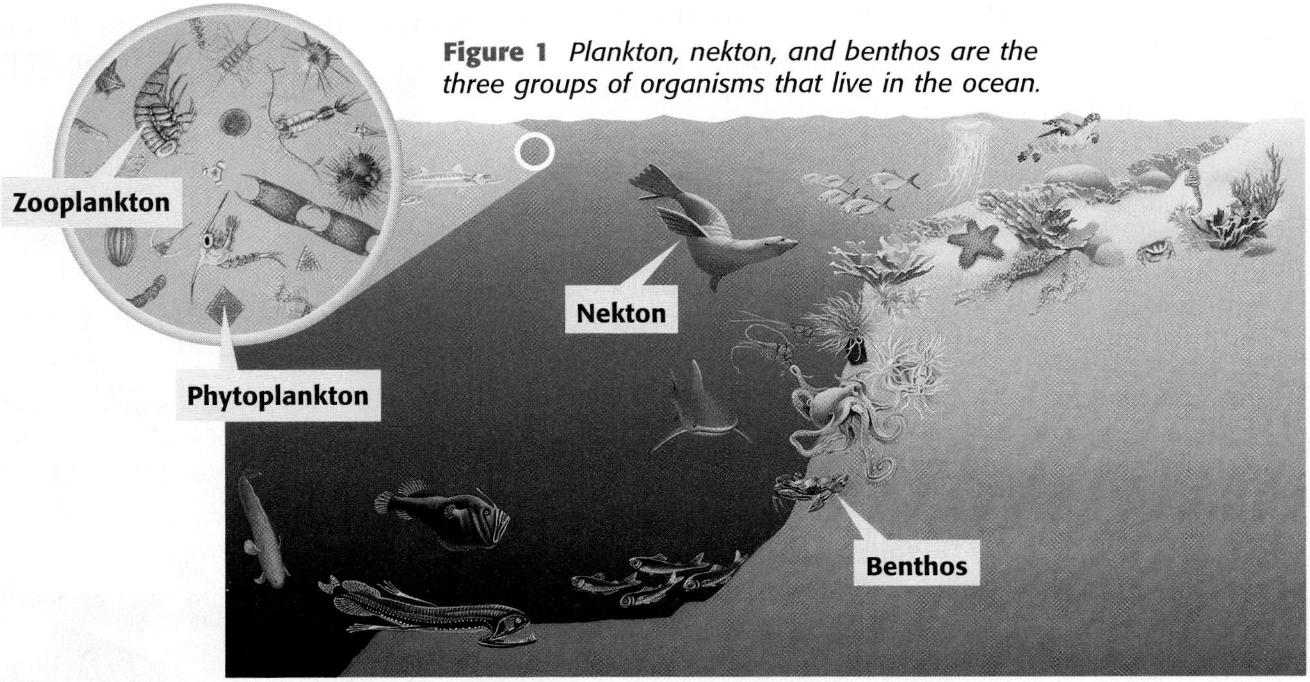

READING WARM-UP

Objectives

● Identify the three groups of marine life.

● Describe the two main ocean environments.

● Identify the ecological zones of the benthic and pelagic environments.

Terms to Learn

plankton
nekton
benthos
benthic environment
pelagic environment

READING STRATEGY

Mnemonics As you read this section, create a mnemonic device to help you remember the ecological zones of the ocean.

Figure 1 *Plankton, nekton, and benthos are the three groups of organisms that live in the ocean.*

Zooplankton

Phytoplankton

Nekton

Benthos

Intertidal zone

Figure 2 *Organisms such as sea anemones and starfish attach themselves to rocks and reefs. These organisms must be able to survive both wet and dry conditions.*

The Benthic Environment

In addition to being divided into zones based on depth, the ocean floor is divided into ecological zones based on where different types of benthos live. These zones are grouped into one major marine environment—the benthic environment. The **benthic environment,** or bottom environment, is the region near the ocean floor and all the organisms that live on or in it.

The Intertidal Zone

The shallowest benthic zone, called the *intertidal zone,* is located between the low-tide and high-tide limits. Twice a day, the intertidal zone changes. As the tide flows in, the zone is covered with ocean water. Then, as the tide flows out, the intertidal zone is exposed to the air and sun.

Because of the change in tides, intertidal organisms must be able to live both underwater and on exposed land. Some organisms, such as the sea anemones and starfish shown in **Figure 2,** attach themselves to rocks and reefs to avoid being washed out to sea during low tide. Other organisms, such as clams, oysters, barnacles, and crabs, have tough shells that give them protection against strong waves during high tide and against harsh sunlight during low tide. Some animals can burrow in sand or between rocks to avoid harsh conditions. Plants also protect themselves from being washed away by strong waves. Plants such as seaweed have strong *holdfasts* (rootlike structures) that allow them to grow in this zone.

✔ **Reading Check** How do clams and oysters survive in the intertidal zone during high tide and low tide? (*See the Appendix for answers to Reading Checks.*)

plankton the mass of mostly microscopic organisms that float or drift freely in freshwater and marine environments

nekton all organisms that swim actively in open water, independent of currents

benthos the organisms that live at the bottom of the sea or ocean

benthic environment the region near the bottom of a pond, lake, or ocean

Figure 3 *Corals, like many other types of organisms, can live in both the sublittoral zone and the intertidal zone. However, they are more common in the sublittoral zone.*

Sublittoral zone

The Sublittoral Zone

The *sublittoral zone* begins where the intertidal zone ends, at the low-tide limit, and extends to the edge of the continental shelf. This zone of the benthic environment is more stable than the intertidal zone. The temperature, water pressure, and amount of sunlight remain fairly constant in the sublittoral zone. Sublittoral organisms, such as corals, shown in **Figure 3,** do not have to cope with as much change as intertidal organisms do. Although the sublittoral zone extends down 200 m below sea level, plants and most animals stay in the upper 100 m, where small amounts of sunlight reaches the ocean floor.

Bathyal zone

The Bathyal Zone

The *bathyal* (BATH ee uhl) *zone* extends from the edge of the continental shelf to the abyssal plain. The depth of this zone ranges from 200 m to 4,000 m below sea level. Because of the lack of sunlight at these depths, plant life is scarce in this part of the benthic environment. Animals in this zone include sponges, brachiopods, sea stars, echinoids, and octopuses, such as the one shown in **Figure 4.**

Figure 4 *Octopuses are one of the animals common to the bathyal zone.*

Figure 5 *Tube worms can tolerate higher temperatures than most other organisms can. These animals survive in water as hot as 81°C.*

Abyssal zone

The Abyssal Zone

No plants and very few animals live in the *abyssal zone,* which is on the abyssal plain. The abyssal zone is the largest ecological zone of the ocean and can reach 4,000 m in depth. Animals such as crabs, sponges, worms, and sea cucumbers live within the abyssal zone. Many of these organisms, such as the tube worms shown in **Figure 5,** live around hot-water vents called *black smokers.* Scientists know very little about this benthic environment because it is so deep and dark.

✓ **Reading Check** What types of animals live in the abyssal zone?

The Hadal Zone

The deepest benthic zone is the *hadal* (HAYD'l) *zone.* This zone consists of the floor of the ocean trenches and any organisms found there. The hadal zone can reach from 6,000 m to 7,000 m in depth. Scientists know even less about the hadal zone than they do about the abyssal zone. So far, scientists have discovered a type of sponge, a few species of worms, and a type of clam, which is shown in **Figure 6.**

Hadal zone

Figure 6 *These clams are one of the few types of organisms known to live in the hadal zone.*

Neritic zone

Figure 7 *Many marine animals, such as these dolphins, live in the neritic zone.*

The Pelagic Environment

The zone near the ocean's surface and at the middle depths of the ocean is called the **pelagic environment.** It is beyond the sublittoral zone and above the abyssal zone. There are two major zones in the pelagic environment—the neritic zone and the oceanic zone.

The Neritic Zone

The *neritic zone* covers the continental shelf. This warm, shallow zone contains the largest concentration of marine life. Fish, plankton, and marine mammals, such as the dolphins in **Figure 7,** are just a few of the animal groups found in this zone. The neritic zone contains diverse marine life because it receives more sunlight than the other zones in the ocean. Sunlight allows plankton, which are food for other marine organisms, to grow. The many animals in the benthic zone below the neritic zone also serve as a food supply.

pelagic environment in the ocean, the zone near the surface or at middle depths, beyond the sublittoral zone and above the abyssal zone

✓ *Reading Check* Why does the neritic zone contain the largest concentration of marine life in the ocean?

CONNECTION TO Language Arts

WRITING SKILL **Water, Water, Everywhere** Samuel Taylor Coleridge wrote "The Rime of the Ancient Mariner" in 1798. The following is an excerpt from the poem:

Water, water, everywhere, / And all the boards did shrink / Water, water, everywhere, / Nor any drop to drink . . . / And every tongue through utter drought, / Was withered at the root; / We could not speak, no more than if / We had been choked with soot.

What do you think this excerpt means? Write a short essay describing the meaning of this passage.

The Oceanic Zone

The *oceanic zone* includes the volume of water that covers the entire sea floor except for the continental shelf. In the deeper parts of the oceanic zone, the water temperature is colder and the pressure is much greater than in the neritic zone. Also, organisms are more spread out in the oceanic zone than in the neritic zone. Although many of the same organisms that live in the neritic zone are found throughout the upper regions, some strange animals lurk in the darker depths, as shown in **Figure 8.** Other animals in the deeper parts of this zone include giant squids and some whale species.

Figure 8 *The angler fish is a predator that uses a wormlike lure attached to its head to attract prey.*

SECTION Review

Summary

● The three main groups of marine life are plankton, nekton, and benthos.

● The two main ocean environments are the benthic environment and the pelagic environment.

● The ecological zones of the benthic environment include the intertidal zone, sublittoral zone, bathyal zone, abyssal zone, and hadal zone.

● The ecological zones of the pelagic environment include the neritic zone and the oceanic zone.

Using Key Terms

The statements below are false. For each statement, replace the underlined term to make a true statement.

1. <u>Plankton</u> are organisms that swim actively in ocean water.

2. The intertidal zone is part of the <u>pelagic zone</u>.

3. Dolphins live in the <u>benthic environment</u>.

Understanding Key Ideas

4. The deepest benthic zone is the
   a. pelagic environment.
   b. hadal zone.
   c. oceanic zone.
   d. abyssal zone.

5. List and briefly describe the three main groups of marine organisms.

6. Name the two ocean environments. In your own words, describe where they are located in the ocean.

Critical Thinking

7. **Making Inferences** Describe why organisms in the intertidal zone must be able to live underwater and on exposed land.

8. **Applying Concepts** How would the ocean's ecological zones change if sea level dropped 300 m?

Interpreting Graphics

Use the diagram below to answer the following question.

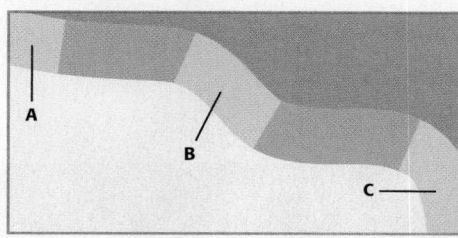

9. Identify the names of the ecological zones of the benthic environment shown above.

For a variety of links related to this chapter, go to www.scilinks.org

Topic: Life in the Oceans
SciLinks code: HSM0874

Resources from the Ocean

The next time you enjoy your favorite ice cream, remember that without seaweed, it would be a runny mess!

The ocean offers a vast supply of resources. These resources are put to a number of uses. For example, a seaweed called *kelp* is used as a thickener for many food products, including ice cream. Food, raw materials, energy, and drinkable water are all harvested from the ocean. And there are probably more resources in unexplored parts of the ocean. As human populations have grown, however, the demand for these resources has increased, while the availability has decreased.

READING WARM-UP

Objectives

● List two ways of harvesting the ocean's living resources.

● Identify three nonliving resources in the ocean.

● Describe the ocean's energy resources.

Terms to Learn

desalination

READING STRATEGY

Paired Summarizing Read this section silently. In pairs, take turns summarizing the material. Stop to discuss ideas that seem confusing.

Living Resources

People have been harvesting plants and animals from the ocean for thousands of years. Many civilizations formed in coastal regions where the ocean offered plenty of food for a growing population. Today, harvesting food from the ocean is a multi-billion-dollar industry.

Fishing the Ocean

Of all the marine organisms, fish are the largest group of organisms that are taken from the ocean. Almost 75 million tons of fish are harvested each year. With improved technology, such as drift nets, fishers have become better at taking fish from the ocean. **Figure 1** shows the large number of fish that can be caught using a drift net. In recent years, many people have become concerned that we are overfishing the ocean. We are taking more fish than can be naturally replaced. Also, animals other than fish, especially dolphins and turtles, can be accidentally caught in drift nets. Today, the fishing industry is making efforts to prevent overfishing and damage to other wildlife from drift nets.

Figure 1 *Drift nets are fishing nets that cover kilometers of ocean. Whole schools of fish can be caught with a single drift net.*

Farming the Ocean

Overfishing reduces fish populations. Recently, laws regulating fishing have become stricter. As a result, it is becoming more difficult to supply our demand for fish. Many people have begun to raise ocean fish in fish farms to help meet the demand. Fish farming requires several holding ponds. Each pond contains fish at a certain level of development. **Figure 2** shows a holding pond in a fish farm. When the fish are old enough, they are harvested and packaged for shipping.

Fish are not the only seafood harvested in a farmlike setting. Shrimp, oysters, crabs, and mussels are raised in enclosed areas near the shore. Mussels and oysters are grown attached to ropes. Huge nets line the nursery area, preventing the animals from being eaten by their natural predators.

✔ **Reading Check** How can fish farms help reduce overfishing? (*See the Appendix for answers to Reading Checks.*)

Figure 2 *Eating fish raised in a fish farm helps lower the number of fish harvested from the ocean.*

Savory Seaweed

Many types of seaweed, which are species of alga, are harvested from the ocean. For example, kelp, shown in **Figure 3,** is a seaweed that grows as much as 33 cm a day. Kelp is harvested and used as a thickener in jellies, ice cream, and similar products. Seaweed is rich in protein. In fact, several species of seaweed are staples of the Japanese diet. For example, some kinds of sushi, a Japanese dish, are wrapped in seaweed.

Figure 3 *Kelp, a type of alga, can grow up to 33 cm a day. It is harvested and used in a number of products, including ice cream.*

Nonliving Resources

Humans also harvest many nonliving resources from the ocean. These resources provide raw materials, drinkable water, and energy for our growing population. Some resources are easy to get, while others are very difficult to harvest.

Oil and Natural Gas

Modern civilization continues to be very dependent on oil and natural gas for energy. Oil and natural gas are *nonrenewable resources*. They are used up faster than they can be replenished naturally. Both oil and natural gas are found under layers of impermeable rock. Petroleum engineers must drill through this rock in order to reach these resources.

✓ Reading Check What are nonrenewable resources? Give an example of a nonrenewable resource.

Searching for Oil

How do engineers know where to drill for oil and natural gas? They use seismic equipment. Special devices send powerful pulses of sound to the ocean floor. The pulses move through the water and penetrate the rocks and sediment below. The pulses are then reflected back toward the ship, where they are recorded by electronic equipment and analyzed by a computer. The computer readings indicate how rock layers are arranged below the ocean floor. Petroleum workers, such as the one in **Figure 4,** use these readings to locate a promising area to drill.

Figure 4 *Petroleum workers, such as the one below, drill for oil and gas in the ocean floor. By using seismic equipment, workers can decide which spot will be best for drilling.*

Figure 5 *Most desalination plants, like this one in Kuwait, use evaporation to separate ocean water from the salt it contains.*

Fresh Water and Desalination

In parts of the world where fresh water is limited, people desalinate ocean water. **Desalination** (DEE SAL uh NAY shuhn) is the process of removing salt from sea water. After the salt is removed, the fresh water is then collected for human use. But desalination is not as simple as it sounds, and it is very expensive. Countries with enough annual rainfall rely on the fresh water provided by precipitation and do not need costly desalination plants. Some countries located in drier parts of the world must build desalination plants to provide enough fresh water. One of these plants is shown in **Figure 5.** Saudi Arabia, located in the desert region of the Middle East, has one of the largest desalination plants in the world.

desalination a process of removing salt from ocean water

✓ Reading Check Explain where desalination plants are most likely to be built.

The Desalination Plant

1. Measure **1,000 mL of warm water** in a **graduated cylinder.** Pour the water in a **large pot.**

2. Carefully, add **35 g of table salt.** Stir the water until all of the salt is dissolved.

3. Place the pot on a **hot plate,** and allow all of the water to boil away.

4. Using a **wooden spoon,** scrape the salt residue from the bottom of the pot.

5. Measure the mass of the salt that was left in the bottom of the pot. How much salt did you separate from the water?

6. How does this activity model what happens in a desalination plant? What would be done differently in a desalination plant?

Figure 6 *Manganese nodules are difficult to mine because they are located on the deep ocean floor.*

Sea-Floor Minerals

Mining companies are interested in mineral nodules that are lying on the ocean floor. These nodules are made mostly of manganese, which can be used to make certain types of steel. They also contain iron, copper, nickel, and cobalt. Other nodules are made of phosphates, which are used to make fertilizer.

Nodules are formed from dissolved substances in sea water that stick to solid objects, such as pebbles. As more substances stick to the coated pebble, a nodule begins to grow. Manganese nodules can be as small as a marble or as large as a soccer ball. The photograph in **Figure 6** shows a number of nodules on the ocean floor. Scientists estimate that 15% of the ocean floor is covered with these nodules. However, these nodules are located in the deeper parts of the ocean, and mining them is costly and difficult.

Tidal Energy

The ocean generates a great deal of energy simply because of its constant movement. The gravitational pulls of the sun and moon cause the ocean to rise and fall as tides. *Tidal energy* is energy generated from the movement of tides. Tidal energy can be an excellent source of power. If the water during high tide can be rushed through a narrow coastal passageway, the water's force can be powerful enough to generate electrical energy. **Figure 7** shows how this process works. Tidal energy is a clean, inexpensive, and renewable resource. A *renewable resource* can be replenished, in time, after being used. Unfortunately, tidal energy is practical only in a few parts of the world. These areas must have a coastline with shallow, narrow channels. For example, the coastline at Cook Inlet, in Alaska, is ideal for generating electrical energy.

Figure 7 Using Tides to Generate Electrical Energy

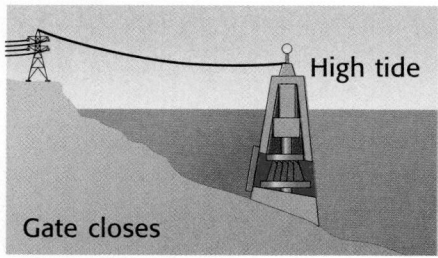

❶ As the tide rises, water enters a bay behind a dam. The gate then closes at high tide.

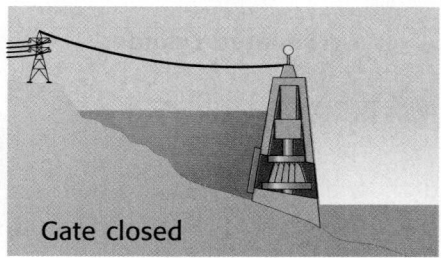

❷ The gate remains closed as the tide lowers.

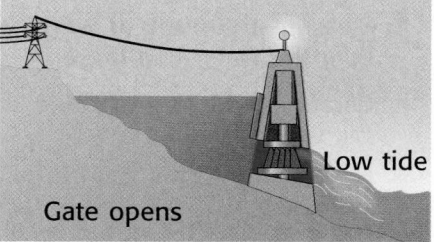

❸ At low tide, the gate opens, and the water rushes through the dam and moves the turbines, which, in turn, generate electrical energy.

Wave Energy

Have you ever stood on the beach and watched as waves crashed on the shore? This constant motion is an energy resource. Wave energy, like tidal energy, is a clean, renewable resource. Recently, computer programs have been developed to analyze wave energy. Researchers have found certain areas of the world where wave energy can generate enough electrical energy to make building power plants worthwhile. Wave energy in the North Sea is strong enough to produce power for parts of Scotland and England.

✓ **Reading Check** Why would wave energy be a good alternative energy resource?

SECTION Review

Summary

- Humans depend on the ocean for living and non-living resources.
- Fish and other marine life are being raised in ocean farms to help feed growing human populations.
- Nonliving ocean resources include oil and natural gas, water, minerals, and tidal and wave energy.

Using Key Terms

1. In your own words, write a definition for the term *desalination*.

Understanding Key Ideas

2. Mineral nodules on the ocean floor are
   a. renewable resources.
   b. easily mined.
   c. used during the process of desalination.
   d. nonliving resources.

3. List two ways of harvesting the ocean's living resources.

4. Name four nonliving resources in the ocean.

5. Explain how fish farms help meet the demand for fish.

6. Explain how engineers decide where to drill for oil and natural gas in the ocean.

Math Skills

7. A kelp plant is 5 cm tall. If it grows an average of 29 cm per day, how tall will the kelp plant be after 2 weeks?

Critical Thinking

8. **Analyzing Processes** Explain why tidal energy and wave energy are considered renewable resources.

9. **Predicting Consequences** Define the term *overfishing* in your own words. What would happen to the population of fish in the ocean if laws did not regulate overfishing? What would happen to the ocean ecosystem?

10. **Analyzing Ideas** What is one benefit and one consequence of building a desalination plant? Would a desalination plant be beneficial to your local area? Explain why or why not.

SCILINKS

NSTA
Developed and maintained by the
National Science Teachers Association

For a variety of links related to this chapter, go to www.scilinks.org

Topic: Ocean Resources
SciLinks code: HSM1065

Ocean Pollution

It's a hot summer day at the beach. You can hardly wait to swim in the ocean. You run to the surf only to be met by piles of trash washed up on the shore. Where did all that trash come from?

Humans have thrown their trash in the ocean for hundreds, if not thousands, of years. This trash has harmed the plants and animals that live in the oceans, as well as the people and animals that depend on them. Fortunately, we are becoming more aware of ocean pollution, and we are learning from our mistakes.

Nonpoint-Source Pollution

There are many sources of ocean pollution. Some of these sources are easily identified, but others are more difficult to pinpoint. **Nonpoint-source pollution** is pollution that comes from many sources rather than just from a single site. Some common sources of nonpoint-source pollutants are shown in **Figure 1.** Most ocean pollution is nonpoint-source pollution. Human activities on land can pollute streams and rivers, which then flow into the ocean and bring the pollutants they carry with them. Because nonpoint-source pollutants can enter bodies of water in many different ways, they are very hard to regulate and control. Nonpoint-source pollution can be reduced by using less lawn chemicals and disposing of used motor oil properly.

Figure 1 Examples of Nonpoint-Source Pollution

Oil and gasoline that have leaked from cars onto streets can wash into storm sewers and then drain into waterways.

Thousands of watercraft, such as boats and personal watercraft, can leak gasoline and oil directly into bodies of water.

Pesticides, herbicides, and fertilizer from residential lawns, golf courses, and farmland can wash into waterways.

Figure 2 *This barge is headed out to the open ocean, where it will dump the trash it carries.*

Point-Source Pollution

Water pollution caused by a leaking oil tanker, a factory, or a wastewater treatment plant is one type of point-source pollution. **Point-source pollution** is pollution that comes from a specific site. Even when the source of pollution is known, cleanup of the pollution is difficult.

Trash Dumping

People dump trash in many places, including the ocean. In the 1980s, scientists became alarmed by the kinds of trash that were washing up on beaches. Bandages, vials of blood, and syringes (needles) were found among the waste. Some of the blood in the vials even contained the AIDS virus. The Environmental Protection Agency (EPA) began an investigation and discovered that hospitals in the United States produce an average of 3 million tons of medical waste each year. Because of stricter laws, much of this medical waste is now buried in sanitary landfills. However, dumping trash in the deeper part of the ocean is still a common practice in many countries. The barge in **Figure 2** will dump the trash it carries into the open ocean.

Effects of Trash Dumping

Trash thrown into the ocean can affect the organisms that live in the ocean and those organisms that depend on the ocean for food. Trash such as plastic can be particularly harmful to ocean organisms. This is because most plastic materials do not break down for thousands of years. Marine animals can mistake plastic materials for food and choke or become strangled. The sea gull in **Figure 3** is tangled up in a piece of plastic trash.

> **Reading Check** What is one effect of trash dumping? (*See the Appendix for answers to Reading Checks.*)

nonpoint-source pollution pollution that comes from many sources rather than from a single, specific site

point-source pollution pollution that comes from a specific site

Figure 3 *Marine animals can be strangled by plastic trash or can choke if they mistake the plastic for food.*

Figure 4 *Sludge is the solid part of waste matter and often carries bacteria. Sludge makes beaches dirty and kills marine animals.*

Sludge Dumping

By 1990, the United States alone had discharged 38 trillion liters of treated sludge into the waters along its coasts. Sludge is part of raw sewage. *Raw sewage* is all the liquid and solid wastes that are flushed down toilets and poured down drains. After collecting in sewer drains, raw sewage is sent through a treatment plant, where it undergoes a cleaning process that removes solid waste. The solid waste is called *sludge,* as shown in **Figure 4.** In many areas, people dump sludge into the ocean several kilometers offshore, intending for it to settle and stay on the ocean floor. Unfortunately, currents can stir the sludge up and move it closer to shore. This sludge can pollute beaches and kill marine life. Many countries have banned sludge dumping, but it continues to occur in many areas of the world.

Oil Spills

Because oil is in such high demand across the world, large tankers must transport billions of barrels of it across the oceans. If not handled properly, these transports can turn disastrous and cause oil spills. **Figure 5** shows some of the major oil spills that have occurred off the coast of North America.

Figure 5 *This map shows some of the major oil spills that have occurred off the coast of North America in the last 30 years.*

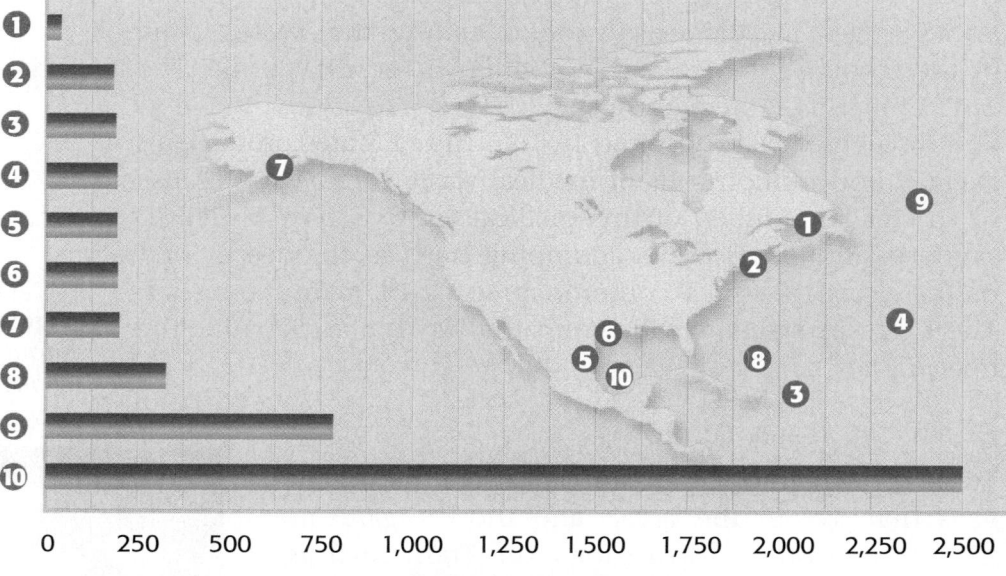

Barrels spilled (in thousands)

❶ *Kurdistan* Gulf of St. Lawrence, Canada, 1979

❷ *Argo Merchant* Nantucket, MA, 1976

❸ Storage Tank Benuelan, Puerto Rico, 1978

❹ *Athenian Venture* Atlantic Ocean, 1988

❺ Unnamed Tanker Tuxpan, Mexico, 1996

❻ *Burmah Agate* Galveston Bay, TX, 1979

❼ *Exxon Valdez* Prince William Sound, AK, 1989

❽ *Epic Colocotronis* Caribbean Sea, 1975

❾ *Odyssey* North Atlantic Ocean, 1988

❿ Exploratory Well Bay of Campeche, 1979

Effects of Oil Spills

One of the oil spills shown on the map in **Figure 5** occurred in Prince William Sound, Alaska, in 1989. The supertanker *Exxon Valdez* struck a reef and spilled more than 260,000 barrels of crude oil along the shorelines of Alaska. The amount of spilled oil is roughly equivalent to 125 olympic-sized swimming pools.

Although some animals were saved, such as the bird in **Figure 6,** many plants and animals died as a result of the spill. Alaskans who made their living from fishing lost their businesses. The Exxon Oil Company spent $2.1 billion to try to clean up the mess. But Alaska's wildlife and economy will continue to suffer for decades.

While oil spills can harm plants, animals, and people, they are responsible for only about 5% of oil pollution in the oceans. Most of the oil that pollutes the oceans is caused by nonpoint-source pollution on land from cities and towns.

Figure 6 *Many oil-covered animals were rescued and cleaned after the* Exxon Valdez *spill.*

Preventing Oil Spills

Today, many oil companies are using new technology to safeguard against oil spills. Tankers are now being built with two hulls instead of one. The inner hull prevents oil from spilling into the ocean if the outer hull of the ship is damaged. **Figure 7** shows the design of a double-hulled tanker.

✓ Reading Check How can two hulls on an oil tanker help prevent an oil spill?

Figure 7 *If the outer hull of a double-hulled tanker is punctured, the oil will still be contained within the inner hull.*

Saving Our Ocean Resources

Although humans have done much to harm the ocean's resources, we have also begun to do more to save them. From international treaties to volunteer cleanups, efforts to conserve the ocean's resources are making an impact around the world.

Nations Take Notice

When ocean pollution reached an all-time high, many countries recognized the need to work together to solve the problem. In 1989, a treaty was passed by 64 countries that prohibits the dumping of certain metals, plastics, oil, and radioactive wastes into the ocean. Even though many other international agreements and laws restricting ocean pollution have been made, waste dumping and oil spills still occur. Therefore, waste continues to wash ashore, as shown in **Figure 8.** Enforcing pollution-preventing laws at all times is often difficult.

Citizens Taking Charge

Citizens of many countries have demanded that their governments do more to solve the growing problem of ocean pollution. Because of public outcry, the United States now spends more than $130 million each year to protect the oceans and beaches. United States citizens have also begun to take the matter into their own hands. In the early 1980s, citizens began organizing beach cleanups. One of the largest cleanups is the semiannual Adopt-a-Beach program, shown in **Figure 8,** which originated with the Texas Coastal Cleanup campaign. Millions of tons of trash have been gathered from the beaches, and people are being educated about the hazards of ocean dumping.

Figure 8 *Making an effort to pick up trash on a beach can help make the beach safer for plants, animals, and people.*

Action in the United States

The United States, like many other countries, has taken additional measures to control local pollution. For example, in 1972, Congress passed the Clean Water Act, which put the Environmental Protection Agency in charge of issuing permits for any dumping of trash into the ocean. Later that year, a stricter law—the U.S. Marine Protection, Research, and Sanctuaries Act—was passed. This act prohibits the dumping of any material that would affect human health or welfare, the marine environment or ecosystems, or businesses that depend on the ocean.

✔ **Reading Check** What is the U.S. Marine Protection, Research, and Sanctuaries Act?

SECTION Review

Summary

- The two main types of ocean pollution are nonpoint-source pollution and point-source pollution.

- Types of nonpoint-source pollution include oil and gasoline from cars, trucks, and watercraft, as well as the use of pesticides, herbicides, and fertilizers.

- Types of point-source ocean pollution include trash dumping, sludge dumping, and oil spills.

- Efforts to save ocean resources include international treaties and volunteer cleanups.

Using Key Terms

1. Use the following terms in the same sentence: *point-source pollution* and *nonpoint-source pollution*.

Understanding Key Ideas

2. Which of the following is an example of nonpoint-source pollution?
   a. a leak from an oil tanker
   b. a trash barge
   c. an unlined landfill
   d. water discharged by industries

3. List three types of ocean pollution. How can each of these types be prevented or minimized?

4. Which part of raw sewage is a type of ocean pollution?

Math Skills

5. Only 3% of Earth's water is drinkable. What portion of Earth's water is not drinkable?

6. A ship spilled 750,000 barrels of oil when it accidentally struck a reef. The oil company was able to recover 65% of the oil spilled. How many barrels of oil were not recovered?

Critical Thinking

7. **Identifying Relationships** List and describe three measures that governments have taken to control ocean pollution.

8. **Evaluating Data** What were two effects of the *Exxon Valdez* oil spill? Describe two ways in which oil spills can be prevented.

9. **Applying Concepts** List two examples of nonpoint-source pollution that occur in your area. Explain why they are nonpoint-source pollution.

10. **Predicting Consequences** How can trash dumping and sludge dumping affect food chains in the ocean?

SCILINKS.

NSTA
Developed and maintained by the National Science Teachers Association

For a variety of links related to this chapter, go to www.scilinks.org

Topic: Ocean Pollution
SciLinks code: HSM1063

Model-Making Lab

OBJECTIVES

Model a method of mapping the ocean floor.

Construct a map of an ocean-floor model.

MATERIALS

- clay, modeling (1 lb)
- pencil, unsharpened (8 of equal length)
- ruler, metric
- scissors
- shoe box with lid

SAFETY

Probing the Depths

In the 1870s, the crew of the ship the HMS *Challenger* used a wire and a weight to discover and map some of the deepest places in the world's oceans. The crew members tied a wire to a weight and dropped the weight overboard. When the weight reached the bottom of the ocean, they hauled the weight back up to the surface and measured the length of the wet wire. In this way, they were eventually able to map the ocean floor. In this activity, you will model this method of mapping by making a map of an ocean-floor model.

Procedure

1. Use the clay to make a model ocean floor in the shoe box. The model ocean floor should have some mountains and valleys.

2. Cut eight holes in a line along the center of the lid. The holes should be just big enough for a pencil to slide through. Place the lid on the box.

3. Exchange boxes with another student or group of students. Do not look into the box.

4. Copy the table shown on the facing page onto a piece of paper. Also, copy the graph shown on the facing page.

5. Measure the length of the probe (pencil) in centimeters. Record the length in your data table.

6. Gently insert the probe into the first hole position in the box until the probe touches the model ocean floor. Do not push the probe down. Pushing the probe down could affect your reading.

7. Make sure that the probe is straight up and down, and measure the length of probe showing above the lid. Record your data in the data table.

8. Use the formula below to calculate the depth in centimeters.

$$\text{length of probe} - \text{length of probe showing (cm)} = \text{depth (cm)}$$

Chapter 13 Exploring the Oceans

Ocean Depth Table				
Hole position	Length of probe	Length of probe showing (cm)	Depth (cm)	Depth (m) scale of 1cm = 200m
1				
2				
3				
4				
5				
6				
7				
8				

DO NOT WRITE IN BOOK

9 To better represent real ocean depths, use the scale 1 cm = 200 m to convert the depth in centimeters to depth in meters. Add the data to your table.

10 Plot the depth in meters for hole position 1 on your graph.

11 Repeat steps 6–10 for the other hole positions.

12 After plotting the data for the eight hole positions, connect the plotted points with a smooth curve.

13 Put a pencil in each of the holes in the shoe box. Compare the rise and fall of the eight pencils with the shape of your graph.

Analyze the Results

1 **Describing Events** How deep was the deepest point of your ocean-floor model? How deep was the shallowest point of your ocean-floor model?

2 **Explaining Events** Did your graph resemble the ocean-floor model, as shown by the pencils in step 13? If not, why not?

Draw Conclusions

3 **Applying Conclusions** Why is measuring the real ocean floor difficult? Explain your answer.

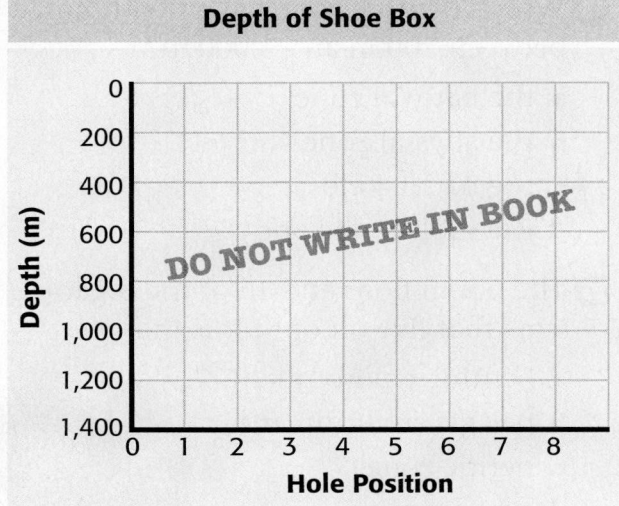

Depth of Shoe Box

Depth (m): 0, 200, 400, 600, 800, 1,000, 1,200, 1,400

DO NOT WRITE IN BOOK

Hole Position: 0 1 2 3 4 5 6 7 8

Chapter Review

USING KEY TERMS

Complete each of the following sentences by choosing the correct term from the word bank.

continental shelf
abyssal plain
salinity
nonpoint-source pollution
continental slope
desalination
benthic environment
point-source pollution

1 The region of the ocean floor that is closest to the shoreline is the ___.

2 ___ is the process of removing salt from sea water.

3 ___ is a measure of the amount of dissolved salts in a liquid.

4 The ___ is the broad, flat part of the deep-ocean basin.

5 The region near the bottom of a pond, lake, or ocean is called the ___.

6 Pollution that comes from many sources rather than a single specific source is called ___.

UNDERSTANDING KEY IDEAS

Multiple Choice

7 The largest ocean is the
 a. Indian Ocean.
 b. Pacific Ocean.
 c. Atlantic Ocean.
 d. Arctic Ocean.

8 One of the most abundant elements in the ocean is
 a. potassium.
 b. calcium.
 c. chlorine.
 d. magnesium.

9 Which of the following affects the ocean's salinity?
 a. fresh water added by rivers
 b. currents
 c. evaporation
 d. All of the above

10 Most precipitation falls
 a. on land.
 b. into lakes and rivers.
 c. into the ocean.
 d. in rain forests.

11 Which of the following is a non-renewable resource in the ocean?
 a. fish
 b. tidal energy
 c. oil
 d. All of the above

12 Which benthic zone has a depth range between 200 m and 4,000 m?
 a. the bathyal zone
 b. the abyssal zone
 c. the hadal zone
 d. the sublittoral zone

13 The ocean floor and all of the organisms that live on or in it is the
 a. benthic environment.
 b. pelagic environment.
 c. neritic zone.
 d. oceanic zone.

Short Answer

⓮ Why does coastal water in areas that have hotter, drier climates typically have a higher salinity than coastal water in cooler, more humid areas does?

⓯ Describe two technologies used for studying the ocean floor.

⓰ Identify the two major regions of the ocean floor, and describe how the continental shelf, the continental slope, and the continental rise are related.

⓱ In your own words, write a definition for each of the following terms: *plankton, nekton,* and *benthos*. Give two examples of each.

⓲ List two living resources and two non-living resources that are harvested from the ocean.

CRITICAL THINKING

⓳ **Concept Mapping** Use the following terms to create a concept map: *water cycle, evaporation, condensation, precipitation, atmosphere,* and *oceans.*

⓴ **Making Inferences** What benefit other than being able to obtain fresh water from salt water comes from desalination?

㉑ **Making Comparisons** Explain the difference between a bathymetric profile and a seismic reading.

㉒ **Analyzing Ideas** In your own words, define *nonpoint-source pollution* and *point-source pollution.* Give an example of each. What is being done to control ocean pollution?

INTERPRETING GRAPHICS

The graph below shows the ecological zones of the ocean. Use the graph below to answer the questions that follow.

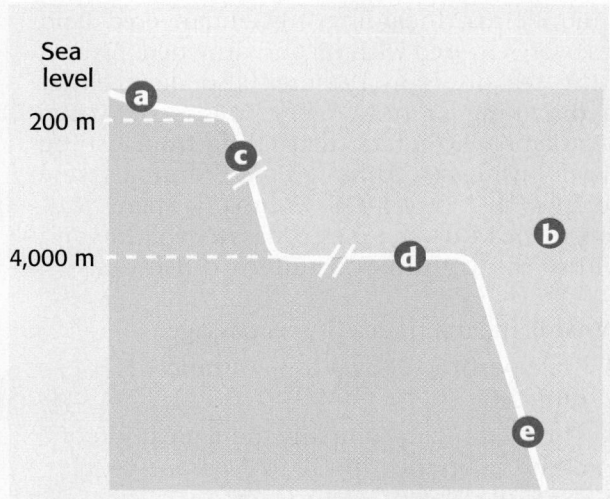

㉓ At which point would you most likely find an anglerfish?

㉔ At which point would you most likely find tube worms?

㉕ Which ecological zone is shown at point c? Which depth zone is shown at point c?

㉖ Name an organism that you might find at point e.

Standardized Test Preparation

Read each of the passages below. Then, answer the questions that follow each passage.

Passage 1 Because oil is in such high demand across the world, large tankers must transport billions of barrels of it across the oceans. If not handled properly, these transports can quickly turn disastrous. In 1989, the supertanker *Exxon Valdez* struck a reef and spilled more than 260,000 barrels of crude oil. The effect of this accident on wildlife was catastrophic. Within the first few weeks of the *Exxon Valdez* oil spill, more than half a million birds, including 109 endangered bald eagles, were covered with oil and drowned. Almost half the sea otters in the area also died, either from drowning or from being poisoned by the oil. Alaskans who made their living from fishing lost their businesses. Although many animals were saved and the Exxon Oil Company spent $2.1 billion to clean up the mess, Alaska's wildlife and economy will continue to suffer for decades.

1. What is the main idea of this passage?
   A Transporting oil over long distances is difficult.
   B The Exxon Oil Company did a great job of cleaning up the oil spill in Alaska.
   C Oil spills such as the *Exxon Valdez* spill can create huge problems.
   D Alaska's economy will suffer because so much oil was lost.

2. In the passage, which of the following problems was said to be a result of the *Exxon Valdez* oil spill?
   F The beach became too slippery to walk on.
   G Many people in Alaska had no oil for their cars.
   H Exxon had to build a new tanker.
   I Many Alaskan fishers lost their businesses.

Passage 2 Whales, dolphins, and porpoises are mammals that belong to the order Cetacea (suh TAY shuh). Cetaceans live throughout the global ocean. They have fishlike bodies and fore-limbs called *flippers*. Cetaceans lack hind limbs but have broad, flat tails that help them swim through the water. Cetaceans breathe through blowholes located on the top of the head. They are completely hairless except for a few bristles on their snout. A thick layer of blubber below the skin helps insulate cetaceans against cold temperatures. Cetaceans are divided into two groups: toothed whales and baleen whales. Toothed whales include sperm whales, beluga whales, narwhals, killer whales, dolphins, and porpoises. Baleen whales, such as blue whales, lack teeth. They filter food from the water by using a meshlike net of baleen that hangs from the roof of their mouth.

1. How are organisms that make up the order Cetacea divided?
   A They are divided into cetaceans that have hair and cetaceans that do not have hair.
   B They are divided into cetaceans that have flippers and cetaceans that do not have flippers.
   C They are divided into cetaceans that have blowholes and cetaceans that do not have blowholes.
   D They are divided into cetaceans that have teeth and cetaceans that do not have teeth.

2. Which of the following statements lists characteristics of all cetaceans?
   F Cetaceans have fur and claws and live in rivers.
   G Cetaceans have flippers and bristles on the snout and live in oceans.
   H Cetaceans have blowholes and flippers and live in lakes.
   I Cetaceans have fur, bristles on the snout, and flippers.

Use the image of the ocean floor below to answer the questions that follow.

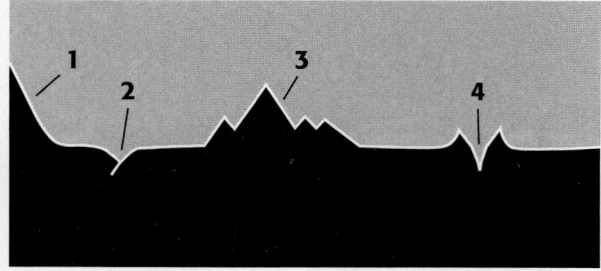

1. At which point are two tectonic plates separating?

A 1

B 2

C 3

D 4

2. Which point shows an ocean trench?

F 1

G 2

H 3

I 4

3. Which feature might eventually become a volcanic island?

A 1

B 2

C 3

D 4

4. Which features are part of the deep-ocean basin?

F 2, 3, and 4

G 1, 2, and 3

H 1, 3, and 4

I 1, 2, and 4

5. Which feature is part of the continental margin?

A 1

B 2

C 3

D 4

Read each question below, and choose the best answer.

1. Imagine that you are in the kelp-farming business and your kelp grows 33 cm per day. You begin harvesting when your plants are 50 cm tall. During the first 7 days of harvest, you cut 10 cm off the top of your kelp plants each day. How tall will your kelp plants be after the seventh day of harvesting?

A 80 cm

B 130 cm

C 210 cm

D 211 cm

2. A sample of ocean water contains 36 g of dissolved solids per 1,000 g of water. So, how many grams of dissolved solids will be in 4 kg of ocean water?

F 36,000 g

G 360 g

H 250 g

I 144 g

3. If the average depth of the Pacific Ocean is 4,250 m and the average depth of the Atlantic Ocean is 4,000 m, what is the average depth of the two oceans?

A 4,250 m

B 4,150 m

C 4,125 m

D 4,000 m

4. *Alvin,* a minisub, starts at −300 m, then rises 20 m, then drops 150 m, and finally reaches the ocean floor by dropping another 218 m. At what depth is *Alvin* when it reaches the ocean floor?

F −648 m

G −88 m

H 88 m

I 648 m

5. The speed of sound in water is 1,500 m/s. How far will sound travel in water in 1 min?

A 25 m

B 1,500 m

C 9,000 m

D 90,000 m

Science in Action

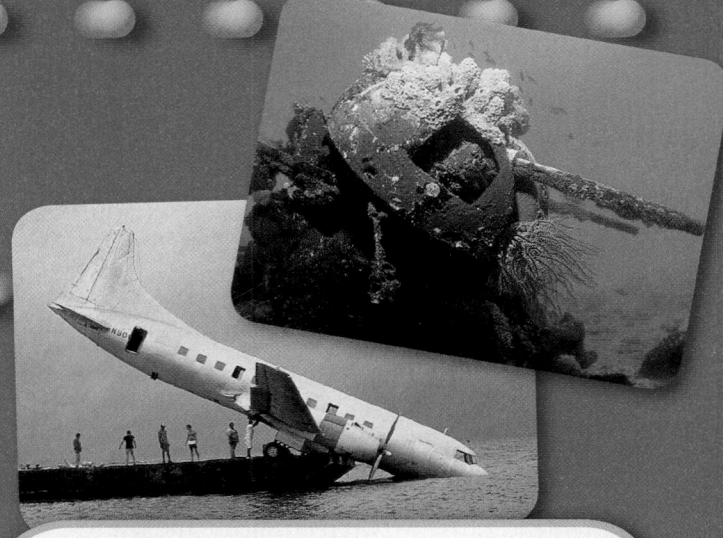

Scientific Discoveries

In Search of the Giant Squid

You might think that giant squids exist only in science fiction novels. You aren't alone, because many people have never seen a giant squid or do not know that giant squids exist. Scientists have not been able to study giant squids in the ocean. They have been able to study only dead or dying squids that have washed ashore or that have been trapped in fishing nets. As the largest of all invertebrates, giant squids range from 8 to 25 m long and have a mass of as much as 2,000 kg. Giant squids are very similar to smaller squids. But a giant squid's body parts are much larger. For example, a giant squid's eye may be as large as a volleyball! Because of the size of giant squids, you may think that they don't have any enemies in the ocean, but they do. They are usually eaten by sperm whales that can weigh 20 tons!

Math ACTIVITY

A giant squid that washed ashore has a mass of 900 kg. A deep-sea squid that washed ashore has a mass that is 93% smaller than the mass of the giant squid. What is the mass in kilograms of the deep-sea squid?

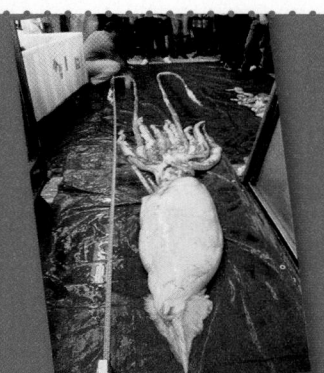

Science, Technology, and Society

Creating Artificial Reefs

If you found a sunken ship, would you look for hidden treasure? Treasure is not the only thing that sunken ships are known for. Hundreds of years ago, people found that the fishing is often good over a sunken ship. The fishing is good because many marine organisms, such as seaweed, corals, and oysters, live only where they can attach to a hard surface in clear water. They attract other organisms to the sunken ship and eventually form a reef community. Thus, in recent years, many human communities have created artificial reefs by sinking objects such as warships, barges, concrete, airplanes, and school buses in the ocean. Like natural reefs, artificial reefs provide a home for organisms and protect organisms from predators.

Social Studies ACTIVITY

WRITING SKILL Research how some artificial reefs are created off the coast of some states in the United States. Write a report that describes some of the objects used to create artificial reefs. In your report also include what countries other than the United States create artificial reefs and what are the benefits and disadvantages of creating artificial reefs.

Jacques Cousteau

Ocean Explorer Jacques Cousteau was born in France in 1910. Cousteau performed his first underwater diving mission at age 10 and became very fascinated with the possibilities of seeing and breathing underwater. As a result, in 1943, Cousteau and Emile Gagnan developed the first aqualung, a self-contained breathing system for underwater exploration. Using the aqualung and other underwater equipment that he developed, Cousteau began making underwater films. In 1950, Cousteau transformed the *Calypso*, a retired minesweeper boat, into an oceanographic vessel and laboratory. For the next 40 years, Cousteau sailed with the *Calypso* around the world to explore and film the world's oceans. Cousteau produced more than 115 films, many of which have won awards.

Jacques Cousteau opened the eyes of countless people to the sea. During his long life, Cousteau explored Earth's oceans and documented the amazing variety of life that they contain. He was an environmentalist, inventor, and teacher who inspired millions with his joy and wonder of the ocean. Cousteau was an outspoken defender of the environment. He campaigned vigorously to protect the oceans and environment. Cousteau died in 1997 at age 87. Before his death, he dedicated the *Calypso II,* a new research vessel, to the children of the world.

Language Arts ACTIVITY

WRITING SKILL Ocean pollution and overfishing are subjects of intense debate. Think about these issues, and discuss them with your classmates. Take notes on what you discuss with your classmates. Then, write an essay in which you try to convince readers of your point of view.

Cousteau sailed his ship, the Calypso, around the world exploring and filming the world's oceans.

To learn more about these Science in Action topics, visit go.hrw.com and type in the keyword **HZ5OCEF.**

Current Science

Check out Current Science® articles related to this chapter by visiting go.hrw.com. Just type in the keyword HZ5CS13.

The Movement of Ocean Water

About the PHOTO

No, this isn't a traffic jam or the result of careless navigation. Hurricane Hugo is to blame for this major boat pile up. When Hurricane Hugo hit South Carolina's coast in 1989, the hurricane's strong winds created large ocean waves. These ocean waves carried these boats right onto the shore.

PRE-READING ACTIVITY

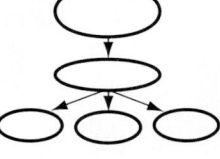

Graphic Organizer

Concept Map Before you read the chapter, create the graphic organizer entitled "Concept Map" described in the **Study Skills** section of the Appendix. As you read the chapter, fill in the concept map with details about each type of ocean water movement.

START-UP ACTIVITY

When Whirls Collide

Some ocean currents flow in a clockwise direction, while other ocean currents flow in a counterclockwise direction. Sometimes these currents collide. In this activity, you and your lab partner will demonstrate how two currents flowing in opposite directions affect one another.

Procedure

1. Fill a large **tub** with **water** 5 cm deep.

2. Add **10 drops of red food coloring** to the water at one end of the tub.

3. Add **10 drops of blue food coloring** to the water at the other end of the tub.

4. Using a **pencil,** quickly stir the water at one end of the tub in a clockwise direction while your partner stirs the water at the other end in a counterclockwise direction. Stir both ends for 5 s.

5. Draw what you see happening in the tub immediately after you stop stirring. (Both ends should be swirling.)

Analysis

1. How did the blue water and the red water interact?

2. How does this activity relate to how ocean currents interact?

Currents

Imagine that you are stranded on a desert island. You stuff a distress message into a bottle and throw it into the ocean. Is there any way to predict where your bottle may land?

Actually, there is a way to predict where the bottle will end up. Ocean water contains streamlike movements of water called **ocean currents.** Currents are influenced by a number of factors, including weather, the Earth's rotation, and the position of the continents. With knowledge of ocean currents, people are able to predict where objects in the open ocean will be carried.

One Way to Explore Currents

In the 1940s, a Norwegian explorer named Thor Heyerdahl tried to answer questions about human migration across the ocean. Heyerdahl theorized that the inhabitants of Polynesia originally sailed from Peru on rafts powered only by the wind and ocean currents. In 1947, Heyerdahl and a crew of five people set sail from Peru on a raft, which is shown in **Figure 1.**

On the 97th day of their expedition, Heyerdahl and his crew landed on an island in Polynesia. Currents had carried the raft westward more than 6,000 km across the South Pacific. This landing supported Heyerdahl's theory that ocean currents carried the ancient Peruvians across the Pacific to Polynesia.

✓ Reading Check What was Heyerdahl's theory, and how did he prove it? (*See the Appendix for answers to Reading Checks.*)

ocean current a movement of ocean water that follows a regular pattern

Figure 1 *The handcrafted Kon-Tiki was made mainly from materials that would have been available to ancient Peruvians.*

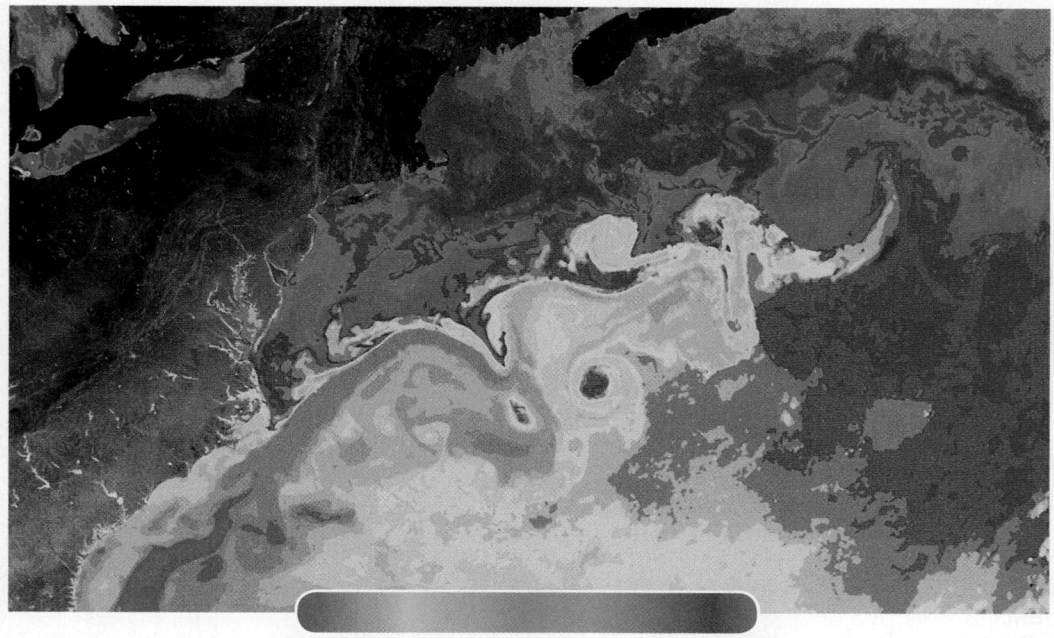

Figure 2 *This infrared satellite image shows the Gulf Stream current moving warm water from lower latitudes to higher latitudes.*

Warm   Cool

Surface Currents

Horizontal, streamlike movements of water that occur at or near the surface of the ocean are called **surface currents.** Surface currents can reach depths of several hundred meters and lengths of several thousand kilometers and can travel across oceans. The Gulf Stream, shown in **Figure 2,** is one of the longest surface currents—it transports 25 times more water than all the rivers in the world.

Surface currents are controlled by three factors: global winds, the Coriolis effect, and continental deflections. These three factors keep surface currents flowing in distinct patterns around the Earth.

Global Winds

Have you ever blown gently on a cup of hot chocolate? You may have noticed ripples moving across the surface, as in **Figure 3.** These ripples are caused by a tiny surface current created by your breath. In much the same way that you create ripples, winds that blow across the Earth's surface create surface currents in the ocean.

Different winds cause currents to flow in different directions. Near the equator, the winds blow ocean water east to west, but closer to the poles, ocean water is blown west to east. Merchant ships often use these currents to travel more quickly back and forth across the oceans.

surface current a horizontal movement of ocean water that is caused by wind and that occurs at or near the ocean's surface

Figure 3 *Winds form surface currents in the ocean, much like blowing on a cup of hot chocolate forms ripples.*

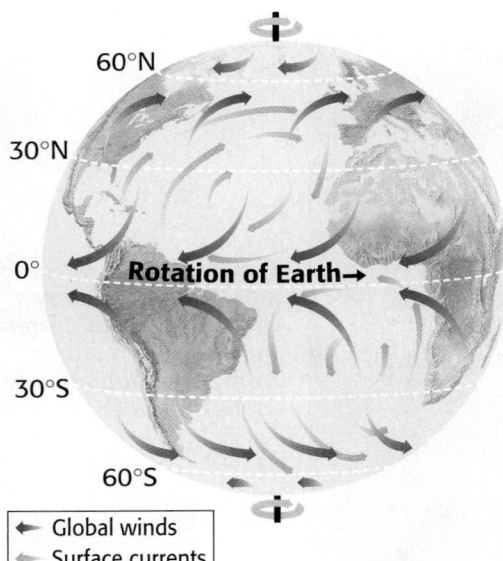

← Global winds
← Surface currents

Figure 4 *The rotation of the Earth causes surface currents (yellow arrows) and global winds (purple arrows) to curve as they move across the Earth's surface.*

Coriolis effect the apparent curving of the path of a moving object from an otherwise straight path due to the Earth's rotation

The Coriolis Effect

The Earth's rotation causes wind and surface currents to move in curved paths rather than in straight lines. The apparent curving of moving objects from a straight path due to the Earth's rotation is called the **Coriolis effect.** To understand the Coriolis effect, imagine trying to roll a ball straight across a turning merry-go-round. Because the merry-go-round is spinning, the path of the ball will curve before it reaches the other side. **Figure 4** shows how the Coriolis effect causes surface currents in the Northern Hemisphere to turn clockwise, and surface currents in the Southern Hemisphere to turn counterclockwise.

✓ *Reading Check* What causes currents to move in curved paths instead of straight lines?

Continental Deflections

If the Earth's surface were covered only with water, surface currents would travel freely across the globe in a very uniform pattern. However, you know that water does not cover the entire surface of the Earth. Continents rise above sea level over roughly one-third of the Earth's surface. When surface currents meet continents, the currents *deflect,* or change direction. Notice in **Figure 5** how the Brazil Current deflects southward as it meets the east coast of South America.

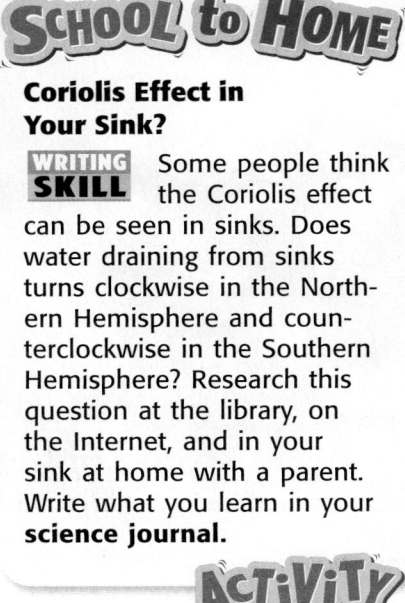

Coriolis Effect in Your Sink?

WRITING SKILL Some people think the Coriolis effect can be seen in sinks. Does water draining from sinks turns clockwise in the Northern Hemisphere and counterclockwise in the Southern Hemisphere? Research this question at the library, on the Internet, and in your sink at home with a parent. Write what you learn in your **science journal.**

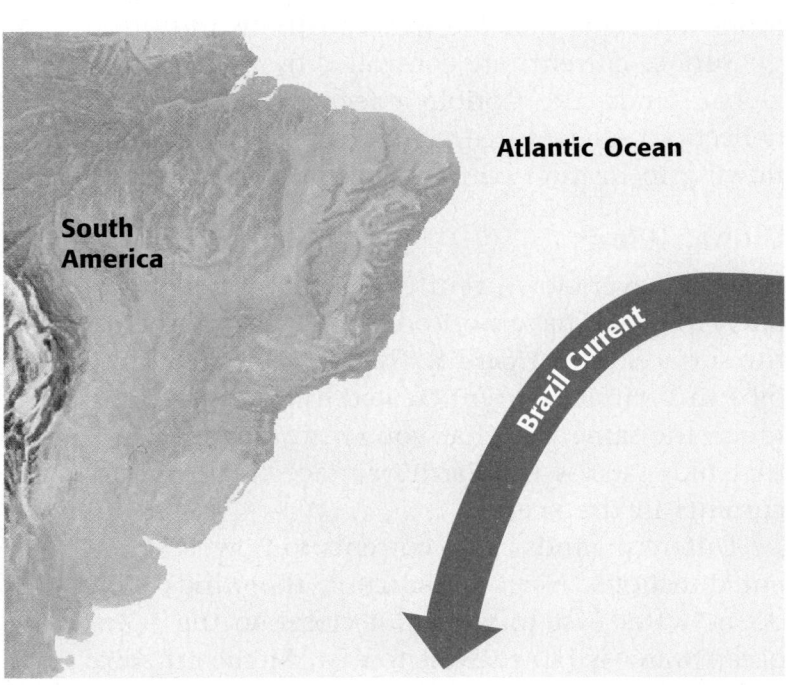

Figure 5 *If South America were not in the way, the Brazil Current would probably flow farther west.*

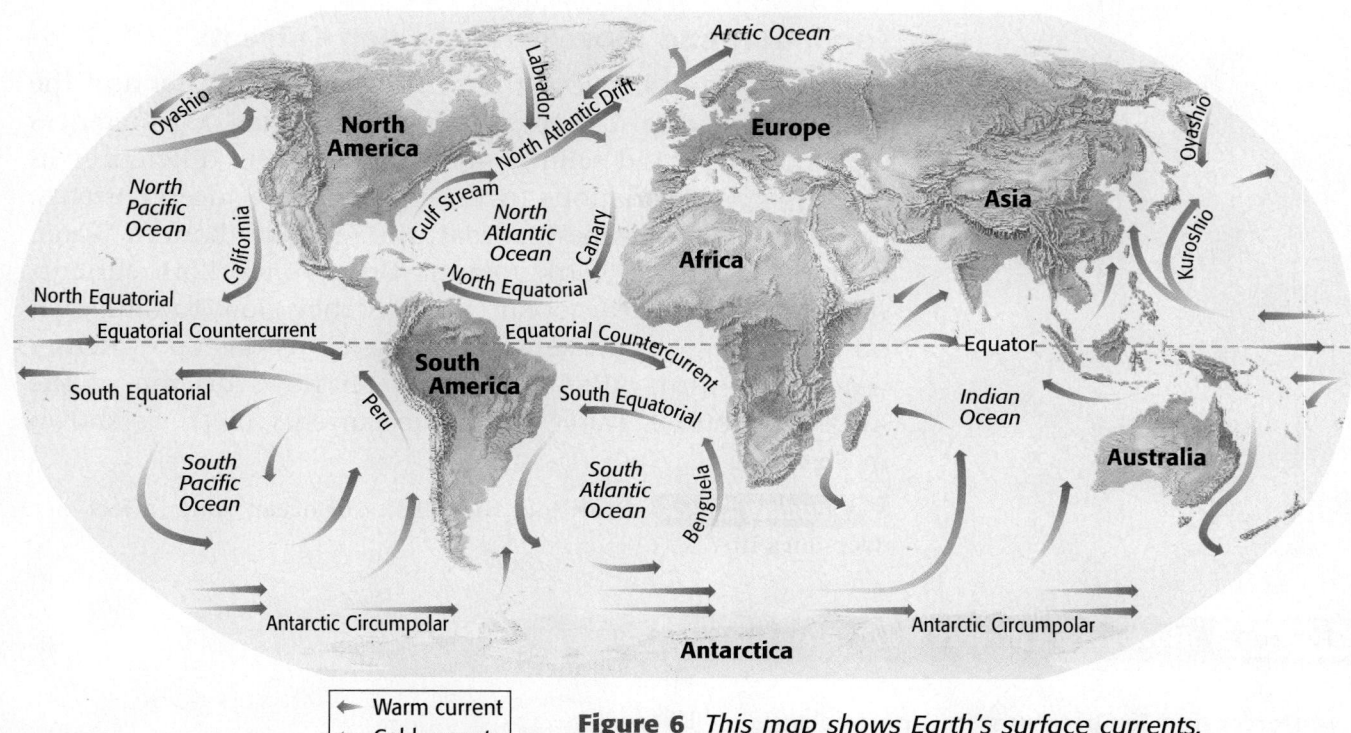

Figure 6 *This map shows Earth's surface currents. Warm-water currents are shown as red arrows, and cold-water currents are shown as blue arrows.*

Taking Temperatures

All three factors—global winds, the Coriolis effect, and continental deflections—work together to form a pattern of surface currents on Earth. But currents are also affected by the temperature of the water in which they form. Warm-water currents begin near the equator and carry warm water to other parts of the ocean. Cold-water currents begin closer to the poles and carry cool water to other parts of the ocean. As you can see on the map in **Figure 6,** all the oceans are connected and both warm-water and cold-water currents travel from one ocean to another.

Reading Check What three factors form a pattern of surface currents on Earth?

Deep Currents

Streamlike movements of ocean water located far below the surface are called **deep currents.** Unlike surface currents, deep currents are not directly controlled by wind. Instead, deep currents form in parts of the ocean where water density increases. *Density* is the amount of matter in a given space, or volume. The density of ocean water is affected by temperature and *salinity*—a measure of the amount of dissolved salts or solids in a liquid. Both decreasing the temperature of ocean water and increasing the water's salinity increase the water's density.

deep current a streamlike movement of ocean water far below the surface

CONNECTION TO Physics

Convection Currents While winds are often responsible for ocean currents, the sun is the initial energy source of the winds and currents. Because the sun heats the Earth more in some places than in others, convection currents are formed. These currents transfer thermal energy. Which ocean currents do you think carry more thermal energy, currents located near the equator or currents located near the poles?

Formation and Movement of Deep Currents

The relationship between the density of ocean water and the formation of deep currents is shown in **Figure 7.** Differences in temperature and salinity—and the resulting differences in density—cause variations in the movement of deep currents. For example, the deepest current, the Antarctic Bottom Water, is denser than the North Atlantic Deep Water. Both currents spread out across the ocean floor as they flow toward each other. Because less-dense water always flows on top of denser water, the North Atlantic Deep Water flows on top of the Antarctic Bottom Water when the currents meet, as shown in **Figure 8.**

✓ **Reading Check** How does the density of ocean water affect deep currents?

Figure 7 **How Deep Currents Form**

Decreasing Temperature In Earth's polar regions, cold air chills the water molecules at the ocean's surface, which causes the molecules to slow down and move closer together. This reaction causes the water's volume to decrease. Thus, the water becomes denser. The dense water sinks and eventually travels toward the equator as a deep current along the ocean floor.

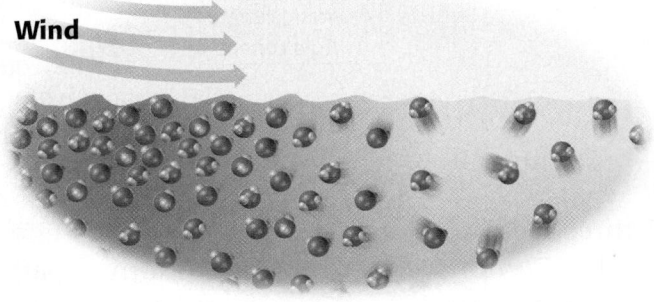

Increasing Salinity Through Freezing If the ocean water freezes at the surface, ice will float on top of the water because ice is less dense than liquid water. The dissolved solids are squeezed out of the ice and enter the liquid water below the ice. This process increases the salinity of the water. As a result of the increased salinity, the water's density increases.

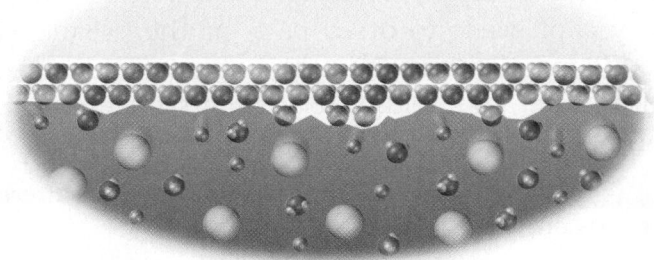

Increasing Salinity Through Evaporation Another way salinity increases is through evaporation of surface water, which removes water but leaves solids behind. This process is especially common in warm climates. Increasing salinity through freezing or evaporation causes water to become denser, to sink to the ocean floor, and to form a deep current.

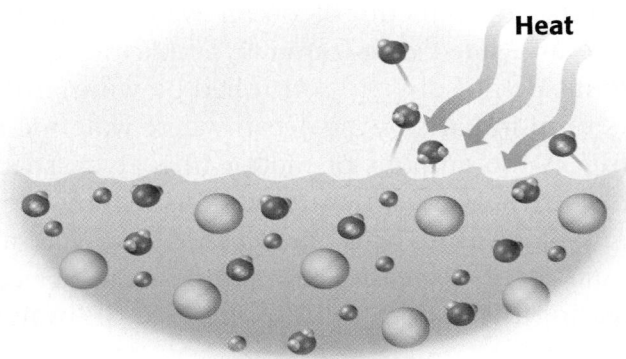

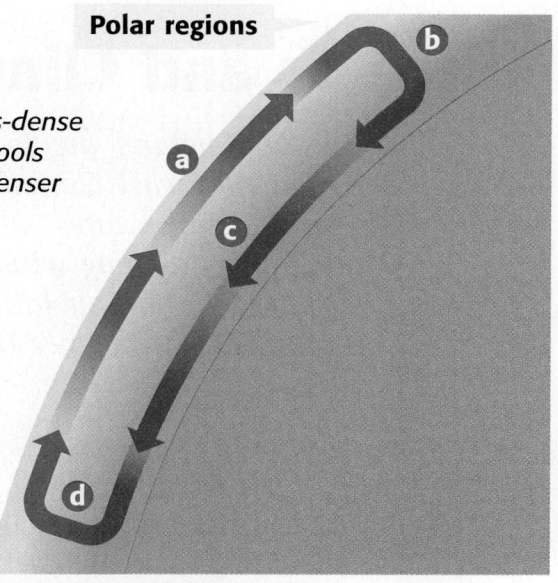

Polar regions

Figure 8 *The warmer, less-dense water in surface currents cools and becomes the colder, denser water in deep currents.*

a Surface currents carry the warmer, less-dense water from other ocean regions to polar regions.

b Warm water from surface currents replaces colder, denser water that sinks to the ocean floor.

c Deep currents carry colder, denser water along the ocean floor from polar regions to other ocean regions.

d Water from deep currents rises to replace water leaving surface currents.

SECTION Review

Summary

- Surface currents are streamlike movements of water at or near the surface of the ocean.

- Surface currents are controlled by three factors: global winds, the Coriolis effect, and continental deflections.

- Deep currents are streamlike movements of ocean water located far below the surface.

- Deep currents form where the density of ocean water increases. Water density depends on temperature and salinity.

Using Key Terms

The statements below are false. For each statement, replace the underlined word to make a true statement.

1. <u>Deep currents</u> are directly controlled by wind.

2. An increase in density in parts of the ocean can cause <u>surface currents</u> to form.

Understanding Key Ideas

3. Surface currents
  a. are formed by wind.
  b. are streamlike movements of water.
  c. can travel across entire oceans.
  d. All of the above

4. List three factors that control surface currents.

5. How does a continent affect the movement of a surface current?

6. Explain how temperature and salinity affect the formation of deep currents.

Math Skills

7. The Gulf Stream flows along the North Carolina coast at 90 million cubic meters per second and at 40 million cubic meters per second when it turns eastward. How much faster is the Gulf Stream flowing along the coast than when it turns eastward?

Critical Thinking

8. Evaluating Conclusions If there were no land on Earth's surface, what would the pattern of surface currents look like? Explain your answer.

9. Making Comparisons Compare the factors that contribute to the formation of surface currents and deep currents.

SCI**L**INKS®

NSTA
Developed and maintained by the National Science Teachers Association

For a variety of links related to this chapter, go to www.scilinks.org

Topic: Ocean Currents
SciLinks code: HSM1061

Currents and Climate

The Scilly Isles in England are located as far north as Newfoundland in northeast Canada. But the Scilly Isles experience warm temperatures almost all year long, while Newfoundland has long winters of frost and snow. How can two places at similar latitudes have completely different climates? This difference in climate is caused by surface currents.

Surface Currents and Climate

Surface currents greatly affect the climate in many parts of the world. Some surface currents warm or cool coastal areas year-round. Other surface currents sometimes change their circulation pattern. Changes in circulation patterns cause changes in atmosphere that affect the climate in many parts of the world.

Warm-Water Currents and Climate

Although surface currents are generally much warmer than deep currents, the temperatures of surface currents do vary. Surface currents are classified as warm-water currents or cold-water currents. Warm-water currents create warmer climates in coastal areas that would otherwise be much cooler. **Figure 1** shows how the Gulf Stream carries warm water from the Tropics to the North Atlantic Ocean. The Gulf Stream flows to the British Isles and creates a relatively mild climate for land at such high latitude. The Gulf Stream is the same current that makes the climate of the Scilly Isles very different from the climate of Newfoundland.

Figure 1 How Warm-Water Currents Affect Climate

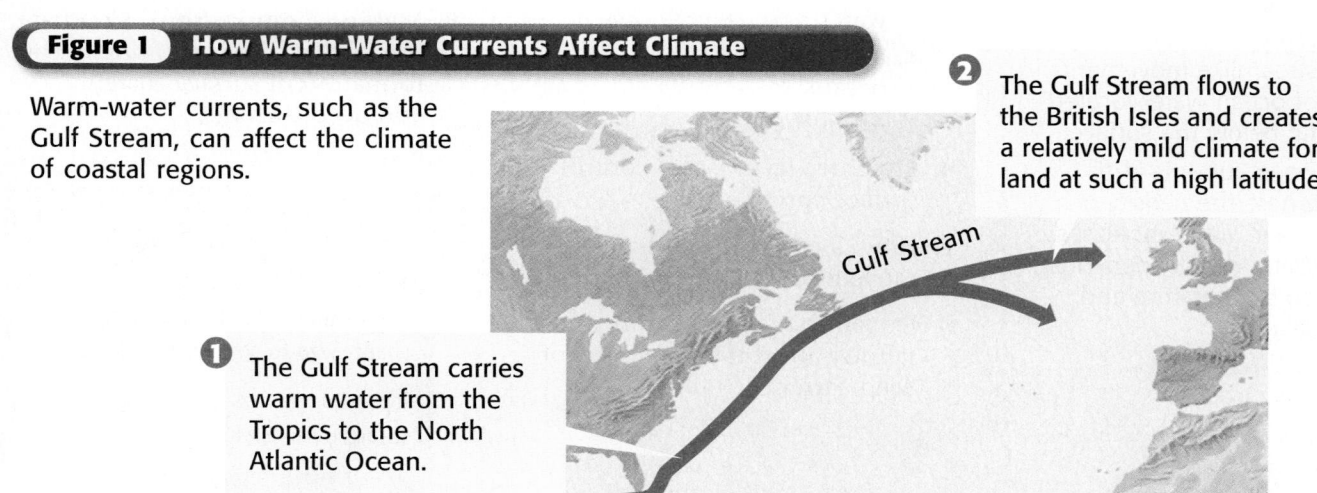

Warm-water currents, such as the Gulf Stream, can affect the climate of coastal regions.

❷ The Gulf Stream flows to the British Isles and creates a relatively mild climate for land at such a high latitude.

Gulf Stream

❶ The Gulf Stream carries warm water from the Tropics to the North Atlantic Ocean.

Figure 2 How Cold-Water Currents Affect Climate

Cold-water currents, such as the California Current, can affect the climate of coastal regions.

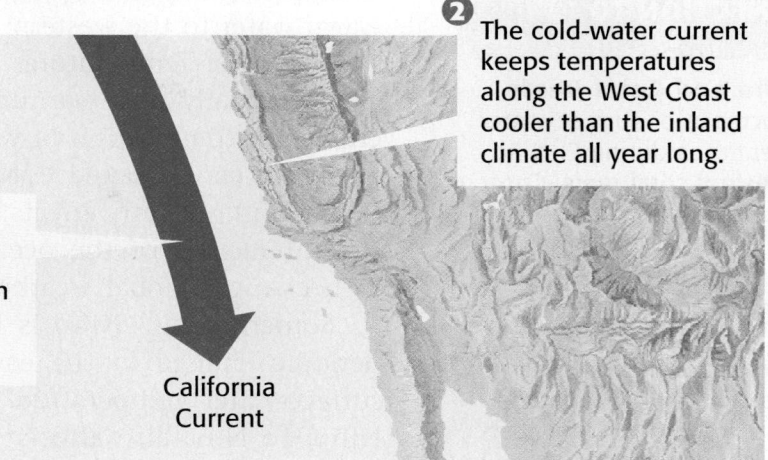

① Cold water from the northern Pacific Ocean is carried south to Mexico by the California Current.

② The cold-water current keeps temperatures along the West Coast cooler than the inland climate all year long.

California Current

Cold-Water Currents and Climate

Cold-water currents also affect the climate of the land near where they flow. **Figure 2** shows how the California Current carries cold water from the North Pacific Ocean southward to Mexico. The cold-water California Current keeps the climate along the West Coast cooler than the inland climate year-round.

✓ Reading Check How do cold-water currents affect coastal regions?

Upwelling

When local wind patterns blow along the northwest coast of South America, they cause local surface currents to move away from the shore. This warm water is then replaced by deep, cold water. This movement causes upwelling to occur in the eastern Pacific. **Upwelling** is a process in which cold, nutrient-rich water from the deep ocean rises to the surface and replaces warm surface water, as shown in **Figure 3.** The nutrients from the deep ocean are made up of elements and chemicals, such as iron and nitrate. When these chemicals are brought to the sunny surface, they help tiny plants grow through the process of photosynthesis.

The process of upwelling is extremely important to organisms. The nutrients that are brought to the surface of the ocean support the growth of phytoplankton and zooplankton. These tiny plants and animals support other organisms such as fish and seabirds.

upwelling the movement of deep, cold, and nutrient-rich water to the surface

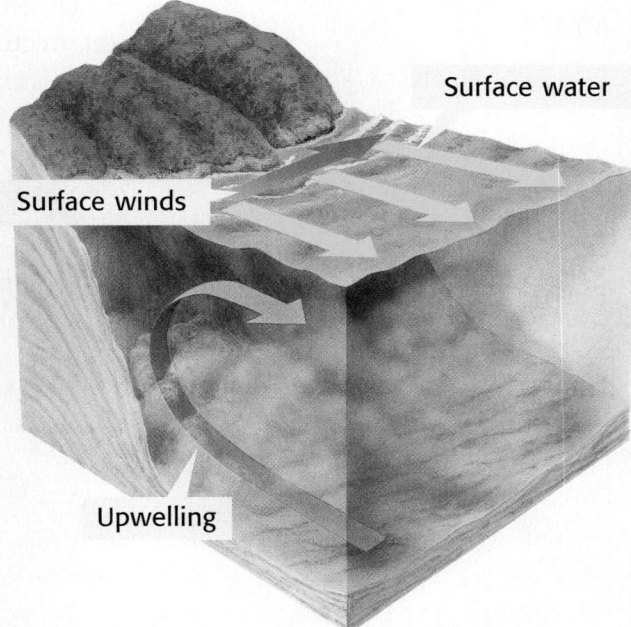

Surface water

Surface winds

Upwelling

Figure 3 *Upwelling causes cold, nutrient-rich water from the deep ocean to rise to the surface.*

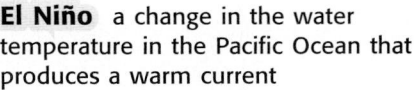

El Niño a change in the water temperature in the Pacific Ocean that produces a warm current

La Niña a change in the eastern Pacific Ocean in which the surface water temperature becomes unusually cool

El Niño

Every 2 to 12 years, the South Pacific trade winds move less warm water to the western Pacific than they usually do. Thus, surface-water temperatures along the coast of South America rise. Gradually, this warming spreads westward. This periodic change in the location of warm and cool surface waters in the Pacific Ocean is called **El Niño.** El Niño can last for a year or longer and not only affects the surface waters but also changes the interaction of the ocean and the atmosphere, which in turn changes global weather patterns.

Sometimes, El Niño is followed by La Niña. **La Niña** is a periodic change in the eastern Pacific Ocean in which the surface-water temperature becomes unusually cool. Like El Niño, La Niña also affects weather patterns.

Effects of El Niño

El Niño alters weather patterns enough to cause disasters. These disasters include flash floods and mudslides in areas of the world that usually receive little rain, such as the southern half of the United States and Peru. **Figure 4** shows homes in Southern California destroyed by a mudslide caused by El Niño. While some regions flood, regions that usually get a lot of rain may experience *droughts,* an unusually long period during which rainfall is below average. During El Niño, severe droughts can occur in Indonesia and Australia. Periods of severe drought can lead to crop failure.

During El Niño, the upwelling of nutrient-rich water does not occur off the coast of South America, which affects the organisms that depend on the nutrients for food.

Figure 4 *This damage in Southern California was the result of excessive rain caused by El Niño in 1997.*

Studying and Predicting El Niño

Because El Niño occurs every 2 to 12 years, studying and predicting it can be difficult. However, it is important for scientists to learn as much as possible about El Niño because of its effects on organisms and land.

One way scientists collect data to predict an El Niño is through a network of buoys operated by the National Oceanic and Atmospheric Administration (NOAA). The buoys, some of which are anchored to the ocean floor, are located along the Earth's equator. The buoys record data about surface temperature, air temperature, currents, and winds. The buoys transmit some of the data on a daily basis to NOAA through a satellite in space.

When the buoys report that the South Pacific trade winds are not as strong as they usually are or that the surface temperatures of the tropical oceans have risen, scientists can predict that an El Niño is likely to occur.

✓ Reading Check Why is it important to study El Niño? Describe one way scientists study El Niño.

INTERNET ACTIVITY

For another activity related to this chapter, go to **go.hrw.com** and type in the keyword **HZ5H20W**.

SECTION Review

Summary

- Surface currents affect the climate of the land near which they flow.
- Warm-water currents bring warmer climates to coastal regions.
- Cold-water currents bring cooler climates to coastal regions.
- During El Niño, warm and cool surface waters change locations.
- El Niño can cause floods, mudslides, and drought.

Using Key Terms

1. Use each of the following terms in a separate sentence: *upwelling, El Niño,* and *La Niña.*

Understanding Key Ideas

2. The Gulf Stream carries warm water to the North Atlantic Ocean, which contributes to
   a. a harsh winter in the British Isles.
   b. a cold-water surface current that flows to the British Isles.
   c. a mild climate for the British Isles.
   d. a warm-water surface current that flows along the coast of California.

3. Why might the climate in Scotland be relatively mild even though the country is located at a high latitude?

4. Name two disasters caused by El Niño.

Math Skills

5. A fisher usually catches 540 kg of anchovies off the coast of Peru. During El Niño, the fisher caught 85% less fish. How many kilograms of fish did the fisher catch during El Niño?

Critical Thinking

6. **Applying Concepts** Many marine organisms depend on upwelling to bring nutrients to the surface. How might El Niño affect a fisher's way of life?

SCiLINKS

NSTA
Developed and maintained by the National Science Teachers Association

For a variety of links related to this chapter, go to www.scilinks.org

Topic: El Niño
SciLinks code: HSM0468

Waves

Have you ever seen a surfer riding waves? Did you ever wonder where the waves come from? And why are some waves big, while others are small?

We all know what ocean waves look like. Even if you've never been to the seashore, you've most likely seen waves on TV. But how do waves form and move? Waves are affected by a number of different factors. They can be formed by something as simple as wind or by something as violent as an earthquake. Ocean waves can travel through water slowly or incredibly quickly. Read on to discover the many forces that affect the formation and movement of ocean waves.

Anatomy of a Wave

Waves are made up of two main parts—crests and troughs. A *crest* is the highest point of a wave. A *trough* is the lowest point of a wave. Imagine a roller coaster designed with many rises and dips. The top of a rise on a roller-coaster track is similar to the crest of a wave, and the bottom of a dip in the track resembles the trough of a wave. The distance between two adjacent wave crests or wave troughs is a *wavelength*. The vertical distance between the crest and trough of a wave is called the *wave height*. **Figure 1** shows the parts of a wave.

Reading Check What is the lowest point of a wave called? *(See the Appendix for answers to Reading Checks.)*

READING WARM-UP

Objectives

- Identify the parts of a wave.
- Explain how the parts of a wave relate to wave movement.
- Describe how ocean waves form and move.
- Classify types of waves.

Terms to Learn

undertow
longshore current
whitecap
swell
tsunami
storm surge

READING STRATEGY

Prediction Guide Before reading this section, write the title of each heading in this section. Next, write what you think you will learn under each heading.

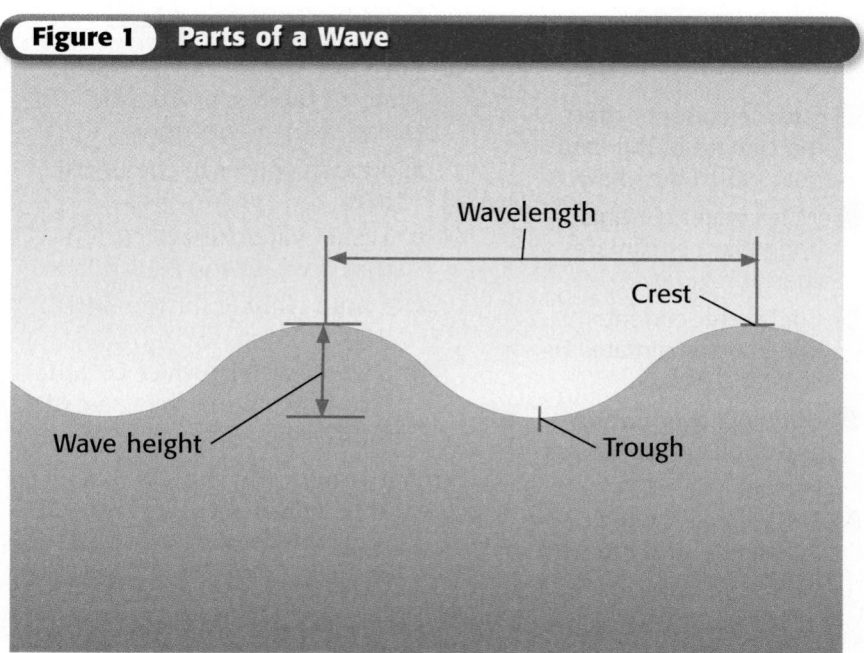

Figure 1 **Parts of a Wave**

Wavelength

Crest

Wave height

Trough

Wave Formation and Movement

If you have watched ocean waves before, you may have noticed that water appears to move across the ocean's surface. However, this movement is only an illusion. Most waves form as wind blows across the water's surface and transfers energy to the water. As the energy moves through the water, so do the waves. But the water itself stays behind, rising and falling in circular movements. Notice in **Figure 2** that the floating bottle remains in the same spot as the waves travel from left to right. This circular motion gets smaller as the water depth increases, because wave energy decreases as the water depth increases. Wave energy reaches only a certain depth. Below that depth, the water is not affected by wave energy.

Specifics of Wave Movement

Waves not only come in different sizes but also travel at different speeds. To calculate wave speed, scientists must know the wavelength and the wave period. *Wave period* is the time between the passage of two wave crests (or troughs) at a fixed point, as shown in **Figure 3.** Dividing wavelength by wave period gives you wave speed, as shown below.

$$\frac{\text{wavelength (m)}}{\text{wave period (s)}} = \text{wave speed (m/s)}$$

For any given wavelength, an increase in the wave period will decrease the wave speed and a decrease in the wave period will increase the wave speed.

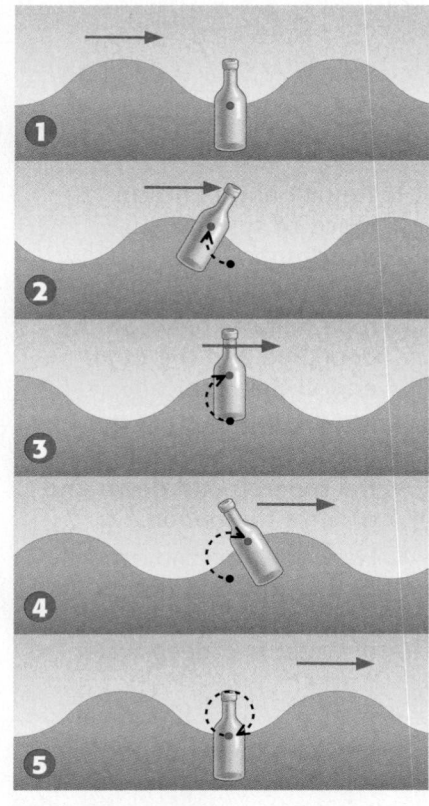

Figure 2 *Like the bottle in this figure, water remains in the same place as waves travel through it.*

Figure 3 Determining Wave Period

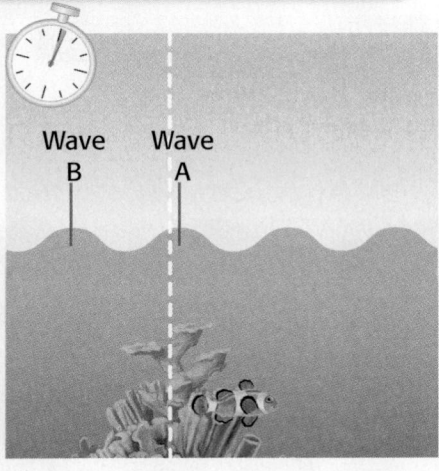

① Notice that the waves are moving from left to right.

② The clock begins running as Wave A passes the reef's peak.

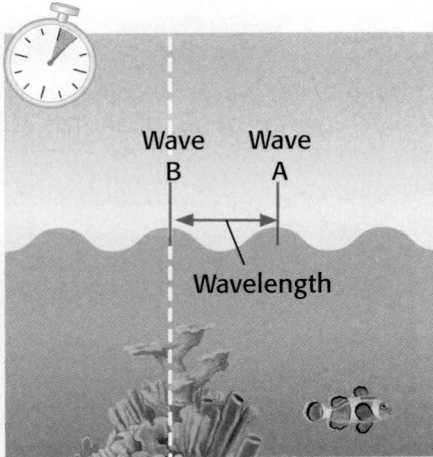

③ The clock stops as Wave B passes the reef's peak. The time shown on the clock (5 s) represents the wave period.

Types of Waves

As you learned earlier in this section, wind forms most ocean waves. Waves can also form by other mechanisms. Underwater earthquakes and landslides as well as impacts by cosmic bodies can form different types of waves. Most waves move in one way regardless of how they are formed. Depending on their size and the angle at which they hit the shore, waves can generate a variety of near-shore events, some of which can be dangerous to humans.

Deep-Water Waves and Shallow-Water Waves

Have you ever wondered why waves increase in height as they approach the shore? The answer has to do with the depth of the water. *Deep-water waves* are waves that move in water deeper than one-half their wavelength. When the waves reach water shallower than one-half their wavelength, they begin to interact with the ocean floor. These waves are called *shallow-water waves*. **Figure 4** shows how deep-water waves become shallow-water waves as they move toward the shore.

As deep-water waves become shallow-water waves, the water particles slow down and build up. This change forces more water between wave crests and increases wave height. Gravity eventually pulls the high wave crests down, which causes them to crash into the ocean floor as *breakers*. The area where waves first begin to tumble downward, or break, is called the *breaker zone*. Waves continue to break as they move from the breaker zone to the shore. The area between the breaker zone and the shore is called the *surf*.

Reading Check How do deep-water waves become shallow-water waves?

Figure 4 **Deep-Water and Shallow-Water Waves**

Deep-water waves become shallow-water waves when they reach depths of less than half of their wavelength.

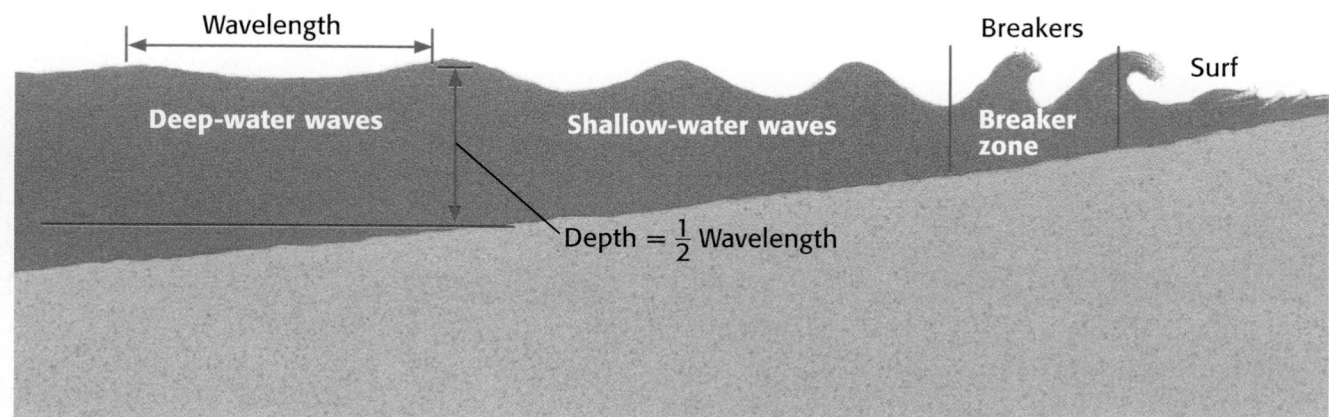

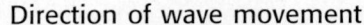

Figure 5 Formation of an Undertow

Head-on waves create an undertow.

Direction of wave movement

Undertow

Shore Currents

When waves crash on the beach head-on, the water they moved through flows back to the ocean underneath new incoming waves. This movement of water, which carries sand, rock particles, and plankton away from the shore, is called an **undertow. Figure 5** illustrates the back-and-forth movement of water at the shore.

Longshore Currents

When waves hit the shore at an angle, they cause water to move along the shore in a current called a **longshore current,** which is shown in **Figure 6.** Longshore currents transport most of the sediment in beach environments. This movement of sand and other sediment both tears down and builds up the coastline. Unfortunately, longshore currents also carry and spread trash and other types of ocean pollution along the shore.

undertow a subsurface current that is near shore and that pulls objects out to sea

longshore current a water current that travels near and parallel to the shoreline

Figure 6 *Longshore currents form where waves approach beaches at an angle.*

Longshore current

Figure 7 *Whitecaps (left) break in the open ocean, while swells, (right), roll gently in the open ocean.*

whitecap the bubbles in the crest of a breaking wave

swell one of a group of long ocean waves that have steadily traveled a great distance from their point of generation

tsunami a giant ocean wave that forms after a volcanic eruption, submarine earthquake, or landslide

Open-Ocean Waves

Sometimes waves called *whitecaps* form in the open ocean. **Whitecaps** are white, foaming waves with very steep crests that break in the open ocean before the waves get close to the shore. These waves usually form during stormy weather, and they are usually short-lived. Winds that are far away from the shore form waves called *swells*. **Swells** are rolling waves that move steadily across the ocean. Swells have longer wavelengths than whitecaps and can travel for thousands of kilometers. **Figure 7** shows how whitecaps and swells differ.

Tsunamis

Professional surfers often travel to Hawaii to catch some of the highest waves in the world. But even the best surfers would not be able to handle a tsunami. **Tsunamis** are waves that form when a large volume of ocean water is suddenly moved up or down. This movement can be caused by underwater earthquakes, volcanic eruptions, landslides, underwater explosions, or the impact of a meteorite or comet. The majority of tsunamis occur in the Pacific Ocean because of the large number of earthquakes in that region. **Figure 8** shows how an earthquake can generate a tsunami.

Figure 8 *An upward shift in the ocean floor creates an earthquake. The energy released by the earthquake pushes a large volume of water upward, which creates a series of tsunamis.*

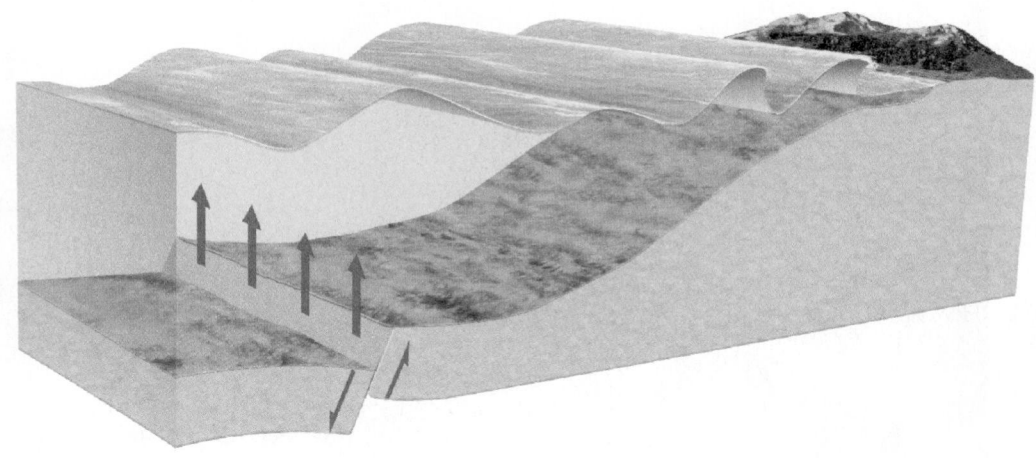

Storm Surges

A local rise in sea level near the shore that is caused by strong winds from a storm, such as a hurricane, is called a **storm surge.** Winds form a storm surge by blowing water into a big pile under the storm. As the storm moves onto shore, so does the giant mass of water beneath it. Storm surges often disappear as quickly as they form, which makes them difficult to study. Storm surges contain a lot of energy and can reach about 8 m in height. Their size and power often make them the most destructive part of hurricanes.

storm surge a local rise in sea level near the shore that is caused by strong winds from a storm, such as those from a hurricane

✓ Reading Check What is a storm surge? Why are storm surges difficult to study?

SECTION Review

Summary

- Waves are made up of two main parts—crests and troughs.
- Waves are usually created by the transfer of the wind's energy across the surface of the ocean.
- Waves travel through water near the water's surface, while the water itself rises and falls in circular movements.
- Wind-generated waves are classified as deep-water or shallow-water waves.
- When waves hit the shore at a certain angle, they can create either an undertow or a longshore current.
- Tsunamis are dangerous waves that can be very destructive to coastal communities.

Using Key Terms

For each pair of terms, explain how the meanings of the terms differ.

1. *whitecap* and *swell*

2. *undertow* and *longshore current*

3. *tsunami* and *storm surge*

Understanding Key Ideas

4. Longshore currents transport sediment
   a. to the open ocean.
   b. along the shore.
   c. only during low tide.
   d. only during high tide.

5. Where do deep-water waves become shallow-water waves?

6. Explain how water moves as waves travel through it.

7. Name five events that can cause a tsunami.

8. Describe the two parts of a wave.

Math Skills

9. If a barrier island that is 1 km wide and 10 km long loses 1.5 m of its width per year to erosion by a longshore current, how long will the island take to lose one-fourth of its width?

Critical Thinking

10. **Analyzing Processes** How would you explain a bottle moving across the water in the same direction that the waves are traveling? Make a drawing of the bottle's movement.

11. **Analyzing Processes** Describe the motion of a wave as it approaches the shore.

12. **Applying Concepts** Explain how energy plays a role in the creation of ocean waves.

13. **Making Comparisons** How does the formation of an undertow differ from the formation of a longshore current? How is sand on the beach affected by each?

SCI LINKS.

NSTA
Developed and maintained by the
National Science Teachers Association

For a variety of links related to this chapter, go to www.scilinks.org

Topic: Ocean Waves
SciLinks code: HSM1066

Tides

If you stand at some ocean shores long enough, you will see the edge of the ocean shrink away from you. Wait longer, and you will see it return to its original place on the shore. Would you believe the moon causes this movement?

You have learned how winds and earthquakes can move ocean water. But less obvious forces move ocean water in regular patterns called tides. **Tides** are daily changes in the level of ocean water. Tides are influenced by the sun and the moon, as shown in **Figure 1,** and they occur in a variety of cycles.

The Lure of the Moon

The phases of the moon and their relationship to the tides were first discovered more than 2,000 years ago by a Greek explorer named *Pytheas.* But Pytheas and other early investigators could not explain the relationship. A scientific explanation was not given until 1687, when Sir Isaac Newton's theories on the principle of gravitation were published.

The gravity of the moon pulls on every particle of the Earth. But the pull on liquids is much more noticeable than on solids, because liquids move more easily. Even the liquid in an open soft drink is slightly pulled by the moon's gravity.

Reading Check How does the moon affect Earth's particles? *(See the Appendix for answers to Reading Checks.)*

High Tide and Low Tide

How often tides occur and the difference in tidal levels depend on the position of the moon as it revolves around the Earth. The moon's pull is strongest on the part of the Earth directly facing the moon.

tide the periodic rise and fall of the water level in the oceans and other large bodies of water

Figure 1 *Although gravitational forces from both the sun and moon continuously pull on the Earth, the moon's gravity is the dominant force on Earth's tides.*

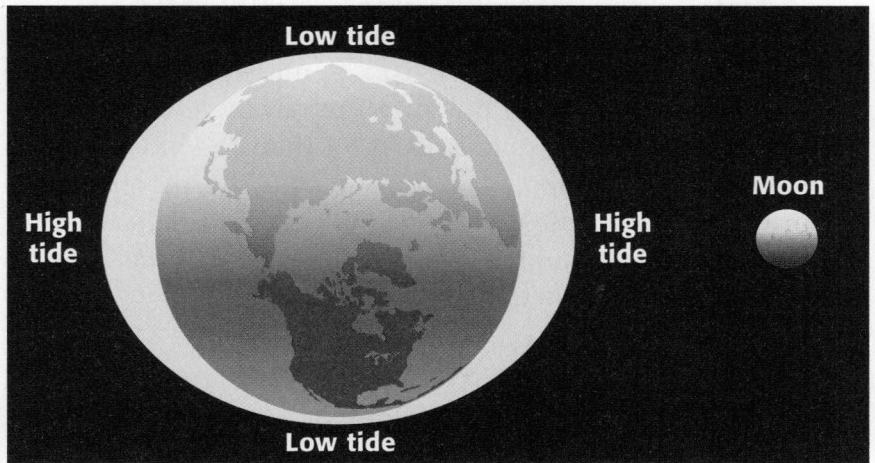

Figure 2 *High tide occurs on the part of Earth that is closest to the moon. At the same time, high tide also occurs on the opposite side of Earth.*

Battle of the Bulge

When part of the ocean is directly facing the moon, the water there bulges toward the moon. At the same time, water on the opposite side of the Earth bulges because of the rotation of the Earth and the motion of the moon around the Earth. These bulges are called *high tides*. Notice in **Figure 2** how the position of the moon causes the water to bulge. Also notice that when high tides occur, water is drawn away from the area between the high tides, which causes *low tides* to form.

Timing the Tides

The rotation of the Earth and the moon's revolution around the Earth determine when tides occur. If the Earth rotated at the same speed that the moon revolves around the Earth, the tides would not alternate between high and low. But the moon revolves around the Earth much more slowly than the Earth rotates. As **Figure 3** shows, a spot on Earth that is facing the moon takes 24 h and 50 m to rotate and face the moon again.

CONNECTION TO Language Arts

WRITING SKILL **Mont-St-Michel Is Sometimes an Island?** Mont-St-Michel is located off the coast of France. Mont-St-Michel experiences extreme tides. The tides are so extreme that during high tide, it is an island and during low tide, it is connected to the mainland. Research the history behind Mont-St-Michel and then write a short story describing what it would be like to live there for a day. Be sure to include a description of Mont-St-Michel at high tide and at low tide.

Figure 3 *Tides occur at different locations on Earth because the Earth rotates more quickly than the moon revolves around the Earth.*

Tuesday, 11:00 AM

Wednesday, 11:50 AM

Tidal Variations

The sun also affects tides. The sun is much larger than the moon, but the sun is also much farther away. As a result, the sun's influence on tides is less powerful than the moon's influence. The combined forces of the sun and the moon on the Earth result in tidal ranges that vary based on the positions of all three bodies. A **tidal range** is the difference between levels of ocean water at high tide and low tide.

√ Reading Check What is a tidal range?

tidal range the difference in levels of ocean water at high tide and low tide

spring tide a tide of increased range that occurs two times a month, at the new and full moons

neap tide a tide of minimum range that occurs during the first and third quarters of the moon

Spring Tides

When the sun, Earth, and moon are aligned, spring tides occur. **Spring tides** are tides with the largest daily tidal range and occur during the new and full moons, or every 14 days. The first time spring tides occur is when the moon is between the sun and Earth. The second time spring tides occur is when the moon and the sun are on opposite sides of the Earth. **Figure 4** shows the positions of the sun, Earth, and moon during spring tides.

Neap Tides

When the sun, Earth, and moon form a 90° angle, neap tides occur. **Neap tides** are tides with the smallest daily tidal range and occur during the first and third quarters of the moon. Neap tides occur halfway between the occurrence of spring tides. When neap tides occur, the gravitational forces on the Earth by the sun and moon work against each other. **Figure 4** shows the positions of the sun, Earth, and moon during neap tides.

Figure 4 **Spring Tides and Neap Tides**

Spring Tides During spring tides, the gravitational forces of the sun and moon pull on the Earth either from the same direction (left) or from opposite directions (right).

Neap Tides During neap tides, the sun and moon are at right angles with respect to the Earth. This arrangement lessens their gravitational effect on the Earth.

Tides and Topography

After a tidal range has been measured, the times that tides occur can be accurately predicted. This information can be useful for people who live near or visit the coast, as shown in **Figure 5.** In some coastal areas that have narrow inlets, movements of water called tidal bores occur. A *tidal bore* is a body of water that rushes up through a narrow bay, estuary, or river channel during the rise of high tide and causes a very sudden tidal rise. Tidal bores occur in coastal areas of China, the British Isles, France, and Canada.

Figure 5 *It's a good thing the people on this beach (left) knew when high tide occurred (right). These photos show the Bay of Fundy, in New Brunswick, Canada. The Bay of Fundy has the greatest tidal range on Earth.*

SECTION
Review

Summary

- Tides are caused by the gravitational forces of the moon and sun on the Earth.

- The moon's gravity is the main force behind the tides.

- The positions of the sun and moon relative to the position of the Earth cause tidal ranges.

- The four different types of tides are: high tides, low tides, spring tides, and neap tides.

Using Key Terms

1. In your own words, write a definition for each of the following terms: *spring tides* and *neap tides*.

Understanding Key Ideas

2. Tides are at their highest during
   a. spring tide.
   b. neap tide.
   c. a tidal bore.
   d. the daytime.

3. Which tides have minimum tidal range? Which tides have maximum tidal range?

4. What causes tidal ranges?

Math Skills

5. If it takes 24 h and 50 min for a spot on Earth that is facing the moon to rotate to face the moon again, how many minutes does it take?

Critical Thinking

6. **Applying Concepts** How many days pass between the minimum and the maximum of the tidal range in any given area? Explain your answer.

7. **Analyzing Processes** Explain how the position of the moon relates to the occurrence of high tides and low tides.

SCiLINKS.

NSTA
Developed and maintained by the National Science Teachers Association

For a variety of links related to this chapter, go to www.scilinks.org

Topic: Tides
SciLinks code: HSM1525

Using Scientific Methods
Skills Practice Lab

OBJECTIVES

Demonstrate the effects of temperature and salinity on the density of water.

Describe why some parts of the ocean turn over, while others do not.

MATERIALS

- beakers, 400 mL (5)
- blue and red food coloring
- bucket of ice
- gloves, heat-resistant
- hot plate
- plastic wrap, 4 pieces, approximately 30 cm × 20 cm
- salt
- spoon
- tap water
- watch or clock

SAFETY

Up from the Depths

Every year, the water in certain parts of the ocean "turns over." That is, the water at the bottom rises to the top and the water at the top falls to the bottom. This yearly change brings fresh nutrients from the bottom of the ocean to the fish living near the surface. However, the water in some parts of the ocean never turns over. By completing this activity, you will find out why not.

Keep in mind that some parts of the ocean are warmer at the bottom, and some are warmer at the top. And sometimes the saltiest water is at the bottom and sometimes not. As you complete this activity, you will investigate how these factors help determine whether the water will turn over.

Ask a Question

1 Why do some parts of the ocean turn over and not others?

Form a Hypothesis

2 Write a hypothesis that is a possible answer to the question above. Explain your reasoning.

Test the Hypothesis

3 Label the beakers 1 through 5. Fill beakers 1 through 4 with tap water.

4 Add a drop of blue food coloring to the water in beakers 1 and 2, and stir with the spoon.

5 Place beaker 1 in the bucket of ice for 10 min.

6 Add a drop of red food coloring to the water in beakers 3 and 4, and stir with the spoon.

7 Set beaker 3 on a hot plate turned to a low setting for 10 min.

8 Add one spoonful of salt to the water in beaker 4, and stir with the spoon.

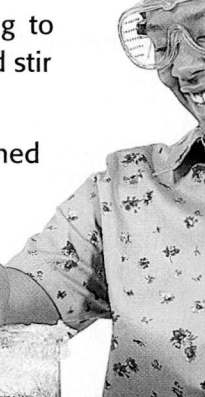

9 While beaker 1 is cooling and beaker 3 is heating, copy the observations table below on a sheet of paper.

Observations Table	
Mixture of water	**Observations**
Warm water placed above cold water	
Cold water placed above warm water	DO NOT WRITE IN BOOK
Salty water placed above fresh water	
Fresh water placed above salty water	

10 Pour half of the water in beaker 1 into beaker 5. Return beaker 1 to the bucket of ice.

11 Tuck a sheet of plastic wrap into beaker 5 so that the plastic rests on the surface of the water and lines the upper half of the beaker.

12 Put on your gloves. Slowly pour half of the water in beaker 3 into the plastic-lined upper half of beaker 5 to form two layers of water. Return beaker 3 to the hot plate, and remove your gloves.

13 Very carefully, pull on one edge of the plastic wrap and remove it so that the warm, red water rests on the cold, blue water.
Caution: The plastic wrap may be warm.

14 Wait about 5 minutes, and then observe the layers in beaker 5. Did one layer remain on top of the other? Was there any mixing or turning over? Record your observations in your observations table.

15 Empty beaker 5, and rinse it with clean tap water.

16 Repeat the procedure used in steps 10–15. This time, pour warm, red water from beaker 3 on the bottom and cold, blue water from beaker 1 on top. (Use gloves when pouring warm water.)

17 Again, repeat the procedure used in steps 10–15. This time, pour blue tap water from beaker 2 on the bottom and red, salty water from beaker 4 on top.

18 Repeat the procedure used in steps 10–15 a third time. This time, pour red, salty water from beaker 4 on the bottom and blue tap water from beaker 2 on top.

Analyze the Results

1 **Analyzing Data** Compare the results of all four trials. Explain why the water turned over in some of the trials but not in all of them.

Draw Conclusions

2 **Evaluating Results** What is the effect of temperature and salinity on the density of water?

3 **Drawing Conclusions** What makes the temperature of ocean water decrease? What could make the salinity of ocean water increase?

4 **Drawing Conclusions** What reasons can you give to explain why some parts of the ocean do not turn over in the spring while some do?

Applying Your Data

Suggest a method for setting up a model that tests the combined effects of temperature and salinity on the density of water. Consider using more than two water samples and dyes.

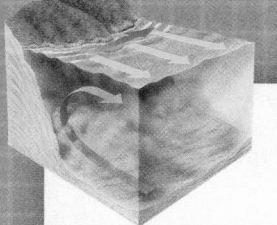

Chapter Review

USING KEY TERMS

For each pair of terms, explain how the meanings of the terms differ.

1 *surface current* and *deep current*

2 *El Niño* and *La Niña*

3 *spring tide* and *neap tide*

4 *tide* and *tidal range*

UNDERSTANDING KEY IDEAS

Multiple Choice

5 Deep currents form when

a. cold air decreases water density.

b. warm air increases water density.

c. the ocean surface freezes and solids from the water underneath are removed.

d. salinity increases.

6 When waves come near the shore,

a. they speed up.

b. they maintain their speed.

c. their wavelength increases.

d. their wave height increases.

7 Whitecaps break

a. in the surf.

b. in the breaker zone.

c. in the open ocean.

d. as their wavelength increases.

8 Tidal range is greatest during

a. spring tide.

b. neap tide.

c. a tidal bore.

d. the daytime.

9 Tides alternate between high and low because the moon revolves around the Earth

a. at the same speed the Earth rotates.

b. at a much faster speed than the Earth rotates.

c. at a much slower speed than the Earth rotates.

d. at different speeds.

10 El Niño can cause

a. droughts to occur in Indonesia and Australia.

b. upwelling to occur off the coast of South America.

c. earthquakes.

d. droughts to occur in the southern half of the United States.

Short Answer

11 Explain the relationship between upwelling and El Niño.

12 Describe the two parts of a wave. Describe how these two parts relate to wavelength and wave height.

13 Compare the relative positions of the Earth, moon, and sun during the spring and neap tides.

14 Explain the difference between the breaker zone and the surf.

15 Describe how warm-water currents affect the climate in the British Isles.

16 Describe the factors that form deep currents.

17 **Concept Mapping** Use the following terms to create a concept map: *wind, deep currents, sun's gravity, types of ocean-water movement, surface currents, tides, increasing water density, waves,* and *moon's gravity*.

18 **Identifying Relationships** Why are tides more noticeable in Earth's oceans than on its land?

19 **Expressing Opinions** Explain why it's important to study El Niño and La Niña.

20 **Applying Concepts** Suppose you and a friend are planning a fishing trip to the ocean. Your friend tells you that the fish bite more in his secret fishing spot during low tide. If low tide occurred at the spot at 7 a.m. today and you are going to fish there in 1 week, at what time will low tide occur in that spot?

21 **Identifying Relationships** Describe how global winds, the Coriolis Effect, and continental deflections form a pattern of surface currents on Earth.

The diagram below shows some of Earth's major surface currents that flow in the Western Hemisphere. Use the diagram to answer the questions that follow.

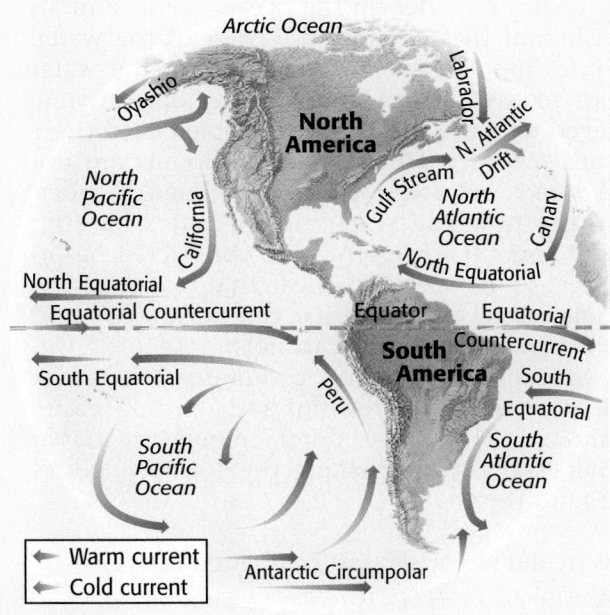

22 List two warm-water currents and two cold-water currents.

23 How do you think the Labrador Current affects the climate of Canada and Greenland?

Standardized Test Preparation

Read each of the passages below. Then, answer the questions that follow each passage.

Passage 1 When certain algae grow rapidly, they clump together on the ocean's surface in an algal bloom that changes the color of the water. Because these algal blooms often turn the water red or reddish brown and tidal conditions were believed to cause the blooms, people called these blooms *red tides*. However, algal blooms are not always red and are not directly related to tides. Scientists now call these algae clusters <u>harmful algal blooms (HABs)</u>. HABs are considered harmful because the species of algae that makes up the blooms produces toxins that can poison fish and shellfish, which in turn can poison people.

Unfortunately, seafood contamination is not noticeable without testing and is not easily eliminated. The toxins don't change the flavor of the seafood, and cooking the seafood doesn't eliminate the toxins.

1. Why did scientists start calling red tides *HABs*?

A The name *HABs* is easier to remember.

B The name *red tides* was not accurate in describing the phenomenon.

C The algal blooms are actually green.

D The term *red tides* did not reflect the danger of the blooms.

2. How can a person tell if seafood has been contaminated by HABs?

F Contaminated seafood has a reddish color.

G HABs change the flavor of the seafood.

H Seafood contaminated by HABs has a strange smell.

I Unfortunately, there is no easy way to tell.

Passage 2 Tsunamis are the most destructive waves in the ocean. Most tsunamis are caused by earthquakes on the ocean floor, but some can be caused by volcanic eruptions and underwater landslides. Tsunamis are sometimes called *tidal waves,* which is <u>misleading</u> because tsunamis have no connection with tides.

Tsunamis commonly have a wave period of about 15 min and a wave speed of about 725 km/h, which is about as fast as a jet airliner. By the time a tsunami reaches the shore, its height may be 30 to 40 m.

In 1960, a tsunami was triggered by an earthquake off the coast of South America. The tsunami was so powerful that it crossed the Pacific Ocean and hit the city of Hilo, on the coast of Hawaii, approximately 10,000 km away. The same tsunami then continued on to strike Japan.

1. The word *misleading* was used in this passage to describe the use of the term *tidal waves* because

A tsunamis are related to tides.

B tsunamis can cause extensive damage to shores.

C tsunamis are related to earthquakes.

D tsunamis are not related to tides.

2. Which of the following statements is a fact from the passage?

F All tsunamis are caused by earthquakes.

G A tsunami can travel as fast as a jet airliner.

H The tsunami of 1960 caused destruction only in Japan.

I Tsunamis are caused by surface currents.

The diagram below shows the possible positions of the moon relative to the Earth and sun during different tidal ranges. Use the diagram below to answer the questions that follow.

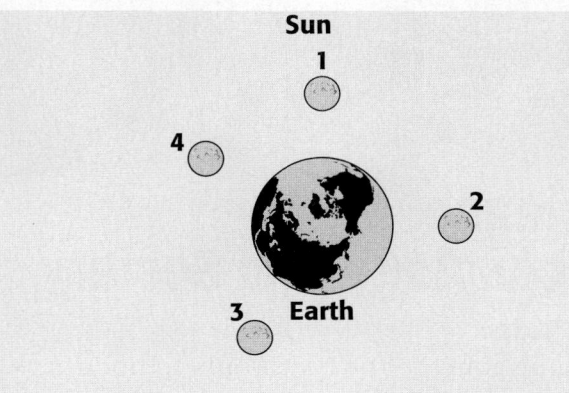

Sun
1
4
2
3 Earth

1. At which position would the moon be during a neap tide?

A 1

B 2

C 3

D 4

2. At which position would the moon be during a spring tide?

F 1

G 2

H 3

I 4

3. The tidal range would be greater when the moon is at position 3 than when the moon is at position 4 because

A position 4 forms a 90° angle with the sun and the Earth.

B position 3 is very near a neap-tide position.

C position 3 is very near a spring-tide position.

D position 4 is very near a spring-tide position.

Read each question below, and choose the best answer.

1. If a wave has a speed of 3 m/s and a wavelength of 12 m, what is its period? Use the following equation to answer the question above:

$$\frac{\text{wavelength (m)}}{\text{wave period (s)}} = \text{wave speed (m/s)}$$

A 36 s

B 4 m

C 24 s

D 4 s

2. Antarctic Bottom Water takes 750 years to move from the Antarctic coast to the equator. If the distance between the equator and the Antarctic coast is about 10,000 km, approximately how many kilometers does the bottom water move each year?

F 13 km

G 200 km

H 75 km

I 1 km

3. A boat is traveling north at 20 km/h against a current that is moving south at 12 km/h. What is the overall speed and direction of the boat?

A 8 km/h north

B 8 km/h south

C 32 km/h north

D 32 km/h south

4. Imagine that you are in a rowboat on the open ocean. You count 2 waves traveling right under your boat in 10 seconds. You estimate the wavelength to be 3 m. What is the wave speed?

F 0.6 m/s

G 6.0 m/s

H 0.3 m/s

I 3.0 m/s

Standardized Test Preparation

Science in Action

Weird Science

Using Toy Ducks to Track Ocean Currents

Accidents can sometimes lead to scientific discovery. For example, on January 10, 1992, 29,000 plastic tub toys spilled overboard when a container ship traveling northwest of Hawaii ran into a storm. In November of that year, those toys began washing up on Alaskan beaches. When oceanographers heard about this, they placed advertisements in newspapers along the Alaskan coast asking people who found the toys to call them. Altogether, hundreds of toys were recovered. Using recovery dates and locations and computer models, oceanographers were able to re-create the toys' drift and figure out which currents carried the toys. As for the remaining toys, currents may carry them to a number of different destinations. Some may travel through the Arctic Ocean and eventually reach Europe!

Math Activity

Between January 10, 1992, and November 16, 1992, some of the toys were carried approximately 3,220 km from the cargo-spill site to the coast of Alaska. Calculate the average distance traveled by these toys per day. (Hint: The year 1992 was a leap year.)

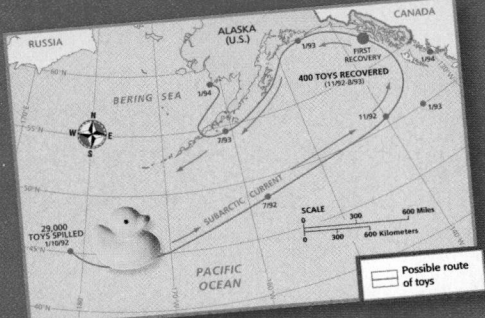

Science, Technology, and Society

Red Tides

Imagine going to the beach only to find that the ocean water has turned red and that a lot of fish are floating belly up. What could cause such damage to the ocean? It may surprise you to find that the answer is single-celled algae. When certain algae grow rapidly, they clump together on the ocean's surface in what are known as algal blooms. These algal blooms have been commonly called *red tides* because the blooms often turn the water red or reddish-brown. The term scientists use for these sudden explosions in algae growth is *harmful algal blooms* (HABs). The blooms are harmful because certain species of algae produce toxins that can poison fish, shellfish, and people who eat poisoned fish or shellfish. Toxic blooms can be carried hundreds of miles on ocean currents. HABs can ride into an area on an ocean current and cause fish to die and people who eat the poisoned fish or shellfish to become ill.

Social Studies Activity

Some scientists think that factors related to human activities, such as agricultural runoff into the ocean, are causing more HABs than occurred in the past. Other scientists disagree. Find out more about this issue, and have a class debate about the roles humans play in creating HABs.

Careers

Cristina Castro

Marine Biologist Have you ever imagined watching whales for a living? Cristina Castro does. Castro works as a marine biologist with the Pacific Whale Foundation in Ecuador. She is studying the migratory patterns of a whale species known as the *humpback whale*. Each year, the humpback whale migrates from feeding grounds in the Antarctic to the warm waters off Ecuador, where the whales breed. Her studies take place largely in the Machalilla National Park. The park is a two-mile stretch of beach that is protected by the government of Ecuador.

In her research, Cristina Castro focuses on the connection between El Niño events and the number of humpback whales in the waters off Ecuador. Castro believes that during an El Niño event, the waters off Ecuador are too hot for the whales. When the whales get hot, they have a difficult time cooling off because they have a thick coat of blubber that provides insulation. So, Castro believes that the whales stay in colder waters during an El Niño event.

Language Arts ACTiViTY

WRITING SKILL Research the humpback whale's migratory route from Antarctica to Ecuador. Write a short story in which you tell of the migration from the point of view of a young whale.

To learn more about these Science in Action topics, visit go.hrw.com and type in the keyword HZ5H2OF.

Current Science

Check out Current Science® articles related to this chapter by visiting go.hrw.com. Just type in the keyword HZ5CS14.

UNIT 6

TIMELINE

Weather and Climate

In this unit, you will learn about Earth's atmosphere, including how it affects conditions on the Earth's surface. The constantly changing weather is always a good topic for conversation, but forecasting the weather is not an easy task. Climate, on the other hand, is much more predictable. This timeline shows some of the events that have occurred as scientists have tried to better understand Earth's atmosphere, weather, and climate.

1281

A sudden typhoon destroys a fleet of Mongolian ships about to reach Japan. This "divine wind," or *kamikaze* in Japanese, saves the country from invasion and conquest.

1778

Carl Scheele concludes that air is mostly made of nitrogen and oxygen.

1838

John James Audubon publishes *The Birds of America.*

1974

Chlorofluorocarbons (CFCs) are recognized as harmful to the ozone layer.

1982

Weather information becomes available 24 hours a day, 7 days a week, on commercial TV.

1655

Saturn's rings are recognized as such. Galileo Galilei had seen them in 1610, but his telescope was not strong enough to show that they were rings.

1718

Gabriel Fahrenheit builds the first mercury thermometer.

1749

Benjamin Franklin explains how updrafts of air are caused by the sun's heating of the local atmosphere.

1920

Serbian scientist Milutin Milankovitch determines that over tens of thousands of years, changes in the Earth's motion through space have profound effects on climate.

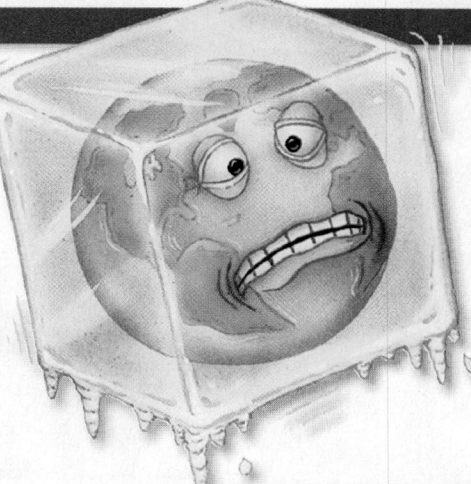

1945

The first atmospheric test of an atomic bomb takes place near Alamogordo, New Mexico.

1985

Scientists discover an ozone hole over Antarctica.

1986

The world's worst nuclear accident takes place at Chernobyl, Ukraine, and spreads radiation through the atmosphere as far as the western United States.

1999

The first nonstop balloon trip around the world is successfully completed when Brian Jones and Bertrand Piccard land in Egypt.

2003

A record 393 tornadoes are observed in the United States during one week in May.

The path of radioactive material released from Chernobyl

The Breitling Orbiter 3 lands in Egypt on March 21, 1999.

The Atmosphere

About the PHOTO

Imagine climbing a mountain and taking only one out of three breaths! As altitude increases, the density of the atmosphere decreases. At the heights shown in this picture, the atmosphere is so thin that it contains only 30% of the amount of oxygen found in the atmosphere at sea level. So, most mountaineers carry part of their atmosphere with them—in the form of oxygen tanks.

PRE-READING ACTIVITY

FOLDNOTES **Booklet** Before you read the chapter, create the FoldNote entitled "Booklet" described in the **Study Skills** section of the Appendix. Label each page of the booklet with a main idea from the chapter. As you read the chapter, write what you learn about each main idea on the appropriate page of the booklet.

START-UP ACTIVITY

Does Air Have Mass?

In this activity, you will compare an inflated balloon with a deflated balloon to find out if air has mass.

Procedure

1. In a **notebook,** answer the following questions: Does air have mass? Will an inflated balloon weigh more than a deflated balloon?

2. Inflate **two large balloons,** and tie the balloons closed. Attach each balloon to opposite ends of a **meterstick** using identical **pushpins.** Balance the meterstick on a **pencil** held by a volunteer. Check that the meterstick is perfectly balanced.

3. Predict what will happen when you pop one balloon. Record your predictions.

4. Put on **safety goggles,** and carefully pop one of the balloons with a **pushpin.**

5. Record your observations.

Analysis

1. Explain your observations. Was your prediction correct?

2. Based on your results, does air have mass? If air has mass, is the atmosphere affected by Earth's gravity? Explain your answers.

Characteristics of the Atmosphere

If you were lost in the desert, you could survive for a few days without food and water. But you wouldn't last more than five minutes without the atmosphere.

The **atmosphere** is a mixture of gases that surrounds Earth. In addition to containing the oxygen you need to breathe, the atmosphere protects you from the sun's damaging rays. The atmosphere is always changing. Every breath you take, every tree that is planted, and every vehicle you ride in affects the atmosphere's composition.

The Composition of the Atmosphere

As you can see in **Figure 1,** the atmosphere is made up mostly of nitrogen gas. The oxygen you breathe makes up a little more than 20% of the atmosphere. In addition to containing nitrogen and oxygen, the atmosphere contains small particles, such as dust, volcanic ash, sea salt, dirt, and smoke. The next time you turn off the lights at night, shine a flashlight, and you will see some of these tiny particles floating in the air.

Water is also found in the atmosphere. Liquid water (water droplets) and solid water (snow and ice crystals) are found in clouds. But most water in the atmosphere exists as an invisible gas called *water vapor*. When atmospheric conditions change, water vapor can change into solid or liquid water, and rain or snow might fall from the sky.

✓ **Reading Check** Describe the three physical states of water in the atmosphere. (*See the Appendix for answers to Reading Checks.*)

READING WARM-UP

Objectives

● Describe the composition of Earth's atmosphere.

● Explain why air pressure changes with altitude.

● Explain how air temperature changes with atmospheric composition.

● Describe the layers of the atmosphere.

Terms to Learn

atmosphere   stratosphere
air pressure   mesosphere
troposphere   thermosphere

READING STRATEGY

Mnemonics As you read this section, create a mnemonic device to help you remember the layers of the Earth's atmosphere.

Figure 1 **Composition of the Atmosphere**

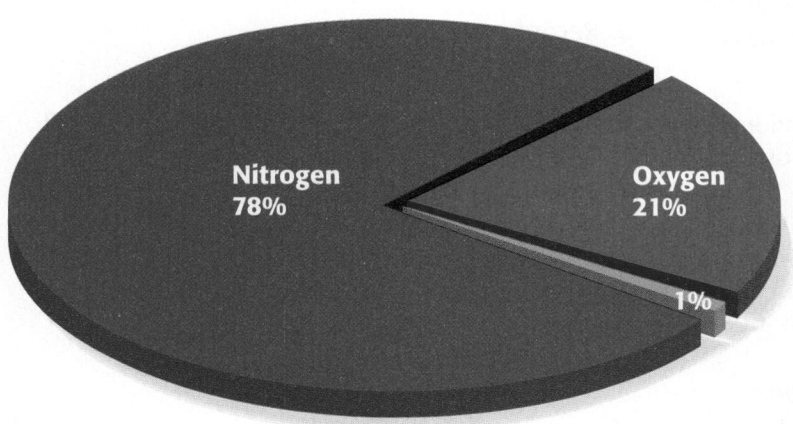

Nitrogen
78%

Oxygen
21%

1%

Nitrogen, the most common atmospheric gas, is released when dead plants and dead animals break down and when volcanoes erupt.

Oxygen, the second most common atmospheric gas, is made by phytoplankton and plants.

The remaining 1% of the atmosphere is made up of argon, carbon dioxide, water vapor, and other gases.

Atmospheric Pressure and Temperature

What would carrying a column of air that is 700 km high feel like? You may be surprised to learn that you carry this load every day. While air is not very heavy, its weight adds up. At sea level, a square inch of surface area is under almost 15 lb of air. Carrying that much air on such a small surface area is like carrying a large bowling ball on the tip of your finger!

As Altitude Increases, Air Pressure Decreases

The atmosphere is held around the Earth by gravity. Gravity pulls gas molecules in the atmosphere toward the Earth's surface, causing air pressure. **Air pressure** is the measure of the force with which air molecules push on a surface. Air pressure is strongest at the Earth's surface because more air is above you. As you move farther away from the Earth's surface, fewer gas molecules are above you. So, as altitude (distance from sea level) increases, air pressure decreases. Think of air pressure as a human pyramid, as shown in **Figure 2.** The people at the bottom of the pyramid can feel all the weight and pressure of the people on top. Air pressure works in a similar way.

Atmospheric Composition Affects Air Temperature

Air temperature also changes as altitude increases. The temperature differences result mainly from the way solar energy is absorbed as it moves through the atmosphere. Some parts of the atmosphere are warmer because they contain a high percentage of gases that absorb solar energy. Other parts of the atmosphere contain less of these gases and are cooler.

atmosphere a mixture of gases that surrounds a planet or moon

air pressure the measure of the force with which air molecules push on a surface

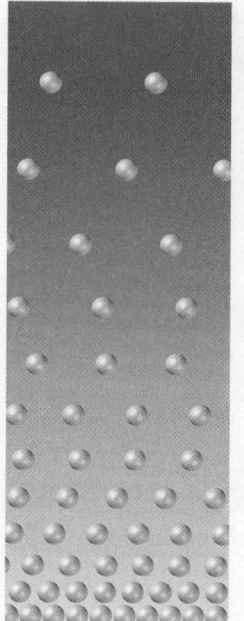

Lower pressure

Higher pressure

Figure 2 *As in a human pyramid, air pressure increases closer to the Earth's surface.*

Layers of the Atmosphere

Based on temperature changes, the Earth's atmosphere is divided into four layers, as shown in **Figure 3.** These layers are the *troposphere, stratosphere, mesosphere,* and *thermosphere.* Although these words might sound complicated, the name of each layer gives you clues about its features.

For example, *-sphere* means "ball," which suggests that each layer of the atmosphere surrounds the Earth like a hollow ball. *Tropo-* means "turning" or "change," and the troposphere is the layer where gases turn and mix. *Strato-* means "layer," and the stratosphere is the sphere where gases are layered and do not mix very much. *Meso-* means "middle," and the mesosphere is the middle layer. Finally, *thermo-* means "heat," and the thermosphere is the sphere where temperatures are highest.

Reading Check What does the name of each atmospheric layer mean?

Figure 3 *The layers of the atmosphere are defined by changes in temperature.*

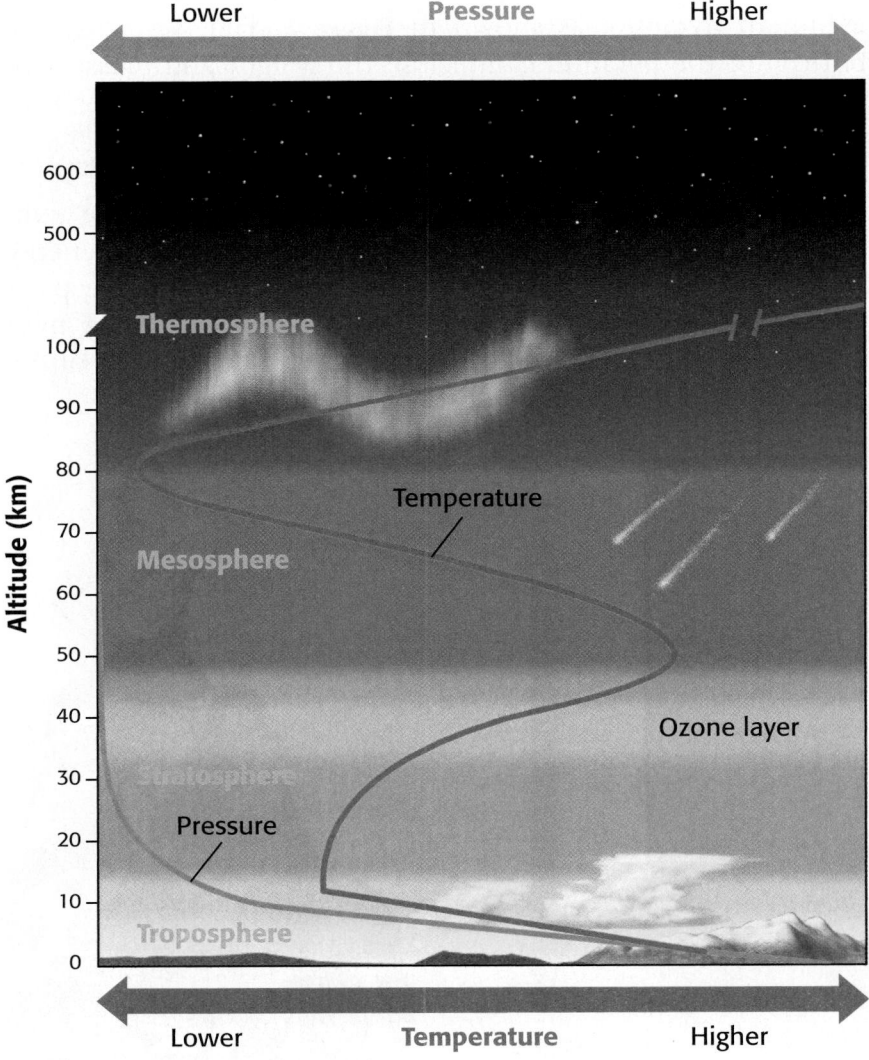

The Troposphere: The Layer in Which We Live

The lowest layer of the atmosphere, which lies next to the Earth's surface, is called the **troposphere.** The troposphere is also the densest atmospheric layer. It contains almost 90% of the atmosphere's total mass! Almost all of the Earth's carbon dioxide, water vapor, clouds, air pollution, weather, and life-forms are in the troposphere. As shown in **Figure 4,** temperatures vary greatly in the troposphere. Differences in air temperature and density cause gases in the troposphere to mix continuously.

The Stratosphere: Home of the Ozone Layer

The atmospheric layer above the troposphere is called the **stratosphere. Figure 5** shows the boundary between the stratosphere and the troposphere. Gases in the stratosphere are layered and do not mix as much as gases in the troposphere. The air is also very thin in the stratosphere and contains little moisture. The lower stratosphere is extremely cold. Its temperature averages –60°C. But temperature rises as altitude increases in the stratosphere. This rise happens because ozone in the stratosphere absorbs ultraviolet radiation from the sun, which warms the air. Almost all of the ozone in the stratosphere is contained in the ozone layer. The *ozone layer* protects life on Earth by absorbing harmful ultraviolet radiation.

The Mesosphere: The Middle Layer

Above the stratosphere is the mesosphere. The **mesosphere** is the middle layer of the atmosphere. It is also the coldest layer. As in the troposphere, the temperature decreases as altitude increases in the mesosphere. Temperatures can be as low as –93°C at the top of the mesosphere.

Figure 4 *As altitude increases in the troposphere, temperature decreases. Snow remains all year on this mountaintop.*

troposphere the lowest layer of the atmosphere, in which temperature decreases at a constant rate as altitude increases

stratosphere the layer of the atmosphere that is above the troposphere and in which temperature increases as altitude increases

mesosphere the layer of the atmosphere between the stratosphere and the thermosphere and in which temperature decreases as altitude increases

Figure 5 *This photograph of Earth's atmosphere was taken from space. The troposphere is the yellow layer; the stratosphere is the white layer.*

The Thermosphere: The Edge of the Atmosphere

The uppermost atmospheric layer is called the **thermosphere.** In the thermosphere, temperature again increases with altitude. Atoms of nitrogen and oxygen absorb high-energy solar radiation and release thermal energy, which causes temperatures in the thermosphere to be 1,000°C or higher.

When you think of an area that has high temperatures, you probably think of a place that is very hot. Although the thermosphere has very high temperatures, it does not feel hot. Temperature is different from heat. Temperature is a measure of the average energy of particles in motion. The high temperature of the thermosphere means that particles in that layer are moving very fast. Heat, however, is the transfer of thermal energy between objects of different temperatures. Particles must touch one another to transfer thermal energy. The space between particles in the thermosphere is so great that particles do not transfer much energy. In other words, the density of the thermosphere is so low that particles do not often collide and transfer energy. **Figure 6** shows how air density affects the heating of the troposphere and the thermosphere.

Reading Check Why doesn't the thermosphere feel hot?

Figure 6 Temperature in the Troposphere and the Thermosphere

The **thermosphere** is less dense than the troposphere. So, although particles are moving very fast, they do not transfer much thermal energy.

The **troposphere** is denser than the thermosphere. So, although particles in the troposphere are moving much slower than particles in the thermosphere, they can transfer much more thermal energy.

The Ionosphere: Home of the Auroras

In the upper mesosphere and the lower thermosphere, nitrogen and oxygen atoms absorb harmful solar energy. As a result, the thermosphere's temperature rises, and gas particles become electrically charged. Electrically charged particles are called *ions*. Therefore, this part of the thermosphere is called the *ionosphere*. As shown in **Figure 7,** in polar regions these ions radiate energy as shimmering lights called *auroras*. The ionosphere also reflects AM radio waves. When conditions are right, an AM radio wave can travel around the world by reflecting off the ionosphere. These radio signals bounce off the ionosphere and are sent back to Earth.

Figure 7 *Charged particles in the ionosphere cause auroras, or northern and southern lights.*

SECTION Review

Summary

- Nitrogen and oxygen make up most of Earth's atmosphere.
- Air pressure decreases as altitude increases.
- The composition of atmospheric layers affects their temperature.
- The troposphere is the lowest atmospheric layer. It is the layer in which we live.
- The stratosphere contains the ozone layer, which protects us from harmful UV radiation.
- The mesosphere is the coldest atmospheric layer.
- The thermosphere is the uppermost layer of the atmosphere.

Using Key Terms

1. Use each of the following terms in a separate sentence: *air pressure, atmosphere, troposphere, stratosphere, mesosphere,* and *thermosphere.*

Understanding Key Ideas

2. Why does the temperature of different layers of the atmosphere vary?
   a. because air temperature increases as altitude increases
   b. because the amount of energy radiated from the sun varies
   c. because of interference by humans
   d. because of the composition of gases in each layer

3. Why does air pressure decrease as altitude increases?

4. How can the thermosphere have high temperatures but not feel hot?

5. What determines the temperature of atmospheric layers?

6. What two gases make up most of the atmosphere?

Math Skills

7. If an average cloud has a density of 0.5 g/m^3 and has a volume of 1,000,000,000 m^3, what is the weight of an average cloud?

Critical Thinking

8. **Applying Concepts** Apply what you know about the relationship between altitude and air pressure to explain why rescue helicopters have a difficult time flying at altitudes above 6,000 m.

9. **Making Inferences** If the upper atmosphere is very thin, why do space vehicles heat up as they enter the atmosphere?

10. **Making Inferences** Explain why gases such as helium can escape Earth's atmosphere.

SECTION 2

Atmospheric Heating

You are lying in a park. Your eyes are closed, and you feel the warmth of the sun on your face. You may have done this before, but have you ever stopped to think that it takes a little more than eight minutes for the energy that warms your face to travel from a star that is 149,000,000 km away?

READING WARM-UP

Objectives

- Describe what happens to solar energy that reaches Earth.
- Summarize the processes of radiation, conduction, and convection.
- Explain the relationship between the greenhouse effect and global warming.

Terms to Learn

radiation
thermal conduction
convection
global warming
greenhouse effect

READING STRATEGY

Reading Organizer As you read this section, make a table comparing radiation, conduction, and convection.

Energy in the Atmosphere

In the scenario above, your face was warmed by energy from the sun. Earth and its atmosphere are also warmed by energy from the sun. In this section, you will find out what happens to solar energy as it enters the atmosphere.

Radiation: Energy Transfer by Waves

The Earth receives energy from the sun by radiation. **Radiation** is the transfer of energy as electromagnetic waves. Although the sun radiates a huge amount of energy, Earth receives only about two-billionths of this energy. But this small fraction of energy is enough to drive the weather cycle and make Earth habitable. **Figure 1** shows what happens to solar energy once it enters the atmosphere.

Figure 1 *Energy from the sun is absorbed by the atmosphere, land, and water and is changed into thermal energy.*

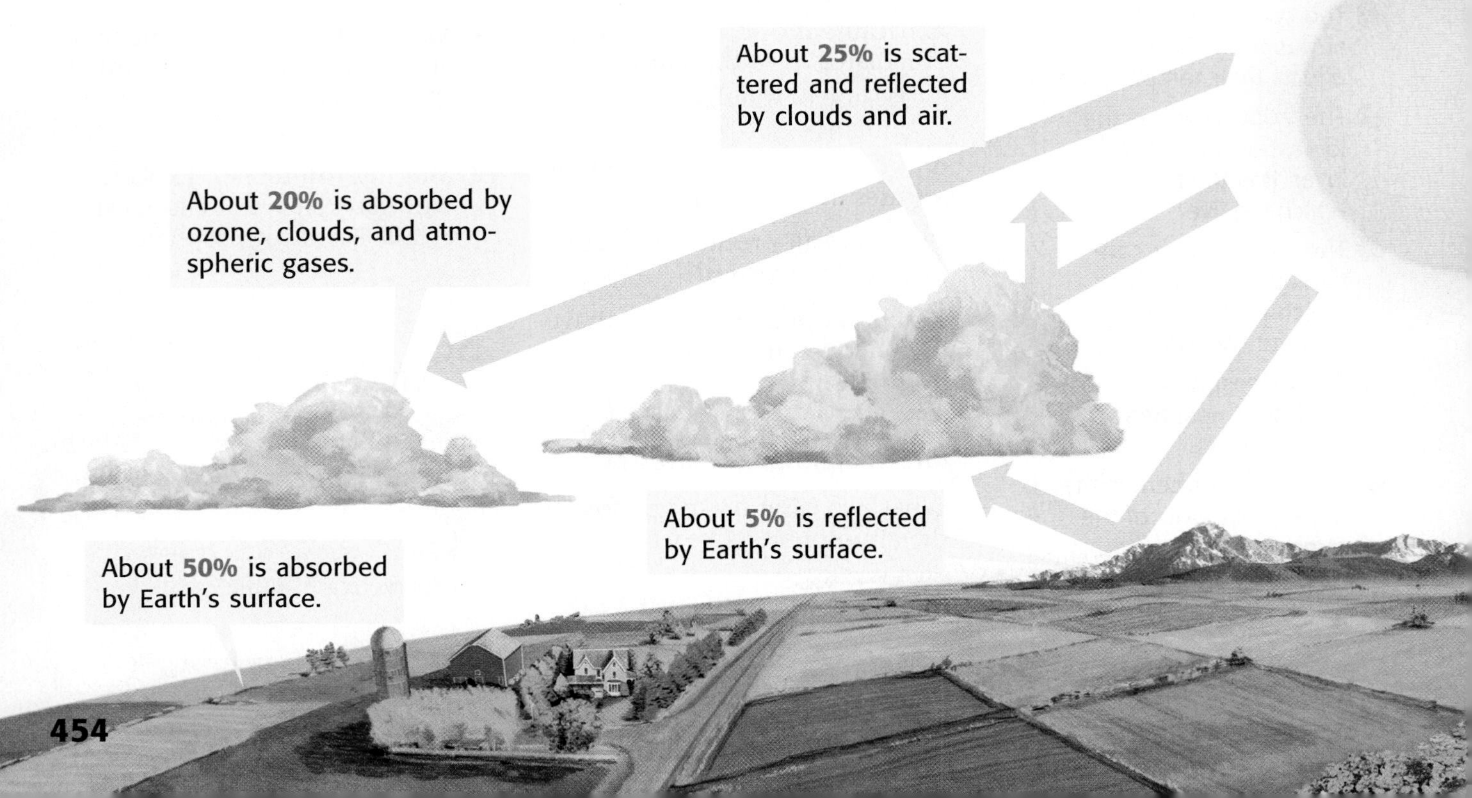

About 25% is scattered and reflected by clouds and air.
About 20% is absorbed by ozone, clouds, and atmospheric gases.
About 5% is reflected by Earth's surface.
About 50% is absorbed by Earth's surface.

Conduction: Energy Transfer by Contact

If you have ever touched something hot, you have experienced the process of conduction. **Thermal conduction** is the transfer of thermal energy through a material. Thermal energy is always transferred from warm to cold areas. When air molecules come into direct contact with the warm surface of Earth, thermal energy is transferred to the atmosphere.

Convection: Energy Transfer by Circulation

If you have ever watched a pot of water boil, you have observed convection. **Convection** is the transfer of thermal energy by the circulation or movement of a liquid or gas. Most thermal energy in the atmosphere is transferred by convection. For example, as air is heated, it becomes less dense and rises. Cool air is denser, so it sinks. As the cool air sinks, it pushes the warm air up. The cool air is eventually heated by the Earth's surface and begins to rise again. This cycle of warm air rising and cool air sinking causes a circular movement of air, called a *convection current,* as shown in **Figure 2.**

✓ Reading Check How do differences in air density cause convection currents? (*See the Appendix for answers to Reading Checks.*)

radiation the transfer of energy as electromagnetic waves

thermal conduction the transfer of energy as heat through a material

convection the transfer of thermal energy by the circulation or movement of a liquid or gas

Figure 2 *The processes of radiation, thermal conduction, and convection heat Earth and its atmosphere.*

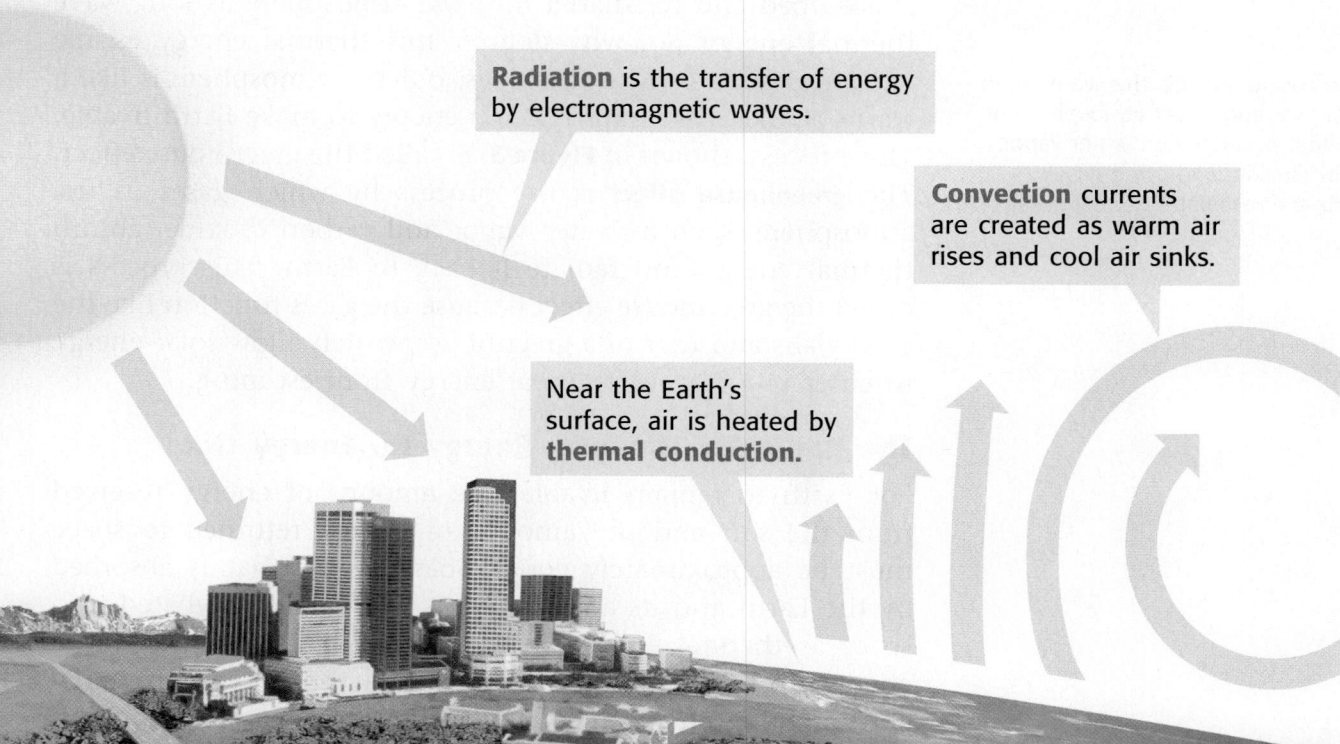

Radiation is the transfer of energy by electromagnetic waves.

Convection currents are created as warm air rises and cool air sinks.

Near the Earth's surface, air is heated by **thermal conduction.**

Figure 3 The Greenhouse Effect

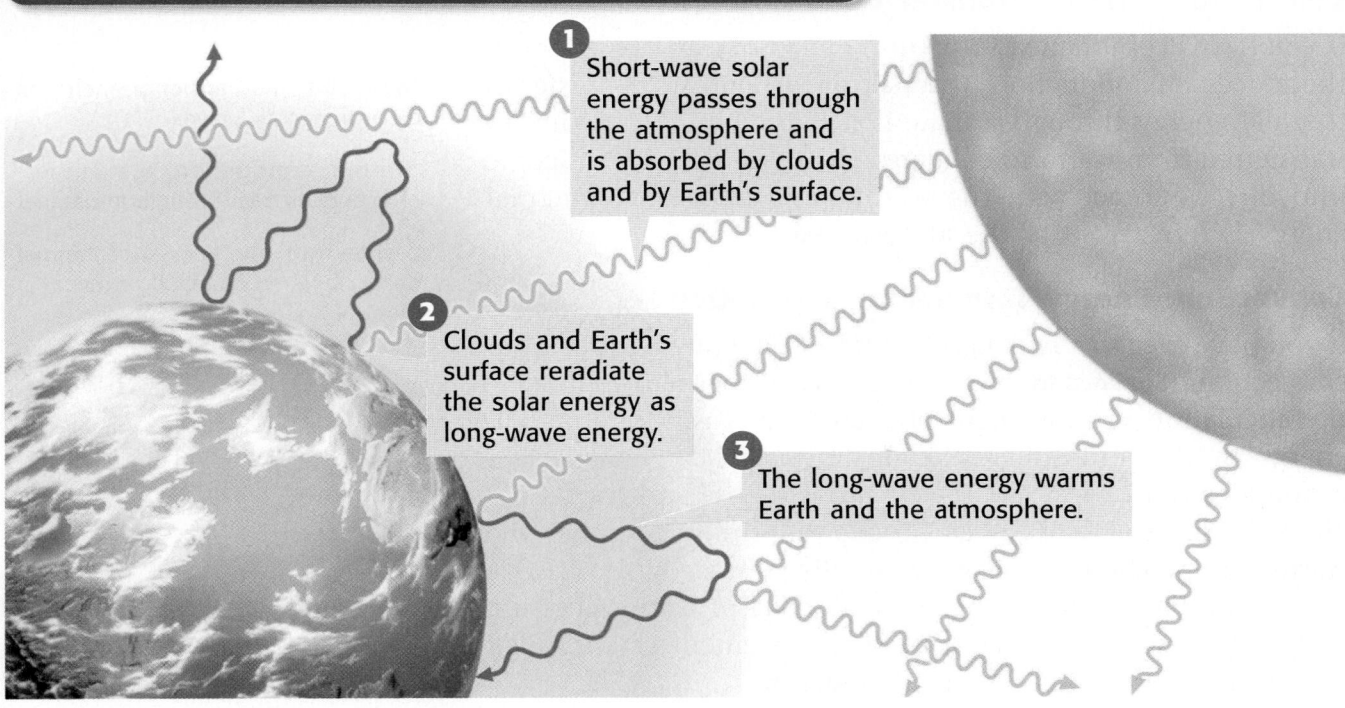

1 Short-wave solar energy passes through the atmosphere and is absorbed by clouds and by Earth's surface.

2 Clouds and Earth's surface reradiate the solar energy as long-wave energy.

3 The long-wave energy warms Earth and the atmosphere.

The Greenhouse Effect and Life on Earth

As you have learned, about 70% of the radiation that enters Earth's atmosphere is absorbed by clouds and by the Earth's surface. This energy is converted into thermal energy that warms the planet. In other words, short-wave visible light is absorbed and reradiated into the atmosphere as long-wave thermal energy. So, why doesn't this thermal energy escape back into space? Most of it does, but the atmosphere is like a warm blanket that traps enough energy to make Earth livable. This process, shown in **Figure 3,** is called the greenhouse effect. The **greenhouse effect** is the process by which gases in the atmosphere, such as water vapor and carbon dioxide, absorb thermal energy and radiate it back to Earth. This process is called the greenhouse effect because the gases function like the glass walls and roof of a greenhouse, which allow solar energy to enter but prevent thermal energy from escaping.

greenhouse effect the warming of the surface and lower atmosphere of Earth that occurs when water vapor, carbon dioxide, and other gases absorb and reradiate thermal energy

The Radiation Balance: Energy In, Energy Out

For Earth to remain livable, the amount of energy received from the sun and the amount of energy returned to space must be approximately equal. Solar energy that is absorbed by the Earth and its atmosphere is eventually reradiated into space as thermal energy. Every day, the Earth receives more energy from the sun. The balance between incoming energy and outgoing energy is known as the *radiation balance.*

Greenhouse Gases and Global Warming

Many scientists have become concerned about data that show that average global temperatures have increased in the past 100 years. Such an increase in average global temperatures is called **global warming.** Some scientists have hypothesized that an increase of greenhouse gases in the atmosphere may be the cause of this warming trend. Greenhouse gases are gases that absorb thermal energy in the atmosphere.

Human activity, such as the burning of fossil fuels and deforestation, may be increasing levels of greenhouse gases, such as carbon dioxide, in the atmosphere. If this hypothesis is correct, increasing levels of greenhouse gases may cause average global temperatures to continue to rise. If global warming continues, global climate patterns could be disrupted. Plants and animals that are adapted to live in specific climates would be affected. However, climate models are extremely complex, and scientists continue to debate whether the global warming trend is the result of an increase in greenhouse gases.

global warming a gradual increase in average global temperature

Reading Check What is a greenhouse gas?

SECTION Review

Summary

- Energy from the sun is transferred through the atmosphere by radiation, thermal conduction, and convection.

- Radiation is energy transfer by electromagnetic waves. Thermal conduction is energy transfer by direct contact. Convection is energy transfer by circulation.

- The greenhouse effect is Earth's natural heating process. Increasing levels of greenhouse gases could cause global warming.

Using Key Terms

1. Use each of the following terms in a separate sentence: *thermal conduction, radiation, convection, greenhouse effect,* and *global warming.*

Understanding Key Ideas

2. Which of the following is the best example of thermal conduction?
   a. a light bulb warming a lampshade
   b. an egg cooking in a frying pan
   c. water boiling in a pot
   d. gases circulating in the atmosphere

3. Describe three ways that energy is transferred in the atmosphere.

4. What is the difference between the greenhouse effect and global warming?

5. What is the radiation balance?

Math Skills

6. Find the average of the following temperatures: 73.2°F, 71.1°F, 54.6°F, 65.5°F, 78.2°F, 81.9°F, and 82.1°F.

Critical Thinking

7. **Identifying Relationships** How does the process of convection rely on radiation?

8. **Applying Concepts** Describe global warming in terms of the radiation balance.

Developed and maintained by the National Science Teachers Association

For a variety of links related to this chapter, go to www.scilinks.org

Topic: Energy in the Atmosphere
SciLinks code: HSM0512

Global Winds and Local Winds

If you open the valve on a bicycle tube, the air rushes out. Why? The air inside the tube is at a higher pressure than the air is outside the tube. In effect, letting air out of the tube created a wind.

Objectives

- Explain the relationship between air pressure and wind direction.
- Describe global wind patterns.
- Explain the causes of local wind patterns.

Terms to Learn

wind	westerlies
Coriolis effect	trade winds
polar easterlies	jet stream

Prediction Guide Before reading this section, write the title of each heading in this section. Next, under each heading, write what you think you will learn.

wind the movement of air caused by differences in air pressure

Why Air Moves

The movement of air caused by differences in air pressure is called **wind.** The greater the pressure difference, the faster the wind moves. The devastation shown in **Figure 1** was caused by winds that resulted from extreme differences in air pressure.

Air Rises at the Equator and Sinks at the Poles

Differences in air pressure are generally caused by the unequal heating of the Earth. The equator receives more direct solar energy than other latitudes, so air at the equator is warmer and less dense than the surrounding air. Warm, less dense air rises and creates an area of low pressure. This warm, rising air flows toward the poles. At the poles, the air is colder and denser than the surrounding air, so it sinks. As the cold air sinks, it creates areas of high pressure around the poles. This cold polar air then flows toward the equator.

Figure 1 *In 1992, Hurricane Andrew became the most destructive hurricane in U.S. history. The winds from the hurricane reached 264 km/h.*

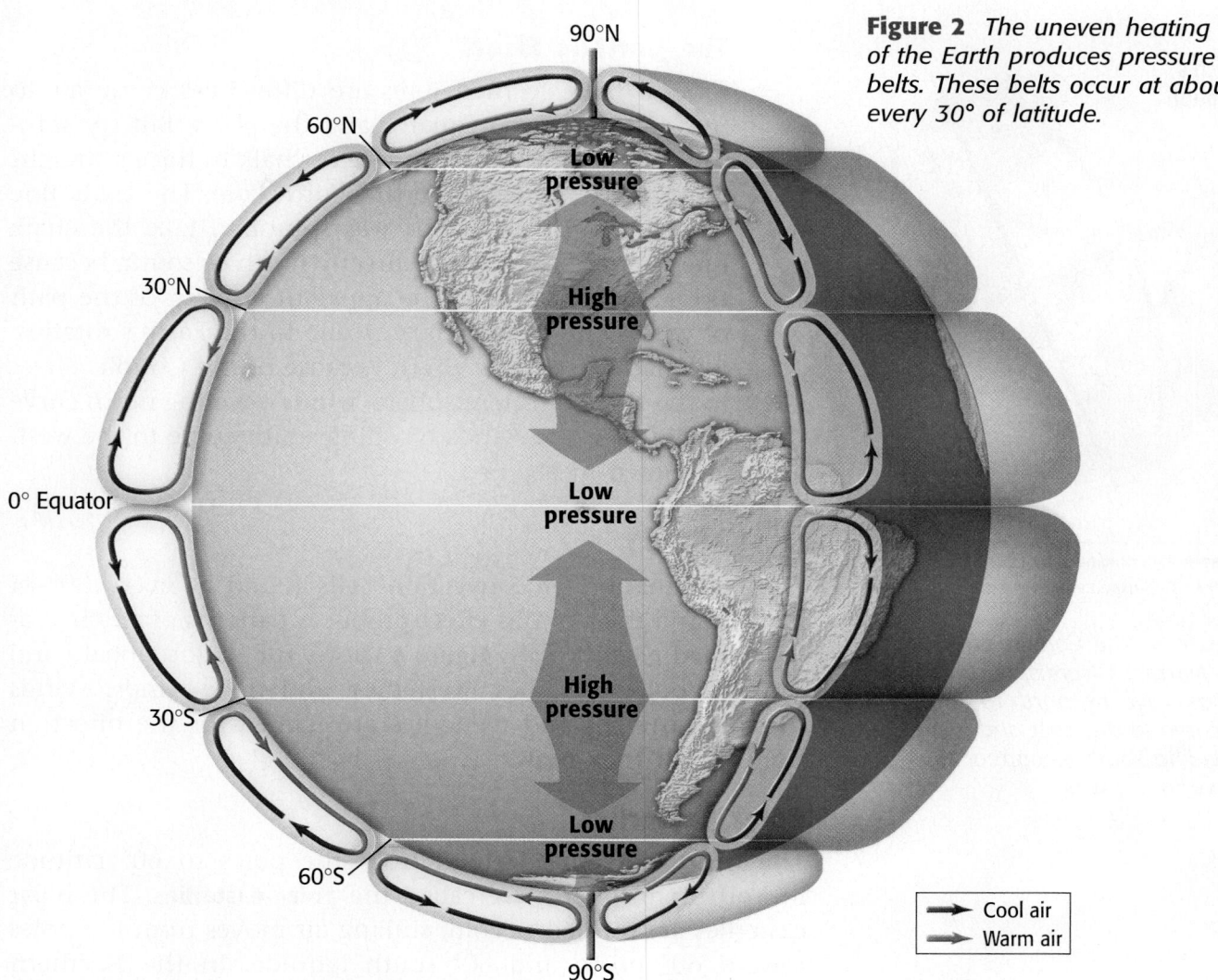

Figure 2 *The uneven heating of the Earth produces pressure belts. These belts occur at about every 30° of latitude.*

90°N
60°N
Low pressure
30°N
High pressure
0° Equator
Low pressure
High pressure
30°S
Low pressure
60°S
90°S

→ Cool air
→ Warm air

Pressure Belts Are Found Every 30°

You may imagine that wind moves in one huge, circular pattern from the poles to the equator. In fact, air travels in many large, circular patterns called *convection cells*. Convection cells are separated by *pressure belts,* bands of high pressure and low pressure found about every 30° of latitude, as shown in **Figure 2.** As warm air rises over the equator and moves toward the poles, the air begins to cool. At about 30° north and 30° south latitude, some of the cool air begins to sink. Cool, sinking air causes high pressure belts near 30° north and 30° south latitude. This cool air flows back to the equator, where it warms and rises again. At the poles, cold air sinks and moves toward the equator. Air warms as it moves away from the poles. Around 60° north and 60° south latitude, the warmer air rises, which creates a low pressure belt. This air flows back to the poles.

✓ Reading Check Why does sinking air cause areas of high pressure? (*See the Appendix for answers to Reading Checks.*)

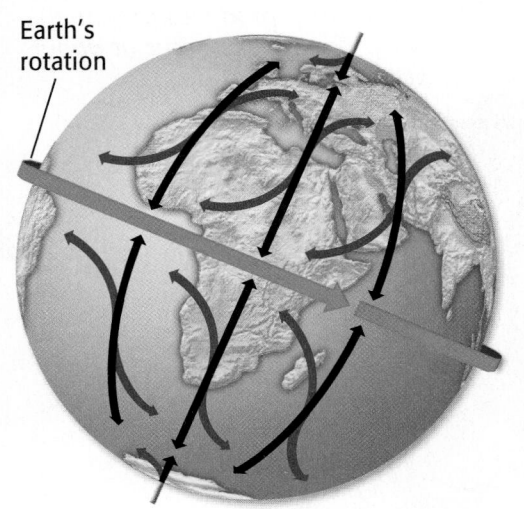

Earth's rotation

→ Path of wind without Coriolis effect
→ Approximate path of wind

Figure 3 *The Coriolis effect in the Northern Hemisphere causes winds traveling north to appear to curve to the east and winds traveling south to appear to curve to the west.*

Coriolis effect the apparent curving of the path of a moving object from an otherwise straight path due to the Earth's rotation

polar easterlies prevailing winds that blow from east to west between 60° and 90° latitude in both hemispheres

westerlies prevailing winds that blow from west to east between 30° and 60° latitude in both hemispheres

trade winds prevailing winds that blow northeast from 30° north latitude to the equator and that blow southeast from 30° south latitude to the equator

The Coriolis Effect

As you have learned, pressure differences cause air to move between the equator and the poles. But try spinning a globe and using a piece of chalk to trace a straight line from the equator to the North Pole. The chalk line curves because the globe was spinning. Like the chalk line, winds do not travel directly north or south, because the Earth is rotating. The apparent curving of the path of winds and ocean currents due to the Earth's rotation is called the **Coriolis effect.** Because of the Coriolis effect in the Northern Hemisphere, winds traveling north curve to the east, and winds traveling south curve to the west, as shown in **Figure 3.**

Global Winds

The combination of convection cells found at every 30° of latitude and the Coriolis effect produces patterns of air circulation called *global winds*. **Figure 4** shows the major global wind systems: polar easterlies, westerlies, and trade winds. Winds such as easterlies and westerlies are named for the direction from which they blow.

Polar Easterlies

The wind belts that extend from the poles to 60° latitude in both hemispheres are called the **polar easterlies.** The polar easterlies are formed as cold, sinking air moves from the poles toward 60° north and 60° south latitude. In the Northern Hemisphere, polar easterlies can carry cold arctic air over the United States, producing snow and freezing weather.

Westerlies

The wind belts found between 30° and 60° latitude in both hemispheres are called the **westerlies.** The westerlies flow toward the poles from west to east. The westerlies can carry moist air over the United States, producing rain and snow.

Trade Winds

In both hemispheres, the winds that blow from 30° latitude almost to the equator are called **trade winds.** The Coriolis effect causes the trade winds to curve to the west in the Northern Hemisphere and to the east in the Southern Hemisphere. Early traders used the trade winds to sail from Europe to the Americas. As a result, the winds became known as "trade winds."

✓ **Reading Check** If the trade winds carried traders from Europe to the Americas, what wind system carried traders back to Europe?

The Doldrums

The trade winds of the Northern and Southern Hemispheres meet in an area around the equator called the *doldrums*. In the doldrums, there is very little wind because the warm, rising air creates an area of low pressure. The name *doldrums* means "dull" or "sluggish."

The Horse Latitudes

At about 30° north and 30° south latitude, sinking air creates an area of high pressure. The winds at these locations are weak. These areas are called the *horse latitudes*. According to legend, this name was given to these areas when sailing ships carried horses from Europe to the Americas. When the ships were stuck in this windless area, horses were sometimes thrown overboard to save drinking water for the sailors. Most of the world's deserts are located in the horse latitudes because the sinking air is very dry.

INTERNET ACTIVITY

For another activity related to this chapter, go to **go.hrw.com** and type in the keyword **HZ5ATMW**.

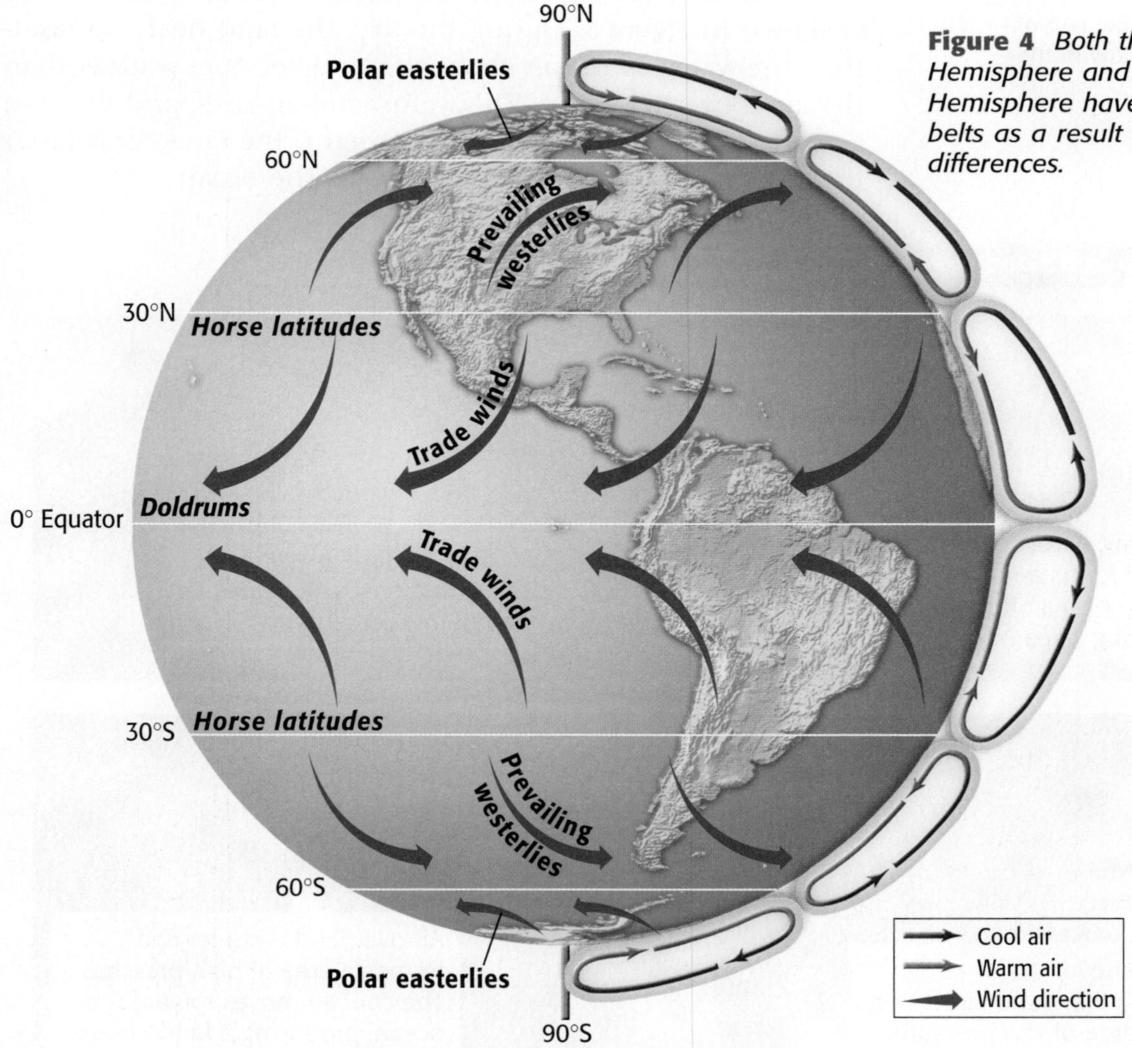

Figure 4 *Both the Northern Hemisphere and the Southern Hemisphere have three wind belts as a result of pressure differences.*

90°N

Polar easterlies

60°N

Prevailing westerlies

30°N **Horse latitudes**

Trade winds

0° Equator **Doldrums**

Trade winds

30°S **Horse latitudes**

Prevailing westerlies

60°S

Polar easterlies

90°S

→ Cool air
→ Warm air
→ Wind direction

Jet Streams: Atmospheric Conveyor Belts

The flight from Seattle to Boston can be 30 minutes faster than the flight from Boston to Seattle. Why? Pilots take advantage of a jet stream similar to the one shown in **Figure 5.** The **jet streams** are narrow belts of high-speed winds that blow in the upper troposphere and lower stratosphere. These winds can reach maximum speeds of 400 km/h. Unlike other global winds, the jet streams do not follow regular paths around the Earth. Knowing the path of a jet stream is important not only to pilots but also to meteorologists. Because jet streams affect the movement of storms, meteorologists can track a storm if they know the location of a jet stream.

Local Winds

Local winds generally move short distances and can blow from any direction. Local geographic features, such as a shoreline or a mountain, can produce temperature differences that cause local winds. For example, the formation of sea and land breezes is shown in **Figure 6.** During the day, the land heats up faster than the water, so the air above the land becomes warmer than the air above the ocean. The warm land air rises, and the cold ocean air flows in to replace it. At night, the land cools faster than water, so the wind blows toward the ocean.

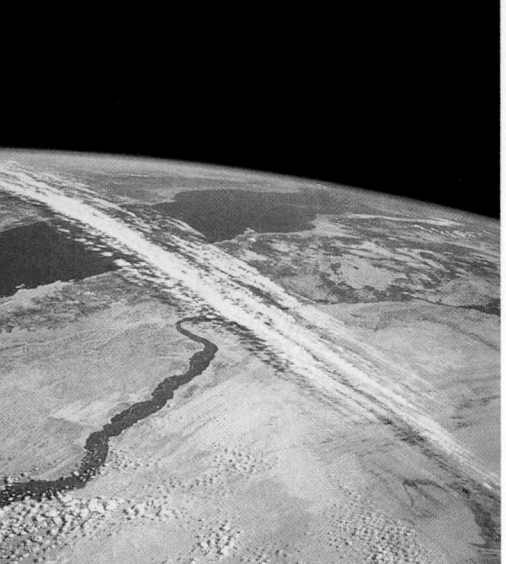

Figure 5 *The jet stream forms this band of clouds as it flows above the Earth.*

jet stream a narrow belt of strong winds that blow in the upper troposphere

Figure 6   Sea and Land Breezes

During the day, air over the ocean is cooler and forms an area of high pressure. The cool air flows to the land, producing a sea breeze.

Air over the land is warmer. As warm air rises, it creates an area of low pressure.

At night, air over the ocean is warmer. As the warm air rises, it forms an area of low pressure.

Air over land is cooler and forms an area of high pressure. The cool air moves toward the ocean, producing a land breeze.

Mountain Breezes and Valley Breezes

Mountain and valley breezes are other examples of local winds caused by an area's geography. Campers in mountainous areas may feel a warm afternoon quickly change into a cold night soon after the sun sets. During the day, the sun warms the air along the mountain slopes. This warm air rises up the mountain slopes, creating a valley breeze. At nightfall, the air along the mountain slopes cools. This cool air moves down the slopes into the valley, producing a mountain breeze.

✓ **Reading Check** Why does the wind tend to blow down from mountains at night?

CONNECTION TO Social Studies

Local Breezes The chinook, the shamal, the sirocco, and the Santa Ana are all local winds. Find out about an interesting local wind, and create a poster-board display that shows how the wind forms and how it affects human cultures.

ACTIVITY

SECTION Review

Summary

- Winds blow from areas of high pressure to areas of low pressure.
- Pressure belts are found approximately every 30° of latitude.
- The Coriolis effect causes wind to appear to curve as it moves across the Earth's surface.
- Global winds include the polar easterlies, the westerlies, and the trade winds.
- Local winds include sea and land breezes and mountain and valley breezes.

Using Key Terms

1. In your own words, write a definition for each of the following terms: *wind, Coriolis effect, jet stream, polar easterlies, westerlies,* and *trade winds*.

Understanding Key Ideas

2. Why does warm air rise and cold air sink?
   a. because warm air is less dense than cold air
   b. because warm air is denser than cold air
   c. because cold air is less dense than warm air
   d. because warm air has less pressure than cold air does

3. What are pressure belts?

4. What causes winds?

5. How does the Coriolis effect affect wind movement?

6. How are sea and land breezes similar to mountain and valley breezes?

7. Would there be winds if the Earth's surface were the same temperature everywhere? Explain your answer.

Math Skills

8. Flying an airplane at 500 km/h, a pilot plans to reach her destination in 5 h. But she finds a jet stream moving 250 km/h in the direction she is traveling. If she gets a boost from the jet stream for 2 h, how long will the flight last?

Critical Thinking

9. **Making Inferences** In the Northern Hemisphere, why do westerlies flow from the west but trade winds flow from the east?

10. **Applying Concepts** Imagine you are near an ocean in the daytime. You want to go to the ocean, but you don't know how to get there. How might a local wind help you find the ocean?

SCILINKS

NSTA Developed and maintained by the National Science Teachers Association

For a variety of links related to this chapter, go to www.scilinks.org

Topic: Atmospheric Pressure and Winds
SciLinks code: HSM0115

air pollution the contamination of the atmosphere by the introduction of pollutants from human and natural sources

Air Pollution

In December 1952, one of London's dreaded "pea souper" fogs settled on the city. But this was no ordinary fog—it was thick with coal smoke and air pollution. It burned people's lungs, and the sky grew so dark that people could not see their hands in front of their faces. When the fog lifted four days later, thousands of people were dead!

London's killer fog shocked the world and caused major changes in England's air-pollution laws. People began to think that air pollution was not simply a part of urban life that had to be endured. Air pollution had to be reduced. Although this event is an extreme example, air pollution is common in many parts of the world. However, nations are taking major steps to reduce air pollution. But what is air pollution? **Air pollution** is the contamination of the atmosphere by the introduction of pollutants from human and natural sources. Air pollutants are classified according to their source as either primary pollutants or secondary pollutants.

Primary Pollutants

Pollutants that are put directly into the air by human or natural activity are *primary pollutants*. Primary pollutants from natural sources include dust, sea salt, volcanic gases and ash, smoke from forest fires, and pollen. Primary pollutants from human sources include carbon monoxide, dust, smoke, and chemicals from paint and other substances. In urban areas, vehicle exhaust is a common source of primary pollutants. Examples of primary pollutants are shown in **Figure 1.**

✓ Reading Check List three primary pollutants from natural sources. (*See the Appendix for answers to Reading Checks.*)

Figure 1 **Examples of Primary Pollutants**

Industrial emissions	Vehicle exhaust	Volcanic ash

Secondary Pollutants

Pollutants that form when primary pollutants react with other primary pollutants or with naturally occurring substances, such as water vapor, are *secondary pollutants*. Ozone and smog are examples of secondary pollutants. Ozone is produced when sunlight reacts with vehicle exhaust and air. You may have heard of "Ozone Action Day" warnings in your community. When such a warning is issued, people are discouraged from outdoor physical activity because ozone can damage their lungs. In the stratosphere, ozone forms a protective layer that absorbs harmful radiation from the sun. Near the Earth's surface, however, ozone is a dangerous pollutant that negatively affects the health of organisms.

The Formation of Smog

Smog forms when ozone and vehicle exhaust react with sunlight, as shown in **Figure 2.** Local geography and weather patterns can also contribute to smog formation. Los Angeles, shown in **Figure 3,** is almost completely surrounded by mountains that trap pollutants and contribute to smog formation. Although pollution controls have reduced levels of smog in Los Angeles, smog remains a problem for Los Angeles and many other large cities.

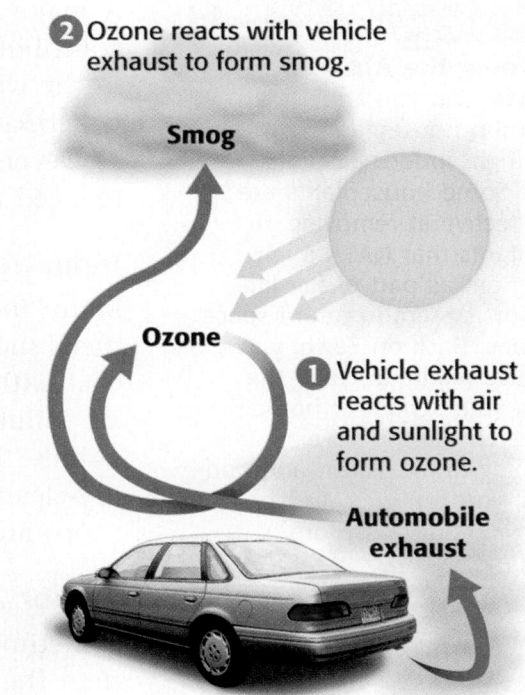

Figure 2 *Smog forms when sunlight reacts with ozone and vehicle exhaust.*

Figure 3 *Smog levels in Los Angeles can vary dramatically. During summer, a layer of warm air can trap smog near the ground. However, in the winter, a storm can quickly clear the air.*

Sources of Human-Caused Air Pollution

Human-caused air pollution comes from a variety of sources. A major source of air pollution today is transportation. Cars contribute about 10% to 20% of the human-caused air pollution in the United States. Vehicle exhaust contains nitrogen oxide, which contributes to smog formation and acid precipitation. However, pollution controls and cleaner gasoline have greatly reduced air pollution from vehicles.

Industrial Air Pollution

Many industrial plants and electric power plants burn fossil fuels, such as coal, to produce energy. Burning some types of coal without pollution controls can release large amounts of air pollutants. Some industries also produce chemicals that can pollute the air. Oil refineries, chemical manufacturing plants, dry-cleaning businesses, furniture refinishers, and auto body shops are all potential sources of air pollution.

Indoor Air Pollution

Sometimes, the air inside a building can be more polluted than the air outside. Some sources of indoor air pollution are shown in **Figure 4.** *Ventilation,* or the mixing of indoor air with outdoor air, can reduce indoor air pollution. Another way to reduce indoor air pollution is to limit the use of chemical solvents and cleaners.

Figure 4 *There are many sources of indoor air pollution. Indoor air pollution can be difficult to detect because it is often invisible.*

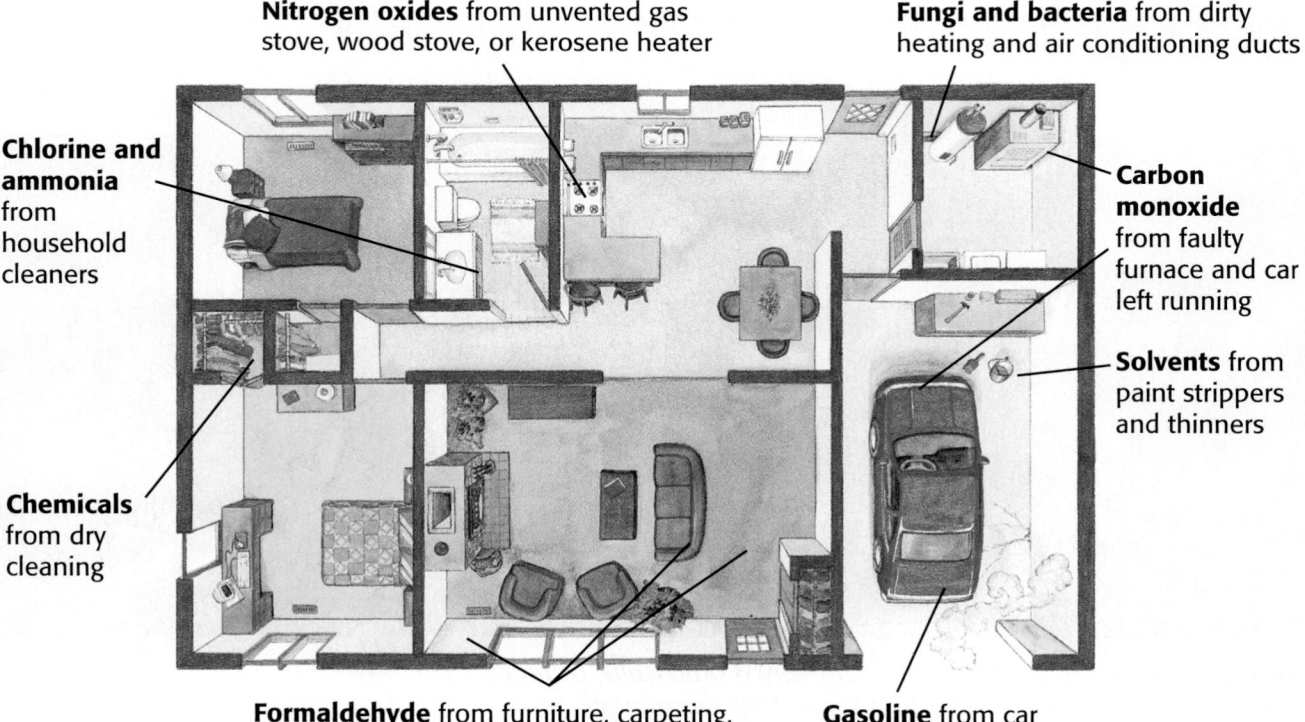

Nitrogen oxides from unvented gas stove, wood stove, or kerosene heater

Fungi and bacteria from dirty heating and air conditioning ducts

Chlorine and ammonia from household cleaners

Carbon monoxide from faulty furnace and car left running

Solvents from paint strippers and thinners

Chemicals from dry cleaning

Formaldehyde from furniture, carpeting, particleboard, and foam insulation

Gasoline from car and lawn mower

Acid Precipitation

Precipitation such as rain, sleet, or snow that contains acids from air pollution is called **acid precipitation.** When fossil fuels are burned, they can release sulfur dioxide and nitrogen oxide into the atmosphere. When these pollutants combine with water in the atmosphere, they form sulfuric acid and nitric acid. Precipitation is naturally acidic, but sulfuric acid and nitric acid can make it so acidic that it can negatively affect the environment. In most areas of the world, pollution controls have helped reduce acid precipitation.

acid precipitation rain, sleet, or snow that contains a high concentration of acids

Acid Precipitation and Plants

Plant communities have adapted over long periods of time to the natural acidity of the soil in which they grow. Acid precipitation can cause the acidity of soil to increase. This process, called *acidification*, changes the balance of a soil's chemistry in several ways. When the acidity of soil increases, some nutrients are dissolved. Nutrients that plants need for growth get washed away by rainwater. Increased acidity also causes aluminum and other toxic metals to be released. Some of these toxic metals are absorbed by the roots of plants.

Reading Check How does acid precipitation affect plants?

The Effects of Acid Precipitation on Forests

Forest ecology is complex. Scientists are still trying to fully understand the long-term effects of acid precipitation on groups of plants and their habitats. In some areas of the world, however, acid precipitation has damaged large areas of forest. The effects of acid precipitation are most noticeable in Eastern Europe, as shown in **Figure 5.** Forests in the northeastern United States and in eastern Canada have also been affected by acid precipitation.

Testing for Particulates

1. Particulates are pollutants such as dust that are extremely small. In this lab, you will measure the amount of particulates in the air. Begin by covering **ten 5 in. × 7 in. index cards** with a thin coat of **petroleum jelly.**

2. Hang the cards in various locations inside and outside your school.

3. One day later, use a **magnifying lens** to count the number of particles on the cards. Which location had the fewest number of particulates? Which location had the highest number of particulates? Hypothesize why.

Figure 5 *This forest in Poland was damaged by acid precipitation.*

Acid Precipitation and Aquatic Ecosystems

Aquatic organisms have adapted to live in water with a particular range of acidity. If acid precipitation increases the acidity of a lake or stream, aquatic plants, fish, and other aquatic organisms may die. The effects of acid precipitation on lakes and rivers are worst in the spring, when the acidic snow that built up in the winter melts and acidic water flows into lakes and rivers. A rapid change in a body of water's acidity is called *acid shock*. Acid shock can cause large numbers of fish to die. Acid shock can also affect the delicate eggs of fish and amphibians.

To reduce the effects of acid precipitation on aquatic ecosystems, some communities spray powdered lime on acidified lakes in the spring, which reduces the acidity of the lakes. Lime, a base, neutralizes the acid in the water. Unfortunately, lime cannot be spread to offset all acid damage to lakes.

✓ Reading Check Why is powdered lime sprayed on lakes in the spring instead of the fall?

The Ozone Hole

In 1985, scientists reported an alarming discovery about the Earth's protective ozone layer. Over the Antarctic regions, the ozone layer was thinning, particularly during the spring. This change was also noted over the Arctic. Chemicals called *CFCs* were causing ozone to break down into oxygen, which does not block the sun's harmful ultraviolet (UV) rays. The thinning of the ozone layer creates an ozone hole, shown in **Figure 6.** The ozone hole allows more UV radiation to reach the Earth's surface. UV radiation is dangerous to organisms because it damages genes and can cause skin cancer.

Cooperation to Reduce the Ozone Hole

In 1987, a group of nations met in Canada and agreed to take action against ozone depletion. Agreements were made to reduce and eventually ban CFC use, and CFC alternatives were quickly developed. Because many countries agreed to take swift action to control CFC use, and because a technological solution was quickly found, many people consider ozone protection an environmental success story. The battle to protect the ozone layer is not over, however. CFC molecules can remain active in the stratosphere for 60 to 120 years. So, CFCs released 30 years ago are still destroying ozone today. Thus, it will take many years for the ozone layer to completely recover.

Figure 6 *Polar weather conditions cause the size of the ozone hole (shown in blue) to vary. In the 2001 image, the ozone hole is larger than North America. One year later, it was 40% smaller.*

September 2001

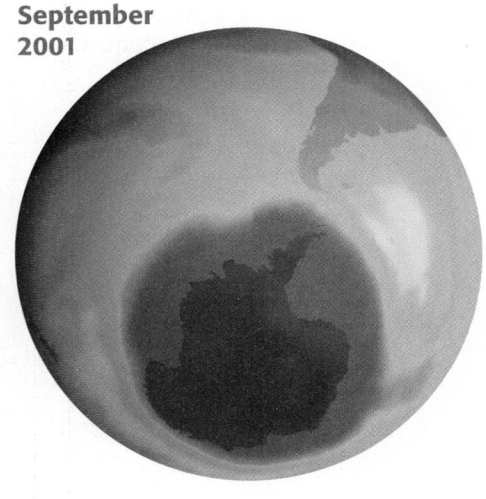

September 2002

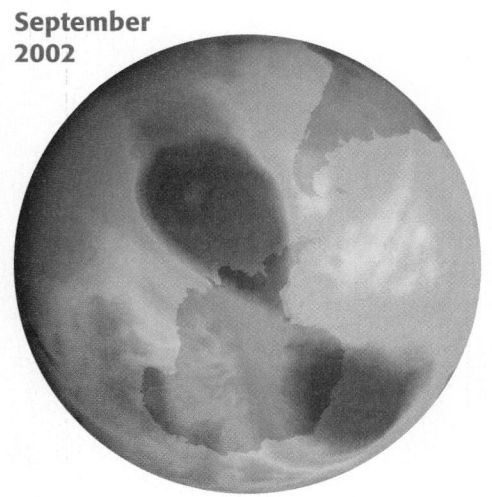

Air Pollution and Human Health

Daily exposure to small amounts of air pollution can cause serious health problems. Children, elderly people, and people with asthma, allergies, lung problems, and heart problems are especially vulnerable to the effects of air pollution. **Table 1** shows some of the effects of air pollution on the human body. The short-term effects of air pollution are immediately noticeable. Coughing, headaches, and increase in asthma-related problems are only a few short-term effects. The long-term effects of air pollution, such as lung cancer, are more dangerous because they may not be noticed until many years after an individual has been exposed to pollutants.

Table 1 Effects of Air Pollution on Human Health	
Short-term effects	headache; nausea; irritation of eyes, nose, and throat; coughing; upper respiratory infections; worsening of asthma and emphysema
Long-term effects	emphysema; lung cancer; permanent lung damage; heart disease

Cleaning Up Air Pollution

Much progress has been made in reducing air pollution. For example, in the United States the Clean Air Act was passed by Congress in 1970. The Clean Air Act is a law that gives the Environmental Protection Agency (EPA) the authority to control the amount of air pollutants that can be released from any source, such as cars and factories. The EPA also checks air quality. If air quality worsens, the EPA can set stricter standards. The Clean Air Act was strengthened in 1990.

Controlling Air Pollution from Industry

The Clean Air Act requires many industries to use pollution-control devices such as scrubbers. A *scrubber* is a device that is used to remove some pollutants before they are released by smokestacks. Scrubbers in coal-burning power plants remove particles such as ash from the smoke. Other industrial plants, such as the power plant shown in **Figure 7,** focus on burning fuel more efficiently so that fewer pollutants are released.

Figure 7 *This power plant in Florida is leading the way in clean-coal technology. The plant turns coal into a gas before it is burned, so fewer pollutants are released.*

Air Pollution Awareness

Work at home with a parent to develop a presentation for an "Air Pollution Awareness Day" at school. Develop a unique way to educate the public about air pollution, but have your presentation approved by your teacher before working on it. On "Air Pollution Awareness Day," your teacher might decide to invite students from another grade or a parent to come see the exhibits.

The Allowance Trading System

The Allowance Trading System is another initiative to reduce air pollution. In this program, the EPA establishes allowances for the amount of a pollutant that companies can release. If a company exceeds their allowance, they must pay a fine. A company that releases less than its allowance can sell some of its allowance to a company that releases more. Allowances are also available for the public to buy. So, organizations seeking to reduce air pollution can buy an allowance of 1,000 tons of sulfur dioxide, thus reducing the total amount of sulfur dioxide released by industries.

Reading Check How does the Allowance Trading System work?

Reducing Air Pollution from Vehicles

A large percentage of air pollution in the United States comes from the vehicles we drive. To reduce air pollution from vehicles, the EPA requires car makers to meet a certain standard for vehicle exhaust. Devices such as catalytic converters remove many pollutants from exhaust and help cars meet this standard. Cleaner fuels and more-efficent engines have also helped reduce air pollution from vehicles. Car manufacturers are also making cars that run on fuels other than gasoline. Some of these cars run on hydrogen or natural gas. Hybrid cars, which are becoming more common, use gasoline and electric power to reduce emissions. Another way to reduce air pollution is to carpool, use public transportation, or bike or walk to your destination, as shown in **Figure 8.**

Figure 8 *In Copenhagen, Denmark, companies loan free bicycles in exchange for publicity. The program helps reduce air pollution and auto traffic.*

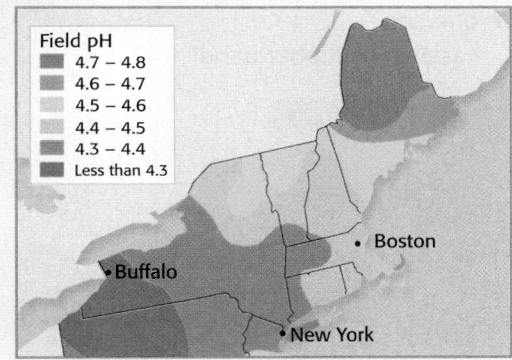

Summary

- Primary pollutants are pollutants that are put directly into the air by human or natural activity.

- Secondary pollutants are pollutants that form when primary pollutants react with other primary pollutants or with naturally occurring substances.

- Transportation, industry, and natural sources are the main sources of air pollution.

- Air pollution can be reduced by legislation, such as the Clean Air Act; by technology, such as scrubbers; and by changes in lifestyle.

Using Key Terms

The statements below are false. For each statement, replace the underlined term to make a true statement.

1. <u>Air pollution</u> is a sudden change in the acidity of a stream or lake.

2. <u>Smog</u> is rain, sleet, or snow that has a high concentration of acid.

Understanding Key Ideas

3. Which of the following results in the formation of smog?

   a. Acids in the air react with ozone.

   b. Ozone reacts with vehicle exhaust.

   c. Vehicle exhaust reacts with sunlight and ozone.

   d. Water vapor reacts with sunlight and ozone.

4. What is the difference between primary and secondary pollutants?

5. Describe five sources of indoor air pollution. Is all air pollution caused by humans? Explain.

6. What is the ozone hole, and why does it form?

7. Describe five effects of air pollution on human health. How can air pollution be reduced?

Critical Thinking

8. **Expressing Opinions** How do you think that nations should resolve air-pollution problems that cross national boundaries?

9. **Making Inferences** Why might establishing a direct link between air pollution and health problems be difficult?

Interpreting Graphics

The map below shows the pH of precipitation measured at field stations in the northeastern U.S. On the pH scale, lower numbers indicate solutions that are more acidic than solutions with higher numbers. Use the map to answer the questions below.

Field pH
- 4.7 – 4.8
- 4.6 – 4.7
- 4.5 – 4.6
- 4.4 – 4.5
- 4.3 – 4.4
- Less than 4.3

Boston
Buffalo
New York

10. Which areas have the most acidic precipitation? Hypothesize why.

11. Boston is a larger city than Buffalo is, but the precipitation measured in Buffalo is more acidic than the precipitation in Boston. Explain why.

SCI LINKS®

NSTA
Developed and maintained by the
National Science Teachers Association

For a variety of links related to this chapter, go to www.scilinks.org

Topic: Air Pollution
SciLinks code: HSM0033

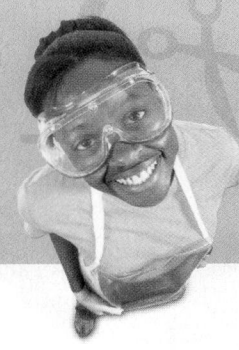

Skills Practice Lab

Under Pressure!

Imagine that you are planning a picnic with your friends, so you look in the newspaper for the weather forecast. The temperature this afternoon should be in the low 80s. This temperature sounds quite comfortable! But you notice that the newspaper's forecast also includes the barometer reading. What's a barometer? And what does the reading tell you? In this activity, you will build your own barometer and will discover what this tool can tell you.

OBJECTIVES

Predict how changes in air pressure affect a barometer.

Build a barometer to test your hypothesis.

MATERIALS

- balloon
- can, coffee, large, empty, 10 cm in diameter
- card, index
- scissors
- straw, drinking
- tape, masking, or rubber band

SAFETY

Ask a Question

1. How can I use a barometer to detect changes in air pressure?

Form a Hypothesis

2. Write a few sentences that answer the question above.

Test the Hypothesis

3. Stretch the balloon a few times. Then, blow up the balloon, and let the air out. This step will make your barometer more sensitive to changes in atmospheric pressure.

4. Cut off the open end of the balloon. Next, stretch the balloon over the open end of the coffee can. Then, attach the balloon to the can with masking tape or a rubber band.

5. Cut one end of the straw at an angle to make a pointer.

6. Place the straw on the stretched balloon so that the pointer is directed away from the center of the balloon. Five centimeters of the end of the straw should hang over the edge of the can. Tape the straw to the balloon as shown in the illustration at right.

7. Tape the index card to the side of the can as shown in the illustration at right. Congratulations! You have just made a barometer!

8. Now, use your barometer to collect and record information about air pressure. Place the barometer outside for 3 or 4 days. On each day, mark on the index card where the tip of the straw points.

Analyze the Results

1. **Explaining Events** What atmospheric factors affect how your barometer works? Explain your answer.

2. **Recognizing Patterns** What does it mean when the straw moves up?

3. **Recognizing Patterns** What does it mean when the straw moves down?

Draw Conclusions

4. **Applying Conclusions** Compare your results with the barometric pressures listed in your local newspaper. What kind of weather is associated with high pressure? What kind of weather is associated with low pressure?

5. **Evaluating Results** Does the barometer you built support your hypothesis? Explain your answer.

Applying Your Data

Now, you can use your barometer to measure the actual air pressure! Get the weather section from your local newspaper for the same 3 or 4 days that you were testing your barometer. Find the barometer reading in the newspaper for each day, and record the reading beside that day's mark on your index card. Use these markings on your card to create a scale with marks at regular intervals. Transfer this scale to a new card and attach it to your barometer.

Chapter Review

USING KEY TERMS

For each pair of terms, explain how the meanings of the terms differ.

1. *air pressure* and *wind*

2. *troposphere* and *thermosphere*

3. *greenhouse effect* and *global warming*

4. *convection* and *thermal conduction*

5. *global wind* and *local wind*

6. *stratosphere* and *mesosphere*

UNDERSTANDING KEY IDEAS

Multiple Choice

7. What is the most abundant gas in the atmosphere?
   - **a.** oxygen
   - **b.** hydrogen
   - **c.** nitrogen
   - **d.** carbon dioxide

8. A major source of oxygen for the Earth's atmosphere is
   - **a.** sea water.
   - **b.** the sun.
   - **c.** plants.
   - **d.** animals.

9. The bottom layer of the atmosphere, where almost all weather occurs, is the
   - **a.** stratosphere.
   - **b.** troposphere.
   - **c.** thermosphere.
   - **d.** mesosphere.

10. What percentage of the solar energy that reaches the outer atmosphere is absorbed at the Earth's surface?
    - **a.** 20% **c.** 50%
    - **b.** 30% **d.** 70%

11. The ozone layer is located in the
    - **a.** stratosphere.
    - **b.** troposphere.
    - **c.** thermosphere.
    - **d.** mesosphere.

12. By which method does most thermal energy in the atmosphere circulate?
    - **a.** conduction
    - **b.** convection
    - **c.** advection
    - **d.** radiation

13. The balance between incoming and outgoing energy is called
    - **a.** the convection balance.
    - **b.** the conduction balance.
    - **c.** the greenhouse effect.
    - **d.** the radiation balance.

14. In which wind belt is most of the United States located?
    - **a.** westerlies
    - **b.** northeast trade winds
    - **c.** southeast trade winds
    - **d.** doldrums

15. Which of the following pollutants is NOT a primary pollutant?
    - **a.** car exhaust
    - **b.** acid precipitation
    - **c.** smoke from a factory
    - **d.** fumes from burning plastic

16 The Clean Air Act

   a. controls the amount of air pollutants that can be released from many sources.

   b. requires cars to run on fuels other than gasoline.

   c. requires many industries to use scrubbers.

   d. Both (a) and (c)

Short Answer

17 Why does the atmosphere become less dense as altitude increases?

18 Explain why air rises when it is heated.

19 What is the main cause of temperature changes in the atmosphere?

20 What are secondary pollutants, and how do they form? Give an example of a secondary pollutant.

21 **Concept Mapping** Use the following terms to create a concept map: *mesosphere, stratosphere, layers, temperature, troposphere,* and *atmosphere.*

22 **Identifying Relationships** What is the relationship between the greenhouse effect and global warming?

23 **Applying Concepts** How do you think the Coriolis effect would change if the Earth rotated twice as fast as it does? Explain.

24 **Making Inferences** The atmosphere of Venus has a very high level of carbon dioxide. How might this fact influence the greenhouse effect on Venus?

Use the diagram below to answer the questions that follow. When answering the questions that follow, assume that ocean currents do not affect the path of the boats.

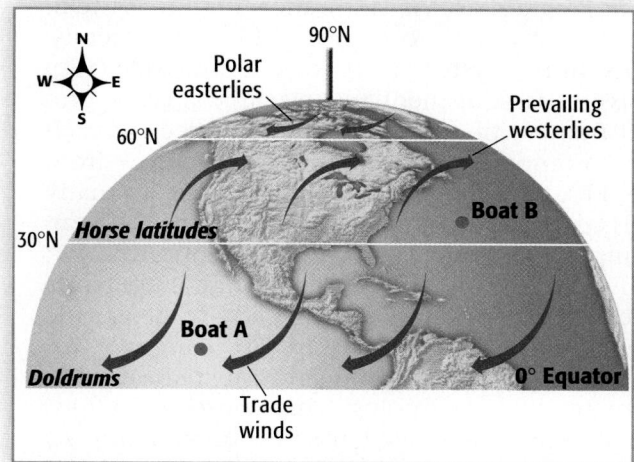

25 If Boat A traveled to 50°N, from which direction would the prevailing winds blow?

26 If Boat B sailed with the prevailing westerlies in the Northern Hemisphere, in which direction would the boat be traveling?

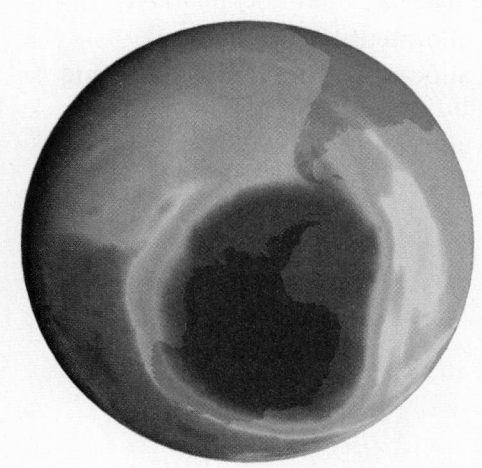

Standardized Test Preparation

Read each of the passages below. Then, answer the questions that follow each passage.

Passage 1 An important part of the EPA's Acid Rain Program is the allowance trading system, which is designed to reduce sulfur dioxide emissions. In this system, 1 ton of sulfur dioxide (SO_2) emission is equivalent to one <u>allowance</u>. A limited number of allowances are allocated for each year. Companies purchase the allowances from the EPA and are allowed to produce as many tons of SO_2 as they have allowances for the year. Companies can buy, sell, or trade allowances, but if they exceed their allowances, they must pay a fine. The system allows a company to determine the most cost-effective ways to comply with the Clean Air Act. A company can reduce emissions by using technology that conserves energy, using renewable energy sources, or updating its pollution-control devices and using low-sulfur fuels.

1. According to the passage, which of the following methods can a company use to reduce emissions?

A preserving wildlife habitat
B lobbying Congress
C using high-sulfur fuels
D using technology that conserves energy

2. In the passage, what does *allowance* mean?

F an allotment for a pollutant
G an allocation of money for reducing pollution
H an alleviation of pollution
I an allegation of pollution

Passage 2 The chinook, or "snow eater," is a dry wind that blows down the eastern side of the Rocky Mountains from New Mexico to Alaska. Arapaho Indians gave the chinook its name because of its ability to melt large amounts of snow very quickly. Chinooks form when moist air is forced over a mountain range. The air cools as it rises. As the air cools, it releases moisture by raining or snowing. As the dry air flows over the mountaintop, it compresses and heats the air below. The warm, dry wind that results is worthy of the name "snow eater" because it melts a half meter of snow in a few hours! The temperature change caused when a chinook rushes down a mountainside can also be dramatic. In 1943 in Spearfish, South Dakota, the temperature at 7:30 in the morning was –4°F. But two minutes later, a chinook caused the temperature to soar 49° to 45°F.

1. Which of the following descriptions best explains why the chinook is called "the snow eater"?

A The chinook is so cold that it prevents the formation of snow in the atmosphere.
B The chinook is so warm that it prevents the formation of snow in the atmosphere.
C The chinook is a warm wind that has high humidity.
D The chinook is a warm wind that has low humidity.

2. According to the passage, at what time did the temperature reach 45°F in Spearfish, South Dakota?

F 7:30 P.M.
G 7:32 P.M.
H 7:30 A.M.
I 7:32 A.M.

INTERPRETING GRAPHICS

Use the illustration below to answer the questions that follow.

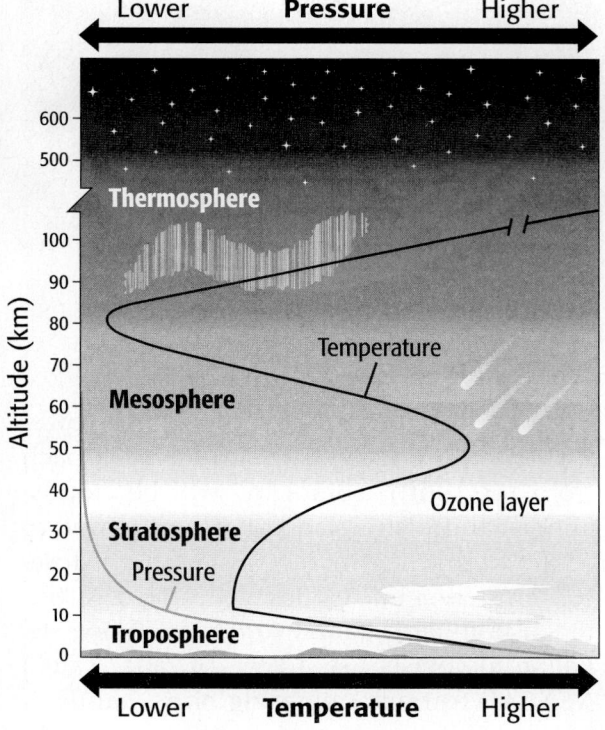

1. Which of the following statements describes how temperature changes in the mesosphere?

   A Temperature increases as altitude increases.

   B Temperature decreases as altitude increases.

   C Temperature decreases as pressure increases.

   D Temperature does not change as pressure increases.

2. In which layers does temperature decrease as pressure decreases?

   F the troposphere and the mesosphere

   G the troposphere and the stratosphere

   H the ozone layer and the troposphere

   I the ozone layer and the thermosphere

3. A research balloon took measurements at 23 km, 35 km, 52 km, 73 km, 86 km, 92 km, 101 km, and 110 km. Which measurements were taken in the mesosphere?

   A measurements at 23 km and 35 km

   B measurements at 52 km and 73 km

   C measurements at 86 km and 92 km

   D measurements at 101 km and 110 km

1. An airplane is flying at a speed of 500 km/h when it encounters a jet stream moving in the same direction at 150 km/h. If the plane flies with the jet stream, how much farther will the plane travel in 1.5 h?

   A 950 km

   B 525 km

   C 225 km

   D 150 km

2. Today's wind speed was measured at 18 km/h. What was the wind speed in meters per hour?

   F 1.8 m/h

   G 180 m/h

   H 1,800 m/h

   I 18,000 m/h

3. Rockport received 24.1 cm of rain on Monday, 12.5 cm of rain on Tuesday, and 5.8 cm of rain on Thursday. The rest of the week, it did not rain. How much rain did Rockport receive during the week?

   A 18.3 cm

   B 36.6 cm

   C 42.4 cm

   D 45.7 cm

4. A weather station recorded the following temperatures during a 5 h period: 15°C, 18°C, 13°C, 15°C, and 20°C. What was the average temperature during this period?

   F 14.2°C

   G 15.2°C

   H 16.2°C

   I 20.2°C

5. The temperature in Waterford, Virginia, increased 1.3°C every hour for 5 h. If the temperature in the morning was –4°C, what was the temperature 4 h later?

   A 2.5°C

   B 2.3°C

   C 1.3°C

   D 1.2°C

Science in Action

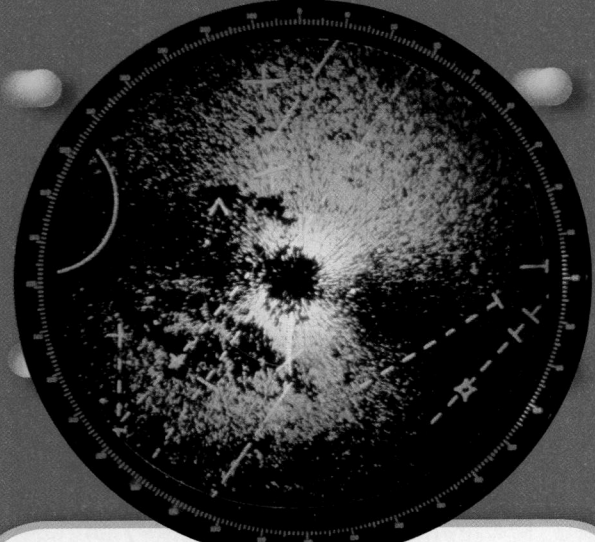

Science, Technology, and Society

The HyperSoar Jet

Imagine traveling from Chicago to Tokyo in 72 minutes. If the HyperSoar jet becomes a reality, you may be able to travel to the other side of the world in less time than it takes to watch a movie! To accomplish this amazing feat, the jet would "skip" across the upper stratosphere. To begin skipping, the jet would climb above the stratosphere, turn off its engines, and glide for about 60 km. Then, gravity would pull the jet down to where the air is denser. The denser air would cause the jet to soar upward. In this way, the jet would skip across a layer of dense air until it was ready to land. Each 2-minute skip would cover about 450 km, and the HyperSoar would be able to fly at Mach 10—a speed of 3 km/s!

Math ACTIVITY

A trip on the HyperSoar from Chicago to Tokyo would require about 18 "skips." Each skip is 450 km. If the trip is 10,123 km, how many kilometers will the jet travel when it is not skipping?

Weird Science

Radar Zoology

"For tonight's forecast, expect a light shower of mayflies. A wave of warblers will approach from the south. Tomorrow will be cloudy, and a band of free-tailed bats will move to the south in the early evening." Such a forecast may not make the evening news, but it is a familiar scenario for radar zoologists. Radar zoologists use a type of radar called *NEXRAD* to track migrating birds, bands of bats, and swarms of insects. NEXRAD tracks animals in the atmosphere in the same way that it tracks storms. The system sends out a microwave signal. If the signal hits an object, some of the energy reflects back to a receiver. NEXRAD has been especially useful to scientists who study bird migration. Birds tend to migrate at night, when the atmosphere is more stable, so until now, nighttime bird migration has been difficult to observe. NEXRAD has also helped identify important bird migration routes and critical stopovers. For example, scientists have discovered that many birds migrate over the Gulf of Mexico instead of around it.

Social Studies ACTIVITY

Geography plays an important role in bird migration. Many birds ride the "thermals" produced by mountain ranges. Find out what thermals are, and create a map of bird migration routes over North America.

Ellen Paneok

Bush Pilot For Ellen Paneok, understanding weather patterns is a matter of life and death. As a bush pilot, she flies mail, supplies, and people to remote villages in Alaska that can be reached only by plane. Bad weather is one of the most serious challenges Paneok faces. "It's beautiful up here," she says, "but it can also be harsh." One dangerous situation is landing a plane in mountainous regions. "On top of a mountain you can't tell which way the wind is blowing," Paneok says. In this case, she flies in a rectangular pattern to determine the wind direction. Landing a plane on the frozen Arctic Ocean is also dangerous. In white-out conditions, the horizon can't be seen because the sky and the ground are the same color. "It's like flying in a milk bottle full of milk," Paneok says. In these conditions, she fills black plastic garbage bags and drops them from the plane to help guide her landing.

Paneok had to overcome many challenges to become a pilot. As a child, she lived in seven foster homes before being placed in an all-girls' home at the age of 14. In the girls' home, she read a magazine about careers in aviation and decided then and there that she wanted to become a pilot. At first, she faced a lot of opposition from people telling her that she wouldn't be able to become a pilot. Now, she encourages young people to pursue their goals. "If you decide you want to go for it, go for it. There may be obstacles in your way, but you've just got to find a way to go over them, get around them, or dig under them," she says.

Ellen Paneok is shown at right with two of her Inupiat passengers.

Language Arts ACTiViTY

Beryl Markham lived an exciting life as a bush pilot delivering mail and supplies to remote areas of Africa. Read about her life or the life of Bessie Coleman, one of the most famous African American women in the history of flying.

To learn more about these Science in Action topics, visit go.hrw.com and type in the keyword **HZ5ATMF.**

Current Science

Check out Current Science® articles related to this chapter by visiting go.hrw.com. Just type in the keyword **HZ5CS15.**

16

Understanding Weather

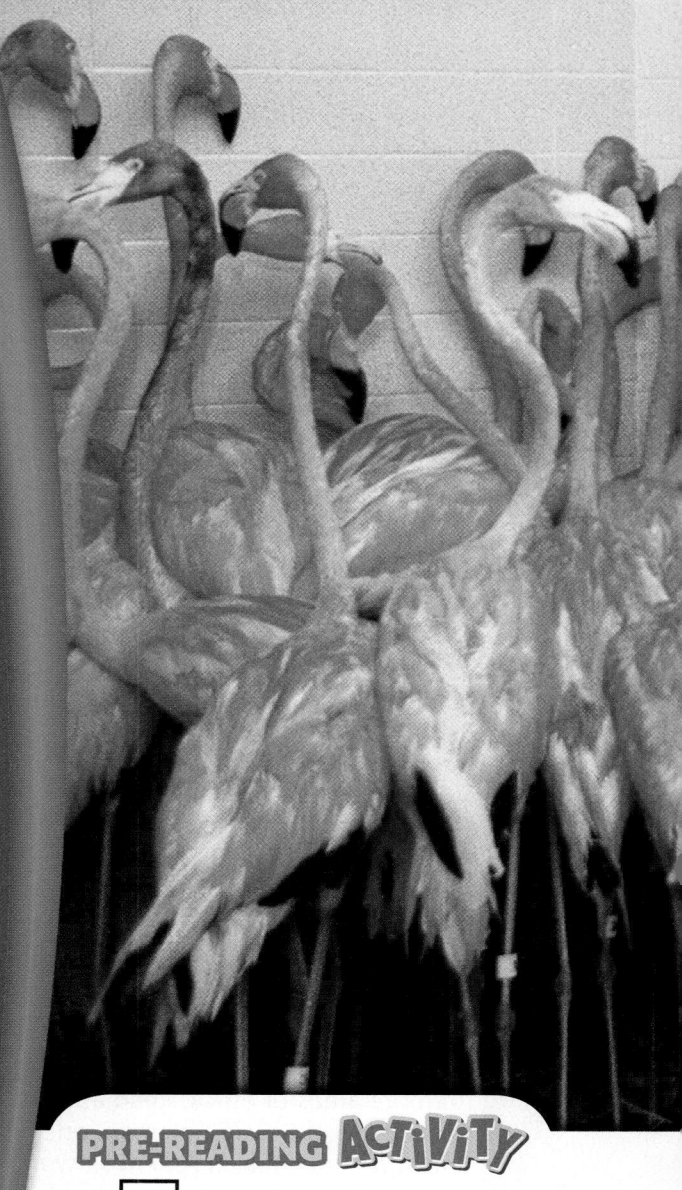

About the PHOTO

Flamingos in the bathroom? This may look like someone's idea of a practical joke, but in fact, it's a practical idea! These flamingos reside at the Miami-Metro Zoo in Florida. They were put in the bathroom for protection against the incredibly dangerous winds of Hurricane Floyd in September of 1999.

PRE-READING ACTIVITY

FOLDNOTES **Four-Corner Fold**
Before you read the chapter, create the FoldNote entitled "Four-Corner Fold" described in the **Study Skills** section of the Appendix. Label the flaps of the four-corner fold with "Water in the air," "Air masses and fronts," "Severe weather," and "Forecasting the weather." Write what you know about each topic under the appropriate flap. As you read the chapter, add other information that you learn.

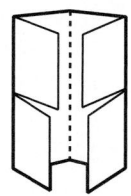

START-UP ACTiViTY

Meeting of the Masses

In this activity, you will model what happens when two air masses that have different temperature characteristics meet.

Procedure

1. Pour **500 mL of water** into a **beaker.** Pour **500 mL of cooking oil** into a **second beaker.** The water represents a dense cold air mass. The cooking oil represents a less dense warm air mass.

2. Predict what would happen to the two liquids if you tried to mix them.

3. Pour the contents of both beakers into a **clear, plastic, rectangular container** at the same time from opposite ends of the container.

4. Observe the interaction of the oil and water.

Analysis

1. What happens when the liquids meet?

2. Does the prediction that you made in step 2 of the Procedure match your results?

3. Using your results, hypothesize what would happen if a cold air mass met a warm air mass.

Water in the Air

What will the weather be this weekend? Depending on what you have planned, knowing the answer to this question could be important. A picnic in the rain can be a mess!

Have you ever wondered what weather is? **Weather** is the condition of the atmosphere at a certain time and place. The condition of the atmosphere is affected by the amount of water in the air. So, to understand weather, you need to understand how water cycles through Earth's atmosphere.

The Water Cycle

Water in liquid, solid, and gaseous states is constantly being recycled through the water cycle. The *water cycle* is the continuous movement of water from sources on Earth's surface—such as lakes, oceans, and plants—into the air, onto and over land, into the ground, and back to the surface. The movement of water through the water cycle is shown in **Figure 1.**

✓ **Reading Check** **What is the water cycle?** (*See the Appendix for answers to Reading Checks.*)

Figure 1 The Water Cycle

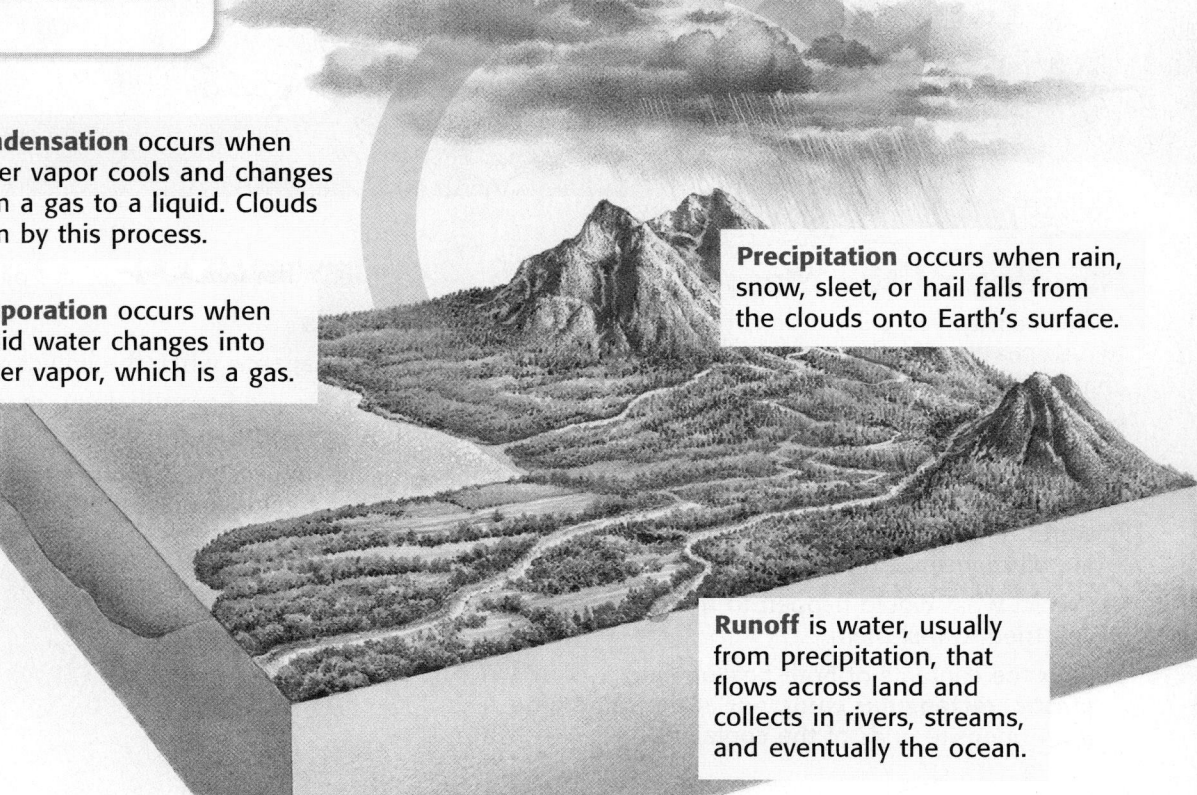

Condensation occurs when water vapor cools and changes from a gas to a liquid. Clouds form by this process.

Evaporation occurs when liquid water changes into water vapor, which is a gas.

Precipitation occurs when rain, snow, sleet, or hail falls from the clouds onto Earth's surface.

Runoff is water, usually from precipitation, that flows across land and collects in rivers, streams, and eventually the ocean.

Amount of Water Vapor Air Can Hold at Various Temperatures

Figure 2 *This graph shows that as air gets warmer, the amount of water vapor that the air can hold increases.*

Humidity

As water evaporates from lakes, oceans, and plants, it becomes *water vapor,* or moisture in the air. Water vapor is invisible. The amount of water vapor in the air is called **humidity.** As water evaporates and becomes water vapor, the humidity of the air increases. The air's ability to hold water vapor changes as the temperature of the air changes. **Figure 2** shows that as the temperature of the air increases, the air's ability to hold water vapor also increases.

weather the short-term state of the atmosphere, including temperature, humidity, precipitation, wind, and visibility

humidity the amount of water vapor in the air

relative humidity the ratio of the amount of water vapor in the air to the maximum amount of water vapor the air can hold at a set temperature

Relative Humidity

One way to express humidity is through relative humidity. **Relative humidity** is the amount of water vapor in the air compared with the maximum amount of water vapor that the air can hold at a certain temperature. So, relative humidity is given as a percentage. When air holds all of the water that it can at a given temperature, it is said to be *saturated.* Saturated air has a relative humidity of 100%. But how do you find the relative humidity of air that is not saturated? If you know the maximum amount of water vapor that air can hold at a given temperature and the actual amount of water vapor in the air, you can calculate the relative humidity.

Suppose that 1 m³ of air at a certain temperature can hold 24 g of water vapor. However, you know that the air actually contains 18 g of water vapor. You can calculate the relative humidity by using the following formula:

$$\frac{actual\ water\ vapor\ content\ (g/m^3)}{saturation\ water\ vapor\ content\ (g/m^3)} \times 100 = relative\ humidity\ (\%)$$

$$\frac{18\ g/m^3}{24\ g/m^3} = 75\%$$

Relative Humidity

Assume that 1 m³ of air at 25°C contains 11 g of water vapor. At this temperature, the air can hold 24 g/m³ of water vapor. Calculate the relative humidity of the air.

INTERNET ACTIVITY

For another activity related to this chapter, go to **go.hrw.com** and type in the keyword **HZ5WEAW**.

Factors Affecting Relative Humidity

Two factors that affect relative humidity are amount of water vapor and temperature. At constant temperature and pressure, as the amount of water vapor in air changes, the relative humidity changes. The more water vapor there is in the air, the higher the relative humidity is. If the amount of water vapor in the air stays the same but the temperature changes, the relative humidity changes. The relative humidity decreases as the temperature rises and increases as the temperature drops.

Measuring Relative Humidity

A *psychrometer* (sie KRAHM uht uhr) is an instrument that is used to measure relative humidity. A psychrometer consists of two thermometers, one of which is a wet-bulb thermometer. The bulb of a wet-bulb thermometer is covered with a damp cloth. The other thermometer is a dry-bulb thermometer.

The difference in temperature readings between the thermometers indicates the amount of water vapor in the air. The larger the difference between the two readings is, the less water vapor the air contains and thus the lower the humidity is. **Figure 3** shows how to use a table of differences between wet-bulb and dry-bulb readings to determine relative humidity.

Reading Check What tool is used to measure relative humidity?

Figure 3 Determining Relative Humidity

Find the relative humidity by locating the column head that is equal to the difference between the wet-bulb and dry-bulb readings. Then, locate the row head that equals the temperature reading on the dry-bulb thermometer. The value that lies where the column and row intersect equals the relative humidity. You can see a psychrometer below.

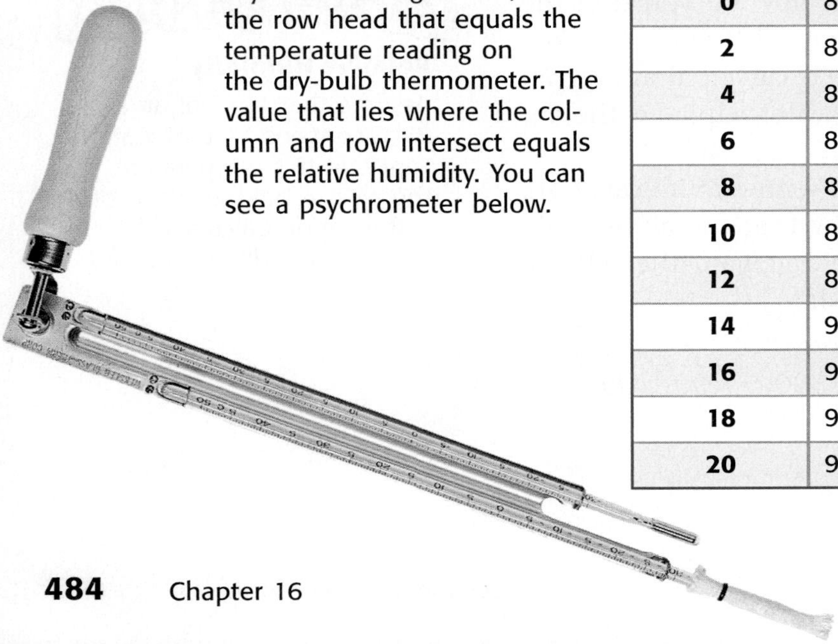

Relative Humidity (%)								
Dry-bulb reading (°C)	Difference between wet-bulb reading and dry-bulb reading (°C)							
	1	2	3	4	5	6	7	8
0	81	64	46	29	13			
2	84	68	52	37	22	7		
4	85	71	57	43	29	16		
6	86	73	60	48	35	24	11	
8	87	75	63	51	40	29	19	8
10	88	77	66	55	44	34	24	15
12	89	78	68	58	48	39	29	21
14	90	79	70	60	51	42	34	26
16	90	81	71	63	54	46	38	30
18	91	82	73	65	57	49	41	34
20	91	83	74	66	59	51	44	37

How a Wet-Bulb Thermometer Works

A wet-bulb thermometer works differently than a dry-bulb thermometer, which measures only air temperature. As air passes over the wet-bulb thermometer, the water in the cloth evaporates. As the water evaporates, the cloth cools. If the humidity is low, the water will evaporate more quickly and the temperature reading on the wet-bulb thermometer will drop. If the humidity is high, only a small amount of water will evaporate from the cloth of the wet-bulb thermometer and the change in temperature will be small.

✓ Reading Check Explain how a wet-bulb thermometer works.

Condensation

You have probably seen water droplets form on the outside of a glass of ice water, as shown in **Figure 4.** Where did those water drops come from? The water came from the surrounding air, and droplets formed as a result of condensation. **Condensation** is the process by which a gas, such as water vapor, becomes a liquid. Before condensation can occur, the air must be saturated, which means that the air must have a relative humidity of 100%. Condensation occurs when saturated air cools.

Dew Point

Air can become saturated when water vapor is added to the air through evaporation. Air can also become saturated when it cools to its dew point. The *dew point* is the temperature at which a gas condenses into a liquid. At its dew point, air is saturated. The ice in the glass of water causes the air surrounding the glass to cool to its dew point.

Before water vapor can condense, though, it must have a surface to condense on. In the case of the glass of ice water, water vapor condenses on the outside of the glass.

Figure 4 *Condensation occurred when the air next to the glass cooled to its dew point.*

condensation the change of state from a gas to a liquid

Out of Thin Air

1. Pour **room-temperature water** into a **plastic container,** such as a drinking cup, until the water level is near the top of the cup.
2. Observe the outside of the container, and record your observations.
3. Add **one or two ice cubes** to the container of water.
4. Watch the outside of the container for any changes.
5. What happened to the outside of the container?
6. What is the liquid on the container?
7. Where did the liquid come from? Explain your answer.

Figure 5 Three Forms of Clouds

Cumulus clouds look like piles of cotton balls.

Stratus clouds are not as tall as cumulus clouds, but they cover more area.

Cirrus clouds are made of ice crystals.

cloud a collection of small water droplets or ice crystals suspended in the air, which forms when the air is cooled and condensation occurs

CONNECTION TO Language Arts

Cloud Clues Did you know that the name of a cloud actually describes the characteristics of the cloud? For example, the word *cumulus* comes from the Latin word meaning "heap." A cumulus cloud is a puffy, white cloud, which could be described as a "heap" of clouds. Use a dictionary or the Internet to find the word origins of the names of the other cloud types you learn about in this section.

Clouds

Have you ever wondered what clouds are and how they form? A **cloud** is a collection of millions of tiny water droplets or ice crystals. Clouds form as warm air rises and cools. As the rising air cools, it becomes saturated. When the air is saturated, the water vapor changes to a liquid or a solid, depending on the air temperature. At temperatures above freezing, water vapor condenses on small particles in the air and forms tiny water droplets. At temperatures below freezing, water vapor changes to a solid to form ice crystals. Clouds are classified by form, as shown in **Figure 5,** and by altitude.

Cumulus Clouds

Puffy, white clouds that tend to have flat bottoms are called *cumulus clouds* (KYOO myoo luhs KLOWDZ). Cumulus clouds form when warm air rises. These clouds generally indicate fair weather. However, when these clouds get larger, they produce thunderstorms. Thunderstorms come from a kind of cumulus cloud called a *cumulonimbus cloud* (KYOO myoo loh NIM buhs KLOWD). Clouds that have names that include *-nimbus* or *nimbo-* are likely to produce precipitation.

Stratus Clouds

Clouds called *stratus clouds* (STRAYT uhs KLOWDZ) are clouds that form in layers. Stratus clouds cover large areas of the sky and often block out the sun. These clouds can be caused by a gentle lifting of a large body of air into the atmosphere. *Nimbostratus clouds* (NIM boh STRAYT uhs KLOWDZ) are dark stratus clouds that usually produce light to heavy, continuous rain. *Fog* is a stratus cloud that has formed near the ground.

Cirrus Clouds

As you can see in **Figure 5,** *cirrus clouds* (SIR uhs KLOWDZ) are thin, feathery, white clouds found at high altitudes. Cirrus clouds form when the wind is strong. If they get thicker, cirrus clouds indicate that a change in the weather is coming.

Clouds and Altitude

Clouds are also classified by the altitude at which they form. **Figure 6** shows two altitude groups used to describe clouds and the altitudes at which they form in the middle latitudes. The prefix *cirro-* is used to describe clouds that form at high altitudes. For example, a cumulus cloud that forms high in the atmosphere is called a *cirrocumulus cloud.* The prefix *alto-* describes clouds that form at middle altitudes. Clouds that form at low altitudes do not have a specific prefix to describe them.

✓ **Reading Check** At what altitude does an altostratus cloud form?

Figure 6 Cloud Types Based on Form and Altitude

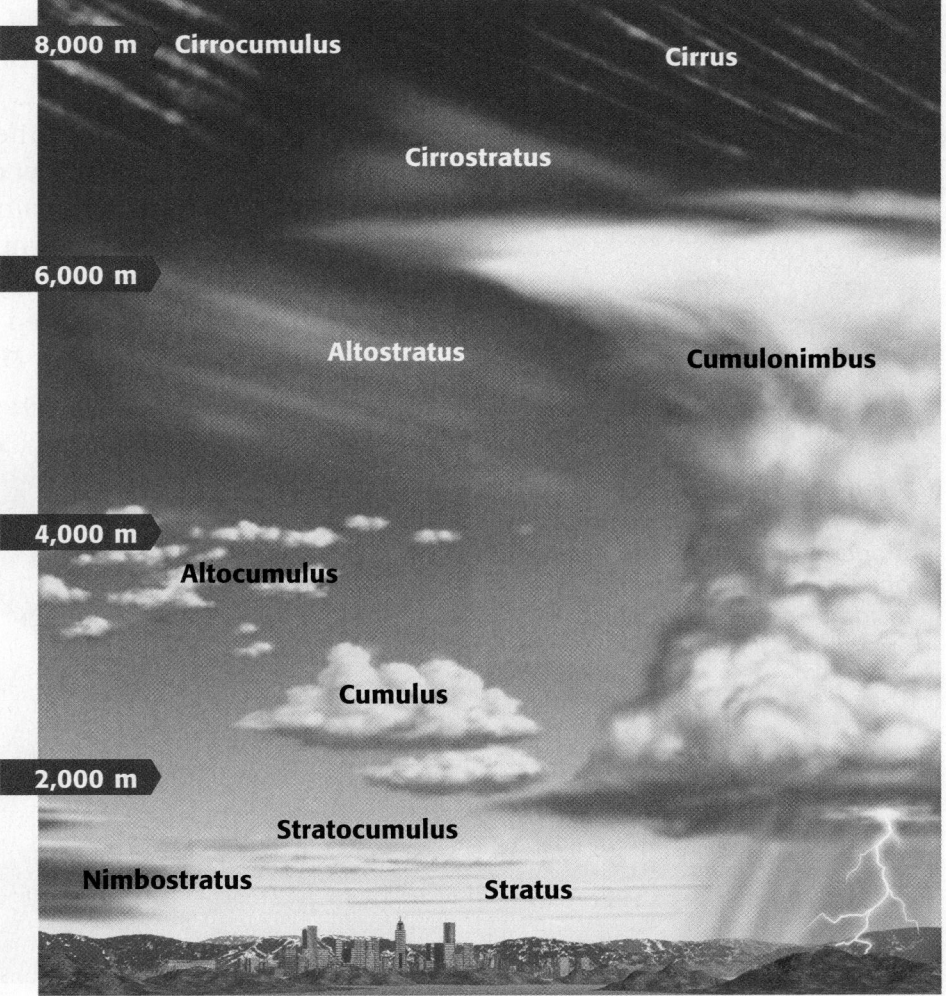

High Clouds Because of the cold temperatures at high altitude, high clouds are made up of ice crystals. The prefix *cirro-* is used to describe high clouds.

Middle Clouds Middle clouds can be made up of both water drops and ice crystals. The prefix *alto-* is used to describe middle clouds.

Low Clouds Low clouds are made up of water drops. There is no specific prefix used to describe low clouds.

8,000 m   Cirrocumulus   Cirrus

Cirrostratus

6,000 m

Altostratus   Cumulonimbus

4,000 m

Altocumulus

Cumulus

2,000 m

Stratocumulus

Nimbostratus   Stratus

Figure 7 *Snowflakes are six-sided ice crystals that can be several millimeters to several centimeters in size.*

Precipitation

When water from the air returns to Earth's surface, it returns as precipitation. **Precipitation** is water, in solid or liquid form, that falls from the air to Earth. There are four major forms of precipitation—rain, snow, sleet, and hail.

Rain

The most common form of precipitation is *rain*. A cloud produces rain when the water drops in the cloud become large enough to fall. A water drop in a cloud begins as a droplet that is smaller than the period at the end of this sentence. Before such a water drop falls as rain, it must become about 100 times its original size.

Sleet and Snow

Sleet forms when rain falls through a layer of freezing air. The rain freezes in the air, which produces falling ice. *Snow* forms when temperatures are so cold that water vapor changes directly to a solid. Snow can fall as single ice crystals or can join to form snowflakes, as shown in **Figure 7.**

Hail

Balls or lumps of ice that fall from clouds are called *hail*. Hail forms in cumulonimbus clouds. When updrafts of air in the clouds carry raindrops high in the clouds, the raindrops freeze and hail forms. As hail falls, water drops coat it. Another updraft of air can send the hail up again. Here, the water drops collected on the hail freeze to form another layer of ice on the hail. This process can happen many times. Eventually, the hail becomes too heavy to be carried by the updrafts and so falls to Earth's surface, as shown in **Figure 8.**

precipitation any form of water that falls to the Earth's surface from the clouds

Figure 8 *The impact of large hailstones can damage property and crops. The inset photograph shows layers inside of a hailstone, which reveal how it formed.*

SECTION Review

Summary

- Weather is the condition of the atmosphere at a certain time and place. Weather is affected by the amount of water vapor in the air.
- The water cycle describes the movement of water above, on, and below Earth's surface.
- Humidity describes the amount of water vapor in the air. Relative humidity is a way to express humidity.
- When the temperature of the air cools to its dew point, the air has reached saturation and condensation occurs.
- Clouds form as air cools to its dew point. Clouds are classified by form and by the altitude at which they form.
- Precipitation occurs when the water vapor that condenses in the atmosphere falls back to Earth in solid or liquid form.

Using Key Terms

1. In your own words, write a definition for each of the following terms: *relative humidity, condensation, cloud,* and *precipitation*.

Understanding Key Ideas

2. Which of the following clouds is most likely to produce light to heavy, continuous rain?
    a. cumulus cloud
    b. cumulonimbus cloud
    c. nimbostratus cloud
    d. cirrus cloud

3. How is relative humidity affected by the amount of water vapor in the air?

4. What does a relative humidity of 75% mean?

5. Describe the path of water through the water cycle.

6. What are four types of precipitation?

Critical Thinking

7. **Applying Concepts** Why are some clouds formed from water droplets, while others are made up of ice crystals?

8. **Applying Concepts** How can rain and hail fall from the same cumulonimbus cloud?

9. **Identifying Relationships** What happens to relative humidity as the air temperature drops below the dew point?

Interpreting Graphics

Use the image below to answer the questions that follow.

10. What type of cloud is shown in the image?

11. How is this type of cloud formed?

12. What type of weather can you expect when you see this type of cloud? Explain.

For a variety of links related to this chapter, go to www.scilinks.org

Topic: The Water Cycle
SciLinks code: HSM1626

Air Masses and Fronts

Have you ever wondered how the weather can change so quickly? For example, the weather may be warm and sunny in the morning and cold and rainy by afternoon.

Changes in weather are caused by the movement and interaction of air masses. An **air mass** is a large body of air where temperature and moisture content are similar throughout. In this section, you will learn about air masses and their effect on weather.

Air Masses

Air masses are characterized by their moisture content and temperature. The moisture content and temperature of an air mass are determined by the area over which the air mass forms. These areas are called *source regions*. An example of a source region is the Gulf of Mexico. An air mass that forms over the Gulf of Mexico is warm and wet because this area is warm and has a lot of water that evaporates. There are many types of air masses, each of which is associated with a particular source region. The characteristics of these air masses are represented on maps by a two-letter symbol, as shown in **Figure 1.** The first letter indicates the moisture content that is characteristic of the air mass. The second letter represents the temperature that is characteristic of the air mass.

READING WARM-UP

Objectives

- Identify the four kinds of air masses that influence weather in the United States.
- Describe the four major types of fronts.
- Explain how fronts cause weather changes.
- Explain how cyclones and anticyclones affect the weather.

Terms to Learn

air mass   cyclone
front   anticyclone

READING STRATEGY

Reading Organizer As you read this section, make a table comparing cold, warm, occluded, and stationary fronts.

Figure 1 Air Masses That Affect Weather in North America

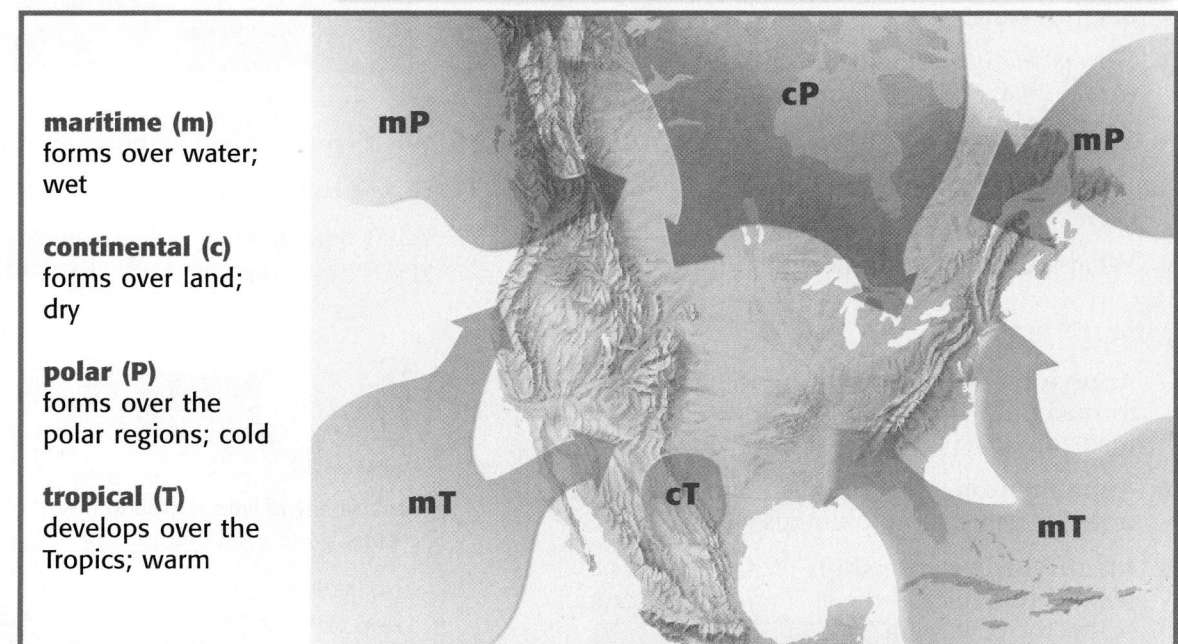

maritime (m) forms over water; wet

continental (c) forms over land; dry

polar (P) forms over the polar regions; cold

tropical (T) develops over the Tropics; warm

Figure 2 *Cold air masses that form over the North Atlantic Ocean can bring severe weather, such as blizzards, in the winter.*

Cold Air Masses

Most of the cold winter weather in the United States is influenced by three polar air masses. A continental polar (cP) air mass forms over northern Canada, which brings extremely cold winter weather to the United States. In the summer, a cP air mass generally brings cool, dry weather.

A maritime polar (mP) air mass that forms over the North Pacific Ocean is cool and very wet. This air mass brings rain and snow to the Pacific Coast in the winter and cool, foggy weather in the summer.

A maritime polar air mass that forms over the North Atlantic Ocean brings cool, cloudy weather and precipitation to New England in the winter, as shown in **Figure 2.** In the summer, the air mass brings cool weather and fog.

air mass a large body of air where temperature and moisture content are constant throughout

Warm Air Masses

Four warm air masses influence the weather in the United States. A maritime tropical (mT) air mass that develops over warm areas in the Pacific Ocean is milder than the maritime polar air mass that forms over the Pacific Ocean.

Other maritime tropical air masses develop over the warm waters of the Gulf of Mexico and the Atlantic Ocean. These air masses move north across the East Coast and into the Midwest. In the summer, they bring hot and humid weather, hurricanes, and thunderstorms, as shown in **Figure 3.** In the winter, they bring mild, often cloudy weather.

A continental tropical (cT) air mass forms over the deserts of northern Mexico and the southwestern United States. This air mass moves northward and brings clear, dry, and hot weather in the summer.

✓ Reading Check What type of air mass contributes to the hot and humid summer weather in the midwestern United States? (*See the Appendix for answers to Reading Checks.*)

Figure 3 *Warm air masses that develop over the Gulf of Mexico bring thunderstorms in the summer.*

Figure 4 Fronts That Affect Weather in North America

Cold Front

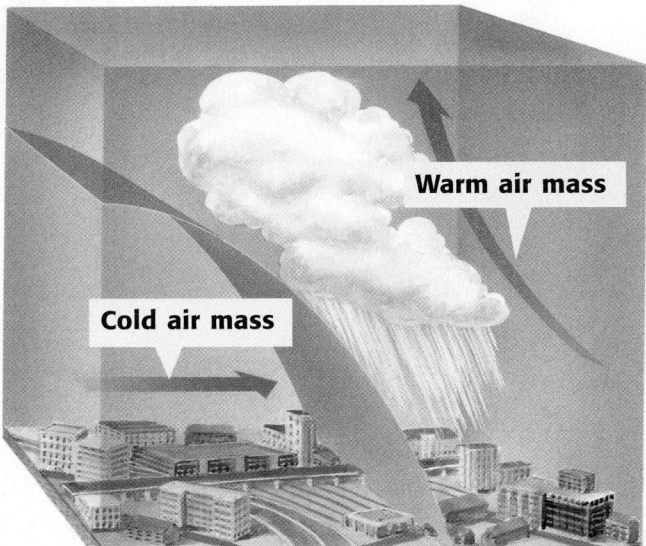

Warm air mass

Cold air mass

Direction of front

Warm Front

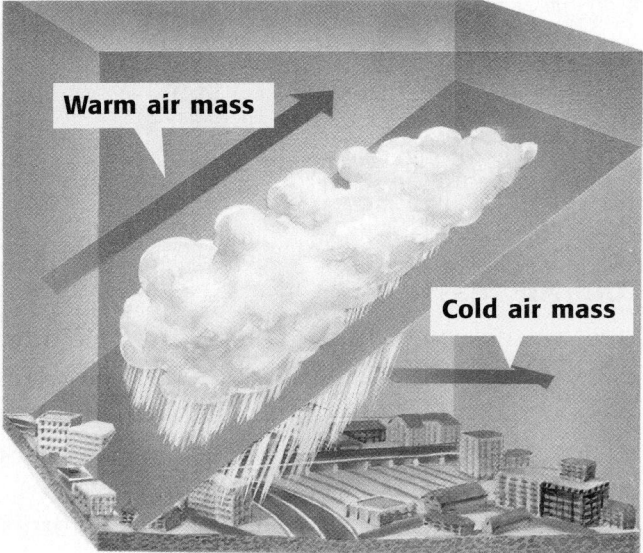

Warm air mass

Cold air mass

Direction of front

Fronts

Air masses that form from different areas often do not mix. The reason is that the air masses have different densities. For example, warm air is less dense than cold air. So, when two types of air masses meet, warm air generally rises. The area in which two types of air masses meet is called a **front**. The four kinds of fronts—cold fronts, warm fronts, occluded fronts, and stationary fronts—are shown in **Figure 4.** Fronts are associated with weather in the middle latitudes.

Cold Front

A cold front forms where cold air moves under warm air, which is less dense, and pushes the warm air up. Cold fronts can move quickly and bring thunderstorms, heavy rain, or snow. Cooler weather usually follows a cold front because the air mass behind the cold front is cooler and drier than the air mass that it is replacing.

Warm Front

A warm front forms where warm air moves over cold, denser air. In a warm front, the warm air gradually replaces the cold air. Warm fronts generally bring drizzly rain and are followed by clear and warm weather.

front the boundary between air masses of different densities and usually different temperatures

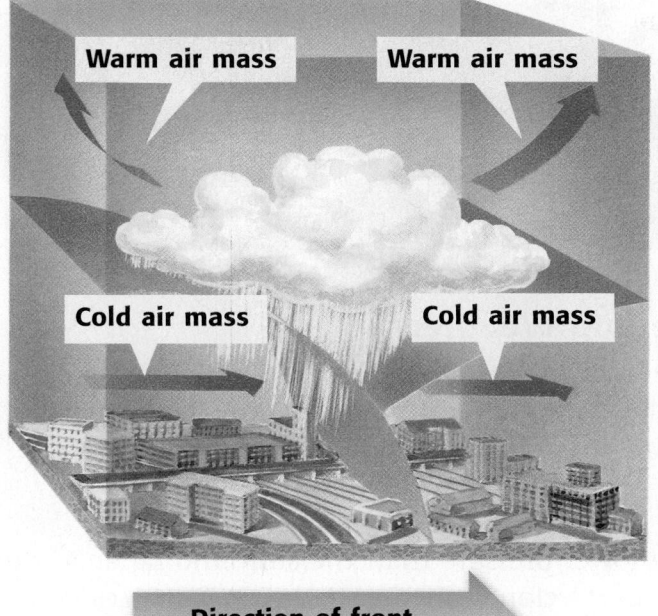

Occluded Front

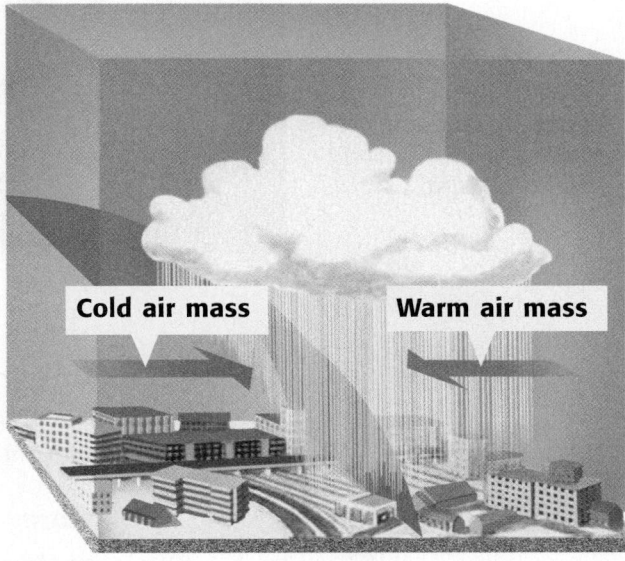

Stationary Front

Occluded Front

An occluded front forms when a warm air mass is caught between two colder air masses. The coldest air mass moves under and pushes up the warm air mass. The coldest air mass then moves forward until it meets a cold air mass that is warmer and less dense. The colder of these two air masses moves under and pushes up the warmer air mass. Sometimes, though, the two colder air masses mix. An occluded front has cool temperatures and large amounts of rain and snow.

✓ *Reading Check* **What type of weather would you expect an occluded front to produce?**

Stationary Front

A stationary front forms when a cold air mass meets a warm air mass. In this case, however, both air masses do not have enough force to lift the warm air mass over the cold air mass. So, the two air masses remain separated. This may happen because there is not enough wind to keep the air masses pushing against each other. A stationary front often brings many days of cloudy, wet weather.

Figure 5 *This satellite image shows a cyclone system forming.*

Air Pressure and Weather

You may have heard a weather reporter on TV or radio talking about areas of low pressure and high pressure. These areas of different pressure affect the weather.

Cyclones

Areas that have lower pressure than the surrounding areas do are called **cyclones.** Cyclones are areas where air masses come together, or converge, and rise. **Figure 5** shows a satellite image of the formation of a cyclone system.

Anticyclones

Areas that have high pressure are called **anticyclones.** Anticyclones are areas where air moves apart, or diverges, and sinks. The sinking air is denser than the surrounding air, and the pressure is higher. Cooler, denser air moves out of the center of these high-pressure areas toward areas of lower pressure. **Figure 6** shows how wind can spiral out of an anticyclone and into a cyclone.

cyclone an area in the atmosphere that has lower pressure than the surrounding areas and has winds that spiral toward the center

anticyclone the rotation of air around a high-pressure center in the direction opposite to Earth's rotation

Figure 6 *As the colder, denser air spirals out of the anticyclone, it moves towards areas of low pressure, which sometimes forms a cyclone.*

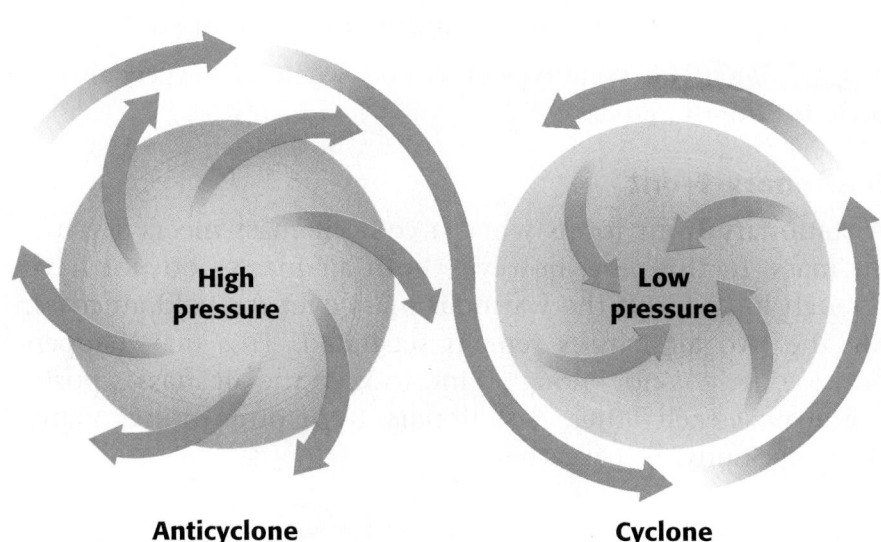

High pressure

Low pressure

Anticyclone

Cyclone

Cyclones, Anticyclones, and Weather

You have learned what cyclones and anticyclones are. So, now you might be wondering how do cyclones and anticyclones affect the weather? As the air in the center of a cyclone rises, it cools and forms clouds and rain. The rising air in a cyclone causes stormy weather. In an anticyclone, the air sinks. As the air sinks, it gets warmer and absorbs moisture. The sinking air in an anticyclone brings dry, clear weather. By keeping track of cyclones and anticyclones, meteorologists can predict the weather.

✔ **Reading Check** Describe the different types of weather that a cyclone and an anticyclone can produce.

CONNECTION TO Astronomy

Storms on Jupiter Cyclones and anticyclones occur on Jupiter, too! Generally, cyclones on Jupiter appear as dark ovals, and anticyclones appear as bright ovals. Jupiter's Great Red Spot is an anticyclone that has existed for centuries. Research the existence of cyclones and anticyclones on other bodies in our solar system.

SECTION Review

Summary

- Air masses are characterized by moisture content and temperature.
- A front occurs where two air masses meet.
- Four major types of fronts are cold, warm, occluded, and stationary fronts.
- Differences in air pressure cause cyclones, which bring stormy weather, and anticyclones, which bring dry, clear weather.

Using Key Terms

For each pair of terms, explain how the meanings of the terms differ.

1. *front* and *air mass*

2. *cyclone* and *anticyclone*

Understanding Key Ideas

3. What kind of front forms when a cold air mass displaces a warm air mass?
   a. a cold front
   b. a warm front
   c. an occluded front
   d. a stationary front

4. What are the major air masses that influence the weather in the United States?

5. What is one source region of a maritime polar air mass?

6. What are the characteristics of an air mass whose two-letter symbol is cP?

7. What are the four major types of fronts?

8. How do fronts cause weather changes?

9. How do cyclones and anticyclones affect the weather?

Math Skills

10. A cold front is moving toward the town of La Porte at 35 km/h. The front is 200 km away from La Porte. How long will it take the front to get to La Porte?

Critical Thinking

11. **Applying Concepts** How do air masses that form over the land and ocean affect weather in the United States?

12. **Identifying Relationships** Why does the Pacific Coast have cool, wet winters and warm, dry summers? Explain.

13. **Applying Concepts** Which air masses influence the weather where you live? Explain.

SCILINKS **NSTA**
Developed and maintained by the
National Science Teachers Association

For a variety of links related to this chapter, go to www.scilinks.org

Topic: Air Masses and Fronts
SciLinks code: HSM0032

Severe Weather

CRAAAACK! BOOM! What made that noise? You didn't expect it, and it sure made you jump.

A big boom of thunder has probably surprised you at one time or another. And the thunder was probably followed by a thunderstorm. A thunderstorm is an example of severe weather. *Severe weather* is weather that can cause property damage and sometimes death.

Thunderstorms

Thunderstorms can be very loud and powerful. **Thunderstorms,** such as the one shown in **Figure 1,** are small, intense weather systems that produce strong winds, heavy rain, lightning, and thunder. Thunderstorms can occur along cold fronts. But thunderstorms can develop in other places, too. There are only two atmospheric conditions required to produce thunderstorms: warm and moist air near Earth's surface and an unstable atmosphere. The atmosphere is unstable when the surrounding air is colder than the rising air mass. The air mass will continue to rise as long as the surrounding air is colder than the air mass.

When the rising warm air reaches its dew point, the water vapor in the air condenses and forms cumulus clouds. If the atmosphere is extremely unstable, the warm air will continue to rise, which causes the cloud to grow into a dark, cumulonimbus cloud. Cumulonimbus clouds can reach heights of more than 15 km.

READING WARM-UP

Objectives

● Describe how lightning forms.
● Describe the formation of thunderstorms, tornadoes, and hurricanes.
● Describe the characteristics of thunderstorms, tornadoes, and hurricanes.
● Explain how to stay safe during severe weather.

Terms to Learn

thunderstorm   tornado
lightning   hurricane
thunder

READING STRATEGY

Reading Organizer As you read this section, create an outline of the section. Use the headings from the section in your outline.

thunderstorm a usually brief, heavy storm that consists of rain, strong winds, lightning, and thunder

Figure 1 *A typical thunderstorm, such as this one over Dallas, Texas, generates an enormous amount of electrical energy.*

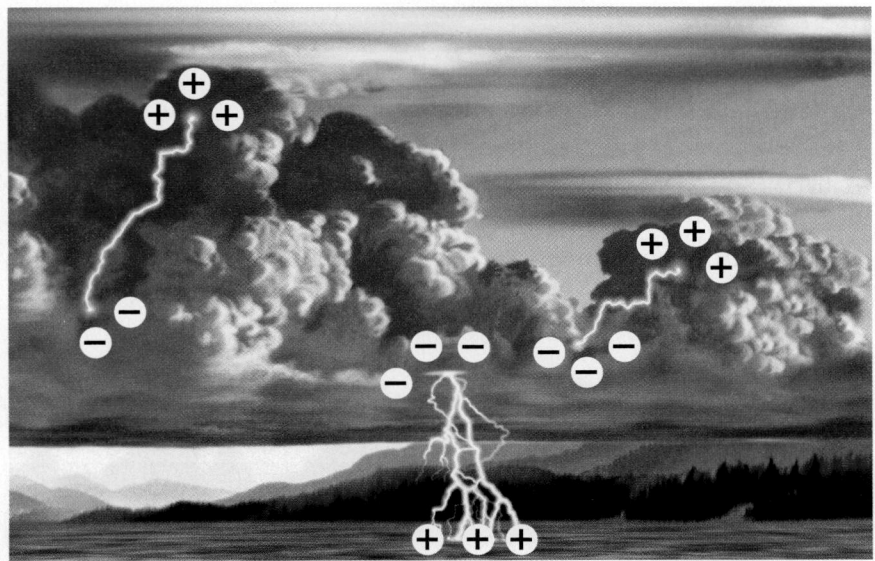

Figure 2 *The upper part of a cloud usually carries a positive electric charge, while the lower part of the cloud carries mainly negative charges.*

Lightning

Thunderstorms are very active electrically. **Lightning** is an electric discharge that occurs between a positively charged area and a negatively charged area, as shown in **Figure 2.** Lightning can happen between two clouds, between Earth and a cloud, or even between two parts of the same cloud. Have you ever touched someone after scuffing your feet on the carpet and received a mild shock? If so, you have experienced how lightning forms. While you walk around, friction between the floor and your shoes builds up an electric charge in your body. When you touch someone else, the charge is released.

When lightning strikes, energy is released. This energy is transferred to the air and causes the air to expand rapidly and send out sound waves. **Thunder** is the sound that results from the rapid expansion of air along the lightning strike.

Severe Thunderstorms

Severe thunderstorms can produce one or more of the following conditions: high winds, hail, flash floods, and tornadoes. Hailstorms damage crops, dent the metal on cars, and break windows. Flash flooding that results from heavy rains causes millions of dollars in property damage annually. And every year, flash flooding is a leading cause of weather-related deaths.

Lightning, as shown in **Figure 3,** happens during all thunderstorms and is very powerful. Lightning is responsible for starting thousands of forest fires each year and for killing or injuring hundreds of people a year in the United States.

✓ **Reading Check** What is a severe thunderstorm? (*See the Appendix for answers to Reading Checks.*)

lightning an electric discharge that takes place between two oppositely charged surfaces, such as between a cloud and the ground, between two clouds, or between two parts of the same cloud

thunder the sound caused by the rapid expansion of air along an electrical strike

Figure 3 *Lightning often strikes the tallest object in an area, such as the Eiffel Tower in Paris, France.*

Tornadoes

tornado a destructive, rotating column of air that has very high wind speeds, is visible as a funnel-shaped cloud, and touches the ground

Tornadoes happen in only 1% of all thunderstorms. A **tornado** is a small, spinning column of air that has high wind speeds and low central pressure and that touches the ground. A tornado starts out as a funnel cloud that pokes through the bottom of a cumulonimbus cloud and hangs in the air. The funnel cloud becomes a tornado when it makes contact with Earth's surface. **Figure 4** shows how a tornado forms.

Figure 4 **How a Tornado Forms**

❶ Wind moving in two directions causes a layer of air in the middle to begin to spin like a roll of toilet paper.

❷ The spinning column of air is turned to a vertical position by strong updrafts of air in the cumulonimbus cloud. The updrafts of air also begin to spin.

❸ The spinning column of air moves to the bottom of the cumulonimbus cloud and forms a funnel cloud.

❹ The funnel cloud becomes a tornado when it touches the ground.

Figure 5 *The tornado that hit Kissimmee, Florida, in 1998 had wind speeds of up to 416 km/h.*

Twists of Terror

About 75% of the world's tornadoes occur in the United States. Most of these tornadoes happen in the spring and early summer when cold, dry air from Canada meets warm, moist air from the Tropics. The size of a tornado's path of destruction is usually about 8 km long and 10 to 60 m wide. Although most tornadoes last only a few minutes, they can cause a lot of damage. Their ability to cause damage is due to their strong spinning winds. The average tornado has wind speeds between 120 and 180 km/h, but rarer, more violent tornadoes can have spinning winds of up to 500 km/h. The winds of tornadoes have been known to uproot trees and destroy buildings, as shown in **Figure 5.** Tornadoes are capable of picking up heavy objects, such as mobile homes and cars, and hurling them through the air.

hurricane a severe storm that develops over tropical oceans and whose strong winds of more than 120 km/h spiral in toward the intensely low-pressure storm center

Hurricanes

A large, rotating tropical weather system that has wind speeds of at least 120 km/h is called a **hurricane,** shown in **Figure 6.** Hurricanes are the most powerful storms on Earth. Hurricanes have different names in different parts of the world. In the western Pacific Ocean, hurricanes are called *typhoons.* Hurricanes that form over the Indian Ocean are called *cyclones.*

Most hurricanes form in the areas between 5° and 20° north latitude and between 5° and 20° south latitude over warm, tropical oceans. At higher latitudes, the water is too cold for hurricanes to form. Hurricanes vary in size from 160 to 1,500 km in diameter and can travel for thousands of kilometers.

✓ Reading Check What are some other names for hurricanes?

Figure 6 *This photograph of Hurricane Fran was taken from space.*

How a Hurricane Forms

A hurricane begins as a group of thunderstorms moving over tropical ocean waters. Winds traveling in two different directions meet and cause the storm to spin. Because of the Coriolis effect, the storm turns counterclockwise in the Northern Hemisphere and clockwise in the Southern Hemisphere.

A hurricane gets its energy from the condensation of water vapor. Once formed, the hurricane is fueled through contact with the warm ocean water. Moisture is added to the warm air by evaporation from the ocean. As the warm, moist air rises, the water vapor condenses and releases large amounts of energy. The hurricane continues to grow as long as it is over its source of warm, moist air. When the hurricane moves into colder waters or over land, it begins to die because it has lost its source of energy. **Figure 7** and **Figure 8** show two views of a hurricane.

Reading Check Where do hurricanes get their energy?

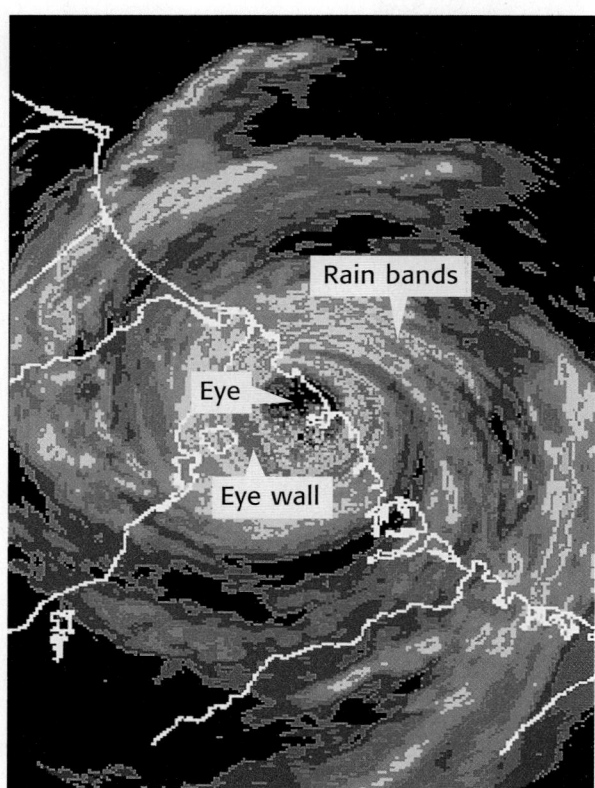

Figure 7 *The photo above gives you a bird's-eye view of a hurricane.*

Rain bands

Eye

Eye wall

Figure 8 Cross Section of a Hurricane

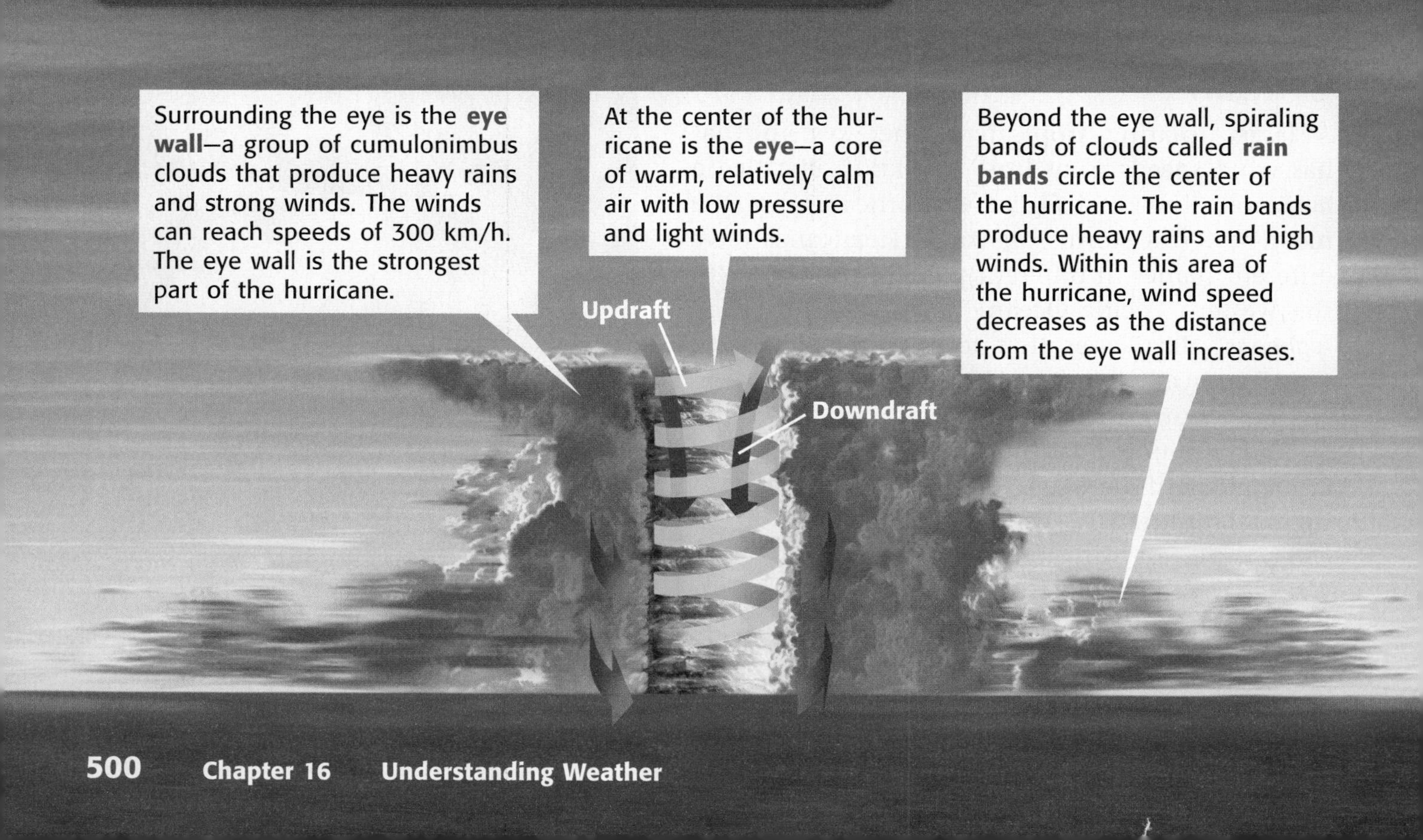

Surrounding the eye is the **eye wall**—a group of cumulonimbus clouds that produce heavy rains and strong winds. The winds can reach speeds of 300 km/h. The eye wall is the strongest part of the hurricane.

At the center of the hurricane is the **eye**—a core of warm, relatively calm air with low pressure and light winds.

Beyond the eye wall, spiraling bands of clouds called **rain bands** circle the center of the hurricane. The rain bands produce heavy rains and high winds. Within this area of the hurricane, wind speed decreases as the distance from the eye wall increases.

Updraft

Downdraft

Damage Caused by Hurricanes

Hurricanes can cause a lot of damage when they move near or onto land. Wind speeds of most hurricanes range from 120 to 150 km/h. Some can reach speeds as high as 300 km/h. Hurricane winds can knock down trees and telephone poles and can damage and destroy buildings and homes.

While high winds cause a great deal of damage, most hurricane damage is caused by flooding associated with heavy rains and storm surges. A *storm surge* is a wall of water that builds up over the ocean because of the strong winds and low atmospheric pressure. The wall of water gets bigger as it nears the shore, and it reaches its greatest height when it crashes onto the shore. Depending on the hurricane's strength, a storm surge can be 1 to 8 m high and 65 to 160 km long. Flooding causes tremendous damage to property and lives when a storm surge moves onto shore, as shown in **Figure 9.**

Severe Weather Safety

Severe weather can be very dangerous, so it is important to keep yourself safe. One way to stay safe is to turn on the radio or TV during a storm. Your local radio and TV stations will let you know if a storm has gotten worse.

Thunderstorm Safety

Lightning is one of the most dangerous parts of a thunderstorm. Lightning is attracted to tall objects. If you are outside, stay away from trees, which can get struck down. If you are in the open, crouch down. Otherwise, you will be the tallest object in the area! Stay away from bodies of water. If lightning hits water while you are in it, you could be hurt or could even die.

Figure 9 *A hurricane's storm surge can cause severe damage to homes near the shoreline.*

Natural Disaster Plan

WRITING SKILL Every family should have a plan to deal with weather emergencies. With a parent, discuss what your family should do in the event of severe weather. Together, write up a plan for your family to follow in case of a natural disaster. Also, make a disaster supply kit that includes enough food and water to last several days.

Figure 10 *During a tornado warning, it is best to protect yourself by crouching against a wall and covering the back of your head and neck with your hands or a book.*

Tornado Safety

Weather forecasters use watches and warnings to let people know about tornadoes. A *watch* is a weather alert that lets people know that a tornado may happen. A *warning* is a weather alert that lets people know that a tornado has been spotted.

If there is a tornado warning for your area, find shelter quickly. The best place to go is a basement or cellar. Or you can go to a windowless room in the center of the building, such as a bathroom, closet, or hallway, as **Figure 10** shows. If you are outside, lie down in a large, open field or a deep ditch.

Flood Safety

An area can get so much rain that it begins to flood. So, like tornadoes, floods have watches and warnings. However, little warning can usually be given. A flash flood is a flood that rises and falls very suddenly. The best thing to do during a flood is to find a high place to wait out the flood. You should always stay out of floodwaters. Even shallow water can be dangerous if it is moving fast.

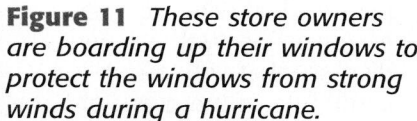

Figure 11 *These store owners are boarding up their windows to protect the windows from strong winds during a hurricane.*

Hurricane Safety

If a hurricane is in your area, your local TV or radio station will keep you updated on its condition. People living on the shore may be asked to evacuate the area. If you live in an area where hurricanes strike, your family should have a disaster supply kit that includes enough water and food to last several days. To protect the windows in your home, you should cover them with plywood, as shown in **Figure 11.** Most important, you must stay indoors during the storm.

Summary

- Thunderstorms are intense weather systems that produce strong winds, heavy rain, lightning, and thunder.

- Lightning is a large electric discharge that occurs between two oppositely charged surfaces. Lightning releases a great deal of energy and can be very dangerous.

- Tornadoes are small, rotating columns of air that touch the ground and can cause severe damage.

- A hurricane is a large, rotating tropical weather system. Hurricanes cause strong winds and can cause severe property damage.

- In the event of severe weather, it is important to stay safe. Listening to your local TV or radio station for updates and remaining indoors and away from windows are good rules to follow.

Using Key Terms

Complete each of the following sentences by choosing the correct term from the word bank.

hurricane   storm surge
tornado   lightning

1. Thunderstorms are very active electrically and often cause ___.

2. A ___ forms when a funnel cloud pokes through the bottom of a cumulonimbus cloud and makes contact with the ground.

Understanding Key Ideas

3. The safest thing to do if you are caught outdoors during a tornado is to
   a. stay near buildings and roads.
   b. head for an open area.
   c. seek shelter near a large tree.
   d. None of the above

4. Describe how tornadoes form.

5. At what latitudes do hurricanes usually form?

6. What is lightning? What happens when lightning strikes?

Critical Thinking

7. **Applying Concepts** What items do you think you would need in a disaster kit? Explain.

8. **Identifying Relationships** What happens to a hurricane as it moves over land? Explain.

Interpreting Graphics

Use the diagram below to answer the questions that follow.

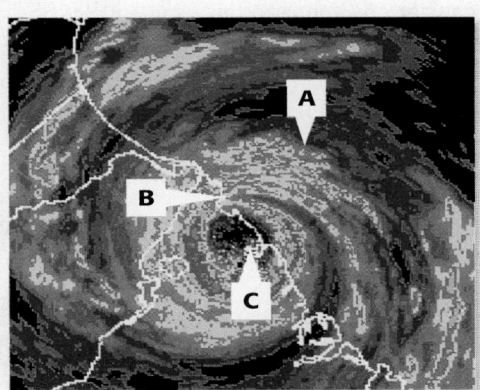

9. Describe what is happening at point C.

10. What is point B?

11. What kind of weather can you expect at point A?

Developed and maintained by the
National Science Teachers Association

For a variety of links related to this chapter, go to www.scilinks.org

Topic: Severe Weather
SciLinks code: HSM1383

Forecasting the Weather

You watch the weather forecast on the evening news. The news is good—there's no rain in sight. But how can the weather forecasters tell that it won't rain?

Weather affects how you dress and how you plan your day, so it is important to get accurate weather forecasts. But where do weather reporters get their information? And how do they predict the weather? A *weather forecast* is a prediction of weather conditions over the next 3 to 5 days. A *meteorologist* is a person who observes and collects data on atmospheric conditions to make weather predictions. In this section, you will learn how weather data are collected and shown.

Weather-Forecasting Technology

To accurately forecast the weather, meteorologists need to measure various atmospheric conditions, such as air pressure, humidity, precipitation, temperature, wind speed, and wind direction. Meteorologists use special instruments to collect data on weather conditions both near and far above Earth's surface.

High in the Sky

Weather balloons carry electronic equipment that can measure weather conditions as high as 30 km above Earth's surface. Weather balloons, such as the one in **Figure 1,** carry equipment that measures temperature, air pressure, and relative humidity. By tracking the balloons, meteorologists can also measure wind speed and direction.

Reading Check How do meteorologists gather data on atmospheric conditions above Earth's surface? (*See the Appendix for answers to Reading Check.*)

Figure 1 *Weather balloons carry radio transmitters that send measurements to stations on the ground.*

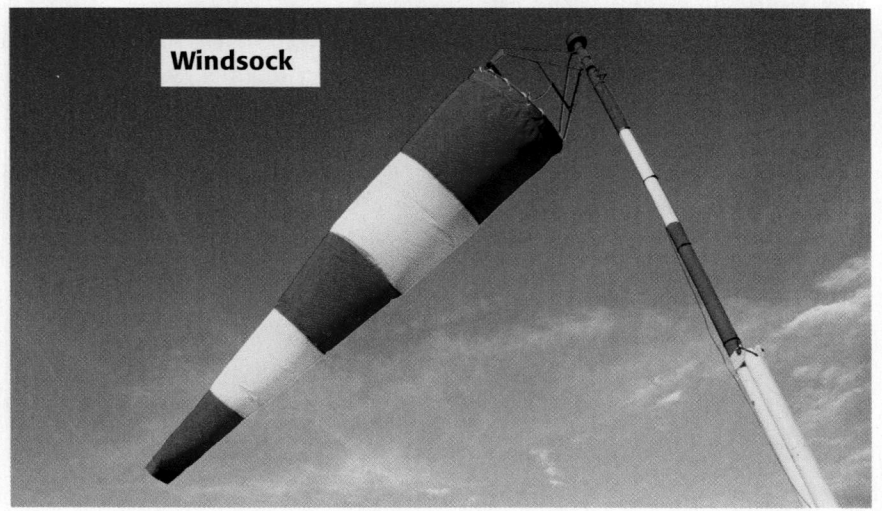
Windsock

Figure 2 *Meteorologists use these tools to collect atmospheric data.*

Thermometer

Measuring Air Temperature and Pressure

A tool used to measure air temperature is called a **thermometer.** Most thermometers use a liquid sealed in a narrow glass tube, as shown in **Figure 2.** When air temperature increases, the liquid expands and moves up the glass tube. As air temperature decreases, the liquid shrinks and moves down the tube.

A **barometer** is an instrument used to measure air pressure. A mercurial barometer consists of a glass tube that is sealed at one end and placed in a container full of mercury. As the air pressure pushes on the mercury inside the container, the mercury moves up the glass tube. The greater the air pressure is, the higher the mercury will rise.

Anemometer
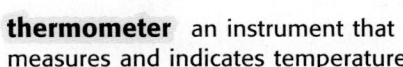

Measuring Wind Direction

Wind direction can be measured by using a windsock or a wind vane. A windsock, shown in **Figure 2,** is a cone-shaped cloth bag open at both ends. The wind enters through the wide end and leaves through the narrow end. Therefore, the wide end points into the wind. A wind vane is shaped like an arrow with a large tail and is attached to a pole. As the wind pushes the tail of the wind vane, the wind vane spins on the pole until the arrow points into the wind.

thermometer an instrument that measures and indicates temperature

barometer an instrument that measures atmospheric pressure

anemometer an instrument used to measure wind speed

Measuring Wind Speed

An instrument used to measure wind speed is called an **anemometer.** An anemometer, as shown in **Figure 2,** consists of three or four cups connected by spokes to a pole. The wind pushes on the hollow sides of the cups and causes the cups to rotate on the pole. The motion sends a weak electric current that is measured and displayed on a dial.

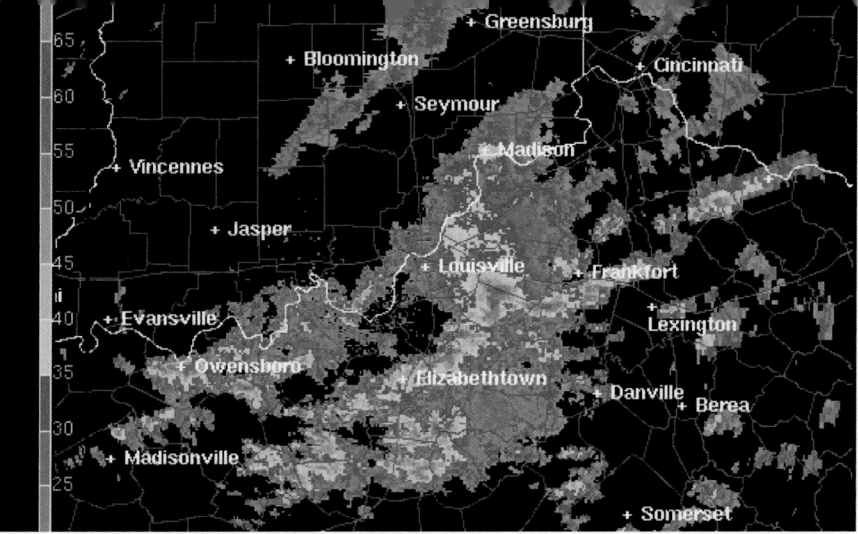

Figure 3 *Using Doppler radar, meteorologists can predict a tornado up to 20 minutes before it touches the ground.*

Radar and Satellites

Radar is used to find the location, movement, and amount of precipitation. It can also detect what form of precipitation a weather system is carrying. You might have seen a kind of radar called *Doppler radar* used in a local TV weather report. **Figure 3** shows how Doppler radar is used to track precipitation. *Weather satellites* that orbit Earth provide the images of weather systems that you see on TV weather reports. Satellites can track storms and measure wind speeds, humidity, and temperatures at different altitudes.

Weather Maps

In the United States, the National Weather Service (NWS) and the National Oceanic and Atmospheric Administration (NOAA) collect and analyze weather data. The NWS produces weather maps based on information gathered from about 1,000 weather stations across the United States. On these maps, each station is represented by a station model. A *station model* is a small circle that shows the location of the weather station. As shown in **Figure 4,** surrounding the small circle is a set of symbols and numbers, which represent the weather data.

Figure 4 **A Station Model**

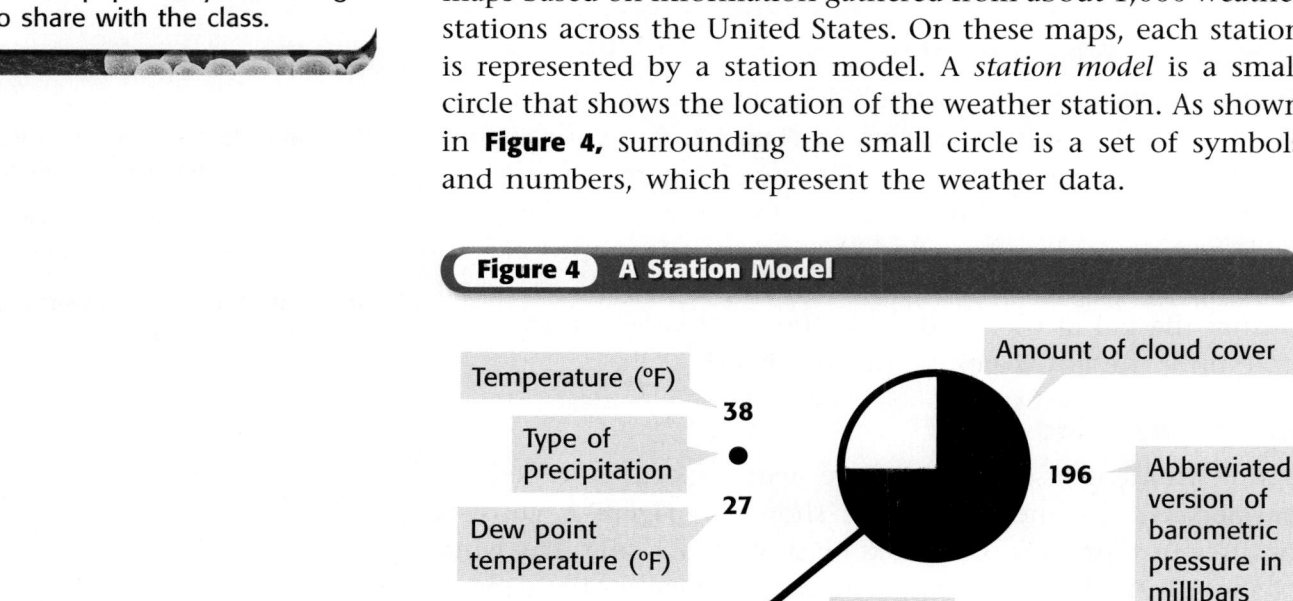

Temperature (°F)

Type of precipitation

Dew point temperature (°F)

Wind speed

Amount of cloud cover

Abbreviated version of barometric pressure in millibars

Wind direction

Reading a Weather Map

Weather maps that you see on TV include lines called *isobars*. Isobars are lines that connect points of equal air pressure. Isobars that form closed circles represent areas of high or low pressure. These areas are usually marked on a map with a capital *H* or *L*. Fronts are also labeled on weather maps, as you can see on the weather map in **Figure 5.**

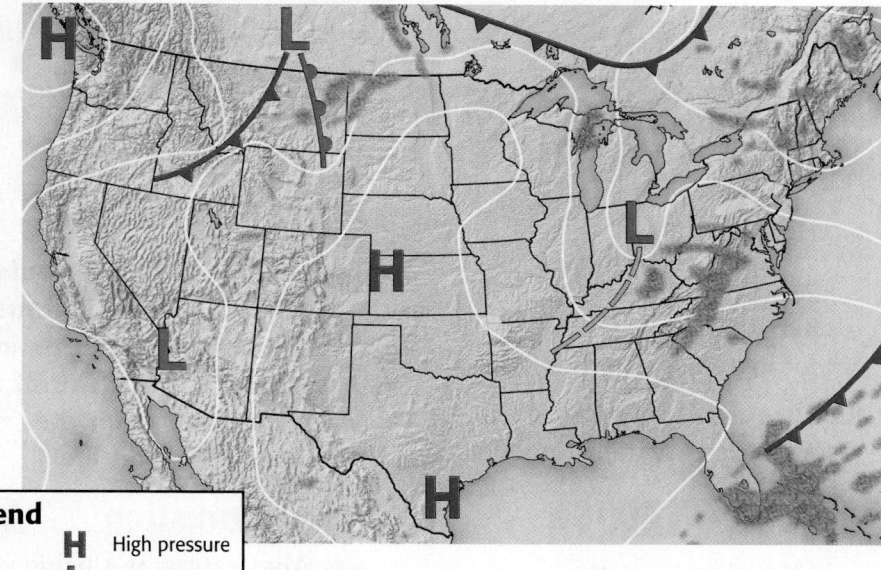

Legend

Cold front		**H**	High pressure
Warm front		**L**	Low pressure
Low pressure trough			Rain
Isobar			Fog

Figure 5 *Can you identify the fronts shown on the weather map?*

SECTION Review

Summary

• Meteorologists use several instruments, such as weather balloons, thermometers, barometers, anemometers, windsocks, weather vanes, radar, and weather satellites, to forecast the weather.

• Station models show the weather conditions at various points across the United States.

• Weather maps show areas of high and low pressure as well as the location of fronts.

Using Key Terms

1. In your own words, write a definition for each of the following terms: *thermometer, barometer,* and *anemometer.*

Understanding Key Ideas

2. Which of the following instruments measures air pressure?

    a. thermometer

    b. barometer

    c. anemometer

    d. windsock

3. How does radar help meteorologists forecast the weather?

4. What does a station model represent?

Math Skills

5. If it is 75°F outside, what is the temperature in degrees Celsius? (Hint: °F = (°C × 9/5) + 32)

Critical Thinking

6. **Applying Concepts** Why would a meteorologist compare a new weather map with one that is 24 h old?

7. **Making Inferences** In the United States, why is weather data gathered from a large number of station models?

8. **Making Inferences** How might several station models from different regions plotted on a map help a meteorologist?

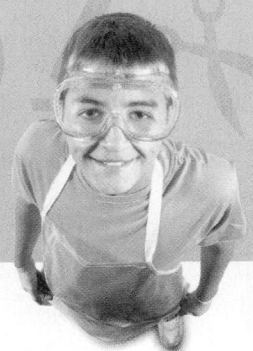

OBJECTIVES

Construct a device that uses water to measure temperature.

Calibrate the new device by using a mercury thermometer.

MATERIALS

- bottle, plastic
- can, aluminum soda
- card, index, 3 in. × 5 in.
- clay, modeling (1 lb)
- container, yogurt, with lid
- cup, plastic-foam, large (2)
- film canister
- food coloring, red (1 bottle)
- funnel, plastic or paper cone
- gloves, heat-resistant
- hot plate
- ice, cube (5 or 6)
- pan, aluminum pie
- pitcher
- plastic tubing, 5 mm diameter, 30 cm long
- ruler, metric
- straw, plastic, inflexible, clear (1)
- tape, transparent (1 roll)
- thermometer, Celsius
- water, tap

SAFETY

Boiling Over!

Safety Industries, Inc., would like to produce and sell thermometers that are safer than mercury thermometers. The company would like your team of inventors to design a thermometer that uses water instead of mercury. The company will offer a contract to the team that creates the best design of a water thermometer. Good luck!

Ask a Question

1 What causes the liquid in a thermometer to rise? How can I use this information to make a thermometer?

Form a Hypothesis

2 Brainstorm with a classmate to design a thermometer that uses only water to measure temperature. Sketch your design. Write a one-sentence hypothesis that describes how your thermometer will work.

Test the Hypothesis

3 Following your design, build a thermometer by using only materials from the materials list. Like a mercury thermometer, your thermometer needs a bulb and a tube. However, the liquid in your thermometer will be water.

4 To test your design, place the aluminum pie pan on a hot plate. Use the pitcher to carefully pour water into the pan until the pan is half full. Turn on the hot plate, and heat the water.

5 Put on your safety goggles and heat-resistant gloves, and carefully place the "bulb" of your thermometer in the hot water. Observe the water level in the tube. Does the water level rise?

6 If the water level does not rise, change your design as necessary and repeat steps 3–5. When the water level in your thermometer does rise, sketch the design of this thermometer as your final design.

7 After you decide on your final design, you must calibrate your thermometer by using a laboratory thermometer. Tape an index card to your thermometer's tube so that the part of the tube that sticks out from the "bulb" of your thermometer touches the card.

8. Place the plastic funnel or the cone-shaped paper funnel into a plastic-foam cup. Carefully pour hot water from the pie pan into the funnel. Be sure that no water splashes or spills.

9. Place your thermometer and a laboratory thermometer in the hot water. As your thermometer's water level rises, mark the level on the index card. At the same time, observe and record the temperature of the laboratory thermometer, and write this value beside your mark on the card.

10. Repeat steps 8–9 using warm tap water.

11. Repeat steps 8–9 using ice water.

12. Draw evenly spaced scale markings between your temperature markings on the index card. Write the temperatures that correspond to the scale marks on the index card.

Analyze the Results

1. **Analyzing Results** How well does your thermometer measure temperature?

Draw Conclusions

2. **Drawing Conclusions** Compare your thermometer design with other students' designs. How would you change your design to make your thermometer measure temperature better?

3. **Applying Conclusions** Take a class vote to see which design should be used by Safety Industries. Why was this thermometer design chosen? How did it differ from other designs in the class?

Chapter Review

USING KEY TERMS

For each pair of terms, explain how the meanings of the terms differ.

1 *relative humidity* and *dew point*

2 *condensation* and *precipitation*

3 *air mass* and *front*

4 *lightning* and *thunder*

5 *tornado* and *hurricane*

6 *barometer* and *anemometer*

UNDERSTANDING KEY IDEAS

Multiple Choice

7 The process in which water changes from a liquid to gas is called

  a. precipitation.

  b. condensation.

  c. evaporation.

  d. water vapor.

8 What is the relative humidity of air at its dew point?

  a. 0% **c.** 75%

  b. 50% **d.** 100%

9 Which of the following is NOT a type of condensation?

  a. fog **c.** snow

  b. cloud **d.** dew

10 High clouds made of ice crystals are called ___ clouds.

  a. stratus **c.** nimbostratus

  b. cumulus **d.** cirrus

11 Large thunderhead clouds that produce precipitation are called ___ clouds.

  a. nimbostratus **c.** cumulus

  b. cumulonimbus **d.** stratus

12 Strong updrafts within a thunderhead can produce

  a. snow. **c.** sleet.

  b. rain. **d.** hail.

13 A maritime tropical air mass contains

  a. warm, wet air. **c.** warm, dry air.

  b. cold, moist air. **d.** cold, dry air.

14 A front that forms when a warm air mass is trapped between cold air masses and is forced to rise is a(n)

  a. stationary front. **c.** occluded front.

  b. warm front. **d.** cold front.

15 A severe storm that forms as a rapidly rotating funnel cloud is called a

  a. hurricane. **c.** typhoon.

  b. tornado. **d.** thunderstorm.

16 The lines connecting points of equal air pressure on a weather map are called

  a. contour lines. **c.** isobars.

  b. highs. **d.** lows.

Short Answer

17 Explain the relationship between condensation and dew point.

18 Describe the conditions along a stationary front.

19 What are the characteristics of an air mass that forms over the Gulf of Mexico?

20 Explain how a hurricane develops.

21 Describe the water cycle, and explain how it affects weather.

22 List the major similarities and differences between hurricanes and tornadoes.

23 Explain how a tornado forms.

24 Describe an interaction between weather and ocean systems.

25 What is a station model? What types of information do station models provide?

26 What type of technology is used to locate and measure the amount of precipitation in an area?

27 List two ways to keep yourself informed during severe weather.

28 Explain why staying away from flood-water is important even when the water is shallow.

CRITICAL THINKING

29 **Concept Mapping** Use the following terms to create a concept map: *evaporation, relative humidity, water vapor, dew, psychrometer, clouds,* and *fog.*

30 **Making Inferences** If both the air temperature and the amount of water vapor in the air change, is it possible for the relative humidity to stay the same? Explain.

31 **Applying Concepts** What can you assume about the amount of water vapor in the air if there is no difference between the wet- and dry-bulb readings of a psychrometer?

32 **Identifying Relationships** Explain why the concept of relative humidity is important to understanding weather.

INTERPRETING GRAPHICS

Use the weather map below to answer the questions that follow.

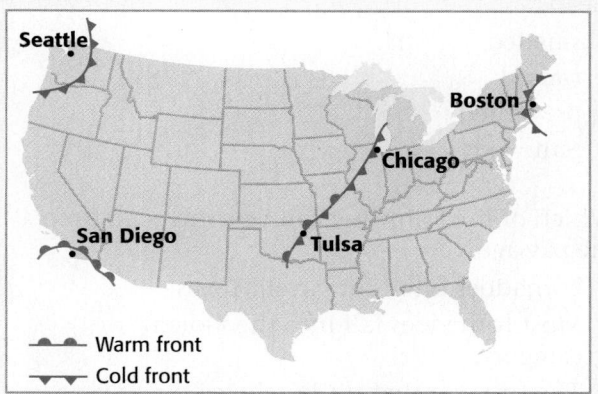

33 Where are thunderstorms most likely to occur? Explain your answer.

34 What are the weather conditions in Tulsa, Oklahoma? Explain your answer.

Standardized Test Preparation

Read each of the passages below. Then, answer the questions that follow each passage.

Passage 1 In May 1997, a springtime tornado <u>wreaked</u> havoc on Jarrell, Texas. The Jarrell tornado was a powerful tornado, whose wind speeds were estimated at more than 410 km/h. The winds of the twister were so strong that they peeled the asphalt from paved roads, stripped fields of corn bare, and destroyed an entire neighborhood. Some tornadoes, such as the one that struck the town of Jarrell, are classified as violent tornadoes. Only 2% of the tornadoes that occur in the United States are categorized as violent tornadoes. Despite the fact that these types of tornadoes do not occur often, 70% of all tornado-related deaths are a result of violent tornadoes.

1. In the passage, what does the word *wreaked* mean?
   A smelled
   B caused
   C prevented
   D removed

2. Which of the following can be concluded from the passage?
   F Tornadoes often hit Jarrell, Texas.
   G Most tornadoes fall into the violent category.
   H The tornado that hit Jarrell was a rare type of tornado.
   I Tornadoes always happen during the spring.

3. Which of the following **best** describes a characteristic of violent tornadoes?
   A Violent tornadoes destroy paved roads.
   B Violent tornadoes damage crops.
   C Violent tornadoes damage homes.
   D Violent tornadoes have extremely strong winds.

Passage 2 Water evaporates into the air from Earth's surface. This water returns to Earth's surface as <u>precipitation</u>. Precipitation is water, in solid or liquid form, that falls from the air to Earth. The four major types of precipitation are rain, snow, sleet, and hail. The most common form of precipitation is rain.

A cloud produces rain when the cloud's water drops become large enough to fall. A raindrop begins as a water droplet that is smaller than the period at the end of this sentence. Before a water drop falls as rain, it must become about 100 times this beginning size. Water drops get larger by joining with other water drops. When the water drops become too heavy, they fall as precipitation.

1. In this passage, what does *precipitation* mean?
   A acceleration
   B haste
   C water that falls from the atmosphere to Earth
   D separating a substance from a solution as a solid

2. What is the main idea of the second paragraph?
   F Rain occurs when the water droplets in clouds become large enough to fall.
   G Raindrops are very small at first.
   H Water droplets join with other water droplets to become larger.
   I Rain is a form of precipitation.

3. According to the passage, which step happens last in the formation of precipitation?
   A Water droplets join.
   B Water droplets fall to the ground.
   C Water droplets become heavy.
   D Water evaporates into the air.

Use each diagram below to answer the question that follows each diagram.

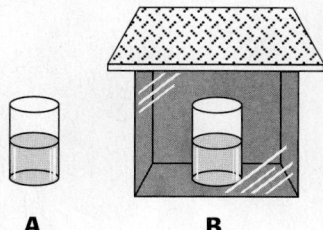

A   B

1. During an experiment, the setup shown in the diagram above is maintained for 72 h. Which of the following is the most likely outcome?

A Beaker A will hold less water than beaker B will.

B The amount of water in beaker A and beaker B will stay the same.

C The amount of water in beaker A and beaker B will change by about the same amount.

D Beaker B will hold less water than beaker A will.

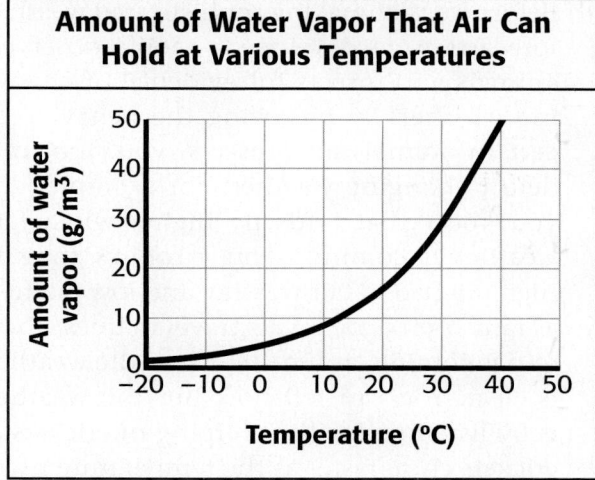

Amount of Water Vapor That Air Can Hold at Various Temperatures

2. Look at the line graph above. Which statement is consistent with the line graph?

F The ability of air to hold moisture increases as temperature increases.

G The ability of air to hold moisture decreases as temperature increases.

H The ability of air to hold moisture decreases and then increases as temperature increases.

I The ability of air to hold moisture stays the same regardless of temperature.

Read each question below, and choose the best answer.

1. The speed of light is 3.00×10^8 m/s. What is another way to express this measure?

A 3,000,000,000 m/s

B 300,000,000 m/s

C 3,000,000 m/s

D 300,000 m/s

2. A hurricane is moving 122 km/h. How long will it take to hit the coast, which is 549 km away?

F 4.2 h

G 4.5 h

H 4.8 h

I 5.2 h

3. A front is moving 15 km/h in an easterly direction. At that rate, how far will the front travel in 12 h?

A 0.8 km

B 1.25 km

C 27 km

D 180 km

4. On average, 2 out of every 100 tornadoes are classified as violent tornadoes. If there are 400 tornadoes in 1 year, which is the best prediction of the number of tornadoes that will be classified as violent tornadoes during that year?

F 2

G 4

H 8

I 16

5. The air temperature in the morning was 27°C. During the day, a front moved into the region and caused the temperature to drop to 18°C. By how many degrees did the temperature drop?

A 1°C

B 9°C

C 11°C

D 19°C

Science in Action

Science Fiction

"All Summer in a Day" by Ray Bradbury

It is raining, just as it has been for seven long years. For the people who live on Venus, constant rain is a fact of life. But today is a special day—a day when the rain stops and the sun shines. This day comes once every seven years. At school, the students have been looking forward to this day for weeks. But Margot longs to see the sun even more than the others do. The reason for her longing makes the other kids jealous, and jealous kids can be cruel. What happens to Margot? Find out by reading Ray Bradbury's "All Summer in a Day" in the *Holt Anthology of Science Fiction*.

Language Arts ACTiViTY

WRITING SKILL What would living in a place where it rained all day and every day for seven years be like? Write a short story describing what your life would be like if you lived in such a place. In your story, describe what you and your friends would do for fun after school.

Weird Science

Can Animals Forecast the Weather?

Before ways of making sophisticated weather forecasts were developed, people observed animals and insects for evidence of changing weather. By observing the behavior of certain animals and insects, you, too, can detect changing weather! For example, did you know that birds fly higher when fair weather is coming? And a robin's song is high pitched in fair weather and low pitched as rain approaches. Ants travel in lines when rain is coming and scatter when the weather is clear. You can tell how hot the weather is by listening for the chirping of crickets— crickets chirp faster as the temperature rises!

Math ACTiViTY

To estimate the outdoor temperature in degrees Fahrenheit, count the number of times that a cricket chirps in 15 s and add 37. If you count 40 chirps in 15 s, what is the estimated temperature?

Cristy Mitchell

Meteorologist Predicting floods, observing a tornado develop inside a storm, watching the growth of a hurricane, and issuing flood warnings are all in a day's work for Cristy Mitchell. As a meteorologist for the National Weather Service, Mitchell spends each working day observing the powerful forces of nature. When asked what made her job interesting, Mitchell replied, "There's nothing like the adrenaline rush you get when you see a tornado coming!"

Perhaps the most familiar field of meteorology is weather forecasting. However, meteorology is also used in air-pollution control, weather control, agricultural planning, and even criminal and civil investigations. Meteorologists also study trends in Earth's climate.

Meteorologists such as Mitchell use high-tech tools—computers and satellites—to collect data. By analyzing such data, Mitchell is able to forecast the weather.

Social Studies ACTIVITY

An almanac is a type of calendar that contains various information, including weather forecasts and astronomical data, for every day of the year. Many people used almanacs before meteorologists started to forecast the weather on TV. Use an almanac from the library to find out what the weather was on the day that you were born.

To learn more about these Science in Action topics, visit go.hrw.com and type in the keyword HZ5WEAF.

Current Science

Check out Current Science® articles related to this chapter by visiting go.hrw.com. Just type in the keyword HZ5CS16.

17

Climate

About the PHOTO

Would you like to hang out on this ice with the penguins? You probably would not. You would be shivering, and your teeth would be chattering. However, these penguins feel comfortable. They have thick feathers and lots of body fat to keep them warm. Like other animals, penguins have adapted to their climate, which allows them to live comfortably in that climate. So, you will never see one of these penguins living comfortably on a hot, sunny beach in Florida!

PRE-READING ACTIVITY

FOLDNOTES **Pyramid** Before you read the chapter, create the FoldNote entitled "Pyramid" described in the **Study Skills** section of the Appendix. Label the sides of the pyramid with "Tropical climate," "Temperate climate," and "Polar climate." As you read the chapter, define each climate zone, and write characteristics of each climate zone on the appropriate pyramid side.

START-UP ACTIVITY

What's Your Angle?

Try this activity to see how the angle of the sun's solar rays influences temperatures on Earth.

Procedure

1. Place a **lamp** 30 cm from a **globe.**

2. Point the lamp so that the light shines directly on the globe's equator.

3. Using **adhesive putty,** attach a **thermometer** to the globe's equator in a vertical position. Attach **another thermometer** to the globe's North Pole so that the tip points toward the lamp.

4. Record the temperature reading of each thermometer.

5. Turn on the lamp, and let the light shine on the globe for 3 minutes.

6. After 3 minutes, turn off the lamp and record the temperature reading of each thermometer again.

Analysis

1. Was there a difference between the final temperature at the globe's North Pole and the final temperature at the globe's equator? If so, what was it?

2. Explain why the temperature readings at the North Pole and the equator may be different.

What Is Climate?

Suppose you receive a call from a friend who is coming to visit you tomorrow. To decide what clothing to bring, he asks about the current weather in your area.

You step outside to see if rain clouds are in the sky and to check the temperature. But what would you do if your friend asked you about the climate in your area? What is the difference between weather and climate?

Climate Vs. Weather

The main difference between weather and climate is the length of time over which both are measured. **Weather** is the condition of the atmosphere at a particular time. Weather conditions vary from day to day and include temperature, humidity, precipitation, wind, and visibility. **Climate,** on the other hand, is the average weather condition in an area over a long period of time. Climate is mostly determined by two factors—temperature and precipitation. Different parts of the world can have different climates, as shown in **Figure 1.** But why are climates so different? The answer is complicated. It includes factors in addition to temperature and precipitation, such as latitude, wind patterns, mountains, large bodies of water, and ocean currents.

✓ *Reading Check* How is climate different from weather? (*See the Appendix for answers to Reading Checks.*)

READING WARM-UP

Objectives

● Explain the difference between weather and climate.

● Identify five factors that determine climates.

● Identify the three climate zones of the world.

Terms to Learn

weather   elevation
climate   surface current
latitude   biome
prevailing winds

READING STRATEGY

Discussion Read this section silently. Write down questions that you have about this section. Discuss your questions in a small group.

Figure 1 *How does the climate in northern Africa differ from the climate where you live?*

North America

South America

Africa

Latitude

Think of the last time you looked at a globe. Do you recall the thin, horizontal lines that circle the globe? Those lines are called lines of latitude. **Latitude** is the distance north or south, measured in degrees, from the equator. In general, the temperature of an area depends on its latitude. The higher the latitude is, the colder the climate tends to be. One of the coldest places on Earth, the North Pole, is 90° north of the equator. However, the equator, at latitude 0°, is usually hot.

As shown in **Figure 2,** if you were to take a trip to different latitudes in the United States, you would experience different climates. For example, the climate in Washington, D.C., which is at a higher latitude, is different from the climate in Texas.

Solar Energy and Latitude

Solar energy, which is energy from the sun, heats the Earth. The amount of direct solar energy a particular area receives is determined by latitude. **Figure 3** shows how the curve of the Earth affects the amount of direct solar energy at different latitudes. Notice that the sun's rays hit the equator directly, at almost a 90° angle. At this angle, a small area of the Earth's surface receives more direct solar energy than at a lesser angle. As a result, that area has high temperatures. However, the sun's rays strike the poles at a lesser angle than they do the equator. At this angle, the same amount of direct solar energy that hits the area at the equator is spread over a larger area at the poles. The result is lower temperatures at the poles.

Figure 2 *Winter in south Texas (top) is different from winter in Washington D.C. (bottom).*

weather the short-term state of the atmosphere, including temperature, humidity, precipitation, wind, and visibility

climate the average weather condition in an area over a long period of time

latitude the distance north or south from the equator; expressed in degrees

Figure 3 The sun's rays strike the Earth's surface at different angles because the surface is curved.

Seasons and Latitude

In most places in the United States, the year consists of four seasons. But there are places in the world that do not have such seasonal changes. For example, areas near the equator have approximately the same temperatures and same amount of daylight year-round. Seasons happen because the Earth is tilted on its axis at a 23.5° angle. This tilt affects how much solar energy an area receives as Earth moves around the sun. **Figure 4** shows how latitude and the tilt of the Earth determine the seasons and the length of the day in a particular area.

✓ Reading Check Why is there less seasonal change near the equator?

Figure 4   The Seasons

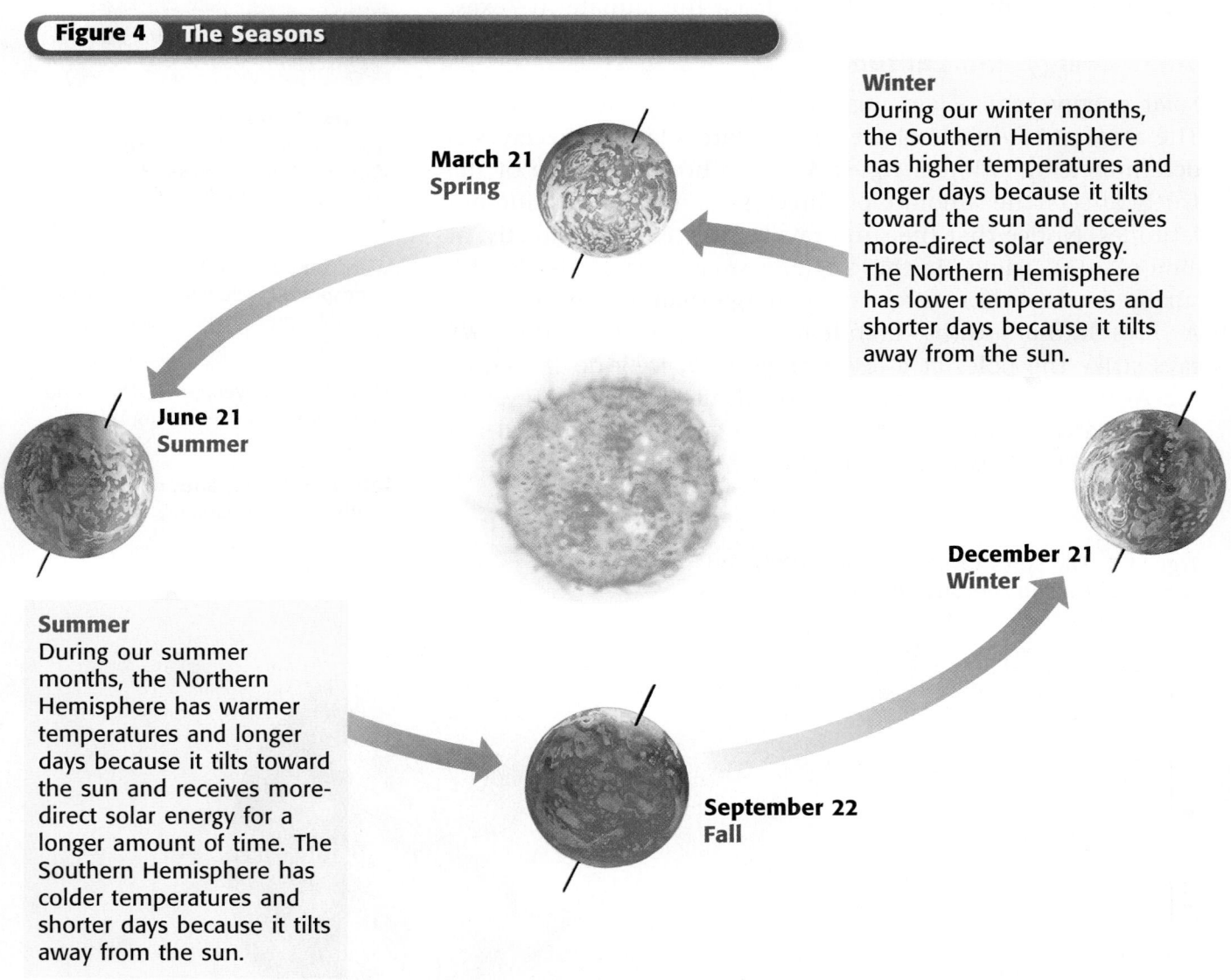

March 21
Spring

Winter
During our winter months, the Southern Hemisphere has higher temperatures and longer days because it tilts toward the sun and receives more-direct solar energy. The Northern Hemisphere has lower temperatures and shorter days because it tilts away from the sun.

June 21
Summer

December 21
Winter

Summer
During our summer months, the Northern Hemisphere has warmer temperatures and longer days because it tilts toward the sun and receives more-direct solar energy for a longer amount of time. The Southern Hemisphere has colder temperatures and shorter days because it tilts away from the sun.

September 22
Fall

Figure 5 The Circulation of Warm Air and Cold Air

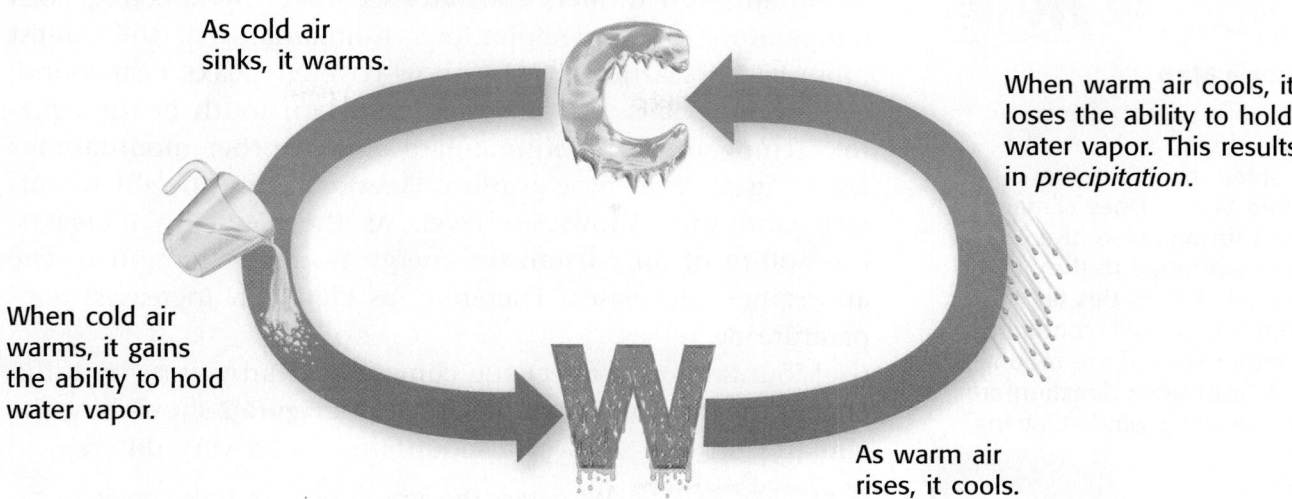

As cold air sinks, it warms.

When warm air cools, it loses the ability to hold water vapor. This results in *precipitation*.

When cold air warms, it gains the ability to hold water vapor.

As warm air rises, it cools.

Prevailing Winds

Winds that blow mainly from one direction are **prevailing winds**. Before you learn how the prevailing winds affect climate, take a look at **Figure 5** to learn about some of the basic properties of air.

Prevailing winds affect the amount of precipitation that a region receives. If the prevailing winds form from warm air, they may carry moisture. If the prevailing winds form from cold air, they will probably be dry.

The amount of moisture in prevailing winds is also affected by whether the winds blow across land or across a large body of water. Winds that travel across large bodies of water absorb moisture. Winds that travel across land tend to be dry. Even if a region borders the ocean, the area might be dry. **Figure 6** shows an example of how dry prevailing winds can cause the land to be dry though the land is near an ocean.

prevailing winds winds that blow mainly from one direction during a given period

A Cool Breeze

1. Hold a **thermometer** next to the top edge of a **cup** of **water** containing two **ice cubes.** Record the temperature next to the cup.

2. Have your lab partner fan the surface of the cup with a **paper fan.** Record the temperature again. Has the temperature changed? Why or why not?

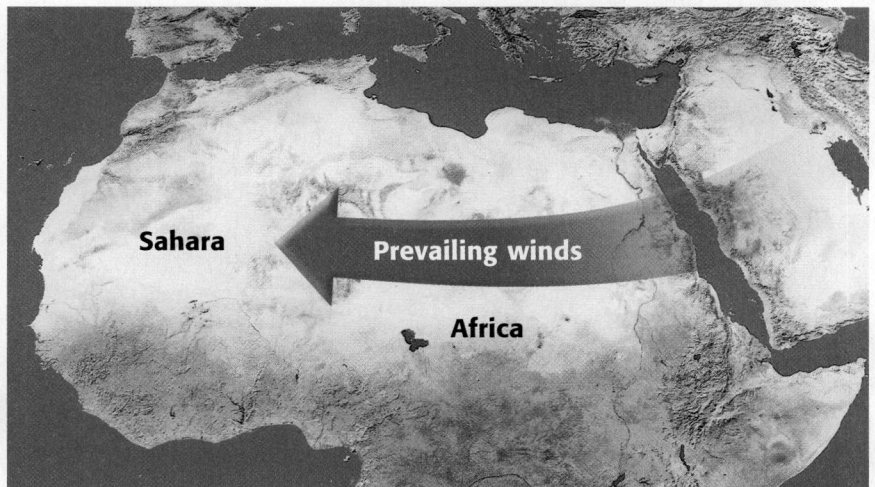

Sahara

Prevailing winds

Africa

Figure 6 *The Sahara Desert, in northern Africa, is extremely dry because of the dry prevailing winds that blow across the continent.*

Using a Map

With your parent, use a physical map to locate the mountain ranges in the United States. Does climate vary from one side of a mountain range to the other? If so, what does this tell you about the climatic conditions on either side of the mountain? From what direction are the prevailing winds blowing?

Mountains

Mountains can influence an area's climate by affecting both temperature and precipitation. Kilimanjaro is the tallest mountain in Africa. It has snow-covered peaks year-round, even though it is only about 3° (320 km) south of the equator. Temperatures on Kilimanjaro and in other mountainous areas are affected by elevation. **Elevation** is the height of surface landforms above sea level. As the elevation increases, the ability of air to transfer energy from the ground to the atmosphere decreases. Therefore, as elevation increases, temperature decreases.

Mountains also affect the climate of nearby areas by influencing the distribution of precipitation. **Figure 7** shows how the climates on two sides of a mountain can be very different.

✓ *Reading Check* Why does the atmosphere become cooler at higher elevations?

Figure 7 *Mountains block the prevailing winds and affect the climate on the other side.*

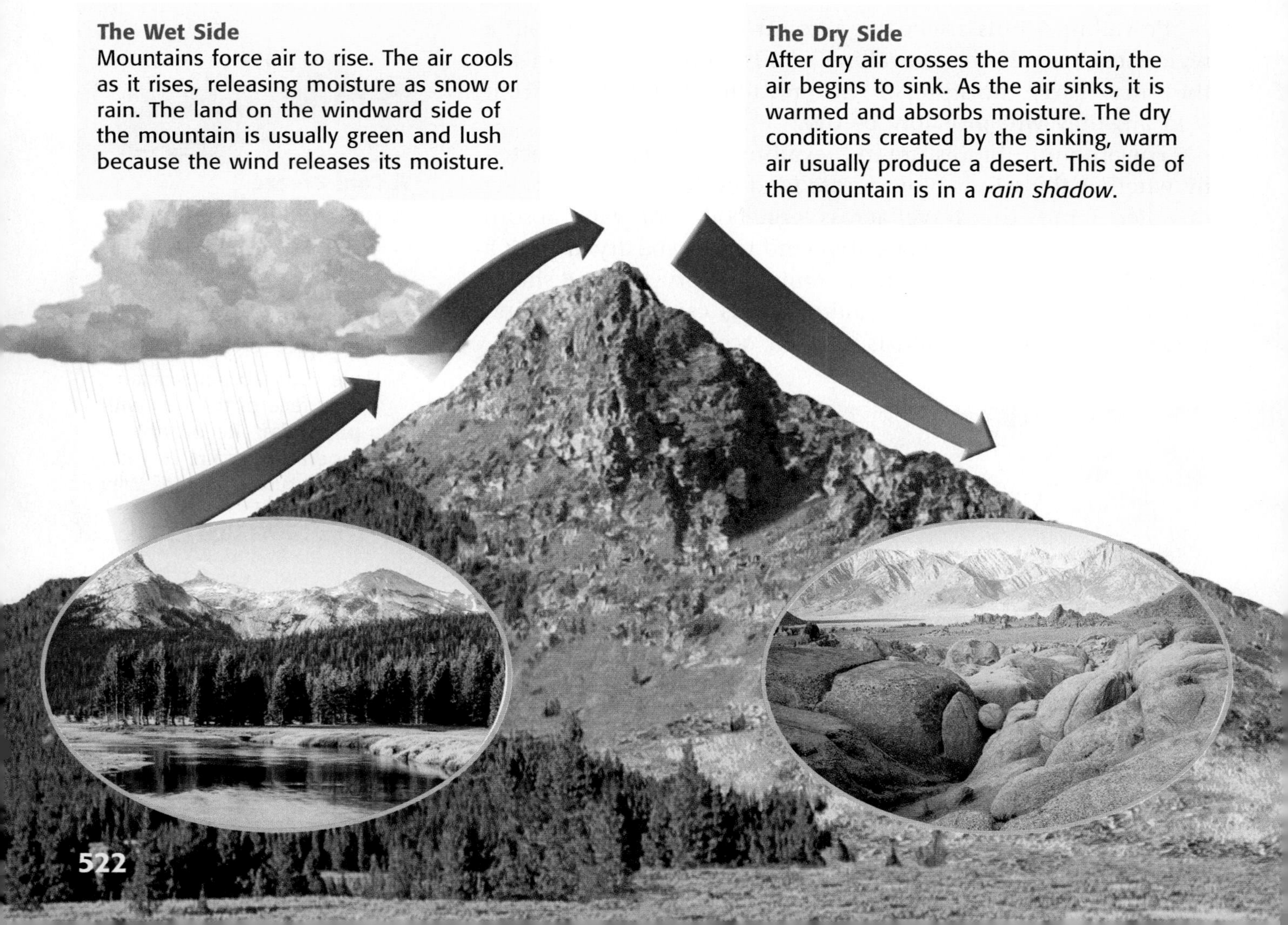

The Wet Side
Mountains force air to rise. The air cools as it rises, releasing moisture as snow or rain. The land on the windward side of the mountain is usually green and lush because the wind releases its moisture.

The Dry Side
After dry air crosses the mountain, the air begins to sink. As the air sinks, it is warmed and absorbs moisture. The dry conditions created by the sinking, warm air usually produce a desert. This side of the mountain is in a *rain shadow*.

Large Bodies of Water

Large bodies of water can influence an area's climate. Water absorbs and releases heat slower than land does. Because of this quality, water helps to moderate the temperatures of the land around it. So, sudden or extreme temperature changes rarely take place on land near large bodies of water. For example, the state of Michigan, which is surrounded by the Great Lakes, has more-moderate temperatures than other places at the same latitude. The lakes also increase the moisture content of the air, which leads to heavy snowfall in the winter. This "lake effect" can cause 350 inches of snow to drop in one year!

Ocean Currents

The circulation of ocean surface currents has a large effect on an area's climate. **Surface currents** are streamlike movements of water that occur at or near the surface of the ocean. **Figure 8** shows the pattern of the major ocean surface currents.

As surface currents move, they carry warm or cool water to different locations. The surface temperature of the water affects the temperature of the air above it. Warm currents heat the surrounding air and cause warmer temperatures. Cool currents cool the surrounding air and cause cooler temperatures. The Gulf Stream current carries warm water northward off the east coast of North America and past Iceland. Iceland is an island country located just below the Arctic Circle. The warm water from the Gulf Stream heats the surrounding air and creates warmer temperatures in southern Iceland. Iceland experiences milder temperatures than Greenland, its neighboring island. Greenland's climate is cooler because Greenland is not influenced by the Gulf Stream.

Reading Check Why does Iceland experience milder temperatures than Greenland?

elevation the height of an object above sea level

surface current a horizontal movement of ocean water that is caused by wind and that occurs at or near the ocean's surface

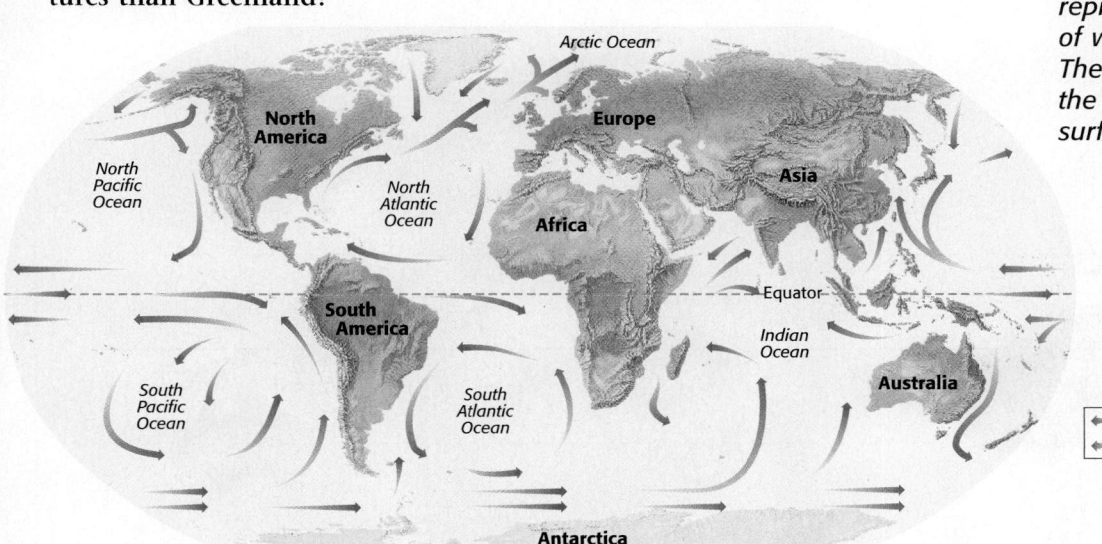

Figure 8 *The red arrows represent the movement of warm surface currents. The blue arrows represent the movement of cold surface currents.*

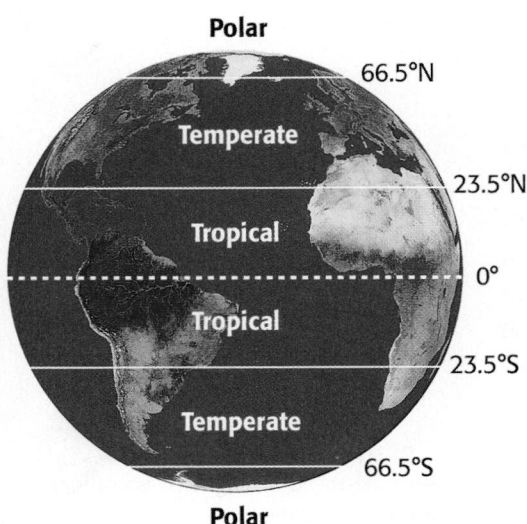

Figure 9 *The three major climate zones are determined by latitude.*

biome a large region characterized by a specific type of climate and certain types of plant and animal communities

Climates of the World

Have you seen any polar bears in your neighborhood lately? You probably have not. That's because polar bears live only in very cold arctic regions. Why are the animals in one part of the world so different from the animals in other parts? One of the differences has to do with climate. Plants and animals that have adapted to one climate may not be able to live in another climate. For example, frogs would not be able to survive at the North Pole.

Climate Zones

The Earth's three major climate zones—tropical, temperate, and polar—are shown in **Figure 9.** Each zone has a temperature range that relates to its latitude. However, in each of these zones, there are several types of climates because of differences in the geography and the amount of precipitation. Because of the various climates in each zone, there are different biomes in each zone. A **biome** is a large region characterized by a specific type of climate and certain types of plant and animal communities. **Figure 10** shows the distribution of the Earth's land biomes. In which biome do you live?

✓ Reading Check What factors distinguish one biome from another biome?

Figure 10   The Earth's Land Biomes

- Tundra
- Taiga
- Temperate forest
- Tropical rain forest
- Temperate grassland
- Tropical savanna
- Temperate desert
- Tropical desert
- Chaparral
- Mountains

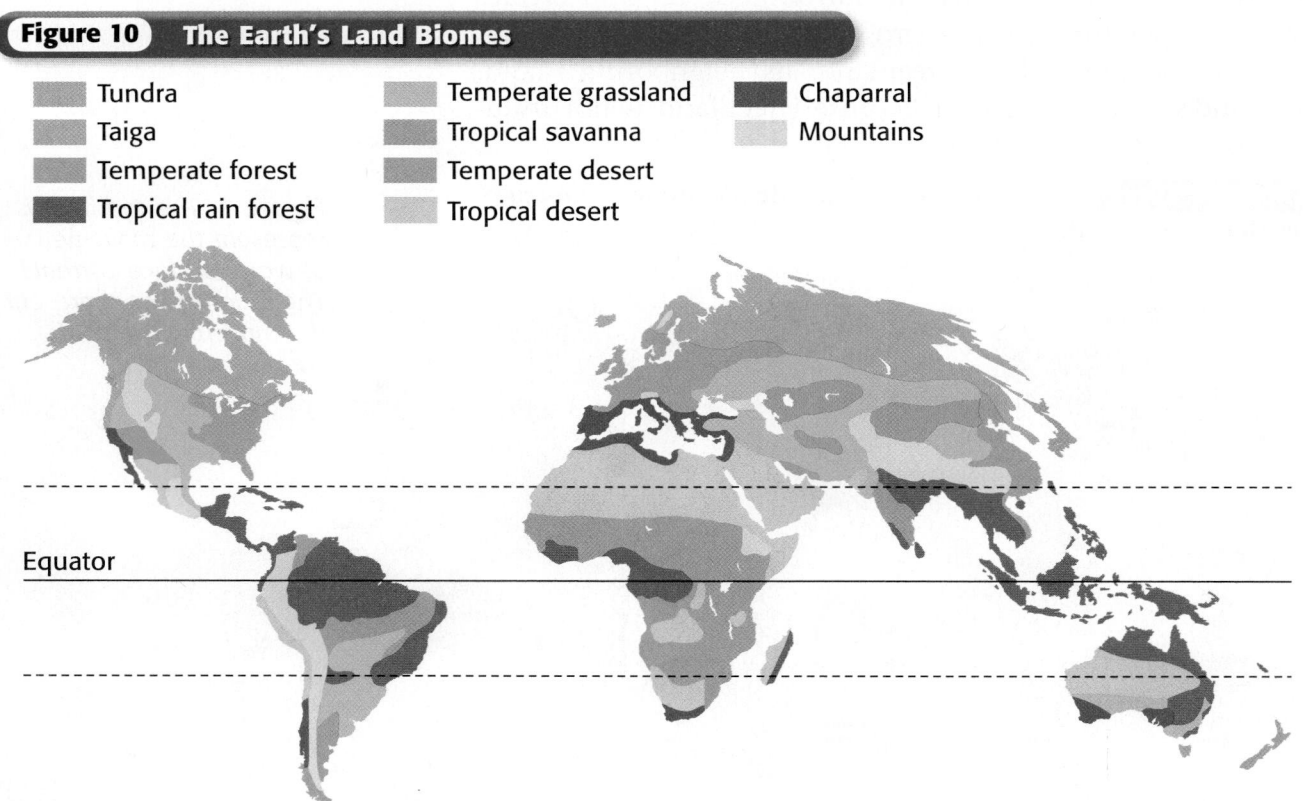

Summary

- Weather is the condition of the atmosphere at a particular time. This condition includes temperature, humidity, precipitation, wind, and visibility.
- Climate is the average weather condition in an area over a long period of time.
- The higher the latitude, the cooler the climate.
- Prevailing winds affect the climate of an area by the amount of moisture they carry.

- Mountains influence an area's climate by affecting both temperature and precipitation.
- Large bodies of water and ocean currents influence the climate of an area by affecting the temperature of the air over the water.
- The three climate zones of the world are the tropical zone, the temperate zone, and the polar zone.

Using Key Terms

1. In your own words, write a definition for each of the following terms: *weather, climate, latitude, prevailing winds, elevation, surface currents,* and *biome.*

Understanding Key Ideas

2. Which of the following affects climate by causing the air to rise?
   a. mountains
   b. ocean currents
   c. large bodies of water
   d. latitude

3. What is the difference between weather and climate?

4. List five factors that determine climates.

5. Explain why there is a difference in climate between areas at 0° latitude and areas at 45° latitude.

6. List the three climate zones of the world.

Critical Thinking

7. **Analyzing Relationships** How would seasons be different if the Earth did not tilt on its axis?

8. **Applying Concepts** During what months does Australia have summer? Explain.

Interpreting Graphics

Use the map below to answer the questions that follow.

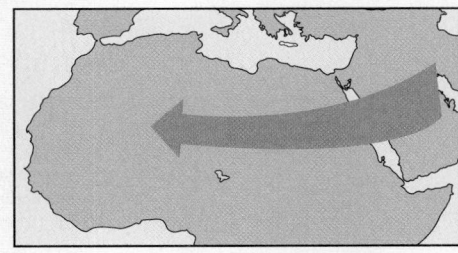

9. Would you expect the area that the arrow points to to be moist or dry? Explain your answer.

10. Describe how the climate of the same area would change if the prevailing winds traveled from the opposite direction. Explain how you came to this conclusion.

SCi LINKS®

Developed and maintained by the
National Science Teachers Association

For a variety of links related to this chapter, go to www.scilinks.org

Topic: What Is Climate?
SciLinks code: HSM1659

The Tropics

Where in the world do you think you could find a flying dragon gliding above you from one treetop to the next?

Don't worry. This flying dragon, or tree lizard, is only about 20 cm long, and it eats only insects. With winglike skin flaps, the flying dragon can glide from one treetop to the next. But, you won't find this kind of animal in the United States. These flying dragons live in Southeast Asia, which is in the tropical zone.

The Tropical Zone

The region that surrounds the equator and that extends from about 23.5° north latitude to 23.5° south latitude is called the **tropical zone.** The tropical zone is also known as the Tropics. Latitudes in the tropical zone receive the most solar radiation. Temperatures are therefore usually hot, except at high elevations.

Within the tropical zone, there are three major types of biomes—tropical rain forest, tropical desert, and tropical savanna. These three biomes have high temperatures. But they differ in the amount of precipitation, soil characteristics, vegetation, and kinds of animals. **Figure 1** shows the distribution of these biomes.

✓ **Reading Check** At what latitudes would you find the tropical zone? (*See the Appendix for answers to Reading Checks.*)

READING WARM-UP

Objectives
- Locate and describe the tropical zone.
- Describe the biomes found in the tropical zone.

Terms to Learn
tropical zone

READING STRATEGY

Reading Organizer As you read this section, make a table comparing *tropical rain forests, tropical savannas,* and *tropical deserts.*

Figure 1 Biomes of the Tropical Zone

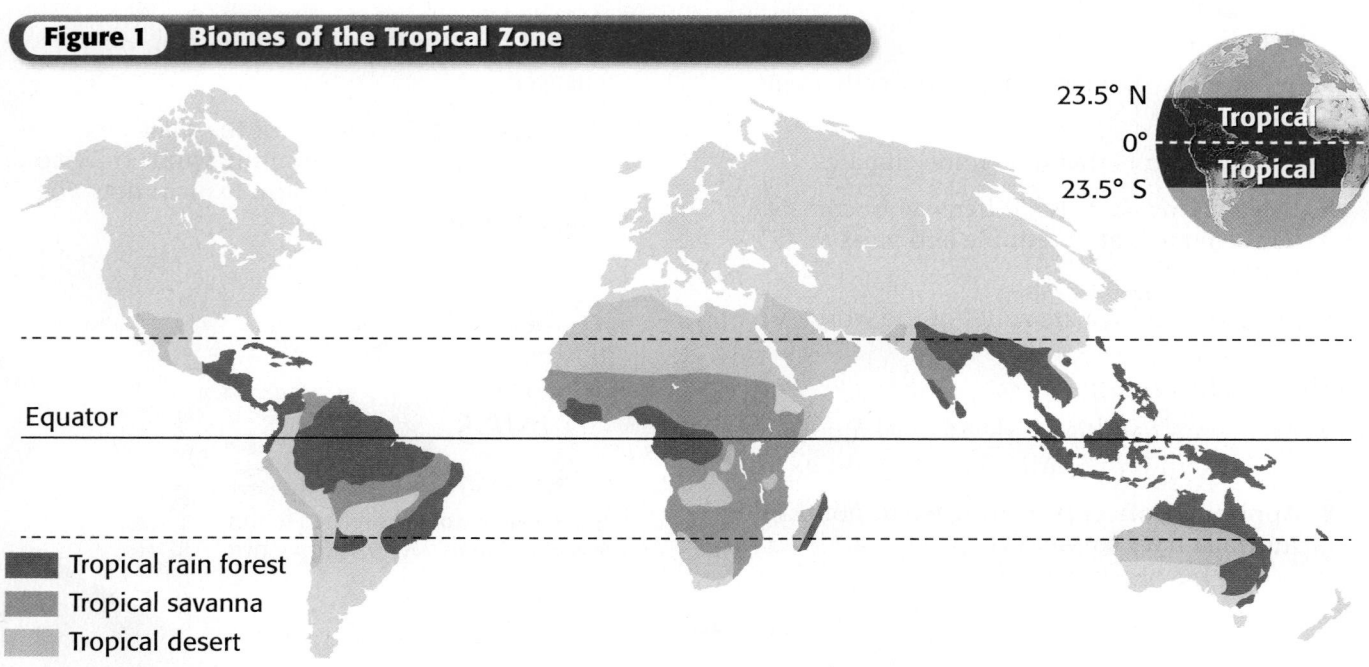

23.5° N
0°
23.5° S

Tropical
Tropical

Equator

■ Tropical rain forest
■ Tropical savanna
■ Tropical desert

Tropical Rain Forest

• Average Temperature Range
  25°C to 28°C (77°F to 82°F)

• Average Yearly Precipitation
  200 cm or more

• Soil Characteristics
  thin and nutrient poor

Tropical Rain Forests

Tropical rain forests are always warm and wet. Because they are located near the equator, they receive strong sunlight year-round. So, there is little difference between seasons in tropical rain forests.

Tropical rain forests contain the greatest number of animal and plant species of any biome. Animals found in tropical rain forests include monkeys, parrots, tree frogs, tigers, and leopards. Plants found in tropical rain forests include mahogany, vines, ferns, and bamboo. But in spite of the lush vegetation, shown in **Figure 2,** the soil in rain forests is poor. The rapid decay of plants and animals returns nutrients to the soil. But these nutrients are quickly absorbed and used by the plants. The nutrients that are not immediately used by the plants are washed away by the heavy rains. The soil is left thin and nutrient poor.

Figure 2 *In tropical rain forests, many of the trees form above-ground roots that provide extra support for the trees in the thin, nutrient-poor soil.*

tropical zone the region that surrounds the equator and that extends from about 23.5° north latitude to 23.5° south latitude

CONNECTION TO Social Studies

WRITING SKILL **Living in the Tropics** The tropical climate is very hot and humid. People who live in the Tropics have had to adapt to feel comfortable in that climate. For example, in the country of Samoa, some people live in homes that have no walls, which are called *fales*. Fales have only a roof, which provides shade. The openness of the home allows cool breezes to flow through the home. Research other countries in the Tropics. See how the climate influences the way the people live in those countries. Then, in your **science journal,** describe how the people's lifestyle helps them adapt to the climate.

Tropical Savanna

- **Average Temperature Range 27°C to 32°C (80°F to 90°F)**
- **Average Yearly Precipitation 100 cm**
- **Soil Characteristics generally nutrient poor**

Figure 3 *The grass of a tropical savanna can be as tall as 5 m.*

Tropical Savannas

Tropical savannas, or grasslands, are composed of tall grasses and a few scattered trees. The climate is usually very warm. Tropical savannas have a dry season that lasts four to eight months and that is followed by short periods of rain. Savanna soils are generally nutrient poor. However, grass fires, which are common during the dry season, leave the soils nutrient enriched. An African savanna is shown in **Figure 3.**

Many plants have adapted to fire and use it to promote development. For example, some species need fire to break open their seeds' outer skin. Only after this skin is broken can each seed grow. For other species, heat from the fire triggers the plants to drop their seeds into the newly enriched soil.

Animals that live in tropical savannas include giraffes, lions, crocodiles, and elephants. Plants include tall grasses, trees, and thorny shrubs.

CONNECTION TO Biology

WRITING SKILL **Animal and Plant Adaptations** Animals and plants adapt to the climate in which they live. These adaptations cause certain animals and plants to be unique to particular biomes. For example, the camel, which is unique to the desert, has adapted to going for long periods of time without water. Research other animals or plants that live in the Tropics. Then, in your **science journal,** describe the characteristics that help them survive in the Tropics.

Tropical Deserts

A desert is an area that receives less than 25 cm of rainfall per year. Because of this low yearly rainfall, deserts are the driest places on Earth. Desert plants, such as those shown in **Figure 4,** are adapted to survive in places that have little water. Animals such as rats, lizards, snakes, and scorpions have also adapted to survive in these deserts.

There are two kinds of deserts—hot deserts and cold deserts. Hot deserts are caused by cool, sinking air masses. Many hot deserts, such as the Sahara, in Africa, are tropical deserts. Daily temperatures in tropical deserts often vary from very hot daytime temperatures (50°C) to cool nighttime temperatures (20°C). Because of the dryness of deserts, the soil is poor in organic matter, which is needed for plants to grow.

Reading Check What animals would you find in a tropical desert?

Tropical Desert

- **Average Temperature Range 16°C to 50°C (61°F to 120°F)**
- **Average Yearly Precipitation 0–25 cm**
- **Soil Characteristics poor in organic matter**

Figure 4 *Plants such as succulents have fleshy stems and leaves to store water.*

SECTION Review

Summary

- The tropical zone is located around the equator, between 23.5° north and 23.5° south latitude.
- Temperatures are usually hot in the tropical zone.
- Tropical rain forests are warm and wet. They have the greatest number of plant and animal species of any biome.
- Tropical savannas are grasslands that have a dry season.
- Tropical deserts are hot and receive little rain.

Using Key Terms

1. In your own words, write a definition for the term *tropical zone*.

Understanding Key Ideas

2. Which of the following tropical biomes has less than 50 cm of precipitation a year?
   a. rain forest   c. grassland
   b. desert   d. savanna

3. What are the soil characteristics of a tropical rain forest?

4. In what ways have savanna vegetation adapted to fire?

Math Skills

5. Suppose that in a tropical savanna, the temperature was recorded every hour for 4 h. The recorded temperatures were 27°C, 28°C, 29°C, and 29°C. Calculate the average temperature for this 4 h period.

Critical Thinking

6. **Analyzing Relationships** How do the tropical biomes differ?

7. **Making Inferences** How would you expect the adaptations of a plant in a tropical rain forest to differ from the adaptations of a tropical desert plant? Explain.

8. **Analyzing Data** An area has a temperature range of 30°C to 40°C and received 10 cm of rain this year. What biome is this area in?

SCiLINKS®

NSTA
Developed and maintained by the National Science Teachers Association

For a variety of links related to this chapter, go to www.scilinks.org

Topic: Climates of the World
SciLinks code: HSM0302

Temperate and Polar Zones

Which season is your favorite? Do you like the change of colors in the fall, the flowers in the spring, or do you prefer the hot days of summer?

If you live in the continental United States, chances are you live in a biome that experiences seasonal change. Seasonal change is one characteristic of the temperate zone. Most of the continental United States is in the temperate zone, which is the climate zone between the Tropics and the polar zone.

The Temperate Zone

The climate zone between the Tropics and the polar zone is the **temperate zone.** Latitudes in the temperate zone receive less solar energy than latitudes in the Tropics do. Because of this, temperatures in the temperate zone tend to be lower than in the Tropics. Some biomes in the temperate zone have a mild change of seasons. Other biomes in the country can experience freezing temperatures in the winter and very hot temperatures in the summer. The temperate zone consists of the following four biomes—temperate forest, temperate grassland, chaparral, and temperate desert. Although these biomes have four distinct seasons, the biomes differ in temperature and precipitation and have different plants and animals. **Figure 1** shows the distribution of the biomes found in the temperate zone.

✓ **Reading Check** **Where is the temperate zone?** (*See the Appendix for answers to Reading Checks.*)

READING WARM-UP

Objectives

● Locate and describe the temperate zone and the polar zone.

● Describe the different biomes found in the temperate zone and the polar zone.

● Explain what a microclimate is.

Terms to Learn

temperate zone
polar zone
microclimate

READING STRATEGY

Reading Organizer As you read this section, create an outline of the section. Use the headings from the section in your outline.

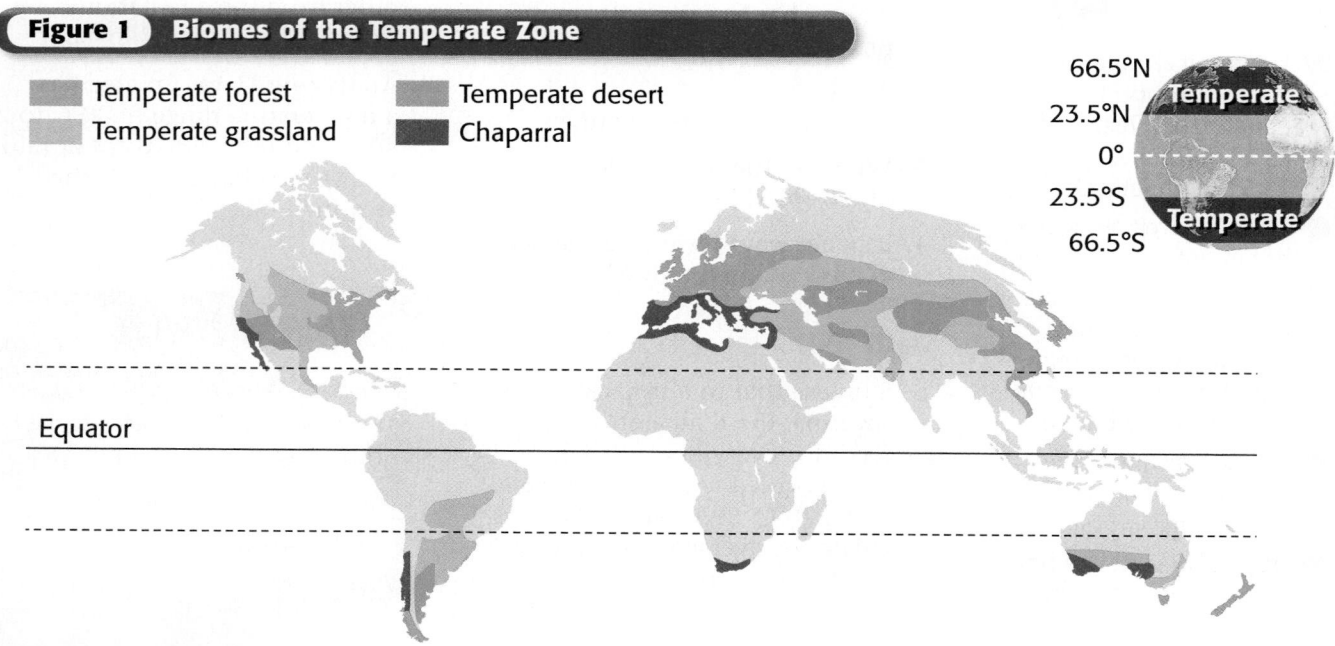

Figure 1 Biomes of the Temperate Zone

- ▇ Temperate forest
- ▇ Temperate grassland
- ▇ Temperate desert
- ▇ Chaparral

66.5°N
23.5°N
0°
23.5°S
66.5°S

Temperate

Temperate

Equator

Temperate Forests

The temperate forest biomes tend to have high amounts of rainfall and seasonal temperature differences. Summers are often warm, and winters are often cold. Animals such as deer, bears, and foxes live in temperate forests. **Figure 2** shows deciduous trees in a temperate forest. *Deciduous* describes trees that lose their leaves at the end of the growing season. The soils in deciduous forests are usually fertile because of the high organic content from decaying leaves that drop every winter. Another type of tree found in the temperate forest is the evergreen. *Evergreens* are trees that keep their leaves year-round.

Figure 2 *Deciduous trees have leaves that change color and drop when temperatures become cold.*

temperate zone the climate zone between the Tropics and the polar zone

Temperate Grasslands

Temperate grasslands, such as those shown in **Figure 3,** are regions that receive too little rainfall for trees to grow. This biome has warm summers and cold winters. Examples of animals that are found in temperate grasslands include bison in North America and kangaroo in Australia. Grasses are the most common kind of plant found in this biome. Because grasslands have the most-fertile soils of all biomes, much of the grassland has been plowed to make room for croplands.

Figure 3 *At one time, the world's grasslands covered about 42% of Earth's total land surface. Today, they occupy only about 12% of the Earth's total land surface.*

- Average Temperature Range 11°C to 26°C (51°F to 78°F)
- Average Yearly Precipitation 48 to 56 cm
- Soil Characteristics rocky, nutrient-poor soils

Figure 4 *Some plant species found in chaparral require fire to reproduce.*

Figure 5 *The Great Basin Desert is in the rain shadow of the Sierra Nevada.*

Chaparrals

Chaparral regions, as shown in **Figure 4,** have cool, wet winters and hot, dry summers. Animals, such as coyotes and mountain lions live in chaparrals. The vegetation is mainly evergreen shrubs. These shrubs are short, woody plants with thick, waxy leaves. The waxy leaves are adaptations that help prevent water loss in dry conditions. These shrubs grow in rocky, nutrient-poor soil. Like tropical-savanna vegetation, chaparral vegetation has adapted to fire. In fact, some plants, such as chamise, can grow back from their roots after a fire.

Temperate Deserts

The temperate desert biomes, like the one shown in **Figure 5,** tend to be cold deserts. Like all deserts, cold deserts receive less than 25 cm of precipitation yearly. Examples of animals that live in temperate deserts are lizards, snakes, bats, and toads. And the types of plants found in temperate deserts include cacti, shrubs, and thorny trees.

Temperate deserts can be very hot in the daytime. But, unlike hot deserts, they are often very cold at night. This large change in temperature between day and night is caused by low humidity and cloudless skies. These conditions allow for a large amount of energy to heat the Earth's surface during the day. However, these same characteristics allow the energy to escape at night. This causes temperatures to drop. You probably rarely think of snow and deserts together. But temperate deserts often receive light snow during the winter.

✓ **Reading Check** Why are temperate deserts cold at night?

Temperate Desert

- Average Temperature Range 1°C to 50°C (34°F to 120°F)
- Average Yearly Precipitation 0 to 25 cm
- Soil Characteristics poor in organic matter

Figure 6 Biomes of the Polar Zone

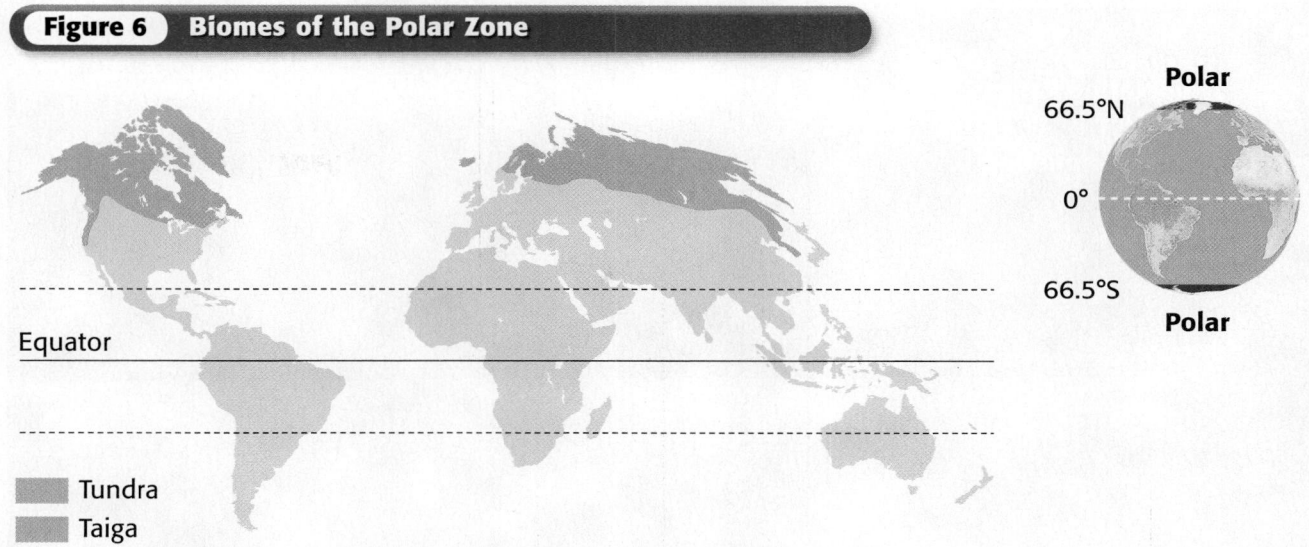

Equator

■ Tundra
■ Taiga

66.5°N Polar

0°

66.5°S

Polar

The Polar Zone

The climate zone located at the North or South Pole and its surrounding area is called the **polar zone.** Polar climates have the coldest average temperatures of all the climate zones. Temperatures in the winter stay below freezing. The temperatures during the summer remain cool. **Figure 6** shows the distribution of the biomes found in the polar zone.

polar zone the North or South Pole and its surrounding area

Tundra

The tundra biome, as shown in **Figure 7,** has long, cold winters with almost 24 hours of night. It also has short, cool summers with almost 24 hours of daylight. In the summer, only the top meter of soil thaws. Underneath the thawed soil lies a permanently frozen layer of soil, called *permafrost*. This frozen layer prevents the water in the thawed soil from draining. Because of the poor drainage, the upper soil layer is muddy. This muddy layer of soil makes a great breeding ground for insects, such as mosquitoes. Many birds migrate to the tundra during the summer to feed on the insects. Other animals that live in the tundra are caribou, reindeer, and polar bears. Plants in this biome include mosses and lichens.

Tundra

• **Average Temperature Range**
  −27°C to 5°C (−17°F to 41°F)

• **Average Yearly Precipitation**
  0 to 25 cm

• **Soil Characteristics**
  frozen

Figure 7 *In the tundra, mosses and lichens cover rocks.*

Figure 8 *The taiga, such as this one in Washington, have mostly evergreens for trees.*

microclimate the climate of a small area

Your Biome With your parents, explore the biome in the area where you live. What kinds of animals and plants live in your area? Write a one-page paper that describes the biome and why the biome of your area has its particular climate.

Taiga (Northern Coniferous Forest)

Just south of the tundra lies the taiga biome. The taiga, as shown in **Figure 8,** has long, cold winters and short, warm summers. Animals commonly found here are moose, bears, and rabbits. The majority of the trees are evergreen needle-leaved trees called *conifers,* such as pine, spruce, and fir trees. The needles and flexible branches allow these trees to shed heavy snow before they can be damaged. Conifer needles are made of acidic substances. When the needles die and fall to the soil, they make the soil acidic. Most plants cannot grow in acidic soil. Because of the acidic soil, the forest floor is bare except for some mosses and lichens.

Microclimates

The climate and the biome of a particular place can also be influenced by local conditions. **Microclimate** is the climate of a small area. The alpine biome is a cold biome found on mountains all around the world. The alpine biome can even be found on mountains in the Tropics! How is this possible? The high elevation affects the area's climate and therefore its biome. As the elevation increases, the air's ability to transfer heat from the ground to the atmosphere by conduction decreases, which causes temperatures to decrease. In winter, the temperatures are below freezing. In summer, average temperatures range from 10°C to 15°C. Plants and animals have had to develop special adaptations to live in this severe climate.

Cities

Cities are also microclimates. In a city, temperatures can be 1°C to 2°C warmer than the surrounding rural areas. Have you ever walked barefoot on a black asphalt street on a hot summer day? Doing so burns your feet because buildings and pavement made of dark materials absorb solar radiation instead of reflecting it. There is also less vegetation in a city to take in the sun's rays. This absorption and re-radiation of heat by buildings and pavement heats the surrounding air. In turn, the temperatures rise.

✓ Reading Check Why do cities have higher temperatures than the surrounding rural areas?

CONNECTION TO
Physics

Hot Roofs! Scientists studied roofs on a sunny day when the air temperature was 13°C. They recorded roof temperatures ranging from 18°C to 61°C depending on color and material of the roof. Place thermometers on outside objects that are made of different types of materials and that are different colors. Please stay off the roof! Is there a difference in temperatures?

ACTIVITY

SECTION
Review

Summary

- The temperate zone is located between the Tropics and the polar zone. It has moderate temperatures.
- Temperate forests, temperate grasslands, and temperate deserts are biomes in the temperate zone.
- The polar zone includes the North or South Pole and its surrounding area. The polar zone has the coldest temperatures.
- The tundra and the taiga are biomes within the polar zone.

Using Key Terms

1. In your own words, write a definition for the term *microclimate*.

Complete each of the following sentences by choosing the correct term from the word bank.

> temperate zone   polar zone
> microclimate

2. The coldest temperatures are found in the ___.

3. The ___ has moderate temperatures.

Understanding Key Ideas

4. Which of the following biomes has the driest climate?
   a. temperate forests
   b. temperate grasslands
   c. chaparrals
   d. temperate deserts

5. Explain why the temperate zone has lower temperatures than the Tropics.

6. Describe how the latitude of the polar zone affects the climate in that area.

7. Explain why the tundra can sometimes experience 24 hours of daylight or 24 hours of night.

8. How do conifers make the soil they grow in too acidic for other plants to grow?

Math Skills

9. Texas has an area of about 700,000 square kilometers. Grasslands compose about 20% of this area. About how many square kilometers of grassland are there in Texas?

Critical Thinking

10. **Identifying Relationships** Which biome would be more suitable for growing crops, temperate forest or taiga? Explain.

11. **Making Inferences** Describe the types of animals and vegetation you might find in the Alpine biome.

SCILINKS

NSTA
Developed and maintained by the National Science Teachers Association

For a variety of links related to this chapter, go to www.scilinks.org

Topic: Modeling Earth's Climate
SciLinks code: HSM0976

Changes in Climate

As you have probably noticed, the weather changes from day to day. Sometimes, the weather can change several times in one day! But have you ever noticed the climate change?

On Saturday, your morning baseball game was canceled because of rain, but by that afternoon the sun was shining. Now, think about the climate where you live. You probably haven't noticed a change in climate, because climates change slowly. What causes climatic change? Studies indicate that human activity may cause climatic change. However, natural factors also can influence changes in the climate.

Ice Ages

The geologic record indicates that the Earth's climate has been much colder than it is today. In fact, much of the Earth was covered by sheets of ice during certain periods. An **ice age** is a period during which ice collects in high latitudes and moves toward lower latitudes. Scientists have found evidence of many major ice ages throughout the Earth's geologic history. The most recent ice age began about 2 million years ago.

Glacial Periods

During an ice age, there are periods of cold and periods of warmth. These periods are called glacial and interglacial periods. During *glacial periods,* the enormous sheets of ice advance. As they advance, they get bigger and cover a larger area, as shown in **Figure 1.** Because a large amount of water is frozen during glacial periods, the sea level drops.

READING WARM-UP

Objectives

● Describe how the Earth's climate has changed over time.

● Summarize four different theories that attempt to explain why the Earth's climate has changed.

● Explain the greenhouse effect and its role in global warming.

Terms to Learn

ice age
global warming
greenhouse effect

READING STRATEGY

Paired Summarizing Read this section silently. In pairs, take turns summarizing the material. Stop to discuss ideas that seem confusing.

ice age a long period of climate cooling during which ice sheets cover large areas of Earth's surface; also known as a glacial period

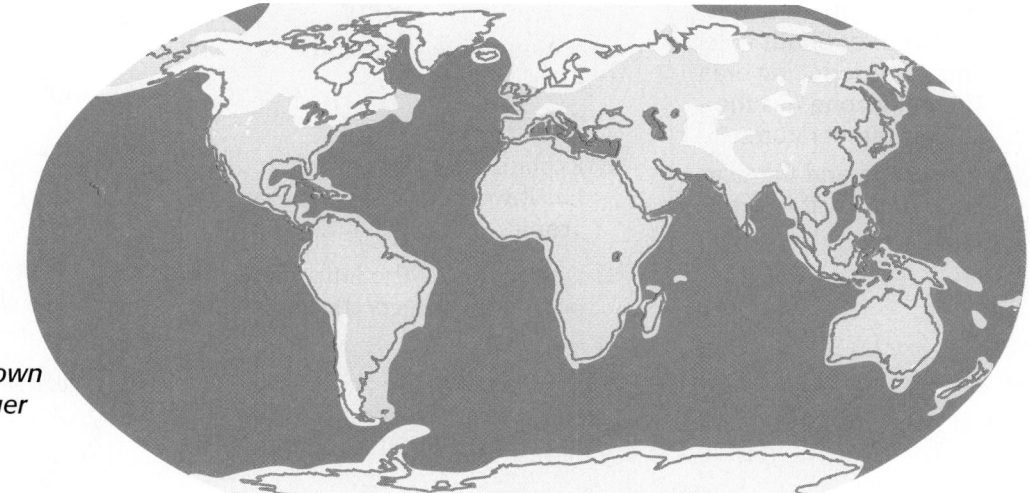

Figure 1 *During glacial periods, ice sheets (as shown in light blue), cover a larger portion of the Earth.*

Interglacial Periods

Warmer times that happen between glacial periods are called *interglacial periods*. During an interglacial period, the ice begins to melt and the sea level rises again. The last interglacial period began 10,000 years ago and is still happening. Why do these periods occur? Will the Earth have another glacial period in the future? These questions have been debated by scientists for the past 200 years.

Motions of the Earth

There are many theories about the causes of ice ages. Each theory tries to explain the gradual cooling that begins an ice age. This cooling leads to the development of large ice sheets that periodically cover large areas of the Earth's surface.

The *Milankovitch theory* explains why an ice age isn't just one long cold spell. Instead, the ice age alternates between cold and warm periods. Milutin Milankovitch, a Yugoslavian scientist, proposed that changes in the Earth's orbit and in the tilt of the Earth's axis cause ice ages. His theory is shown in **Figure 2.** In a 100,000 year period, the Earth's orbit changes from elliptical to circular. This changes the Earth's distance from the sun. In turn, it changes the temperature on Earth. Changes in the tilt of the Earth also influence the climate. The more the Earth is tilted, the closer the poles are to the sun.

✔ **Reading Check** What are the two things Milankovitch says causes ice ages? (*See the Appendix for answers to Reading Checks.*)

INTERNET ACTIVITY

For another activity related to this chapter, go to **go.hrw.com** and type in the keyword **HZ5CLMW.**

Figure 2   The Milankovitch Theory

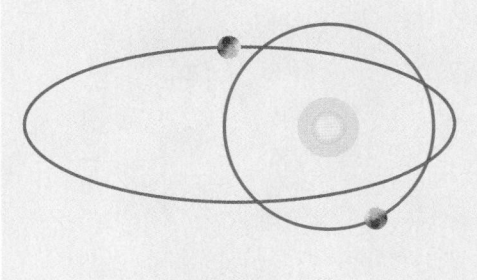

1 Over a period of 100,000 years, the Earth's orbit slowly changes from a more circular shape to a more elliptical shape and back again. When Earth's orbit is elliptical, Earth receives more energy from the sun. When its orbit is more circular, Earth receives less energy from the sun.

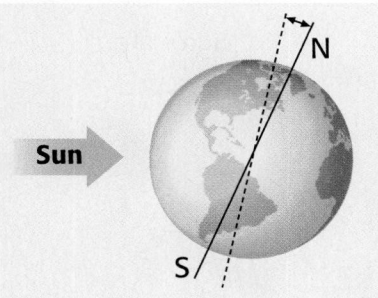

2 Over a period of 41,000 years, the tilt of the Earth's axis varies between 22.2° and 24.5°. When the tilt is at 24.5°, the poles receive more solar energy.

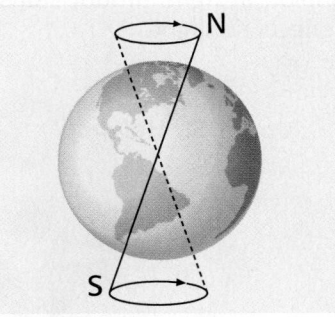

3 The Earth's axis traces a complete circle every 26,000 years. The circular motion of the Earth's axis determines the time of year that the Earth is closest to the sun.

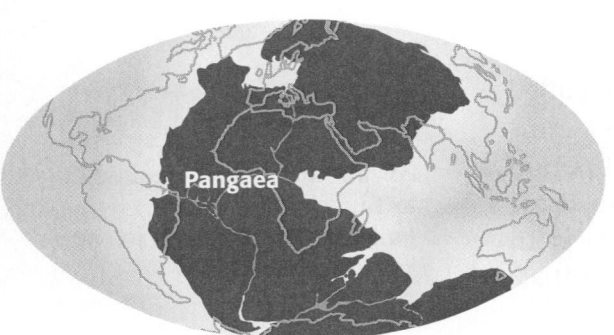

Figure 3 *Much of Pangaea—the part that is now Africa, South America, India, Antarctica, Australia, and Saudi Arabia—was covered by continental ice sheets.*

Plate Tectonics

The Earth's climate is further influenced by plate tectonics and continental drift. One theory proposes that ice ages happen when the continents are positioned closer to the polar regions. About 250 million years ago, all the continents were connected near the South Pole in one giant landmass called *Pangaea,* as shown in **Figure 3.** During this time, ice covered a large area of the Earth's surface. As Pangaea broke apart, the continents moved toward the equator, and the ice age ended. During the last ice age, many large landmasses were positioned in the polar zones. Antarctica, northern North America, Europe, and Asia were covered by large sheets of ice.

Volcanic Eruptions

Many natural factors can affect global climate. Catastrophic events, such as volcanic eruptions, can influence climate. Volcanic eruptions send large amounts of dust, ash, and smoke into the atmosphere. Once in the atmosphere, the dust, smoke, and ash particles act as a shield. This shield blocks the sun's rays, which causes the Earth to cool. **Figure 4** shows how dust particles from a volcanic eruption block the sun.

Reading Check How can volcanoes change the climate?

Figure 4   Volcanic Dust in the Atmosphere

Volcanic eruptions, such as the 1980 eruption of Mount St. Helens, as shown at right, produce dust that reflects sunlight.

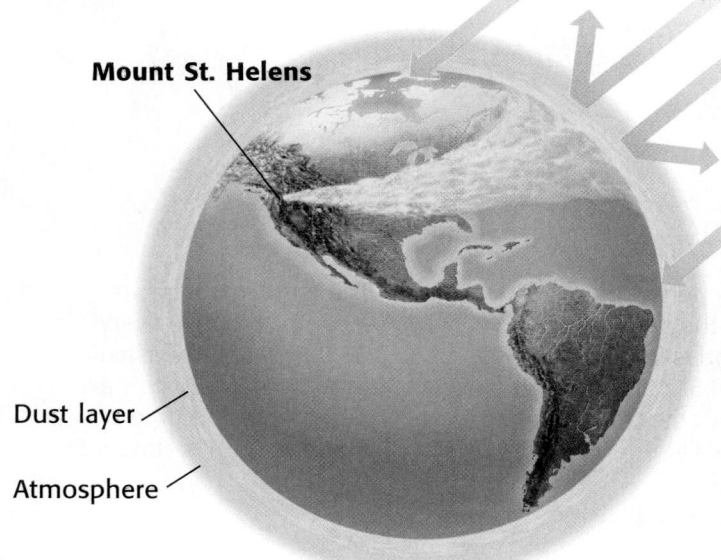

Sun's rays

Mount St. Helens

Dust layer

Atmosphere

Figure 5 *Some scientists believe that a 10 km chunk of rock smashed into the Earth 65 million years ago, which caused the climatic change that resulted in the extinction of dinosaurs.*

Asteroid Impact

Imagine a rock the size of a car flying in from outer space and crashing in your neighborhood. This rock, like the one shown in **Figure 5,** is called an asteroid. An *asteroid* is a small, rocky object that orbits the sun. Sometimes, asteroids enter our atmosphere and crash into the Earth. What would happen if an asteroid 1 km wide, which is more than half a mile long, hit the Earth? Scientists believe that if an asteroid this big hit the Earth, it could change the climate of the entire world.

When a large piece of rock slams into the Earth, it causes debris to shoot into the atmosphere. *Debris* is dust and smaller rocks. This debris can block some of the sunlight and thermal energy. This would lower average temperatures, which would change the climate. Plants wouldn't get the sunlight they needed to grow, and animals would find surviving difficult. Scientists believe such an event is what caused dinosaurs to become extinct 65 million years ago when a 10 km asteroid slammed into the Earth and changed the Earth's climate.

The Sun's Cycle

Some changes in the climate can be linked to changes in the sun. You might think that the sun always stays the same. However, the sun follows an 11-year cycle. During this cycle, the sun changes from a solar maximum to a solar minimum. During a solar minimum, the sun produces a low percentage of high-energy radiation. But when the sun is at its solar maximum, it produces a large percentage of high-energy radiation. This increase in high-energy radiation warms the winds in the atmosphere. This change in turn affects climate patterns around the world.

CONNECTION TO Astronomy

Sunspots Sunspots are dark areas on the sun's surface. The number of sunspots changes with the sun's cycle. When the cycle is at a solar maximum, there are many sunspots. When the cycle is at a solar minimum, there are fewer sunspots. If the number of sunspots was low in 1997, in what year will the next low point in the cycle happen?

global warming a gradual increase in the average global temperature

greenhouse effect the warming of the surface and lower atmosphere of Earth that occurs when carbon dioxide, water vapor, and other gases in the air absorb and trap thermal energy

Global Warming

A gradual increase in the average global temperature that is due to a higher concentration of gases, such as carbon dioxide in the atmosphere, is called **global warming.** To understand how global warming works, you must first learn about the greenhouse effect.

Greenhouse Effect

The Earth's natural heating process, in which gases in the atmosphere trap thermal energy, is called the **greenhouse effect.** The car in **Figure 6** shows how the greenhouse effect works. The car's windows stop most of the thermal energy from escaping, and the inside of the car gets hot. On Earth, instead of glass stopping the thermal energy, atmospheric gases absorb the thermal energy. When this happens, the thermal energy stays in the atmosphere and keeps the Earth warm. Many scientists believe that the rise in global temperatures is due to an increase of carbon dioxide, an atmospheric gas. Most evidence shows that the increase in carbon dioxide is caused by the burning of fossil fuels.

Another factor that may add to global warming is the clearing of forests. In many countries, forests are being burned to clear land for farming. Burning of the forests releases more carbon dioxide. Because plants use carbon dioxide to make food, destroying the trees decreases a natural way of removing carbon dioxide from the atmosphere.

Figure 6 *Sunlight streams into the car through the clear, glass windows. The seats absorb the radiant energy and change it into thermal energy. The energy is then trapped in the car.*

Consequences of Global Warming

Many scientists think that if the global temperature continues to rise, the ice caps will melt and cause flooding. Melted ice-caps would raise the sea level and flood low-lying areas, such as the coasts.

Areas that receive little rainfall, such as deserts, might receive even less because of increased evaporation. Desert animals and plants would find surviving harder. Warmer and drier climates could harm crops in the Midwest of the United States. But farther north, such as in Canada, weather conditions for farming could improve.

Reading Check How would warmer temperatures affect deserts?

SCHOOL to HOME

Reducing Pollution
Your city just received a warning from the Environmental Protection Agency for exceeding the automobile fuel emissions standards. Discuss with your parent ways that the city can reduce the amount of automobile emissions.

ACTIVITY

SECTION Review

Summary

- The Earth's climate experiences glacial and inter-glacial periods.
- The Milankovitch theory states that the Earth's climate changes as its orbit and the tilt of its axis change.
- Climate changes can be caused by volcanic eruptions, asteroid impact, the sun's cycle, and by global warming.
- Excess carbon dioxide is believed to contribute to global warming.

Using Key Terms

1. Use the following term in a sentence: *ice age*.

2. In your own words, write a definition for each of the following terms: *global warming* and *greenhouse effect*.

Understanding Key Ideas

3. Describe the possible causes of an ice age.

4. Which of the following can cause a change in the climate due to dust particles?
   a. volcanic eruptions
   b. plate tectonics
   c. solar cycles
   d. ice ages

5. How has the Earth's climate changed over time?

6. What might have caused the Earth's climate to change?

7. Which period of an ice age are we in currently? Explain.

8. Explain how the greenhouse effect warms the Earth.

Math Skills

9. After a volcanic eruption, the average temperature in a region dropped from 30° to 18°C. By how many degrees Celsius did the temperature drop?

Critical Thinking

10. **Analyzing Relationships** How will the warming of the Earth affect agriculture in different parts of the world? Explain.

11. **Predicting Consequences** How would deforestation (the cutting of trees) affect global warming?

SCILINKS

NSTA
Developed and maintained by the
National Science Teachers Association

For a variety of links related to this chapter, go to www.scilinks.org

Topic: Changes in Climate
SciLinks code: HSM0252

Skills Practice Lab

Biome Business

You have just been hired as an assistant to a world-famous botanist. You have been provided with climatographs for three biomes. A *climatograph* is a graph that shows the monthly temperature and precipitation of an area in a year.

You can use the information provided in the three graphs to determine what type of climate each biome has. Next to the climatograph for each biome is an unlabeled map of the biome. Using the maps and the information provided in the graphs, you must figure out what the environment is like in each biome. You can find the exact location of each biome by tracing the map of the biome and matching it to the map at the bottom of the page.

OBJECTIVES

Interpret data in a climatograph.

Identify the biome for each climatograph.

Procedure

1 Look at each climatograph. The shaded areas show the average precipitation for the biome. The red line shows the average temperature.

2 Use the climatographs to determine the climate patterns for each biome. Compare the map of each biome with the map below to find the exact location of each biome.

Tundra
Taiga
Temperate forest
Tropical rain forest
Temperate grassland
Tropical savanna
Temperate desert
Tropical desert
Chaparral
Mountains

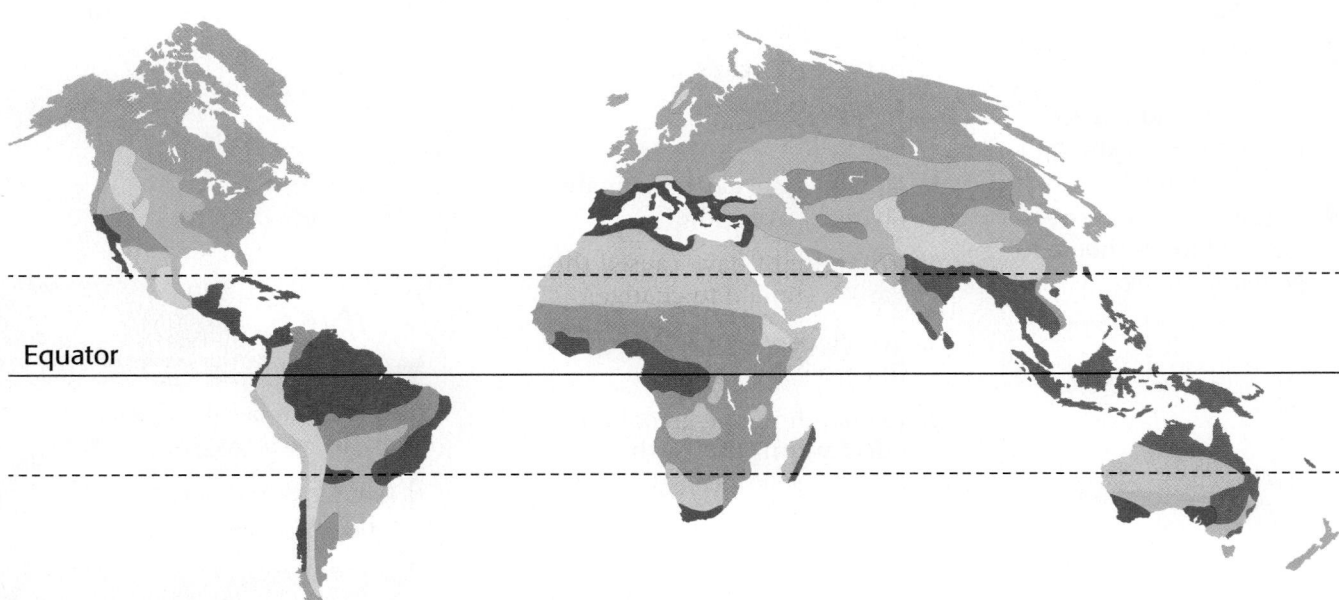

Equator

Analyze Results

1 **Analyzing Data** Describe the precipitation patterns of each biome by answering the following questions:

    a. In which month does the biome receive the most precipitation?

    b. Do you think that the biome is dry, or do you think that it is wet from frequent rains?

2 **Analyzing Data** Describe the temperature patterns of each biome by answering the following questions:

    a. In the biome, which months are warmest?

    b. Does the biome seem to have temperature cycles, like seasons, or is the temperature almost always the same?

    c. Do you think that the biome is warm or cold? Explain.

Draw Conclusions

3 **Drawing Conclusions** Name each biome.

4 **Applying Conclusions** Where is each biome located?

Biome B

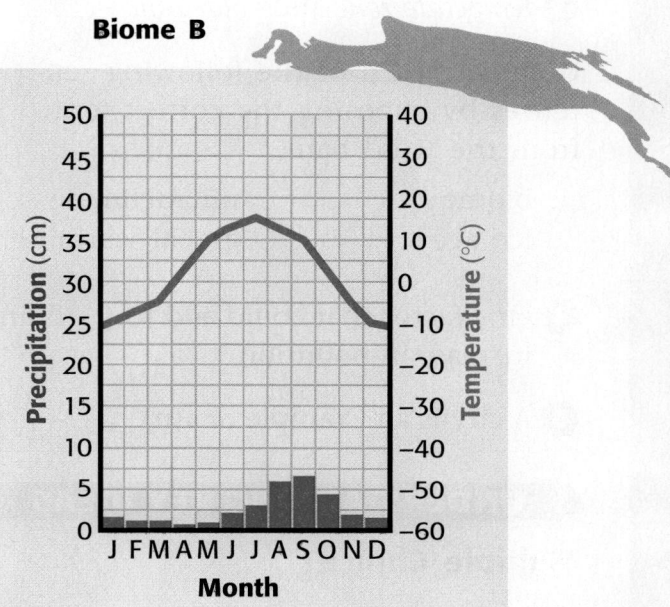

Biome A

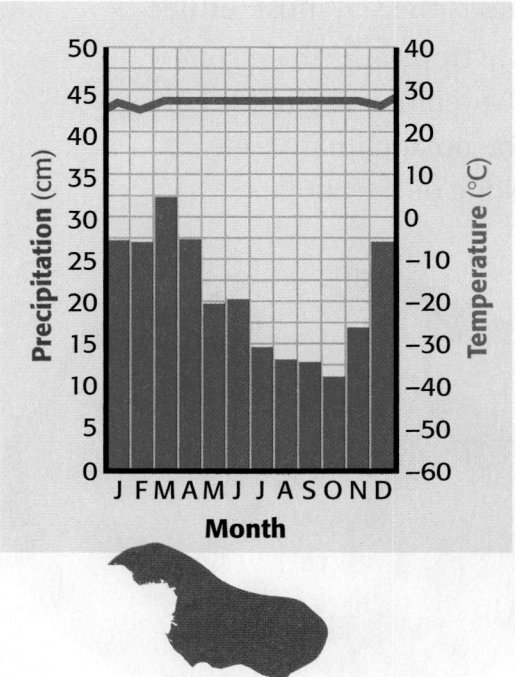

Biome C

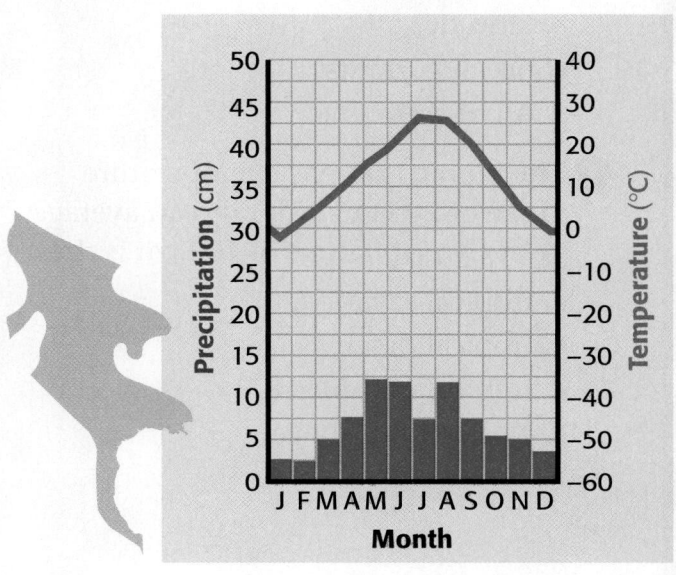

Chapter Review

USING KEY TERMS

For each pair of terms, explain how the meanings of the terms differ.

1 *biome* and *tropical zone*

2 *weather* and *climate*

3 *temperate zone* and *polar zone*

Complete each of the following sentences by choosing the correct term from the word bank.

biome	microclimate
ice age	global warming

4 One factor that could add to ___ is an increase in pollution.

5 A city is an example of a(n) ___.

UNDERSTANDING KEY IDEAS

Multiple Choice

6 Which of the following is a factor that affects climate?

a. prevailing winds

b. latitude

c. ocean currents

d. All of the above

7 The biome that has a temperature range of 28°C to 32°C and an average yearly precipitation of 100 cm is the

a. tropical savanna.

b. tropical desert.

c. tropical rain forest.

d. None of the above

8 Which of the following biomes is NOT found in the temperate zone?

a. temperate forest

b. taiga

c. chaparral

d. temperate grassland

9 In which of the following is the tilt of the Earth's axis considered to have an effect on climate?

a. global warming

b. the sun's cycle

c. the Milankovitch theory

d. asteroid impact

10 Which of the following substances contributes to the greenhouse effect?

a. smoke

b. smog

c. carbon dioxide

d. All of the above

11 In which of the following climate zones is the soil most fertile?

a. the tropical climate zone

b. the temperate climate zone

c. the polar climate zone

d. None of the above

Short Answer

12 Why do higher latitudes receive less solar radiation than lower latitudes do?

13 How does wind influence precipitation patterns?

14 Give an example of a microclimate. What causes the unique temperature and precipitation characteristics of this area?

15 How are tundras and deserts similar?

16 How does deforestation influence global warming?

17 **Concept Mapping** Use the following terms to create a concept map: *global warming, deforestation, changes in climate, greenhouse effect, ice ages,* and *the Milankovitch theory.*

18 **Analyzing Processes** Explain how ocean surface currents cause milder climates.

19 **Identifying Relationships** Describe how the tilt of the Earth's axis affects seasonal changes in different latitudes.

20 **Evaluating Conclusions** Explain why the climate on the eastern side of the Rocky Mountains differs drastically from the climate on the western side.

21 **Applying Concepts** What are some steps you and your family can take to reduce the amount of carbon dioxide that is released into the atmosphere?

22 **Applying Concepts** If you wanted to live in a warm, dry area, which biome would you choose to live in?

23 **Evaluating Data** Explain why the vegetation in areas that have a tundra climate is sparse even though these areas receive precipitation that is adequate to support life.

Use the diagram below to answer the questions that follow.

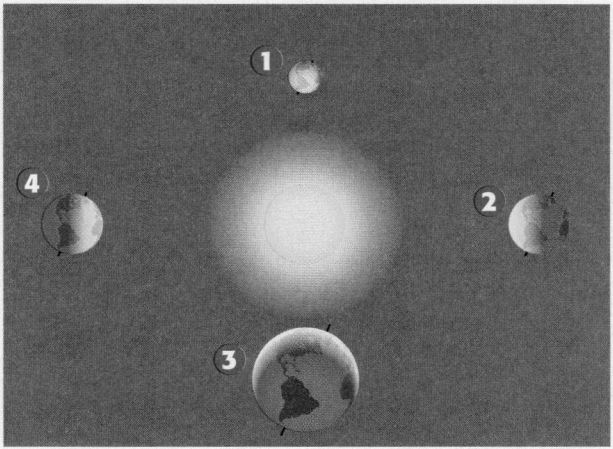

24 At what position—1, 2, 3, or 4—is it spring in the Southern Hemisphere?

25 At what position does the South Pole receive almost 24 hours of daylight?

26 Explain what is happening in each climate zone in both the Northern and Southern Hemispheres at position 4.

Standardized Test Preparation

Read each of the passages below. Then, answer the questions that follow each passage.

Passage 1 Earth's climate has gone through many changes. For example, 6,000 years ago today's desert in North Africa was grassland and shallow lakes. Hippopotamuses, crocodiles, and early Stone Age people shared the shallow lakes that covered the area. For many years, scientists have known that Earth's climate has changed. What they didn't know was why it changed. Today, scientists can use supercomputers and complex computer programs to help them find the answer. Now, scientists may be able to <u>decipher</u> why North Africa's lakes and grasslands became a desert. And that information may be useful for predicting future heat waves and ice ages.

1. In this passage, what does *decipher* mean?

   A to question

   B to cover up

   C to explain

   D to calculate

2. According to the passage, which of the following statements is true?

   F Scientists did not know that Earth's climate has changed.

   G Scientists have known that Earth's climate has changed.

   H Scientists have known why Earth's climate has changed.

   I Scientists know that North Africa was always desert.

3. Which of the following is a fact in the passage?

   A North African desert areas never had lakes.

   B North American desert areas never had lakes.

   C North African desert areas had shallow lakes.

   D North Africa is covered with shallow lakes.

Passage 2 El Niño, which is Spanish for "the child," is the name of a weather event that occurs in the Pacific Ocean. Every 2 to 12 years, the interaction between the ocean surface and atmospheric winds creates El Niño. This event influences weather patterns in many regions of the world. For example, in Indonesia and Malaysia, El Niño meant <u>drought</u> and forest fires in 1998. Thousands of people in these countries suffered respiratory ailments caused by breathing the smoke from these fires. Heavy rains in San Francisco created extremely high mold-spore counts. These spores caused problems for people who have allergies. In San Francisco, the spore count in February is usually between 0 and 100. In 1998, the count was often higher than 8,000.

1. In this passage, what does *drought* mean?

   A windy weather

   B stormy weather

   C long period of dry weather

   D rainy weather

2. What can you infer about mold spores from reading the passage?

   F Some people in San Francisco are allergic to mold spores.

   G Mold spores are only in San Francisco.

   H A higher mold-spore count helps people with allergies.

   I The mold-spore count was low in 1998.

3. According to the passage, which of the following statements is true?

   A El Niño causes droughts in Indonesia and Malaysia.

   B El Niño occurs every year.

   C El Niño causes fires in San Francisco.

   D El Niño last occurred in 1998.

The chart below shows types of organisms in an unknown biome. Use the chart below to answer the questions that follow.

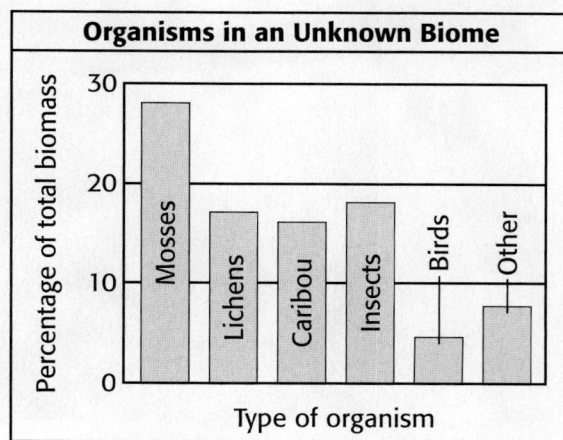

Organisms in an Unknown Biome

1. *Biomass* is a term that means "the total mass of all living things in a certain area." The graph above shows the relative percentages of the total biomass for different plants and animals in a given area. What type of biome does the graph represent?

   A rain forest
   B chaparral
   C tundra
   D taiga

2. Approximately what percentage of biomass is made up of caribou?

   F 28%
   G 25%
   H 16%
   I 5%

3. Approximately what percentage of biomass is made up of lichens and mosses?

   A 45%
   B 35%
   C 25%
   D 16%

Read each question below, and choose the best answer.

1. In a certain area of the savanna that is 12 km long and 5 km wide, there are 180 giraffes. How many giraffes are there per square kilometer in this area?

   A 12
   B 6
   C 4
   D 3

2. If the air temperature near the shore of a lake measures 24°C and the temperature increases by 0.055°C every 10 m traveled away from the lake, what would the air temperature 1 km from the lake be?

   F 5°C
   G 25°C
   H 29.5°C
   I 35°C

3. In a temperate desert, the temperature dropped from 50°C at noon to 37°C by nightfall. By how many degrees Celsius did the noon temperature drop?

   A 13°C
   B 20°C
   C 26°C
   D 50°C

4. Earth is tilted on its axis at a 23.5° angle. What is the measure of the angle that is complementary to a 23.5° angle?

   F 66.5°
   G 67.5°
   H 156.5°
   I 336.5°

5. After a volcanic eruption, the average temperature in a region dropped from 30°C to 18°C. By what percentage did the temperature drop?

   A 30%
   B 25%
   C 40%
   D 15%

Standardized Test Preparation

Science in Action

Scientific Debate

Global Warming

Many scientists believe that pollution from burning fossil fuels is causing temperatures on Earth to rise. Higher average temperatures can cause significant changes in climate. These changes may make survival difficult for animals and plants that have adapted to a biome.

However, other scientists believe that there isn't enough evidence to prove that global warming exists. They argue that any increase in temperatures around the world can be caused by a number of factors other than pollution, such as the sun's cycle.

Language Arts ActiViTY

WRITING SKILL Read articles that present a variety of viewpoints on global warming. Then, write your own article supporting your viewpoint on global warming.

Science, Technology, and Society

Ice Cores

How do scientists know what Earth's climate was like thousands of years ago? Scientists learn about Earth's past climates by studying ice cores. An ice core is collected by drilling a tube of ice from glaciers and polar ice sheets. Layers in the ice core contain substances that landed in the snow during a particular year or season, such as dust from desert storms, ash from volcanic eruptions, and carbon dioxide from pollution. By studying the layers of the ice cores, scientists can learn what factors influenced the past climates.

Math ActiViTY

An area has an average yearly rainfall of 20 cm. In 1,000 years, if the average yearly rainfall decreases by 6%, what would the new average yearly rainfall be?

Mercedes Pascual

Climate Change and Disease Mercedes Pascual is a theoretical ecologist at the University of Michigan. Pascual has been able to help the people of Bangladesh save lives by using information about climate changes to predict outbreaks of the disease cholera. Cholera can be a deadly disease that people usually contract by drinking contaminated water. Pascual knew that in Bangladesh, outbreaks of cholera peak every 3.7 years. She noticed that this period matches the frequency of the El Niño Southern Oscillations, which is a weather event that occurs in the Pacific Ocean. El Niño affects weather patterns in many regions of the world, including Bangladesh. El Niño increases the temperatures of the sea off the coast of Bangladesh. Pascual found that increased sea temperatures lead to higher numbers of the bacteria that cause cholera. In turn, more people contract cholera. But because of the research conducted by Pascual and other scientists, the people of Bangladesh can better predict and prepare for outbreaks of cholera.

Social Studies ACTIVITY

WRITING SKILL Research the effects of El Niño. Write a report describing El Niño and its affect on a country other than Bangladesh.

go.hrw.com

To learn more about these Science in Action topics, visit go.hrw.com and type in the keyword **HZ5CLMF.**

Current Science

Check out Current Science® articles related to this chapter by visiting go.hrw.com. Just type in the keyword **HZ5CS17.**

UNIT 7

TIMELINE

Astronomy

In this unit, you will learn about the science of astronomy. Long before science was called science, people looked up at the night sky and tried to understand the meaning of the twinkling lights above. Early astronomers charted the stars and built calendars based on the movement of the sun, moon, and planets. Today, scientists from around the world have come together to place a space station in orbit around the Earth. This timeline shows some of the events that have occurred throughout human history as scientists have come to understand more about our planet's "neighborhood" in space.

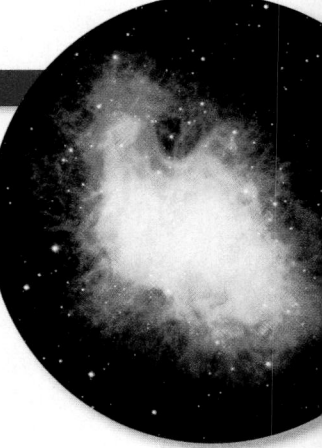

1054

Chinese and Korean astronomers record the appearance of a supernova, an exploding star. Strangely, no European observations of this event have ever been found.

The Crab Nebula

Andromeda Nebula

1924

An astronomer named Edwin Hubble confirms the existence of other galaxies.

1983

Sally Ride becomes the first American woman to travel in space.

1582

Ten days are dropped from October as the Julian calendar is replaced by the Gregorian calendar.

1666

Using a prism, Isaac Newton discovers that white light is composed of different colors.

1898

The War of the Worlds, by H. G. Wells, is published.

1958

The National Aeronautics and Space Administration (NASA) is established to oversee the exploration of space.

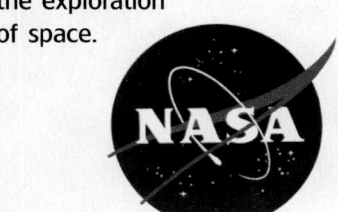

1970

Apollo 13 is damaged shortly after leaving orbit. The spacecraft's three astronauts navigate around the moon to return safely to the Earth.

1977

Voyager 1 and *Voyager 2* are launched on missions to Jupiter, Saturn, and beyond. Now more than 10 billion kilometers away from the Earth, they are still sending back information about space.

Voyager 2

1992

Astronomers discover the first planet outside the solar system.

1998

John Glenn becomes the oldest human in space. His second trip into space comes 36 years after he became the first American to orbit the Earth.

2003

Astronomers discover three distant quasars that date back to a time when the universe was only 800 million years old. It takes light 13 billion years to reach Earth from the farthest of the three quasars.

18

Studying Space

About the PHOTO ⟳

This time-exposure photograph was taken at an observatory located high in the mountains of Chile. As the night passed, the photograph recorded the stars as they circled the southern celestial pole. Just as Earth's rotation causes the sun to appear to move across the sky during the day, Earth's rotation also causes the stars to appear to move across the night sky.

PRE-READING ACTIVITY

FOLDNOTES **Three-Panel Flip Chart**
Before you read the chapter, create the FoldNote entitled "Three-Panel Flip Chart" described in the **Study Skills** section of the Appendix. Label the flaps of the three-panel flip chart with "Astronomy," "Telescopes," and "Mapping the stars." As you read the chapter, write information you learn about each category under the appropriate flap.

START-UP ACTIVITY

Making an Astrolabe

In this activity, you will make an astronomical device called an *astrolabe* (AS troh LAYB). Ancient astronomers used astrolabes to measure the location of stars in the sky. You will use the astrolabe to measure the angle, or altitude, of an object.

Procedure

1. Tie one end of a **piece of thread** that is 15 cm long to the center of the straight edge of a **protractor.** Attach a **paper clip** to the other end of the string.

2. Tape a **soda straw** lengthwise along the straight edge of the protractor. Your astrolabe is complete!

3. Go outside, and hold the astrolabe in front of you.

4. Look through the straw at a distant object, such as a treetop. The curve of the astrolabe should point toward the ground.

5. Hold the astrolabe still, and carefully pinch the string between your thumb and the protractor. Count the number of degrees between the string and the 90° marker on the protractor. This angle is the altitude of the object.

Analysis

1. What is the altitude of the object? How would the altitude change if you moved closer to the object?

2. Explain how you would use an astrolabe to find the altitude of a star. What are the advantages and disadvantages of this method of measurement?

Astronomy: The Original Science

astronomy the study of the universe

year the time required for the Earth to orbit once around the sun

Imagine that it is 5,000 years ago. Clocks and modern calendars have not been invented. How would you tell the time or know what day it is? One way to tell the time is to study the movement of stars, planets, and the moon.

People in ancient cultures used the seasonal cycles of the stars, planets, and the moon to mark the passage of time. For example, by observing these yearly cycles, early farmers learned the best times of year to plant and harvest various crops. Studying the movement of objects in the sky was so important to ancient people that they built observatories, such as the one shown in **Figure 1.** Over time, the study of the night sky became the science of astronomy. **Astronomy** is the study of the universe. Although ancient cultures did not fully understand how the planets, moons, and stars move in relation to each other, their observations led to the first calendars.

Our Modern Calendar

The years, months, and days of our modern calendar are based on the observation of bodies in our solar system. A **year** is the time required for the Earth to orbit once around the sun. A **month** is roughly the amount of time required for the moon to orbit once around the Earth. (The word *month* comes from the word *moon.*) A **day** is the time required for the Earth to rotate once on its axis.

Figure 1 *This building is located at Chichén Itzá in the Yucatán, Mexico. It is thought to be an ancient Mayan observatory.*

Who's Who of Early Astronomy

Astronomical observations have given us much more than the modern calendar that we use. The careful work of early astronomers helped people understand their place in the universe. The earliest astronomers had only oral histories to learn from. Almost everything they knew about the universe came from what they could discover with their eyes and minds. Not surprisingly, most early astronomers thought that the universe consisted of the sun, the moon, and the planets. They thought that the stars were at the edge of the universe. Claudius Ptolemy (KLAW dee uhs TAHL uh mee) and Nicolaus Copernicus (NIK uh LAY uhs koh PUHR ni kuhs) were two early scientists who influenced the way that people thought about the structure of the universe.

month a division of the year that is based on the orbit of the moon around the Earth

day the time required for Earth to rotate once on its axis

Ptolemy: An Earth-Centered Universe

In 140 CE, Ptolemy, a Greek astronomer, wrote a book that combined all of the ancient knowledge of astronomy that he could find. He expanded ancient theories with careful mathematical calculations in what was called the *Ptolemaic theory*. Ptolemy thought that the Earth was at the center of the universe and that the other planets and the sun revolved around the Earth. Although the Ptolemaic theory, shown in **Figure 2,** was incorrect, it predicted the motions of the planets better than any other theory at the time did. For over 1,500 years in Europe, the Ptolemaic theory was the most popular theory for the structure of the universe.

Figure 2 *According to the Ptolemaic theory, the Earth is at the center of the universe.*

Copernicus: A Sun-Centered Universe

In 1543, a Polish astronomer named Copernicus published a new theory that would eventually revolutionize astronomy. According to his theory, which is shown in **Figure 3,** the sun is at the center of the universe, and all of the planets—including the Earth—orbit the sun. Although Copernicus correctly thought that the planets orbit the sun, his theory did not replace the Ptolemaic theory immediately. When Copernicus's theory was accepted, major changes in science and society called the *Copernican revolution* took place.

✔ **Reading Check** What was Copernicus's theory?
(*See the Appendix for answers to Reading Checks.*)

Figure 3 *According to Copernicus's theory, the sun is at the center of the universe.*

Tycho Brahe: A Wealth of Data

In the late-1500s, Danish astronomer Tycho Brahe (TIE koh BRAW uh) used several large tools, including the one shown in **Figure 4,** to make the most detailed astronomical observations that had been recorded so far. Brahe favored a theory of an Earth-centered universe that was different from the Ptolemaic theory. Brahe thought that the sun and the moon revolved around the Earth and that the other planets revolved around the sun. While his theory was not correct, Brahe recorded very precise observations of the planets and stars that helped future astronomers.

Johannes Kepler: Laws of Planetary Motion

After Brahe died, his assistant, Johannes Kepler, continued Brahe's work. Kepler did not agree with Brahe's theory, but he recognized how valuable Brahe's data were. In 1609, after analyzing the data, Kepler announced that all of the planets revolve around the sun in elliptical orbits and that the sun is not in the exact center of the orbits. Kepler also stated three laws of planetary motion. These laws are still used today.

Figure 4 *Brahe (upper right) used a mural quadrant, which is a large quarter-circle on a wall, to measure the positions of stars and planets.*

Galileo: Turning a Telescope to the Sky

In 1609, Galileo Galilei became one of the first people to use a telescope to observe objects in space. Galileo discovered craters and mountains on the Earth's moon, four of Jupiter's moons, sunspots on the sun, and the phases of Venus. These discoveries showed that the planets are not "wandering stars" but are physical bodies like the Earth.

Isaac Newton: The Laws of Gravity

In 1687, a scientist named Sir Isaac Newton showed that all objects in the universe attract each other through gravitational force. The force of gravity depends on the mass of the objects and the distance between them. Newton's law of gravity explained why all of the planets orbit the most massive object in the solar system—the sun. Thus, Newton helped explain the observations of the scientists who came before him.

✓ Reading Check How did the work of Isaac Newton help explain the observations of earlier scientists?

Modern Astronomy

The invention of the telescope and the description of gravity were two milestones in the development of modern astronomy. In the 200 years following Newton's discoveries, scientists made many discoveries about our solar system. But they did not learn that our galaxy has cosmic neighbors until the 1920s.

Edwin Hubble: Beyond the Edge of the Milky Way

Before the 1920s, many astronomers thought that our galaxy, the Milky Way, included every object in space. In 1924, Edwin Hubble proved that other galaxies existed beyond the edge of the Milky Way. His data confirmed the beliefs of some astronomers that the universe is much larger than our galaxy. Today, larger and better telescopes on the Earth and in space, new models of the universe, and spacecraft help astronomers study space. Computers, shown in **Figure 5,** help process data and control the movement of telescopes. These tools have helped answer many questions about the universe. Yet new technology has presented questions that were unthinkable even 10 years ago.

Figure 5 *Computers are used to control telescopes and process large amounts of data.*

SECTION Review

Summary

- Astronomy, the study of the universe, is one of the oldest sciences.
- The units of the modern calendar—days, months, and years—are based on observations of objects in space.
- Ptolemaic theory states that the Earth is at the center of the universe.
- Copernican theory states that the sun is at the center of the universe.
- Modern astronomy has shown that there are billions of galaxies.

Using Key Terms

1. Use each of the following terms in a separate sentence: *year, day, month,* and *astronomy.*

Understanding Key Ideas

2. What happens in 1 year?
   a. The moon completes one orbit around the Earth.
   b. The sun travels once around the Earth.
   c. The Earth revolves once on its axis.
   d. The Earth completes one orbit around the sun.

3. What is the difference between the Ptolemaic and Copernican theories? Who was more accurate: Ptolemy or Copernicus?

4. What contributions did Brahe and Kepler make to astronomy?

5. What contributions did Galileo, Newton, and Hubble make to astronomy?

Math Skills

6. How many times did Earth orbit the sun between 140 CE, when Ptolemy introduced his theories, and 1543, when Copernicus introduced his theories?

Critical Thinking

7. **Analyzing Relationships** What advantage did Galileo have over earlier astronomers?

8. **Making Inferences** Why is astronomy such an old science?

SCiLINKS.

NSTA
Developed and maintained by the
National Science Teachers Association

For a variety of links related to this chapter, go to www.scilinks.org
Topic: The Stars and Keeping Time; Early Theories in Astronomy
SciLinks code: HSM1449; HSM0444

Telescopes

What color are Saturn's rings? What does the surface of the moon look like? To answer these questions, you could use a device called a telescope.

For professional astronomers and amateur stargazers, the telescope is the standard tool for observing the sky. A **telescope** is an instrument that gathers electromagnetic radiation from objects in space and concentrates it for better observation.

Optical Telescopes

Optical telescopes, which are the most common type of telescope, are used to study visible light from objects in the universe. Without using an optical telescope, you can see at most about 3,000 stars in the night sky. Using an optical telescope, however, you can see millions of stars and other objects.

An optical telescope collects visible light and focuses it to a focal point for closer observation. A *focal point* is the point where the rays of light that pass through a lens or that reflect from a mirror converge. The simplest optical telescope has two lenses. One lens, called the *objective lens,* collects light and forms an image at the back of the telescope. The bigger the objective lens is, the more light the telescope can gather. The second lens is located in the eyepiece of the telescope. This lens magnifies the image produced by the objective lens. **Figure 1** shows how much more of the moon you can see by using an optical telescope.

Reading Check What are the functions of the two lenses in an optical telescope? (*See the Appendix for answers to Reading Checks.*)

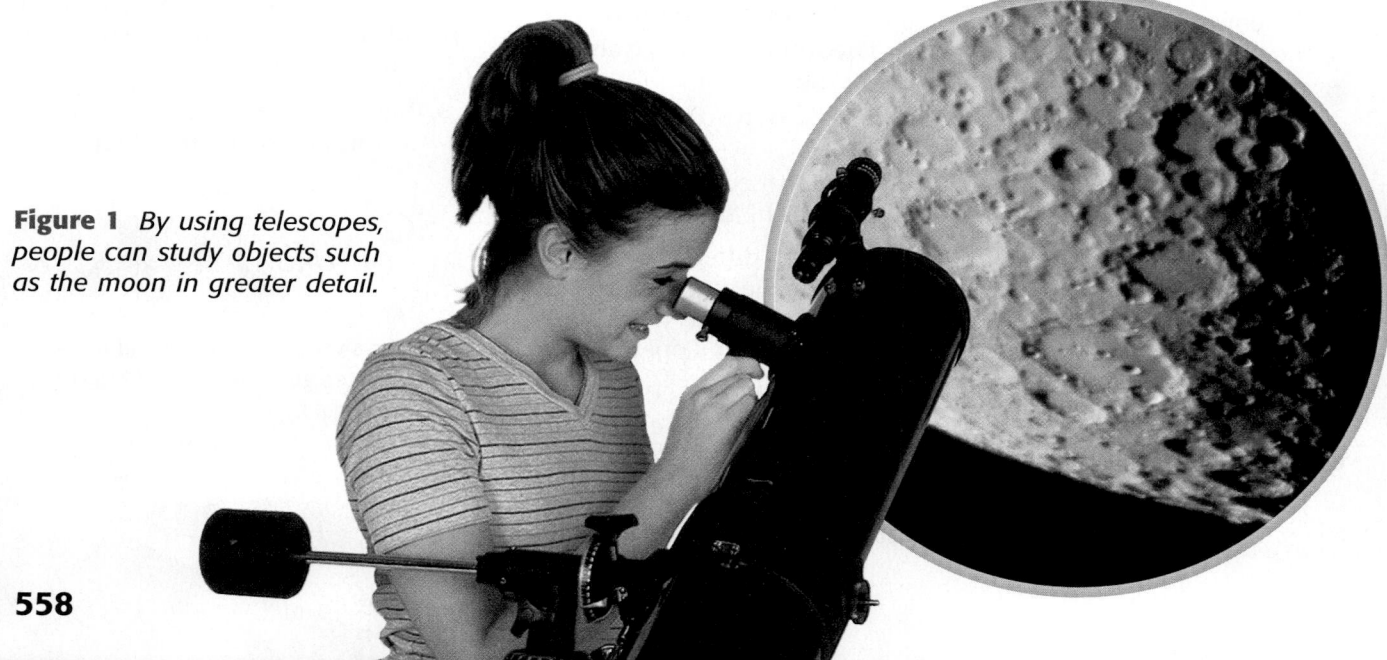

Figure 1 *By using telescopes, people can study objects such as the moon in greater detail.*

Figure 2 Refracting and Reflecting Telescopes

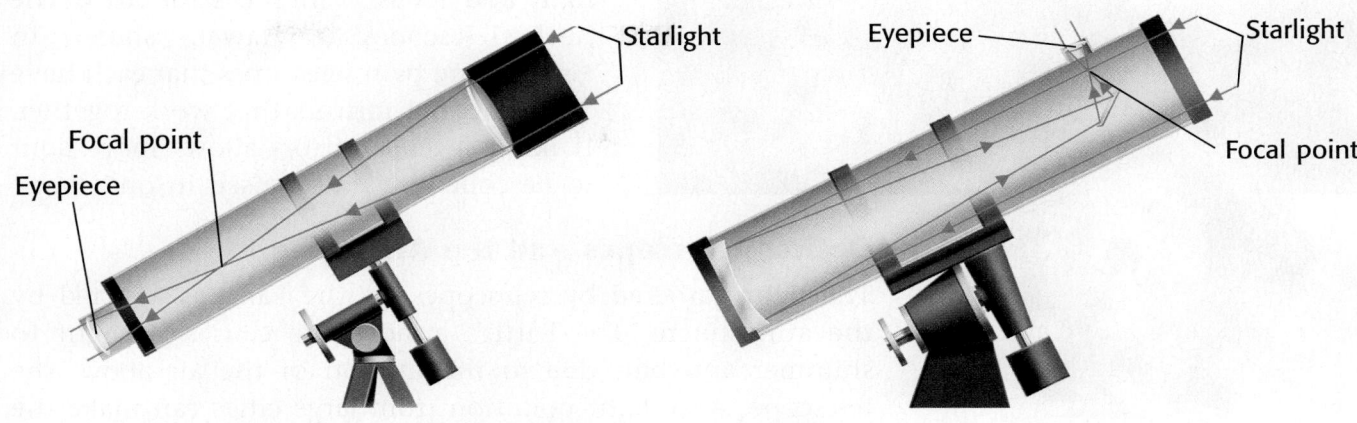

Refracting telescopes use lenses to gather and focus light.

Reflecting telescopes use mirrors to gather and focus light.

Refracting Telescopes

Telescopes that use lenses to gather and focus light are called **refracting telescopes.** As shown in **Figure 2,** a refracting telescope has an objective lens that bends light that passes through it and focuses the light to be magnified by an eyepiece. Refracting telescopes have two disadvantages. First, lenses focus different colors of light at slightly different distances, so images cannot be perfectly focused. Second, the size of a refracting telescope is also limited by the size of the objective lens. If the lens is too large, the glass sags under its own weight and images are distorted. These limitations are two reasons that most professional astronomers use reflecting telescopes.

Reflecting Telescopes

A telescope that uses a curved mirror to gather and focus light is called a **reflecting telescope.** Light enters the telescope and is reflected from a large, curved mirror to a flat mirror. As shown in **Figure 2,** the flat mirror focuses the image and reflects the light to be magnified by the eyepiece.

One advantage of reflecting telescopes is that the mirrors can be very large. Large mirrors allow reflecting telescopes to gather more light than refracting telescopes do. Another advantage is that curved mirrors are polished on their curved side, which prevents light from entering the glass. Thus, any flaws in the glass do not affect the light. A third advantage is that mirrors can focus all colors of light to the same focal point. Therefore, reflecting telescopes allow all colors of light from an object to be seen in focus at the same time.

telescope an instrument that collects electromagnetic radiation from the sky and concentrates it for better observation

refracting telescope a telescope that uses a set of lenses to gather and focus light from distant objects

reflecting telescope a telescope that uses a curved mirror to gather and focus light from distant objects

Very Large Reflecting Telescopes

In some very large reflecting telescopes, several mirrors work together to collect light and focus it in the same area. The Keck Telescopes in Hawaii, shown in **Figure 3,** are twin telescopes that each have 36 hexagonal mirrors that work together. Linking several mirrors allows more light to be collected and focused in one spot.

Figure 3 *The Keck Telescopes are in Hawaii. The 36 hexagonal mirrors in each telescope (shown in the inset) combine to form a light-reflecting surface that is 10 m across.*

Optical Telescopes and the Atmosphere

The light gathered by telescopes on the Earth is affected by the atmosphere. The Earth's atmosphere causes starlight to shimmer and blur due to the motion of the air above the telescope. Also, light pollution from large cities can make the sky look bright. As a result, an observer's ability to view faint objects is limited. Astronomers often place telescopes in dry areas to avoid moisture in the air. Mountaintops are also good locations for telescopes because the air is thinner at higher elevations. In addition, mountaintops generally have less air pollution and light pollution than other areas do.

Reading Check How does the atmosphere affect the images produced by optical telescopes?

Optical Telescopes in Space

To avoid interference by the atmosphere, scientists have put telescopes in space. Although the mirror in the *Hubble Space Telescope,* shown in **Figure 4,** is only 2.4 m across, this optical telescope can detect very faint objects in space.

Figure 4 *The* Hubble Space Telescope *has produced very clear images of objects in deep space.*

The Electromagnetic Spectrum

For thousands of years, humans have used their eyes to observe stars and planets. But scientists eventually discovered that visible light, the light that we can see, is not the only form of radiation. In 1852, James Clerk Maxwell proved that visible light is a part of the electromagnetic spectrum. The **electromagnetic spectrum** is made up of all of the wavelengths of electromagnetic radiation.

Detecting Electromagnetic Radiation

Each color of light is a different wavelength of electromagnetic radiation. Humans can see radiation from red light, which has a long wavelength, to blue light, which has a shorter wavelength. But visible light is only a small part of the electromagnetic spectrum, as shown in **Figure 5.** The rest of the electromagnetic spectrum—radio waves, microwaves, infrared light, ultraviolet light, X rays, and gamma rays—is invisible. The Earth's atmosphere blocks most invisible radiation from objects in space. In this way, the atmosphere functions as a protective shield around the Earth. Radiation that can pass through the atmosphere includes some radio waves, microwaves, infrared light, visible light, and some ultraviolet light.

electromagnetic spectrum all of the frequencies or wavelengths of electromagnetic radiation

Figure 5 *Visible light is only a small band of the electromagnetic spectrum. Radio waves have the longest wavelengths, and gamma rays have the shortest wavelengths.*

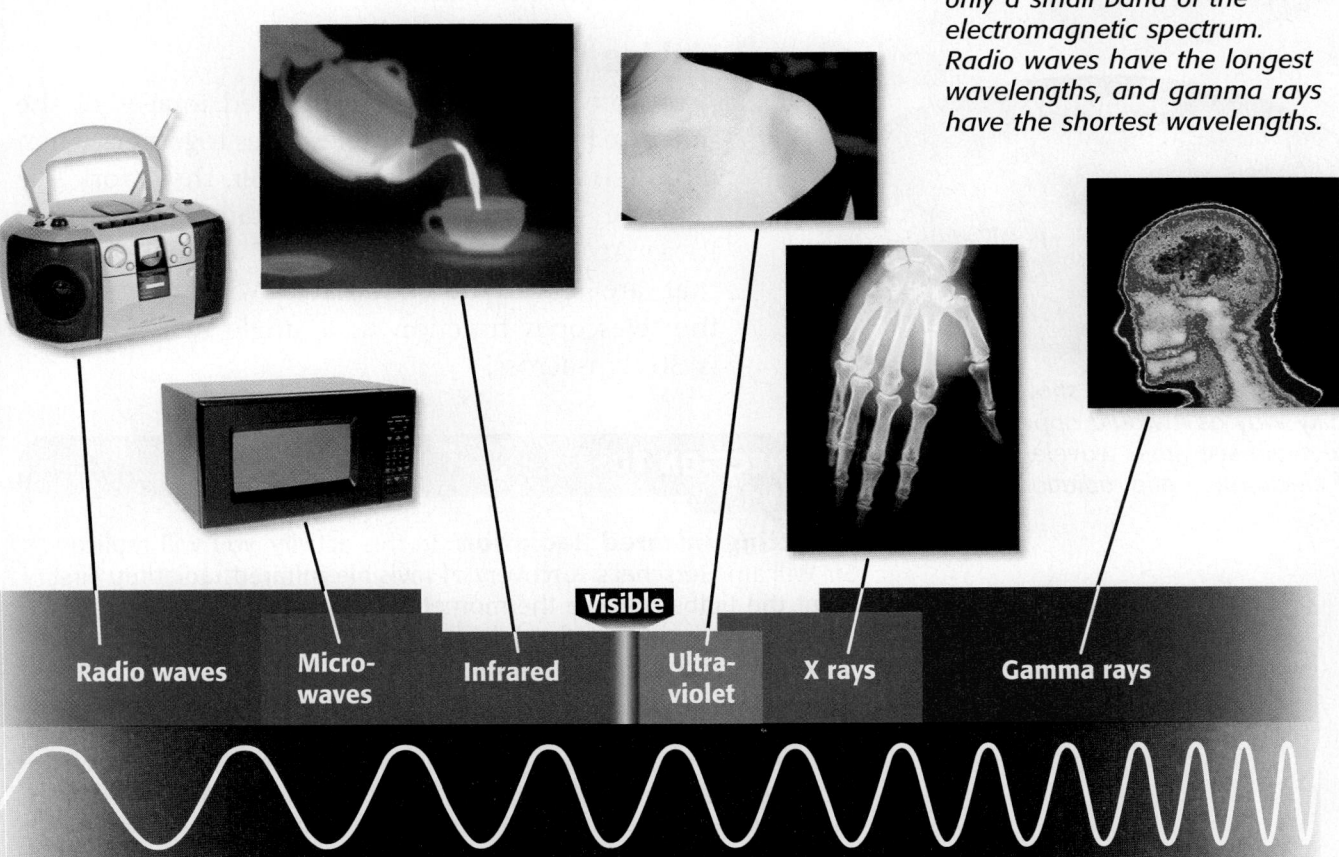

Radio waves | Micro-waves | Infrared | **Visible** | Ultra-violet | X rays | Gamma rays

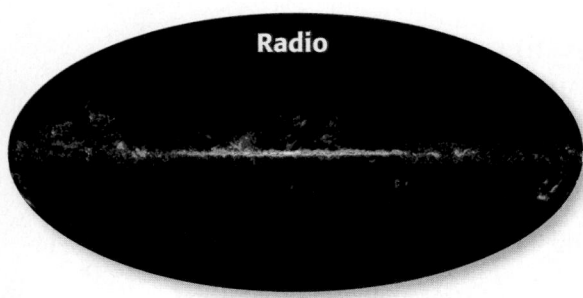

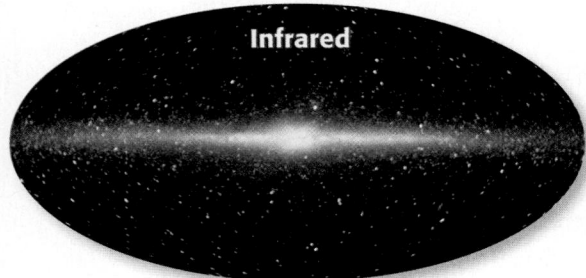

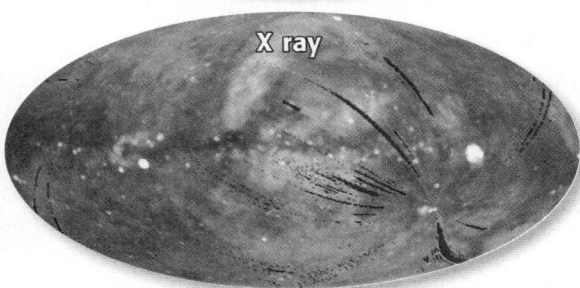

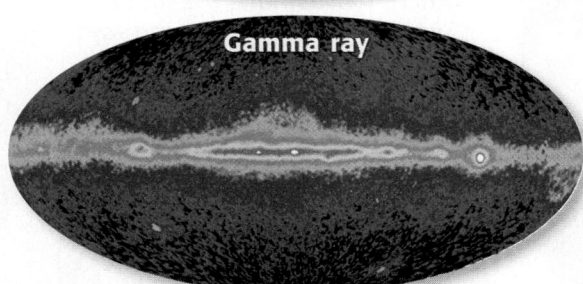

Figure 6 *Each image shows the Milky Way as it would appear if we could see other wavelengths of electromagnetic radiation.*

Nonoptical Telescopes

To study invisible radiation, scientists use nonoptical telescopes. Nonoptical telescopes detect radiation that cannot be seen by the human eye. Astronomers study the entire electromagnetic spectrum because each type of radiation reveals different clues about an object. As **Figure 6** shows, our galaxy looks very different when it is observed at various wavelengths. A different type of telescope was used to produce each image. The "cloud" that goes across the image is the Milky Way galaxy.

Radio Telescopes

Radio telescopes detect radio waves. Radio telescopes have to be much larger than optical telescopes because radio wavelengths are about 1 million times longer than optical wavelengths. Most radio radiation reaches the ground and can be detected both during the day and night. The surface of radio telescopes does not have to be as flawless as the lenses and mirrors of optical telescopes. In fact, the surface of a radio telescope does not have to be solid.

Linking Radio Telescopes

Astronomers can get more detailed images of the universe by linking radio telescopes together. When radio telescopes are linked together, they work like a single giant telescope. For example, the Very Large Array (VLA) consists of 27 radio telescopes that are spread over 30 km. Working together, the telescopes function as a single telescope that is 30 km across!

CONNECTION TO Physics

Detecting Infrared Radiation In this activity, you will replicate Sir William Herschel's discovery of invisible infrared radiation. First, paint the bulbs of three thermometers black. Place a sheet of white paper inside a tall cardboard box. Tape the thermometers parallel to each other, and place them inside the box. Cut a small notch in the top of the box, and position a small glass prism so that a spectrum is projected inside the box. Arrange the thermometers so that one is just outside the red end of the spectrum, with no direct light on it. After 10 min, record the temperatures. Which thermometer recorded the highest temperature? Explain why.

ACTiViTY

Nonoptical Telescopes in Space

Because most electromagnetic waves are blocked by the Earth's atmosphere, scientists have placed ultraviolet telescopes, infrared telescopes, gamma-ray telescopes, and X-ray telescopes in space. The *Chandra X-Ray Observatory*, a space-based telescope that detects X rays, is illustrated in **Figure 7.** X-ray telescopes in space can be much more sensitive than optical telescopes. For example, NASA has tested an X-ray telescope that can detect an object that is the size of a frisbee on the surface of the sun. If an optical telescope had a similar power, it could detect a hair on the head of an astronaut on the moon!

Reading Check Why are X-ray telescopes placed in space?

Figure 7 *The* Chandra X-Ray Observatory *can detect black holes and some of the most distant objects in the universe.*

SECTION Review

Summary

- Refracting telescopes use lenses to gather and focus light.
- Reflecting telescopes use mirrors to gather and focus light.
- Astronomers study all wavelengths of the electromagnetic spectrum, including radio waves, microwaves, infrared light, visible light, ultraviolet light, X rays, and gamma rays.
- The atmosphere blocks most forms of electromagnetic radiation from reaching the Earth. To overcome this limitation, astronomers place telescopes in space.

Using Key Terms

For each pair of terms, explain how the meanings of the terms differ.

1. *refracting telescope* and *reflecting telescope*

2. *telescope* and *electromagnetic spectrum*

Understanding Key Ideas

3. How does the atmosphere affect astronomical observations?
   a. It focuses visible light.
   b. It blocks most electromagnetic radiation.
   c. It blocks all radio waves.
   d. It does not affect astronomical observations.

4. Describe how reflecting and refracting telescopes work.

5. What limits the size of a refracting telescope? Explain.

6. What advantages do reflecting telescopes have over refracting telescopes?

7. List the types of radiation in the electromagnetic spectrum, from the longest wavelength to the shortest wavelength. Then, describe how astronomers study each type of radiation.

Math Skills

8. A telescope's light-gathering power is proportional to the area of its objective lens or mirror. If the diameter of a lens is 1 m, what is the area of the lens? (Hint: $area = 3.1416 \times radius^2$)

Critical Thinking

9. **Applying Concepts** Describe three reasons why Hawaii is a good location for a telescope.

10. **Making Inferences** Why doesn't the surface of a radio telescope have to be as flawless as the surface of a mirror in an optical telescope?

11. **Making Inferences** What limitation of a refracting telescope could be overcome by placing the telescope in space?

SC*i*LINKS.

NSTA
Developed and maintained by the
National Science Teachers Association

For a variety of links related to this chapter, go to www.scilinks.org

Topic: Telescopes
SciLinks code: HSM1500

Mapping the Stars

Have you ever seen Orion the Hunter or the Big Dipper in the night sky? Ancient cultures linked stars together to form patterns that represented characters from myths and objects in their lives.

Today, we can see the same star patterns that people in ancient cultures saw. Modern astronomers still use many of the names given to stars centuries ago. But astronomers can now describe a star's location precisely. Advances in astronomy have led to a better understanding of how far away stars are and how big the universe is.

Patterns in the Sky

When people in ancient cultures connected stars in patterns, they named sections of the sky based on the patterns. These patterns are called *constellations*. **Constellations** are sections of the sky that contain recognizable star patterns. Understanding the location and movement of constellations helped people navigate and keep track of time.

Different civilizations had different names for the same constellations. For example, where the Greeks saw a hunter (Orion) in the northern sky, the Japanese saw a drum, as shown in **Figure 1.** Today, different cultures still interpret the sky in different ways, but astronomers have agreed on the names and locations of the constellations.

READING WARM-UP

Objectives

- Explain how constellations are used to organize the night sky.
- Describe how the altitude of a star is measured.
- Explain how the celestial sphere is used to describe the location of objects in the sky.
- Compare size and scale in the universe, and explain how red shift indicates that the universe is expanding.

Terms to Learn

constellation   horizon
zenith   light-year
altitude

READING STRATEGY

Paired Summarizing Read this section silently. In pairs, take turns summarizing the material. Stop to discuss ideas that seem confusing.

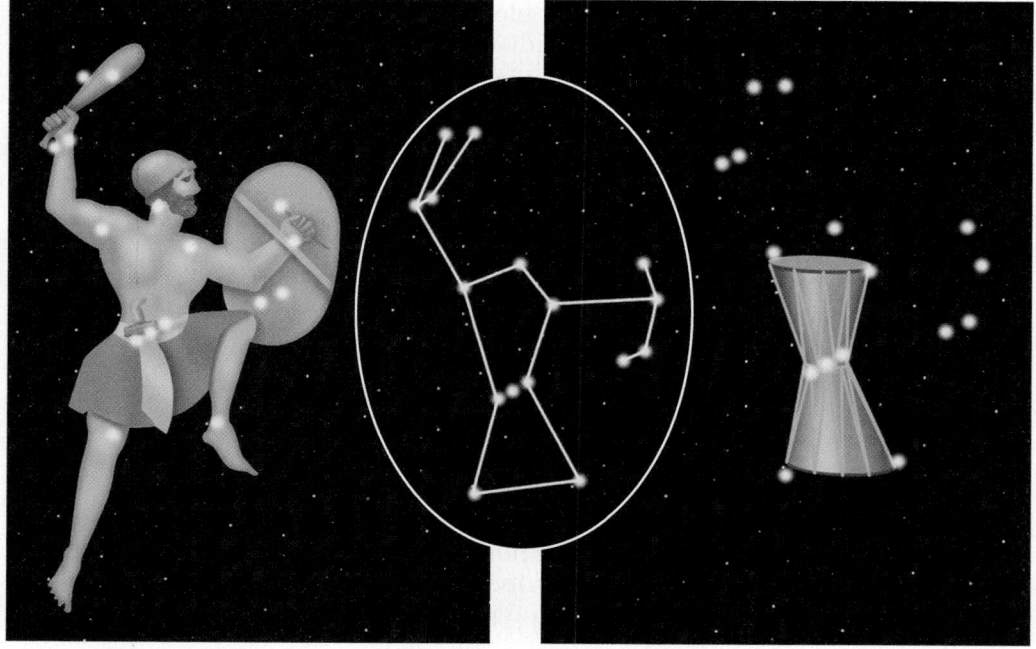

Figure 1 *The ancient Greeks saw Orion as a hunter, but the Japanese saw the same set of stars as a drum.*

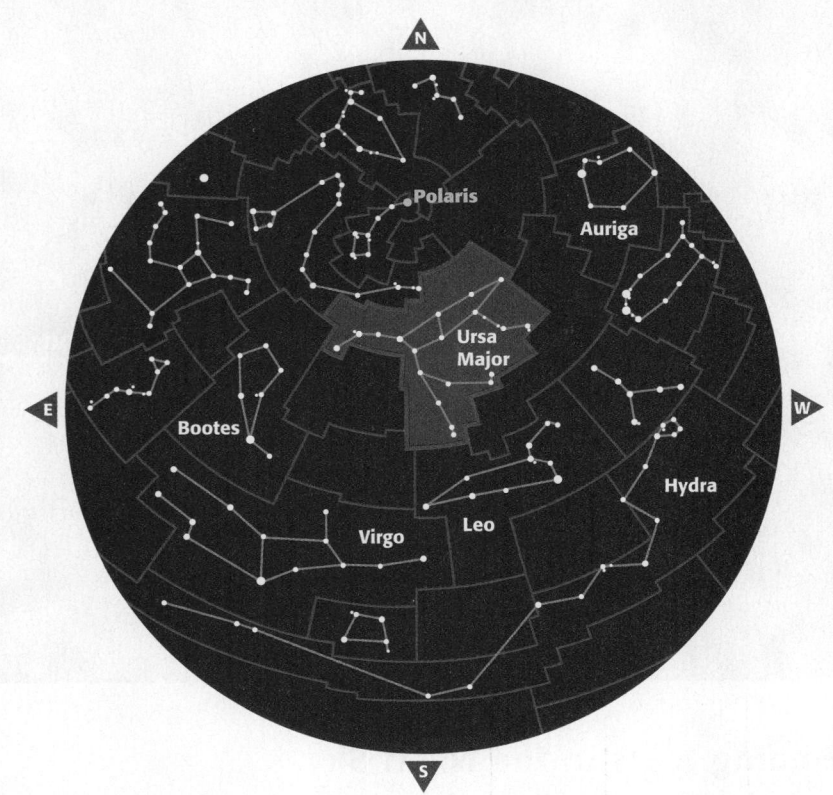

Figure 2 *This sky map shows some of the constellations in the Northern Hemisphere at midnight in the spring. Ursa Major (the Great Bear) is a region of the sky that includes all of the stars that make up that constellation.*

constellation a region of the sky that contains a recognizable star pattern and that is used to describe the location of objects in space

Constellations Help Organize the Sky

When you think of constellations, you probably think of the stick figures made by connecting bright stars with imaginary lines. To an astronomer, however, a constellation is something more. As you can see in **Figure 2,** a constellation is a region of the sky. Each constellation shares a border with neighboring constellations. For example, in the same way that the state of Texas is a region of the United States, Ursa Major is a region of the sky. Every star or galaxy is located within 1 of 88 constellations.

Seasonal Changes

The sky map in **Figure 2** shows what the midnight sky in the Northern Hemisphere looks like in the spring. But as the Earth revolves around the sun, the apparent locations of the constellations change from season to season. In addition, different constellations are visible in the Southern Hemisphere. Thus, a child in Chile can see different constellations than you can. Therefore, this map is not accurate for the other three seasons or for the Southern Hemisphere. Sky maps for summer, fall, and winter in the Northern Hemisphere appear in the Appendix of this book.

✓ Reading Check Why are different constellations visible in the Northern and Southern Hemispheres? (*See the Appendix for answers to Reading Checks.*)

Using a Sky Map

1. Hold your **textbook** over your head with the cover facing upward. Turn the book so that the direction at the bottom of the sky map is the same as the direction you are facing.

2. Notice the locations of the constellations in relation to each other.

3. If you look up at the sky at night in the spring, you should see the stars positioned as they are on your map.

4. Why are *E* and *W* on sky maps the reverse of how they appear on land maps?

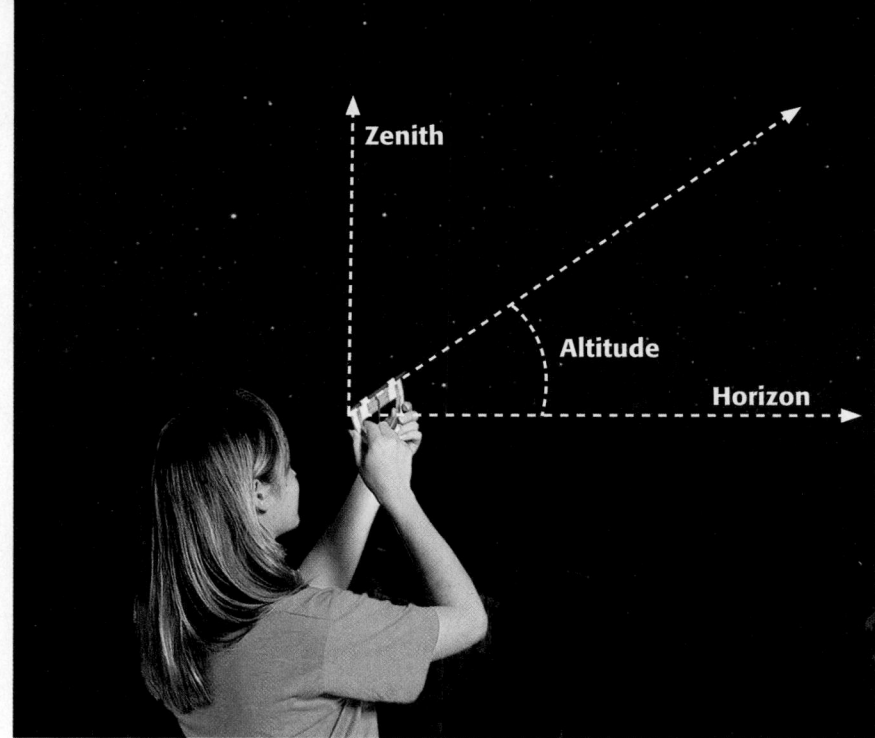

Figure 3 *Using an astrolabe, you can determine the altitude of a star by measuring the angle between the horizon and a star. The altitude of any object depends on where you are and when you look.*

zenith the point in the sky directly above an observer on Earth

altitude the angle between an object in the sky and the horizon

horizon the line where the sky and the Earth appear to meet

Finding Stars in the Night Sky

Have you ever tried to show someone a star by pointing to it? Did the person miss what you were seeing? If you use an instrument called an *astrolabe,* shown in **Figure 3,** you can describe the location of a star or planet. To use an astrolabe correctly, you need to understand the three points of reference shown in **Figure 4.** This method is useful to describe the location of a star relative to where you are. But if you want to describe a star's location in relation to the Earth, you need to use the celestial sphere, shown in **Figure 5.**

Figure 4 Zenith, Altitude, and Horizon

The **zenith** is an imaginary point in the sky directly above an observer on Earth. The zenith always has an altitude of 90°.

An object's **altitude** is the angle between the object and the horizon.

The **horizon** is the line where the sky and the Earth appear to meet.

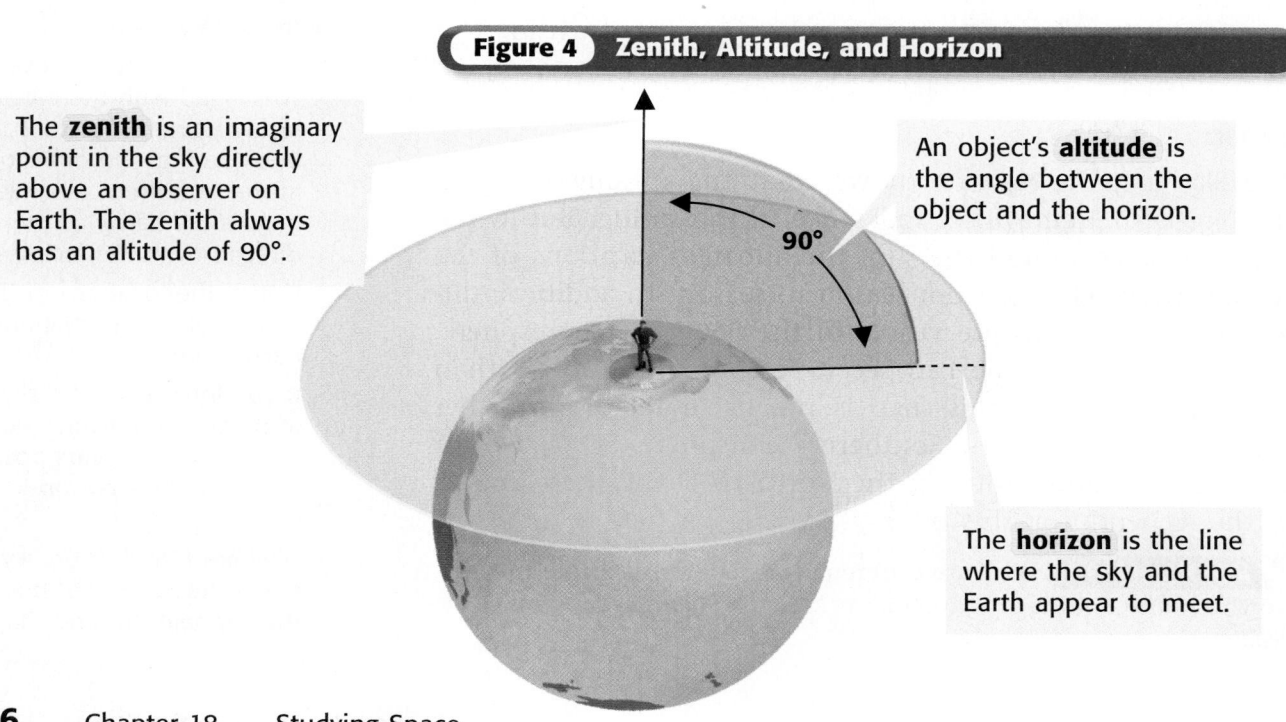

Figure 5 The Celestial Sphere

To talk to each other about the location of a star, astronomers must have a common method of describing a star's location. The method that astronomers have invented is based on a reference system known as the *celestial sphere*. The celestial sphere is an imaginary sphere that surrounds the Earth. Just as we use latitude and longitude to plot positions on Earth, astronomers use right ascension and declination to plot positions in the sky. *Right ascension* is a measure of how far east an object is from the *vernal equinox,* the location of the sun on the first day of spring. *Declination* is a measure of how far north or south an object is from the celestial equator.

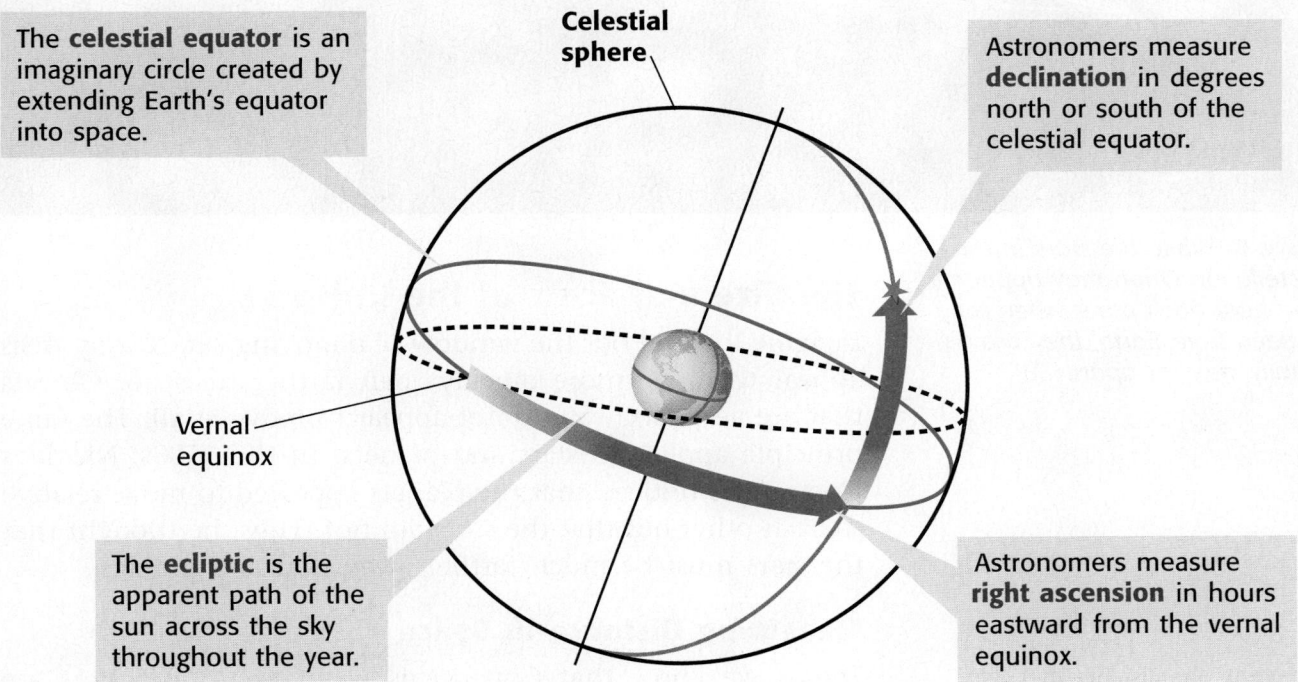

The **celestial equator** is an imaginary circle created by extending Earth's equator into space.

Celestial sphere

Astronomers measure **declination** in degrees north or south of the celestial equator.

Vernal equinox

The **ecliptic** is the apparent path of the sun across the sky throughout the year.

Astronomers measure **right ascension** in hours eastward from the vernal equinox.

The Path of Stars Across the Sky

Just as the sun appears to move across the sky during the day, most stars and planets rise and set throughout the night. This apparent motion is caused by the Earth's rotation. As the Earth spins on its axis, stars and planets appear to move. Near the poles, however, stars are circumpolar. *Circumpolar stars* are stars that can be seen at all times of year and all times of night. These stars never set, and they appear to circle the celestial poles. You also see different stars in the sky depending on the time of year. Why? The reason is that as the Earth travels around the sun, different areas of the universe are visible.

✔ *Reading Check* How is the apparent movement of the sun similar to the apparent movement of most stars during the night?

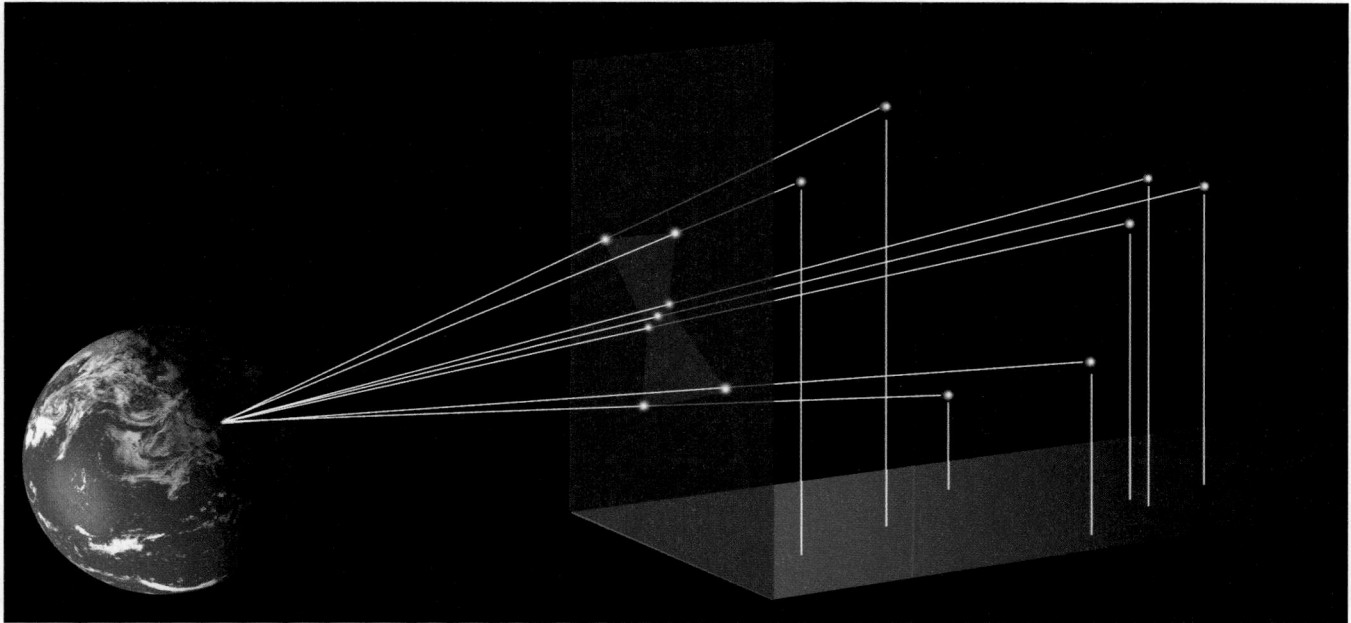

Figure 6 *While the stars in the constellation Orion may appear to be near each other when they are seen from Earth, they are actually very far apart.*

light-year the distance that light travels in one year; about 9.46 trillion kilometers

INTERNET ACTIVITY

For another activity related to this chapter, go to **go.hrw.com** and type in the keyword **HZ5OBSW.**

The Size and Scale of the Universe

Imagine looking out the window of a moving car. Nearby trees appear to move more quickly than farther trees do. Objects that are very far away do not appear to move at all. The same principle applies to stars and planets. In the 1500s, Nicolaus Copernicus noticed that the planets appeared to move relative to each other but that the stars did not. Thus, he thought that the stars must be much farther away than the planets.

Measuring Distance in Space

Today, we know that Copernicus was correct. The stars are much farther away than the planets are. In fact, stars are so distant that a new unit of length—the light-year—was created to measure their distance. A **light-year** is a unit of length equal to the distance that light travels in 1 year. One light-year is equal to about 9.46 trillion kilometers! The farthest objects we can observe are more than 10 billion light-years away. Although the stars may appear to be at similar distances from Earth, their distances vary greatly. For example, **Figure 6** shows how far away the stars that make up part of Orion are.

Reading Check **How far does light travel in 1 year?**

Considering Scale in the Universe

When you think about the universe and all of the objects it contains, it is important to consider scale. For example, stars appear to be very small in the night sky. But we know that most stars are a lot larger than Earth. **Figure 7** will help you understand the scale of objects in the universe.

Figure 7 From Home Plate to 10 Million Light-Years Away

1 Let's start with home plate in a baseball stadium. You are looking down from a distance of about 10 m.

2 At 1,000 m (1 km) away, you can see the baseball stadium and the surrounding neighborhood.

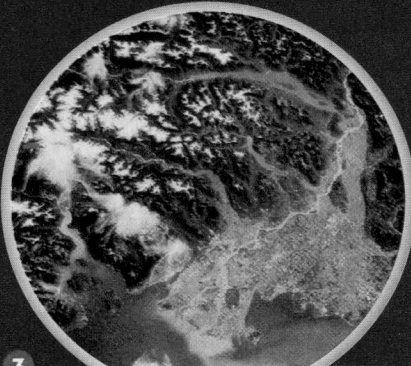

3 At 100 km away, you see the city that contains the stadium and the countryside around the city.

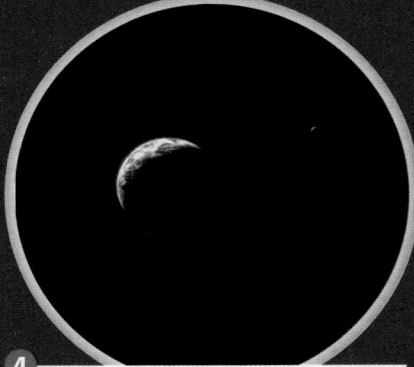

4 At 100,000 km away, you can see the Earth and the moon.

5 At 1,500,000,000 km (83 light-minutes) away, you can look back at the sun and the inner planets.

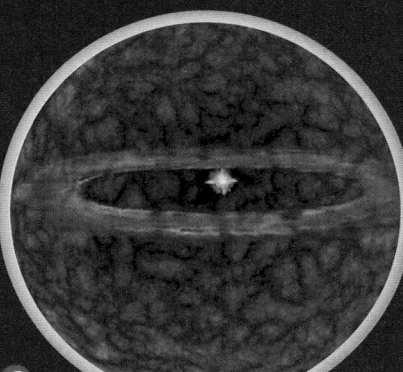

6 At 150 light-days, the solar system, surrounded by a cloud of comets and other icy debris, can be seen.

7 By the time you are 10 light-years away, the sun resembles any other star in space.

8 At 1 million light-years away, our galaxy looks like the Andromeda galaxy, a cloud of stars set in the blackness of space.

9 At 10 million light-years away, you can see a handful of galaxies called the *Local Group*.

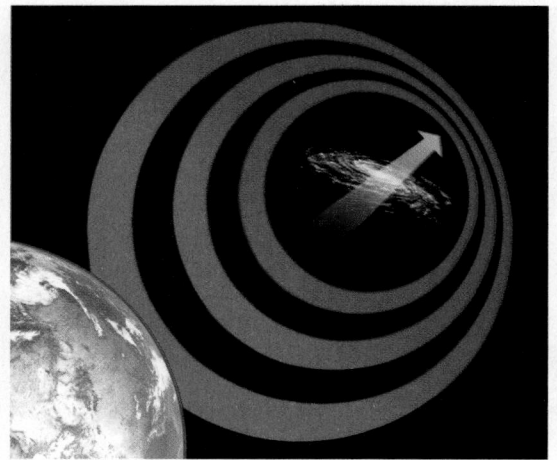

Figure 8 *As an object moves away from an observer at a high speed, the light from the object appears redder. As the object moves toward the observer, the light from the object appears bluer.*

The Doppler Effect

Have you ever noticed that when a driver in an approaching car blows the horn, the horn sounds higher pitched as the car approaches and lower pitched after the car passes? This effect is called the *Doppler effect*. As shown in **Figure 8,** the Doppler effect also occurs with light. If a light source, such as a star or galaxy, is moving quickly away from an observer, the light emitted looks redder than it normally does. This effect is called *redshift*. If a star or galaxy is moving quickly toward an observer, its light appears bluer than it normally does. This effect is known as *blueshift*.

An Expanding Universe

After discovering that the universe is made up of many other galaxies like our own, Edwin Hubble analyzed the light from galaxies and stars to study the general direction that objects in the universe are moving. Hubble soon made another startling discovery—the light from all galaxies except our close neighbors is affected by redshift. This means that galaxies are rapidly moving apart from each other. In other words, because all galaxies except our close neighbors are moving apart, the universe must be expanding. **Figure 9** shows evidence of redshift recorded by the *Hubble Space Telescope* in 2002.

✓ Reading Check What logical conclusion could be made if the light from all of the galaxies were affected by blueshift?

Figure 9 *The galaxy that is cut off at the bottom of this image is moving away from us at a much slower speed than the other galaxies are. Distant galaxies are visible as faint disks.*

SECTION Review

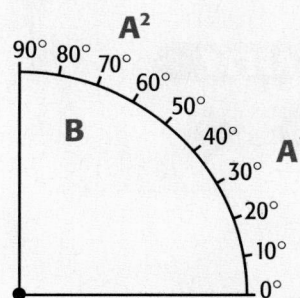

Summary

- Astronomers use constellations to organize the sky.
- Altitude, or the angle between an object and the horizon, can be used to describe the location of an object in the sky.
- The celestial sphere is an imaginary sphere that surrounds the Earth. Using the celestial sphere, astronomers can accurately describe the location of an object without reference to an observer.
- A light-year is the distance that light travels in 1 year.
- The Doppler effect causes the light emitted by objects that are moving away from an observer to appear to shift toward the red end of the spectrum. Objects moving toward an observer are shifted to the blue end of the spectrum.
- Observations of redshift and blueshift indicate that the universe is expanding.

Using Key Terms

The statements below are false. For each statement, replace the underlined term to make a true statement.

1. <u>Zenith</u> is the angle between an object and the horizon.

2. The distance that light travels in 1 year is called a <u>light-meter</u>.

Understanding Key Ideas

3. Stars appear to move across the night sky because of
   a. the rotation of Earth on its axis.
   b. the movement of the Milky Way galaxy.
   c. the movement of stars in the universe.
   d. the revolution of Earth around the sun.

4. How do astronomers use the celestial sphere to plot a star's exact position?

5. How do constellations relate to patterns of stars? How are constellations like states?

6. Why are different sky maps needed for different times of the year?

7. What are redshift and blueshift? Why are these effects useful in the study of the universe?

Critical Thinking

8. **Applying Concepts** Light from the Andromeda galaxy is affected by blueshift. What can you conclude about this galaxy?

9. **Making Comparisons** Explain how Copernicus concluded that stars were farther away than planets. Draw a diagram showing how this principle applies to another example.

Interpreting Graphics

The diagram below shows the altitude of Star A and Star B. Use the diagram below to answer the questions that follow.

A^2
90° 80° 70°
60°
B 50°
40° A^1
30°
20°
10°
0°

10. What is the approximate altitude of star B?

11. In 4 h, star A moved from A^1 to A^2. How many degrees did the star move each hour?

SCI**LINKS**.

Developed and maintained by the
National Science Teachers Association

For a variety of links related to this chapter, go to www.scilinks.org

Topic: Constellations
SciLinks code: HSM0347

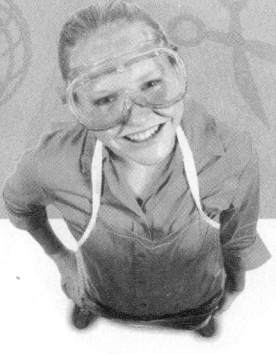

Skills Practice Lab

Through the Looking Glass

Have you ever looked toward the horizon or up into the sky and wished that you could see farther? Do you think that a telescope might help you see farther? Astronomers use huge telescopes to study the universe. You can build your own telescope to get a glimpse of how these enormous, technologically advanced telescopes help astronomers see distant objects.

OBJECTIVES

Construct a simple model of a refracting telescope.

Observe distant objects by using your telescope.

MATERIALS

- clay, modeling (1 stick)
- convex lens, 3 cm in diameter (2 of different focal length)
- lamp, desk
- paper, white (1 sheet)
- ruler, metric
- scissors
- tape, masking (1 roll)
- toilet-paper tube, cardboard
- wrapping paper tube, cardboard

SAFETY

Procedure

1. Use modeling clay to form a base that holds one of the lenses upright on your desktop. When the lights are turned off, your teacher will turn on a lamp at the front of the classroom. Rotate your lens so that the light from the lamp passes through the lens.

2. Hold the paper so that the light passing through the lens lands on the paper. To sharpen the image of the light on the paper, slowly move the paper closer to or farther from the lens. Hold the paper in the position in which the image is sharpest.

3. Using the metric ruler, measure the distance between the lens and the paper. Record this distance.

4. How far is the paper from the lens? This distance, called the *focal length,* is the distance that the paper has to be from the lens for the image to be in focus.

5. Repeat steps 1–4 using the other lens.

6. Measuring from one end of the long cardboard tube, mark the focal length of the lens that has the longer focal length. Place a mark 2 cm past this line toward the other end of the tube, and label the mark "Cut."

7. Measuring from one end of the short cardboard tube, mark the focal length of the lens that has the shorter focal length. Place a mark 2 cm past this line toward the other end of the tube, and label the mark "Cut."

8. Shorten the tubes by cutting along the marks labeled "Cut." Wear safety goggles when you make these cuts.

9. Tape the lens that has the longer focal length to one end of the longer tube. Tape the other lens to one end of the shorter tube. Slip the empty end of one tube inside the empty end of the other tube. Be sure that there is one lens at each end of this new, longer tube.

10. Congratulations! You have just constructed a telescope. To use your telescope, look through the short tube (the eyepiece) and point the long end at various objects in the room. You can focus the telescope by adjusting its length. Are the images right side up or upside down? Observe birds, insects, trees, or other outside objects. Record the images that you see. **Caution:** NEVER look directly at the sun! Looking directly at the sun could cause permanent blindness.

Analyze the Results

1. **Analyzing Results** Which type of telescope did you just construct: a refracting telescope or a reflecting telescope? What makes your telescope one type and not the other?

2. **Identifying Patterns** What factor determines the focal length of a lens?

Draw Conclusions

3. **Evaluating Results** How would you improve your telescope?

Chapter Review

USING KEY TERMS

1 Use each of the following terms in a separate sentence: *year, month, day, astronomy, electromagnetic spectrum, constellation,* and *altitude.*

For each pair of terms, explain how the meanings of the terms differ.

2 *reflecting telescope* and *refracting telescope*

3 *zenith* and *horizon*

4 *year* and *light-year*

UNDERSTANDING KEY IDEAS

Multiple Choice

5 Which of the following answer choices lists types of electromagnetic radiation from longest wavelength to shortest wavelength?

a. radio waves, ultraviolet light, infrared light

b. infrared light, microwaves, X rays

c. X rays, ultraviolet light, gamma rays

d. microwaves, infrared light, visible light

6 The length of a day is based on the amount of time that

a. Earth takes to orbit the sun one time.

b. Earth takes to rotate once on its axis.

c. the moon takes to orbit Earth one time.

d. the moon takes to rotate once on its axis.

7 Which of the following statements about X rays and radio waves from objects in space is true?

a. Both types of radiation can be observed by using the same telescope.

b. Separate telescopes are needed to observe each type of radiation, but both telescopes can be on Earth.

c. Separate telescopes are needed to observe each type of radiation, but both telescopes must be in space.

d. Separate telescopes are needed to observe each type of radiation, but only one of the telescopes must be in space.

8 According to ___, Earth is at the center of the universe.

a. the Ptolemaic theory

b. Copernicus's theory

c. Galileo's theory

d. None of the above

9 Which scientist was one of the first scientists to successfully use a telescope to observe the night sky?

a. Brahe   c. Hubble

b. Galileo   d. Kepler

10 Astronomers divide the sky into

a. galaxies.   c. zeniths.

b. constellations.   d. phases.

11 ___ determines which stars you see in the sky.

a. Your latitude

b. The time of year

c. The time of night

d. All of the above

12 The altitude of an object in the sky is the object's angular distance

    a. above the horizon.

    b. from the north celestial pole.

    c. from the zenith.

    d. from the prime meridian.

13 Right ascension is a measure of how far east an object in the sky is from

    a. the observer.

    b. the vernal equinox.

    c. the moon.

    d. Venus.

14 Telescopes that work on Earth's surface include all of the following EXCEPT

    a. radio telescopes.

    b. refracting telescopes.

    c. X-ray telescopes.

    d. reflecting telescopes.

Short Answer

15 Explain how right ascension and declination are similar to latitude and longitude.

16 How does a reflecting telescope work?

CRITICAL THINKING

17 **Concept Mapping** Use the following terms to create a concept map: *right ascension, declination, celestial sphere, degrees, hours, celestial equator,* and *vernal equinox.*

18 **Making Inferences** Why was seeing objects in the sky easier for people in ancient cultures than it is for most people today? What tools help modern people study objects in space in greater detail than was possible in the past?

19 **Making Inferences** Because many forms of radiation from space do not penetrate Earth's atmosphere, astronomers' ability to detect this radiation is limited. But how does the protection of the atmosphere benefit humans?

20 **Analyzing Ideas** Explain why the Ptolemaic theory seems logical based on daily observations of the rising and setting of the sun.

INTERPRETING GRAPHICS

Use the sky map below to answer the questions that follow. (Example: The star Aldebaran is located at about 4 h, 30 min right ascension, 16° declination.)

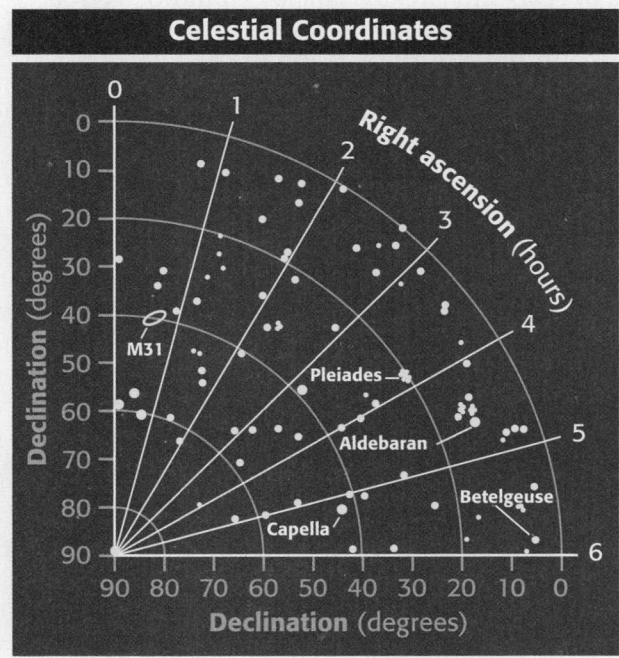

21 What object is located near 5 h, 55 min right ascension, and 7° declination?

22 What are the celestial coordinates for the Andromeda galaxy (M31)? Round off the right ascension to the nearest half-hour.

READING

Read each of the passages below. Then, answer the questions that follow each passage.

Passage 1 In the early Roman calendar, a year had exactly 365 days. The calendar worked well until people realized that the seasons were beginning and ending later each year. To fix this problem, Julius Caesar developed the Julian calendar based on a 365.25-day calendar year. He added 90 days to the year 46 BCE and added an extra day every 4 years. A year in which an extra day is added to the calendar is called a *leap year*. In the mid-1500s, astronomers determined that there are actually 365.2422 days in a year, so Pope Gregory XIII developed the Gregorian calendar. He dropped 10 days from the year 1582 and restricted leap years to years that are divisible by 4 but not by 100 (except for years that are divisible by 400). Today, most countries use the Gregorian calendar.

1. According to the passage, which of the following years is a leap year?
   A 46 BCE
   B 1582
   C 1600
   D 1800

2. How long is a year?
   F 365 days
   G 365.224 days
   H 365.2422 days
   I 365.25 days

3. Why did Julius Caesar change the early Roman calendar?
   A to deal with the fact that the seasons were beginning and ending later each year
   B to compete with the Gregorian calendar
   C to add an extra day every year
   D to shorten the length of a year

Passage 2 The earliest known evidence of astronomical observations is a group of stones near Nabta in southern Egypt that is between 6,000 and 7,000 years old. According to <u>archeoastronomers</u>, some of the stones are positioned such that they would have lined up with the sun during the summer solstice 6,000 years ago. The summer solstice occurs on the longest day of the year. At the Nabta site, the noonday sun is at its zenith (directly overhead) for about three weeks before and after the summer solstice. When the sun is at its zenith, upright objects do not cast shadows. For many civilizations in the Tropics, the zenith sun has had ceremonial significance for thousands of years. The same is probably true for the civilizations that used the Nabta site. Artifacts found at the site near Nabta suggest that the site was created by African cattle herders. These people probably used the site for many purposes, including trade, social bonding, and ritual.

1. In the passage, what does *archeoastronomer* mean?
   A an archeologist that studies Egyptian culture
   B an astronomer that studies the zenith sun
   C an archeologist that studies ancient astronomy
   D an astronomer that studies archeologists

2. Why don't upright objects cast a shadow when the sun is at its zenith?
   F because the sun is directly overhead
   G because the summer solstice is occurring
   H because the sun is below the horizon
   I because the sun is at its zenith on the longest day of the year

The diagram below shows a galaxy moving in relation to four observers. The concentric circles illustrate the Doppler effect at each location. Use the diagram below to answer the questions that follow.

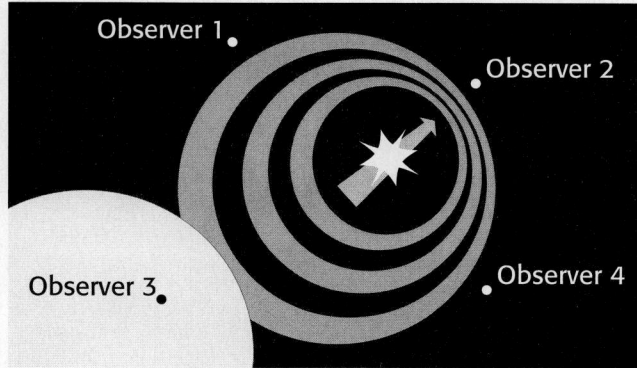

1. Which of the following observers would see the light from the galaxy affected by redshift?

  A observers 1 and 2

  B observer 3

  C observers 3 and 4

  D observers 1 and 4

2. Which of the following observers would see the light from the galaxy affected by blueshift?

  F observer 1

  G observers 2 and 4

  H observers 3 and 4

  I observer 2

3. How would the wavelengths of light detected by observer 4 appear?

  A The wavelengths would appear shorter than they really are.

  B The wavelengths would appear longer than they really are.

  C The wavelengths would appear unchanged.

  D The wavelengths would alternate between blue and red.

Read each question below, and choose the best answer.

1. If light travels 300,000 km/s, how long does light reflected from Mars take to reach Earth when Mars is 65,000,000 km away ?

  A 22 s

  B 217 s

  C 2,170 s

  D 2,200 s

2. Star A is 8 million kilometers from star B. What is this distance expressed in meters?

  F 0.8 m

  G 8,000 m

  H 8×10^6 m

  I 8×10^9 m

3. If each hexagonal mirror in the Keck Telescopes is 1.8 m across, how many mirrors would be needed to create a light-reflecting surface that is 10.8 m across?

  A 3.2

  B 5

  C 6

  D 6.2

4. If the altitude of a star is 37°, what is the angle between the star and the zenith?

  F 143°

  G 90°

  H 53°

  I 37°

5. You are studying an image made by the *Hubble Space Telescope*. If you observe 90 stars in an area that is 1 cm², which of the following estimates is the best estimate for the number of stars in 15 cm²?

  A 700

  B 900

  C 1,200

  D 1,350

Science in Action

Science Fiction

"Why I Left Harry's All-Night Hamburgers" by Lawrence Watt-Evans

The main character was 16, and he needed to find a job. So, he began working at Harry's All-Night Hamburgers. His shift was from midnight to 7:30 A.M. so that he could still go to school. Harry's All-Night Hamburgers was pretty quiet most nights, but once in a while some unusual characters came by. For example, one guy came in dressed for Arctic weather even though it was April. Then there were the folks who parked a very strange vehicle in the parking lot for anyone to see. The main character starts questioning the visitors, and what he learns startles and fascinates him. Soon, he's thinking about leaving Harry's. Find out why when you read "Why I Left Harry's All-Night Hamburgers," in the *Holt Anthology of Science Fiction*.

Social Studies ACTIVITY

WRITING SKILL The main character in the story learns that Earth is a pretty strange place. Find out about some of the places mentioned in the story, and create an illustrated travel guide that describes some of the foreign places that interest you.

Science, Technology, and Society

Light Pollution

When your parents were your age, they could look up at the night sky and see many more stars than you can now. In a large city, seeing more than 50 stars or planets in the night sky can be difficult. Light pollution is a growing—or you could say "glowing"—problem. If you have ever seen a white glow over the horizon in the night sky, you have seen the effects of light pollution. Most light pollution comes from outdoor lights that are excessively bright or misdirected. Light pollution not only limits the number of stars that the average person can see but also limits what astronomers can detect. Light pollution affects migrating animals, too. Luckily, there are ways to reduce light pollution. The International Dark Sky Association is working to reduce light pollution around the world. Find out how you can reduce light pollution in your community or home.

Math ACTIVITY

A Virginia high school student named Jennifer Barlow started "National Dark Sky Week." If light pollution is reduced for 1 week each year, for what percentage of the year would light pollution be reduced?

Neil deGrasse Tyson

Star Writer When Neil deGrasse Tyson was nine years old, he visited a planetarium for the first time. Tyson was so affected by the experience he decided at that moment to dedicate his life to studying the universe. Tyson began studying the stars through a telescope on the roof of his apartment building. This interest led Tyson to attend the Bronx High School of Science, where he studied astronomy and physics. Tyson's passion for astronomy continued when he was a student at Harvard. However, Tyson soon realized that he wanted to share his love of astronomy with the public. So, today Tyson is America's best-known astrophysicist. When something really exciting happens in the universe, such as the discovery of evidence of water on Mars, Tyson is often asked to explain the discovery to the public. He has been interviewed hundreds of times on TV programs and has written several books. Tyson also writes a monthly column in the magazine *Natural History*. But writing and appearing on TV isn't even his day job! Tyson is the director of the Hayden Planetarium in New York—the same planetarium that ignited his interest in astronomy when he was nine years old!

Language Arts ACTIVITY

WRITING SKILL Be a star writer! Visit a planetarium or find a Web site that offers a virtual tour of the universe. Write a magazine-style article about the experience.

To learn more about these Science in Action topics, visit go.hrw.com and type in the keyword HZ5OBSF.

Current Science

Check out Current Science® articles related to this chapter by visiting go.hrw.com. Just type in the keyword HZ5CS18.

19

Stars, Galaxies, and the Universe

About the PHOTO

This image was taken by the *Hubble Space Telescope* and shows the IC 2163 galaxy (right) swinging past the NGC 2207 galaxy (left). Strong forces from NGC 2207 have caused stars and gas to fling out of IC 2163 into long streamers.

PRE-READING ACTIVITY

Three-Panel Flip Chart
Before you read the chapter, create the FoldNote entitled "Three-Panel Flip Chart" described in the **Study Skills** section of the Appendix. Label the flaps of the three-panel flip chart with "Stars," "Galaxies," and "The universe." As you read the chapter, write information you learn about each category under the appropriate flap.

Exploring the Movement of Galaxies in the Universe

Not all galaxies are the same. Galaxies can differ by size, shape, and how they move in space. In this activity, you will explore how the galaxies in the photo move in space.

Procedure

1. Fill a **one-quart glass jar** three-fourths of the way with **water.**
2. Take a pinch of **glitter,** and sprinkle it on the surface of the water.
3. Quickly stir the water with a **wooden spoon.** Be sure to stir the water in a circular pattern.
4. After you stop stirring, look at the water from the sides of the jar and from the top of the jar.

Analysis

1. What kind of motion did the water make after you stopped stirring the water?
2. How is the motion similar to the galaxies in the photo?
3. Make up a name that describes the galaxies in the photo.

Stars

Do you remember the children's song "Twinkle, Twinkle Little Star"? In the song, you sing "How I wonder what you are!" Well, what are stars? And what are they made of?

Most stars look like faint dots of light in the night sky. But stars are actually huge, hot, bright balls of gas that are trillions of kilometers away from Earth. How do astronomers learn about stars when the stars are too far away to visit? Astronomers study starlight!

Color of Stars

Look at the flames on the candle and the Bunsen burner shown in **Figure 1.** Which flame is hottest? How can you tell? Although red and yellow may be thought of as "warm" colors and blue may be thought of as a "cool" color, scientists consider red and yellow to be cool colors and blue to be a warm color. For example, the blue flame of the Bunsen burner is much hotter than the yellow flame of the candle.

If you look carefully at the night sky, you might notice the different colors of some stars. Betelgeuse (BET uhl JOOZ), which is red, and Rigel (RIE juhl), which is blue, are the stars that form two corners of the constellation Orion, shown in **Figure 1.** Because these two stars are different colors, we can conclude that they have different temperatures.

✓ **Reading Check** Which star is hotter, Betelgeuse or Rigel? **Explain your answer.** (*See the Appendix for answers to Reading Checks.*)

READING WARM-UP

Objectives

- Describe how color indicates the temperature of a star.
- Explain how a scientist can identify a of star's composition.
- Describe how scientists classify stars.
- Compare absolute magnitude with apparent magnitude.
- Identify how astronomers measure distances from Earth to stars.
- Describe the difference between the apparent motion and the actual motion of stars.

Terms to Learn

spectrum
apparent magnitude
absolute magnitude
light-year
parallax

READING STRATEGY

Prediction Guide Before reading this section, write the title of each heading in this section. Next, under each heading, write what you think you will learn.

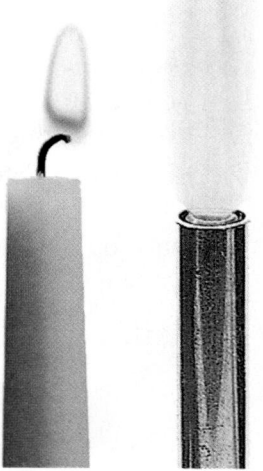

Figure 1 *In the same way that we know the blue flame of the Bunsen burner is hotter than the yellow flame of the candle, astronomers know that Rigel is hotter than Betelgeuse.*

Betelgeuse

Rigel

Composition of Stars

A star is made up of different elements in the form of gases. The inner layers of a star are very dense and hot. But the outer layers of a star, or a star's atmosphere, are made up of cool gases. Elements in a star's atmosphere absorb some of the light that radiates from the star. Because different elements absorb different wavelengths of light, astronomers can tell what elements a star is made of from the light they observe from the star.

The Colors of Light

When you look at white light through a glass prism, you see a rainbow of colors called a **spectrum.** The spectrum consists of millions of colors, including red, orange, yellow, green, blue, indigo, and violet. A hot, solid object, such as the glowing wire inside a light bulb, gives off a *continuous spectrum*—a spectrum that shows all the colors. However, the spectrum of a star is different. Astronomers use an instrument called a *spectrograph* to break a star's light into a spectrum. The spectrum gives astronomers information about the composition and temperature of a star. To understand how to read a star's spectrum, think about something more familiar—a neon sign.

Making an ID

Many restaurants use neon signs to attract customers. The gas in a neon sign glows when an electric current flows through the gas. If you were to look at the sign with a spectrograph, you would not see a continuous spectrum. Instead, you would see *emission lines*. Emission lines are lines that are made when certain wavelengths of light, or colors, are given off by hot gases. When an element emits light, only some colors in the spectrum show up, while all the other colors are missing. Each element has a unique set of bright emission lines. Emission lines are like fingerprints for the elements. You can see emission lines for four elements in **Figure 2.**

CONNECTION TO
Physics

WRITING SKILL **Fingerprinting Cars**
Police use spectrographs to "fingerprint" cars. Car makers put trace elements in the paint of cars. Each make of car has a special paint and thus its own combination of trace elements. When a car is in a hit-and-run accident, police officers can identify the make of the car by the paint left behind. Using a spectrograph to identify a car is one of many scientific methods that police use to solve crimes. Solving crimes by using scientific equipment and methods is part of a science called *forensic science*. Research the topic of forensic science. In your **science journal,** write a short paragraph about the other scientific methods that forensic scientists use to solve crimes.

spectrum the band of color produced when white light passes through a prism

Ne (neon)

H (hydrogen)

He (helium)

Na (sodium)

Figure 2 *Neon gas produces a unique set of emission lines, as do the elements hydrogen, helium, and sodium.*

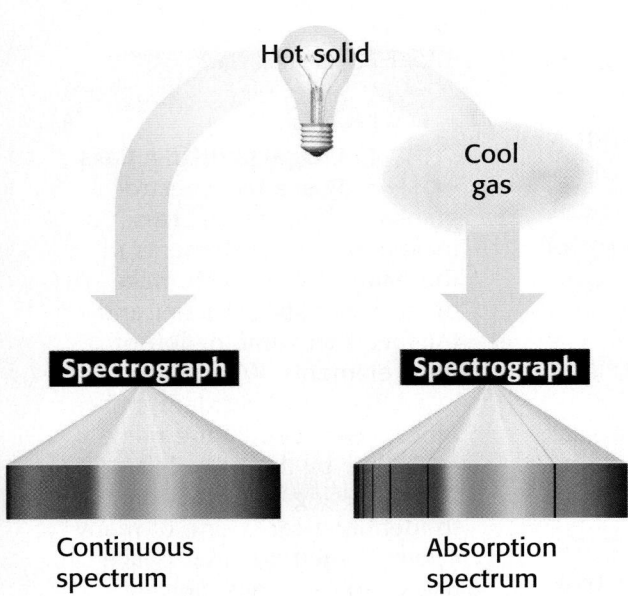

Hot solid

Cool gas

Spectrograph

Spectrograph

Continuous spectrum

Absorption spectrum

Figure 3 *A continuous spectrum (left) shows all colors while an absorption spectrum (right) absorbs some colors. Black lines appear in the spectrum where colors are absorbed.*

CONNECTION TO Biology

Rods, Cones, and Stars

WRITING SKILL Have you ever wondered why it's hard to see the different colors of stars? Our eyes are not sensitive to colors when light levels are low. There are two types of light-sensitive cells in the eye: rods and cones. Research the functions of rods and cones. In your **science journal,** write a paragraph that explains why we can't see colors well in low light.

Trapping the Light—Cosmic Detective Work

Like an element that is charged by an electric current, a star also produces a spectrum. However, while the spectrum of an electrically charged element is made of bright emission lines, a star's spectrum is made of dark emission lines. A star's atmosphere absorbs certain colors of light in the spectrum, which causes black lines to appear.

Identifying Elements Using Dark Lines

Because a star's atmosphere absorbs colors of light instead of emitting them, the spectrum of a star is called an *absorption spectrum.* An absorption spectrum is produced when light from a hot solid or dense gas passes through a cooler gas. Therefore, a star gives off an absorption spectrum because a star's atmosphere is cooler than the inner layers of the star. The black lines of a star's spectrum represent places where less light gets through. **Figure 3** compares a continuous spectrum and an absorption spectrum. What do you notice about the absorption spectrum that is different?

The pattern of lines in a star's absorption spectrum shows some of the elements that are in the star's atmosphere. If a star were made of one element, we could easily identify the element from the star's absorption spectrum. But a star is a mixture of elements and all the different sets of lines for a star's elements appear together in its spectrum. Sorting the patterns is often a puzzle.

✓ **Reading Check** What does a star's absorption spectrum show?

Classifying Stars

In the 1800s, astronomers started to collect and classify the spectra of many stars. At first, letters were assigned to each type of spectra. Stars were classified according to the elements of which they were made. Later, scientists realized that the stars were classified in the wrong order.

Differences in Temperature

Stars are now classified by how hot they are. Temperature differences between stars result in color differences that you can see. For example, the original class O stars are blue—the hottest stars. Look at **Table 1.** Notice that the stars are arranged in order from highest temperature to lowest temperature.

Table 1 Types of Stars

Class	Color	Surface temperature (°C)	Elements detected	Examples of stars
O	blue	above 30,000	helium	10 Lacertae
B	blue-white	10,000–30,000	helium and hydrogen	Rigel, Spica
A	blue-white	7,500–10,000	hydrogen	Vega, Sirius
F	yellow-white	6,000–7,500	hydrogen and heavier elements	Canopus, Procyon
G	yellow	5,000–6,000	calcium and other metals	the sun, Capella
K	orange	3,500–5,000	calcium and molecules	Arcturus, Aldebaran
M	red	less than 3,500	molecules	Betelgeuse, Antares

Differences in Brightness

With only their eyes to aid them, early astronomers created a system to classify stars based on their brightness. They called the brightest stars in the sky *first-magnitude* stars and the dimmest stars *sixth-magnitude* stars. But when they began to use telescopes, astronomers were able to see many stars that had been too dim to see before. Rather than replace the old system of magnitudes, they added to it. Positive numbers represent dimmer stars, and negative numbers represent brighter stars. For example, by using large telescopes, astronomers can see stars as dim as 29th magnitude. And the brightest star in the night sky, Sirius, has a magnitude of -1.4. The Big Dipper, shown in **Figure 4,** contains both bright stars and dim stars.

Figure 4 *The Big Dipper contains both bright stars and dim stars. What is the magnitude of the brightest star in the Big Dipper?*

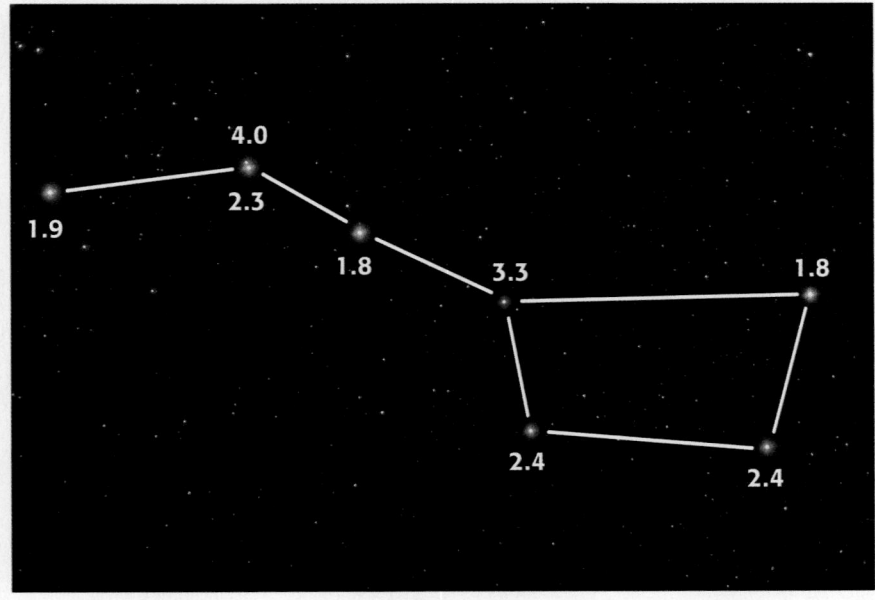

Stargazing

WRITING SKILL Someone looking at the night sky in a city would not see as many stars as someone looking at the sky in the country. With a parent, research why this is true. Try to find a place near your home that would be ideal for stargazing. If you find one, schedule a night to stargaze. Write down what you see in the night sky.

Figure 5 *You can estimate how far away each street light is by looking at its apparent brightness. Does this process work when estimating the distance of stars from Earth?*

apparent magnitude the brightness of a star as seen from the Earth

absolute magnitude the brightness that a star would have at a distance of 32.6 light-years from Earth

Starlight, Star Bright

Magnitude is used to show how bright one object is compared with another object. Every five magnitudes is equal to a factor of 100 times in brightness. The brightest blue stars, for example, have an absolute magnitude of −10. The sun has an absolute magnitude of about +5. How much brighter is a blue star than the sun? Because each five magnitudes is a factor of 100 and the blue star is 15 magnitudes greater than the sun, the blue star must be 100 × 100 × 100, or 1,000,000 (1 million), times brighter than the sun!

How Bright Is That Star?

If you look at a row of street lights, such as those shown in **Figure 5,** do they all look the same? Of course not! The nearest ones look bright, and the farthest ones look dim.

Apparent Magnitude

The brightness of a light or star is called **apparent magnitude.** If you measure the brightness of a street light with a light meter, you will find that the light's brightness depends on the square of the ratio between the light and the light meter. For example, a light that is 10 m away from you will appear 4 (2×2, or 2^2) times brighter than a light that is 20 m away from you. The same light will appear 9 (3×3, or 3^2) times brighter than a light that is 30 m away. But unlike street lights, some stars are brighter than other stars because of their size or energy output, not because of their distance from Earth. So, how can you tell how bright a star is and why?

✓ Reading Check What is apparent magnitude?

Absolute Magnitude

Astronomers use a star's apparent magnitude and its distance from Earth to calculate its absolute magnitude. **Absolute magnitude** is the actual brightness of a star. If all stars were the same distance away, their absolute magnitudes would be the same as their apparent magnitudes. The sun, for example, has an absolute magnitude of +4.8, which is ordinary for a star. But because the sun is so close to Earth, the sun's apparent magnitude is −26.8, which makes it the brightest object in the sky.

Figure 6 Measuring a Star's Parallax

Very distant stars

Apparent position in July

Apparent position in January

Nearer Star

Parallax

Earth in January

Sun

Earth in July

light-year the distance that light travels in one year; about 9.5 trillion kilometers

parallax an apparent shift in the position of an object when viewed from different locations

Distance to the Stars

Because stars are so far away, astronomers use light-years to measure the distances from Earth to the stars. A **light-year** is the distance that light travels in one year. Obviously, it would be easier to give the distance to the North Star as 431 light-years than as 4,080,000,000,000,000 km. But how do astronomers measure a star's distance from Earth?

Stars near the Earth seem to move, while more-distant stars seem to stay in one place as Earth revolves around the sun, as shown in **Figure 6.** A star's apparent shift in position is called **parallax.** Notice that the location of the nearer star in **Figure 6** seems to shift in relation to the pattern of more-distant stars. This shift can be seen only through telescopes. Astronomers use parallax and simple trigonometry (a type of math) to find the actual distance to stars that are close to Earth.

Reading Check What is a light-year?

Motions of Stars

As you know, daytime and nighttime are caused by the Earth's rotation. The Earth's tilt and revolution around the sun cause the seasons. During each season, the Earth faces a different part of the sky at night. Look again at **Figure 6.** In January, the Earth's night side faces a different part of the sky than it faces in July. This is why you see a different set of constellations at different times of the year.

Not All Thumbs!

1. Hold your thumb in front of your face at arm's length.
2. Close one eye, and focus on an **object** some distance behind your thumb.
3. Slowly turn your head side to side a small amount. Notice how your thumb seems to be moving compared with the background you are looking at.
4. Now, move your thumb in close to your face, and move your head the same amount. Does your thumb seem to move more?

Figure 7 *As Earth rotates on its axis, the stars appear to rotate around Polaris.*

For another activity related to this chapter, go to **go.hrw.com** and type in the keyword **HZ5UNVW.**

The Apparent Motion of Stars

Because of Earth's rotation, the sun appears to move across the sky. Likewise, if you look at the night sky long enough, the stars also appear to move. In fact, at night you can observe that the whole sky is rotating above us. Look at **Figure 7.** All the stars you see appear to rotate around Polaris, the North Star, which is almost directly above Earth's North Pole. Because of Earth's rotation, all of the stars in the sky appear to make one complete circle around Polaris every 24 h.

The Actual Motion of Stars

You now know that the apparent motion of the sun and stars in our sky is due to Earth's rotation. But each star is also moving in space. Because stars are so distant, however, their actual motion is hard to see. If you could put thousands of years into one hour, a star's movement would be obvious. **Figure 8** shows how familiar star patterns slowly change their shapes.

Reading Check Why is the actual motion of stars hard to see?

Figure 8 *Over time, the shapes of star patterns, such as the Big Dipper and other groups, change.*

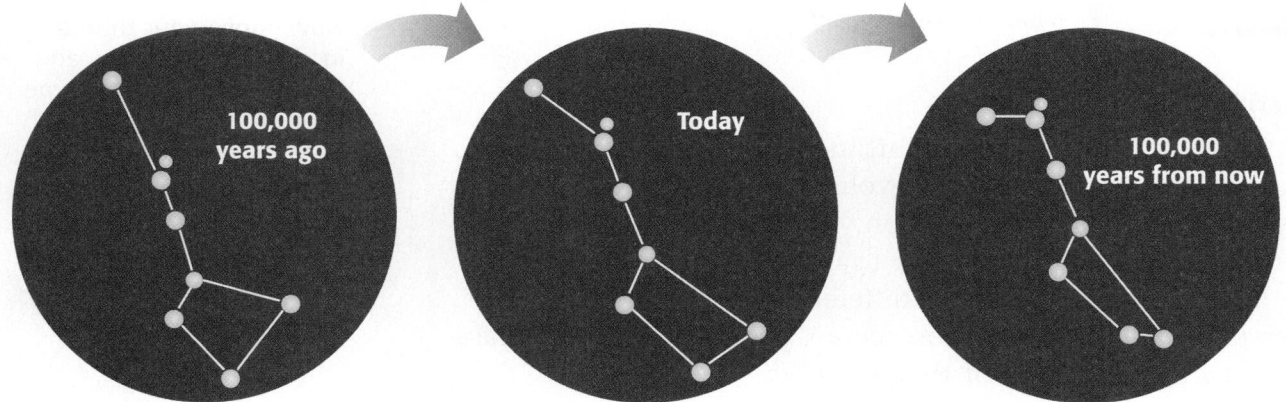

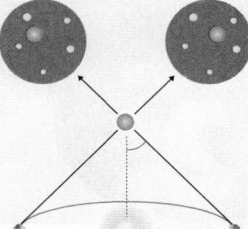

Summary

- The color of a star depends on its temperature. Hot stars are blue. Cool stars are red.
- The spectrum of a star shows the composition of a star.
- Scientists classify stars by temperature and brightness.
- Apparent magnitude is the brightness of a star as seen from Earth.

- Absolute magnitude is the measured brightness of a star at a distance of 32.6 light-years.
- Astronomers use parallax and trigonometry to measure distances from Earth to stars.
- Stars appear to move because of Earth's rotation. However, the actual motion of stars is very hard to see because stars are so distant.

Using Key Terms

1. Use the following terms in the same sentence: *apparent magnitude* and *absolute magnitude*.

2. Use each of the following terms in a separate sentence: *spectrum, light-year,* and *parallax*.

Understanding Key Ideas

3. When you look at white light through a glass prism, you see a rainbow of colors called a
   a. spectograph.
   b. spectrum.
   c. parallax.
   d. light-year.

4. Class F stars are
   a. blue.
   b. yellow.
   c. yellow-white.
   d. red.

5. Describe how scientists classify stars.

6. Explain how color indicates the temperature of a star.

Critical Thinking

7. **Applying Concepts** If a certain star displayed a large parallax, what could you say about the star's distance from Earth?

8. **Making Comparisons** Compare a continuous spectrum with an absorption spectrum. Then, explain how an absorption spectrum can identify a star's composition.

9. **Making Comparisons** Compare apparent motion with actual motion.

Interpreting Graphics

10. Look at the two figures below. How many hours passed between the first image and the second image? Explain your answer.

For a variety of links related to this chapter, go to www.scilinks.org

Topic: Stars
SciLinks code: HSM1448

The Life Cycle of Stars

Some stars exist for billions of years. But how are they born? And what happens when a star dies?

Because stars exist for billions of years, scientists cannot observe a star throughout its entire life. Therefore, scientists have developed theories about the life cycle of stars by studying them in different stages of development.

READING WARM-UP

Objectives
- Describe different types of stars.
- Describe the quantities that are plotted in the H-R diagram.
- Explain how stars at different stages in their life cycle appear on the H-R diagram.

Terms to Learn

red giant	supernova
white dwarf	neutron star
H-R diagram	pulsar
main sequence	black hole

READING STRATEGY

Paired Summarizing Read this section silently. In pairs, take turns summarizing the material. Stop to discuss ideas that seem confusing.

The Beginning and End of Stars

A star enters the first stage of its life cycle as a ball of gas and dust. Gravity pulls the gas and dust together into a sphere. As the sphere becomes denser, it gets hotter and the hydrogen changes to helium in a process called *nuclear fusion*.

As stars get older, they lose some of their material. Stars usually lose material slowly, but sometimes they can lose material in a big explosion. Either way, when a star dies, much of its material returns to space. In space, some of the material combines with more gas and dust to form new stars.

Different Types of Stars

Stars can be classified by their size, mass, brightness, color, temperature, spectrum, and age. Some types of stars include *main-sequence stars*, *giants*, *supergiants*, and *white dwarf stars*. A star can be classified as one type of star early in its life cycle and then can be classified as another star when it gets older. For example, the star shown in **Figure 1** has reached the final stage in its life cycle. It has run out of fuel, which has caused the central parts of the star to collapse inward.

Figure 1 *This star (center) has entered the last stage of its life cycle.*

Main-Sequence Stars

After a star forms, it enters the second and longest stage of its life cycle known as the main sequence. During this stage, energy is generated in the core of the star as hydrogen atoms fuse into helium atoms. This process releases an enormous amount of energy. The size of a main-sequence star will change very little as long as the star has a continuous supply of hydrogen atoms to fuse into helium atoms.

Giants and Supergiants

After the main-sequence stage, a star can enter the third stage of its life cycle. In this third stage, a star can become a red giant. A **red giant** is a star that expands and cools once it uses all of its hydrogen. Eventually, the loss of hydrogen causes the center of the star to shrink. As the center of the star shrinks, the atmosphere of the star grows very large and cools to form a red giant or a red supergiant, as shown in **Figure 2.** Red giants can be 10 or more times bigger than the sun. Supergiants are at least 100 times bigger than the sun.

✓ Reading Check What is the difference between a red giant star and a red supergiant star? *(See the Appendix for answers to Reading Checks.)*

White Dwarfs

In the final stages of a star's life cycle, a star that has the same mass as the sun or smaller can be classified as a white dwarf. A **white dwarf** is a small hot star that is the leftover center of an older star. A white dwarf has no hydrogen left and can no longer generate energy by fusing hydrogen atoms into helium atoms. White dwarfs can shine for billions of years before they cool completely.

Figure 2 *The red supergiant star Antares is shown above. Antares is located in the constellation of Scorpius.*

red giant a large, reddish star late in its life cycle

white dwarf a small, hot, dim star that is the leftover center of an old star

CONNECTION TO Astronomy

WRITING SKILL **Long Live the Sun** Our sun probably took about 10 million years to become a main-sequence star. It has been shining for about 5 billion years. In another 5 billion years, our sun will burn up most of its hydrogen and expand to become a red giant. When this change happens, the sun's diameter will increase. How will this change affect Earth and our solar system? Use the Internet or library resources to find out what might happen as the sun gets older and how the changes in the sun might affect our solar system. Gather your findings, and write a report on what you find out about the life cycle the sun.

A Tool for Studying Stars

In 1911, a Danish astronomer named Ejnar Hertzsprung (IE nawr HUHRTS sproong) compared the brightness and temperature of stars on a graph. Two years later, American astronomer Henry Norris Russell made some similar graphs. Although these astronomers used different data, they had similar results. The combination of their ideas is now called the Hertzsprung-Russell diagram, or H-R diagram. The **H-R diagram** is a graph that shows the relationship between a star's surface temperature and its absolute magnitude. Over the years, the H-R diagram has become a tool for studying the lives of stars. It shows not only how stars are classified by brightness and temperature but also how stars change over time.

H-R diagram Hertzsprung-Russell diagram, a graph that shows the relationship between a star's surface temperature and absolute magnitude

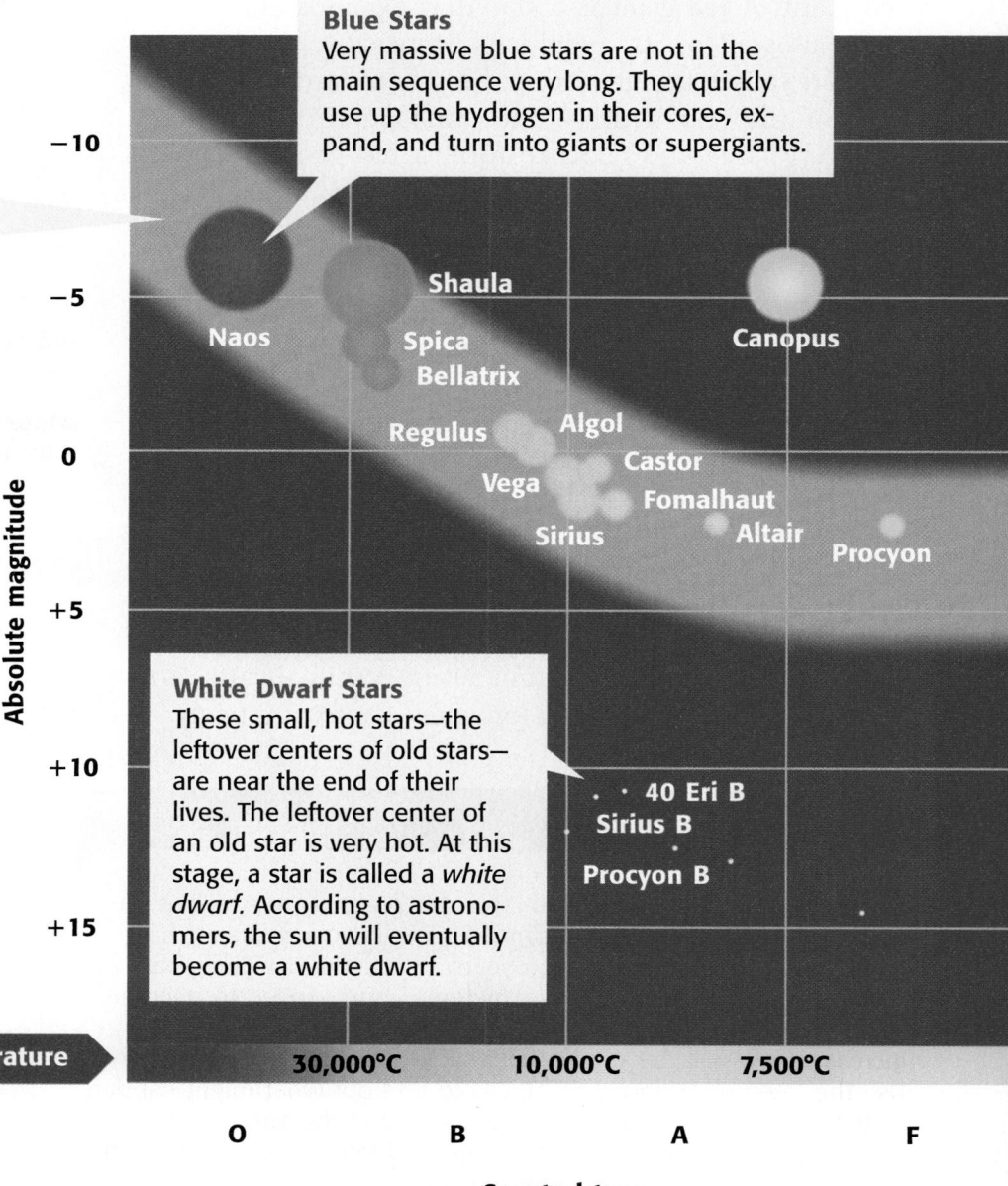

Main-Sequence Stars
Stars in the main sequence form a band that runs along the middle of the H-R diagram. The sun is a main-sequence star. The sun has been shining for about 5 billion years. Scientists think the sun is in midlife and that it will remain on the main sequence for another 5 billion years.

Blue Stars
Very massive blue stars are not in the main sequence very long. They quickly use up the hydrogen in their cores, expand, and turn into giants or supergiants.

White Dwarf Stars
These small, hot stars—the leftover centers of old stars—are near the end of their lives. The leftover center of an old star is very hot. At this stage, a star is called a *white dwarf*. According to astronomers, the sun will eventually become a white dwarf.

Reading the H-R Diagram

The modern H-R diagram is shown below. Temperature is given along the bottom of the diagram and absolute magnitude, or brightness, is given along the left side. Hot (blue) stars are located on the left, and cool (red) stars are on the right. Bright stars are at the top, and dim stars are at the bottom. The brightest stars are 1 million times brighter than the sun. The dimmest stars are 1/10,000 as bright as the sun. The diagonal pattern on the H-R diagram where most stars lie, is called the **main sequence.** A star spends most of its lifetime in the main sequence. As main-sequence stars age, they move up and to the right on the H-R diagram to become giants or supergiants and then down and to the left to become white dwarfs.

main sequence the location on the H-R diagram where most stars lie

Giants and Supergiants
When a star runs out of hydrogen in its core, the center of the star shrinks inward and the outer parts expand outward. For a star the size of our sun, the star's atmosphere will grow very large and become cool. When this change happens, the star becomes a *red giant.* If the star is very massive, it becomes a supergiant.

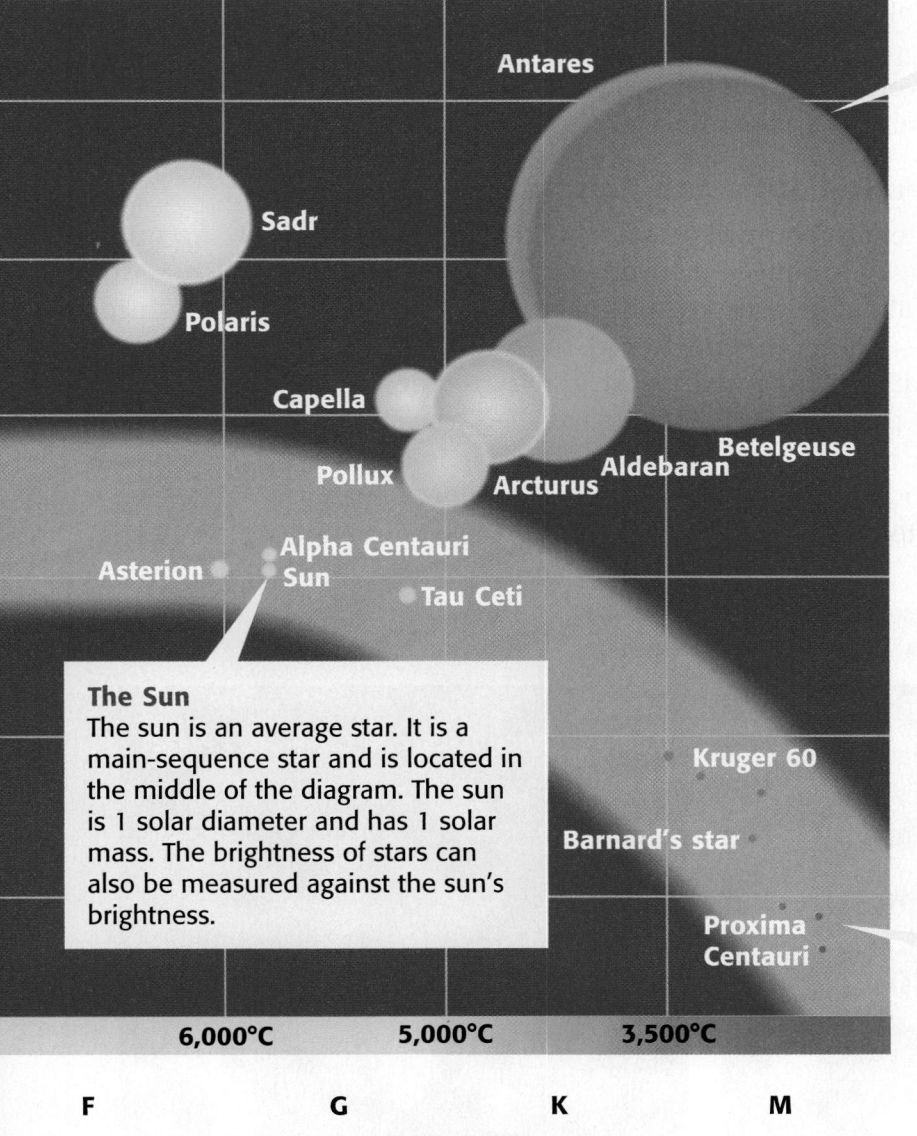

The Sun
The sun is an average star. It is a main-sequence star and is located in the middle of the diagram. The sun is 1 solar diameter and has 1 solar mass. The brightness of stars can also be measured against the sun's brightness.

Red Dwarf Stars
At the lower end of the main sequence are the red dwarf stars, which are low-mass stars. Low-mass stars remain on the main sequence a long time. The stars that have the lowest mass are among the oldest stars in the universe.

When Stars Get Old

Although stars may stay on the main sequence for a long time, they don't stay there forever. Average stars, such as the sun, become red giants and then white dwarfs. However, stars that are more massive than the sun may explode with such intensity that they become a variety of strange objects such as supernovas, neutron stars, pulsars, and black holes.

Supernovas

Massive blue stars use their hydrogen much faster than stars like the sun do. Therefore, blue stars generate more energy than stars like the sun do, which makes blue stars very hot and blue! And compared with other stars, blue stars don't have long lives. At the end of its life, a blue star may explode in a large, bright flash called a *supernova*. A **supernova** is a gigantic explosion in which a massive star collapses. The explosion is so powerful that it can be brighter than an entire galaxy for several days. The ringed structure shown in **Figure 3** is the result of a supernova explosion.

Neutron Stars and Pulsars

After a supernova occurs, the materials in the center of a supernova are squeezed together to form a new star. This new star is about two times the mass of the sun. The particles inside the star's core are forced together to form neutrons. A star that has collapsed under gravity to the point at which all of its particles are neutrons is called a **neutron star.**

If a neutron star is spinning, it is called a **pulsar.** A pulsar sends out a beam of radiation that spins very rapidly. The beam is detected on Earth by radio telescopes as rapid clicks, or pulses.

supernova a gigantic explosion in which a massive star collapses and throws its outer layers into space

neutron star a star that has collapsed under gravity to the point that the electrons and protons have smashed together to form neutrons

pulsar a rapidly spinning neutron star that emits rapid pulses of radio and optical energy

---

Figure 3 Explosion of a Supernova

Supernova 1987A was the first supernova visible to the unaided eye in 400 years. The first image shows what the original star must have looked like only a few hours before the explosion. Today, the star's remains form a double ring of gas and dust, as shown at right.

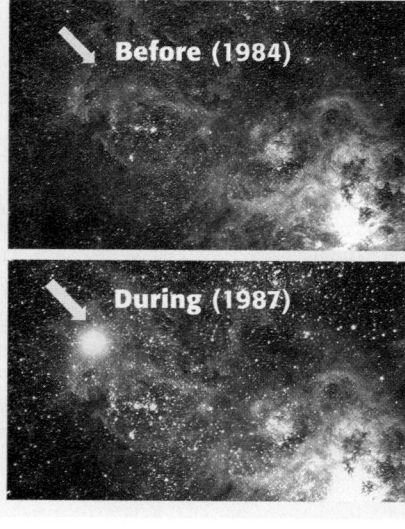
Before (1984)

During (1987)

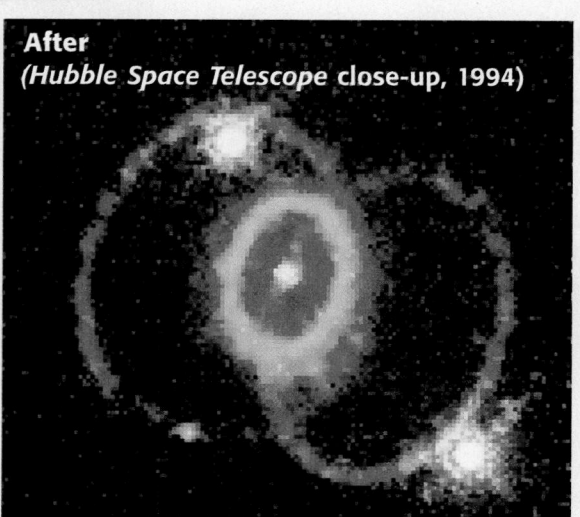
After
(Hubble Space Telescope close-up, 1994)

Black Holes

Sometimes the leftovers of a supernova are so massive that they collapse to form a black hole. A **black hole** is an object that is so massive that even light cannot escape its gravity. So, it is called a *black hole*. A black hole doesn't gobble up other stars like some movies show. Because black holes do not give off light, locating them is difficult. If a star is nearby, some gas or dust from the star will spiral into the black hole and give off X rays. These X rays allow astronomers to detect the existence of black holes.

black hole an object so massive and dense that even light cannot escape its gravity

✓ **Reading Check** What is a black hole? How do astronomers detect the presence of black holes?

SECTION Review

Summary

- New stars form from the material of old stars that have gone through their lives.

- Types of stars include main-sequence stars, giants and supergiants, and white dwarf stars.

- The H-R diagram shows the brightness of a star in relation to the temperature of a star. It also shows the life cycle of stars.

- Most stars are main-sequence stars.

- Massive stars become supernovas. Their cores can change into neutron stars or black holes.

Using Key Terms

For each pair of terms, explain how the meanings of the terms differ.

1. *white dwarf* and *red giant*

2. *supernova* and *neutron star*

3. *pulsar* and *black hole*

Understanding Key Ideas

4. The sun is a
   a. white dwarf.
   b. main-sequence star.
   c. red giant.
   d. red dwarf.

5. A star begins as a ball of gas and dust pulled together by
   a. black holes.
   b. electrons and protons.
   c. heavy metals.
   d. gravity.

6. Are blue stars young or old? How can you tell?

7. In main-sequence stars, what is the relationship between brightness and temperature?

8. Arrange the following stages in order of their appearance in the life cycle of a star: white dwarf, red giant, and main-sequence star. Explain your answer.

Math Skills

9. The sun's present radius is 700,000 km. If the sun's radius increased by 150 times, what would its radius be?

Critical Thinking

10. **Applying Concepts** Given that there are more low-mass stars than high-mass stars in the universe, do you think there are more white dwarfs or more black holes in the universe? Explain.

11. **Analyzing Processes** Describe what might happen to a star after it becomes a supernova.

12. **Evaluating Data** How does the H-R diagram explain the life cycle of a star?

Developed and maintained by the National Science Teachers Association

For a variety of links related to this chapter, go to www.scilinks.org

Topic: Supernova
SciLinks code: HSM1482

Galaxies

Your complete address is part of a much larger system than your street, city, state, country, and even the planet Earth. You also live in the Milky Way galaxy.

Large groups of stars, dust, and gas are called **galaxies.** Galaxies come in a variety of sizes and shapes. The largest galaxies contain more than a trillion stars. Astronomers don't count the stars, of course. They estimate how many sun-sized stars the galaxy might have by studying the size and brightness of the galaxy.

Types of Galaxies

There are many different types of galaxies. Edwin Hubble, the astronomer for whom the *Hubble Space Telescope* is named, began to classify galaxies, mostly by their shapes, in the 1920s. Astronomers still use the galaxy classification that Hubble developed.

Spiral Galaxies

When someone says the word *galaxy,* most people probably think of a spiral galaxy. *Spiral galaxies,* such as the one shown in **Figure 1,** have a bulge at the center and spiral arms. The spiral arms are made up of gas, dust, and new stars that have formed in these denser regions of gas and dust.

✓ **Reading Check** What are two characteristics of spiral galaxies? What makes up the arms of a spiral galaxy? (*See the Appendix for answers to Reading Checks.*)

READING WARM-UP

Objectives

● Identify three types of galaxies.

● Describe the contents and characteristics of galaxies.

● Explain why looking at distant galaxies reveals what young galaxies looked like.

Terms to Learn

galaxy
nebula
globular cluster
open cluster
quasar

READING STRATEGY

Reading Organizer As you read this section, make a table comparing the different types of galaxies.

galaxy a collection of stars, dust, and gas bound together by gravity

---

Figure 1 **Types of Galaxies**

▼ **Spiral Galaxy**
The Andromeda galaxy is a spiral galaxy that looks similar to what our galaxy, the Milky Way, is thought to look like.

The Milky Way

It is hard to tell what type of galaxy we live in because the gas, dust, and stars keep astronomers from having a good view of our galaxy. Observing other galaxies and making measurements inside our galaxy, the Milky Way, has led astronomers to think that our solar system is in a spiral galaxy.

Elliptical Galaxies

About one-third of all galaxies are simply massive blobs of stars. Many look like spheres, and others are more stretched out. Because we don't know how they are oriented, some of these galaxies could be cucumber shaped, with the round end facing our galaxy. These galaxies are called *elliptical galaxies*. Elliptical galaxies usually have very bright centers and very little dust and gas. Elliptical galaxies contain mostly old stars. Because there is so little free-flowing gas in an elliptical galaxy, few new stars form. Some elliptical galaxies, such as M87, shown in **Figure 1,** are huge and are called *giant elliptical galaxies*. Other elliptical galaxies are much smaller and are called *dwarf elliptical galaxies*.

Irregular Galaxies

When Hubble first classified galaxies, he had a group of leftovers. He named the leftovers "irregulars." *Irregular galaxies* are galaxies that don't fit into any other class. As their name suggests, their shape is irregular. Many of these galaxies, such as the Large Magellanic Cloud, shown in **Figure 1,** are close companions of large spiral galaxies. The large spiral galaxies may be distorting the shape of these irregular galaxies.

Elliptical Galaxy
Unlike the Milky Way, the galaxy known as M87 has no spiral arms.

Irregular Galaxy
The Large Magellanic Cloud, an irregular galaxy, is located within our galactic neighborhood.

Contents of Galaxies

Galaxies are composed of billions of stars and some planetary systems, too. Some of these stars form large features, such as gas clouds and star clusters, as shown in **Figure 2.**

Gas Clouds

nebula a large cloud of dust and gas in interstellar space; a region in space where stars are born or where stars explode at the end of their lives

The Latin word for "cloud" is *nebula*. In space, **nebulas** (or nebulae) are large clouds of gas and dust. Some types of nebulas glow, while others absorb light and hide stars. Still, other nebulas reflect starlight and produce some amazing images. Some nebulas are regions in which new stars form. **Figure 2** shows part of the Eagle nebula. Spiral galaxies usually contain nebulas, but elliptical galaxies contain very few.

Star Clusters

globular cluster a tight group of stars that looks like a ball and contains up to 1 million stars

Globular clusters are groups of older stars. A **globular cluster** is a group of stars that looks like a ball, as shown in **Figure 2.** There may be up to one million stars in a globular cluster. Globular clusters are located in a spherical *halo* that surrounds spiral galaxies such as the Milky Way. Globular clusters are also common near giant elliptical galaxies.

open cluster a group of stars that are close together relative to surrounding stars

Open clusters are groups of closely grouped stars that are usually located along the spiral disk of a galaxy. Newly formed open clusters have many bright blue stars, as shown in **Figure 2.** There may be a few hundred to a few thousand stars in an open cluster.

✓ Reading Check What is the difference between a globular cluster and an open cluster?

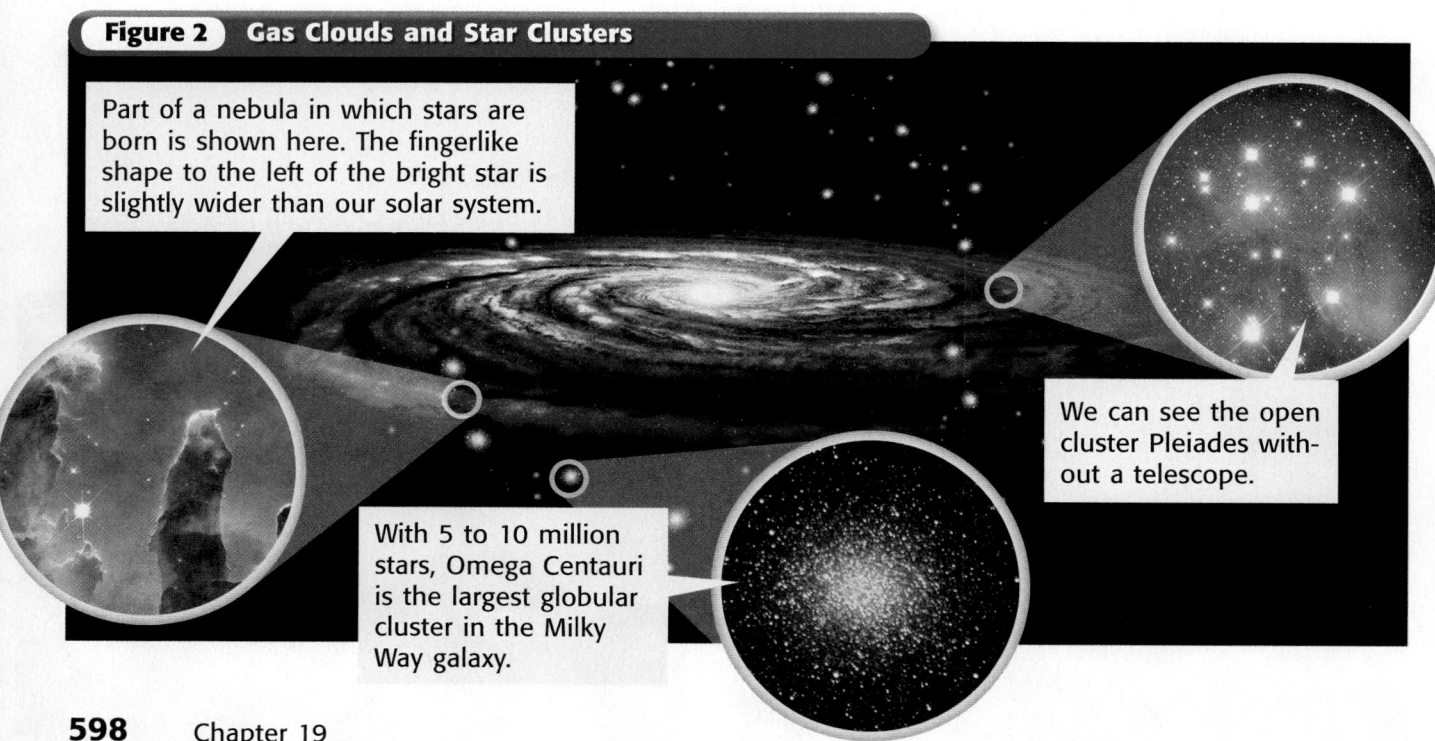

Figure 2 Gas Clouds and Star Clusters

Part of a nebula in which stars are born is shown here. The fingerlike shape to the left of the bright star is slightly wider than our solar system.

With 5 to 10 million stars, Omega Centauri is the largest globular cluster in the Milky Way galaxy.

We can see the open cluster Pleiades without a telescope.

Origin of Galaxies

Scientists investigate the early universe by observing objects that are extremely far away in space. Because it takes time for light to travel through space, looking through a telescope is like looking back in time. Looking at distant galaxies reveals what early galaxies looked like. This information gives scientists an idea of how galaxies change over time and may give them insight about what caused the galaxies to form.

Quasars

Among the most distant objects are quasars. **Quasars** are starlike sources of light that are extremely far away. They are among the most powerful energy sources in the universe. Some scientists think that quasars may be caused by massive black holes in the cores of some galaxies. **Figure 3** shows a quasar that is 6 billion light-years away.

Reading Check What are quasars? What do some scientists think quasars might be?

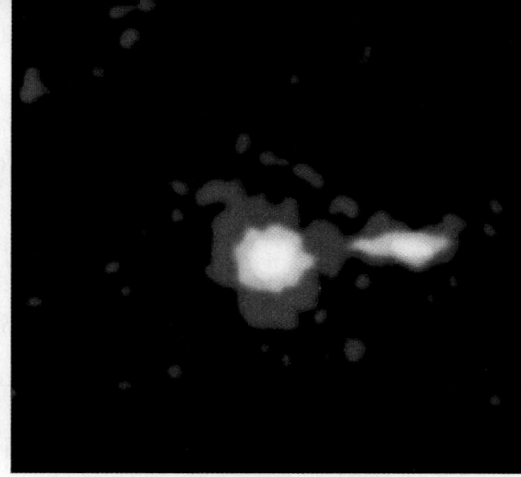

Figure 3 *The quasar known as PKS 0637-752 is as massive as 10 billion suns.*

quasar a very luminous, starlike object that generates energy at a high rate; quasars are thought to be the most distant objects in the universe

---

SECTION Review

Summary

- Edwin Hubble classified galaxies according to their shape including spiral, elliptical, and irregular galaxies.

- Some galaxies consist of nebulas and star clusters.

- Nebulas are large clouds of gas and dust. Globular clusters are tightly grouped stars. Open clusters are closely grouped stars.

- Scientists look at distant galaxies to learn what early galaxies looked like.

Using Key Terms

1. Use the following terms in the same sentence: *nebula, globular cluster,* and *open cluster.*

Understanding Key Ideas

2. Arrange the following galaxies in order of decreasing size: spiral, giant elliptical, dwarf elliptical, and irregular.

3. All of the following are shapes used to classify galaxies EXCEPT
   a. elliptical.
   b. irregular.
   c. spiral.
   d. triangular.

Critical Thinking

4. **Making Comparisons** Describe the difference between an elliptical galaxy and a globular cluster.

5. **Identifying Relationships** Explain how looking through a telescope is like looking back in time.

Math Skills

6. The quasar known as PKS 0637-752 is 6 billion light-years away from Earth. The North Star is 431 light-years away from Earth. What is the ratio of the distances in kilometers these two celestial objects are from Earth? (Hint: One light-year is equal to 9.46 trillion km.)

Formation of the Universe

Imagine explosions, bright lights, and intense energy. Does that scene sound like an action movie? This scene could also describe a theory about the formation of the universe.

The study of the origin, structure, and future of the universe is called **cosmology.** Like other scientific theories, theories about the beginning and end of the universe must be tested by observations or experiments.

Universal Expansion

To understand how the universe formed, scientists study the movement of galaxies. Careful measurements have shown that most galaxies are moving apart.

A Raisin-Bread Model

To understand how the galaxies are moving, imagine a loaf of raisin bread before it is baked. Inside the dough, each raisin is a certain distance from every other raisin. As the dough gets warm and rises, it expands and all of the raisins begin to move apart. No matter which raisin you observe, the other raisins are moving farther away from it. The universe, like the rising bread dough, is expanding. Think of the raisins as galaxies. As the universe expands, the galaxies move farther apart.

The Big Bang Theory

With the discovery that the universe is expanding, scientists began to wonder what it would be like to watch the formation of the universe in reverse. The universe would appear to be contracting, not expanding. All matter would eventually come together at a single point. Thinking about what would happen if all of the matter in the universe were squeezed into such a small space led scientists to the big bang theory.

READING WARM-UP

Objectives

- Describe the big bang theory.
- Explain evidence used to support the big bang theory.
- Describe the structure of the universe.
- Describe two ways scientists calculate the age of the universe.
- Explain what will happen if the universe expands forever.

Terms to Learn

cosmology
big bang theory

READING STRATEGY

Prediction Guide Before reading this section, write the title of each heading in this section. Next, under each heading, write what you think you will learn.

cosmology the study of the origin, properties, processes, and evolution of the universe

Figure 1 *Some astronomers think the big bang caused the universe to expand in all directions.*

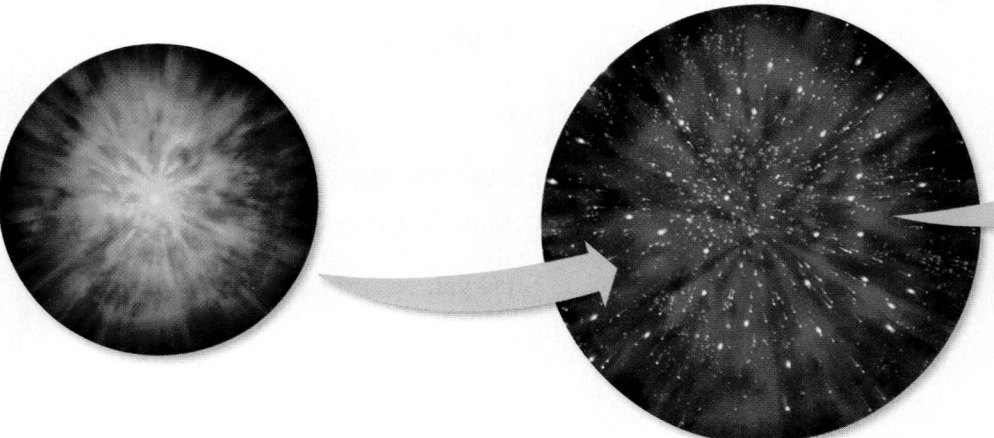

A Tremendous Explosion

The theory that the universe began with a tremendous explosion is called the **big bang theory.** According to the theory, 13.7 billion years ago all the contents of the universe was compressed under extreme pressure, temperature, and density in a very tiny spot. Then, the universe rapidly expanded, and matter began to come together and form galaxies. **Figure 1** illustrates what the big bang might have looked like.

big bang theory the theory that states the universe began with a tremendous explosion 13.7 billion years ago

Cosmic Background Radiation

In 1964, two scientists using a huge antenna accidentally found radiation coming from all directions in space. One explanation for this radiation is that it is *cosmic background radiation* left over from the big bang. To understand the connection between the big bang theory and cosmic background radiation, think about a kitchen oven. When an oven door is left open after the oven has been used, thermal energy is transferred throughout the kitchen and the oven cools. Eventually, the room and the oven are the same temperature. According to the big bang theory, the thermal energy from the original explosion was distributed in every direction as the universe expanded. This cosmic background radiation now fills all of space.

Reading Check Explain the relationship between cosmic background radiation and the big bang theory. (*See the Appendix for answers to Reading Checks.*)

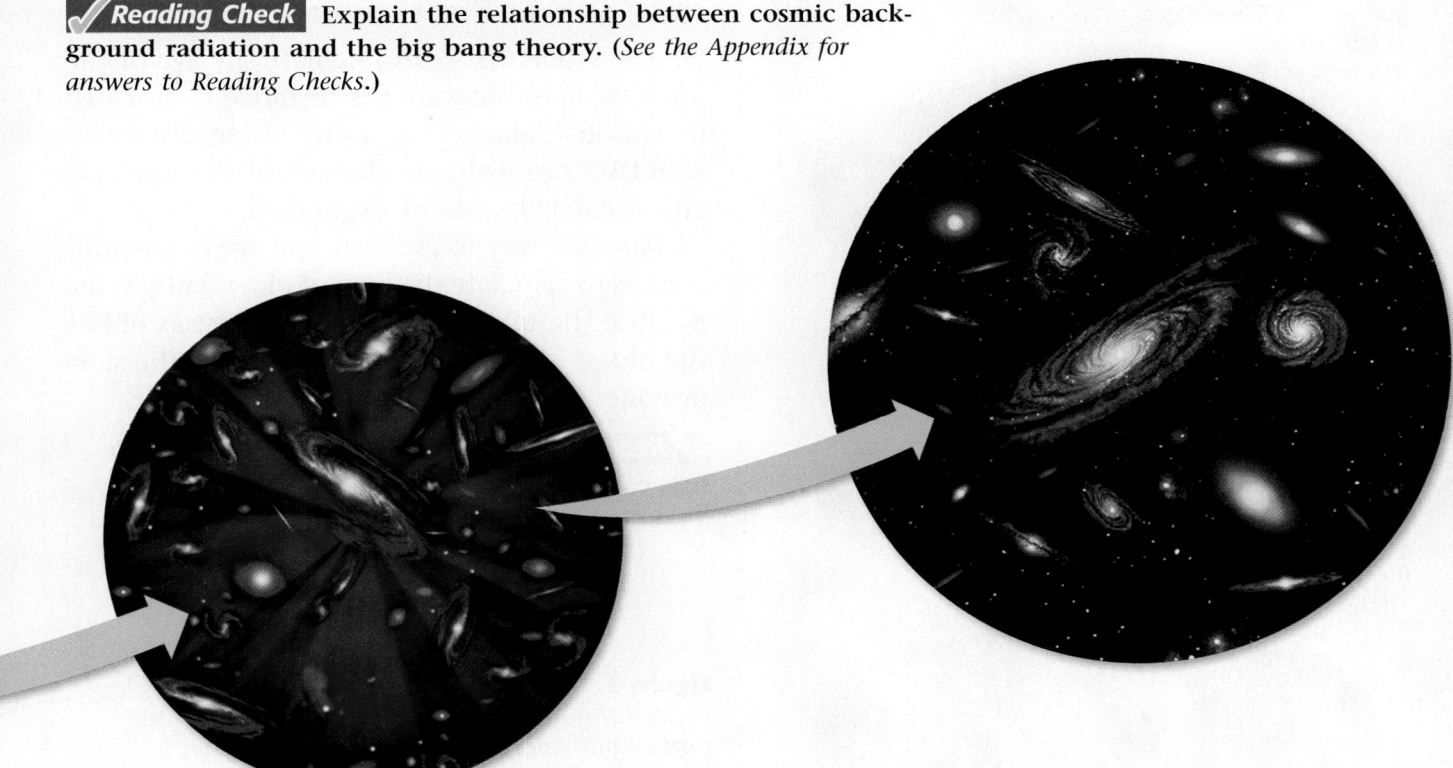

Structure of the Universe

From our home on Earth, the universe stretches out farther than astronomers can see with their most advanced instruments. The universe contains a variety of objects. But these objects in the universe are not simply scattered through the universe in a random pattern. The universe has a structure that is loosely repeated over and over again.

A Cosmic Repetition

Every object in the universe is part of a larger system. As illustrated in **Figure 2,** a cluster or group of galaxies can be made up of smaller star clusters and galaxies. Galaxies, such as the Milky Way, can include planetary systems, such as our solar system. Earth is part of our solar system. Although our solar system is the planetary system that we are most familiar with, other planets have been detected in orbit around other stars. Scientists think that planetary systems are common in the universe.

How Old Is the Universe?

One way scientists can calculate the age of the universe is to measure the distance from Earth to various galaxies. By using these distances, scientists can estimate the age of the universe and predict its rate of expansion.

Another way to estimate the age of the universe is to calculate the ages of old, nearby stars. Because the universe must be at least as old as the oldest stars it contains, the ages of the stars provide a clue to the age of the universe.

Reading Check What is one way that scientists calculate the age of the universe?

Figure 2 *Every object in the universe is part of a larger system. Earth is part of our solar system, which is in turn part of the Milky Way galaxy.*

A Forever Expanding Universe

What will happen to the universe? As the galaxies move farther apart, they get older and stop forming stars. The farther galaxies move apart from each other, the less visible to us they will become. The expansion of the universe depends on how much matter the universe contains. Scientists predict that if there is enough matter, gravity could eventually stop the expansion of the universe. If the universe stops expanding, it could start collapsing to its original state. This process would be a reverse of what might have happened during the big bang.

However, scientists now think that there may not be enough matter in the universe, so the universe will continue to expand forever. Therefore, stars will age and die, and the universe will probably become cold and dark after many billions of years. Even after the universe becomes cold and dark, it will continue to expand forever.

✓ Reading Check If the universe expanded to the point at which gravity stopped the expansion, what would happen? What will happen if the expansion of the universe continues forever?

CONNECTION TO Physics

WRITING SKILL **Origin of the Universe** The big bang theory is one scientific theory about the origin of the universe. Use library resources to research these other scientific theories. In your **science journal,** describe in your own words the different theories of the origin of the universe. Use charts or tables to examine and evaluate these differences.

SECTION Review

Summary

- Observations show that the universe is expanding.
- The big bang theory states that the universe began with an explosion about 13.7 billion years ago.
- Cosmic background radiation helps support the big bang theory.
- Scientists use different ways to calculate the age of the universe.
- Scientists think that the universe may expand forever.

Using Key Terms

1. In your own words, write a definition for the following terms: *cosmology* and *big bang theory*.

Understanding Key Ideas

2. Describe two ways scientists calculate the age of the universe.

3. The expansion of the universe can be compared to
   a. cosmology.
   b. raisin bread baking in an oven.
   c. thermal energy leaving an oven as the oven cools.
   d. bread pudding.

4. How does cosmic background radiation support the big bang theory?

5. What do scientists think will eventually happen to the universe?

Math Skills

6. The North Star is 4.08×10^{12} km from Earth. What is this number written in its long form?

Critical Thinking

7. **Applying Concepts** Explain how every object in the universe is part of a larger system.

8. **Analyzing Ideas** Why do scientists think that the universe will expand forever?

SCILINKS®

NSTA
Developed and maintained by the National Science Teachers Association

For a variety of links related to this chapter, go to www.scilinks.org

Topic: Structure of the Universe
SciLinks code: HSM1469

Skills Practice Lab

OBJECTIVES

Discover what the color of a glowing object reveals about the temperature of the object.

Describe how the color and temperature of a star are related.

MATERIALS

- battery, D cell (2)
- battery, D cell, weak
- flashlight bulb
- tape, electrical
- wire, insulated copper, with ends stripped, 20 cm long (2)

SAFETY

Red Hot, or Not?

When you look at the night sky, some stars are brighter than others. Some are even different colors. For example, Betelgeuse, a bright star in the constellation Orion, glows red. Sirius, one of the brightest stars in the sky, glows bluish white. Astronomers use color to estimate the temperature of stars. In this activity, you will experiment with a light bulb and some batteries to discover what the color of a glowing object reveals about the temperature of the object.

Ask a Question

1 How are the color and temperature of a star related?

Form a Hypothesis

2 On a sheet of paper, change the question above into a statement that gives your best guess about the relationship between a star's color and temperature.

Test the Hypothesis

③ Tape one end of an insulated copper wire to the positive pole of the weak D cell. Tape one end of the second wire to the negative pole.

④ Touch the free end of each wire to the light bulb. Hold one of the wires against the bottom tip of the light bulb. Hold the second wire against the side of the metal portion of the bulb. The bulb should light.

⑤ Record the color of the filament in the light bulb. Carefully touch your hand to the bulb. Observe the temperature of the bulb. Record your observations.

⑥ Repeat steps 3–5 with one of the two fresh D cells.

⑦ Use the electrical tape to connect two fresh D cells so that the positive pole of the first cell is connected to the negative pole of the second cell.

⑧ Repeat steps 3–5 using the fresh D cells that are taped together.

Analyze the Results

① **Describing Events** What was the color of the filament in each of the three trials? For each trial, compare the bulb temperature to the temperature of the bulb in the other two trials.

② **Analyzing Results** What information does the color of a star tell you about the star?

③ **Classifying** What color are stars that have relatively high surface temperatures? What color are stars that have relatively low surface temperatures?

Draw Conclusions

④ **Applying Conclusions** Arrange the following stars in order from highest to lowest surface temperature: Sirius, which is bluish white; Aldebaran, which is orange; Procyon, which is yellow-white; Capella, which is yellow; and Betelgeuse, which is red.

Chapter Review

USING KEY TERMS

The statements below are false. For each statement, replace the underlined term to make a true statement.

1 The distance that light travels in space in 1 year is called <u>apparent magnitude</u>.

2 <u>Globular clusters</u> are groups of stars that are usually located along the spiral disk of a galaxy.

3 Galaxies that have very bright centers and very little dust and gas are called <u>spiral galaxies</u>.

4 When you look at white light through a glass prism, you see a rainbow of colors called a <u>supernova</u>.

UNDERSTANDING KEY IDEAS

Multiple Choice

5 A scientist can identify a star's composition by looking at

  a. the star's prism.

  b. the star's continuous spectrum.

  c. the star's absorption spectrum.

  d. the star's color.

6 If the universe expands forever,

  a. the universe will collapse.

  b. the universe will repeat itself.

  c. the universe will remain just as it is today.

  d. stars will age and die and the universe will become cold and dark.

7 The majority of stars in our galaxy are

  a. blue stars.

  b. white dwarfs.

  c. main-sequence stars.

  d. red giants.

8 Which of the following is used to measure the distance between objects in space?

  a. parallax   **c.** zenith

  b. magnitude   **d.** altitude

9 Which of the following stars would be seen as the brightest star?

  a. Alcyone, which has an apparent magnitude of 3

  b. Alpheratz, which has an apparent magnitude of 2

  c. Deneb, which has an apparent magnitude of 1

  d. Rigel, which has an apparent magnitude of 0

Short Answer

10 Describe how scientists classify stars.

11 Describe the structure of the universe.

12 Explain how stars at different stages in their life cycle appear on the H-R diagram.

13 Explain the difference between the apparent motion and actual motion of stars.

14 Describe how color indicates the temperature of a star.

15 Describe two ways that scientists calculate the age of the universe.

CRITICAL THINKING

16 Concept Mapping Use the following terms to create a concept map: *main-sequence star, nebula, red giant, white dwarf, neutron star,* and *black hole*.

17 Evaluating Conclusions While looking through a telescope, you see a galaxy that doesn't appear to contain any blue stars. What kind of galaxy is it most likely to be? Explain your answer.

18 Making Comparisons Explain the differences between main-sequence stars, giant stars, supergiant stars, and white dwarfs.

19 Evaluating Data Why do astronomers use absolute magnitudes to plot stars? Why don't astronomers use apparent magnitudes to plot stars?

20 Evaluating Sources According to the big bang theory, how did the universe begin? What evidence supports this theory?

21 Evaluating Data If a certain star displayed a large parallax, what could you say about the star's distance from Earth?

INTERPRETING GRAPHICS

The graph below shows Hubble's law, which relates how far galaxies are from Earth and how fast they are moving away from Earth. Use the graph below to answer the questions that follow.

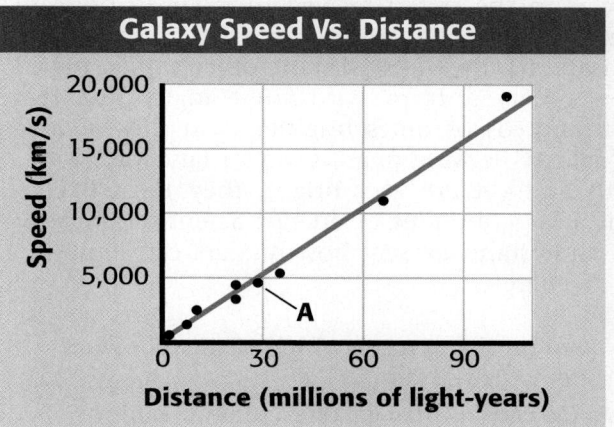

Galaxy Speed Vs. Distance

22 Look at the point that represents galaxy A in the graph. How far is galaxy A from Earth, and how fast is it moving away from Earth?

23 If a galaxy is moving away from Earth at 15,000 km/s, how far is the galaxy from Earth?

24 If a galaxy is 90,000,000 light-years from Earth, how fast is it moving away from Earth?

Standardized Test Preparation

Read each of the passages below. Then, answer the questions that follow each passage.

Passage 1 Quasars are some of the most puzzling objects in the sky. If viewed through an optical telescope, a quasar appears as a small, dim star. Quasars are the most distant objects that have been observed from Earth. But many quasars are hundreds of times brighter than the brightest galaxy. Because quasars are so far away from Earth and yet are very bright, they most likely emit a large amount of energy. Scientists do not yet understand exactly how quasars can emit so much energy.

1. Based on the passage, which of the following statements is a fact?
   A Quasars, unlike galaxies, include billions of bright objects.
   B Galaxies are brighter than quasars.
   C Quasars are hundreds of times brighter than the brightest galaxy.
   D Galaxies are the most distant objects observed from Earth.

2. Based on the information in the passage, what can the reader conclude?
   F Quasars are the same as galaxies.
   G Quasars appear as small, dim stars, but they emit a large amount of energy.
   H Quasars can be viewed only by using an optical telescope.
   I Quasars will never be understood.

3. Why do scientists think that quasars emit a large amount of energy?
   A because quasars are the brightest stars in the universe
   B because quasars can be viewed only through an optical telescope
   C because quasars are very far away and are still bright
   D because quasars are larger than galaxies

Passage 2 If you live away from bright outdoor lights, you may be able to see a faint, narrow band of light and dark patches across the sky. This band is called the Milky Way. Our galaxy, the Milky Way, consists of stars, gases, and dust. Between the stars of the Milky Way are clouds of gas and dust called <u>interstellar matter</u>. These clouds provide materials that form new stars.

Every star that you can see in the night sky is a part of the Milky Way, because our solar system is inside the Milky Way. Because we are inside the galaxy, we cannot see the entire galaxy. But scientists can use astronomical data to create a picture of the Milky Way.

1. In the passage, what does the term *interstellar matter* mean?
   A stars in the Milky Way
   B the Milky Way
   C a narrow band of light and dark patches across the sky
   D the clouds of gas and dust between the stars in the Milky Way

2. Based on the information in the passage, what can the reader conclude?
   F The Milky Way can be seen in the night sky near a large city.
   G The entire Milky Way can be seen all at once.
   H Every star that is seen in the night sky is a part of the Milky Way.
   I Scientists have no idea what the entire Milky Way looks like.

The graph below shows the relationship between a star's age and mass. Use the graph below to answer the questions that follow.

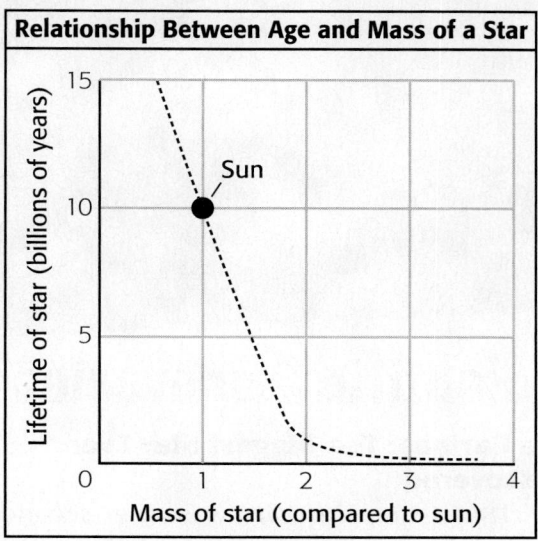

Relationship Between Age and Mass of a Star

1. How long does a star that has 1.2 times the mass of the sun live?
   A 10 billion years
   B 8 billion years
   C 6 billion years
   D 5 billion years

2. How long does a star that has 2 times the mass of the sun live?
   F 4 billion years
   G 1 billion years
   H 10 billion years
   I 5 billion years

3. If the sun's mass was reduced by half, how long would the sun live?
   A 2 billion years
   B 8 billion years
   C 10 billion years
   D more than 15 billion years

4. According to the graph, how long is the sun predicted to live?
   F 15 billion years
   G 10 billion years
   H 5 billion years
   I 2 billion years

Read each question below, and choose the best answer.

1. How many kilometers away from Earth is an object that is 8 light-years away from Earth? (Hint: One light-year is equal to 9.46 trillion kilometers.)
   A 77 trillion kilometers
   B 76 trillion kilometers
   C 7.66 trillion kilometers
   D 7.6 trillion kilometers

2. An astronomer observes two stars of about the same temperature and size. Alpha Centauri B is about 4 light-years away from Earth, and Sigma 2 Eridani A is about 16 light-years away from Earth. How many times as bright as Sigma 2 Eridani A does Alpha Centauri B appear? (Hint: One light-year is equal to 9.46 trillion kilometers.)
   F 2 times as bright
   G 4 times as bright
   H 16 times as bright
   I 32 times as bright

3. Star A is 5 million kilometers from Star B. What is this distance expressed in meters?
   A 0.5 m
   B 5,000 m
   C 5×10^6 m
   D 5×10^9 m

4. In the vacuum of space, light travels 3×10^8 m/s. How far does light travel in 1 h in space?
   F 3,600 m
   G 1.80×10^{10} m
   H 1.08×10^{12} m
   I 1.08×10^{16} m

5. The mass of the known universe is about 10^{23} solar masses, which is 10^{50} metric tons. How many metric tons is one solar mass?
   A 10^{27} solar masses
   B 10^{27} metric tons
   C 10^{73} solar masses
   D 10^{73} metric tons

Science in Action

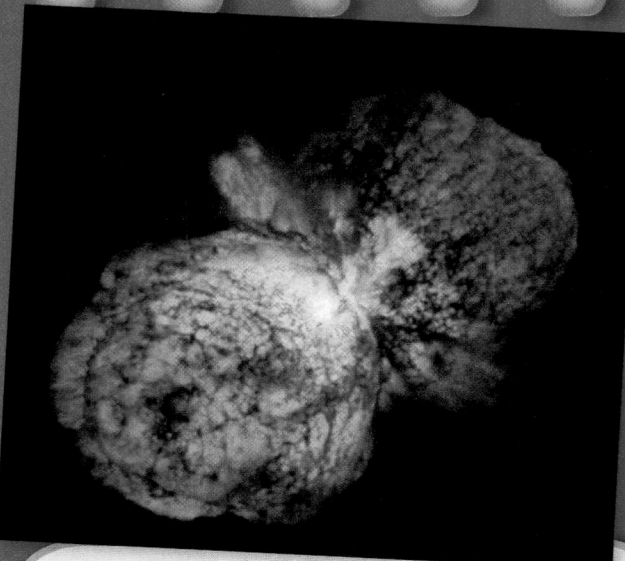

Weird Science

Holes Where Stars Once Were

An invisible phantom lurks in space, ready to swallow everything that comes near it. Once trapped in its grasp, matter is stretched, torn, and crushed into oblivion. Does this tale sound like a horror story? Guess again! Scientists call this phantom a *black hole*. As a star runs out of fuel, it cools and eventually collapses under the force of its own gravity. If the collapsing star is massive enough, it may shrink to become a black hole. The resulting gravitational attraction is so strong that even light cannot escape! Many astronomers think that black holes lie at the heart of many galaxies. Some scientists suggest that there is a giant black hole at the center of our own Milky Way.

Scientific Discoveries

Eta Carinae: The Biggest Star Ever Discovered

In 1841, Eta Carinae was the second-brightest star in the night sky. Why is this observation a part of history? Eta Carinae's brightness is historic because before 1837, Eta Carinae wasn't even visible to the naked eye! Strangely, a few years later Eta Carinae faded again and disappeared from the night sky. Something unusual was happening to Eta Carinae, and scientists wanted to know what it was. As soon as scientists had telescopes with which they could see far into space, they took a closer look at Eta Carinae. Scientists discovered that this star is highly unstable and prone to violent outbursts. These outbursts, the last of which was seen in 1841, can be seen on Earth. Scientists also discovered that Eta Carinae is 150 times as big as our sun and about 4 million times as bright. Eta Carinae is the biggest and brightest star ever found!

Language Arts ACTiViTY

WRITING SKILL Can you imagine traveling through a black hole? Write a short story that describes what you would see if you led a space mission to a black hole.

Math ACTiViTY

If Eta Carinae is 8,000 light-years from our solar system, how many kilometers is Eta Carinae from our solar system? (Hint: One light-year is equal to 9.46 trillion kilometers.)

Jocelyn Bell-Burnell

Astrophysicist Imagine getting a signal from far out in space and not knowing what or whom it's coming from. That's what happened to astrophysicist Jocelyn Bell-Burnell. Bell-Burnell is known for discovering pulsars, objects in space that emit radio waves at short, regular intervals. But before she and her advisor discovered that the signals came from pulsars, they thought that the signals may have come from aliens!

Born in 1943 in Belfast, Northern Ireland, Jocelyn Bell-Burnell became interested in astronomy at an early age. At Cambridge University in 1967, Bell-Burnell, who was a graduate student, and her advisor, Anthony Hewish, completed work on a huge radio telescope designed to pick up signals from quasars. Bell-Burnell's job was to operate the telescope and analyze its chart paper recordings on a graph. Each day, the telescope recordings used 29.2 m of chart paper! After a month, Bell-Burnell noticed that the recordings showed a few "bits of scruff"—very short, pulsating radio signals—that she could not explain. Bell-Burnell and Hewish struggled to find the source of the mysterious signal. They checked the equipment and began eliminating possible sources of the signal, such as satellites, television, and radar. Shortly after finding the first signal, Bell-Burnell discovered a second. The second signal was similar to the first but came from a different position in the sky. By January 1968, Bell-Burnell had discovered two more pulsating signals. In March of 1968, her findings that the signals were from a new kind of star were published and amazed the scientific community. The scientific press named the newly discovered stars *pulsars*.

Today, Bell-Burnell is a leading expert in the field of astrophysics and the study of stars. She is currently head of the physics department at the Open University, in Milton Keynes, England.

Social Studies ACTiViTY

Use the Internet or library resources to research historical events that occurred during 1967 and 1968. Find out if the prediction that the signals from pulsars were coming from aliens affected historical events during this time.

go.hrw.com
To learn more about these Science in Action topics, visit **go.hrw.com** and type in the keyword **HZ5UNVF.**

Current Science
Check out Current Science® articles related to this chapter by visiting **go.hrw.com.** Just type in the keyword **HZ5CS19.**

20

Formation of the Solar System

About the PHOTO

The Orion Nebula, a vast cloud of dust and gas that is 35 trillion miles wide, is part of the familiar Orion constellation. Here, swirling clouds of dust and gas give birth to systems like our own solar system.

PRE-READING ACTIVITY

Graphic Organizer

Chain-of-Events Chart Before you read the chapter, create the graphic organizer entitled "Chain-of-Events Chart" described in the **Study Skills** section of the Appendix. As you read the chapter, fill in the chart with details about each step of the formation of the solar system.

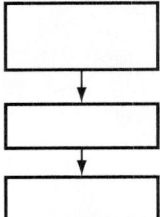

START-UP ACTIVITY

Strange Gravity

If you drop a heavy object, will it fall faster than a lighter one? According to the law of gravity, the answer is no. In 1971, *Apollo 15* astronaut David Scott stood on the moon and dropped a feather and a hammer. Television audiences were amazed to see both objects strike the moon's surface at the same time. Now, you can perform a similar experiment.

Procedure

1. Select **two pieces of identical notebook paper.** Crumple one piece of paper into a ball.

2. Place the flat piece of paper on top of a **book** and the paper ball on top of the flat piece of paper.

3. Hold the book waist high, and then drop it to the floor.

Analysis

1. Which piece of paper reached the bottom first? Did either piece of paper fall slower than the book? Explain your observations.

2. Now, hold the crumpled paper in one hand and the flat piece of paper in the other. Drop both pieces of paper at the same time. Besides gravity, what affected the speed of the falling paper? Record your observations.

A Solar System Is Born

As you read this sentence, you are traveling at a speed of about 30 km/s around an incredibly hot star shining in the vastness of space!

Earth is not the only planet orbiting the sun. In fact, Earth has eight fellow travelers in its cosmic neighborhood. The solar system includes a star we call the sun, nine planets, and many moons and small bodies that travel around the sun. For almost 5 billion years, planets have been orbiting the sun. But how did the solar system come to be?

The Solar Nebula

All of the ingredients for building planets, moons, and stars are found in the vast, seemingly empty regions of space between the stars. Just as there are clouds in the sky, there are clouds in space. These clouds are called nebulas. **Nebulas** (or nebulae) are mixtures of gases—mainly hydrogen and helium—and dust made of elements such as carbon and iron. Although nebulas are normally dark and invisible to optical telescopes, they can be seen when nearby stars illuminate them. So, how can a cloud of gas and dust such as the Horsehead Nebula, shown in **Figure 1,** form planets and stars? To answer this question, you must explore two forces that interact in nebulas—gravity and pressure.

Gravity Pulls Matter Together

The gas and dust that make up nebulas are made of matter. The matter of a nebula is held together by the force of gravity. In most nebulas, there is a lot of space between the particles. In fact, nebulas are less dense than air! Thus, the gravitational attraction between the particles in a nebula is very weak. The force is just enough to keep the nebula from drifting apart.

READING WARM-UP

Objectives

- Explain the relationship between gravity and pressure in a nebula.
- Describe how the solar system formed.

Terms to Learn

nebula
solar nebula

READING STRATEGY

Reading Organizer As you read this section, make a flowchart of the steps of the formation of a solar system.

nebula a large cloud of gas and dust in interstellar space; a region in space where stars are born or where stars explode at the end of their lives

Figure 1 *The Horsehead Nebula is a cold, dark cloud of gas and dust. But observations suggest that it is also a site where stars form.*

Figure 2 Gravity and Pressure in a Nebula

❶ Gravity causes the particles in a nebula to be attracted to each other.

❷ As particles move closer together, collisions cause pressure to increase and particles are pushed apart.

❸ If the inward force of gravity is balanced by outward pressure, the nebula becomes stable.

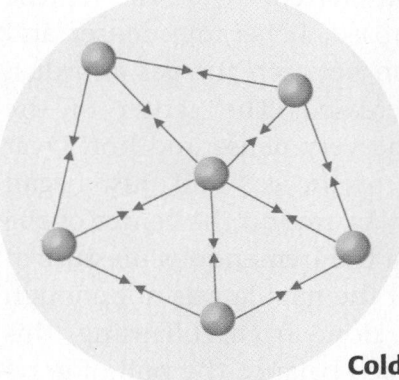

Cold

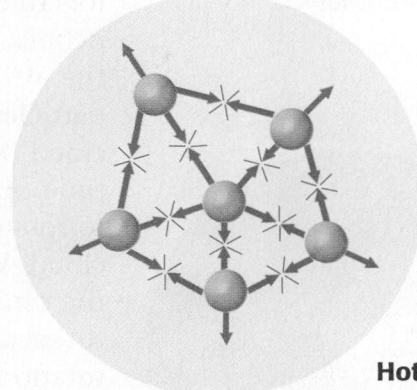

Hot

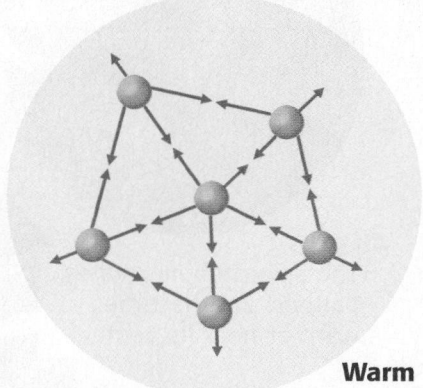

Warm

Pressure Pushes Matter Apart

If gravity pulls on all of the particles in a nebula, why don't nebulas slowly collapse? The answer has to do with the relationship between temperature and pressure in a nebula. *Temperature* is a measure of the average kinetic energy, or the energy of motion, of the particles in an object. If the particles in a nebula have little kinetic energy, they move slowly and the temperature of the cloud is very low. If the particles move fast, the temperature of the cloud is high. As particles move around, they sometimes crash into each other. As shown in **Figure 2,** these collisions cause particles to push away from each other, which creates *pressure*. If you have ever blown up a balloon, you understand how pressure works—pressure keeps a balloon from collapsing. In a nebula, outward pressure balances the inward gravitational pull and keeps the cloud from collapsing.

Upsetting the Balance

The balance between gravity and pressure in a nebula can be upset if two nebulas collide or a nearby star explodes. These events compress, or push together, small regions of a nebula called *globules,* or gas clouds. Globules can become so dense that they contract under their own gravity. As the matter in a globule collapses inward, the temperature increases and the stage is set for stars to form. The **solar nebula**—the cloud of gas and dust that formed our solar system—may have formed in this way.

solar nebula the cloud of gas and dust that formed our solar system

✓ **Reading Check** What is the solar nebula? (*See the Appendix for answers to Reading Checks.*)

Figure 3 The Formation of the Solar System

① The young solar nebula begins to collapse.

② The solar nebula rotates, flattens, and becomes warmer near its center.

③ Planetesimals begin to form within the swirling disk.

④ As the largest planetesimals grow in size, their gravity attracts more gas and dust.

⑤ Smaller planetesimals collide with the larger ones, and planets begin to grow.

⑥ A star is born, and the remaining gas and dust are blown out of the new solar system.

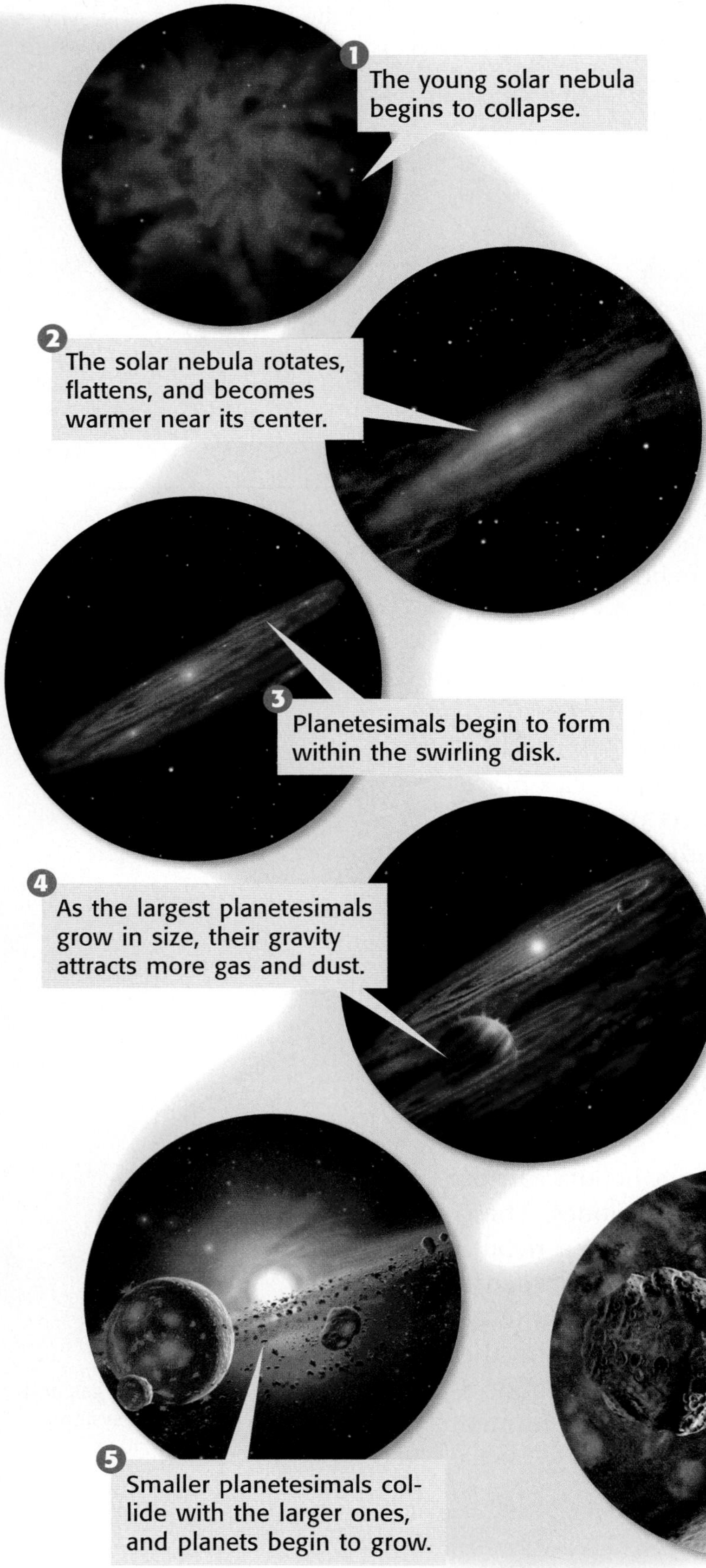

How the Solar System Formed

The events that may have led to the formation of the solar system are shown in **Figure 3.** After the solar nebula began to collapse, it took about 10 million years for the solar system to form. As the nebula collapsed, it became denser and the attraction between the gas and dust particles increased. The center of the cloud became very dense and hot. Over time, much of the gas and dust began to rotate slowly around the center of the cloud. While the tremendous pressure at the center of the nebula was not enough to keep the cloud from collapsing, this rotation helped balance the pull of gravity. Over time, the solar nebula flattened into a rotating disk. All of the planets still follow this rotation.

From Planetesimals to Planets

As bits of dust circled the center of the solar nebula, some collided and stuck together to form golf ball–sized bodies. These bodies eventually drifted into the solar nebula, where further collisions caused them to grow to kilometer-wide bodies. As more collisions happened, some of these bodies grew to hundreds of kilometers wide. The largest of these bodies are called *planetesimals,* or small planets. Some of these planetesimals are part of the cores of current planets, while others collided with forming planets to create enormous craters.

Gas Giant or Rocky Planet?

The largest planetesimals formed near the outside of the rotating solar disk, where hydrogen and helium were located. These planetesimals were far enough from the solar disk that their gravity could attract the nebula gases. These outer planets grew to huge sizes and became the gas giants—Jupiter, Saturn, Uranus, and Neptune. Closer to the center of the nebula, where Mercury, Venus, Earth, and Mars formed, temperatures were too hot for gases to remain. Therefore, the inner planets in our solar system are made mostly of rocky material.

Reading Check Which planets are gas giants?

The Birth of a Star

As the planets were forming, other matter in the solar nebula was traveling toward the center. The center became so dense and hot that hydrogen atoms began to fuse, or join, to form helium. Fusion released huge amounts of energy and created enough outward pressure to balance the inward pull of gravity. At this point, when the gas stopped collapsing, our sun was born and the new solar system was complete!

SECTION Review

Summary

- The solar system formed out of a vast cloud of gas and dust called the *nebula*.
- Gravity and pressure were balanced until something upset the balance. Then, the nebula began to collapse.
- Collapse of the solar nebula caused heating at the center, while planetesimals formed in surrounding space.
- The central mass of the nebula became the sun. Planets formed from the surrounding materials.

Using Key Terms

1. In your own words, write a definition for each of the following terms: *nebula* and *solar nebula*.

Understanding Key Ideas

2. What is the relationship between gravity and pressure in a nebula?
   a. Gravity reduces pressure.
   b. Pressure balances gravity.
   c. Pressure increases gravity.
   d. None of the above

3. Describe how our solar system formed.

4. Compare the inner planets with the outer planets.

Math Skills

5. If the planets, moons, and other bodies make up 0.15% of the solar system's mass, what percentage does the sun make up?

Critical Thinking

6. **Evaluating Hypotheses** Pluto, the outermost planet, is small and rocky. Some scientists argue that Pluto is a captured asteroid, not a planet. Use what you know about how solar systems form to evaluate this hypothesis.

7. **Making Inferences** Why do all of the planets go around the sun in the same direction, and why do the planets lie on a relatively flat plane?

SCLINKS

NSTA
Developed and maintained by the National Science Teachers Association

For a variety of links related to this chapter, go to www.scilinks.org

Topic: The Planets
SciLinks code: HSM1152

The Sun: Our Very Own Star

Can you imagine what life on Earth would be like if there were no sun? Without the sun, life on Earth would be impossible!

Energy from the sun lights and heats Earth's surface. Energy from the sun even drives the weather. Making up more than 99% of the solar system's mass, the sun is the dominant member of our solar system. The sun is basically a large ball of gas made mostly of hydrogen and helium held together by gravity. But what does the inside of the sun look like?

The Structure of the Sun

Although the sun may appear to have a solid surface, it does not. When you see a picture of the sun, you are really seeing through the sun's outer atmosphere. The visible surface of the sun starts at the point where the gas becomes so thick that you cannot see through it. As **Figure 1** shows, the sun is made of several layers.

Figure 1 The Structure and Atmosphere of the Sun

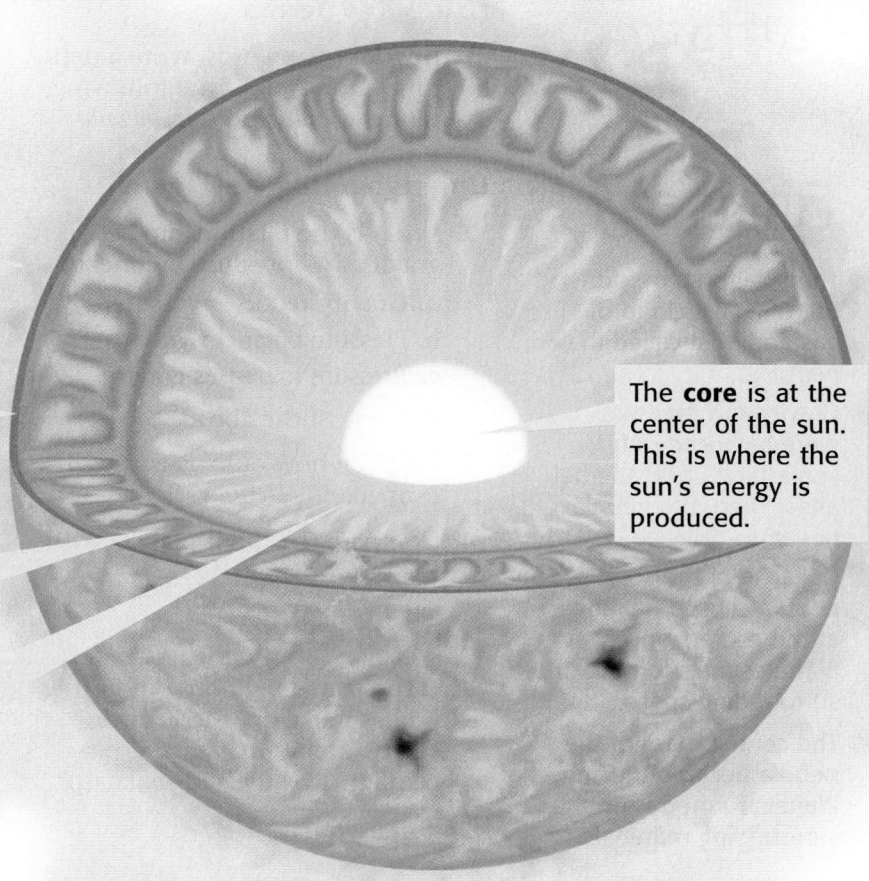

The **corona** forms the sun's outer atmosphere.

The **chromosphere** is a thin region below the corona, only 30,000 km thick.

The **photosphere** is the visible part of the sun that we can see from Earth.

The **convective zone** is a region about 200,000 km thick where gases circulate.

The **radiative zone** is a very dense region about 300,000 km thick.

The **core** is at the center of the sun. This is where the sun's energy is produced.

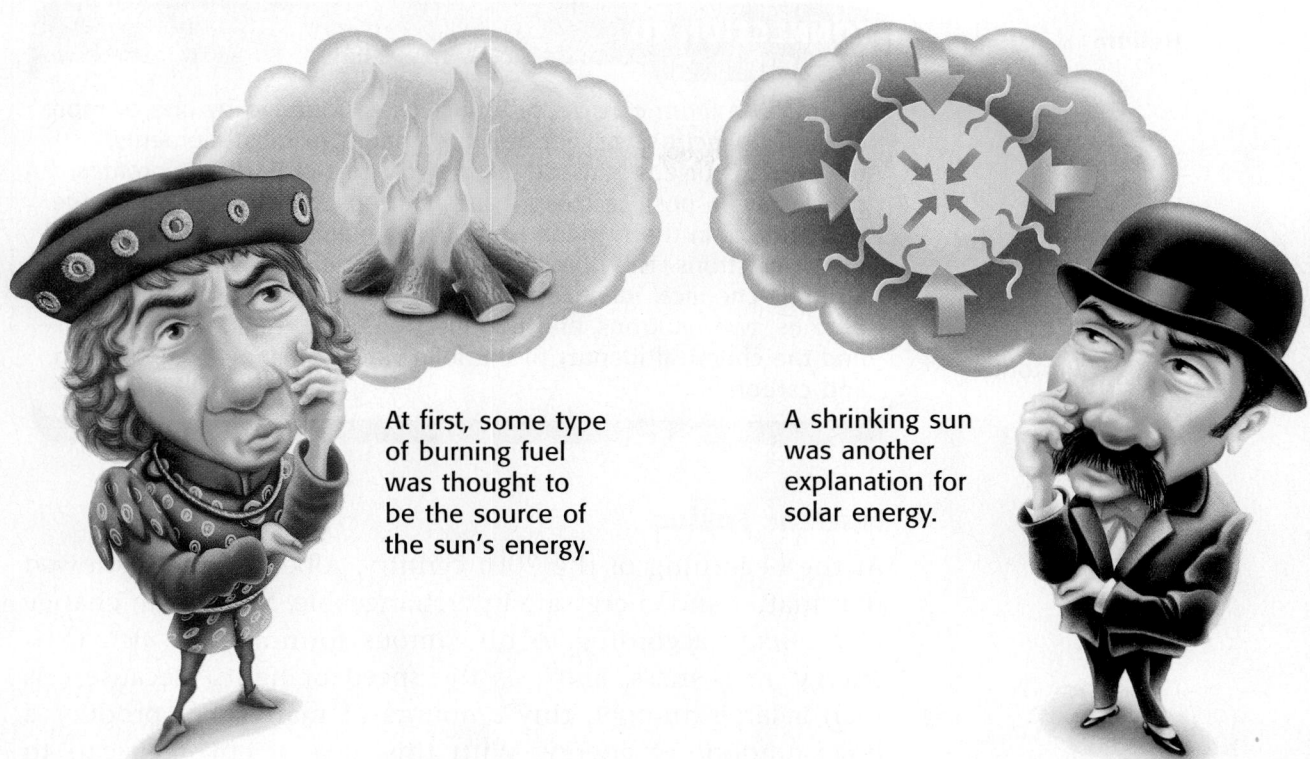

At first, some type of burning fuel was thought to be the source of the sun's energy.

A shrinking sun was another explanation for solar energy.

Figure 2 *Ideas about the source of the sun's energy have changed over time.*

Energy Production in the Sun

The sun has been shining on Earth for about 4.6 billion years. How can the sun stay hot for so long? And what makes it shine? **Figure 2** shows two theories that were proposed to answer these questions. Many scientists thought that the sun burned fuel to generate its energy. But the amount of energy that is released by burning would not be enough to power the sun. If the sun were simply burning, it would last for only 10,000 years.

Burning or Shrinking?

It eventually became clear to scientists that burning wouldn't last long enough to keep the sun shining. Then, scientists began to think that gravity was causing the sun to slowly shrink. They thought that perhaps gravity would release enough energy to heat the sun. While the release of gravitational energy is more powerful than burning, it is not enough to power the sun. If all of the sun's gravitational energy were released, the sun would last for only 45 million years. However, fossils that have been discovered prove that dinosaurs roamed the Earth more than 65 million years ago, so this couldn't be the case. Therefore, something even more powerful than gravity was needed.

✓ Reading Check Why isn't energy from gravity enough to power the sun? (*See the Appendix for answers to Reading Checks.*)

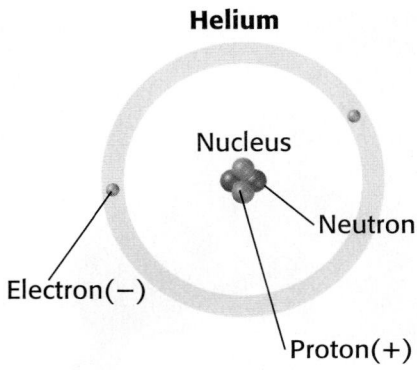

Helium

Nucleus

Neutron

Electron(−)

Proton(+)

Atoms An atom consists of a nucleus surrounded by one or more electrons. Electrons have a negative charge. In most elements, the atom's nucleus is made up of two types of particles: *protons,* which have a positive charge, and *neutrons,* which have no charge. The protons in the nucleus are usually balanced by an equal number of electrons. The number of protons and electrons gives the atom its chemical identity. A helium atom, shown at left, has two protons, two neutrons, and two electrons. Use a Periodic Table to find the chemical identity of the following atoms: nitrogen, oxygen, and carbon.

Nuclear Fusion

At the beginning of the 20th century, Albert Einstein showed that matter and energy are interchangeable. Matter can change into energy according to his famous formula: $E = mc^2$. (E is energy, m is mass, and c is the speed of light.) Because c is such a large number, tiny amounts of matter can produce a huge amount of energy. With this idea, scientists began to understand a very powerful source of energy.

nuclear fusion the combination of the nuclei of small atoms to form a larger nucleus; releases energy

Nuclear fusion is the process by which two or more low-mass nuclei join together, or fuse, to form another nucleus. In this way, four hydrogen nuclei can fuse to form a single nucleus of helium. During the process, energy is produced. Scientists now know that the sun gets its energy from nuclear fusion. Einstein's equation, shown in **Figure 3,** changed ideas about the sun's energy source by equating mass and energy.

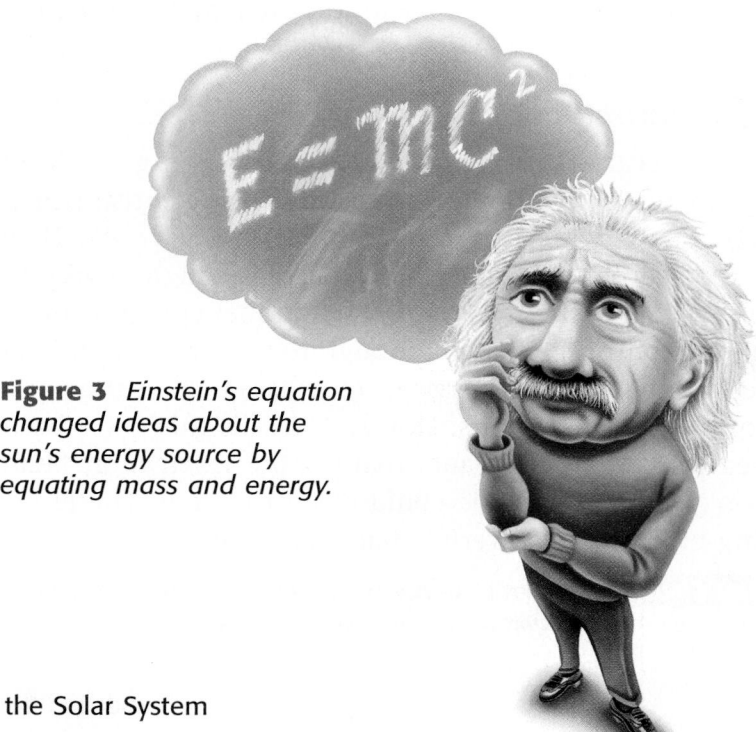

Figure 3 *Einstein's equation changed ideas about the sun's energy source by equating mass and energy.*

Fusion in the Sun

During fusion, under normal conditions, the nuclei of hydrogen atoms never get close enough to combine. The reason is that they are positively charged. Like charges repel each other, as shown in **Figure 4.** In the center of the sun, however, the temperature and pressure are very high. As a result, the hydrogen nuclei have enough energy to overcome the repulsive force, and hydrogen fuses into helium, as shown in **Figure 5.**

The energy produced in the center, or core of the sun takes millions of years to reach the sun's surface. The energy passes from the core through a very dense region called the *radiative zone*. The matter in the radiative zone is so crowded that the light and energy are blocked and sent in different directions. Eventually, the energy reaches the *convective zone*. Gases circulate in the convective zone, which is about 200,000 km thick. Hot gases in the convective zone carry the energy up to the *photosphere,* the visible surface of the sun. From there, the energy leaves the sun as light, which takes only 8.3 min to reach Earth.

Figure 4 *Like charges repel just as similar poles on a pair of magnets do.*

✓ Reading Check What causes the nuclei of hydrogen atoms to repel each other?

Figure 5 **Fusion of Hydrogen in the Sun**

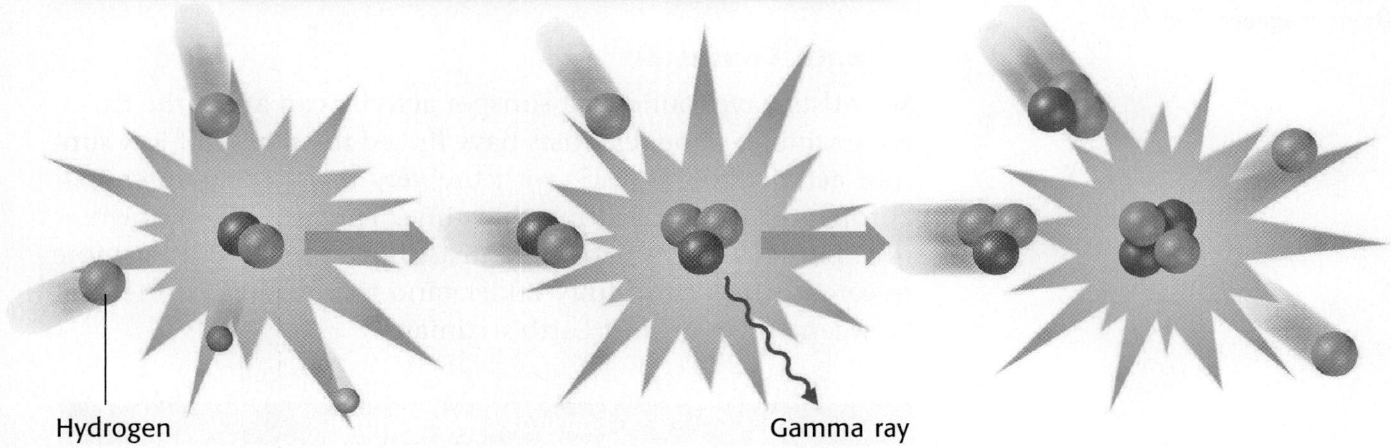

Hydrogen

Gamma ray

❶ **Deuterium** Two hydrogen nuclei (protons) collide. One proton emits particles and energy and then becomes a neutron. The proton and neutron combine to produce a heavy form of hydrogen called *deuterium*.

❷ **Helium-3** Deuterium combines with another hydrogen nucleus to form a variety of helium called *helium-3*. More energy, as well as gamma rays, is released.

❸ **Helium-4** Two helium-3 atoms then combine to form ordinary helium-4, which releases more energy and a pair of hydrogen nuclei.

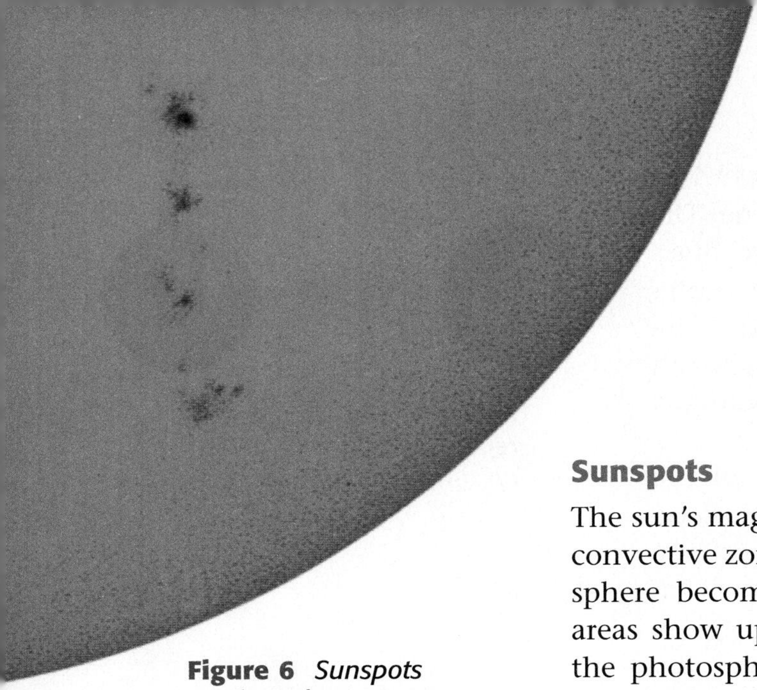

Solar Activity

The photosphere is an ever-changing place. Thermal energy moves from the sun's interior by the circulation of gases in the convective zone. This movement of energy causes the gas in the photosphere to boil and churn. This circulation, combined with the sun's rotation, creates magnetic fields that reach far out into space.

Sunspots

The sun's magnetic fields tend to slow down the activity in the convective zone. When activity slows down, areas of the photosphere become cooler than surrounding areas. These cooler areas show up as sunspots. **Sunspots** are cooler, dark spots of the photosphere of the sun, as shown in **Figure 6.** Sunspots can vary in shape and size. Some sunspots can be as large as 50,000 miles in diameter.

The numbers and locations of sunspots on the sun change in a regular cycle. Scientists have found that the sunspot cycle lasts about 11 years. Every 11 years, the amount of sunspot activity in the sun reaches a peak intensity and then decreases. **Figure 7** shows the sunspot cycle since 1610, excluding the years 1645–1715, which was a period of unusually low sunspot activity.

✔ **Reading Check** What are sunspots? What causes sunspots to occur?

Climate Confusion

Scientists have found that sunspot activity can affect the Earth. For example, some scientists have linked the period of low sunspot activity, 1645–1715, with the very low temperatures that Europe experienced during that time. This period is known as the "Little Ice Age." Most scientists, however, think that more research is needed to fully understand the possible connection between sunspots and Earth's climate.

Figure 6 *Sunspots mark cooler areas on the sun's surface. They are related to changes in the magnetic properties of the sun.*

sunspot a dark area of the photosphere of the sun that is cooler than the surrounding areas and that has a strong magnetic field

Figure 7 *This graph shows the number of sunspots that have occurred each year since Galileo's first observation in 1610.*

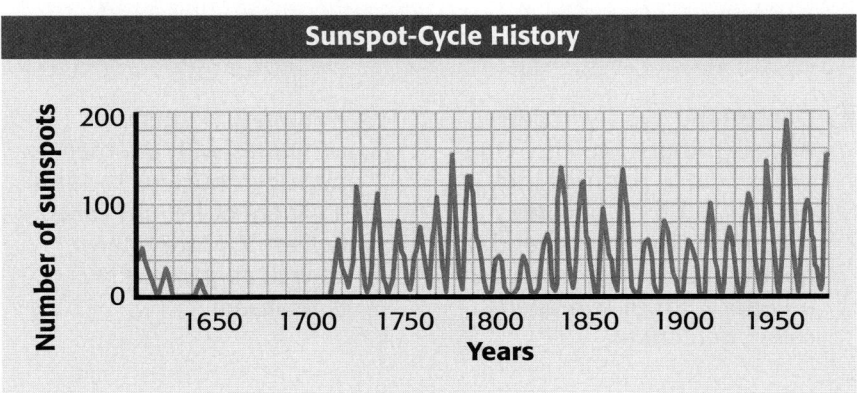

Solar Flares

The magnetic fields that cause sunspots also cause solar flares. *Solar flares,* as shown in **Figure 8,** are regions of extremely high temperature and brightness that develop on the sun's surface. When a solar flare erupts, it sends huge streams of electrically charged particles into the solar system. Solar flares can extend upward several thousand kilometers within minutes. Solar flares are usually associated with sunspots and can interrupt radio communications on Earth and in orbit. Scientists are trying to find ways to give advance warning of solar flares.

Figure 8 *Solar flares are giant eruptions on the sun's surface.*

SECTION Review

Summary

- The sun is a large ball of gas made mostly of hydrogen and helium. The sun consists of many layers.

- The sun's energy comes from nuclear fusion that takes place in the center of the sun.

- The visible surface of the sun, or the photosphere, is very active.

- Sunspots and solar flares are the result of the sun's magnetic fields that reach space.

- Sunspot activity may affect Earth's climate, and solar flares can interact with Earth's atmosphere.

Using Key Terms

1. In your own words, write a definition for each of the following terms: *sunspot* and *nuclear fusion.*

Understanding Key Ideas

2. Which of the following statements describes how energy is produced in the sun?
   a. The sun burns fuels to generate energy.
   b. As hydrogen changes into helium deep inside the sun, a great deal of energy is made.
   c. Energy is released as the sun shrinks because of gravity.
   d. None of the above

3. Describe the composition of the sun.

4. Name and describe the layers of the sun.

5. In which area of the sun do sunspots appear?

6. Explain how sunspots form.

7. Describe how sunspots can affect the Earth.

8. What are solar flares, and how do they form?

Math Skills

9. If the equatorial diameter of the sun is 1.39 million kilometers, how many kilometers is the sun's radius?

Critical Thinking

10. **Applying Concepts** If nuclear fusion in the sun's core suddenly stopped today, would the sky be dark in the daytime tomorrow? Explain.

11. **Making Comparisons** Compare the theories that scientists proposed about the source of the sun's energy with the process of nuclear fusion in the sun.

SCILINKS. **NSTA**
Developed and maintained by the
National Science Teachers Association

For a variety of links related to this chapter, go to www.scilinks.org

Topic: The Sun
SciLinks code: HSM1477

The Earth Takes Shape

In many ways, Earth seems to be a perfect place for life.

We live on the third planet from the sun. The Earth, shown in **Figure 1,** is mostly made of rock, and nearly three-fourths of its surface is covered with water. It is surrounded by a protective atmosphere of mostly nitrogen and oxygen and smaller amounts of other gases. But Earth has not always been such an oasis in the solar system.

Formation of the Solid Earth

The Earth formed as planetesimals in the solar system collided and combined. From what scientists can tell, the Earth formed within the first 10 million years of the collapse of the solar nebula!

The Effects of Gravity

When a young planet is still small, it can have an irregular shape, somewhat like a potato. But as the planet gains more matter, the force of gravity increases. When a rocky planet, such as Earth, reaches a diameter of about 350 km, the force of gravity becomes greater than the strength of the rock. As the Earth grew to this size, the rock at its center was crushed by gravity and the planet started to become round.

The Effects of Heat

As the Earth was changing shape, it was also heating up. Planetesimals continued to collide with the Earth, and the energy of their motion heated the planet. Radioactive material, which was present in the Earth as it formed, also heated the young planet. After Earth reached a certain size, the temperature rose faster than the interior could cool, and the rocky material inside began to melt. Today, the Earth is still cooling from the energy that was generated when it formed. Volcanoes, earthquakes, and hot springs are effects of this energy trapped inside the Earth. As you will learn later, the effects of heat and gravity also helped form the Earth's layers when the Earth was very young.

✓ Reading Check What factors heated the Earth during its early formation? (*See the Appendix for answers to Reading Checks.*)

Figure 1 *When Earth is seen from space, one of its unique features—the presence of water—is apparent.*

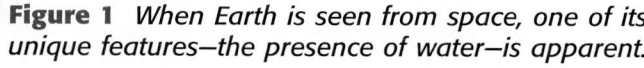

How the Earth's Layers Formed

Have you ever watched the oil separate from vinegar in a bottle of salad dressing? The vinegar sinks because it is denser than oil. The Earth's layers formed in much the same way. As rocks melted, denser materials, such as nickel and iron, sank to the center of the Earth and formed the core. Less dense materials floated to the surface and became the crust. This process is shown in **Figure 2.**

The **crust** is the thin, outermost layer of the Earth. It is 5 to 100 km thick. Crustal rock is made of materials that have low densities, such as oxygen, silicon, and aluminum. The **mantle** is the layer of Earth beneath the crust. It extends 2,900 km below the surface. Mantle rock is made of materials such as magnesium and iron and is denser than crustal rock. The **core** is the central part of the Earth below the mantle. It contains the densest materials (nickel and iron) and extends to the center of the Earth—almost 6,400 km below the surface.

crust the thin and solid outermost layer of the Earth above the mantle

mantle the layer of rock between the Earth's crust and core

core the central part of the Earth below the mantle

Figure 2 The Formation of Earth's Layers

❶ All materials in the early Earth are randomly mixed.

❷ Rocks melt, and denser materials sink toward the center. Less dense elements rise and form layers.

❸ According to composition, the Earth is divided into three layers: the crust, the mantle, and the core.

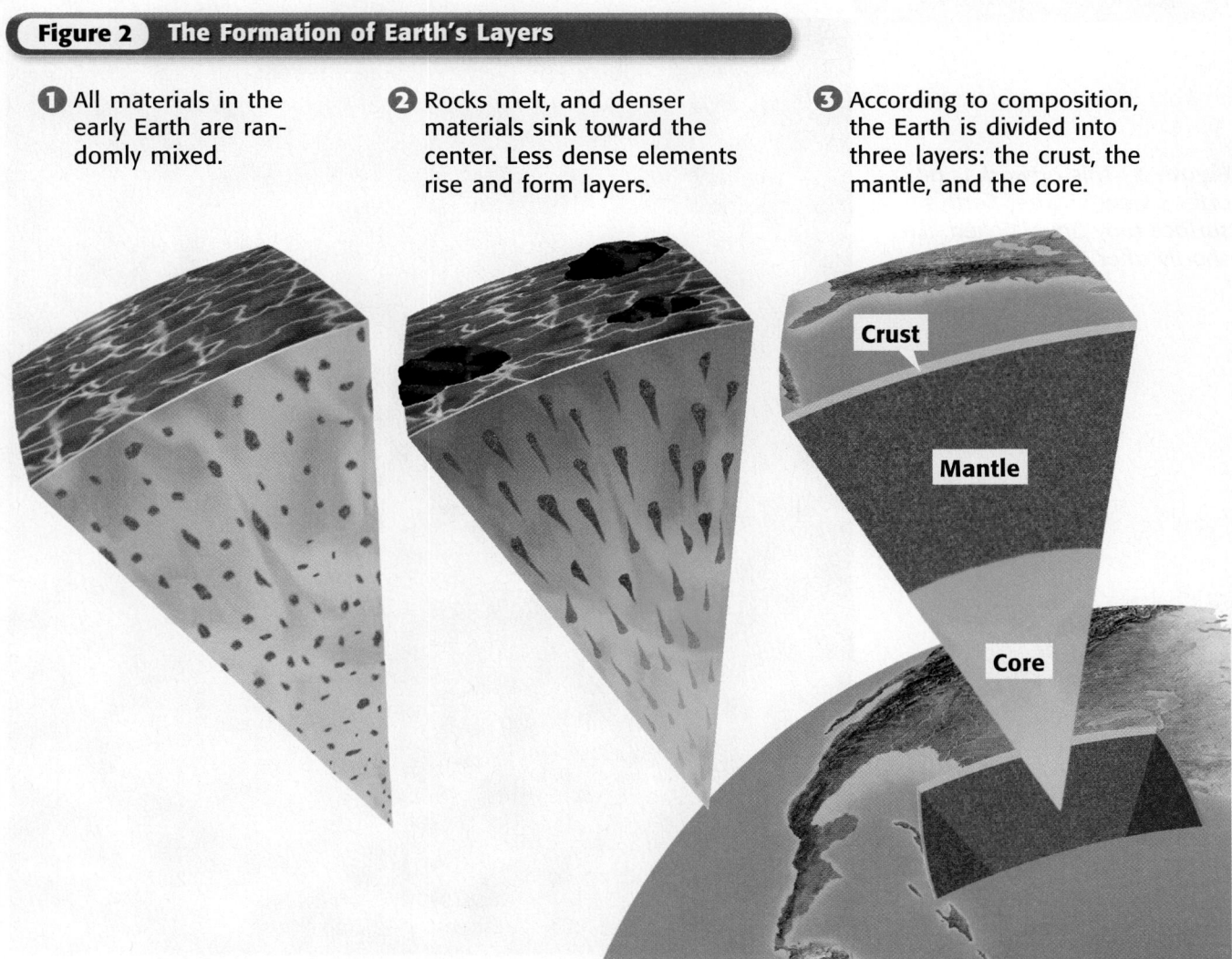

Crust

Mantle

Core

Formation of the Earth's Atmosphere

Today, Earth's atmosphere is 78% nitrogen, 21% oxygen, and about 1% argon. (There are tiny amounts of many other gases.) Did you know that the Earth's atmosphere did not always contain the oxygen that you need to live? The Earth's atmosphere is constantly changing. Scientists think that the Earth's earliest atmosphere was very different than it is today.

Earth's Early Atmosphere

Scientists think that Earth's early atmosphere was a mixture of gases that were released as Earth cooled. During the final stages of the Earth's formation, its surface was very hot—even molten in places—as shown in **Figure 3.** The molten rock released large amounts of carbon dioxide and water vapor. Therefore, scientists think that Earth's early atmosphere was a steamy mixture of carbon dioxide and water vapor.

✔ **Reading Check** Describe Earth's early atmosphere.

**CONNECTION TO
Environmental Science**

WRITING SKILL **The Greenhouse Effect** Carbon dioxide is a greenhouse gas. Greenhouse gases are gases that absorb thermal energy and radiate it back to Earth. This process is called the greenhouse effect because the gases function like the walls and roof of a greenhouse, which allow solar energy to enter but prevent thermal energy from escaping. Do research to find the percentage of carbon dioxide that is thought to make up Earth's early atmosphere. Write a report, and share your findings with your class.

Figure 3 *This artwork is an artist's view of what Earth's surface may have looked like shortly after the Earth formed.*

Figure 4 *As this volcano in Hawaii shows, a large amount of gas is released during an eruption.*

Earth's Changing Atmosphere

As the Earth cooled and its layers formed, the Earth's atmosphere changed again. This atmosphere probably formed from volcanic gases. Volcanoes, such as the one in **Figure 4,** released chlorine, nitrogen, and sulfur in addition to large amounts of carbon dioxide and water vapor. Some of this water vapor may have condensed to form the Earth's first oceans.

Comets, which are planetesimals made of ice, also may have contributed to this change of Earth's atmosphere. As comets crashed into the Earth, they brought in a range of elements, such as carbon, hydrogen, oxygen, and nitrogen. Comets also may have brought some of the water that helped form the oceans.

The Role of Life

How did this change of Earth's atmosphere become the air you are breathing right now? The answer is related to the appearance of life on Earth.

Ultraviolet Radiation

Scientists think that ultraviolet (UV) radiation, the same radiation that causes sunburns, helped produce the conditions necessary for life. Because UV light has a lot of energy, it can break apart molecules in your skin and in the air. Today, we are shielded from most of the sun's UV rays by Earth's protective ozone layer. But Earth's early atmosphere probably did not have ozone, so many molecules in the air and at Earth's surface were broken apart. Over time, this material collected in the Earth's waters. Water offered protection from the effects of UV radiation. In these sheltered pools of water, chemicals may have combined to form the complex molecules that made life possible. The first life-forms were very simple and did not need oxygen to live.

Comets and Meteors
What is the difference between a comet and a meteor? With a parent, research the difference between comets and meteors. Then, find out if you can view meteor showers in your area!

The Source of Oxygen

Sometime before 3.4 billion years ago, organisms that produced food by photosynthesis appeared. *Photosynthesis* is the process of absorbing energy from the sun and carbon dioxide from the atmosphere to make food. During the process of making food, these organisms released oxygen—a gas that was not abundant in the atmosphere at that time. Scientists think that the descendants of these early life-forms are still around today, as shown in **Figure 5.**

Photosynthetic organisms played a major role in changing Earth's atmosphere to become the mixture of gases you breathe today. Over the next hundreds of millions of years, more and more oxygen was added to the atmosphere. At the same time, carbon dioxide was removed. As oxygen levels increased, some of the oxygen formed a layer of ozone in the upper atmosphere. This ozone blocked most of the UV radiation and made it possible for life, in the form of simple plants, to move onto land about 2.2 billion years ago.

Reading Check How did photosynthesis contribute to Earth's current atmosphere?

Formation of Oceans and Continents

Scientists think that the oceans probably formed during Earth's second atmosphere, when the Earth was cool enough for rain to fall and remain on the surface. After millions of years of rainfall, water began to cover the Earth. By 4 billion years ago, a global ocean covered the planet.

For the first few hundred million years of Earth's history, there may not have been any continents. Given the composition of the rocks that make up the continents, scientists know that these rocks have melted and cooled many times in the past. Each time the rocks melted, the heavier elements sank and the lighter ones rose to the surface.

Figure 5 *Stromatolites, mats of fossilized algae (left), are among the earliest evidence of life. Blue-green algae (right) living today are thought to be similar to the first life-forms on Earth.*

The Growth of Continents

After a while, some of the rocks were light enough to pile up on the surface. These rocks were the beginning of the earliest continents. The continents gradually thickened and slowly rose above the surface of the ocean. These scattered young continents did not stay in the same place, however. The slow transfer of thermal energy in the mantle pushed them around. Approximately 2.5 billion years ago, continents really started to grow. And by 1.5 billion years ago, the upper mantle had cooled and had become denser and heavier. At this time, it was easier for the cooler parts of the mantle to sink. These conditions made it easier for the continents to move in the same way that they do today.

INTERNET ACTIVITY

For another activity related to this chapter, go to **go.hrw.com** and type in the keyword **HZ5SOLW**.

SECTION Review

Summary

- The effects of gravity and heat created the shape and structure of Earth.
- The Earth is divided into three main layers based on composition: the crust, mantle, and core.
- The presence of life dramatically changed Earth's atmosphere by adding free oxygen.
- Earth's oceans formed shortly after the Earth did, when it had cooled off enough for rain to fall. Continents formed when lighter materials gathered on the surface and rose above sea level.

Using Key Terms

1. Use each of the following terms in a separate sentence: *crust*, *mantle*, and *core*.

Understanding Key Ideas

2. Earth's first atmosphere was mostly made of
   a. nitrogen and oxygen.
   b. chlorine, nitrogen, and sulfur.
   c. carbon dioxide and water vapor.
   d. water vapor and oxygen.

3. Describe the structure of the Earth.

4. Why did the Earth separate into distinct layers?

5. Describe the development of Earth's atmosphere. How did life affect Earth's atmosphere?

6. Explain how Earth's oceans and continents formed.

Critical Thinking

7. **Applying Concepts** How did the effects of gravity help shape the Earth?

8. **Making Inferences** How would the removal of forests affect the Earth's atmosphere?

Interpreting Graphics

Use the illustration below to answer the questions that follow.

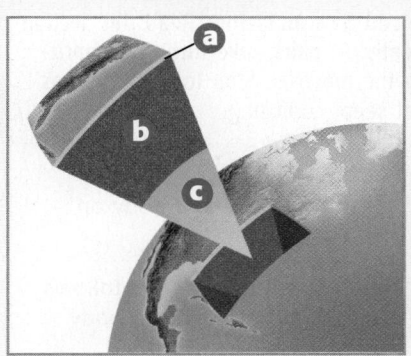

9. Which of the layers is composed mostly of the elements magnesium and iron?

10. Which of the layers is composed mostly of the elements iron and nickel?

SCILINKS

NSTA
Developed and maintained by the National Science Teachers Association

For a variety of links related to this chapter, go to www.scilinks.org

Topic: The Layers of the Earth; The Oceans
SciLinks code: HSM0862; HSM1069

Planetary Motion

Why do the planets revolve around the sun? Why don't they fly off into space? Does something hold them in their paths?

To answer these questions, you need to go back in time to look at the discoveries made by the scientists of the 1500s and 1600s. Danish astronomer Tycho Brahe (TIE koh BRAH uh) carefully observed the positions of planets for more than 25 years. When Brahe died in 1601, a German astronomer named Johannes Kepler (yoh HAHN uhs KEP luhr) continued Brahe's work. Kepler set out to understand the motions of planets and to describe the solar system.

A Revolution in Astronomy

Each planet spins on its axis. The spinning of a body, such as a planet, on its axis is called **rotation.** As the Earth rotates, only one-half of the Earth faces the sun. The half facing the sun is light (day). The half that faces away from the sun is dark (night).

The path that a body follows as it travels around another body in space is called the **orbit.** One complete trip along an orbit is called a **revolution.** The amount of time a planet takes to complete a single trip around the sun is called a *period of revolution.* Each planet takes a different amount of time to circle the sun. Earth's period of revolution is about 365.25 days (a year), but Mercury orbits the sun in only 88 days. **Figure 1** illustrates the orbit and revolution of the Earth around the sun as well as the rotation of the Earth on its axis.

Figure 1 *A planet rotates on its own axis and revolves around the sun in a path called an* orbit.

rotation the spin of a body on its axis

orbit the path that a body follows as it travels around another body in space

revolution the motion of a body that travels around another body in space; one complete trip along an orbit

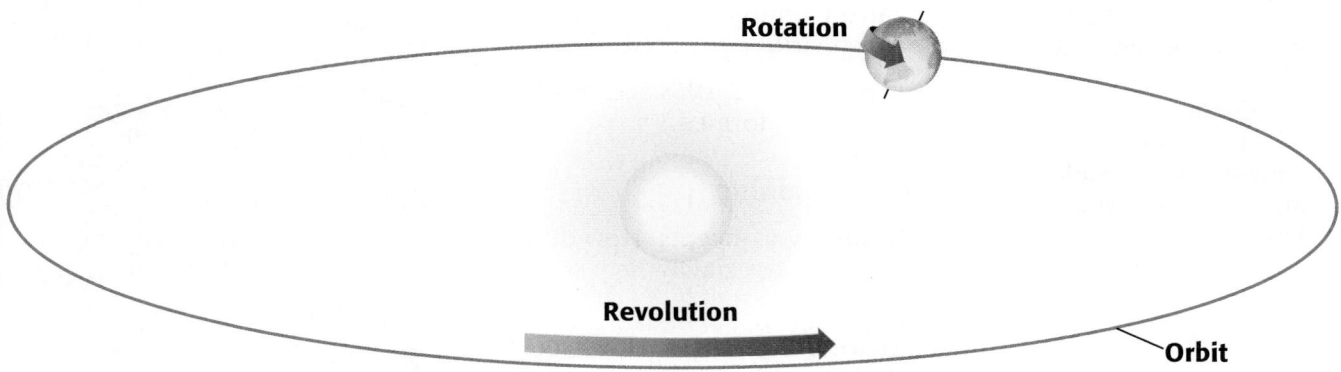

Figure 2 Parts of an Ellipse

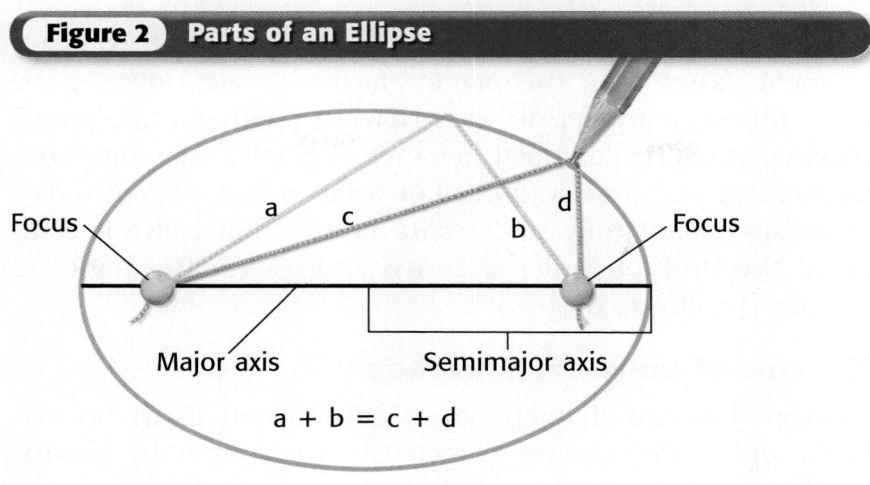

Focus

Major axis

Semimajor axis

Focus

a

c

b

d

$$a + b = c + d$$

Kepler's First Law of Motion

Kepler's first discovery came from his careful study of Mars. Kepler discovered that Mars did not move in a circle around the sun but moved in an elongated circle called an *ellipse*. This finding became Kepler's first law of motion. An ellipse is a closed curve in which the sum of the distances from the edge of the curve to two points inside the ellipse is always the same, as shown in **Figure 2.** An ellipse's maximum length is called its *major axis*. Half of this distance is the *semimajor axis*, which is usually used to describe the size of an ellipse. The semimajor axis of Earth's orbit—the maximum distance between Earth and the sun—is about 150 million kilometers.

Kepler's Second Law of Motion

Kepler's second discovery, or second law of motion, was that the planets seemed to move faster when they are close to the sun and slower when they are farther away. To understand this idea, imagine that a planet is attached to the sun by a string, as modeled in **Figure 3.** When the string is shorter, the planet must move faster to cover the same area.

Kepler's Third Law of Motion

Kepler noticed that planets that are more distant from the sun, such as Saturn, take longer to orbit the sun. This finding was Kepler's third law of motion, which explains the relationship between the period of a planet's revolution and its semimajor axis. Knowing how long a planet takes to orbit the sun, Kepler was able to calculate the planet's distance from the sun.

✓ **Reading Check** Describe Kepler's third law of motion. (*See the Appendix for answers to Reading Checks.*)

MATH PRACTICE

Kepler's Formula

Kepler's third law can be expressed with the formula

$$P^2 = a^3$$

where P is the period of revolution and a is the semimajor axis of an orbiting body. For example, Mars's period is 1.88 years, and its semimajor axis is 1.523 AU. Thus, $1.88^2 = 1.523^3 = 3.53$. Calculate a planet's period of revolution if the semimajor axis is 5.74 AU.

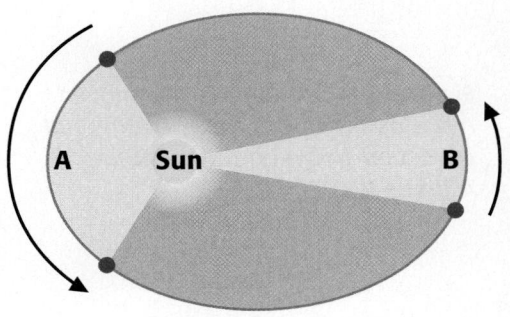

Figure 3 *According to Kepler's second law, to keep the area of* A *equal to the area of* B, *the planet must move faster in its orbit when it is closer to the sun.*

Newton to the Rescue!

Kepler wondered what caused the planets closest to the sun to move faster than the planets farther away. However, he never found an answer. Sir Isaac Newton finally put the puzzle together when he described the force of gravity. Newton didn't understand why gravity worked or what caused it. Even today, scientists do not fully understand gravity. But Newton combined the work of earlier scientists and used mathematics to explain the effects of gravity.

The Law of Universal Gravitation

Newton reasoned that an object falls toward Earth because Earth and the object are attracted to each other by gravity. He discovered that this attraction depends on the masses of the objects and the distance between the objects.

Newton's *law of universal gravitation* states that the force of gravity depends on the product of the masses of the objects divided by the square of the distance between the objects. The larger the masses of two objects and the closer together the objects are, the greater the force of gravity between the objects. For example, if two objects are moved twice as far apart, the gravitational attraction between them will decrease by 2×2 (a factor of 4), as shown in **Figure 4.** If two objects are moved 10 times as far apart, the gravitational attraction between them will decrease by 10×10 (a factor of 100).

Both Earth and the moon are attracted to each other. Although it may seem as if Earth does not orbit the moon, Earth and the moon actually orbit each other.

✓ Reading Check Explain Newton's law of universal gravitation.

Staying in Focus

1. Take a **short piece of string,** and pin both ends to a **piece of paper** by using **two thumbtacks.**

2. Keeping the string stretched tight at all times, use a **pencil** to trace the path of an ellipse.

3. Change the distance between the thumbtacks to change the shape of the ellipse.

4. How does the position of the thumbtacks (foci) affect the ellipse?

Figure 4 *If two objects are moved twice as far apart, the gravitational attraction between them will be 4 times less.*

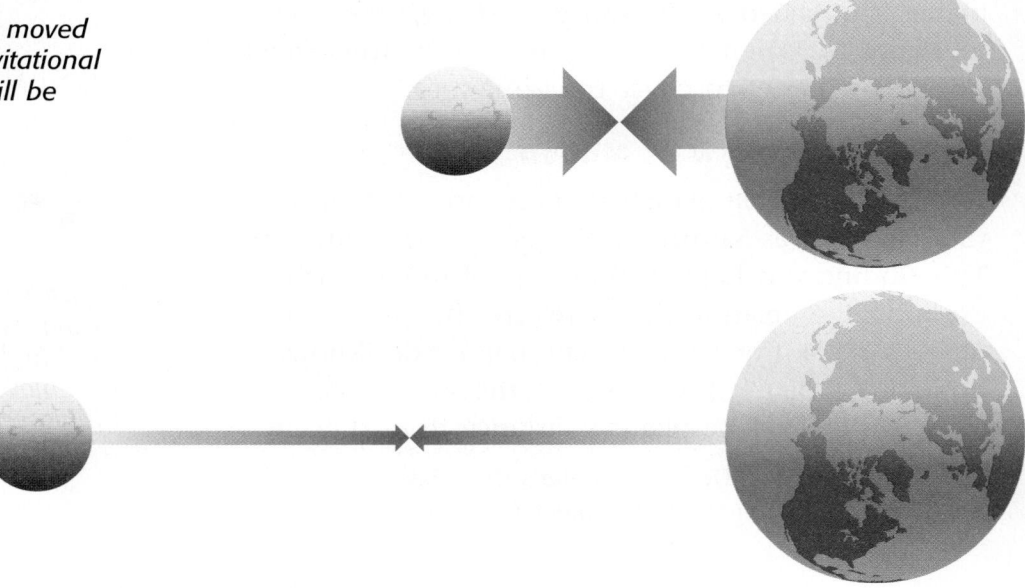

Orbits Falling Down and Around

If you drop a rock, it falls to the ground. So, why doesn't the moon come crashing into the Earth? The answer has to do with the moon's inertia. *Inertia* is an object's resistance in speed or direction until an outside force acts on the object. In space, there isn't any air to cause resistance and slow down the moving moon. Therefore, the moon continues to move, but gravity keeps the moon in orbit, as **Figure 5** shows.

Imagine twirling a ball on the end of a string. As long as you hold the string, the ball will orbit your hand. As soon as you let go of the string, the ball will fly off in a straight path. This same principle applies to the moon. Gravity keeps the moon from flying off in a straight path. This principle holds true for all bodies in orbit, including the Earth and other planets in our solar system.

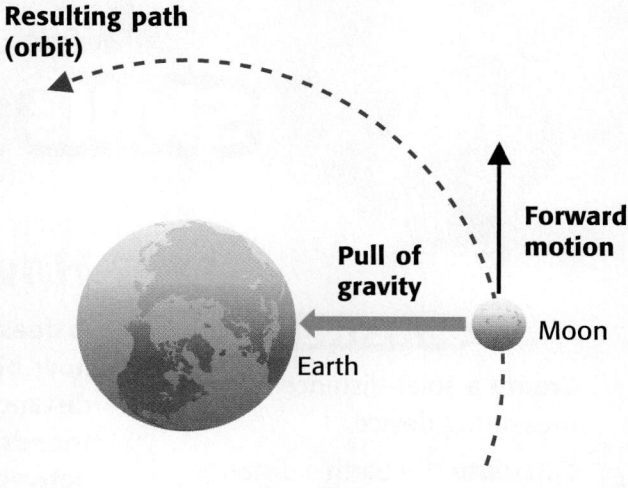

Figure 5 *Gravity causes the moon to fall toward the Earth and changes a straight-line path into a curved orbit.*

SECTION Review

Summary

- Rotation is the spinning of a planet on its axis, and revolution is one complete trip along an orbit.

- Planets move in an ellipse around the sun. The closer they are to the sun, the faster they move. The period of a planet's revolution depends on the planet's semimajor axis.

- Gravitational attraction decreases as distance increases and as mass decreases.

Using Key Terms

1. In your own words, write a definition for each of the following terms: *revolution* and *rotation*.

Understanding Key Ideas

2. Kepler discovered that planets move faster when they
   a. are farther from the sun.
   b. are closer to the sun.
   c. have more mass.
   d. rotate faster.

3. On what properties does the force of gravity between two objects depend?

4. How does gravity keep a planet moving in an orbit around the sun?

Math Skills

5. The Earth's period of revolution is 365.25 days. Convert this period of revolution into hours.

Critical Thinking

6. **Applying Concepts** If a planet had two moons and one moon was twice as far from the planet as the other, which moon would complete a revolution of the planet first? Explain your answer.

7. **Making Comparisons** Describe the three laws of planetary motion. How is each law related to the other laws?

SCiLINKS®

NSTA
Developed and maintained by the
National Science Teachers Association

For a variety of links related to this chapter, go to www.scilinks.org

Topic: Kepler's Laws
SciLinks code: HSM0216

Skills Practice Lab

OBJECTIVES

Create a solar-distance measuring device.

Calculate the Earth's distance from the sun.

MATERIALS

- aluminum foil, 5 cm × 5 cm
- card, index
- meterstick
- poster board
- ruler, metric
- scissors
- tape, masking
- thumbtack

SAFETY

How Far Is the Sun?

It doesn't slice, it doesn't dice, but it can give you an idea of how big our universe is! You can build your very own solar-distance measuring device from household items. Amaze your friends by figuring out how many metersticks can be placed between the Earth and the sun.

Ask a Question

1 How many metersticks could I place between the Earth and the sun?

Form a Hypothesis

2 Write a hypothesis that answers the question above.

Test the Hypothesis

3 Measure and cut a 4 cm × 4 cm square from the middle of the poster board. Tape the foil square over the hole in the center of the poster board.

4 Using a thumbtack, carefully prick the foil to form a tiny hole in the center. Congratulations! You have just constructed your very own solar-distance measuring device!

5 Tape the device to a window facing the sun so that sunlight shines directly through the pinhole. **Caution:** Do not look directly into the sun.

6 Place one end of the meterstick against the window and beneath the foil square. Steady the meterstick with one hand.

7 With the other hand, hold the index card close to the pinhole. You should be able to see a circular image on the card. This image is an image of the sun.

8 Move the card back until the image is large enough to measure. Be sure to keep the image on the card sharply focused. Reposition the meterstick so that it touches the bottom of the card.

Analyze the Results

1 **Analyzing Results** According to your calculations, how far from the Earth is the sun? Don't forget to convert your measurements to meters.

Draw Conclusions

2 **Evaluating Data** You could put 150 billion metersticks between the Earth and the sun. Compare this information with your result in step 11. Do you think that this activity was a good way to measure the Earth's distance from the sun? Support your answer.

9 Ask your partner to measure the diameter of the image on the card by using the metric ruler. Record the diameter of the image in millimeters.

10 Record the distance between the window and the index card by reading the point at which the card rests on the meterstick.

11 Calculate the distance between Earth and the sun by using the following formula:

$$\text{distance between the sun and Earth} = \text{sun's diameter} \times \frac{\text{distance to the image}}{\text{image's diameter}}$$

1 cm = 10 mm
1 m = 100 cm
1 km = 1,000 m

(Hint: The sun's diameter is 1,392,000,000 m.)

Chapter Review

USING KEY TERMS

Complete each of the following sentences by choosing the correct term from the word bank.

nebula   crust

mantle   solar nebula

1 A ___ is a large cloud of gas and dust in interstellar space.

2 The ___ lies between the core and the crust of the Earth.

For each pair of terms, explain how the meanings of the terms differ.

3 *nebula* and *solar nebula*

4 *crust* and *mantle*

5 *rotation* and *revolution*

6 *nuclear fusion* and *sunspot*

UNDERSTANDING KEY IDEAS

Multiple Choice

7 To determine a planet's period of revolution, you must know its

a. size.

b. mass.

c. orbit.

d. All of the above

8 During Earth's formation, materials such as nickel and iron sank to the

a. mantle.

b. core.

c. crust.

d. All of the above

9 Planetary orbits are shaped like

a. orbits.

b. spirals.

c. ellipses.

d. periods of revolution.

10 Impacts in the early solar system

a. brought new materials to the planets.

b. released energy.

c. dug craters.

d. All of the above

11 Organisms that photosynthesize get their energy from

a. nitrogen.   c. the sun.

b. oxygen.   d. water.

12 Which of the following planets has the shortest period of revolution?

a. Pluto   c. Mercury

b. Earth   d. Jupiter

13 Which gas in Earth's atmosphere suggests that there is life on Earth?

a. hydrogen   c. carbon dioxide

b. oxygen   d. nitrogen

14 Which layer of the Earth has the lowest density?

a. the core

b. the mantle

c. the crust

d. None of the above

15 What is the measure of the average kinetic energy of particles in an object?

a. temperature   c. gravity

b. pressure   d. force

Short Answer

16 Compare a sunspot with a solar flare.

17 Describe how the Earth's oceans and continents formed.

18 Explain how pressure and gravity may have become unbalanced in the solar nebula.

19 Define *nuclear fusion* in your own words. Describe how nuclear fusion generates the sun's energy.

CRITICAL THINKING

20 **Concept Mapping** Use the following terms to create a concept map: *solar nebula, solar system, planetesimals, sun, photosphere, core, nuclear fusion, planets,* and *Earth*.

21 **Making Comparisons** How did Newton's law of universal gravitation help explain the work of Johannes Kepler?

22 **Predicting Consequences** Using what you know about the relationship between living things and the development of Earth's atmosphere, explain how the formation of ozone holes in Earth's atmosphere could affect living things.

23 **Identifying Relationships** Describe Kepler's three laws of motion in your own words. Describe how each law relates to either the revolution, rotation, or orbit of a planetary body.

INTERPRETING GRAPHICS

Use the illustration below to answer the questions that follow.

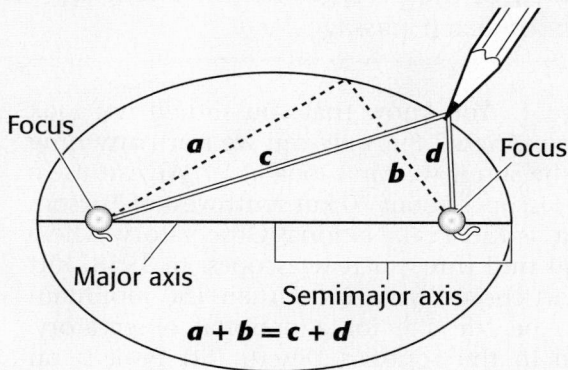

24 Which of Kepler's laws of motion does the illustration represent?

25 How does the equation shown above support the law?

26 What is an ellipse's maximum length called?

Standardized Test Preparation

Read each of the passages below. Then, answer the questions that follow each passage.

Passage 1 You know that you should not look at the sun, right? But how can we learn anything about the sun if we can't look at it? We can use a solar telescope! About 70 km southwest of Tucson, Arizona, is Kitt Peak National Observatory, where you will find three solar telescopes. In 1958, Kitt Peak was chosen from more than 150 mountain sites to be the site for a national observatory. Located in the Sonoran Desert, Kitt Peak is on land belonging to the Tohono O'odham Indian nation. On this site, the McMath-Pierce Facility houses the three largest solar telescopes in the world. Astronomers come from around the globe to use these telescopes. The largest of the three, the McMath-Pierce solar telescope, produces an image of the sun that is almost 1 m wide!

1. Which of the following is the largest telescope in the world?

A Kitt Peak

B Tohono O'odham

C McMath-Pierce

D Tucson

2. According to the passage, how can you learn about the sun?

F You can look at it.

G You can study it by using a solar telescope.

H You can go to Kitt Peak National Observatory.

I You can study to be an astronomer.

3. Which of the following is a fact in the passage?

A One hundred fifty mountain sites contain solar telescopes.

B Kitt Peak is the location of the smallest solar telescope in the world.

C In 1958, Tucson, Arizona, was chosen for a national observatory.

D Kitt Peak is the location of the largest solar telescope in the world.

Passage 2 Sunlight that has been focused can produce a great amount of thermal energy—enough to start a fire. Now, imagine focusing the sun's rays by using a magnifying glass that is 1.6 m in diameter. The resulting heat could melt metal. If a <u>conventional</u> telescope were pointed directly at the sun, it would melt. To avoid a meltdown, the McMath-Pierce solar telescope uses a mirror that produces a large image of the sun. This mirror directs the sun's rays down a diagonal shaft to another mirror, which is 50 m underground. This mirror is adjustable to focus the sunlight. The sunlight is then directed to a third mirror, which directs the light to an observing room and instrument shaft.

1. In this passage, what does the word *conventional* mean?

A special

B solar

C unusual

D ordinary

2. What can you infer from reading the passage?

F Focused sunlight can avoid a meltdown.

G Unfocused sunlight produces little energy.

H A magnifying glass can focus sunlight to produce a great amount of thermal energy.

I Mirrors increase the intensity of sunlight.

3. According to the passage, which of the following statements about solar telescopes is true?

A Solar telescopes make it safe for scientists to observe the sun.

B Solar telescopes don't need to use mirrors.

C Solar telescopes are built 50 m underground.

D Solar telescopes are 1.6 m in diameter.

The diagram below models the moon's orbit around the Earth. Use the diagram below to answer the questions that follow.

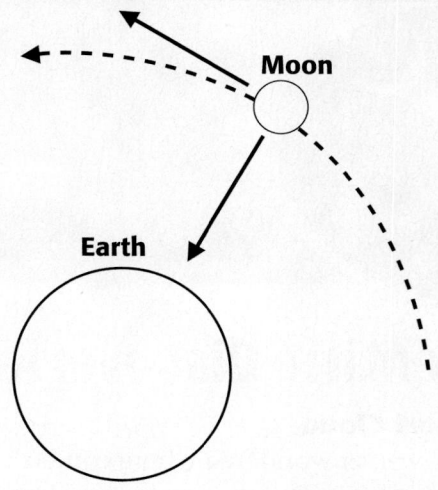

1. Which statement best describes the diagram?

   A Orbits are straight lines.

   B The force of gravity does not affect orbits.

   C Orbits result from a combination of gravitational attraction and inertia.

   D The moon moves in three different directions depending on its speed.

2. In which direction does gravity pull the moon?

   F toward the Earth

   G around the Earth

   H away from the Earth

   I toward and away from the Earth

3. If the moon stopped moving, what would happen?

   A It would fly off into space.

   B It would continue to orbit the Earth.

   C It would stay where it is in space.

   D It would move toward the Earth.

Read each question below, and choose the best answer.

1. An astronomer found 3 planetary systems in the nebula that she was studying. One system had 6 planets, another had 2 planets, and the third had 7 planets. What is the average number of planets in all 3 systems?

   A 3

   B 5

   C 8

   D 16

2. A newly discovered planet has a period of rotation of 270 Earth years. How many Earth days are in 270 Earth years?

   F 3,240

   G 8,100

   H 9,855

   I 98,550

3. A planet has seven rings. The first ring is 20,000 km from the center of the planet. Each ring is 50,000 km wide and 500 km apart. What is the total radius of the ring system from the planet's center?

   A 353,000 km

   B 373,000 km

   C 373,500 km

   D 370,000 km

4. If you bought a telescope for $87.75 and received a $10 bill, two $1 bills, and a quarter as change, how much money did you give the clerk?

   F $100

   G $99

   H $98

   I $90

Standardized Test Preparation

Science in Action

Science, Technology, and Society

Don't Look at the Sun!

How can we learn anything about the sun if we can't look at it? The answer is to use a special telescope called a *solar telescope*. The three largest solar telescopes in the world are located at Kitt Peak National Observatory near Tucson, Arizona. The largest of these telescopes, the McMath-Pierce solar telescope, creates an image of the sun that is almost 1 m wide! How is the image created? The McMath-Pierce solar telescope uses a mirror that is more than 2 m in diameter to direct the sun's rays down a diagonal shaft to another mirror, which is 152 m underground. This mirror is adjustable to focus the sunlight. The sunlight is then directed to a third mirror, which directs the light to an observing room and instrument shaft.

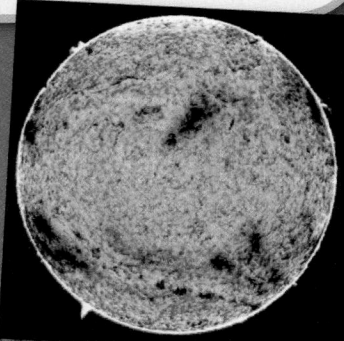

Scientific Discoveries

The Oort Cloud

Have you ever wondered where comets come from? In 1950, Dutch astronomer Jan Oort decided to find out where comets originated. Oort studied 19 comets. He found that none of these comets had orbits indicating that the comets had come from outside the solar system. Oort thought that all of the comets had come from an area at the far edge of the solar system. In addition, he believed that the comets had entered the planetary system from different directions. These conclusions led Oort to theorize that the area from which comets come surrounds the solar system like a sphere and that comets can come from any point within the sphere. Today, this spherical zone at the edge of the solar system is called the *Oort Cloud*. Astronomers believe that billions or even trillions of comets may exist within the Oort Cloud.

Math Activity

The outer skin of the McMath-Pierce solar telescope consists of 140 copper panels that measure 10.4 m × 2.4 m each. How many square meters of copper were used to construct the outer skin of the telescope?

Social Studies Activity

WRITING SKILL Before astronomers understood the nature of comets, comets were a source of much fear and misunderstanding among humans. Research some of the myths that humans have created about comets. Summarize your findings in a short essay.

Subrahmanyan Chandrasekhar

From White Dwarfs to Black Holes You may be familiar with the *Chandra X-Ray Observatory*. Launched by NASA in July 1999 to search for x-ray sources in space, the observatory is the most powerful x-ray telescope that has ever been built. However, you may not know how the observatory got its name. The *Chandra X-Ray Observatory* was named after the Indian American astrophysicist Subrahmanyan Chandrasekhar (SOOB ruh MAHN yuhn CHUHN druh SAY kuhr).

One of the most influential astrophysicists of the 20th century, Chandrasekhar was simply known as "Chandra" by his fellow scientists. Chandrasekhar made many contributions to physics and astrophysics. The contribution for which Chandrasekhar is best known was made in 1933, when he was a 23-year-old graduate student at Cambridge University in England. At the time, astrophysicists thought that all stars eventually became planet-sized stars known as *white dwarfs*. But from his calculations, Chandrasekhar believed that not all stars ended their lives as white dwarfs. He determined that the upper limit to the mass of a white dwarf was 1.4 times the mass of the sun. Stars that were more massive would collapse and would become very dense objects. These objects are now known as *black holes*. Chandrasekhar's ideas revolutionized astrophysics. In 1983, at the age of 73, Chandrasekhar was awarded the Nobel Prize in physics for his work on the evolution of stars.

Language Arts ACTIVITY

WRITING SKILL Using the Internet or another source, research the meaning of the word *chandra*. Write a paragraph describing your findings.

go.hrw.com

To learn more about these Science in Action topics, visit **go.hrw.com** and type in the keyword **HZ5SOLF.**

Current Science

Check out Current Science® articles related to this chapter by visiting go.hrw.com. Just type in the keyword **HZ5CS20.**

21

A Family of Planets

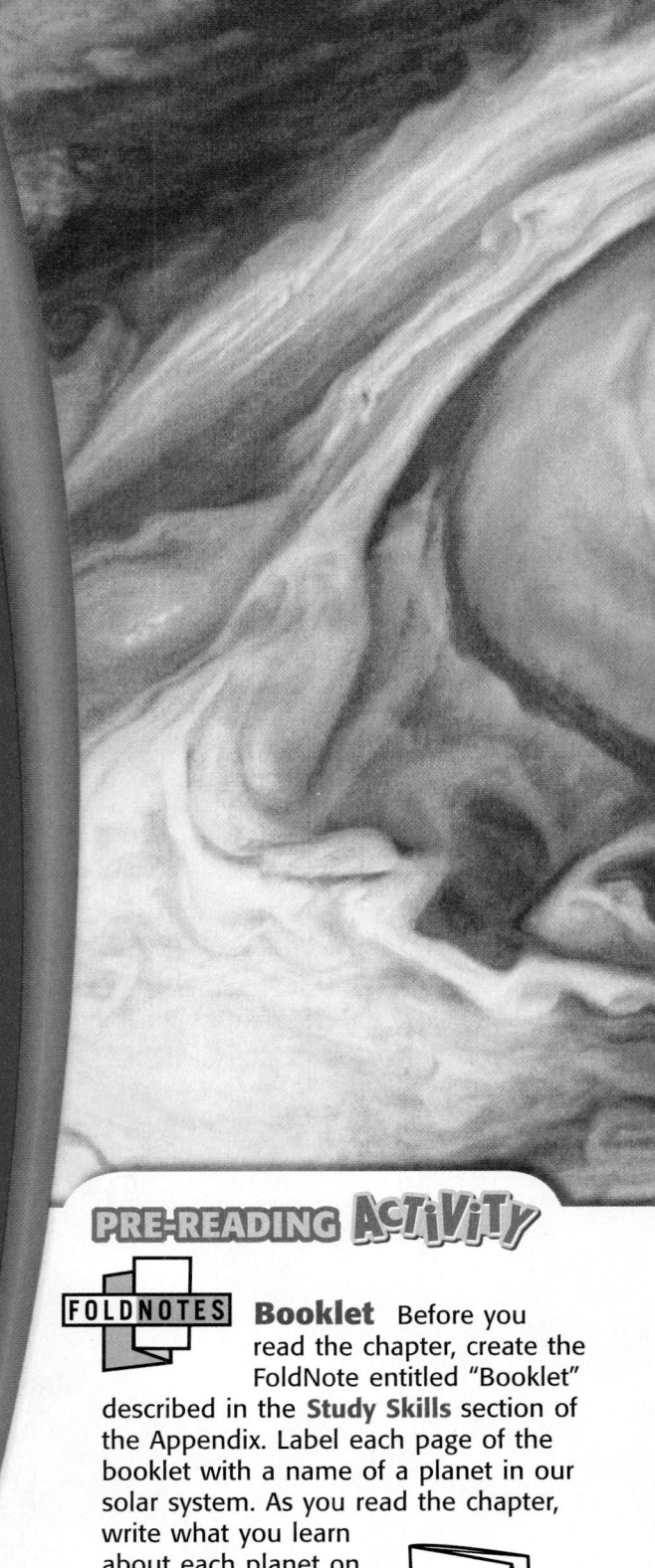

About the PHOTO

These rich swirls of color may remind you of a painting you might see in an art museum. But this photograph is of the planet Jupiter. The red swirl, called the Great Red Spot, is actually a hurricane-like storm system that is 3 times the diameter of Earth!

PRE-READING ACTIVITY

FOLDNOTES **Booklet** Before you read the chapter, create the FoldNote entitled "Booklet" described in the **Study Skills** section of the Appendix. Label each page of the booklet with a name of a planet in our solar system. As you read the chapter, write what you learn about each planet on the appropriate page of the booklet.

START-UP ACTIVITY

Measuring Space

Do the following activity to get a better idea of your solar neighborhood.

Procedure

1. Use a **meterstick** and some **chalk** to draw a line 2 m long on a **chalkboard.** Draw a large dot at one end of the line. This dot represents the sun.

2. Draw smaller dots on the line to represent the relative distances of each of the planets from the sun, based on information in the table.

Analysis

1. What do you notice about how the planets are spaced?

Planet	Distance from sun	
	Millions of km	**Scaled to cm**
Mercury	57.9	2
Venus	108.2	4
Earth	149.6	5
Mars	227.9	8
Jupiter	778.4	26
Saturn	1,424.0	48
Uranus	2,827.0	97
Neptune	4,499.0	151
Pluto	5,943.0	200

The Nine Planets

Did you know that planets, when viewed from Earth, look like stars to the naked eye? Ancient astronomers were intrigued by these "stars" which seemed to wander in the sky.

Ancient astronomers named these "stars" planets, which means "wanderers" in Greek. These astronomers knew planets were physical bodies and could predict their motions. But scientists did not begin to explore these worlds until the 17th century, when Galileo used the telescope to study planets and stars. Now, scientists have completed more than 150 successful missions to moons, planets, comets, and asteroids in our cosmic neighborhood.

READING WARM-UP

Objectives

- List the planets in the order in which they orbit the sun.
- Explain how scientists measure distances in space.
- Describe how the planets in our solar system were discovered.
- Describe three ways in which the inner planets and outer planets differ.

Terms to Learn

astronomical unit

READING STRATEGY

Paired Summarizing Read this section silently. In pairs, take turns summarizing the material. Stop to discuss ideas that seem confusing.

Our Solar System

Our *solar system,* shown in **Figure 1,** includes the sun, the planets, and many smaller objects. In some cases, these bodies may be organized into smaller systems of their own. For example, the Saturn system is made of the planet Saturn and the several moons that orbit Saturn. In this way, our solar system is a combination of many smaller systems.

Figure 1 *These images show the relative diameters of the planets and the sun.*

Mercury
4,879 km

Venus
12,104 km

Earth
12,756 km

Mars
6,794 km

Sun
1,392,000 km

Jupiter
142,984 km

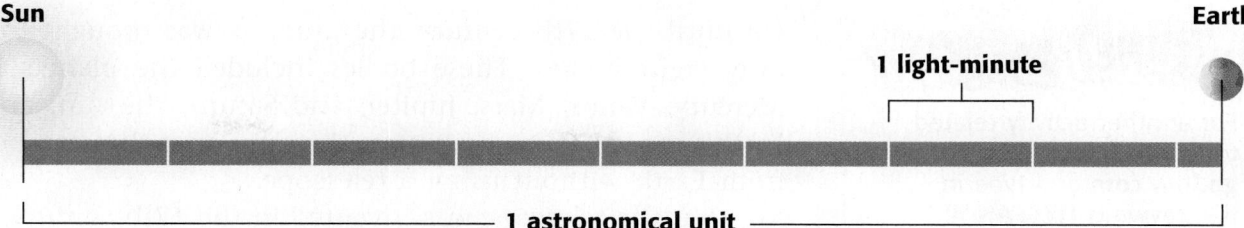

Sun · 1 light-minute · 1 astronomical unit · Earth

Figure 2 *One astronomical unit equals about 8.3 light-minutes.*

Measuring Interplanetary Distances

One way that scientists measure distances in space is by using the astronomical unit. One **astronomical unit** (AU) is the average distance between the sun and Earth, or approximately 150,000,000 km. Another way to measure distances in space is by using the speed of light. Light travels at about 300,000 km/s in space. This means that in 1 s, light travels 300,000 km.

In 1 min, light travels nearly 18,000,000 km. This distance is also called a *light-minute*. Look at **Figure 2.** Light from the sun takes 8.3 min to reach Earth. So, the distance from Earth to the sun, or 1 AU, is 8.3 light-minutes. Distances in the solar system can be measured in light-minutes and light-hours.

✔ Reading Check How far does light travel in 1 s? (*See the Appendix for answers to Reading Checks.*)

astronomical unit the average distance between the Earth and the sun; approximately 150 million kilometers (symbol, AU)

Saturn
120,536 km

Uranus
51,118 km

Neptune
49,528 km

Pluto
2,390 km

For another activity related to this chapter, go to **go.hrw.com** and type in the keyword **HZ5FAMW.**

The Discovery of the Solar System

Up until the 17th century, the universe was thought to have only eight bodies. These bodies included the planets Earth, Mercury, Venus, Mars, Jupiter, and Saturn, the sun, and the Earth's moon. These bodies are the only ones that can be seen from Earth without using a telescope.

After the telescope was invented in the 17th century, however, more discoveries were made. By the end of the 17th century, nine more large bodies were discovered. These bodies were moons of Jupiter and Saturn.

By the 18th century, the planet Uranus, along with two of its moons and two more of Saturn's moons, was discovered. In the 19th century, Neptune, as well as moons of several other planets, was discovered. Finally, in the 20th century, the ninth planet, Pluto, was discovered.

The Inner and Outer Solar Systems

The solar system is divided into two main parts: the inner solar system and the outer solar system. The inner solar system contains the four planets that are closest to the sun. The outer solar system contains the planets that are farthest from the sun.

The Inner Planets

The planets of the inner solar system, shown in **Figure 3,** are more closely spaced than the planets of the outer solar system. The inner planets are also known as the *terrestrial planets* because their surfaces are dense and rocky. However, each of the inner planets is unique.

Figure 3 *The inner planets are the planets that are closest to the sun.*

The Outer Planets

The planets of the outer solar system include Jupiter, Saturn, Uranus, Neptune, and Pluto. The outer planets are very different from the inner planets, as you will soon find out.

Unlike the inner planets, the outer planets, except for Pluto, are large and are composed mostly of gases. Because of this, Jupiter, Saturn, Uranus, and Neptune are known as gas giants. The atmospheres of these planets blend smoothly into the denser layers of their interiors. The icy planet Pluto is the only planet of the outer solar system that is small, dense, and rocky. You can see a diagram of the outer solar system in **Figure 4.**

✓ *Reading Check* **Which planets are in the outer solar system?**

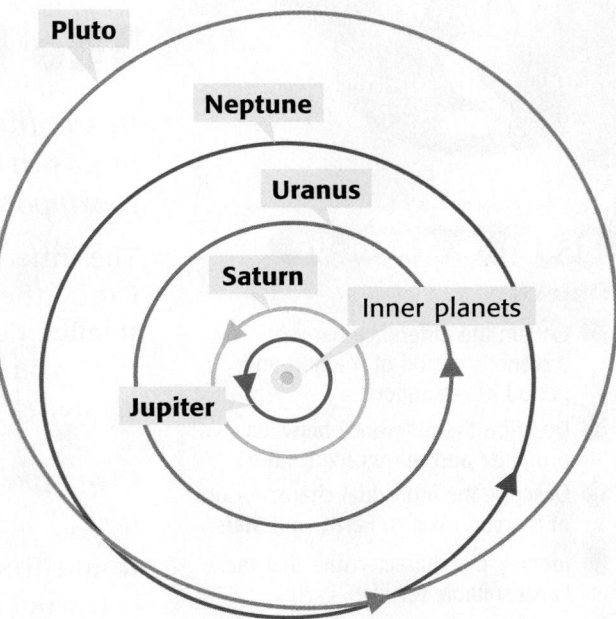

Figure 4 The planets of the outer solar system are the farthest from the sun.

SECTION Review

Summary

- In the order in which they orbit the sun, the nine planets are Mercury, Venus, Earth, Mars, Jupiter, Saturn, Uranus, Neptune, and Pluto.

- Two ways in which scientists measure distances in space are to use astronomical units and to use light-years.

- The inner planets are spaced more closely together, are smaller, and are rockier than the outer planets.

Using Key Terms

1. In your own words, write a definition for the term *astronomical unit*.

Understanding Key Ideas

2. When was the planet Uranus discovered?
   a. before the 17th century
   b. in the 18th century
   c. in the 19th century
   d. in the 20th century

3. The invention of what instrument helped early scientists discover more bodies in the solar system?

4. Which of the nine planets are included in the outer solar system?

5. Describe how the inner planets are different from the outer planets.

Math Skills

6. If Venus is 6.0 light-minutes from the sun, what is Venus's distance from the sun in astronomical units?

Critical Thinking

7. **Analyzing Methods** The distance between Earth and the sun is measured in light-minutes, but the distance between Pluto and the sun is measured in light-hours. Explain why.

SCiLINKS®

NSTA
Developed and maintained by the National Science Teachers Association

For a variety of links related to this chapter, go to www.scilinks.org

Topic: The Nine Planets
SciLinks code: HSM1033

SECTION 2

The Inner Planets

In the inner solar system, you will find one of the hottest places in our solar system as well as the only planet known to support life.

READING WARM-UP

Objectives

- Explain the difference between a planet's period of rotation and period of revolution.
- Describe the difference between prograde and retrograde rotation.
- Describe the individual characteristics of Mercury, Venus, Earth, and Mars.
- Identify the characteristics that make Earth suitable for life.

Terms to Learn

terrestrial planet
prograde rotation
retrograde rotation

READING STRATEGY

Reading Organizer As you read this section, create an outline of the section. Use the headings from the section in your outline.

terrestrial planet one of the highly dense planets nearest to the sun; Mercury, Venus, Mars, and Earth

The inner planets are also called **terrestrial planets** because, like Earth, they are very dense and rocky. The inner planets are smaller, denser, and rockier than the outer planets. In this section, you will learn more about the individual characteristics of Mercury, Venus, Earth, and Mars.

Mercury: Closest to the Sun

If you visited the planet Mercury, shown in **Figure 1,** you would find a very strange world. For one thing, on Mercury you would weigh only 38% of what you weigh on Earth. The weight you have on Earth is due to surface gravity, which is less on less massive planets. Also, because of Mercury's slow rotation, a day on Mercury is almost 59 Earth days long! The amount of time that an object takes to rotate once is called its *period of rotation.* So, Mercury's period of rotation is almost 59 Earth days long.

A Year on Mercury

Another curious thing about Mercury is that its year is only 88 Earth days long. As you know, a *year* is the time that a planet takes to go around the sun once. The motion of a body orbiting another body in space is called *revolution.* The time an object takes to revolve around the sun once is called its *period of revolution.* Every 88 Earth days, or 1.5 Mercurian days, Mercury revolves once around the sun.

Figure 1 *This image of Mercury was taken by the* Mariner 10 *spacecraft on March 24, 1974, from a distance of 5,380,000 km.*

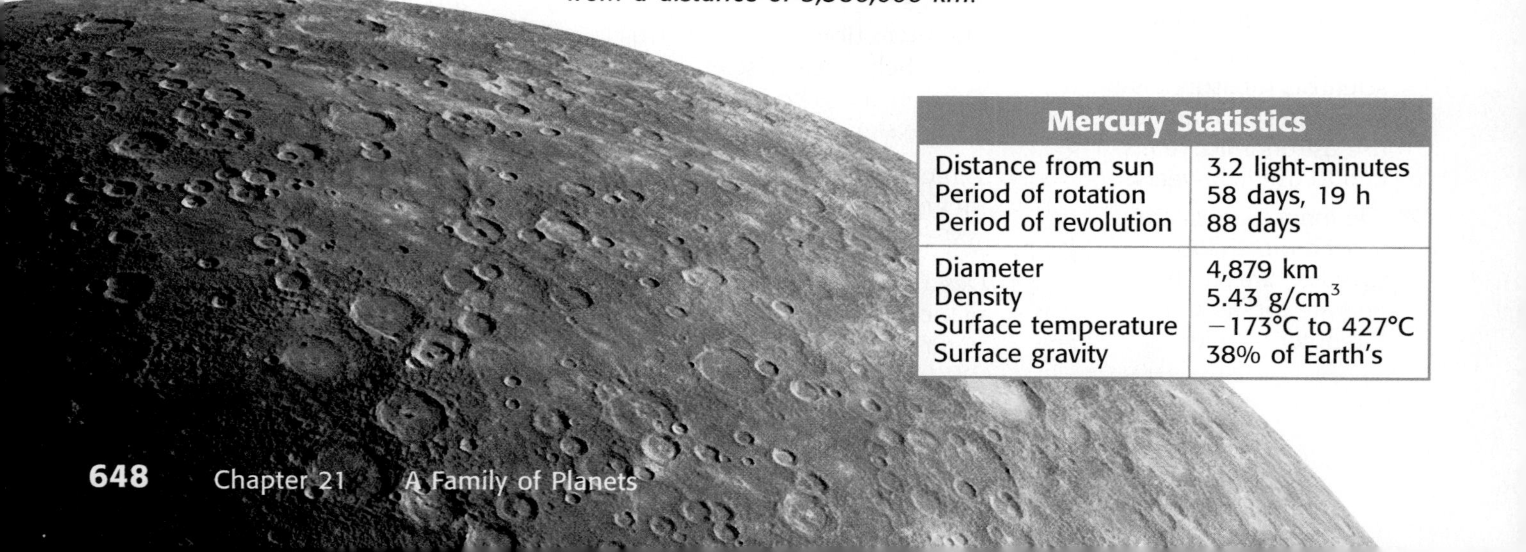

Mercury Statistics	
Distance from sun	3.2 light-minutes
Period of rotation	58 days, 19 h
Period of revolution	88 days
Diameter	4,879 km
Density	5.43 g/cm^3
Surface temperature	−173°C to 427°C
Surface gravity	38% of Earth's

Venus Statistics	
Distance from sun	6.0 light-minutes
Period of rotation	243 days, 16 h (R)*
Period of revolution	224 days, 17 h
Diameter	12,104 km
Density	5.24 g/cm³
Surface temperature	464°C
Surface gravity	91% of Earth's

*R = retrograde rotation

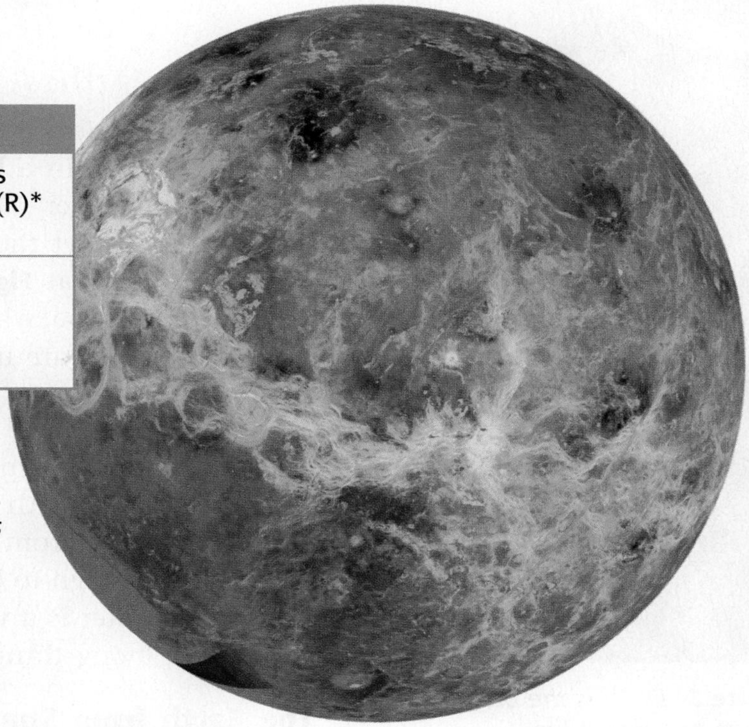

Figure 2 *This image of Venus was taken by Mariner 10 on February 5, 1974. The uppermost layer of clouds contains sulfuric acid.*

Venus: Earth's Twin?

Look at **Figure 2.** In many ways, Venus is more like Earth than any other planet. Venus is only slightly smaller, less massive, and less dense than Earth. But in other ways, Venus is very different from Earth. On Venus, the sun rises in the west and sets in the east. The reason is that Venus and Earth rotate in opposite directions. Earth is said to have **prograde rotation** because it appears to spin in a *counterclockwise* direction when it is viewed from above its North Pole. If a planet spins in a *clockwise* direction, the planet is said to have **retrograde rotation.**

The Atmosphere of Venus

Of the terrestrial planets, Venus has the densest atmosphere. Venus's atmosphere has 90 times the pressure of Earth's atmosphere! The air on Venus is mostly carbon dioxide, but the air is also made of some of the most destructive acids known. The carbon dioxide traps thermal energy from sunlight in a process called the *greenhouse effect*. The greenhouse effect causes Venus's surface temperature to be very high. At 464°C, Venus has the hottest surface of any planet in the solar system.

Mapping Venus's Surface

Between 1990 and 1992, the *Magellan* spacecraft mapped the surface of Venus by using radar waves. The radar waves traveled through the clouds and bounced off the planet's surface. Data gathered from the radar waves showed that Venus, like Earth, has volcanoes.

Reading Check What technology was used to map the surface of Venus? (*See the Appendix for answers to Reading Checks.*)

prograde rotation the counterclockwise spin of a planet or moon as seen from above the planet's North Pole; rotation in the same direction as the sun's rotation

retrograde rotation the clockwise spin of a planet or moon as seen from above the planet's North Pole

Figure 3 *Earth is the only planet known to support life.*

Earth: An Oasis in Space

As viewed from space, Earth is like a sparkling blue oasis in a black sea of stars. Constantly changing weather patterns create the swirls of clouds that blanket the blue and brown sphere we call home. Look at **Figure 3.** Why did Earth have such good fortune, while its two nearest neighbors, Venus and Mars, are unsuitable for life as we know it?

Water on Earth

Earth formed at just the right distance from the sun. Earth is warm enough to keep most of its water from freezing. But unlike Venus, Earth is cool enough to keep its water from boiling away. Liquid water is a vital part of the chemical processes that living things depend on for survival.

The Earth from Space

The picture of Earth shown in **Figure 4** was taken from space. You might think that the only goal of space exploration is to make discoveries beyond Earth. But the National Aeronautics and Space Administration (NASA) has a program to study Earth by using satellites in the same way that scientists study other planets. This program is called the Earth Science Enterprise. Its goal is to study the Earth as a global system that is made of smaller systems. These smaller systems include the atmosphere, land, ice, the oceans, and life. The program will also help us understand how humans affect the global environment. By studying Earth from space, scientists hope to understand how different parts of the global system interact.

Reading Check What is the Earth Science Enterprise?

Earth Statistics	
Distance from sun	8.3 light-minutes
Period of rotation	23 h, 56 min
Period of revolution	365 days, 6 h
Diameter	12,756 km
Density	5.52 g/cm³
Surface temperature	−13°C to 37°C
Surface gravity	100% of Earth's

Figure 4 *This image of Earth was taken on December 7, 1972, by the crew of the* Apollo 17 *spacecraft while on their way to the moon.*

Mars Statistics	
Distance from sun	12.7 light-minutes
Period of rotation	24 h, 40 min
Period of revolution	1 year, 322 days
Diameter	6,794 km
Density	3.93 g/cm^3
Surface temperature	−123°C to 37°C
Surface gravity	38% of Earth's

Mars: Our Intriguing Neighbor

Mars, shown in **Figure 5,** is perhaps the most studied planet in the solar system other than Earth. Much of our knowledge of Mars has come from information gathered by spacecraft. *Viking 1* and *Viking 2* landed on Mars in 1976, and *Mars Pathfinder* landed on Mars in 1997.

The Atmosphere of Mars

Because of its thinner atmosphere and greater distance from the sun, Mars is a cold planet. Midsummer temperatures recorded by the *Mars Pathfinder* range from –13°C to –77°C. Martian air is so thin that the air pressure on the surface of Mars is about the same as it is 30 km above Earth's surface. This distance is about 3 times higher than most planes fly! The air pressure is so low that any liquid water would quickly boil away. The only water found on the surface of Mars is in the form of ice.

Figure 5 *This Viking orbiter image shows the eastern hemisphere of Mars. The large circular feature in the center is the impact crater Schiaparelli, which has a diameter of 450 km.*

Water on Mars

Even though liquid water cannot exist on Mars's surface today, there is strong evidence that it existed there in the past. **Figure 6** shows an area on Mars with features that might have resulted from deposition of sediment in a lake. This finding means that in the past Mars might have been a warmer place and had a thicker atmosphere.

Figure 6 *The origin of the features shown in this image is unknown. The features might have resulted from deposition of sediment in a lake.*

WRITING SKILL **Boiling Point on Mars** At sea level on Earth's surface, water boils at 100°C. But if you try to boil water on top of a high mountain, you will find that the boiling point is lower than 100°C. Do some research to find out why. Then, in your own words, explain why liquid water cannot exist on Mars, based on what you learned.

Where Is the Water Now?

Mars has two polar icecaps made of both frozen water and frozen carbon dioxide. But the polar icecaps do not have enough water to create a thick atmosphere or rivers. Looking closely at the walls of some Martian craters, scientists have found that the debris around the craters looks as if it were made by the flow of mud rather than by dry soil. In this case, where might some of the "lost" Martian water have gone? Many scientists think that it is frozen beneath the Martian soil.

Martian Volcanoes

Mars has a rich volcanic history. Unlike Earth, where volcanoes exist in many places, Mars has only two large volcanic systems. The largest, the Tharsis region, stretches 8,000 km across the planet. The largest mountain in the solar system, Olympus Mons, is an extinct shield volcano similar to Mauna Kea on the island of Hawaii. Mars not only is smaller and cooler than Earth but also has a slightly different chemical makeup. This makeup may have kept the Martian crust from moving around as Earth's crust does. As a result, the volcanoes kept building up in the same spots on Mars. Images and data sent back by probes such as the *Sojourner* rover, shown in **Figure 7,** are helping to explain Mars's mysterious past.

Reading Check What characteristics of Mars may explain why Mars has only two large volcanic systems?

Figure 7 *The* Sojourner *rover, part of the Mars Pathfinder mission, is shown here creeping up to a rock named Yogi to measure its composition. The solar panel on the rover's back collected the solar energy used to power the rover's motor.*

Missions to Mars

Scientists are still intrigued by the mysteries of Mars. Several recent missions to Mars were launched to gain a better understanding of the Martian world. **Figure 8** shows the *Mars Express Orbiter,* which was launched by the European Space Agency (ESA) in 2003, and was designed to help scientists determine the composition of the Martian atmosphere and Martian climate. Also, in 2003, NASA launched the Twin Rover mission to Mars. These exploration rovers are designed to gather information that may help scientists determine if life ever existed on Mars. In addition, information collected by these rovers may help scientists prepare for human exploration on Mars.

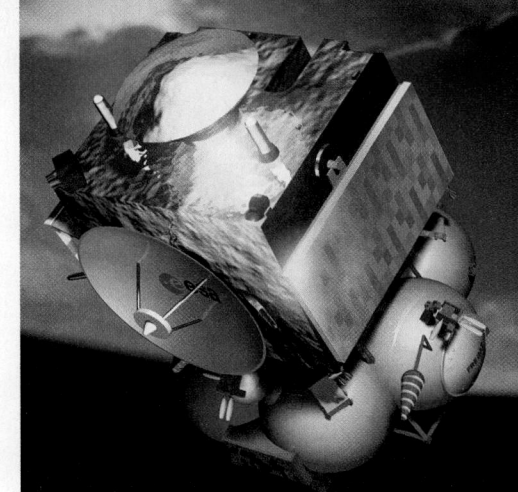

Figure 8 *The Mars Express Orbiter will help scientists study Mars's atmosphere.*

SECTION Review

Summary

- A period of rotation is the length of time that an object takes to rotate once on its axis.

- A period of revolution is the length of time that an object takes to revolve around the sun.

- Mercury is the planet closest to the sun. Of all the terrestrial planets, Venus has the densest atmosphere. Earth is the only planet known to support life. Mars has a rich volcanic history and shows evidence of once having had water.

Using Key Terms

1. In your own words, write a definition for the term *terrestrial planet.*

For the pair of terms below, explain how the meanings of the terms differ.

2. *prograde rotation* and *retrograde rotation*

Understanding Key Ideas

3. Scientists believe that the water on Mars now exists as

   a. polar icecaps.

   b. dry riverbeds.

   c. ice beneath the Martian soil.

   d. Both (a) and (c)

4. List three differences between and three similarities of Venus and Earth.

5. What is the difference between a planet's period of rotation and its period of revolution?

6. What are some of the characteristics of Earth that make it suitable for life?

7. Explain why the surface temperature of Venus is higher than the surface temperatures of the other planets in our solar system.

Math Skills

8. Mercury has a period of rotation equal to 58.67 Earth days. Mercury's period of revolution is equal to 88 Earth days. How many times does Mercury rotate during one revolution around the sun?

Critical Thinking

9. **Making Inferences** What type of information can we get by studying Earth from space?

10. **Analyzing Ideas** What type of evidence found on Mars suggests that Mars may have been a warmer place and had a thicker atmosphere?

SC**LINKS**®

NSTA

Developed and maintained by the
National Science Teachers Association

For a variety of links related to this chapter, go to www.scilinks.org

Topic: The Inner Planets
SciLinks code: HSM0798

SECTION 3

The Outer Planets

What do all the outer planets except for Pluto have in common?

Except for Pluto, the outer planets are very large planets that are made mostly of gases. These planets are called gas giants. **Gas giants** are planets that have deep, massive atmospheres rather than hard and rocky surfaces like those of the inner planets.

READING WARM-UP

Objectives

- Explain how gas giants are different from terrestrial planets.
- Describe the individual characteristics of Jupiter, Saturn, Uranus, Neptune, and Pluto.

Terms to Learn

gas giant

READING STRATEGY

Prediction Guide Before reading this section, write the title of each heading in this section. Next, under each heading write what you think you will learn.

gas giant a planet that has a deep, massive atmosphere, such as Jupiter, Saturn, Uranus, or Neptune

Jupiter: A Giant Among Giants

Jupiter is the largest planet in our solar system. Like the sun, Jupiter is made mostly of hydrogen and helium. The outer part of Jupiter's atmosphere is made of layered clouds of water, methane, and ammonia. The beautiful colors you see in **Figure 1** are probably due to small amounts of organic compounds. At a depth of about 10,000 km into Jupiter's atmosphere, the pressure is high enough to change hydrogen gas into a liquid. Deeper still, the pressure changes the liquid hydrogen into a liquid, metallic state. Unlike most planets, Jupiter radiates much more energy into space than it receives from the sun. The reason is that Jupiter's interior is very hot. Another striking feature of Jupiter is the Great Red Spot, a storm system that is more than 400 years old and is about 3 times the diameter of Earth!

NASA Missions to Jupiter

NASA has sent five missions to Jupiter. These include two Pioneer missions, two Voyager missions, and the recent Galileo mission. The *Voyager 1* and *Voyager 2* spacecraft sent back images that revealed a thin, faint ring around Jupiter. The Voyager missions also gave us the first detailed images of Jupiter's moons. The *Galileo* spacecraft reached Jupiter in 1995 and sent a probe into Jupiter's atmosphere. The probe sent back data on Jupiter's composition, temperature, and pressure.

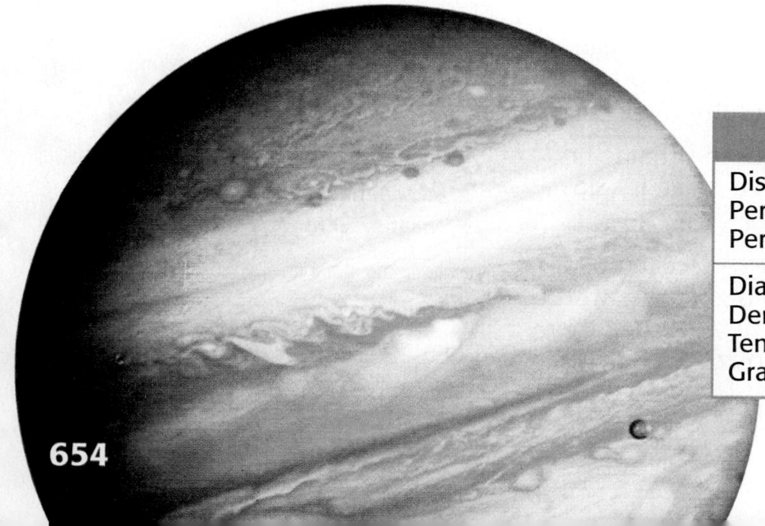

Figure 1 *This* Voyager 2 *image of Jupiter was taken at a distance of 28.4 million kilometers. Io, one of Jupiter's largest moons, can also be seen in this image.*

Jupiter Statistics	
Distance from sun	43.3 light-minutes
Period of rotation	9 h, 54 min
Period of revolution	11 years, 313 days
Diameter	142,984 km
Density	1.33 g/cm^3
Temperature	−110°C
Gravity	236% of Earth's

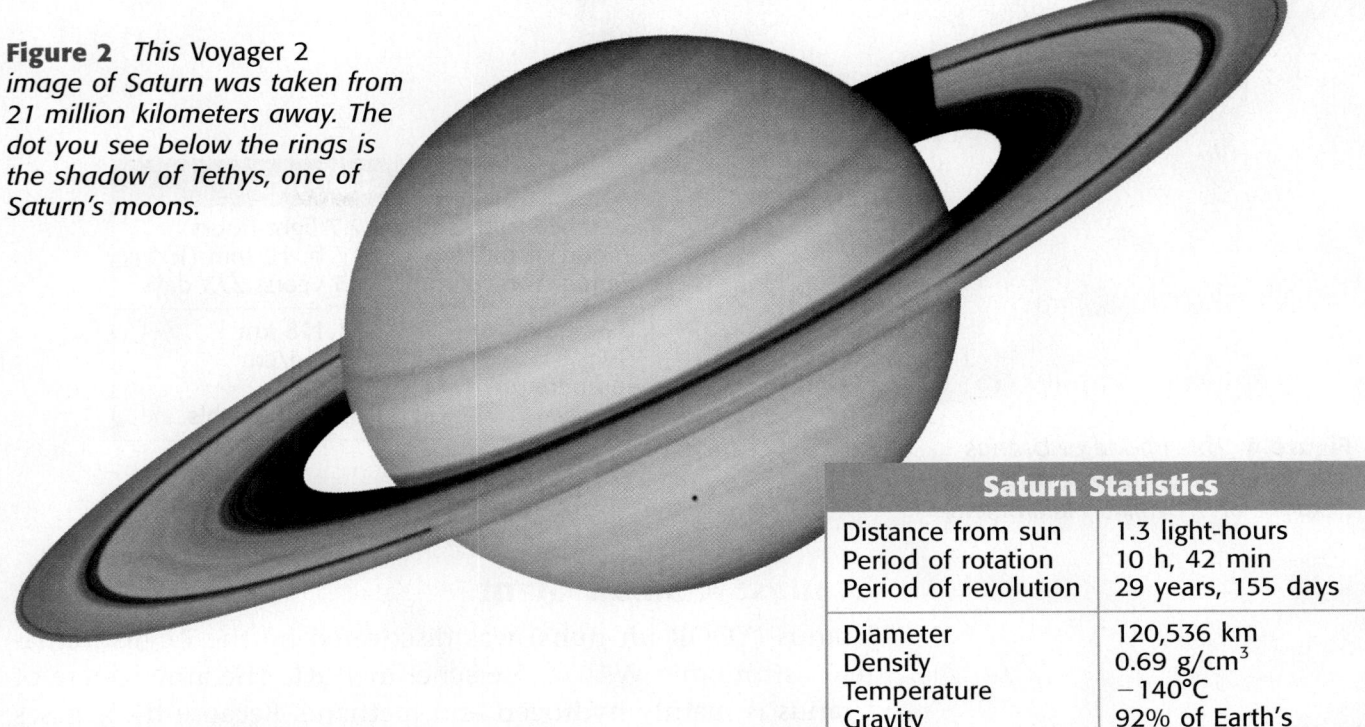

Figure 2 *This Voyager 2 image of Saturn was taken from 21 million kilometers away. The dot you see below the rings is the shadow of Tethys, one of Saturn's moons.*

Saturn Statistics	
Distance from sun	1.3 light-hours
Period of rotation	10 h, 42 min
Period of revolution	29 years, 155 days
Diameter	120,536 km
Density	0.69 g/cm^3
Temperature	−140°C
Gravity	92% of Earth's

Saturn: Still Forming

Saturn, shown in **Figure 2,** is the second-largest planet in the solar system. Saturn has roughly 764 times the volume of Earth and is 95 times more massive than Earth. Its overall composition, like Jupiter's, is mostly hydrogen and helium. But methane, ammonia, and ethane are found in the upper atmosphere. Saturn's interior is probably much like Jupiter's. Also, like Jupiter, Saturn gives off much more energy than it receives from the sun. Scientists think that Saturn's extra energy comes from helium falling out of the atmosphere and sinking to the core. In other words, Saturn is still forming!

The Rings of Saturn

Although all of the gas giants have rings, Saturn's rings are the largest. Saturn's rings have a total diameter of 272,000 km. Yet, Saturn's rings are only a few hundred meters thick. The rings are made of icy particles that range in size from a few centimeters to several meters wide. **Figure 3** shows a close-up view of Saturn's rings.

✓ *Reading Check* What are Saturn's rings made of? (*See the Appendix for answers to Reading Checks.*)

NASA's Exploration of Saturn

Launched in 1997, the *Cassini* spacecraft is designed to study Saturn's rings, moons, and atmosphere. The spacecraft is also designed to return more than 300,000 color images of Saturn.

Figure 3 *The different colors in this* Voyager 2 *image of Saturn's rings show differences in the rings' chemical composition.*

Uranus Statistics	
Distance from sun	2.7 light-hours
Period of rotation	17 h, 12 min (R)*
Period of revolution	83 years, 273 days
Diameter	51,118 km
Density	1.27 g/cm³
Temperature	−195°C
Gravity	89% of Earth's

*R = retrograde rotation

Figure 4 *This image of Uranus was taken by Voyager 2 at a distance of 9.1 million kilometers.*

Uranus: A Small Giant

Uranus (YOOR uh nuhs) was discovered by the English amateur astronomer William Herschel in 1781. The atmosphere of Uranus is mainly hydrogen and methane. Because these gases absorb the red part of sunlight very strongly, Uranus appears blue-green in color, as shown in **Figure 4.** Uranus and Neptune have much less mass than Jupiter, but their densities are similar. This suggests that their compositions are different from Jupiter's. They may have lower percentages of light elements and a greater percentage of water.

A Tilted Planet

Unlike most other planets, Uranus is tipped over on its side. So, its axis of rotation is tilted by almost 90° and lies almost in the plane of its orbit, as shown in **Figure 5.** For part of a Uranus year, one pole points toward the sun while the other pole is in darkness. At the other end of Uranus's orbit, the poles are reversed. Some scientists think that early in its history, Uranus may have been hit by a massive object that tipped the planet over.

Figure 5 *Uranus's axis of rotation is tilted so that the axis is nearly parallel to the plane of Uranus's orbit. In contrast, the axes of most other planets are closer to being perpendicular to the plane of the planets' orbits.*

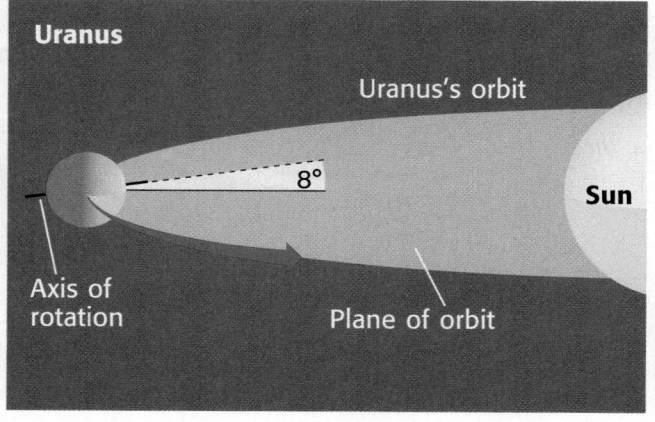

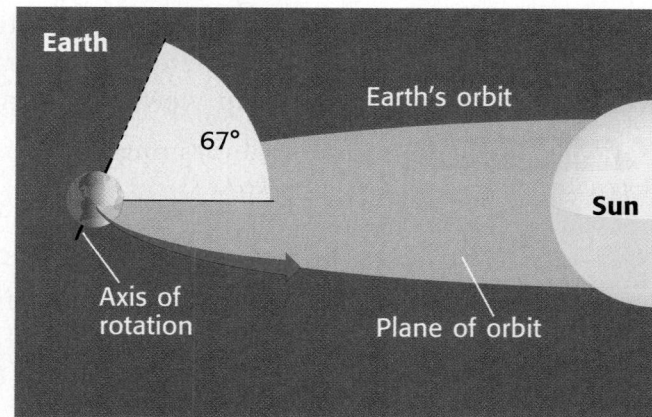

Neptune: The Blue World

Irregularities in the orbit of Uranus suggested to early astronomers that there must be another planet beyond it. They thought that the gravity of this new planet pulled Uranus off its predicted path. By using the predictions of the new planet's orbit, astronomers discovered the planet Neptune in 1846. Neptune is shown in **Figure 6.**

The Atmosphere of Neptune

The *Voyager 2* spacecraft sent back images that provided much new information about Neptune's atmosphere. Although the composition of Neptune's atmosphere is similar to that of Uranus's atmosphere, Neptune's atmosphere has belts of clouds that are much more visible. At the time of *Voyager 2*'s visit, Neptune had a Great Dark Spot like the Great Red Spot on Jupiter. And like the interiors of Jupiter and Saturn, Neptune's interior releases thermal energy to its outer layers. This release of energy helps the warm gases rise and the cool gases sink, which sets up the wind patterns in the atmosphere that create the belts of clouds. *Voyager 2* images also revealed that Neptune has a set of very narrow rings.

Reading Check What characteristic of Neptune's interior accounts for the belts of clouds in Neptune's atmosphere?

Figure 6 *This* Voyager 2 *image of Neptune, taken at a distance of more than 7 million kilometers, shows the Great Dark Spot as well as some bright cloud bands.*

Neptune Statistics	
Distance from sun	4.2 light-hours
Period of rotation	16 h, 6 min
Period of revolution	163 years, 263 days
Diameter	49,528 km
Density	1.64 g/cm³
Temperature	−200°C
Gravity	112% of Earth's

Pluto Statistics	
Distance from sun	5.4 light-hours
Period of rotation	6 days, 10 h (R)*
Period of revolution	248 years, 4 days
Diameter	2,390 km
Density	1.75 g/cm³
Surface temperature	−225°C
Surface gravity	6% of Earth's

*R = retrograde rotation

Figure 7 *This* Hubble Space Telescope *image is one of the clearest ever taken of Pluto* (left) *and its moon, Charon* (right).

Pluto: The Mystery Planet

Further study of Neptune showed some irregularities in Neptune's orbit. This finding led many scientists to believe there was yet another planet beyond Neptune. The mystery planet was finally discovered in 1930.

A Small World

The mystery planet, now called Pluto, is the farthest planet from the sun. Less than half the size of Mercury, Pluto is also the smallest planet. Pluto's moon, Charon (KER uhn), is more than half its size! In fact, Charon is the largest satellite relative to its planet in the solar system. **Figure 7** shows Pluto and Charon together. From Earth, it is hard to separate the images of Pluto and Charon because the bodies are so far away. **Figure 8** shows how far from the sun Pluto and Charon really are. From Pluto, the sun looks like a very distant bright star.

From calculations of Pluto's density, scientists know that Pluto must be made of rock and ice. Pluto is covered by frozen nitrogen, but Charon is covered by frozen water. Scientists believe Pluto has a thin atmosphere of methane.

Figure 8 *An artist's view of the sun and Charon from Pluto shows just how little light and heat Pluto receives from the sun.*

A True Planet?

Because Pluto is so small and is so unusual, some scientists think that it should not be classified as a planet. In fact, some scientists agree that Pluto could be considered a large asteroid or comet—large enough to have its own satellite. However, because Pluto was historically classified as a planet, it most likely will remain so.

Pluto is the only planet that has not been visited by a NASA mission. However, plans are underway to visit Pluto and Charon in 2006. During this mission, scientists hope to learn more about this unusual planet and map the surface of both Pluto and Charon.

SCHOOL to HOME

Surviving Space

WRITING SKILL Imagine it is the year 2150 and you are flying a spacecraft to Pluto. Suddenly, your systems fail, giving you only one chance to land safely. You can't head back to Earth. With a parent, write a paragraph explaining which planet you would choose to land on.

ACTIVITY

SECTION Review

Summary

- Jupiter is the largest planet in our solar system. Energy from the interior of Jupiter is transferred to its exterior.
- Saturn is the second-largest planet and, in some ways, is still forming as a planet.
- Uranus's axis of rotation is tilted by almost 90°.
- Neptune has a faint ring, and its atmosphere contains belts of clouds.
- Pluto is the smallest planet, and its moon, Charon, is more than half its size.

Using Key Terms

1. In your own words, write a definition for the term *gas giant*.

Understanding Key Ideas

2. The many colors of Jupiter's atmosphere are probably caused by _____ in the atmosphere.
   a. clouds of water
   b. methane
   c. ammonia
   d. organic compounds

3. Why do scientists claim that Saturn, in a way, is still forming?

4. Why does Uranus have a blue green color?

5. What is unusual about Pluto's moon, Charon?

6. What is the Great Red Spot?

7. Explain why Jupiter radiates more energy into space than it receives from the sun.

8. How do the gas giants differ from the terrestrial planets?

9. What is so unusual about Uranus's axis of rotation?

Math Skills

10. Pluto is 5.5 light-hours from the sun. How far is Pluto from the sun in astronomical units? (Hint: 1 AU = 8.3 light-minutes)

11. If Jupiter is 43.3 light-minutes from the sun and Neptune is 4.2 light-hours from the sun, how far from Jupiter is Neptune?

Critical Thinking

12. **Evaluating Data** What conclusions can your draw about the properties of a planet just by knowing how far it is from the sun?

13. **Applying Concepts** Why isn't the word *surface* included in the statistics for the gas giants?

SCiLINKS **NSTA**
Developed and maintained by the National Science Teachers Association

For a variety of links related to this chapter, go to www.scilinks.org

Topic: The Outer Planets
SciLinks code: HSM1091

Moons

If you could, which moon would you visit? With volcanoes, craters, and possible underground oceans, the moons in our solar system would be interesting places to visit.

Natural or artificial bodies that revolve around larger bodies such as planets are called **satellites.** Except for Mercury and Venus, all of the planets have natural satellites called *moons.*

Luna: The Moon of Earth

Scientists have learned a lot from studying Earth's moon, which is also called *Luna.* The lunar rocks brought back during the Apollo missions were found to be about 4.6 billion years old. Because these rocks have hardly changed since they formed, scientists know the solar system itself is about 4.6 billion years old.

The Surface of the Moon

As you can see in **Figure 1,** the moon's history is written on its face. The surfaces of bodies that have no atmospheres preserve a record of almost all of the impacts that the bodies have had. Because scientists now know the age of the moon, they can count the number of impact craters to find the rate of cratering since the birth of our solar system. By knowing the rate of cratering, scientists are able to use the number of craters on any body to estimate how old the body's surface is. That way, scientists don't need to bring back rock samples.

READING WARM-UP

Objectives

- Describe the current theory of the origin of Earth's moon.
- Explain what causes the phases of Earth's moon.
- Describe the difference between a solar eclipse and a lunar eclipse.
- Describe the individual characteristics of the moons of other planets.

Terms to Learn

satellite
phase
eclipse

READING STRATEGY

Reading Organizer As you read this section, make a table comparing solar eclipses and lunar eclipses.

Figure 1 *This image of the moon was taken by the* Galileo *spacecraft while on its way to Jupiter. The large, dark areas are lava plains called* maria.

Moon Statistics	
Period of rotation	27 days, 9 hours
Period of revolution	27 days, 7 hours
Diameter	3,475 km
Density	3.34 g/cm^3
Surface temperature	-170 to $134°C$
Surface gravity	16% of Earth's

Lunar Origins

Before scientists had rock samples from the moon, there were three popular explanations for the moon's formation: (1) The moon was a separate body captured by Earth's gravity, (2) the moon formed at the same time and from the same materials as the Earth, and (3) the newly formed Earth was spinning so fast that a piece flew off and became the moon.

When rock samples of the moon were brought back from the Apollo mission, the mystery was solved. Scientists found that the composition of the moon was similar to that of Earth's mantle. This evidence from the lunar rock samples supported the third explanation for the moon's formation.

The current theory is that a large, Mars-sized object collided with Earth while the Earth was still forming, as shown in **Figure 2.** The collision was so violent that part of the Earth's mantle was blasted into orbit around Earth to form the moon.

✓ Reading Check What is the current explanation for the formation of the moon? (*See the Appendix for answers to Reading Checks.*)

satellite a natural or artificial body that revolves around a planet

---

Figure 2 Formation of the Moon

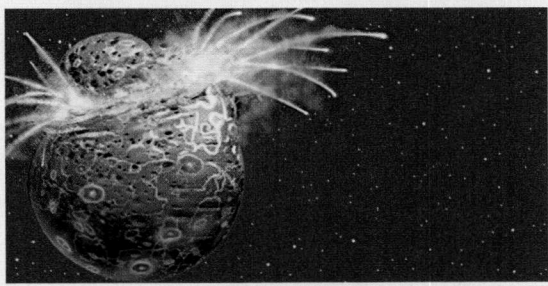

❶ Impact
About 4.6 billion years ago, when Earth was still mostly molten, a large body collided with Earth. Scientists reason that the object must have been large enough to blast part of Earth's mantle into space, because the composition of the moon is similar to that of Earth's mantle.

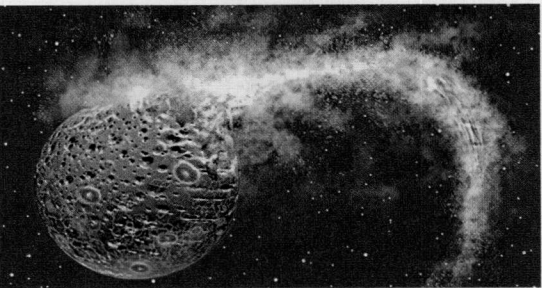

❷ Ejection
The resulting debris began to revolve around the Earth within a few hours of the impact. This debris consisted of mantle material from Earth and from the impacting body as well as part of the iron core of the impacting body.

❸ Formation
Soon after the giant impact, the clumps of material ejected into orbit around Earth began to join together to form the moon. Much later, as the moon cooled, additional impacts created deep basins and fractured the moon's surface. Lunar lava flowed from those cracks and flooded the basins to form the lunar maria that we see today.

Phases of the Moon

From Earth, one of the most noticeable aspects of the moon is its continually changing appearance. Within a month, the moon's Earthward face changes from a fully lit circle to a thin crescent and then back to a circle. These different appearances of the moon result from its changing position relative to Earth and the sun. As the moon revolves around Earth, the amount of sunlight on the side of the moon that faces Earth changes. The different appearances of the moon due to its changing position are called **phases.** The phases of the moon are shown in **Figure 3.**

phase the change in the sunlit area of one celestial body as seen from another celestial body

Waxing and Waning

When the moon is *waxing,* the sunlit fraction that we can see from Earth is getting larger. When the moon is *waning,* the sunlit fraction is getting smaller. Notice in **Figure 3** that even as the phases of the moon change, the total amount of sunlight that the moon gets remains the same. Half the moon is always in sunlight, just as half the Earth is always in sunlight. But because the moon's period of rotation is the same as its period of revolution, on Earth you always see the same side of the moon. If you lived on the far side of the moon, you would see the sun for half of each lunar day, but you would never see the Earth!

Figure 3 *The positions of the moon, sun, and Earth determine which phase the moon is in. The photo insets show how the moon looks from Earth at each phase.*

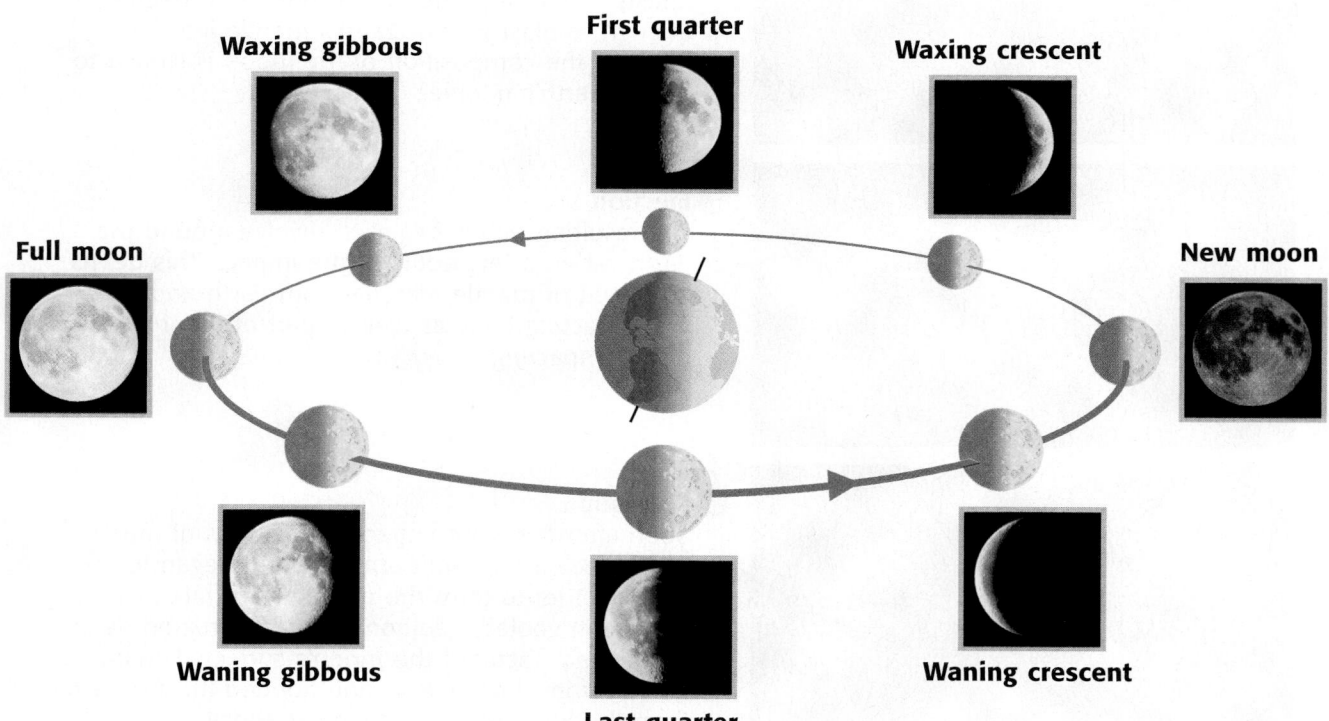

Waxing gibbous

First quarter

Waxing crescent

Full moon

New moon

Waning gibbous

Waning crescent

Last quarter

Solar eclipse

NEVER look directly at the sun! You can permanently damage your eyes.

Eclipses

When the shadow of one celestial body falls on another, an **eclipse** occurs. A *solar eclipse* happens when the moon comes between Earth and the sun and the shadow of the moon falls on part of Earth. A *lunar eclipse* happens when Earth comes between the sun and the moon and the shadow of Earth falls on the moon.

Solar Eclipses

Because the moon's orbit is elliptical, the distance between the moon and the Earth changes. During an *annular eclipse*, the moon is farther from the Earth. The disk of the moon does not completely cover the disk of the sun. A thin ring of the sun shows around the moon's outer edge. When the moon is closer to the Earth, the moon appears to be the same size as the sun. During a *total solar eclipse*, the disk of the moon completely covers the disk of the sun, as shown in **Figure 4.**

✔ **Reading Check** Describe what happens during a solar eclipse.

Figure 4 *On the left is a diagram of the positions of the Earth and the moon during a solar eclipse. On the right is a picture of the sun's outer atmosphere, or* corona, *which is visible only when the entire disk of the sun is blocked by the moon.*

eclipse an event in which the shadow of one celestial body falls on another

Clever Insight

1. Cut out a circle of **heavy, white paper.** This circle will represent Earth.
2. Find **two spherical objects** and **several other objects** of different shapes.
3. Hold up each object in front of a **lamp** (which represents the sun) so that the object's shadow falls on the white paper circle.
4. Rotate your objects in all directions, and record the shapes of the shadows that the objects make.
5. Which objects always cast a curved shadow?

Lunar eclipse

Figure 5 *On the left, you can see that the moon can have a reddish color during a lunar eclipse. On the right, you can see the positions of Earth and the moon during a lunar eclipse.*

Lunar Eclipses

As shown in **Figure 5,** the view during a lunar eclipse is spectacular. Earth's atmosphere acts like a lens and bends some of the sunlight into the Earth's shadow. When sunlight hits the particles in the atmosphere, blue light is filtered out. As a result, most of the remaining light that lights the moon is red.

The Tilted Orbit of the Moon

You may be wondering why you don't see solar and lunar eclipses every month. The reason is that the moon's orbit around Earth is tilted—by about 5°—relative to the orbit of Earth around the sun. This tilt is enough to place the moon out of Earth's shadow for most full moons and Earth out of the moon's shadow for most new moons.

✓ Reading Check Explain why you don't see solar and lunar eclipses every month.

The Moons of Other Planets

The moons of the other planets range in size from very small to as large as terrestrial planets. All of the gas giants have multiple moons, and scientists are still discovering new moons. Some moons have very elongated, or elliptical, orbits, and some moons even orbit their planet backward! Many of the very small moons may be captured asteroids. As scientists are learning from recent space missions, moons may be some of the most bizarre and interesting places in the solar system!

The Moons of Mars

Mars's two moons, Phobos and Deimos, are small, oddly shaped satellites. Both moons are very dark. Their surface materials are much like those of some asteroids—large, rocky bodies in space. Scientists think that these two moons are asteroids caught by Mars's gravity.

The Moons of Jupiter

Jupiter has dozens of moons. The four largest moons—Ganymede, Callisto, Io, and Europa—were discovered in 1610 by Galileo. They are known as the *Galilean satellites*. The largest moon, Ganymede, is even larger than the planet Mercury! Many of the smaller moons probably are captured asteroids.

The Galilean satellite closest to Jupiter is Io, a truly bizarre world. Io is caught in a gravitational tug of war between Jupiter and Io's nearest neighbor, the moon Europa. This constant tugging stretches Io a little and causes it to heat up. As a result, Io is the most volcanically active body in the solar system!

Recent pictures of the moon Europa, shown in **Figure 6,** support the idea that liquid water may lie beneath the moon's icy surface. This idea makes many scientists wonder if life could have evolved in the underground oceans of Europa.

The Moons of Saturn

Like Jupiter, Saturn has dozens of moons. Most of these moons are small bodies that are made mostly of frozen water but contain some rocky material. The largest satellite, Titan, was discovered in 1655 by Christiaan Huygens. In 1980, the *Voyager 1* spacecraft flew past Titan and discovered a hazy orange atmosphere, as shown in **Figure 7.** Earth's early atmosphere may have been much like Titan's is now. In 1997, NASA launched the *Cassini* spacecraft to study Saturn and its moons, including Titan. By studying Titan, scientists hope to learn more about how life began on Earth.

✓ Reading Check How can scientists learn more about how life began on Earth by studying Titan?

Figure 6 *Europa, Jupiter's fourth largest moon, might have liquid water beneath the moon's icy surface.*

Figure 7 *Titan is Saturn's largest moon.*

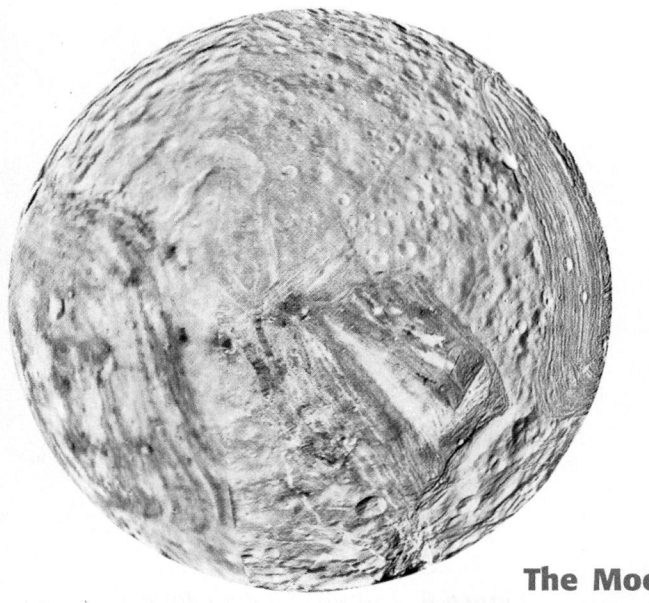

Figure 8 *This* Voyager 2 *image shows Miranda, the most unusual moon of Uranus. Its patchwork terrain indicates that it has had a violent history.*

The Moons of Uranus

Uranus has several moons. Like the moons of Saturn, Uranus's largest moons are made of ice and rock and are heavily cratered. The small moon Miranda, shown in **Figure 8,** has some of the strangest features in the solar system. Miranda's surface has smooth, cratered plains as well as regions that have grooves and cliffs. Scientists think that Miranda may have been hit and broken apart in the past. Gravity pulled the pieces together again, leaving a patchwork surface.

The Moons of Neptune

Neptune has several known moons, only one of which is large. This large moon, Triton, is shown in **Figure 9.** It revolves around the planet in a *retrograde,* or "backward," orbit. This orbit suggests that Triton may have been captured by Neptune's gravity. Triton has a very thin atmosphere made mostly of nitrogen gas. Triton's surface is mostly frozen nitrogen and methane. *Voyager 2* images reveal that Triton is geologically active. "Ice volcanoes," or geysers, eject nitrogen gas high into the atmosphere. The other moons of Neptune are small, rocky worlds much like the smaller moons of Saturn and Jupiter.

The Moon of Pluto

Pluto's only known moon, Charon, was discovered in 1978. Charon's period of revolution is the same as Pluto's period of rotation—about 6.4 days. So, one side of Pluto always faces Charon. In other words, if you stood on the surface of Pluto, Charon would always occupy the same place in the sky. Charon's orbit around Pluto is tilted relative to Pluto's orbit around the sun. As a result, Pluto, as seen from Earth, is sometimes eclipsed by Charon. But don't hold your breath; this eclipse happens only once every 120 years!

Reading Check How often is Pluto eclipsed by Charon?

Figure 9 *This* Voyager 2 *image shows Neptune's largest moon, Triton. The polar icecap currently facing the sun may have a slowly evaporating layer of nitrogen ice, adding to Triton's thin atmosphere.*

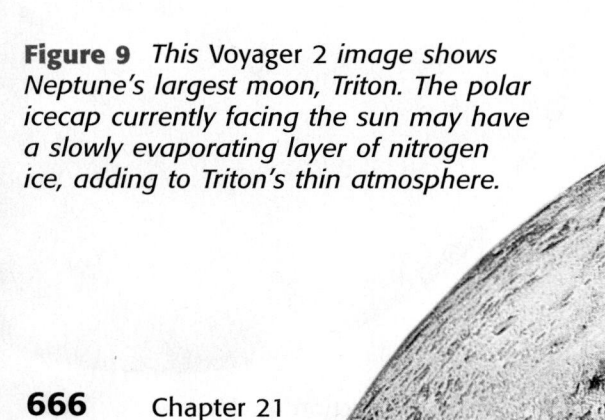

SECTION Review

Summary

- Scientists reason that the moon formed from the debris that was created after a large body collided with Earth.
- As the moon revolves around Earth, the amount of sunlight on the side of the moon changes. Because the amount of sunlight on the side of the moon changes, the moon's appearance from Earth changes. These changes in appearance are the phases of the moon.
- A solar eclipse happens when the shadow of the moon falls on Earth.
- A lunar eclipse happens when the shadow of Earth falls on the moon.
- Mars has 2 moons: Phobos and Deimos.
- Jupiter has dozens of moons. Ganymede, Io, Callisto, and Europa are the largest.
- Saturn has dozens of moons. Titan is the largest.
- Uranus has several moons.
- Neptune has several moons. Triton is the largest.
- Pluto has 1 known moon, Charon.

Using Key Terms

Complete each of the following sentences by choosing the correct term from the word bank.

satellite   eclipse

1. A(n) _____, or a body that revolves around a larger body, can be either artificial or natural.

2. A(n) _____ occurs when the shadow of one body in space falls on another body.

Understanding Key Ideas

3. Which of the following is a Galilean satellite?
   a. Phobos
   b. Deimos
   c. Ganymede
   d. Charon

4. Describe the current theory for the origin of Earth's moon.

5. What is the difference between a solar eclipse and a lunar eclipse?

6. What causes the phases of Earth's moon?

Critical Thinking

7. **Analyzing Methods** How can astronomers use the age of a lunar rock to estimate the age of the surface of a planet such as Mercury?

8. **Identifying Relationships** Charon stays in the same place in Pluto's sky, but the moon moves across Earth's sky. What causes this difference?

Interpreting Graphics

Use the diagram below to answer the questions that follow.

9. What type of eclipse is shown in the diagram?

10. Describe what is happening in the diagram.

11. Make a sketch of the type of eclipse that is not shown in the diagram.

SCLINKS®

NSTA

Developed and maintained by the National Science Teachers Association

For a variety of links related to this chapter, go to www.scilinks.org

Topic: Moons of Other Planets
SciLinks code: HSM0993

Small Bodies in the Solar System

Imagine you are traveling in a spacecraft to explore the edge of our solar system. You see several small bodies, as well as the planets and their satellites, moving through space.

The solar system contains not only planets and moons but other small bodies, including comets, asteroids, and meteoroids. Scientists study these objects to learn about the composition of the solar system.

Comets

A small body of ice, rock, and cosmic dust loosely packed together is called a **comet**. Some scientists refer to comets as "dirty snowballs" because of their composition. Comets formed in the cold, outer solar system. Nothing much has happened to comets since the birth of the solar system 4.6 billion years ago. Comets are probably left over from the time when the planets formed. As a result, each comet is a sample of the early solar system. Scientists want to learn more about comets to piece together the history of our solar system.

Comet Tails

When a comet passes close enough to the sun, solar radiation heats the ice so that the comet gives off gas and dust in the form of a long tail, as shown in **Figure 1**. Sometimes, a comet has two tails—an *ion tail* and a *dust tail*. The ion tail is made of electrically charged particles called *ions*. The solid center of a comet is called its *nucleus*. Comet nuclei can range in size from less than half a kilometer to more than 100 km in diameter.

READING WARM-UP

Objectives

- Explain why comets, asteroids, and meteoroids are important to the study of the formation of the solar system.
- Describe the similarities of and differences between asteroids and meteoroids.
- Explain how cosmic impacts may affect life on Earth.

Terms to Learn

comet	meteoroid
asteroid	meteorite
asteroid belt	meteor

READING STRATEGY

Discussion Read this section silently. Write down questions that you have about this section. Discuss your questions in a small group.

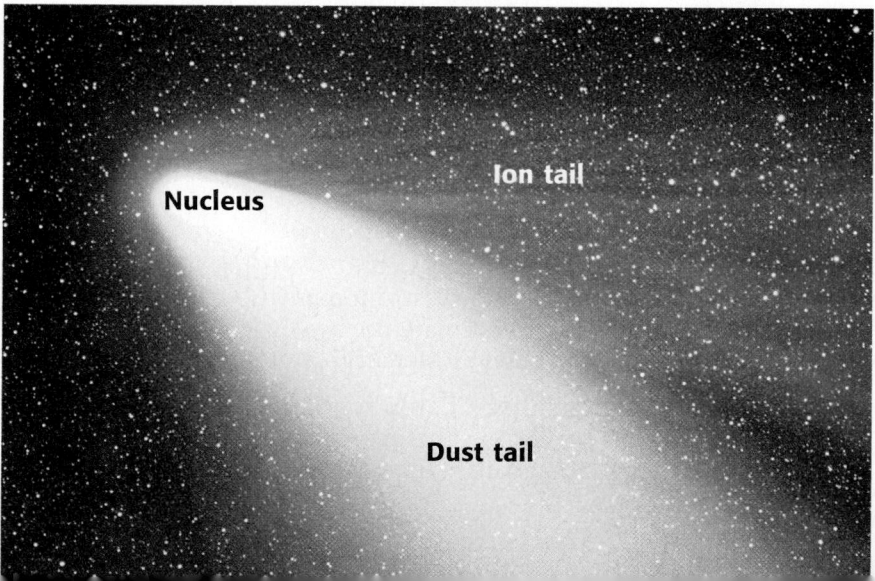

Figure 1 *This image shows the physical features of a comet when it is close to the sun. The nucleus of a comet is hidden by brightly lit gases and dust.*

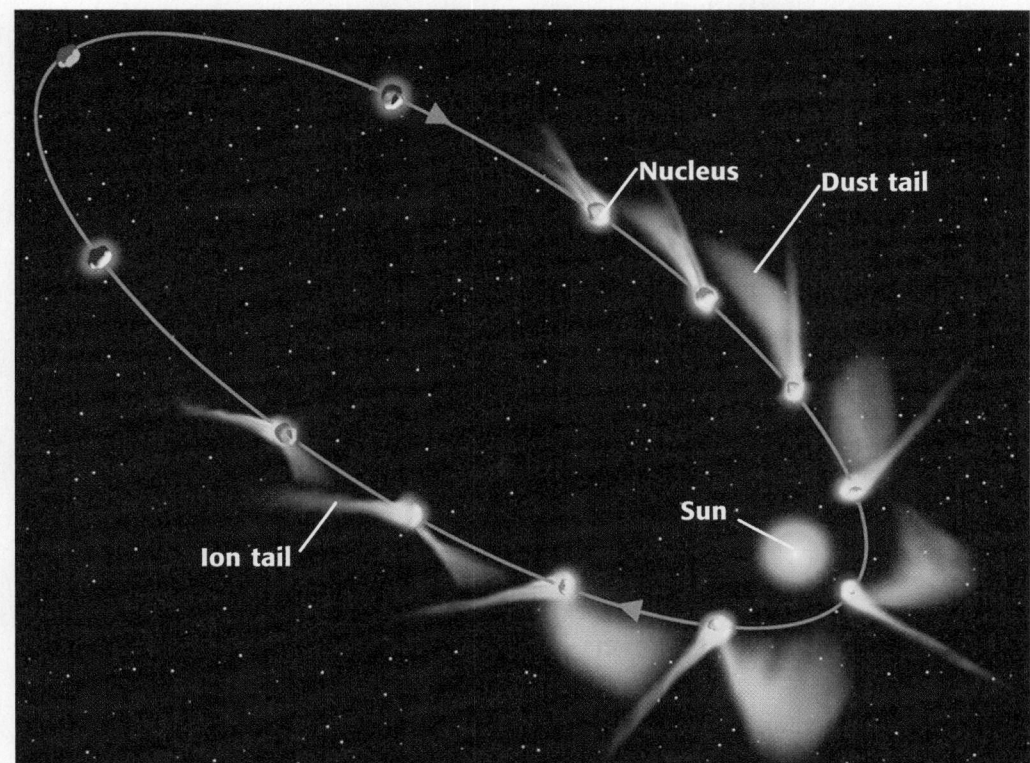

Figure 2 *Comets have very elongated orbits. When a comet gets close to the sun, the comet can develop one or two tails.*

Labels in figure: Nucleus, Dust tail, Ion tail, Sun

Comet Orbits

The orbits of all bodies that move around the sun are ellipses. *Ellipses* are circles that are somewhat stretched out of shape. The orbits of most planets are close to perfect circles, but the orbits of comets are very elongated.

Notice in **Figure 2** that a comet's ion tail always points away from the sun. The reason is that the ion tail is blown away from the sun by *solar wind*, which is also made of ions. The dust tail tends to follow the comet's orbit around the sun. Dust tails do not always point away from the sun. When a comet is close to the sun, its tail can extend millions of kilometers through space!

Comet Origins

Where do comets come from? Many scientists think that comets come from the Oort (AWRT) cloud, a spherical region that surrounds the solar system. When the gravity of a passing planet or star disturbs part of this cloud, comets can be pulled toward the sun. Another recently discovered region where comets exist is the Kuiper (KIE puhr) belt, which is the region outside the orbit of Neptune.

✔ **Reading Check** From which two regions do comets come? (*See the Appendix for answers to Reading Checks*.)

comet a small body of ice, rock, and cosmic dust that follows an elliptical orbit around the sun and that gives off gas and dust in the form of a tail as it passes close to the sun

CONNECTION TO Language Arts

WRITING SKILL **Interplanetary Journalist** In 1994, the world watched in awe as parts of the comet Shoemaker-Levy 9 collided with Jupiter, which caused enormous explosions. Imagine you were an interplanetary journalist who traveled through space to observe the comet during this time. Write an article describing your adventure.

Asteroids

asteroid a small, rocky object that orbits the sun, usually in a band between the orbits of Mars and Jupiter

asteroid belt the region of the solar system that is between the orbits of Mars and Jupiter and in which most asteroids orbit

Small, rocky bodies that revolve around the sun are called **asteroids.** They range in size from a few meters to more than 900 km in diameter. Asteroids have irregular shapes, although some of the larger ones are spherical. Most asteroids orbit the sun in the asteroid belt. The **asteroid belt** is a wide region between the orbits of Mars and Jupiter. Like comets, asteroids are thought to be material left over from the formation of the solar system.

Types of Asteroids

The composition of asteroids varies depending on where they are located within the asteroid belt. In the outermost region of the asteroid belt, asteroids have dark reddish brown to black surfaces. This coloring may indicate that the asteroids are rich in organic material. Asteroids that have dark gray surfaces are rich in carbon. In the innermost part of the asteroid belt are light gray asteroids that have either a stony or metallic composition. **Figure 3** shows three asteroids: Hektor, Ceres, and Vesta.

Figure 3 The Asteroid Belt

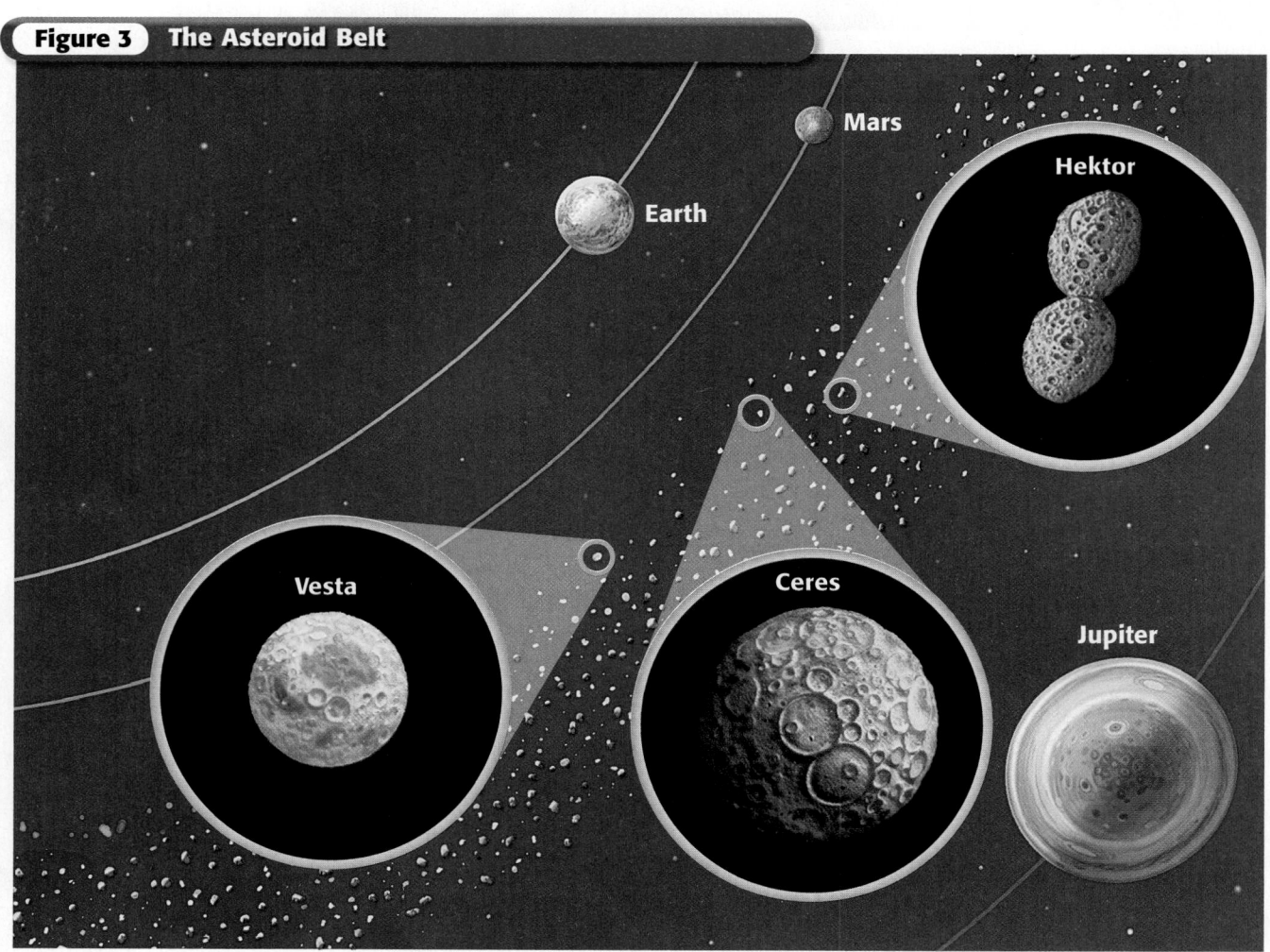

Meteoroids

Meteoroids are similar to but much smaller than asteroids. A **meteoroid** is a small, rocky body that revolves around the sun. Most meteoroids are probably pieces of asteroids. A meteoroid that enters Earth's atmosphere and strikes the ground is called a **meteorite.** As a meteoroid falls into Earth's atmosphere, the meteoroid moves so fast that its surface melts. As the meteoroid burns up, it gives off an enormous amount of light and thermal energy. From the ground, you see a spectacular streak of light, or a shooting star. A **meteor** is the bright streak of light caused by a meteoroid or comet dust burning up in the atmosphere.

meteoroid a relatively small, rocky body that travels through space

meteorite a meteoroid that reaches the Earth's surface without burning up completely

meteor a bright streak of light that results when a meteoroid burns up in the Earth's atmosphere

Meteor Showers

Many of the meteors that we see come from very small (dust-sized to pebble-sized) rocks. Even so, meteors can be seen on almost any night if you are far enough away from a city to avoid the glare of its lights. At certain times of the year, you can see large numbers of meteors, as shown in **Figure 4.** These events are called *meteor showers*. Meteor showers happen when Earth passes through the dusty debris that comets leave behind.

Types of Meteorites

Like their asteroid relatives, meteorites have different compositions. The three major types of meteorites—stony, metallic, and stony-iron meteorites—are shown in **Figure 5.** Many of the stony meteorites probably come from carbon-rich asteroids. Stony meteorites may contain organic materials and water. Scientists use meteorites to study the early solar system. Like comets and asteroids, meteorites are some of the building blocks of planets.

Figure 4 *Meteors are the streaks of light caused by meteoroids as they burn up in Earth's atmosphere.*

✔ **Reading Check** What are the major types of meteorites?

Figure 5   Three Major Types of Meteorites

Stony meteorite
rocky material

Metallic meteorite
iron and nickel

Stony-iron meteorite
rocky material, iron, and nickel

The Role of Impacts in the Solar System

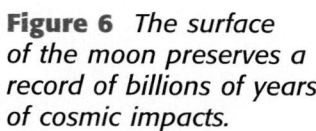

CONNECTION TO
Biology

WRITING SKILL **Mass Extinctions** Throughout Earth's history, there have been times when large numbers of species suddenly became extinct. Many scientists think that these mass extinctions may have been caused by impacts of large objects on Earth. However, other scientists are not so sure. Use the Internet or another source to research this idea. In your **science journal,** write a paragraph describing the different theories scientists have for past mass extinctions.

The Role of Impacts in the Solar System

An impact happens when an object in space collides with another object in space. Often, the result of such a collision is an impact crater. Many planets and moons have visible impact craters. In fact, several planets and moons have many more impact craters than Earth does. Planets and moons that do not have atmospheres have more impact craters than do planets and moons that have atmospheres.

Look at **Figure 6.** Earth's moon has many more impact craters than the Earth does because the moon has no atmosphere to slow objects down. Fewer objects strike Earth because Earth's atmosphere acts as a shield. Smaller objects burn up before they ever reach the surface. Also, most craters left on Earth are no longer visible because of weathering, erosion, and tectonic activity.

Future Impacts on Earth?

Most objects that come close to Earth are small and usually burn up in the atmosphere. However, larger objects are more likely to strike Earth's surface. Scientists estimate that impacts that are powerful enough to cause a natural disaster might happen once every few thousand years. An impact that is large enough to cause a global catastrophe is estimated to happen once every few hundred thousand years, on average.

Reading Check How often do large objects strike Earth?

Figure 6 *The surface of the moon preserves a record of billions of years of cosmic impacts.*

The Torino Scale

The Torino scale is a system that allows scientists to rate the hazard level of an object moving toward Earth. The object is carefully observed and then assigned a number from the scale. The scale ranges from 0 to 10. Zero indicates that the object has a very small chance of striking Earth. Ten indicates that the object will definitely strike Earth and cause a global disaster. The Torino scale is also color coded. White represents 0, and green represents 1. White and green objects rarely strike Earth. Yellow represents 2, 3, and 4 and indicates a higher chance that objects will hit Earth. Orange, which represents 5, 6, and 7, refers to objects highly likely to hit Earth. Red refers to objects that will definitely hit Earth.

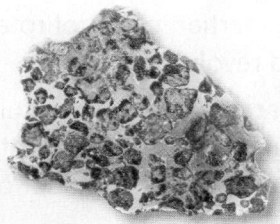

SECTION Review

Summary

- Studying comets, asteroids, and meteoroids can help scientists understand more about the formation of the solar system.

- Asteroids are small bodies that orbit the sun. Meteoroids are similar to but smaller than asteroids. Most meteoroids come from asteroids.

- Most objects that collide with Earth burn up in the atmosphere. Large impacts, however, may cause a global catastrophe.

Using Key Terms

For each pair of terms, explain how the meanings of the terms differ.

1. *comet* and *asteroid*

2. *meteor* and *meteorite*

Understanding Key Ideas

3. Which of the following is NOT a type of meteorite?
   a. stony meteorite
   b. rocky-iron meteorite
   c. stony-iron meteorite
   d. metallic meteorite

4. Why is the study of comets, asteroids, and meteoroids important in understanding the formation of the solar system?

5. Why do a comet's two tails often point in different directions?

6. How can a cosmic impact affect life on Earth?

7. What is the difference between an asteroid and a meteoroid?

8. Where is the asteroid belt located?

9. What is the Torino scale?

10. Describe why we see several impact craters on the moon but few on Earth.

Math Skills

11. The diameter of comet A's nucleus is 55 km. If the diameter of comet B's nucleus is 30% larger than comet A's nucleus, what is the diameter of comet B's nucleus?

Critical Thinking

12. **Expressing Opinions** Do you think the government should spend money on programs to search for asteroids and comets that have Earth-crossing orbits? Explain.

13. **Making Inferences** What is the likelihood that scientists will discover an object belonging in the red category of the Torino scale in the next 500 years? Explain your answer.

SCI LINKS.

NSTA
Developed and maintained by the
National Science Teachers Association

For a variety of links related to this chapter, go to www.scilinks.org
Topic: Comets, Asteroids, and Meteoroids
SciLinks code: HSM0317

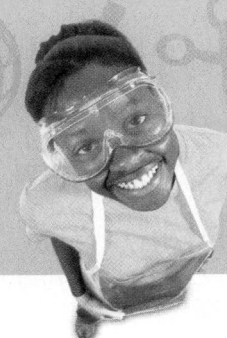

Inquiry Lab

Create a Calendar

OBJECTIVES

Create a calendar based on the Martian cycles of rotation and revolution.

Describe why it is useful to have a calendar that matches the cycles of the planet on which you live.

MATERIALS

- calculator (optional)
- marker
- pencils, assorted colors
- poster board
- ruler, metric

Imagine that you live in the first colony on Mars. You have been trying to follow the Earth calendar, but it just isn't working anymore. Mars takes almost 2 Earth years to revolve around the sun—almost 687 Earth days to be exact! That means that there are only two Martian seasons for every Earth calendar year. On Mars, in one Earth year, you get winter and spring, but the next year, you get only summer and fall! And Martian days are longer than Earth days. Mars takes 24.6 Earth hours to rotate on its axis. Although they are similar, Earth days and Martian days just don't match. You need a new calendar!

Ask a Question

1 How can I create a calendar based on the Martian cycles of rotation and revolution that includes months, weeks, and days?

Form a Hypothesis

2 Write a few sentences that answer your question.

Test the Hypothesis

3 Use the following formulas to determine the number of Martian days in a Martian year:

$$\frac{687 \text{ Earth days}}{1 \text{ Martian year}} \times \frac{24 \text{ Earth hours}}{1 \text{ Earth day}} = \text{Earth hours per Martian year}$$

$$\text{Earth hours per Martian year} \times \frac{1 \text{ Martian day}}{24.6 \text{ Earth hours}} = \text{Martian days per Martian year}$$

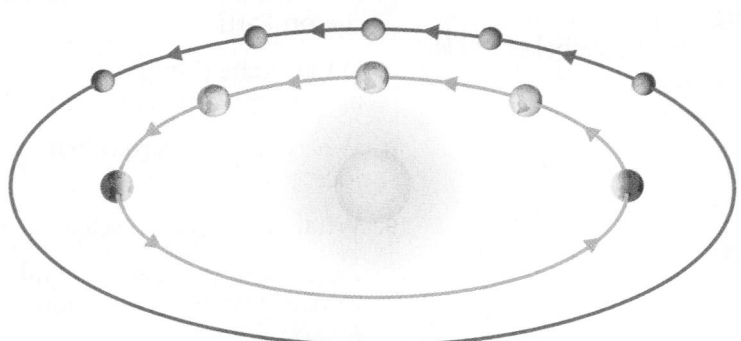

4 Decide how to divide your calendar into a system of Martian months, weeks, and days. Will you have a leap day, a leap week, a leap month, or a leap year? How often will it occur?

5 Choose names for the months and days of your calendar. Explain why you chose each name. If you have time, explain how you would number the Martian years. For instance, would the first year correspond to a certain Earth year?

6 Follow your design to create your own calendar for Mars. Construct your calendar by using a computer to help organize your data. Draw the calendar on your piece of poster board. Make sure it is brightly colored and easy to follow.

7 Present your calendar to the class. Explain how you chose your months, weeks, and days.

Analyze the Results

1 **Analyzing Results** What advantages does your calendar design have? Are there any disadvantages to your design?

2 **Classifying** Which student or group created the most original calendar? Which design was the most useful? Explain.

3 **Analyzing Results** What might you do to improve your calendar?

Draw Conclusions

4 **Evaluating Models** Take a class vote to decide which design should be chosen as the new calendar for Mars. Why was this calendar chosen? How did it differ from the other designs?

5 **Drawing Conclusions** Why is it useful to have a calendar that matches the cycles of the planet on which you live?

Chapter Review

USING KEY TERMS

For each pair of terms, explain how the meanings of the terms differ.

1 *terrestrial planet* and *gas giant*

2 *asteroid* and *comet*

3 *meteor* and *meteorite*

Complete each of the following sentences by choosing the correct term from the word bank.

astronomical unit	meteorite
meteoroid	prograde
retrograde	satellite

4 The average distance between the sun and Earth is 1 ___.

5 A small rock in space is called a(n) ___.

6 When viewed from above its north pole, a body that moves in a counter-clockwise direction is said to have ___ rotation.

7 A(n) ___ is a natural or artificial body that revolves around a planet.

UNDERSTANDING KEY IDEAS

Multiple Choice

8 Of the following, which is the largest body?

a. the moon

b. Pluto

c. Mercury

d. Ganymede

9 Which of the following planets have retrograde rotation?

a. the terrestrial planets

b. the gas giants

c. Mercury, Venus, and Uranus

d. Venus, Uranus, and Pluto

10 Which of the following planets does NOT have any moons?

a. Mercury

b. Mars

c. Uranus

d. None of the above

11 Why can liquid water NOT exist on the surface of Mars?

a. The temperature is too high.

b. Liquid water once existed there.

c. The gravity of Mars is too weak.

d. The atmospheric pressure is too low.

Short Answer

12 List the names of the planets in the order the planets orbit the sun.

13 Describe three ways in which the inner planets are different from the outer planets.

14 What are the gas giants? How are the gas giants different from the terrestrial planets?

15 What is the difference between asteroids and meteoroids?

16 What is the difference between a planet's period of rotation and period of revolution?

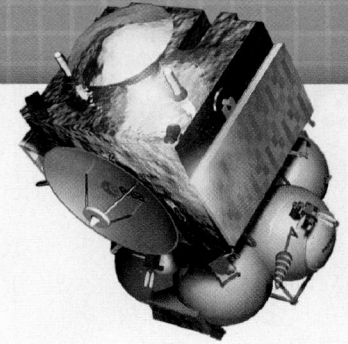

17 Explain the difference between prograde rotation and retrograde rotation.

18 Which characteristics of Earth make it suitable for life?

19 Describe the current theory for the origin of Earth's moon.

20 What causes the phases of the moon?

CRITICAL THINKING

21 **Concept Mapping** Use the following terms to create a concept map: *solar system, terrestrial planets, gas giants, moons, comets, asteroids,* and *meteoroids.*

22 **Applying Concepts** Even though we haven't yet retrieved any rock samples from Mercury's surface for radiometric dating, scientists know that the surface of Mercury is much older than that of Earth. How do scientists know this?

23 **Making Inferences** Where in the solar system might scientists search for life, and why?

24 **Analyzing Ideas** Is the far side of the moon always dark? Explain your answer.

25 **Predicting Consequences** If scientists could somehow bring Europa as close to the sun as the Earth is, 1 AU, how do you think Europa would be affected?

26 **Identifying Relationships** How did variations in the orbit of Uranus help scientists discover Neptune?

INTERPRETING GRAPHICS

The graph below shows density versus mass for Earth, Uranus, and Neptune. Mass is given in Earth masses—the mass of Earth is equal to 1 Earth mass. The relative volumes for the planets are shown by the size of each circle. Use the graph below to answer the questions that follow.

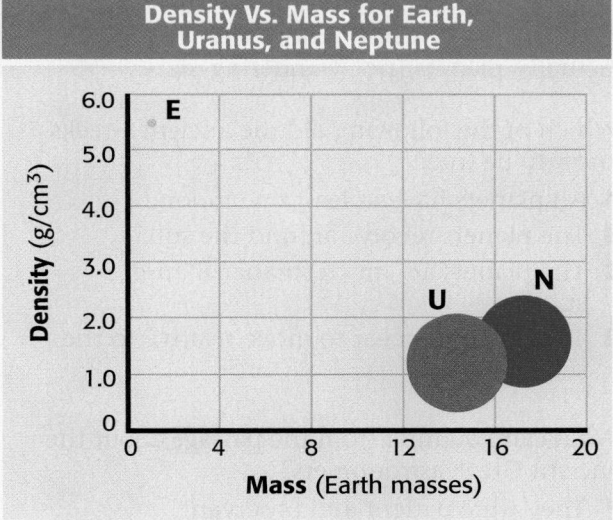

Density Vs. Mass for Earth, Uranus, and Neptune

27 Which planet is denser, Uranus or Neptune? How can you tell?

28 You can see that although Earth has the smallest mass, it has the highest density of the three planets. How can Earth be the densest of the three when Uranus and Neptune have so much more mass than Earth does?

Standardized Test Preparation

Read each of the passages below. Then, answer the questions that follow each passage.

Passage 1 Imagine that it is 200 BCE and you are an apprentice to a Greek astronomer. After years of observing the sky, the astronomer knows all of the constellations as well as the back of his hand. He shows you how the stars all move together—the whole sky spins slowly as the night goes on. He also shows you that among the thousands of stars in the sky, some of the brighter ones slowly change their position relative to the other stars. He names these stars *planetai*, the Greek word for "wanderers." Building on the observations of the ancient Greeks, we now know that the *planetai* are actually planets, not wandering stars.

1. Which of the following did the ancient Greeks know to be true?

A All planets have at least one moon.

B The planets revolve around the sun.

C The planets are much smaller than the stars.

D The planets appear to move relative to the stars.

2. What can you infer from the passage about the ancient Greek astronomers?

F They were patient and observant.

G They knew much more about astronomy than we do.

H They spent all their time counting stars.

I They invented astrology.

3. What does the word *planetai* mean in Greek?

A planets

B wanderers

C stars

D moons

Passage 2 To explain the source of short-period comets (comets that have a relatively short orbit), the Dutch-American astronomer Gerard Kuiper proposed in 1949 that a belt of icy bodies must lie beyond the orbits of Pluto and Neptune. Kuiper argued that comets were icy <u>planetesimals</u> that formed from the condensation that happened during the formation of our galaxy. Because the icy bodies are so far from any large planet's gravitational field (30 to 100 AU), they can remain on the fringe of the solar system. Some theorists speculate that the large moons Triton and Charon were once members of the Kuiper belt before they were captured by Neptune and Pluto. These moons and short-period comets have similar physical and chemical properties.

1. According to the passage, why can icy bodies remain at the edge of the solar system?

A The icy bodies are so small that they naturally float to the edge of the solar system.

B The icy bodies have weak gravitational fields and therefore do not orbit individual planets.

C The icy bodies are short-period comets, which can reside only at the edge of the solar system.

D The icy bodies are so far away from any large planet's gravitational field that they can remain at the edge of the solar system.

2. According to the passage, which of the following best describes the meaning of the word *planetesimal*?

F a small object that existed during the early development of the solar system

G an extremely tiny object in space

H a particle that was once part of a planet

I an extremely large satellite that was the result of a collision of two objects

Use the diagrams below to answer the questions that follow.

Planet A 115 craters/km²

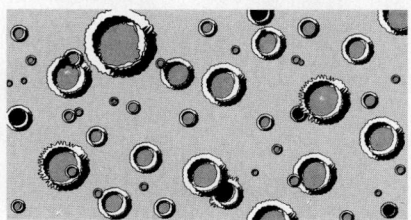

Planet B 75 craters/km²

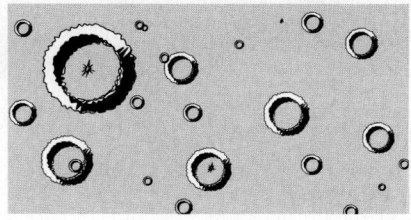

Planet C 121 craters/km²

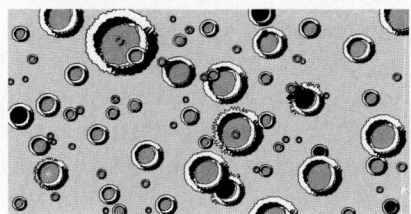

Planet D 97 craters/km²

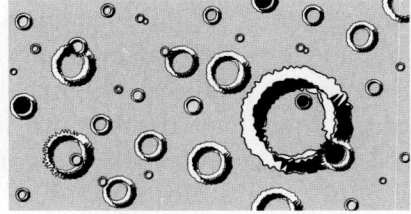

1. According to the information above, which planet has the oldest surface?

A planet A

B planet B

C planet C

D planet D

2. How many more craters per square kilometer are there on planet C than on planet B?

F 46 craters per square kilometer

G 24 craters per square kilometer

H 22 craters per square kilometer

I 6 craters per square kilometer

Read each question below, and choose the best answer.

1. Venus's surface gravity is 91% of Earth's. If an object weighs 12 N on Earth, how much would it weigh on Venus?

A 53 N

B 13 N

C 11 N

D 8 N

2. Earth's overall density is 5.52 g/cm³, while Saturn's density is 0.69 g/cm³. How many times denser is Earth than Saturn?

F 8 times

G 9 times

H 11 times

I 12 times

3. If Earth's history spans 4.6 billion years and the Phanerozoic eon was 543 million years, what percentage of Earth's history does the Phanerozoic eon represent?

A about 6%

B about 12%

C about 18%

D about 24%

4. The diameter of Venus is 12,104 km. The diameter of Mars is 6,794 km. What is the difference between the diameter of Venus and the diameter of Mars?

F 5,400 km

G 5,310 km

H 4,890 km

I 890 km

Standardized Test Preparation

Science in Action

Science Fiction

"The Mad Moon" by Stanley Weinbaum

The third largest moon of Jupiter, called Io, can be a hard place to live. Grant Calthorpe is finding this out the hard way. Although living comfortably is possible in the small cities at the polar regions of Io, Grant has to spend most of his time in the moon's hot and humid jungles. Grant treks into the jungles of Io to gather ferva leaves so that they can be converted into useful medications for humans. During Grant's quest, he encounters loonies and slinkers, and he has to avoid blancha, a kind of tropical fever that causes hallucinations, weakness, and vicious headaches. Without proper medication a person with blancha can go mad or even die. In "The Mad Moon," you'll discover a dozen adventures with Grant Calthorpe as he struggles to stay alive—and sane.

Language Arts ACTiViTY

WRITING SKILL Read "The Mad Moon" by Stanley Weinbaum. Write a short story describing the adventures that you would have on Io if you were chosen as Grant Calthorpe's assistant.

HOLT ANTHOLOGY OF
Science Fiction
HOLT, RINEHART AND WINSTON

Scientific Debate

Is Pluto a Planet?

Is it possible that Pluto isn't a planet? Some scientists think so! Since 1930, Pluto has been included as one of the nine planets in our solar system. But observations in the 1990s led many astronomers to refer to Pluto as an object, not a planet. Other astronomers disagree with this change. Astronomers that refer to Pluto as an object do not think that it fits well with the other outer planets. Unlike the other outer planets, which are large and gaseous, Pluto is small and made of rock and ice. Pluto also has a very elliptical orbit that is unlike its neighboring planets. Astronomers that think Pluto is a planet point out that Pluto, like all other planets, has its own atmosphere and its own moon, called Charon. These and other factors have fueled a debate as to whether Pluto should be classified as a planet.

Math ACTiViTY

How many more kilometers is Earth's diameter compared to Pluto's diameter if Earth's diameter is 12,756 km and Pluto's diameter is 2,390 km?

Adriana C. Ocampo

Planetary Geologist Sixty-five million years ago, in what is now Mexico, a giant meteor at least six miles wide struck Earth. The meteor made a hole nine miles deep and over 100 miles wide. The meteor sent billions of tons of dust into Earth's atmosphere. This dust formed thick clouds. After forming, these clouds may have left the planet in total darkness for six months, and the temperature near freezing for ten years. Some scientists think that this meteor crash and its effect on the Earth's climate led to the extinction of the dinosaurs. Adriana Ocampo studies the site in Mexico made by the crater known as the Chicxulub (cheeks OO loob) impact crater. Ocampo is a planetary geologist and has been interested in space exploration since she was young. Ocampo's specialty is studying "impact craters." "Impact craters are formed when an asteroid or a comet collides with the Earth or any other terrestrial planet," explains Ocampo. Ocampo visits crater sites around the world to collect data. She also uses computers to create models of how the impact affected the planet. Ocampo has worked for NASA and has helped plan space exploration missions to Mars, Jupiter, Saturn, and Mercury. Ocampo currently works for the European Space Agency (ESA) and is part of the team getting ready to launch the next spacecraft that will go to Mars.

Social Studies ACTiViTY

Research information about impact craters. Find the different locations around the world where impact craters have been found. Make a world map that highlights these locations.

The circle on the map shows the site in Mexico made by the Chicxulub impact crater.

go.hrw.com
To learn more about these Science in Action topics, visit go.hrw.com and type in the keyword HZ5FAMF.

Current Science
Check out Current Science® articles related to this chapter by visiting go.hrw.com. Just type in the keyword HZ5CS21.

22

Exploring Space

About the PHOTO

Although the astronauts in the photo appear to be motionless, they are orbiting the Earth at almost 28,000 km/h! The astronauts reached orbit—about 300 km above the Earth's sur-face—in a space shuttle. Space shuttles are the first vehicles in a new generation of reusable spacecraft. They have opened an era of space exploration in which missions to space are more common than ever before.

PRE-READING ACTIVITY

Graphic Organizer

Chain-of-Events Chart Before you read the chapter, create the graphic organizer entitled "Chain-of-Events Chart" described in the **Study Skills** section of the Appendix. As you read the chapter, fill in the chart with a timeline that describes the exploration of space from the theories of Konstantin Tsiolkovsky to the future of space exploration.

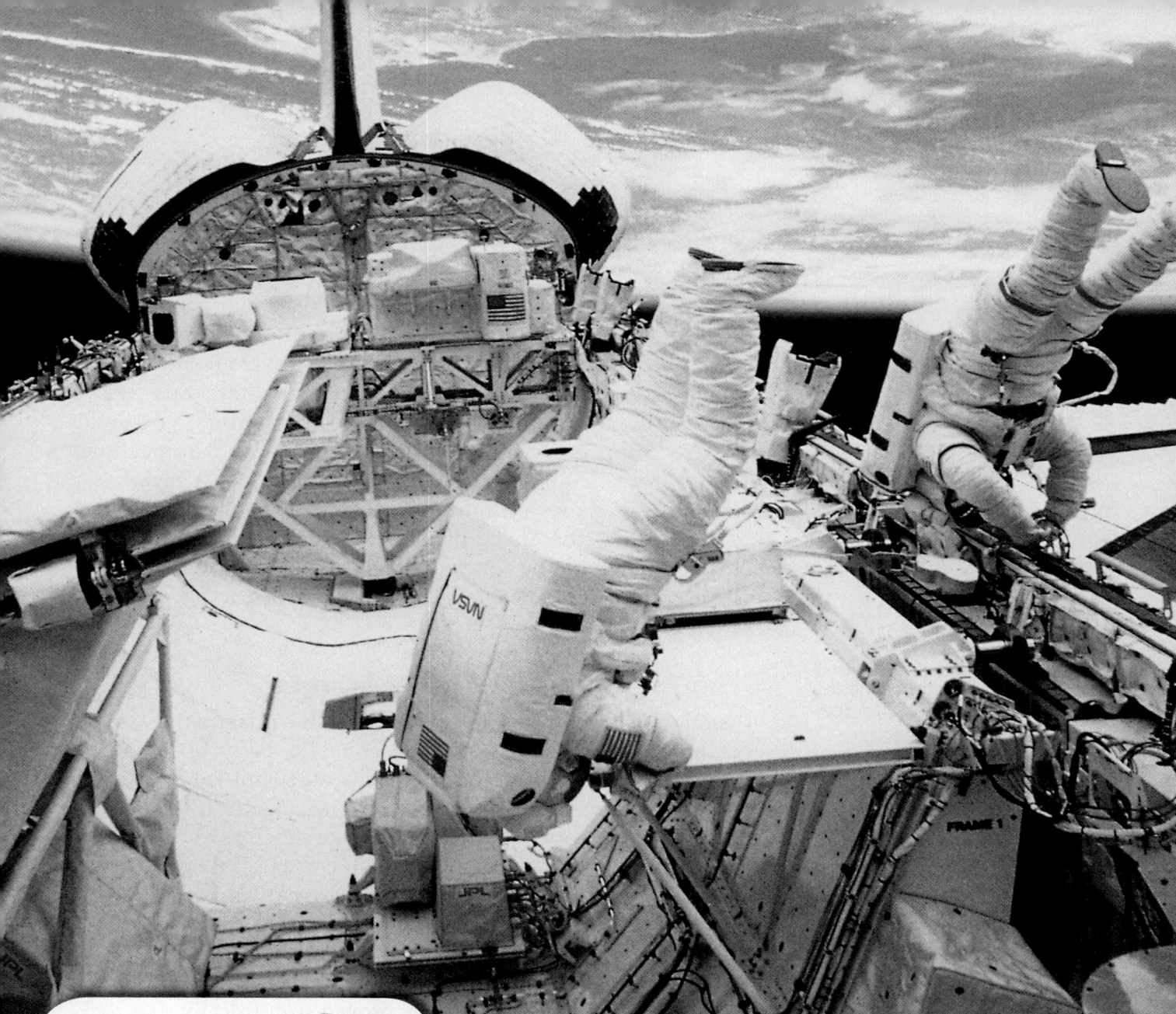

START-UP ACTIVITY

Balloon Rockets

In this activity you will launch a balloon "rocket" to learn about how rockets move.

Procedure

1. Insert a **2 m thread** through a **drinking straw,** and tie it between two objects that won't move, such as **chairs.** Make sure that the thread is tight.

2. Inflate a **large balloon.** Do not tie the neck of the balloon closed. Hold the neck of the balloon closed, and **tape** the balloon firmly to the straw, parallel to the thread.

3. Move the balloon to one end of the thread, and then release the neck of the balloon. Use a **meterstick** to record the distance the balloon traveled.

4. Repeat steps 2–3. This time, hold a piece of **poster board** behind the balloon.

Analysis

1. Did the poster board affect the distance that the balloon traveled? Explain your answer.

2. Newton's third law of motion states that for every action there is an equal and opposite reaction. Apply this idea and your observations of the balloon to explain how rockets accelerate. Do rockets move by "pushing off" a launch pad? Explain your answer.

Rocket Science

If you could pack all of your friends in a car and drive to the moon, it would take about 165 days to get there. And that doesn't include stopping for gas or food!

The moon is incredibly far away, and years ago people could only dream of traveling into space. The problem was that no machine could generate enough force to overcome Earth's gravity and reach outer space. But about 100 years ago, a Russian high school teacher named Konstantin Tsiolkovsky (KAHN stuhn TEEN TSI uhl KAHV skee) proposed that machines called *rockets* could take people to outer space. A **rocket** is a machine that uses escaping gas to move. Tsiolkovsky stated, "The Earth is the cradle of mankind. But one does not have to live in the cradle forever." Rockets would become the key to leaving the cradle of Earth and starting the age of space exploration.

The Beginnings of Rocket Science

Tsiolkovsky's inspiration came from the imaginative stories of Jules Verne. In Verne's book *From the Earth to the Moon*, characters reached the moon in a capsule shot from an enormous cannon. Although this idea would not work, Tsiolkovsky proved—in theory—that rockets could generate enough force to reach outer space. He also suggested the use of liquid rocket fuel to increase a rocket's range. For his vision and careful work, Tsiolkovsky is known as the father of rocket theory.

A Boost for Modern Rocketry

Although Tsiolkovsky proved scientifically that rockets could reach outer space, he never built any rockets himself. That task was left to American physicist and inventor Robert Goddard, shown in **Figure 1.** Goddard launched the first successful liquid-fuel rocket in 1926. Goddard tested more than 150 rocket engines, and by the time of World War II, Goddard's work began to interest the United States military. His work drew much attention because of a terrifying new weapon that the German army had developed.

Reading Check How did Tsiolkovsky and Goddard contribute to the development of rockets? (*See the Appendix for answers to Reading Checks.*)

Figure 1 *Robert Goddard is known as the father of modern rocketry.*

From Rocket Bombs to Rocket Ships

Toward the end of World War II, Germany developed a new weapon known as the V-2 rocket. The V-2 rocket, shown in **Figure 2,** could deliver explosives from German military bases to London—a distance of about 350 km. The V-2 rocket was developed by a team led by Wernher von Braun, a young Ph.D. student whose research was supported by the German military. But in 1945, near the end of the war, von Braun and his entire research team surrendered to the advancing Americans. The United States thus gained 127 of the best German rocket scientists. With this gain, rocket research in the United States boomed in the 1950s.

The Birth of NASA

The end of World War II marked the beginning of the *Cold War*—a long period of political tension between the United States and the Soviet Union. The Cold War was marked by an arms race and by competition in space technology. In response to Soviet advances in space, the U.S. government formed the National Aeronautics and Space Administration, or **NASA,** in 1958. NASA combined all of the rocket-development teams in the United States. Their cooperation led to the development of many rockets, including those shown in **Figure 3.**

Figure 2 *The V-2 rocket is the ancestor of all modern rockets.*

rocket a machine that uses escaping gas from burning fuel to move

NASA the **N**ational **A**eronautics and **S**pace **A**dministration

---

Figure 3 40 Years of NASA Rockets

A rocket's payload is the amount of material the rocket is able to carry into space.

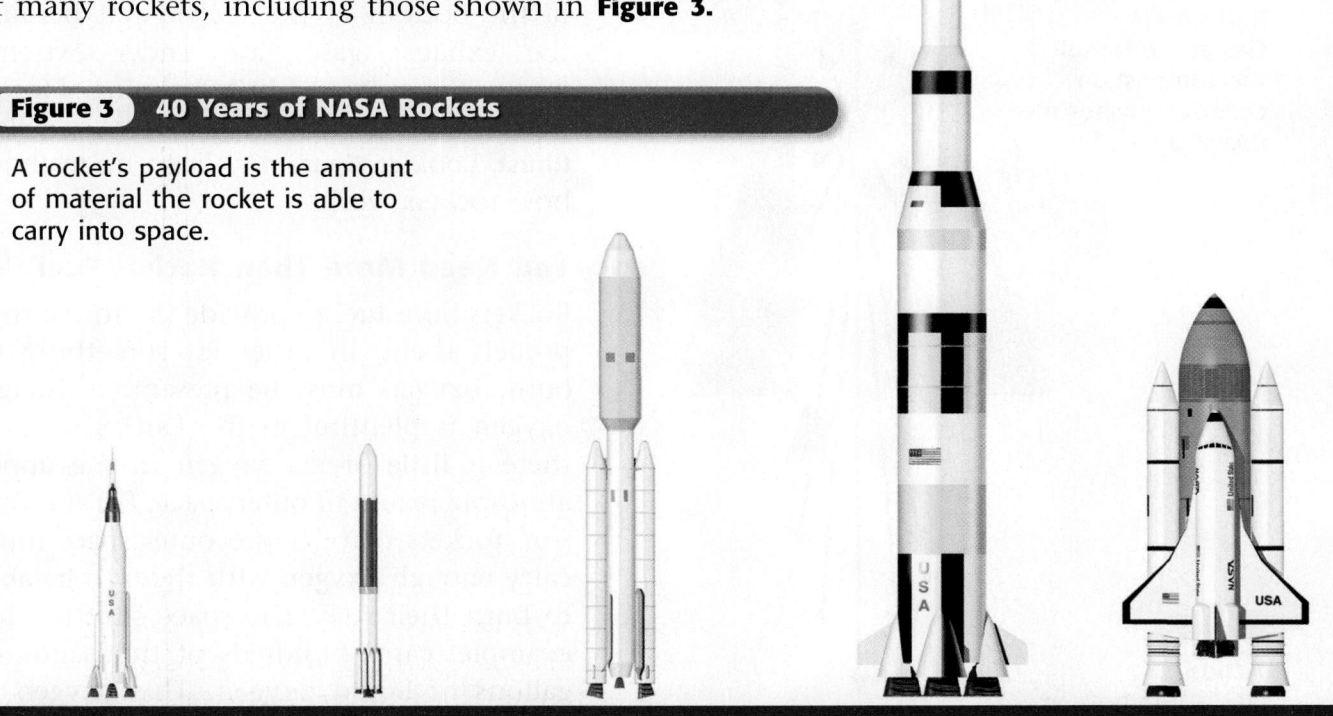

| *Mercury-Atlas*
Height: 29 m
Payload: 1,400 kg | *Delta*
Height: 36 m
Payload: 1,770 kg | *Titan IV*
Height: 62 m
Payload: 18,000 kg | *Saturn V*
Height: 111 m
Payload: 129,300 kg | **Space shuttle and boosters**
Height: 56 m
Payload: 29,500 kg |

How Rockets Work

thrust the pushing or pulling force exerted by the engine of an aircraft or rocket

If you are sitting in a chair that has wheels and you want to move, you would probably push away from a table or kick yourself along with your feet. Many people think that rockets move in a similar way—by pushing off of a launch pad. But if rockets moved in this way, how would they accelerate in the vacuum of space where there is nothing to push against?

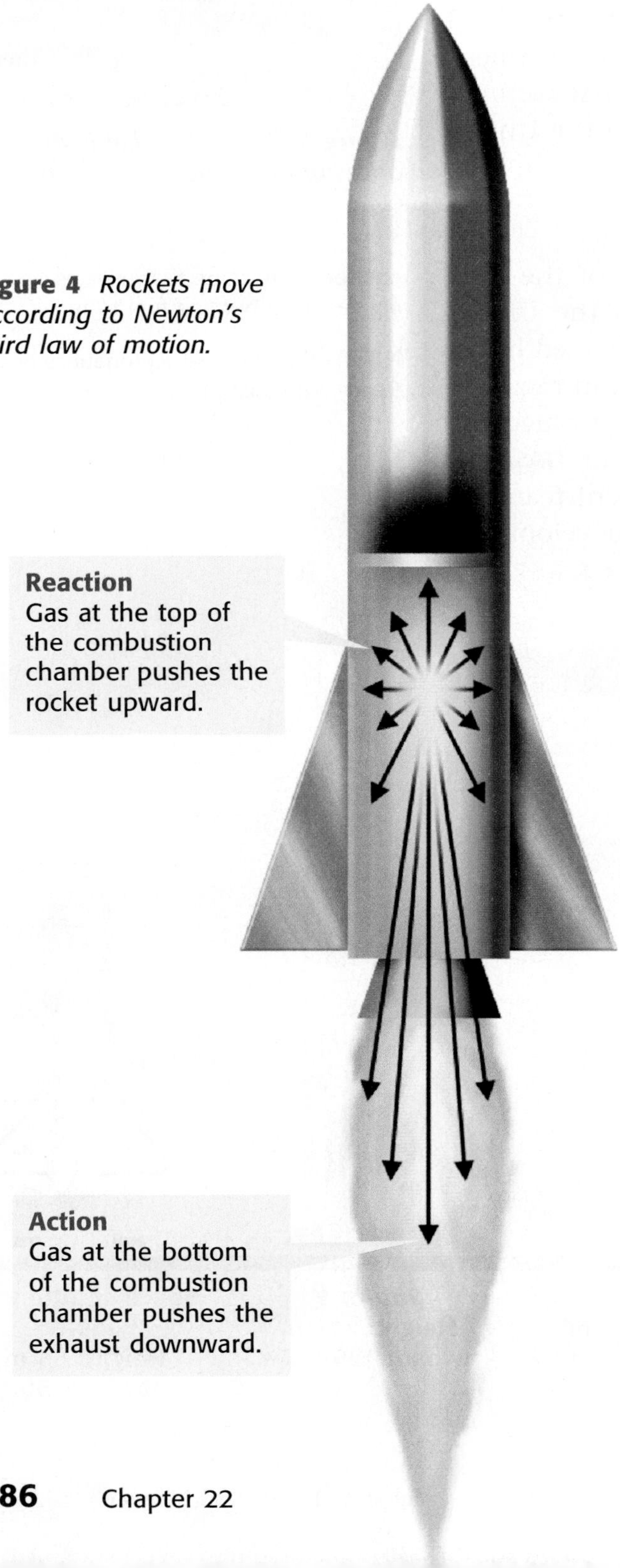

For Every Action . . .

As you saw in the Start-Up Activity, the balloon moved according to Newton's third law of motion. This law states that for every action there is an equal and opposite reaction. For example, the air rushing backward from a balloon (the action) results in the forward motion of the balloon (the reaction). Rockets work in the same way. In fact, rockets were once called *reaction devices*.

However, in the case of rockets, the action and the reaction may not be obvious. The mass of a rocket—including all of the fuel it carries—is much greater than the mass of the hot gases that come out of the bottom of the rocket. But because the exhaust gases are under extreme pressure, they exert a huge amount of force. The force that accelerates a rocket is called **thrust.** Look at **Figure 4** to learn more about how rockets work.

Figure 4 *Rockets move according to Newton's third law of motion.*

Reaction
Gas at the top of the combustion chamber pushes the rocket upward.

Action
Gas at the bottom of the combustion chamber pushes the exhaust downward.

You Need More Than Rocket Fuel

Rockets burn fuel to provide the thrust that propels them. In order for something to burn, oxygen must be present. Although oxygen is plentiful at the Earth's surface, there is little or no oxygen in the upper atmosphere and in outer space. For this reason, rockets that go into outer space must carry enough oxygen with them to be able to burn their fuel. The space shuttles, for example, carry hundreds of thousands of gallons of liquid oxygen. This oxygen is needed to burn the shuttle's rocket fuel.

Reading Check Why do rockets carry oxygen in addition to fuel?

686 Chapter 22

How to Leave the Earth

The gravitational pull of the Earth is the main factor that a rocket must overcome. As shown in **Figure 5,** a rocket must reach a certain *velocity*, or speed and direction, to orbit or escape the Earth.

Orbital Velocity and Escape Velocity

For a rocket to orbit the Earth, it must have enough thrust to reach orbital velocity. *Orbital velocity* is the speed and direction a rocket must travel in order to orbit a planet or moon. The lowest possible speed a rocket may go and still orbit the Earth is about 8 km/s (17,927 mi/h). If the rocket goes any slower, it will fall back to Earth. For a rocket to travel beyond Earth orbit, the rocket must achieve escape velocity. *Escape velocity* is the speed and direction a rocket must travel to completely break away from a planet's gravitational pull. The speed a rocket must reach to escape the Earth is about 11 km/s (24,606 mi/h).

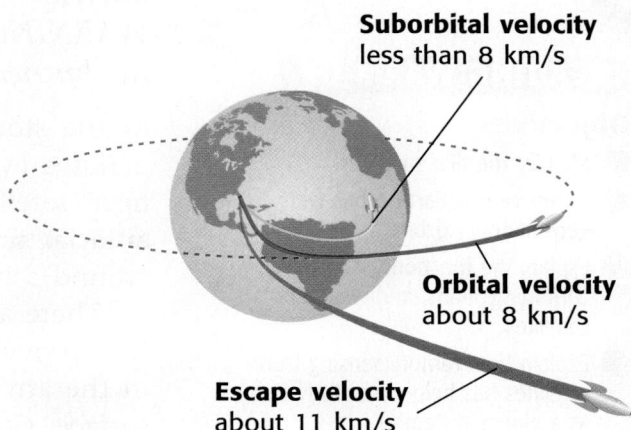

Suborbital velocity
less than 8 km/s

Orbital velocity
about 8 km/s

Escape velocity
about 11 km/s

Figure 5 *A rocket must travel very fast to escape the gravitational pull of the Earth.*

SECTION Review

Summary

- Tsiolkovsky and Goddard were pioneers of rocket science.

- The outcome of WWII and the political pressures of the Cold War helped advance rocket science.

- Rockets work according to Newton's third law of motion—for every action there is an equal and opposite reaction.

- Rockets need to reach different velocities to attain orbit and to escape a planet's gravitational attraction.

Using Key Terms

1. Use each of the following terms in a separate sentence: *rocket, thrust,* and *NASA.*

Understanding Key Ideas

2. What factor must a rocket overcome to reach escape velocity?
   a. Earth's axial tilt
   b. Earth's gravity
   c. the thrust of its engines
   d. Newton's third law of motion

3. Describe the contributions of Tsiolkovsky and Goddard to modern rocketry.

4. Use Newton's third law of motion to describe how rockets work.

5. What is the difference between orbital and escape velocity?

6. How did the Cold War accelerate the U.S. space program?

Math Skills

7. If you travel at 60 mi/h, it takes about 165 days to reach the moon. Approximately how far away is the moon?

Critical Thinking

8. **Applying Concepts** How do rockets accelerate in space?

9. **Making Inferences** Why does escape velocity vary depending on the planet from which a rocket is launched?

SCiLINKS.

NSTA
Developed and maintained by the
National Science Teachers Association

For a variety of links related to this chapter, go to www.scilinks.org

Topic: Rocket Technology
SciLinks code: HSM1323

READING WARM-UP

Objectives

● Identify the first satellites.

● Compare low Earth orbits with geostationary orbits.

● Explain the functions of military, communications, and weather satellites.

● Explain how remote sensing from satellites has helped us study Earth as a global system.

Terms to Learn

artificial satellite
low Earth orbit
geostationary orbit

READING STRATEGY

Reading Organizer As you read this section, make a table comparing the advantages and disadvantages of low Earth orbits and geostationary orbits.

Artificial Satellites

You are watching TV, and suddenly a weather bulletin interrupts your favorite show. There is a HURRICANE WARNING! You grab a cell phone and call your friend—the hurricane is headed straight for where she lives!

In the story above, the TV show, the weather bulletin, and perhaps even the phone call were all made possible by artificial satellites orbiting thousands of miles above Earth! An **artificial satellite** is any human-made object placed in orbit around a body in space.

There are many kinds of artificial satellites. Weather satellites provide continuous updates on the movement of gases in the atmosphere so that we can predict weather on Earth's surface. Communications satellites relay TV programs, phone calls, and computer data. Remote-sensing satellites monitor changes in the environment. Perhaps more than the exploration of space, satellites have changed the way we live.

The First Satellites

The first artificial satellite, *Sputnik 1,* was launched by the Soviets in 1957. **Figure 1** shows a model of *Sputnik 1,* which orbited for 57 days before it fell back to Earth and burned up in the atmosphere. Two months later, *Sputnik 2* carried the first living being into space—a dog named Laika. The United States followed with the launch of its first satellite, *Explorer 1,* in 1958. The development of new satellites increased quickly. By 1964, communications satellite networks were able to send messages around the world. Today, thousands of satellites orbit the Earth, and more are launched every year.

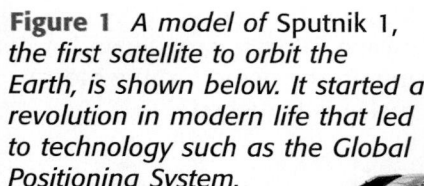

Figure 1 *A model of* Sputnik 1, *the first satellite to orbit the Earth, is shown below. It started a revolution in modern life that led to technology such as the Global Positioning System.*

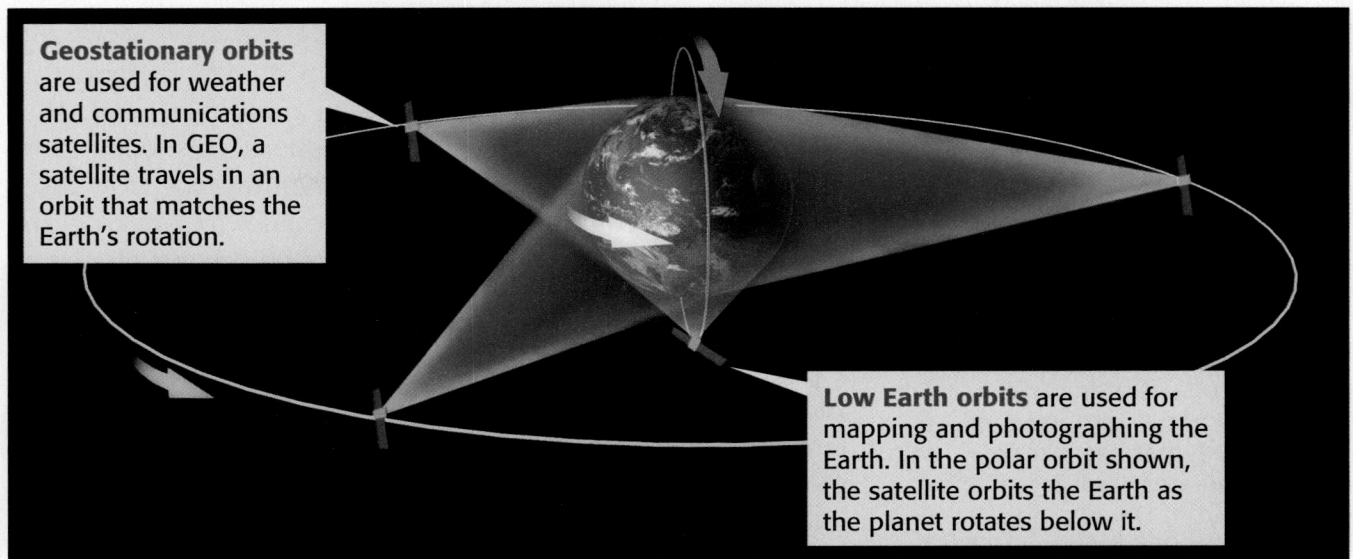

Geostationary orbits are used for weather and communications satellites. In GEO, a satellite travels in an orbit that matches the Earth's rotation.

Low Earth orbits are used for mapping and photographing the Earth. In the polar orbit shown, the satellite orbits the Earth as the planet rotates below it.

Choosing Your Orbit

Satellites are placed in different types of orbits, as shown in **Figure 2.** All of the early satellites were placed in **low Earth orbit** (LEO), which is a few hundred kilometers above the Earth's surface. A satellite in LEO moves around the Earth very quickly and can provide clear images of Earth. However, this motion can place a satellite out of contact much of the time.

Most communications satellites and weather satellites orbit much farther from Earth. In this orbit, called a **geostationary orbit** (GEO), a satellite travels in an orbit that exactly matches the Earth's rotation. Thus, the satellite is always above the same spot on Earth. Ground stations are in continuous contact with these satellites so that TV programs and other communications will not be interrupted.

✓ **Reading Check** What is the difference between GEO and LEO? (*See the Appendix for answers to Reading Checks.*)

Figure 2 *Low Earth orbits are in the upper reaches of Earth's atmosphere, while geostationary orbits are about 36,000 km from Earth's surface.*

artificial satellite any human-made object placed in orbit around a body in space

low Earth orbit an orbit less than 1,500 km above the Earth's surface

geostationary orbit an orbit that is about 36,000 km above the Earth's surface and in which a satellite is above a fixed spot on the equator

Modeling LEO and GEO

1. Use a **length of thread** to measure 300 km on the scale of a **globe.**

2. Use another **length of thread** to measure 36,000 km on the globe's scale.

3. Use the short thread to measure the distance of LEO from the surface of the globe and the long thread to measure the distance of GEO from the surface of the globe.

4. Your teacher will turn off the lights. One student will spin the globe, while other students will hold **penlights** at LEO and GEO orbits.

5. Was more of the globe illuminated by the penlights in LEO or GEO?

6. Which orbit is better for communications satellites? Which orbit is better for spy satellites?

Triangulation

GPS uses the principle of triangulation. To practice triangulation, use a drawing compass and a photocopy of a U.S. map that has a scale. Try to find a city that is 980 km from Detroit and Miami, and 950 km from Baltimore. For each city named, adjust the compass to the correct distance on the map's scale. Then, place the compass point on the city's location. Draw a circle with a radius equal to the given distance. Where do the circles overlap? Once you have solved this riddle, write one for a friend!

ACTIVITY

Military Satellites

Some satellites placed in LEO are equipped with cameras that can photograph the Earth's surface in amazing detail. It is possible to photograph objects as small as this book from LEO. While photographs taken by satellites are now used for everything from developing real estate to tracking the movements of dolphins, the technology was first developed by the military. Because satellites can take very detailed photos from hundreds of kilometers above the Earth's surface, they are ideal for defense purposes. The United States and the Soviet Union developed satellites to spy on each other right up to the end of the Cold War. **Figure 3,** for example, is a photo of San Francisco taken by a Soviet spy satellite in 1989. Even though the Cold War is over, spy satellites continue to play an important role in the military defense of many countries.

The Global Positioning System

In the past, people invented very complicated ways to keep from getting lost. Now, for less than $100, people can find out their exact location on Earth by using a Global Positioning System (GPS) receiver. GPS is another example of military satellite technology that has become a part of everyday life. The GPS consists of 27 solar-powered satellites that continuously send radio signals to Earth. From the amount of time it takes the signals to reach Earth, the hand-held receiver can calculate its distance from the satellites. Using the distance from four satellites, a GPS receiver can determine a person's location with great accuracy.

Figure 3 *This photo was taken in 1989 by a Soviet spy satellite in LEO about 220 km above San Francisco. Can you identify any objects on the ground?*

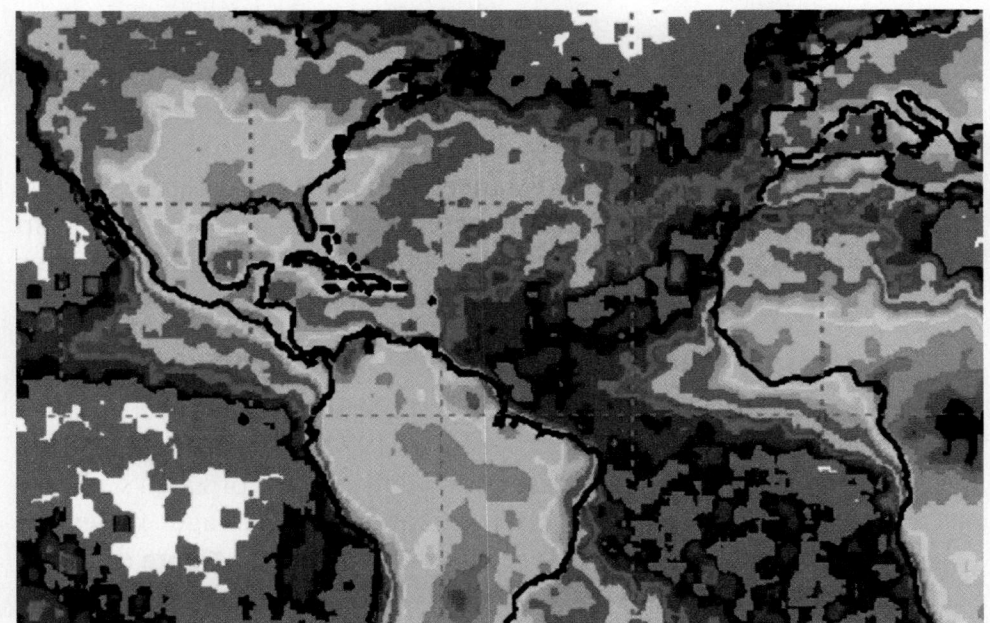

Figure 4 *This map shows average annual lightning strikes around the world. Red and black indicate a high number of strikes. Cooler colors, such as purple and blue, indicate fewer strikes.*

Weather Satellites

It is hard to imagine life without reliable weather forecasts. Every day, millions of people make decisions based on information provided by weather satellites. Weather satellites in GEO provide a big-picture view of the Earth's atmosphere. These satellites constantly monitor the atmosphere for the "triggers" that lead to severe weather conditions. Weather satellites in GEO created the map of world lightning strikes shown in **Figure 4.** Weather satellites in LEO are usually placed in polar orbits. Satellites in polar orbits revolve around the Earth in a north or south direction as the Earth rotates beneath them. These satellites, which orbit between 830 km and 870 km above the Earth, provide a much closer look at weather patterns.

Communications Satellites

Many types of modern communications use radio waves or microwaves to relay messages. Radio waves and microwaves are ideal for communications because they can travel through the air. The problem is that the Earth is round, but the waves travel in a straight line. So how do you send a message to someone on the other side of the Earth? Communications satellites in GEO solve this problem by relaying information from one point on Earth's surface to another. The signals are transmitted to a satellite and then sent to receivers around the world. Communications satellites relay computer data, and some television and radio broadcasts.

✓ Reading Check How do communications satellites relay information from one point on Earth's surface to another?

SCHOOL to HOME

Tracking Satellites

A comfortable lawn chair and a clear night sky are all you need to track satellites. Just after sunset or before sunrise, satellites in LEO are easy to track. They look like slow-moving stars, and they generally move in a west to east direction. With a little practice, you should be able to find one or two satellites a minute. A pair of binoculars will help you get a closer look. Satellites in GEO are difficult to see because they do not appear to move. You and a parent can find out more about how to track specific satellites and space stations on the Internet.

ACTIVITY

Remote Sensing and Environmental Change

Using satellites, scientists have been able to study the Earth in ways that were never before possible. Satellites gather information by *remote sensing*. Remote sensing is the gathering of images and data from a distance. Remote-sensing satellites measure light and other forms of energy that are reflected from Earth. Some satellites use radar, which bounces high-frequency radio waves off the Earth and measures the returned signal.

Landsat: Monitoring the Earth from Orbit

One of the most successful remote-sensing projects is the Landsat program, which began in 1972 and continues today. It has given us the longest continuous record of Earth's surface as seen from space. Landsat satellites gather images in several wavelengths—from visible light to infrared. **Figure 5** shows Landsat images of part of the Mississippi Delta. One image was taken in 1973, and the other was taken in 2003. The two images reveal a pattern of environmental change over a 30-year period. The main change is a dramatic reduction in the amount of silt that is reaching the delta. A comparison of the images also reveals a large-scale loss of wetlands in the bottom left of the delta in 2003. The loss of wetlands affects plants and animals living on the delta and the fishing industry.

Figure 5 **The Loss of Wetlands in the Mississippi Delta**

Silt reaching the Mississippi Delta is shown in blue. In 1973 (left), the amount of silt reaching the delta was much greater than in 2003 (right). This reduction led to the rapid loss of wetlands, which are green in this image. Notice the lower left corner of the delta in both images. Areas of wetland loss are black.

1973

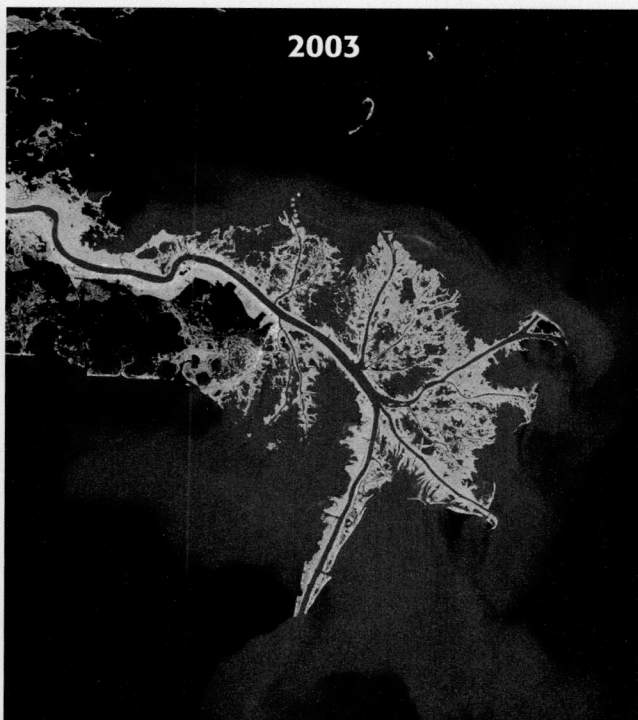

2003

A New Generation of Remote-Sensing Satellites

The Landsat program has produced millions of images that are used to identify and track environmental change on Earth. Satellite remote sensing allows scientists to perform large-scale mapping, look at changes in patterns of vegetation growth, map the spread of urban development, and study the effect of humans on the global environment. In 1999, NASA launched *Terra 1*, the first satellite in NASA's Earth Observing System (EOS) program. Satellites in the EOS program are designed to work together so that they can gather integrated data on environmental change on the land, in the atmosphere, in the oceans, and on the icecaps.

✓ **Reading Check** What is unique about the EOS program?

INTERNET ACTIVITY

For another activity related to this chapter, go to **go.hrw.com** and type in the keyword **HZ5EXPW**.

SECTION Review

Summary

- *Sputnik 1* was the first artificial satellite. *Explorer 1* was the first U.S. satellite.
- Low Earth orbits are used for making detailed images of the Earth.
- Geostationary orbits are used for communications, navigation, and weather satellites.
- Satellites with remote sensing technology have helped us understand the Earth as a global system.

Using Key Terms

1. Use each of the following terms in a separate sentence: *artificial satellite, low Earth orbit,* and *geostationary orbit.*

Understanding Key Ideas

2. In a low Earth orbit, the speed of a satellite is
   a. slower than the rotational speed of the Earth.
   b. equal to the rotational speed of the Earth.
   c. faster than the rotational speed of the Earth.
   d. None of the above

3. What was the name of the first satellite placed in orbit?

4. List three ways that satellites benefit human society.

5. What was the *Explorer 1*?

6. Explain the differences between LEO and GEO satellites.

7. How does the Global Positioning System work?

8. How do communications satellites relay signals around the curved surface of Earth?

Math Skills

9. The speed required to reach Earth orbit is 8 km/s. What does this equal in *meters per hour*?

Critical Thinking

10. **Applying Concepts** The *Hubble Space Telescope* is located in LEO. Does the telescope move faster or slower around the Earth compared with a geostationary weather satellite? Explain.

11. **Applying Concepts** To triangulate your location on a map, you need to know your distance from three points. If you knew your distance from two points, how many possible places could you occupy?

SCI LINKS.

NSTA

Developed and maintained by the National Science Teachers Association

For a variety of links related to this chapter, go to www.scilinks.org

Topic: Artificial Satellites
SciLinks code: HSM0101

Space Probes

What does the surface of Mars look like? Does life exist anywhere else in the solar system?

To answer questions like these, scientists send space probes to explore the solar system. A **space probe** is an uncrewed vehicle that carries scientific instruments to planets or other bodies in space. Unlike satellites, which stay in Earth orbit, space probes travel away from the Earth. Space probes are valuable because they can complete missions that would be very dangerous and expensive for humans to undertake.

Visits to the Inner Solar System

Because Earth's moon and the inner planets are much closer than the other planets and moons in the solar system, they were the first to be explored by space probes. Let's take a closer look at some missions to the moon, Venus, and Mars.

Luna and Clementine: Missions to the Moon

Luna 1, the first space probe, was launched by the Soviets in 1959 to fly past the moon. In 1966, *Luna 9* made the first soft landing on the moon's surface. During the next 10 years, the United States and the Soviet Union completed more than 30 lunar missions. Thousands of images of the moon's surface were taken. In 1994, the United States probe *Clementine* discovered that craters of the moon may contain water left by comet impacts. In 1998, the *Lunar Prospector* confirmed that frozen water exists on the moon. This ice would be very valuable to a human colony on the moon.

READING WARM-UP

Objectives

- Describe five discoveries made by space probes.
- Explain how space-probe missions help us better understand the Earth.
- Describe how NASA's new strategy of "faster, cheaper, and better" relates to space probes.

Terms to Learn

space probe

READING STRATEGY

Reading Organizer As you read this section, make a concept map showing the space probes, the planetary bodies they visited, and their discoveries.

space probe an uncrewed vehicle that carries scientific instruments into space to collect scientific data

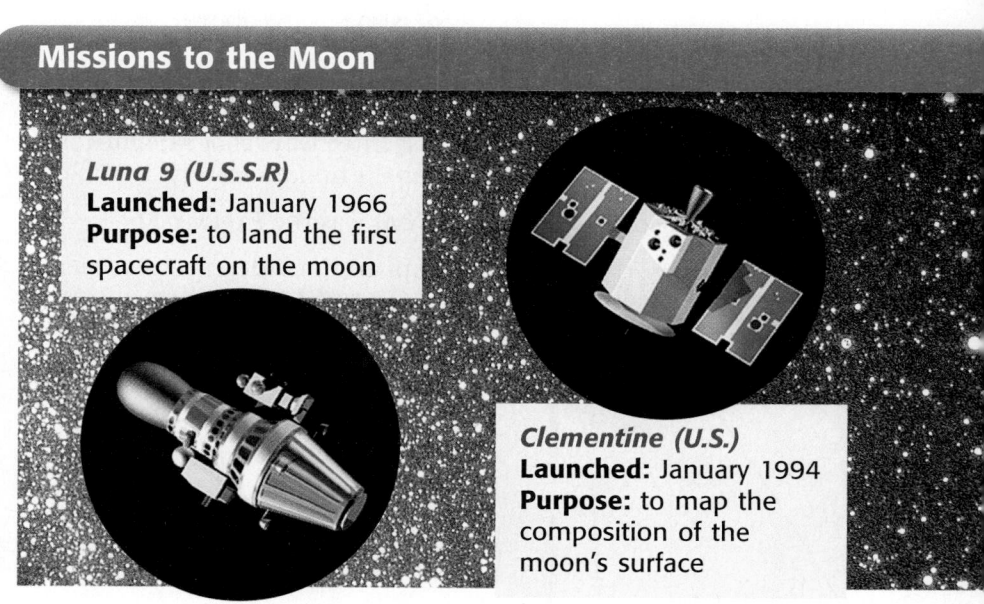

Missions to the Moon

Luna 9 (U.S.S.R)
Launched: January 1966
Purpose: to land the first spacecraft on the moon

Clementine (U.S.)
Launched: January 1994
Purpose: to map the composition of the moon's surface

Venera 9: The First Probe to Land on Venus

The Soviet probe *Venera 9* was the first probe to land on Venus. The probe parachuted into Venus's atmosphere and transmitted images of the surface to Earth. *Venera 9* found that the surface temperature and atmospheric pressure on Venus are much higher than on Earth. The surface temperature of Venus is an average of 464°C—hot enough to melt lead! *Venera 9* also found that the chemistry of the surface rocks on Venus is similar to that of Earth rocks. Perhaps most important, *Venera 9* and earlier missions revealed that Venus has a severe greenhouse effect. Scientists study Venus's atmosphere to learn about the effects of increased greenhouse gases in Earth's atmosphere.

The Magellan Mission: Mapping Venus

In 1989, the United States launched the *Magellan* probe, which used radar to map 98% of the surface of Venus. The radar data were transmitted back to Earth where computers used the data to generate three-dimensional images like the one shown in **Figure 1.** The Magellan mission showed that, in many ways, the geology of Venus is similar to that of Earth. Venus has features that suggest plate tectonics occurs there, as it does on Earth. Venus also has volcanoes, and some of them may be active.

Reading Check What discoveries were made by *Magellan*? (*See the Appendix for answers to Reading Checks.*)

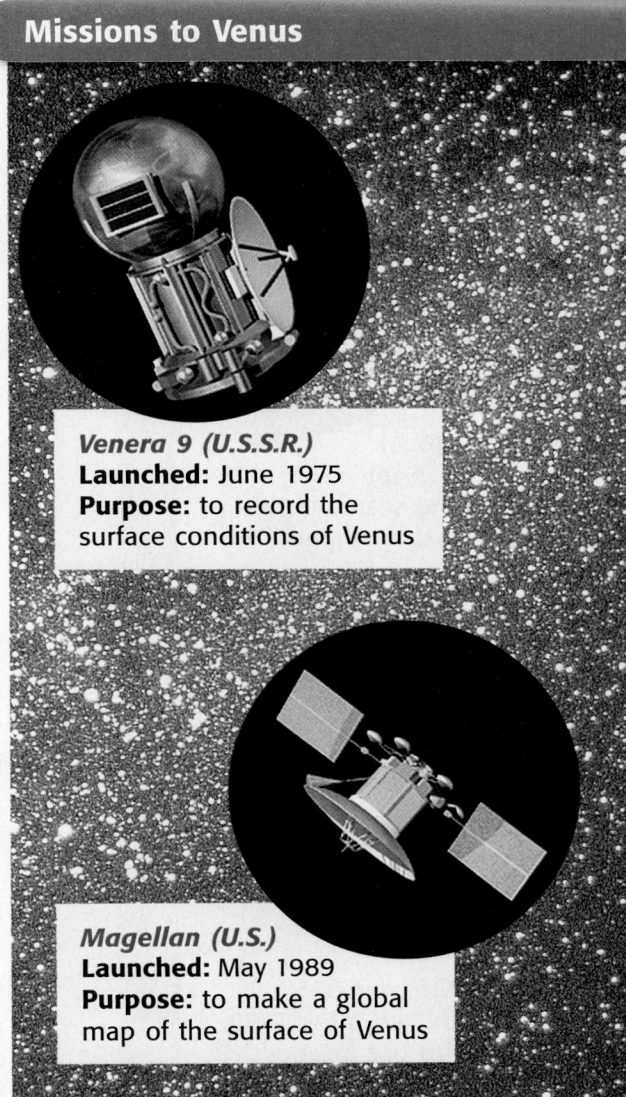

Missions to Venus

Venera 9 (U.S.S.R.)
Launched: June 1975
Purpose: to record the surface conditions of Venus

Magellan (U.S.)
Launched: May 1989
Purpose: to make a global map of the surface of Venus

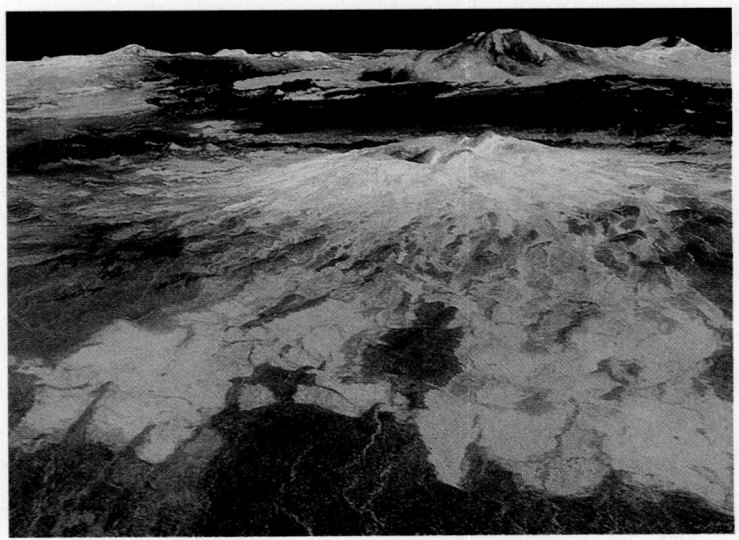

Figure 1 *This false-color image of volcanoes on the surface of Venus was made with radar data transmitted to Earth by* Magellan.

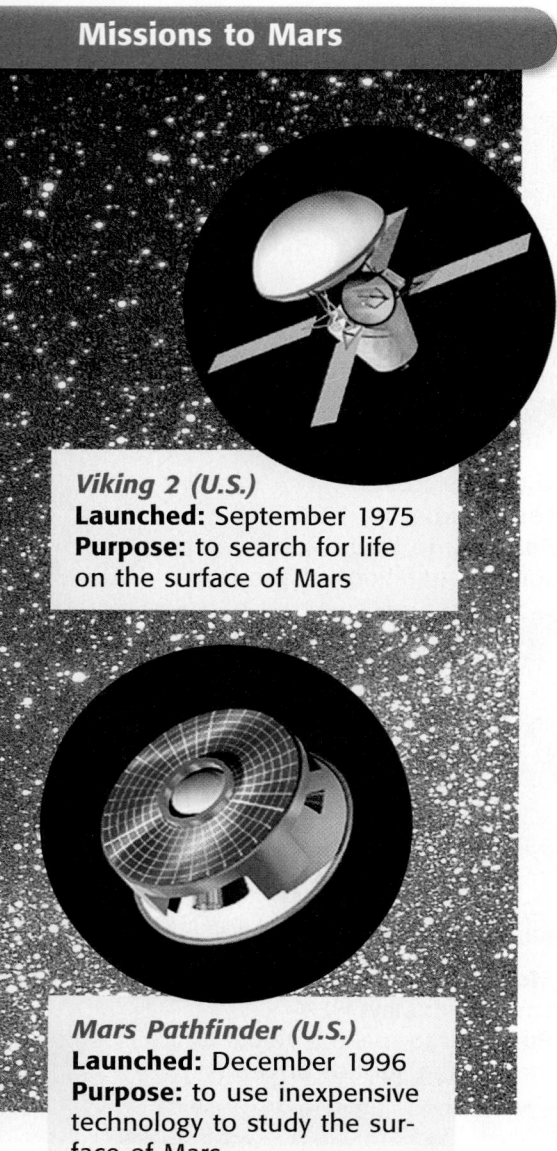

Viking 2 (U.S.)
Launched: September 1975
Purpose: to search for life on the surface of Mars

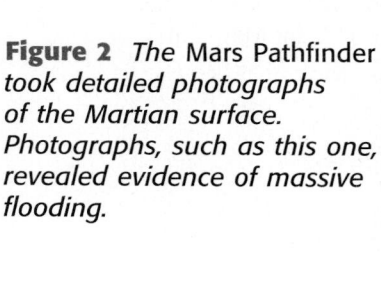

Mars Pathfinder (U.S.)
Launched: December 1996
Purpose: to use inexpensive technology to study the surface of Mars

The Viking Missions: Exploring Mars

In 1975, the United States sent a pair of probes—*Viking 1* and *Viking 2*—to Mars. The surface of Mars is more like the Earth's surface than that of any other planet. For this reason, one of the main goals of the Viking missions was to look for signs of life. The probes contained instruments designed to gather soil and test it for evidence of life. However, no hard evidence was found. The Viking missions did find evidence that Mars was once much warmer and wetter than it is now. This discovery led scientists to ask even more questions about Mars. Did the Martian climate once support life? Why and when did the Martian climate change?

The Mars Pathfinder Mission: Revisiting Mars

More than 20 years later, in 1997, the surface of Mars was visited again by a NASA space probe. The goal of the Mars Pathfinder mission was to show that Martian exploration is possible at a much lower cost than the Viking missions. The probe sent back detailed images of dry water channels on the planet's surface. These images, such as the one shown in **Figure 2**, suggest that massive floods flowed across the surface of Mars relatively recently in the planet's past. The *Mars Pathfinder* successfully landed on Mars and deployed the *Sojourner* rover. *Sojourner* traveled across the surface of Mars for almost three months, collecting data and recording images. The European Space Agency and NASA have many more Mars missions planned for the near future. These missions will pave the way for a crewed mission to Mars that may occur in your lifetime!

✓ Reading Check What discoveries were made by the Mars Pathfinder mission?

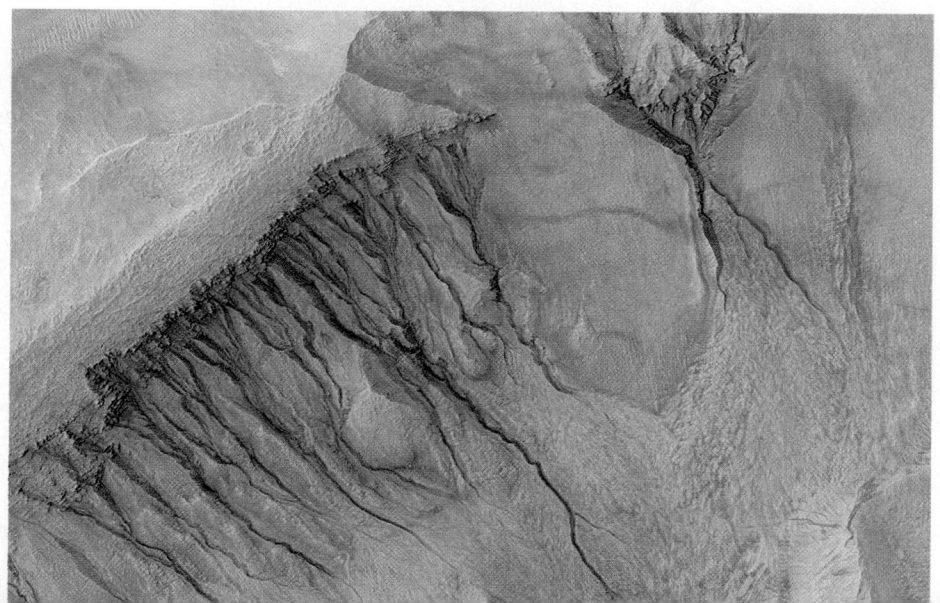

Figure 2 *The Mars Pathfinder took detailed photographs of the Martian surface. Photographs, such as this one, revealed evidence of massive flooding.*

696 Chapter 22

Visits to the Outer Solar System

The planets in the outer solar system—Jupiter, Saturn, Uranus, Neptune, and Pluto—are very far away. Probes such as those described below can take 10 years or more to complete their missions.

Pioneer and Voyager: To Jupiter and Beyond

The *Pioneer 10* and *Pioneer 11* space probes were the first to visit the outer planets. Among other things, these probes sampled the *solar wind*—the flow of particles coming from the sun. The Pioneer probes also found that the dark belts on Jupiter provide deep views into Jupiter's atmosphere. In 1983, *Pioneer 10* became the first probe to travel past the orbit of Pluto, the outermost planet.

The Voyager space probes were the first to detect Jupiter's faint rings, and *Voyager 2* was the first probe to fly by the four gas giants—Jupiter, Saturn, Uranus, and Neptune. The paths of the Pioneer and Voyager space probes are shown in **Figure 3.** Today, they are near the solar system's edge and some are still sending back data.

The Galileo Mission: A Return to Jupiter

The *Galileo* probe arrived at Jupiter in 1995. While *Galileo* itself began a long tour of Jupiter's moons, it sent a smaller probe into Jupiter's atmosphere to measure its composition, density, temperature, and cloud structure. *Galileo* gathered data about the geology of Jupiter's major moons and Jupiter's magnetic properties. The moons of Jupiter proved to be far more exciting than the earlier Pioneer and Voyager images had suggested. *Galileo* discovered that two of Jupiter's moons have magnetic fields and that one of its moons, Europa, may have an ocean of liquid water under its icy surface.

Missions to the Outer Solar System

Pioneer 10 (U.S.)
Launched: March 1972
Purpose: to study Jupiter and the outer solar system

Galileo (U.S.)
Launched: October 1989
Purpose: to study Jupiter and its moons

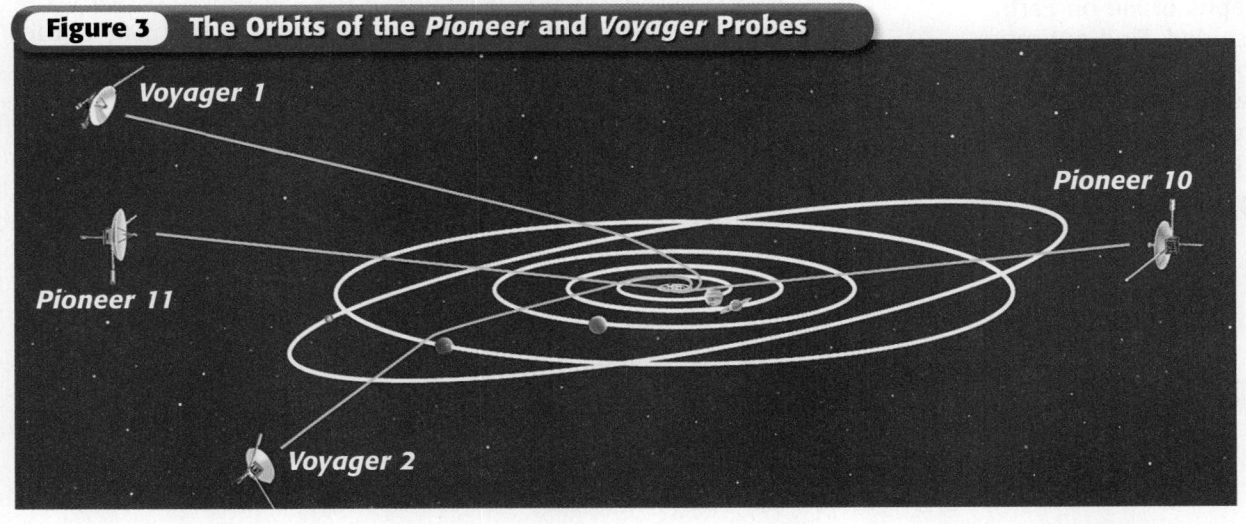

Figure 3 The Orbits of the *Pioneer* and *Voyager* Probes

Voyager 1

Pioneer 10

Pioneer 11

Voyager 2

Figure 4 *This artist's view shows the* Huygens *probe parachuting to the surface of Saturn's moon Titan. Saturn and* Cassini *are in the background.*

CONNECTION TO Social Studies

Cosmic Message in a Bottle
When the Voyager space probes were launched in 1977, they carried a variety of messages intended for alien civilizations that might find them. In addition to greetings spoken in 55 different languages, a variety of songs, nature sounds, a diagram of the solar system, and photographs of life on Earth were included. Find out more about the message carried by the Voyager missions, and then create your own cosmic message in a bottle.

ACTIVITY

The Cassini Mission: Exploring Saturn's Moons

In 1997, the *Cassini* space probe was launched on a seven-year journey to Saturn where it will make a grand tour of Saturn's moons. As shown in **Figure 4,** a smaller probe, called the *Huygens* probe, will detach itself from *Cassini* and descend into the atmosphere of Saturn's moon Titan. Scientists are interested in Titan's atmosphere because it may be similar to the Earth's early atmosphere. Titan's atmosphere may reveal clues about how life developed on Earth.

Faster, Cheaper, and Better

The early space probe missions were very large and costly. Probes such as *Voyager 2* and *Galileo* took years to develop. Now, NASA has a vision for missions that are "faster, cheaper, and better." One new program, called Discovery, seeks proposals for smaller science programs. The first six approved Discovery missions include sending small space probes to asteroids, landing on Mars again, studying the moon, and returning comet dust to Earth.

Stardust: Comet Detective

Launched in 1999, the *Stardust* space probe is the first probe to focus only on a comet. The probe will arrive at the comet in 2004 and gather samples of the comet's dust tail. It will return the samples to Earth in 2006. For the first time, pure samples from beyond the orbit of the moon will be brought back to Earth. The comet dust should help scientists better understand how the solar system formed.

✓ **Reading Check** What is the mission of the *Stardust* probe?

Deep Space 1: Testing Ion Propulsion

Another NASA project is the New Millennium program. Its purpose is to test new technologies that can be used in the future. *Deep Space 1,* shown in **Figure 5,** is the first mission of this program. It is a space probe with an ion-propulsion system. Instead of burning chemical fuel, an ion rocket uses charged particles that exit the vehicle at high speed. An ion rocket follows Newton's third law of motion, but it does so using a unique source of propulsion. Ion propulsion is like sitting on the back of a truck and shooting peas out of a straw. If there were no friction, the truck would gradually accelerate to tremendous speeds.

Figure 5 Deep Space 1 *uses a revolutionary type of propulsion— an ion rocket.*

SECTION Review

Summary

- Exploration with space probes began with missions to the moon. Space probes then explored other bodies in the inner solar system.

- Space-probe missions to Mars have focused on the search for signs of water and life.

- The Pioneer and Voyager programs explored the outer solar system.

- Space probe missions have helped us understand Earth's formation and environment.

- NASA's new strategy of "faster, cheaper, and better" seeks to create space-probe missions that are smaller than those of the past.

Using Key Terms

The statements below are false. For each statement, replace the underlined term to make a true statement.

1. <u>Luna 1</u> discovered evidence of water on the moon.

2. <u>Venera 9</u> helped map 98% of Venus's surface.

3. <u>Stardust</u> uses ion propulsion to accelerate.

Understanding Key Ideas

4. What is the significance of the discovery of evidence of water on the moon?
   a. Water is responsible for the formation of craters.
   b. Water was left by early space probes.
   c. Water could be used by future moon colonies.
   d. The existence of water proves that there is life on the moon.

5. Describe three discoveries that have been made by space probes.

6. How do missions to Venus, Mars, and Titan help us understand Earth's environment?

Math Skills

7. Traveling at the speed of light, signals from *Voyager 1* take about 12 h to reach Earth. The speed of light is about 299,793 km/s, how far away is the probe?

Critical Thinking

8. **Making Inferences** Why did we need space probes to discover water channels on Mars and evidence of ice on Europa?

9. **Expressing Opinions** What are the advantages of the new Discovery program over the older space-probe missions, and what are the disadvantages?

10. **Applying Concepts** How does *Deep Space 1* use Newton's third law of motion to accelerate?

SCILINKS®

NSTA
Developed and maintained by the
National Science Teachers Association

For a variety of links related to this chapter, go to www.scilinks.org

Topic: Space Probes
SciLinks code: HSM1342

People in Space

One April morning in 1961, a rocket stood on a launch pad in a remote part of the Soviet Union. Inside, a 27-year-old cosmonaut named Yuri Gagarin sat and waited. He was about to do what no human had done before—travel to outer space. No one knew if the human brain would function in space or if he would be instantly killed by radiation.

On April 12, 1961, Yuri Gagarin, shown in **Figure 1,** became the first human to orbit Earth. The flight lasted 108 minutes. An old woman, her granddaughter, and a cow were the first to see Gagarin as he safely parachuted back to Earth, but the news of his success was quickly broadcast around the world.

The Race Is On

The Soviets were first once again, and the Americans were concerned that their rivals were winning the space race. Therefore, on May 25, 1961, President Kennedy announced, "I believe that the nation should commit itself to achieving the goal, before this decade is out, of landing a man on the moon and returning him safely to the Earth. No single project in this period will be more impressive to mankind, or more important for the long range exploration of space."

Kennedy's speech took everyone by surprise—even NASA's leaders. Go to the moon? We had not even reached orbit yet! In response to Kennedy's challenge, a new spaceport called Kennedy Space Center was built in Florida and Mission Control was established in Houston, Texas. In February 1962, John Glenn became the first American to orbit the Earth.

Figure 1 *In 1961, Yuri Gagarin (left) became the first person in space. In 1962, John Glenn (right) became the first American to orbit the Earth.*

"The Eagle Has Landed"

Seven years later, on July 20, 1969, Kennedy's challenge was met. The world watched on television as the *Apollo 11* landing module—the *Eagle,* shown in **Figure 2**—landed on the moon. Neil Armstrong became the first human to set foot on a world other than Earth. This moment forever changed the way we view ourselves and our planet. The Apollo missions also contributed to the advancement of science. *Apollo 11* returned moon rocks to Earth for study. Its crew also put devices on the moon to study moonquakes and the solar wind.

The Space Shuttle

The Saturn V rockets, which carried the Apollo astronauts to the moon, were huge and very expensive. They were longer than a football field, and each could be used only once. To save money, NASA began to develop the space shuttle program in 1972. A **space shuttle** is a reusable space vehicle that takes off like a rocket and lands like an airplane.

The Space Shuttle Gets off the Ground

Columbia, the first space shuttle, was launched on April 12, 1981. Since then, NASA has completed more than 100 successful shuttle missions. If you look at the shuttle *Endeavour* in **Figure 3,** you can see its main parts. The orbiter is about the size of an airplane. It carries the astronauts and payload into space. The liquid-fuel tank is the large red column. Two white solid-fuel booster rockets help the shuttle reach orbit. Then they fall back to Earth along with the fuel tank. The booster rockets are reused, the fuel tank is not. After completing a mission, the orbiter returns to Earth and lands like an airplane.

✓ Reading Check What are the main parts of the shuttle? (*See the Appendix for answers to Reading Checks.*)

Shuttle Tragedies

On January 28, 1986, the booster rocket on the space shuttle *Challenger* exploded just after takeoff, killing all seven of its astronauts. On board was Christa McAuliffe, who would have been the first teacher in space. Investigations found that cold weather on the morning of the launch had caused rubber gaskets in the solid fuel booster rockets to stiffen and fail. The failure of the gaskets led to the explosion. The shuttle program resumed in 1988. In 2003, however, the space shuttle *Columbia* exploded as it reentered the atmosphere. All seven astronauts onboard were killed. These disasters emphasize the dangers of space exploration that continue to challenge scientists and engineers.

Figure 2 *Neil Armstrong took this photo of Edwin "Buzz" Aldrin as Aldrin was about to become the second human to set foot on the moon.*

space shuttle a reusable space vehicle that takes off like a rocket and lands like an airplane

Figure 3 *The space shuttles are the first reusable space vehicles.*

Figure 4 *As this illustration shows, space planes may provide transportation to outer space and around the world.*

Space Planes: The Shuttles of the Future?

NASA is working to develop advanced space systems, such as a space plane. This craft will fly like a normal airplane, but it will have rocket engines for use in space. Once in operation, space planes, such as the one shown in **Figure 4,** may lower the cost of getting material to LEO by 90%. Private companies are also becoming interested in developing space vehicles for commercial use and to make space travel cheaper, easier, and safer.

Space Stations—People Working in Space

space station a long-term orbiting platform from which other vehicles can be launched or scientific research can be carried out

A long-term orbiting platform in space is called a **space station.** On April 19, 1971, the Soviets became the first to successfully place a space station in orbit. A crew of three Soviet cosmonauts conducted a 23-day mission aboard the station, which was called *Salyut 1*. By 1982, the Soviets had put up seven space stations. Because of this experience, the Soviet Union became a leader in space-station development and in the study of the effects of weightlessness on humans. Their discoveries will be important for future flights to other planets—journeys that will take years to complete.

Skylab and *Mir*

Skylab, the United States' first space station, was a science and engineering lab used to conduct a wide variety of scientific studies. These studies included experiments in biology and space manufacturing and astronomical observations. Three different crews spent a total of 171 days on *Skylab* before it was abandoned. In 1986, the Soviets began to launch the pieces for a much more ambitious space station called *Mir* (meaning "peace"). Astronauts on *Mir* conducted a wide range of experiments, made many astronomical observations, and studied manufacturing in space. After 15 years, *Mir* was abandoned and it burned up in the Earth's atmosphere in 2001.

CONNECTION TO Biology

Effects of Weightlessness
When a human body stays in space for long periods of time without having to work against gravity, the bones lose mass and muscles become weaker. Find out about the exercises to reduce the loss of bone mass used by astronauts aboard the *International Space Station*. Create an "Astronaut Exercise Book" to share with your friends.

The *International Space Station*

The *International Space Station (ISS)*, the newest space station, is being constructed in LEO. Russia, the United States, and 14 other countries are designing and building different parts of the station. **Figure 5** shows what the *ISS* will look like when it is completed. The *ISS* is being built with materials brought up on the space shuttles and by Russian rockets. The United States is providing lab modules, the supporting frame, solar panels, living quarters, and a biomedical laboratory. The Russians are contributing a service module, docking modules, life-support and research modules, and transportation to and from the station. Other components will come from Japan, Canada, and several European countries.

Reading Check What contributions are the Americans and Russians making to the *ISS*?

Research on the *International Space Station*

The *ISS* will provide many benefits—some of which we cannot predict. What scientists do know is that it will be a unique, space-based facility to perform space-science experiments and to test new technologies. Much of the space race involved political and military rivalry between the Soviet Union and the United States. Hopefully, the *ISS* will promote cooperation between countries while continuing the pioneering spirit of the first astronauts and cosmonauts.

CONNECTION TO
Social Studies

Oral Histories The exciting times of the Apollo moon missions thrilled the nation. Interview adults in your community about their memories of those times. Prepare a list of questions first, and have your questions and contacts approved by your teacher. If possible, use a tape recorder or video camera to record the interviews. As a class, create a library of your oral histories for future students.

ACTIVITY

Figure 5 *When the* International Space Station *is completed, it will be about the size of a soccer field and will weigh about 500 tons.*

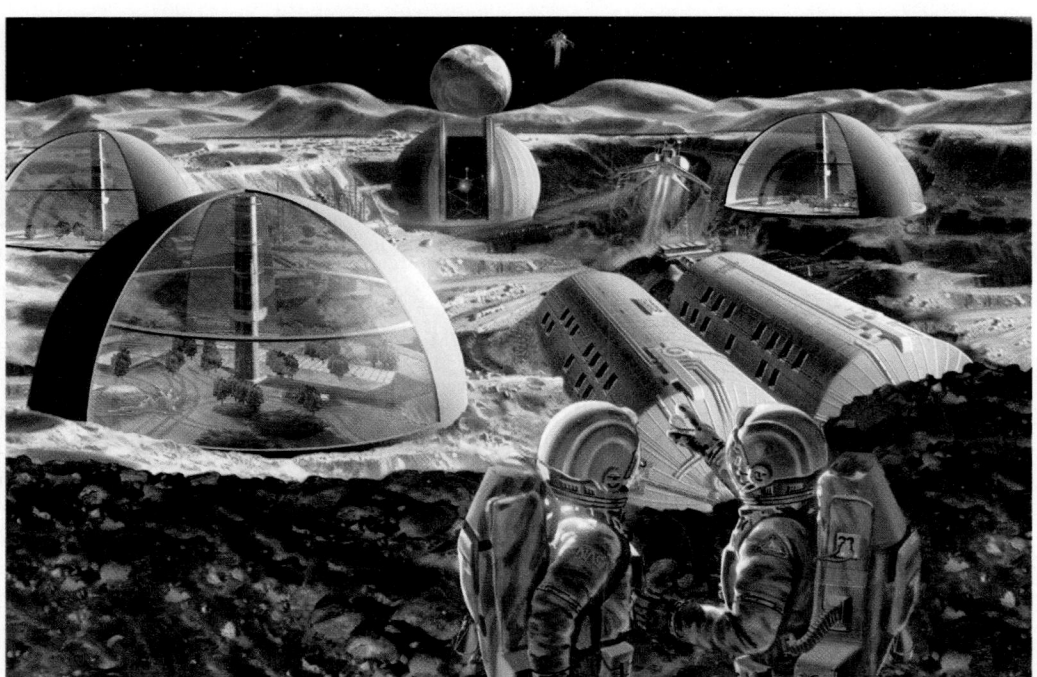

Figure 6 As shown in this illustration, humans may eventually establish a colony on the moon or on Mars.

To the Moon, Mars, and Beyond

We may eventually need resources beyond what Earth can offer. Space offers many such resources. For example, a rare form of helium is found on the moon. If this helium could be used in nuclear fusion reactors, it would produce no radioactive waste! A base on the moon similar to the one shown in **Figure 6** could be used to manufacture materials in low gravity or in a vacuum. A colony on the moon or on Mars could be an important link to bringing space resources to Earth. It would also be a good base for exploring the rest of the solar system. The key will be to make these missions economically worthwhile.

The Benefits of the Space Program

Space exploration is expensive, and it has cost several human lives since the time that Yuri Gagarin and John Glenn first left the Earth more than 40 years ago. We have visited the moon, and we have sent probes outside the solar system. So why should we continue to explore space? There are many answers to this question. Space exploration has expanded our scientific knowledge of everything from the most massive stars to the smallest particles. Life-saving technologies have also resulted from the space missions. For example, artificial heart pumps use a turbine developed to pump fuel in the space shuttles. NASA's aerogel, shown in **Figure 7,** may become an energy-saving replacement for windows in the future. All of the scientific benefits of the space programs cannot be predicted. However, the exploration of space is also a challenge to human courage and a quest for new knowledge of ourselves and the universe.

Figure 7 Aerogel is the lightest solid on Earth. Aerogel is only 3 times heavier than air, and has 39 times the insulating properties of the best fiberglass insulation.

Space-Age Spinoffs

Technologies that were developed for the space programs but are now used in everyday life are called space-age spinoffs. There are dozens of examples of common items that were first developed for the space programs. Cordless power tools, for example, were first developed for use on the moon by the Apollo astronauts. Hand-held cameras that were developed to study the heat emitted from the space shuttle are used by firefighters to detect dangerous hot spots in fires. A few other examples of space-age spinoffs are shown in **Table 1.**

✔ **Reading Check** What are space-age spinoffs?

Table 1 Space-Age Spinoffs
smoke detectors
bar coding on merchandise
pacemakers
artificial heart pumps
land mine removal devices
medical lasers
fire fighting equipment
invisible braces
video game joysticks
ear thermometers

SECTION Review

Summary

- In 1961, the Soviet cosmonaut Yuri Gagarin became the first person in space. In 1969, Neil Armstrong became the first person on the moon.

- During the 1970s, the United States focused on developing the space shuttle. The Soviets focused on developing space stations.

- The United States, Russia, and 14 other countries are currently developing the *International Space Station.*

- There have been many scientific, economic, and social benefits of the space programs.

Using Key Terms

1. Use each of the following terms in a separate sentence: *space shuttle* and *space station.*

Using Key Ideas

2. What is the main difference between the space shuttles and other space vehicles?
   a. The space shuttles are powered by liquid rocket fuel.
   b. The space shuttles take off like a plane and land like a rocket.
   c. The space shuttles are reusable.
   d. The space shuttles are not reusable.

3. Describe the history and future of human spaceflight. How was the race to explore space influenced by the Cold War?

4. Describe five "space-age spinoffs."

5. How will space stations help in the exploration of space?

6. In the 1970s, what was the main difference in the focus of the space programs in the United States and in the Soviet Union?

Math Skills

7. When it is fueled, a space shuttle has a mass of about 2,000,000 kg. About 80% of that mass is fuel and oxygen. Calculate the mass of a space shuttle's fuel and oxygen.

Critical Thinking

8. **Making Inferences** Why did the United States stop sending people to the moon after the Apollo program ended?

9. **Expressing Opinions** Imagine that you are a U.S. senator reviewing NASA's proposed budget. Write a two-paragraph position statement expressing your opinion about increasing or decreasing funding for NASA.

SCILINKS®

NSTA
Developed and maintained by the National Science Teachers Association

For a variety of links related to this chapter, go to www.scilinks.org
Topic: Space Exploration and Space Stations
SciLinks code: HSM1340

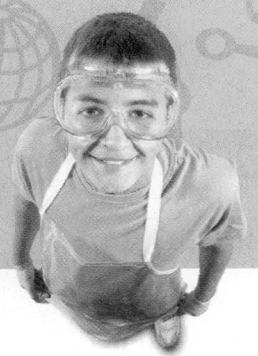

Inquiry Lab

OBJECTIVES

Predict which design features would improve a rocket's flight.

Design and build a rocket that includes your design features.

Test your rocket design, and evaluate your results.

MATERIALS

- bottle, soda, 2 L
- clay, modeling
- foam board
- rocket launcher
- scissors
- tape, duct
- watch or clock that indicates seconds
- water

SAFETY

Water Rockets Save the Day!

Imagine that for the big Fourth of July celebration, you and your friends had planned a full day of swimming, volleyball, and fireworks at the lake. You've just learned, however, that the city passed a law that bans all fireworks within city limits. But you do not give up so easily on having fun. Last year at summer camp, you learned how to build water rockets. And you have kept the launcher in your garage since then. With a little bit of creativity, you and your friends are going to celebrate with a splash!

Ask a Question

1 What is the most efficient design for a water rocket?

Form a Hypothesis

2 Write a hypothesis that provides a possible answer to the question above.

Test the Hypothesis

3 Decide how your rocket will look, and then draw a sketch.

4 Using only the materials listed, decide how to build your rocket. Write a description of your plan, and have your teacher approve your plan. Keep in mind that you will need to leave the opening of your bottle clear. The bottle opening will be placed over a rubber stopper on the rocket launcher.

5 Fins are often used to stabilize rockets. Do you want fins on your water rocket? Decide on the best shape for the fins, and then decide how many fins your rocket needs. Use the foam board to construct the fins.

6 Your rocket must be heavy enough to fly in a controlled manner. Consider using clay in the body of your rocket to provide some additional weight and stability.

7 Pour water into your rocket until the rocket is one-third to one-half full.

8 Your teacher will provide the launcher and will assist you during blastoff. Attach your rocket to the launcher by placing the opening of the bottle on the rubber stopper.

9 When the rocket is in place, clear the immediate area and begin pumping air into your rocket. Watch the pump gauge, and take note of how much pressure is needed for liftoff. **Caution:** Be sure to step back from the launch site. You should be several meters away from the bottle when you launch it.

10 Use the watch to time your rocket's flight. How long was your rocket in the air?

11 Make small changes in your rocket design that you think will improve the rocket's performance. Consider using different amounts of water and clay or experimenting with different fins. You may also want to compare your design with those of your classmates.

Analyze the Results

1 **Describing Events** How did your rocket perform? If you used fins, do you think they helped your flight? Explain your answer.

2 **Explaining Results** What do you think propelled your rocket? Use Newton's third law of motion to explain your answer.

3 **Analyzing Results** How did the amount of water in your rocket affect the launch?

Draw Conclusions

4 **Drawing Conclusions** What modifications made your rocket fly for the longest time? How did the design help the rockets fly so far?

5 **Evaluating Results** Which group's rocket was the most stable? How did the design help the rocket fly straight?

6 **Making Predictions** How can you improve your design to make your rocket perform even better?

Chapter Review

USING KEY TERMS

For each pair of terms, explain how the meanings of the terms differ.

1 *geostationary orbit* and *low Earth orbit*

2 *space probe* and *space station*

3 *artificial satellite* and *moon*

Complete each of the following sentences by choosing the correct term from the word bank.

escape velocity	oxygen
nitrogen	thrust

4 The force that accelerates a rocket is called ___.

5 Rockets need to have ___ in order to burn fuel.

UNDERSTANDING KEY IDEAS

Multiple Choice

6 Whose rocket research team surrendered to the Americans at the end of World War II?

a. Konstantin Tsiolkovsky's
b. Robert Goddard's
c. Wernher von Braun's
d. Yuri Gargarin's

7 Rockets work according to Newton's

a. first law of motion.
b. second law of motion.
c. third law of motion.
d. law of universal gravitation.

8 The first artificial satellite to orbit the Earth was

a. *Pioneer 4.*   c. *Voyager 2.*
b. *Explorer 1.*   d. *Sputnik 1.*

9 Communications satellites are able to transfer TV signals between continents because communications satellites

a. are located in LEO.
b. relay signals past the horizon.
c. travel quickly around Earth.
d. can be used during the day and night.

10 GEO is a better orbit for communications satellites because satellites that are in GEO

a. remain in position over one spot.
b. have polar orbits.
c. do not revolve around the Earth.
d. orbit a few hundred kilometers above the Earth.

11 Which space probe discovered evidence of water at the moon's south pole?

a. *Luna 9*
b. *Viking 1*
c. *Clementine*
d. *Magellan*

12 When did humans first set foot on the moon?

a. 1959   c. 1969
b. 1964   d. 1973

13 Which of the following planets has not yet been visited by space probes?

a. Venus   c. Mars
b. Neptune   d. Pluto

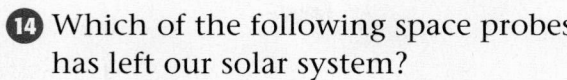

14 Which of the following space probes has left our solar system?

a. *Galileo*

c. *Viking 10*

b. *Magellan*

d. *Pioneer 10*

15 Based on space-probe data, which of the following is the most likely place in our solar system to find liquid water?

a. the moon

c. Europa

b. Mercury

d. Venus

Short Answer

16 Describe how Newton's third law of motion relates to the movement of rockets.

17 What is one disadvantage that objects in LEO have?

18 Why did the United States develop the space shuttle?

19 How does data from satellites help us understand the Earth's environment?

CRITICAL THINKING

20 Concept Mapping Use the following terms to create a concept map: *orbital velocity, thrust, LEO, artificial satellites, escape velocity, space probes, GEO,* and *rockets.*

21 Making Inferences What is the difference between speed and velocity?

22 Applying Concepts Why must rockets that travel in outer space carry oxygen with them?

23 Expressing Opinions What impact has space research had on scientific thought, on society, and on the environment?

INTERPRETING GRAPHICS

The diagram below illustrates suborbital velocity, orbital velocity, and escape velocity. Use the diagram below to answer the questions that follow.

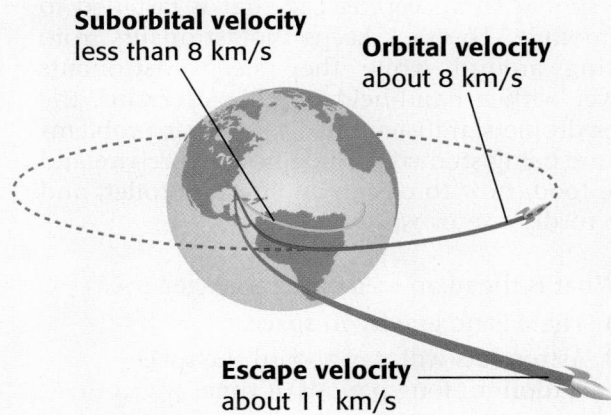

Suborbital velocity less than 8 km/s

Orbital velocity about 8 km/s

Escape velocity about 11 km/s

24 Could a rocket traveling at 6 km/s reach orbital velocity?

25 If a rocket traveled for 3 days at the minimum escape velocity, how far would the rocket travel?

26 How much faster would a rocket traveling in orbital velocity need to travel to reach escape velocity?

27 If the escape velocity for a planet was 9 km/s, would you assume that the mass of the planet was more or less than the mass of Earth?

Standardized Test Preparation

Read each of the passages below. Then, answer the questions that follow each passage.

Passage 1 One of the strange things about living in space is free fall, the reduced effect of gravity. Everything inside the *International Space Station* that is not fastened down will float! The engineers who designed the space station have come up with some <u>intriguing</u> solutions to this problem. For example, each astronaut sleeps in a sack similar to a sleeping bag that is fastened to the module. The sack keeps the astronauts from floating around while they sleep. Astronauts shower with a hand-held nozzle. Afterward, the water droplets are vacuumed up. Other problems that are being studied include how to prepare and serve food, how to design an effective toilet, and how to dispose of waste.

1. What is the main idea of the passage?
   A There is no gravity in space.
   B Astronauts will stay aboard the space station for long periods of time.
   C Living in free fall presents interesting problems.
   D Sleeping bags are needed to keep astronauts warm in space.

2. Which of the following is a problem mentioned in the passage?
   F how to dissipate the heat of reentry
   G how to maintain air pressure
   H how to serve food
   I how to listen to music

3. Which of the following words is the best antonym for *intriguing*?
   A authentic
   B boring
   C interesting
   D unsolvable

Passage 2 In 1999, the crew of the space station *Mir* tried to place a large, umbrella-like mirror in orbit. The mirror was designed to reflect sunlight to Siberia. The experiment failed because the crew was unable to unfold the mirror. If things had gone as planned, the beam of reflected sunlight would have been 5 to 10 times brighter than the light from the moon! If the first space mirror had worked, Russia was planning to place many more mirrors in orbit to lengthen winter days in Siberia, extend the growing season, and even reduce the amount of electricity needed for lighting. Luckily, the experiment failed. If it had succeeded, the environmental effects of extra daylight in Siberia would have been catastrophic. Astronomers were concerned that the mirrors would cause light pollution and obstruct their view of the universe. Outer space should belong to all of humanity, and any project of this kind, including placing advertisements on the moon, should be banned.

1. Which of the following is a statement of opinion?
   A Astronomers were concerned about the effects of the space mirror.
   B Outer space should belong to all of humanity.
   C The experiment failed because the mirror could not unfold.
   D Russia was planning to place many more mirrors in orbit.

2. What can you infer about the location of Siberia?
   F It is near the equator.
   G It is closer to the equator than it is to the North Pole.
   H It is closer to the North Pole than it is to the equator.
   I It is the same distance from the equator as it is from the North Pole.

The diagram below shows the location of satellites in LEO and GEO. Use the diagram below to answer the questions that follow.

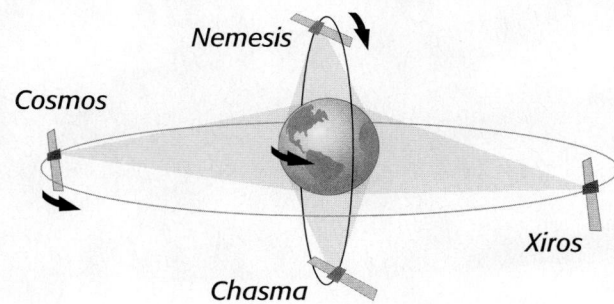

1. Which satellites are always located over the same spot on Earth?

   A Xiros and Chasma

   B Xiros and Cosmos

   C Nemesis and Cosmos

   D Chasma and Nemesis

2. Which satellites are likely to be spy satellites?

   F Xiros and Cosmos

   G Xiros and Chasma

   H Chasma and Nemesis

   I Nemesis and Cosmos

3. Which satellites are likely to be communications satellites?

   A Chasma and Nemesis

   B Nemesis and Cosmos

   C Xiros and Cosmos

   D Xiros and Chasma

4. Which satellites are traveling in an orbit that is 90° with respect to the direction of Earth's rotation?

   F Nemesis and Cosmos

   G Xiros and Chasma

   H Nemesis and Chasma

   I Xiros and Cosmos

Read each question below, and choose the best answer.

1. To escape Earth's gravity, a rocket must travel at least 11 km/s. About how many hours would it take to get to the moon at this speed? (On average, the moon is about 384,500 km away from Earth.)

   A 1 h

   B 7 h

   C 8 h

   D 10 h

2. The Saturn V launch vehicle, which carried the Apollo astronauts into space, had a mass of about 2.7 million kilograms and carried about 2.5 million kilograms of propellant. What percentage of Saturn V's mass was propellant?

   F 9.25%

   G 9%

   H 92.5%

   I 90%

3. Scientists discovered that when a person is in orbit, bone mass in the lower hip and spine is lost at a rate of 1.2% per month. At that rate, how long would it take for 7.2% of bone mass to be lost?

   A 4 months

   B 6 months

   C 7.2 months

   D 8 months

4. The space shuttle can carry 25,400 kg of cargo into orbit. Assume that the average astronaut has a mass of 75 kg and that each satellite has a mass of 4,300 kg. If a shuttle mission is already carrying 9,000 kg of equipment and 10 astronauts, how many satellites can the shuttle carry?

   F 2

   G 3

   H 4

   I 5

Standardized Test Preparation

Science in Action

Science, Technology, and Society

Mission to Mars

In spring 2003, two cutting-edge NASA rovers were sent on a mission to Mars. When they reach their destination, they will parachute through the thin Martian atmosphere and land on the surface. First, the rovers will use video and infrared cameras to look around. Then, for at least 92 Earth days (90 Martian days), the rovers will explore the surface of Mars. They will gather geologic evidence of liquid water because liquid water may have enabled Mars to support life in the past. Each rover will carry five scientific tools and a Rock Abrasion Tool, or "RAT," which will grind away rock surfaces to expose the rock interiors for scientific tests. Stay tuned for more news from Mars!

Weird Science

Flashline Mars Arctic Research Station

If you wanted to visit a place on Earth that is like the surface of Mars, where would you go? You might head to an impact crater on Devon Island, close to the Arctic circle. The rugged terrain and harsh weather there resemble what explorers will find on Mars, although Mars has no breathable air and is a lot colder. In the summer, volunteers from the Mars Society live in an experimental base in the crater and test technology that might be used on Mars. The volunteers try to simulate the experience of explorers on Mars. For example, the volunteers wear spacesuits when they go outside, and they explore the landscape by using rovers. They even communicate with the outside world using types of technology likely to be used on Mars. These dedicated volunteers have already made discoveries that will help NASA plan a crewed mission to Mars!

Language Arts ACTiViTY

Watch for stories about this mission in newspapers and magazines. If you read about a discovery on Mars, bring a copy of the article to share with your class. As a class, compile a scrapbook entitled "Mars in the News."

Social Studies ACTiViTY

A Mars mission could require astronauts to endure nearly two years of extreme isolation. Research how NASA would prepare astronauts for the psychological pressures of a mission to Mars.

Careers

Franklin Chang-Diaz

Astronaut You have to wear a suit, but the commute is not too long. In fact, it is only about eight and a half minutes, and what a view on your way to work! Astronauts, such as Franklin Chang-Diaz, have one of the most exciting jobs on Earth—or in space. Chang-Diaz has flown on seven space shuttle missions and has completed three space walks. Since the time he became an astronaut in 1981, Chang-Diaz has spent more than 1,601 hours (66 days) in space.

Chang-Diaz was born in San Jose, Costa Rica. He earned a degree in mechanical engineering in 1973 and received a doctorate in applied plasma physics from the Massachusetts Institute of Technology (MIT) in 1977. His work in physics attracted the attention of NASA, and he began training at the Johnson Space Center in Houston, Texas. In addition to doing research on the space shuttle, Chang-Diaz has worked on developing plasma propulsion systems for long space flights. He has also helped create closer ties between astronauts and scientists by starting organizations such as the Astronaut Science Colloquium Program and the Astronaut Science Support Group. If you want to find out more about what it takes to be an astronaut, look on NASA's Web site.

Math ACTiViTY

If 1 out of 120 people interviewed by NASA is selected for astronaut training, how many people will be selected for training if 10,680 people are interviewed?

As this mission patch shows, Chang-Diaz flew on the 111th space shuttle mission.

To learn more about these Science in Action topics, visit **go.hrw.com** and type in the keyword **HZ5EXPF.**

Current Science

Check out Current Science® articles related to this chapter by visiting go.hrw.com. Just type in the keyword HZ5CS22.

LabBook

Contents

Inquiry Lab

Orient Yourself!

You have been invited to attend an orienteering event with your neighbors. In orienteering events, participants use maps and compasses to find their way along a course. There are several control points that each participant must reach. The object is to reach each control point and then the finish line. Orienteering events are often timed competitions. In order to find the fastest route through the course, the participants must read the map and use their compass correctly. Being the fastest runner does not necessarily guarantee finishing first. You also must choose the most direct route to follow.

Your neighbors participate in several orienteering events each year. They always come home raving about how much fun they had. You would like to join them, but you will need to learn how to use your compass first.

MATERIALS

- compass, magnetic
- course map
- pencils (or markers), colored (2)
- ruler

Procedure

1. Together as a class, go outside to the orienteering course your teacher has made.

2. Hold your compass flat in your hand. Turn the compass until the N is pointing straight in front of you. (The needle in your compass will always point north.) Turn your body until the needle lines up with the N on your compass. You are now facing north.

3. Regardless of which direction you want to face, you should always align the end of the needle with the N on your compass. If you are facing south, the needle will be pointing directly toward your body. When the N is aligned with the needle, the S will be directly in front of you, and you will be facing south.

4. Use your compass to face east. Align the needle with the N. Where is the E? Turn to face that direction. You are facing east when the needle and the N are aligned and the E is directly in front of you.

5. In an orienteering competition, you will need to know how to determine which direction you are traveling. Now, face any direction you choose.

6. Do not move, but rotate the compass to align the needle on your compass with the N. What direction are you facing? You are probably not facing directly north, south, east, or west. If you are facing between north and west, you are facing northwest. If you are facing between north and east, you are facing northeast.

7. Find a partner or partners to follow the course your teacher has made. Get a copy of the course map from your teacher. It will show several control points. You must stop at each one. You will need to follow this map to find your way through the course. Find and stand at the starting point.

8. Face the next control point on your map. Rotate your compass to align the needle on your compass with the N. What direction are you facing?

9. Use the ruler to draw a line on your map between the two control points. On your map, write the direction between the starting point and the next control point.

10. Walk toward the control point. Keep your eyes on the horizon, not on your compass. You might need to go around an obstacle, such as a fence or a building. Use the map to find the easiest way around.

11. Next to the control point symbol on your map, record the color or code word you find at the control point.

12. Repeat steps 8–11 for each control point. Follow the points in order as they are labeled. For example, determine the direction from control point 1 to control point 2. Be sure to include the direction between the final control point and the starting point.

Analyze the Results

1. The object of an orienteering competition is to arrive at the finish line first. The maps provided at these events do not instruct the participants to follow a specific path. In one form of orienteering, called *score orienteering*, competitors may find the control points in any order. Look at your map. If this course were used for a score-orienteering competition, would you change your route? Explain.

Draw Conclusions

2. If there is time, follow the map again. This time, use your own path to find the control points. Draw this path and the directions on your map in a different color. Do you believe this route was faster? Why?

Applying Your Data

Do some research to find out about orienteering events in your area. The Internet and local newspapers may be good sources for the information. Are there any events that you would like to attend?

Skills Practice Lab

Topographic Tuber

Imagine that you live on top of a tall mountain and often look down on the lake below. Every summer, an island appears. You call it Sometimes Island because it goes away again during heavy fall rains. This summer, you begin to wonder if you could make a topographic map of Sometimes Island. You don't have fancy equipment to make the map, but you have an idea. What if you place a meterstick with the 0 m mark at the water level in the summer? Then, as the expected fall rains come, you could draw the island from above as the water rises. Would this idea really work?

- container, clear plastic storage, with transparent lid
- marker, transparency
- paper, tracing
- potato, cut in half
- ruler, metric
- water

Ask a Question

1 How do I make a topographic map?

Form a Hypothesis

2 Write a hypothesis that is a possible answer to the question above. Describe the method you would use.

Test the Hypothesis

3 Place a mark at the storage container's base. Label this mark "0 cm" with a transparency marker.

4 Measure and mark 1 cm increments up the side of the container until you reach the top of the container. Label these marks "1 cm," "2 cm," "3 cm," and so on.

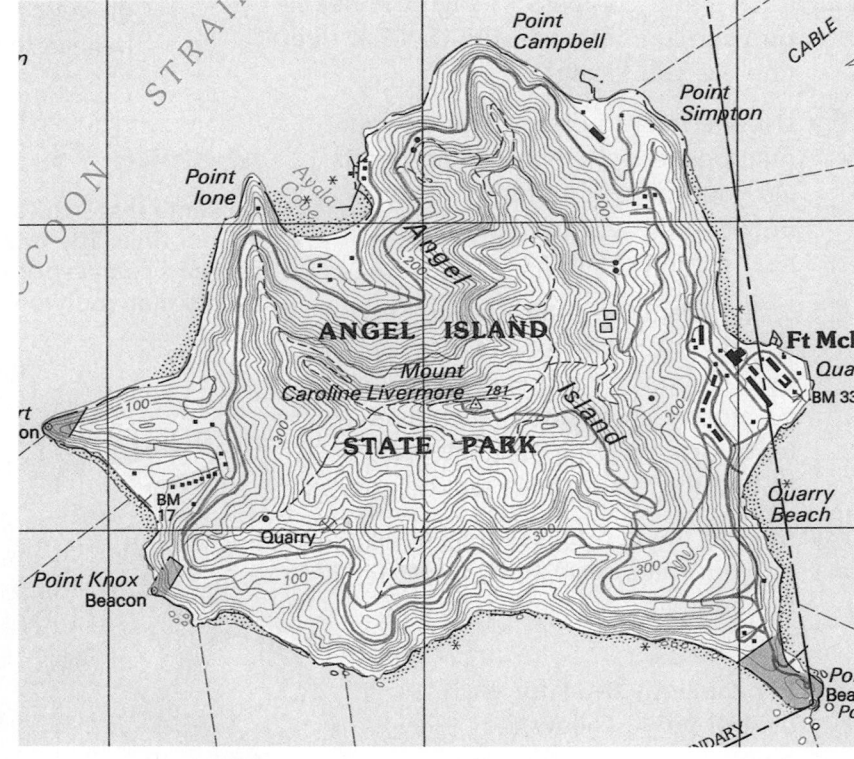

5 The scale for your map will be 1 cm = 10 m. Draw a line 2 cm long in the bottom right-hand corner of the lid. Place hash marks at 0 cm, 1 cm, and 2 cm. Label these marks "0 m," "10 m," and "20 m."

6 Place the potato, flat side down, in the center of the container.

7 Place the lid on the container, and seal it.

8. Viewing the potato from above, use the transparency marker to trace the outline of the potato where it rests on the bottom of the container. The floor of the container corresponds to the summer water level in the lake.

9. Label this contour "0 m." (For this activity, assume that the water level in the lake during the summer is the same as sea level.)

10. Pour water into the container until it reaches the line labeled "1 cm."

11. Again, place the lid on the container, and seal it. Part of the potato will be sticking out above the water. Viewing the potato from above, trace the part of the potato that touches the top of the water.

12. Label the elevation of the contour line you drew in step 11. According to the scale, the elevation is 10 m.

13. Remove the lid. Carefully pour water into the container until it reaches the line labeled "2 cm."

14. Place the lid on the container, and seal it. Viewing the potato from above, trace the part of the potato that touches the top of the water at this level.

15. Use the scale to calculate the elevation of this line. Label the elevation on your drawing.

16. Repeat steps 13–15, adding 1 cm to the depth of the water each time. Stop when the potato is completely covered.

17. Remove the lid, and set it on a tabletop. Place tracing paper on top of the lid. Trace the contours from the lid onto the paper. Label the elevation of each contour line. Congratulations! You have just made a topographic map!

Analyze the Results

1. What is the contour interval of this topographic map?

2. By looking at the contour lines, how can you tell which parts of the potato are steeper?

3. What is the elevation of the highest point on your map?

Draw Conclusions

4. Do all topographic maps have a 0 m elevation contour line as a starting point? How would this affect a topographic map of Sometimes Island? Explain your answer.

5. Would this method of measuring elevation be an effective way to make a topographic map of an actual area on Earth's surface? Why or why not?

Applying Your Data

Place all of the potatoes on a table or desk at the front of the room. Your teacher will mix up the potatoes as you trade topographic maps with another group. By reading the topographic map you just received, can you pick out the matching potato?

Skills Practice Lab

Mysterious Minerals

Imagine sitting on a rocky hilltop, gazing at the ground below you. You can see dozens of different types of rocks. How can scientists possibly identify the countless variations? It's a mystery!

In this activity, you'll use your powers of observation and a few simple tests to determine the identities of rocks and minerals. Take a look at the Mineral Identification Key on the next page. That key will help you use clues to discover the identity of several minerals.

MATERIALS

- gloves, protective
- iron filings
- minerals, samples
- slides, microscope, glass
- streak plate

SAFETY

Procedure

1. On a separate sheet of paper, create a data chart like the one below.

2. Choose one mineral sample, and locate its column in your data chart.

3. Follow the Mineral Identification Key to find the identity of your sample. When you are finished, record the mineral's name and primary characteristics in the appropriate column in your data chart. **Caution:** Put on your safety goggles and gloves when scratching the glass slide.

4. Select another mineral sample, and repeat steps 2 and 3 until your data table is complete.

Analyze the Results

1. Were some minerals easier to identify than others? Explain.

2. A streak test is a better indicator of a mineral's true color than visual observation is. Why isn't a streak test used to help identify every mineral?

3. On a separate sheet of paper, summarize what you learned about the various characteristics of each mineral sample you identified.

Mineral Summary Chart						
Characteristics	**1**	**2**	**3**	**4**	**5**	**6**
Mineral name						
Luster						
Color						
Streak			DO NOT WRITE IN BOOK			
Hardness						
Cleavage						
Special properties						

Mineral Identification Key

1. **a.** If your mineral has a metallic luster, **GO TO STEP 2.**
   b. If your mineral has a nonmetallic luster, **GO TO STEP 3.**

2. **a.** If your mineral is black, **GO TO STEP 4.**
   b. If your mineral is yellow, it is **PYRITE.**
   c. If your mineral is silver, it is **GALENA.**

3. **a.** If your mineral is light in color, **GO TO STEP 5.**
   b. If your mineral is dark in color, **GO TO STEP 6.**

4. **a.** If your mineral leaves a red-brown line on the streak plate, it is **HEMATITE.**
   b. If your mineral leaves a black line on the streak plate, it is **MAGNETITE.** Test your sample for its magnetic properties by holding it near some iron filings.

5. **a.** If your mineral scratches the glass microscope slide, **GO TO STEP 7.**
   b. If your mineral does not scratch the glass microscope slide, **GO TO STEP 8.**

6. **a.** If your mineral scratches the glass slide, **GO TO STEP 9.**
   b. If your mineral does not scratch the glass slide, **GO TO STEP 10.**

7. **a.** If your mineral shows signs of cleavage, it is **ORTHOCLASE FELDSPAR.**
   b. If your mineral does not show signs of cleavage, it is **QUARTZ.**

8. **a.** If your mineral shows signs of cleavage, it is **MUSCOVITE.** Examine this sample for twin sheets.
   b. If your mineral does not show signs of cleavage, it is **GYPSUM.**

9. **a.** If your mineral shows signs of cleavage, it is **HORNBLENDE.**
   b. If your mineral does not show signs of cleavage, it is **GARNET.**

10. **a.** If your mineral shows signs of cleavage, it is **BIOTITE.** Examine your sample for twin sheets.
    b. If your mineral does not show signs of cleavage, it is **GRAPHITE.**

Applying Your Data

Using your textbook and other reference books, research other methods of identifying different types of minerals. Based on your findings, create a new identification key. Give the key and a few sample minerals to a friend, and see if your friend can unravel the mystery!

Skills Practice Lab

Crystal Growth

Magma forms deep below the Earth's surface at depths of 25 km to 160 km and at extremely high temperatures. Some magma reaches the surface and cools quickly. Other magma gets trapped in cracks or magma chambers beneath the surface and cools very slowly. When magma cools slowly, large, well-developed crystals form. But when magma erupts onto the surface, it cools more quickly. There is not enough time for large crystals to grow. The size of the crystals found in igneous rocks gives geologists clues about where and how the rocks formed.

In this experiment, you will demonstrate how the rate of cooling affects the size of crystals in igneous rocks by cooling crystals of magnesium sulfate at two different rates.

Ask a Question

1 How does temperature affect the formation of crystals?

Form a Hypothesis

2 Suppose you have two solutions that are identical in every way except for temperature. How will the temperature of a solution affect the size of the crystals and the rate at which they form?

Test the Hypothesis

3 Put on your gloves, apron, and goggles.

4 Fill the beaker halfway with tap water. Place the beaker on the hot plate, and let it begin to warm. The temperature of the water should be between 40°C and 50°C. **Caution:** Make sure the hot plate is away from the edge of the lab table.

5 Examine two or three crystals of the magnesium sulfate with your magnifying lens. On a separate sheet of paper, describe the color, shape, luster, and other interesting features of the crystals.

6 On a separate sheet of paper, draw a sketch of the magnesium sulfate crystals.

- aluminum foil
- basalt
- beaker, 400 mL
- gloves, heat-resistant
- granite
- hot plate
- laboratory scoop, pointed
- magnesium sulfate (MgSO$_4$) (Epsom salts)
- magnifying lens
- marker, dark
- pumice
- tape, masking
- test tube, medium-sized
- thermometer, Celsius
- tongs, test-tube
- watch (or clock)
- water, distilled
- water, tap, 200 mL

SAFETY

7 Use the pointed laboratory scoop to fill the test tube about halfway with the magnesium sulfate. Add an equal amount of distilled water.

8 Hold the test tube in one hand, and use one finger from your other hand to tap the test tube gently. Observe the solution mixing as you continue to tap the test tube.

9 Place the test tube in the beaker of hot water, and heat it for approximately 3 min. **Caution:** Be sure to direct the opening of the test tube away from you and other students.

10 While the test tube is heating, shape your aluminum foil into two small boatlike containers by doubling the foil and turning up each edge.

11 If all the magnesium sulfate is not dissolved after 3 min, tap the test tube again, and heat it for 3 min longer. **Caution:** Use the test-tube tongs to handle the hot test tube.

12 With a marker and a piece of masking tape, label one of your aluminum boats "Sample 1," and place it on the hot plate. Turn the hot plate off.

13 Label the other aluminum boat "Sample 2," and place it on the lab table.

14 Using the test-tube tongs, remove the test tube from the beaker of water, and evenly distribute the contents to each of your foil boats. Carefully pour the hot water in the beaker down the drain. Do not move or disturb either of your foil boats.

15 Copy the table below onto a separate sheet of paper. Using the magnifying lens, carefully observe the foil boats. Record the time it takes for the first crystals to appear.

Crystal-Formation Table			
Crystal formation	Time	Size and appearance of crystals	Sketch of crystals
Sample 1			
Sample 2		DO NOT WRITE IN BOOK	

16 If crystals have not formed in the boats before class is over, carefully place the boats in a safe place. You may then record the time in days instead of in minutes.

17 When crystals have formed in both boats, use your magnifying lens to examine the crystals carefully.

Analyze the Results

1 Was your prediction correct? Explain.

2 Compare the size and shape of the crystals in Samples 1 and 2 with the size and shape of the crystals you examined in step 5. How long do you think the formation of the original crystals must have taken?

Draw Conclusions

3 Granite, basalt, and pumice are all igneous rocks. The most distinctive feature of each is the size of its crystals. Different igneous rocks form when magma cools at different rates. Examine a sample of each with your magnifying lens.

4 Copy the table below onto a separate sheet of paper, and sketch each rock sample.

5 Use what you have learned in this activity to explain how each rock sample formed and how long it took for the crystals to form. Record your answers in your table.

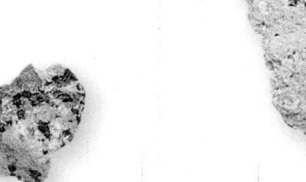  

Igneous Rock Observations			
	Granite	**Basalt**	**Pumice**
Sketch			
How did the rock sample form?		DO NOT WRITE IN BOOK	
Rate of cooling			

Communicating Your Data

Describe the size and shape of the crystals you would expect to find when a volcano erupts and sends material into the air and when magma oozes down the volcano's slope.

Model-Making Lab

Metamorphic Mash

Metamorphism is a complex process that takes place deep within the Earth, where the temperature and pressure would turn a human into a crispy pancake. The effects of this extreme temperature and pressure are obvious in some metamorphic rocks. One of these effects is the reorganization of mineral grains within the rock. In this activity, you will investigate the process of metamorphism without being charred, flattened, or buried.

MATERIALS

- cardboard (or plywood), very stiff, small pieces
- clay, modeling
- knife, plastic
- sequins (or other small flat objects)

SAFETY

Procedure

1. Flatten the clay into a layer about 1 cm thick. Sprinkle the surface with sequins.

2. Roll the corners of the clay toward the middle to form a neat ball.

3. Carefully use the plastic knife to cut the ball in half. On a separate sheet of paper, describe the position and location of the sequins inside the ball.

4. Put the ball back together, and use the sheets of cardboard or plywood to flatten the ball until it is about 2 cm thick.

5. Using the plastic knife, slice open the slab of clay in several places. Describe the position and location of the sequins in the slab.

Analyze the Results

1. What physical process does flattening the ball represent?

2. Describe any changes in the position and location of the sequins that occurred as the clay ball was flattened into a slab.

Draw Conclusions

3. How are the sequins oriented in relation to the force you put on the ball to flatten it?

4. Do you think the orientation of the mineral grains in a foliated metamorphic rock tells you anything about the rock? Defend your answer.

Applying Your Data

Suppose you find a foliated metamorphic rock that has grains running in two distinct directions. Use what you have learned in this activity to offer a possible explanation for this observation.

Skills Practice Lab

Power of the Sun

The sun radiates energy in every direction. Like the sun, the energy radiated by a light bulb spreads out in all directions. But how much energy an object receives depends on how close that object is to the source. As you move farther from the source, the amount of energy you receive decreases. For example, if you measure the amount of energy that reaches you from a light and then move three times farther away, you will discover that nine times less energy will reach you at your second position. Energy from the sun travels as light energy. When light energy is absorbed by an object it is converted into thermal energy. Power is the rate at which one form of energy is converted to another, and it is measured in watts. Because power is related to distance, nearby objects can be used to measure the power of far-away objects. In this lab you will calculate the power of the sun using an ordinary 100-watt light bulb.

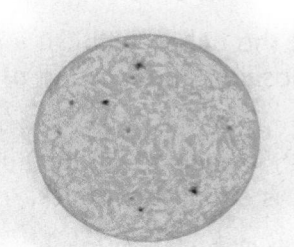

MATERIALS

- aluminum strip, 2 × 8 cm
- calculator, scientific
- clay, modeling
- desk lamp with a 100 W bulb and removable shade
- gloves, protective
- marker, black permanent
- mason jar, cap, and lid with hole in center
- pencil
- ruler, metric
- thermometer, Celsius
- watch (or clock) that indicates seconds

SAFETY

Procedure

1. Gently shape the piece of aluminum around a pencil so that it holds on in the middle and has two wings, one on either side of the pencil.

2. Bend the wings outward so that they can catch as much sunlight as possible.

3. Use the marker to color both wings on one side of the aluminum strip black.

4. Remove the pencil and place the aluminum snugly around the thermometer near the bulb. **Caution:** Do not press too hard—you do not want to break the thermometer! Wear protective gloves when working with the thermometer and the aluminum.

5. Carefully slide the top of the thermometer through the hole in the lid. Place the lid on the jar so that the thermometer bulb is inside the jar, and screw down the cap.

6. Secure the thermometer to the jar lid by molding clay around the thermometer on the outside of the lid. The aluminum wings should be in the center of the jar.

7. Read the temperature on the thermometer. Record this as room temperature.

8. Place the jar on a windowsill in the sunlight. Turn the jar so that the black wings are angled toward the sun.

9. Watch the thermometer until the temperature reading stops rising. Record the temperature.

10. Remove the jar from direct sunlight, and allow it to return to room temperature.

11. Remove any shade or reflector from the lamp. Place the lamp at one end of a table.

12. Place the jar about 30 cm from the lamp. Turn the jar so that the wings are angled toward the lamp.

13 Turn on the lamp, and wait about 1 minute.

14 Move the jar a few centimeters toward the lamp until the temperature reading starts to rise. When the temperature stops rising, compare it with the reading you took in step 9.

15 Repeat step 14 until the temperature matches the temperature you recorded in step 9.

16 If the temperature reading rises too high, move the jar away from the lamp and allow it to cool. Once the reading has dropped to at least 5°C below the temperature you recorded in step 9, you may begin again at step 12.

17 When the temperature in the jar matches the temperature you recorded in step 9, record the distance between the center of the light bulb and the thermometer bulb.

Analyze the Results

1 The thermometer measured the same amount of energy absorbed by the jar at the distance you measured to the lamp. In other words, your jar absorbed as much energy from the sun at a distance of 150 million kilometers as it did from the 100 W light bulb at the distance you recorded in step 17.

2 Use the following formula to calculate the power of the sun (be sure to show your work):

$$\frac{\text{power of the sun}}{(\text{distance to the sun})^2} = \frac{\text{power of the lamp}}{(\text{distance to the lamp})^2}$$

Hint: $(\text{distance})^2$ means that you multiply the distance by itself. If you found that the lamp was 5 cm away from the jar, for example, the $(\text{distance})^2$ would be 25.

Hint: Convert 150,000,000 km to 15,000,000,000,000 cm.

3 Review the discussion of scientific notation in the Math Refresher found in the Appendix at the back of this book. You will need to understand this technique for writing large numbers in order to compare your calculation with the actual figure. For practice, convert the distance to the sun given above in step 2 of Analyze the Results to scientific notation.

15,000,000,000,000 cm = $1.5 \times 10^{?}$ cm

Draw Conclusions

4 The sun emits 3.7×10^{26} W of power. Compare your answer in step 2 with this value. Was this a good way to calculate the power of the sun? Explain.

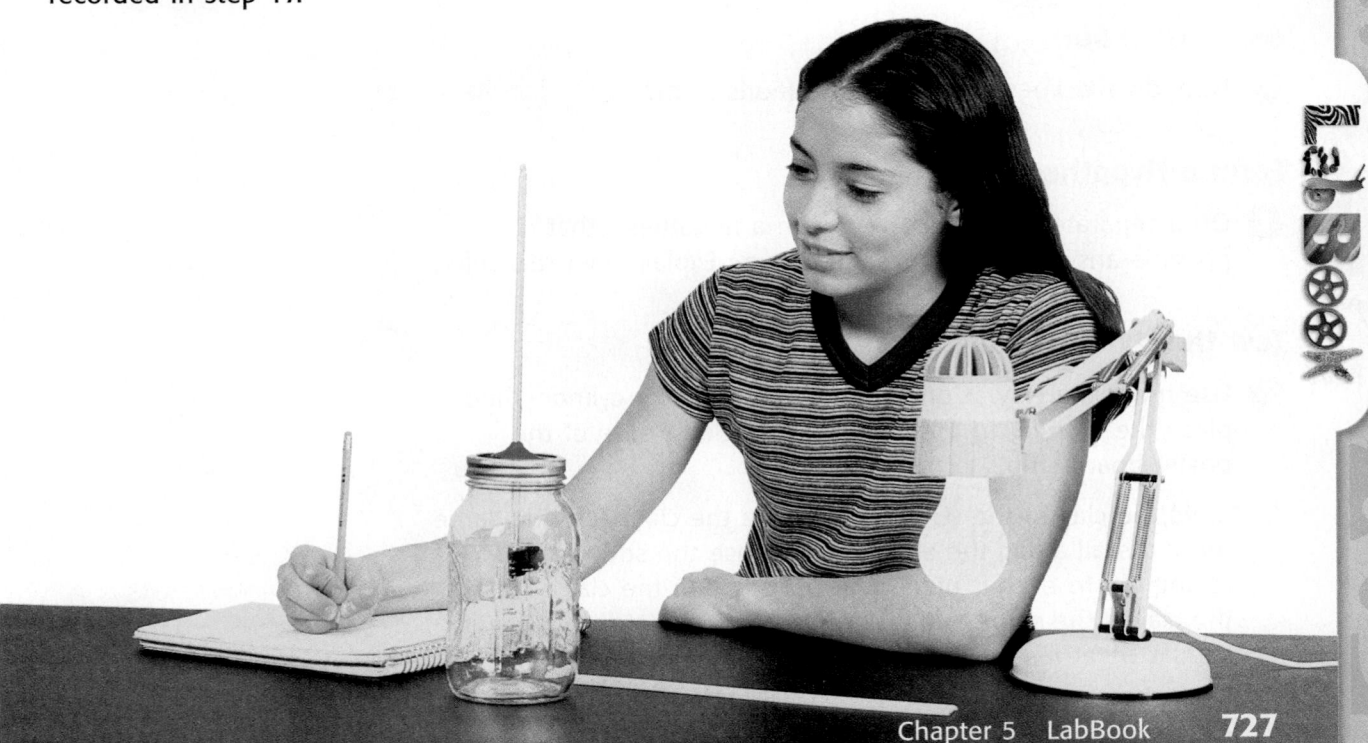

Model-Making Lab

Oh, the Pressure!

When scientists want to understand natural processes, such as mountain formation, they often make models to help them. Models are useful in studying how rocks react to the forces of plate tectonics. A model can demonstrate in a short amount of time geological processes that take millions of years. Do the following activity to find out how folding and faulting occur in the Earth's crust.

MATERIALS

- can, soup (or rolling pin)
- clay, modeling, 4 colors
- knife, plastic
- newspaper
- pencils, colored
- poster board, 5 cm × 5 cm squares (2)
- poster board, 5 cm × 15 cm strip

SAFETY

Ask a Question

❶ How do synclines, anticlines, and faults form?

Form a Hypothesis

❷ On a separate piece of paper, write a hypothesis that is a possible answer to the question above. Explain your reasoning.

Test the Hypothesis

❸ Use modeling clay of one color to form a long cylinder, and place the cylinder in the center of the glossy side of the poster-board strip.

❹ Mold the clay to the strip. Try to make the clay layer the same thickness all along the strip; you can use the soup can or rolling pin to even it out. Pinch the sides of the clay so that the clay is the same width and length as the strip. Your strip should be at least 15 cm long and 5 cm wide.

5 Flip the strip over on the newspaper your teacher has placed across your desk. Carefully peel the strip from the modeling clay.

6 Repeat steps 3–5 with the other colors of modeling clay. Each person should have a turn molding the clay. Each time you flip the strip over, stack the new clay layer on top of the previous one. When you are finished, you should have a block of clay made of four layers.

7 Lift the block of clay, and hold it parallel to and just above the tabletop. Push gently on the block from opposite sides, as shown below.

8 Use the colored pencils to draw the results of step 6. Use the terms *syncline* and *anticline* to label your diagram. Draw arrows to show the direction that each edge of the clay was pushed.

9 Repeat steps 3–6 to form a second block of clay.

10 Cut the second block of clay in two at a 45° angle as seen from the side of the block.

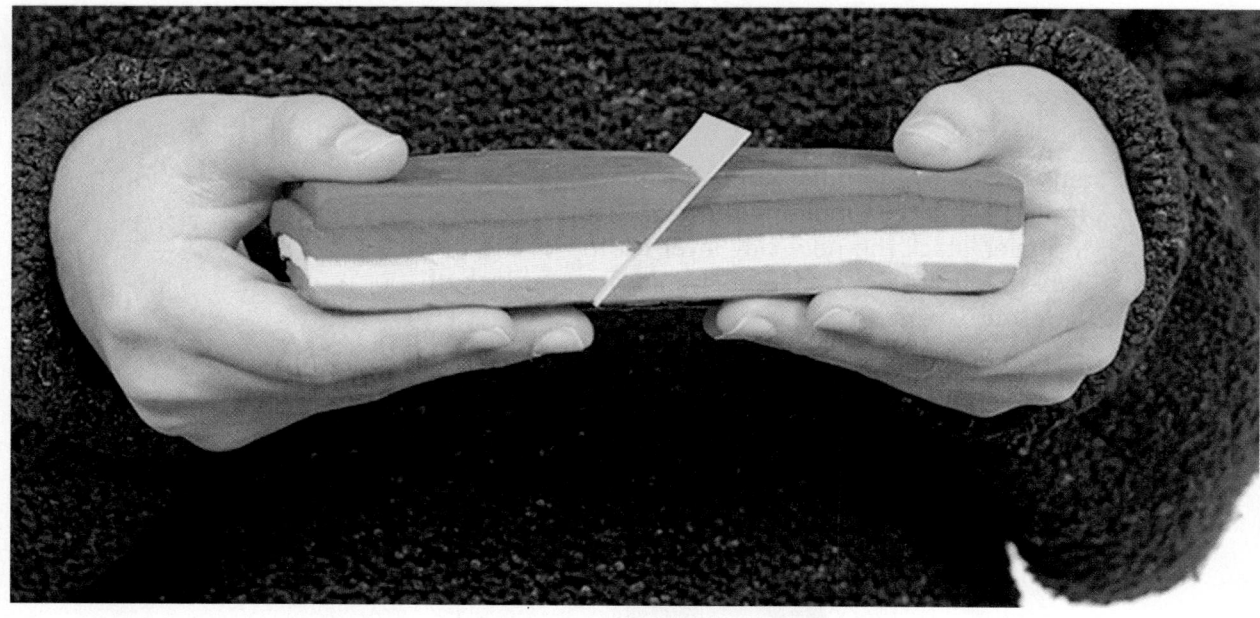

11 Press one poster-board square on the angled end of each of the block's two pieces. The poster board represents a fault. The two angled ends represent a hanging wall and a footwall. The model should resemble the one in the photograph above.

12 Keeping the angled edges together, lift the blocks, and hold them parallel to and just above the tabletop. Push gently on the two blocks until they move. Record your observations.

13 Now, hold the two pieces of the clay block in their original position, and slowly pull them apart, allowing the hanging wall to move downward. Record your observations.

Analyze the Results

1 What happened to the first block of clay in step 7? What kind of force did you apply to the block of clay?

2 What happened to the pieces of the second block of clay in step 12? What kind of force did you apply to them?

3 What happened to the pieces of the second block of clay in step 13? Describe the forces that acted on the block and the way the pieces of the block reacted.

Draw Conclusions

4 Summarize how the forces you applied to the blocks of clay relate to the way tectonic forces affect rock layers. Be sure to use the terms *fold, fault, anticline, syncline, hanging wall, footwall, tension,* and *compression* in your summary.

Skills Practice Lab

Earthquake Waves

The energy from an earthquake travels as seismic waves in all directions through the Earth. Seismologists can use the properties of certain types of seismic waves to find the epicenter of an earthquake.

P waves travel more quickly than S waves and are always detected first. The average speed of P waves in the Earth's crust is 6.1 km/s. The average speed of S waves in the Earth's crust is 4.1 km/s. The difference in arrival time between P waves and S waves is called *lag time.*

In this activity, you will use the S-P-time method to determine the location of an earthquake's epicenter.

MATERIALS

- calculator (optional)
- compass
- ruler, metric

SAFETY

Procedure

1 The illustration below shows seismographic records made in three cities following an earthquake. These traces begin at the left and show the arrival of P waves at time zero. The second set of waves on each record represents the arrival of S waves.

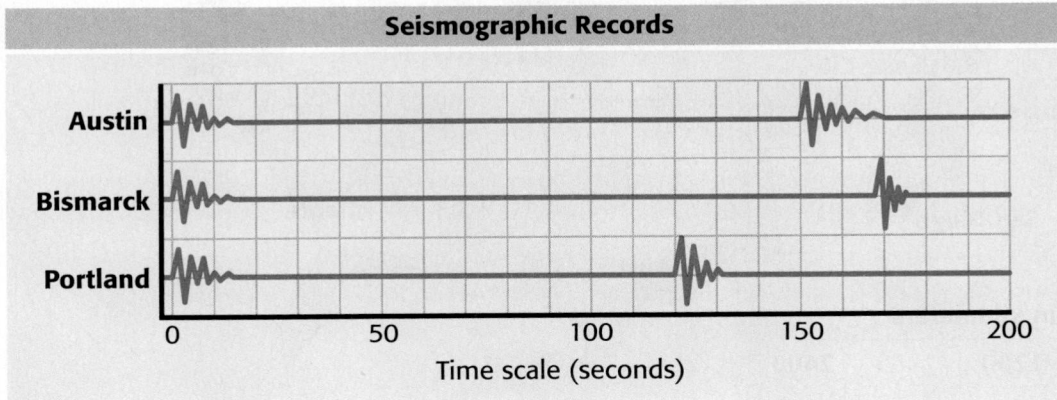

Seismographic Records

Austin

Bismarck

Portland

Time scale (seconds)

2 Copy the data table on the next page.

3 Use the time scale provided with the seismographic records to find the lag time between the P waves and the S waves for each city. Remember that the lag time is the time between the moment when the first P wave arrives and the moment when the first S wave arrives. Record this data in your table.

4 Use the following equation to calculate how long it takes each wave type to travel 100 km:

$$100 \text{ km} \div \textit{average speed of the wave} = \textit{time}$$

5 To find lag time for earthquake waves at 100 km, subtract the time it takes P waves to travel 100 km from the time it takes S waves to travel 100 km. Record the lag time.

6 Use the following formula to find the distance from each city to the epicenter:

$$distance = \frac{measured\ lag\ time\ (s) \times 100\ km}{lag\ time\ for\ 100\ km\ (s)}$$

In your data table, record the distance from each city to the epicenter.

7 Trace the map below onto a separate sheet of paper.

8 Use the scale to adjust your compass so that the radius of a circle with Austin at the center is equal to the distance between Austin and the epicenter of the earthquake.

Epicenter Data Table		
City	Lag time (seconds)	Distance to the epicenter (km)
Austin, TX		
Bismarck, ND	DO NOT WRITE IN BOOK	
Portland, OR		

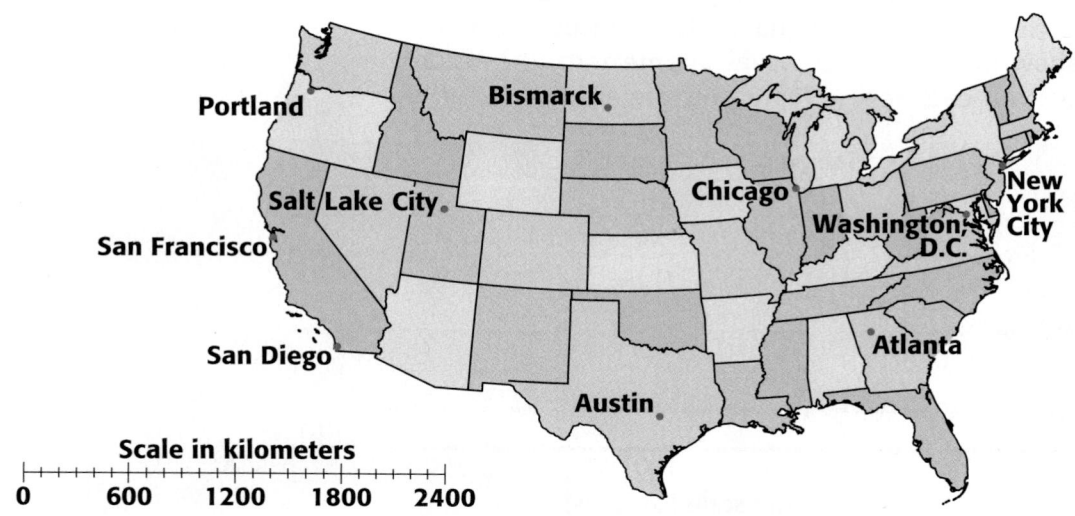

Scale in kilometers
0   600   1200   1800   2400

9 Put the point of your compass at Austin on your copy of the map, and draw a circle.

10 Repeat steps 8 and 9 for Bismarck and Portland. The epicenter of the earthquake is located near the point where the three circles meet.

Anayze the Results

1 Which city is closest to the epicenter?

Draw Conclusions

2 Why do seismologists need measurements from three different locations to find the epicenter of an earthquake?

Skills Practice Lab

Some Go "Pop," Some Do Not

Volcanic eruptions range from mild to violent. When volcanoes erupt, the materials left behind provide information to scientists studying the Earth's crust. Mild, or nonexplosive, eruptions produce thin, runny lava that is low in silica. During nonexplosive eruptions, lava simply flows down the side of the volcano. Explosive eruptions, on the other hand, do not produce much lava. Instead, the explosions hurl ash and debris into the air. The materials left behind are light in color and high in silica. These materials help geologists determine the composition of the crust underneath the volcanoes.

MATERIALS

- paper, graph (1 sheet)
- pencils (or markers), red, yellow, and orange
- ruler, metric

Procedure

1. Copy the map below onto graph paper. Take care to line the grid up properly.

2. Locate each volcano from the list on the next page by drawing a circle with a diameter of about 2 mm in the proper location on your copy of the map. Use the latitude and longitude grids to help you.

3. Review all the eruptions for each volcano. For each explosive eruption, color the circle red. For each quiet volcano, color the circle yellow. For volcanoes that have erupted in both ways, color the circle orange.

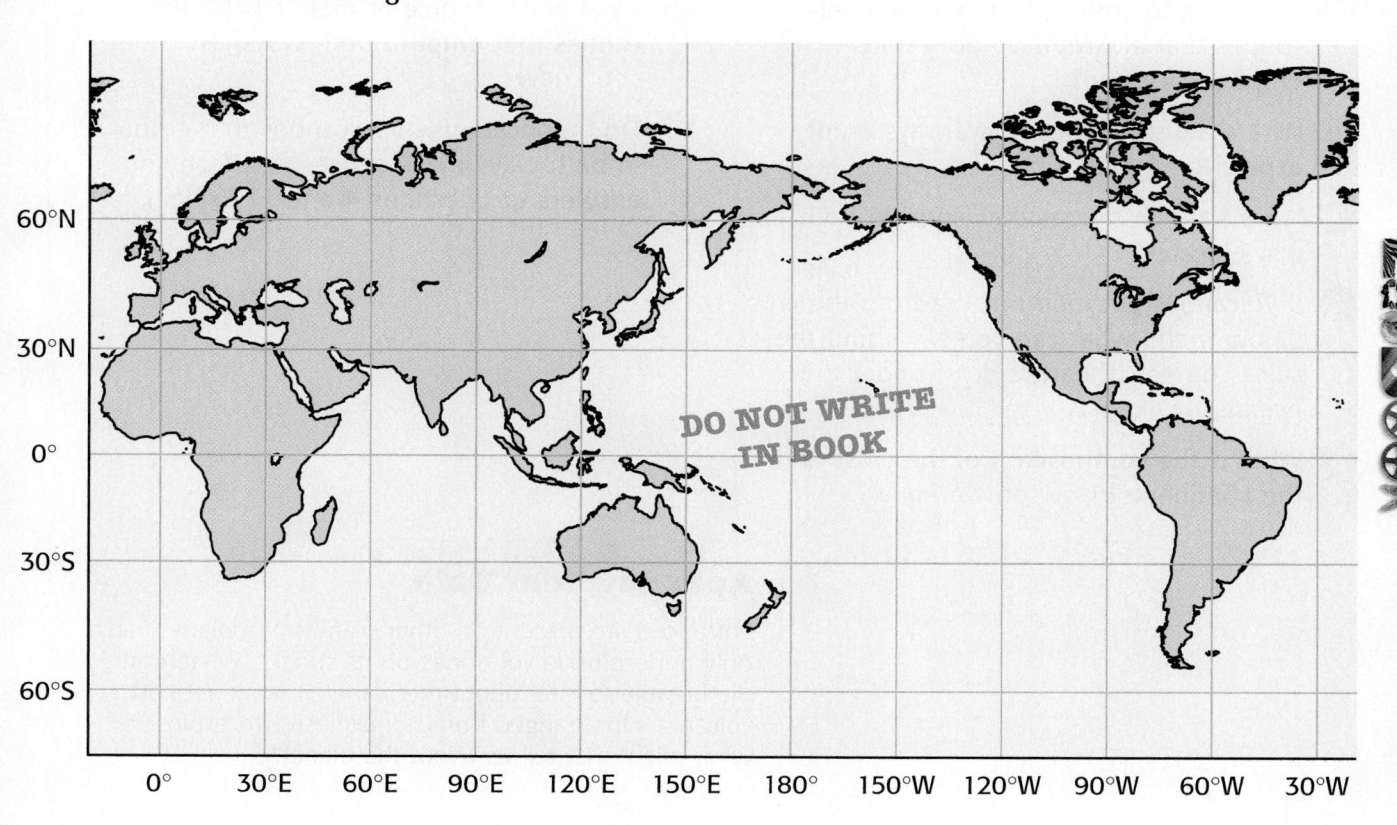

DO NOT WRITE IN BOOK

Volcanic Activity Chart

Volcano name	Location	Description
Mount St. Helens	46°N 122°W	An explosive eruption blew the top off the mountain. Light-colored ash covered thousands of square kilometers. Another eruption sent a lava flow down the southeast side of the mountain.
Kilauea	19°N 155°W	One small eruption sent a lava flow along 12 km of highway.
Rabaul caldera	4°S 152°E	Explosive eruptions have caused tsunamis and have left 1–2 m of ash on nearby buildings.
Popocatépetl	19°N 98°W	During one explosion, Mexico City closed the airport for 14 hours because huge columns of ash made it too difficult for pilots to see. Eruptions from this volcano have also caused damaging avalanches.
Soufriere Hills	16°N 62°W	Small eruptions have sent lava flows down the hills. Other explosive eruptions have sent large columns of ash into the air.
Long Valley caldera	37°N 119°W	Explosive eruptions have sent ash into the air.
Okmok	53°N 168°W	Recently, there have been slow lava flows from this volcano. Twenty-five hundred years ago, ash and debris exploded from the top of this volcano.
Pavlof	55°N 161°W	Eruption clouds have been sent 200 m above the summit. Eruptions have sent ash columns 10 km into the air. Occasionally, small eruptions have caused lava flows.
Fernandina	42°N 12°E	Eruptions have ejected large blocks of rock from this volcano.
Mount Pinatubo	15°N 120°E	Ash and debris from an explosive eruption destroyed homes, crops, and roads within 52,000 km² around the volcano.

Analyze the Results

1 According to your map, where are volcanoes that always have nonexplosive eruptions located?

2 Where are volcanoes that always erupt explosively located?

3 Where are volcanoes that erupt in both ways located?

4 If volcanoes get their magma from the crust below them, what can you say about the silica content of Earth's crust under the oceans?

5 What is the composition of the crust under the continents? How do we know?

Draw Conclusions

6 What is the source of materials for volcanoes that erupt in both ways? How do you know?

7 Do the locations of volcanoes that erupt in both ways make sense, based on your answers to questions 4 and 5? Explain.

Applying Your Data

Volcanoes are present on other planets. If a planet had only nonexplosive volcanoes on its surface, what would we be able to infer about the planet? If a planet had volcanoes that ranged from nonexplosive to explosive, what might that tell us about the planet?

Skills Practice Lab

Great Ice Escape

Did you know that ice acts as a natural wrecking ball? Even rocks don't stand a chance against the power of ice. When water trapped in rock freezes, a process called *ice wedging* occurs. The water volume increases, and the rock cracks to "get out of the way." This expansion can fragment a rock into several pieces. In this exercise, you will see how this natural wrecker works, and you will try to stop the great ice escape.

Ask a Question

1 If a plastic jar is filled with water, is there a way to prevent the jar from breaking when the water freezes?

Form a Hypothesis

2 Write a hypothesis that is a possible answer to the question above. Explain your reasoning.

Test the Hypothesis

3 Fill three identical jars to overflowing with water, and close two of them securely.

4 Measure the height of the water in the unsealed container. Record the height.

5 Tightly wrap one of the closed jars with tape, string, or other items to reinforce the jar. These items must be removable.

6 Place all three jars in resealable sandwich bags, and leave them in the freezer overnight. (Make sure the open jar does not spill.)

7 Remove the jars from the freezer, and carefully remove the wrapping from the reinforced jar.

8 Did your reinforced jar crack? Why or why not?

9 What does each jar look like? Record your observations.

10 Record the height of the ice in the unsealed jar. How does the new height compare with the height you measured in step 4?

Analyze the Results

1 Do you think it is possible to stop the ice from breaking the sealed jars? Why or why not?

2 How could ice wedging affect soil formation?

MATERIALS

- bags, sandwich resealable (3)
- freezer
- jars, hard plastic with screw-on lids, such as spice containers (3)
- ruler, metric
- tape, strings, rubber bands, and other items to bind or reinforce the jars
- water

SAFETY

Skills Practice Lab

Clean Up Your Act

When you wash dishes, the family car, the bathroom sink, or your clothes, you wash them with water. But have you ever wondered how water gets clean? Two major methods of purifying water are filtration and evaporation. In this activity, you will use both of these methods to test how well they remove pollutants from water. You will test detritus (decaying plant matter), soil, vinegar, and detergent. Your teacher may also ask you to test other pollutants.

Form a Hypothesis

1 Form a hypothesis about whether filtration and evaporation will clean each of the four pollutants from the water and how well they might do it. Then, use the procedures below to test your hypothesis.

Part A: Filtration

Filtration is a common method of removing various pollutants from water. Filtration requires very little energy—gravity pulls water down through the layers of filter material. See how well this energy-efficient method works to clean your sample of polluted water.

Test the Hypothesis

2 Put on your gloves and goggles. Use scissors to carefully cut the bottom out of the empty soda bottle.

3 Using a small nail and hammer, carefully punch four or five small holes through the plastic cap of the bottle. Screw the plastic cap onto the bottle.

4 Turn the bottle upside down, and set its neck in a ring on a ring stand, as shown on the next page. Put a handful of gravel into the inverted bottle. Add a layer of activated charcoal, followed by thick layers of sand and gravel. Place a 400 mL beaker under the neck of the bottle.

5 Fill each of the large beakers with 1,000 mL of clean water. Set one beaker aside to serve as the control. Add three or four spoonfuls of each of the following pollutants to the other beaker: detritus, soil, household vinegar, and dishwashing detergent.

6 Copy the table on the next page, and record your observations for each beaker in the columns labeled "Before cleaning."

7 Observe the color of the water in each beaker.

8 Use a hand lens to examine the water for visible particles.

Part A
- charcoal, activated
- goggles
- gravel
- hammer and small nail
- sand
- scissors
- soda bottle, plastic, with cap, 2 L

Part B
- bag, plastic sandwich, sealable
- flask, Erlenmeyer
- gloves, heat-resistant
- hot plate
- ice
- stopper, rubber, one-hole, with a glass tube
- tubing, plastic, 1.5 m

Parts A and B
- beaker, 400 mL
- beaker, 1,000 mL (2)
- detergent, dishwashing
- detritus (grass and leaf clippings)
- hand lens
- pH test strips
- ring stand with ring
- soil
- spoons, plastic (2)
- vinegar, household
- water, 2,000 mL

SAFETY

9 Smell the water, and note any unusual odors.

10 Stir the water in each beaker rapidly with a plastic spoon, and check for suds. Use a different spoon for each sample.

11 Use a pH test strip to find the pH of the water.

12 Gently stir the clean water, and then pour half of it through the filtration device.

13 Observe the water in the collection beaker for color, particles, odors, suds, and pH. Be patient. It may take several minutes for the water to travel through the filtration device.

14 Record your observations in the appropriate "After filtration" column in your table.

15 Repeat steps 12–14 using the polluted water.

Analyze the Results

1 How did the color of the polluted water change after the filtration? Did the color of the clean water change?

2 Did the filtration method remove all of the particles from the polluted water? Explain.

3 How much did the pH of the polluted water change? Did the pH of the clean water change? Was the final pH of the polluted water the same as the pH of the clean water before cleaning? Explain.

Results Table						
	Before cleaning (clean water)	Before cleaning (polluted water)	After filtration (clean water)	After filtration (polluted water)	After evaporation (clean water)	After evaporation (polluted water)
Color						
Particles						
Odor			DO NOT WRITE IN BOOK			
Suds						
pH						

Part B: Evaporation

Cleaning water by evaporation is more expensive than cleaning water by filtration. Evaporation requires more energy, which can come from a variety of sources. In this activity, you will use an electric hot plate as the energy source. See how well this method works to clean your sample of polluted water.

Form a Hypothesis

1 Write a hypothesis about which method you think will work better for water purification. Explain your reasoning.

Test the Hypothesis

2 Fill an Erlenmeyer flask with about 250 mL of the clean water, and insert the rubber stopper and glass tube into the flask.

3 Wearing goggles and gloves, connect about 1.5 m of plastic tubing to the glass tube.

4 Set the flask on the hot plate, and run the plastic tubing up and around the ring and down into a clean, empty 400 mL collection beaker.

5 Fill the sandwich bag with ice, seal the bag, and place the bag on the ring stand. Be sure the plastic bag and the tubing touch, as shown below.

6 Bring the water in the flask to a slow boil. As the water vapor passes by the bag of ice, the vapor will condense and drip into the collection beaker.

7 Observe the water in the collection beaker for color, particles, odor, suds, and pH. Record your observations in the "After evaporation" column in your data table.

8 Repeat steps 2–7 using the polluted water.

Analyze the Results

1 How did the color of the polluted water change after evaporation? Did the color of the clean water change after evaporation?

2 Did the evaporation method remove all of the particles from the polluted water? Explain.

3 How much did the pH of the polluted water change? Did the pH of the final clean water change? Was the final pH of the polluted water the same as the pH of the clean water before it was cleaned? Explain.

Draw Conclusions: Parts A and B

4 Which method—filtration or evaporation— removed the most pollutants from the water? Explain your reasoning.

5 Describe any changes that occurred in the clean water during this experiment.

6 What do you think are the advantages and disadvantages of each method?

7 Explain how you think each material (sand, gravel, and charcoal) used in the filtration system helped clean the water.

8 List areas of the country where you think each method of purification would be the most and the least beneficial. Explain your reasoning.

Applying Your Data

Do you think either purification method would remove oil from water? If time permits, repeat your experiment using several spoonfuls of cooking oil as the pollutant.

Filtration is only one step in the purification of water at water treatment plants. Research other methods used to purify public water supplies.

Model-Making Lab

Dune Movement

Wind moves the sand by a process called *saltation*. The sand skips and bounces along the ground in the same direction as the wind is blowing. As sand is blown across a beach, the dunes change. In this activity, you will investigate the effect wind has on a model sand dune.

MATERIALS

- bag, paper, large enough to hold half the box
- box, cardboard, shallow
- hair dryer
- marker
- mask, filter
- ruler, metric
- sand, fine

SAFETY

Procedure

1. Use the marker to draw and label vertical lines 5 cm apart along one side of the box.

2. Fill the box about halfway with sand. Brush the sand into a dune shape about 10 cm from the end of the box.

3. Use the lines you drew along the edge of the box to measure the location of the dune's peak to the nearest centimeter.

4. Slide the box into the paper bag until only about half the box is exposed, as shown below.

5. Put on your safety goggles and filter mask. Hold the hair dryer so that it is level with the peak of the dune and about 10–20 cm from the open end of the box.

6. Turn on the hair dryer at the lowest speed, and direct the air toward the model sand dune for 1 min.

7. Record the new location of the model dune.

8. Repeat steps 5 and 6 three times. After each trial, measure and record the location of the dune's peak.

Analyze the Results

1. How far did the dune move during each trial?

2. How far did the dune move overall?

Draw Conclusions

3. How might the dune's movement be affected if you were to turn the hair dryer to the highest speed?

Applying Your Data

Flatten the sand. Place a barrier, such as a rock, in the sand. Position the hair dryer level with the top of the sand's surface. How does the rock affect the dune's movement?

Skills Practice Lab

Creating a Kettle

As glaciers recede, they leave huge amounts of rock material behind. Sometimes receding glaciers form moraines by depositing some of the rock material in ridges. At other times, glaciers leave chunks of ice that form depressions called *kettles*. As the ice melts, these depressions may form ponds or lakes. In this activity, you will discover how kettles are formed by creating your own.

MATERIALS

- ice, cubes of various sizes (4–5)
- ruler, metric
- sand
- tub, small

Ask a Question

1 How are kettles formed?

Form a Hypothesis

2 Write a hypothesis that could answer the question above.

Test the Hypothesis

3 Fill the tub three-quarters full with sand.

4 Describe the size and shape of each ice cube.

5 Push the ice cubes to various depths in the sand.

6 Put the tub where it won't be disturbed overnight.

7 Closely observe the sand around the area where you left each ice cube.

8 What happened to the ice cubes?

9 Use a metric ruler to measure the depth and diameter of the indentation left by each ice cube.

Analyze the Results

1 How does this model relate to the size and shape of a natural kettle?

2 In what ways are your model kettles similar to real ones? How are they different?

Draw Conclusions

3 Based on your model, what can you conclude about the formation of kettles by receding glaciers?

Skills Practice Lab

Investigating an Oil Spill

Have you ever wondered why it is important to recycle motor oil rather than pour it down the drain or sewer? Or have you ever wondered why a seemingly small oil spill can cause so much damage? The reason is that a little oil goes a long way.

Observing Oil and Water

Maybe you've heard the phrase "Oil and water don't mix." Oil dropped in water will spread out thinly over the surface of the water. In this activity, you'll learn how far a drop of oil can spread.

Ask a Question

1 How far will one drop of oil spread in a pan of water?

Form a Hypothesis

2 Write a hypothesis that could answer the question above.

Test the Hypothesis

3 Use a pipet to place one drop of oil into the middle of a pan of water. **Caution:** Machine oil is poisonous. Wear goggles and gloves. Keep materials that have contacted oil out of your mouth and eyes.

4 Observe what happens to the drop of oil for the next few seconds. Record your observations.

5 Using a metric ruler, measure the diameter of the oil slick to the nearest centimeter.

6 Determine the area of the oil slick in square centimeters. Use the formula below to find the area of a circle ($A = \pi r^2$). The radius (r) is equal to the diameter you measured in step 5 divided by 2. Multiply the radius by itself to get the square of the radius (r^2). Pi (π) is equal to 3.14. Record your answer.

> **Example**
>
> If your diameter is 10 cm,
>
> $r = 5$ cm, $r^2 = 25$ cm^2, $\pi = 3.14$
>
> $A = \pi r^2$
>
> $A = 3.14 \times 25$ cm^2
>
> $A = 78.5$ cm^2

MATERIALS

- calculator (optional)
- gloves, protective
- goggles
- graduated cylinder
- oil, light machine, 15 mL
- pan, large, at least 22 cm in diameter
- pipet
- ruler, metric
- water

SAFETY

Analyze the Results

1 What happened to the drop of oil when it came in contact with the water?

2 What total surface area was covered by the oil slick? (Show your calculations.)

Draw Conclusions

3 What can you conclude about the density of oil compared with the density of water?

Finding the Number of Drops in a Liter

"It's only a few drops," you may think as you spill something toxic on the ground. But those drops eventually add up. Just how many drops does it take to make a difference? In this activity, you'll learn just what an impact a few drops can have.

Procedure

1 Using a clean pipet, count the number of water drops it takes to fill the graduated cylinder to 10 mL. Be sure to add the drops slowly so you get an accurate count.

2 Since there are 1,000 mL in a liter, multiply the number of drops in 10 mL by 100. The result is the number of drops in a liter.

Analyze the Results

1 How many drops of water from your pipet did it take to fill a 1 L container?

2 What would happen if someone spilled 4 L of oil into a lake?

Applying Your Data

Can you devise a way to clean the oil from the water? Get permission from your teacher before testing your cleaning method.

Do you think oil behaves the same way in ocean water? Devise an experiment to test your hypothesis.

Model-Making Lab

Turning the Tides

Daily tides are caused by two "bulges" on the ocean's surface—one on the side of the Earth facing the moon and the other on the opposite side of the Earth. The bulge on the side facing the moon is caused by the moon's gravitational pull on the water. But the bulge on the opposite side of the Earth is slightly more difficult to explain. Whereas the moon pulls the water on one side of the Earth, the combined rotation of the Earth and the moon "pushes" the water on the opposite side of the Earth. In this activity, you will model the motion of the Earth and the moon to investigate the tidal bulge on the side of Earth facing away from the moon.

MATERIALS

- cardboard, 1 cm × 1 cm piece
- corrugated cardboard, one large and one small, with centers marked (2 disks)
- dowel, $\frac{1}{4}$ in. in diameter and 36 cm long
- glue, white
- pencil, sharp
- stapler with staples
- string, 5 cm length

SAFETY

Procedure

1. Draw a line from the center of each disk along the folds in the cardboard to the edge of the disk. This line is the radius.

2. Place a drop of white glue on one end of the dowel. Lay the larger disk flat, and align the dowel with the line for the radius you drew in step 1. Insert about 2.5 cm of the dowel into the edge of the disk.

3. Add a drop of glue to the other end of the dowel, and push that end into the smaller disk, again along its radius. The setup should look like a large, two-headed lollipop, as shown below. This setup is a model of the Earth-moon system.

4. Staple the string to the edge of the large disk on the side opposite the dowel. Staple the cardboard square to the other end of the string. This smaller piece of cardboard represents the Earth's oceans that face away from the moon.

5. Place the tip of the pencil at the center of the large disk, as shown in the figure on the next page, and spin the model. You may poke a small hole in the bottom of the disk with your pencil, but DO NOT poke all the way through the cardboard. Record your observations. **Caution:** Be sure you are at a safe distance from other people before spinning your model.

6 Now, find your model's center of mass. The center of mass is the point at which the model can be balanced on the end of the pencil. (Hint: It might be easier to find the center of mass by using the eraser end. Then, use the sharpened end of the pencil to balance the model.) This balance point should be just inside the edge of the larger disk.

7 Place the pencil at the center of mass, and spin the model around the pencil. Again, you may wish to poke a small hole in the disk. Record your observations.

Analyze the Results

1 What happened when you tried to spin the model around the center of the large disk? This model, called the Earth-centered model, represents the incorrect view that the moon orbits the center of the Earth.

2 What happened when you tried to spin the model around its center of mass? This point, called the *barycenter,* is the point around which both the Earth and the moon rotate.

3 In each case, what happened to the string and cardboard square when the model was spun?

Draw Conclusions

4 Which model—the Earth-centered model or the barycentric model—explains why the Earth has a tidal bulge on the side opposite the moon? Explain.

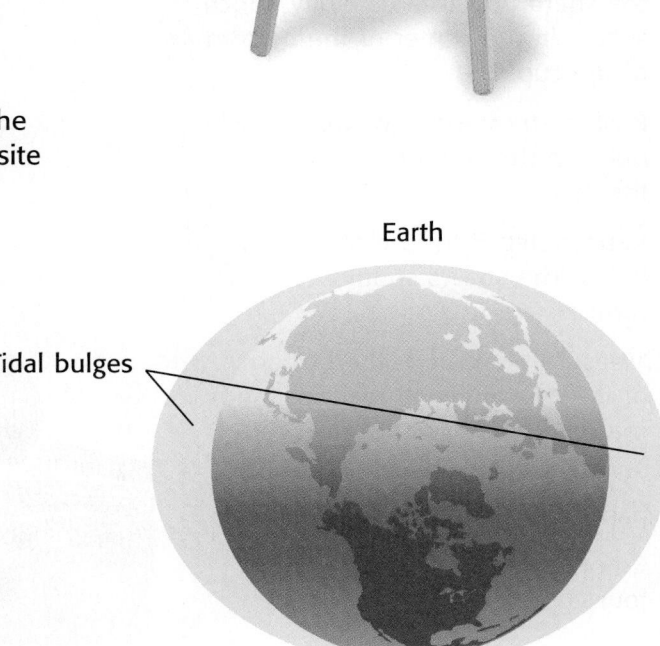

Earth

Tidal bulges

Moon

Skills Practice Lab

Go Fly a Bike!

Your friend Daniel just invented a bicycle that can fly! Trouble is, the bike can fly only when the wind speed is between 3 m/s and 10 m/s. If the wind is not blowing hard enough, the bike won't get enough lift to rise into the air, and if the wind is blowing too hard, the bike is difficult to control. Daniel needs to know if he can fly his bike today. Can you build a device that can estimate how fast the wind is blowing?

Ask a Question

① How can I construct a device to measure wind speed?

Form a Hypothesis

② Write a possible answer for the question above. Explain your reasoning.

Test the Hypothesis

③ Cut off the rolled edges of all five paper cups. They will then be lighter so that they can spin more easily.

④ Measure and place four equally spaced markings 1 cm below the rim of one of the paper cups.

⑤ Use the hole punch to punch a hole at each mark so that the cup has four equally spaced holes. Use the sharp pencil to carefully punch a hole in the center of the bottom of the cup.

⑥ Push a straw through two opposite holes in the side of the cup.

⑦ Repeat step 5 for the other two holes. The straws should form an X.

⑧ Measure 3 cm from the bottom of the remaining paper cups, and mark each spot with a dot.

⑨ At each dot, punch a hole in the paper cups with the hole punch.

⑩ Color the outside of one of the four cups.

MATERIALS

- clay, modeling
- cups, paper, small (5)
- hole punch
- marker, colored
- pencil, sharp, with an eraser
- ruler, metric
- scissors
- stapler, small
- straws, straight plastic (2)
- tape, masking
- thumbtack
- watch (or clock) that indicates seconds

SAFETY

11. Slide a cup on one of the straws by pushing the straw through the punched hole. Rotate the cup so that the bottom faces to the right.

12. Fold the end of the straw, and staple it to the inside of the cup directly across from the hole.

13. Repeat steps 11–12 for each of the remaining cups.

14. Push the tack through the intersection of the two straws.

15. Push the eraser end of a pencil through the bottom hole in the center cup. Push the tack as far as it will go into the end of the eraser.

16. Push the sharpened end of the pencil into some modeling clay to form a base. The device will then be able to stand up without being knocked over, as shown at right.

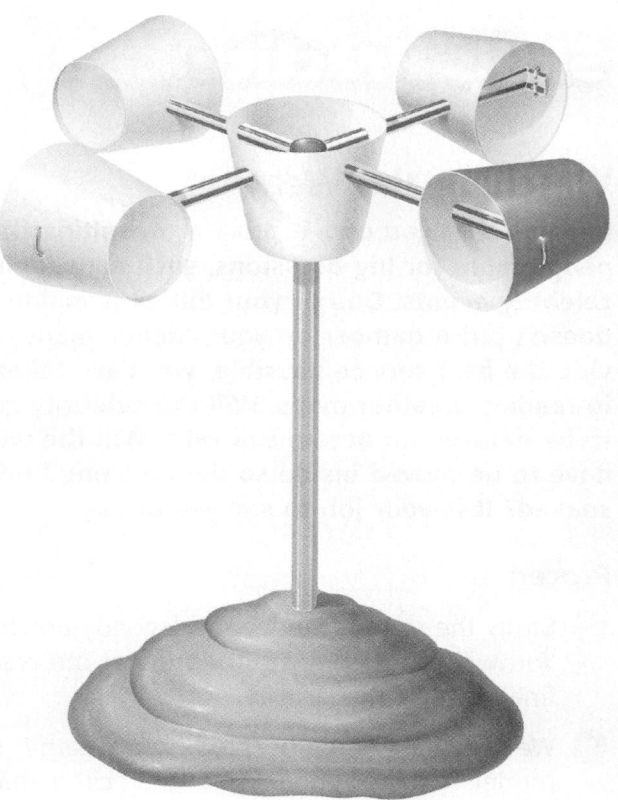

17. Blow into the cups so that they spin. Adjust the tack so that the cups can freely spin without wobbling or falling apart. Congratulations! You have just constructed an anemometer.

18. Find a suitable area outside to place the anemometer vertically on a surface away from objects that would obstruct the wind, such as buildings and trees.

19. Mark the surface at the base of the anemometer with masking tape. Label the tape "starting point."

20. Hold the colored cup over the starting point while your partner holds the watch.

21. Release the colored cup. At the same time, your partner should look at the watch or clock. As the cups spin, count the number of times the colored cup crosses the starting point in 10 s.

Analyze the Results

1. How many times did the colored cup cross the starting point in 10 s?

2. Divide your answer in step 21 by 10 to get the number of revolutions in 1 s.

3. Measure the diameter of your anemometer (the distance between the outside edges of two opposite cups) in centimeters. Multiply this number by 3.14 to get the circumference of the circle made by the cups of your anemometer.

4. Multiply your answer from step 3 by the number of revolutions per second (step 2). Divide that answer by 100 to get wind speed in meters per second.

5. Compare your results with those of your classmates. Did you get the same results? What could account for any slight differences in your results?

Draw Conclusions

6. Could Daniel fly his bicycle today? Why or why not?

Skills Practice Lab

Watching the Weather

MATERIALS

• pencil

Imagine that you own a private consulting firm that helps people plan for big occasions, such as weddings, parties, and celebrity events. One of your duties is making sure the weather doesn't put a damper on your clients' plans. In order to provide the best service possible, you have taken a crash course in reading weather maps. Will the celebrity golf match have to be delayed on account of rain? Will the wedding ceremony have to be moved inside so the blushing bride doesn't get soaked? It is your job to say yea or nay.

Procedure

1 Study the station model and legend shown on the next page. You will use the legend to interpret the weather map on the final page of this activity.

2 Weather data is represented on a weather map by a station model. A station model is a small circle that shows the location of the weather station along with a set of symbols and numbers around the circle that represent the data collected at the weather station. Study the table below.

Weather-Map Symbols		
Weather conditions	**Cloud cover**	**Wind speed (mph)**
•• Light rain	◯ No clouds	◉ Calm
∴ Moderate rain	◐ One-tenth or less	⌐ 3–8
⁘ Heavy rain	◓ Two- to three-tenths	⌐ 9–14
, Drizzle	◕ Broken	⌐ 15–20
✳ ✳ Light snow	◑ Nine-tenths	⌐ 21–25
✳✳✳ Moderate snow	● Overcast	⌐ 32–37
� Thunderstorm	⊗ Sky obscured	⌐ 44–48
∿ Freezing rain	**Special Symbols**	⌐ 55–60
∞ Haze	▲▲▲▲ Cold front	⌐ 66–71
☰ Fog	●●●● Warm front	
	H High pressure	
	L Low pressure	
	𝓢 Hurricane	

Station Model

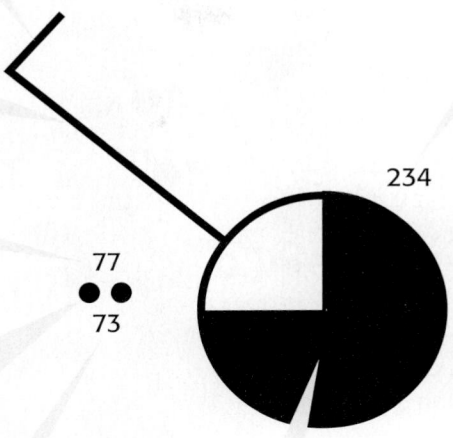

Wind speed is represented by whole and half tails.

A line indicates the direction the wind is coming from.

Air temperature

A symbol represents the current weather conditions. If there is no symbol, there is no precipitation.

Dew point temperature

Shading indicates the cloud coverage.

Atmospheric pressure in millibars (mbar). This number has been shortened on the station model. To read the number properly you must follow a few simple rules.

- If the first number is greater than 5, place a 9 in front of the number and a decimal point between the last two digits.

- If the first number is less than or equal to 5, place a 10 in front of the number and a decimal point between the last two digits.

234

77
73

Interpreting Station Models

The station model below is for Boston, Massachusetts. The current temperature in Boston is 42°F, and the dew point is 39°F. The barometric pressure is 1011.0 mbar. The sky is overcast, and there is moderate rainfall. The wind is coming from the southwest at 15–20 mph.

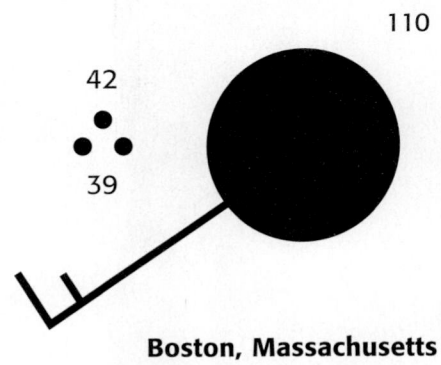

110

42

39

Boston, Massachusetts

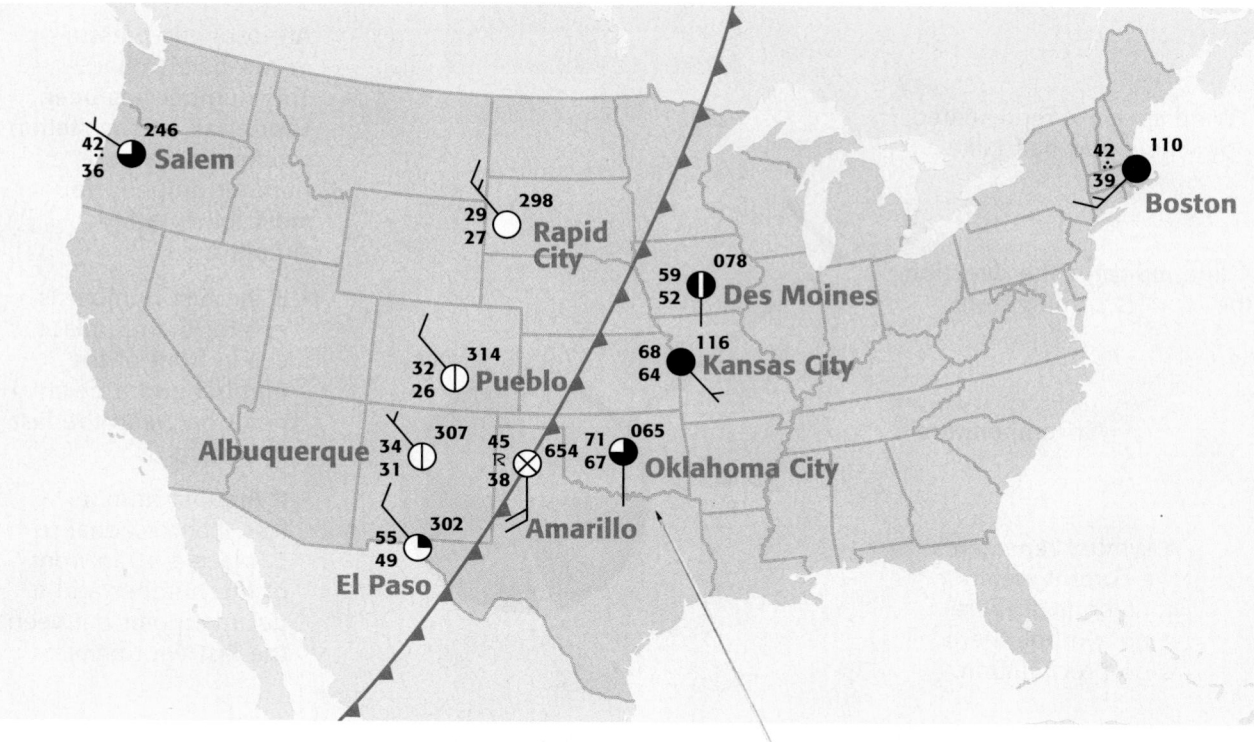

Analyze the Results

1. Based on the weather for the entire United States, what time of year is it? Explain your answer.

2. Interpret the station model for Salem, Oregon. What is the temperature, dew point, cloud coverage, wind direction, wind speed, and atmospheric pressure? Is there any precipitation? If so, what kind?

3. What is happening to wind direction, temperature, and pressure as the cold front approaches? as it passes?

Draw Conclusions

4. Interpret the station model for Amarillo, Texas.

Skills Practice Lab

Let It Snow!

Although an inch of rain might be good for your garden, 7 cm or 8 cm could cause an unwelcome flood. But what about snow? How much snow is too much? A blizzard might drop 40 cm of snow overnight. Sure it's up to your knees, but how does this much snow compare with rain? This activity will help you find out.

MATERIALS

- beaker, 100 mL
- gloves, heat-resistant
- graduated cylinder
- hot plate
- ice, shaved, 150 mL
- ruler, metric

SAFETY

Procedure

1. Pour 50 mL of shaved ice into your beaker. Do not pack the ice into the beaker. This ice will represent your snowfall.

2. Use the ruler to measure the height of the snow in the beaker.

3. Turn on the hot plate to a low setting. **Caution:** Wear heat-resistant gloves and goggles when working with the hot plate.

4. Place the beaker on the hot plate, and leave it there until all of the snow melts.

5. Pour the water into the graduated cylinder, and record the height and volume of the water.

6. Repeat steps 1–5 two more times.

Analysis

1. What was the difference in height before and after the snow melted in each of your three trials? What was the average difference?

2. Why did the volume change after the ice melted?

3. What was the ratio of snow height to water height?

4. Use the ratio you found in step 3 of the Analysis to calculate how much water 50 cm of this snow would produce. Use the following equation to help.

$$\frac{\text{measured height of snow}}{\text{measured height of water}} = \frac{50 \text{ cm of snow}}{? \text{ cm of water}}$$

5. Why is it important to know the water content of a snowfall?

Applying Your Data

Shaved ice isn't really snow. Research to find out how much water real snow would produce. Does every snowfall produce the same ratio of snow height to water depth?

Model-Making Lab

Gone with the Wind

Pilots at the Fly Away Airport need your help—fast! Last night, lightning destroyed the orange windsock. This windsock helped pilots measure which direction the wind was blowing. But now the windsock is gone with the wind, and an incoming airplane needs to land. The pilot must know which direction the wind is blowing and is counting on you to make a device that can measure wind direction.

MATERIALS

- card, index
- compass, drawing
- compass, magnetic
- pencil, sharpened
- plate, paper
- protractor
- rock, small
- ruler, metric
- scissors
- stapler
- straw, straight plastic
- thumbtack (or pushpin)

SAFETY

Ask a Question

1. How can I measure wind direction?

Form a Hypothesis

2. Write a possible answer to the question above.

Test the Hypothesis

3. Find the center of the plate by tracing around its edge with a drawing compass. The pointed end of the compass should poke a small hole in the center of the plate.

4. Use a ruler to draw a line across the center of the plate.

5. Use a protractor to help you draw a second line through the center of the plate. This new line should be at a 90° angle to the line you drew in step 4.

6. Moving clockwise, label each line "N," "E," "S," and "W."

7. Use a protractor to help you draw two more lines through the center of the plate. These lines should be at a 45° angle to the lines you drew in steps 4 and 5.

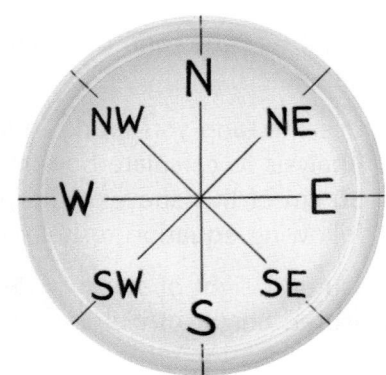

8. Moving clockwise from *N*, label these new lines "NE," "SE," "SW," and "NW." The plate now resembles the face of a magnetic compass. The plate will be the base of your wind-direction indicator. It will help you read the direction of the wind at a glance.

9. Measure and mark a 5 cm × 5 cm square on an index card, and cut out the square. Fold the square in half to form a triangle.

10. Staple an open edge of the triangle to the straw so that one point of the triangle touches the end of the straw.

11. Hold the pencil at a 90° angle to the straw. The eraser should touch the balance point of the straw. Push a thumbtack or pushpin through the straw and into the eraser. The straw should spin without falling off.

12. Find a suitable area outside to measure the wind direction. The area should be clear of trees and buildings.

13. Press the sharpened end of the pencil through the center hole of the plate and into the ground. The labels on your paper plate should be facing the sky, as shown on this page.

14. Use a compass to find magnetic north. Rotate the plate so that the *N* on the plate points north. Place a small rock on top of the plate so that the plate does not turn.

15. Watch the straw as it rotates. The triangle will point in the direction the wind is blowing.

Analyze the Results

1. From which direction is the wind coming?

2. In which direction is the wind blowing?

Draw Conclusions

3. Would this be an effective way for pilots to measure wind direction? Why or why not?

4. What improvements would you suggest to Fly Away Airport to measure wind direction more accurately?

Applying Your Data

Use this tool to measure and record wind direction for several days. What changes in wind direction occur as a front approaches? as a front passes?

Review magnetic declination in the chapter entitled "Maps as Models of the Earth." How might magnetic declination affect your design for a tool to measure wind direction?

Skills Practice Lab

Global Impact

For years, scientists have debated the topic of global warming. Is the temperature of the Earth actually getting warmer? In this activity, you will examine a table to determine if the data indicate any trends. Be sure to notice how much the trends seem to change as you analyze different sets of data.

MATERIALS

• pencils, colored (4)
• ruler, metric

Procedure

1. The table below shows average global temperatures recorded over the last 100 years.

2. Draw a graph. Label the horizontal axis "Time." Mark the grid in 5-year intervals. Label the vertical axis "Temperature (°C)," with values ranging from 13°C to 15°C.

3. Starting with 1900, use the numbers in red to plot the temperature in 20-year intervals. Connect the dots with straight lines.

4. Using a ruler, estimate the average slope for the temperatures. Draw a red line to represent the slope.

5. Using different colors, plot the temperatures at 10-year intervals and 5-year intervals on the same graph. Connect each set of dots, and draw the average slope for each set.

Analyze the Results

1. Examine your completed graph, and explain any trends you see in the graphed data. Was there an increase or a decrease in average temperature over the last 100 years?

2. What similarities and differences did you see between each set of graphed data?

Draw Conclusions

3. What conclusions can you draw from the data you graphed in this activity?

4. What would happen if your graph were plotted in 1-year intervals? Try it!

Average Global Temperatures

Year	°C	Year	°C	Year	°C	Year	°C	Year	°C	Year	°C
1900	14.0	1917	13.6	1934	14.0	1951	14.0	1968	13.9	1985	14.1
1901	13.9	1918	13.6	1935	13.9	1952	14.0	1969	14.0	1986	14.2
1902	13.8	1919	13.8	1936	14.0	1953	14.1	1970	14.0	1987	14.3
1903	13.6	1920	13.8	1937	14.1	1954	13.9	1971	13.9	1988	14.4
1904	13.5	1921	13.9	1938	14.1	1955	13.9	1972	13.9	1989	14.2
1905	13.7	1922	13.9	1939	14.0	1956	13.8	1973	14.2	1990	14.5
1906	13.8	1923	13.8	1940	14.1	1957	14.1	1974	13.9	1991	14.4
1907	13.6	1924	13.8	1941	14.1	1958	14.1	1975	14.0	1992	14.1
1908	13.7	1925	13.8	1942	14.1	1959	14.0	1976	13.8	1993	14.2
1909	13.7	1926	14.1	1943	14.0	1960	14.0	1977	14.2	1994	14.3
1910	13.7	1927	14.0	1944	14.1	1961	14.1	1978	14.1	1995	14.5
1911	13.7	1928	14.0	1945	14.0	1962	14.0	1979	14.1	1996	14.4
1912	13.7	1929	13.8	1946	14.0	1963	14.0	1980	14.3	1997	14.4
1913	13.8	1930	13.9	1947	14.1	1964	13.7	1981	14.4	1998	14.5
1914	14.0	1931	14.0	1948	14.0	1965	13.8	1982	14.1	1999	14.5
1915	14.0	1932	14.0	1949	13.9	1966	13.9	1983	14.3	2000	14.5
1916	13.8	1933	13.9	1950	13.8	1967	14.0	1984	14.1	2001	14.5

Skills Practice Lab

For the Birds

You and a partner have a new business building birdhouses. But your first clients have told you that birds do not want to live in the birdhouses you have made. The clients want their money back unless you can solve the problem. You need to come up with a solution right away!

You remember reading an article about microclimates in a science magazine. Cities often heat up because the pavement and buildings absorb so much solar radiation. Maybe the houses are too warm! How can the houses be kept cooler?

You decide to investigate the roofs; after all, changing the roofs would be a lot easier than building new houses. In order to help your clients and the birds, you decide to test different roof colors and materials to see how these variables affect a roof's ability to absorb the sun's rays.

One partner will test the color, and the other partner will test the materials. You will then share your results and make a recommendation together.

MATERIALS

- cardboard (4 pieces)
- paint, black, white, and light blue tempera
- rubber, beige or tan
- thermometers, Celsius (4)
- watch (or clock)
- wood, beige or tan

SAFETY

Part A: Color Test

Ask a Question

1 What color would be the best choice for the roof of a birdhouse?

Form a Hypothesis

2 Write down the color you think will keep a birdhouse coolest.

Test the Hypothesis

3 Paint one piece of cardboard black, another piece white, and a third light blue.

4 After the paint has dried, take the three pieces of cardboard outside, and place a thermometer on each piece.

5 In an area where there is no shade, place each piece at the same height so that all three receive the same amount of sunlight. Leave the pieces in the sunlight for 15 min.

6 Leave a fourth thermometer outside in the shade to measure the temperature of the air.

7 Record the reading of the thermometer on each piece of cardboard. Also, record the outside temperature.

Analyze the Results

1 Did each of the three thermometers record the same temperature after 15 min? Explain.

2 Were the temperature readings on each of the three pieces of cardboard the same as the reading for the outside temperature? Explain.

Draw Conclusions

3 How do your observations compare with your hypothesis?

Part B: Material Test

Ask a Question

1 Which material would be the best choice for the roof of a birdhouse?

Form a Hypothesis

2 Write down the material you think will keep a birdhouse coolest.

Test the Hypothesis

3 Take the rubber, wood, and the fourth piece of cardboard outside, and place a thermometer on each.

4 In an area where there is no shade, place each material at the same height so that they all receive the same amount of sunlight. Leave the materials in the sunlight for 15 min.

5 Leave a fourth thermometer outside in the shade to measure the temperature of the air.

6 Record the temperature of each material. Also, record the outside temperature. After you and your partner have finished your investigations, take a few minutes to share your results.

Analyze the Results

1. Did each of the thermometers on the three materials record the same temperature after 15 min? Explain.

2. Were the temperature readings on the rubber, wood, and cardboard the same as the reading for the outside temperature? Explain.

Draw Conclusions

3. How do your observations compare with your hypothesis?

4. Which material would you use to build the roofs for your birdhouses? Why?

5. Which color would you use to paint the new roofs? Why?

Applying Your Data

Make three different-colored samples for each of the three materials. When you measure the temperatures for each sample, how do the colors compare for each material? Is the same color best for all three materials? How do your results compare with what you concluded in steps 4 and 5 under Draw Conclusions of this activity? What's more important, color or material?

Skills Practice Lab

The Sun's Yearly Trip Through the Zodiac

During the course of a year, the sun appears to move through a circle of 12 constellations in the sky. The 12 constellations make up a "belt" in the sky called the *zodiac.* Each month, the sun appears to be in a different constellation. The ancient Babylonians developed a 12-month calendar based on the idea that the sun moved through this circle of constellations as it revolved around the Earth. They believed that the constellations of stars were fixed in position and that the sun and planets moved past the stars. Later, Copernicus developed a model of the solar system in which the Earth and the planets revolve around the sun. But how can Copernicus's model of the solar system be correct when the sun appears to move through the zodiac?

MATERIALS

- ball, inflated
- box, cardboard, large
- cards, index (12)
- chairs (12)
- tape, masking (1 roll)

Ask a Question

1 If the sun is at the center of the solar system, why does it appear to move with respect to the stars in the sky?

Form a Hypothesis

2 Write a possible answer to the question above. Explain your reasoning.

Test the Hypothesis

3 Set the chairs in a large circle so that the backs of the chairs all face the center of the circle. Make sure that the chairs are equally spaced, like the numbers on the face of a clock.

4 Write the name of each constellation in the zodiac on the index cards. You should have one card for each constellation.

5 Stand inside the circle with the masking tape and the index cards. Moving counterclockwise, attach the cards to the backs of the chairs in the following order: Aries, Taurus, Gemini, Cancer, Leo, Virgo, Libra, Scorpio, Sagittarius, Capricorn, Aquarius, and Pisces.

6 Use masking tape to label the ball "Sun."

7 Place the large, closed box in the center of the circle. Set the roll of masking tape flat on top of the box.

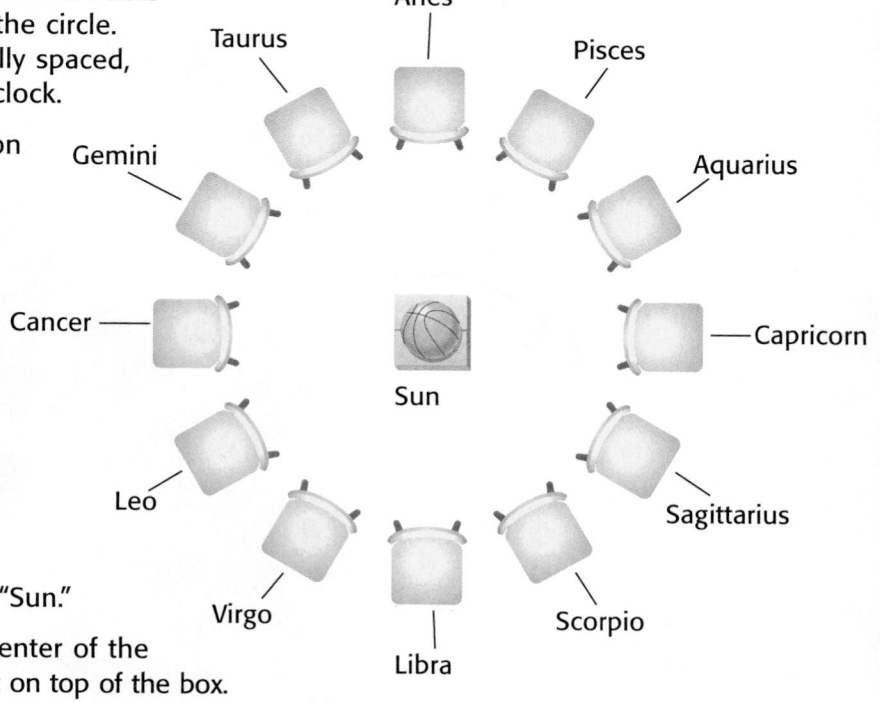

8 Place the ball on top of the roll of masking tape so that the ball stays in place.

9 Stand inside the circle of chairs. You will represent the Earth. As you move around the ball, you will model the Earth's orbit around the sun. Notice that even though only the "Earth" is moving, as seen from the Earth, the sun appears to move through the entire zodiac!

10 Stand in front of the chair labeled "Aries." Look at the ball representing the sun. Then, look past the ball to the chair at the opposite side of the circle. Where in the zodiac does the sun appear to be?

11 Move to the next chair on your right (counterclockwise). Where does the sun appear to be? Is it in the same constellation? Explain your answer.

12 Repeat step 10 until you have observed the position of the sun from each chair in the circle.

Analyze the Results

1 Did the sun appear to move through the 12 constellations, even though the Earth was orbiting around the sun? How can you explain this apparent movement?

Draw Conclusions

2 How does Copernicus's model of the solar system explain the apparent movement of the sun through the constellations of the zodiac?

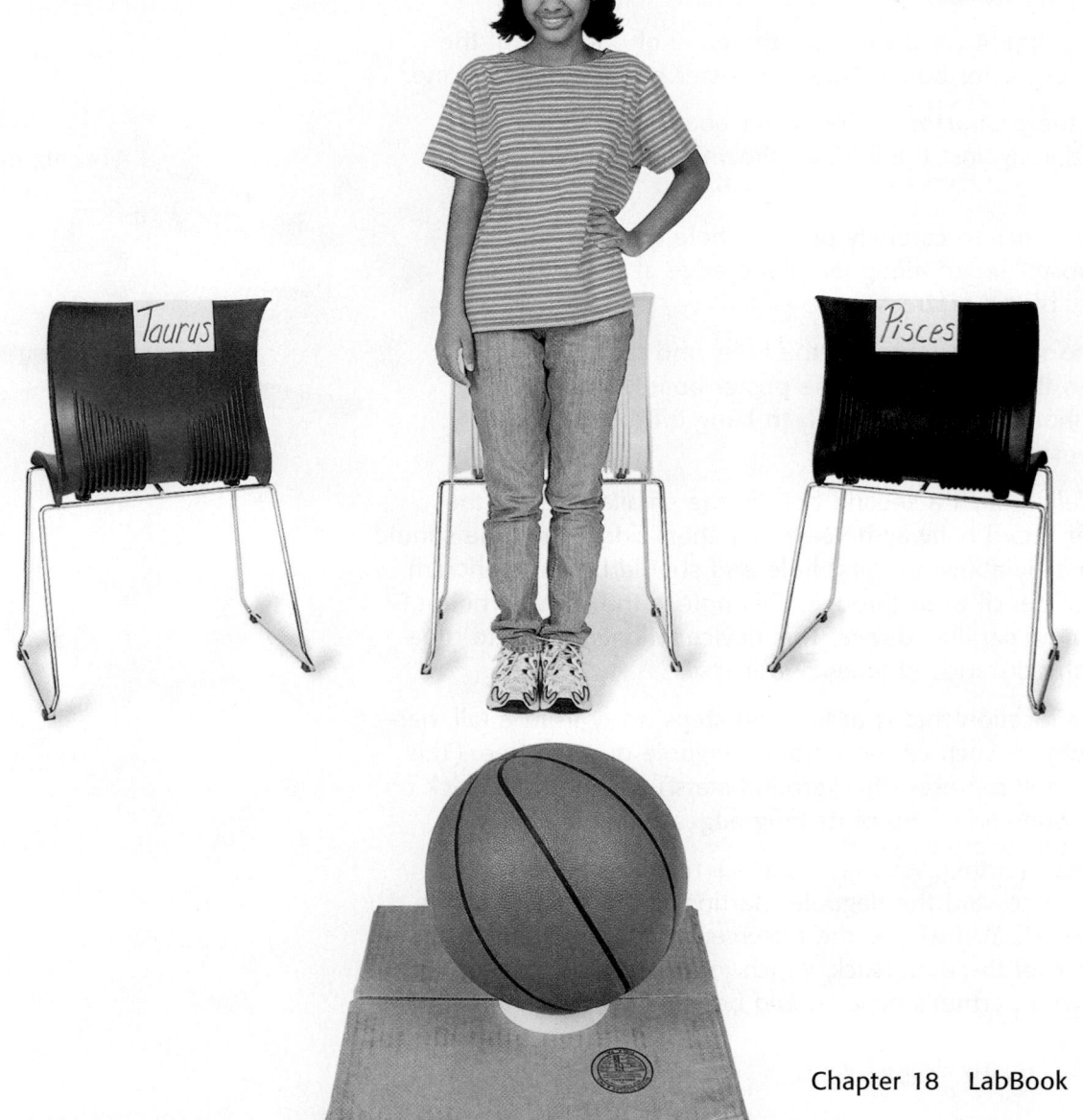

Skills Practice Lab

I See the Light!

How do you find the distance to an object you can't reach? You can do it by measuring something you can reach, finding a few angles, and using mathematics. In this activity, you'll practice measuring the distances of objects here on Earth. When you get used to it, you can take your skills to the stars!

Ask a Question

1 How can you measure the distance to a star?

Form a Hypothesis

2 Write a hypothesis that might answer this question. Explain your reasoning.

Test the Hypothesis

3 Draw a line 4 cm away from the edge of one side of the piece of poster board. Fold the poster board along this line.

4 Tape the protractor to the poster board with its flat edge against the fold, as shown in the photo below.

5 Use a pencil to carefully punch a hole through the poster board along its folded edge at the center of the protractor.

6 Thread the string through the hole, and tape one end to the underside of the poster board. The other end should be long enough to hang off the far end of the poster board.

7 Carefully punch a second hole in the smaller area of the poster board halfway between its short sides. The hole should be directly above the first hole and should be large enough for the pencil to fit through. This hole is the viewing hole of your new parallax device. This device will allow you to measure the distance of faraway objects.

8 Find a location that is at least 50 steps away from a tall, narrow object, such as the school's flagpole or a tall tree. (This object will represent background stars.) Set the meterstick on the ground with one of its long edges facing the flagpole.

9 Ask your partner, who represents a nearby star, to take 10 steps toward the flagpole, starting at the left end of the meterstick. You will be the observer. When you stand at the left end of the meterstick, which represents the location of the sun, your partner's nose should be lined up with the flagpole.

MATERIALS

- calculator, scientific
- meterstick
- pencil, sharp
- poster board, 16 × 16 cm
- protractor
- ruler, metric
- scissors
- string, 30 cm
- tape measure, metric
- tape, transparent

SAFETY

Viewing hole

10. Move to the other end of the meterstick, which represents the location of Earth. Does your partner appear to the left or right of the flagpole? Record your observations.

11. Hold the string so that it runs straight from the viewing hole to the 90° mark on the protractor. Using one eye, look through the viewing hole along the string, and point the device at your partner's nose.

12. Holding the device still, slowly move your head until you can see the flagpole through the viewing hole. Move the string so that it lines up between your eye and the flagpole. Make sure the string is taut, and hold it tightly against the protractor.

13. Read and record the angle made by the string and the string's original position at 90° (count the number of degrees between 90° and the string's new position).

14. Use the measuring tape to find and record the distance from the left end of the meterstick to your partner's nose.

15. Now, find a place outside that is at least 100 steps away from the flagpole. Set the meterstick on the ground as before, and repeat steps 9–14.

Analyze the Results

1. The angle you recorded in step 13 is called the *parallax angle.* The distance from one end of the meterstick to the other is called the *baseline.* With this angle and the length of your baseline, you can calculate the distance to your partner.

2. To calculate the distance (*d*) to your partner, use the following equation:

$$d = b/\tan A$$

In this equation, *A* is the parallax angle, and *b* is the length of the baseline (1 m). (Tan *A* means the tangent of angle *A,* which you will learn more about in math classes.)

3. To find *d,* enter 1 (the length of your baseline in meters) into the calculator, press the division key, enter the value of *A* (the parallax angle you recorded), then press the tan key. Finally, press the equals key.

4. Record this result. It is the distance in meters between the left end of the meterstick and your partner. You may want to use a table like the one below.

5. How close is this calculated distance to the distance you measured?

6. Repeat steps 1–3 under Analyze the Results using the angle you found when the flagpole was 100 steps away.

Draw Conclusions

7. At which position, 50 steps or 100 steps from the flagpole, did your calculated distance better match the actual distance as measured?

8. What do you think would happen if you were even farther from the flagpole?

9. When astronomers use parallax, their "flagpoles" are distant stars. Might this affect the accuracy of their parallax readings?

Distance by Parallax Versus Measuring Tape		
	At 50 steps	**At 100 steps**
Parallax angle		
Distance (calculated)		
Distance (measured)		

Model-Making Lab

Why Do They Wander?

MATERIALS

- compass, drawing
- paper, white
- pencils, colored
- ruler, metric

SAFETY

Before the discoveries of Nicholas Copernicus in the early 1500s, most people thought that the planets and the sun revolved around the Earth and that the Earth was the center of the solar system. But Copernicus observed that the sun is the center of the solar system and that all the planets, including Earth, revolve around the sun. He also explained a puzzling aspect of the movement of planets across the night sky.

If you watch a planet every night for several months, you'll notice that it appears to "wander" among the stars. While the stars remain in fixed positions relative to each other, the planets appear to move independently of the stars. Mars first travels to the left, then back to the right, and then again to the left.

In this lab, you will make your own model of part of the solar system to find out how Copernicus's model of the solar system explained this zigzag motion of the planets.

Ask a Question

1. Why do the planets appear to move back and forth in the Earth's night sky?

Form a Hypothesis

2. Write a possible answer to the question above.

Test the Hypothesis

3. Use the compass to draw a circle with a diameter of 9 cm on the paper. This circle will represent the orbit of the Earth around the sun. (Note: The orbits of the planets are actually slightly elliptical, but circles will work for this activity.)

4. Using the same center point, draw a circle with a diameter of 12 cm. This circle will represent the orbit of Mars.

5. Using a blue pencil, draw three parallel lines diagonally across one end of your paper, as shown at right. These lines will help you plot the path Mars appears to travel in Earth's night sky. Turn your paper so the diagonal lines are at the top of the page.

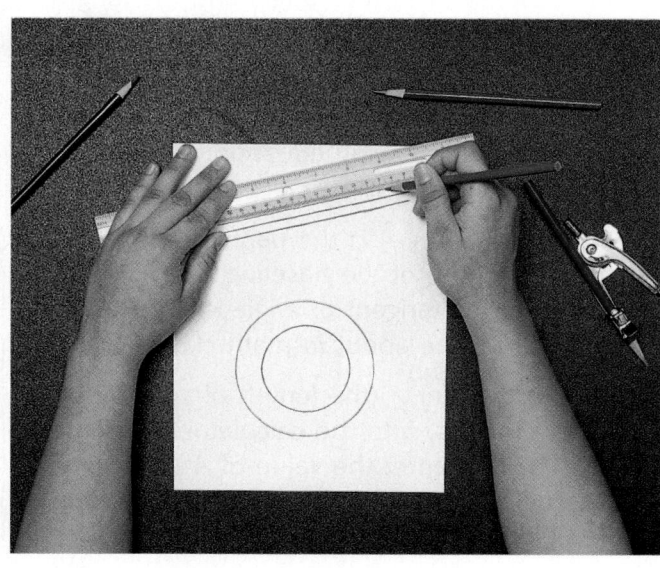

6. Place 11 dots 2.5 cm apart from each other on your Earth orbit. Number the dots 1 through 11. These dots will represent Earth's position from month to month.

7. Now, place 11 dots along the top of your Mars orbit 0.5 cm apart from each other. Number the dots as shown. These dots will represent the position of Mars at the same time intervals. Notice that Mars travels slower than Earth.

8. Draw a green line to connect the first dot on Earth's orbit to the first dot on Mars's orbit. Extend this line to the first diagonal line at the top of your paper. Place a green dot where the green line meets the first blue diagonal line. Label the green dot "1."

9. Now, connect the second dot on Earth's orbit to the second dot on Mars's orbit, and extend the line all the way to the first diagonal at the top of your paper. Place a green dot where this line meets the first blue diagonal line, and label this dot "2."

10. Continue drawing green lines from Earth's orbit through Mars's orbit and finally to the blue diagonal lines. Pay attention to the pattern of dots you are adding to the diagonal lines. When the direction of the dots changes, extend the green line to the next diagonal line, and add the dots to that line instead.

11. When you are finished adding green lines, draw a red line to connect all the green dots on the blue diagonal lines in the order you drew them.

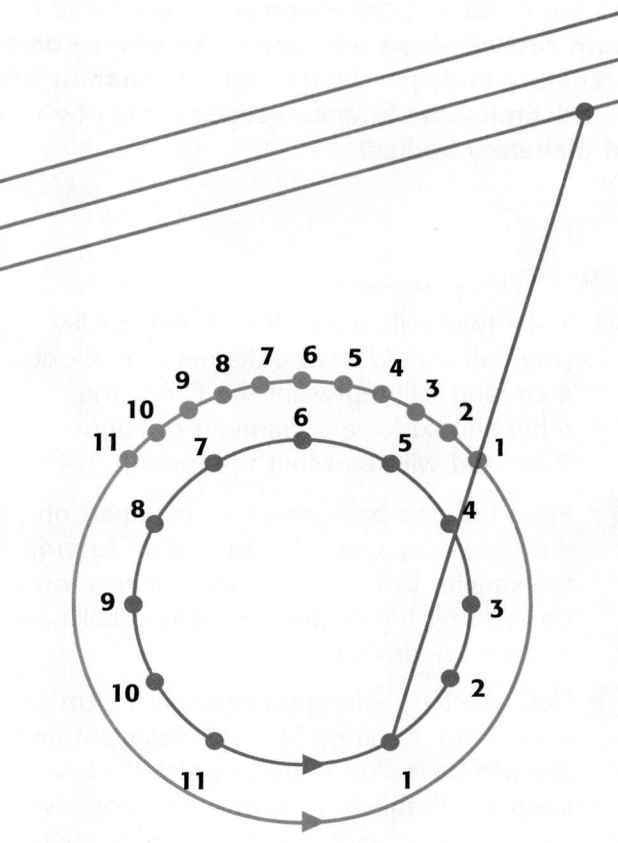

Analyze the Results

1. What do the green lines connecting points along Earth's orbit and Mars's orbit represent?

2. What does the red line connectir.g the dots along the diagonal lines look like? How can you explain this?

Draw Conclusions

3. What does this demonstration show about the motion of Mars?

4. Why do planets appear to move back and forth across the sky?

5. Were the Greeks justified in calling the planets *wanderers*? Explain.

Model-Making Lab

Eclipses

As the Earth and the moon revolve around the sun, they both cast shadows into space. An eclipse occurs when one planetary body passes through the shadow of another. You can demonstrate how an eclipse occurs by using clay models of planetary bodies.

MATERIALS

- clay, modeling
- flashlight, small
- paper, notebook (1 sheet)
- ruler, metric

Procedure

1. Make two balls out of the modeling clay. One ball should have a diameter of about 4 cm and will represent the Earth. The other should have a diameter of about 1 cm and will represent the moon.

2. Place the two balls about 15 cm apart on the sheet of paper. (You may want to prop the smaller ball up on folded paper or on clay so that the centers of the two balls are at the same level.)

3. Hold the flashlight approximately 15 cm away from the large ball. The flashlight and the two balls should be in a straight line. Keep the flashlight at about the same level as the clay. When the whole class is ready, your teacher will turn off the lights.

4. Turn on your flashlight. Shine the light on the larger ball, and sketch your model. Include the beam of light in your drawing.

5. Move the flashlight to the opposite side of the paper. The flashlight should now be approximately 15 cm away from the smaller clay ball. Repeat step 4.

Analyze the Results

1. What does the flashlight in your model represent?

2. As viewed from Earth, what event did your model represent in step 4?

3. As viewed from the moon, what event did your model represent in step 4?

4. As viewed from Earth, what event did your model represent in step 5?

5. As viewed from the moon, what event did your model represent in step 5?

6. According to your model, how often would solar and lunar eclipses occur? Is this accurate? Explain.

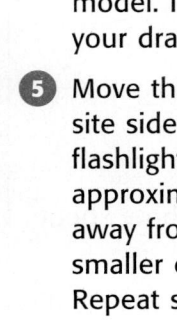

Skills Practice Lab

Phases of the Moon

It's easy to see when the moon is full. But you may have wondered exactly what happens when the moon appears as a crescent or when you cannot see the moon at all. Does the Earth cast its shadow on the moon? In this activity, you will discover how and why the moon appears as it does in each phase.

MATERIALS
- ball, plastic-foam
- globe, world
- light source

SAFETY

Procedure

1 Place your globe near the light source. Be sure that the north pole is tilted toward the light. Rotate the globe so that your state faces the light.

2 Using the ball as your model of the moon, move the moon between the Earth (the globe) and the sun (the light). The side of the moon that faces the Earth will be in darkness. Write your observations of this new-moon phase.

3 Continue to move the moon in its orbit around the Earth. When part of the moon is illuminated by the light, as viewed from Earth, the moon is in the crescent phase. Record your observations.

4 If you have time, you may draw your own moon-phase diagram.

Analyze the Results

1 About 2 weeks after the new moon appears, the entire moon is visible in the sky. Move the ball to show this event.

2 What other phases can you add to your diagram? For example, when does the quarter moon appear?

3 Explain why the moon sometimes appears as a crescent to viewers on Earth.

Model-Making Lab

Reach for the Stars

Have you ever thought about living and working in space? Well, in order for you to do so, you would have to learn to cope with the new environment and surroundings. At the same time that astronauts are adjusting to the topsy-turvy conditions of space travel, they are also dealing with special tools used to repair and build space stations. In this activity, you will get the chance to model one tool that might help astronauts work in space.

MATERIALS

- ball, plastic-foam
- box, cardboard
- hole punch
- paper brads (2)
- paper clips, jumbo (2)
- ruler, metric
- scissors
- wire, metal

SAFETY

Ask a Question

1. How can I build a piece of equipment that models how astronauts work in space?

Form a Hypothesis

2. Write a possible answer for the question above. Describe a possible tool that would help astronauts work in space.

Test the Hypothesis

3. Cut three strips from the cardboard box. Each strip should be about 5 cm wide. The strips should be at least 20 cm long but not longer than 40 cm.

4. Punch holes near the center of each end of the three cardboard strips. The holes should be about 3 cm from the end of each strip.

5. Lay the strips end to end along your table. Slide the second strip toward the first strip so that a hole in the first strip lines up with a hole in the second strip. Slip a paper brad through the holes, and bend its ends out to attach the cardboard strips.

6. Use another brad to attach the third cardboard strip to the free end of the second strip. Now, you have your mechanical arm. The paper brads create joints where the cardboard strips meet.

7. Straighten the wire, and slide it through the hole in one end of your mechanical arm. Bend about 3 cm of the wire in a 90° angle so that it will not slide back out of the hole.

8. Now, try to move the arm by holding the free ends of the cardboard and wire. The arm should bend and straighten at the joints. If it is difficult to move your mechanical arm, adjust the design. Consider loosening the brads, for example.

9. Your mechanical arm now needs a hand. Otherwise, it won't be able to pick things up! Straighten one paper clip, and slide it through the hole where you attached the wire in step 7. Bend one end of the paper clip to form a loop around the cardboard and the other end to form a hook. You will use this hook to pick things up.

10. Bend a second paper clip into a U shape. Stick the straight end of this paper clip into the foam ball. Leave the ball on your desk.

11. Move your mechanical arm so that you can lift the foam ball. The paper-clip hook on the mechanical arm will have to catch the paper clip on the ball.

Analyze the Results

1. Did you have any trouble moving the mechanical arm in step 8? What adjustments did you make?

2. Did you have trouble picking up the foam ball? What might have made picking up the ball easier?

Draw Conclusions

3. What improvements could you make to your mechanical arm that might make it easier to use?

4. How would a tool like this one help astronauts work in space?

Applying Your Data

Adjust the design for your mechanical arm. Can you find a way to lift objects other than the foam ball? For example, can you lift heavier objects or objects that do not have a loop attached? How?

Research the tools that astronauts use on space stations and on the space shuttle. How do their tools help them work in the special conditions of space?

Contents

Inch

Yard

Fathom

Foot

Appendix

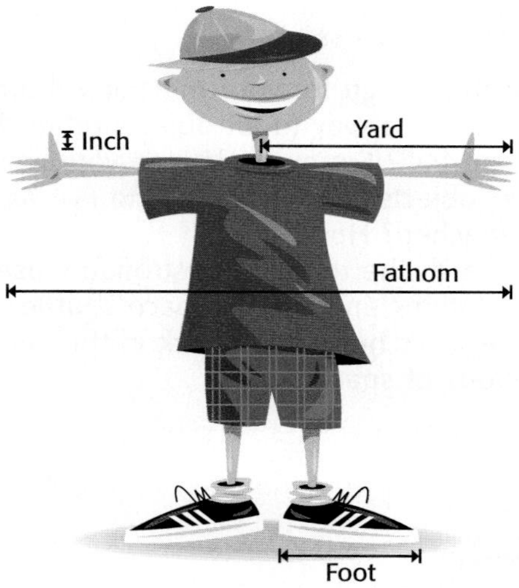

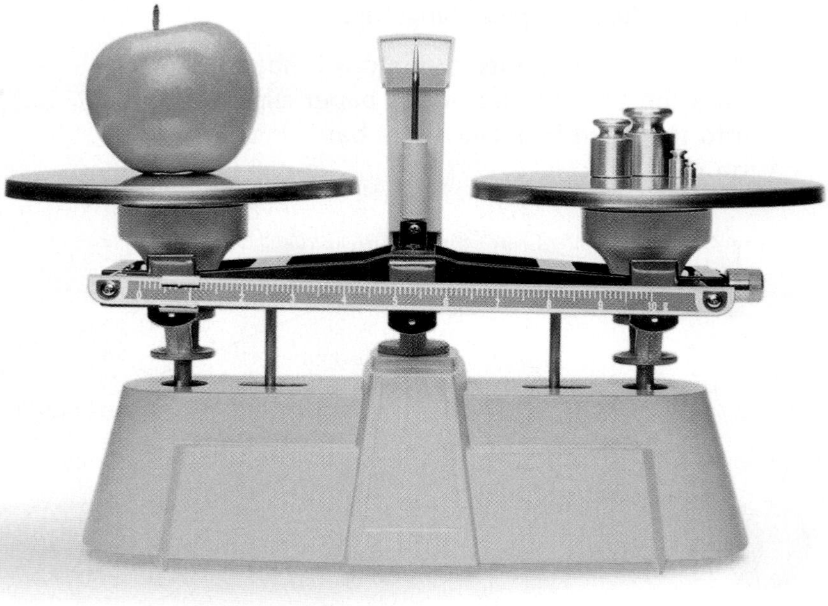

✔ Reading Check Answers

Chapter 1   The World of Earth Science

Section 1
Page 7: Four areas of oceanography are physical oceanography, biological oceanography, geological oceanography, and chemical oceanography.

Page 9: Astronomers study stars, asteroids, planets, and everything else in space.

Page 11: Cartographers make maps.

Section 2
Page 12: Scientists begin to learn about things by asking questions.

Page 15: Scientists create graphs and tables to organize and summarize their data.

Page 16: It is important for the scientific community to review new evidence so that scientists can evaluate and question the evidence for accuracy.

Section 3
Page 19: The big bang theory is an explanation of the creation of the universe.

Page 21: A climate model is complicated because there are so many variables that affect climate.

Section 4
Page 22: The International System of Units was developed to create a standard measurement system.

Page 25: Before you start a science investigation, obtain your teacher's permission and read the lab procedures carefully.

Chapter 2   Maps as Models of the Earth

Section 1
Page 37: A reference point is a fixed place on the Earth's surface from which direction and location can be described.

Page 38: True north is the direction to the geographic North Pole.

Page 40: lines of longitude

Section 2
Page 42: Distortions are inaccuracies produced when information is transferred from a curved surface to a flat surface.

Page 45: Azimuthal and conic projections are similar because they are both ways to represent the curved surface of the Earth on a flat map. Azimuthal projections show the surface of a globe transferred to a flat plane, whereas conic projections show the surface of a globe transferred to a cone.

Page 46: Every map should have a title, a compass rose, a scale, the date, and a legend.

Page 48: A GIS stores information in layers.

Section 3
Page 51: An index contour is a darker contour line that is usually every fifth line. Index contours make it easier to read a map.

Chapter 3   Minerals of the Earth's Crust

Section 1
Page 67: An element is a pure substance that cannot be broken down into simpler substances by ordinary chemical means. A compound is a substance made of two or more elements that have been chemically bonded.

Page 68: Answers may vary. Silicate minerals contain a combination of silicon and oxygen; nonsilicate minerals do not contain a combination of silicon and oxygen.

Section 2
Page 71: A mineral's streak is not affected by air or water, but a mineral's color may be affected by air or water.

Page 72: Scratch the mineral with a series of 10 reference minerals. If the reference mineral scratches the unidentified mineral, the reference mineral is harder than the unidentified mineral.

Section 3
Page 77: Surface mining is used to remove mineral deposits that are at or near the Earth's surface. Subsurface mining is used to remove mineral deposits that are too deep to be removed by surface mining.

Page 79: Sample answer: Gemstones are nonmetallic minerals that are valued for their beauty and rarity rather than for their usefulness.

Chapter 4   Rocks: Mineral Mixtures

Section 1
Page 90: Types of rocks that have been used by humans to construct buildings include granite, limestone, marble, sandstone, and slate.

Page 94: Rock within the Earth is affected by temperature and pressure.

Page 95: The minerals that a rock contains determine a rock's composition.

Page 96: Fine-grained rocks are made of small grains, such as silt or clay particles. Medium-grained rocks are made of medium-sized grains, such as sand. Coarse-grained rocks are made of large grains, such as pebbles.

Section 2
Page 99: Felsic rocks are light-colored igneous rocks rich in aluminum, potassium, silicon, and sodium. Mafic rocks are dark-colored igneous rocks rich in calcium, iron, and magnesium.

Page 101: New sea floor forms when lava that flows from fissures on the ocean floor cools and hardens.

Section 3
Page 103: Halite forms when sodium and chlorine ions in shallow bodies of water become so concentrated that halite crystallizes from solution.

Page 105: Ripple marks are the marks left by wind and water waves on lakes, seas, rivers, and sand dunes.

Section 4

Page 107: Regional metamorphism occurs when pressure builds up in rock that is buried deep below other rock formations or when large pieces of the Earth's crust collide. The increased pressure can cause thousands of square miles of rock to become deformed and chemically changed.

Page 108: An index mineral is a metamorphic mineral that forms only at certain temperatures and pressures and therefore can be used by scientists to estimate the temperature, pressure, and depth at which a rock undergoes metamorphosis.

Page 111: Deformation causes metamorphic structures, such as folds.

Chapter 5   Energy Resources

Section 1

Page 123: A renewable resource is a natural resource that can be replaced at the same rate at which the resource is used.

Page 125: Answers may vary. Sample answer: newspapers, plastic containers, and cardboard boxes.

Section 2

Page 127: Natural gas is most often used for heating and for generating electrical energy.

Page 128: Coal was most commonly used to power trains.

Page 131: Natural gas and petroleum are removed from the Earth by drilling wells into rock that contains petroleum and natural gas.

Page 132: The sulfur dioxide released from the burning coal combines with moisture in the air to produce acid rain.

Section 3

Page 135: Fusion produces few dangerous wastes.

Page 136: The energy of fossil fuels comes from the sun.

Page 138: Hydroelectric energy is renewable because water is constantly recycled.

Page 140: Geothermal power plants obtain energy from the Earth by pumping steam and hot water from wells drilled into the rock.

Chapter 6   The Rock and Fossil Record

Section 1

Page 153: Catastrophists believed that all geologic change occurs rapidly.

Page 154: A global catastrophe can cause the extinction of species.

Section 2

Page 157: Geologists use the geologic column to interpret rock sequences and to identify layers in puzzling rock sequences.

Page 159: An unconformity is a surface that represents a missing part of the geologic column.

Page 160: A disconformity is found where part of a sequence of parallel rock layers is missing. A nonconformity is found where horizontal sedimentary rock layers lie on top of an eroded surface of igneous or metamorphic rock. Angular unconformities are found between horizontal sedimentary rock layers and rock layers that have been tilted or folded.

Section 3

Page 163: A half-life is the time it takes one-half of a radioactive sample to decay.

Page 164: strontium-87

Section 4

Page 166: An organism is caught in soft, sticky tree sap, which hardens and preserves the organism.

Page 168: A mold is a cavity in rock where a plant or an animal was buried. A cast is an object created when sediment fills a mold and becomes rock.

Page 170: To fill in missing information about changes in organisms in the fossil record, paleontologists look for similarities between fossilized organisms or between fossilized organisms and their closest living relatives.

Page 171: *Phacops* can be used to establish the age of rock layers because *Phacops* lived during a relatively short, well-defined time span and is found in rock layers throughout the world.

Section 5

Page 173: approximately 2 billion years

Page 174: The geological time scale is a scale that divides Earth's 4.6 billion—year history into distinct intervals of time.

Page 176: The Mesozoic era is known as the *Age of Reptiles* because reptiles, including the dinosaurs, were the dominant organisms on land.

Chapter 7   Plate Tectonics

Section 1

Page 191: The crust is the thin, outermost layer of the Earth. It is 5 km to 100 km thick and is mainly made up of the elements oxygen, silicon, and aluminum. The mantle is the layer between the crust and core. It is 2,900 km thick, is denser than the crust, and contains most of the Earth's mass. The core is the Earth's innermost layer. The core has a radius of 3,430 km and is made mostly of iron.

Page 192: The five physical layers of the Earth are the lithosphere, asthenosphere, mesosphere, outer core, and inner core.

Page 195: Although continental lithosphere is less dense than oceanic lithosphere is, continental lithosphere has a greater mass because of its greater thickness and will displace more asthenosphere than oceanic lithosphere.

Page 196: Answers may vary. A seismic wave traveling through a solid will go faster than a seismic wave traveling through a liquid.

Section 2

Page 198: Similar fossils were found on landmasses that are very far apart. The best explanation for this phenomenon is that the landmasses were once joined.

Page 201: The molten rock at mid-ocean ridges contains tiny grains of magnetic minerals. The minerals align with the Earth's magnetic field before the rock cools and hardens. When the Earth's magnetic field reverses, the orientation of the mineral grains in the rocks will also change.

Section 3

Page 203: A transform boundary forms when two tectonic plates slide past each other horizontally.

Page 204: The circulation of thermal energy causes changes in density in the asthenosphere. As rock is heated, it expands, becomes less dense, and rises. As rock cools, it contracts, becomes denser, and sinks.

Section 4

Page 206: Compression can cause rocks to be pushed into mountain ranges as tectonic plates collide at convergent boundaries. Tension can pull rocks apart as tectonic plates separate at divergent boundaries.

Page 208: In a normal fault, the hanging wall moves down. In a reverse fault, the hanging wall moves up.

Page 210: Folded mountains form when rock layers are squeezed together and pushed upward.

Chapter 8   Earthquakes

Section 1

Page 225: During elastic rebound, rock releases energy. Some of this energy travels as seismic waves that cause earthquakes.

Page 227: Earthquake zones are usually located along tectonic plate boundaries.

Page 229: Surface waves travel more slowly than body waves but are more destructive.

Section 2

Page 231: Seismologists determine an earthquake's start time by comparing seismograms and noting differences in arrival times of P and S waves.

Page 232: Each time the magnitude increases by 1 unit, the amount of ground motion increases by 10 times.

Section 3

Page 235: With a decrease of one unit in earthquake magnitude, the number of earthquakes occurring annually increases by about 10 times.

Page 236: Retrofitting is the process of making older structures more earthquake resistant.

Page 238: You should crouch or lie face down under a table or desk.

Chapter 9   Volcanoes

Section 1

Page 251: Nonexplosive eruptions are common, and they feature relatively calm flows of lava. Explosive eruptions are less common and produce large, explosive clouds of ash and gases.

Page 252: Because silica-rich magma has a high viscosity, it tends to trap gases and plug volcanic vents. This causes pressure to build up and can result in an explosive eruption.

Page 254: Volcanic bombs are large blobs of magma that harden in the air. Lapilli are small pieces of magma that harden in the air. Volcanic blocks are pieces of solid rock erupted from a volcano. Ash forms when gases in stiff magma expand rapidly and the walls of the gas bubbles shatter into tiny glasslike slivers.

Section 2

Page 256: Eruptions release large quantities of ash and gases, which can block sunlight and cause global temperatures to drop.

Page 258: Calderas form when a magma chamber partially empties and the roof overlying the chamber collapses.

Section 3

Page 261: Volcanic activity is common at tectonic plate boundaries because magma tends to form at plate boundaries.

Page 263: When a tectonic plate subducts, it becomes hotter and releases water. The water lowers the melting point of the rock above the plate, causing magma to form.

Page 264: According to one theory, a rising body of magma, called a mantle plume, causes a chain of volcanoes to form on a moving tectonic plate. According to another theory, a chain of volcanoes forms along cracks in the Earth's crust.

Chapter 10   Weathering and Soil Formation

Section 1

Page 279: Wind, water, and gravity can cause abrasion.

Page 280: Answers may vary. Sample answer: ants, worms, mice, coyotes, and rabbits.

Page 283: Oxidation occurs when oxygen combines with an element to form an oxide.

Section 2

Page 285: As the surface area increases, the rate of weathering also increases.

Page 286: Warm, humid climates have higher rates of weathering because oxidation happens faster when temperatures are higher and when water is present.

Page 287: Mountains weather faster because they are exposed to more wind, rain, and ice, which are agents of weathering.

Section 3

Page 288: Soil is formed from parent rock, organic material, water, and air.

Page 291: Heavy rains leach precious nutrients into deeper layers of soil, resulting in a very thin layer of topsoil.

Page 292: Temperate climates have the most productive soil.

Section 4

Page 294: Soil provides nutrients to plants, houses for animals, and stores water.

Page 297: They restore important nutrients to the soil and provide cover to prevent erosion.

Chapter 11 The Flow of Fresh Water

Section 1
Page 308: The Colorado River eroded the rock over millions of years.

Page 310: A divide is the boundary that separates drainage areas, whereas a watershed is the area of land that is drained by a water system.

Page 311: An increase in a stream's gradient and discharge can cause the stream to flow faster.

Page 313: A mature river erodes its channel wider rather than deeper. It is not steep and has fewer falls and rapids. It also has good drainage and more discharge than a youthful river does.

Page 314: Rejuvenated rivers form when the land is raised by tectonic forces.

Section 2
Page 317: Deltas are made of the deposited load of the river, which is mostly mud.

Page 319: The flow of water can be controlled by dams and levees.

Section 3
Page 320: The zone of aeration is located underground. It is the area above the water table.

Page 322: The size of the recharge zone depends on how permeable rock is at the surface.

Page 323: A well must be deeper than the water table for it to be able to reach water.

Page 324: Deposition is the process that causes the formation of stalactites and stalagmites.

Section 4
Page 326: Nonpoint-source pollution is the hardest to control.

Page 329: Less than 8% of water in our homes is used for drinking.

Page 330: Drip irrigation systems deliver small amounts of water directly to the roots of the plant so that the plant absorbs the water before it can evaporate or runoff.

Page 331: Answers may vary. Sample answer: taking shorter showers, avoiding running water while brushing your teeth, and using the dishwasher only when it is full.

Chapter 12 Agents of Erosion and Deposition

Section 1
Page 343: The amount of energy released from breaking waves causes rock to break down, eventually forming sand.

Page 345: Large waves are more capable of moving large rocks on a shoreline because they have more energy than normal waves do.

Page 346: Beach material is material deposited by waves.

Section 2
Page 349: Deflation hollows form in areas where there is little vegetation.

Page 351: Dunes move in the direction of strong winds.

Section 3
Page 352: Alpine glaciers form in mountainous areas.

Page 357: A till deposit is made up of unsorted material, while stratified drift is made up of sorted material.

Section 4
Page 359: A slump is the result of a landslide in which a block of material moves downslope over a curved surface.

Page 360: A lahar is caused by the eruption of an ice-covered volcano, which melts ice and causes a hot mudflow.

Chapter 13 Exploring the Oceans

Section 1
Page 375: The first oceans began to form sometime before 4 billion years ago as the Earth cooled enough for water vapor to condense and fall as rain.

Page 376: Coastal water in places with hotter, drier climates has a higher salinity because less fresh water runs into the ocean in drier areas and because heat increases the evaporation rate.

Page 378: Parts of the ocean along the equator are warmer because they receive more sunlight per year.

Page 380: If the ocean did not release thermal energy so slowly, the air temperature on land would vary greatly from above 100°C during the day to below 100°C at night.

Section 2
Page 383: Satellite photos from *Seasat* send images of the ocean back to Earth. These images allow scientists to measure the direction and speed of ocean currents. Satellite photos and information from *Geosat* have been used to measure slight changes in the height of the ocean's surface.

Page 384: 64,000 km; on the ocean floor

Page 385: continental shelf, continental slope, and continental rise

Page 386: It is unique because some organisms living around the vent do not rely on photosynthesis for energy.

Section 3
Page 389: The tough shells of clams and oysters protect the organisms against strong waves and harsh sunlight.

Page 391: crabs, sponges, worms, and sea cucumbers

Page 392: The neritic zone contains the largest concentration of marine life in the ocean because it receives more sunlight than the other zones in the ocean.

Section 4
Page 395: Fish farms can help reduce overfishing because the fish are raised instead of fished directly out of the ocean.

Page 396: Nonrenewable resources are resources that cannot be replenished. Oil and natural gas are nonrenewable resources.

Page 397: Desalination plants are most likely to be built in drier parts of the world, and where governments can afford to buy expensive equipment. Most desalination plants are in the Middle East, where the fuel needed to run the plants is relatively inexpensive.

Page 399: Wave energy would be a good alternative energy resource because it is a clean and renewable resource.

Section 5
Page 401: One effect of trash dumping is that plastic materials may harm and kill marine animals because these animals may mistake the trash for food.

Page 403: An oil tanker that has two hulls can prevent an oil spill, because if the outer hull is damaged, the inner hull will prevent oil from spilling into the ocean.

Page 405: The U.S. Marine Protection, Research, and Sanctuaries Act prohibits the dumping of any material that would affect human health or welfare, the marine environment or ecosystems, or businesses that depend on the ocean.

Chapter 14   The Movement of Ocean Water
Section 1
Page 416: Heyerdahl theorized that the inhabitants of Polynesia originally sailed from Peru on rafts powered only by the wind and ocean currents. Heyerdahl proved his theory by sailing from Peru to Polynesia on a raft powered only by wind and ocean currents.

Page 418: The Earth's rotation causes surface currents to move in curved paths rather than in straight lines.

Page 419: The three factors that form a pattern of surface currents on Earth are global winds, the Coriolis effect, and continental deflections.

Page 420: Density causes variations in the movement of deep currents.

Section 2
Page 423: Cold-water currents keep coastal climates cooler than inland climates all year long.

Page 425: Answers may vary. Sample answer: It is important to study El Niño because El Niño can greatly affect organisms and land. One way that scientists study El Niño is through a network of buoys located along the equator. These buoys record information that helps scientists predict when an El Niño is likely to occur.

Section 3
Page 426: The lowest point of a wave is called a *trough*.

Page 428: Deep-water waves become shallow-water waves as they move toward the shore and reach water that is shallower than one-half their wavelength.

Page 431: A storm surge is a local rise in sea level near the shore and is caused by strong winds from a storm, such as a hurricane. Storm surges are difficult to study because they disappear as quickly as they form.

Section 4
Page 432: The gravity of the moon pulls on every particle of the Earth.

Page 434: A tidal range is the difference between levels of ocean water at high tide and low tide.

Chapter 15   The Atmosphere
Section 1
Page 448: Water can be liquid (rain), solid (snow or ice), or gas (water vapor).

Page 450: The troposphere is the layer of turning or change. The stratosphere is the layer in which gases are layered and do not mix vertically. The mesosphere is the middle layer. The thermosphere is the layer in which temperatures are highest.

Page 452: The thermosphere does not feel hot because air molecules are spaced far apart and cannot collide to transfer much thermal energy.

Section 2
Page 455: Cold air is more dense than warm air, so cold air sinks and warm air rises. This produces convection currents.

Page 457: A greenhouse gas is a gas that absorbs thermal energy in the atmosphere.

Section 3
Page 459: Sinking air causes areas of high pressure because sinking air presses down on the air beneath it.

Page 460: the westerlies

Page 463: At night, the air along the mountain slopes cools. This cool air moves down the slopes into the valley and produces a mountain breeze.

Section 4
Page 464: Sample answer: smoke, dust and sea salt

Page 467: Answers may vary. Acid precipitation may decrease the soil nutrients that are available to plants.

Page 468: Powdered lime is used to counteract the effects of acidic snowmelt from snow that accumulated during the winter.

Page 470: Allowance trading establishes allowances for a certain type of pollutant. Companies are permitted to release their allowance of the pollutant, but if they exceed the allowance, they must buy additional allowances or pay a fine.

Chapter 16   Understanding Weather
Section 1
Page 482: The water cycle is the continuous movement of water from Earth's oceans and rivers into the atmosphere, into the ground, and back into the oceans and rivers.

Page 484: A psychrometer is used to measure relative humidity.

Page 485: The bulb of a wet-bulb thermometer is covered with moistened material. The bulb cools as water evaporates from the material. If the air is dry, more water will evaporate from the material, and the temperature recorded by the thermometer will be low. If the air is humid, less water will evaporate from the material, and the temperature recorded by the thermometer will be higher.

Page 487: Altostratus clouds form at middle altitudes.

Section 2
Page 491: A maritime tropical air mass causes hot and humid summer weather in the midwestern United States.

Page 493: An occluded front produces cool temperatures and large amounts of rain.

Page 495: An anticyclone can produce dry, clear weather.

Section 3

Page 497: A severe thunderstorm is a thunderstorm that produces high winds, hail, flash floods, or tornadoes.

Page 499: Hurricanes are also called *typhoons* or *cyclones.*

Page 500: Hurricanes get their energy from the condensation of water vapor.

Section 4

Page 504: Meteorologists use weather balloons to collect atmospheric data above Earth's surface.

Chapter 17   Climate

Section 1

Page 518: Climate is the average weather condition in an area over a long period of time. Weather is the condition of the atmosphere at a particular time.

Page 520: Locations near the equator have less seasonal variation because the tilt of the Earth does not change the amount of energy these locations receive from the sun.

Page 522: The atmosphere becomes less dense and loses its ability to absorb and hold thermal energy, at higher elevations.

Page 523: The Gulf Stream current carries warm water past Iceland, which heats the air and causes milder temperatures.

Page 524: Each biome has a different climate and different plant and animals communities.

Section 2

Page 526: You would find the tropical zone from 23.5° north latitude to 23.5° south latitude.

Page 529: Answers may vary. Sample answer: rats, lizards, snakes, and scorpions.

Section 3

Page 530: The temperate zone is located between the Tropics and the polar zone.

Page 532: Temperate deserts are cold at night because low humidity and cloudless skies allow energy to escape.

Page 535: Cities have higher temperatures than the surrounding rural areas because buildings and pavement absorb solar radiation instead of reflecting it.

Section 4

Page 537: Changes in the Earth's orbit and the tilt of the Earth's axis are the two things that Milankovitch says cause ice ages.

Page 538: Dust, ash, and smoke from volcanic eruptions block the sun's rays, which causes the Earth to cool.

Page 541: The deserts would receive less rainfall, making it harder for plants and animals in the desert to survive.

Chapter 18   Studying Space

Section 1

Page 555: Copernicus believed in a sun-centered universe.

Page 556: Newton's law of gravity helped explain why the planets orbit the sun and moons orbit planets.

Section 2

Page 558: The objective lens collects light and forms an image at the back of the telescope. The eyepiece magnifies the image produced by the objective lens.

Page 560: The motion of air, air pollution, water vapor, and light pollution distort the images produced by optical telescopes.

Page 563: because the atmosphere blocks most X-ray radiation from space

Section 3

Page 565: Different constellations are visible in the Northern and Southern Hemispheres because different portions of the sky are visible from the Northern and Southern hemispheres.

Page 567: The apparent movement of the sun and stars is caused by the Earth's rotation on its axis.

Page 568: 9.46 trillion kilometers

Page 570: One might conclude that all of the galaxies are traveling toward the Earth and that the universe is contracting.

Chapter 19   Stars, Galaxies, and the Universe

Section 1

Page 582: Rigel is hotter than Betelgeuse because blue stars are hotter than red stars.

Page 584: A star's absorption spectrum indicates some of the elements that are in the star's atmosphere.

Page 586: Apparent magnitude is the brightness of a light or star.

Page 587: A light-year is the distance that light travels in 1 year.

Page 588: The actual motion of stars is hard to see because the stars are so distant.

Section 2

Page 591: A red giant star is a star that expands and cools once it uses all of its hydrogen. As the center of a star continues to shrink a red giant star can become a red supergiant star.

Page 595: A black hole is an object that is so massive that even light cannot escape its gravity. A black hole can be detected when it gives off X rays.

Section 3

Page 596: Spiral galaxies have a bulge at the center and spiral arms. The arms of spiral galaxies are made up of gas, dust, and new stars.

Page 598: A globular cluster is a tight group of up to 1 million stars that looks like a ball. An open cluster is a group of closely grouped stars that are usually located along the spiral disk of a galaxy.

Page 599: Quasars are starlike sources of light that are extremely far away. Some scientists think that quasars may be the core of young galaxies that are in the process of forming.

Section 4

Page 601: Cosmic background radiation is radiation that is left over from the big bang. After the big bang, cosmic background radiation was distributed everywhere and filled all of space.

Page 602: One way to calculate the age of the universe is to measure the distance from Earth to various galaxies.

Page 603: If gravity stops the expansion of the universe, the universe might collapse. If the expansion of the universe continues forever, stars will age and die. The universe will eventually become cold and dark.

Chapter 20 Formation of the Solar System

Section 1
Page 615: The solar nebula is the cloud of gas and dust that formed our solar system.

Page 617: Jupiter, Saturn, Uranus, and Neptune

Section 2
Page 619: Energy from gravity is not enough to power the sun, because if all of the sun's gravitational energy were released, the sun would last for only 45 million years.

Page 621: The nuclei of hydrogen atoms repel each other because they are positively charged and like charges repel each other.

Page 622: Sunspots are cooler, dark spots on the sun. They occur because when activity slows down in the convective zone, areas of the photosphere become cooler.

Section 3
Page 624: During Earth's early formation, planetesimals collided with the Earth. The energy of their motion heated the planet.

Page 626: Scientists think that the Earth's first atmosphere was a mixture of CO_2 and water vapor.

Page 628: When photosynthetic organisms appeared on Earth, they released oxygen into the Earth's atmosphere. Over several million years, more and more oxygen was added to the atmosphere, which helped form Earth's current atmosphere.

Section 4
Page 631: Kepler's third law of motion states that planets that are farther away from the sun take longer to orbit the sun.

Page 632: Newton's law of universal gravitation states that the force of gravity depends on the product of the masses of the objects divided by the square of the distance between the objects.

Chapter 21 A Family of Planets

Section 1
Page 645: Light travels about 300,000 km/s.

Page 647: Jupiter, Saturn, Uranus, Neptune, and Pluto are in the outer solar system.

Section 2
Page 649: Radar technology was used to map the surface of Venus.

Page 650: Earth Science Enterprise is a NASA program that uses satellites to study Earth's atmosphere, land, oceans, life, and ice. This program will help scientists understand how humans affect the environment and how different parts of the global system interact.

Page 652: Mars' crust is chemically different from Earth's crust, so the Martian crust does not move. As a result, volcanoes build up in the same spots on Mars.

Section 3
Page 655: Saturn's rings are made of icy particles ranging in size from a few cm to several m wide.

Page 657: Neptune's interior releases energy to its outer layers, which creates belts of clouds in Neptune's atmosphere.

Section 4
Page 661: The moon formed from a piece of Earth's mantle, which broke off during a collision between Earth and a large object.

Page 663: During a solar eclipse, the moon blocks out the sun and casts a shadow on Earth.

Page 664: We don't see solar and lunar eclipses every month because the moon's orbit around Earth is tilted.

Page 665: Because Titan's atmosphere is similar to the atmosphere on Earth before life evolved, scientists can study Titan's atmosphere to learn how life began.

Page 666: Pluto is eclipsed by Charon every 120 years.

Section 5
Page 669: Comets come from the Oort cloud and the Kuiper belt.

Page 671: The major types of meteorites are stony, metallic, and stony-iron meteorites.

Page 672: Large objects strike Earth every few thousand years.

Chapter 22 Exploring Space

Section 1
Page 684: Tsiolkovsky helped develop rocket theory. Goddard developed the first rockets.

Page 686: Rockets carry oxygen so that their fuel can be burned.

Section 2
Page 689: Answers may vary. LEO is much closer to the Earth than GEO.

Page 691: Information from one location is transmitted to a communications satellite. The satellite then sends the information to another location on Earth.

Page 693: Satellites in the EOS program are designed to work together so that many different types of data can be integrated.

Section 3
Page 695: The Magellan mission showed that, in many ways, the surface of Venus is similar to the surface of Earth.

Page 696: The Mars Pathfinder mission found evidence suggesting that water once flowed across the surface of Mars.

Page 698: The mission of the Stardust probe is to gather samples from a comet's tail and return them to Earth.

Section 4
Page 701: the orbiter, the liquid-fuel tank, and the solid-fuel booster rockets

Page 703: The Russians are supplying a service module, docking modules, life-support and research modules, and transportation to and from the station. The Americans are providing lab modules, the supporting frame, solar panels, living quarters, and a biomedical laboratory.

Page 705: Space-age spinoffs are technologies that were developed for the space program but are now used in everyday life.

Study Skills

FoldNote Instructions

Have you ever tried to study for a test or quiz but didn't know where to start? Or have you read a chapter and found that you can remember only a few ideas? Well, FoldNotes are a fun and exciting way to help you learn and remember the ideas you encounter as you learn science!

FoldNotes are tools that you can use to organize concepts. By focusing on a few main concepts, FoldNotes help you learn and remember how the concepts fit together. They can help you see the "big picture." Below you will find instructions for building 10 different FoldNotes.

Pyramid

1. Place a sheet of paper in front of you. Fold the lower left-hand corner of the paper diagonally to the opposite edge of the paper.

2. Cut off the tab of paper created by the fold (at the top).

3. Open the paper so that it is a square. Fold the lower right-hand corner of the paper diagonally to the opposite corner to form a triangle.

4. Open the paper. The creases of the two folds will have created an X.

5. Using scissors, cut along one of the creases. Start from any corner, and stop at the center point to create two flaps. Use tape or glue to attach one of the flaps on top of the other flap.

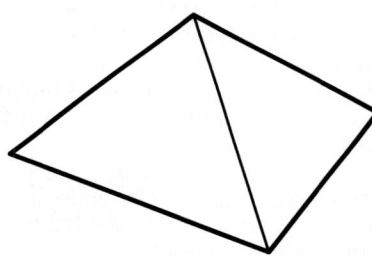

Double Door

1. Fold a sheet of paper in half from the top to the bottom. Then, unfold the paper.

2. Fold the top and bottom edges of the paper to the crease.

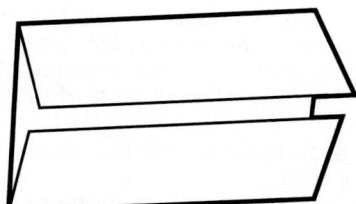

Booklet

1. Fold a sheet of paper in half from left to right. Then, unfold the paper.

2. Fold the sheet of paper in half again from the top to the bottom. Then, unfold the paper.

3. Refold the sheet of paper in half from left to right.

4. Fold the top and bottom edges to the center crease.

5. Completely unfold the paper.

6. Refold the paper from top to bottom.

7. Using scissors, cut a slit along the center crease of the sheet from the folded edge to the creases made in step 4. Do not cut the entire sheet in half.

8. Fold the sheet of paper in half from left to right. While holding the bottom and top edges of the paper, push the bottom and top edges together so that the center collapses at the center slit. Fold the four flaps to form a four-page book.

Layered Book

1. Lay one sheet of paper on top of another sheet. Slide the top sheet up so that 2 cm of the bottom sheet is showing.

2. Hold the two sheets together, fold down the top of the two sheets so that you see four 2 cm tabs along the bottom.

3. Using a stapler, staple the top of the FoldNote.

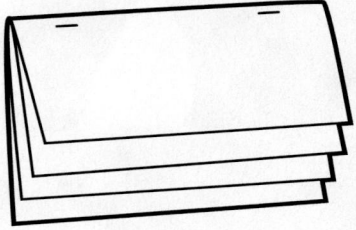

Key-Term Fold

1. Fold a sheet of lined notebook paper in half from left to right.

2. Using scissors, cut along every third line from the right edge of the paper to the center fold to make tabs.

Four-Corner Fold

1. Fold a sheet of paper in half from left to right. Then, unfold the paper.

2. Fold each side of the paper to the crease in the center of the paper.

3. Fold the paper in half from the top to the bottom. Then, unfold the paper.

4. Using scissors, cut the top flap creases made in step 3 to form four flaps.

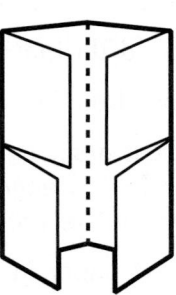

Three-Panel Flip Chart

1. Fold a piece of paper in half from the top to the bottom.

2. Fold the paper in thirds from side to side. Then, unfold the paper so that you can see the three sections.

3. From the top of the paper, cut along each of the vertical fold lines to the fold in the middle of the paper. You will now have three flaps.

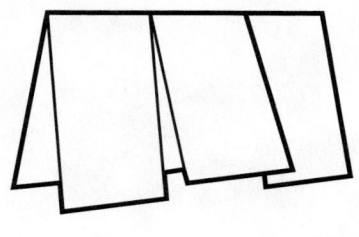

Appendix

Table Fold

1. Fold a piece of paper in half from the top to the bottom. Then, fold the paper in half again.

2. Fold the paper in thirds from side to side.

3. Unfold the paper completely. Carefully trace the fold lines by using a pen or pencil.

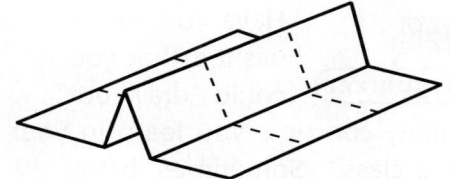

Two-Panel Flip Chart

1. Fold a piece of paper in half from the top to the bottom.

2. Fold the paper in half from side to side. Then, unfold the paper so that you can see the two sections.

3. From the top of the paper, cut along the vertical fold line to the fold in the middle of the paper. You will now have two flaps.

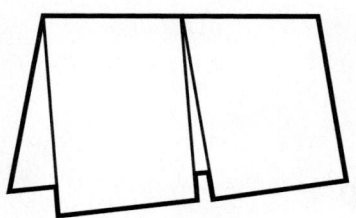

Tri-Fold

1. Fold a piece a paper in thirds from the top to the bottom.

2. Unfold the paper so that you can see the three sections. Then, turn the paper sideways so that the three sections form vertical columns.

3. Trace the fold lines by using a pen or pencil. Label the columns "Know," "Want," and "Learn."

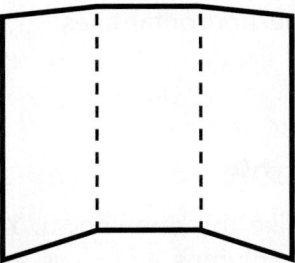

Graphic Organizer Instructions

 Have you ever wished that you could "draw out" the many concepts you learn in your science class? Sometimes, being able to *see* how concepts are related really helps you remember what you've learned. Graphic Organizers do just that! They give you a way to draw or map out concepts.

All you need to make a Graphic Organizer is a piece of paper and a pencil. Below you will find instructions for four different Graphic Organizers designed to help you organize the concepts you'll learn in this book.

Spider Map

1. Draw a diagram like the one shown. In the circle, write the main topic.

2. From the circle, draw legs to represent different categories of the main topic. You can have as many categories as you want.

3. From the category legs, draw horizontal lines. As you read the chapter, write details about each category on the horizontal lines.

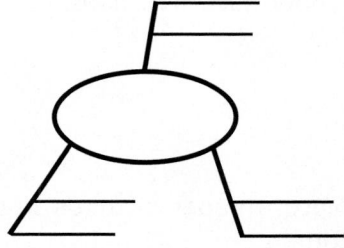

Comparison Table

1. Draw a chart like the one shown. Your chart can have as many columns and rows as you want.

2. In the top row, write the topics that you want to compare.

3. In the left column, write characteristics of the topics that you want to compare. As you read the chapter, fill in the characteristics for each topic in the appropriate boxes.

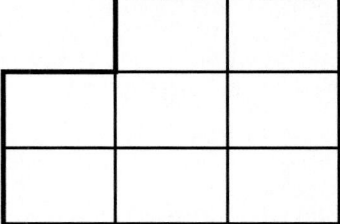

Chain-of-Events-Chart

1. Draw a box. In the box, write the first step of a process or the first event of a timeline.

2. Under the box, draw another box, and use an arrow to connect the two boxes. In the second box, write the next step of the process or the next event in the timeline.

3. Continue adding boxes until the process or timeline is finished.

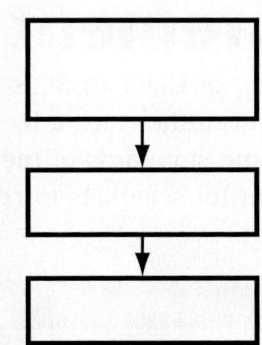

Concept Map

1. Draw a circle in the center of a piece of paper. Write the main idea of the chapter in the center of the circle.

2. From the circle, draw other circles. In those circles, write characteristics of the main idea. Draw arrows from the center circle to the circles that contain the characteristics.

3. From each circle that contains a characteristic, draw other circles. In those circles, write specific details about the characteristic. Draw arrows from each circle that contains a characteristic to the circles that contain specific details. You may draw as many circles as you want.

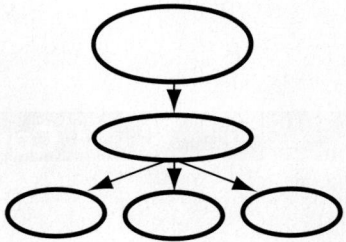

SI Measurement

The International System of Units, or SI, is the standard system of measurement used by many scientists. Using the same standards of measurement makes it easier for scientists to communicate with one another.

SI works by combining prefixes and base units. Each base unit can be used with different prefixes to define smaller and larger quantities. The table below lists common SI prefixes.

SI Prefixes

Prefix	Symbol	Factor	Example
kilo-	k	1,000	kilogram, 1 kg = 1,000 g
hecto-	h	100	hectoliter, 1 hL = 100 L
deka-	da	10	dekameter, 1 dam = 10 m
		1	meter, liter, gram
deci-	d	0.1	decigram, 1 dg = 0.1 g
centi-	c	0.01	centimeter, 1 cm = 0.01 m
milli-	m	0.001	milliliter, 1 mL = 0.001 L
micro-	μ	0.000 001	micrometer, 1 μm = 0.000 001 m

SI Conversion Table

SI units	From SI to English	From English to SI
Length		
kilometer (km) = 1,000 m	1 km = 0.621 mi	1 mi = 1.609 km
meter (m) = 100 cm	1 m = 3.281 ft	1 ft = 0.305 m
centimeter (cm) = 0.01 m	1 cm = 0.394 in.	1 in. = 2.540 cm
millimeter (mm) = 0.001 m	1 mm = 0.039 in.	
micrometer (μm) = 0.000 001 m		
nanometer (nm) = 0.000 000 001 m		
Area		
square kilometer (km^2) = 100 hectares	1 km^2 = 0.386 mi^2	1 mi^2 = 2.590 km^2
hectare (ha) = 10,000 m^2	1 ha = 2.471 acres	1 acre = 0.405 ha
square meter (m^2) = 10,000 cm^2	1 m^2 = 10.764 ft^2	1 ft^2 = 0.093 m^2
square centimeter (cm^2) = 100 mm^2	1 cm^2 = 0.155 in.^{2}	1 in.^{2} = 6.452 cm^2
Volume		
liter (L) = 1,000 mL = 1 dm^3	1 L = 1.057 fl qt	1 fl qt = 0.946 L
milliliter (mL) = 0.001 L = 1 cm^3	1 mL = 0.034 fl oz	1 fl oz = 29.574 mL
microliter (μL) = 0.000 001 L		
Mass		
kilogram (kg) = 1,000 g	1 kg = 2.205 lb	1 lb = 0.454 kg
gram (g) = 1,000 mg	1 g = 0.035 oz	1 oz = 28.350 g
milligram (mg) = 0.001 g		
microgram (μg) = 0.000 001 g		

Temperature Scales

Temperature can be expressed by using three different scales: Fahrenheit, Celsius, and Kelvin. The SI unit for temperature is the kelvin (K).

Although 0 K is much colder than 0°C, a change of 1 K is equal to a change of 1°C.

Three Temperature Scales

	Fahrenheit	Celsius	Kelvin
Water boils	212°	100°	373
Body temperature	98.6°	37°	310
Room temperature	68°	20°	293
Water freezes	32°	0°	273

Temperature Conversions Table		
To convert	**Use this equation:**	**Example**
Celsius to Fahrenheit °C → °F	$°F = \left(\dfrac{9}{5} \times °C\right) + 32$	Convert 45°C to °F. $°F = \left(\dfrac{9}{5} \times 45°C\right) + 32 = 113°F$
Fahrenheit to Celsius °F → °C	$°C = \dfrac{5}{9} \times (°F - 32)$	Convert 68°F to °C. $°C = \dfrac{5}{9} \times (68°F - 32) = 20°C$
Celsius to Kelvin °C → K	$K = °C + 273$	Convert 45°C to K. $K = 45°C + 273 = 318\ K$
Kelvin to Celsius K → °C	$°C = K - 273$	Convert 32 K to °C. $°C = 32K - 273 = -241°C$

Appendix

Measuring Skills

Using a Graduated Cylinder

When using a graduated cylinder to measure volume, keep the following procedures in mind:

1. Place the cylinder on a flat, level surface before measuring liquid.

2. Move your head so that your eye is level with the surface of the liquid.

3. Read the mark closest to the liquid level. On glass graduated cylinders, read the mark closest to the center of the curve in the liquid's surface.

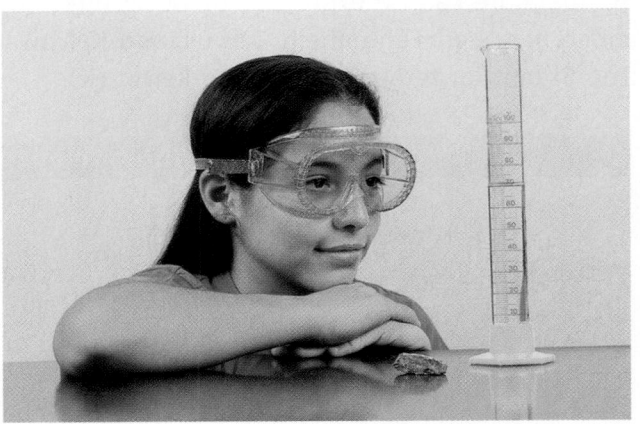

Using a Meterstick or Metric Ruler

When using a meterstick or metric ruler to measure length, keep the following procedures in mind:

1. Place the ruler firmly against the object that you are measuring.

2. Align one edge of the object exactly with the 0 end of the ruler.

3. Look at the other edge of the object to see which of the marks on the ruler is closest to that edge. (Note: Each small slash between the centimeters represents a millimeter, which is one-tenth of a centimeter.)

Using a Triple-Beam Balance

When using a triple-beam balance to measure mass, keep the following procedures in mind:

1. Make sure the balance is on a level surface.

2. Place all of the countermasses at 0. Adjust the balancing knob until the pointer rests at 0.

3. Place the object you wish to measure on the pan. **Caution:** Do not place hot objects or chemicals directly on the balance pan.

4. Move the largest countermass along the beam to the right until it is at the last notch that does not tip the balance. Follow the same procedure with the next-largest countermass. Then, move the smallest countermass until the pointer rests at 0.

5. Add the readings from the three beams together to determine the mass of the object.

6. When determining the mass of crystals or powders, first find the mass of a piece of filter paper. Then, add the crystals or powder to the paper, and remeasure. The actual mass of the crystals or powder is the total mass minus the mass of the paper. When finding the mass of liquids, first find the mass of the empty container. Then, find the combined mass of the liquid and container. The mass of the liquid is the total mass minus the mass of the container.

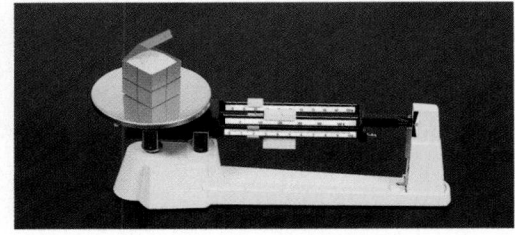

Scientific Methods

The ways in which scientists answer questions and solve problems are called **scientific methods.** The same steps are often used by scientists as they look for answers. However, there is more than one way to use these steps. Scientists may use all of the steps or just some of the steps during an investigation. They may even repeat some of the steps. The goal of using scientific methods is to come up with reliable answers and solutions.

Six Steps of Scientific Methods

1 Ask a Question

Good questions come from careful **observations.** You make observations by using your senses to gather information. Sometimes, you may use instruments, such as microscopes and telescopes, to extend the range of your senses. As you observe the natural world, you will discover that you have many more questions than answers. These questions drive investigations.

Questions beginning with *what, why, how,* and *when* are important in focusing an investigation. Here is an example of a question that could lead to an investigation.

Question: How does acid rain affect plant growth?

2 Form a Hypothesis

After you ask a question, you need to form a **hypothesis.** A hypothesis is a clear statement of what you expect the answer to your question to be. Your hypothesis will represent your best "educated guess" based on what you have observed and what you already know. A good hypothesis is testable. Otherwise, the investigation can go no further. Here is a hypothesis based on the question, "How does acid rain affect plant growth?"

Hypothesis: Acid rain slows plant growth.

The hypothesis can lead to predictions. A prediction is what you think the outcome of your experiment or data collection will be. Predictions are usually stated in an if-then format. Here is a sample prediction for the hypothesis that acid rain slows plant growth.

Prediction: If a plant is watered with only acid rain (which has a pH of 4), then the plant will grow at half its normal rate.

3 Test the Hypothesis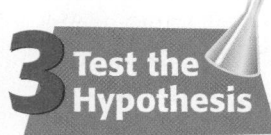

After you have formed a hypothesis and made a prediction, your hypothesis should be tested. One way to test a hypothesis is with a controlled experiment. A **controlled experiment** tests only one factor at a time. In an experiment to test the effect of acid rain on plant growth, the **control group** would be watered with normal rain water. The **experimental group** would be watered with acid rain. All of the plants should receive the same amount of sunlight and water each day. The air temperature should be the same for all groups. However, the acidity of the water will be a variable. In fact, any factor that is different from one group to another is a **variable.** If your hypothesis is correct, then the acidity of the water and plant growth are *dependant variables.* The amount a plant grows is dependent on the acidity of the water. However, the amount of water each plant receives and the amount of sunlight each plant receives are *independent variables.* Either of these factors could change without affecting the other factor.

Sometimes, the nature of an investigation makes a controlled experiment impossible. For example, the Earth's core is surrounded by thousands of meters of rock. Under such circumstances, a hypothesis may be tested by making detailed observations.

4 Analyze the Results

After you have completed your experiments, made your observations, and collected your data, you must analyze all the information you have gathered. Tables and graphs are often used in this step to organize the data.

Appendix

5 Draw Conclusions

After analyzing your data, you can determine if your results support your hypothesis. If your hypothesis is supported, you (or others) might want to repeat the observations or experiments to verify your results. If your hypothesis is not supported by the data, you may have to check your procedure for errors. You may even have to reject your hypothesis and make a new one. If you cannot draw a conclusion from your results, you may have to try the investigation again or carry out further observations or experiments.

6 Communicate Results

After any scientific investigation, you should report your results. By preparing a written or oral report, you let others know what you have learned. They may repeat your investigation to see if they get the same results. Your report may even lead to another question and then to another investigation.

Scientific Methods in Action

Scientific methods contain loops in which several steps may be repeated over and over again. In some cases, certain steps are unnecessary. Thus, there is not a "straight line" of steps. For example, sometimes scientists find that testing one hypothesis raises new questions and new hypotheses to be tested. And sometimes, testing the hypothesis leads directly to a conclusion. Furthermore, the steps in scientific methods are not always used in the same order. Follow the steps in the diagram, and see how many different directions scientific methods can take you.

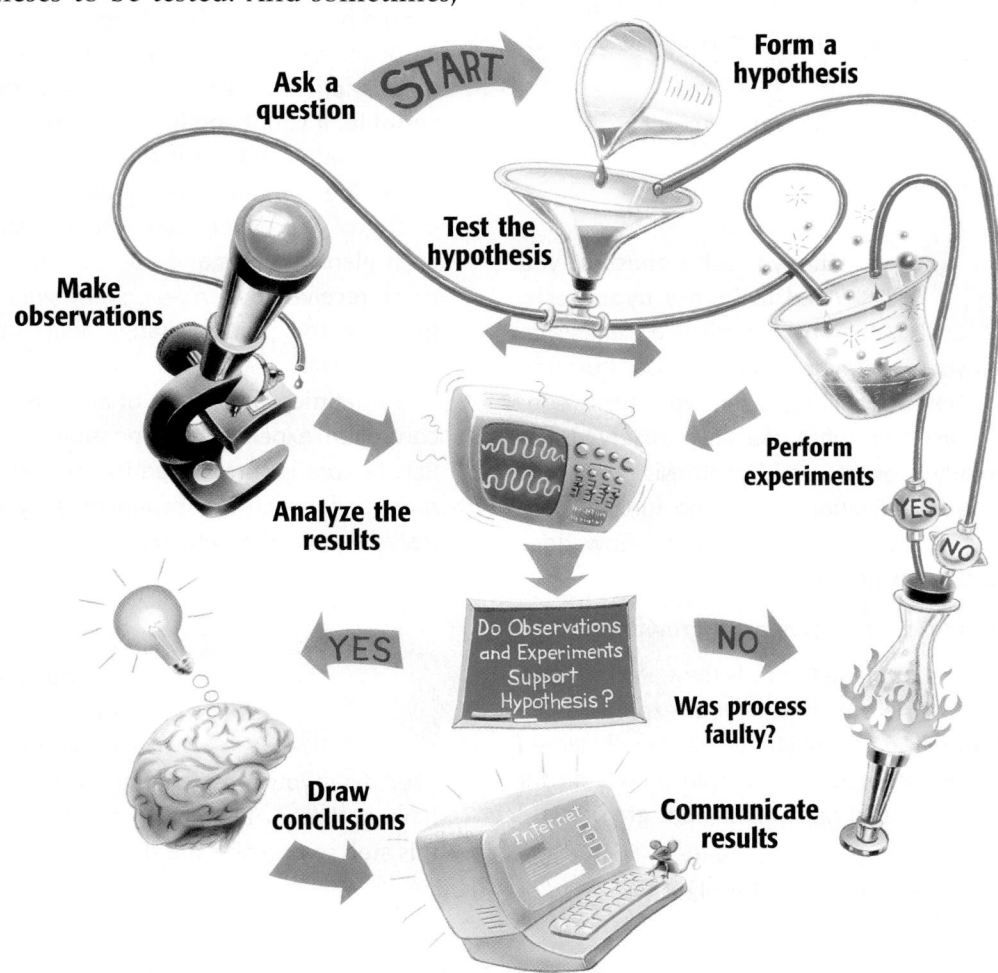

Making Charts and Graphs

Pie Charts

A pie chart shows how each group of data relates to all of the data. Each part of the circle forming the chart represents a category of the data. The entire circle represents all of the data. For example, a biologist studying a hardwood forest in Wisconsin found that there were five different types of trees. The data table at right summarizes the biologist's findings.

Wisconsin Hardwood Trees	
Type of tree	**Number found**
Oak	600
Maple	750
Beech	300
Birch	1,200
Hickory	150
Total	3,000

How to Make a Pie Chart

1 To make a pie chart of these data, first find the percentage of each type of tree. Divide the number of trees of each type by the total number of trees, and multiply by 100.

$$\frac{600 \text{ oak}}{3{,}000 \text{ trees}} \times 100 = 20\%$$

$$\frac{750 \text{ maple}}{3{,}000 \text{ trees}} \times 100 = 25\%$$

$$\frac{300 \text{ beech}}{3{,}000 \text{ trees}} \times 100 = 10\%$$

$$\frac{1{,}200 \text{ birch}}{3{,}000 \text{ trees}} \times 100 = 40\%$$

$$\frac{150 \text{ hickory}}{3{,}000 \text{ trees}} \times 100 = 5\%$$

2 Now, determine the size of the wedges that make up the pie chart. Multiply each percentage by 360°. Remember that a circle contains 360°.

$20\% \times 360° = 72°$ $25\% \times 360° = 90°$

$10\% \times 360° = 36°$ $40\% \times 360° = 144°$

$5\% \times 360° = 18°$

3 Check that the sum of the percentages is 100 and the sum of the degrees is 360.

$20\% + 25\% + 10\% + 40\% + 5\% = 100\%$

$72° + 90° + 36° + 144° + 18° = 360°$

4 Use a compass to draw a circle and mark the center of the circle.

5 Then, use a protractor to draw angles of 72°, 90°, 36°, 144°, and 18° in the circle.

6 Finally, label each part of the chart, and choose an appropriate title.

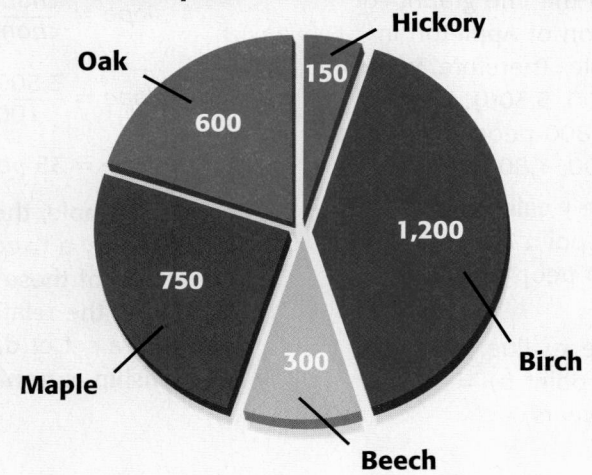
A Community of Wisconsin Hardwood Trees

Line Graphs

Line graphs are most often used to demonstrate continuous change. For example, Mr. Smith's students analyzed the population records for their hometown, Appleton, between 1900 and 2000. Examine the data at right.

Because the year and the population change, they are the *variables*. The population is determined by, or dependent on, the year. Therefore, the population is called the **dependent variable,** and the year is called the **independent variable.** Each set of data is called a **data pair.** To prepare a line graph, you must first organize data pairs into a table like the one at right.

Population of Appleton, 1900–2000	
Year	Population
1900	1,800
1920	2,500
1940	3,200
1960	3,900
1980	4,600
2000	5,300

How to Make a Line Graph

1. Place the independent variable along the horizontal (*x*) axis. Place the dependent variable along the vertical (*y*) axis.

2. Label the *x*-axis "Year" and the *y*-axis "Population." Look at your largest and smallest values for the population. For the *y*-axis, determine a scale that will provide enough space to show these values. You must use the same scale for the entire length of the axis. Next, find an appropriate scale for the *x*-axis.

3. Choose reasonable starting points for each axis.

4. Plot the data pairs as accurately as possible.

5. Choose a title that accurately represents the data.

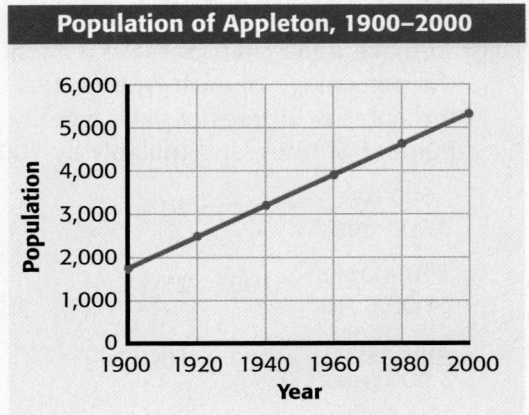

How to Determine Slope

Slope is the ratio of the change in the *y*-value to the change in the *x*-value, or "rise over run."

1. Choose two points on the line graph. For example, the population of Appleton in 2000 was 5,300 people. Therefore, you can define point *a* as (2000, 5,300). In 1900, the population was 1,800 people. You can define point *b* as (1900, 1,800).

2. Find the change in the *y*-value. (*y* at point *a*) − (*y* at point *b*) = 5,300 people − 1,800 people = 3,500 people

3. Find the change in the *x*-value. (*x* at point *a*) − (*x* at point *b*) = 2000 − 1900 = 100 years

4. Calculate the slope of the graph by dividing the change in *y* by the change in *x*.

$$slope = \frac{change\ in\ y}{change\ in\ x}$$

$$slope = \frac{3,500\ people}{100\ years}$$

$$slope = 35\ people\ per\ year$$

In this example, the population in Appleton increased by a fixed amount each year. The graph of these data is a straight line. Therefore, the relationship is **linear.** When the graph of a set of data is not a straight line, the relationship is **nonlinear.**

Using Algebra to Determine Slope

The equation in step 4 may also be arranged to be

$$y = kx$$

where y represents the change in the y-value, k represents the slope, and x represents the change in the x-value.

$$slope = \frac{change\ in\ y}{change\ in\ x}$$

$$k = \frac{y}{x}$$

$$k \times x = \frac{y \times x}{x}$$

$$kx = y$$

Bar Graphs

Bar graphs are used to demonstrate change that is not continuous. These graphs can be used to indicate trends when the data cover a long period of time. A meteorologist gathered the precipitation data shown here for Hartford, Connecticut, for April 1–15, 1996, and used a bar graph to represent the data.

Precipitation in Hartford, Connecticut April 1–15, 1996			
Date	Precipitation (cm)	Date	Precipitation (cm)
April 1	0.5	April 9	0.25
April 2	1.25	April 10	0.0
April 3	0.0	April 11	1.0
April 4	0.0	April 12	0.0
April 5	0.0	April 13	0.25
April 6	0.0	April 14	0.0
April 7	0.0	April 15	6.50
April 8	1.75		

How to Make a Bar Graph

1 Use an appropriate scale and a reasonable starting point for each axis.

2 Label the axes, and plot the data.

3 Choose a title that accurately represents the data.

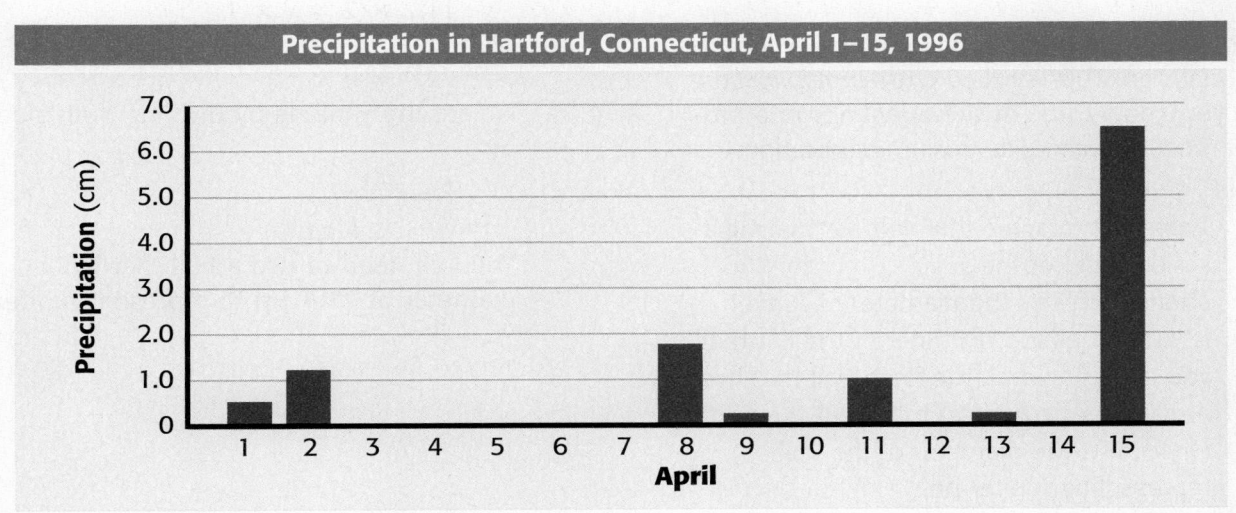

Precipitation in Hartford, Connecticut, April 1–15, 1996

Math Refresher

Science requires an understanding of many math concepts. The following pages will help you review some important math skills.

Averages

An **average**, or **mean**, simplifies a set of numbers into a single number that *approximates* the value of the set.

> **Example:** Find the average of the following set of numbers: 5, 4, 7, and 8.

Step 1: Find the sum.

$$5 + 4 + 7 + 8 = 24$$

Step 2: Divide the sum by the number of numbers in your set. Because there are four numbers in this example, divide the sum by 4.

$$\frac{24}{4} = 6$$

The average, or mean, is **6.**

Ratios

A **ratio** is a comparison between numbers, and it is usually written as a fraction.

> **Example:** Find the ratio of thermometers to students if you have 36 thermometers and 48 students in your class.

Step 1: Make the ratio.

$$\frac{36 \text{ thermometers}}{48 \text{ students}}$$

Step 2: Reduce the fraction to its simplest form.

$$\frac{36}{48} = \frac{36 \div 12}{48 \div 12} = \frac{3}{4}$$

The ratio of thermometers to students is **3 to 4,** or $\frac{3}{4}$. The ratio may also be written in the form 3:4.

Proportions

A **proportion** is an equation that states that two ratios are equal.

$$\frac{3}{1} = \frac{12}{4}$$

To solve a proportion, first multiply across the equal sign. This is called *cross-multiplication*. If you know three of the quantities in a proportion, you can use cross-multiplication to find the fourth.

> **Example:** Imagine that you are making a scale model of the solar system for your science project. The diameter of Jupiter is 11.2 times the diameter of the Earth. If you are using a plastic-foam ball that has a diameter of 2 cm to represent the Earth, what must the diameter of the ball representing Jupiter be?
>
> $$\frac{11.2}{1} = \frac{x}{2 \text{ cm}}$$

Step 1: Cross-multiply.

$$\frac{11.2}{1} \diagdown\!\!\!\!\diagup \frac{x}{2}$$

$$11.2 \times 2 = x \times 1$$

Step 2: Multiply.

$$22.4 = x \times 1$$

Step 3: Isolate the variable by dividing both sides by 1.

$$x = \frac{22.4}{1}$$

$$x = 22.4 \text{ cm}$$

You will need to use a ball that has a diameter of **22.4** cm to represent Jupiter.

Percentages

A **percentage** is a ratio of a given number to 100.

> **Example:** What is 85% of 40?

Step 1: Rewrite the percentage by moving the decimal point two places to the left.

$$0.\overset{\frown}{8}\overset{\frown}{5}$$

Step 2: Multiply the decimal by the number that you are calculating the percentage of.

$$0.85 \times 40 = 34$$

85% of 40 is **34.**

Decimals

To **add** or **subtract decimals,** line up the digits vertically so that the decimal points line up. Then, add or subtract the columns from right to left. Carry or borrow numbers as necessary.

> **Example:** Add the following numbers: 3.1415 and 2.96.

Step 1: Line up the digits vertically so that the decimal points line up.

$$\begin{array}{r} 3.1415 \\ + \ 2.96 \\ \hline \end{array}$$

Step 2: Add the columns from right to left, and carry when necessary.

$$\begin{array}{r} {}^{1}\ {}^{1} \\ 3.1415 \\ + \ 2.96 \\ \hline 6.1015 \end{array}$$

The sum is **6.1015.**

Fractions

Numbers tell you how many; **fractions** tell you *how much of a whole*.

> **Example:** Your class has 24 plants. Your teacher instructs you to put 5 plants in a shady spot. What fraction of the plants in your class will you put in a shady spot?

Step 1: In the denominator, write the total number of parts in the whole.

$$\frac{?}{24}$$

Step 2: In the numerator, write the number of parts of the whole that are being considered.

$$\frac{5}{24}$$

So, $\frac{5}{24}$ of the plants will be in the shade.

Reducing Fractions

It is usually best to express a fraction in its simplest form. Expressing a fraction in its simplest form is called *reducing* a fraction.

> **Example:** Reduce the fraction $\frac{30}{45}$ to its simplest form.

Step 1: Find the largest whole number that will divide evenly into both the numerator and denominator. This number is called the *greatest common factor* (GCF).

Factors of the numerator 30:
  1, 2, 3, 5, 6, 10, **15,** 30

Factors of the denominator 45:
  1, 3, 5, 9, **15,** 45

Step 2: Divide both the numerator and the denominator by the GCF, which in this case is 15.

$$\frac{30}{45} = \frac{30 \div 15}{45 \div 15} = \frac{2}{3}$$

Thus, $\frac{30}{45}$ reduced to its simplest form is $\frac{2}{3}$.

Appendix

Adding and Subtracting Fractions

To **add** or **subtract fractions** that have the **same denominator,** simply add or subtract the numerators.

Examples:

$$\frac{3}{5} + \frac{1}{5} = ? \text{ and } \frac{3}{4} - \frac{1}{4} = ?$$

Step 1: Add or subtract the numerators.

$$\frac{3}{5} + \frac{1}{5} = \frac{4}{} \text{ and } \frac{3}{4} - \frac{1}{4} = \frac{2}{}$$

Step 2: Write the sum or difference over the denominator.

$$\frac{3}{5} + \frac{1}{5} = \frac{4}{5} \text{ and } \frac{3}{4} - \frac{1}{4} = \frac{2}{4}$$

Step 3: If necessary, reduce the fraction to its simplest form.

$\frac{4}{5}$ cannot be reduced, and $\frac{2}{4} = \frac{1}{2}$.

To **add** or **subtract fractions** that have **different denominators,** first find the least common denominator (LCD).

Examples:

$$\frac{1}{2} + \frac{1}{6} = ? \text{ and } \frac{3}{4} - \frac{2}{3} = ?$$

Step 1: Write the equivalent fractions that have a common denominator.

$$\frac{3}{6} + \frac{1}{6} = ? \text{ and } \frac{9}{12} - \frac{8}{12} = ?$$

Step 2: Add or subtract the fractions.

$$\frac{3}{6} + \frac{1}{6} = \frac{4}{6} \text{ and } \frac{9}{12} - \frac{8}{12} = \frac{1}{12}$$

Step 3: If necessary, reduce the fraction to its simplest form.

The fraction $\frac{4}{6} = \frac{2}{3}$, and $\frac{1}{12}$ cannot be reduced.

Multiplying Fractions

To **multiply fractions,** multiply the numerators and the denominators together, and then reduce the fraction to its simplest form.

Example:

$$\frac{5}{9} \times \frac{7}{10} = ?$$

Step 1: Multiply the numerators and denominators.

$$\frac{5}{9} \times \frac{7}{10} = \frac{5 \times 7}{9 \times 10} = \frac{35}{90}$$

Step 2: Reduce the fraction.

$$\frac{35}{90} = \frac{35 \div 5}{90 \div 5} = \frac{7}{18}$$

Dividing Fractions

To **divide fractions,** first rewrite the divisor (the number you divide by) upside down. This number is called the *reciprocal* of the divisor. Then multiply and reduce if necessary.

Example:

$$\frac{5}{8} \div \frac{3}{2} = ?$$

Step 1: Rewrite the divisor as its reciprocal.

$$\frac{3}{2} \rightarrow \frac{2}{3}$$

Step 2: Multiply the fractions.

$$\frac{5}{8} \times \frac{2}{3} = \frac{5 \times 2}{8 \times 3} = \frac{10}{24}$$

Step 3: Reduce the fraction.

$$\frac{10}{24} = \frac{10 \div 2}{24 \div 2} = \frac{5}{12}$$

Scientific Notation

Scientific notation is a short way of representing very large and very small numbers without writing all of the place-holding zeros.

Example: Write 653,000,000 in scientific notation.

Step 1: Write the number without the place-holding zeros.

653

Step 2: Place the decimal point after the first digit.

6.53

Step 3: Find the exponent by counting the number of places that you moved the decimal point.

6.53000000

The decimal point was moved eight places to the left. Therefore, the exponent of 10 is positive 8. If you had moved the decimal point to the right, the exponent would be negative.

Step 4: Write the number in scientific notation.

$$\mathbf{6.53 \times 10^8}$$

Area

Area is the number of square units needed to cover the surface of an object.

Formulas:

area of a square = side × side
area of a rectangle = length × width
area of a triangle = $\frac{1}{2}$ × base × height

Examples: Find the areas.

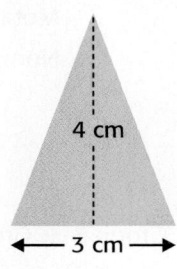

Triangle

area = $\frac{1}{2}$ × base × height
area = $\frac{1}{2}$ × 3 cm × 4 cm
area = **6 cm²**

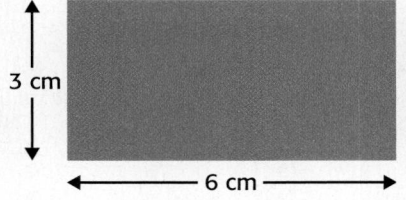

Rectangle

area = length × width
area = 6 cm × 3 cm
area = **18 cm²**

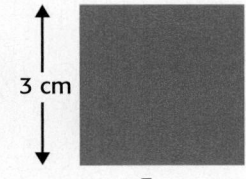

Square

area = side × side
area = 3 cm × 3 cm
area = **9 cm²**

Volume

Volume is the amount of space that something occupies.

Formulas:

volume of a cube = side × side × side

volume of a prism = area of base × height

Examples:

Find the volume of the solids.

Cube

volume = side × side × side
volume = 4 cm × 4 cm × 4 cm
volume = **64 cm³**

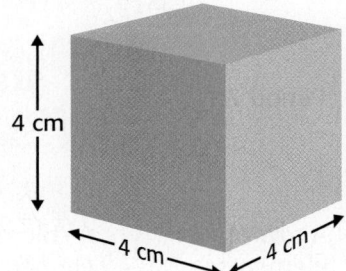

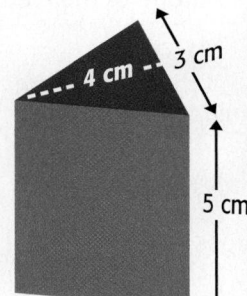

Prism

volume = area of base × height
volume = (area of triangle) × height
volume = ($\frac{1}{2}$ × 3 cm × 4 cm) × 5 cm
volume = 6 cm² × 5 cm
volume = **30 cm³**

Appendix

Periodic Table of the Elements

Each square on the table includes an element's name, chemical symbol, atomic number, and atomic mass.

The color of the chemical symbol indicates the physical state at room temperature. Carbon is a solid.

| 6 |
| C |
| Carbon |
| 12.0 |

Atomic number
Chemical symbol
Element name
Atomic mass

The background color indicates the type of element. Carbon is a nonmetal.

Background
- Metals
- Metalloids
- Nonmetals

Chemical symbol
- Solid
- Liquid
- Gas

Period 1

| 1 |
| H |
| Hydrogen |
| 1.0 |

	Group 1	Group 2	Group 3	Group 4	Group 5	Group 6	Group 7	Group 8	Group 9
Period 2	3 Li Lithium 6.9	4 Be Beryllium 9.0							
Period 3	11 Na Sodium 23.0	12 Mg Magnesium 24.3							
Period 4	19 K Potassium 39.1	20 Ca Calcium 40.1	21 Sc Scandium 45.0	22 Ti Titanium 47.9	23 V Vanadium 50.9	24 Cr Chromium 52.0	25 Mn Manganese 54.9	26 Fe Iron 55.8	27 Co Cobalt 58.9
Period 5	37 Rb Rubidium 85.5	38 Sr Strontium 87.6	39 Y Yttrium 88.9	40 Zr Zirconium 91.2	41 Nb Niobium 92.9	42 Mo Molybdenum 95.9	43 Tc Technetium (98)	44 Ru Ruthenium 101.1	45 Rh Rhodium 102.9
Period 6	55 Cs Cesium 132.9	56 Ba Barium 137.3	57 La Lanthanum 138.9	72 Hf Hafnium 178.5	73 Ta Tantalum 180.9	74 W Tungsten 183.8	75 Re Rhenium 186.2	76 Os Osmium 190.2	77 Ir Iridium 192.2
Period 7	87 Fr Francium (223)	88 Ra Radium (226)	89 Ac Actinium (227)	104 Rf Rutherfordium (261)	105 Db Dubnium (262)	106 Sg Seaborgium (263)	107 Bh Bohrium (264)	108 Hs Hassium (265)[†]	109 Mt Meitnerium (268)[†]

† Estimated from currently available IUPAC data.

A row of elements is called a *period*.

A column of elements is called a *group* or *family*.

Values in parentheses are of the most stable isotope of the element.

These elements are placed below the table to allow the table to be narrower.

Lanthanides

58 Ce Cerium 140.1	59 Pr Praseodymium 140.9	60 Nd Neodymium 144.2	61 Pm Promethium (145)	62 Sm Samarium 150.4

Actinides

90 Th Thorium 232.0	91 Pa Protactinium 231.0	92 U Uranium 238.0	93 Np Neptunium (237)	94 Pu Plutonium (244)

Topic: **Periodic Table**
Go To: **go.hrw.com**
Keyword: **HN0 PERIODIC**
Visit the HRW Web site for
updates on the periodic table.

Group 18

2	
He	
Helium	
4.0	

Group 13	Group 14	Group 15	Group 16	Group 17
5	6	7	8	9
B	**C**	**N**	**O**	**F**
Boron	Carbon	Nitrogen	Oxygen	Fluorine
10.8	12.0	14.0	16.0	19.0

> This zigzag line reminds you where the metals, nonmetals, and metalloids are.

10
Ne
Neon
20.2

13	14	15	16	17	18
Al	**Si**	**P**	**S**	**Cl**	**Ar**
Aluminum	Silicon	Phosphorus	Sulfur	Chlorine	Argon
27.0	28.1	31.0	32.1	35.5	39.9

Group 10	Group 11	Group 12						
28	29	30	31	32	33	34	35	36
Ni	**Cu**	**Zn**	**Ga**	**Ge**	**As**	**Se**	**Br**	**Kr**
Nickel	Copper	Zinc	Gallium	Germanium	Arsenic	Selenium	Bromine	Krypton
58.7	63.5	65.4	69.7	72.6	74.9	79.0	79.9	83.8
46	47	48	49	50	51	52	53	54
Pd	**Ag**	**Cd**	**In**	**Sn**	**Sb**	**Te**	**I**	**Xe**
Palladium	Silver	Cadmium	Indium	Tin	Antimony	Tellurium	Iodine	Xenon
106.4	107.9	112.4	114.8	118.7	121.8	127.6	126.9	131.3
78	79	80	81	82	83	84	85	86
Pt	**Au**	**Hg**	**Tl**	**Pb**	**Bi**	**Po**	**At**	**Rn**
Platinum	Gold	Mercury	Thallium	Lead	Bismuth	Polonium	Astatine	Radon
195.1	197.0	200.6	204.4	207.2	209.0	(209)	(210)	(222)
110	111	112		114				
Ds	**Uuu**	**Uub**		**Uuq**				
Darmstadtium	Unununium	Ununbium		Ununquadium				
(269)†	(272)†	(277)†		(285)†				

> The names and three-letter symbols of elements are temporary. They are based on the atomic numbers of the elements. Official names and symbols will be approved by an international committee of scientists.

63	64	65	66	67	68	69	70	71
Eu	**Gd**	**Tb**	**Dy**	**Ho**	**Er**	**Tm**	**Yb**	**Lu**
Europium	Gadolinium	Terbium	Dysprosium	Holmium	Erbium	Thulium	Ytterbium	Lutetium
152.0	157.2	158.9	162.5	164.9	167.3	168.9	173.0	175.0
95	96	97	98	99	100	101	102	103
Am	**Cm**	**Bk**	**Cf**	**Es**	**Fm**	**Md**	**No**	**Lr**
Americium	Curium	Berkelium	Californium	Einsteinium	Fermium	Mendelevium	Nobelium	Lawrencium
(243)	(247)	(247)	(251)	(252)	(257)	(258)	(259)	(262)

Appendix

Appendix   **795**

Physical Science Refresher

Atoms and Elements

Every object in the universe is made up of particles of some kind of matter. **Matter** is anything that takes up space and has mass. All matter is made up of elements. An **element** is a substance that cannot be separated into simpler components by ordinary chemical means. This is because each element consists of only one kind of atom. An **atom** is the smallest unit of an element that has all of the properties of that element.

Atomic Structure

Atoms are made up of small particles called subatomic particles. The three major types of subatomic particles are **electrons, protons, and neutrons.** Electrons have a negative electric charge, protons have a positive charge, and neutrons have no electric charge. The protons and neutrons are packed close to one another to form the **nucleus.** The protons give the nucleus a positive charge. Electrons are most likely to be found in regions around the nucleus called **electron clouds.** The negatively charged electrons are attracted to the positively charged nucleus. An atom may have several energy levels in which electrons are located.

Atomic Number

To help in the identification of elements, scientists have assigned an **atomic number** to each kind of atom. The atomic number is the number of protons in the atom. Atoms with the same number of protons are all the same kind of element. In an uncharged, or electrically neutral, atom there are an equal number of protons and electrons. Therefore, the atomic number equals the number of electrons in an uncharged atom. The number of neutrons, however, can vary for a given element. Atoms of the same element that have different numbers of neutrons are called **isotopes.**

Periodic Table of the Elements

In the periodic table, the elements are arranged from left to right in order of increasing atomic number. Each element in the table is in a separate box. An uncharged atom of each element has one more electron and one more proton than an uncharged atom of the element to its left. Each horizontal row of the table is called a **period.** Changes in chemical properties of elements across a period correspond to changes in the electron arrangements of their atoms. Each vertical column of the table, known as a **group,** lists elements with similar properties. The elements in a group have similar chemical properties because their atoms have the same number of electrons in their outer energy level. For example, the elements helium, neon, argon, krypton, xenon, and radon all have similar properties and are known as the noble gases.

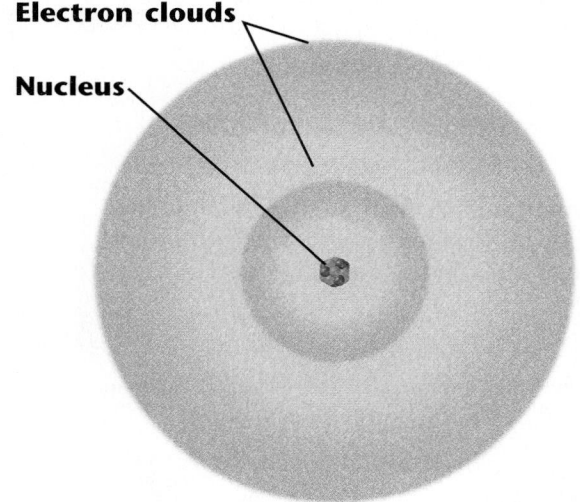

Electron clouds

Nucleus

Molecules and Compounds

When two or more elements are joined chemically, the resulting substance is called a **compound.** A compound is a new substance with properties different from those of the elements that compose it. For example, water, H_2O, is a compound formed when hydrogen (H) and oxygen (O) combine. The smallest complete unit of a compound that has the properties of that compound is called a **molecule.** A chemical formula indicates the elements in a compound. It also indicates the relative number of atoms of each element present. The chemical formula for water is H_2O, which indicates that each water molecule consists of two atoms of hydrogen and one atom of oxygen. The subscript number after the symbol for an element indicates how many atoms of that element are in a single molecule of the compound.

Acids, Bases, and pH

An ion is an atom or group of atoms that has an electric charge because it has lost or gained one or more electrons. When an acid, such as hydrochloric acid, HCl, is mixed with water, it separates into ions. An **acid** is a compound that produces hydrogen ions, H+, in water. The hydrogen ions then combine with a water molecule to form a hydronium ion, H_3O^+. A **base,** on the other hand, is a substance that produces hydroxide ions, OH^-, in water.

To determine whether a solution is acidic or basic, scientists use pH. The **pH** is a measure of the hydronium ion concentration in a solution. The pH scale ranges from 0 to 14. The middle point, pH = 7, is neutral, neither acidic nor basic. Acids have a pH less than 7; bases have a pH greater than 7. The lower the number is, the more acidic the solution. The higher the number is, the more basic the solution.

Chemical Equations

A chemical reaction occurs when a chemical change takes place. (In a chemical change, new substances with new properties are formed.) A chemical equation is a useful way of describing a chemical reaction by means of chemical formulas. The equation indicates what substances react and what the products are. For example, when carbon and oxygen combine, they can form carbon dioxide. The equation for the reaction is as follows: $C + O_2 \rightarrow CO_2$.

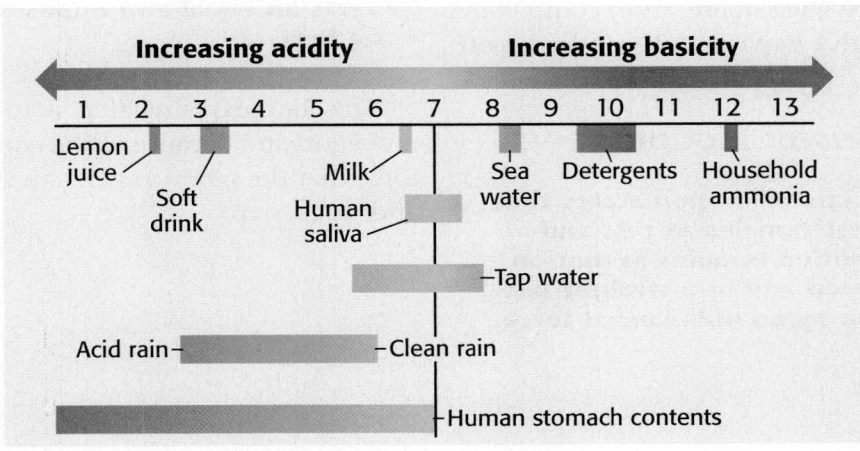

| Increasing acidity | | | | | | | Increasing basicity | | | | | |
| 1 | 2 | 3 | 4 | 5 | 6 | 7 | 8 | 9 | 10 | 11 | 12 | 13 |

Lemon juice
Soft drink
Milk
Human saliva
Sea water
Detergents
Household ammonia
Tap water
Acid rain — Clean rain
Human stomach contents

Physical Science Laws and Equations

Law of Conservation of Energy

The law of conservation of energy states that energy can be neither created nor destroyed.

The total amount of energy in a closed system is always the same. Energy can be changed from one form to another, but all of the different forms of energy in a system always add up to the same total amount of energy no matter how many energy conversions occur.

Law of Universal Gravitation

The law of universal gravitation states that all objects in the universe attract each other by a force called *gravity*. The size of the force depends on the masses of the objects and the distance between objects.

The first part of the law explains why a bowling ball is much harder to lift than a table-tennis ball. Because the bowling ball has a much larger mass than the table-tennis ball does, the amount of gravity between the Earth and the bowling ball is greater than the amount of gravity between the Earth and the table-tennis ball.

The second part of the law explains why a satellite can remain in orbit around the Earth. The satellite is carefully placed at a distance great enough to prevent the Earth's gravity from immediately pulling the satellite down but small enough to prevent the satellite from completely escaping the Earth's gravity and wandering off into space.

Newton's Laws of Motion

Newton's first law of motion states that an object at rest remains at rest and an object in motion remains in motion at constant speed and in a straight line unless acted on by an unbalanced force.

The first part of the law explains why a football will remain on a tee until it is kicked off or until a gust of wind blows it off.

The second part of the law explains why a bike rider will continue moving forward after the bike comes to an abrupt stop. Gravity and the friction of the sidewalk will eventually stop the rider.

Newton's second law of motion states that the acceleration of an object depends on the mass of the object and the amount of force applied.

The first part of the law explains why the acceleration of a 4 kg bowling ball will be greater than the acceleration of a 6 kg bowling ball if the same force is applied to both.

The second part of the law explains why the acceleration of a bowling ball will be larger if a larger force is applied to the bowling ball.

The relationship of acceleration (a) to mass (m) and force (F) can be expressed mathematically by the following equation:

$$acceleration = \frac{force}{mass}, \text{ or } a = \frac{F}{m}$$

This equation is often rearranged to the form

$$force = mass \times acceleration$$
$$or$$
$$F = m \times a$$

Newton's third law of motion states that whenever one object exerts a force on a second object, the second object exerts an equal and opposite force on the first.

This law explains that a runner is able to move forward because of the equal and opposite force that the ground exerts on the runner's foot after each step.

Useful Equations

Average speed

$$\text{average speed} = \frac{\text{total distance}}{\text{total time}}$$

Example: A bicycle messenger traveled a distance of 136 km in 8 h. What was the messenger's average speed?

$$\frac{136 \text{ km}}{8 \text{ h}} = 17 \text{ km/h}$$

The messenger's average speed was **17 km/h.**

Average acceleration

$$\frac{\text{average}}{\text{acceleration}} = \frac{\text{final velocity} - \text{starting velocity}}{\text{time it takes to change velocity}}$$

Example: Calculate the average acceleration of an Olympic 100 m dash sprinter who reaches a velocity of 20 m/s south at the finish line. The race was in a straight line and lasted 10 s.

$$\frac{20 \text{ m/s} - 0 \text{ m/s}}{10 \text{ s}} = 2 \text{ m/s/s}$$

The sprinter's average acceleration is **2 m/s/s south.**

Net force

Forces in the Same Direction

When forces are in the same direction, add the forces together to determine the net force.

Example: Calculate the net force on a stalled car that is being pushed by two people. One person is pushing with a force of 13 N northwest, and the other person is pushing with a force of 8 N in the same direction.

$$13 \text{ N} + 8 \text{ N} = 21 \text{ N}$$

The net force is **21 N northwest.**

Forces in Opposite Directions

When forces are in opposite directions, subtract the smaller force from the larger force to determine the net force. The net force will be in the direction of the larger force.

Net force (continued)

Example: Calculate the net force on a rope that is being pulled on each end. One person is pulling on one end of the rope with a force of 12 N south. Another person is pulling on the opposite end of the rope with a force of 7 N north.

$$12 \text{ N} - 7 \text{ N} = 5 \text{ N}$$

The net force is **5 N south.**

Density

$$\text{density} = \frac{\text{mass}}{\text{volume}}$$

Example: Calculate the density of a sponge that has a mass of 10 g and a volume of 40 cm^3.

$$\frac{10 \text{ g}}{40 \text{ cm}^3} = \frac{0.25 \text{g}}{\text{cm}^3}$$

The density of the sponge is **0.25 g/cm^3.**

Pressure

Pressure is the force exerted over a given area. The SI unit for pressure is the pascal, whose symbol is Pa.

$$\text{pressure} = \frac{\text{force}}{\text{area}}$$

Example: Calculate the pressure of the air in a soccer ball if the air exerts a force of 10 N over an area of 0.5 m^2.

$$\text{pressure} = \frac{10 \text{ N}}{0.5 \text{ m}^2} = \frac{20 \text{ N}}{\text{m}^2} = 20 \text{ Pa}$$

The pressure of the air inside the soccer ball is **20 Pa.**

Concentration

$$\text{concentration} = \frac{\text{mass of solute}}{\text{volume of solvent}}$$

Example: Calculate the concentration of a solution in which 10 g of sugar is dissolved in 125 mL of water.

$$\frac{10 \text{ g of sugar}}{125 \text{ mL of water}} = \frac{0.08 \text{ g}}{\text{mL}}$$

The concentration of this solution is **0.08 g/mL.**

Properties of Common Minerals

Silicate Minerals

Mineral	Color	Luster	Streak	Hardness
Beryl	deep green, pink, white, bluish green, or yellow	vitreous	white	7.5–8
Chlorite	green	vitreous to pearly	pale green	2–2.5
Garnet	green, red, brown, black	vitreous	white	6.5–7.5
Hornblende	dark green, brown, or black	vitreous	none	5–6
Muscovite	colorless, silvery white, or brown	vitreous or pearly	white	2–2.5
Olivine	olive green, yellow	vitreous	white or none	6.5–7
Orthoclase	colorless, white, pink, or other colors	vitreous	white or none	6
Plagioclase	colorless, white, yellow, pink, green	vitreous	white	6
Quartz	colorless or white; any color when not pure	vitreous or waxy	white or none	7

Nonsilicate Minerals

Native Elements

Mineral	Color	Luster	Streak	Hardness
Copper	copper-red	metallic	copper-red	2.5–3
Diamond	pale yellow or colorless	adamantine	none	10
Graphite	black to gray	submetallic	black	1–2

Carbonates

Mineral	Color	Luster	Streak	Hardness
Aragonite	colorless, white, or pale yellow	vitreous	white	3.5–4
Calcite	colorless or white to tan	vitreous	white	3

Halides

Mineral	Color	Luster	Streak	Hardness
Fluorite	light green, yellow, purple, bluish green, or other colors	vitreous	none	4
Halite	white	vitreous	white	2.0–2.5

Oxides

Mineral	Color	Luster	Streak	Hardness
Hematite	reddish brown to black	metallic to earthy	dark red to red-brown	5.6–6.5
Magnetite	iron-black	metallic	black	5.5–6.5

Sulfates

Mineral	Color	Luster	Streak	Hardness
Anhydrite	colorless, bluish, or violet	vitreous to pearly	white	3–3.5
Gypsum	white, pink, gray, or colorless	vitreous, pearly, or silky	white	2.0

Sulfides

Mineral	Color	Luster	Streak	Hardness
Galena	lead-gray	metallic	lead-gray to black	2.5–2.8
Pyrite	brassy yellow	metallic	greenish, brownish, or black	6–6.5

Density (g/cm³)	Cleavage, Fracture, Special Properties	Common Uses
2.6–2.8	1 cleavage direction; irregular fracture; some varieties fluoresce in ultraviolet light	gemstones, ore of the metal beryllium
2.6–3.3	1 cleavage direction; irregular fracture	
4.2	no cleavage; conchoidal to splintery fracture	gemstones, abrasives
3.0–3.4	2 cleavage directions; hackly to splintery fracture	
2.7–3	1 cleavage direction; irregular fracture	electrical insulation, wallpaper, fireproofing material, lubricant
3.2–3.3	no cleavage; conchoidal fracture	gemstones, casting
2.6	2 cleavage directions; irregular fracture	porcelain
2.6–2.7	2 cleavage directions; irregular fracture	ceramics
2.6	no cleavage; conchoidal fracture	gemstones, concrete, glass, porcelain, sandpaper, lenses
8.9	no cleavage; hackly fracture	wiring, brass, bronze, coins
3.5	4 cleavage directions; irregular to conchoidal fracture	gemstones, drilling
2.3	1 cleavage direction; irregular fracture	pencils, paints, lubricants, batteries
2.95	2 cleavage directions; irregular fracture; reacts with hydrochloric acid	no important industrial uses
2.7	3 cleavage directions; irregular fracture; reacts with weak acid; double refraction	cements, soil conditioner, whitewash, construction materials
3.0–3.3	4 cleavage directions; irregular fracture; some varieties fluoresce	hydrofluoric acid, steel, glass, fiberglass, pottery, enamel
2.1–2.2	3 cleavage directions; splintery to conchoidal fracture; salty taste	tanning hides, salting icy roads, food preservation
5.2–5.3	no cleavage; splintery fracture; magnetic when heated	iron ore for steel, pigments
5.2	no cleavage; splintery fracture; magnetic	iron ore
3.0	3 cleavage directions; conchoidal to splintery fracture	soil conditioner, sulfuric acid
2.3	3 cleavage directions; conchoidal to splintery fracture	plaster of Paris, wallboard, soil conditioner
7.4–7.6	3 cleavage directions; irregular fracture	batteries, paints
5	no cleavage; conchoidal to splintery fracture	sulfuric acid

Sky Maps

Spring

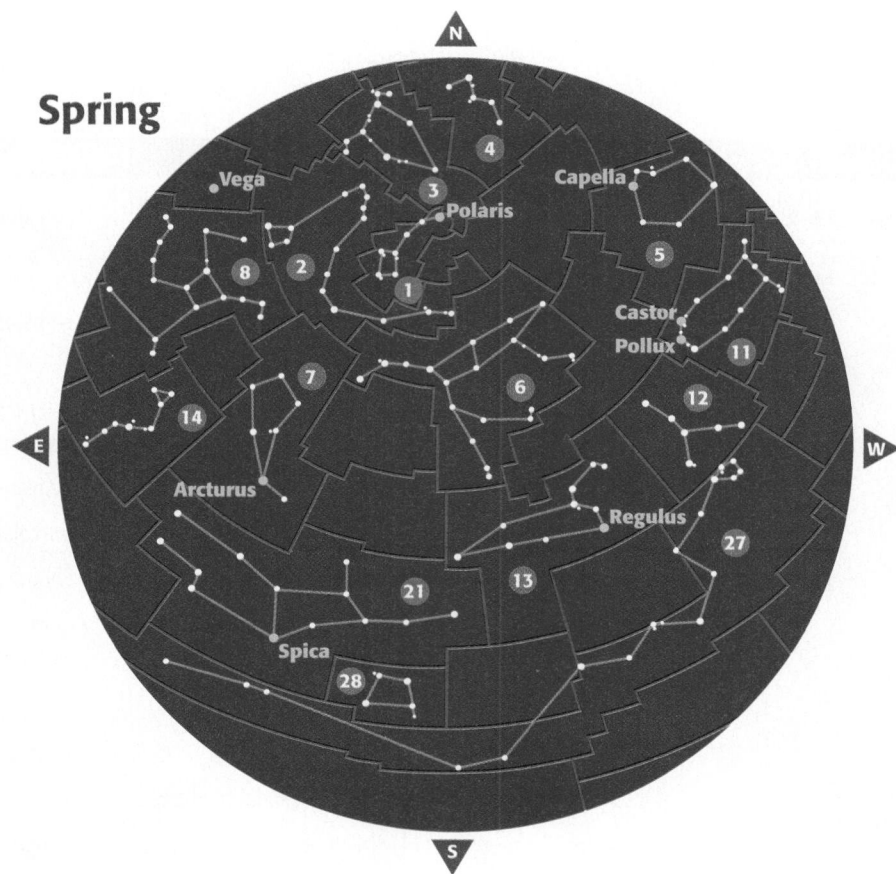

Summer

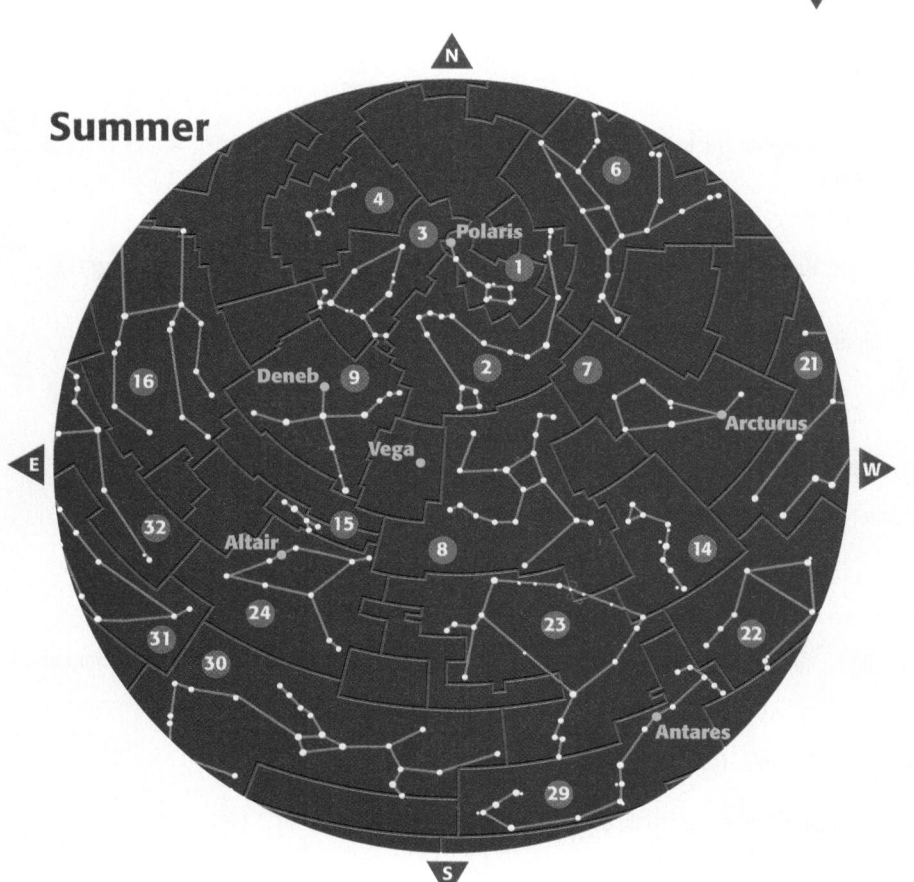

Constellations

1 **Ursa Minor**
2 **Draco**
3 **Cepheus**
4 **Cassiopeia**
5 **Auriga**
6 **Ursa Major**
7 **Bootes**
8 **Hercules**
9 **Cygnus**
10 **Perseus**
11 **Gemini**
12 **Cancer**
13 **Leo**
14 **Serpens**
15 **Sagitta**
16 **Pegasus**
17 **Pisces**

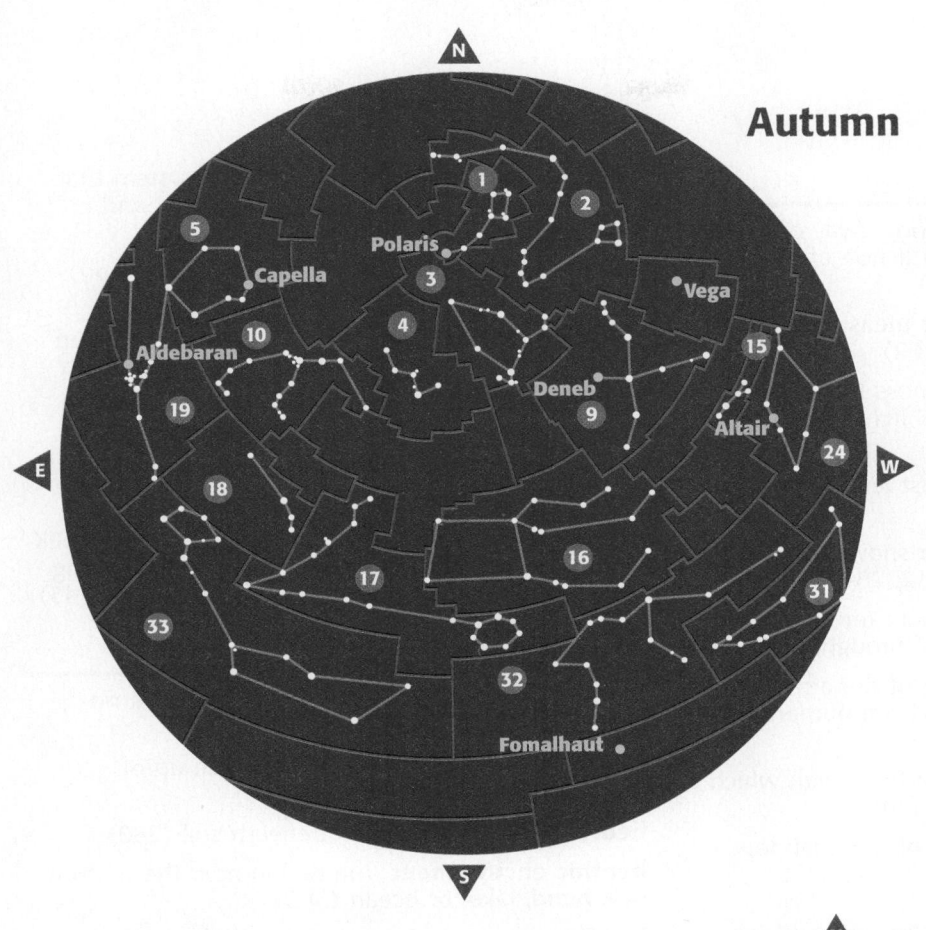

Autumn

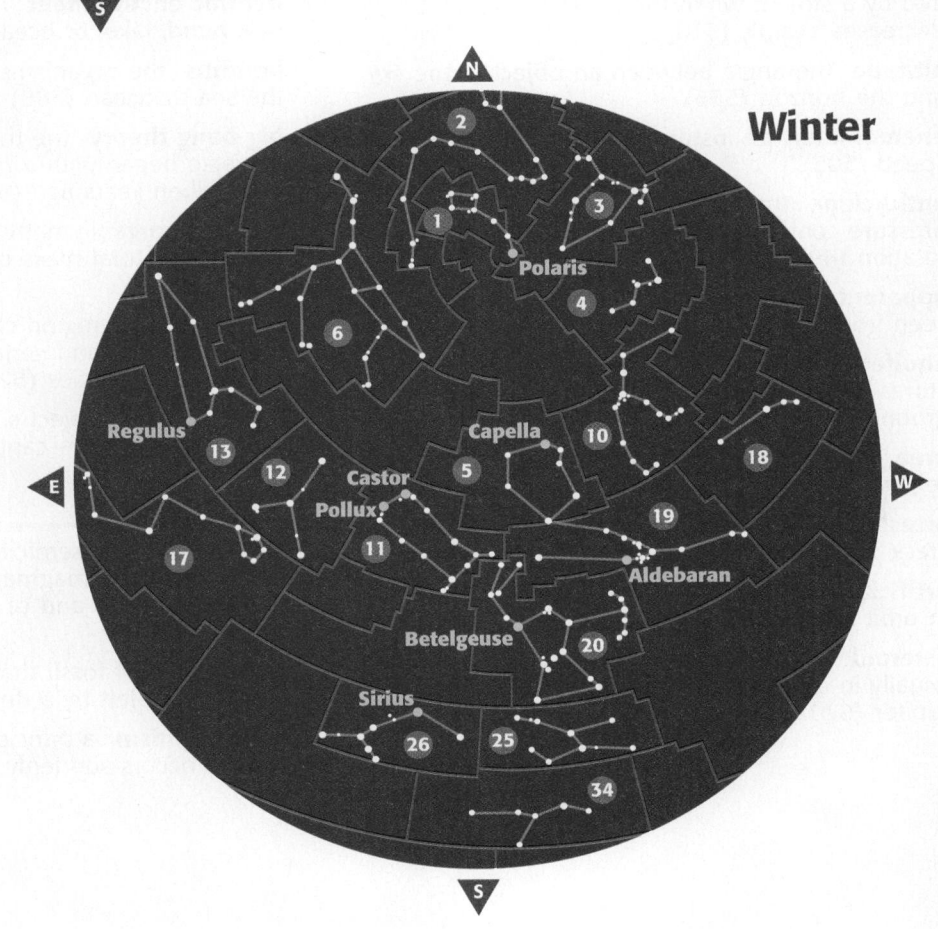

Winter

Constellations

18 **Aries**
19 **Taurus**
20 **Orion**
21 **Virgo**
22 **Libra**
23 **Ophiuchus**
24 **Aquila**
25 **Lepus**
26 **Canis Major**
27 **Hydra**
28 **Corvus**
29 **Scorpius**
30 **Sagittarius**
31 **Capricornus**
32 **Aquarius**
33 **Cetus**
34 **Columba**

Glossary

A

abrasion the grinding and wearing away of rock surfaces through the mechanical action of other rock or sand particles (279, 349)

absolute dating any method of measuring the age of an event or object in years (162)

absolute magnitude the brightness that a star would have at a distance of 32.6 light-years from Earth (586)

abyssal plain a large, flat, almost level area of the deep-ocean basin (384)

acid precipitation rain, sleet, or snow that contains a high concentration of acids (132, 281, 467)

air mass a large body of air where temperature and moisture content are similar throughout (490)

air pollution the contamination of the atmosphere by the introduction of pollutants from human and natural sources (464)

air pressure the measure of the force with which air molecules push on a surface (449)

alluvial fan a fan-shaped mass of material deposited by a stream when the slope of the land decreases sharply (318)

altitude the angle between an object in the sky and the horizon (566)

anemometer an instrument used to measure wind speed (505)

anticyclone the rotation of air around a high-pressure center in the direction opposite to Earth's rotation (494)

apparent magnitude the brightness of a star as seen from the Earth (586)

aquifer a body of rock or sediment that stores groundwater and allows the flow of groundwater (321)

area a measure of the size of a surface or a region (24)

artesian spring a spring whose water flows from a crack in the cap rock over the aquifer (323)

artificial satellite any human-made object placed in orbit around a body in space (688)

asteroid a small, rocky object that orbits the sun, usually in a band between the orbits of Mars and Jupiter (670)

asteroid belt the region of the solar system that is between the orbits of Mars and Jupiter and in which most asteroids orbit (670)

asthenosphere the soft layer of the mantle on which the tectonic plates move (192)

astronomical unit the average distance between the Earth and the sun; approximately 150 million kilometers (symbol, AU) (645)

astronomy the study of the universe (9, 554)

atmosphere a mixture of gases that surrounds a planet or moon (448)

azimuthal projection (az uh MYOOTH uhl proh JEK shuhn) a map projection that is made by moving the surface features of the globe onto a plane (45)

B

barometer an instrument that measures atmospheric pressure (505)

beach an area of the shoreline made up of material deposited by waves (346)

bedrock the layer of rock beneath soil (288)

benthic environment the region near the bottom of a pond, lake, or ocean (389)

benthos the organisms that live at the bottom of the sea or ocean (388)

big bang theory the theory that states that the universe began with a tremendous explosion about 13.7 billion years ago (601)

biomass organic matter that can be a source of energy; the total mass of the organisms in a given area (139)

biome a large region characterized by a specific type of climate and certain types of plant and animal communities (524)

black hole an object so massive and dense that even light cannot escape its gravity (595)

C

caldera a large, semicircular depression that forms when the magma chamber below a volcano partially empties and causes the ground above to sink (258)

cast a type of fossil that forms when sediments fill in the cavity left by a decomposed organism (168)

catastrophism a principle that states that geologic change occurs suddenly (153)

channel the path that a stream follows (311)

chemical energy the energy released when a chemical compound reacts to produce new compounds (136)

chemical weathering the process by which rocks break down as a result of chemical reactions (281)

cleavage the splitting of a mineral along smooth, flat surfaces (71)

climate the average weather conditions in an area over a long period of time (518)

cloud a collection of small water droplets or ice crystals suspended in the air, which forms when the air is cooled and condensation occurs (486)

coal a fossil fuel that forms underground from partially decomposed plant material (128)

comet a small body of ice, rock, and cosmic dust that follows an elliptical orbit around the sun and that gives off gas and dust in the form of a tail as it passes close to the sun (668)

composition the chemical makeup of a rock; describes either the minerals or other materials in the rock (95)

compound a substance made up of atoms of two or more different elements joined by chemical bonds (67)

compression stress that occurs when forces act to squeeze an object (206)

condensation the change of state from a gas to a liquid (485)

conic projection a map projection that is made by moving the surface features of the globe onto a cone (44)

constellation a region of the sky that contains a recognizable star pattern and that is used to describe the location of objects in space (564)

continental drift the hypothesis that states that the continents once formed a single landmass, broke up, and drifted to their present locations (198)

continental rise the gently sloping section of the continental margin located between the continental slope and the abyssal plain (384)

continental shelf the gently sloping section of the continental margin located between the shoreline and the continental slope (384)

continental slope the steeply inclined section of the continental margin located between the continental rise and the continental shelf (384)

contour interval the difference in elevation between one contour line and the next (51)

contour line a line that connects points of equal elevation (50)

convection the transfer of thermal energy by the circulation or movement of a liquid or gas (455)

convergent boundary the boundary formed by the collision of two lithospheric plates (203)

core the central part of the Earth below the mantle (191, 627)

Coriolis effect the apparent curving of the path of a moving object from an otherwise straight path due to the Earth's rotation (418, 460)

cosmology the study of the origin, properties, processes, and evolution of the universe (600)

crater a funnel-shaped pit near the top of the central vent of a volcano (258)

creep the slow downhill movement of weathered rock material (361)

crust the thin and solid outermost layer of the Earth above the mantle (190, 625)

crystal a solid whose atoms, ions, or molecules are arranged in a definite pattern (67)

cyclone an area in the atmosphere that has lower pressure than the surrounding areas and has winds that spiral toward the center (494)

cylindrical projection (suh LIN dri kuhl proh JEK shuhn) a map projection that is made by moving the surface features of the globe onto a cylinder (43)

D

day the time required for Earth to rotate once on its axis (554)

deep current a streamlike movement of ocean water far below the surface (419)

deflation a form of wind erosion in which fine, dry soil particles are blown away (349)

deformation the bending, tilting, and breaking of the Earth's crust; the change in the shape of rock in response to stress (225)

delta a fan-shaped mass of material deposited at the mouth of a stream (317)

density the ratio of the mass of a substance to the volume of the substance (25, 72)

deposition the process in which material is laid down (91, 316)

desalination (DEE SAL uh NAY shuhn) a process of removing salt from ocean water (397)

differential weathering the process by which softer, less weather resistant rocks wear away and leave harder, more weather resistant rocks behind (284)

divergent boundary the boundary between two tectonic plates that are moving away from each other (203)

divide the boundary between drainage areas that have streams that flow in opposite directions (310)

dune a mound of wind-deposited sand that keeps its shape even though it moves (350)

E

eclipse an event in which the shadow of one celestial body falls on another (663)

elastic rebound the sudden return of elastically deformed rock to its undeformed shape (225)

electromagnetic spectrum all of the frequencies or wavelengths of electromagnetic radiation (561)

element a substance that cannot be separated or broken down into simpler substances by chemical means (66)

elevation the height of an object above sea level (50, 522)

El Niño a change in the surface water temperature in the Pacific Ocean that produces a warm current (424)

eon (EE AHN) the largest division of geologic time (175)

epicenter the point on Earth's surface directly above an earthquake's starting point, or focus (230)

epoch (EP uhk) a subdivision of a geologic period (175)

equator the imaginary circle halfway between the poles that divides the Earth into the Northern and Southern Hemispheres (39)

era a unit of geologic time that includes two or more periods (175)

erosion the process by which wind, water, ice, or gravity transports soil and sediment from one location to another (91, 295, 308)

extinction the death of every member of a species (175)

extrusive igneous rock rock that forms as a result of volcanic activity at or near the Earth's surface (101)

F

fault a break in a body of rock along which one block slides relative to another (208)

floodplain an area along a river that forms from sediments deposited when the river overflows its banks (318)

focus the point along a fault at which the first motion of an earthquake occurs (230)

folding the bending of rock layers due to stress (207)

foliated describes the texture of metamorphic rock in which the mineral grains are arranged in planes or bands (109)

fossil the remains or physical evidence of an organism preserved by geological processes (166)

fossil fuel a nonrenewable energy resource formed from the remains of organisms that lived long ago (126)

fracture the manner in which a mineral breaks along either curved or irregular surfaces (71)

front the boundary between air masses of different densities and usually different temperatures (492)

G

galaxy a collection of stars, dust, and gas bound together by gravity (596)

gap hypothesis a hypothesis that is based on the idea that a major earthquake is more likely to occur along the part of an active fault where no earthquakes have occurred for a certain period of time (235)

gas giant a planet that has a deep, massive atmosphere, such as Jupiter, Saturn, Uranus, or Neptune (654)

gasohol a mixture of gasoline and alcohol that is used as a fuel (139)

geologic column an arrangement of rock layers in which the oldest rocks are at the bottom (157)

geologic time scale the standard method used to divide the Earth's long natural history into manageable parts (174)

geology the study of the origin, history, and structure of the Earth and the processes that shape the Earth (6)

geostationary orbit an orbit that is about 36,000 km above the Earth's surface and in which a satellite is above a fixed spot on the equator (689)

geothermal energy the energy produced by heat within the Earth (140)

glacial drift the rock material carried and deposited by glaciers (356)

glacier a large mass of moving ice (352)

global warming a gradual increase in average global temperature (457, 540)

globular cluster a tight group of stars that looks like a ball and contains up to 1 million stars (598)

greenhouse effect the warming of the surface and lower atmosphere of Earth that occurs when water vapor, carbon dioxide, and other gases absorb and reradiate thermal energy (456, 540)

H

half-life the time needed for half of a sample of a radioactive substance to undergo radioactive decay (163)

hardness a measure of the ability of a mineral to resist scratching (72)

horizon the line where the sky and the Earth appear to meet (566)

hot spot a volcanically active area of Earth's surface far from a tectonic plate boundary (264)

H-R diagram Hertzsprung-Russell diagram, a graph that shows the relationship between a star's surface temperature and absolute magnitude (592)

humidity the amount of water vapor in the air (483)

humus dark, organic material formed in soil from the decayed remains of plants and animals (290)

hurricane a severe storm that develops over tropical oceans and whose strong winds of more than 120 km/h spiral in toward the intensely low-pressure storm center (499)

hydroelectric energy electrical energy produced by falling water (138)

hypothesis (hie PAHTH uh sis) an explanation that is based on prior scientific research or observations and that can be tested (14)

I

ice age a long period of climate cooling during which ice sheets cover large areas of Earth's surface; also known as a *glacial period* (536)

index contour on a map, a darker, heavier contour line that is usually every fifth line and that indicates a change in elevation (51)

index fossil a fossil that is found in the rock layers of only one geologic age and that is used to establish the age of the rock layers (170)

intrusive igneous rock rock formed from the cooling and solidification of magma beneath the Earth's surface (100)

isobar a line that is drawn on a weather map and that connects points of equal pressure (507)

isotope an atom that has the same number of protons (or the same atomic number) as other atoms of the same element do but that has a different number of neutrons (and thus a different atomic mass) (162)

J

jet stream a narrow belt of strong winds that blow in the upper troposphere (462)

L

landslide the sudden movement of rock and soil down a slope (359)

La Niña a change in the eastern Pacific Ocean in which the surface water temperature becomes unusually cool (424)

latitude the distance north or south from the equator; expressed in degrees (39, 519)

lava plateau a wide, flat landform that results from repeated nonexplosive eruptions of lava that spread over a large area (259)

leaching the removal of substances that can be dissolved from rock, ore, or layers of soil due to the passing of water (290)

lightning an electric discharge that takes place between two oppositely charged surfaces, such as between a cloud and the ground, between two clouds, or between two parts of the same cloud (497)

light-year the distance that light travels in one year; about 9.46 trillion kilometers (568, 587)

lithosphere the solid, outer layer of the Earth that consists of the crust and the rigid upper part of the mantle (192)

load the materials carried by a stream; *also* the mass of rock overlying a geological structure (312)

loess (LOH ES) very fertile sediments of quartz, feldspar, hornblende, mica, and clay deposited by the wind (350)

longitude the distance east and west from the prime meridian; expressed in degrees (40)

longshore current a water current that travels near and parallel to the shoreline (429)

low earth orbit an orbit that is less than 1,500 km above the Earth's surface (689)

luster the way in which a mineral reflects light (70)

M

magma chamber the body of molten rock that feeds a volcano (252)

magnetic declination the difference between the magnetic north and the true north (38)

main sequence the location on the H-R diagram where most stars lie; it has a diagonal pattern from the lower right (low temperature and luminosity) to the upper left (high temperature and luminosity) (593)

mantle the layer of rock between the Earth's crust and core (191, 625)

map a representation of the features of a physical body such as Earth (36)

mass a measure of the amount of matter in an object (24)

mass movement a movement of a section of land down a slope (358)

mechanical weathering the breakdown of rock into smaller pieces by physical means (278)

mesosphere the strong, lower part of the mantle between the asthenosphere and the outer core (193); *also* the layer of the atmosphere between the stratosphere and the thermosphere and in which temperature decreases as altitude increases (451)

meteor a bright streak of light that results when a meteoroid burns up in the Earth's atmosphere (671)

meteorite a meteoroid that reaches the Earth's surface without burning up completely (671)

meteoroid a relatively small, rocky body that travels through space (671)

meteorology the scientific study of the Earth's atmosphere, especially in relation to weather and climate (8)

meter the basic unit of length in the SI (symbol, m) (23)

microclimate the climate of a small area (534)

mid-ocean ridge a long, undersea mountain chain that forms along the floor of the major oceans (385)

mineral a naturally formed, inorganic solid that has a definite chemical structure (66)

model a pattern, plan, representation, or description designed to show the structure or workings of an object, system, or concept (18)

mold a mark or cavity made in a sedimentary surface by a shell or other body (168)

month a division of the year that is based on the orbit of the moon around the Earth (554)

mudflow the flow of a mass of mud or rock and soil mixed with a large amount of water (360)

N

NASA the **N**ational **A**eronautics and **S**pace **A**dministration (685)

natural gas a mixture of gaseous hydrocarbons located under the surface of the Earth, often near petroleum deposits; used as a fuel (127)

natural resource any natural material that is used by humans, such as water, petroleum, minerals, forests, and animals (122)

neap tide a tide of minimum range that occurs during the first and third quarters of the moon (434)

nebula a large cloud of gas and dust in interstellar space; a region in space where stars are born or where stars explode at the end of their lives (598, 614)

nekton all organisms that swim actively in open water, independent of currents (388)

neutron star a star that has collapsed under gravity to the point that the electrons and protons have smashed together to form neutrons (594)

nonfoliated describes the texture of metamorphic rock in which the mineral grains are not arranged in planes or bands (110)

nonpoint-source pollution pollution that comes from many sources rather than from a single, specific site (326, 400)

nonrenewable resource a resource that forms at a rate that is much slower than the rate at which it is consumed (123)

nonsilicate mineral a mineral that does not contain compounds of silicon and oxygen (68)

nuclear energy the energy released by a fission or fusion reaction; the binding energy of the atomic nucleus (134)

nuclear fusion the combination of the nuclei of small atoms to form a larger nucleus; releases energy (620)

O

ocean current a movement of ocean water that follows a regular pattern (416)

oceanography the scientific study of the sea (7)

ocean trench a steep and long depression in the deep-sea floor that runs parallel to a chain of volcanic islands or a continental margin (385)

open cluster a group of stars that are close together relative to surrounding stars (598)

orbit the path that a body follows as it travels around another body in space (630)

ore a natural material whose concentration of economically valuable minerals is high enough for the material to be mined profitably (76)

P

paleontology the scientific study of fossils (154)

parallax an apparent shift in the position of an object when viewed from different locations (587)

parent rock a rock formation that is the source of soil (288)

pelagic environment in the ocean, the zone near the surface or at middle depths, beyond the sublittoral zone and above the abyssal zone (392)

period a unit of geologic time into which eras are divided (175)

permeability the ability of a rock or sediment to let fluids pass through its open spaces, or pores (321)

petroleum a liquid mixture of complex hydrocarbon compounds; used widely as a fuel source (127)

phase the change in the sunlit area of one celestial body as seen from another celestial body (662)

plankton the mass of mostly microscopic organisms that float or drift freely in freshwater and marine environments (388)

plate tectonics the theory that explains how large pieces of the Earth's outermost layer, called *tectonic plates,* move and change shape (202)

point-source pollution pollution that comes from a specific site (326, 401)

polar easterlies prevailing winds that blow from east to west between 60° and 90° latitude in both hemispheres (460)

polar zone the North or South Pole and the surrounding region (533)

porosity the percentage of the total volume of a rock or sediment that consists of open spaces (321)

precipitation any form of water that falls to the Earth's surface from the clouds (488)

prevailing winds winds that blow mainly from one direction during a given period (521)

prime meridian the meridian, or line of longitude, that is designated as 0° longitude (40)

prograde rotation the counterclockwise spin of a planet or moon as seen from above the planet's North Pole; rotation in the same direction as the sun's rotation (649)

pulsar a rapidly spinning neutron star that emits rapid pulses of radio and optical energy (594)

P wave a seismic wave that causes particles of rock to move in a back-and-forth direction (228)

Q

quasar a very luminous, starlike object that generates energy at a high rate; quasars are thought to be the most distant objects in the universe (599)

R

radiation the transfer of energy as electromagnetic waves (454)

radioactive decay the process in which a radioactive isotope tends to break down into a stable isotope of the same element or another element (162)

radiometric dating a method of determining the age of an object by estimating the relative percentages of a radioactive (parent) isotope and a stable (daughter) isotope (163)

recharge zone an area in which water travels downward to become part of an aquifer (322)

reclamation the process of returning land to its original condition after mining is completed (77)

recycling the process of recovering valuable or useful materials from waste or scrap; the process of reusing some items (125)

red giant a large, reddish star late in its life cycle (591)

reflecting telescope a telescope that uses a curved mirror to gather and focus light from distant objects (559)

refracting telescope a telescope that uses a set of lenses to gather and focus light from distant objects (559)

relative dating any method of determining whether an event or object is older or younger than other events or objects (156)

relative humidity the ratio of the amount of water vapor in the air to the maximum amount of water vapor the air can hold at a set temperature (483)

relief the variations in elevation of a land surface (51)

remote sensing the process of gathering and analyzing information about an object without physically being in touch with the object (47)

renewable resource a natural resource that can be replaced at the same rate at which the resource is consumed (123)

retrograde rotation the clockwise spin of a planet or moon as seen from above the planet's North Pole (649)

revolution the motion of a body that travels around another body in space; one complete trip along an orbit (630)

rift valley a long, narrow valley that forms as tectonic plates separate (385)

rift zone an area of deep cracks that forms between two tectonic plates that are pulling away from each other (262)

rock a naturally occurring solid mixture of one or more minerals or organic matter (90)

rock cycle the series of processes in which a rock forms, changes from one type to another, is destroyed, and forms again by geological processes (90)

rocket a machine that uses escaping gas from burning fuel to move (684)

rock fall the rapid mass movement of rock down a steep slope or cliff (359)

rotation the spin of a body on its axis (630)

S

salinity a measure of the amount of dissolved salts in a given amount of liquid (376)

saltation the movement of sand or other sediments by short jumps and bounces that is caused by wind or water (348)

satellite a natural or artificial body that revolves around a planet (660)

scientific methods a series of steps followed to solve problems (13)

sea-floor spreading the process by which new oceanic lithosphere forms as magma rises toward the surface and solidifies (200)

seamount a submerged mountain on the ocean floor that is at least 1,000 m high and that has a volcanic origin (385)

seismic gap an area along a fault where relatively few earthquakes have occurred recently but where strong earthquakes have occurred in the past (235)

seismic wave a wave of energy that travels through the Earth and away from an earthquake in all directions (228)

seismogram a tracing of earthquake motion that is created by a seismograph (230)

seismograph an instrument that records vibrations in the ground and determines the location and strength of an earthquake (230)

seismology (siez MAHL uh jee) the study of earthquakes (224)

septic tank a tank that separates solid waste from liquids and that has bacteria that break down the solid waste (329)

sewage treatment plant a facility that cleans the waste materials found in water that comes from sewers or drains (328)

shoreline the boundary between land and a body of water (342)

silicate mineral a mineral that contains a combination of silicon, oxygen, and one or more metals (68)

smog photochemical haze that forms when sunlight acts on industrial pollutants and burning fuels (132)

soil a loose mixture of rock fragments, organic material, water, and air that can support the growth of vegetation (288)

soil conservation a method to maintain the fertility of the soil by protecting the soil from erosion and nutrient loss (294)

soil structure the arrangement of soil particles (289)

soil texture the soil quality that is based on the proportions of soil particles (289)

solar energy the energy received by the Earth from the sun in the form of radiation (136)

solar nebula the cloud of gas and dust that formed our solar system (615)

space probe an uncrewed vehicle that carries scientific instruments into space to collect scientific data (694)

space shuttle a reusable space vehicle that takes off like a rocket and lands like an airplane (701)

space station a long-term orbiting platform from which other vehicles can be launched or scientific research can be carried out (702)

spectrum the band of colors produced when white light passes through a prism (583)

spring tide a tide of increased range that occurs two times a month, at the new and full moons (434)

storm surge a local rise in sea level near the shore that is caused by strong winds from a storm, such as those from a hurricane (431)

strata layers of rock (singular, *stratum*) (102)

stratification the process in which sedimentary rocks are arranged in layers (105)

stratified drift a glacial deposit that has been sorted and layered by the action of streams or meltwater (357)

stratosphere the layer of the atmosphere that is above the troposphere and in which temperature increases as altitude increases (451)

streak the color of the powder of a mineral (71)

subsidence (suhb SIED'ns) the sinking of regions of the Earth's crust to lower elevations (212)

sunspot a dark area of the photosphere of the sun that is cooler than the surrounding areas and that has a strong magnetic field (622)

supernova a gigantic explosion in which a massive star collapses and throws its outer layers into space (594)

superposition a principle that states that younger rocks lie above older rocks if the layers have not been disturbed (156)

surface current a horizontal movement of ocean water that is caused by wind and that occurs at or near the ocean's surface (417, 523)

S wave a seismic wave that causes particles of rock to move in a side-to-side direction (228)

swell one of a group of long ocean waves that have steadily traveled a great distance from their point of generation (430)

T

tectonic plate a block of lithosphere that consists of the crust and the rigid, outermost part of the mantle (194)

telescope an instrument that collects electromagnetic radiation from the sky and concentrates it for better observation (558)

temperate zone the climate zone between the Tropics and the polar zone (530)

temperature a measure of how hot (or cold) something is; specifically, a measure of the average kinetic energy of the particles in an object (24)

tension stress that occurs when forces act to stretch an object (206)

terrestrial planet one of the highly dense planets nearest to the sun; Mercury, Venus, Mars, and Earth (648)

texture the quality of a rock that is based on the sizes, shapes, and positions of the rock's grains (96)

theory an explanation that ties together many hypotheses and observations (20)

thermal conduction the transfer of energy as heat through a material (455)

thermometer an instrument that measures and indicates temperature (505)

thermosphere the uppermost layer of the atmosphere, in which temperature increases as altitude increases (452)

thrust the pushing or pulling force exerted by the engine of an aircraft or rocket (686)

thunder the sound caused by the rapid expansion of air along an electrical strike (497)

thunderstorm a usually brief, heavy storm that consists of rain, strong winds, lightning, and thunder (496)

tidal range the difference in levels of ocean water at high tide and low tide (434)

tide the periodic rise and fall of the water level in the oceans and other large bodies of water (432)

till unsorted rock material that is deposited directly by a melting glacier (356)

topographic map (TAHP uh GRAF ik MAP) a map that shows the surface features of Earth (50)

tornado a destructive, rotating column of air that has very high wind speeds, is visible as a funnel-shaped cloud, and touches the ground (498)

trace fossil a fossilized mark that is formed in soft sediment by the movement of an animal (168)

trade winds prevailing winds that blow northeast from 30° north latitude to the equator and that blow southeast from 30° south latitude to the equator (460)

transform boundary the boundary between tectonic plates that are sliding past each other horizontally (203)

tributary a stream that flows into a lake or into a larger stream (310)

tropical zone the region that surrounds the equator and that extends from about 23° north latitude to 23° south latitude (526)

troposphere the lowest layer of the atmosphere, in which temperature decreases at a constant rate as altitude increases (451)

true north the direction to the geographic North Pole (38)

tsunami a giant ocean wave that forms after a volcanic eruption, submarine earthquake, or landslide (430)

U

unconformity a break in the geologic record created when rock layers are eroded or when sediment is not deposited for a long period of time (159)

undertow a subsurface current that is near shore and that pulls objects out to sea (429)

uniformitarianism a principle that states that geologic processes that occurred in the past can be explained by current geologic processes (153)

uplift the rising of regions of the Earth's crust to higher elevations (212)

upwelling the movement of deep, cold, and nutrient-rich water to the surface (423)

V

vent an opening at the surface of the Earth through which volcanic material passes (252)

volcano a vent or fissure in the Earth's surface through which magma and gases are expelled (250)

volume a measure of the size of a body or region in three-dimensional space (23)

W

water cycle the continuous movement of water from the ocean to the atmosphere to the land and back to the ocean (309, 379)

watershed the area of land that is drained by a water system (310)

water table the upper surface of underground water; the upper boundary of the zone of saturation (320)

weather the short-term state of the atmosphere, including temperature, humidity, precipitation, wind, and visibility (482, 518)

weathering the process by which rock materials are broken down by the action of physical or chemical processes (278)

westerlies prevailing winds that blow from west to east between 30° and 60° latitude in both hemispheres (460)

whitecap the bubbles in the crest of a breaking wave (430)

white dwarf a small, hot, dim star that is the left-over center of an old star (591)

wind the movement of air caused by differences in air pressure (458)

wind power the use of a windmill to drive an electric generator (137)

Y

year the time required for the Earth to orbit once around the sun (554)

Z

zenith the point in the sky directly above an observer on Earth (566)

Spanish Glossary

A

abrasion/abrasión proceso por el cual las superficies de las rocas se muelen o desgastan por medio de la acción mecánica de otras rocas y partículas de arena (279, 349)

absolute dating/datación absoluta cualquier método que sirve para determinar la edad de un suceso u objeto en años (162)

absolute magnitude/magnitud absoluta el brillo que una estrella tendría a una distancia de 32.6 años luz de la Tierra (586)

abyssal plain/llanura abisal un área amplia, llana y casi plana de la cuenca oceánica profunda (384)

acid precipitation/precipitación ácida lluvia, aguanieve o nieve que contiene una alta concentración de ácidos (132, 281, 467)

air mass/masa de aire un gran volumen de aire que tiene una temperatura y contenido de humedad similar en toda su extensión (490)

air pollution/contaminación del aire la contaminación de la atmósfera debido a la introducción de contaminantes provenientes de fuentes humanas y naturales (464)

air pressure/presión del aire la medida de la fuerza con la que las moléculas del aire empujan contra una superficie (449)

alluvial fan/abanico aluvial masa de materiales rocosos en forma de abanico, depositados por un arroyo cuando la pendiente del terreno disminuye bruscamente (318)

altitude/altitud el ángulo que se forma entre un objeto en el cielo y el horizonte (566)

anemometer/anemómetro un instrumento que se usa para medir la rapidez del viento (505)

anticyclone/anticiclón la rotación del aire alrededor de un centro de alta presión en dirección opuesta a la rotación de la Tierra (494)

apparent magnitude/magnitud aparente el brillo de una estrella como se percibe desde la Tierra (586)

aquifer/acuífero un cuerpo rocoso o sedimento que almacena agua subterránea y permite que fluya (321)

area/área una medida del tamaño de una superficie o región (24)

artesian spring/manantial artesiano un manantial en el que el agua fluye a partir de una grieta en la capa de rocas que se encuentra sobre el acuífero (323)

artificial satellite/satélite artificial cualquier objeto hecho por los seres humanos y colocado en órbita alrededor de un cuerpo en el espacio (688)

asteroid/asteroide un objeto pequeño y rocoso que se encuentra en órbita alrededor del Sol, normalmente en una banda entre las órbitas de Marte y Júpiter (670)

asteroid belt/cinturón de asteroides la región del Sistema Solar que está entre las órbitas de Marte y Júpiter, en la que la mayoría de los asteroides se encuentran en órbita (670)

asthenosphere/astenosfera la capa blanda del manto sobre la que se mueven las placas tectónicas (192)

astronomical unit/unidad astronómica la distancia promedio entre la Tierra y el Sol; aproximadamente 150 millones de kilómetros (símbolo: UA) (645)

astronomy/astronomía el estudio del universo (9, 554)

atmosphere/atmósfera una mezcla de gases que rodea un planeta o una luna (448)

azimuthal projection/proyección azimutal una proyección cartográfica que se hace al transferir las características de la superficie del globo a un plano (45)

B

barometer/barómetro un instrumento que mide la presión atmosférica (505)

beach/playa un área de la costa formada por materiales depositados por las olas (346)

bedrock/lecho de roca la capa de rocas que está debajo del suelo (288)

benthic environment/ambiente béntico la región que se encuentra cerca del fondo de una laguna, lago u océano (389)

benthos/benthos los organismos que viven en el fondo del mar o del océano (388)

big bang theory/teoría del Big Bang la teoría que establece que el universo comenzó con una tremenda explosión hace aproximadamente 13.7 mil millones de años (601)

biomass/biomasa materia orgánica que puede ser una fuente de energía; la masa total de los organismos en un área determinada (139)

biome/bioma una región extensa caracterizada por un tipo de clima específico y ciertos tipos de comunidades de plantas y animales (524)

black hole/hoyo negro un objeto tan masivo y denso que ni siquiera la luz puede salir de su campo gravitacional (595)

C

caldera/caldera una depresión grande y semicircular que se forma cuando se vacía parcialmente la cámara de magma que hay debajo de un volcán, lo cual hace que el suelo se hunda (258)

cast/molde un tipo de fósil que se forma cuando un organismo descompuesto deja una cavidad que es llenada por sedimentos (168)

catastrophism/catastrofismo un principio que establece que los cambios geológicos ocurren súbitamente (153)

channel/canal el camino que sigue un arroyo (311)

chemical energy/energía química la energía que se libera cuando un compuesto químico reacciona para producir nuevos compuestos (136)

chemical weathering/desgaste químico el proceso por medio del cual las rocas se fragmentan como resultado de reacciones químicas (281)

cleavage/exfoliación el agrietamiento de un mineral en sus superficies lisas y planas (71)

climate/clima las condiciones promedio del tiempo en un área durante un largo período de tiempo (518)

cloud/nube un conjunto de pequeñas gotitas de agua o cristales de hielo suspendidos en el aire, que se forma cuando el aire se enfría y ocurre condensación (486)

coal/carbón un combustible fósil que se forma en el subsuelo a partir de materiales vegetales parcialmente descompuestos (128)

comet/cometa un cuerpo pequeño formado por hielo, roca y polvo cósmico que sigue una órbita elíptica alrededor del Sol y que libera gas y polvo, los cuales forman una cola al pasar cerca del Sol (668)

composition/composición la constitución química de una roca; describe los minerales u otros materiales presentes en ella (95)

compound/compuesto una substancia formada por átomos de dos o más elementos diferentes unidos por enlaces químicos (67)

compression/compresión estrés que se produce cuando distintas fuerzas actúan para estrechar un objeto (206)

condensation/condensación el cambio de estado de gas a líquido (485)

conic projection/proyección cónica una proyección cartográfica que se hace al transferir las características de la superficie del globo a un cono (44)

constellation/constelación una región del cielo que contiene un patrón reconocible de estrellas y que se utiliza para describir la ubicación de los objetos en el espacio (564)

continental drift/deriva continental la hipótesis que establece que alguna vez los continentes formaron una sola masa de tierra, se dividieron y se fueron a la deriva hasta terminar en sus ubicaciones actuales (198)

continental rise/elevación continental la sección del margen continental que tiene un ligero declive, ubicada entre el talud continental y la llanura abisal (384)

continental shelf/plataforma continental la sección del margen continental que tiene un ligero declive, ubicada entre la costa y el talud continental (384)

continental slope/talud continental la sección del margen continental que tiene una gran inclinación, ubicada entre la elevación continental y la plataforma continental (384)

contour interval/distancia entre las curvas de nivel la diferencia en elevación entre una curva de nivel y la siguiente (51)

contour line/curva de nivel una línea que une puntos que tienen la misma elevación (50)

convection/convección la transferencia de energía térmica mediante la circulación o el movimiento de un líquido o gas (455)

convergent boundary/límite convergente el límite que se forma debido al choque de dos placas de la litosfera (203)

core/núcleo la parte central de la Tierra, debajo del manto (191, 627)

Coriolis effect/efecto de Coriolis la desviación aparente de la trayectoria recta que experimentan los objetos en movimiento debido a la rotación de la Tierra (418, 460)

Spanish Glossary

cosmology/cosmología el estudio del origen, propiedades, procesos y evolución del universo (600)

crater/cráter una depresión con forma de embudo que se encuentra cerca de la parte superior de la chimenea central de un volcán (258)

creep/arrastre el movimiento lento y descendente de materiales rocosos desgastados (361)

crust/corteza la capa externa, delgada y sólida de la Tierra, que se encuentra sobre el manto (190, 625)

crystal/cristal un sólido cuyos átomos, iones o moléculas están ordenados en un patrón definido (67)

cyclone/ciclón un área de la atmósfera que tiene una presión menor que la de las áreas circundantes y que tiene vientos que giran en espiral hacia el centro (494)

cylindrical projection/proyección cilíndrica una proyección cartográfica que se hace al transferir las características de la superficie del globo a un cilindro (43)

D

day/día el tiempo que se requiere para que la Tierra rote una vez sobre su eje (554)

deep current/corriente profunda un movimiento del agua del océano que es similar a una corriente y ocurre debajo de la superficie (419)

deflation/deflación una forma de erosión del viento en la que se mueven partículas de suelo finas y secas (349)

deformation/deformación el proceso de doblar, inclinar y romper la corteza de la Tierra; el cambio en la forma de una roca en respuesta a la tensión (225)

delta/delta un depósito de materiales rocosos en forma de abanico ubicado en la desembocadura de un río (317)

density/densidad la relación entre la masa de una substancia y su volumen (25, 72)

deposition/deposición el proceso por medio del cual un material se deposita (91, 316)

desalination/desalación (o desalinización) un proceso de remoción de sal del agua del océano (397)

differential weathering/desgaste diferencial el proceso por medio cual las rocas más suaves y menos resistentes al clima se desgastan y las rocas más duras y resistentes al clima permanecen (284)

divergent boundary/límite divergente el límite entre dos placas tectónicas que se están separando una de la otra (203)

divide/división el límite entre áreas de drenaje que tienen corrientes que fluyen en direcciones opuestas (310)

dune/duna un montículo de arena depositada por el viendo que conserva su forma incluso cuando se mueve (350)

E

eclipse/eclipse un suceso en el que la sombra de un cuerpo celeste cubre otro cuerpo celeste (663)

elastic rebound/rebote elástico ocurre cuando una roca deformada elásticamente vuelve súbitamente a su forma no deformada (225)

electromagnetic spectrum/espectro electromagnético todas las frecuencias o longitudes de onda de la radiación electromagnética (561)

element/elemento una substancia que no se puede separar o descomponer en substancias más simples por medio de métodos químicos (66)

elevation/elevación la altura de un objeto sobre el nivel del mar (50, 522)

El Niño/El Niño un cambio en la temperatura del agua superficial del océano Pacífico que produce una corriente caliente (424)

eon/eón la mayor división del tiempo geológico (175)

epicenter/epicentro el punto de la superficie de la Tierra que queda justo arriba del punto de inicio, o foco, de un terremoto (230)

epoch/época una subdivisión de un período geológico (175)

equator/ecuador el círculo imaginario que se encuentra a la mitad entre los polos y divide a la Tierra en los hemisferios norte y sur (39)

era/era una unidad de tiempo geológico que incluye dos o más períodos (175)

erosion/erosión el proceso por medio del cual el viento, el agua, el hielo o la gravedad transporta tierra y sedimentos de un lugar a otro (91, 295, 308)

extinction/extinción la muerte de todos los miembros de una especie (175)

extrusive igneous rock/roca ígnea extrusiva una roca que se forma como resultado de la actividad volcánica en la superficie de la Tierra o cerca de ella (101)

F

fault/falla una grieta en un cuerpo rocoso a lo largo de la cual un bloque se desliza respecto a otro (208)

floodplain/llanura de inundación un área a lo largo de un río formada por sedimentos que se depositan cuando el río se desborda (318)

focus/foco el punto a lo largo de una falla donde ocurre el primer movimiento de un terremoto (230)

folding/plegamiento fenómeno que ocurre cuando las capas de roca se doblan debido a la compresión (207)

foliated/foliada término que describe la textura de una roca metamórfica en la que los granos de mineral están ordenados en planos o bandas (109)

fossil/fósil los restos o las pruebas físicas de un organismo preservados por los procesos geológicos (166)

fossil fuel/combustible fósil un recurso energético no renovable formado a partir de los restos de organismos que vivieron hace mucho tiempo (126)

fracture/fractura la forma en la que se rompe un mineral a lo largo de superficies curvas o irregulares (71)

front/frente el límite entre masas de aire de diferentes desidades y, normalmente, diferentes temperaturas (492)

G

galaxy/galaxia un conjunto de estrellas, polvo y gas unidos por la gravedad (596)

gap hypothesis/hipótesis del intervalo una hipótesis que se basa en la idea de que es más probable que ocurra un terremoto importante a lo largo de la parte de una falla activa donde no se han producido terremotos durante un determinado período de tiempo (235)

gas giant/gigante gaseoso un planeta con una atmósfera masiva y profunda, como por ejemplo, Júpiter, Saturno, Urano o Neptuno (654)

gasohol/gasohol una mezcla de gasolina y alcohol que se usa como combustible (139)

geologic column/columna geológica un arreglo de las capas de roca en el que las rocas más antiguas están al fondo (157)

geologic time scale/escala de tiempo geológico el método estándar que se usa para dividir la larga historia natural de la Tierra en partes razonables (174)

geology/geología el estudio del origen, historia y estructura del planeta Tierra y los procesos que le dan forma (6)

geostationary orbit/órbita geoestacionaria una órbita que está a aproximadamente 36,000 km de la superficie terrestre, en la que un satélite permanece sobre un punto fijo en el ecuador (689)

geothermal energy/energía geotérmica la energía producida por el calor del interior de la Tierra (140)

glacial drift/deriva glacial el material rocoso que es transportado y depositado por los glaciares (356)

glacier/glaciar una masa grande de hielo en movimiento (352)

global warming/calentamiento global un aumento gradual de la temperatura global promedio (457, 540)

globular cluster/cúmulo globular un grupo compacto de estrellas que parece una bola y contiene hasta un millón de estrellas (598)

greenhouse effect/efecto de invernadero el calentamiento de la superficie y de la parte más baja de la atmósfera, el cual se produce cuando el vapor de agua, el dióxido de carbono y otros gases absorben y vuelven a irradiar la energía térmica (456, 540)

H

half-life/vida media el tiempo que tarda la mitad de la muestra de una substancia radiactiva en desintegrarse por desintegración radiactiva (163)

hardness/dureza una medida de la capacidad de un mineral de resistir ser rayado (72)

horizon/horizonte la línea donde parece que el cielo y la Tierra se unen (566)

hot spot/mancha caliente un área volcánicamente activa de la superficie de la Tierra que se encuentra lejos de un límite entre placas tectónicas (264)

H-R diagram/diagrama H-R diagrama de Hertzsprung-Russell; una gráfica que muestra la relación entre la temperatura de la superficie de una estrella y su magnitud absoluta (592)

humidity/humedad la cantidad de vapor de agua que hay en el aire (483)

humus/humus material orgánico obscuro que se forma en la tierra a partir de restos de plantas y animales en descomposición (290)

hurricane/huracán tormenta severa que se desarrolla sobre océanos tropicales, con vientos fuertes que soplan a más de 120 km/h y que se mueven en espiral hacia el centro de presión extremadamente baja de la tormenta (499)

hydroelectric energy/energía hidroeléctrica energía eléctrica producida por agua en caída (138)

hypothesis/hipótesis una explicación que se basa en observaciones o investigaciones científicas previas y que se puede probar (14)

I

ice age/edad de hielo un largo período de tiempo frío durante el cual grandes áreas de la superficie terrestre están cubiertas por capas de hielo; también conocido como período glacial (536)

index contour/índice de las curvas de nivel en un mapa, la curva de nivel que es más gruesa y oscura, la cual normalmente se encuentra cada quinta línea e indica un cambio en la elevación (51)

index fossil/fósil guía un fósil que se encuentra en las capas de roca de una sola era geológica y que se usa para establecer la edad de las capas de roca (170)

intrusive igneous rock/roca ígnea intrusiva una roca formada a partir del enfriamiento y solidificación del magma debajo de la superficie terrestre (100)

isobar/isobara una línea que se dibuja en un mapa meteorológico y conecta puntos de igual presión (507)

isotope/isótopo un átomo que tiene el mismo número de protones (o el mismo número atómico) que otros átomos del mismo elemento, pero que tiene un número diferente de neutrones (y, por lo tanto, otra masa atómica) (162)

J

jet stream/corriente en chorro un cinturón delgado de vientos fuertes que soplan en la parte superior de la troposfera (462)

L

landslide/derrumbamiento el movimiento súbito hacia abajo de rocas y suelo por una pendiente (359)

La Niña/La Niña un cambio en el océano Pacífico oriental por el cual el agua superficial se vuelve más fría que de costumbre (424)

latitude/latitud la distancia hacia el norte o hacia el sur del ecuador; se expresa en grados (39, 519)

lava plateau/meseta de lava un accidente geográfico amplio y plano que se forma debido a repetidas erupciones no explosivas de lava que se expanden por un área extensa (259)

leaching/lixiviación la remoción de substancias que pueden disolverse de rocas, menas o capas de suelo debido al paso del agua (290)

lightning/relámpago una descarga eléctrica que ocurre entre dos superficies que tienen carga opuesta, como por ejemplo, entre una nube y el suelo, entre dos nubes o entres dos partes de la misma nube (497)

light-year/año luz la distancia que viaja la luz en un año; aproximadamente 9.46 trillones de kilómetros (568, 587)

lithosphere/litosfera la capa externa y sólida de la Tierra que está formada por la corteza y la parte superior y rígida del manto (192)

load/carga los materiales que lleva un arroyo; también, la masa de rocas que recubre una estructura geológica (312)

loess/loess sedimentos muy fértiles de cuarzo, feldespato, horneblenda, mica y arcilla depositados por el viento (350)

longitude/longitud la distancia hacia el este y hacia el oeste del primer meridiano; se expresa en grados (40)

longshore current/corriente de ribera una corriente de agua que se desplaza cerca de la costa y paralela a ella (429)

low earth orbit/órbita terrestre baja una órbita ubicada a menos de 1,500 km sobre la superficie terrestre (689)

luster/brillo la forma en que un mineral refleja la luz (70)

M

magma chamber/cámara de magma la masa de roca fundida que alimenta un volcán (252)

magnetic declination/declinación magnética la diferencia entre el norte magnético y el norte verdadero (38)

main sequence/secuencia principal la ubicación en el diagrama H-R donde se encuentran la mayoría de las estrellas; tiene un patrón diagonal de la parte inferior derecha (baja temperatura y luminosidad) a la parte superior izquierda (alta temperatura y luminosidad) (593)

mantle/manto la capa de roca que se encuentra entre la corteza terrestre y el núcleo (191, 625)

map/mapa una representación de las características de un cuerpo físico, tal como la Tierra (36)

mass/masa una medida de la cantidad de materia que tiene un objeto (24)

mass movement/movimiento masivo un movimiento hacia abajo de una sección de terreno por una pendiente (358)

mechanical weathering/desgaste mecánico el rompimiento de una roca en pedazos más pequeños mediante medios físicos (278)

mesosphere/mesosfera la parte fuerte e inferior del manto que se encuentra entre la astenosfera y el núcleo externo (193); *también,* la capa de la atmósfera que se encuentra entre la estratosfera y la termosfera, en la cual la temperatura disminuye al aumentar la altitud (451)

meteor/meteoro un rayo de luz brillante que se produce cuando un meteoroide se quema en la atmósfera de la Tierra (671)

meteorite/meteorito un meteoroide que llega a la superficie de la Tierra sin quemarse por completo (671)

meteoroid/meteoroide un cuerpo rocoso relativamente pequeño que viaja en el espacio (671)

meteorology/meteorología el estudio científico de la atmósfera de la Tierra, sobre todo en lo que se relaciona al tiempo y al clima (8)

meter/metro la unidad fundamental de longitud en el sistema internacional de unidades (símbolo: m) (23)

microclimate/microclima el clima de un área pequeña (534)

mid-ocean ridge/dorsal oceánica una larga cadena submarina de montañas que se forma en el suelo de los principales océanos (385)

mineral/mineral un sólido natural e inorgánico que tiene una estructura química definida (66)

model/modelo un diseño, plan, representación o descripción cuyo objetivo es mostrar la estructura o funcionamiento de un objeto, sistema o concepto (18)

mold/molde una marca o cavidad hecha en una superficie sedimentaria por una concha u otro cuerpo (168)

month/mes una división del año que se basa en la órbita de la Luna alrededor de la Tierra (554)

mudflow/flujo de lodo el flujo de una masa de lodo o roca y suelo mezclados con una gran cantidad de agua (360)

N

NASA/NASA la Administración Nacional de Aeronáutica y del Espacio (685)

natural gas/gas natural una mezcla de hidrocarburos gaseosos que se encuentran debajo de la superficie de la Tierra, normalmente cerca de los depósitos de petróleo, y los cuales se usan como combustible (127)

natural resource/recurso natural cualquier material natural que es utilizado por los seres humanos, como agua, petróleo, minerales, bosques y animales (122)

neap tide/marea muerta una marea que tiene un rango mínimo, la cual ocurre durante el primer y el tercer cuartos de la Luna (434)

nebula/nebulosa una nube grande de gas y polvo en el espacio interestelar; una región en el espacio donde las estrellas nacen o donde explotan al final de su vida (598, 614)

nekton/necton todos los organismos que nadan activamente en las aguas abiertas, de manera independiente de las corrientes (388)

neutron star/estrella de neutrones una estrella que se ha colapsado debido a la gravedad hasta el punto en que los electrones y protones han chocado unos contra otros para formar neutrones (594)

nonfoliated/no foliada término que describe la textura de una roca metamórfica en la que los granos de mineral no están ordenados en planos ni bandas (110)

nonpoint-source pollution/contaminación no puntual contaminación que proviene de muchas fuentes, en lugar de provenir de un solo sitio específico (326, 400)

nonrenewable resource/recurso no renovable un recurso que se forma a una tasa que es mucho más lenta que la tasa a la que se consume (123)

nonsilicate mineral/mineral no-silicato un mineral que no contiene compuestos de sílice y oxígeno (68)

nuclear energy/energía nuclear la energía liberada por una reacción de fisión o fusión; la energía de enlace del núcleo atómico (134)

nuclear fusion/fusión nuclear combinación de los núcleos de átomos pequeños para formar un núcleo más grande; libera energía (620)

O

ocean current/corriente oceánica un movimiento del agua del océano que sigue un patrón regular (416)

oceanography/oceanografía el estudio científico del mar (7)

ocean trench/fosa oceánica una depresión empinada y larga del suelo marino profundo, paralela a una cadena de islas volcánicas o al margen continental (385)

open cluster/conglomerado abierto un grupo de estrellas que se encuentran juntas respecto a las estrellas que las rodean (598)

orbit/órbita la trayectoria que sigue un cuerpo al desplazarse alrededor de otro cuerpo en el espacio (630)

ore/mena un material natural cuya concentración de minerales con valor económico es suficientemente alta como para que el material pueda ser explotado de manera rentable (76)

P

paleontology/paleontología el estudio científico de los fósiles (154)

parallax/paralaje un cambio aparente en la posición de un objeto cuando se ve desde lugares distintos (587)

parent rock/roca precursora una formación rocosa que es la fuente a partir de la cual se origina el suelo (288)

pelagic environment/ambiente pelágico en el océano, la zona ubicada cerca de la superficie o en profundidades medias, más allá de la zona sublitoral y por encima de la zona abisal (392)

period/período una unidad de tiempo geológico en la que se dividen las eras (175)

permeability/permeabilidad la capacidad de una roca o sedimento de permitir que los fluidos pasen a través de sus espacios abiertos o poros (321)

petroleum/petróleo una mezcla líquida de compuestos hidrocarburos complejos; se usa ampliamente como una fuente de combustible (127)

phase/fase el cambio en el área iluminada de un cuerpo celeste según se ve desde otro cuerpo celeste (662)

plankton/plancton la masa de organismos en su mayoría microscópicos que flotan o se encuentran a la deriva en ambientes de agua dulce o marina (388)

plate tectonics/tectónica de placas la teoría que explica cómo se mueven y cambian de forma las placas tectónicas, que son grandes porciones de la capa más externa de la Tierra (202)

point-source pollution/contaminación puntual contaminación que proviene de un lugar específico (326, 401)

polar easterlies/vientos polares del este vientos preponderantes que soplan de este a oeste entre los 60° y los 90° de latitud en ambos hemisferios (460)

polar zone/zona polar el Polo Norte y el Polo Sur y la región circundante (533)

porosity/porosidad el porcentaje del volumen total de una roca o sedimento que está formado por espacios abiertos (321)

precipitation/precipitación cualquier forma de agua que cae de las nubes a la superficie de la Tierra (488)

prevailing winds/vientos prevalecientes vientos que soplan principalmente de una dirección durante un período de tiempo determinado (521)

prime meridian/meridiano de Greenwich el meridiano, o línea de longitud, que se designa como longitud 0° (40)

prograde rotation/rotación progresiva el giro en contra de las manecillas del reloj de un planeta o de una luna según lo vería un observador ubicado encima del Polo Norte del planeta; rotación en la misma dirección que la rotación del Sol (649)

pulsar/pulsar una estrella de neutrones que gira rápidamente y emite pulsaciones rápidas de energía radioeléctrica y óptica (594)

P wave/onda P una onda sísmica que hace que las partículas de roca se muevan en una dirección de atrás hacia delante (228)

Q

quasar/cuasar un objeto muy luminoso, parecido a una estrella, que genera energía a una gran velocidad; se piensa que los cuásares son los objetos más distantes del universo (599)

R

radiation/radiación la transferencia de energía en forma de ondas electromagnéticas (454)

radioactive decay/desintegración radiactiva el proceso por medio del cual un isótopo radiactivo tiende a desintegrarse y formar un isótopo estable del mismo elemento o de otro elemento (162)

radiometric dating/datación radiométrica un método para determinar la edad de un objeto estimando los porcentajes relativos de un isótopo radiactivo (precursor) y un isótopo estable (hijo) (163)

recharge zone/zona de recarga un área en la que el agua se desplaza hacia abajo para convertirse en parte de un acuífero (322)

reclamation/restauración el proceso de hacer que la tierra vuelva a su condición original después de que se terminan las actividades de explotación minera (77)

recycling/reciclar el proceso de recuperar materiales valiosos o útiles de los desechos o de la basura; el proceso de reutilizar algunas cosas (125)

red giant/gigante roja una estrella grande de color rojizo que se encuentra en una etapa avanzada de su vida (591)

reflecting telescope/telescopio reflector un telescopio que utiliza un espejo curvo para captar y enfocar la luz de objetos lejanos (559)

refracting telescope/telescopio refractante un telescopio que utiliza un conjunto de lentes para captar y enfocar la luz de objetos lejanos (559)

relative dating/datación relativa cualquier método que se utiliza para determinar si un acontecimiento u objeto es más viejo o más joven que otros acontecimientos u objetos (156)

relative humidity/humedad relativa la proporción de la cantidad de vapor de agua que hay en el aire respecto a la cantidad máxima de vapor de agua que el aire puede contener a una temperatura dada (483)

relief/relieve las variaciones en elevación de una superficie de terreno (51)

remote sensing/teledetección el proceso de recopilar y analizar información acerca de un objeto sin estar en contacto físico con el objeto (47)

renewable resource/recurso renovable un recurso natural que puede reemplazarse a la misma tasa a la que se consume (123)

retrograde rotation/rotación retrógrada el giro en el sentido de las manecillas del reloj de un planeta o de una luna según lo vería un observador ubicado encima del Polo Norte del planeta (649)

revolution/revolución el movimiento de un cuerpo que viaja alrededor de otro cuerpo en el espacio; un viaje completo a lo largo de una órbita (630)

rift valley/fosa tectónica un valle largo y estrecho que se forma cuando se separan las placas tectónicas (385)

rift zone/zona de rift un área de grietas profundas que se forma entre dos placas tectónicas que se están alejando una de la otra (262)

rock/roca una mezcla sólida de uno o más minerales o de materia orgánica que se produce de forma natural (90)

rock cycle/ciclo de las rocas la serie de procesos por medio de los cuales una roca se forma, cambia de un tipo a otro, se destruye y se forma nuevamente por procesos geológicos (90)

rocket/cohete un aparato que para moverse utiliza el gas de escape que se origina a partir de la combustión (684)

rock fall/desprendimiento de rocas el movimiento rápido y masivo de rocas por una pendiente empinada o un precipicio (359)

rotation/rotación el giro de un cuerpo alrededor de su eje (630)

S

salinity/salinidad una medida de la cantidad de sales disueltas en una cantidad determinada de líquido (376)

saltation/saltación el movimiento de la arena u otros sedimentos por medio de saltos pequeños y rebotes debido al viento o al agua (348)

satellite/satélite un cuerpo natural o artificial que gira alrededor de un planeta (660)

scientific methods/métodos científicos una serie de pasos que se siguen para solucionar problemas (13)

sea-floor spreading/expansión del suelo marino el proceso por medio del cual se forma nueva litosfera oceánica a medida que el magma se eleva hacia la superficie y se solidifica (200)

seamount/montaña submarina una montaña sumergida que se encuentra en el fondo del océano, la cual tiene por lo menos 1,000 m de altura y cuyo origen es volcánico (385)

seismic gap/brecha sísmica un área a lo largo de una falla donde han ocurrido relativamente pocos terremotos recientemente, pero donde se han producido terremotos fuertes en el pasado (235)

seismic wave/onda sísmica una onda de energía que viaja a través de la Tierra y se aleja de un terremoto en todas direcciones (228)

seismogram/sismograma una gráfica del movimiento de un terremoto elaborada por un sismógrafo (230)

seismograph/sismógrafo un instrumento que registra las vibraciones en el suelo y determina la ubicación y la fuerza de un terremoto (230)

seismology/sismología el estudio de los terremotos (224)

septic tank/tanque séptico un tanque que separa los desechos sólidos de los líquidos y que tiene bacterias que descomponen los desechos sólidos (329)

sewage treatment plant/planta de tratamiento de residuos una instalación que limpia los materiales de desecho que se encuentran en el agua procedente de cloacas o alcantarillas (328)

shoreline/orilla el límite entre la tierra y una masa de agua (342)

silicate mineral/mineral silicato un mineral que contiene una combinación de sílice, oxígeno y uno o más metales (68)

smog/esmog bruma fotoquímica que se forma cuando la luz solar actúa sobre contaminantes industriales y combustibles (132)

soil/suelo una mezcla suelta de fragmentos de roca, material orgánico, agua y aire en la que puede crecer vegetación (288)

soil conservation/conservación del suelo un método para mantener la fertilidad del suelo protegiéndolo de la erosión y la pérdida de nutrientes (294)

soil structure/estructura del suelo la organización de las partículas del suelo (289)

soil texture/textura del suelo la cualidad del suelo que se basa en las proporciones de sus partículas (289)

solar energy/energía solar la energía que la Tierra recibe del Sol en forma de radiación (136)

solar nebula/nebulosa solar la nube de gas y polvo que formó nuestro Sistema Solar (615)

space probe/sonda espacial un vehículo no tripulado que lleva instrumentos científicos al espacio con el fin de recopilar información científica (694)

space shuttle/transbordador espacial un vehículo espacial reutilizable que despega como un cohete y aterriza como un avión (701)

space station/estación espacial una plataforma orbital de largo plazo desde la cual pueden lanzarse otros vehículos o en la que pueden realizarse investigaciones científicas (702)

spectrum/espectro la banda de colores que se produce cuando la luz blanca pasa a través de un prisma (583)

spring tide/marea muerta una marea de mayor rango que ocurre dos veces al mes, durante la luna nueva y la luna llena (434)

storm surge/marea de tempestad un levantamiento local del nivel del mar cerca de la costa, el cual es resultado de los fuertes vientos de una tormenta, como por ejemplo, los vientos de un huracán (431)

strata/estratos capas de roca (102)

stratification/estratificación el proceso por medio del cual las rocas sedimentarias se acomodan en capas (105)

stratified drift/deriva estratificada un depósito glacial que ha formado capas debido a la acción de los arroyos o de las aguas de ablación (357)

stratosphere/estratosfera la capa de la atmósfera que se encuentra encima de la troposfera y en la que la temperatura aumenta al aumentar la altitud (451)

streak/veta el color del polvo de un mineral (71)

subsidence/hundimiento del terreno el hundimiento de regiones de la corteza terrestre a elevaciones más bajas (212)

sunspot/mancha solar un área oscura en la fotosfera del Sol que es más fría que las áreas que la rodean y que tiene un campo magnético fuerte (622)

supernova/supernova una explosión gigantesca en la que una estrella masiva se colapsa y lanza sus capas externas hacia el espacio (594)

superposition/superposición un principio que establece que las rocas más jóvenes se encontrarán sobre las rocas más viejas si las capas no han sido alteradas (156)

surface current/corriente superficial un movimiento horizontal del agua del océano que es producido por el viento y que ocurre en la superficie del océano o cerca de ella (417, 523)

S wave/onda S una onda sísmica que hace que las partículas de roca se muevan en una dirección de lado a lado (228)

swell/mar de leva un grupo de olas oceánicas grandes que se han desplazado una gran distancia desde el punto en el que se originaron (430)

T

tectonic plate/placa tectónica un bloque de litosfera formado por la corteza y la parte rígida y más externa del manto (194)

telescope/telescopio un instrumento que capta la radiación electromagnética del cielo y la concentra para mejorar la observación (558)

temperate zone/zona templada la zona climática ubicada entre los trópicos y la zona polar (530)

temperature/temperatura una medida de qué tan caliente (o frío) está algo; específicamente, una medida de la energía cinética promedio de las partículas de un objeto (24)

tension/tensión estrés que se produce cuando distintas fuerzas actúan para estirar un objeto (206)

terrestrial planet/planeta terrestre uno de los planetas muy densos que se encuentran más cerca del Sol; Mercurio, Venus, Marte y la Tierra (648)

texture/textura la cualidad de una roca que se basa en el tamaño, la forma y la posición de los granos que la forman (96)

theory/teoría una explicación que relaciona muchas hipótesis y observaciones (20)

thermal conduction/conducción térmica la transferencia de energía en forma de calor a través de un material (455)

thermometer/termómetro un instrumento que mide e indica la temperatura (505)

thermosphere/termosfera la capa más alta de la atmósfera, en la cual la temperatura aumenta a medida que la altitud aumenta (452)

thrust/empuje la fuerza de empuje o arrastre ejercida por el motor de un avión o cohete (686)

thunder/trueno el sonido producido por la expansión rápida del aire a lo largo de una descarga eléctrica (497)

thunderstorm/tormenta eléctrica una tormenta fuerte y normalmente breve que consiste en lluvia, vientos fuertes, relámpagos y truenos (496)

tidal range/rango de marea la diferencia en los niveles del agua del océano entre la marea alta y la marea baja (434)

tide/marea el ascenso y descenso periódico del nivel del agua en los océanos y otras masas grandes de agua (432)

till/arcilla glaciárica material rocoso desordenado que deposita directamente un glaciar que se está derritiendo (356)

topographic map/mapa topográfico un mapa que muestra las características superficiales de la Tierra (50)

tornado/tornado una columna destructiva de aire en rotación cuyos vientos se mueven a velocidades muy altas; se ve como una nube con forma de embudo y toca el suelo (498)

trace fossil/fósil traza una marca fosilizada que se forma en un sedimento blando debido al movimiento de un animal (168)

trade winds/vientos alisios vientos preponderantes que soplan hacia el noreste a partir de los 30° de latitud norte hacia el ecuador y que soplan hacia el sureste a partir de los 30° de latitud sur hacia el ecuador (460)

transform boundary/límite de transformación el límite entre placas tectónicas que se están deslizando horizontalmente una sobre otra (203)

tributary/afluente un arroyo que fluye a un lago o a otro arroyo más grande (310)

tropical zone/zona tropical la región que rodea el ecuador y se extiende desde aproximadamente 23° de latitud norte hasta 23° de latitud sur (526)

troposphere/troposfera la capa inferior de la atmósfera, en la que la temperatura disminuye a una tasa constante a medida que la altitud aumenta (451)

true north/norte verdadero la dirección al Polo Norte geográfico (38)

tsunami/tsunami una ola gigante del océano que se forma después de una erupción volcánica, terremoto submarino o desprendimiento de tierras (430)

U

unconformity/disconformidad una ruptura en el registro geológico, creada cuando las capas de roca se erosionan o cuando el sedimento no se deposita durante un largo período de tiempo (159)

undertow/resaca un corriente subsuperficial que está cerca de la orilla y que arrastra los objetos hacia el mar (429)

uniformitarianism/uniformitarianismo un principio que establece que es posible explicar los procesos geológicos que ocurrieron en el pasado en función de los procesos geológicos actuales (153)

uplift/levantamiento la elevación de regiones de la corteza terrestre a elevaciones más altas (212)

upwelling/surgencia el movimiento de las aguas profundas, frías y ricas en nutrientes hacia la superficie (423)

V

vent/chimenea una abertura en la superficie de la Tierra a través de la cual pasa material volcánico (252)

volcano/volcán una chimenea o fisura en la superficie de la Tierra a través de la cual se expulsan magma y gases (250)

volume/volumen una medida del tamaño de un cuerpo o región en un espacio de tres dimensiones (23)

W

water cycle/ciclo del agua el movimiento continuo del agua: del océano a la atmósfera, de la atmósfera a la tierra y de la tierra al océano (309, 379)

watershed/cuenca hidrográfica el área del terreno que es drenada por un sistema de agua (310)

water table/capa freática el nivel más alto del agua subterránea; el límite superior de la zona de saturación (320)

weather/tiempo el estado de la atmósfera a corto plazo que incluye la temperatura, la humedad, la precipitación, el viento y la visibilidad (482, 518)

weathering/meteorización el proceso por el cual se desintegran los materiales que forman las rocas debido a la acción de procesos físicos o químicos (278)

westerlies/vientos del oeste vientos preponderantes que soplan de oeste a este entre 30° y 60° de latitud en ambos hemisferios (460)

whitecap/cabrillas las burbujas de la cresta de una ola rompiente (430)

white dwarf/enana blanca una estrella pequeña, caliente y tenue que es el centro sobrante de una estrella vieja (591)

wind/viento el movimiento de aire producido por diferencias en la presión barométrica (458)

wind power/potencia eólica el uso de un molino de viento para hacer funcionar un generador eléctrico (137)

Y

year/año el tiempo que se requiere para que la Tierra le dé la vuelta al Sol una vez (554)

Z

zenith/cenit el punto del cielo situado directamente sobre un observador en la Tierra (566)

Index

Boldface page numbers refer to illustrative material, such as figures, tables, margin elements, photographs, and illustrations.

A

aa lava, 253, **253**
abrasion, 279, **279**, 298–299, 349, **349**
absolute dating, 162, **162**
   radioactive decay, 162–163, **162**
   radiometric dating, 163–165, **163, 164, 165**
absolute magnitude, 585, 586, **586,** 592, **592–593**
absorption spectrum, 584, **584**
abyssal plains, **384**, 385
abyssal zone, 391, **391**
acceleration, 798, 799
acidification, 467
acid precipitation, 281, **281**, 467–468, **467, 468**
   aquatic ecosystems and, 468, **468**
   effects on forests, 467, **467**
   from fossil fuels, 132, **132**
   weathering from, 281
acids, 797. *See also* pH
acid shock, 468
active tendon systems, **237**
active volcanoes, 264. *See also* volcanoes
adaptations, **528**, 529, 532
adding decimals, 791
adding fractions, 792
Adopt-a-Beach program, 404, **404**
aeration, zone of, 320, **320**
aerogels, **704**
aftershocks, **236**
agents of weathering, 278, 281
Age of Mammals (Cenozoic era), **174**, 177, **177**
Age of Reptiles (Mesozoic era), **174**, 176, **176**
ages
   geologic time scale, 174–177
   ice, 536–538, **536, 537, 538**
   of the universe, 602
agriculture, water use by, 330, **330**
air, weathering from, 283, **283**. *See also* acid precipitation
air masses, 490–495, **491**
   cold, 491, **491, 492–493**
   fronts and, 492–493, **492–493, 507**

source regions, 490, **490**
   warm, 491, **491, 492–493**
air pollution, 464–471
   acid precipitation from, 281, 467–468, **467, 468**
   awareness of, **470**
   cleaning up, 469–470, **469, 470**
   human health and, 469, **469**
   human sources of, 466, **466**
   indoor, 466, **466**
   lab on, **467**
   ozone hole and, 468, **468**
   particulate testing of, **467**
   plants and, **466**
   primary pollutants, 464, **464**
   secondary pollutants, 465, **465**
   smog, 132, **132**, 465, **465**
air pressure, 449, **449**. *See also* atmosphere
   calculation of, 799
   isobars, 507, **507**
   lab on, 471–472
   measurement of, 505, **505**
   pressure belts, 459, **459**
   sea breezes and, 462, **462**
   land breezes and, 462, **462**
   weather and, 494–495, **494**
Alaska Volcano Observatory, 273
alcohol, as fuel, 139, **139**
Aldrin, Edwin "Buzz," **701**
algae, 442, **628**
alkalinity, 327, **327**
Allowance Trading System, 470
"All Summer in a Day," 514
alluvial fans, 318, **318**
alpine glaciers, 352, **352,** 354, **354, 355**
alpines, 534
Alps, 210
alternative energy resources, 134–141
   biomass, 139, **139**
   fission, 134–135, **134, 135**
   fuel cells, 136, **136**
   fusion, 135, **135,** 149
   gasohol, 139, **139**
   geothermal, 140, **140**
   hydroelectric, 138, **138,** 148
   solar, 136–137, **136, 137**
   wind, 137, **137**
altitude, 565, **566**
   atmosphere and, 451, **451**
   clouds and, 487, **487**
   star location from, 566, **566**
altocumulus clouds, **487**
altostratus clouds, **487**
aluminum, 68, **69,** 77, **78**
Alvin, 7, 386

amber, 166, **166**
ammonia, **466**
ammonites, 168, **168,** 169, **169**
Andes Mountains, **210**
Andrew, Hurricane, 8, **8, 458**
Andromeda galaxy, **596**
anemometers, 505, **505**
angle of repose, 358, **358**
angler fish, **393**
angular unconformities, 160, **160**
anhydrite, **800–801**
animals
   earthquake prediction by, 246
   magnetite in, **68**
   weather forecasting by, **506,** 514
   weathering by, 280, **280**
Ankarana National Park, 338
annular eclipses, 663, **663**
Antarctica, 353, 468, **468**
Antarctic Bottom Water, 420
anthracite, 130, **130**
anticlines, 207, **207**
anticyclones, 494–495, **494, 495**
ants, weather and, 514
apatite, **72**
Apollo missions, 660, 701
Appalachian Mountains, 210, **210**
apparent magnitude, 585, 586, **586**
aqualung, 413
aquamarines, 79
aquatic ecosystems, 468, **468, 692.** *See also* marine life
aquifers, 321–322, **321, 322,** 330, **330.** *See also* groundwater
aragonite, **800–801**
Archean Eon, **174,** 175
arctic climates, 293, **293**
area, 24, **24**
   of squares or rectangles, 24, **24,** 793
   surface, 285, **285**
   of triangles, 793
   units of, **782**
Arecibo radio telescope, 562
arêtes, **355**
argon, **164**
Armstrong, Neil, 701, **701**
artesian formations, 323, **323**
artesian springs, 322–323, **323**
artifacts, American Indian, **15**
artificial reefs, 412
artificial satellites, 688–693, **689, 691**
   communications, 691
   earliest, 688, **688**
   lab on, **689**
   military, 690, **690**
   observing, **691**

Index

erosion (continued)
load and, 312, **312**
from ocean waves, 343, 344–345, **344–345**
from overgrazing, 305
from rivers, 308, **308,** 311–312, **311, 312**
rock cycle and, **91–92,** 92–93, **93,** 94
of shorelines, 342–347
of soil, 295, **295**
stages of rivers and, 313, **313**
unconformities and, 159–160, **159, 160**
underground, 324–325, **324, 325,** 338
wind, 279, **279,** 348–351, **348, 349, 350**
eruptions
climate change and, 256, **256,** 538, **538**
explosive, 251, **251,** 252, **252, 254**
gas release from, 264, 627, **627**
lab on, 266–267
lava flows from, 101, **101,** 250, **250, 251**
magma in, 252, **252**
nonexplosive, 250, **250,** 253
predicting, 264–265, 266–267
pyroclastic flows from, 253–255, **254**
water in, 252, 263, **263**
escape velocity, 687, **687**
Eta Carinae, 610, **610**
Europa, 665, 697
European Space Agency (ESA), 653, 681
evaporation
mineral formation from, **74**
of ocean water, 376, **379,** 397, **397, 420**
in the water cycle, **309, 379, 482**
evergreen trees, 531, 534
expansion of the universe, 570, 600–603
experimental groups, 786
experiments, controlled, 14
Explorer 1, 688
extinctions, 175–177, **175,** 539, **672**
of dinosaurs, 154, **154,** 177, 539
extinct volcanoes, 264
extrusive igneous rock, 101, **101**
Exxon Valdez oil spill, 402–403, **402, 403**
eyes, of hurricanes, **500**
eyes, rods and cones in, **584**
eye wall, **500**

F

Fahrenheit scale, 24, **24, 783**
fales, **527**
fault-block mountains, 211, **211**
fault blocks, 208, **208,** 210, 212, **212**
faults, 208, **208**
earthquakes and, 224, 226–227, **226–227**
effect on rock layers, 158, **158**
normal and reverse, 208–209, **208, 209,** 211, **211, 226, 227**
in rift zones, 212, **212**
strike-slip, 209, **209,** 226, **226**
types of, 226, **226–227**
feathered dinosaurs, 184
feldspar, **68, 75**
felsic rocks, 99, **99**
fine-grained texture, 96, **96,** 99, **99**
fingerprinting cars, **583**
first law of motion, Newton's, 798
fish, raining, 32
fish farming, 395, **395**
fishing, 394–395, **394, 395,** 412
fission, 134–135, **134, 135**
fissures, 101
flash floods, 319
Flashline Mars Arctic Research Station (FMARS), 712
flexible pipes, **237**
FLIP (Floating Instrument Platform), 32
flood plains, 314, **314,** 318–319, **318, 319**
floods, safety during, 502
fluorescence, **73**
fluorine, 68, **69**
fluorite, **69, 72, 800–801**
FMARS (Flashline Mars Arctic Research Station), 712
focus, earthquake, 230, **230**
fog, 486
folded mountains, 207, **207,** 210, **210**
folding, 158, **158,** 207, **207**
FoldNote instructions, 776–778, **776, 777, 778**
folds, 111, **111**
foliated rock, 109, **109**
Folk, Robert L., 119, **119**
fool's gold (pyrite), 70, **75,** 80–81, **800–801**
footwalls, 208–209, **208**
force, net, 799
forecasting earthquakes, 235–236, **235, 236,** 246
forecasting weather, 504–507, **504, 505, 506, 507,** 514
forensic science, **583**

forests
acid precipitation and, 467, **467**
cave formations in, 338
deforestation, **291**
northern coniferous, **533,** 534, **534**
temperate, 292, **292, 530,** 531, **531**
tropical rain, 291, **291,** 526, **526,** 527, **527**
formaldehyde, **466**
fossil fuels, 126–133, **126.** *See also* energy resources
coal, 76, 128, **128,** 469 (*see also* coal)
formation of, 129–130, **129, 130**
lab on, **129**
location of, 131, **131**
natural gas, 127, **127,** 129, **129,** 131
obtaining, 131, **131**
petroleum, 127, **127,** 129, **129,** 131–132
problems with, 132, **132,** 548
fossiliferous limestone, 104, **104**
fossils, 166–171, **166**
absolute dating of, 162–165, **162, 163, 164, 165**
casts, 168, **168**
dinosaur, 33, 168, **168,** 172, **172,** 184
fossilized organisms, 166–167, **166, 167**
frozen, 167, **167,** 184
geologic time and, 172–173, **172, 173**
index, 170–171, **170–171**
information from, 169–170
labs on, **157, 169,** 178–179
limestone from, 104, **104**
mineral replacement in, 167
molds, 168, **168**
record, 173, **173**
relative dating of, 156–161, **156, 157, 158, 159, 160**
trace, 168, **168**
four-corner fold instructions (FoldNote), 778, **778**
fractionation, **127**
fractions, 791
fracture, mineral, 71, **71, 801**
Fran, Hurricane, **499**
France, tidal bores in, 435
Frank landslide of 1903, 368
freezing, ocean currents and, **420**
freezing points, **24,** 98, **783**
friction, permeability and, 321, **321**
frogs, raining, 32
Fronk, Robert, 6
fronts, air, 492–493, **492–493,** 507
frost action, 278, **278**
frozen fossils, 167, **167,** 184
fuel cells, 136, **136**

Index

Index

Index

Index

Index

Index

rockets, definition of, 685, **685**
rocket science
  beginnings of, 684, **684**
  birth of NASA, 685, **685**
  development of, 684–687
  how rockets work, 686, **686**
  ion propulsion, 699, **699**
  orbital and escape velocities, 687, **687**
  water rockets, 706–707
  World War II and the development of, 685, **685**
rock falls, 359, **359**
rock salt, 67, **67**
Rocky Mountains, **207**
room temperature, **783**
rotation, planetary, 630, **630**, 648–649, **649, 656**
rubidium-strontium dating method, 164
rubies, 79
runoff, **309, 482**
Russell, Henry Norris, 591
rust, 283, **283**

S

safety, 22–25, 501–502, **502**
safety symbols, **25**
SAFOD (San Andreas Fault Observatory at Depth), 246
Saglet Fjord (Labrador), **111**
Sahara Desert, **521**, 529
salinity, 376–377, **376, 377,** 419, **420**
saltation, 348, **348**
salts
  desalination, 397, **397**
  mining of, 86
  salinity of ocean water, 376–377, **376, 377,** 419, **420**
  sodium chloride, 103, 376, **376**
  in soils, 292, **292**
Salyut 1, 702
Samoa, **527**
San Andreas Fault, 203, 209, **225,** 236, **236**
San Andreas Fault Observatory at Depth (SAFOD), 246
San Andreas Fault Zone, 227
sand, **289,** 346, **346**
sandbars, 347, **347**
sandstone, 96, **96,** 102–103, **102**
San Francisco, earthquake of 1906, 233, **233,** 240
Santa Ana wind, **463**
sapphires, 79
Sargasso Sea, **377**
satellite images, 383, **383**
satellite laser ranging (SLR), 220

satellites, 660, **660.** *See also* moon
  moons of other planets, 660–667, **665, 666**
satellites, artificial, 688–693
  communications, 691
  earliest, 688, **688**
  lab on, 689
  military, 690, **690**
  observing, **691**
  orbits for, 664, 688, **688,** 689, **689**
  remote sensing by, 47, **47,** 692–693, **692**
  weather, 506, 691
saturated air, 483
saturation, zone of, 320, **320**
Saturn
  atmosphere of, 655
  missions to, 655, 697–698, **697, 698**
  moons of, 665, **665**
  relative size of, **644**
  rings of, 655, **655**
  statistics, **655**
Saturn V rockets, **685,** 701
Saudi Arabia, desalination in, 397
scale, of a map, **46**
scanning electron microscopes, 118
Schiaparelli crater, **651**
schist, 109, **109**
scientific methods, 12–17, **13,** 26–27
  analyzing results, 15, 786
  asking questions, 13, 785
  communicating results, 16, 786
  drawing conclusions, 16, 786
  forming hypotheses, 14, 785
  summary of steps in, **13,** 785–786
  testing hypotheses, 14–15, 785–786
scientific models, 18–21, **19**
  choosing, 20, **20**
  climate models, 21, **21**
  conceptual, 19
  of the Earth, 20, **20,** 192
  lab on, 214–215
  mathematical, 19, **19,** 21, **21**
  physical, 18, **18**
  of the solar system, 555–556, **555**
  station, 506, **506**
scientific notation, 793
scientific theories, 20, **20**
sea anemones, **389**
sea arches, **344**
sea breezes, 462, **462**
sea caves, **344**
sea cliffs, **344**
sea-floor spreading, 199–201, **200, 201**
seamounts, 385, **385**

seasons, 520, **520,** 565, **802–803**
sea stacks, **344**
seaweed, 389, 395, **395**
secondary pollutants, 465, **465**
secondary treatment, 328, **328**
secondary waves, 228, **228**
second law of planetary motion, Kepler's, 631, **631**
second law of motion, Newton's, 798
sediment. *See also* deposition; erosion
  deposition in water, 316–317, **316, 317**
  deposition process and, 94, **94**
  erosion process and, 94, **94**
  formation of rock from, 102
sedimentary rock, 102–105
  composition of, 103–104, **104**
  lab on, 112–113
  metamorphism of, 94, 109
  origins of, 102, **102**
  in the rock cycle, **91–92,** 92–94, 93
  stratification of, 104, **104,** 156
  texture of, 96, **96,** 103
seismic gaps, 235–236, **235, 236**
seismic waves, 228, **228**
  in earthquakes, 228–229, **228, 229**
  elastic rebound and, 225, **225**
  lab on, **228**
  long period, 247
seismograms, 230
seismographs, 230, **230, 231**
seismologists, 6, 247
seismology, 224, **225.** *See also* earthquakes
Seismosaurus hallorum, 12, **12, 16, 17**
semimajor axis, 631, **631**
SEMs (scanning electron microscopes), 118
septic tanks, 329, **329**
sewage sludge dumping, 402, **402**
sewage treatment plants, 328, **328**
shale, 103, 109, **109**
shallow-water waves, 428, **428**
shamal, **463**
Shasta, Mount, 257
shellfish, toxins in, 442
shield volcanoes, 257, **257**
shock metamorphism, 118
Shoemaker-Levy 9 comet, **669**
shore currents, 429, **429**
shorelines, 342, **342**
  beaches, 346, **346,** 401
  dunes, 350–351, **350, 351**
  erosion of, 342–347
  landforms at, **344–345**
  wave energy and, 342–343, **343**
  wave trains and, 343, **343**

stars (continued)
  circumpolar, 567
  classification of, 584–585, **585**
  color of, 582, **582, 585,** 592, **592**
  composition of, 583–584, **583, 584, 585,** 590
  in constellations, 564–565, **564, 565,** 802–803
  distance to, 568, **568, 569,** 587, **587**
  Doppler effects from, 570, **570**
  elements in, **585**
  Eta Carinae, 610, **610**
  formation of, 593, 616–617, **616**
  giants, 591, **593**
  in Hertzsprung-Russell diagram, 591–592, **591, 592–593**
  labs on, **565, 587**
  life cycle of, 590–595, **590, 591, 592–593, 594**
  locating, 564–571, **566, 567,** 802–803
  magnitudes, 585–586, **586, 592–593**
  main-sequence, 590, **590, 592–593**
  mass of, 641
  motion of, 587–588, **588**
  neutron stars and pulsars, 594, **594**
  number of, 9, **9**
  parallax and, 587, **587**
  path across sky, 567
  red dwarf, **593**
  star clusters, 598, **598**
  supergiants, 591, **593**
  supernovas, 594, **594**
  white dwarf, 590–591, **590, 591, 592,** 641
stationary fronts, 493, **493**
station models, 506, **506**
St. Helens, Mount, **251,** 257, 538, **538**
stocks, **100**
storms
  hurricanes, 8, **8, 458,** 499–501, **499, 500, 501**
  on Jupiter, **495**
  thunderstorms, 486, 491, **491,** 496–497, **496, 497,** 501, 691
  tornadoes, 8, **8,** 32, 498, **498,** 499, **499,** 502, **502**
storm surges, 431, **431,** 501, **501**
strata, (singular, *stratum*) 102, **102,** 104
stratification, 104, **104,** 105, **105,** 156, **156**
stratified drift, 357, **357**
stratocumulus clouds, **487**
stratosphere, **450,** 451, **451**
stratovolcanoes, 257, **257**
stratus clouds, 486, **486, 487**
streak, 71, **71,** 800
streak plates, 71

stream discharge, 311
stream ecosystems, 468. *See also* rivers
streams, 316–319
stress, 206, **206, 207, 261**
strike-slip faults, 209, **209,** 226, **226**
strip mining, 76, 131
stromatolites, **628**
strontium, 164
subduction zones
  at convergent boundaries, 202, **202,** 203, **203**
  magma formation at, 260–261, **260,** 263, **263**
  mountain building and, 210–211
  sea-floor spreading towards, 200
sublittoral zone, 390, **390**
submarine volcanoes, **378, 385**
submetallic luster, 70, **70**
suborbital velocity, 687, **687**
subsidence, 212, **212**
subsurface mining, 77, **77**
subtracting decimals, 791
subtracting fractions, 792
succulents, **529**
Sue (fossil dinosaur), 33
sulfates, **69, 800–801**
sulfides, **69, 800–801**
sulfur, 68, **69, 75**
sulfuric acid, 649, **649**
sun, 618–623
  age of, 619
  distance from Earth, 634–635
  eclipses of, 663–664, **663**
  formation of, 616–617, **616**
  fusion in, 617, 620–621, **620, 621**
  gravity and, 619
  in H-R diagram, **593**
  radiation from, 454
  size of, **644**
  solar activity, 539, **539,** 622–623, **622, 623**
  solar telescopes, 640
  solar wind, 669
  structure of, 618, **618**
  theories of energy production in, 619, **619**
  tides and, 434, **434**
sunspots, 539, **539,** 622–623, **622**
supergiants, 591, **593**
supernovas, 594, **594**
superposition, principle of, 156–157, **156,** 178
surf, 428, **428.** *See also* waves, ocean
surface area–to-volume ratio, 285, **285**
surface coal mining, 76, **76,** 131
surface currents, 417, **417,** 523, **523.** *See also* ocean currents
  in Atlantic Ocean, **417, 418, 419**

  climate and, 422–423, **422, 423,** 523, **523**
  cold-water, 419, **419,** 423, **423**
  continental deflections, 418, **418**
  Coriolis effect and, 418, **418**
  deep currents and, **421**
  El Niño and, 424–425, **424,** 443, 549
  global winds and, 417, **417**
  La Niña and, 424–425, **424**
  shore currents, 429, **429**
  upwelling and, 423, **423**
  warm-water, 419, **419, 421,** 422, **422**
surface waves, seismic, 228–229, **229**
surface zone, oceanic, **377**
Surtsey, 262
suspended load, **312**
S waves, 228, **228**
swells, 430, **430**
symbols, safety, **25**
synclines, 207, **207**

T

table fold instructions (FoldNote), 779, **779**
taiga, **533,** 534, **534**
talc, **72, 74**
Tambora, Mount, 256
tar pits, 167
tectonic plates, 194, **194.** *See also* plate tectonics
  causes of motion of, 204, **204**
  close-up of, 195, **195**
  earthquakes at boundaries of, 224, **224,** 226, **226–227**
  fault types at boundaries of, 226, **226–227**
  labs on, **195,** 214–215
  lithosphere and, 195, 202–204, **202–203, 204**
  map of, 194, **194**
  tracking motion of, 205, **205**
  types of tectonic boundaries, 202–203, **202–203**
  volcanoes at boundaries of, 261–263, **261, 262, 263**
telescopes, 558–563, **559**
  atmospheric effects on, 560
  electomagnetic spectrum and, 561, **561**
  importance to astronomy, 9, **9**
  lab on, 572–573
  nonoptical, 561–563, **561, 562, 563**
  optical, 9, 558–560, **558, 559, 560**
  radio, 9, **9,** 562, **562,** 611
  reflecting, 559–560, **559, 560**
  refracting, 559, **559**

water vapor, 448, 483, **483**
water wheels, 138, **138**, 142–143
Watt-Evans, Lawrence, 578
wave-cut terraces, 345
wave energy, 342–343, **343**, 399
wave height, 426, **426**
wavelengths, 426–428, **426, 427, 428**
wave periods, 427, **427**
waves, ocean, 426–431
    breakers, 428, **428**
    deep-water and shallow-water, 428, **428**
    energy of, 342–343, **343**, 399
    formation and movement of, 427, **427**
    lab on, **429**
    longshore currents, 429, **429**
    open-ocean, 430, **430**
    parts of, 426, **426**
    periods, 343, **343**
    shore currents, 429, **429**
    speed of, 427, **427**
    storm surges, 431, **431**, 501, **501**
    wave-cut terraces, **345**
    wave deposits, 346–347, **346, 347**
    wave trains, 343, **343**
wave speed, 427, **427**
wave troughs, 426, **426**
waxing moon, 662, **662**
waxy luster, **70**
weather, 482–507, **483**, 518, **518.** *See also* climate
    air masses and, 490–491, **490, 491**
    anticyclones, 494–495, **494, 495**
    birds and, 514
    clouds and, 486–488, **486, 487**
    condensation and, **309, 482,** 485, **485**
    cyclones, 494–495, **494, 495**
    forecasting, 504–507, **504, 505, 506, 507,** 514
    fronts and, 492–493, **492–493, 507**
    humidity and, 483–485, **483, 484**
    hurricanes, 499–501, **499, 500, 501**
    labs on, **485**, 508–509
    precipitation, **482**, 488, **488**
    safety during severe, 501–502, **502**
    thunderstorms, 486, 491, **491,** 496–497, **496, 497**
    tornadoes, **8,** 32, 498–499, **498, 499**
    water cycle and, 482, **482**
weather balloons, 504, **504**

weather forecasting
    animal and plant signs in, **506,** 514
    meteorologists, 8, **8,** 504, 515
    technology for, 504–505, **504, 505**
    weather maps, 506–507, **506, 507**
    weather satellites in, 506, 691
weathering, 278–287, **278.** *See also* soil
    chemical, 280, 281–283, **281, 282, 283**
    climate and, 286, **286**
    differential, 284, **284**
    elevation and, 287, **287**
    labs on, **282,** 298–299
    mechanical, 278–280, **278, 279, 280**
    from organisms, 282
    from oxidation, 283, **283,** 286, **286**
    patterns from, 304
    in the rock cycle, **91,** 93, **93**
    surface area and, 285, **285**
weather maps, 506–507, **506, 507**
weather satellites, 506, 691
Wegener, Alfred, 198–199, 221
weightlessness, 702, **702**
Weinbaum, Stanley, 680
wells, 323, **323**
westerlies, 460, **460, 461**
wet-bulb thermometers, 484–485, **484**
wetland ecosystems, **692**
whales, humpback, 443
whitecaps, 430, **430**
white dwarf stars, 590–591, **590, 591, 592,** 641
"Why I Left Harry's All-Night Hamburgers," 578
Wieliczka salt mine, 86
Williamson, Jack, 86
Wilson, Robert, **601**
wind erosion, 279, **279,** 348–351, **348, 349, 350**
wind power, 137, **137**
winds, 458–463, **458**
    causes of, 458–460, **458, 459, 460**
    Coriolis effect on, 417–418, **418,** 460, **460**
    deposition by, 350–351, **350, 351**
    direction, measurement of, 505, **505**
    global, 417, **417, 418,** 460–461, **461**
    in hurricanes, **500,** 501
    in jet streams, 462, **462**
    local, 462–463, **462, 463**
    prevailing, 521, **521**

    solar, 669
    in storms, **458**
    trade, 460, **460, 461**
wind socks, 505, **505**
wind turbines, **122,** 137, **137**
wind vanes, 505
woolly mammoths, 167, **167,** 184
world population growth, **19**

X

X-ray telescopes, **562,** 563, **563,** 641

Y

years, 554, **554,** 630
Yellowstone National Park, 258, **313**
Yoho National Park, **169**

Z

zenith, 566, **566**
zone of aeration, 320, **320**
zone of saturation, 320, **320**
zoology, radar, 478
zooplankton, 388, **388**

Acknowledgments

continued from page ii

Joel S. Leventhal, Ph.D.
Emeritus Scientist
U.S. Geological Survey
Lakewood, Colorado

Madeline Micceri Mignone, Ph.D.
Assistant Professor
Natural Science
Dominican College
Orangeburg, New York

Sten Odenwald, Ph.D.
Astronomer
NASA Goddard Space Flight
Center and Raytheon
ITSS
Greenbelt, Maryland

Kenneth K. Peace
Manager of Transportation
WestArch Coal, Inc.
St. Louis, Missouri

Kenneth H. Rubin, Ph.D.
Associate Professor
Department of Geology &
Geophysics
University of Hawaii at
Manoa
Honolulu, Hawaii

Dork Sahagian, Ph.D.
Research Professor
Department of Earth
Sciences
Institute for the Study of
Earth, Oceans, and Space
University of New
Hampshire
Durham, New Hampshire

Daniel Z. Sui, Ph.D.
Professor
Department of Geography
Texas A&M University
College Station, Texas

Colin D. Sumrall, Ph.D.
Lecturer of Paleontology
Earth and Planetary
Sciences
The University of Tennessee
Knoxville, Tennessee

Vatche P. Tchakerian, Ph.D.
Professor
Department of Geography
& Geology
Texas A&M University
College Station, Texas

Peter W. Weigand, Ph.D.
Professor Emeritus
Department of Geological
Sciences
California State University
Northridge, California

Teacher Reviewers

Diedre S. Adams
Physical Science Instructor
Science Department
West Vigo Middle School
West Terre Haute, Indiana

Laura Buchanan
*Science Teacher and
Department Chairperson*
Corkran Middle School
Glen Burnie, Maryland

Robin K. Clanton
Science Department Head
Berrien Middle School
Nashville, Georgia

Randy Dye, M.S.
*Middle School Science
Department Head*
Earth Science
Wood Middle School
Waynesville School District
#6, Missouri

Meredith Hanson
Science Teacher
Westside Middle School
Rocky Face, Georgia

James Kerr
*Oklahoma Teacher of the Year
2002–2003*
Oklahoma State
Department of Education
Union Public Schools
Tulsa, Oklahoma

Laura Kitselman
*Science Teacher and
Coordinator*
Loudoun Country Day
School
Leesburg, Virginia

Deborah L. Kronsteiner
Teacher
Science Department
Spring Grove Area Middle
School
Spring Grove, Pennsylvania

Jennifer L. Lamkie
Science Teacher
Thomas Jefferson Middle
School
Edison, New Jersey

Sally M. Lesley
ESL Science Teacher
Burnet Middle School
Austin, Texas

Susan H. Robinson
Science Teacher
Oglethorpe County Middle
School
Lexington, Georgia

Marci L. Stadiem
Department Head
Science Department
Cascade Middle School,
Highline School District
Seattle, Washington

Lab Development

Kenneth E. Creese
Science Teacher
White Mountain Junior
High School
Rock Spring, Wyoming

Linda A. Culp
*Science Teacher and
Department Chair*
Thorndale High School
Thorndale, Texas

Bruce M. Jones
*Science Teacher and
Department Chair*
The Blake School
Minneapolis, Minnesota

Shannon Miller
Science and Math Teacher
Llano Junior High School
Llano, Texas

Robert Stephen Ricks
Special Services Teacher
Department of Classroom
Improvement
Alabama State Department
of Education
Montgomery, Alabama

James J. Secosky
Science Teacher
Bloomfield Central School
Bloomfield, New York

Lab Testing

Barry L. Bishop
*Science Teacher and
Department Chair*
San Rafael Junior High
Ferron, Utah

Daniel Bugenhagen
*Science Teacher and
Department Chair*
Yutan Jr.–Sr. high
Yutan, Nebraska

Kenneth Creese
Science Teacher
White Mountain Junior
High
Rock Springs, Wyoming

Susan Gorman
Science Teacher
North Ridge Middle School
North Richmond Hills,
Texas

C. John Graves
Science Teacher
Monforton Middle School
Bozeman, Montana

Janel Guse
*Science Teacher and
Department Chair*
West Central Middle School
Hartford, South Dakota

Norman Holcomb
Science Teacher
Marion Local Schools
Maria Stein, Ohio

Tracy Jahn
Science Teacher
Berkshire Jr–Sr. High
Canaan, New York

David Jones
Science Teacher
Andrew Jackson Middle
School
Cross Lanes, West Virginia

Michael E. Kral
Science Teacher
West Hardin Middle School
Cecilia, Kentucky

Kathy McKee
Science Teacher
Hoyt Middle School
Des Moines, Iowa

Alyson, Mike
Science Teacher
East Valley Middle School
East Helena, Montana

Jan Nelson
Science Teacher
East Valley Middle School
East Helena, Montana

Dwight Patton
Science Teacher
Carrol T. Welch Middle
School
Horizon City, Texas

Joseph Price
*Chairman—Science
Department*
H.M. Browne Junior High
Washington, D.C.

Terry J. Rakes
Science Teacher
Elmwood Junior High
Rogers, Arkansas

Helen Schiller
Science Teacher
Northwood Middle School
Taylors, South Carolina

Bert Sherwood
Science Teacher
Socorro Middle School
El Paso, Texas

David M. Sparks
Science Teacher
Redwater Junior High
School
Redwater, Texas

Larry Tackett
*Science Teacher and
Department Chair*
Andrew Jackson Middle
School
Cross Lanes, West Virginia

Walter Woolbaugh
Science Teacher
Manhattan School System
Manhattan, Montana

Gordon Zibelman
Science Teacher
Drexel Hill Middle School
Drexel Hill, Pennsylvania

Answer Checking
Catherine Podeszwa
Duluth, Minnesota

Feature Development
Katy Z. Allen
Hatim Belyamani
John A. Benner
David Bradford
Jennifer Childers
Mickey Coakley
Susan Feldkamp
Jane Gardner
Erik Hahn
Christopher Hess
Deena Kalai

Charlotte W. Luongo, MSc
Michael May
Persis Mehta, Ph.D.
Eileen Nehme, MPH
Catherine Podeszwa
Dennis Rathnaw
Daniel B. Sharp
John Stokes
April Smith West
Molly F. Wetterschneider

Staff Credits

Editorial
Robert Todd, *Vice President,
Editorial Science*
Debbie Starr, *Managing
Editor*
Leigh Ann García, *Senior
Editor*

**Editorial Development
Team**
Jen Driscoll
Amy Fry
Angela Hemmeter
Shari Husain
Bill Rader
Jim Ratcliffe

Copyeditors
Dawn Marie Spinozza,
Copyediting Manager
Anne-Marie De Witt
Jane A. Kirschman
Kira J. Watkins

Editorial Support Staff
Mary Anderson
Suzanne Krejci
Shannon Oehler

Online Products
Bob Tucek,
Executive Editor
Wesley M. Bain

Design
Book Design
Kay Selke,
Director of Book Design
Sonya Mendeke, *Designer*
Mercedes Newman,
Designer
Holly Whittaker, *Project
Administrator*

Media Design
Richard Metzger, *Design
Director*
Chris Smith, *Senior Designer*

Image Acquisitions
Curtis Riker, *Director*
Jeannie Taylor,
Photo Research Manager
Andy Christiansen, *Photo
Researcher*
Elaine Tate,
Art Buyer Supervisor
Angela Boehm,
Senior Art Buyer

Design New Media
Edwin Blake, *Director*
Kimberly Cammerata, *Design
Manager*
Michael Rinella,
Senior Designer

Cover Design
Bill Smith Studio

Publishing Services
Carol Martin, *Director*

Graphic Services
Bruce Bond, *Director*
Jeff Bowers, *Graphic Services
Manager*
JoAnn Stringer, *Senior
Graphics Specialist II*
Cathy Murphy, *Senior
Graphics Specialist*
Nanda Patel, *Graphics
Specialist*
Katrina Gnader, *Graphics
Specialist*

Technology Services
Laura Likon, *Director*
Juan Baquera, *Technology
Services Manager*
Lana Kaupp, *Senior
Technology Services Analyst*
Margaret Sanchez, *Senior
Technology Services Analyst*
Sara Buller, *Technology
Services Analyst*
Patty Zepeda, *Technology
Services Analyst*
Jeff Robinson, *Ancillary
Design Manager*

New Media
Armin Gutzmer, *Director*
Melanie Baccus,
New Media Coordinator

Lydia Doty, *Senior Project
Manager*
Cathy Kuhles, *Technical
Assistant*
Marsh Flournoy, *Quality
Assurance Analyst*
Tara F. Ross, *Senior Project
Manager*

Production
Eddie Dawson, *Production
Manager*
Sherry Sprague, *Senior
Production Coordinator*
Suzanne Brooks, *Production
Coordinator*

Teacher Edition
Alicia Sullivan
David Hernandez
April Litz

Manufacturing and
Inventory
Wilonda Ieans
Ivania Quant Lee

Ancillary
Development
and Production
General Learning
Communications,
Northbrook, Illinois

Acknowledgments **847**

Credits

Abbreviations used: (t) top, (c) center, (b) bottom, (l) left, (r) right, (bkgd) background

PHOTOGRAPHY

Front Cover (tl), Paul & Lindamarie Ambrose/Getty Images; (tr), NASA Goddard Space Flight Center. Image by Reto Stöckli (land surface, shallow water, clouds). Enhancements by Robert Simmon (ocean color, compositing, 3D globes, animation). Data and technical support: MODIS Land Group; MODIS Science Data Support Team; (cr), Larry Landolfi/Photo Researchers, Inc.; (c), Steve Niedirf Photography/Getty Images; (bl), Corel; (owl), Kim Taylor/Bruce Coleman

Skills Practice Lab Teens Sam Dudgeon/HRW

Connection to Astronomy Corbis Images; **Connection to Biology** David M. Phillips/Visuals Unlimited; **Connection to Chemistry** Digital Image copyright © 2005 PhotoDisc; **Connection to Environment** Digital Image copyright © 2005 PhotoDisc; **Connection to Geology** Letraset Phototone; **Connection to Language Arts** Digital Image copyright © 2005 PhotoDisc; **Connection to Meteorology** Digital Image copyright © 2005 PhotoDisc; **Connection to Oceanography** © ICONOTEC; **Connection to Physics** Digital Image copyright © 2005 PhotoDisc

Table of Contents iii (t), Sam Dudgeon/HRW; iii (b), NASA; iv (t), Howard B. Bluestein; iv (bl), Tom Pantages Photography; v (t), E. R. Degginger/Color-Pic, Inc.; v (green), Dr. E.R. Degginger/Bruce Coleman Inc.; v (purple), Mark A. Schneider/Photo Researchers, Inc.; v, CORBIS Images/HRW; vi, Laurent Gillieron/Keystone/AP/Wide World Photos; vi (b), The G.R. "Dick" Roberts Photo Library; viii (t), National Geographic Image Collection/Robert W. Madden; viii (b), Bob Krueger/Photo Researchers, Inc.; ix (t), Glenn M. Oliver/Visuals Unlimited; ix (b) Tom Bean/CORBIS; x (t), Stuart Westmorland/CORBIS; xi (t), Goddard Space Flight Center Scientific Visualization Studio/NASA; xi (b), NASA; xii (tl), Index Stock; xii (c), MSFC/NASA; xii (bl), Peter Van Steen/HRW; xiii (t), Bill & Sally Fletcher/Tom Stack & Associates; xiii (b), NASA/TSADO/Tom Stack & Associates; xiv (t), NASA/Peter Arnold, Inc.; xv; Sam Dudgeon/HRW; xvi, Victoria Smith/HRW; xviii, xix, xx, xxii, Victoria Smith/HRW; xxvi, Sam Dudgeon/HRW; xxvii (t), John Langford/HRW; xxvii (b), xxviii (t, bl), Sam Dudgeon/HRW; xxviii (bl), Stephanie Morris/HRW; xxix (tl), Sam Dudgeon/HRW; xxix (tr), Jana Birchum/HRW; xxix (b), Sam Dudgeon/HRW

Unit One 2 (tl), Ed Reschke/Peter Arnold, Inc.; 2 (c), Francois Gohier; 2 (b), Smithsonian Air and Space Museum; 2 (tl), T.A. Wiewandt/DRK Photo; 3 (tl), Uwe Fink/University of Arizona, Department of Planetary Sciences, Lunar & Planetary Laboratory; 3 (tr), Hulton Archive/Getty Images; 3 (stone), Adam Woolfitt/British Museum/Woodfin Camp & Assocites, Inc.; 3 (volcano), K. Segerstrom/USGS; 3 (bl), NASA; 3 (br), Iziko Museums of Cape Town

Chapter One 4-5, © Louie Psihoyos/psihoyos.com; 6, James W. Rozzi; 7, Woods Hole Oceanographic Institute; 8 (t), Marit Jentoft-Nilsen and Fritz Hasler/NASA Goddard Laboratory for Atmospheres; 8 (b), Howard B. Bluestein; 9, Jean Miele/Corbis Stock Market; 10 (bl, br), Andy Christiansen/HRW; 10, Mark Howard/Westfall Eco Images; 11, Annie Griffiths Belt/CORBIS; 14, Dr. David Gillette; 17, Paul Fraughton/HRW; 18 (r), Jim Sugar Photography/CORBIS; 18 (l), Sam Dudgeon/HRW; 20 (l), AKG Photo, London; 20 (r), Image Copyright ©2005 PhotoDisc, Inc.; 21, Andy Newman/AP/Wide World Photos; 23 (l, r), Peter Van Steen/HRW; 26, Victoria Smith/HRW; 29 (b), Andy Christiansen/HRW; 29 (l), Peter Van Steen/HRW; 32 (tl), Scripps Institution of Oceanography; 32 (tr), The Stuart News, Carl Rivenbark/AP/Wide World Photos; 33, AFP/CORBIS; 33 (b), AFP/CORBIS

Chapter Two 34-35, JPL/NASA; 36, Royal Geographical Society, London ,UK./The Bridgeman Art Library; 37 (t), Sam Dudgeon/HRW; 37 (b), Tom Pantages Photography; 38, Sam Dudgeon/HRW; 42 (bl, br), Andy Christiansen/HRW; 46, Texas Department of Transportaion; 47, Spaceimaging.com/Getty Images/NewsCom; 48 (bl, bc, br), Strategic Planning Office, City of Seattle; 48 (tl), HO/NewsCom; 49, Andy Christiansen/HRW; 50, USGS; 51 (tl), USGS; 51 (tr), USGS; 52, USGS; 55, Sam Dudgeon/HRW ; 57, USGS; 57 (br), Strategic Planning Office, City of Seattle; 60 (r), JPL/NASA; 60 (l), Victoria Smith/HRW; 61 (r), Bettman/CORBIS; 61 (bl), Layne Kennedy/CORBIS

Unit Two 62 (tl), Science Photo Library/Photo Researchers, Inc; 62 (c), Francois Gohier; 62 (bl), © UPI/ Bettmann/CORBIS; 62 (br), Thomas Laird/Peter Arnold, Inc; 63 (tl), Science VU/Visuals Unlimited; 63 (tr), SuperStock; 63 (cl), AP/Wide World Photos; 63 (cr), NASA/Image State; 63 (br), File/AP/Wide World Photos

Chapter Three 64-65, Terry Wilson; 66, Sam Dudgeon/HRW; 67, Dr. Rainer Bode/Bode-Verlag Gmb; 68 (tr), Victoria Smith/HRW; 68 (bc), Sam Dudgeon/HRW; 68 (tl), Sam Dudgeon/HRW; 69, (copper), E. R. Degginger/Color-Pic, Inc.; 69, (calcite), E. R. Degginger/Color-Pic, Inc.; 69, (fluorite), E. R. Degginger/Color-Pic, Inc.; 69, (corundum), E. R. Degginger/Color-Pic, Inc.; 69, (gypsum), SuperStock; 69, (galena), Visuals Unlimited/Ken Lucas; 70, (vitreous), Biophoto Associates/Photo Researchers, Inc.; 70, (waxy), Biophoto Associates/Photo Researchers, Inc.; 70, (silky), Dr. E.R. Degginger/Bruce Coleman Inc.; 70, (submetallic), John Cancalosi 1989/DRK Photo; 70 (bl), Kosmatsu Mining Systems; 70, (resinous), Charles D. Winters/Photo Researchers, Inc.; 70, (pearly), Victoria Smith/HRW; 70, (metallic), Victoria Smith/HRW; 70, (earthy), Sam Dudgeon/HRW; 71 (tr, c, bl), Sam Dudgeon/HRW; 71, Tom Pantages; 72, (1), Visuals Unlimited/Ken Lucas; 72, (3), Visuals Unlimited/Dane S. Johnson; 72, (7), Carlyn Iverson/Absolute Science Illustration and Photography; 72, (8), Mark A. Schneider/Visuals Unlimited; 72, (9), Charles D. Winters/Photo Researchers, Inc.; 72, (10), Bard Wrisley; 72, (5), Biophoto Associates/Photo Researchers, Inc.; 72, (6), Victoria Smith/HRW; 72, (4), Mark A. Schneider/Photo Researchers, Inc.; 72, (2), Sam Dudgeon/HRW; 73 (tc), Sam Dudgeon/HRW; 73 (tr), Sam Dudgeon/HRW, Courtesy Science Stuff, Austin, TX; 73 (br), Tom Pantages Photography; 73 (bc), Sam Dudgeon/HRW; 73 (tl), Mark A. Schneider/Photo Researchers, Inc.; 73 (tl), Mark A. Schneider/Photo Researchers, Inc.; 73 (bl), 74 (t), Sam Dudgeon/HRW, Victoria Smith/HRW Photo, Courtesy Science Stuff, Austin, TX; 74 (c), Breck P. Kent; 75 (br), Sam Dudgeon/HRW; 75 (c), Breck P. Kent; 75 (t), Visuals Unlimited/Ken Lucas; 76 (br), Wernher Krutein; 77, Stewart Cohen/Index Stock Photography, Inc.; 78, Digital Image copyright © 2005 PhotoDisc; 79, Historic Royal Palaces; 80 (c), Russell Dian/HRW; 80 (b), 81 (tr), Sam Dudgeon/HRW; 82, Digital Image copyright © 2005 PhotoDisc; 83 (b), E. R. Degginger/Color-Pic, Inc.; 86 (t), Stephan Edelbroich; 87 (t), Will & Dennie McIntyre/McIntyre Photography; 87 (b), Mark Schneider/Visuals Unlimited

Chapter Four 88-89, Tom Till; 90 (bl), Michael Melford/Getty Images/The Image Bank; 90 (br), Joseph Sohm; Visions of America/CORBIS; 91, CORBIS Images/HRW; 94 (t), Joyce Photographics/Photo Researchers, Inc.; 94 (l), Pat Lanza/Bruce Coleman Inc.; 94 (r), Sam Dudgeon/HRW ; 94 (b), James Watt/Animals Animals/Earth Scenes; 94 (l), Pat Lanza/Bruce Coleman Inc.; 95, (granite), Pat Lanza/Bruce Coleman Inc.; 95, (mica), E. R. Degginger/Color-Pic, Inc.; 95, (aragonite), Breck P. Kent; 95, (limestone), Breck P. Kent; 95, (calcite), Mark Schneider/Visuals Unlimited; 95, (feldspar), Mark Schneider/Visuals Unlimited; 95, (quartz), Digital Image copyright © 2005 PhotoDisc; 96 (tl), Sam Dudgeon/HRW; 96 (tc), Dorling Kindersley; 96 (tr, br), Breck P. Kent; 96 (bl), E. R. Degginger/Color-Pic, Inc.; 97, Joseph Sohm; Visions of America/CORBIS; 98 (l), E. R. Degginger/Color-Pic, Inc.; 99 (tr, tl, bl), Breck P. Kent; 99 (br), Victoria Smith/HRW; 101, J.D. Griggs/USGS; 102, CORBIS Images/HRW; 103, (conglomerate), Breck P. Kent; 103, (siltstone), Sam Dudgeon/HRW; 103, (sandstone), Joyce Photographics/Photo Researchers, Inc.; 103, (shale), Sam Dudgeon/HRW; 104 (tl), Stephen Frink/Corbis; 104 (br), Breck P. Kent; 104 (bc), David Muench/CORBIS; 105, Franklin P. OSF/Animals Animals/Earth Scenes; 106, George Wuerthner; 108, (calcite), Dane S. Johnson/Visuals Unlimited; 108, (quartz), Carlyn Iverson/Absolute Science Illustration and Photography; 108, (hematite), Breck P. Kent; 108, (garnet), Breck P. Kent/Animals Animals/Earth Scenes; 108, (chlorite), Sam Dudgeon/HRW; 108, (mica), Tom Pantages; 109, (shale), Ken Karp/HRW; 109, (slate), Sam Dudgeon/HRW; 109, (phyllite), Sam Dudgeon/HRW; 109, (gneiss), Breck P. Kent; 109, (schist), Sam Dudgeon/HRW; 110 (tl), E. R. Degginger/Color-Pic, Inc.; 110 (bl), Ray Simmons/Photo Researchers, Inc.; 110 (tr), The Natural History Museum, London; 110 (br), Breck P. Kent; 111, Jim Wark/Airphoto; 113 (t), Sam Dudgeon/HRW; 113 (b), James Tallon; 118 (l), Wolfgang Kaehler/CORBIS; 118 (tr), Dr. David Kring/Science Photo Library/Photo Researchers, Inc.; 119 (r), James Miller/Courtesy Robert Folk, Department of Geological Sciences, University of Texas at Austin; 119 (l), Dr. Philppa Uwins, Whistler Research PTY/SPL/Photo Researchers, Inc.; 120 (inset), Roger Ressmeyer/CORBIS;

Chapter Five 120-121 (inset), Novovitch/Liaison/Getty Images; 122 (tc), Andy Christiansen/HRW; 122 (tl), John Blaustein/Liaison/Getty Images; 122 (tr), Mark Lewis/Getty Images/Stone; 123 (tl), James Randklev/Getty Images/Stone; 123 (b), Ed Malles/Liaison/Newsmakers/Getty Images; 123 (tr), Myrleen Furgusson Cate/PhotoEdit; 124, Victoria Smith/HRW; 126, Data courtesy Marc Imhoff of NASA/GSFC and Christopher Elvidge of NOAA/NGDC. Image by Craig Mayhew and Robert Simmon, NASA/GSFC.; 127 (b), John Zoiner; 127 (t), Mark Green/Getty Images/Taxi; 128, John Zoiner; 130, 2, Paolo Koch/Photo Researchers, Inc.; 130, 1, Horst Schafer/Peter Arnold, Inc.; 130, 3, Brian Parker/Tom Stack & Associates; 130, 4, C. Kuhn/Getty Images/The Image Bank; 130, 4, Alberto Incrocci/Getty Images/The Image Bank; 132 (inset), ©1994 NYC Parks Photo Archive/Fundamental Photographs; 132 (tl), © 1994 Kristen Brochman/Fundamental Photographs; 132, Martin Harvey; 135 (tr), Tom Myers/Photo Researchers, Inc; 136 (l), Laurent Gillieron/Keystone/AP/Wide World Photos; 137 (b), Terry W. Eggers/CORBIS; 138 (t), Craig Sands/National Geographic Image Collection/Getty Images; 138 (b), Caio Coronel/Reuters/NewsCom; 139, G.R. Roberts Photo Library; 141, Laurent Gillieron/Keystone/AP/Wide World Photos; 143, Sam Dudgeon/HRW; 144, HRW; 145; 132, Martin Harvey; 148 (t), Junko Kimura/Getty Images; 148 (b), STR/AP/Wide World Photos; 149 (t), Courtesy of Los Alamos National Laboratories; 149 (b), Corbis Images

848 Credits